Street by Stree[t]

BIRMINGH[AM] WOLVERHAMPT[ON]

DUDLEY, SOLIHULL, STOURBRIDGE, WALSALL, WEST BROMWICH

Aldridge, Brownhills, Codsall, Coleshill, Dorridge, Halesowen, Knowle, Pelsall, Sutton Coldfield, Wombourne

3rd edition November 2007
© Automobile Association Developments Limited
2007

Original edition printed May 2001

 This product includes map data licensed from Ordnance Survey® with the permission of the Controller of Her Majesty's Stationery Office. © Crown copyright 2007. All rights reserved. Licence number 100021153.

The copyright in all PAF is owned by Royal Mail Group plc.

Published by AA Publishing (a trading name of Automobile Association Developments Limited, whose registered office is Fanum House, Basing View, Basingstoke, Hampshire RG21 4EA. Registered number 1878835).

Produced by the Mapping Services Department of The Automobile Association. (A03490)

A CIP Catalogue record for this book is available from the British Library.

Printed by Oriental Press in Dubai

The contents of this atlas are believed to be correct at the time of the latest revision. However, the publishers cannot be held responsible or liable for any loss or damage occasioned to any person acting or refraining from action as a result of any use or reliance on any material in this atlas, nor for any errors, omissions or changes in such material. This does not affect your statutory rights. The publishers would welcome information to correct any errors or omissions and to keep this atlas up to date. Please write to Publishing, The Automobile Association, Fanum House, Basing View, Basingstoke, Hampshire, RG21 4EA. E-mail: *streetbystreet@theaa.com*

Ref: ML33y

Key to map pages	ii-iii
Key to map symbols	iv-1
Enlarged map pages	2-7
Main map pages	8-199
Index – towns & villages	200
Index – streets	201-243
Index – featured places	243-252
Acknowledgements	252

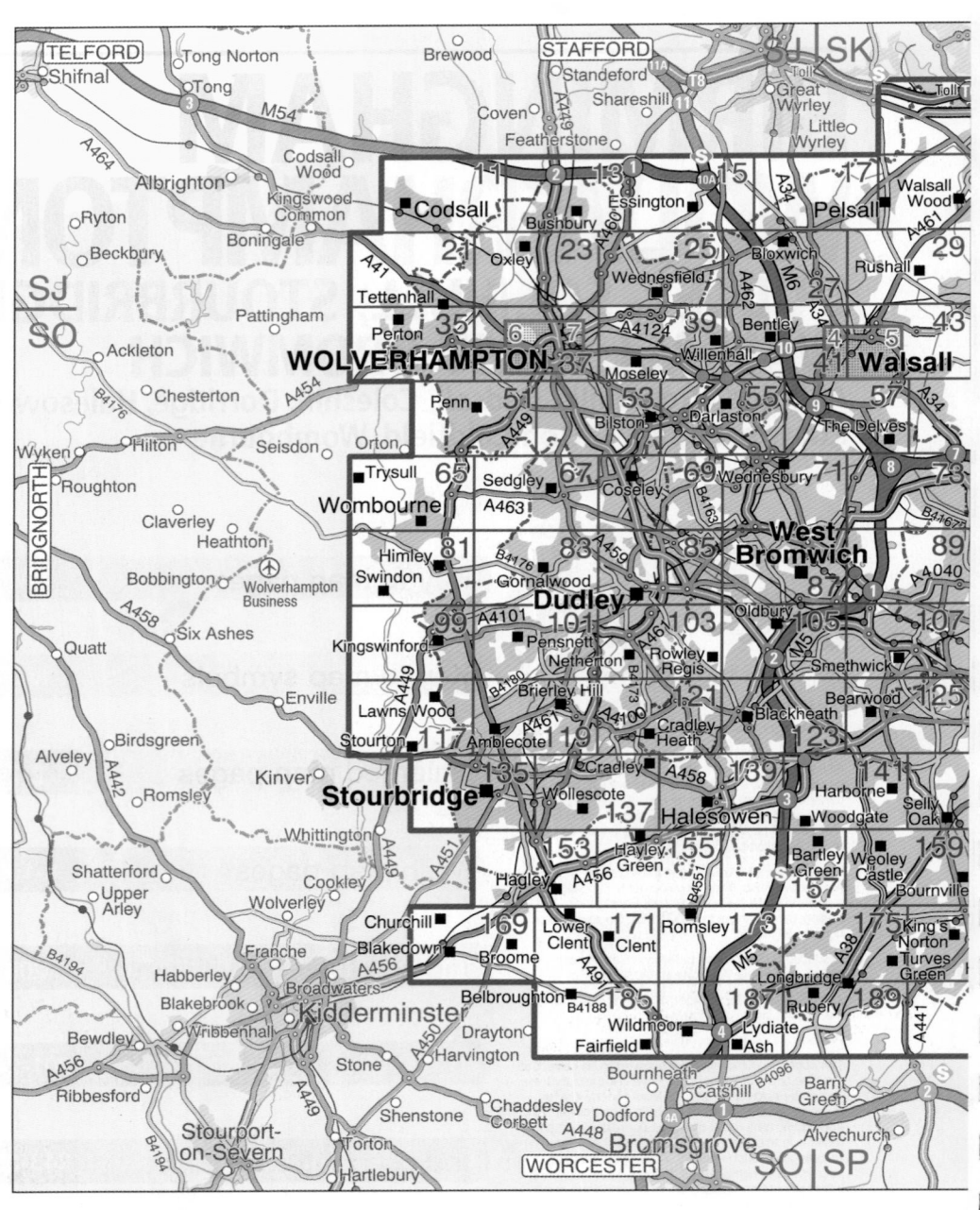

ii

0   1/4   miles   1/2

0   1/4   1/2   kilometres   3/4   1

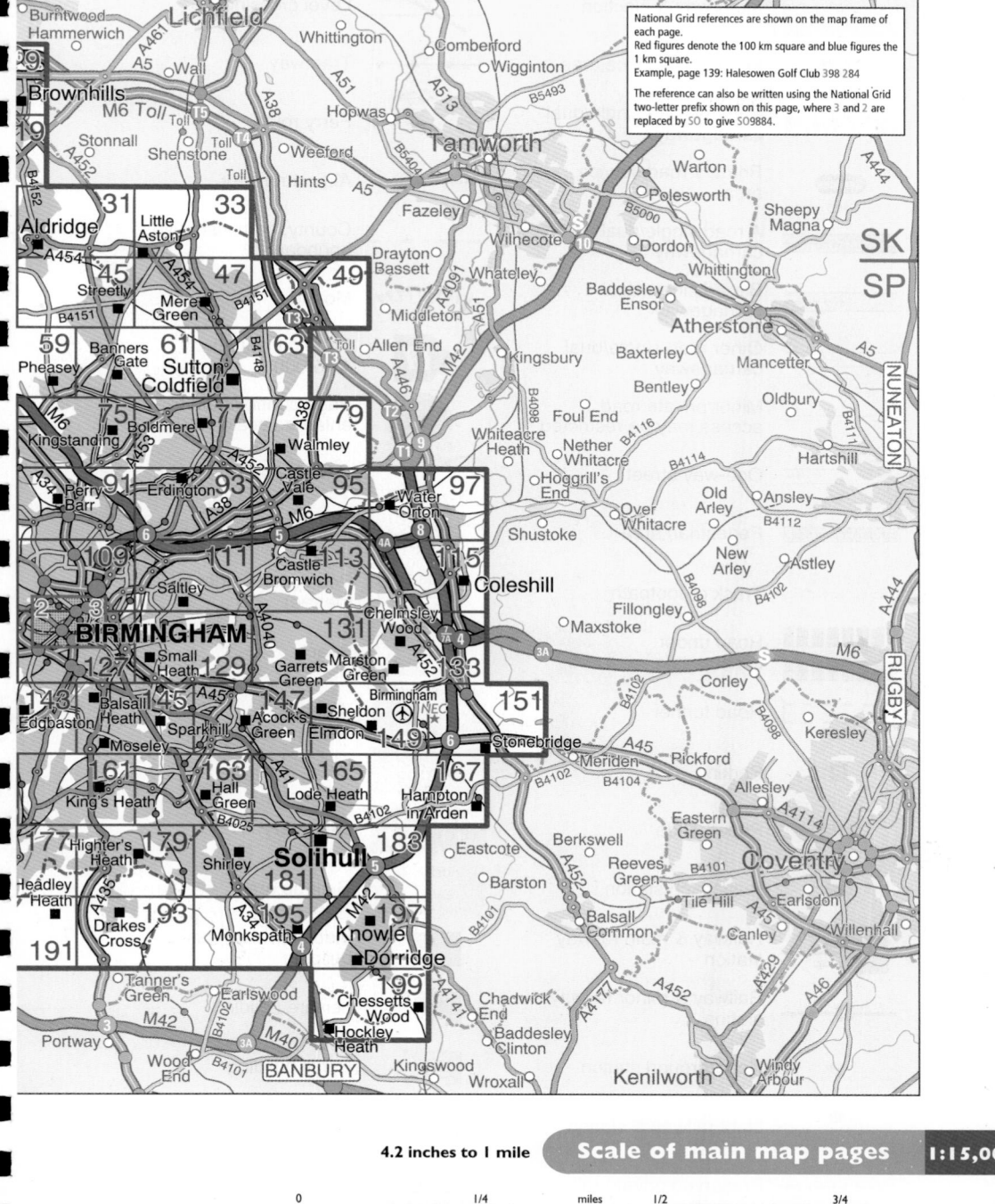

National Grid references are shown on the map frame of each page.
Red figures denote the 100 km square and blue figures the 1 km square.
Example, page 139: Halesowen Golf Club 398 284

The reference can also be written using the National Grid two-letter prefix shown on this page, where 3 and 2 are replaced by SO to give SO9884.

4.2 inches to 1 mile

Scale of main map pages 1:15,000

miles
0   1/4   1/2   3/4   1

kilometres
0   1/4   1/2   3/4   1   1 1/4   1 1/2

iv

Junction 9	Motorway & junction	LC	Level crossing
Services	Motorway service area		Tramway
	Primary road single/dual carriageway		Ferry route
Services	Primary road service area		Airport runway
	A road single/dual carriageway		County, administrative boundary
	B road single/dual carriageway		Mounds
	Other road single/dual carriageway	17	Page continuation 1:15,000
	Minor/private road, access may be restricted	3	Page continuation to enlarged scale 1:10,000
	One-way street		River/canal, lake, pier
	Pedestrian area		Aqueduct, lock, weir
	Track or footpath	465 Winter Hill	Peak (with height in metres)
	Road under construction		Beach
	Road tunnel		Woodland
P	Parking		Park
P+	Park & Ride		Cemetery
	Bus/coach station		Built-up area
	Railway & main railway station		Industrial/business building
	Railway & minor railway station		Leisure building
	Underground station		Retail building
	Light railway & station		Other building
	Preserved private railway	IKEA	IKEA store

City wall	City wall	Castle	Castle
A&E	Hospital with 24-hour A&E department		Historic house or building
PO	Post Office	Wakehurst Place (NT)	National Trust property
	Public library	M	Museum or art gallery
i	Tourist Information Centre		Roman antiquity
i	Seasonal Tourist Information Centre		Ancient site, battlefield or monument
	Petrol station, 24 hour Major suppliers only		Industrial interest
†	Church/chapel		Garden
	Public toilets		Garden Centre Garden Centre Association Member
	Toilet with disabled facilities		Garden Centre Wyevale Garden Centre
PH	Public house AA recommended		Arboretum
	Restaurant AA inspected		Farm or animal centre
Madeira Hotel	Hotel AA inspected		Zoological or wildlife collection
	Theatre or performing arts centre		Bird collection
	Cinema		Nature reserve
	Golf course		Aquarium
▲	Camping AA inspected	V	Visitor or heritage centre
	Caravan site AA inspected		Country park
	Camping & caravan site AA inspected		Cave
	Theme park		Windmill
	Abbey, cathedral or priory		Distillery, brewery or vineyard

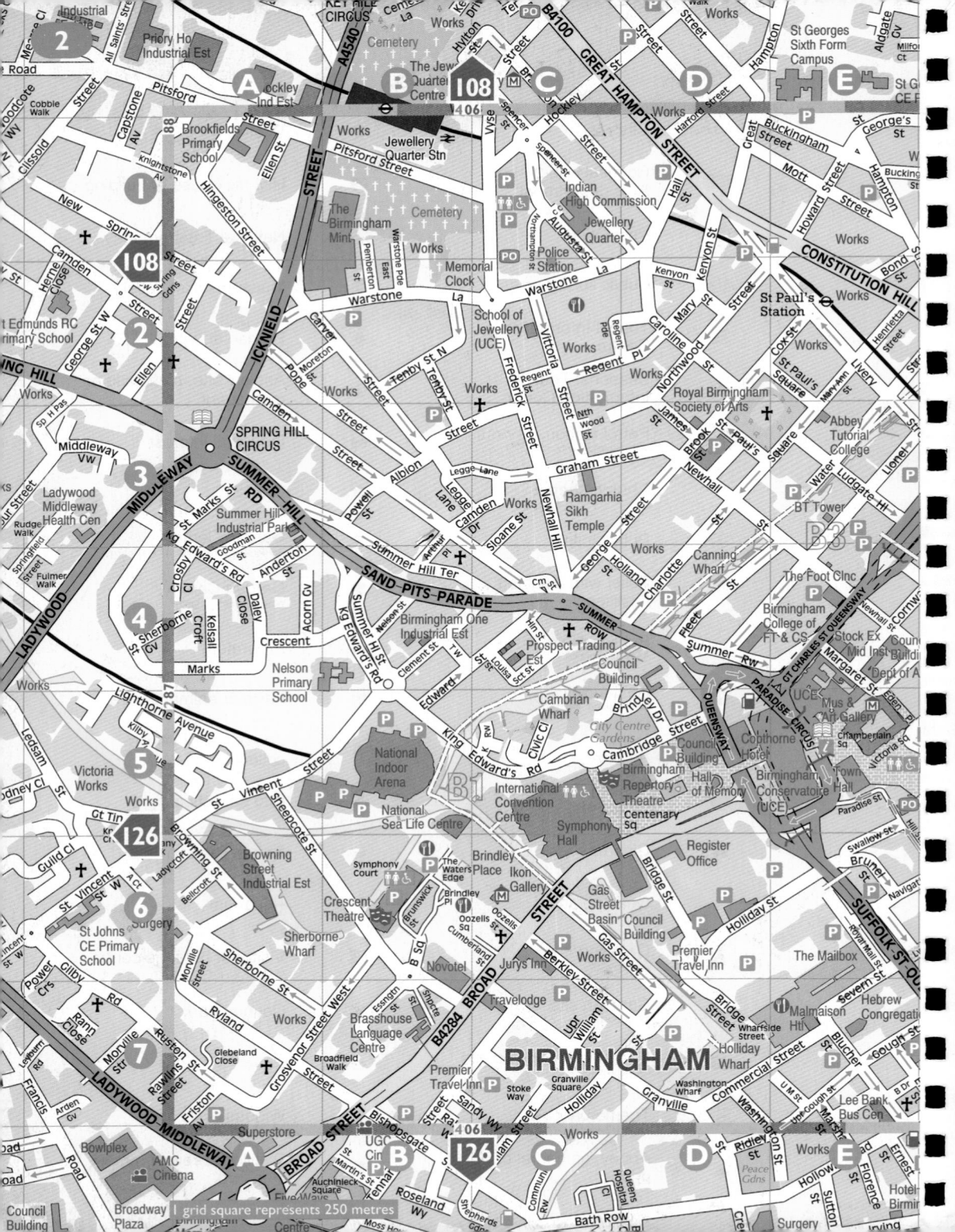

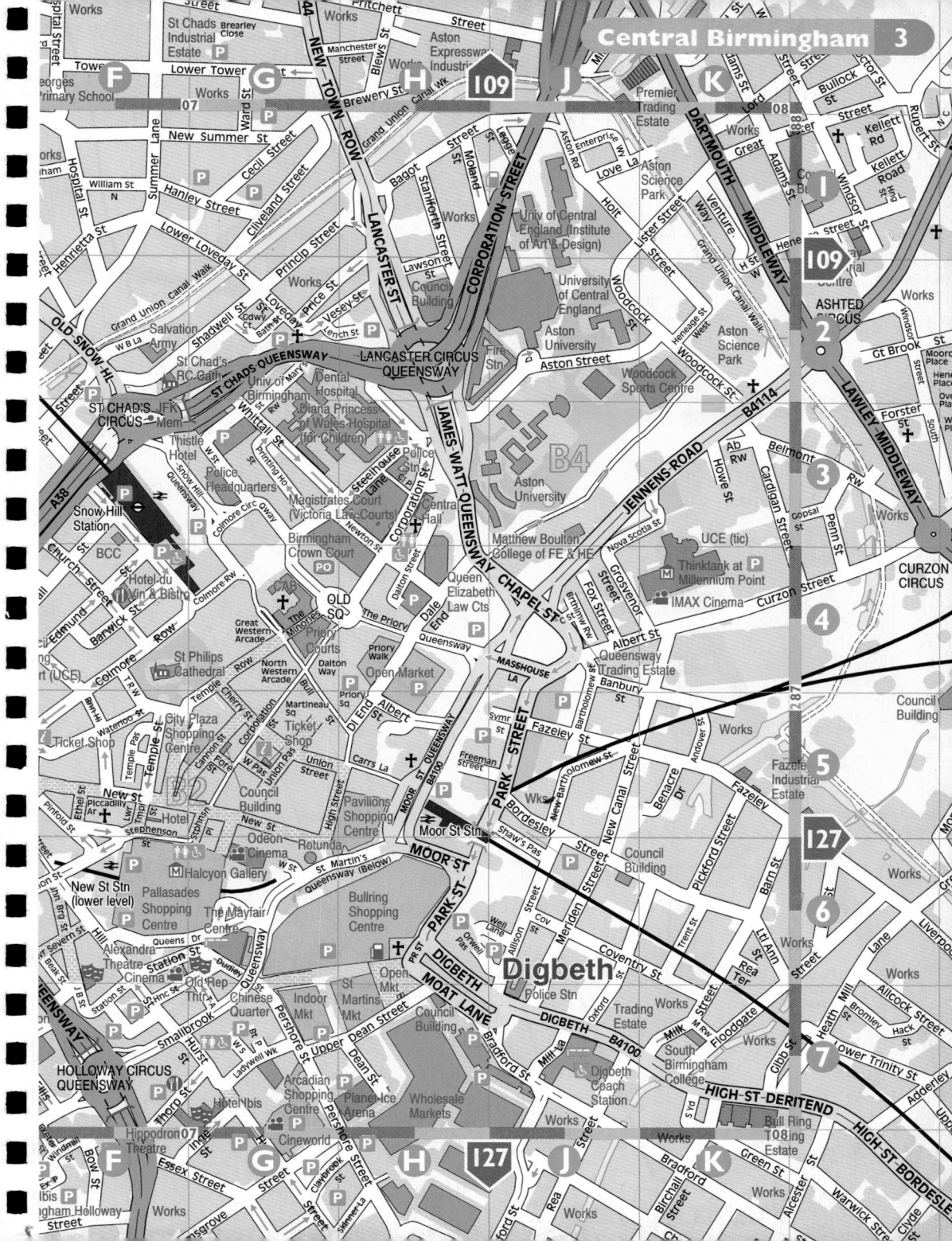

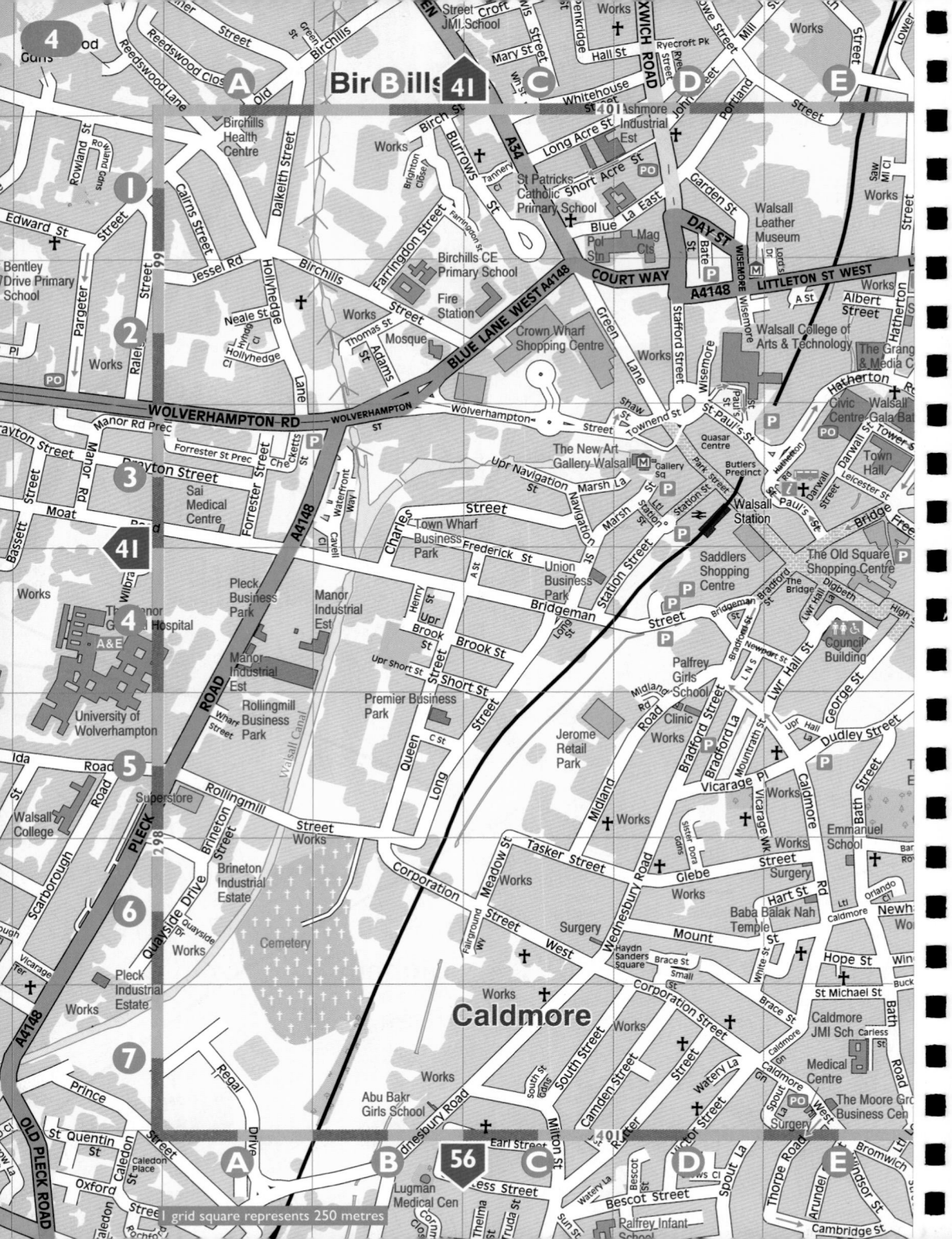

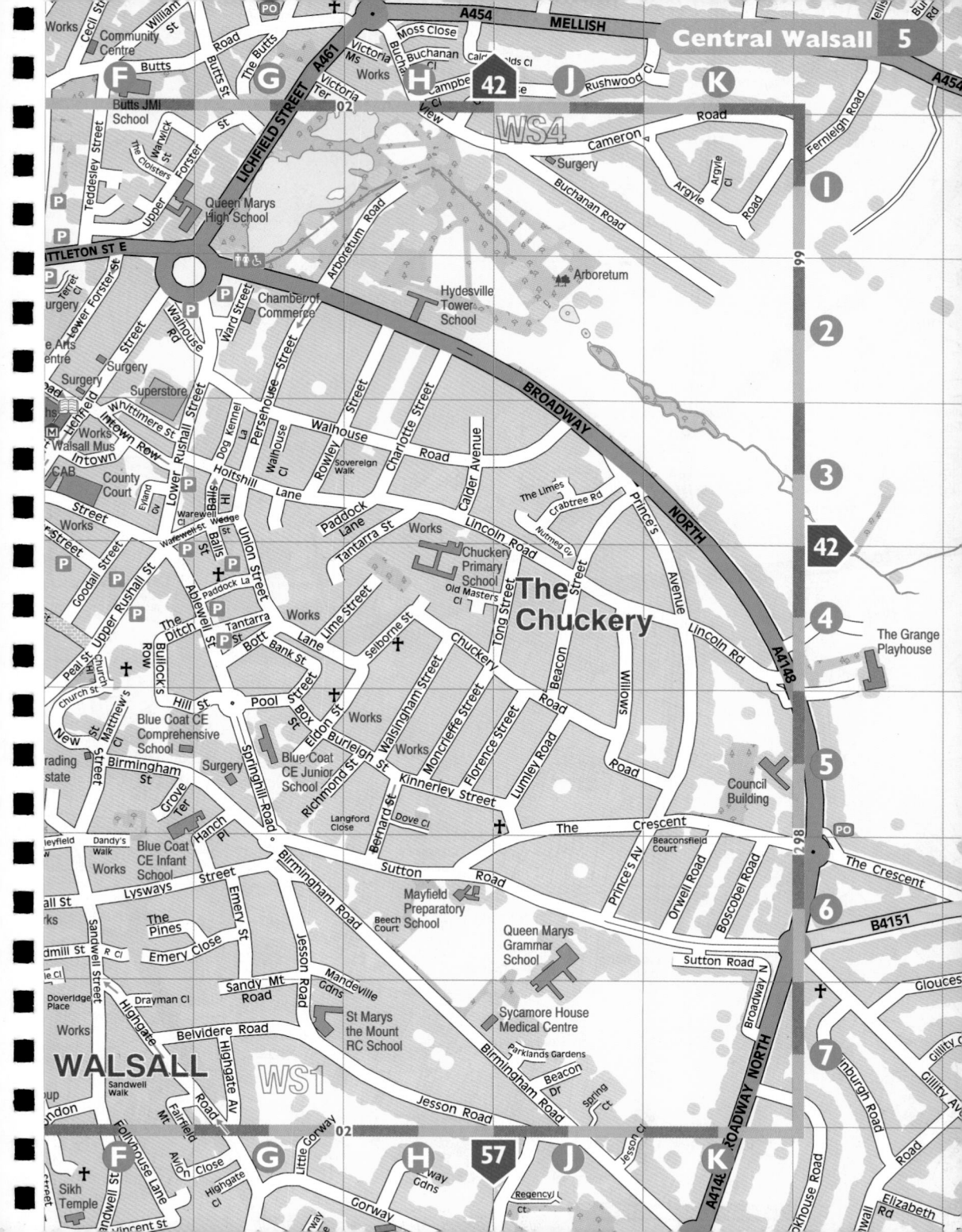

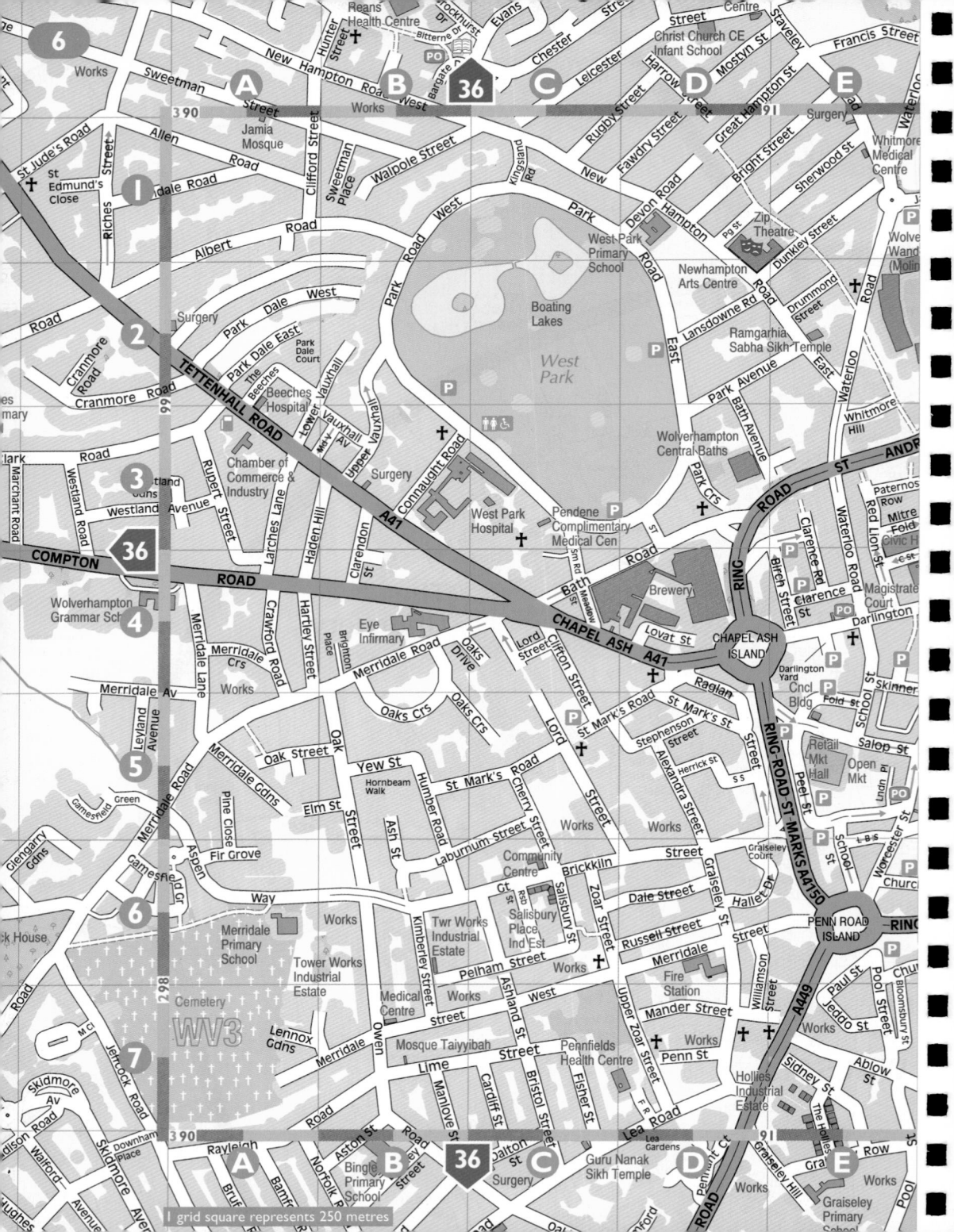

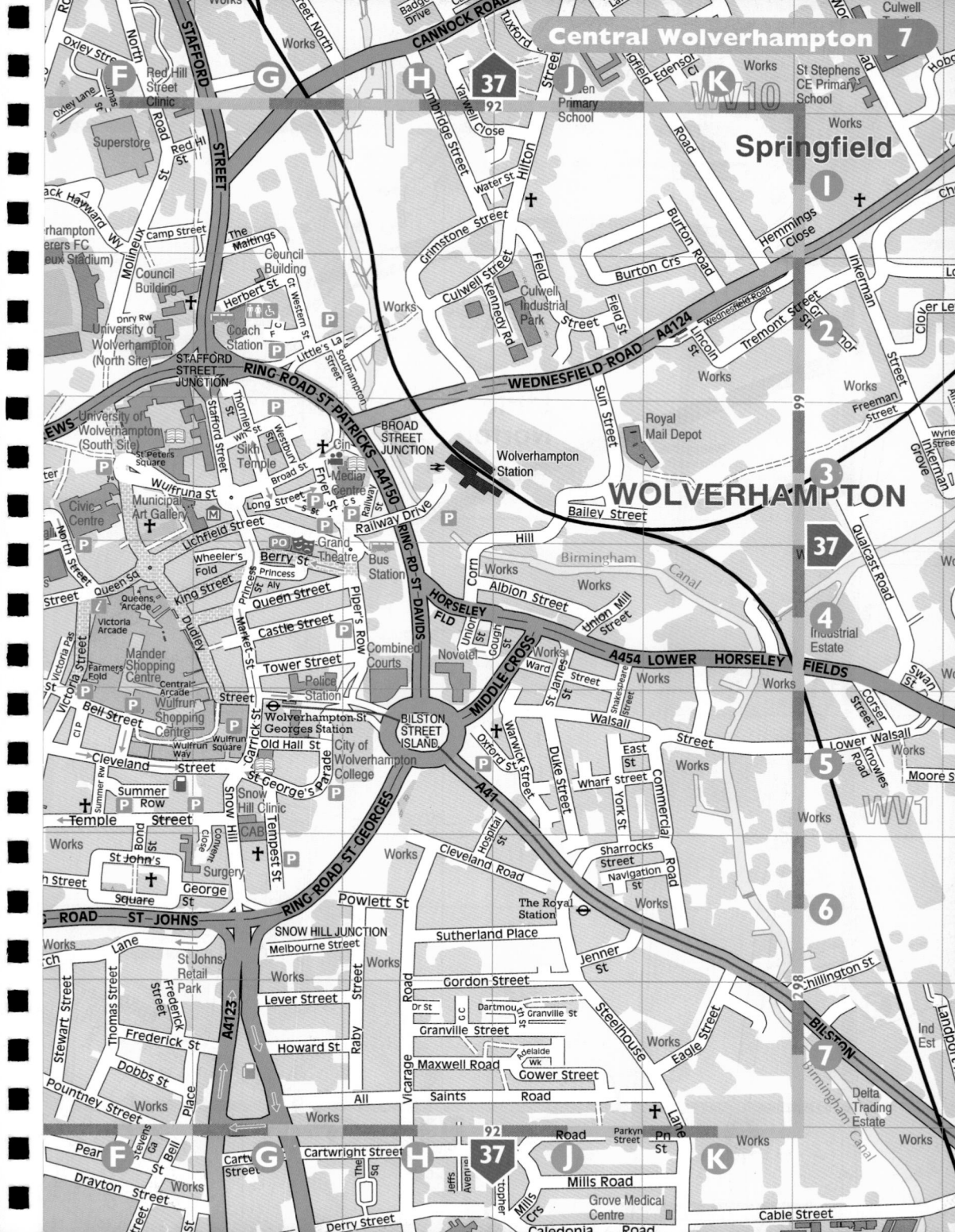

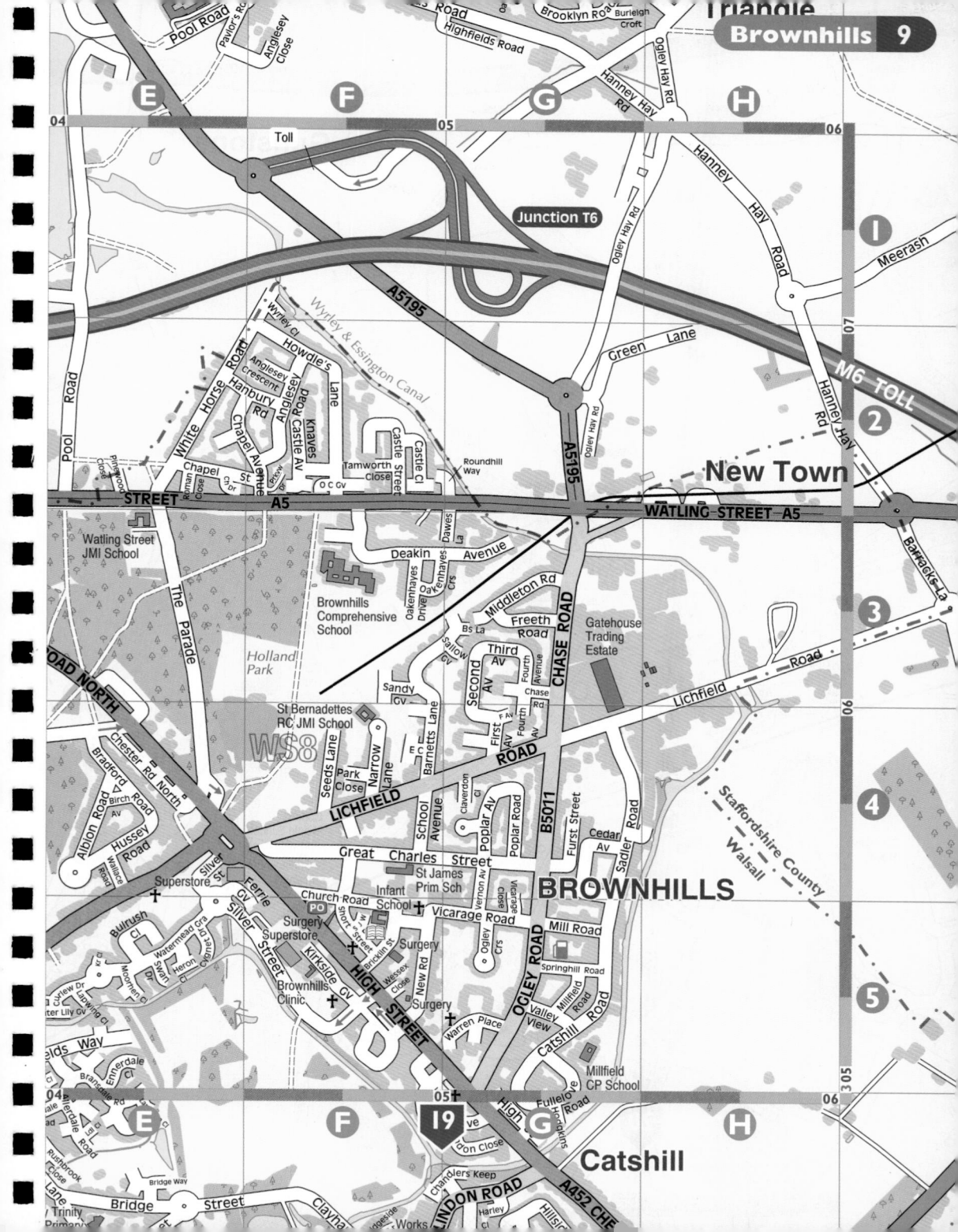

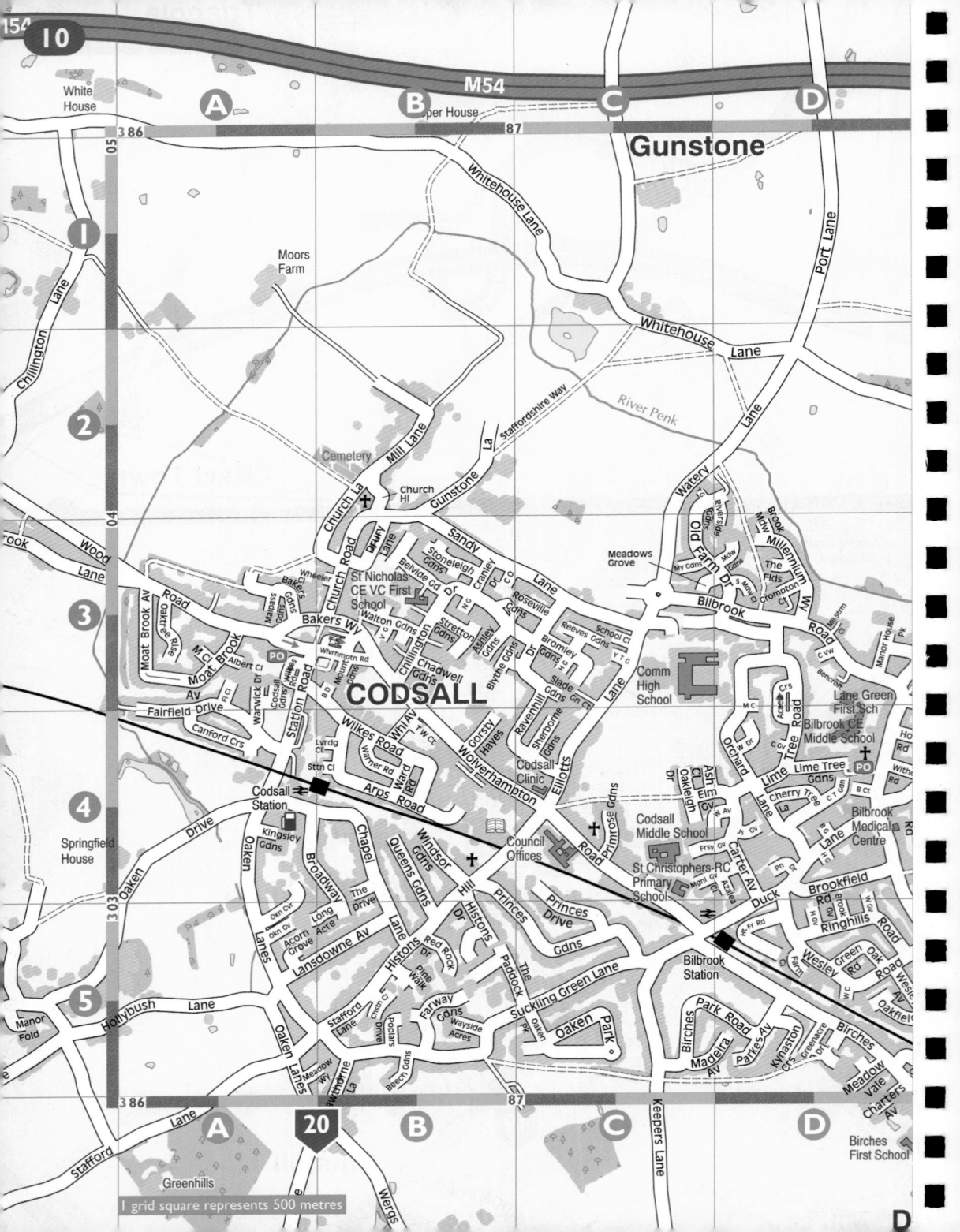

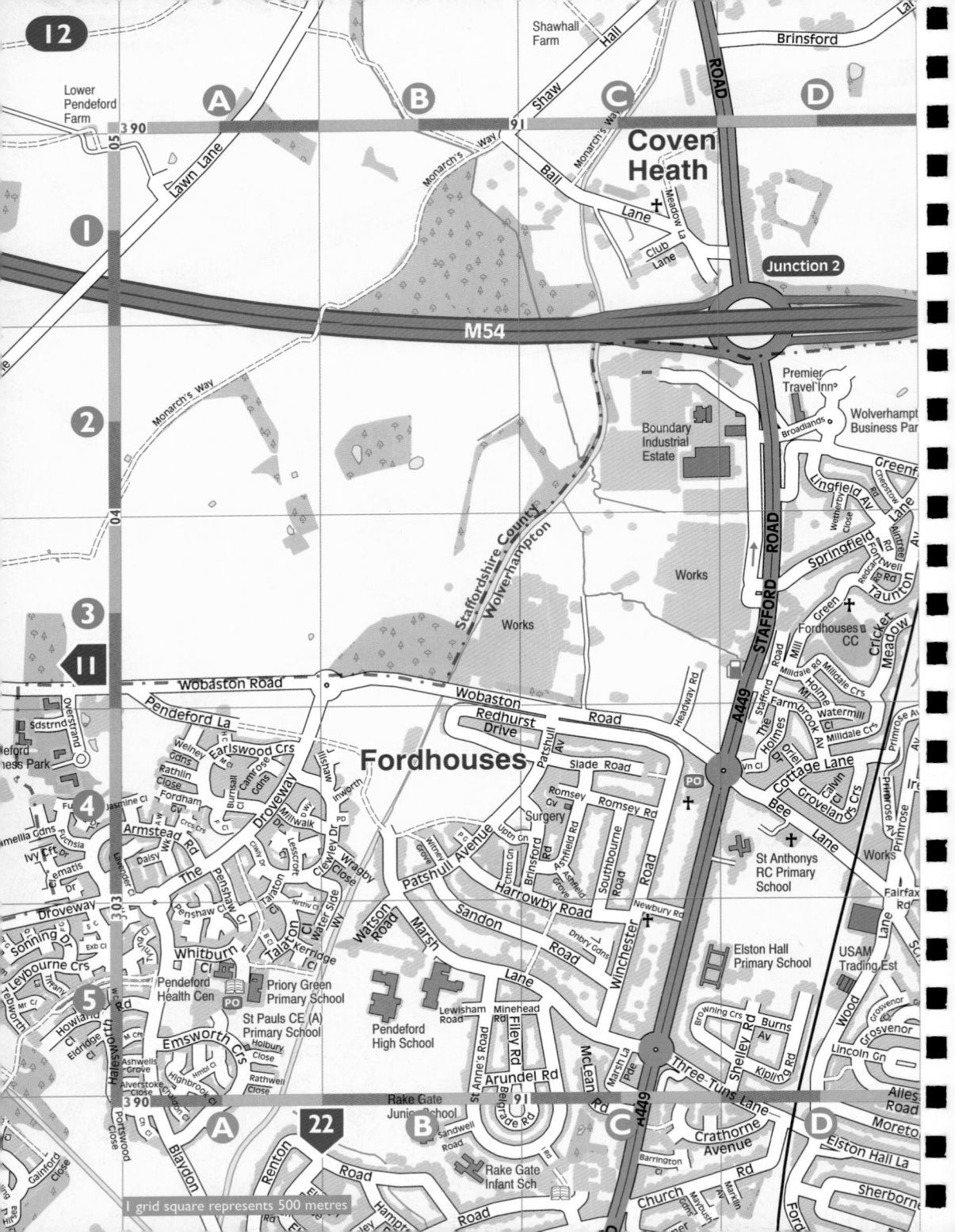

12

Lower
Pendeford
Farm

Shawhall
Farm

Brinsford

A ₀₅ 3 90 **B** 91 **C** **D**

Shaw

Ball

Monarch's Way

Coven
Heath

Meadow La

Lawn Lane

Club
Lane

Junction 2

I

M54

Premier
Travel Inn

2 Monarch's Way

Boundary
Industrial
Estate

Broadlands

Wolverhampton
Business Park

Greenf

Lingfield Av

Wetherby

Chepstow
Close

Fortwell Rd

₀₄

Staffordshire County
Wolverhampton

Works

Springfield

Redcar

Taunton

3

Works

Green
Fordhouses
CC

Cricket

Meadow

II

Wobaston Road

Mill

Mildale Rd

Milldale Crs

STAFFORD ROAD

A449

Pendeford La

Wobaston

Redhurst
Drive

Road

Headway Rd

The
Holmes

Watermill
Cl

Farmbrook Av

Milldale Crs

Overstrand

Sdstrnd

Fordhouses

Earlswood Crs

Welney
Gdns

Camrose
Gdns

Ilsham

Patshull
Av

Slade Road

vn Cl

Homle

Cottage Lane

eford
ess Park

Rathlin
Close

Burnsall

Inworth

Oriel

Calvin

Grovelan

Bee
Lane

Fordham
Gv

Crs Crs

PD

Romsey
Gv

Romsey Rd

PO

Grovean Crs

Iro

Primrose

4

Jasmine Cl

Droveway

Millwalk
Dr

Clewley Dr

Surgery

Uplyn Gn

Ashfield Rd

Ashfield
Grove

Southbourne
Road

Road

St Anthonys
RC Primary
School

Primrose

Armstead
Rd

Daisy

Lesscroft

Chwy Dr

Brinsford

Witney Rd

Patshull Avenue

Crntln Gn

Dnbry Gdns

Newbury Rd

Works

Fairfax
Rd

Camelia Gdns

Ivy Cft

Fuchsia

ematis

Dr

The
Penshaw

Talaton
Cl

Water Side

Wragby
Cl

Harrowby Road

5

Droveway

₃₀₃

Penshaw
Cl

Nrthiv Cl

Watson
Road

Marsh

Sandon

Road

Elston Hall
Primary
School

USAM
Trading Est

Sonning Dr

Exp Cl

Kerridge
Cl

Road

Lane

Newbury Rd

Browning Crs

Grosvenor

Leybourne Crs

Whitburn
Cl

Pendeford
Health Cen

PO

Priory Green
Primary School

Lewisham
Road

Minehead
Rd

Shelley Rd

Burns
Av

Kipling Rd

Wood

Grosvenor

Howland
Cl

Eldridge

Emsworth Crs

St Pauls CE (A)
Primary School

Holbury
Close

Pendeford
High School

Filey Rd

Lincoln Gn

Tebwood

Mr Cl

Falelworth

A449

W Cft

Ashwells
Grove

Rathwell
Close

St Anne's Road

Arundel Rd

McLean Rd

Three Tuns Lane

Alles
Road

Highbrook

Hmbl D

₀₅ 3 90 91

Moreto

Alverstoke
Close

A **22** **B** **C** A449 **D**

Blaydon

Renton

Road

Rake Gate
Junior School

Belgrade Rd

Sandwell
Road

Marsh La
Pde

Crathorne
Avenue

Elston Hall La

Portswood
Close

Gainsford
Close

Barrington
Rd

sherborne

Rake Gate
Infant Sch

Church

Hampt

Road

1 grid square represents 500 metres

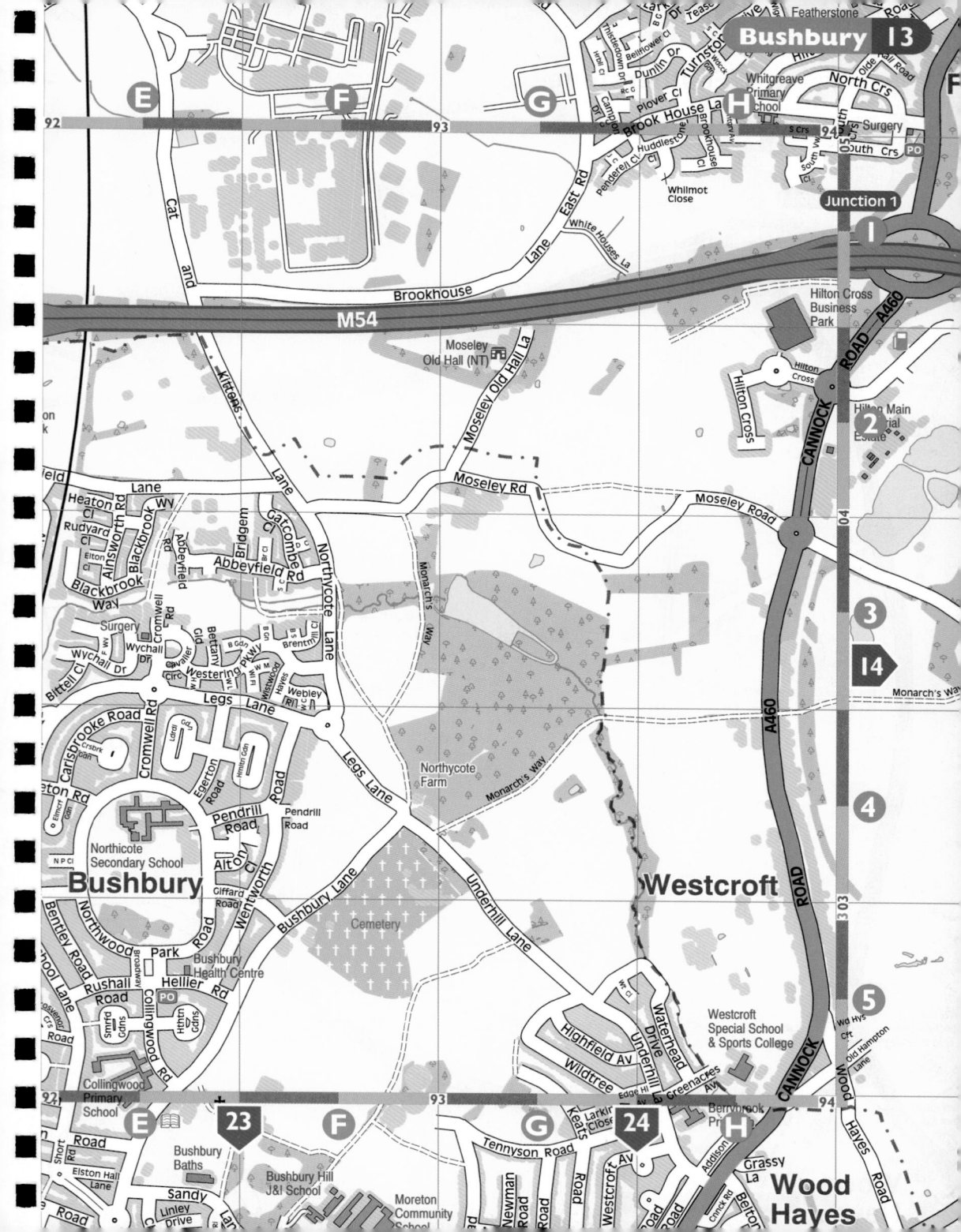

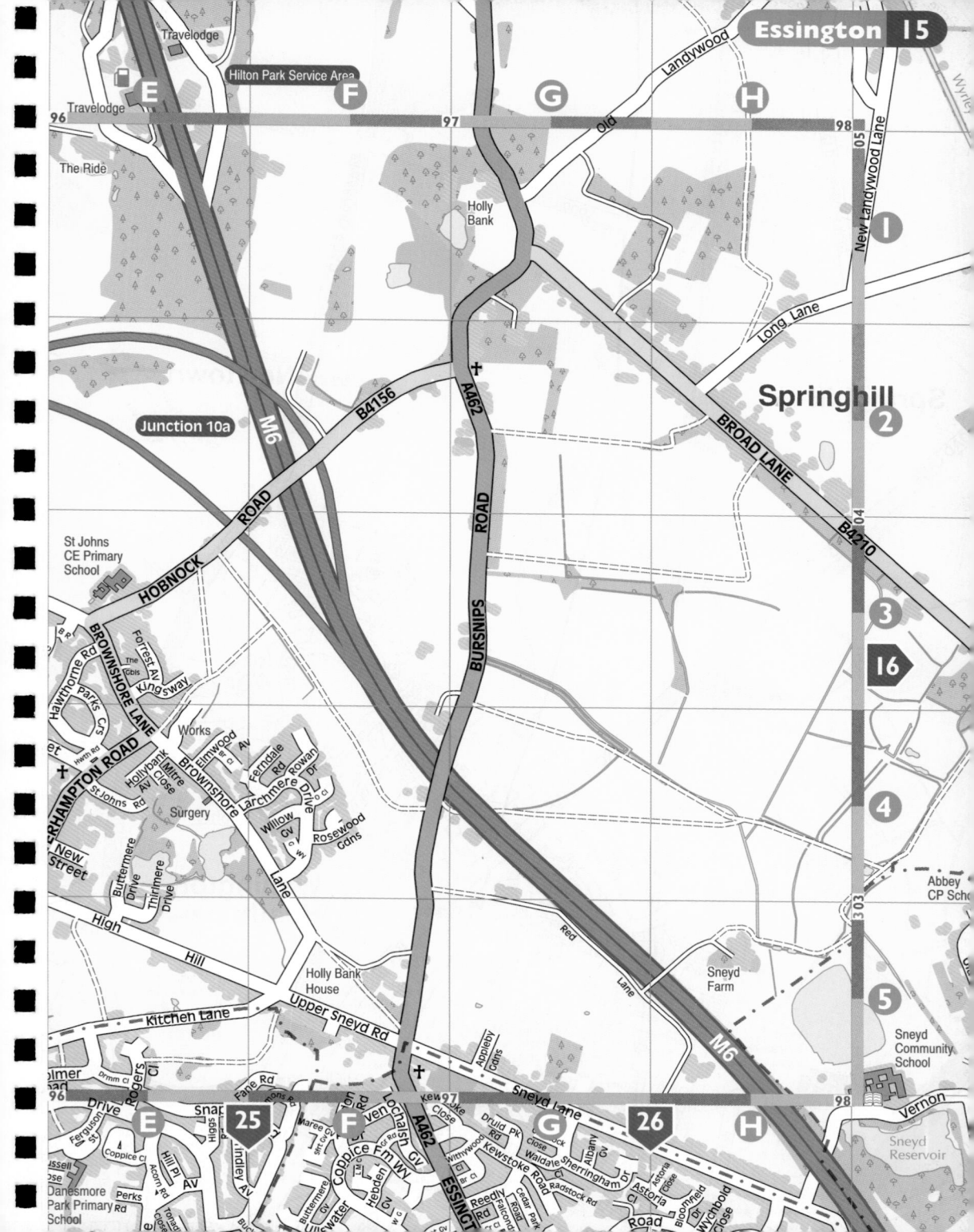

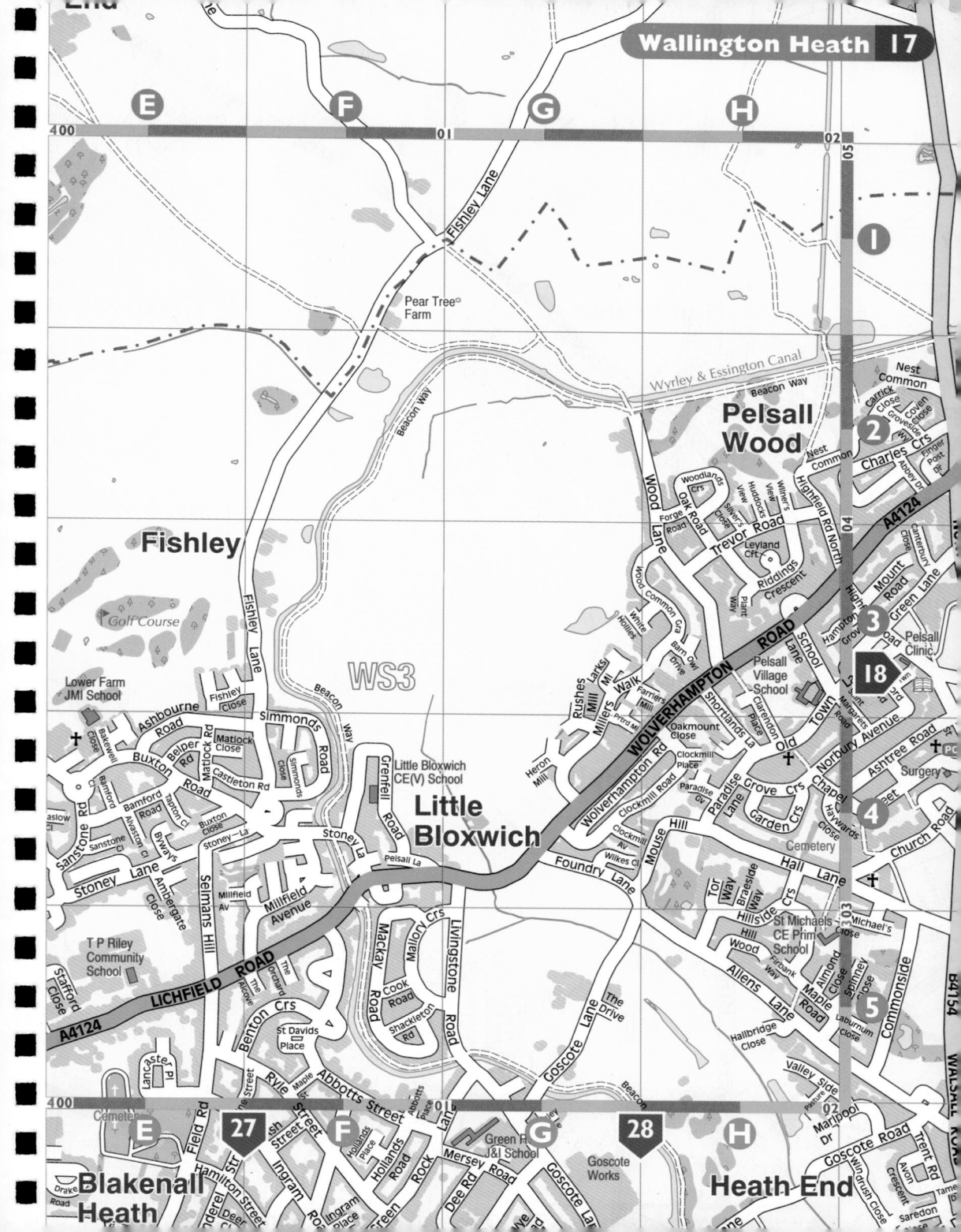

E   F   G   H

400   01   02   05

I

Fishley Lane

Pear Tree Farm

Wyrley & Essington Canal

Beacon Way

Pelsall Wood

Nest Common

Carrick Close
Coven Close
Grovesde

2

Charles Crs

Finger Post Dr

Abbey Dr

Fishley

Wood Lane

Oak Road

Woodlands Crs

Witter's View
Hudocks View
Silver's Way
Riddings Crescent

Trevor Road

Leyland Cft

Plant Way

Highfield Rd North

A4124

Mount Road

Centenary Close

Canterbury Close

Golf Course

Wood Common Gra

White Hollies

Hollies Mil
Larks

Rushes

Mill Walk

Barn Owl Drive

Farrier Mil

Petro Mi

Highmill Grove

Hampton Lane

School Lane

3

Pelsall Clinic.

Green Lane

WS3

Little Bloxwich

Fishley Lane

Beacon Way

Simmonds Road

Fishley Close

Grenfell Road

Little Bloxwich CE(V) School

Heron Mill

WOLVERHAMPTON ROAD

Pelsall Village School

Shortlands Lane

Clarendon

Old TOWN

Margaret's

18

Norbury Avenue

Ashtree Road

PO

Surgery

Lower Farm JMI School

Ashbourne Road

Belper Rd

Matlock Close

Castleton Rd

Matlock Rd

Simmonds Close

Oakmount Close

Clockmill Place

Paradise Lane

Chapel

Haywards Grove Crs

4

Church Road

Buxton Road

Bamford Road

Thorton Ct

Buxton Close

Stoney —La

Stoney La

Pelsall La

Clockmill Road

Clockmill

Wilkes Ct

Mouse Hill

Paradise Gv

Garden

Cemetery

Hall Lane

B4203

Michael's Close

Bamford

Sanstone Rd

Sanstone

Anston Cl

Byways

Millfield Av

Stoney Lane

Amergate Close

Selmans Hill

Millfield Avenue

Little Bloxwich

Foundry Lane

The Drive

Goscote Lane

Beacon

Tor Way

Braeside Way

Hillside

Hill Wood

Allens Lane

Almond Close

Maple Road

Spinney

Commonside

St Michaels CE Prim School

Firbank Way

5

T P Riley Community School

LICHFIELD ROAD

A4124

Stafford Close

The Orchard

The Arrow

Benton Crs

St Davids Place

Mackay Road

Cook Road

Mallory Crs

Shackleton Rd

Livingstone Road

Laburnum Close

Hallbridge Close

Valley Side

Pasture

Goscote Road

B4154

Trent Rd

Cemetery

Lancaster Pl

Field Rd

Str   Street

Ingram Road

Rock

Hollands Place

Mersey Road

Dee Rd

Green R J&I School

Goscote Lane

Goscote Works

Maripool Dr

Goscote Road

Windrush Close

Avon Crescent

Saredon

28

Heath End

27

E   F   G   H

400   01

Blakenall Heath

Drake Road

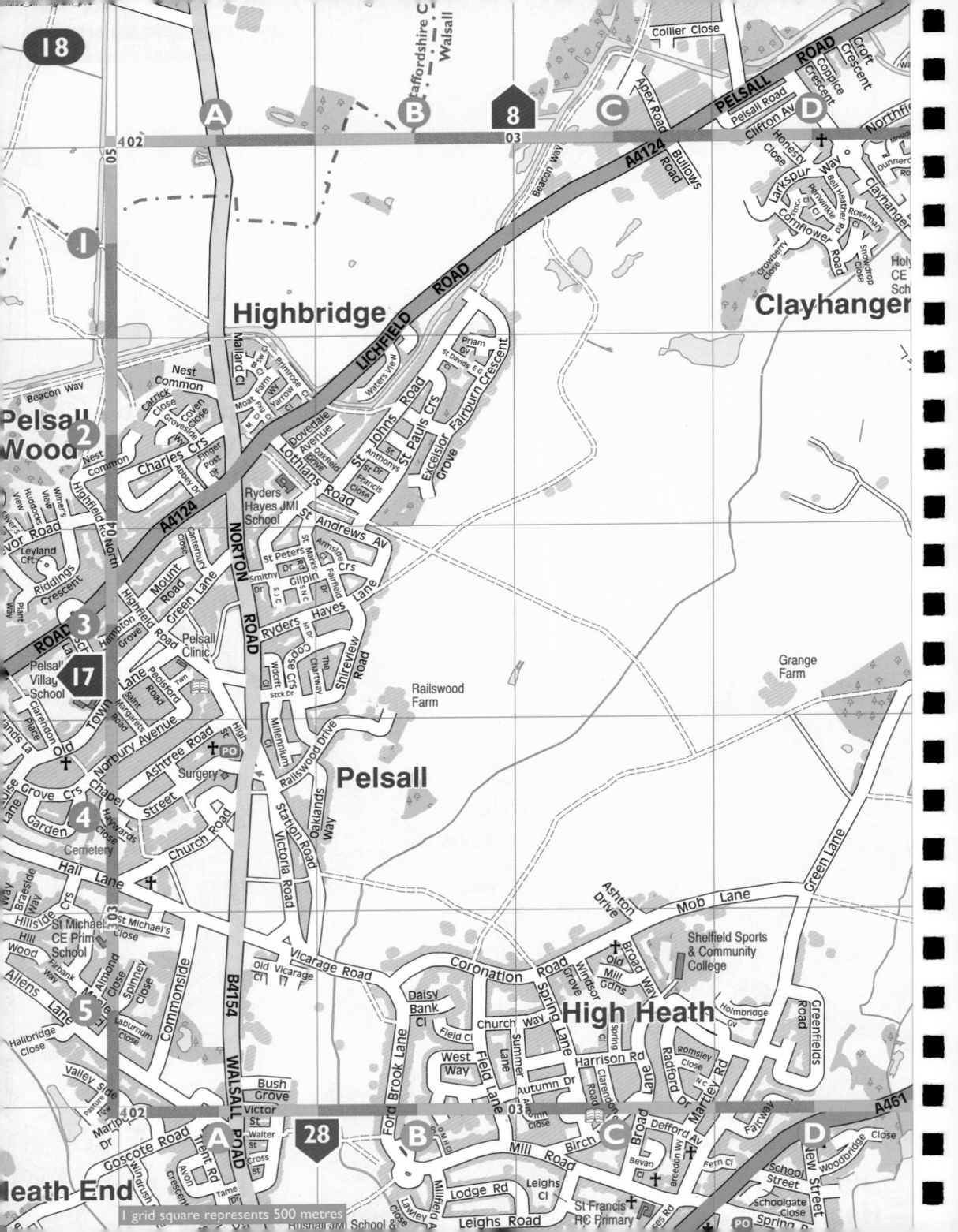

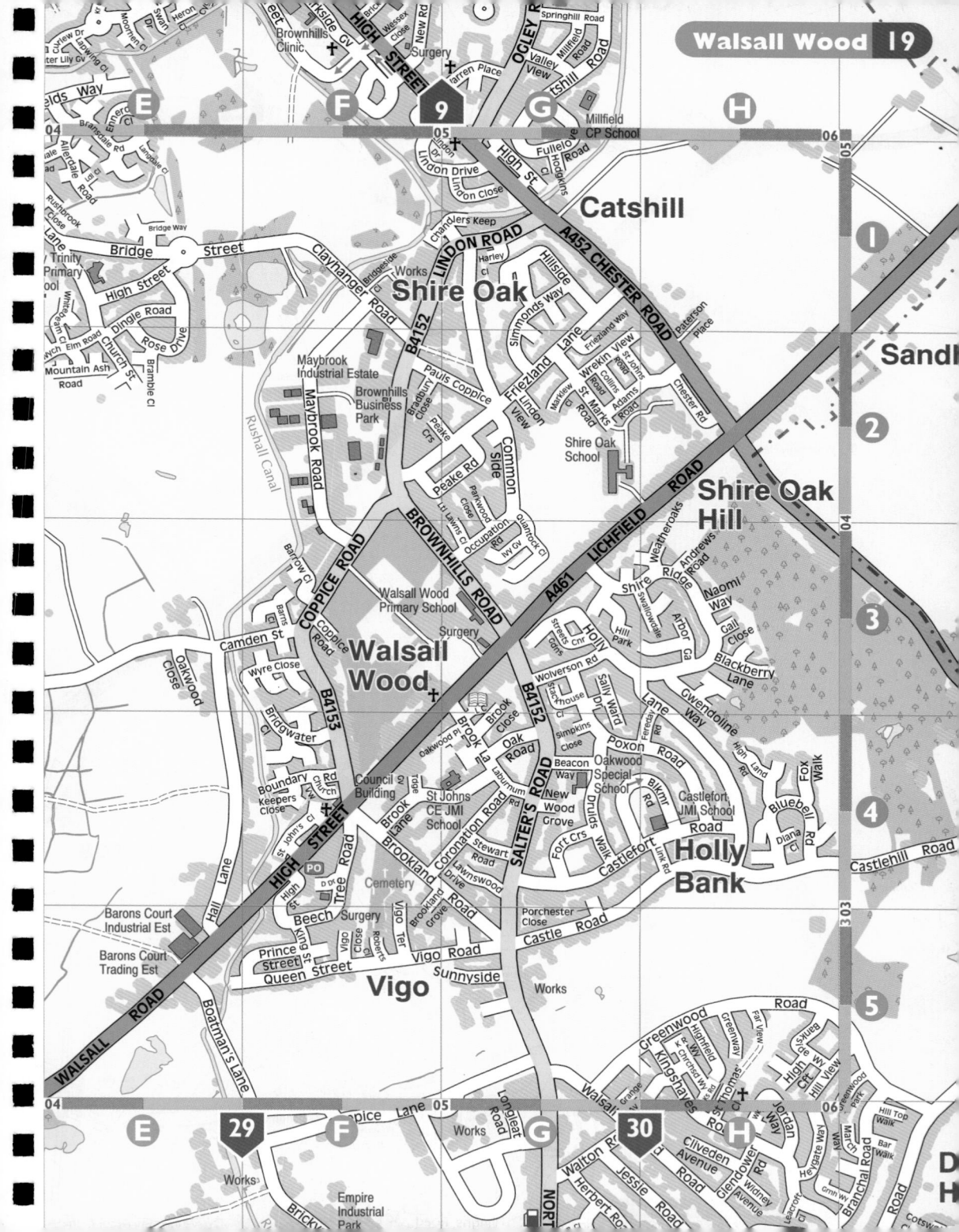

Catshill

Shire Oak

Shire Oak Hill

Walsall Wood

Holly Bank

Vigo

Sandl

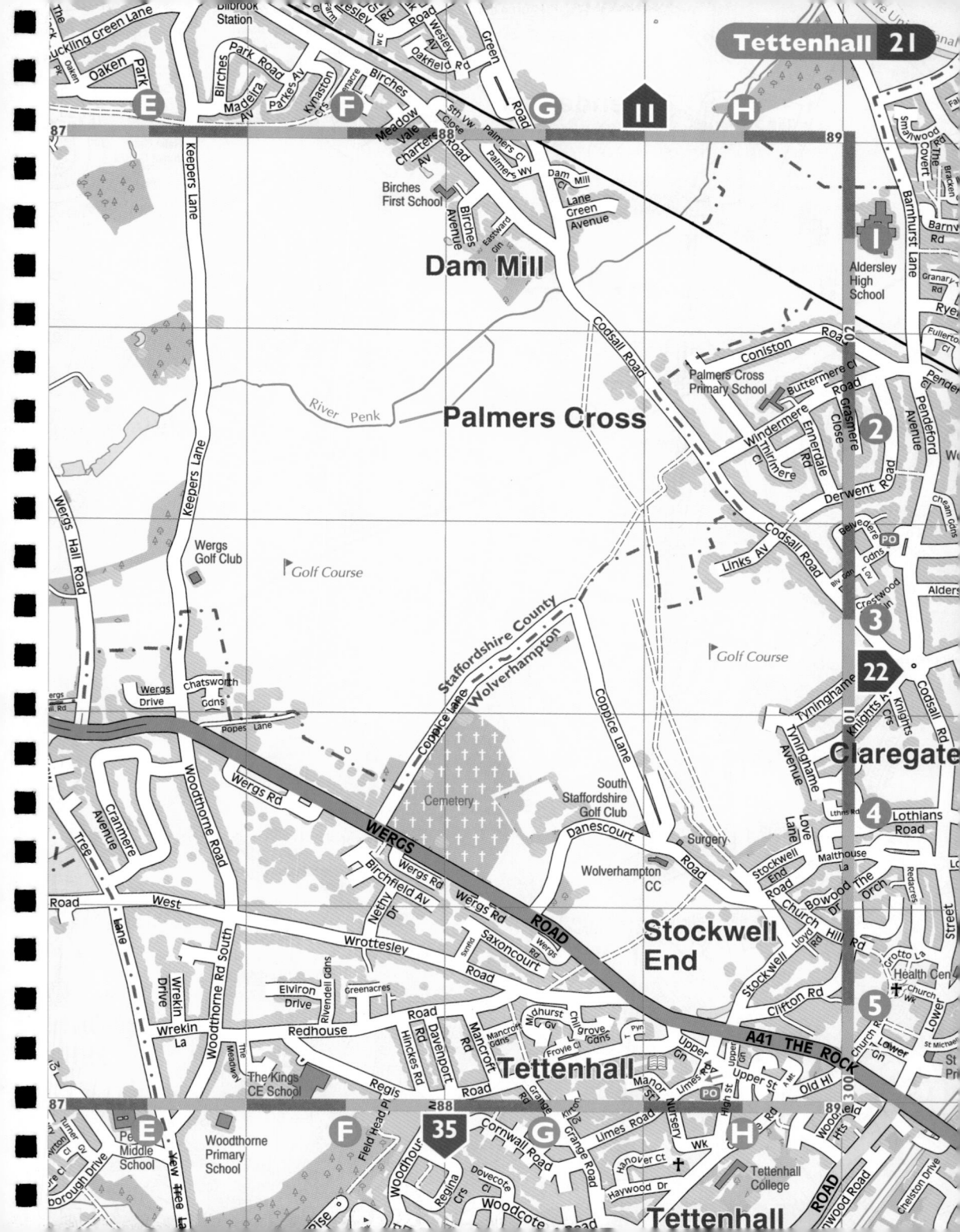

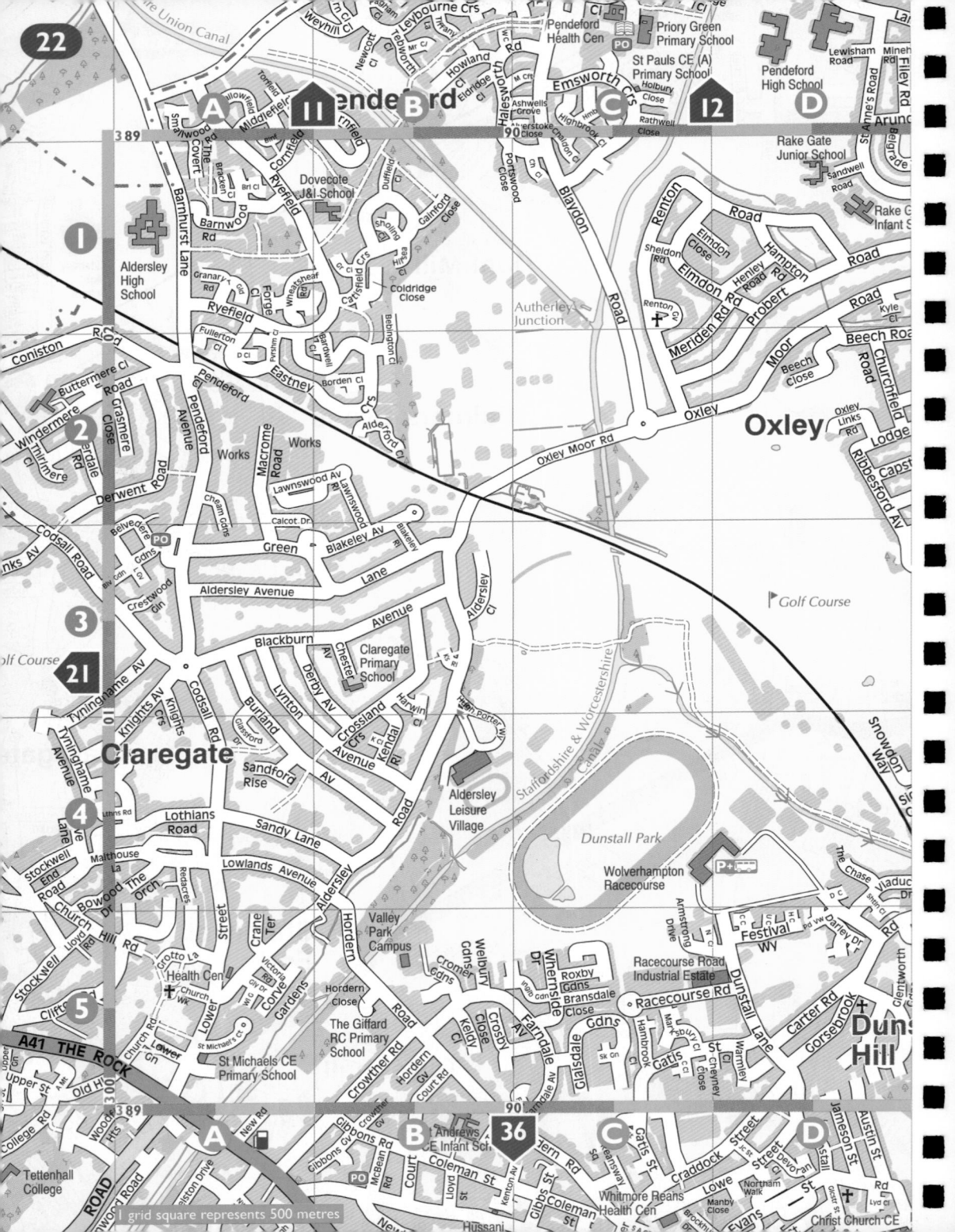

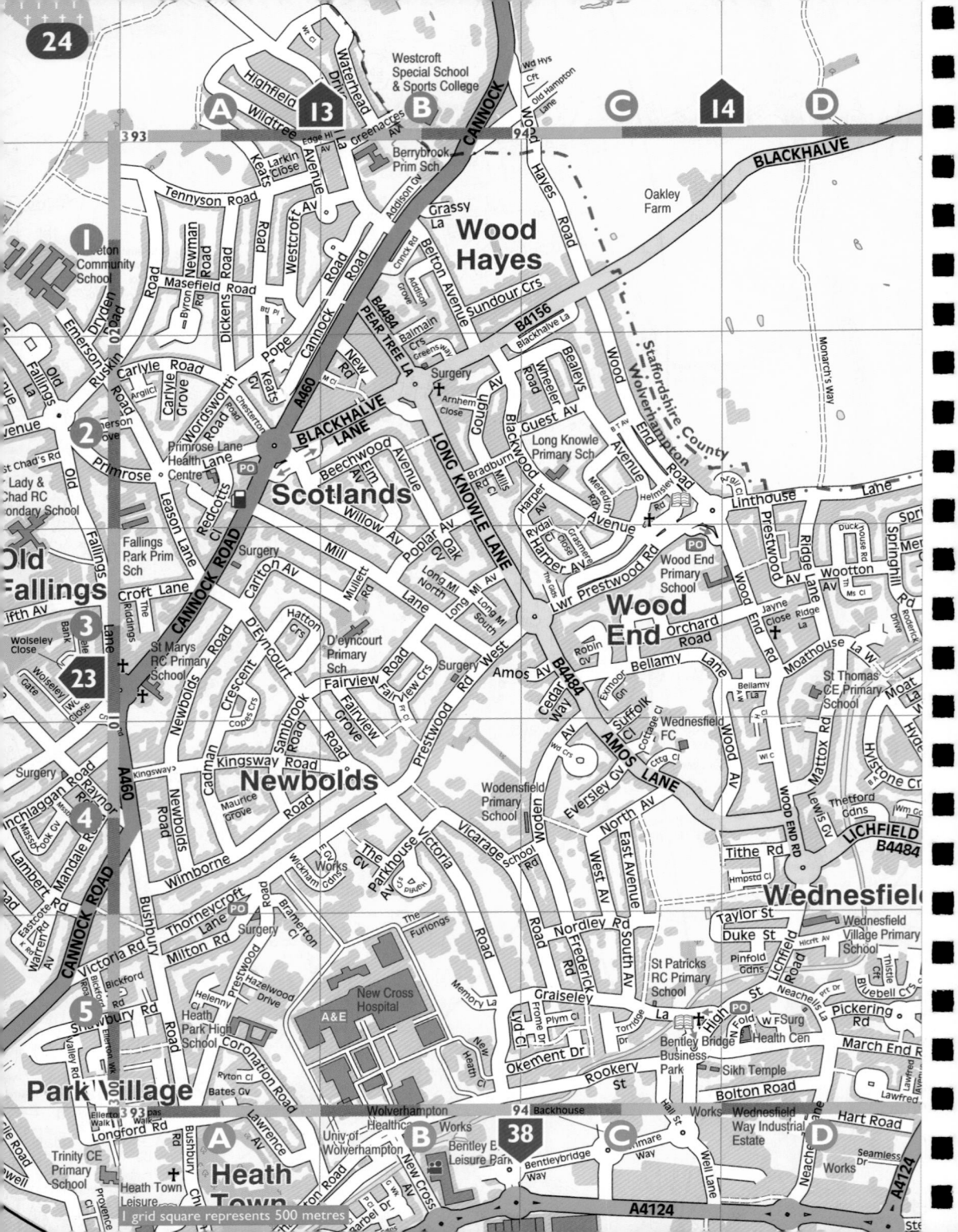

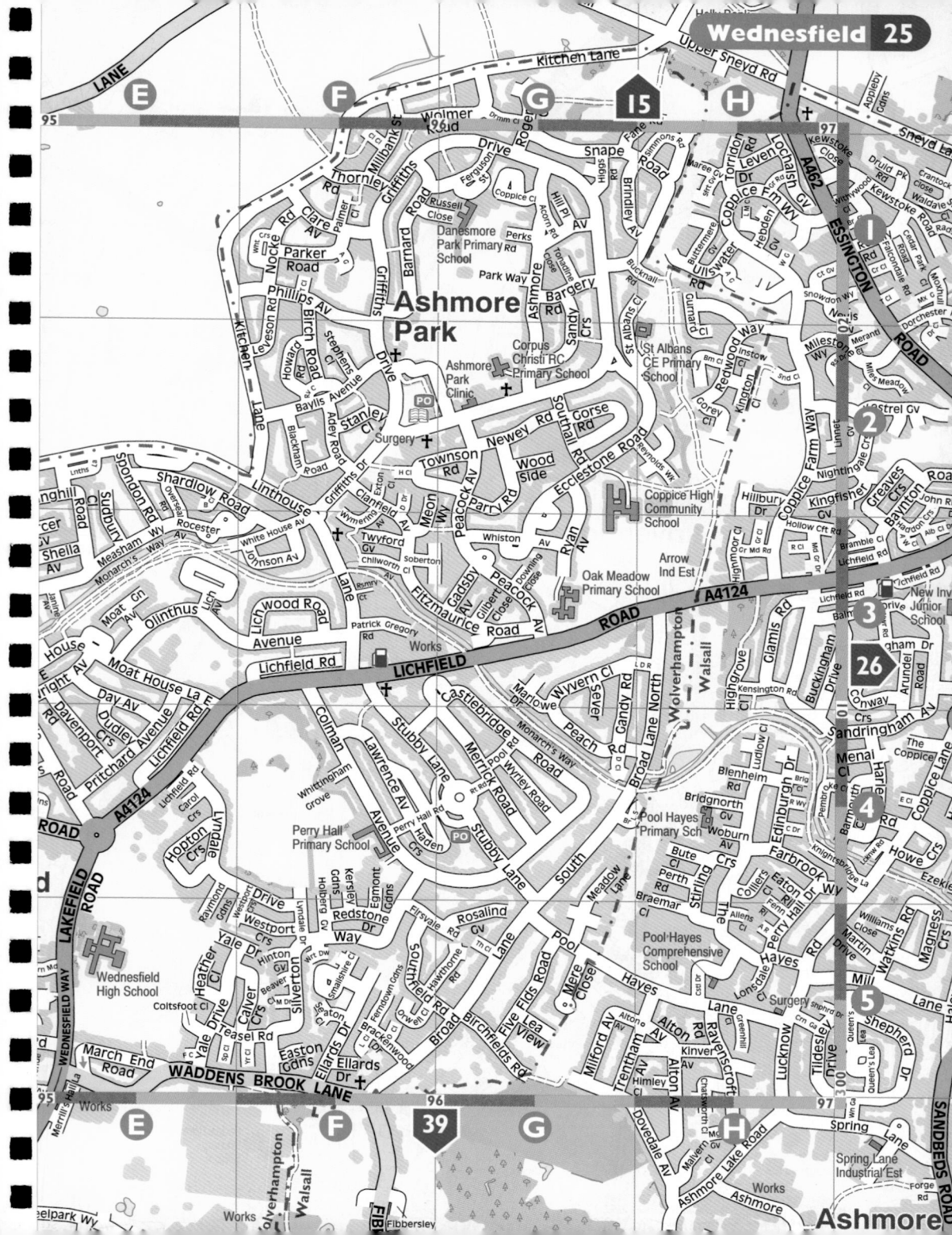

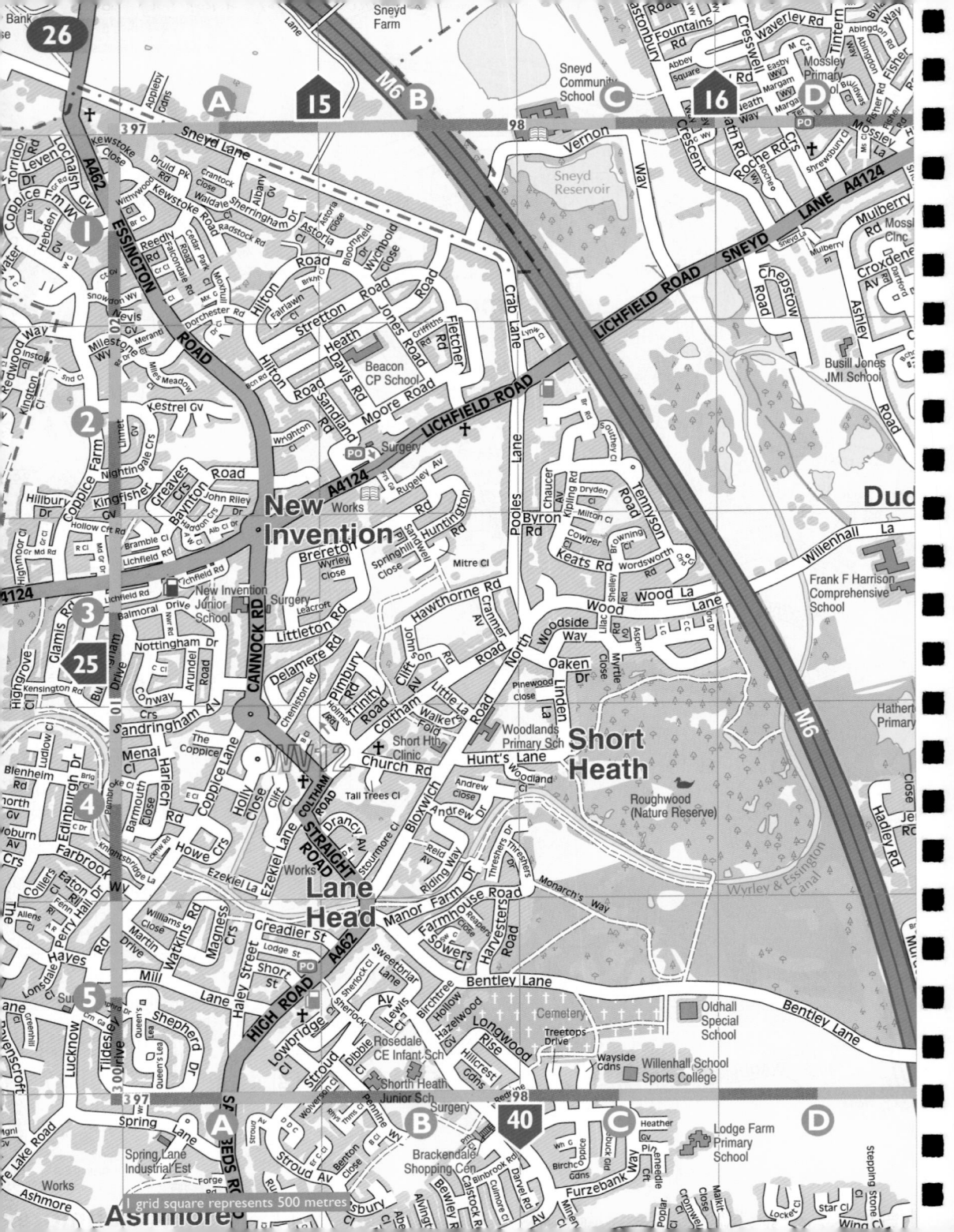

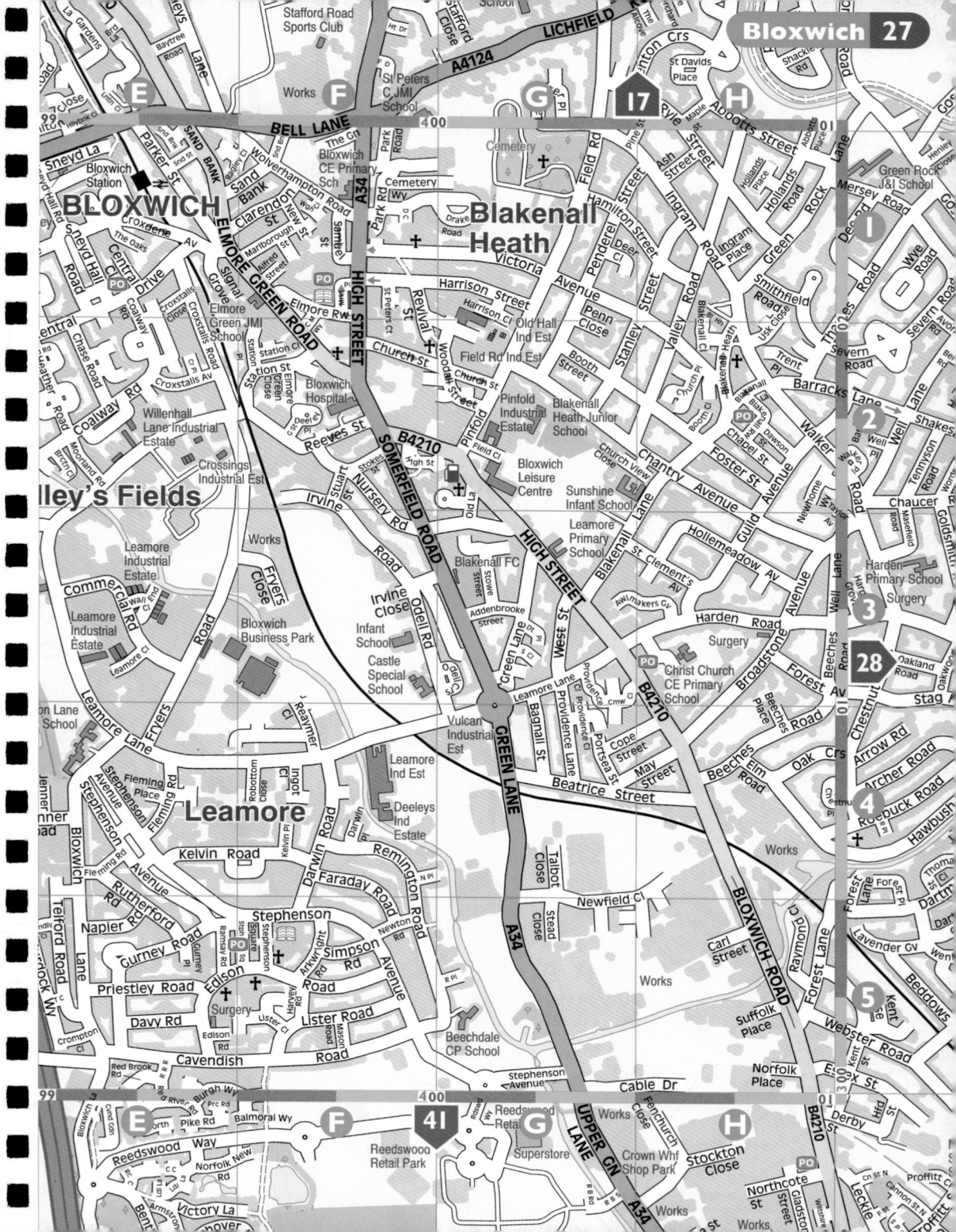

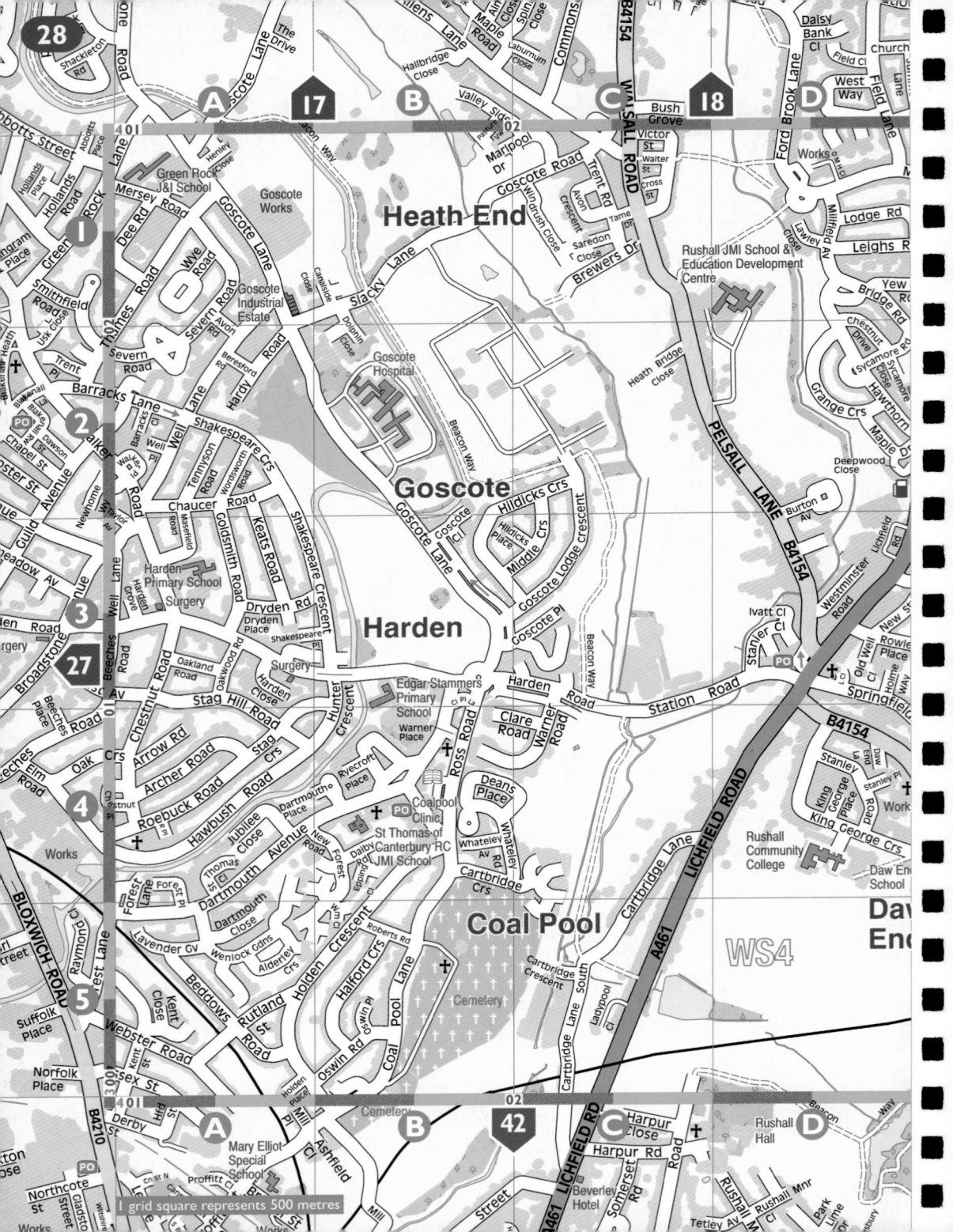

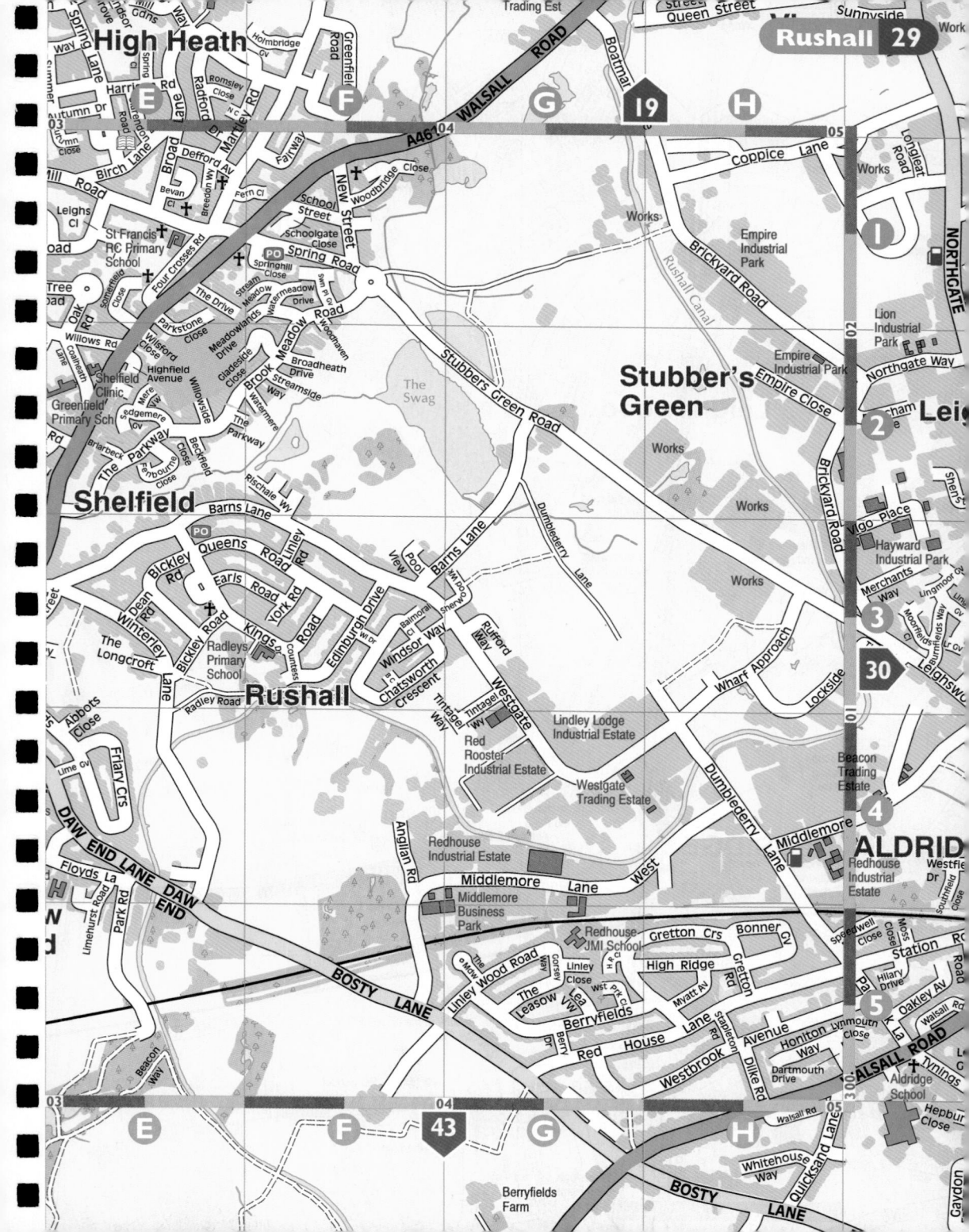

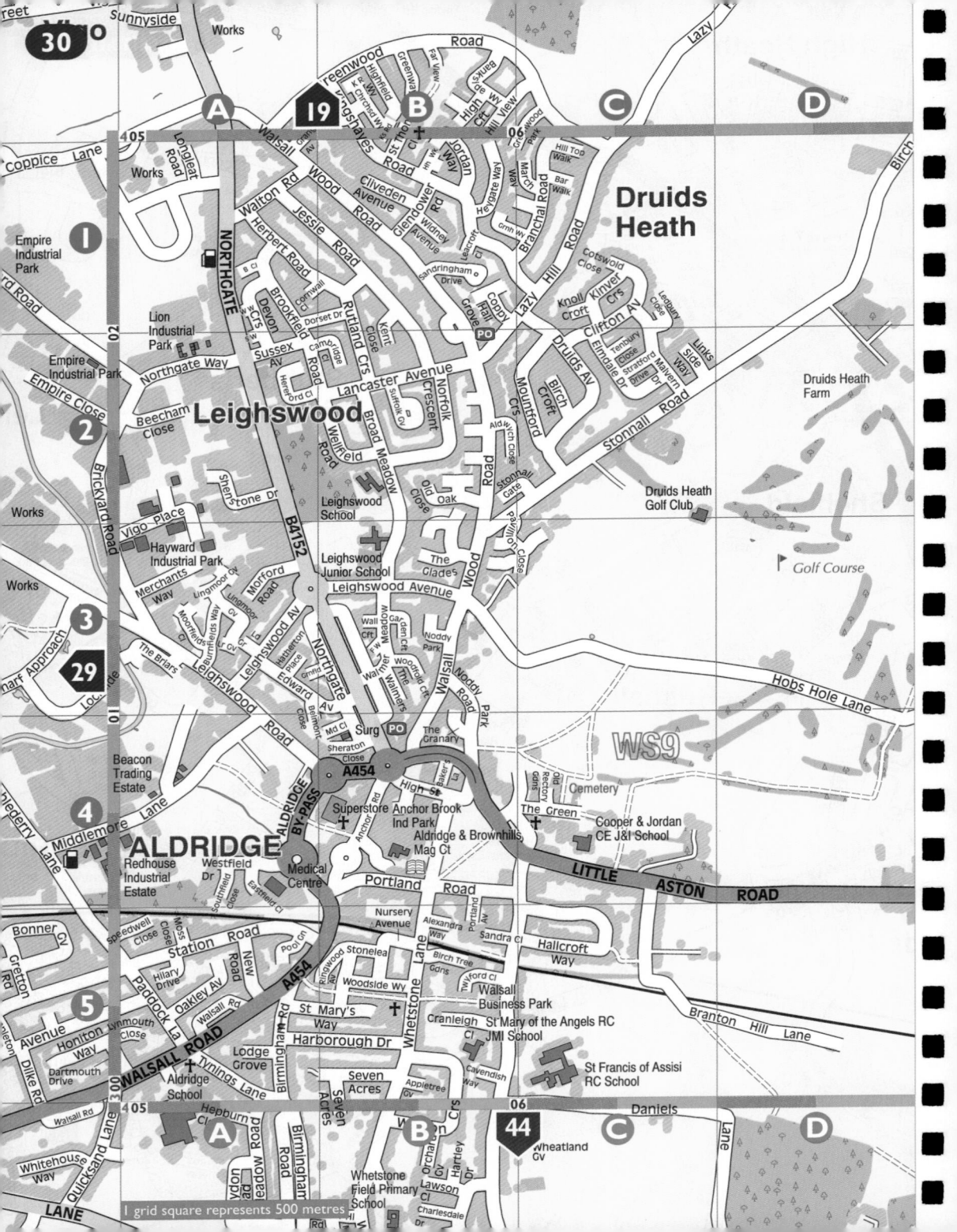

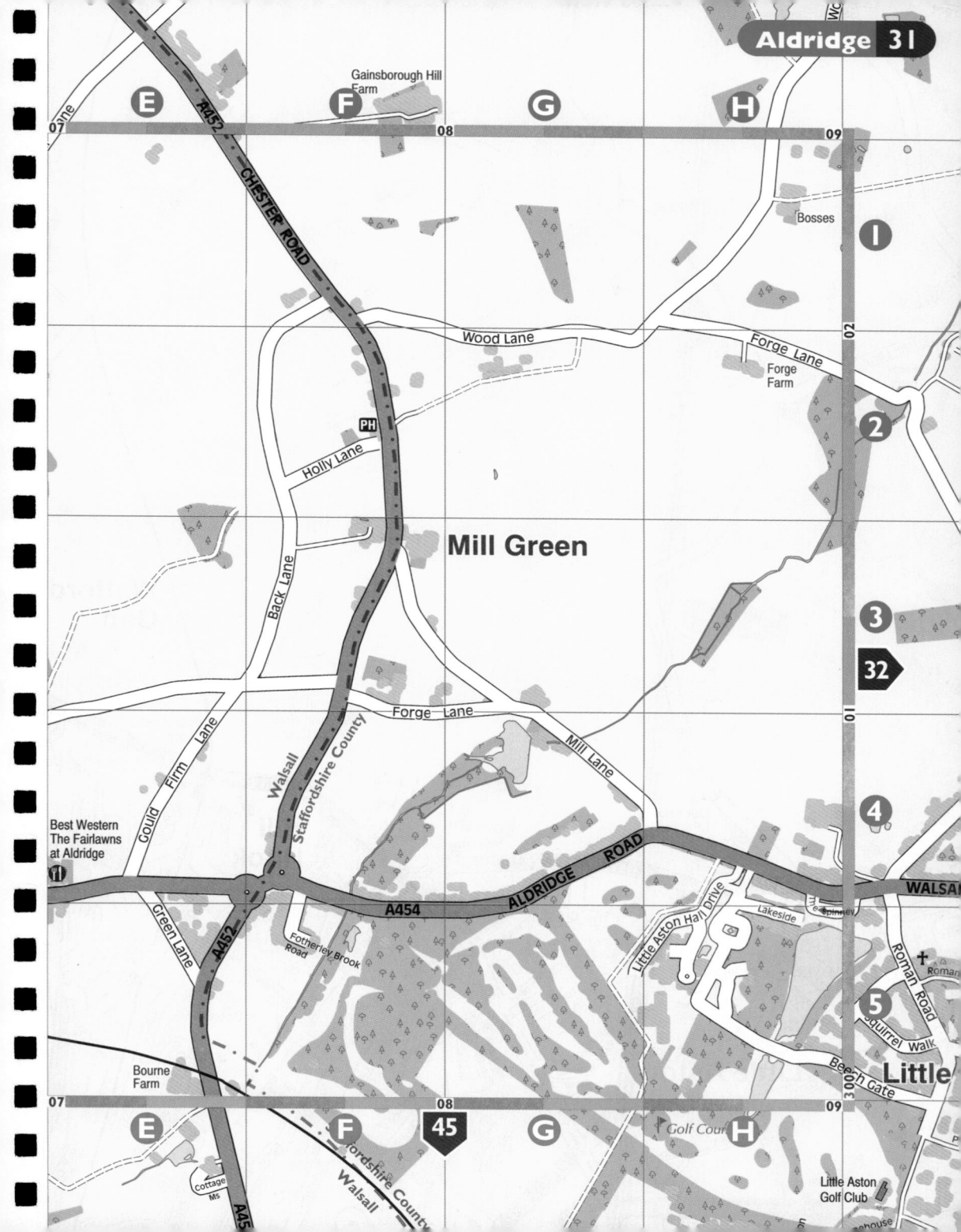

Gainsborough Hill Farm

E   A452   F   G   H

07   08   09

CHESTER ROAD

Bosses

I

Wood Lane

Forge Lane

02

Forge Farm

PH

2

Holly Lane

Mill Green

Back Lane

3

32

Forge Lane

Mill Lane

01

Gould Firm Lane

Walsall

Staffordshire County

4

Best Western
The Fairlawns
at Aldridge

Little Aston Hall Drive   Lakeside   The Spinney

WALSA

Green Lane

A452

Fotherley Brook
Road

A454   ALDRIDGE   ROAD

Roman Road   Roman

300th

5   Squirrel Walk

Beech gate

Little

Bourne
Farm

07   08   09

E   F   45   G   Golf Cour   H

Cottage
Ms

Walsall

Staffordshire County

A45

Little Aston
Golf Club

32

Ⓐ   Ⓑ   Ⓒ   Ⓓ

409

① Bosses

Forge Lane
Forge
Farm

② 02

Golf Course

③ 03

31

Watford
Gap

Aston Wood
Golf Club

Blake Street
Station

Back Lane

Footherley Lane

Moor La

A4026
B Cft

Tennyson
AV

Shelley Drive

Beighton
Close

Saxton Drive

Vaughan
Close

Kts Cl

STREET

④ Little Aston
CP School

Council
Building

Little Aston
Lane

Hill
Hook

HILL

HOOK

ROAD

Netherstone CV

Cranmer

Bishops
Way

Bishops K & Cr

Becker Ct

Vernon Close

Bickley Av

Blackberry Lane

Clarence Road

St Georges
Ct

Four Oaks Saints
CC

Lyola
Cft

Lowercroft
Way

Regency Wy

Poplar Rise
Rosemary
Nook

LITTLE ASTON LANE

WALSALL ROAD

The Grove

⑤ Lakeside
Spinney

Roman Road

Roman Cr

Woodside
Drive

Squirrel Walk

Keepers Road

A454

Beechwood
Cft

Hornton
Close

Birch Drive

Loxton Close

Knighton
Road

Silver Birch
Coppice

Kesterton
Road

Harrison Road

Ensford
Close

Aylesford
Drive

Kensington
Dr

Sandhurst
Dr

Balmoral Road

Bdfd'rs gate Rd

Bridgate
Drive

Little Aston

Beech Gate

Longfield
Dr

Park
Drive

Selwyn
Wk

WALSALL ROA

Chartwell
Dr

Woodstock
Dr

46

Edge Hill Road

Dockswell Road

1 Rd

White Farm
Road

Blackberry

Harcrft

Weymouth
Dr

Kn
Bridge

Clarence

Chelsea

Wall Dr

Little Aston
Golf Club

Four Oaks
J&I School

Ⓐ   Ⓑ   Ⓒ   Ⓓ

409

1 grid square represents 500 metres

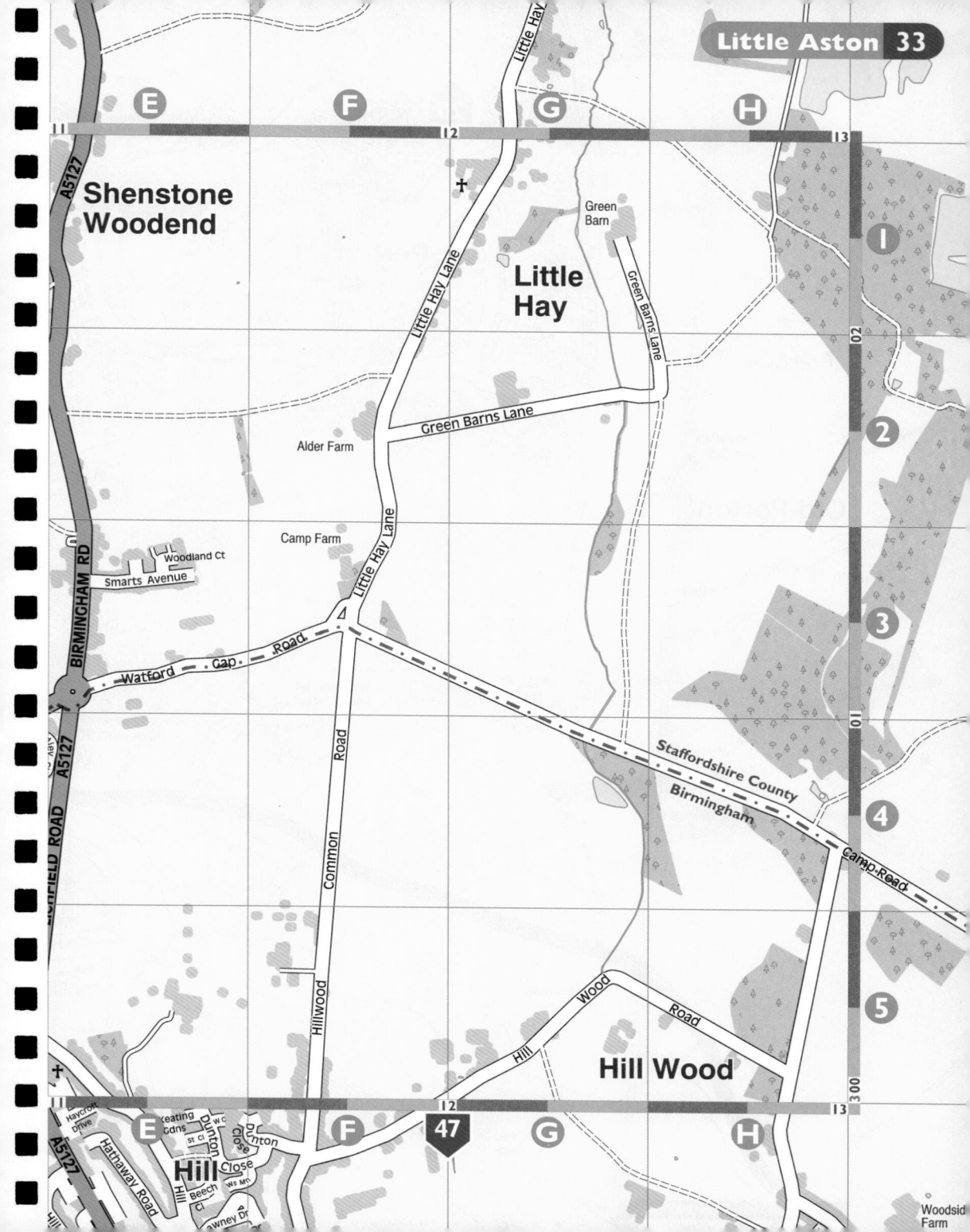

E   F   G   H

Shenstone
Woodend

Little Hay Lane

Green Barn

Little
Hay

Green Barns Lane

I

02

2

Alder Farm

Green Barns Lane

Camp Farm

Little Hay Lane

3

Woodland Ct

Smarts Avenue

BIRMINGHAM RD

01

Watford   Gap   Road

Staffordshire County

Birmingham

4

Common   Road

A5127

Camp Road

5

Hillwood

Wood   Road

Hill

Hill Wood

300

Haycroft Drive

Keating Gdns

Dunton Close

Dunton Close

E   F   47   G   H

A5127

Hathaway Road

Hill

Beech Cl

Ws Mw

Sawney Dr

Woodsid
Farm

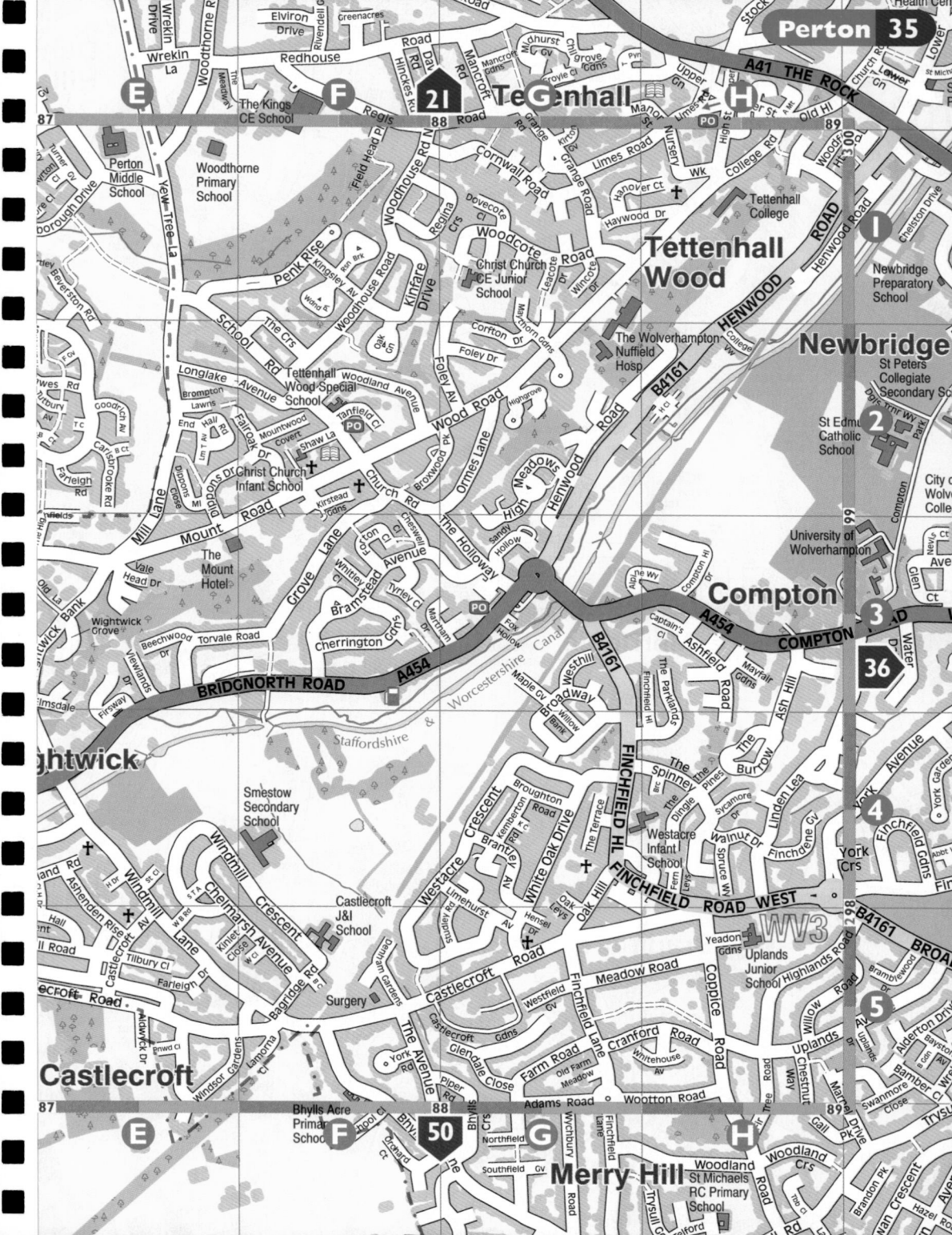

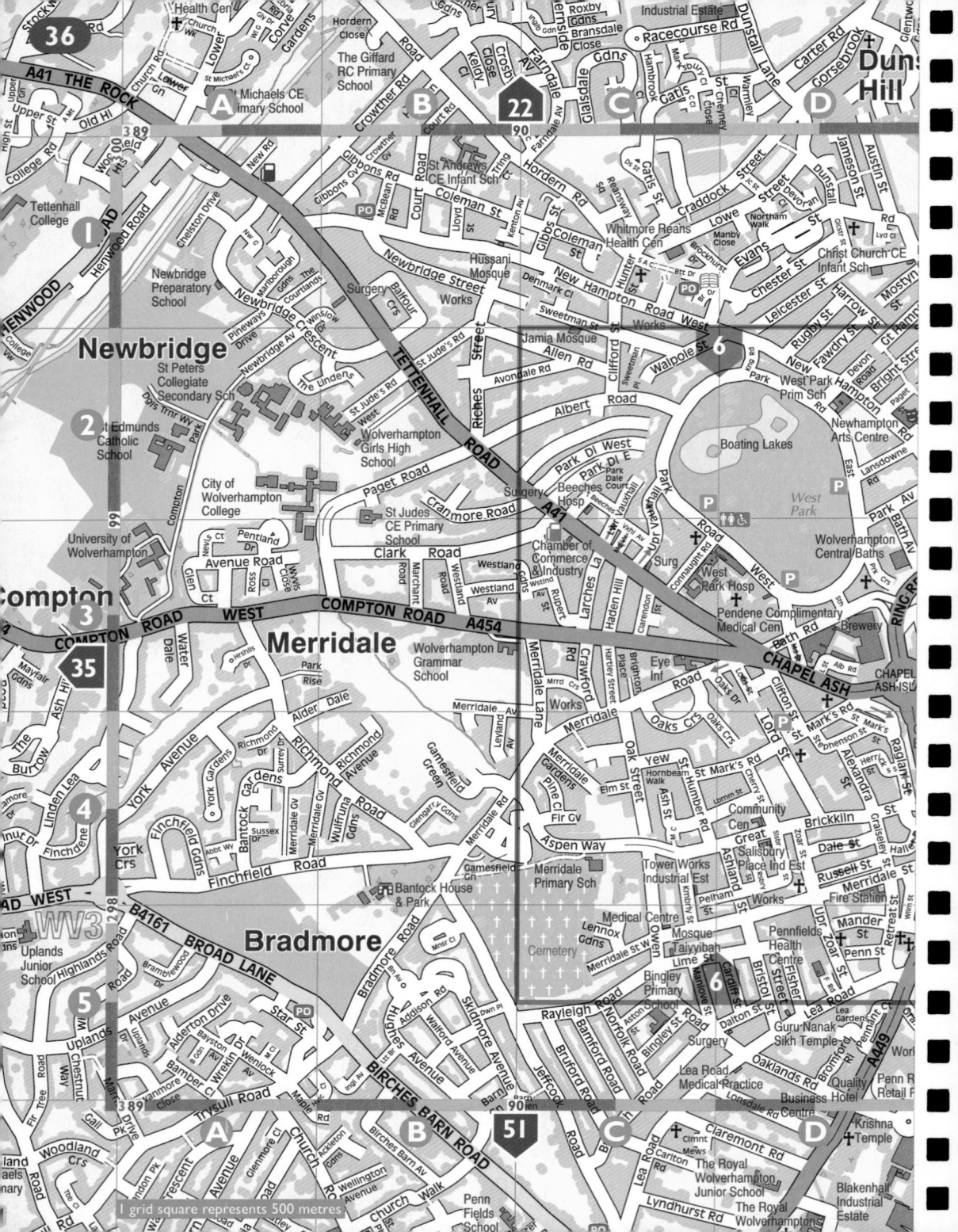

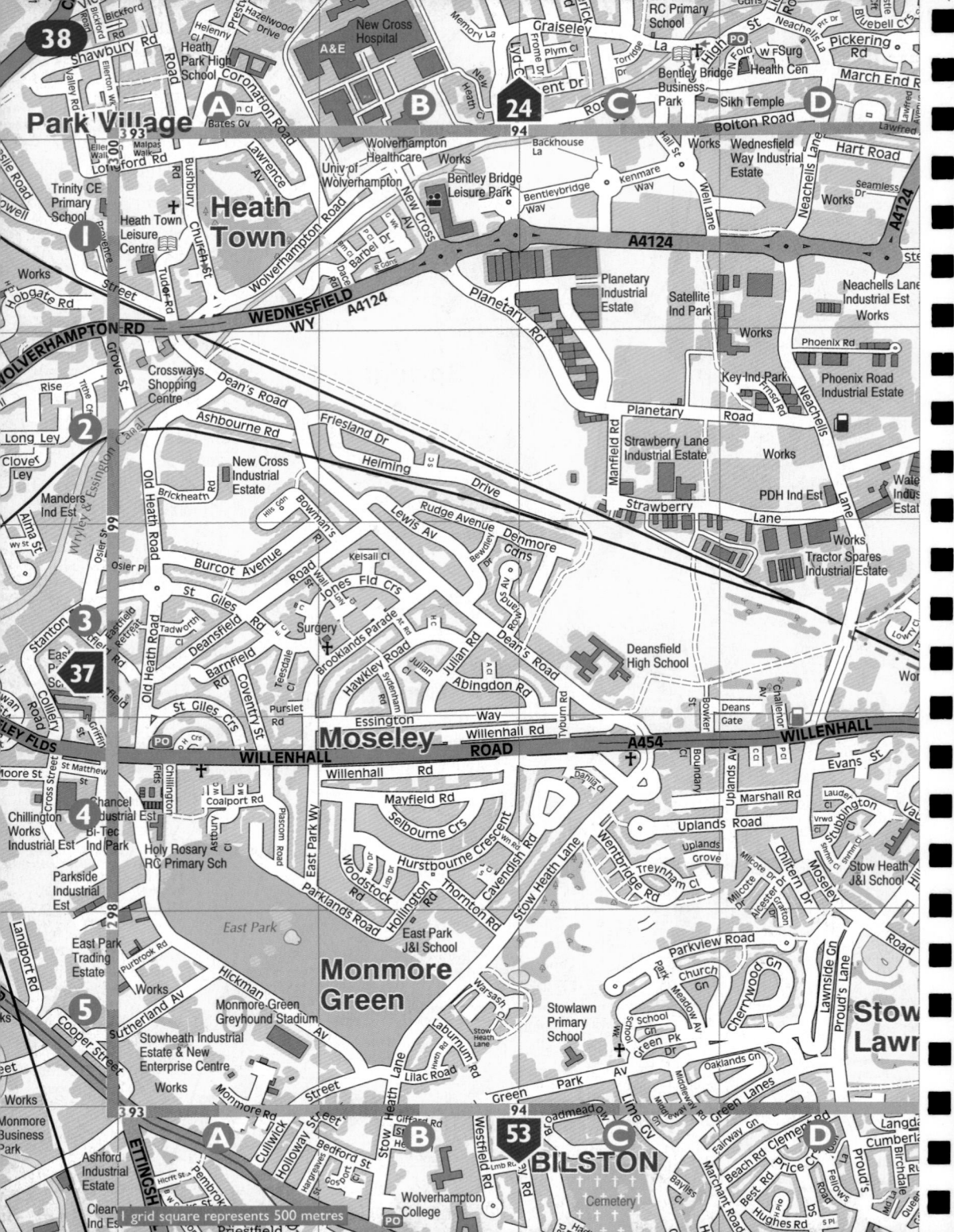

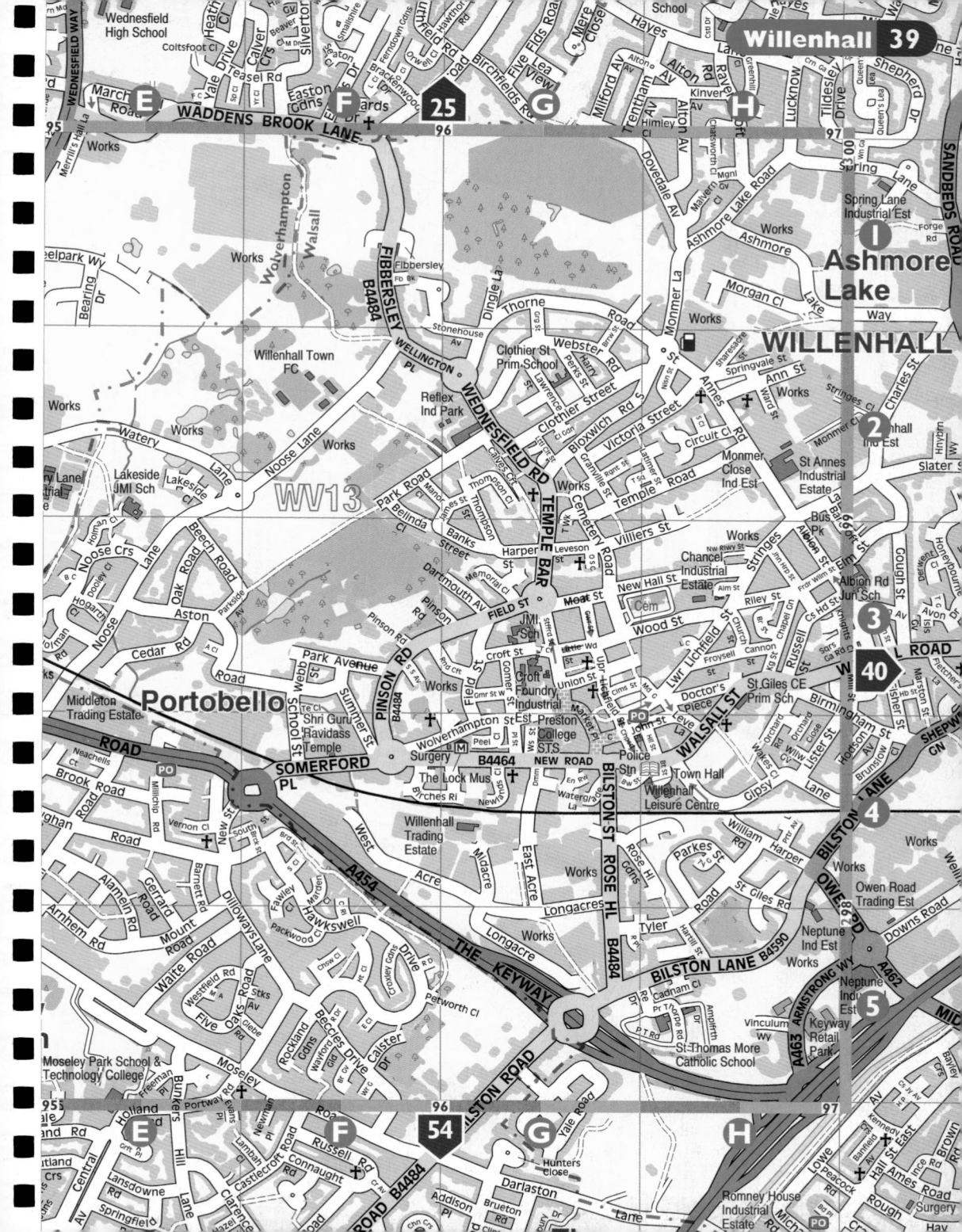

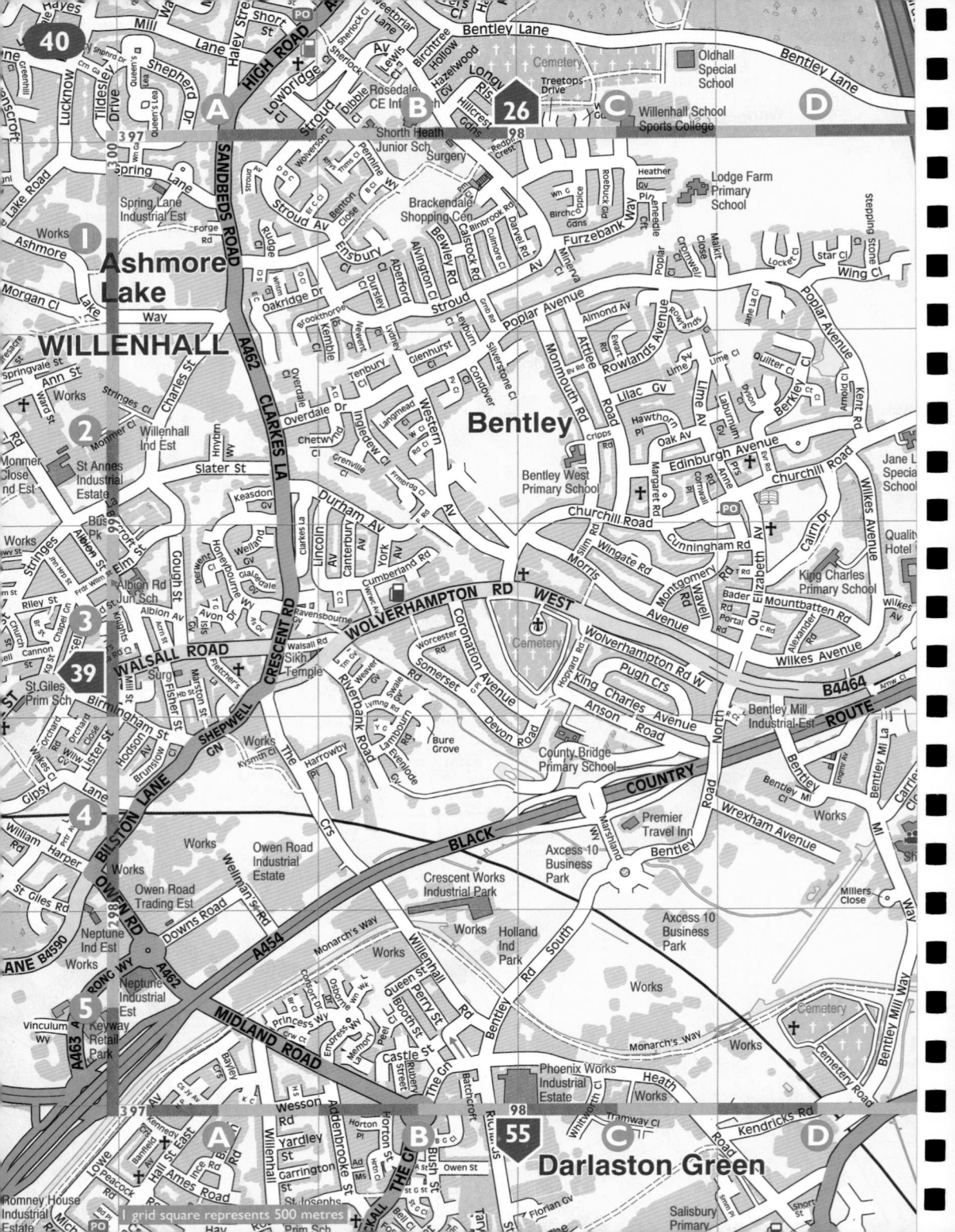

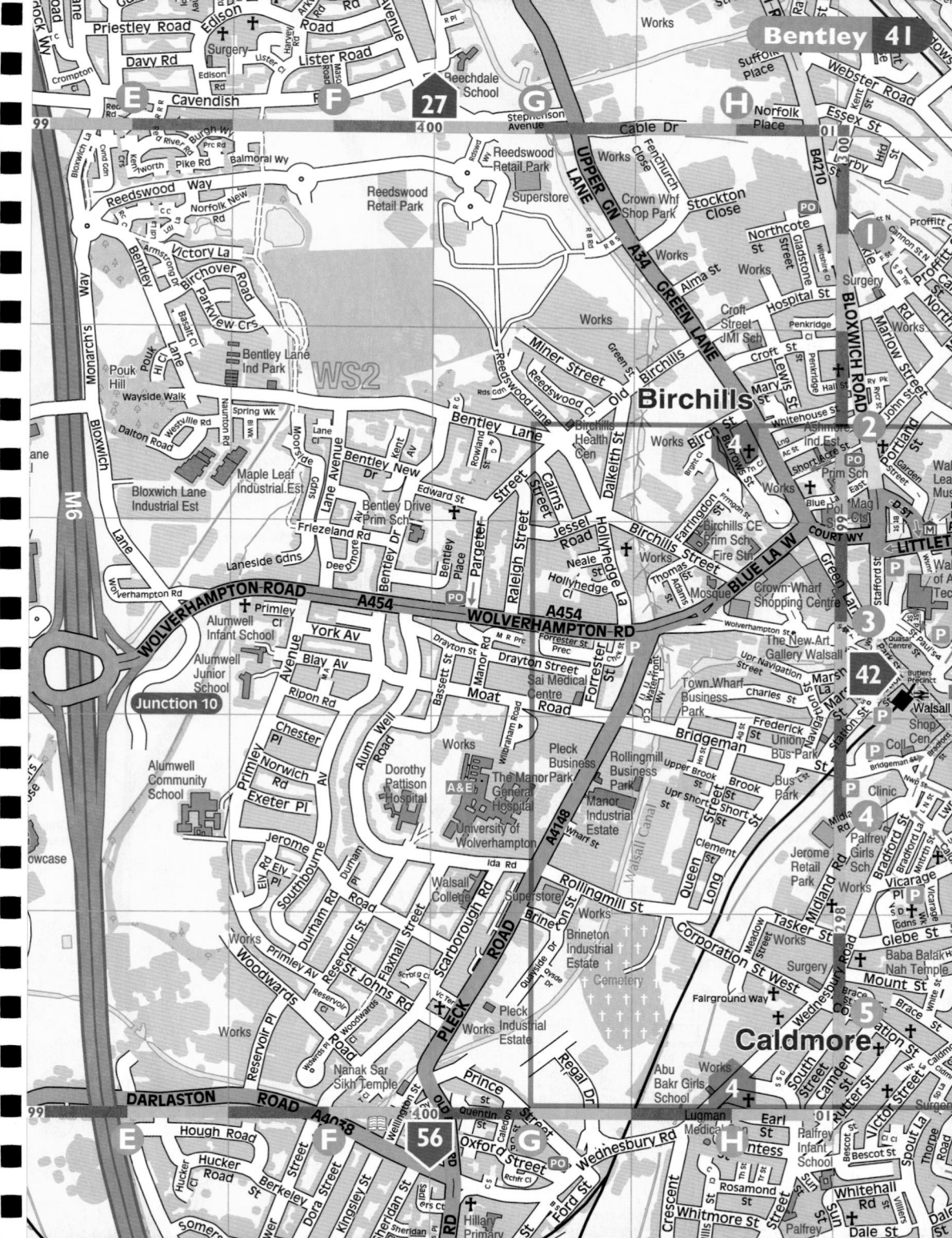

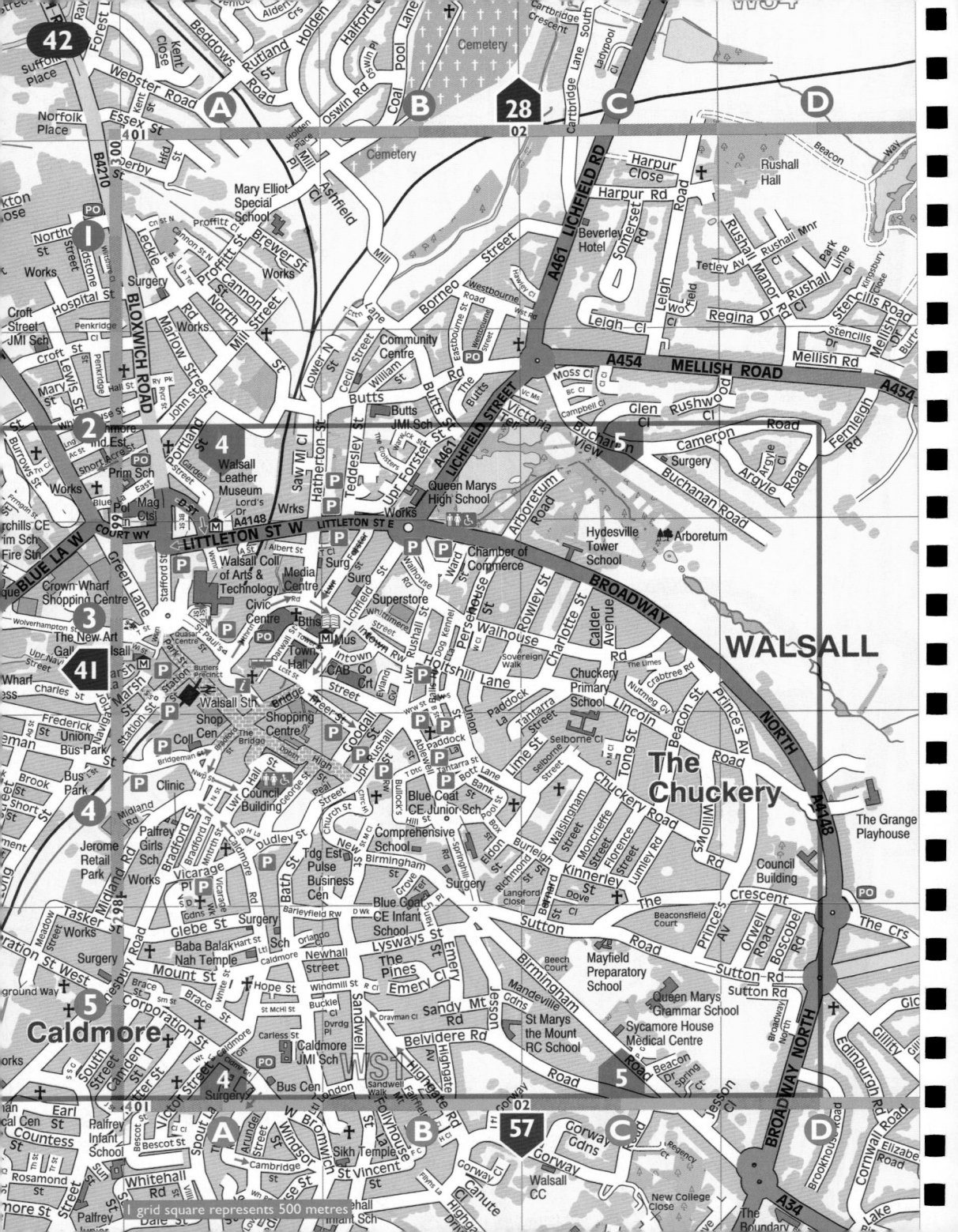

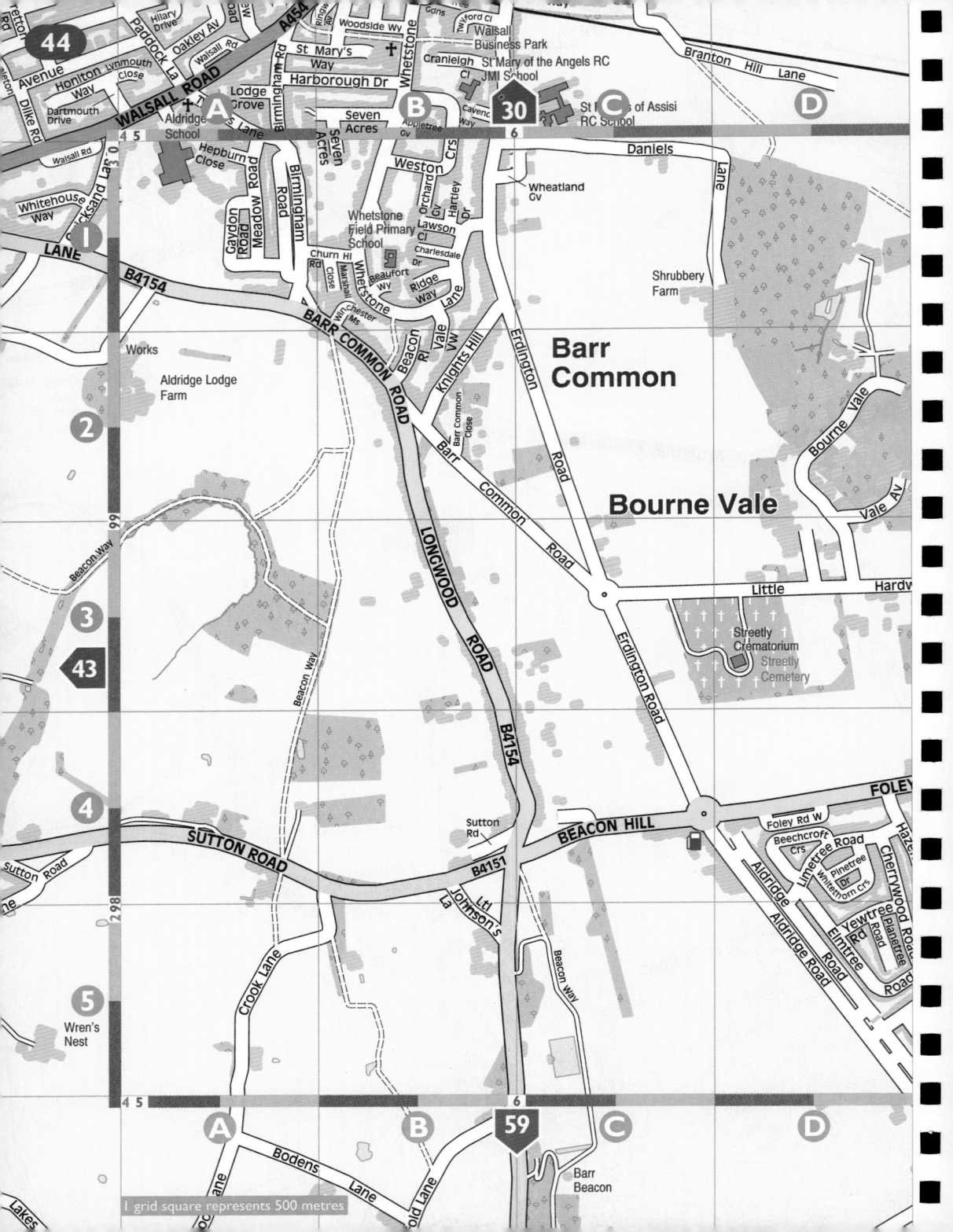

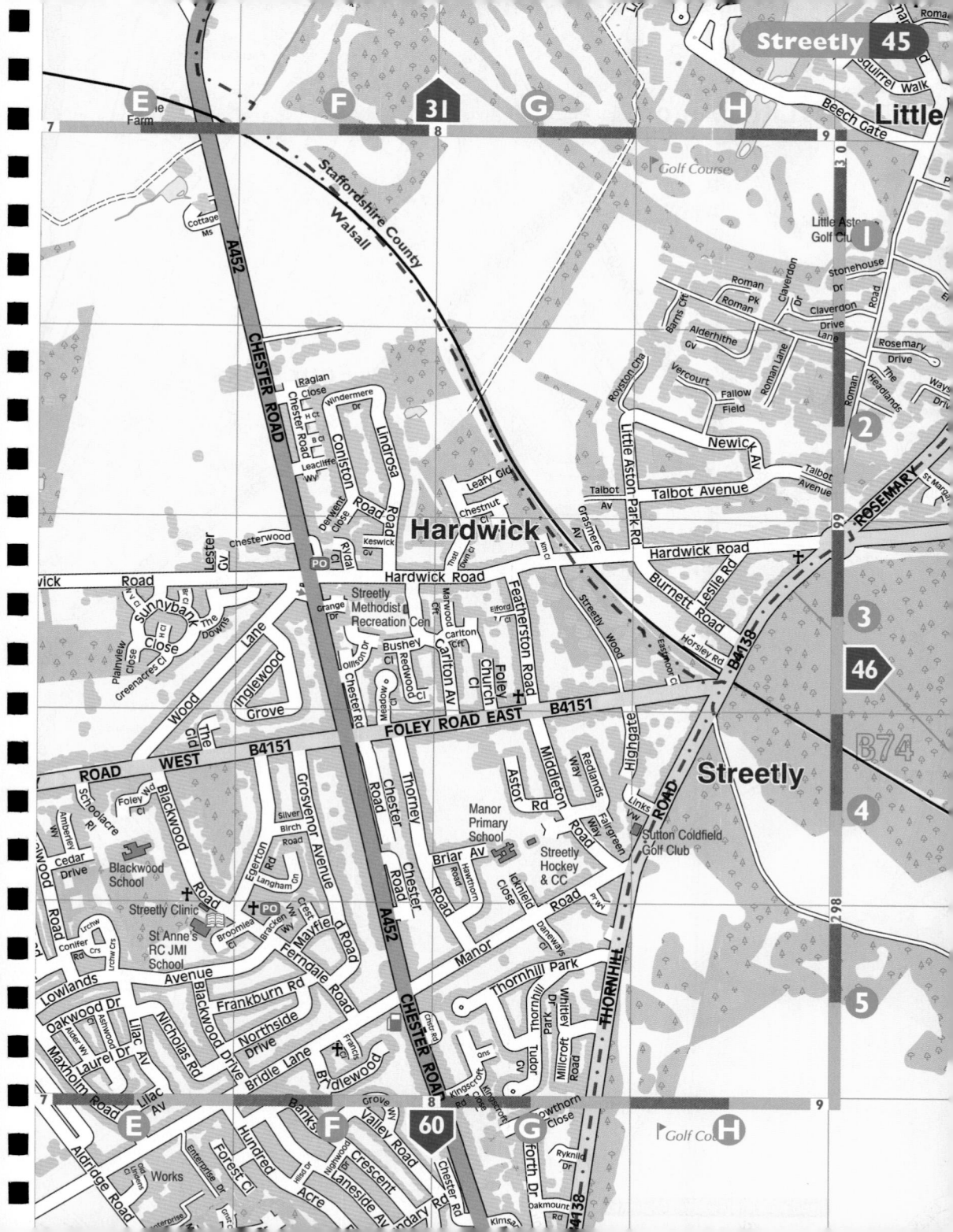

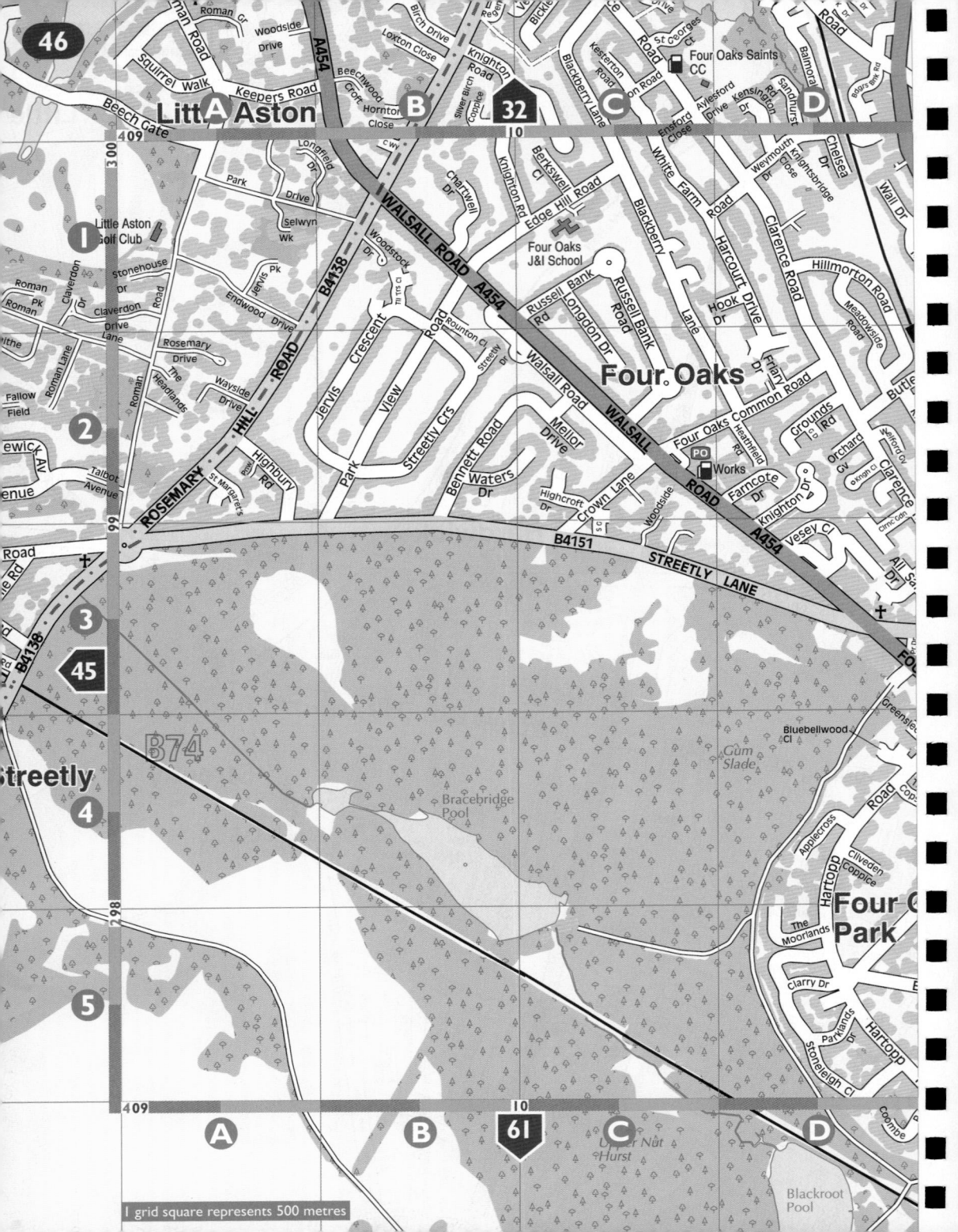

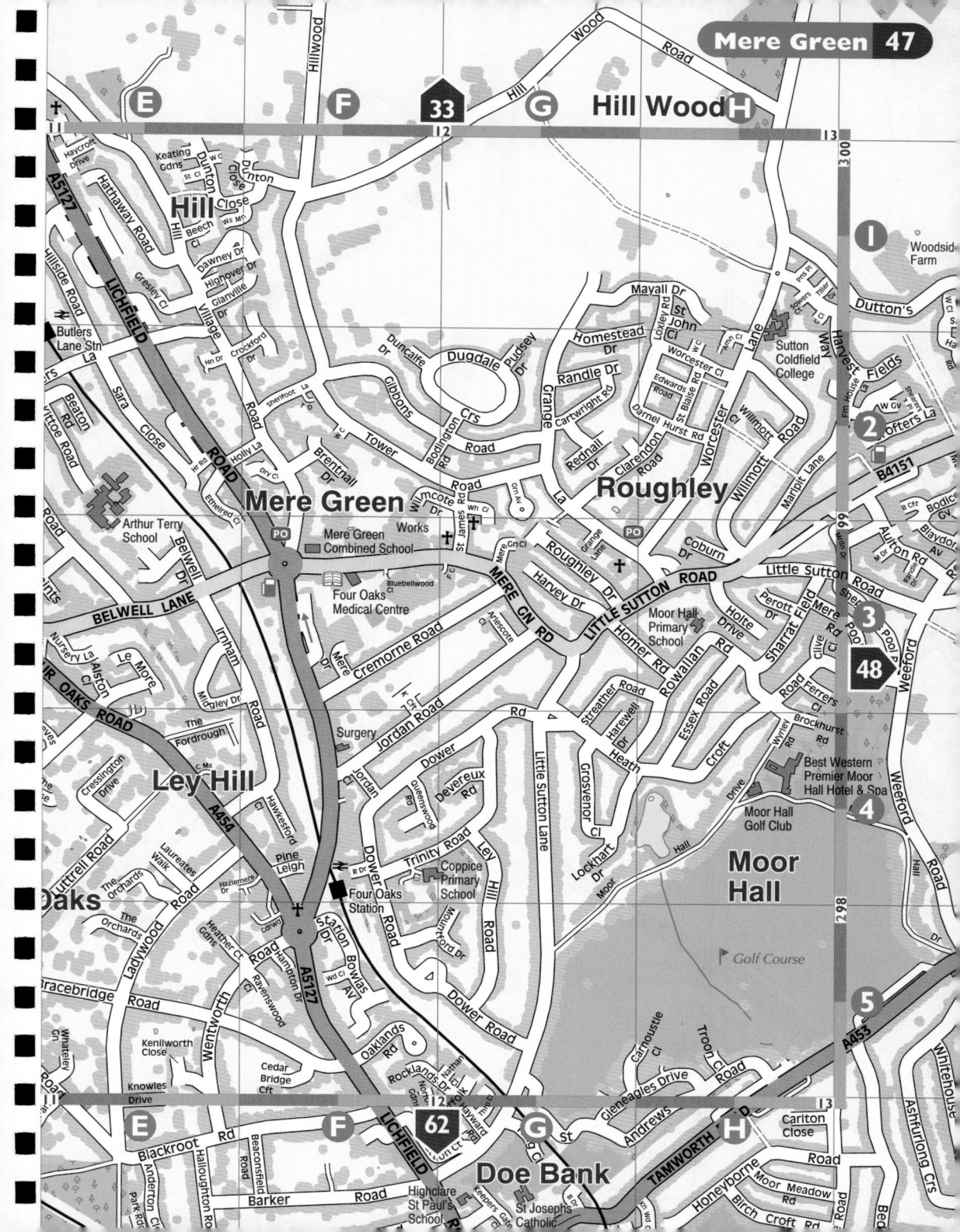

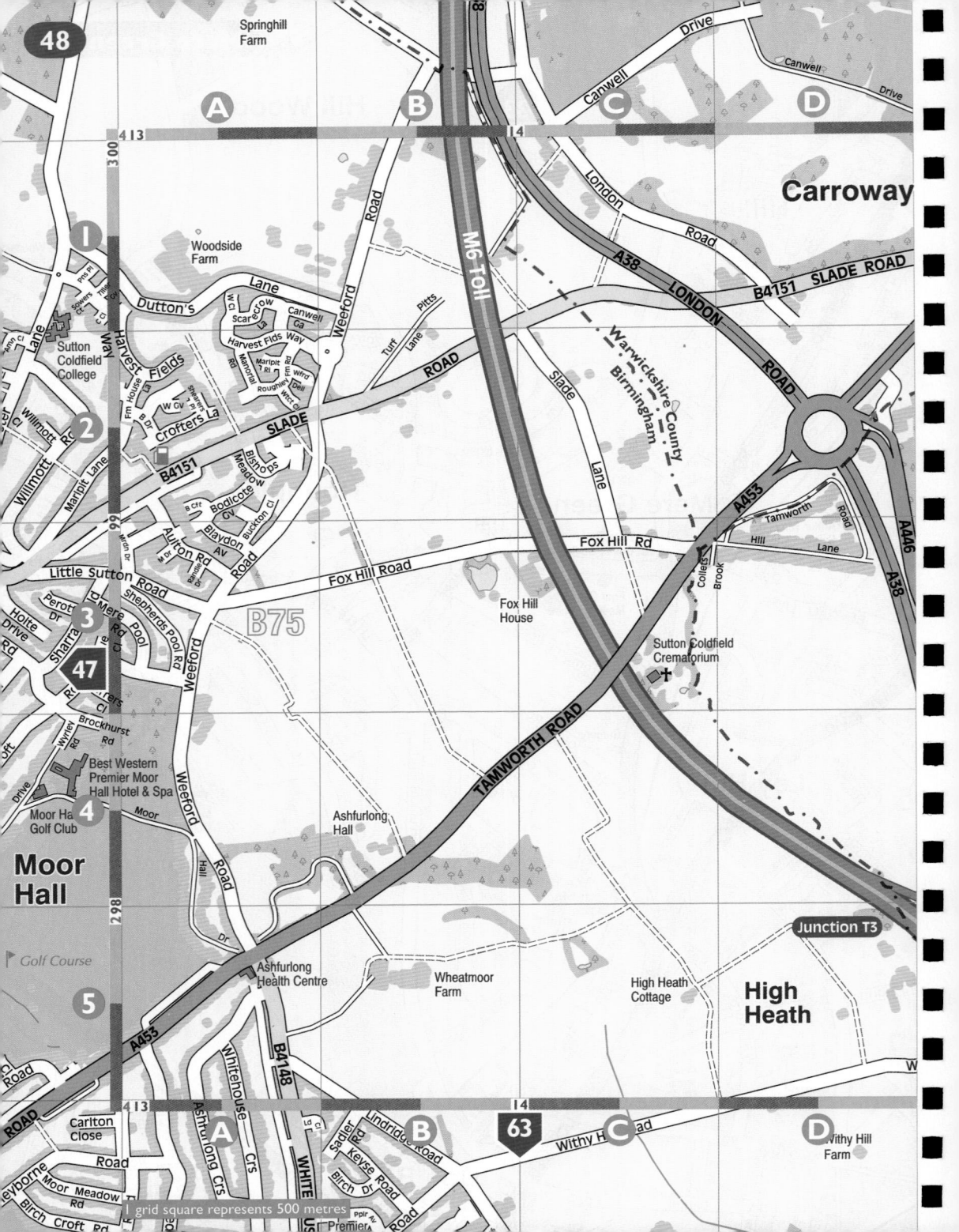

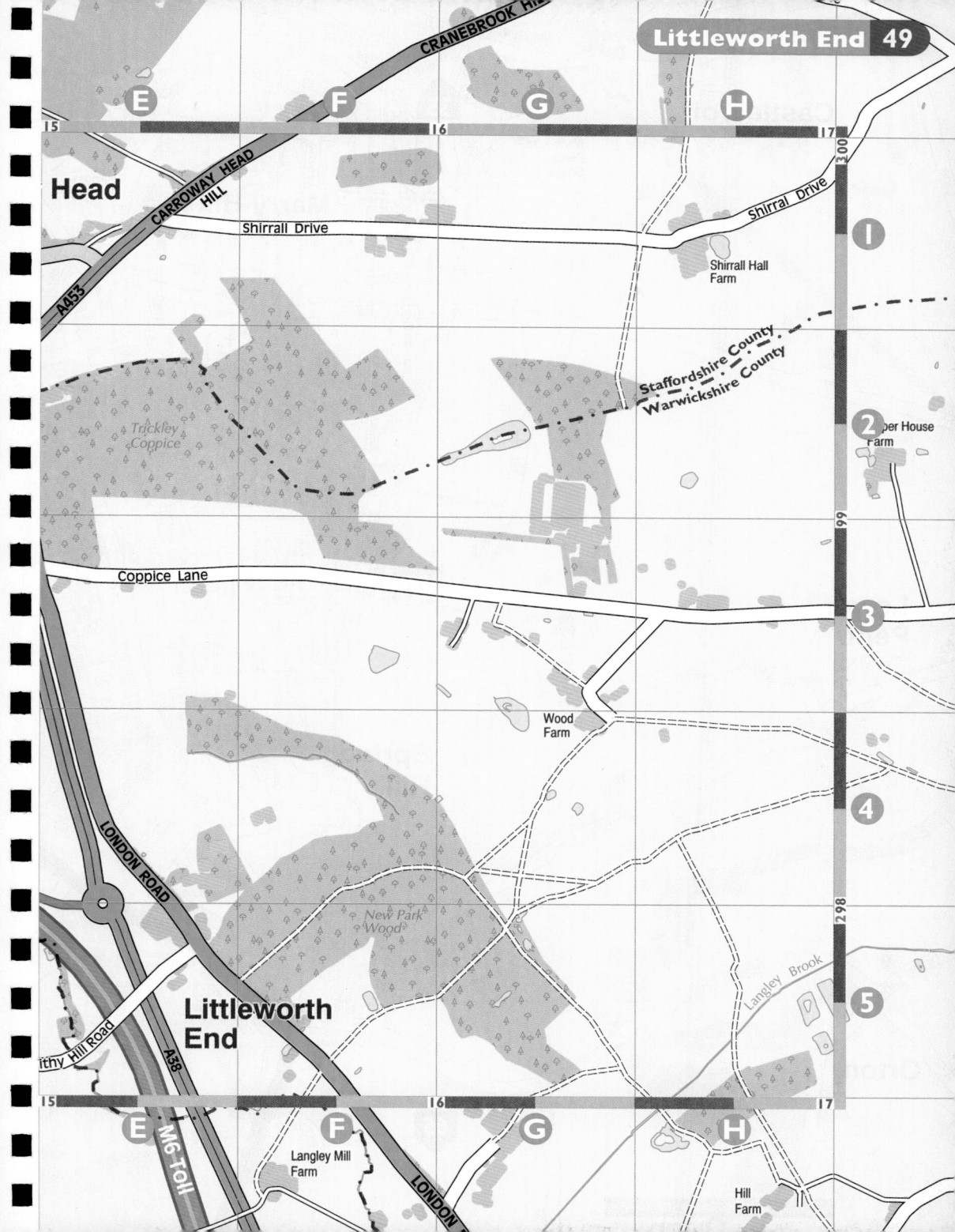

E F G H

15 16 17

300

Head

CRANEBROOK Hi

CARROWAY HEAD HILL

Shirral Drive

Shirral Drive

I

A453

Shirrall Hall Farm

Staffordshire County
Warwickshire County

Trickley Coppice

2 per House Farm

99

Coppice Lane

3

Wood Farm

4

298

LONDON ROAD

New Park Wood

Langley Brook

5

Littleworth End

ithy Hill Road

A38

15 16 17

E F G H

M6 Toll

Langley Mill Farm

LONDON

Hill Farm

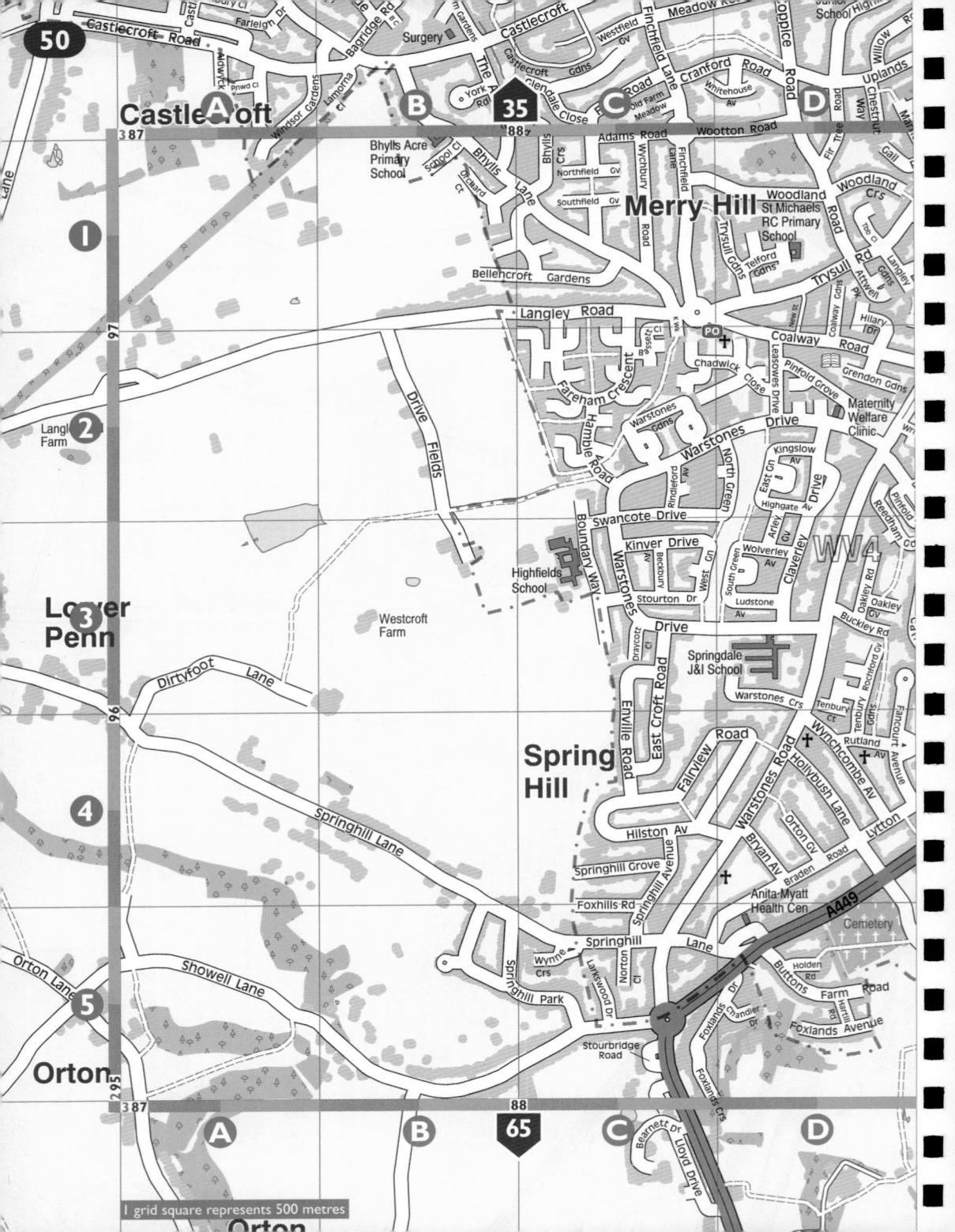

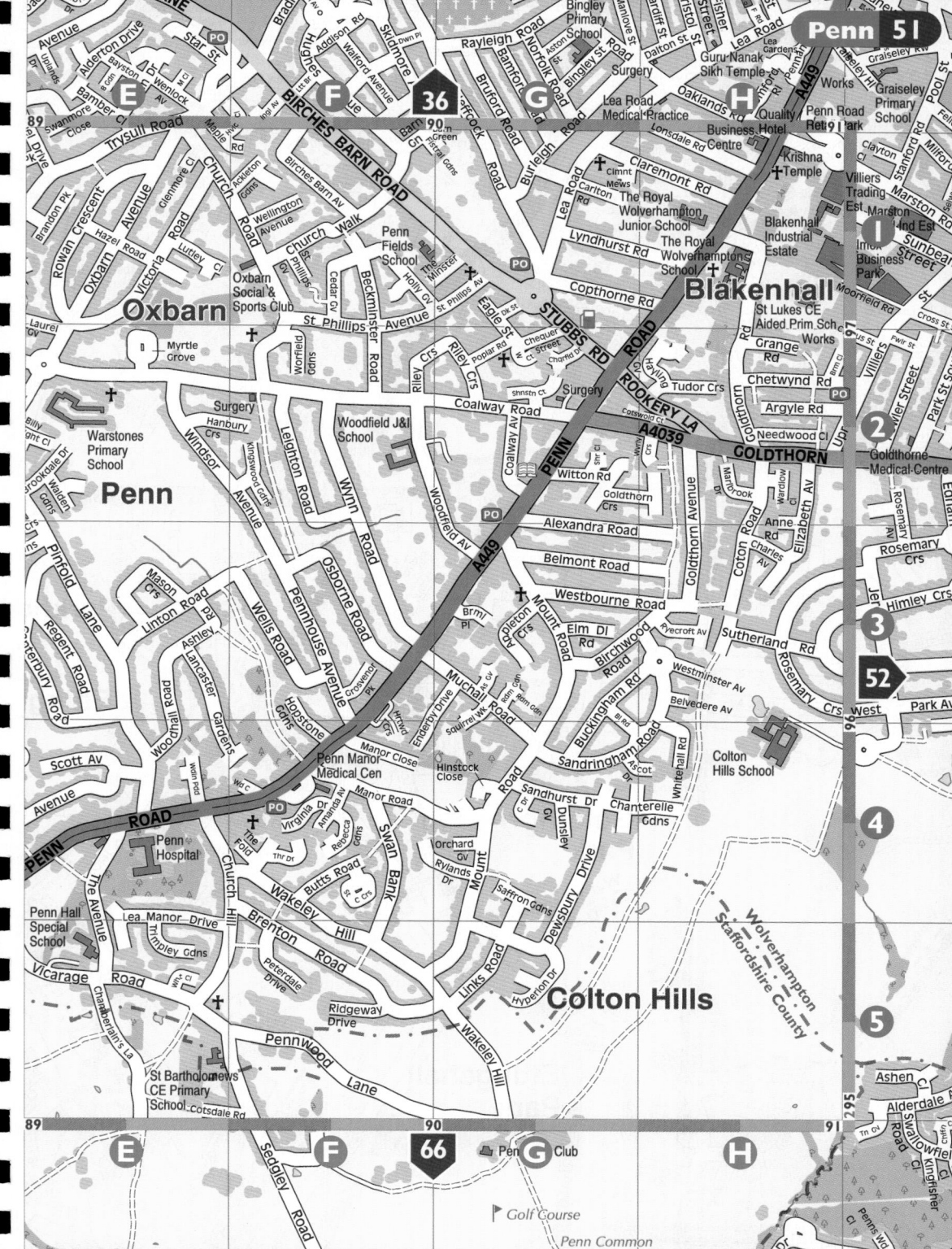

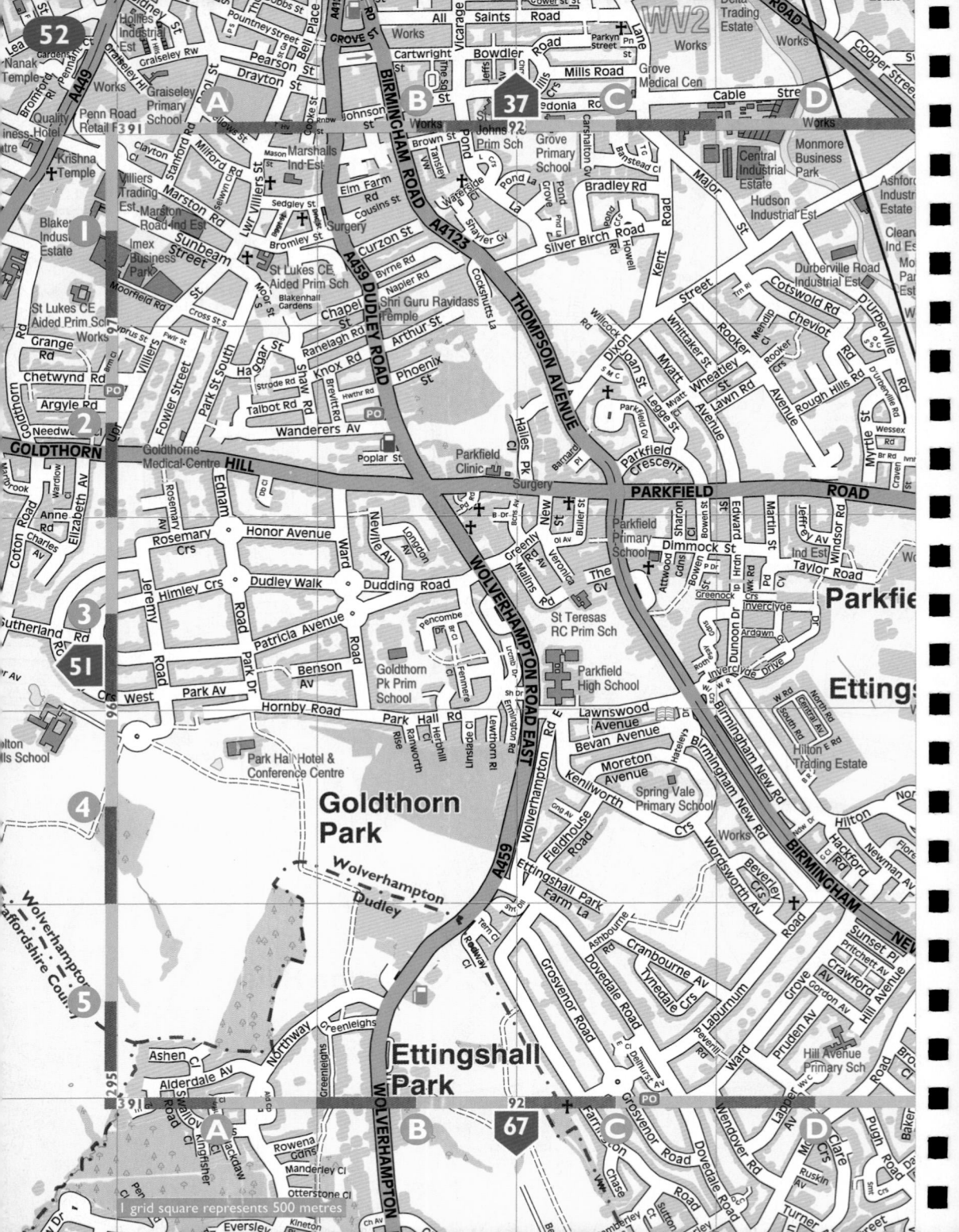

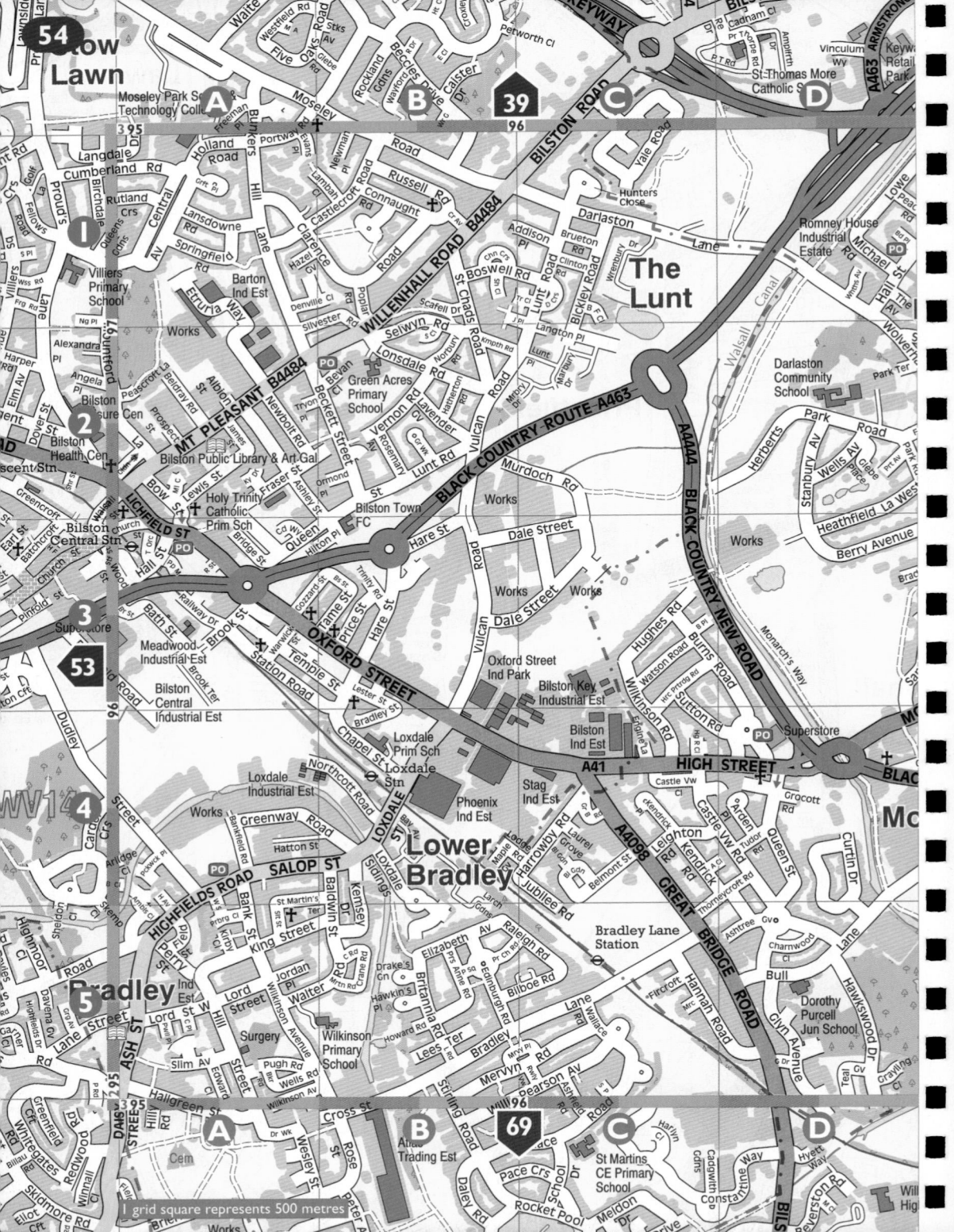

1 grid square represents 500 metres

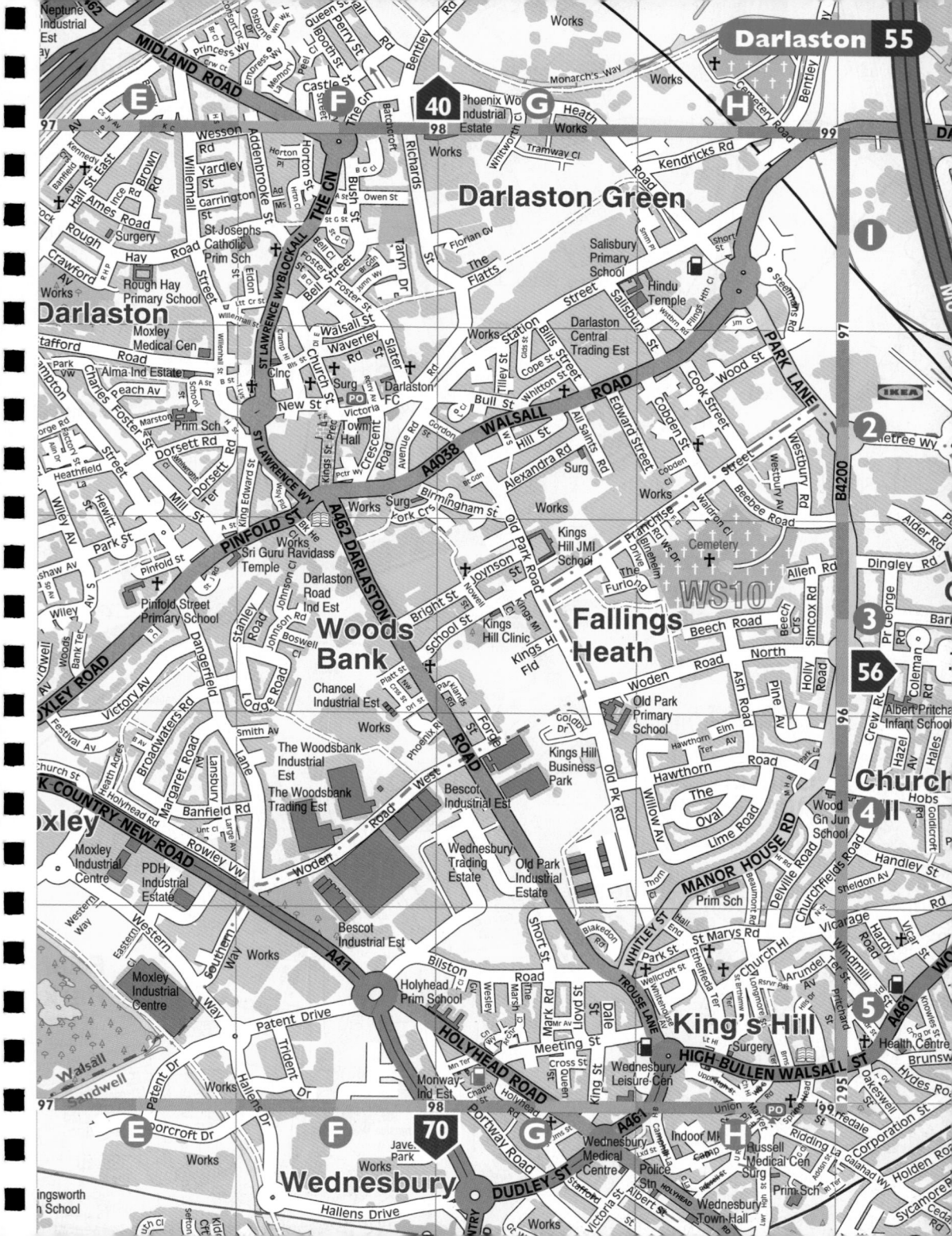

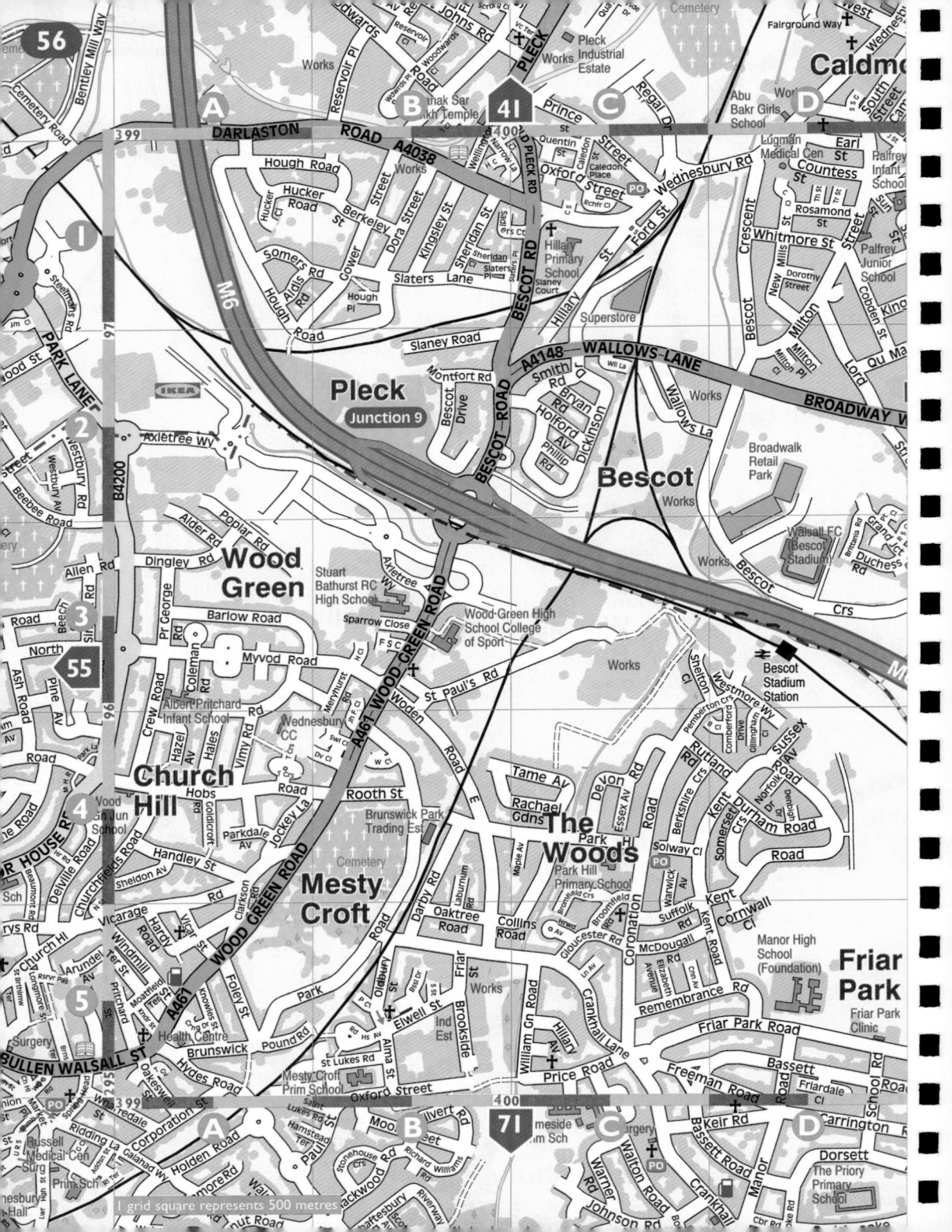

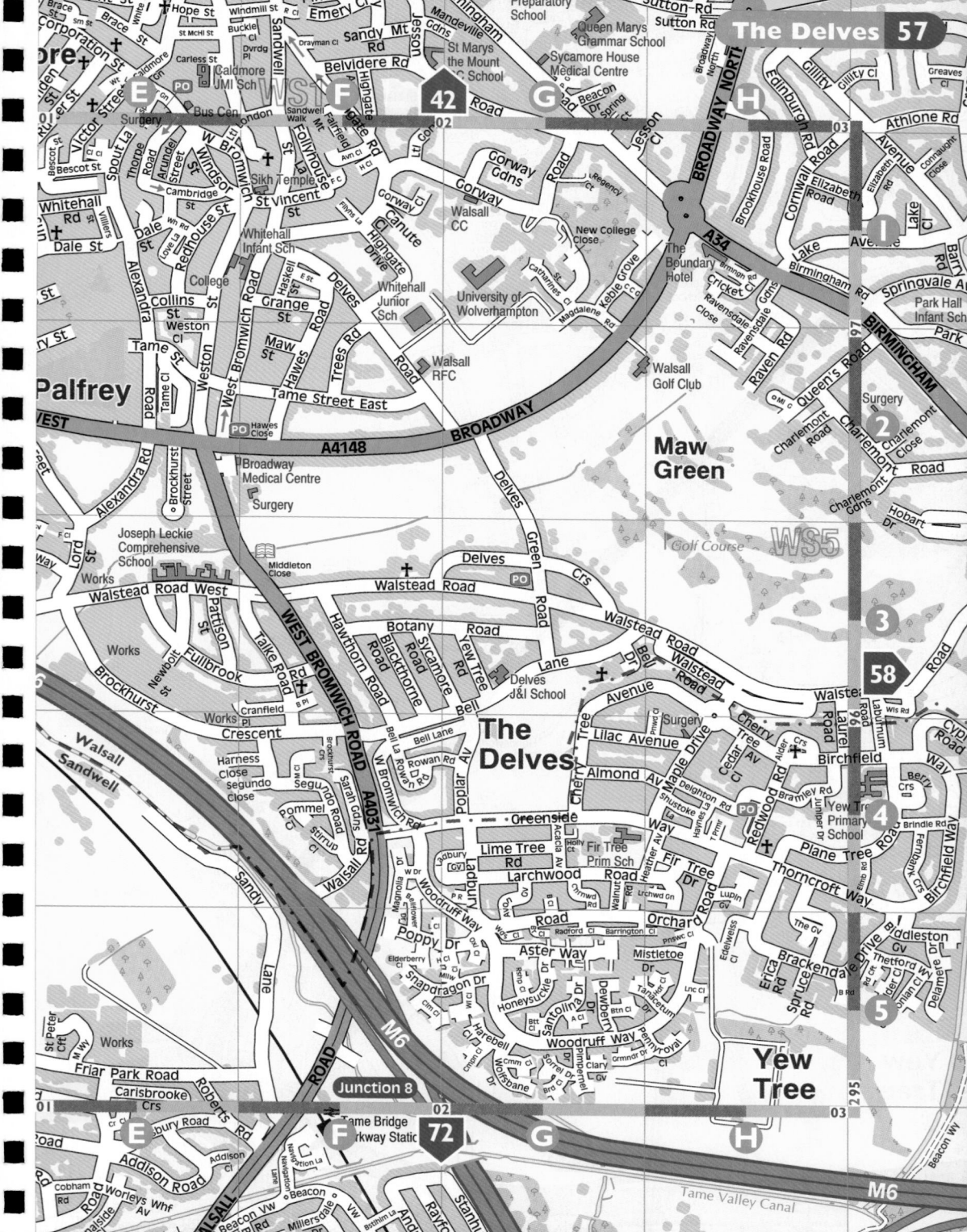

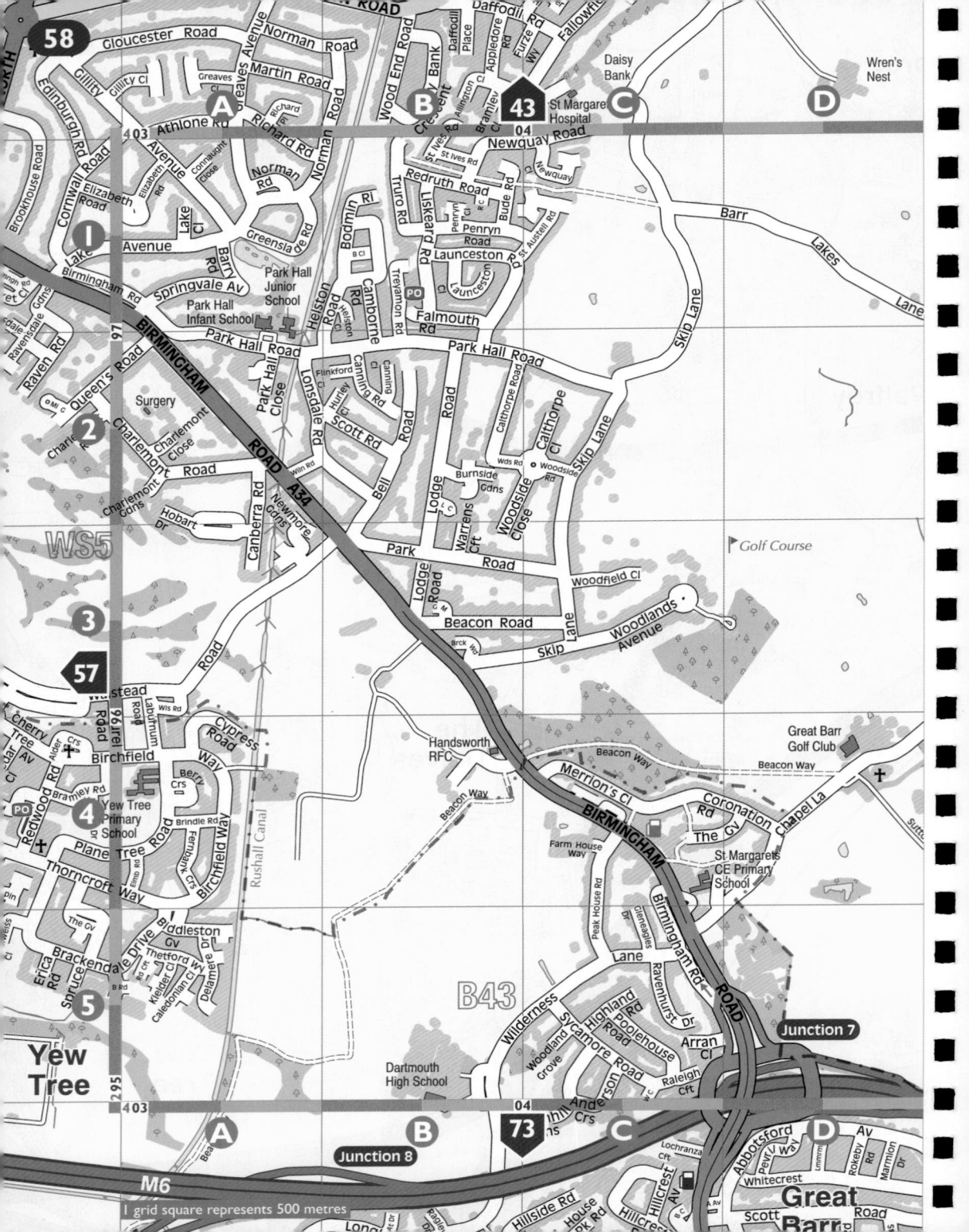

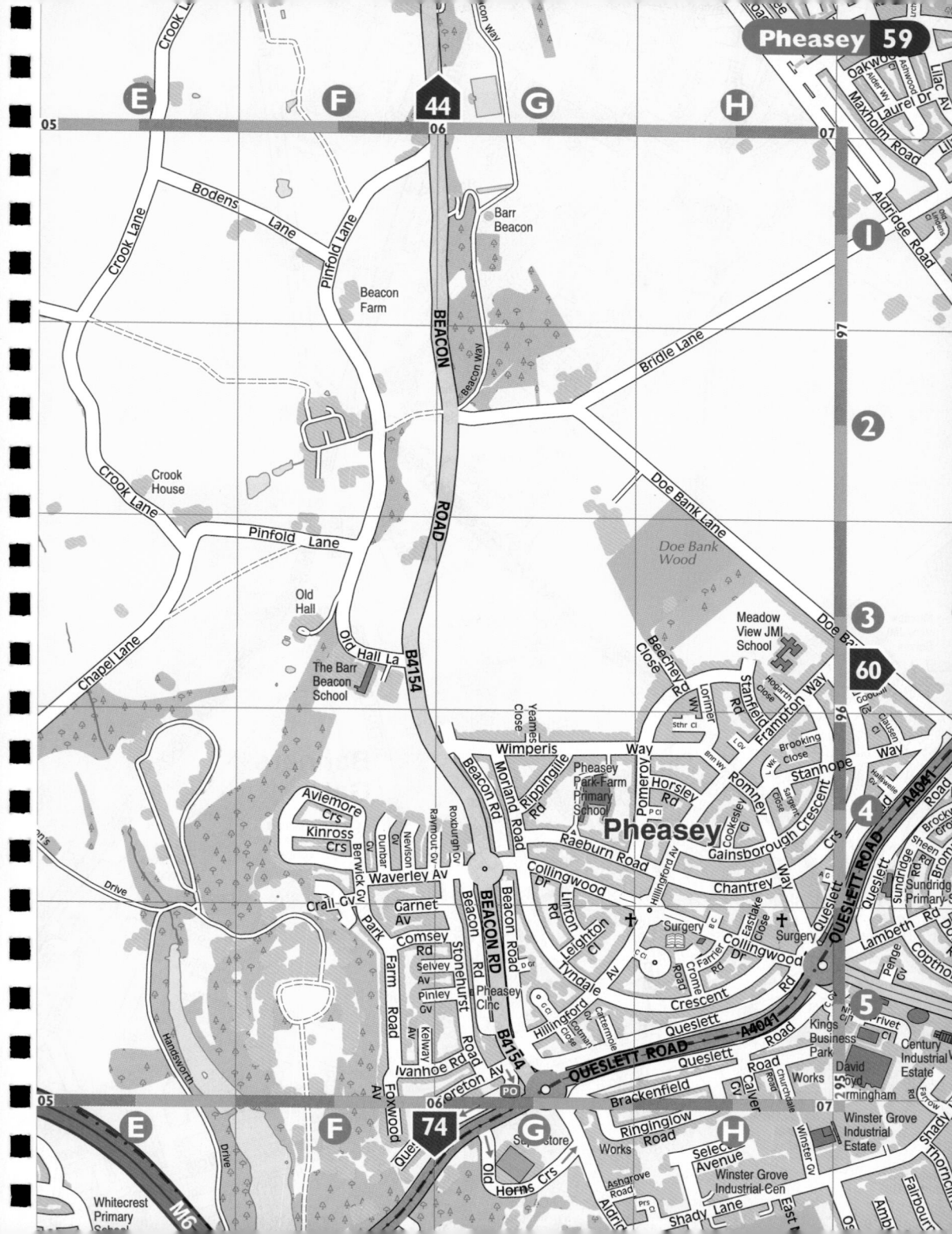

E F **46** G H

9 10 I

Upper Nut Hurst

Blackroot Pool

Sutton Park

2

Keeper's Pool

Rowton's Well

Holly Hurst

3

62

Wyn Leis Cen

W Sw Ba

Wyndle

4

Wyndle Pool

Monmouth

Golf Course

Powell's Pool

Monmouth Drive

5

Rushbrooke Dr

Durley Dr

Lowe Dr

Alcester Dr

Avery Road

Alcester Dr

Drive

Jevons

Markham Road

Dunchurch Cres

Milcote Dr

Grendon Drive

Road

Halton Road

Stonehouse Rd

Boldmere Golf Club

Monmouth Drive

Elw Roxburgh Rd

A452

Denholm R

B73

Corbridge Road

Stonehouse Road

Mo Road

Greenway Dr

smans

Welshmans Hl

Welshmans Rd

CHESTER ROAD NORTH

Lapworth Dr

Avery Road

Warwic

Churchill

Tudor Cl

E F **76** G H

9 10

Falstone Rd

Dalkeith Rd

Carnwath Rd

Melrose Avenue

Braemar Road

Matre Av

Honile

Parkwood Dr

Superstore

Stirling

JOCKEY

St Nicholas RC JMI School

A453

Wakefield

Braemar

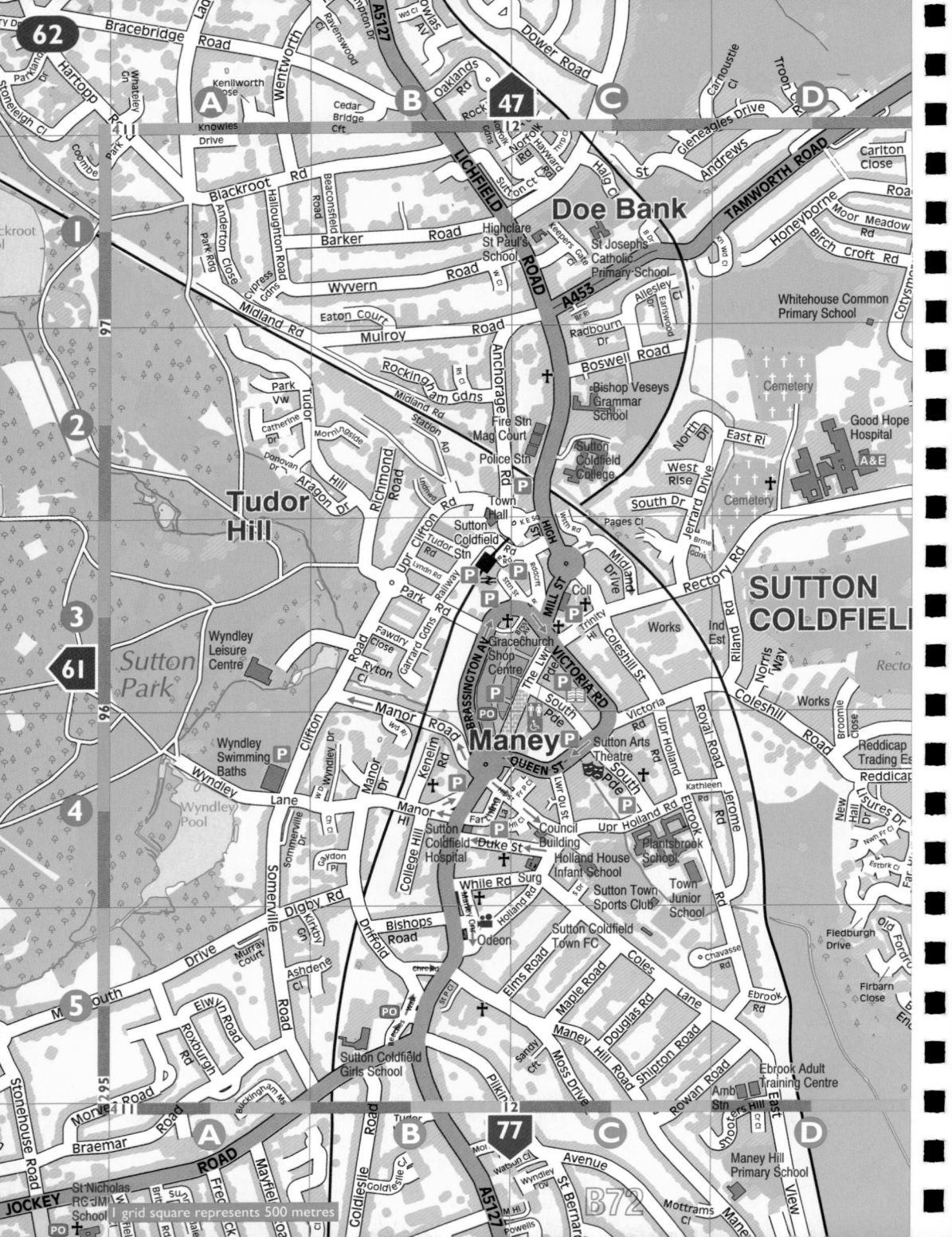

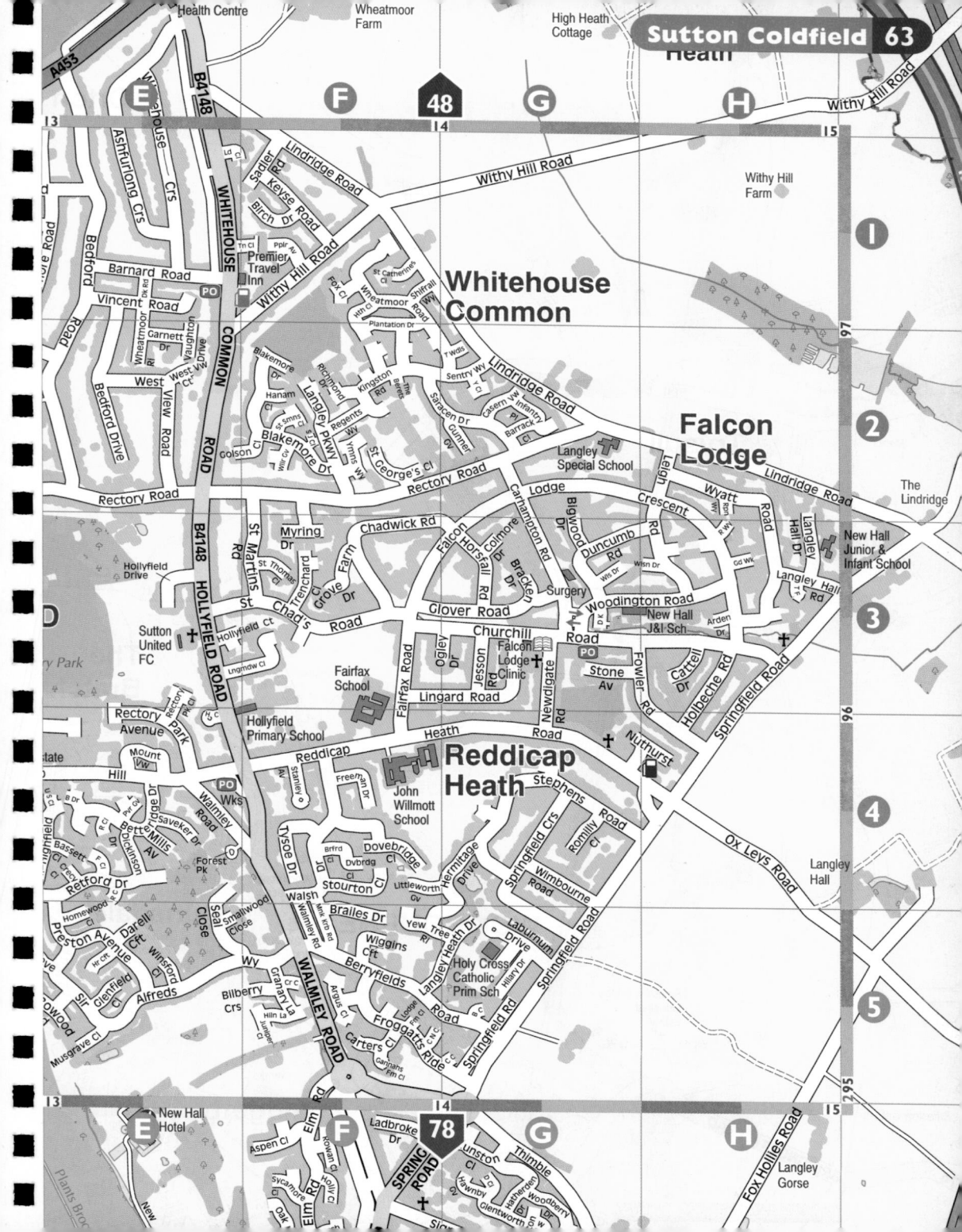

Health Centre
Wheatmoor Farm
High Heath Cottage
Heath

A453
B4148
WHITEHOUSE
Withy Hill Road

E **F** 48 **G** **H**

13 14 15

Withy Hill Road

Withy Hill Farm

Ashfurlong Crs
Whitehouse Crs
Sadler
Keyse Road
Lindridge Road
Birch Dr
Barnard Road
Tn Cl
Pplr Av
Premier Travel Inn
St Catherine's Cl
Wheatmoor Rd
Shifnall
Hth Cl
Vincent Road
PO
Fdy Cl
Plantation Dr
Garnett Dr
Vaughton
Bridge
I

Bedford Road

Wheatmoor Dr
West View Ct

Whitehouse Common

West View Road
Bedford Drive

Blakemore Dr
Richmond Dr
Kingston Rd
T Wdls
Sentry Wy
Infantry
Hanam
Langley Pkwy
Regents Wy
St Smns
Saracen Dr
Casern Vw
Barrack Cl
Lindridge Road
Falcon Lodge
The Lindridge

2

Blakemore Dr
Golson
St Geo Cl
Wllr Vw
Gunner Vw
Langley Special School
Lindridge Road

97

Rectory Road

Lodge
Crescent
Wyatt Rd
Leigh Rd
Langley Hall Dr

B4148
HOLLYFIELD ROAD
St Martins Rd
Myring Dr
Chadwick Rd
Falcon
Horsall Rd
Colmore
Bracken
Carhampton Rd
Bigwood Dr
Duncumb Rd
Wls Dr
Wisn Dr
Gd Wk
Langley Hall Rd
New Hall Junior & Infant School

Hollyfield Drive
St Thomas
Grove Farm
Trenchard Dr
Glover Road
Surgery
Woodington Road
New Hall J&I Sch
Arden Dr

3

Sutton United FC
Hollyfield Ct
St Chad's Road
Lngmdw Cl
Ogley Dr
Fairfax Road
Churchill Road
Newdigate Rd
Falcon Lodge Clinic
PO
Stone Av
Fowler Rd
Cattell Dr
Holbeche Rd
Springfield Road

96

ry Park
Rectory Park
Fairfax School
Jesson Dr
Lingard Road
Heath Road
Nuthurst

Rectory Avenue
Mount Vw
Hollyfield Primary School
Reddicap Heath
Reddicap Heath
Stephens Road

4

Hill
PO
Wks
Walmley Road
Stanley
Freeman Dr
John Willmott School
Springfield Crs
Romilly Cl
Wimbourne Road
Ox Leys Road
Langley Hall

Mount Vw
Bassett Cl
Bette Mills Av
Dickenson
Forest Pk
Tysoe Dr
Brfrd
Dvbrdg
Dovebridge
Littleworth Gv
Stourton Cl
Hermitage Drive

Homewood
Darell Cft
Winsford Close
Walsh
Walmley Rd
Brailes Dr
Yew Tree Rd
Langley Heath Dr
Laburnum Drive

5

Preston Avenue
Glenfield
Alfreds
Wiggins Cft
Berryfields
Argus Cl
Lodge Rd
Hilary Cr
Holy Cross Catholic Prim Sch
Springfield Rd
Springfield Road

Retford Dr
Bilberry Crs
Granary La
Hiln La
Jumber Cl
Carters
Froggatts Ride
Gannans Fm Cl

Musgrave Cl

295

13 14 78 15

E **F** Ladbroke Dr **G** **H**

New Hall Hotel
Aspen Cl
Elm Rd
Rowan Cl
Gunston Cl
Holly
Thimble
SPRING ROAD
Hawnby
Hathersage
Woodberry
Fox Hollies Road
Langley Gorse

Plants Brook
Sycamore
Oak
New
Clentworth

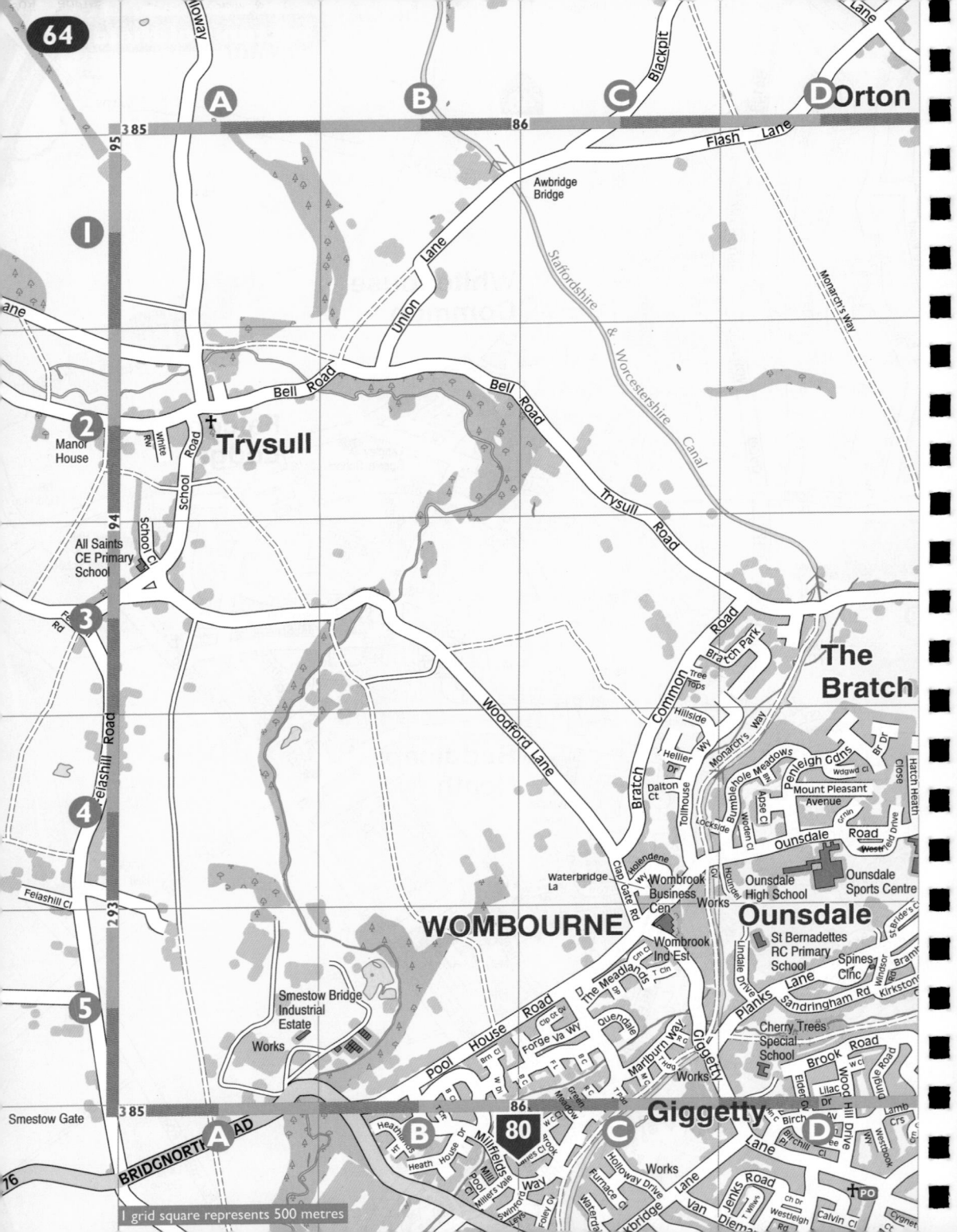

A   B   C   D **O**rton

385   86

95

Blackpit

Lane

Flash Lane

Awbridge
Bridge

Union Lane

I

Staffordshire & Worcestershire Canal

Monarch's Way

Bell Road

Bell Road

Trysull Road

2   Manor
House

White

RW

† **Trysull**

School Road

94

School Cl

All Saints
CE Primary
School

3

Rd

Felashill Road

Woodford Lane

Bratch Park

Common Road

Tree
Tops

Hillside

**The
Bratch**

Hellier
Dr

Dalton
Ct

Tollhouse

Monarch's Way

Bumblehole Meadows

Penleigh Gdns

Wdgwd Cl

Apse Cl

Woden Cl

Lockside

Br Dr

Close

Hatch Heath

Mount Pleasant
Avenue

Cl Grn

4

293

Felashill Cl

Ounsdale Road

West

High Houlder

Ounsdale
High School

Ounsdale
Sports Centre

St bride's Cl

Bramble

Kirkstone

5

Waterbridge
La

Clap Gate Rd

Volendene

Wombrook
Business
Cen

Works

Wombrook
Ind Est

St Bernadettes
RC Primary
School

Windsor Av

Spines
Clnc

WOMBOURNE

Ounsdale

Lindale drive

Planks Lane

Sandringham Rd

Smestow Bridge
Industrial
Estate

Works

Pool House Road

The Meadlans
Dr

Forge va Wy

Quendale

Brn Cl

Cherry Trees
Special
School

Brook Road

Wy Cl

Elder Av

Lilac
Dr

Wood Hill Drive

Smestow Gate

385

86

80

BRIDGNORTH
A R**AD**

B

C

D

Giggetty

76

Heathfield

Ht

Heath House Dr

Millfields Way

Miller's vale

Swinford

Foley Cl

Holloway Drive

Furnace Ln

Waterfall

bridge

Van Diemans

Works

Jenks Road

Lane

Ch Dr

T Wks

Westleigh
Cl

Birch
Cl

Birchill Cl

Calvin Cl

Lamb
Crs

Westbrook

Cygnet

† PO

I grid square represents 500 metres

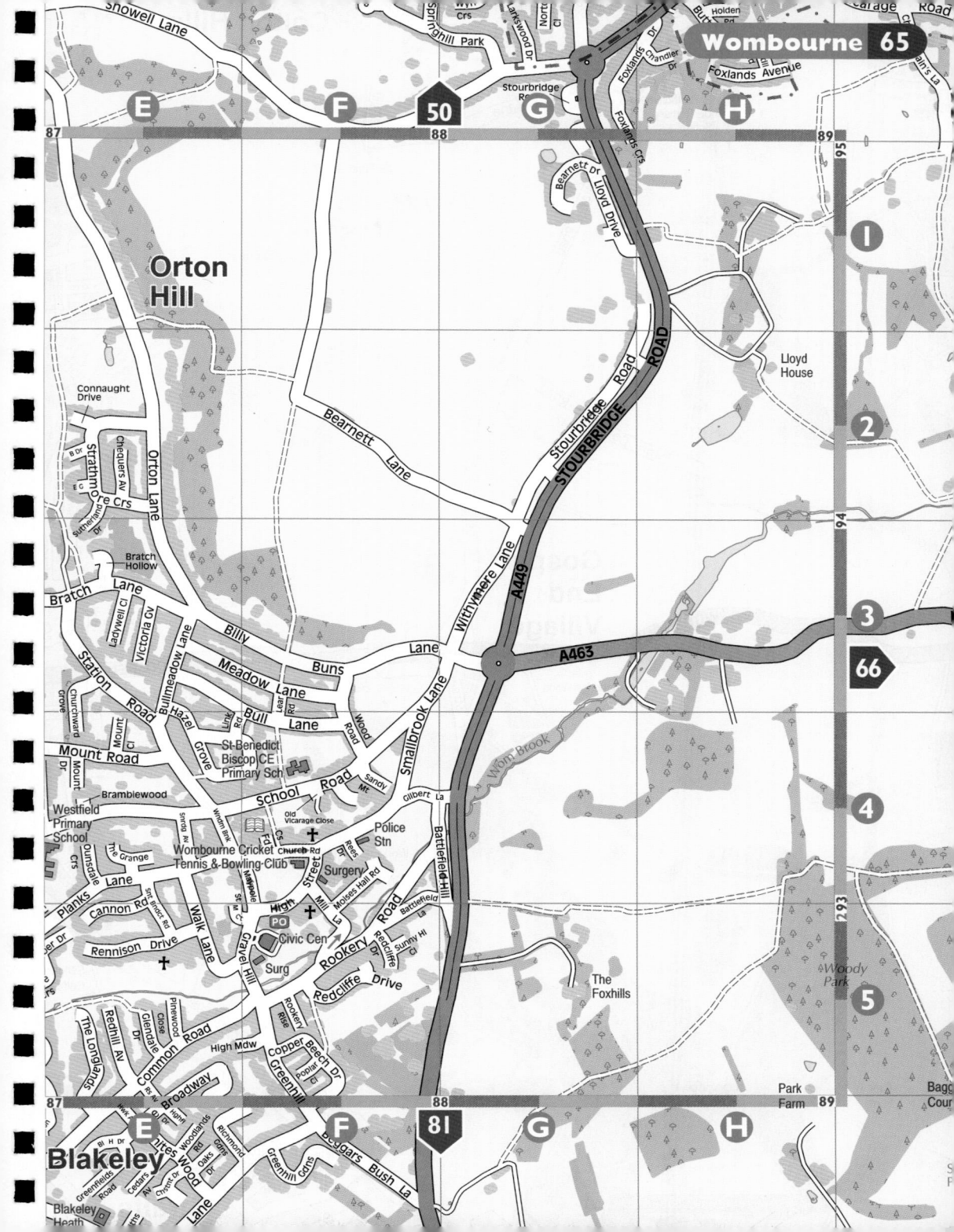

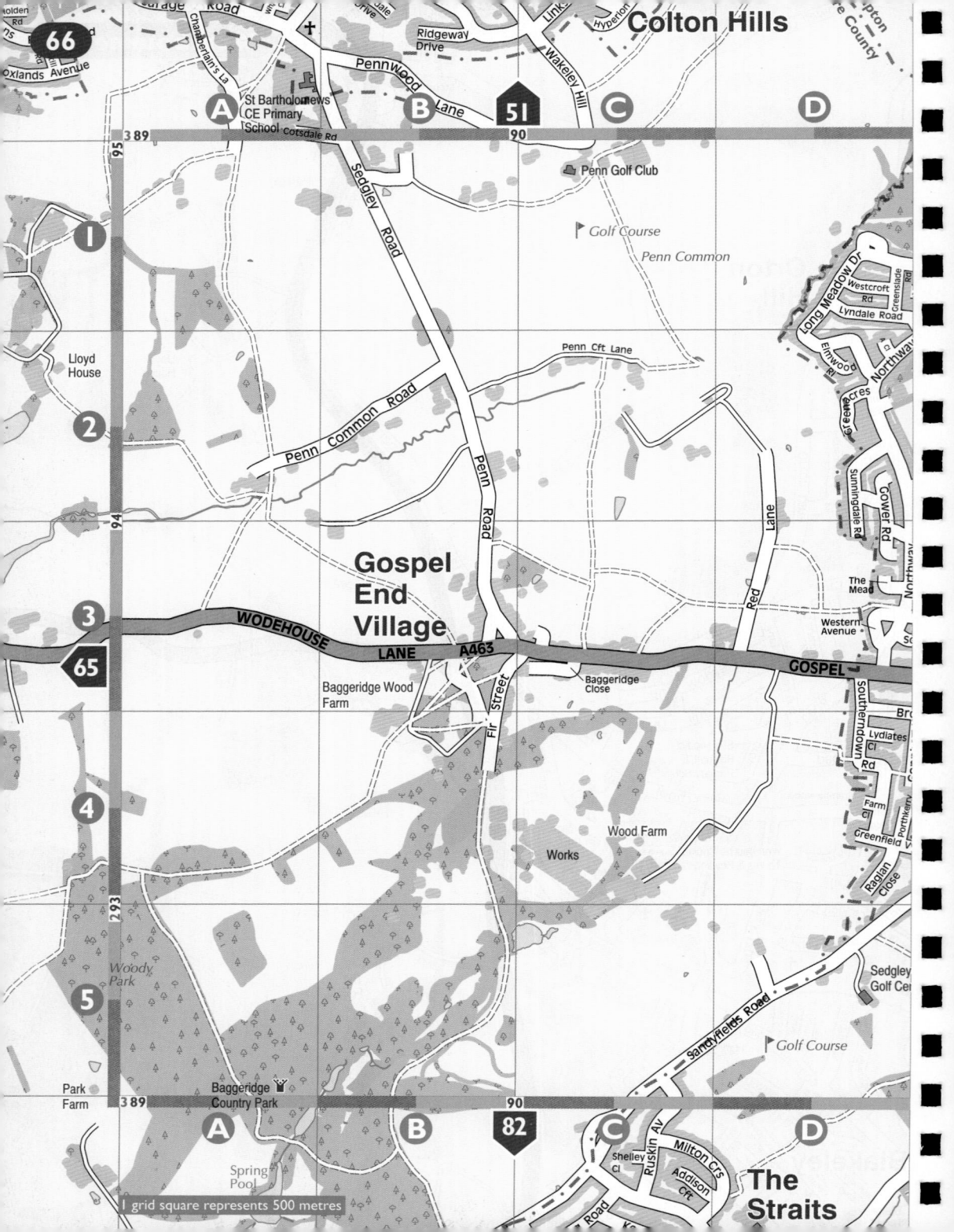

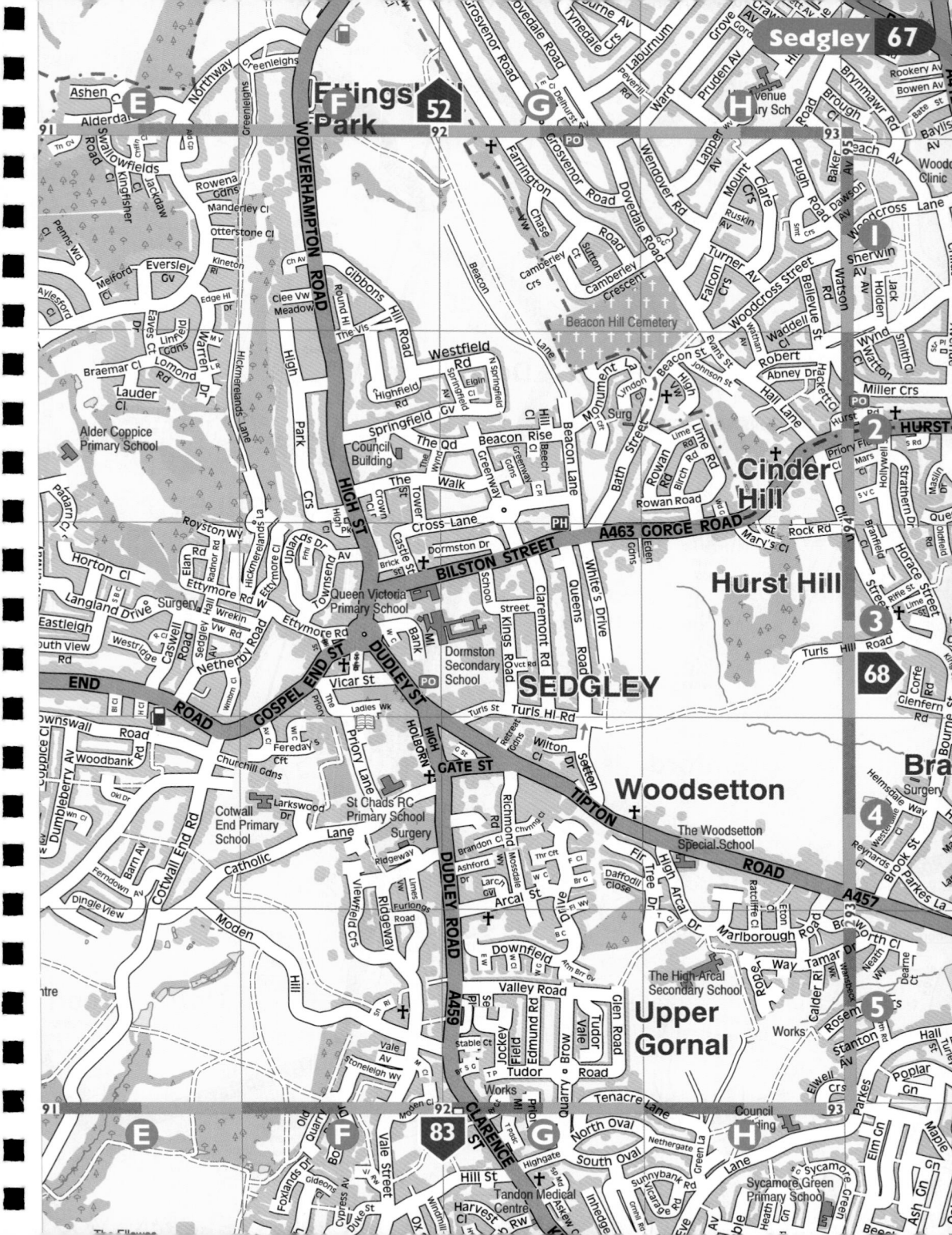

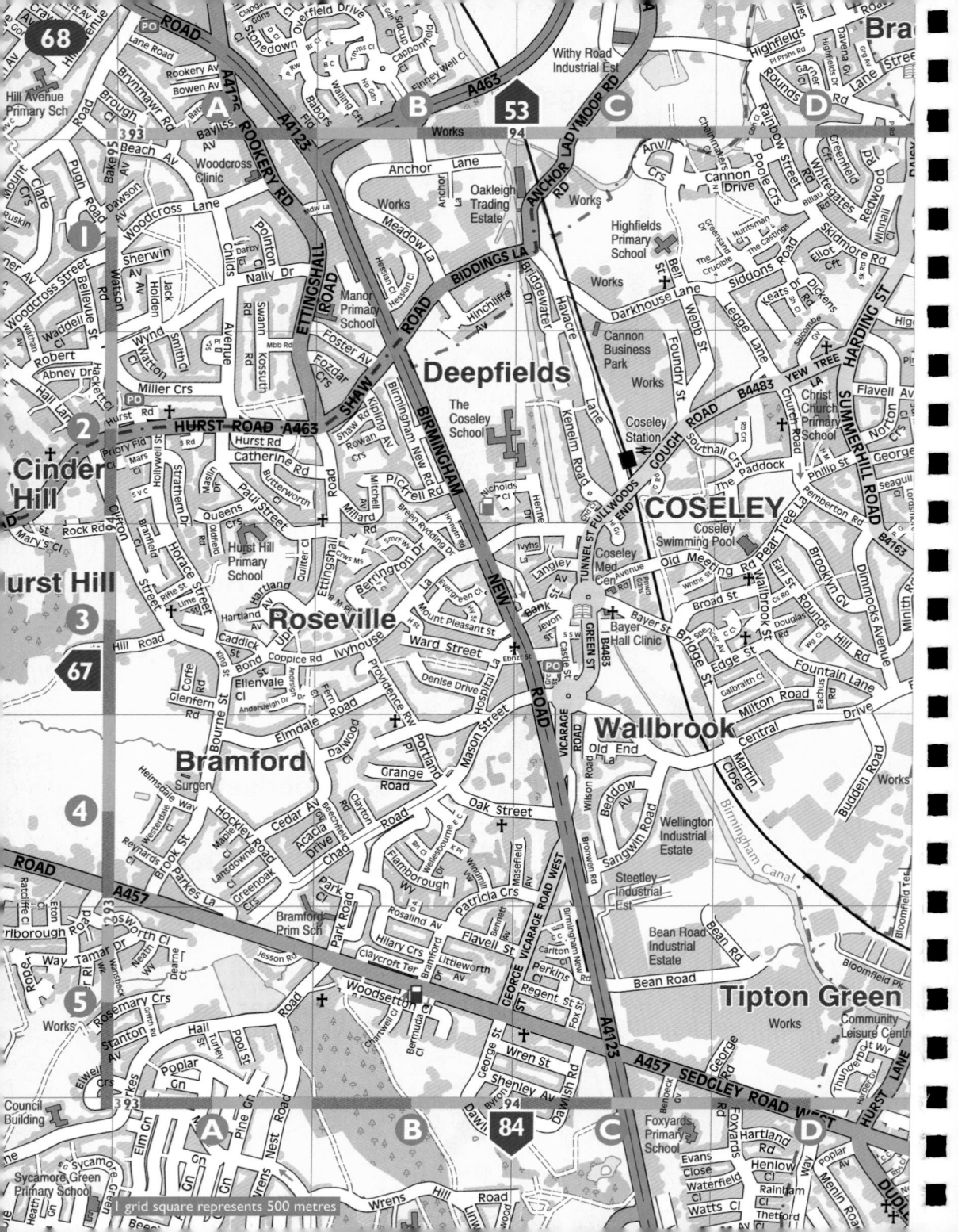

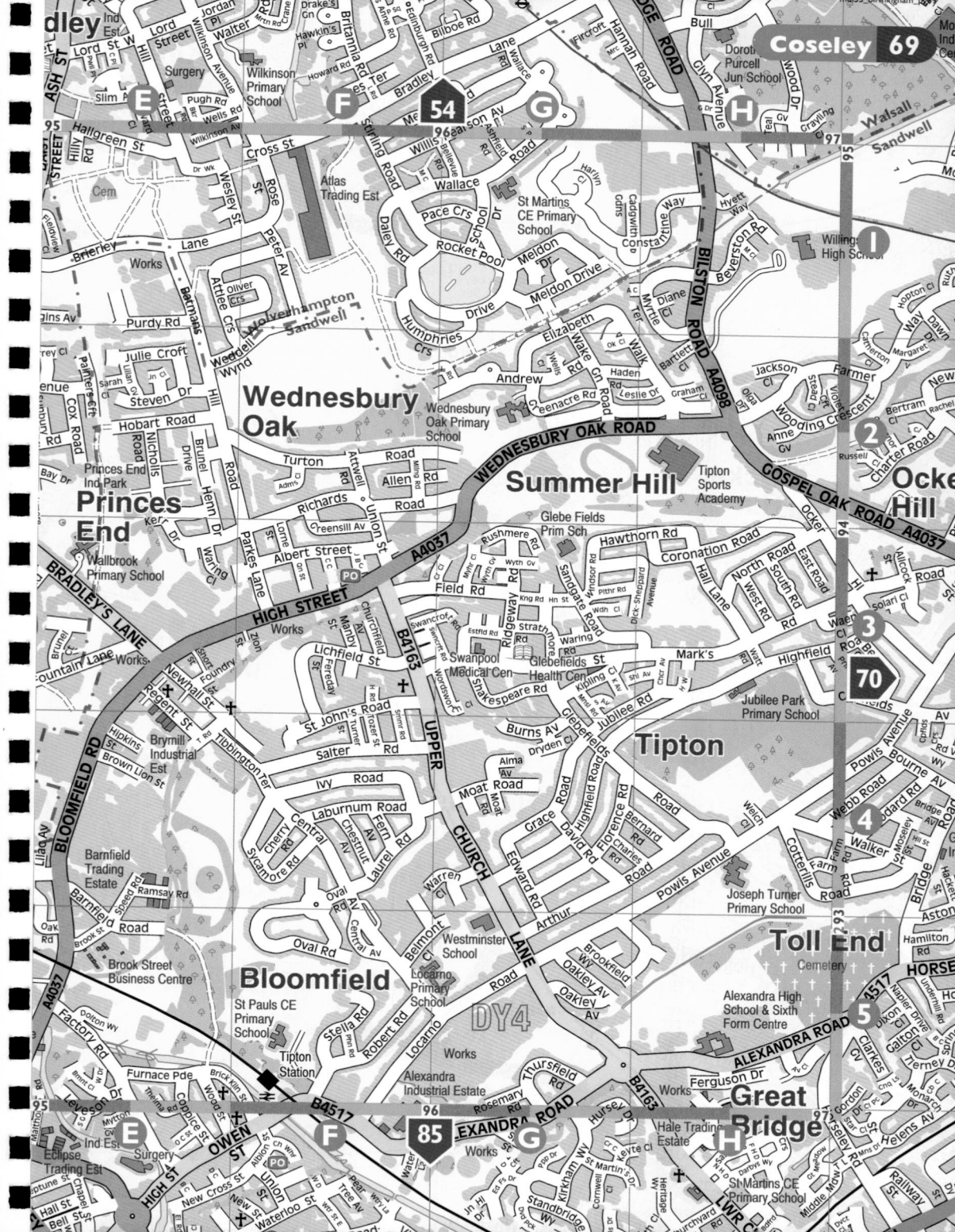

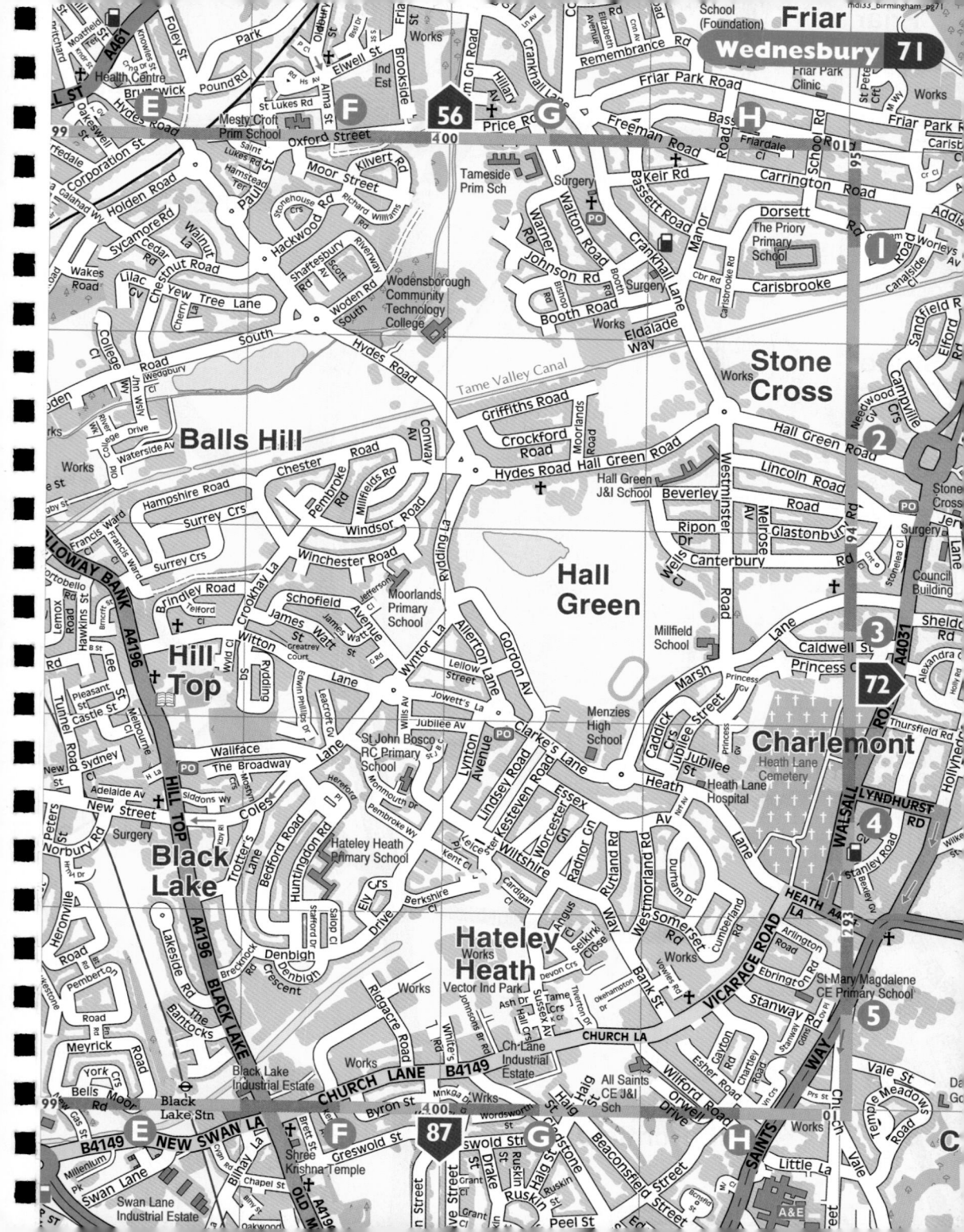

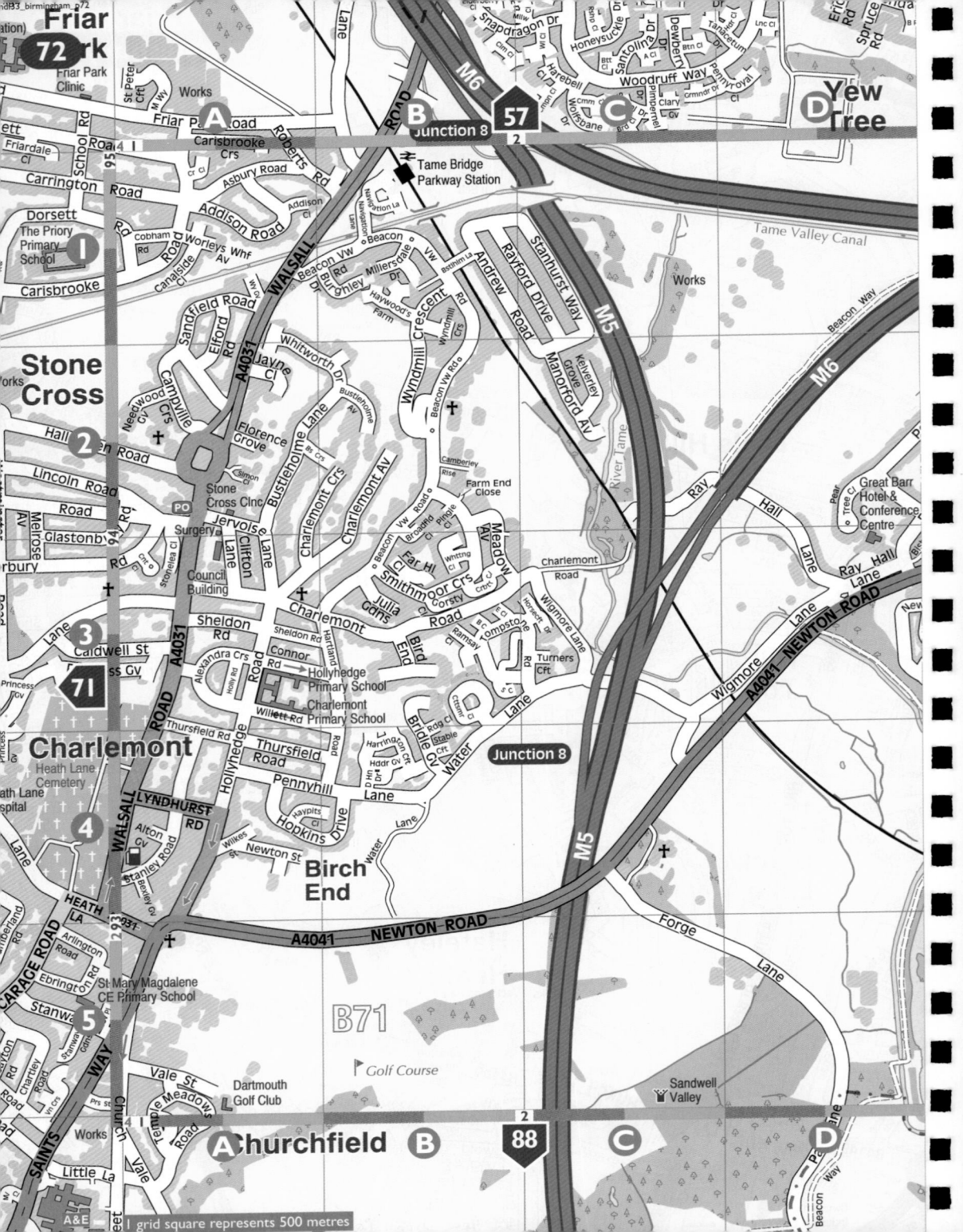

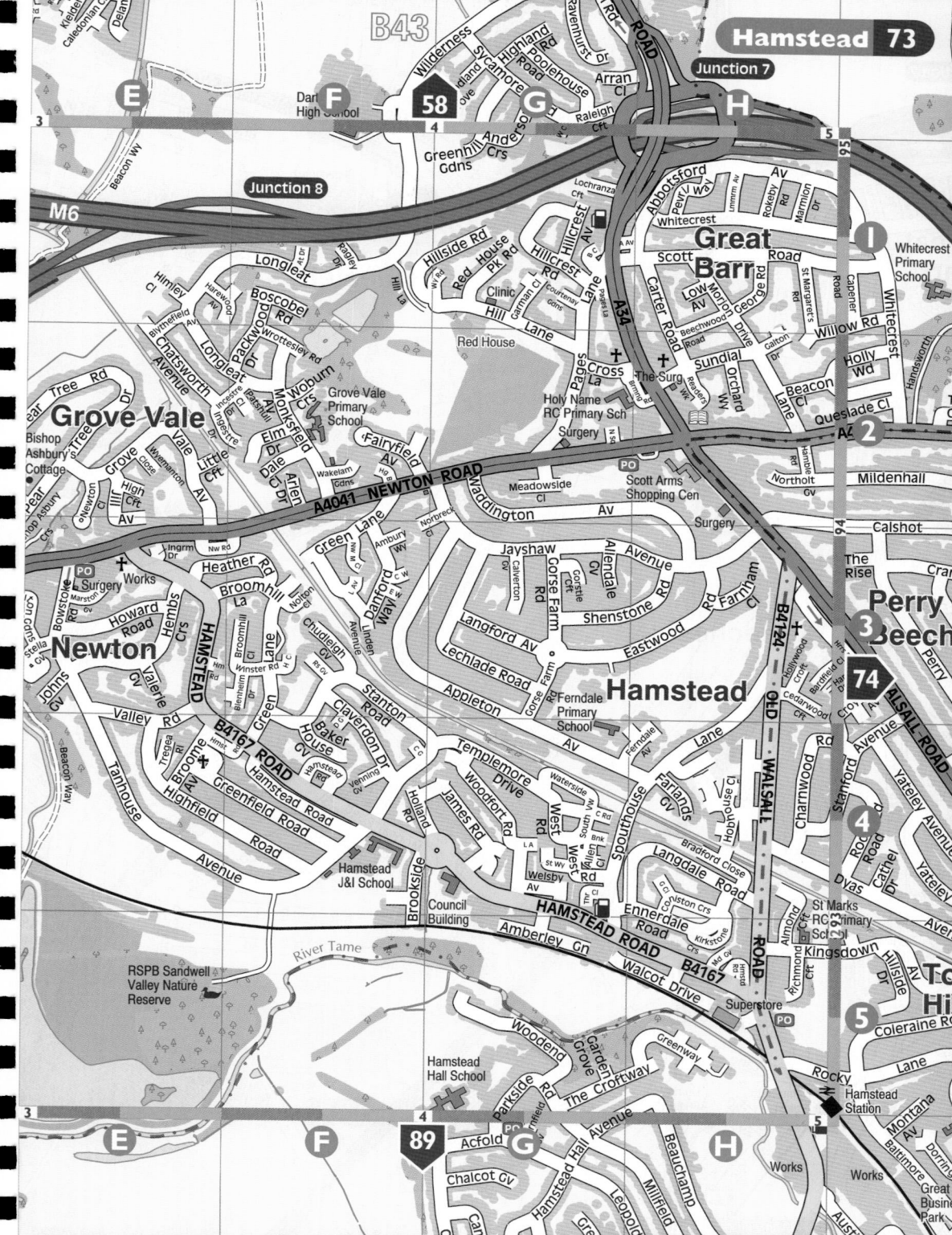

B43

Junction 8

M6

58

E F G H

I

Wilderness
Highland Rd
Poolehouse
Sycamore
Arran Cl
Raleigh Cft
Dart High School
Greenhill Gdns
Anders
Greenhill Crs

Abbotsford
Whitecrest
Great Barr
Scott
Abbotsford Road
Low Av
George Rd
St Margaret's
Beechwood Road
Carter Road
Morton Drive
Sundial Orchard
Calton
Beacon Cl
Queslade Cl

Capener
Willow Rd
Holly Wd
Whitecrest
Handsworth

Whitecrest Primary School

Hillside Rd
Red House Pk Rd
Hillcrest Rd
Hillcrest Rd
Clinic
Hill Lane
Cross La
Pages
Holy Name RC Primary Sch
Surgery
The Surg
Reader's

Longleat
Boscobel Rd
Woburn
Wrottesley Rd
Hill La
Red House

Grove Vale
Bishop Ashbury's Cottage
Chatsworth Avenue
Longleat
Packwood Dr
Monsfield Crs
Elm Dale Dr
Arlen
Wakelam Gdns
Fairyfield Av

Grove Vale Primary School

A4041 NEWTON ROAD
Meadowside Cl
Scott Arms Shopping Cen
Surgery
PO

2
A4
Mildenhall
Calshot
The Rise

Waddington Av

Newton
PO
Surgery
Works
Heather Rd
Broomhill La
Howard Road
Hembs Crs
HAMSTEAD
Broomhill
Chudleigh
Linden
Avenue
Green Lane
Stanton Road

Green Lane
Ambury Wy
Norbreck
Danford Way
Jayshaw Av
Calverton
Corse Cft
Corse Farm Rd
Alendale
Shenstone Rd
Eastwood
Rd
Farnham
Avenue
B4124
Perry Beech
Surgery
Northolt Gv
94

Langford Av
Lechlade Road
Appleton
Gorse Farm Rd
Hamstead
Ferndale Primary School
Ferndale Av
Lane

3
74
A34
Old
WALSALL
Stanford Avenue
ALSALL ROAD
Perry
Yateley Avenue

Valerie
Valley Rd
B4167 ROAD
Baker House
Claverdon Dr
Venning Gv
Templemore Drive
Woodfort Rd
Waterside
West Rd
South Vw
Spouthouse
Farlands Gv
Charnwood Rd
Rock Road
Cathel
Dyas
Yateley
Aven

4

Tregea
Broome Av
Greenfield Road
Highfield Road
Avenue
Holland
James Rd
West
Welsby
Allen Rd
Bradford Close
Hobhouse Cl
Langdale Road
Cedarwood
St Marks RC Primary School
Almond
Cft

Hamstead J&I School
Council Building
Brookside
Amberley Gn
HAMSTEAD ROAD
Ennerdale Road
Kirkstone
Kingsdown
Richmond Cft
PO
5
Coleraine Rd
Montana Av

RSPB Sandwell Valley Nature Reserve
River Tame
Walcot Drive
B4167
Superstore
PO
Rocky Lane
Hamstead Station

Woodend
Garden Grove
Greenway
Works

Hamstead Hall School
Parkside Rd
The Croftway
Hamstead Hall Avenue
Beauchamp
Leopold
Works
Baltimore

89
Acfold
Chalcot Gv
Green
Austin

E F G H

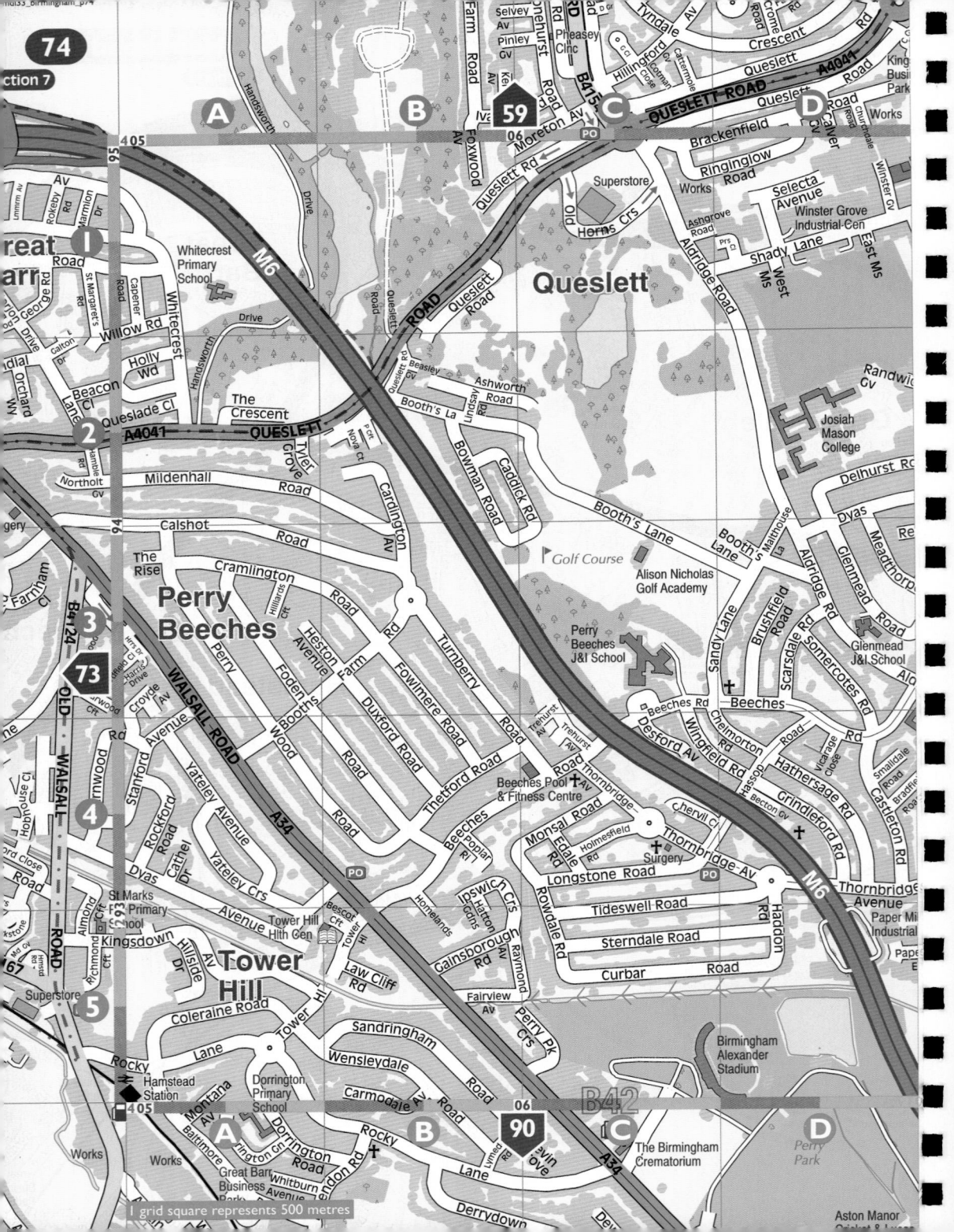

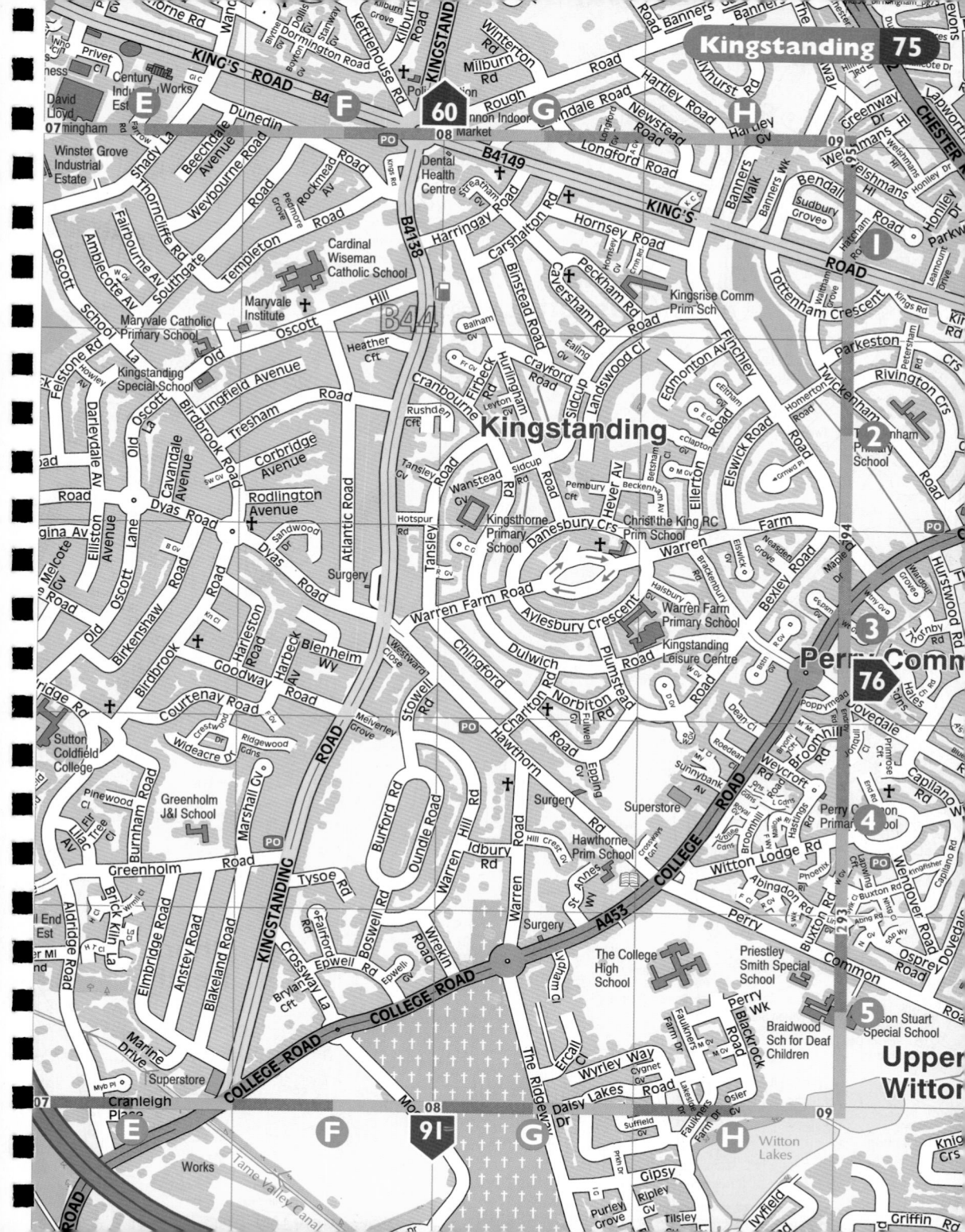

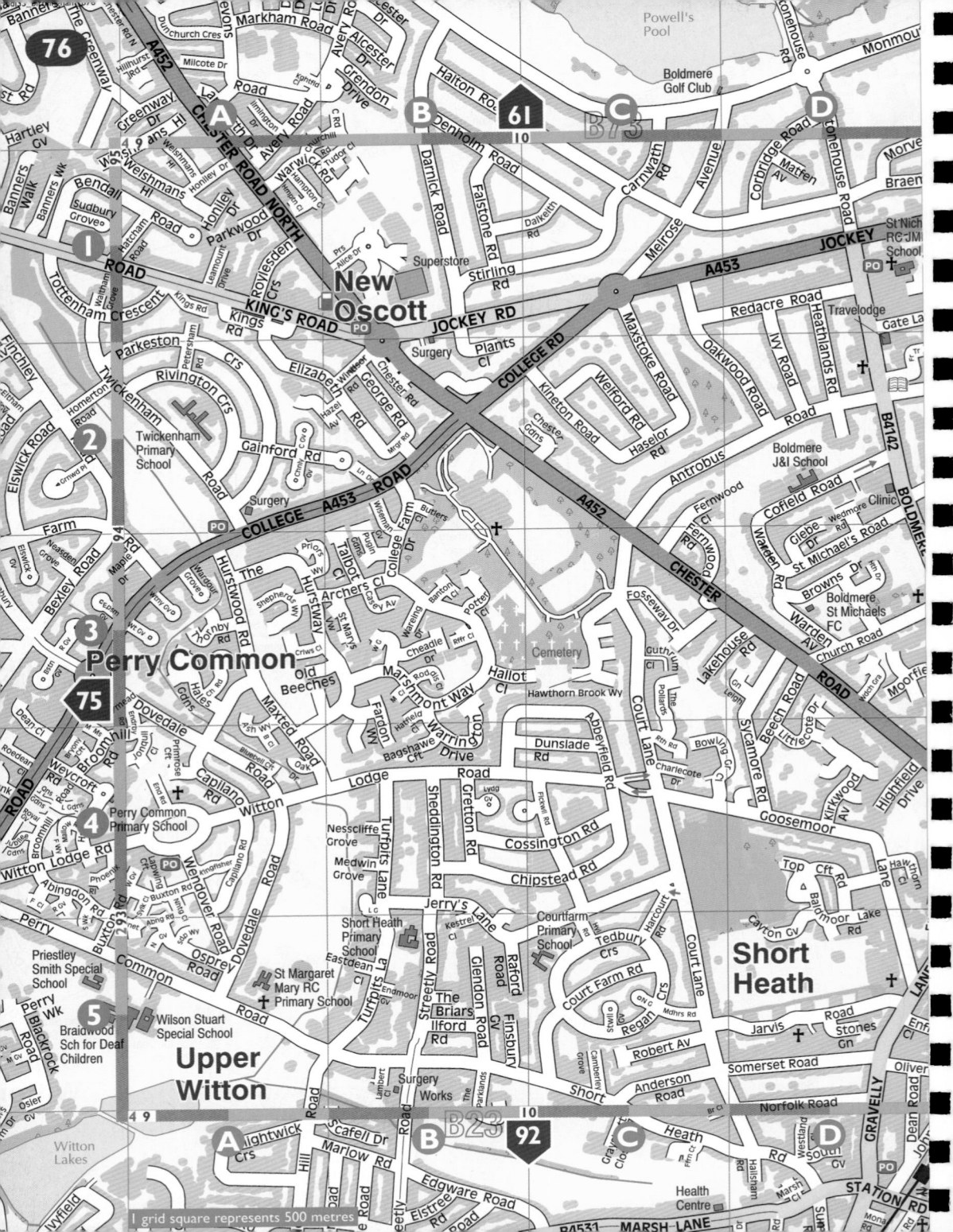

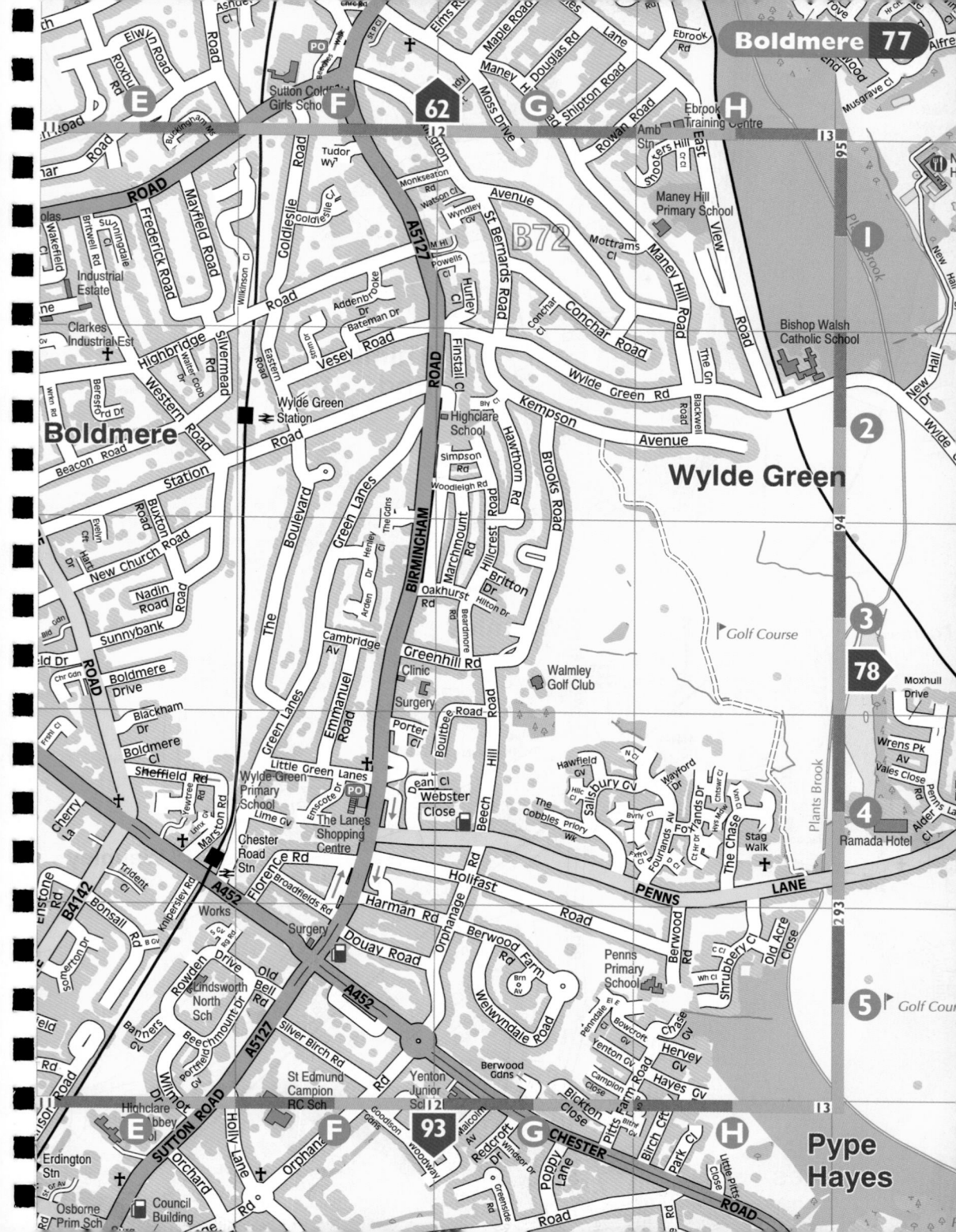

E F Ox Leys Farm G x Leys Road H Grove

15 16 **Grove** **End** 17

Golf Course

Fairview Farm

Wishaw Golf Course

A38

Bull's Lane

Grove Lane

Church Lane

2 **B76**

Over Green

Curdworth Lane

Golf Course

Peddimore Hall

Wishaw Lane

Wiggins Hill Road

Warwickshire County Birmingham

3

4

Peddimore

A38

Peddimore Lane

Wiggins Hill Farm

Peddimore Lane

Hurst Green Farm

5

Superstore

Far Rd

Vale Gv

Thorney Cl

Lindridge Dr

Beaumont Way

Cottage Lane

Oxall Close

Hurst Gn Rd

Summer La

Lawrence Drive

W Dr

Longley Av

Kingsbury Close

Birmingham & Fazeley Canal

Kingsbury Business Park

The Greaves

K

Stockton Cl

Minworth Industrial Park

E oakenhayes Crs

KINGSBURY ROAD

Old Kingsbury Road

F

95 orks **A4097** **G** **H**

16 17

Midpoint Bvd

Minworth

Water Orton La

Minworth J&I School

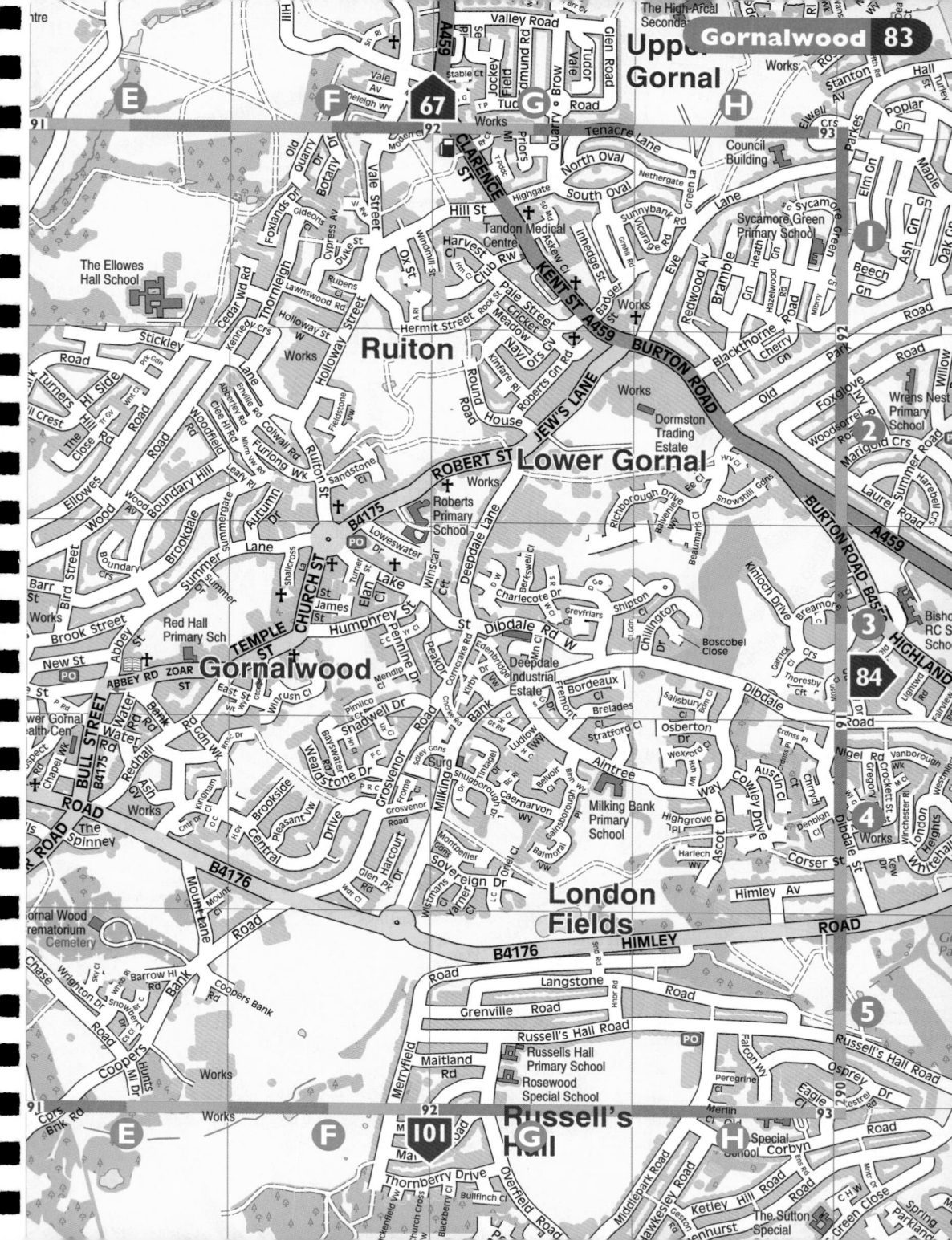

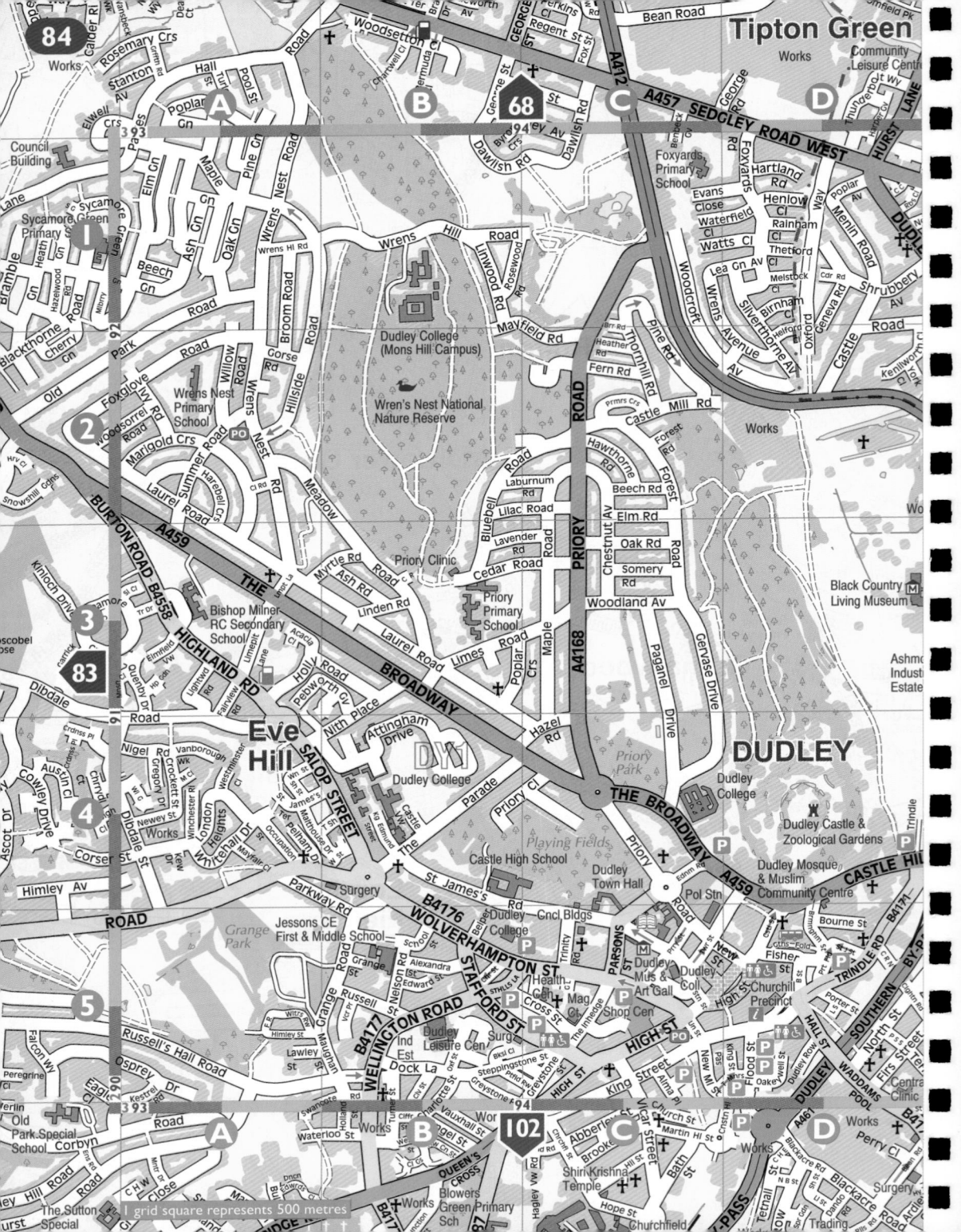

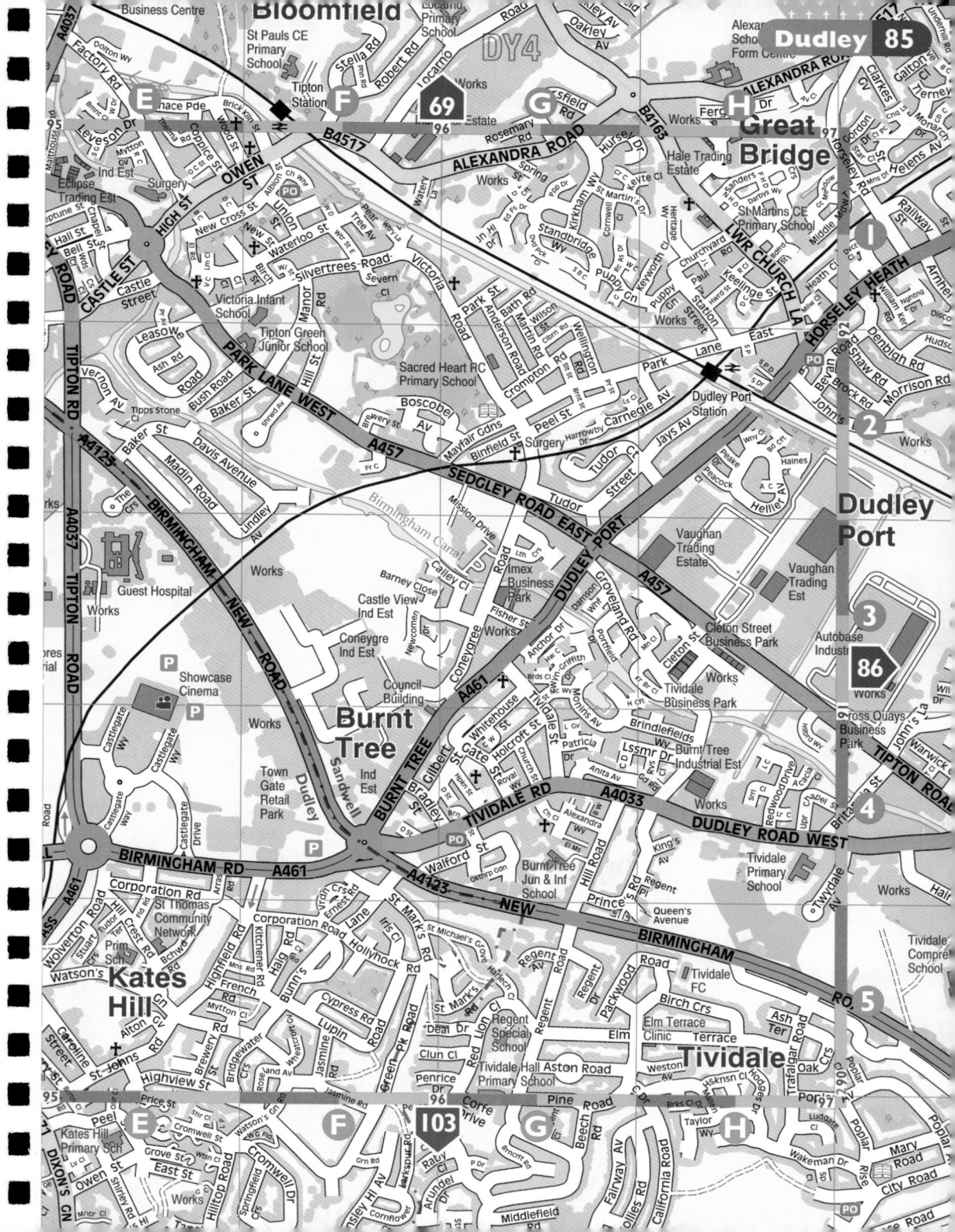

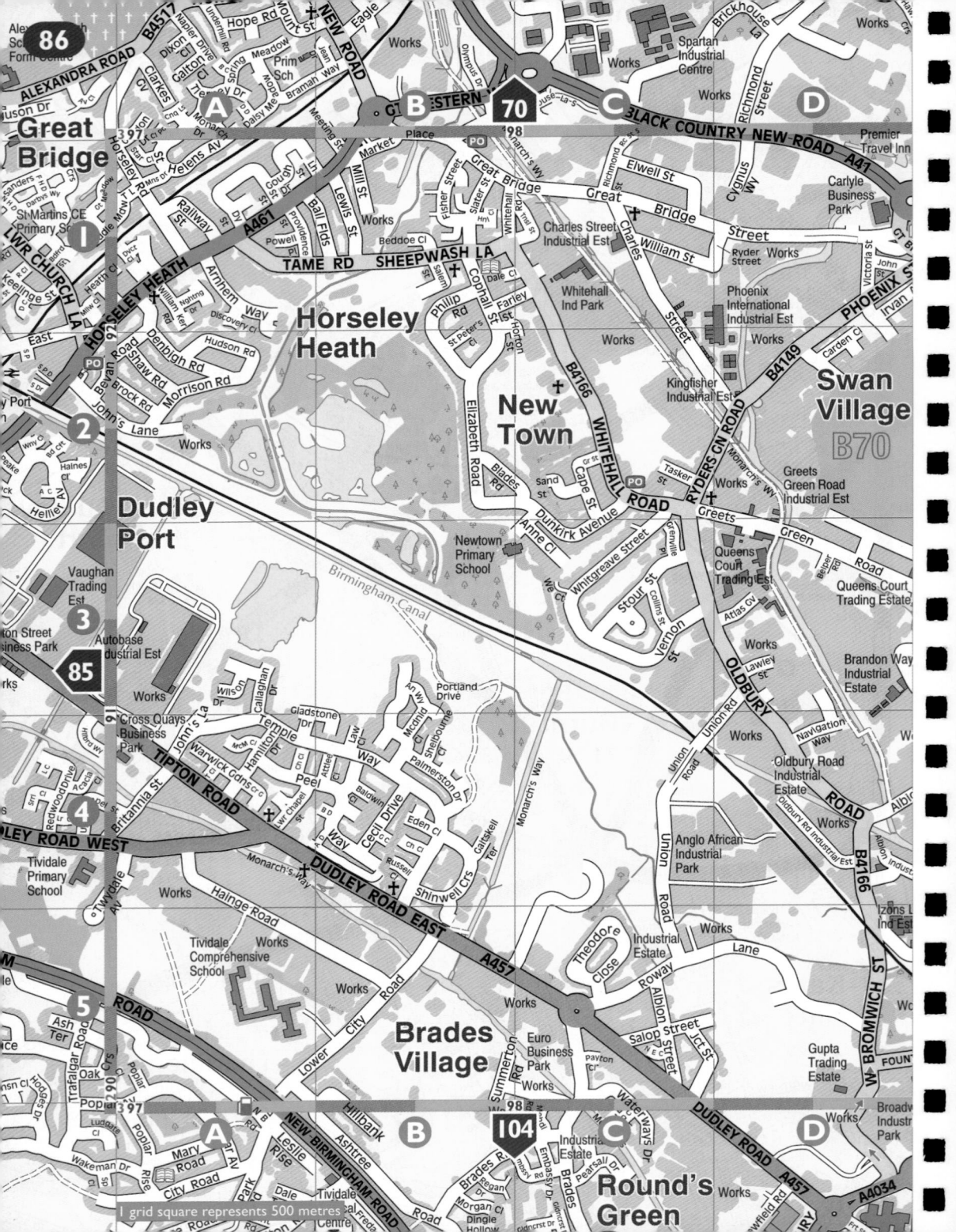

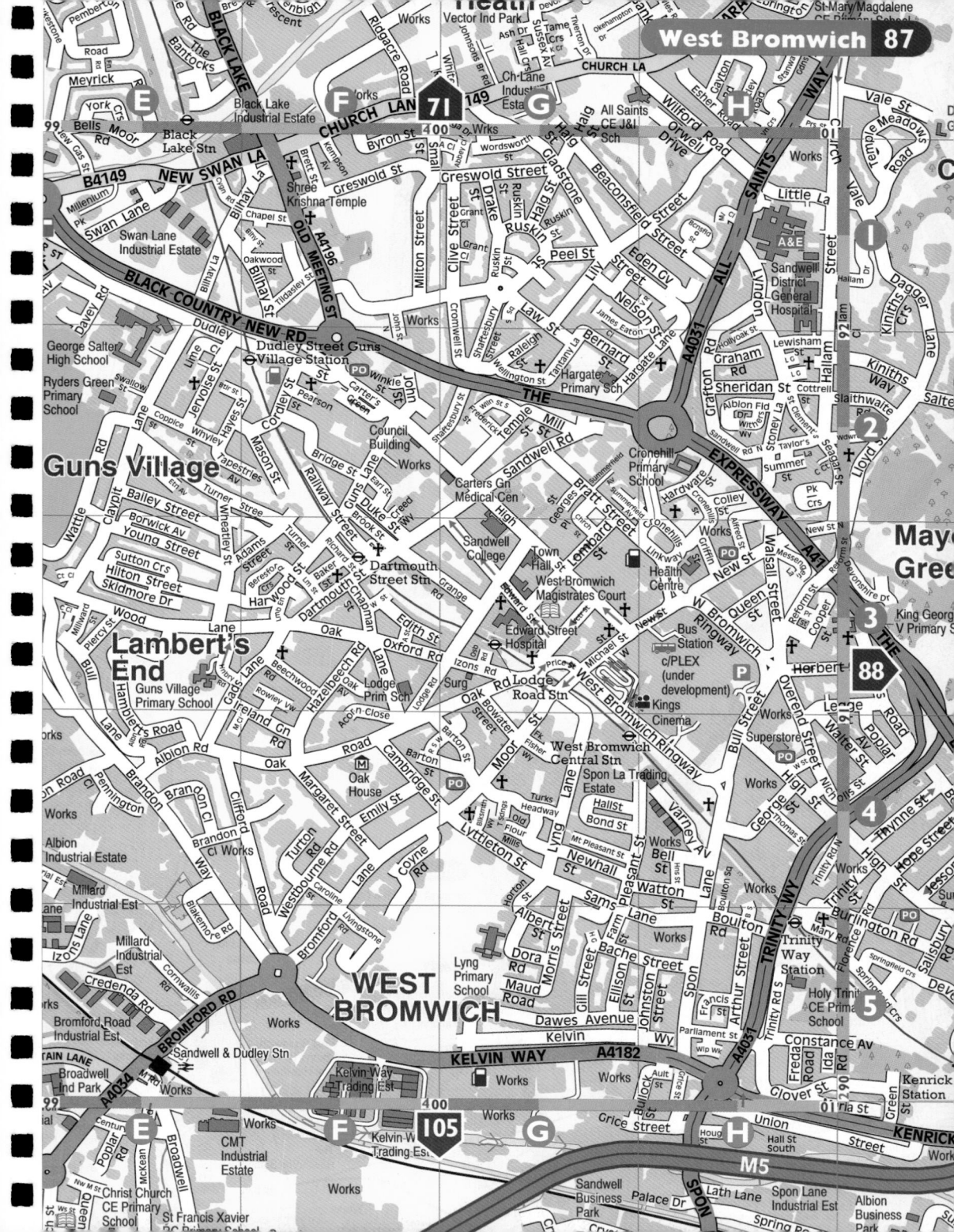

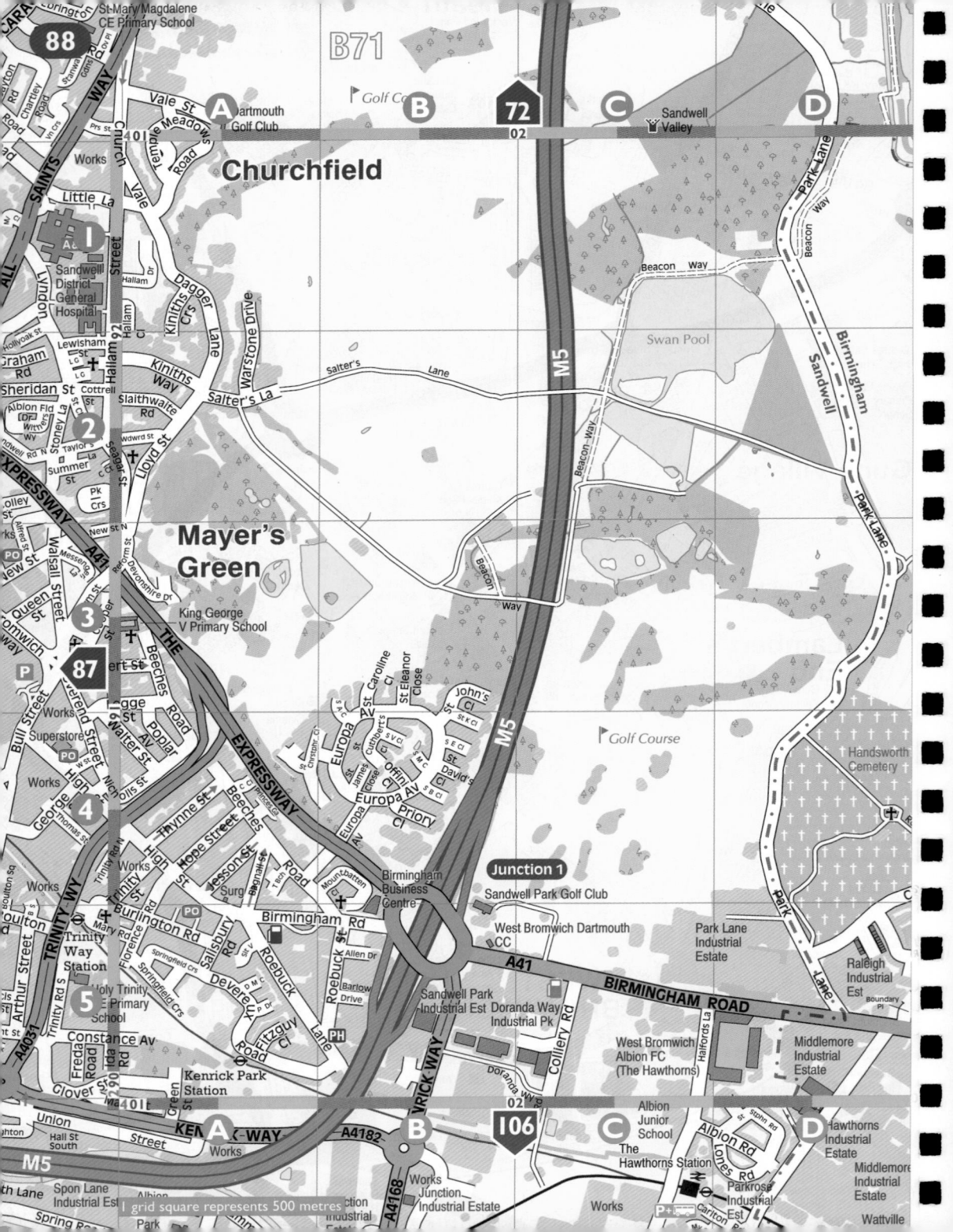

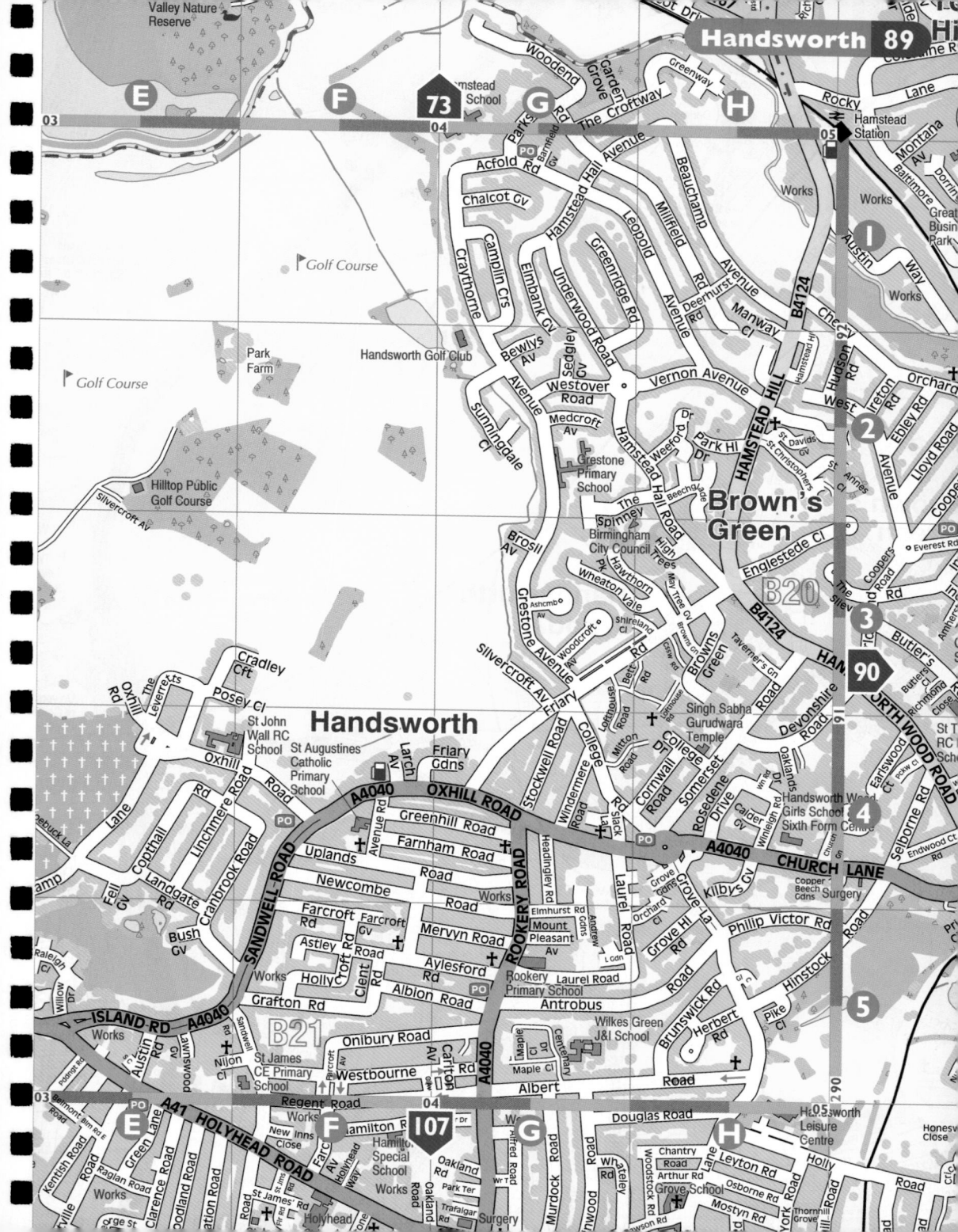

Valley Nature Reserve

E   F   73   G   H

03   04   05

Golf Course

Golf Course

Park Farm

Hilltop Public Golf Course

Silvercroft Av

Hamstead School

Woodend

Garden Grove

The Croftway

Greenway

Rocky Lane

Hamstead Station

Parks Rd

Montana

Acfold Rd

Barnfield

PO

Baltimore

Dornie

Chalcot Gv

Hamstead Hall Avenue

Beauchamp

Works

Works

Great Busin Park

Crawthorne

Camplin Crs

Leopold

Millfield Rd

Avenue

Austin

Way

Works

I

Elmbank Gv

Greenridge Rd

Deernhurst Rd

Manway Cl

Hudson

West

Treton Rd

Orchard

Bewlys Av

Sedgley

Underwood Road

Vernon Avenue

St Davids Gv

St Christophers

Annes

Ebley Rd

Lloyd Road

2

Westover Road

Dr

Park Hl

Dr

Avenue

Cooper

Medcroft Av

Weeford

Beechd

Brown's Green

PO

Everest Rd

Sunningdale Cl

Grestone Primary School

The Spinney

Birmingham City Council

High Trees

Englestede Cl

The

Coopers Road

3

Brosil Av

Hawthorn

May Tree Cl

B20

Butler's

Grestone Avenue

Ashcmb Av

Wheaton Vale

Pk

Browns Green

B4124

HAM

90

Silvercroft Av

Woodcroft

Shireland Cl

Battr

Eskw Rd

Taverner's Gn

ORTH WOOD ROAD

Butler's

Richmond

Close

Cradley Cft

Oxhill Rd

The Leverets

Posey Cl

Friary

Loughouse

Mitton Rd

Singh Sabha Gurudwara Temple

Devonshire Road

St

RC

Earlswood Ct

Selborne Rd

Handsworth

St John Wall RC School

St Augustines Catholic Primary School

Larch Av

Friary Gdns

Stockwell Road

College

Cornwall Road

Somerset Rd

Rosedene Drive

Handsworth Wood Girls School & Sixth Form Centre

Endwood Ct Rd

4

Oxhill Road

PO

A4040 OXHILL ROAD

Avenue Rd

Greenhill Road

Windermere Road

College Road

Calder Gv

A4040

CHURCH LANE

290

Uplands

Farnham Road

Laurel Road

Grove Hl

Kilbys

Copper Beech Gdns

Surgery

Newcombe

Road

Road

Works

Elmnurst Rd

Mount Pleasant Rd

Andrew Gdns

Grove Gdns

Orchard

Grove Hl Rd

Philip Victor Road

Hinstock

5

Farcroft Rd

Farcroft Gv

Mervyn Road

Aylesford Road

Rookery Primary School

Laurel Road

Brunswick Rd

Herbert Rd

Pike Cl

Astley Rd

Clent Rd

Hollycroft Rd

Albion Rd

Grafton Rd

Antrobus

Wilkes Green J&I School

Road

ISLAND RD A4040

Fell Gv

Landgate Rd

Bush Gv

Works

Sandwell Rd

B21

Onibury Road

Carlton Av

A4040

Centenary

Maple Cl

Raleigh Rd

Willow

Austin Rd

Nijon

St James CE Primary School

Westbourne

Albert

Road

Douglas Road

Handsworth Leisure Centre

Honeswo Close

E   F   107   G   H

HOLYHEAD ROAD

A41

Regent Road

Works

New Inns Close

Hamilton Rd

Hamilton Special School

Oakland Road

Park Ter

Alfred Road

Whateley Rd

Chantry Road

Arthur Rd

Grove School

Leyton Rd

Osborne Rd

Holly

Green Lane

Kentish Road

Raglan Road

Clarence Road

Works

Trafalgar

Surgery

Murdock Rd

Woodstock Rd

York Rd

Mostyn Rd

Thornhill

Road

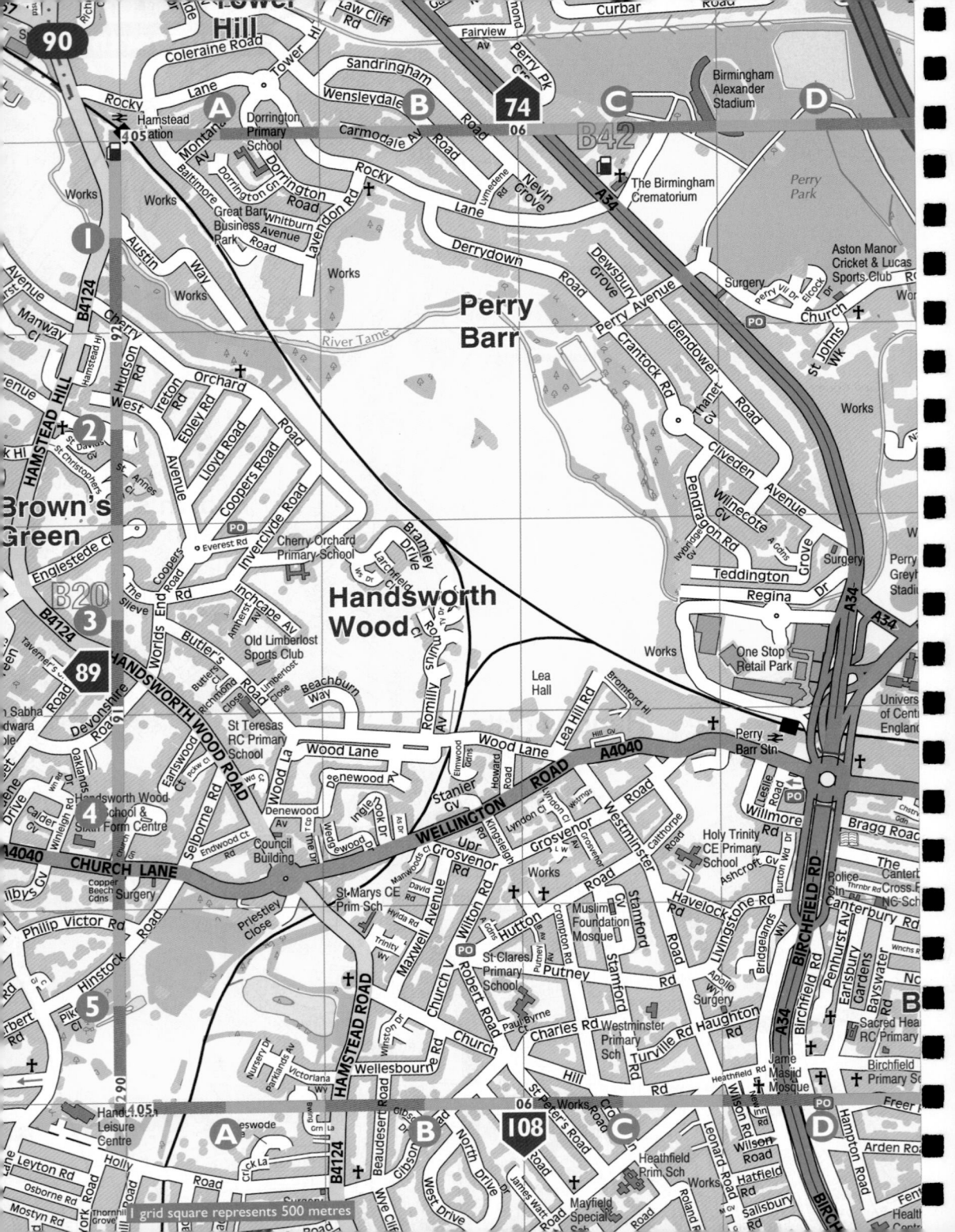

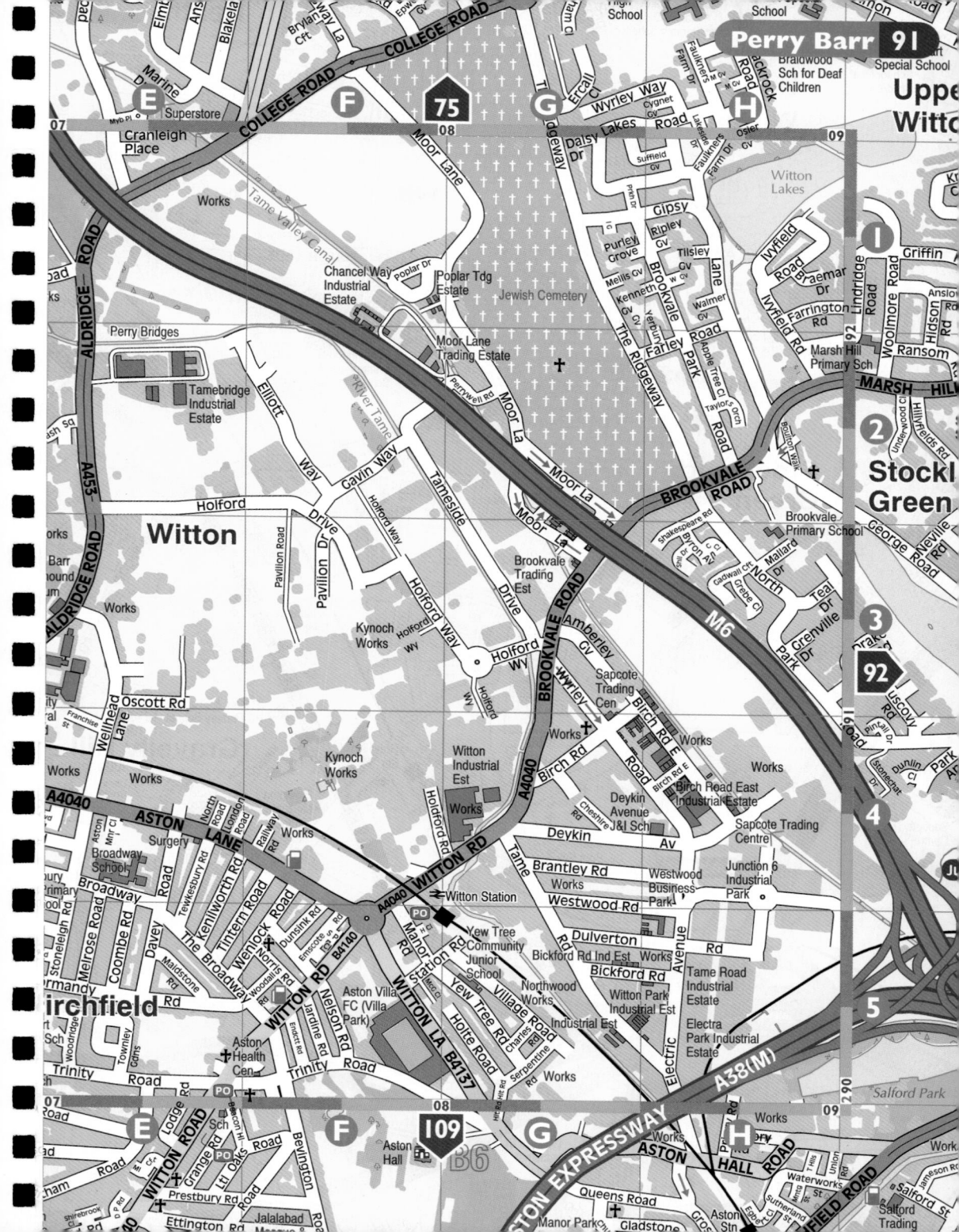

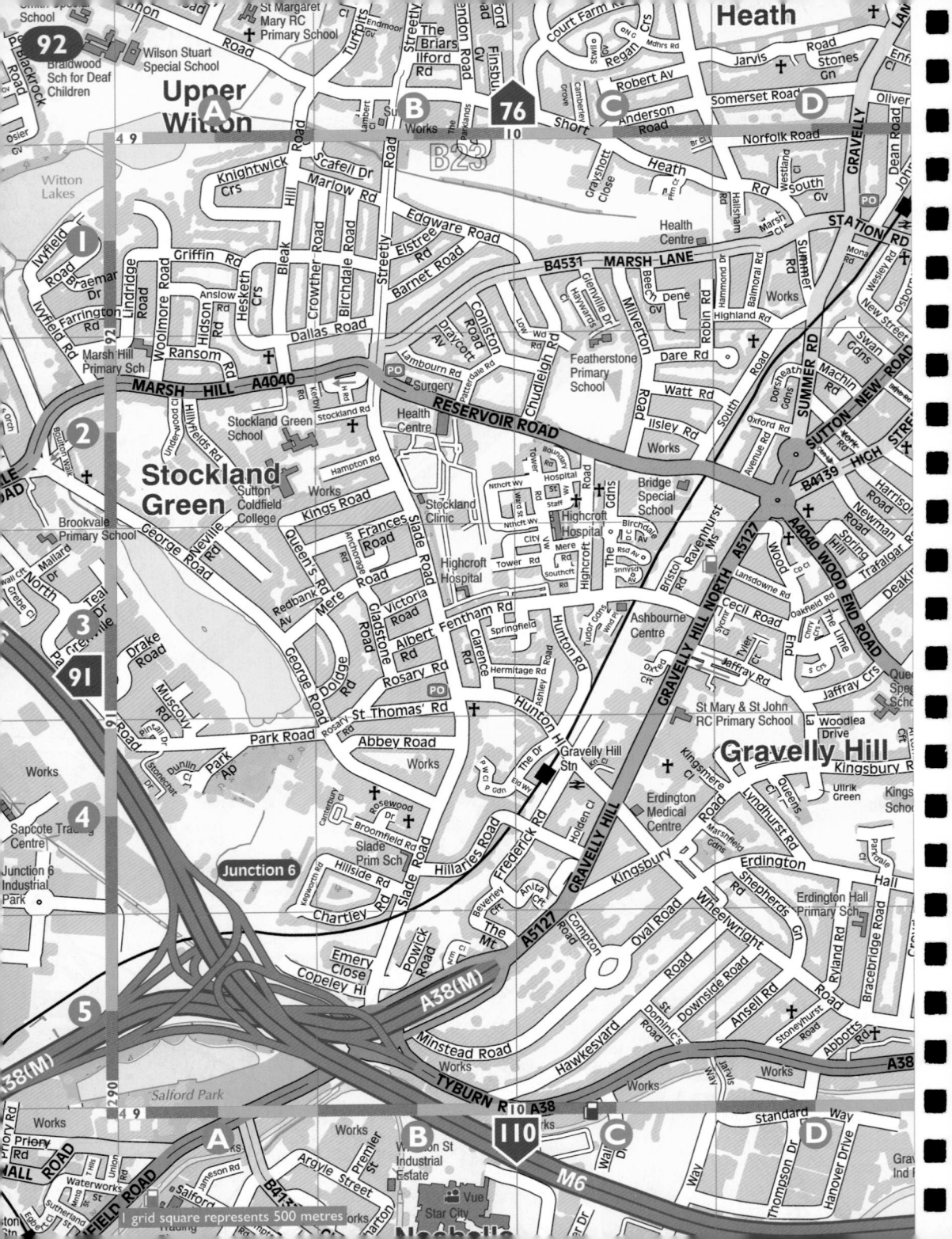

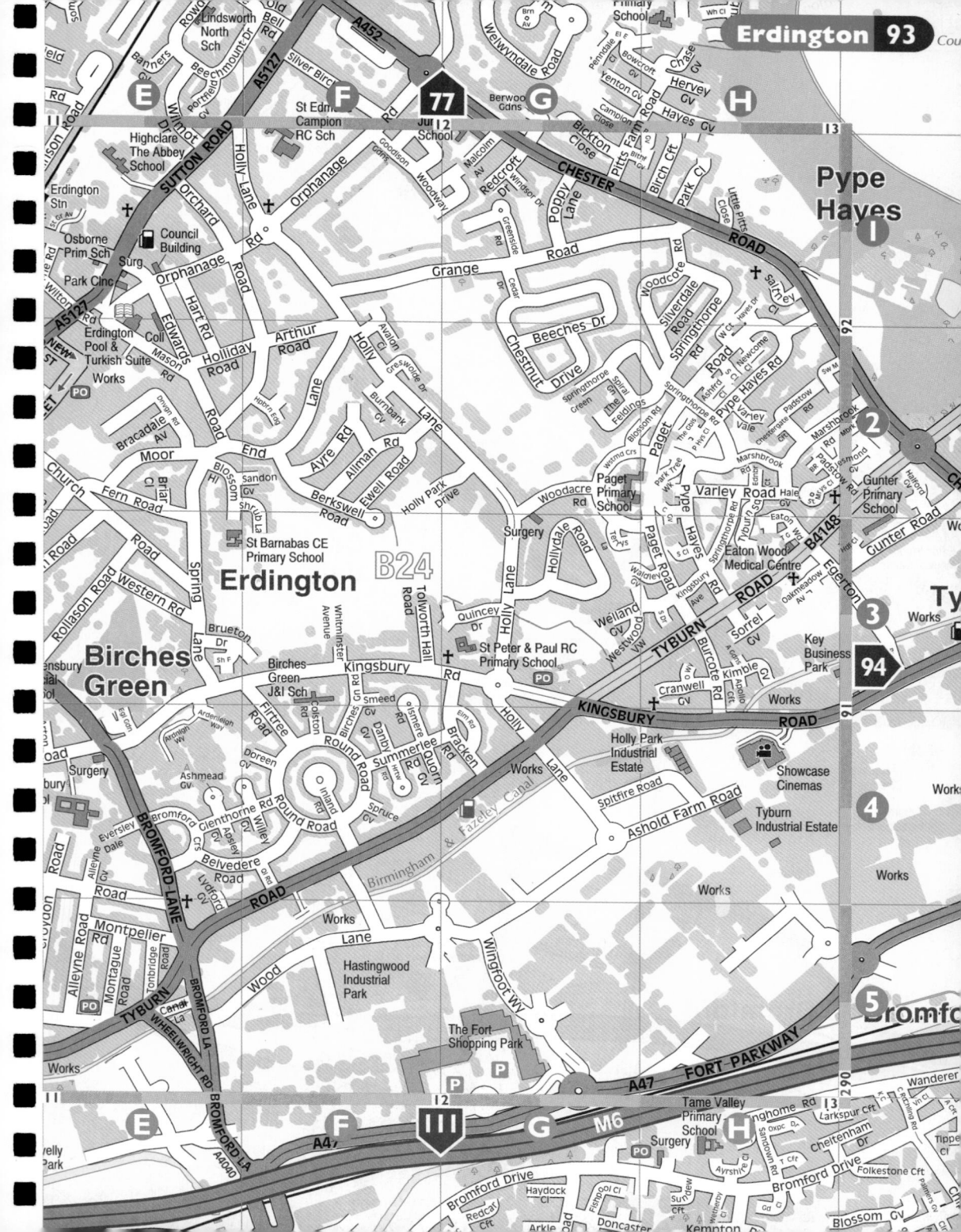

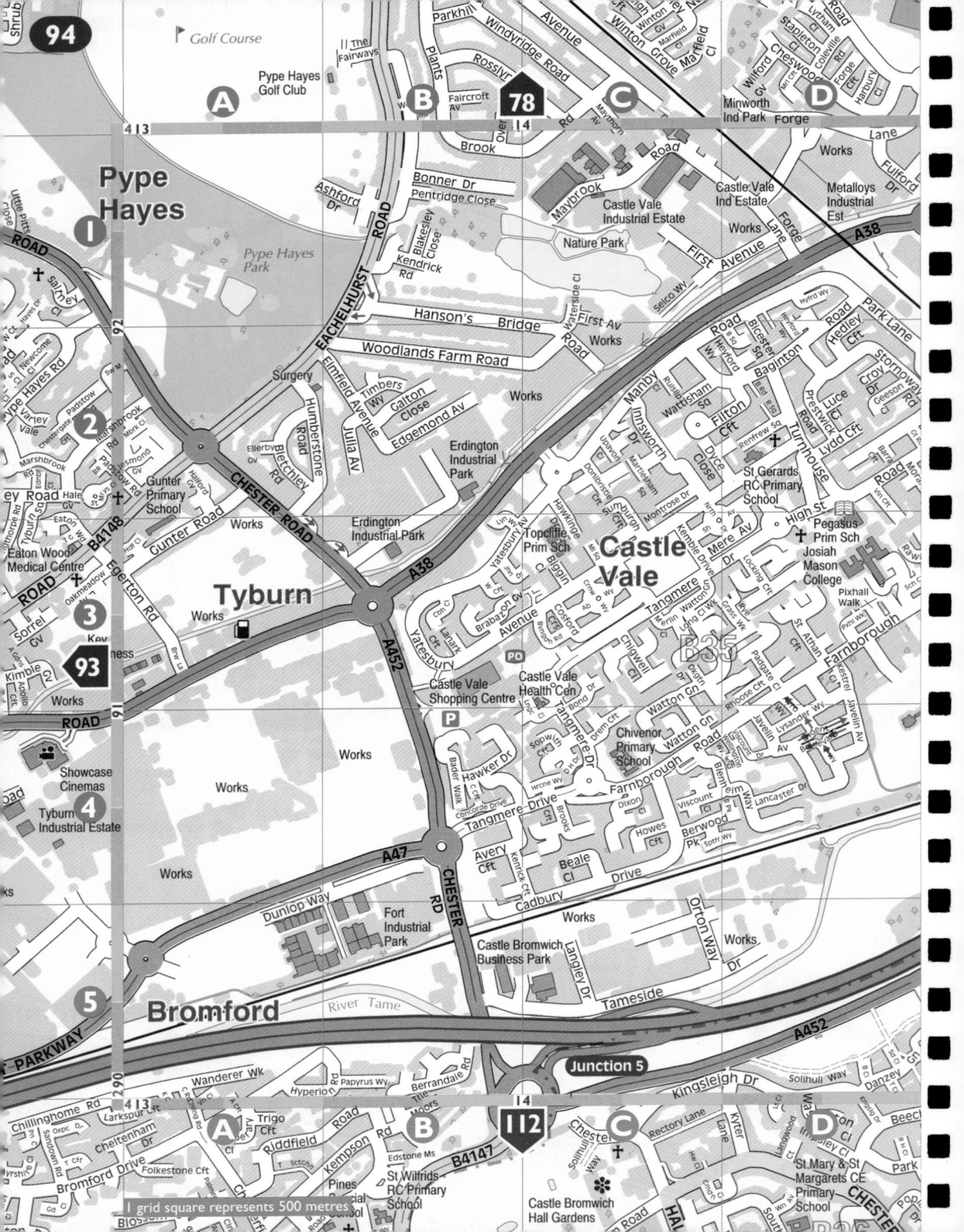

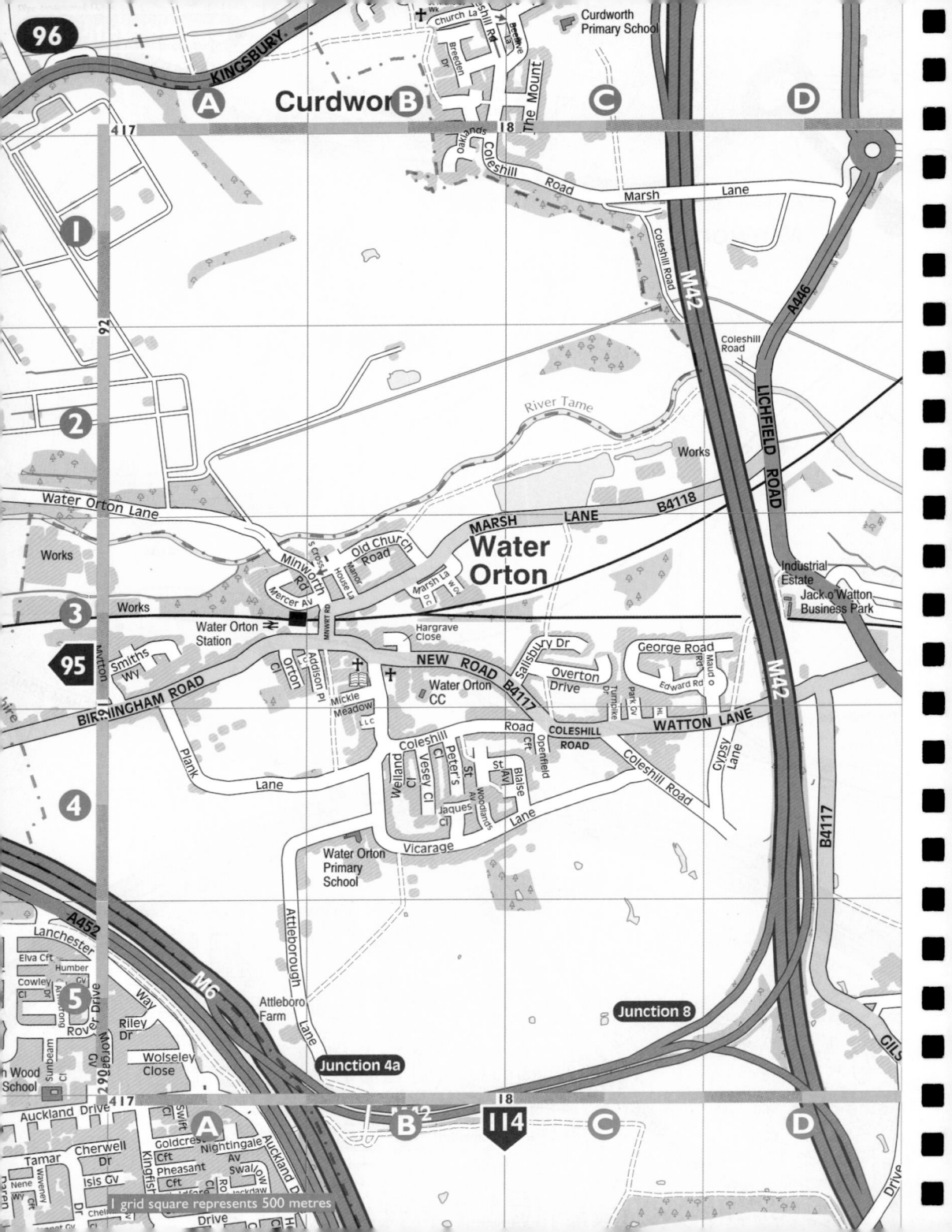

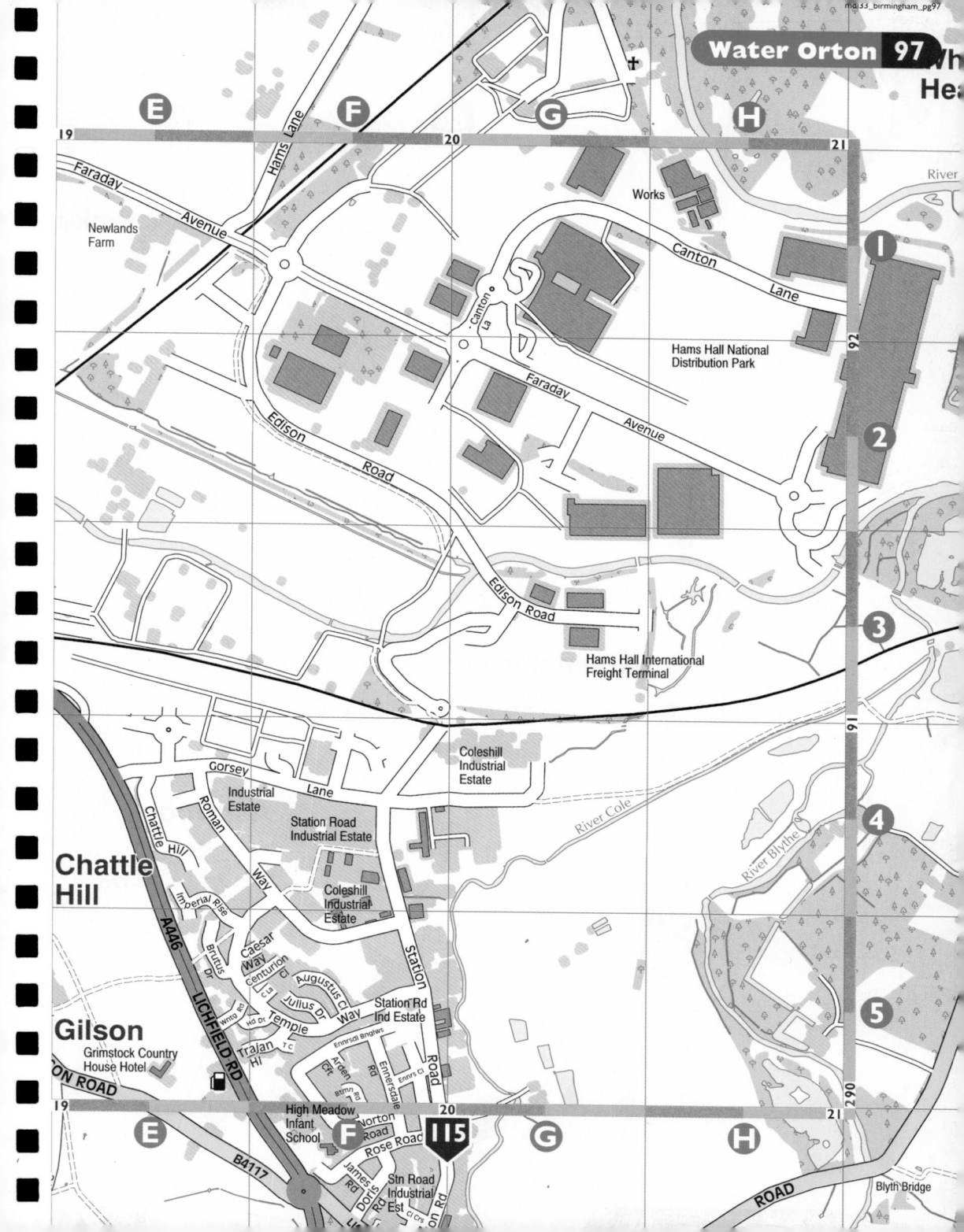

Wh
Hea

River

Works

Canton Lane

Faraday Avenue

Newlands Farm

Canton La

Hams Hall National Distribution Park

Edison Road

Faraday Avenue

Edison Road

Hams Hall International Freight Terminal

Coleshill Industrial Estate

River Cole

Gorsey Lane

Industrial Estate

Station Road Industrial Estate

River Blythe

Chattle Hill

Roman Way

Imperial Rise

Coleshill Industrial Estate

Chattle Hill

A446

Gilson

Grimstock Country House Hotel

Brutus Dr

Caesar Way

Centurion Cl

Augustus Cl

Julius Dr

Temple

Trajan Hi

Wng Rd

Hd Dr

TC

TC

Station Road

Station Rd Ind Estate

Ennrsdl Bnglws

Ennrs Cl

Ennersdale Rd

LICHFIELD RD

ON ROAD

High Meadow Infant School

Norton Road

Rose Road

James Rd

Doris Rd

Arden Cl

Cft

Bttmn Rd

Cft

Stn Road Industrial Est

Cl Crs

115

B4117

ROAD

Blyth Bridge

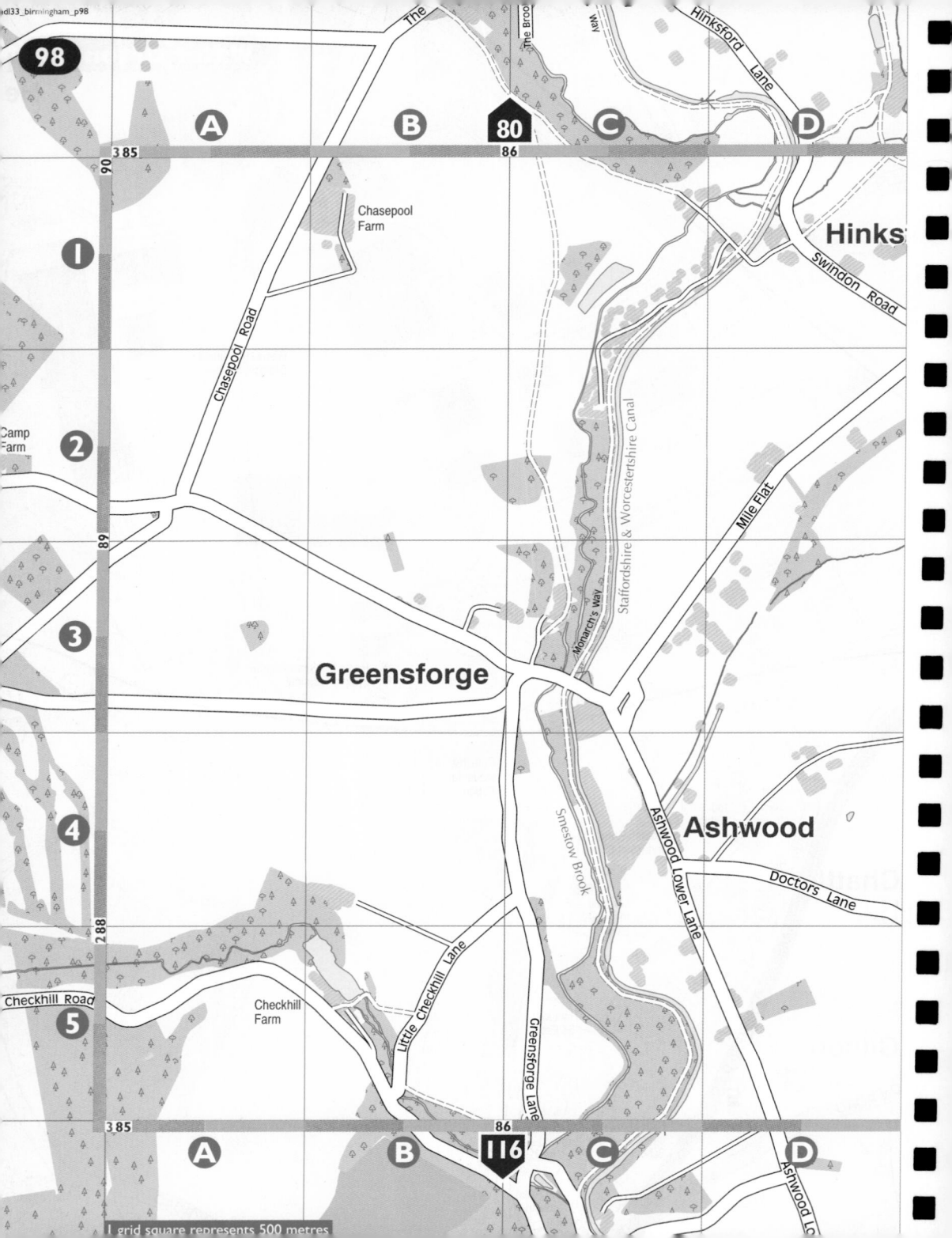

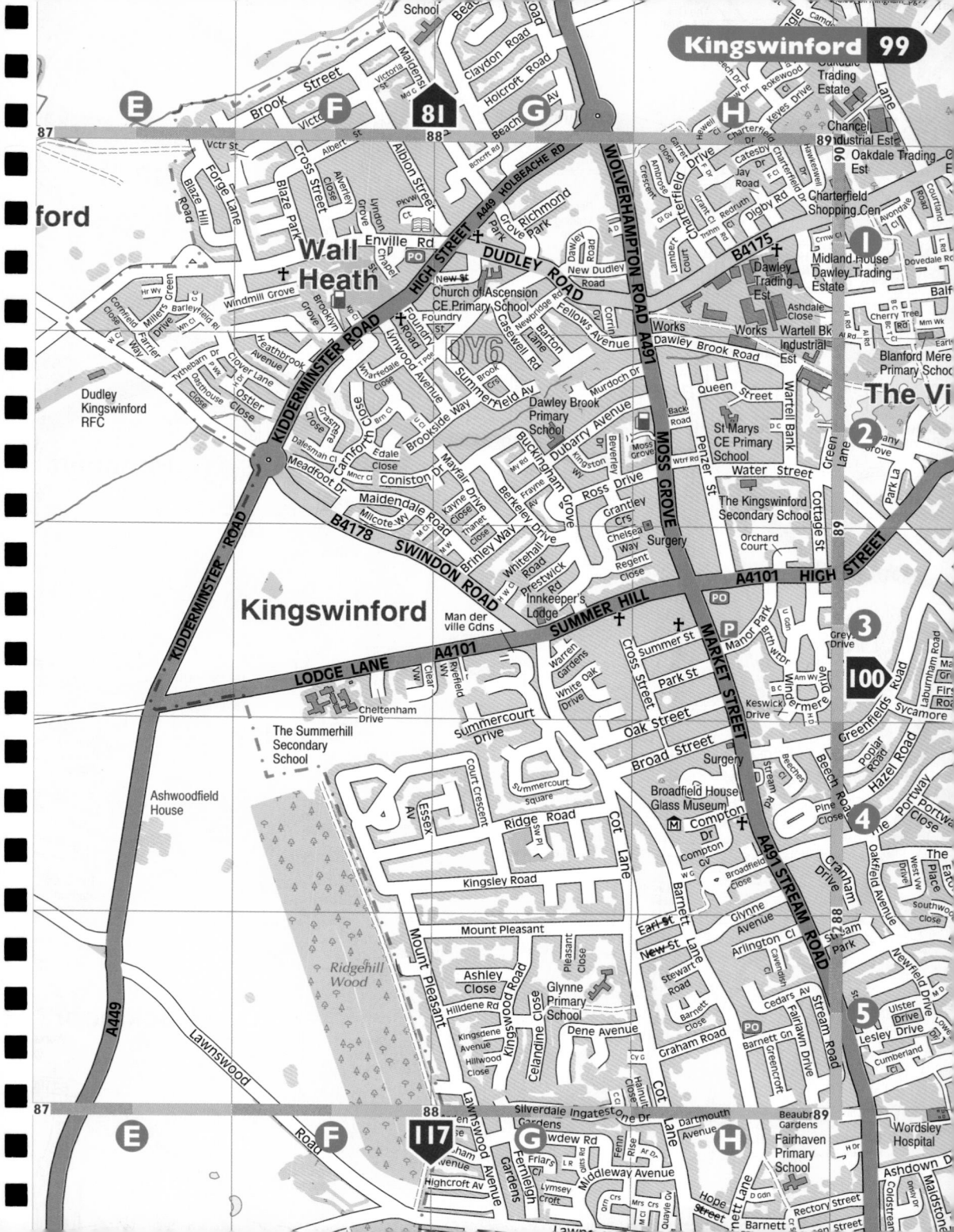

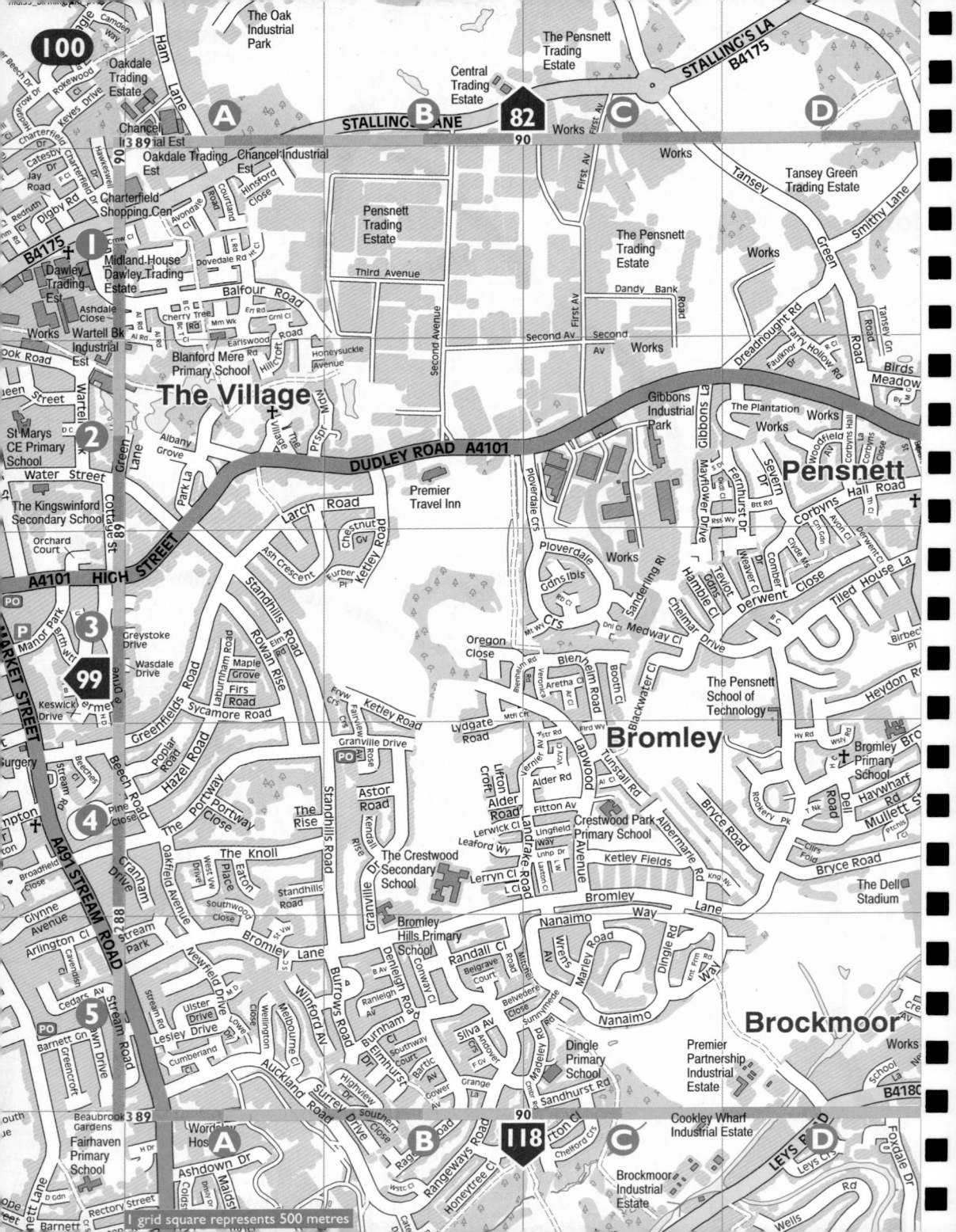

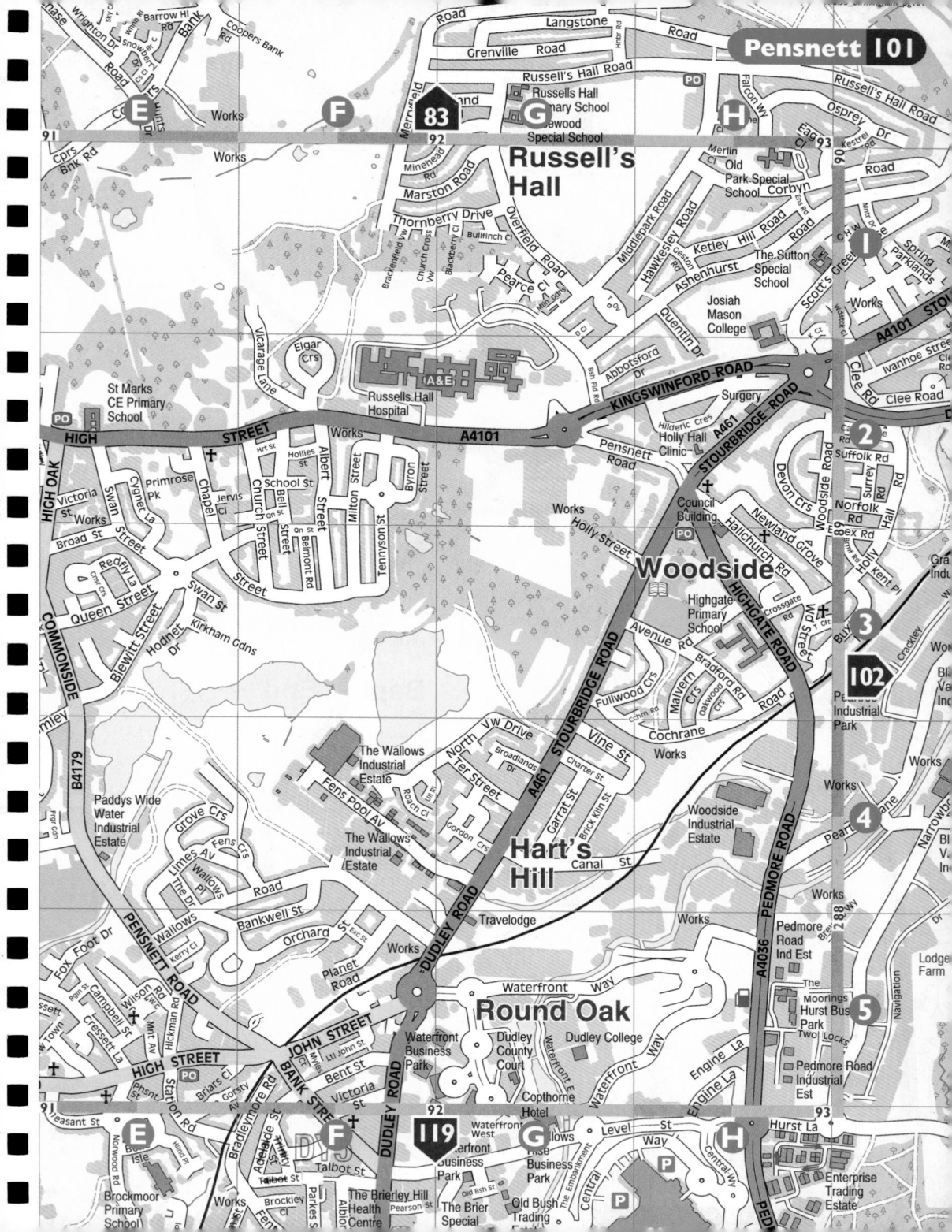

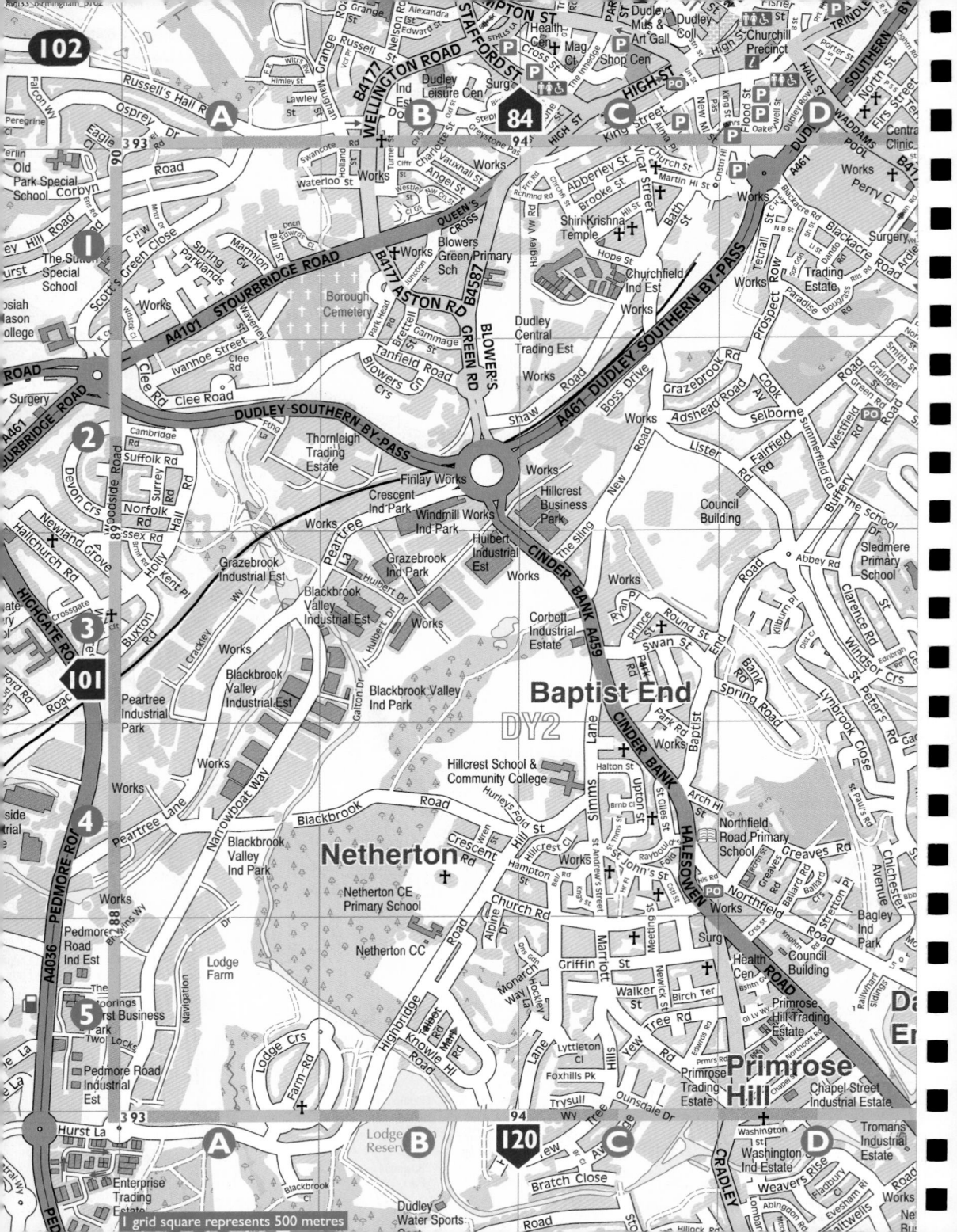

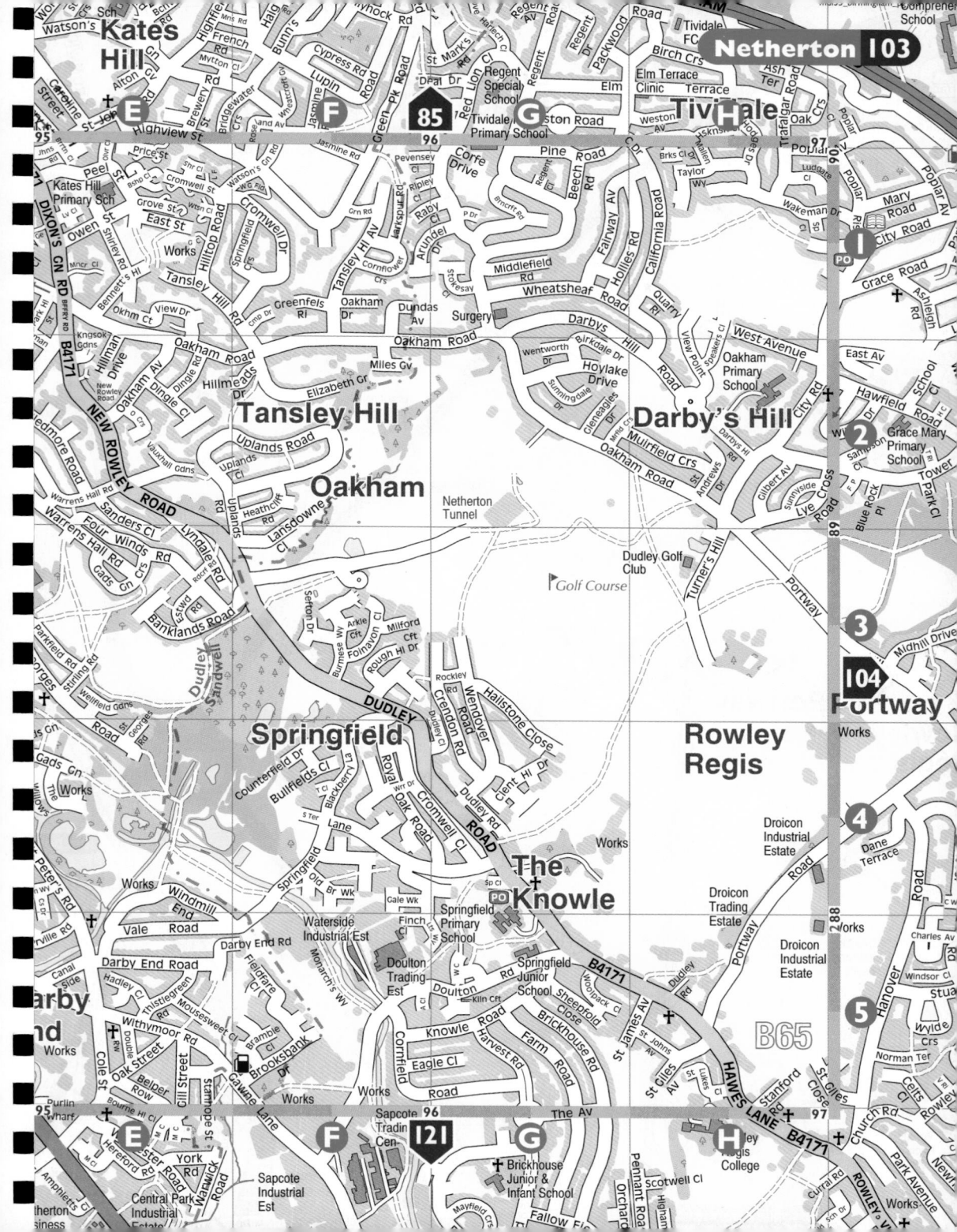

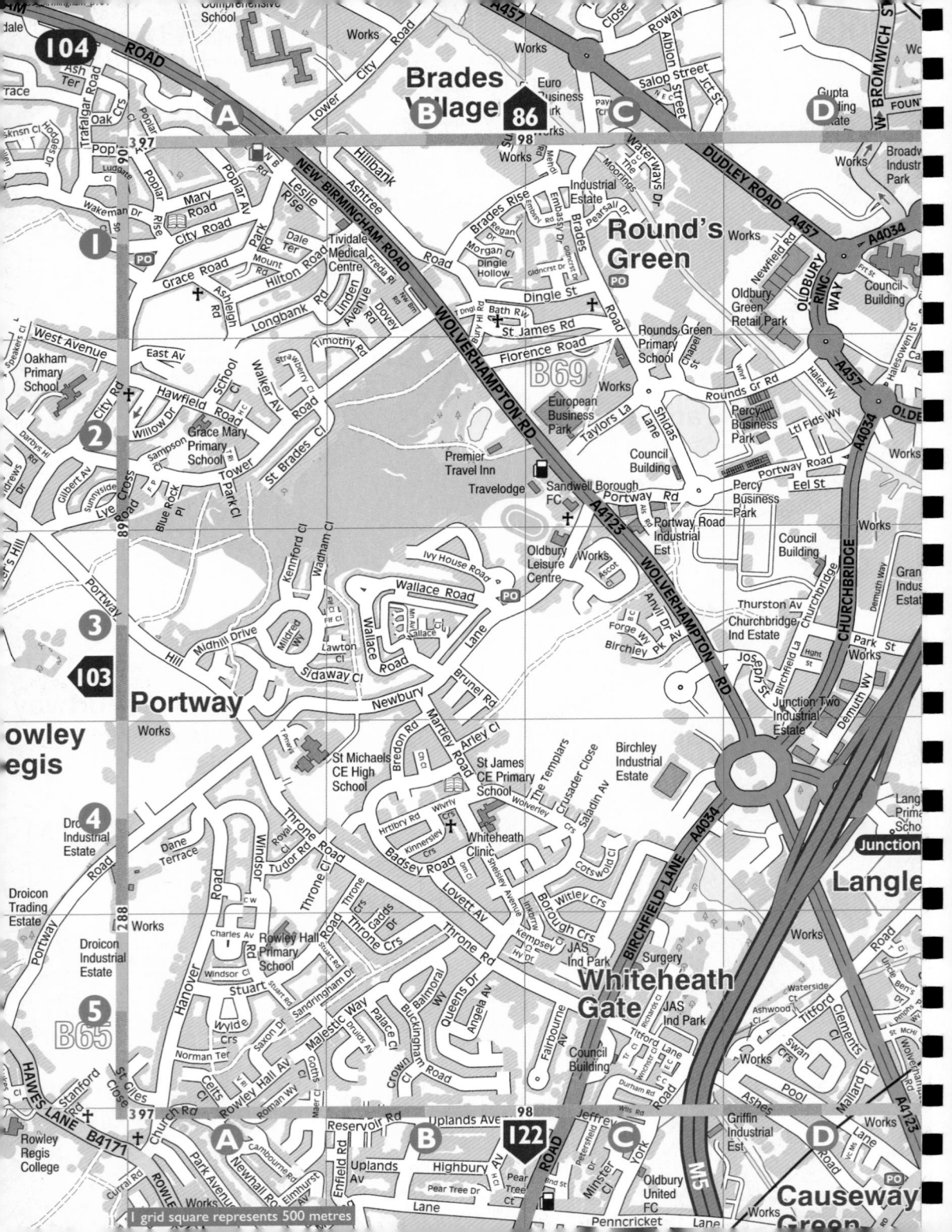

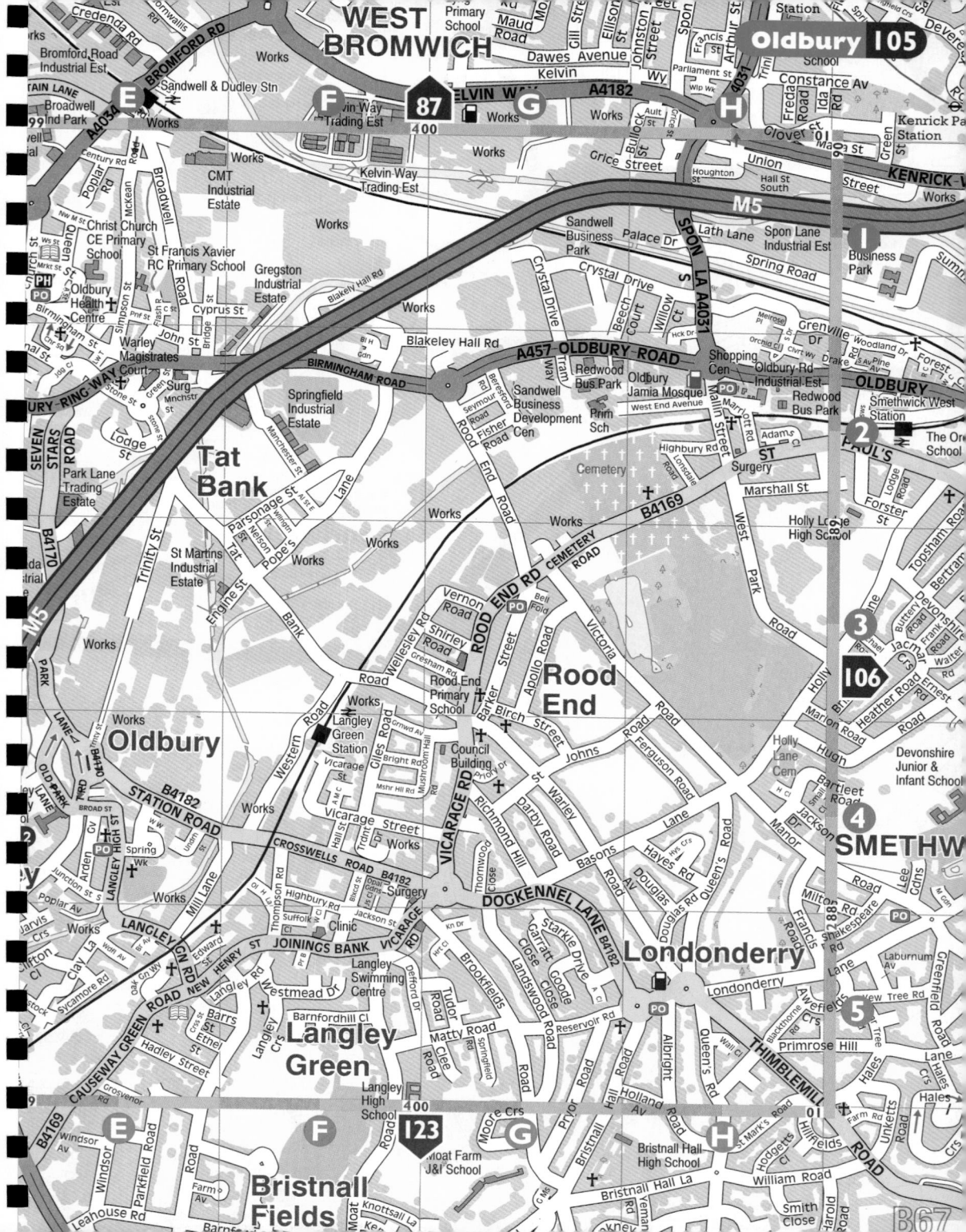

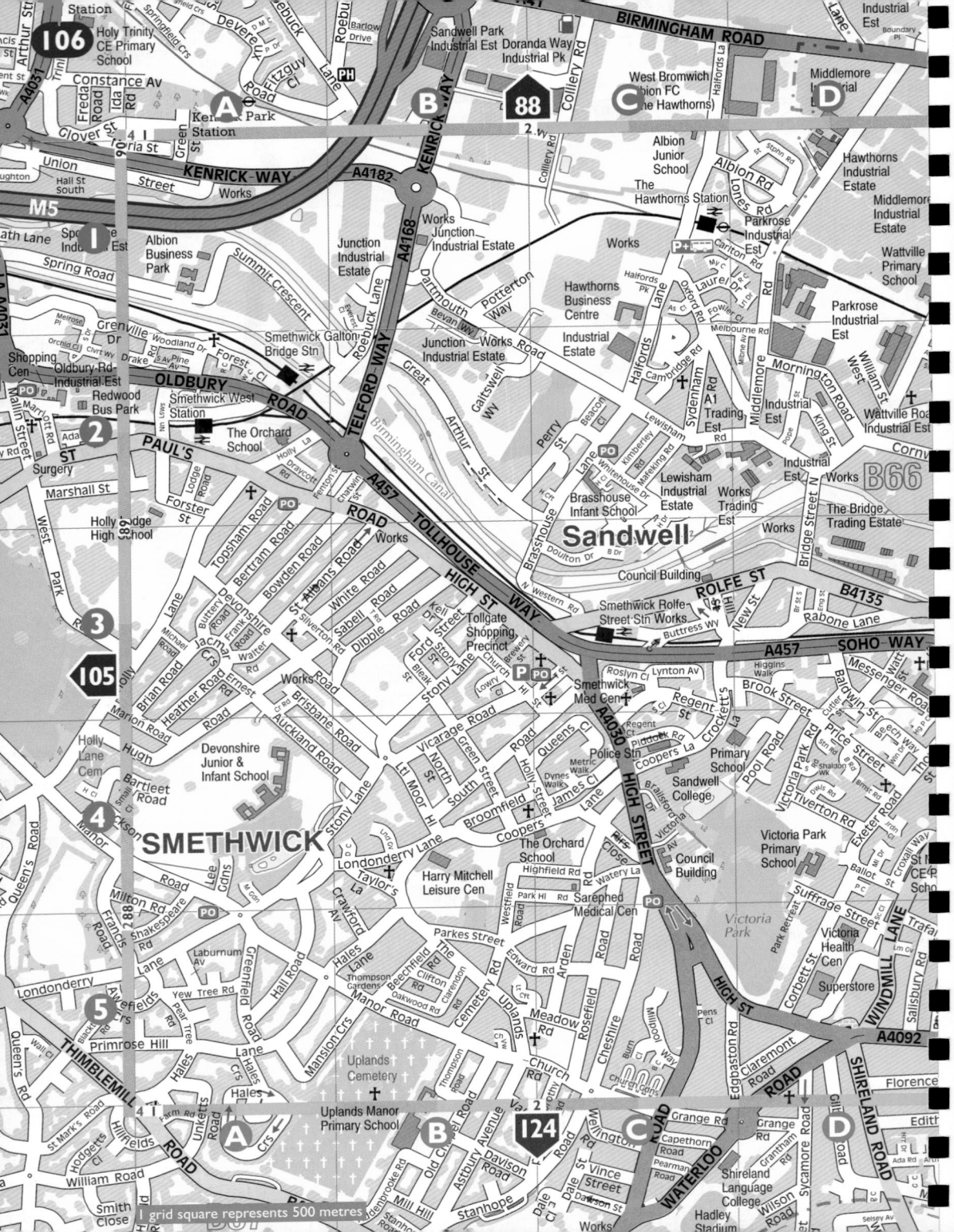

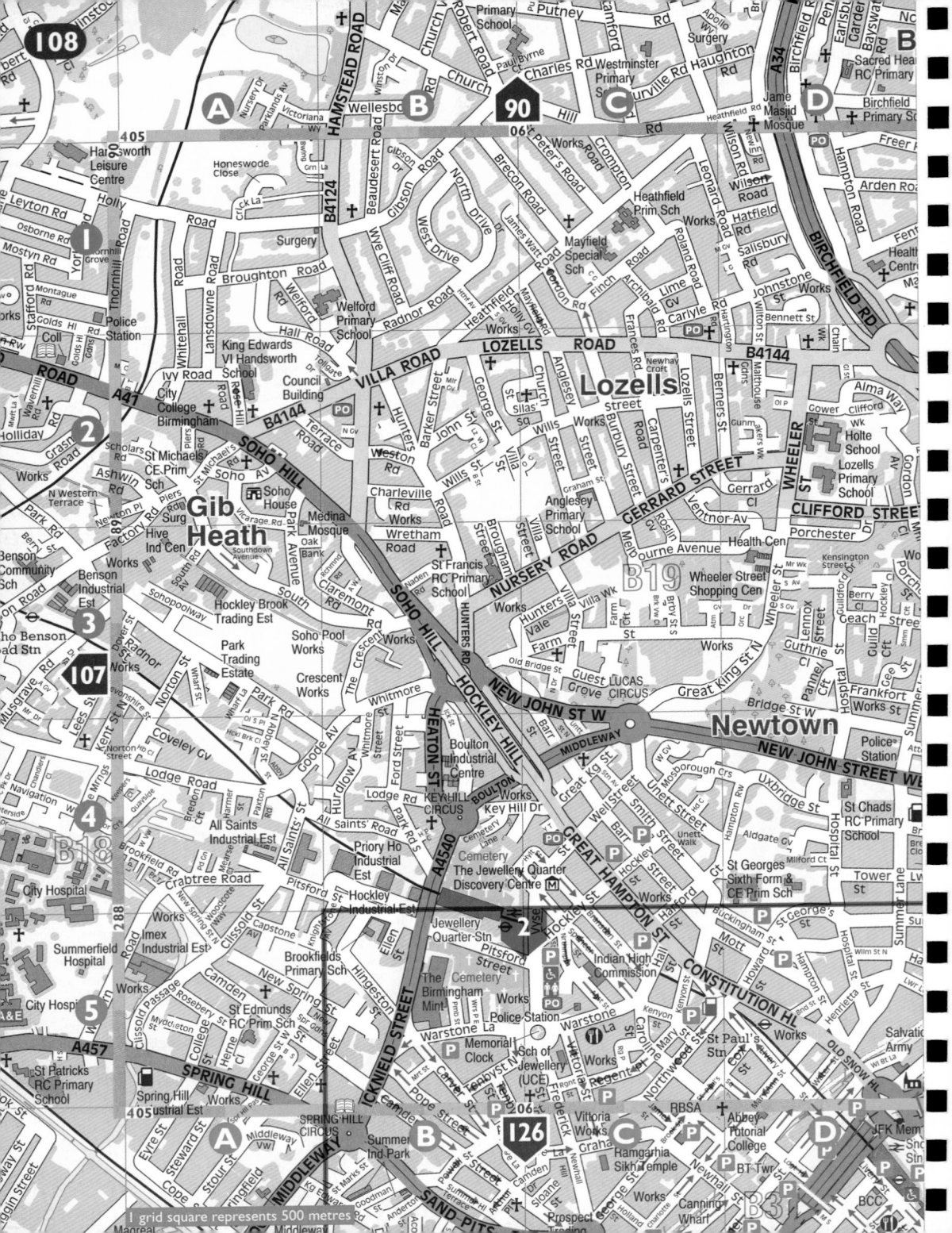

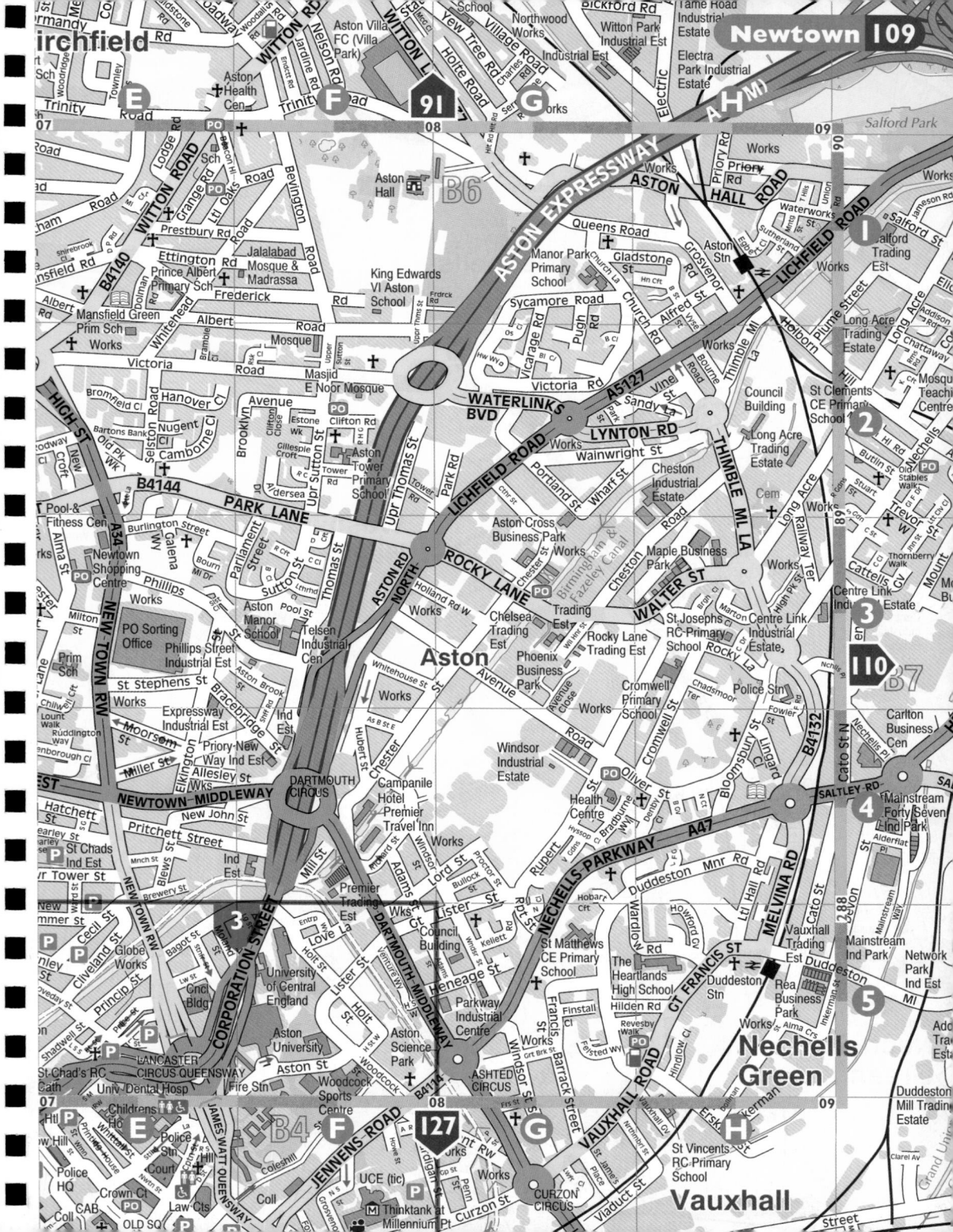

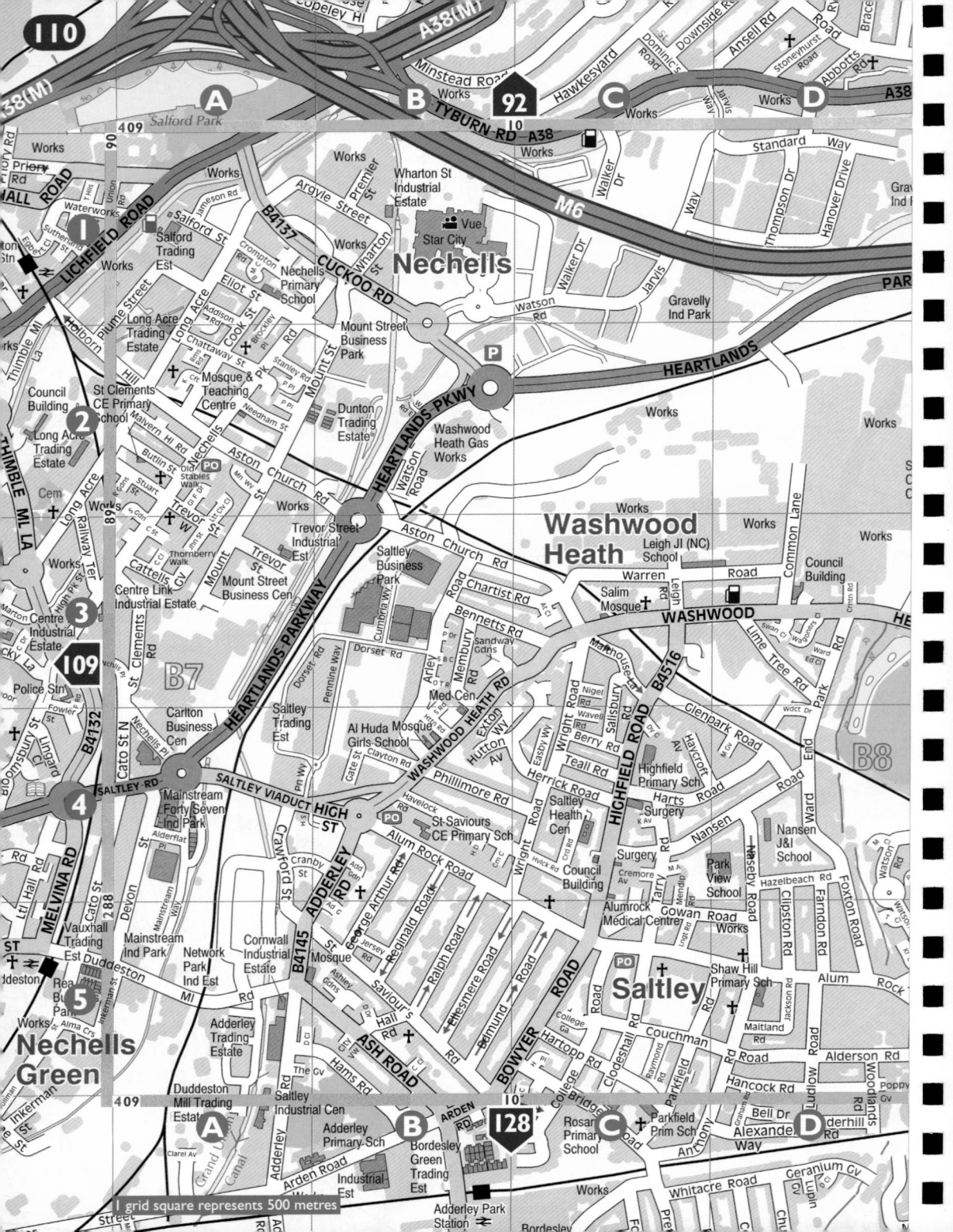

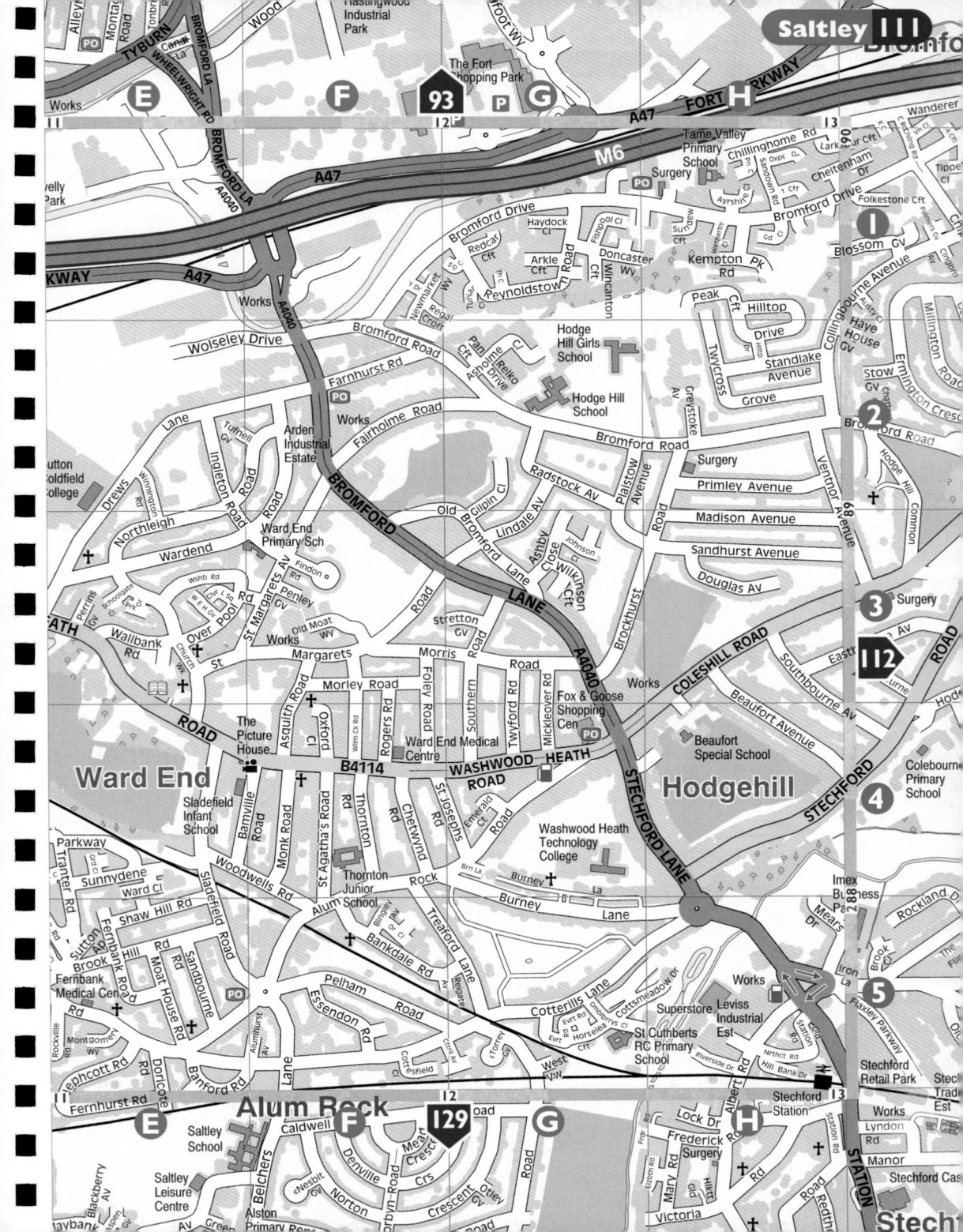

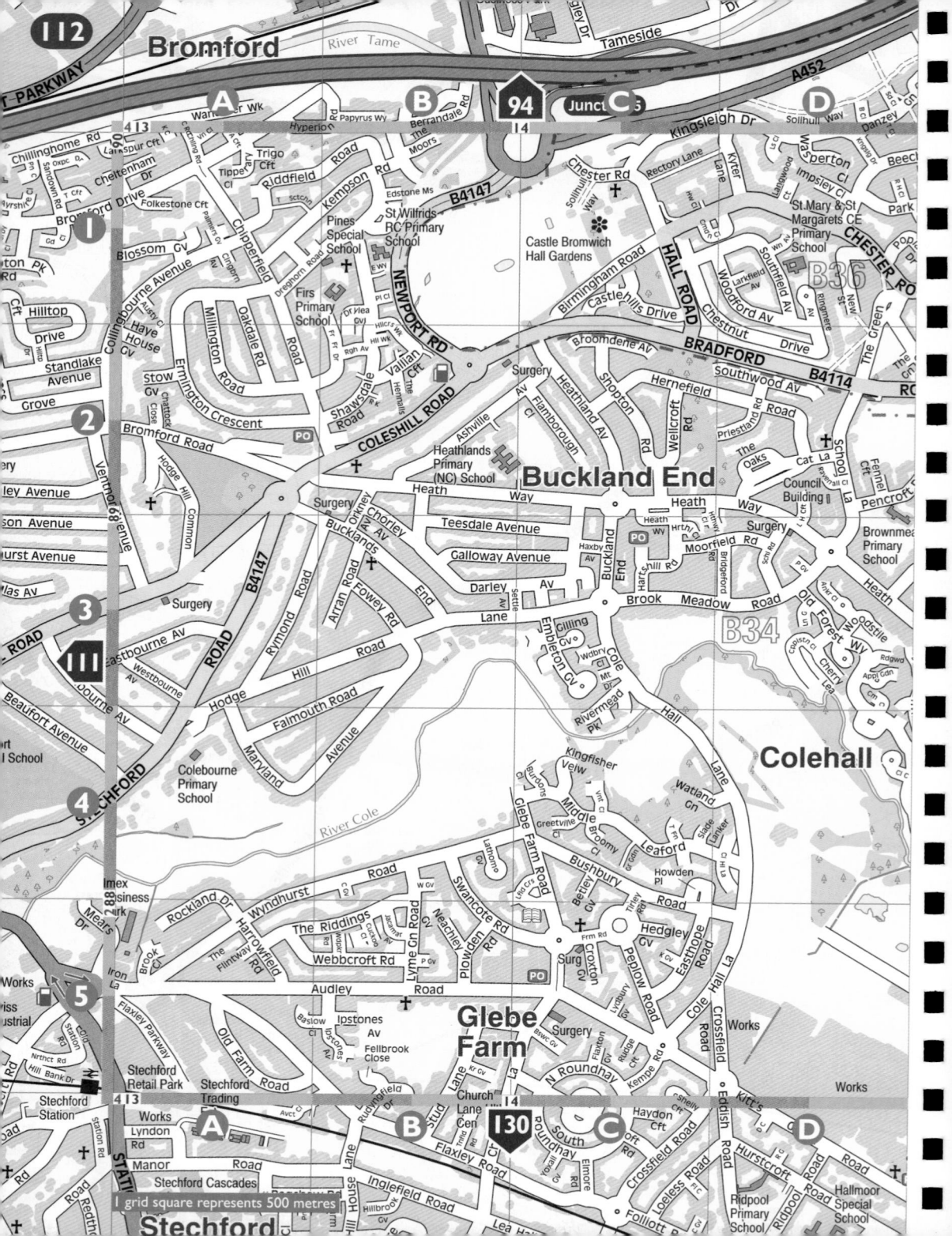

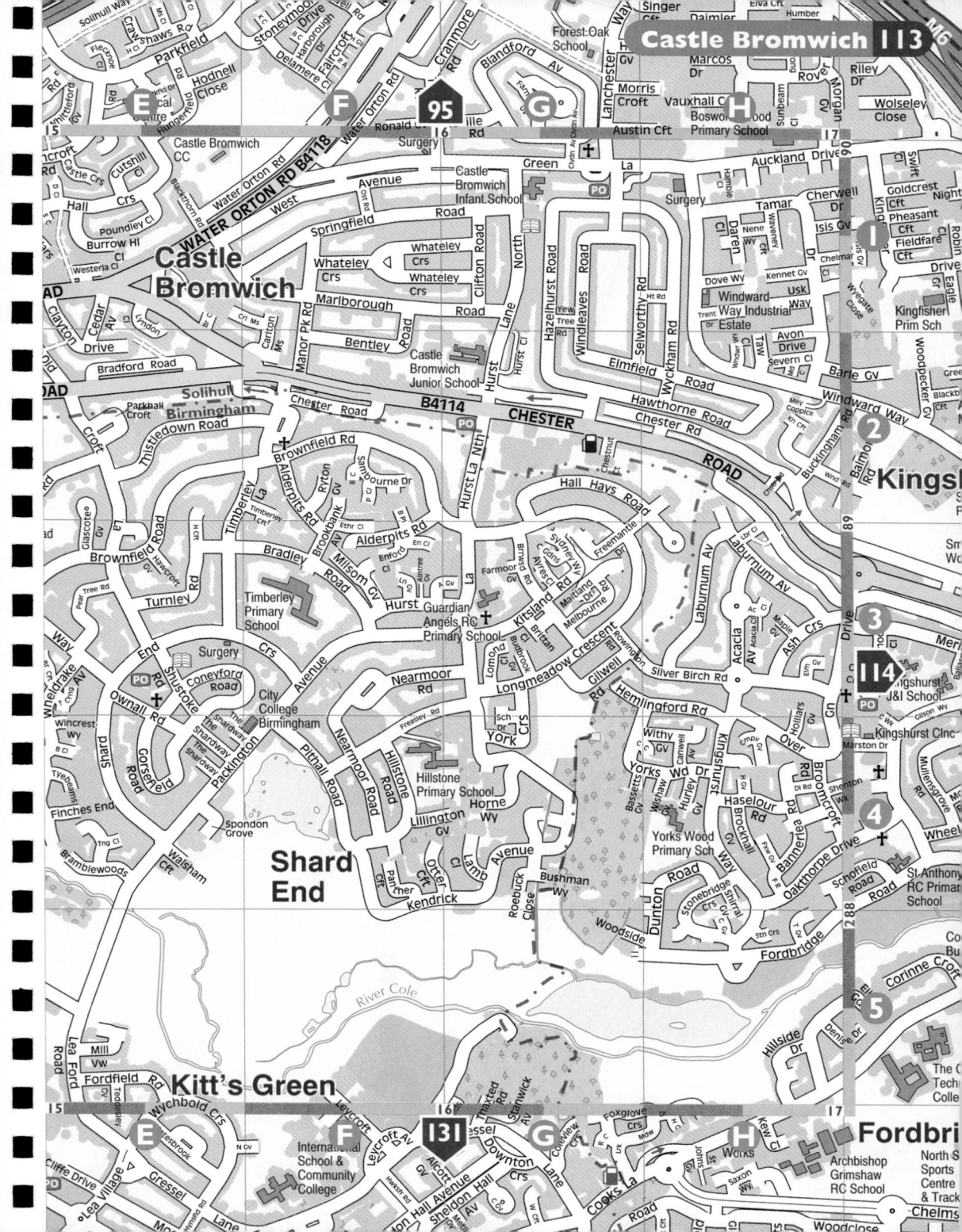

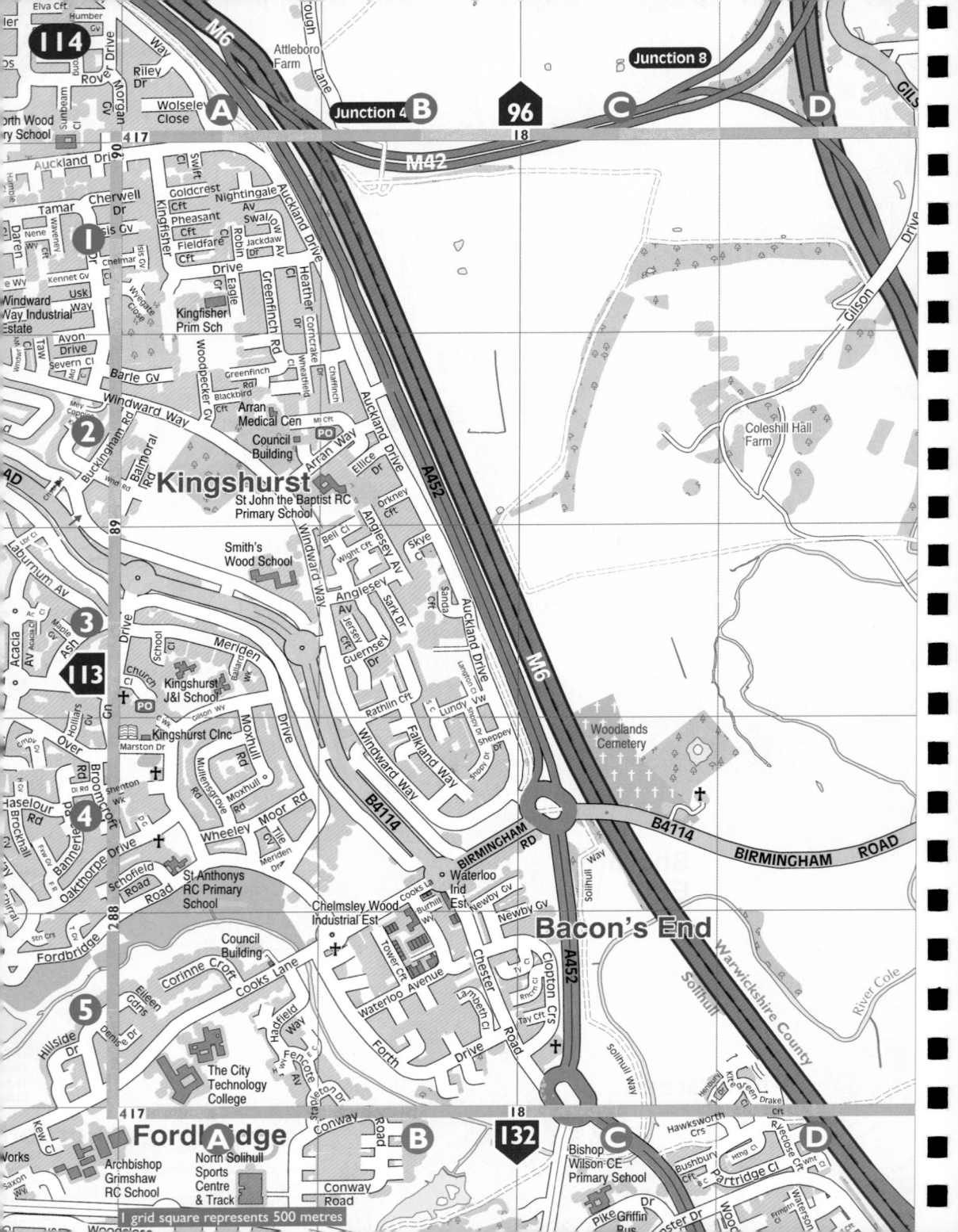

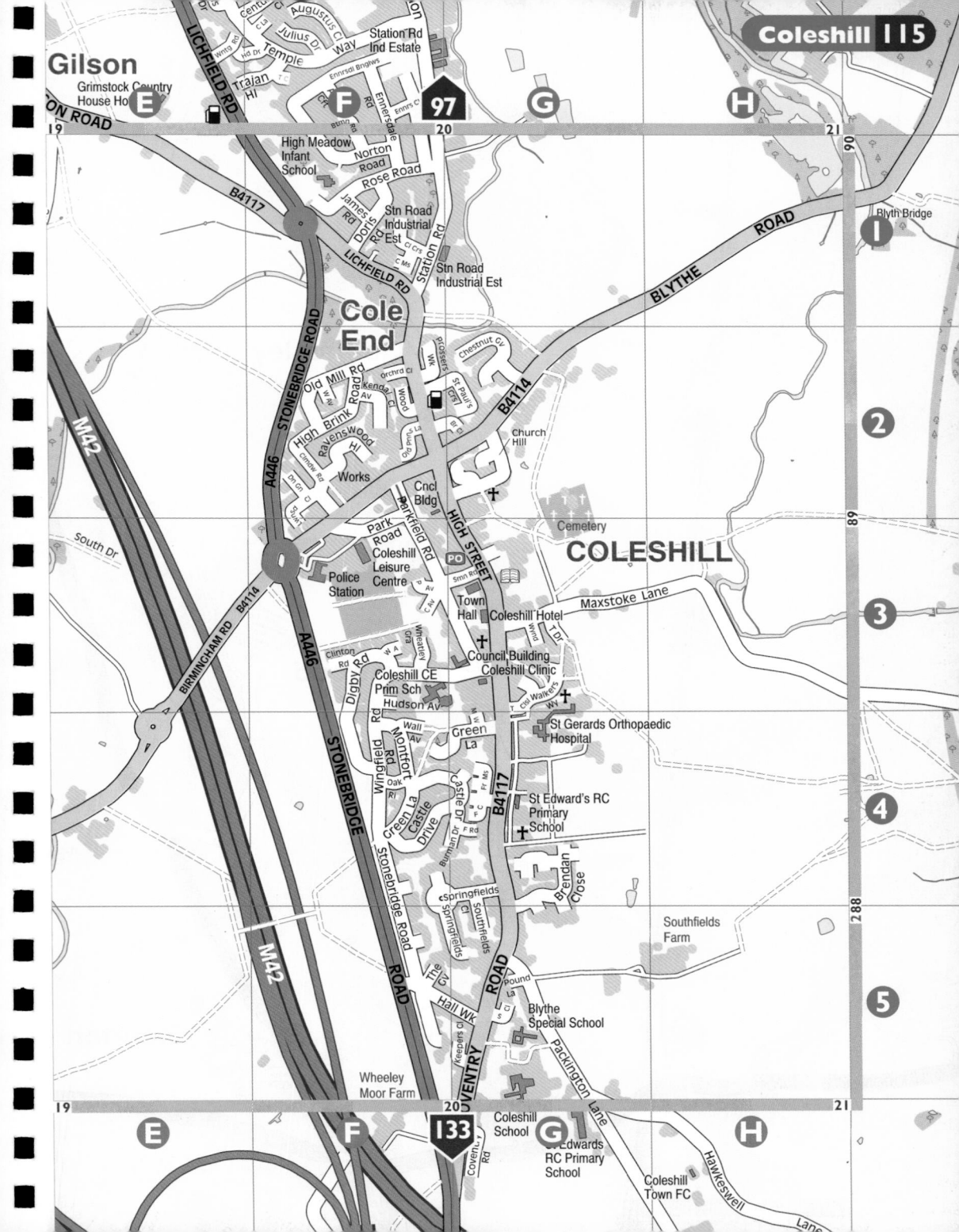

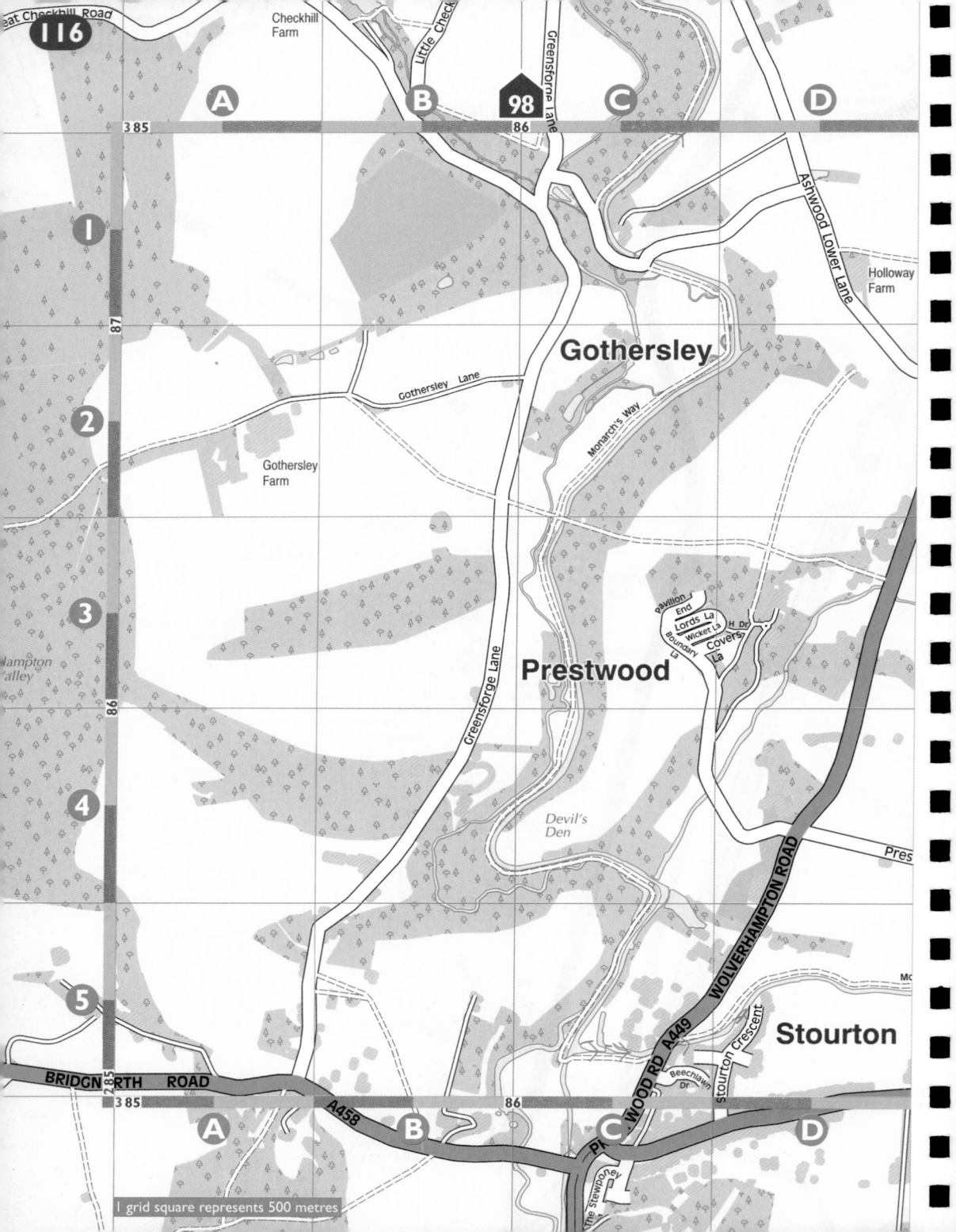

116

A   B   98   C   D
86

3 85

1

87

Checkhill Farm

Great Checkhill Road

Little Check

Greensforne Lane

Ashwood Lower Lane

Holloway Farm

Gothersley

86

2

Gothersley Lane

Monarch's Way

Gothersley Farm

Greensforge Lane

3

ampton alley

Pavilion
End
Lords La
Wicket La
Boundary
La   Covers
La

Prestwood

H Dr

4

Devil's Den

Pres

WOLVERHAMPTON ROAD

5

Stourton

Stourton Crescent

BRIDGNRTH ROAD

3 85

A458

86

Mo

WOOD RD A449

Beechlawn Dr

A   B   A458   C   D

The Stewponey

I grid square represents 500 metres

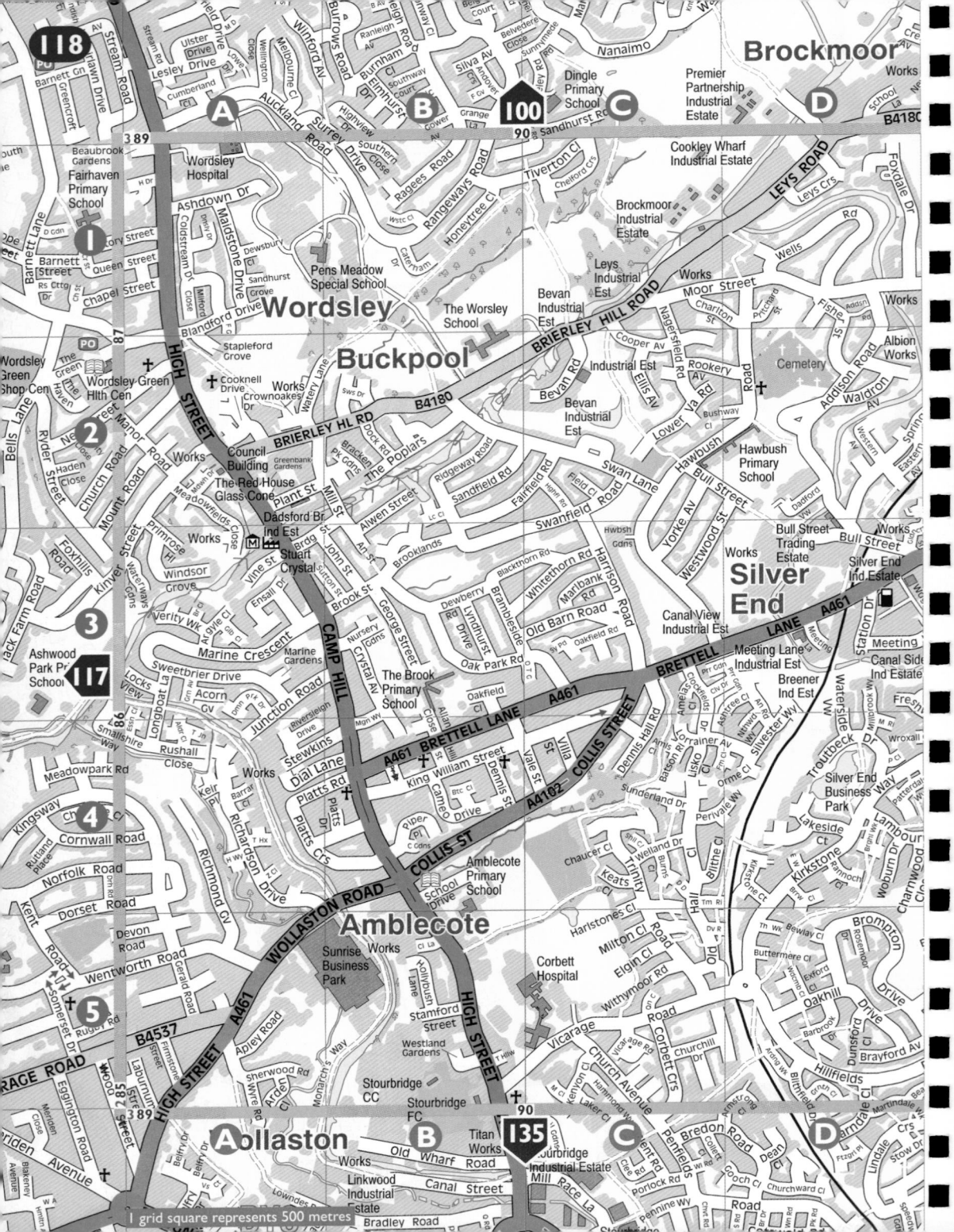

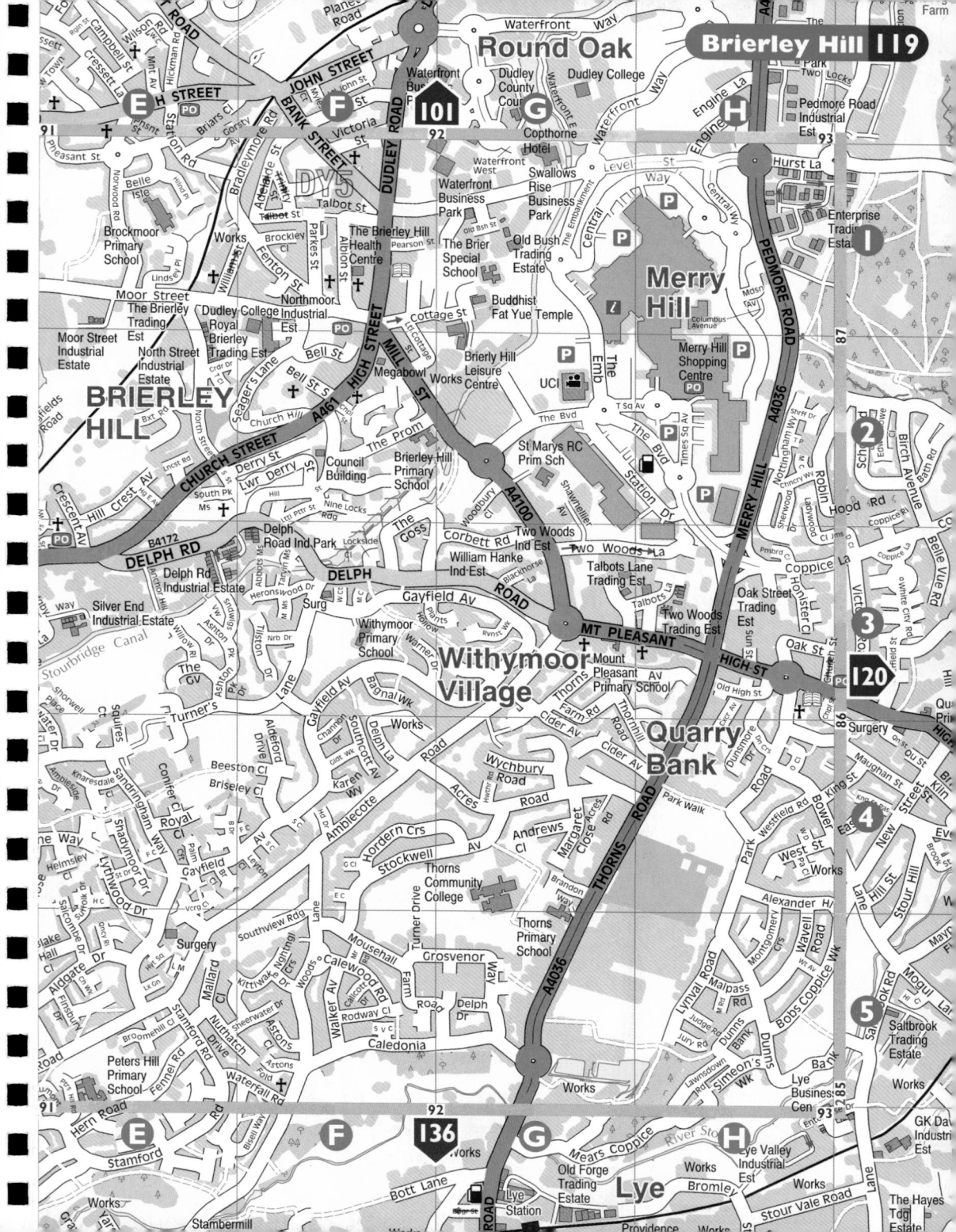

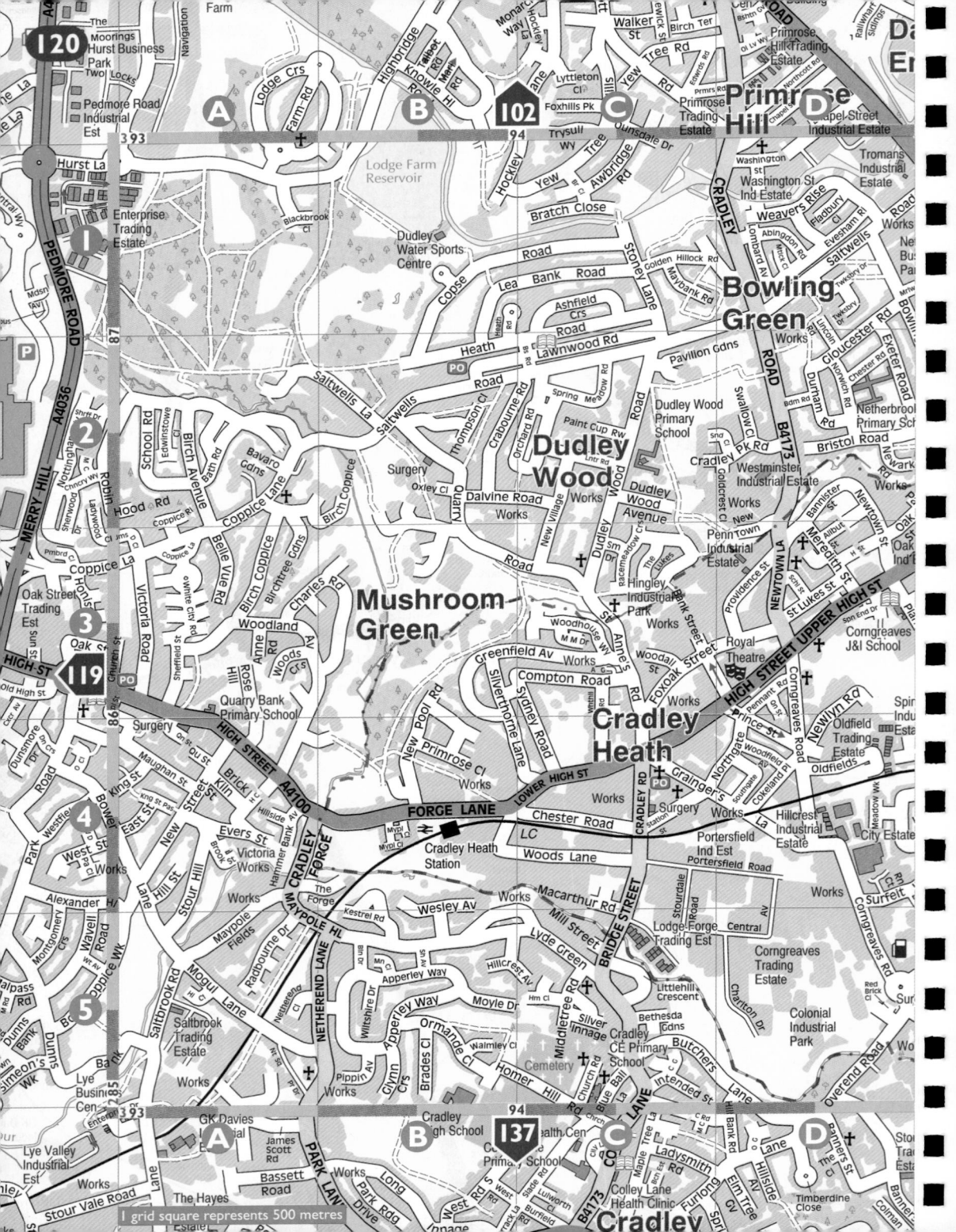

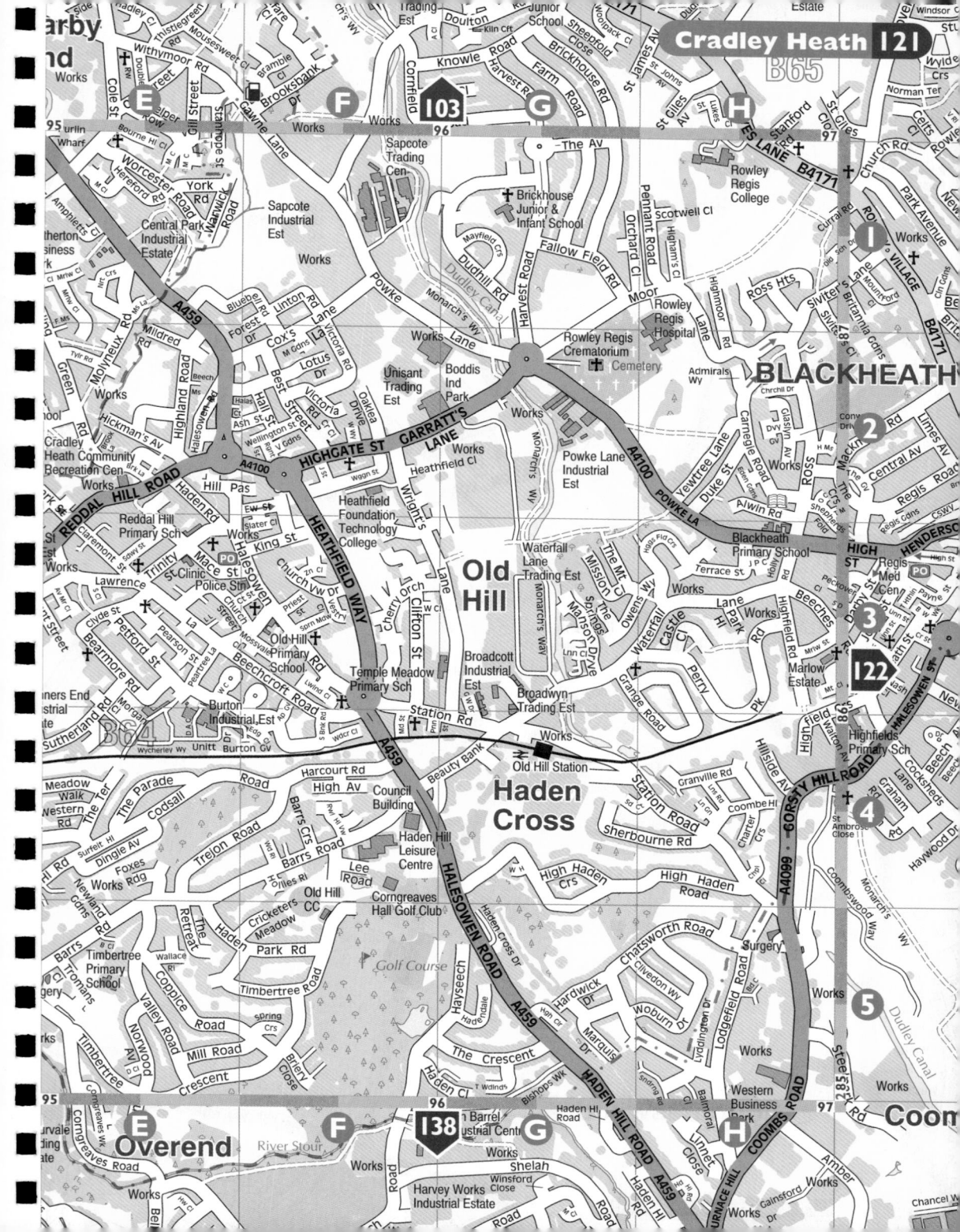

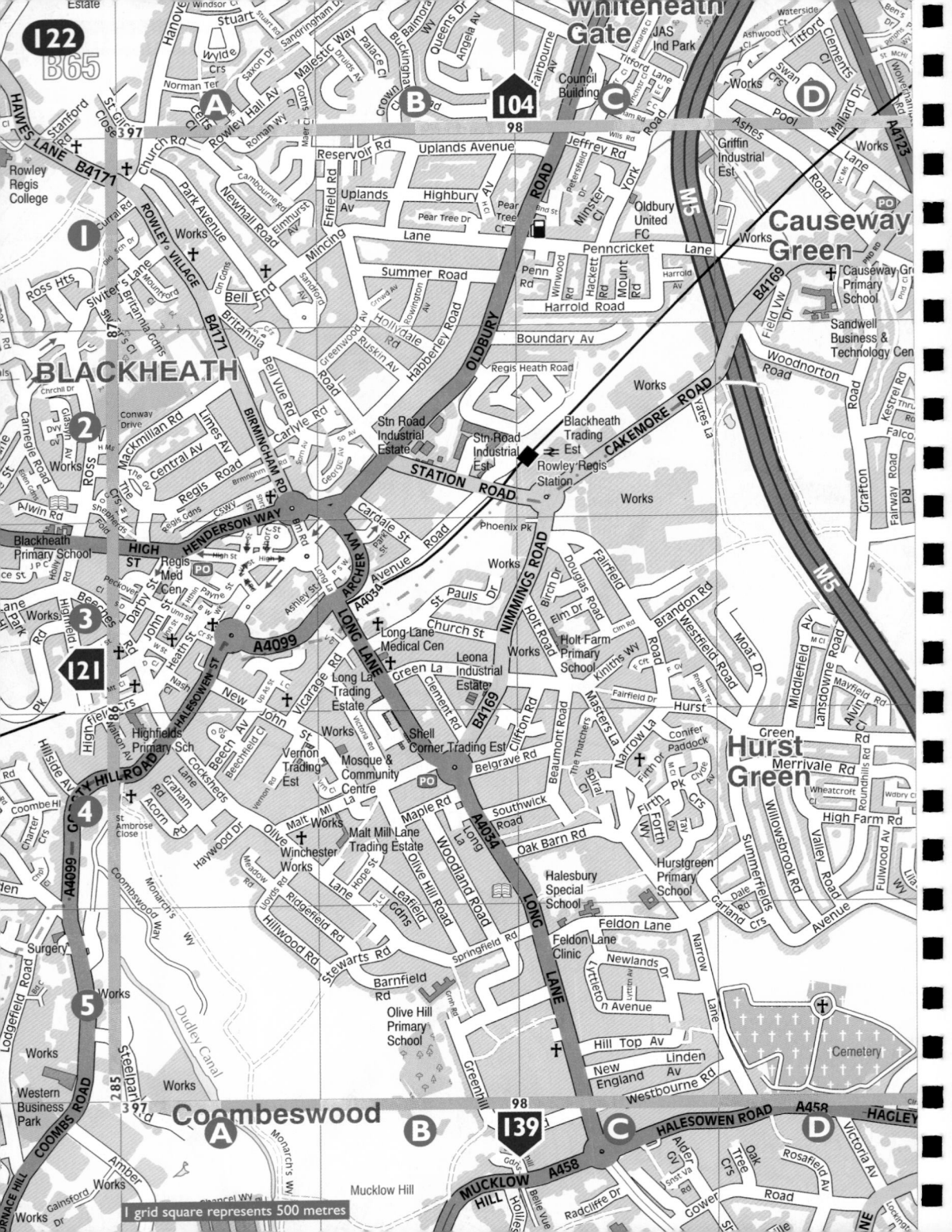

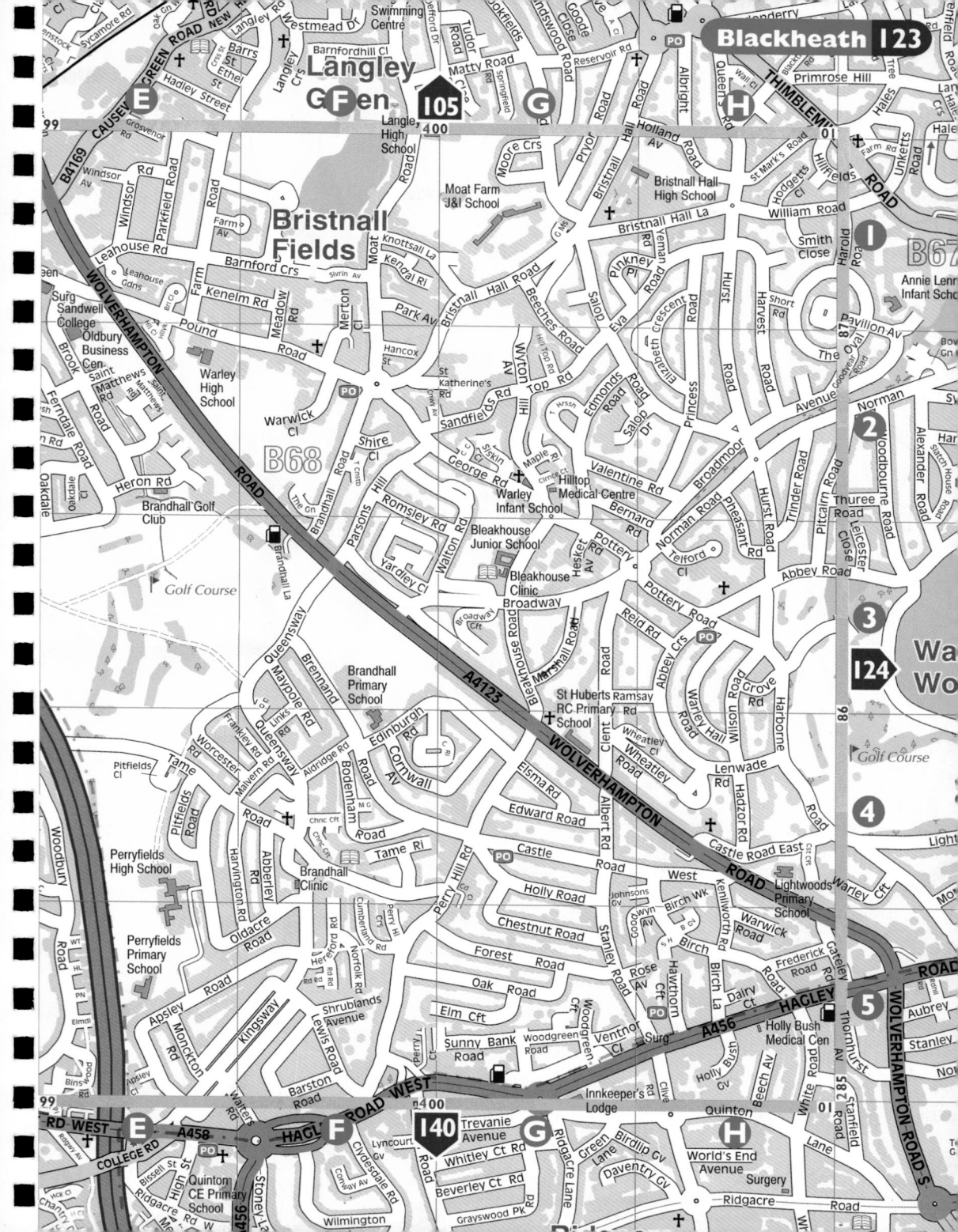

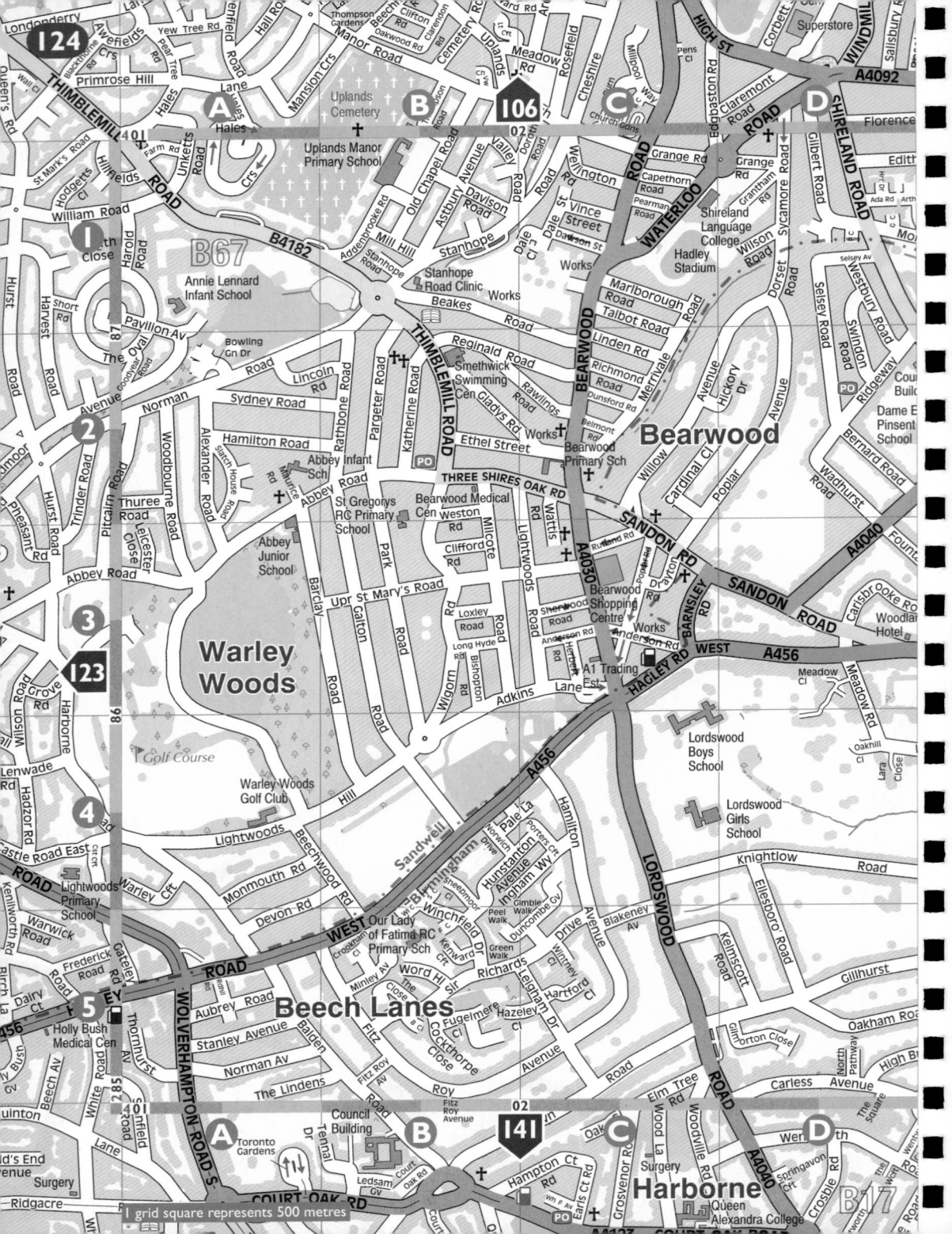

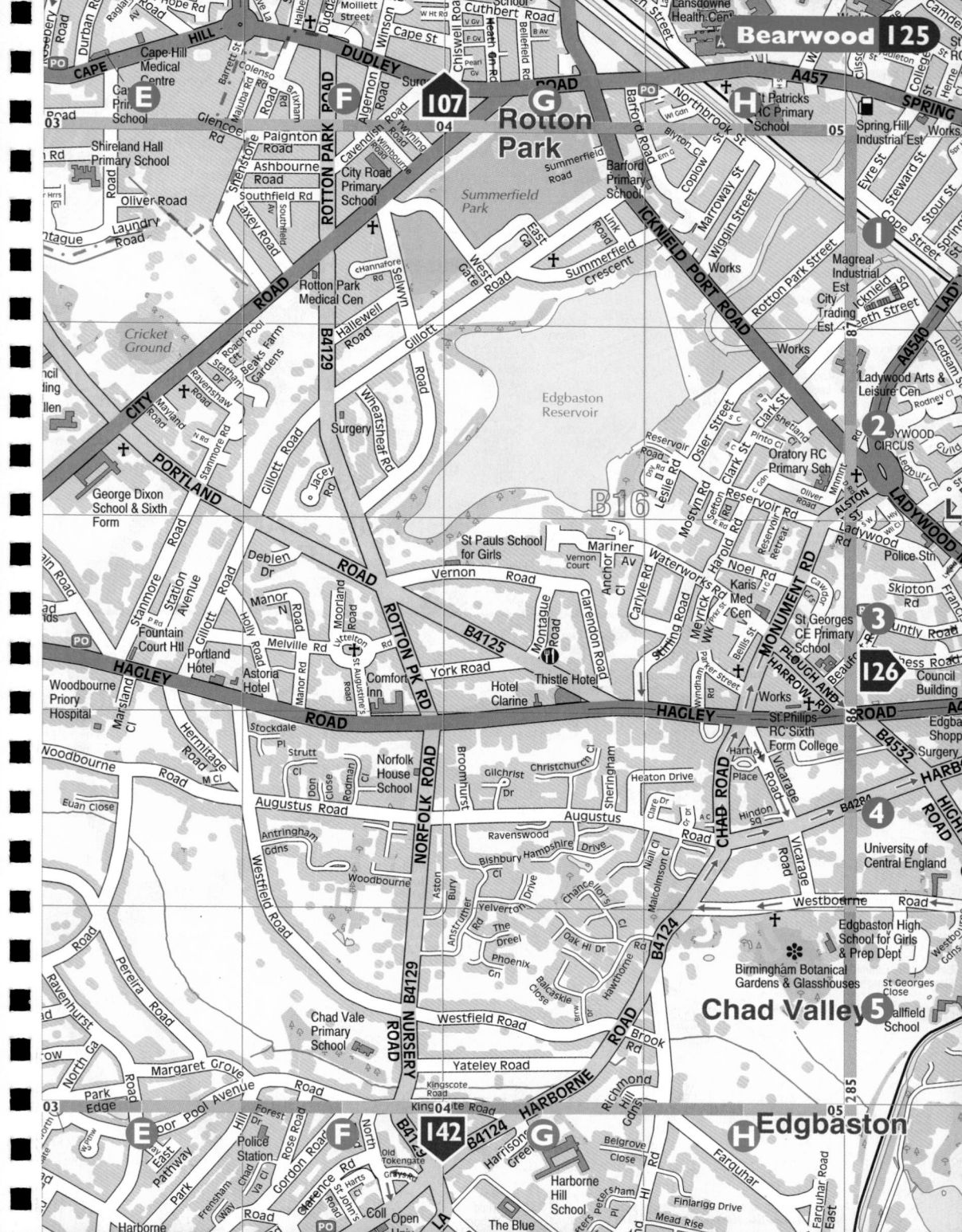

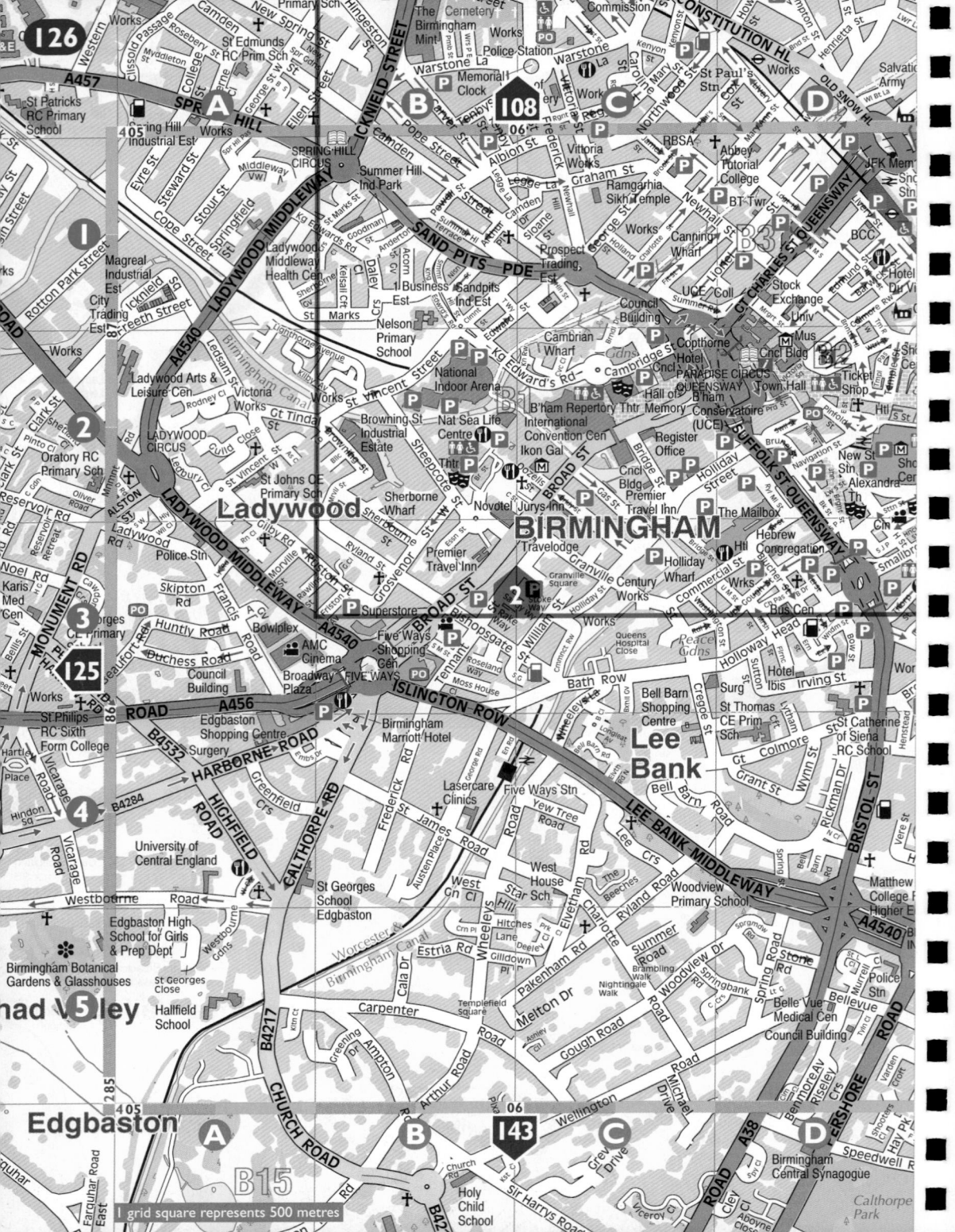

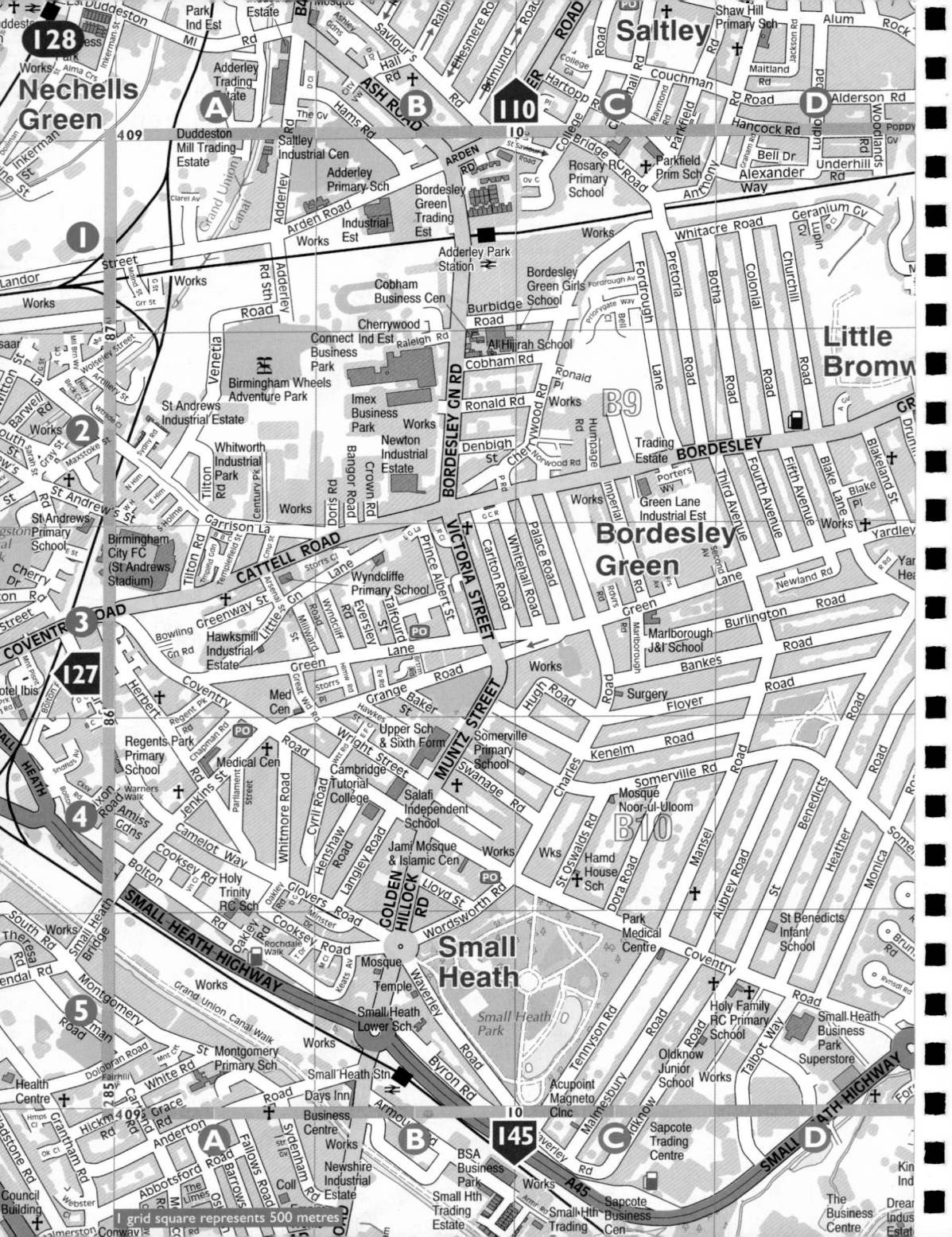

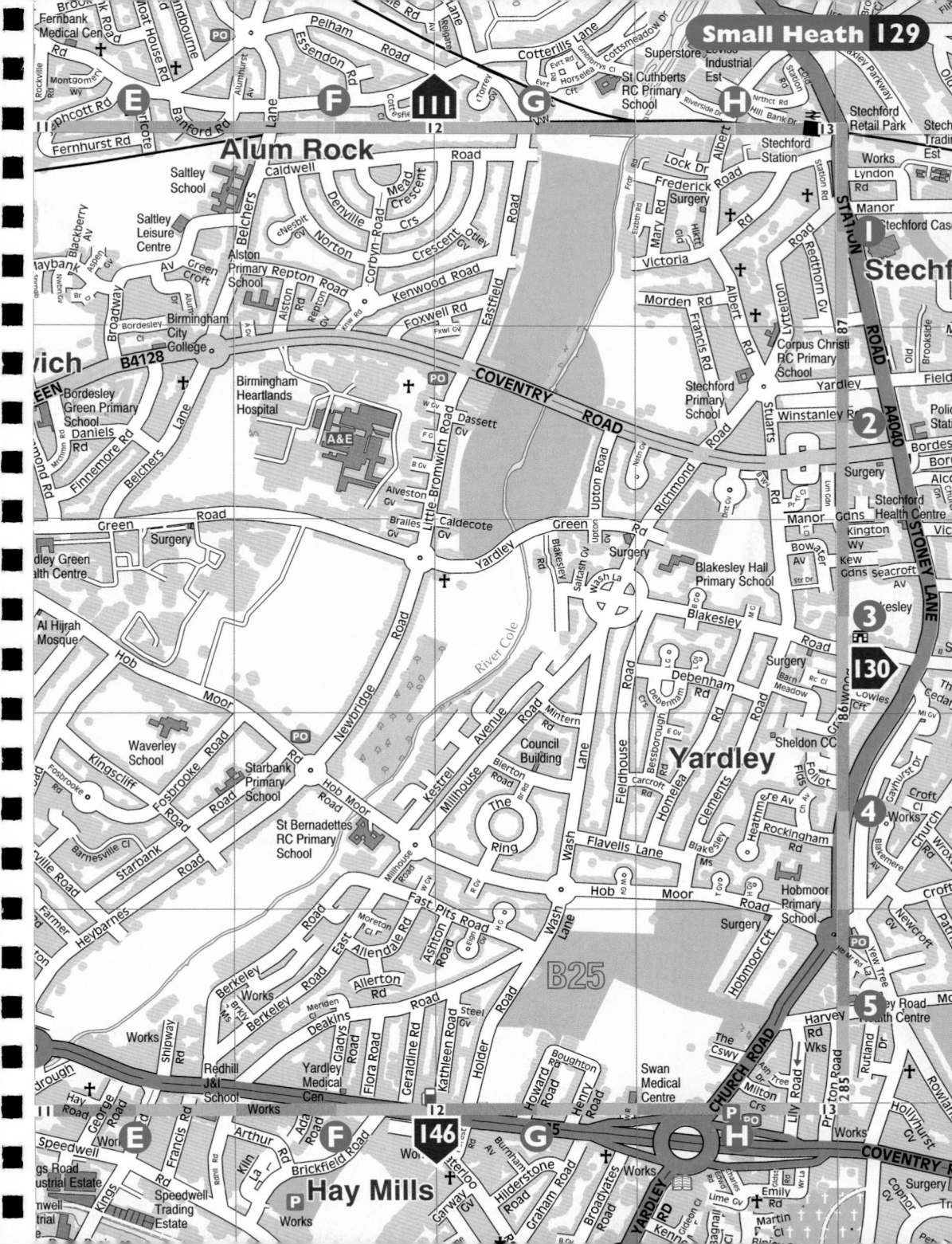

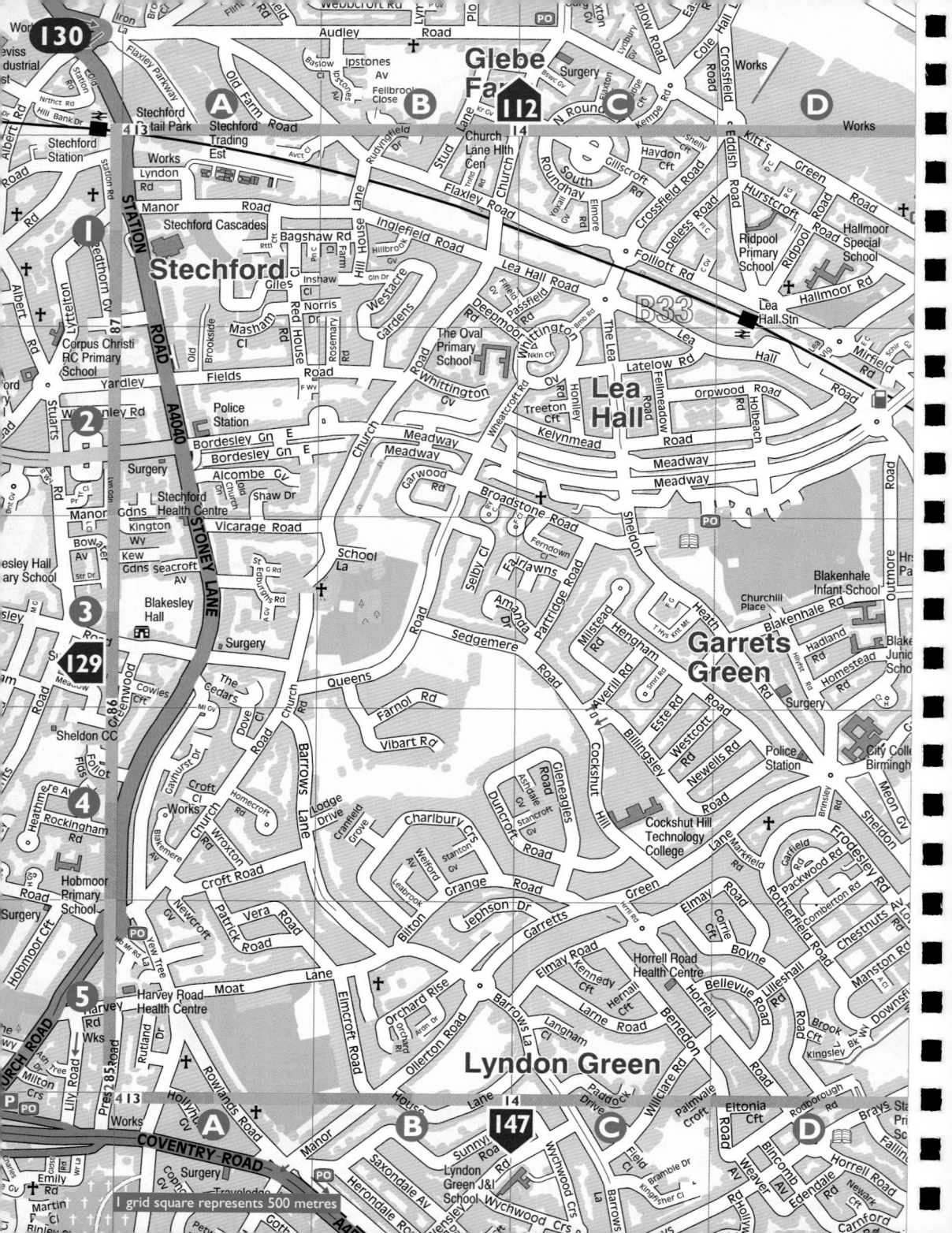

I 130

Glebe Farm

I 12

Stechford Retail Park
Stechford Trading Est
A
Stechford Station
Works
Lyndon Rd
Manor Road
Stechford Cascades
Bagshaw Rd
Stechford
Corpus Christi RC Primary School
Yardley
2
Surgery
Bordesley Gn E
Bordesley Gn E
Alcombe Gv
Manor
Kington Wy
Kew Gdns
Seacroft Av
3
Blakesley Hall
Surgery
Esley Hall ary School
S
I 129
Sheldon CC
4
Rockingham Rd
Hobmoor Primary School
Surgery
5
Harvey Road Health Centre
P
PO
413

Police Station
Meadway
Meadway
Garwood Rd
The Oval Primary School
Whittington Gv
Vicarage Road
School La
Sedgemere
Queens
Farnol Rd
Vibart Rd
The Gedars
Selby Cl
Fairlawns
Amanda
Partridge Road
Broadstone Road
Ferndown Rd
Charlbury Crs
Duncroft Road
Grange Road
Bilton
Jephson Dr
Garretts
Orchard Rise
Barrows Lane
Ollerton Road
Lyndon Green
Coventry Road
Lyndon Green J&I School
I 147

Inglefield Road
Flaxley Road
Lea Hall Road
Lea Hall Stn
B33
Follott Rd
Latelow Rd
Ridpool Primary School
Hallmoor Special School
Hallmoor Rd
Mirfield Rd
Lea Hall
Kelynmead
Meadway
Meadway
Sheldon
PO
Blakenhale Infant School
Churchill Place
Blakenhale Rd
Garrets Green
Hadland Rd
Homestead Rd
Surgery
Cleneagles Road
Cockshut Hill
Cockshut Hill Technology College
Police Station
City College Birmingham
Este Rd
Westcott Rd
Newells Rd
Horrell Road Health Centre
Kennedy Cft
Larne Road
Langham Cl
Frodesley Rd
Sheldon
Chestnuts Av
Manston Rd
Rotherfield Road
Bellevue Road
Lilleshall Road
Willclare Rd
Paddock Drive
Palmvale Cft
Eltonia Cft
Roatborough
Horrell Road
D

1 grid square represents 500 metres

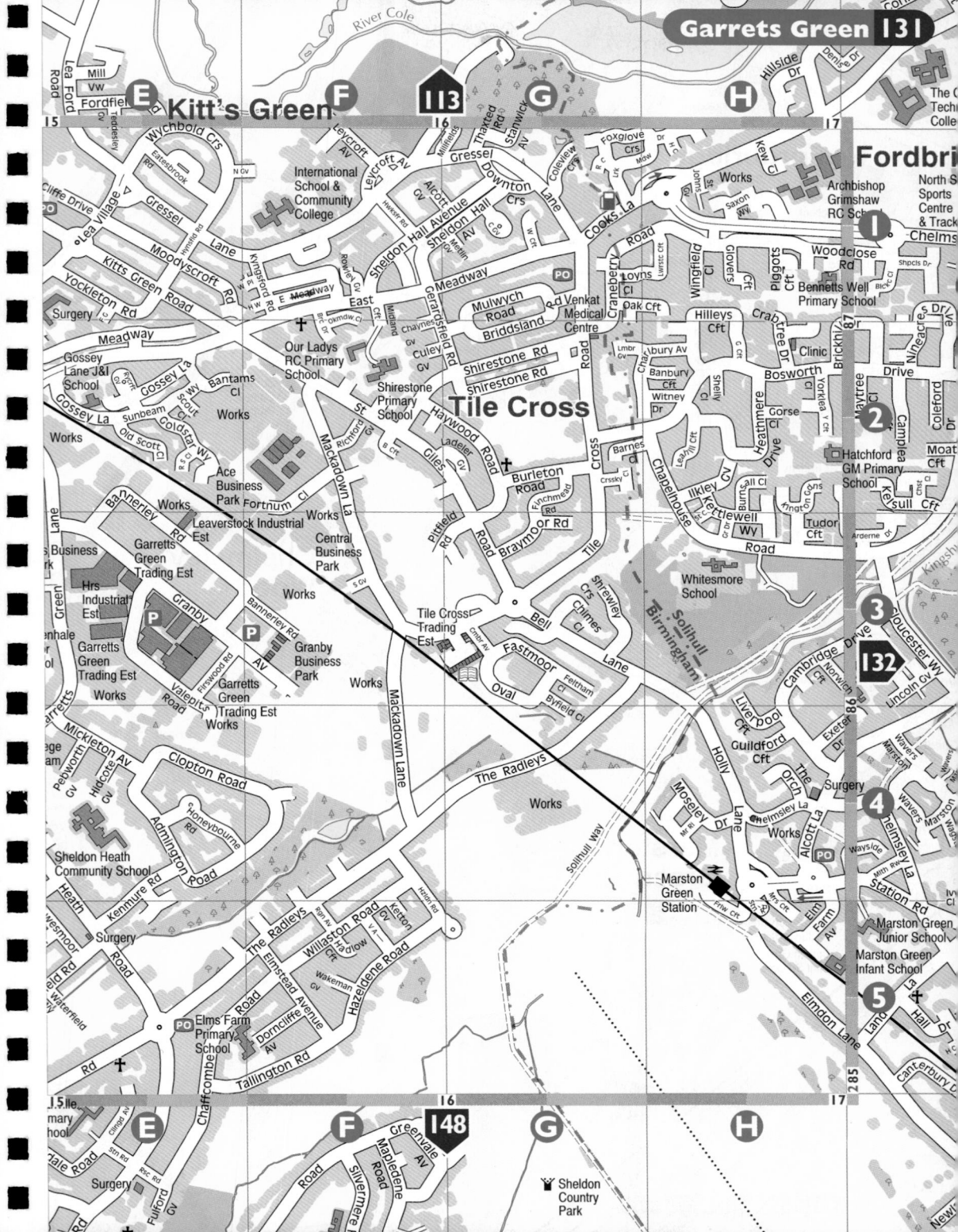

Kitt's Green

E **F** **G** **H**

15 16 17

113

Fordbri

Fordfiel

Mill Vw

Lea Ford Road

Wychbold Crs

Eatesbrook Rd

N Gv

Leycroft Av

Gressel Lane

Thaxted Rd

Stanwick Av

Coleview

Foxglove Crs

Kew Cl

Hillside Dr

The O Tech Colle

International School & Community College

Leycroft Av

Downton Crs

Millfield

Cooks La

Works

Saxon Wy

Archbishop Grimshaw RC Schl

North S Sports Centre & Track

Chelms

Cliffe Drive

Lea Village

Gressel Lane

Moodyscroft Rd

Kingstone Rd

Sheldon Hall Av

Alcott Av

Merlin

Cranebery Road

Wingfield Cl

Glovers

Piggots Cft

Woodclose Rd

Bennetts Well Primary School

I

Kitts Green Road

Yockleton Rd

E Meadway

Meadway

East

Midland

Chaynes

Gerard Road

Mulwych Road

Venkat Medical Centre

Oak Cft

Hilleys Cft

Banbury Cft

Clinic

Maytree Dr

Coleford

2

Gossey Lane J&I School

Gossey La

Sunbeam

Bantams Cl

Scout

Works

Our Ladys RC Primary School

Shirestone Primary School

Shirestone Rd

shirestone rd

Tile Cross

Heathmere Drive

Bosworth

Gorse Cl

Ninacres Dr

Drive

Witney Dr

Campian Cft

Gossey La

Works

Coldstar Wy

Old Scott

Ace Business Park

Fortnum Cl

Mackadown La

Richford St

Haywood Road

Ladeler Gv

Giles

Burleton Road

Finchmead Rd

Cross Road

Barnes

Chapelhouse Road

Hatchford GM Primary School

Kirtlewell Wy

Tudor Cft

Moat Cft

Sull Cft

3

132

98

Bannerley

Leaverstock Industrial Est

Garretts Green Trading Est

Hrs Industrial Est

Granby

Bannerley Rd

Central Business Park

Pitfield Rd

Braymor Road

Tile Road

Whitesmore School

Solihull Birmingham

Gloucester Drive

Lincoln Gv

P

Firswood Rd

P

Granby Av

Granby Business Park

Works

Valepits Road

Garretts Green Trading Est

Works

Tile Cross Trading Est

Bell

Fastmoor Oval

Shrewley Crs

Chimes Cl

Feltham

Byfield Cl

Liverpool Cft

Exeter Dr

Norwich Cft

Cambridge Drive

Wavers

Mickleton Av

Pebworth Gv

Hidcote Gv

Clopton Road

Honeybourne Rd

Admington Road

Mackadown Lane

The Radleys

Works

Guildford Cft

Holly Lane

Moseley Dr

Chelmsley La

Works

Surgery

4

Heimsley La

Wavers

Marston

Station Rd

Sheldon Heath Community School

Kenmure Rd

The Radleys

Willaston Road

Ketton

Elmstead Avenue

Solihull Way

Marston Green Station

Elm Farm

PO

Wayside

Marston Green Junior School

Marston Green Infant School

5

Surgery

Road

Hazeldene Road

Wakeman Gv

Dorncliffe Av

Elms Farm Primary School

PO

Chaffcombe Road

Tallington Rd

Elmdon Lane

Hall Dr

Canterbury Rd

285

E **F** 148 **G** **H**

16 17

Greenvale Av

Mapledene Road

Silvermere Road

Sheldon Country Park

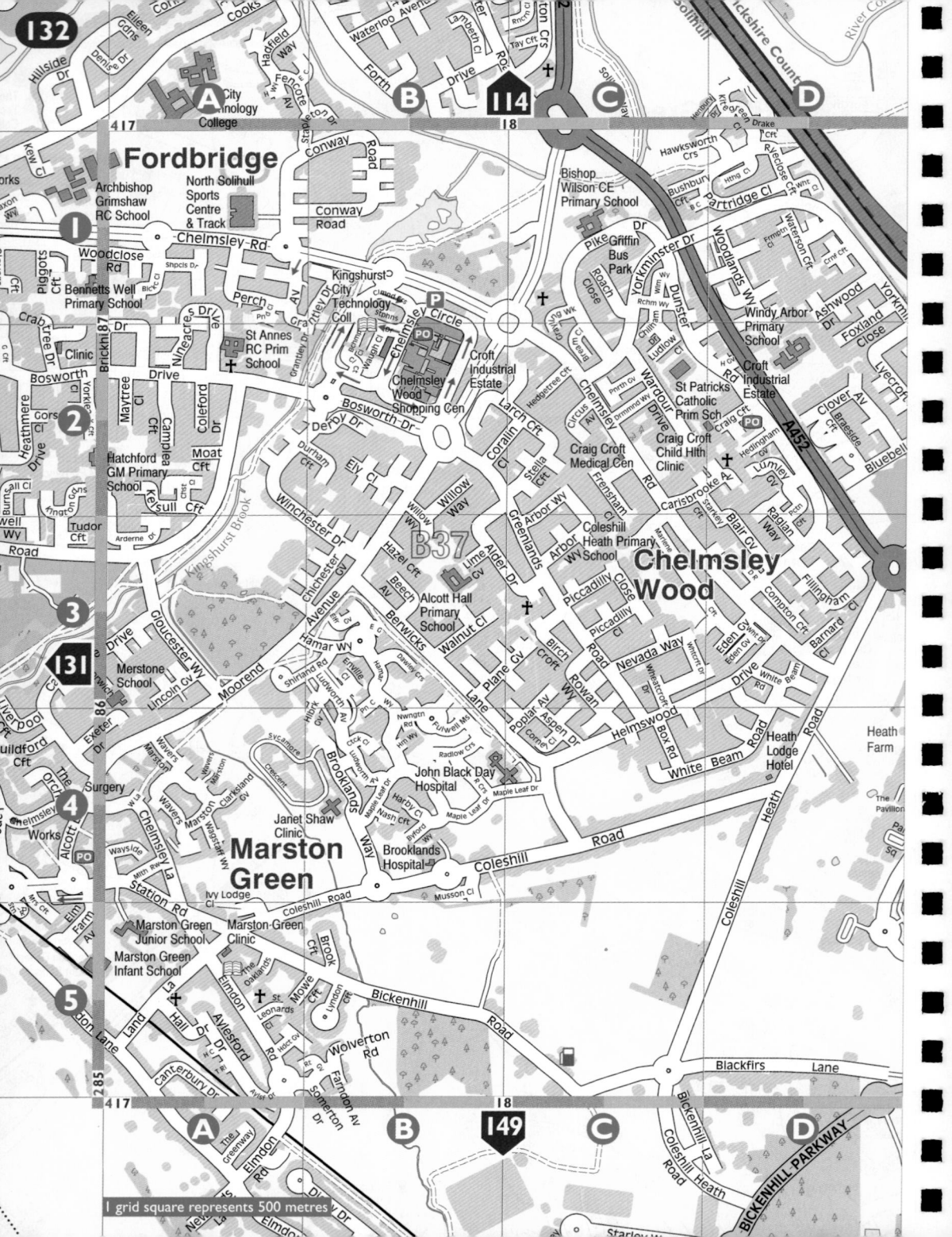

E   F   115   G   H

19   20   21

Blythe Special School

Wheeley Moor Farm

Coleshill School

St Edwards RC Primary School

Coleshill Town FC

Hawkeswell Lane

Packington Lane

I

Packington Lane Farm

Hawkeswell Farm

Hawk La

87

Pool Farm

M6

M6

2

A446

M42

Heath

M6

Junction 4

Road

Coleshill

Junction 7/7a

Packington Lane

Coleshill Pool

86

Banneyley Pool

3

King's Court

CHESTER ROAD

The Crescent

Solihull Parkway

Trident Court

Bishop's Court

A452

Knights Court

Birmingham Business Park

Lakeside

STONEBRIDGE

4

Solihull Pkwy

M42

ROAD

5

Solihull   Parkway

285

Lane

Premier Travel Inn

Blackfirs

B4438

Garden Centre

A4

19   20   150   452   G   21

E   F   H

Little

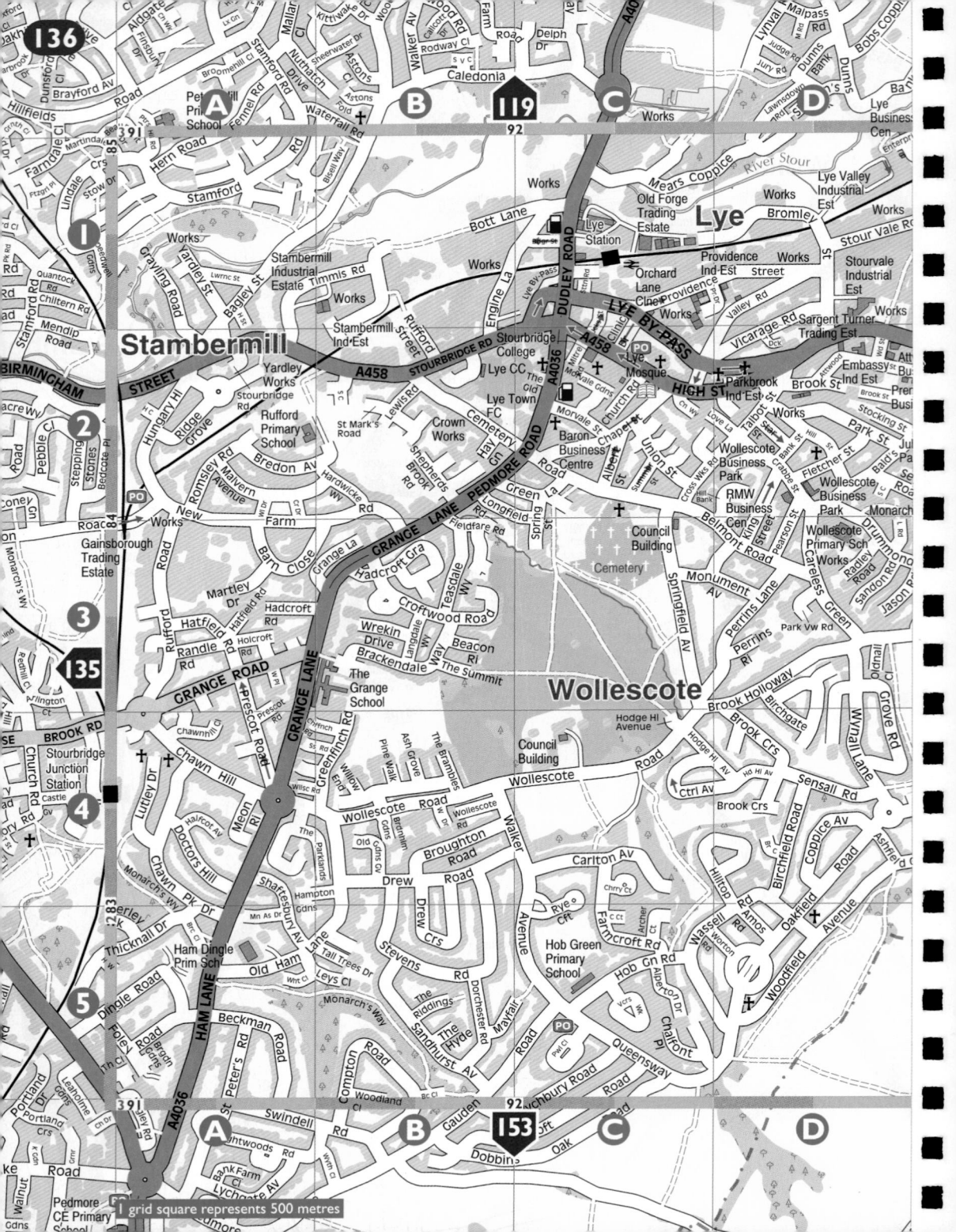

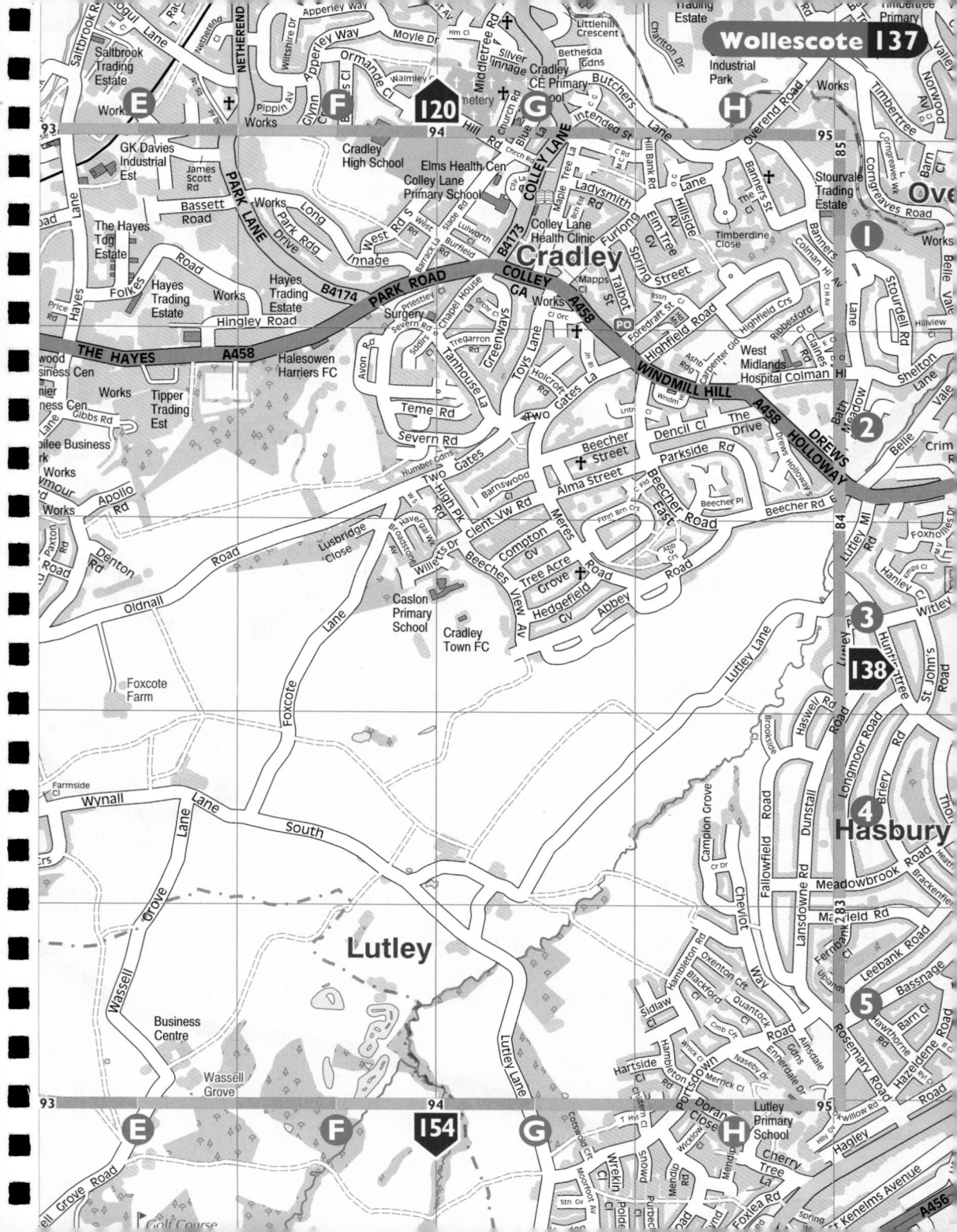

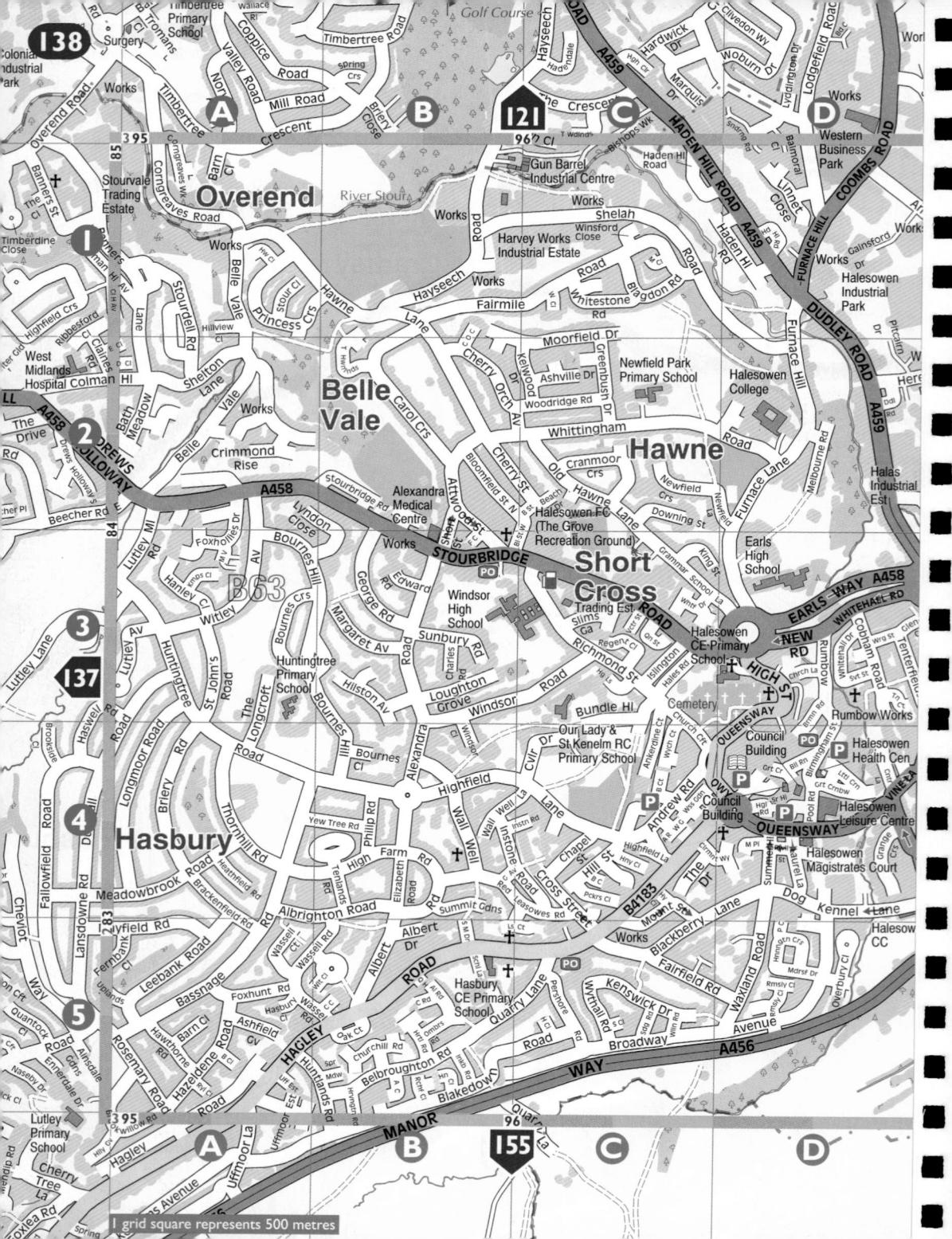

I grid square represents 500 metres

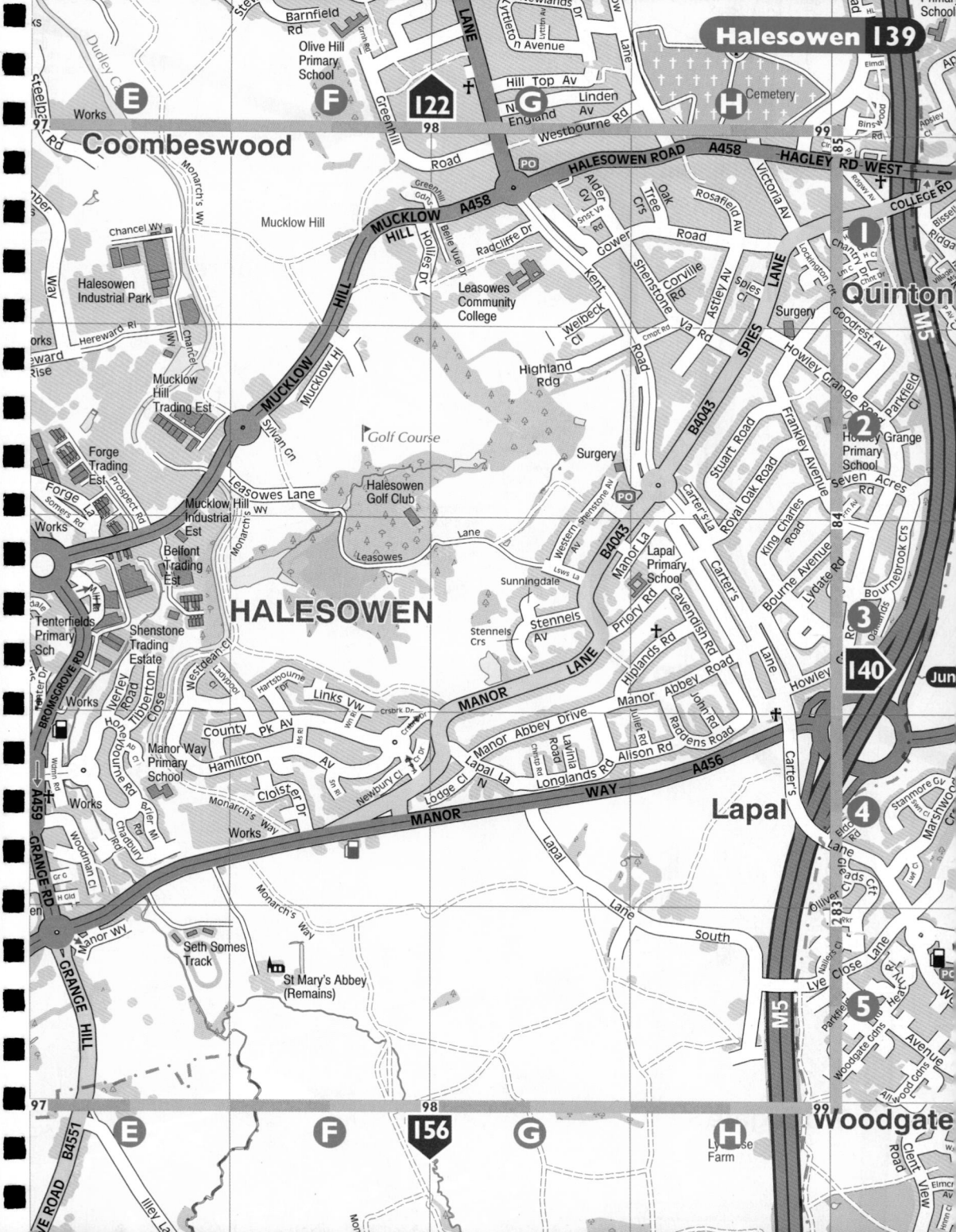

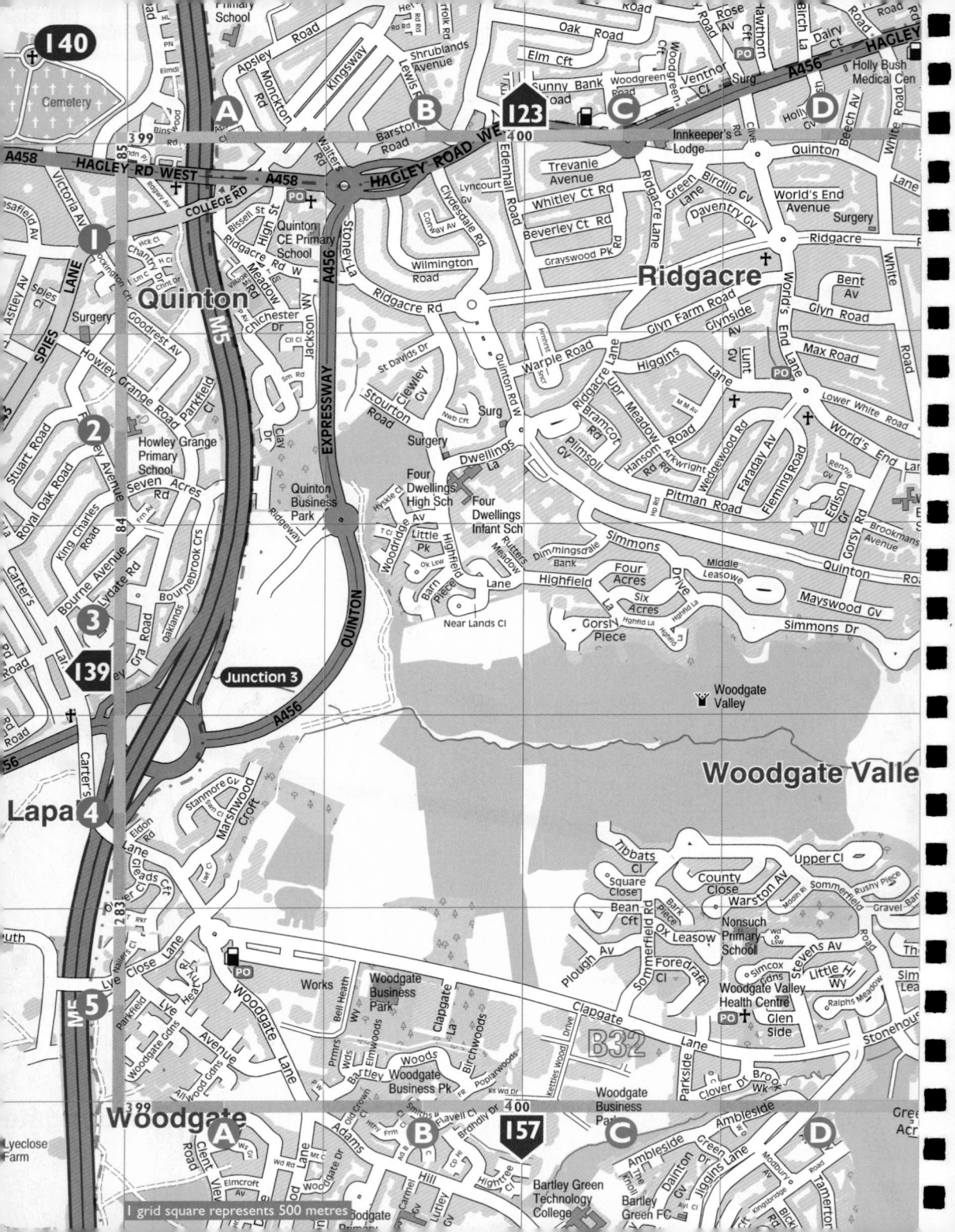

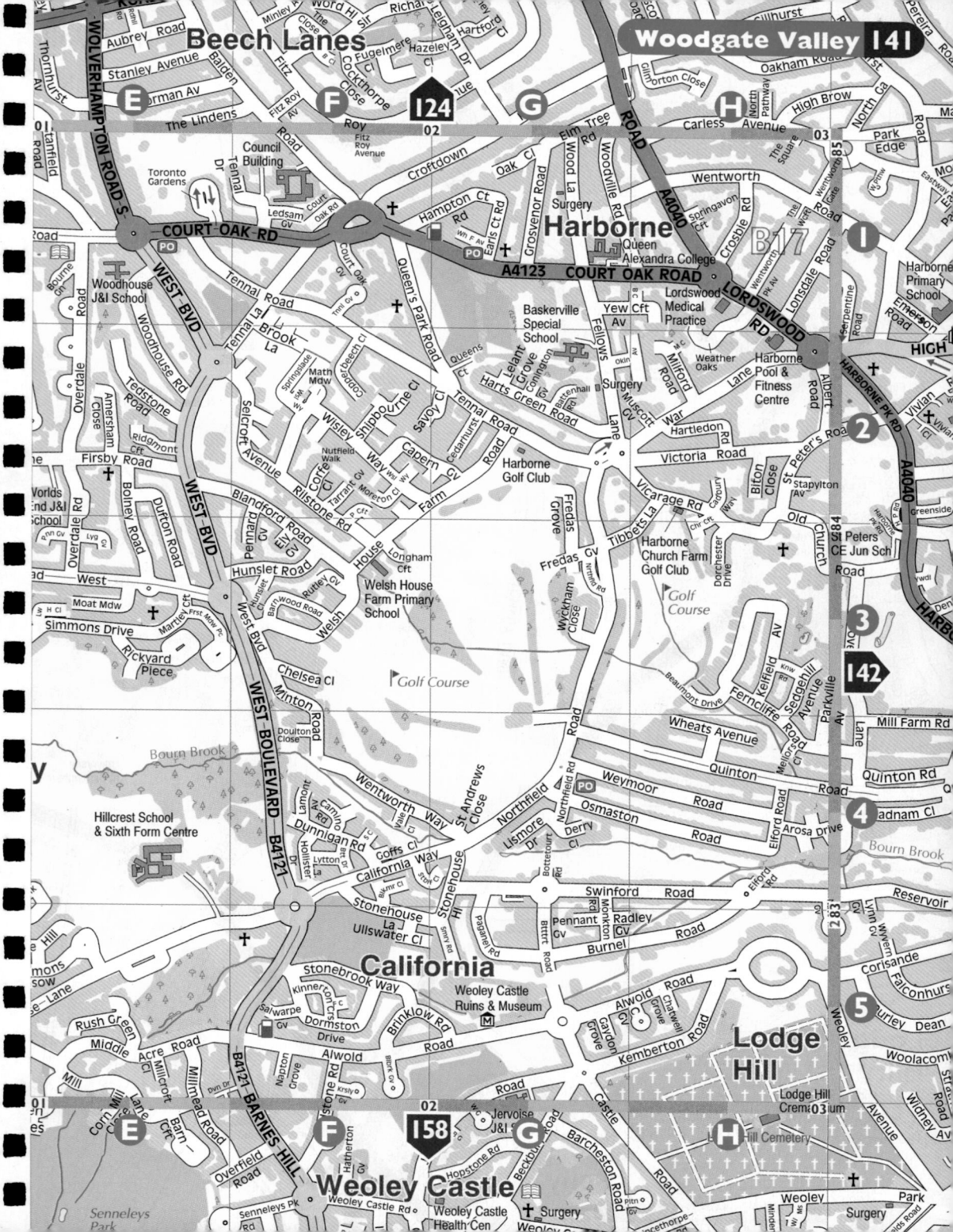

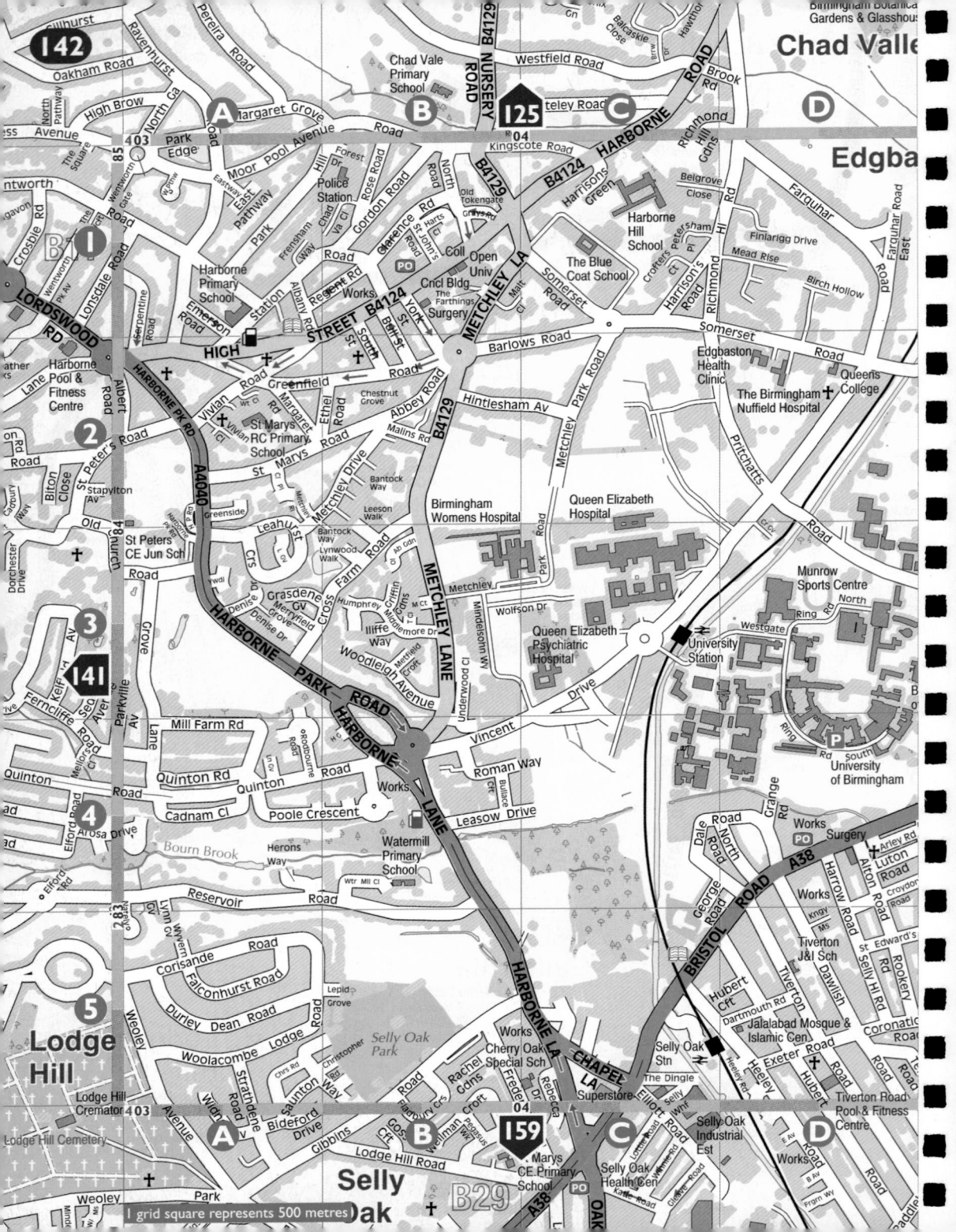

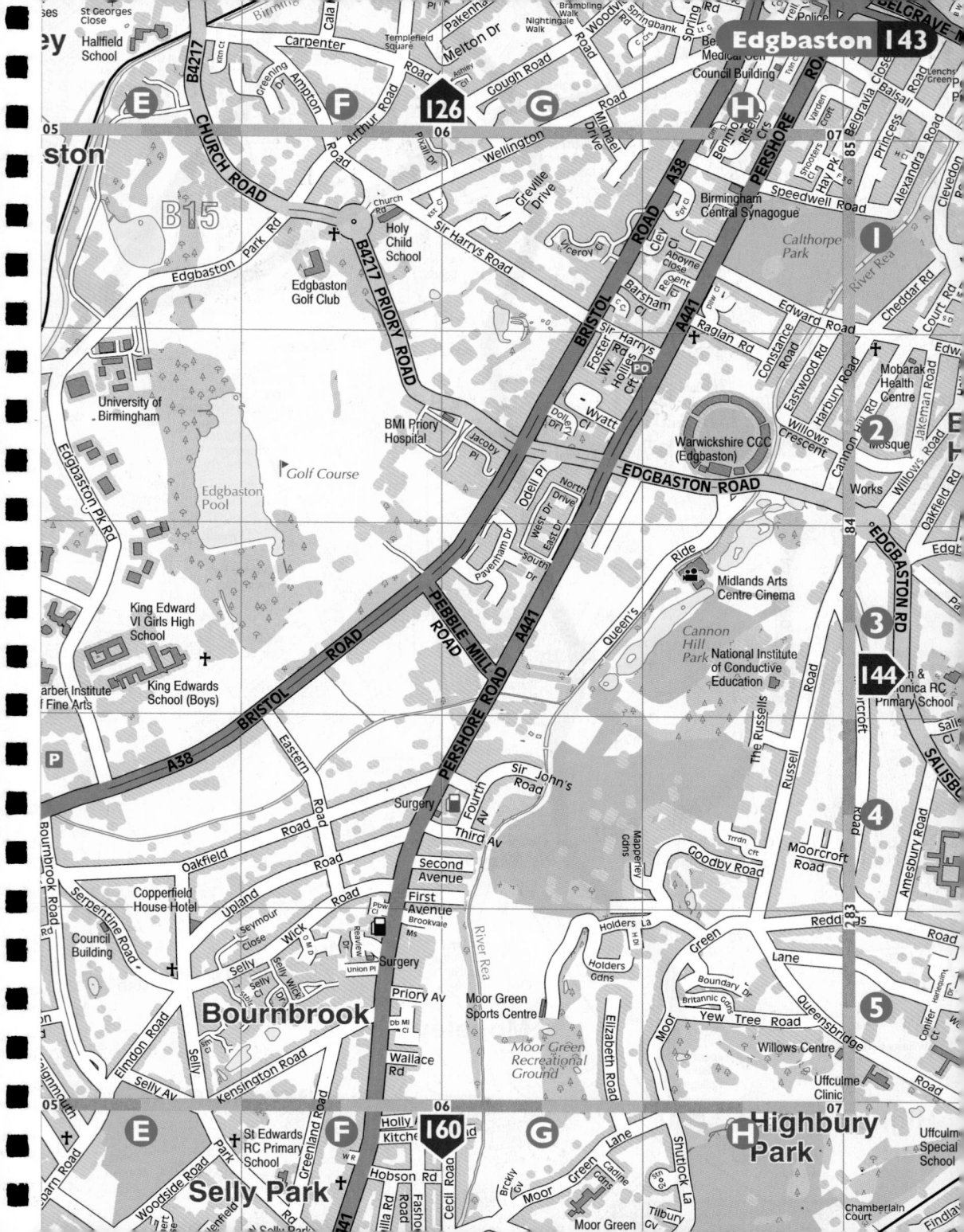

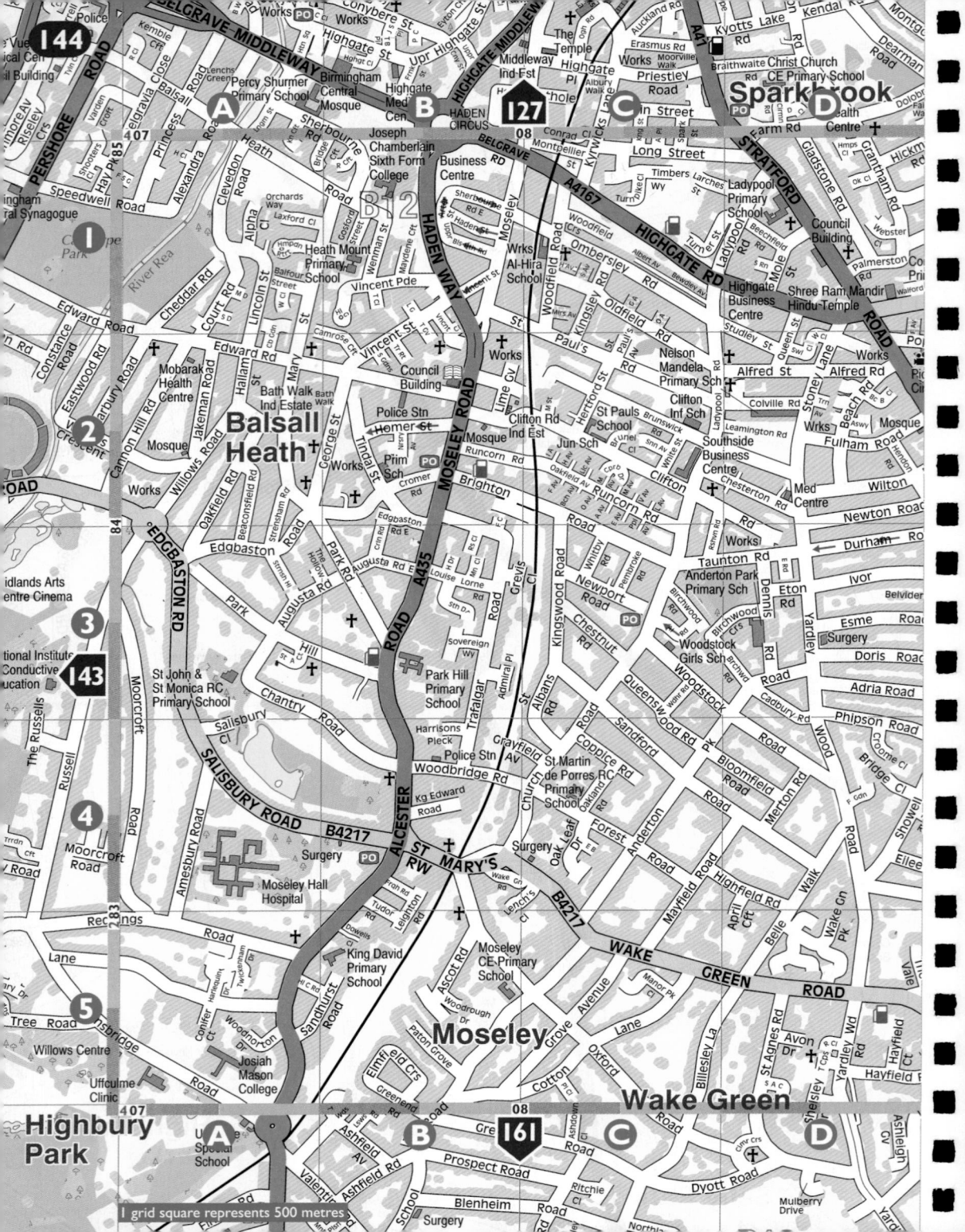

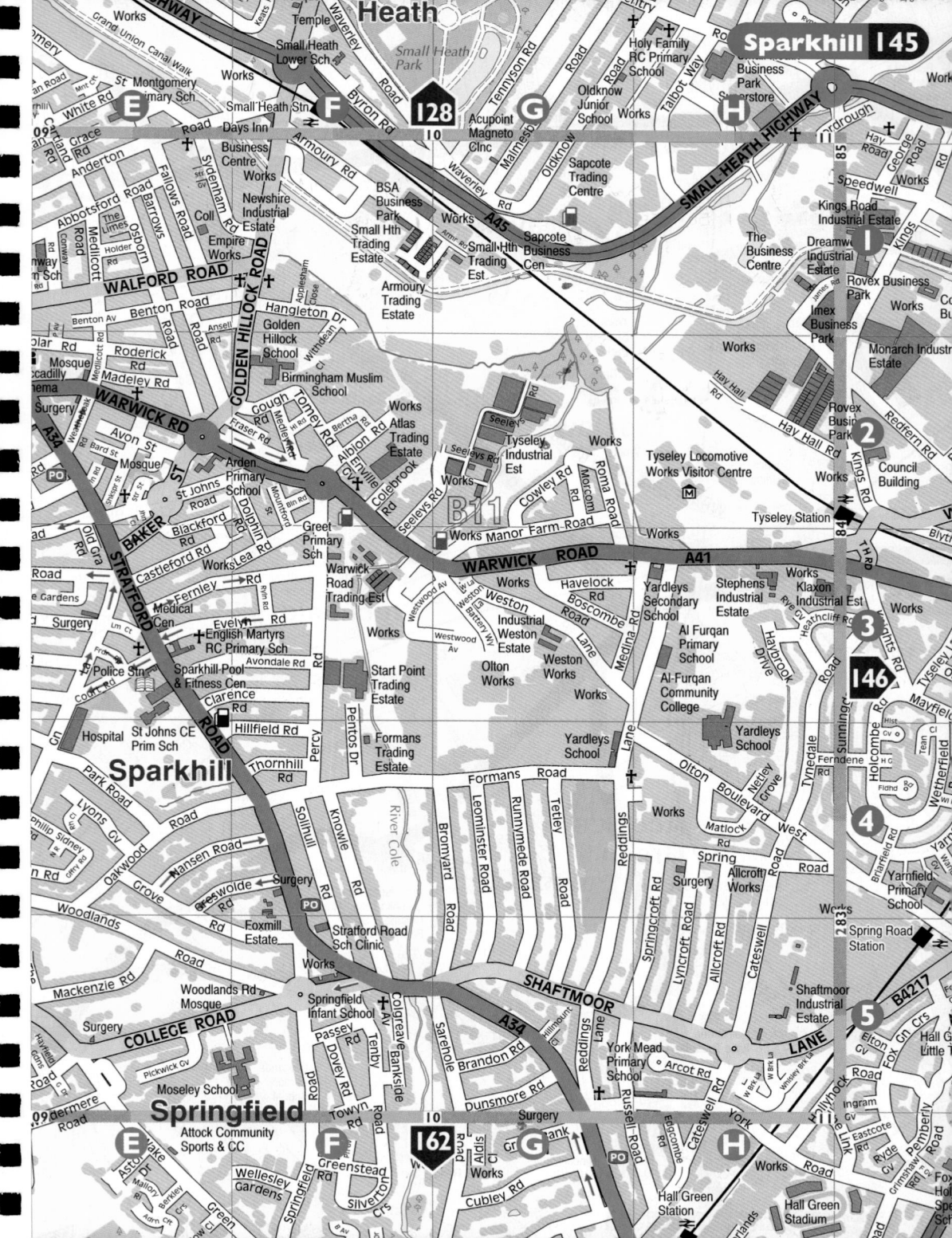

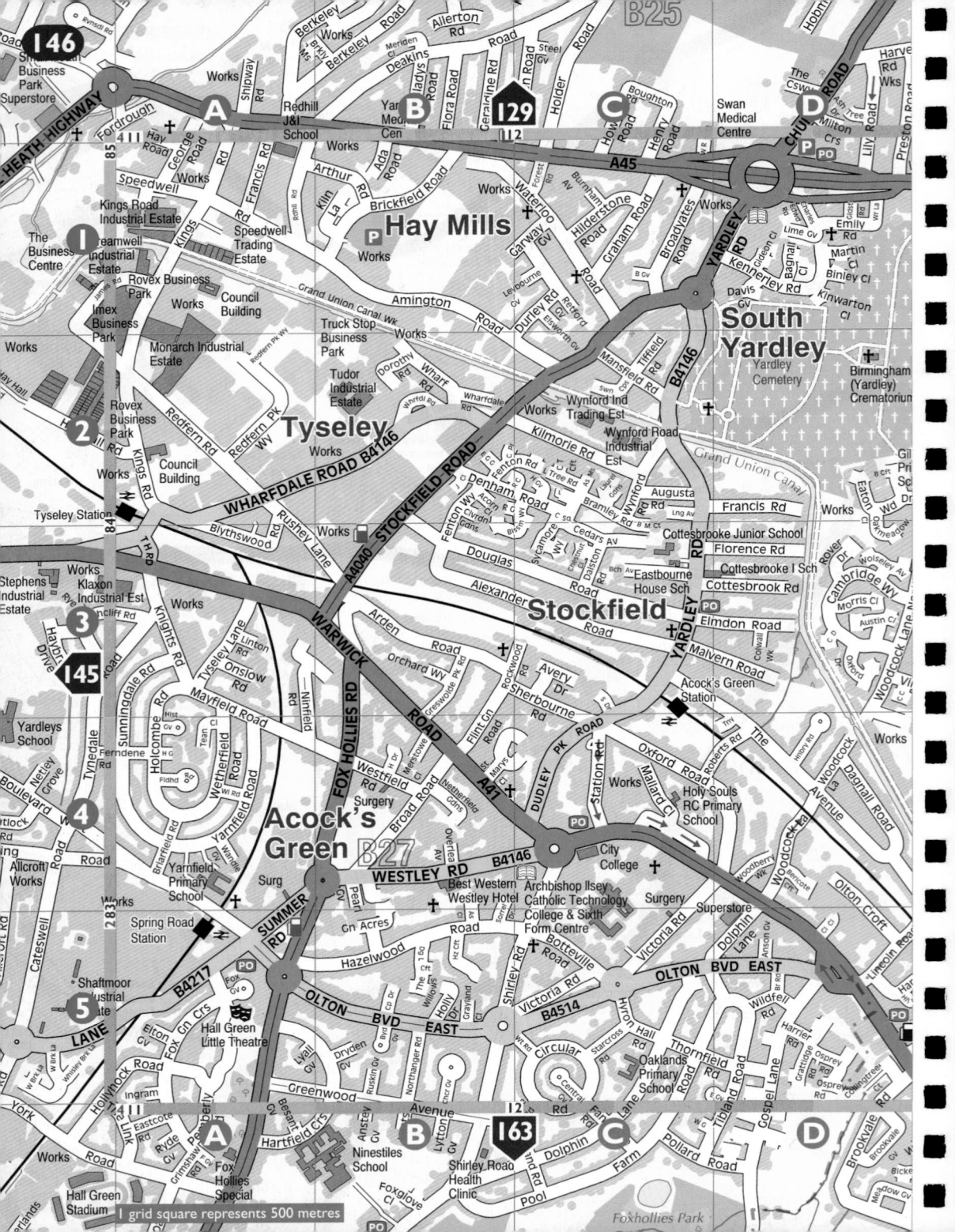

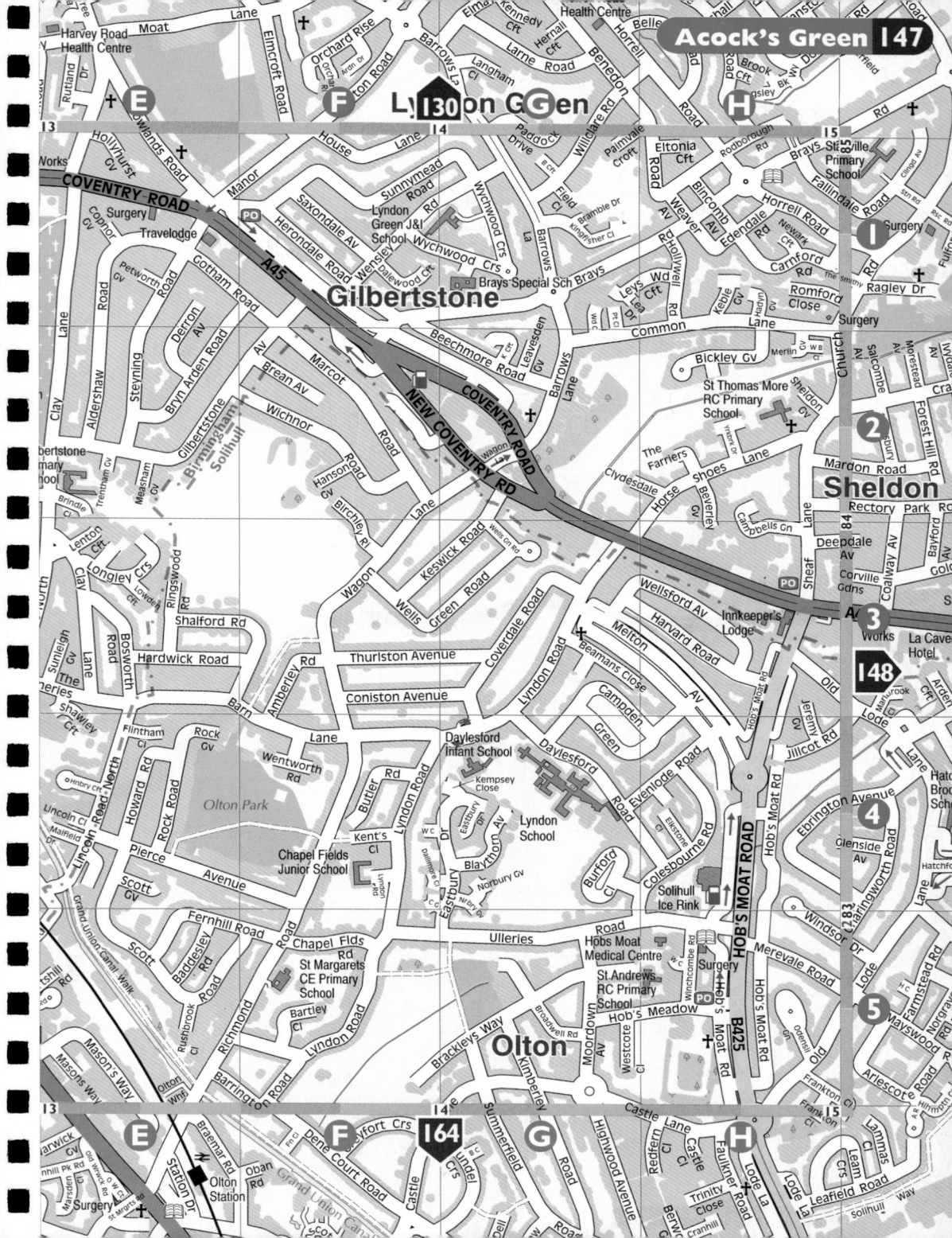

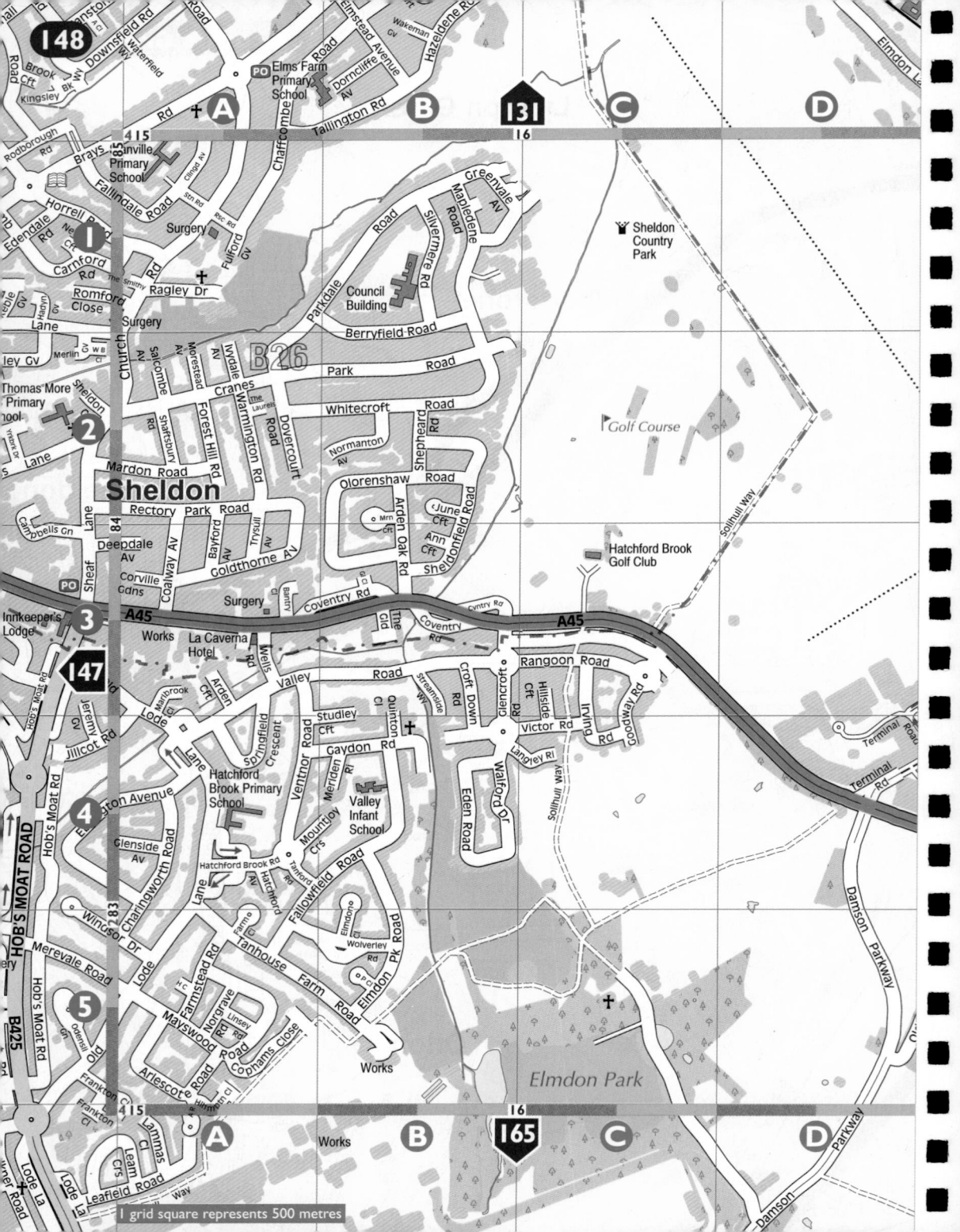

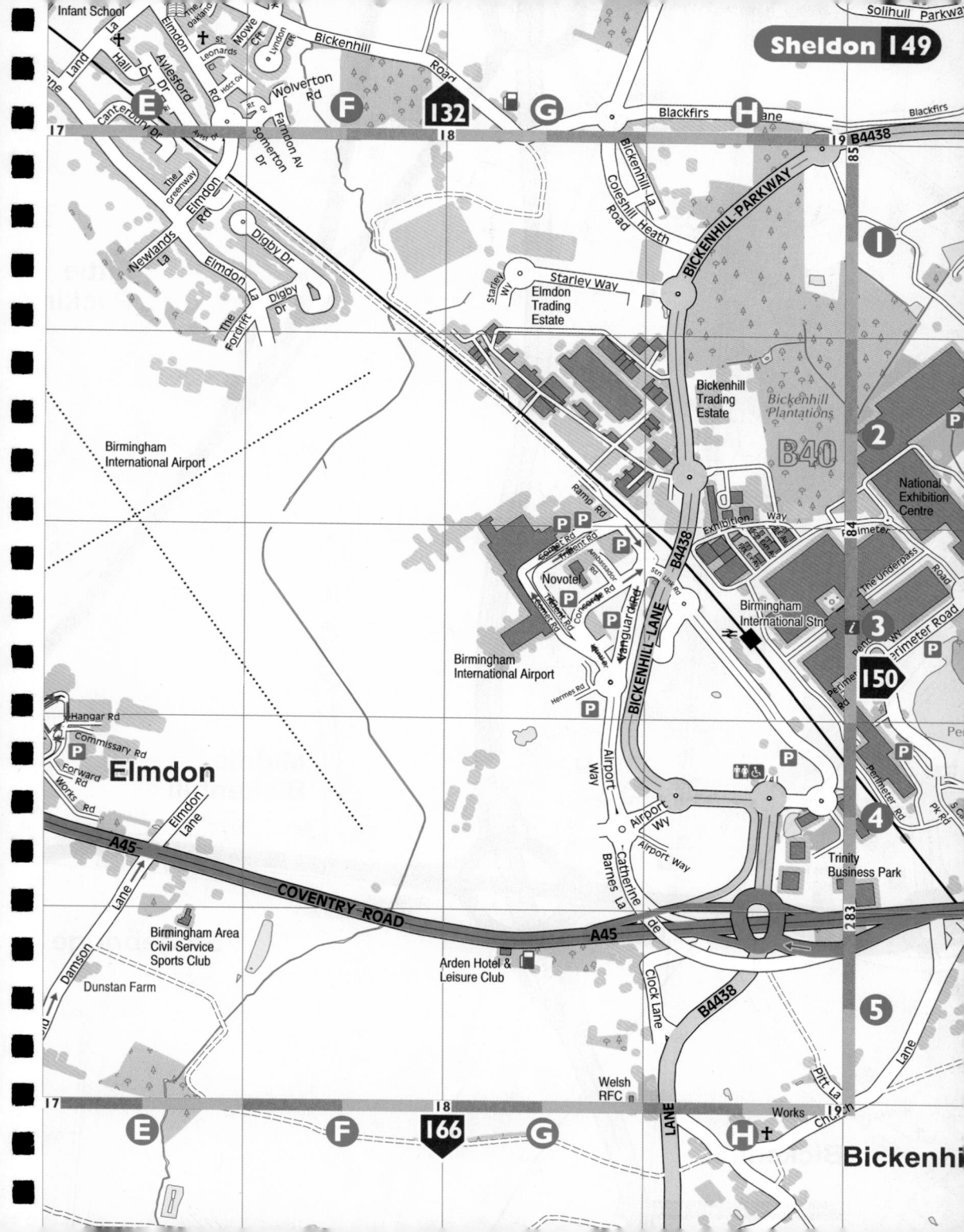

Infant School

Bickenhill

Solihull Parkway

Wolverton Rd

132

Blackfirs

Blackfirs

E

F

G

H

17

18

19

85 B4438

Canterbury Dr

Aylesford Rd

Hall Dr

Elmdon Rd

St Leonards

Lyndon Gr

Mowe

Farnton Av

Somerton Dr

Bickenhill Rd

Coleshill Heath Road

BICKENHILL PARKWAY

The Greenway

Elmdon Rd

Newlands La

Elmdon La

Digby Dr

The Fordrift

Digby Dr

Starley Wy

Starley Way

Elmdon Trading Estate

Bickenhill Trading Estate

Bickenhill Plantations

B40

2

I

Birmingham International Airport

Ramp Rd

Trent Rd

P P

P

Novotel

Ambassador Rd

Concorde Rd

P

P

P

Stn Lane Rd

B4438

Exhibition Way

National Exhibition Centre

Perimeter Rd

The Underpass

Road

Birmingham International Airport

Hermes Rd

Vanguard Rd

BICKENHILL LANE

Birmingham International Stn

3

150

Perimeter Rd

Perimeter Road

PK Rd

Pe

P

Hangar Rd

Commissary Rd

P

Forward Rd

Works Rd

Elmdon

Elmdon Lane

Airport Way

Airport Wy

P

4

Trinity Business Park

A45

COVENTRY ROAD

A45

Catherine de Barnes La

Airport Way

283

Damson Lane

Birmingham Area Civil Service Sports Club

Dunstan Farm

Arden Hotel & Leisure Club

Clock Lane

B4438

Pitt La

Lane

5

Welsh RFC

E

F

G

H

Bickenhi

17

18

166

LANE

Ch Lch

Works

19 ch

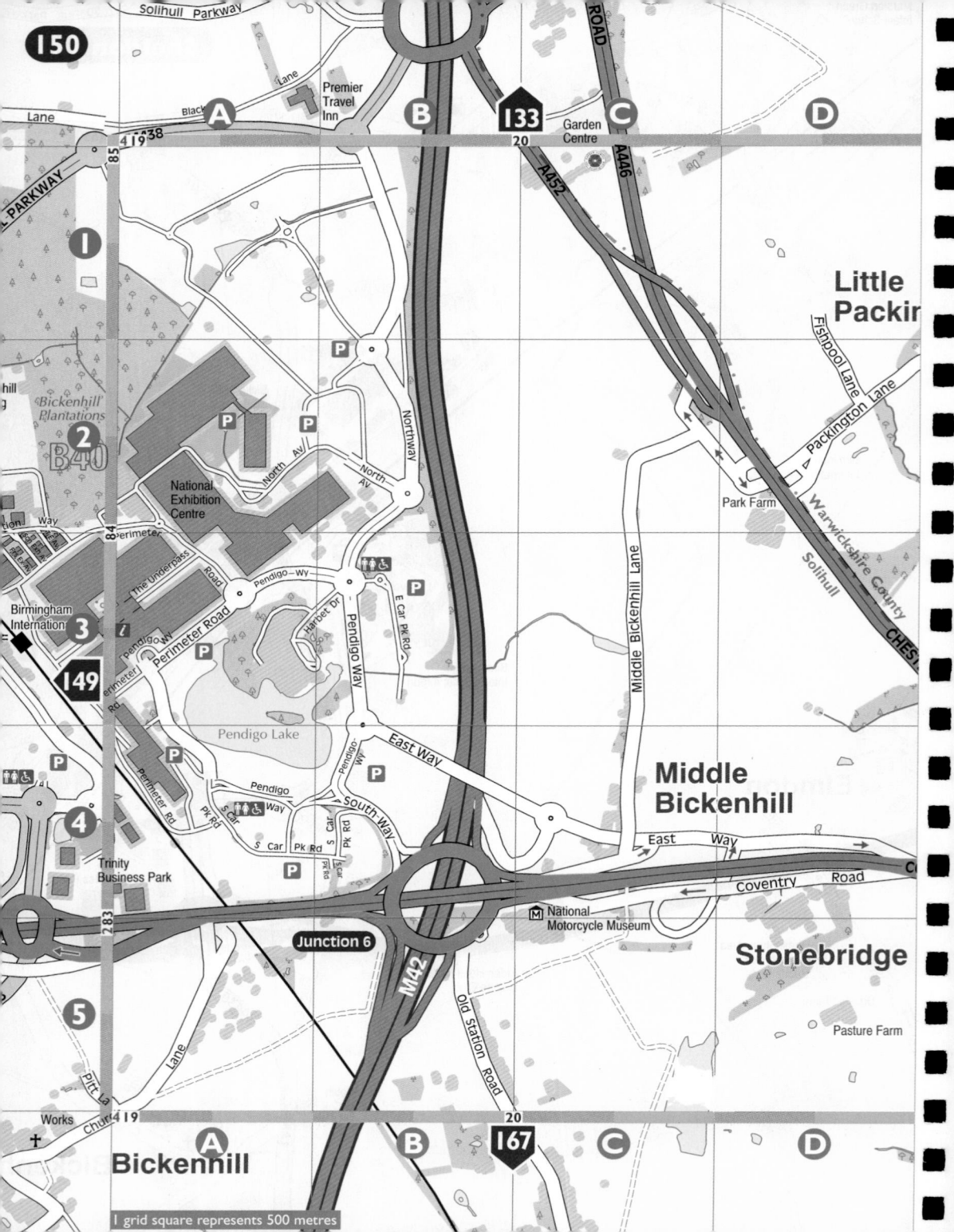

150

Solihull Parkway

Lane

Black A 41 38

Premier Travel Inn

B

133
20

Garden Centre

C

D

Little Packin

I

Bickenhill Plantations

2
B40

National Exhibition Centre

Birmingham International

3

149

4

5

Trinity Business Park

Pendigo Lake

The Underpass

Perimeter Road

Pendigo Wy

Northway

North Av

North Av

Pendigo Way

Harbet Dr

E Car Pk Rd

P

East Way

South Way

S Car Pk Rd

Pendigo Way

Pendigo Way

Pendigo Way

S Car Pk Rd

Pendigo Pk Rd

S Car Pk Rd

Junction 6

M42

National Motorcycle Museum

East Way

Middle Bickenhill

Middle Bickenhill Lane

Park Farm

Fishpool Lane

Packington Lane

Warwickshire County

Solihull

CHES

Coventry Road

Stonebridge

Pasture Farm

Pitt La

Lane

Works

Chur 419

Old Station Road

283

A
Bickenhill

B

167
20

C

D

1 grid square represents 500 metres

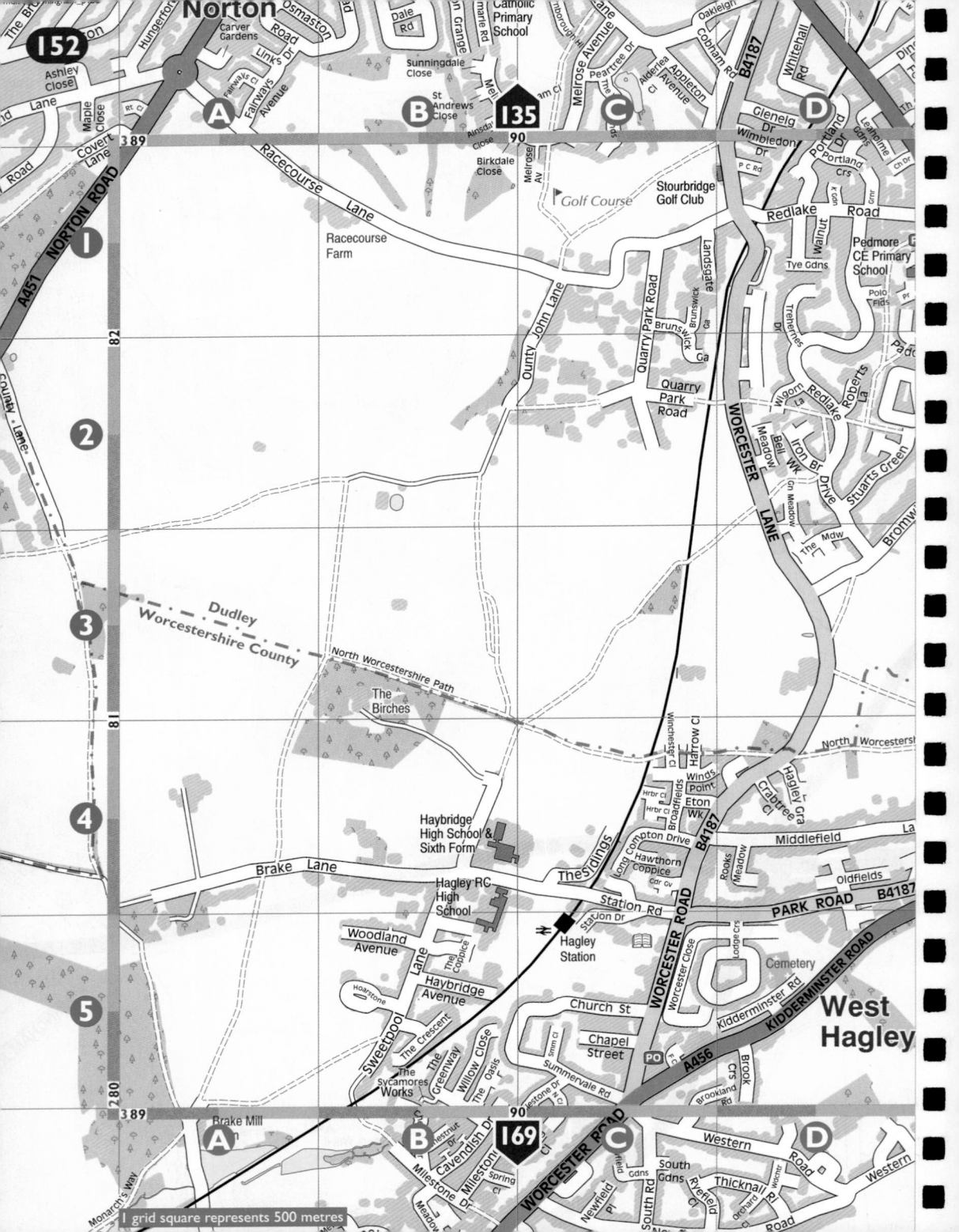

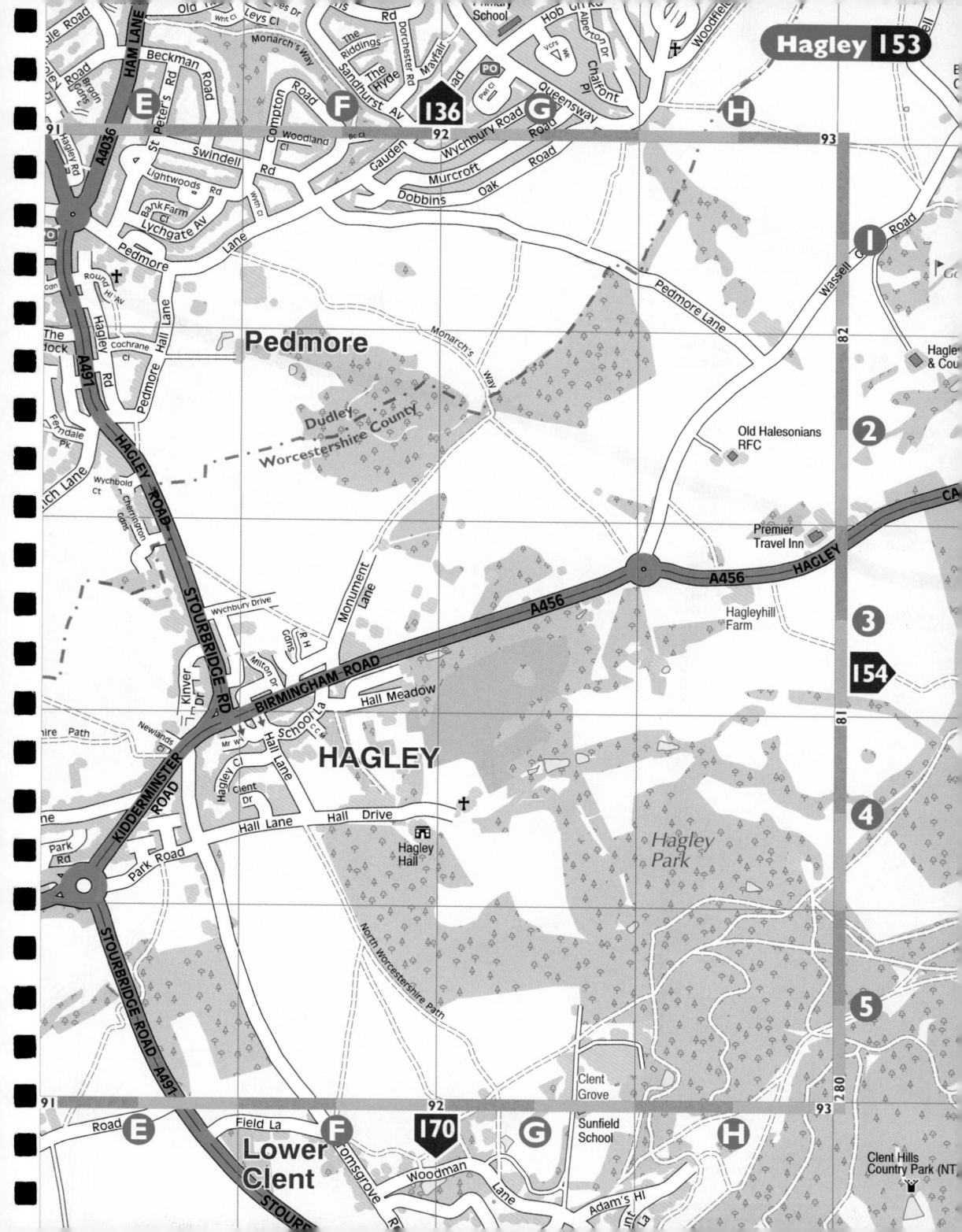

Hagley 153

Pedmore

Dudley
Worcestershire County

HAGLEY

Hagley
Hall

*Hagley
Park*

Old Halesonians
RFC

Premier
Travel Inn

Hagleyhill
Farm

Clent
Grove

Sunfield
School

**Lower
Clent**

Clent Hills
Country Park (NT)

136

92

93

154

170

E F G H I

HAM LANE
Beckman
Road
Monarch's Way
The
Riddings
The
Hyde
Mayfair
Sandhurst Av
Compton
Road
Woodland
Cl
Gauden
Murcroft
Road
Dobbins
Oak
Road
Wychbury Road
Queensway
Chalfont
Pl
Woodfield

Swindell
Rd
Lightwoods Rd
Bank Farm Cl
Lychgate Av
St Peter's Rd

Pedmore

Pedmore Hall Lane
Cochrane
Cl
Wychbold
Ct
Cherrington
Gdns
Wychbury Drive

Monarch's
Way

Pedmore Lane

Wassell Rd

A4036
A491
Hagley Rd
HAGLEY ROAD
STOURBRIDGE RD
KIDDERMINSTER ROAD
STOURBRIDGE ROAD A491
BIRMINGHAM ROAD
A456
A456 HAGLEY

Monument
Lane
R H
Gdns
Milton
School La
Hall Meadow
Newlands
Mr W's
Hagley
Cl
Clent
Dr
Hall Lane
Hall Lane
Hall Drive
Hall Drive
Kinver
Dr
Park
Rd
Park Road
North Worcestershire Path

Field La
Romsgrove
Road
Woodman
Lane
Adam's Hl

91 92 93
81 82 280

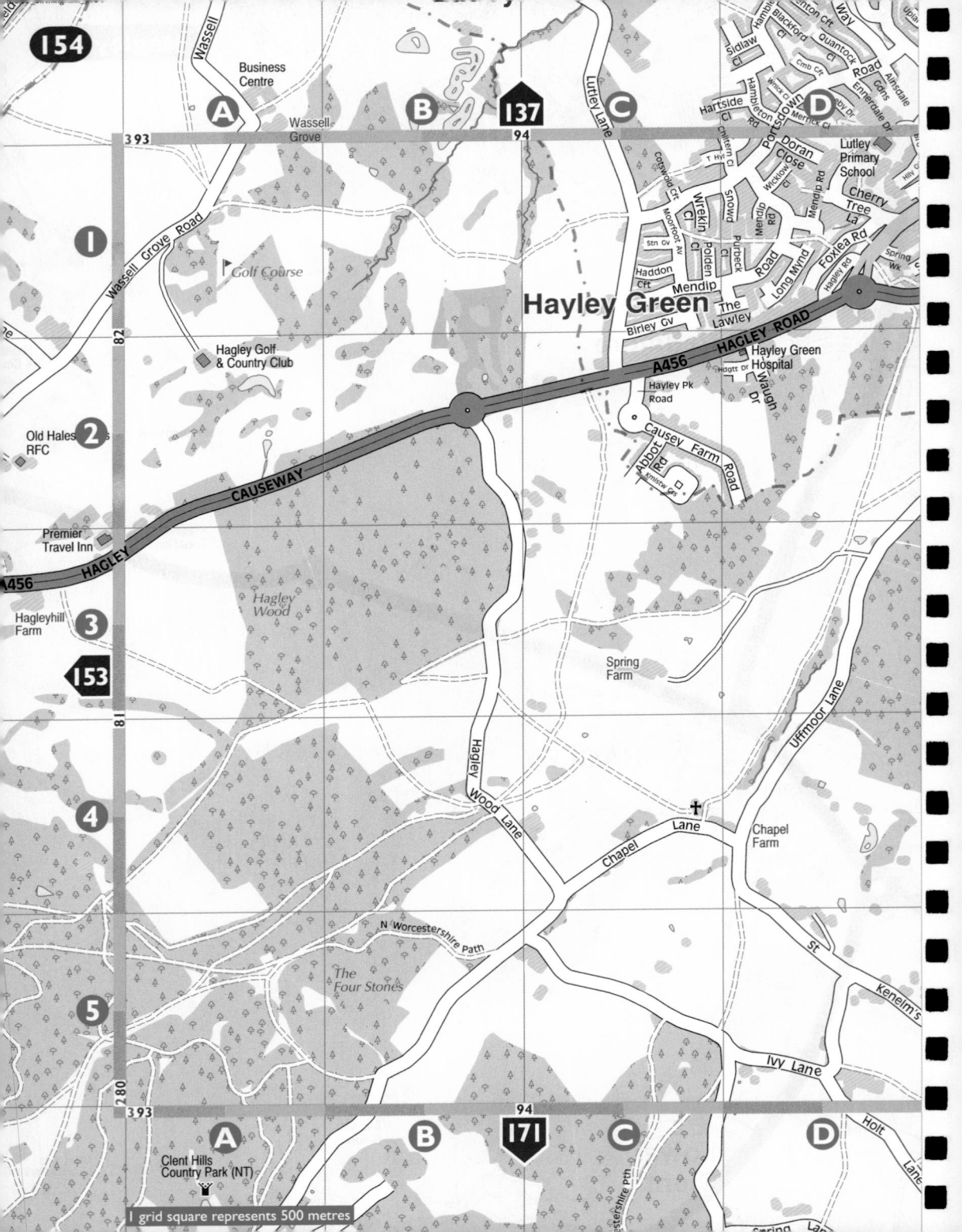

A 393
Wassell

Business
Centre

B
Wassell
Grove

94

137

C
Lutley Lane

Hartside
Cl

Cotswold Cft

D
Portsdown
Doran
Close
Lutley
Primary
School

I
Wassell Grove Road

82

Golf Course

Moorfoot Av
Chiltern Cl
T Hyl
Stn Rd

Snowd
Wrekin
Cft
Purbeck
Haddon
Cft
Mendip
Rd
Long Mynd
Mendip
Road

Wickow Rd

Cherry
Tree
La

Foxlea Rd

Spring
Wk

Hagley Golf
& Country Club

Birley Gv
Mendip
The
Lawley

Hayley Green

A456 HAGLEY ROAD

Hayley Green
Hospital

Hagtt Dr
Waugh Dr

2
Old Hales
RFC

CAUSEWAY

Hayley Pk
Road

Causey Farm Road

Abbot Dr
Kristin Ct

456 HAGLEY

Premier
Travel Inn

Hagley
Wood

Spring
Farm

Uffmoor Lane

3
Hagleyhill
Farm

153

81

Hagley
Wood Lane

4

Chapel Lane

Chapel
Farm

St

5

N Worcestershire Path

The
Four Stones

Chapel

Kenelm's

Ivy Lane

2 80 393

A
Clent Hills
Country Park (NT)

B

94

171

C

D
Holt
Lane

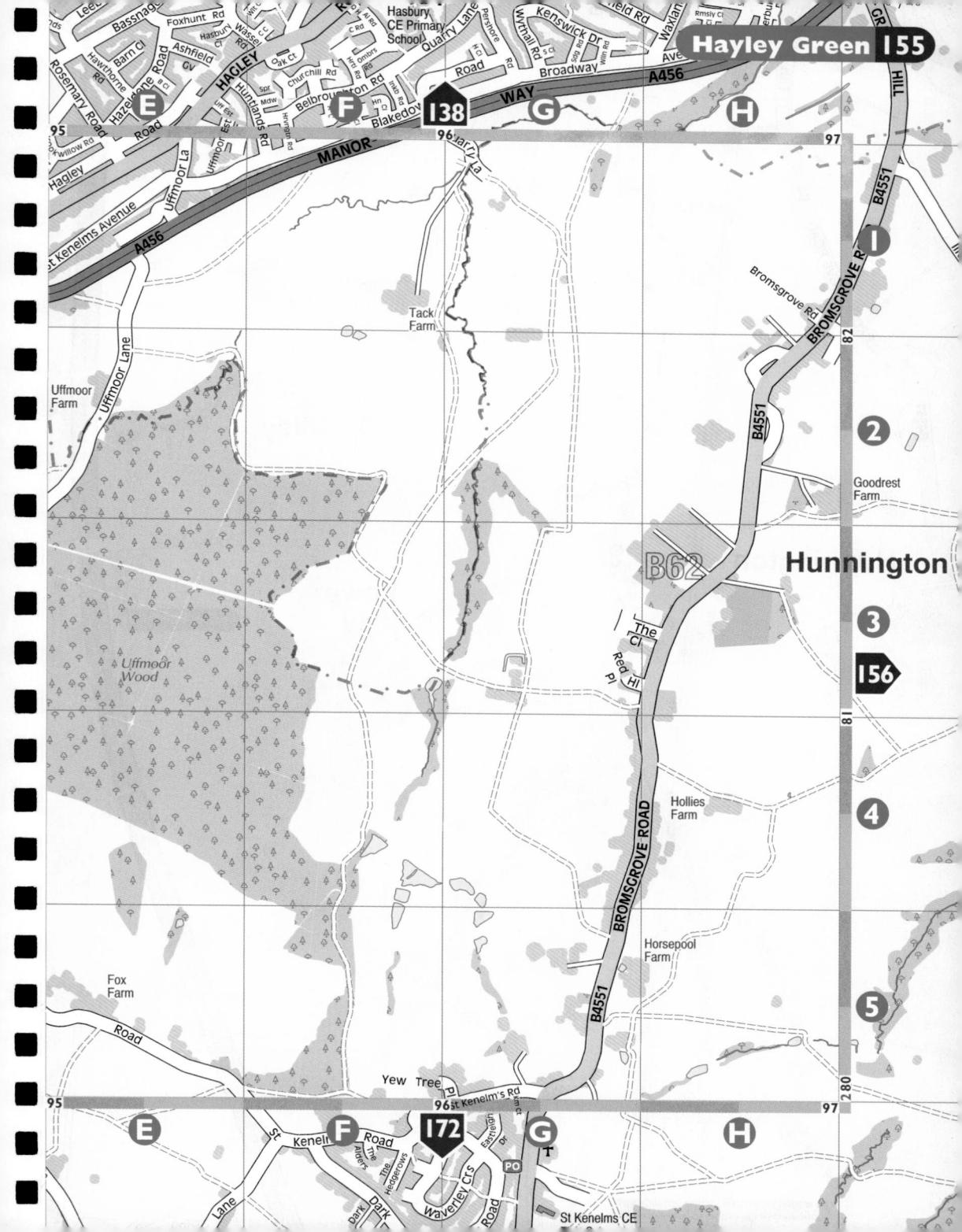

Leek
Bassnage
Foxhunt Rd
Hasbury CE Primary School
Kenswick Dr
Rmsly Ct

Rosemary Rd
Hawthorne Rd
Barn Cl
Ashfield Ov
Quarry Lane
Prestare Rd
Wrthall Rd
St Cl
Waxlan
Broadway

Hawthorne Rd
HAGLEY
Hazeldene Road
Huntlands Rd
Belbroughton Rd
Blakedown
Broadway
A456

E   **F**   **138**   WAY   **G**   **H**

Willow Rd
Hagley
95
MANOR
96 arly La
97
B4551

St Kenelms Avenue
A456
Uffmoor Lane

Bromsgrove Rd
I
B4551

Tack Farm
BROMSGROVE Rd
82
B4551
Uffmoor Farm
2

Goodrest Farm

Uffmoor Wood
B62
Hunnington

The Cl
Red Hl
3

156

81

Hollies Farm
4

Fox Farm
Road
Horsepool Farm

B4551
5

280
Yew Tree
95
96 St Kenelm's Rd
97

E   **F**   **172**   **G**   **H**

Kenelm
Road
Eastreign
Dr
PO
The Alders
The Hedgerows
Waverley Crs
Road
St Kenelms CE
Lane
Dark

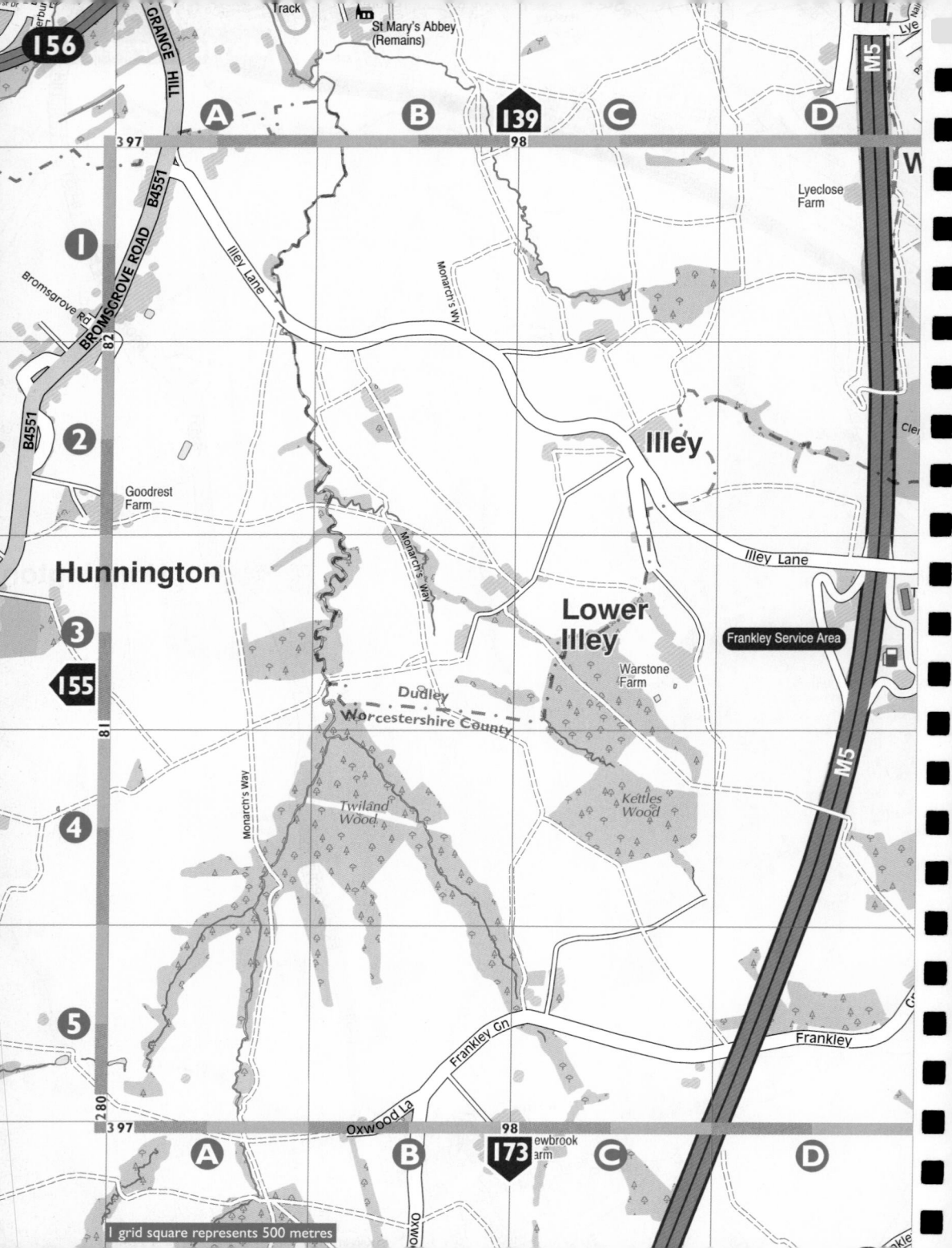

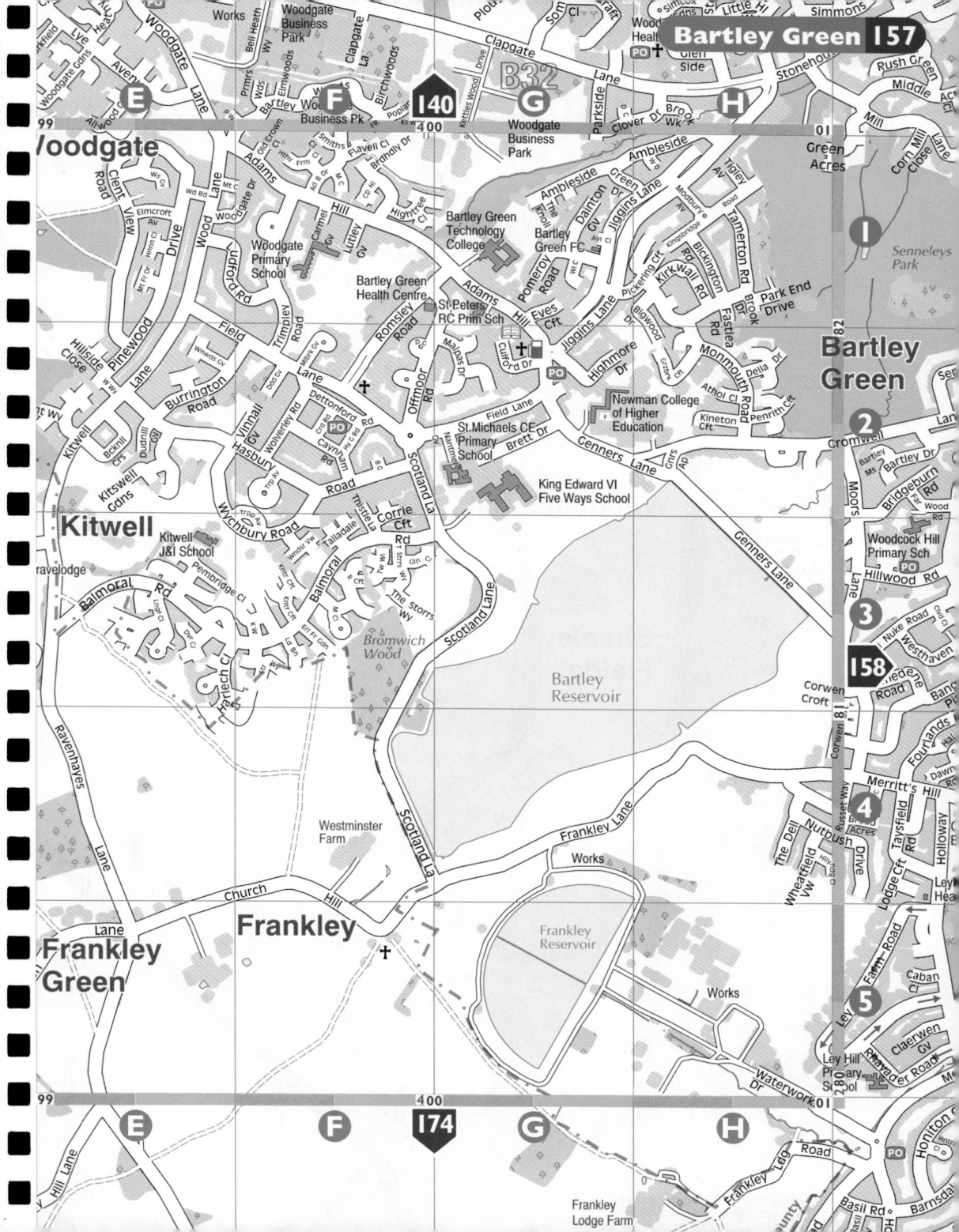

B32

140

158

174

Woodgate

Bartley Green

Kitwell

Travelodge

Frankley Green

Frankley

Woodgate

Woodgate Business Park

Bell Heath Wy

Woodgate Lane

Works

Clapgate Lane

Woodgate Health

PO

Glen Side

Stonehouse

Little Hl

Simmons

Rush Grn

Middle Acre

Mill

Green Acres

Senneleys Park

Bartley Green

Clent View

Elmcroft Av

Cluford Rd

Woodgate Primary School

Adams Hill

Carmel Gv

Lutley Gv

Bartley Green Technology College

Bartley Green Health Centre

St Peters RC Prim Sch

Ambleside

The Knoll

Dainton Gv

Jiggins Lane

Ambleside

Bartley Green FC

Pomeroy Road

Eves Cft

Jiggins Lane

Highmore Dr

Tigley Av

Modbury

Bickington Rd

Kirk Wall Rd

Tamerton Rd

Fastlea Rd

Park End Drive

Hillside Close

Pinewood Drive

Field Lane

Burrington Road

Vimall Gv

Hasbury

Wychbury Road

Dettonford Rd

Romsley Road

Offmoor Rd

Malpas Dr

Cluford Dr

Jiggins Lane

Highmore Dr

St Michaels CE Primary School

Field Lane

Brett Dr

Newman College of Higher Education

Kineton Cft

Monmouth Road

Athol Cl

Penrith Cft

Della Dr

Bartley Green

Cromwell

Moors

Bartley Ms

Bartley Dr

Bridgeburn Rd

Wood Rd

Woodcock Hill Primary Sch

PO

Hillwood Rd

Westhaven

Corwen Croft

Kitwell Gdns

Kitwell J&I School

Balmoral Rd

Pembridge Cl

Corrie Cft Rd

Talladale

The Storrs Wy

Bromwich Wood

Scotland Lane

Genners Lane

King Edward VI Five Ways School

Bartley Reservoir

Corwen Road

Fourlands

Merritt's Hill

Broad Acres

Russet Way

Taysfield Rd

Wheatfield Vw

Nutpush

The Dell

Ravenhayes Lane

Church Hill

Westminster Farm

Scotland La

Frankley Lane

Works

Frankley Reservoir

Works

Lodge Cft

Ley Farm Road

Caban Cl

Claerwen Gv

Rhayader Road

Ley Hill Primary School

Ley Hill

Waterwork Dr

Honiton

Frankley Lodge Road

Basil Rd

Frankley Lodge Farm

Hill Lane

Ravenhayes Lane

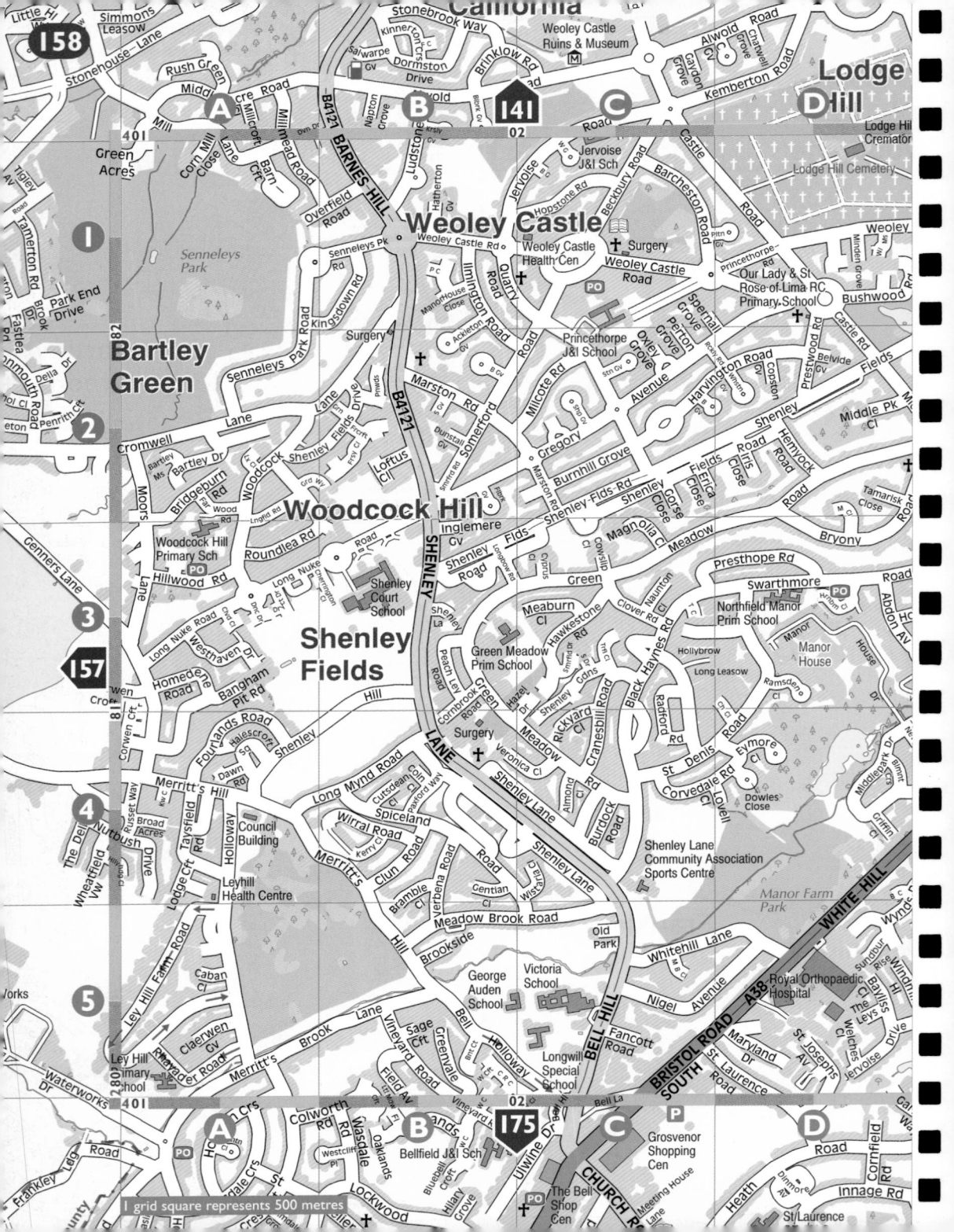

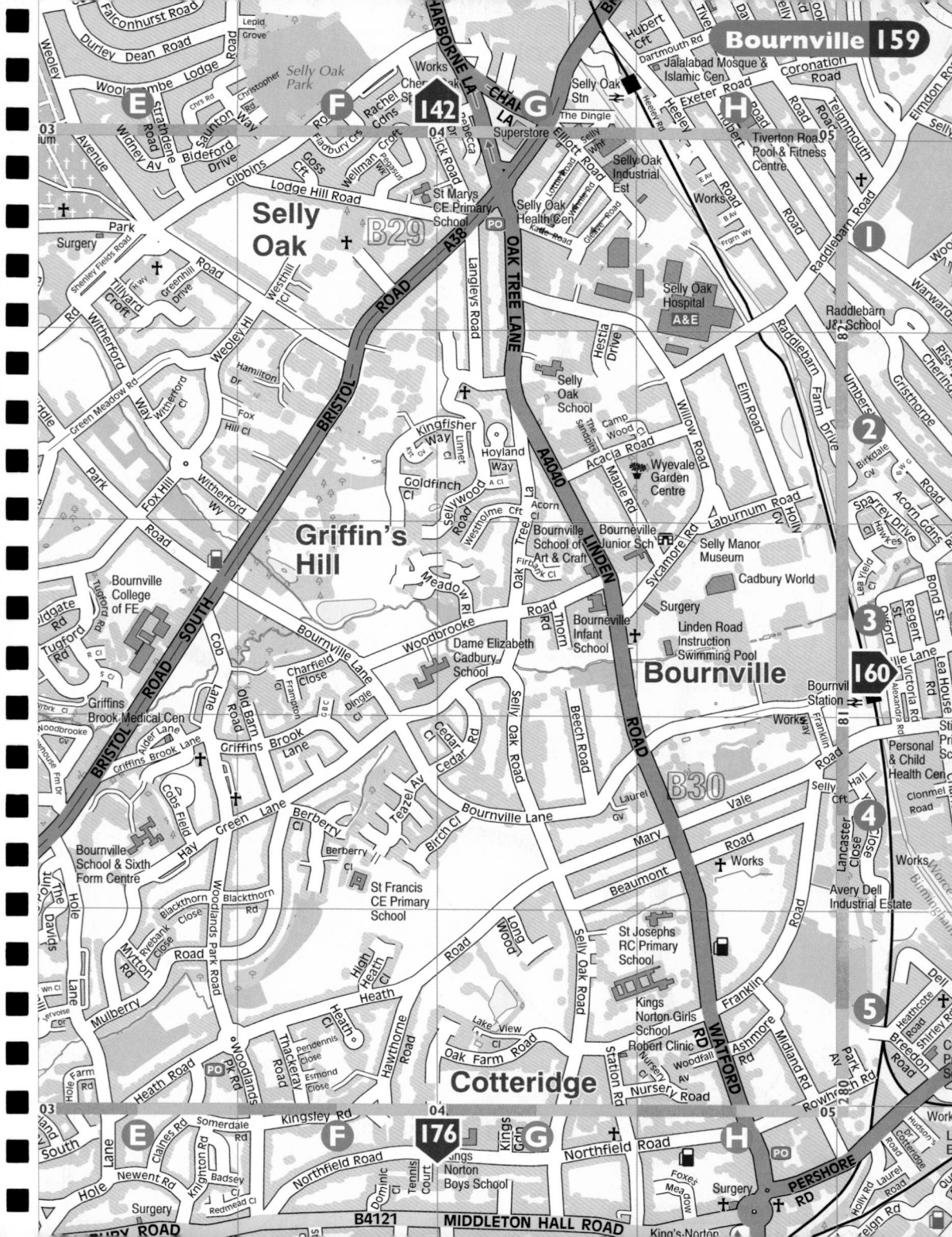

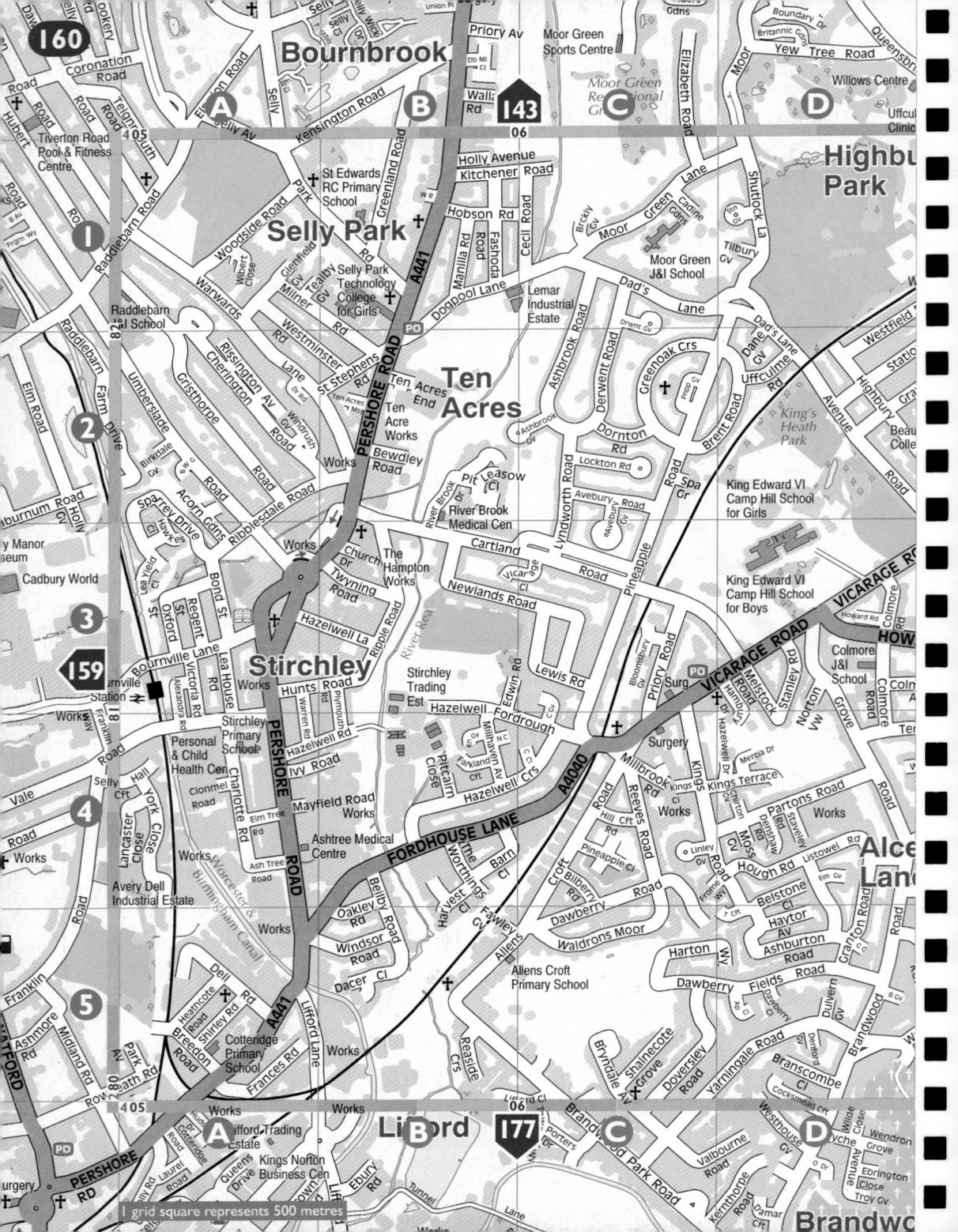

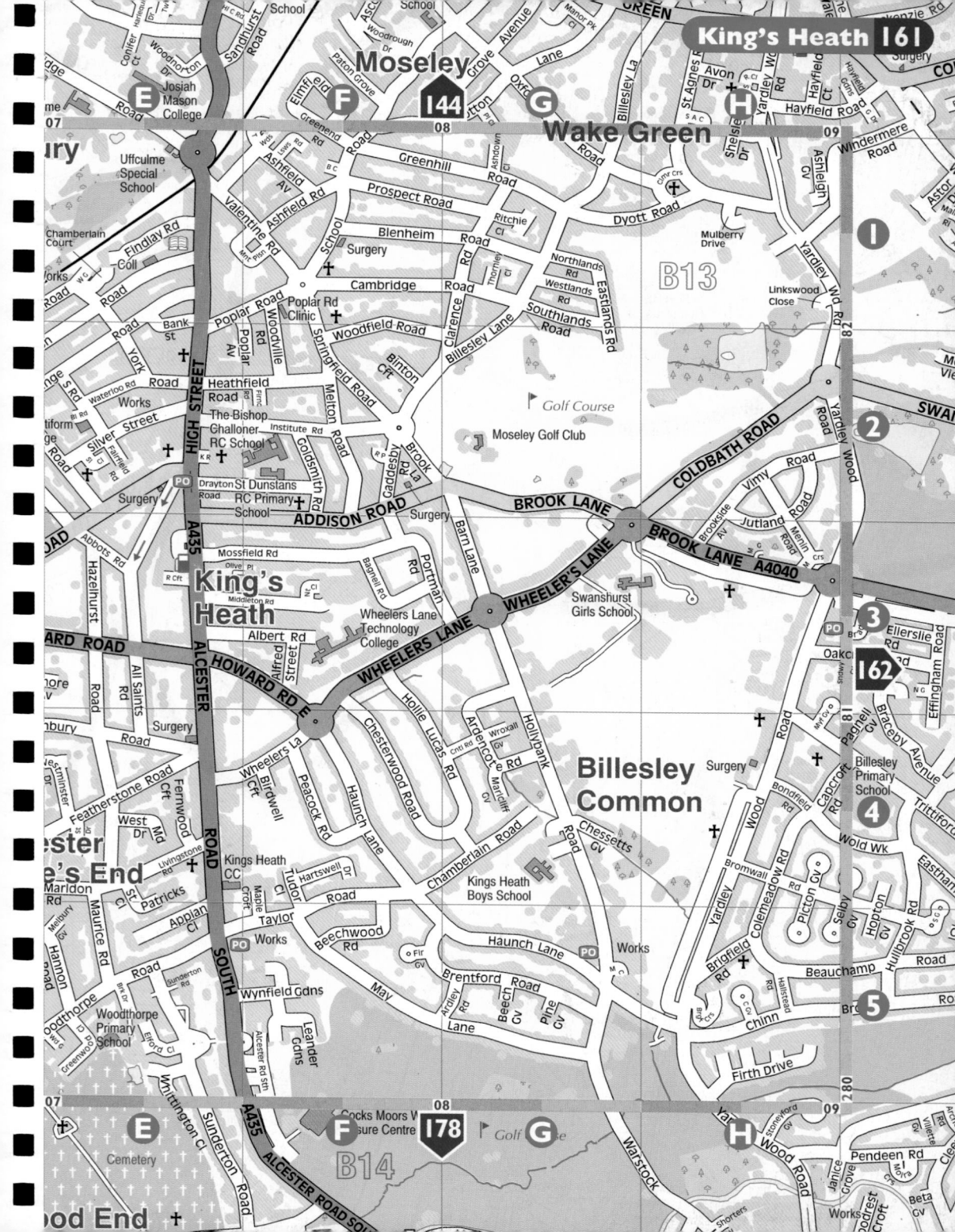

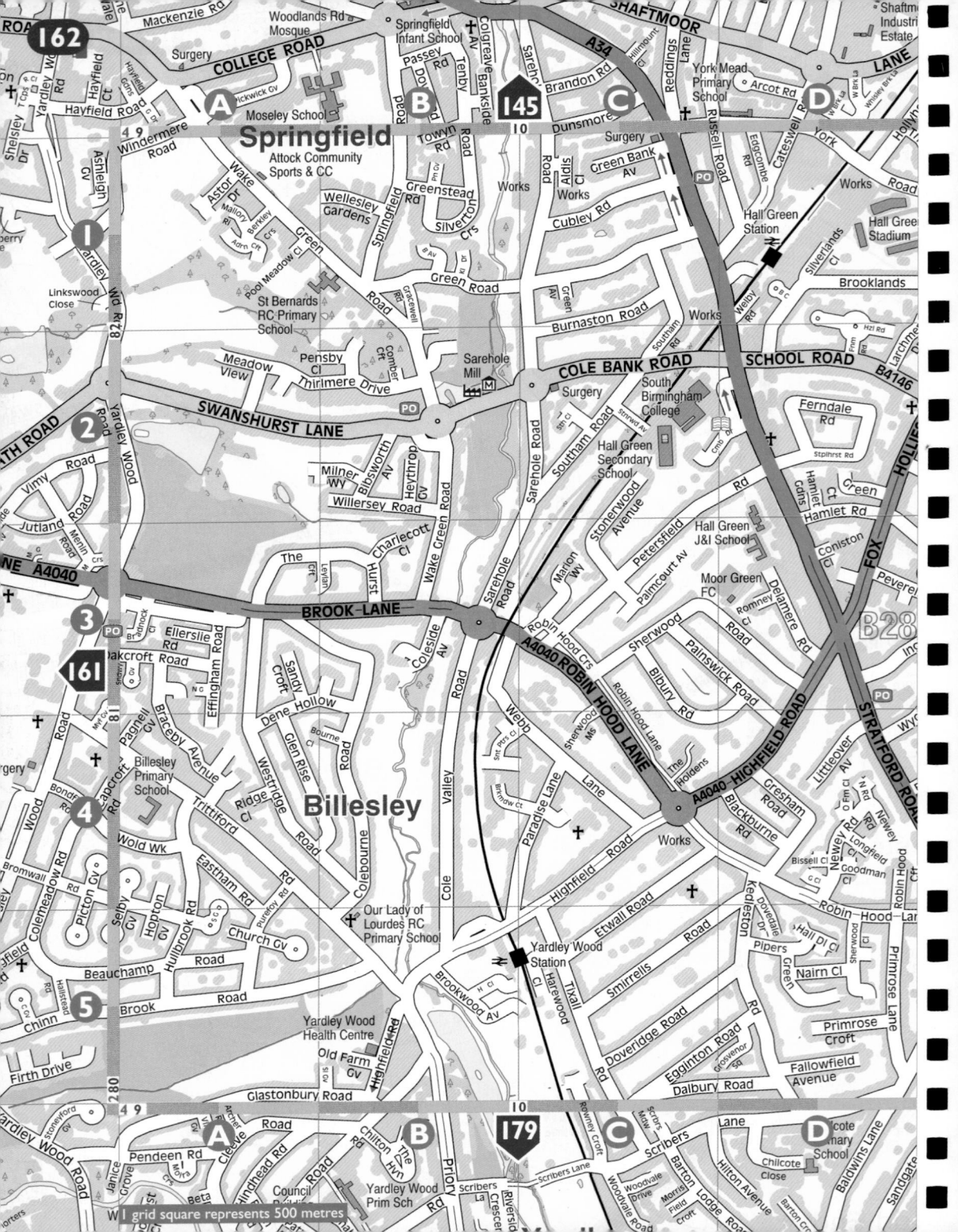

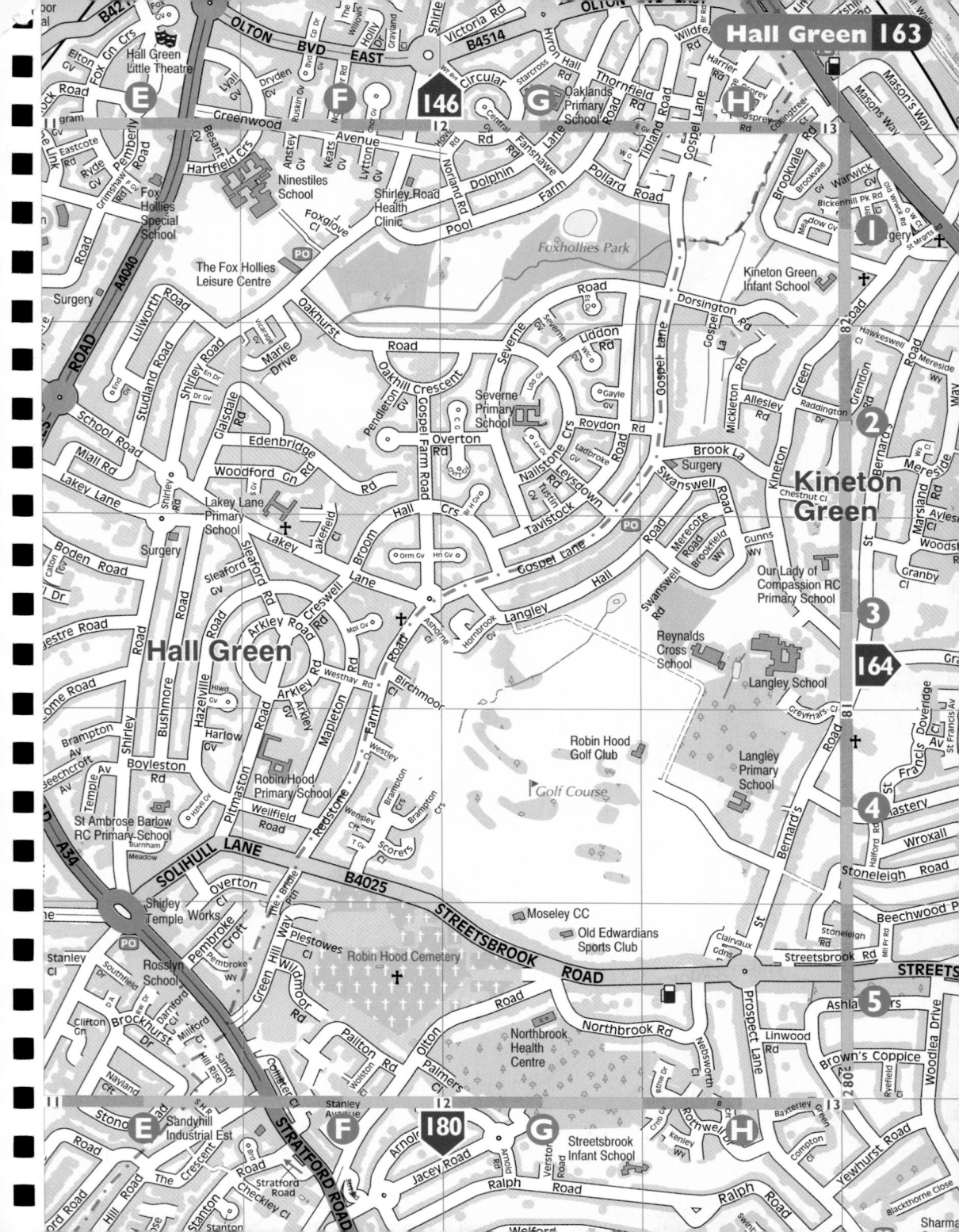

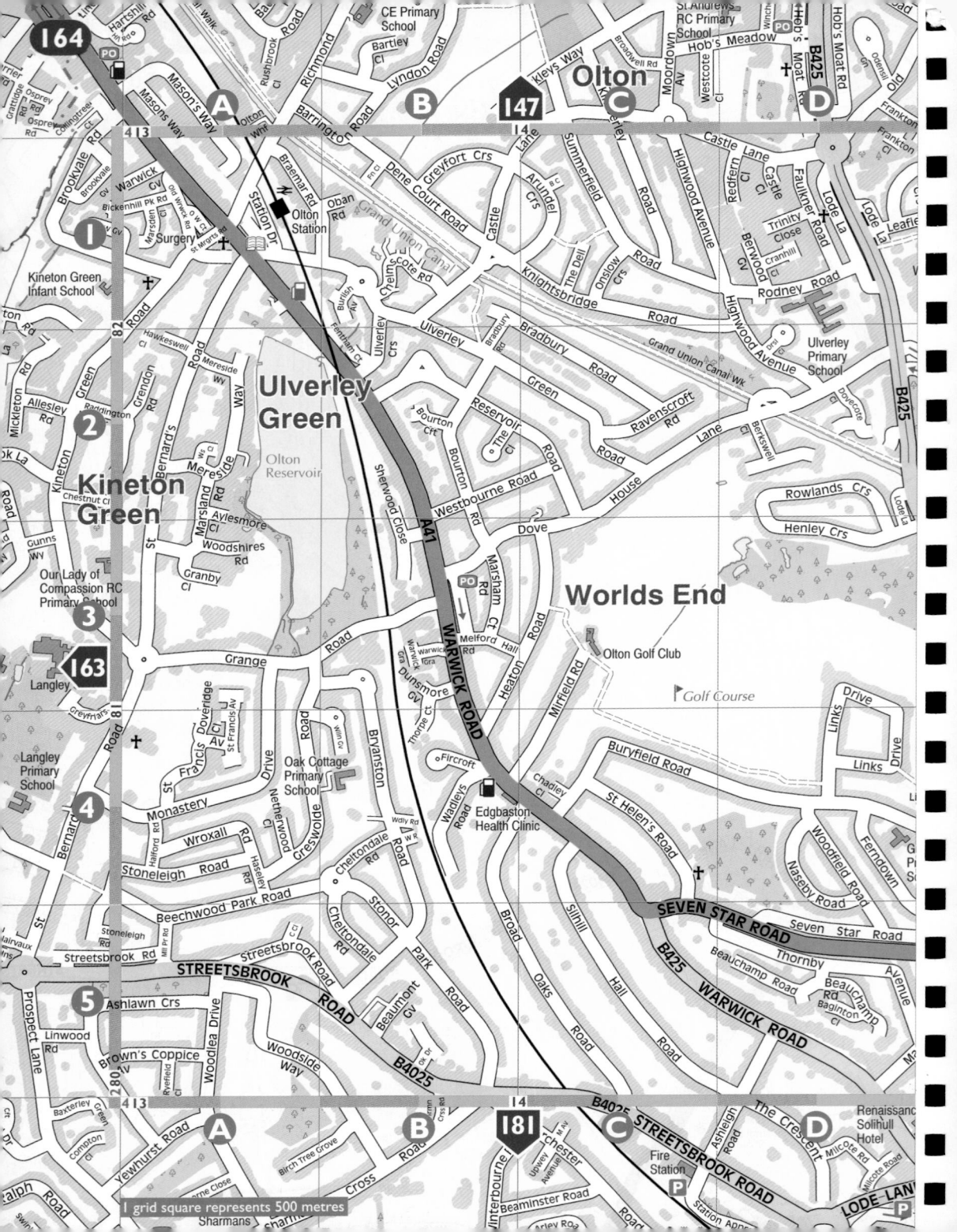

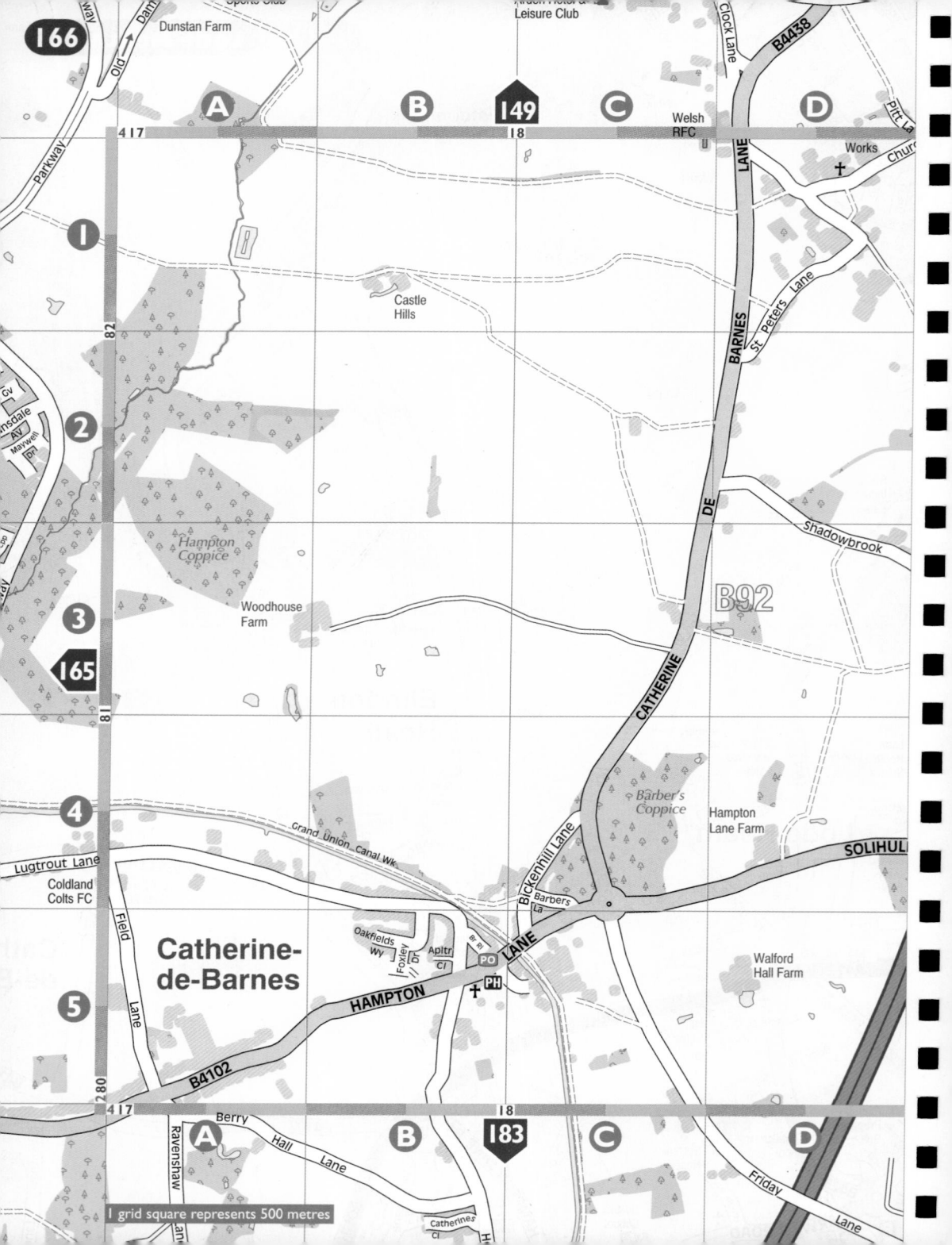

Pasture Farm

Bickenhill

The Grove

Hampton in Arden

Fiddlers Green

Meriden Rd

Meriden Rd

Corberts Close

Lapwing Drive

Nesfield Grove

MERIDEN RD

Hampton in Arden Station

The Crescent

HIGH STREET

Station Road

Fentham Road

Meadow Drive

Fentham

Hampton Manor Homes

George Fentham Endowed Primary School

Elm Tree Rd

Peel Close

PH

PO

Bellemere Road

Belle Vue Ter

Surgery

ROAD

B4102

Eastcote Lane

Lane

Eastcote Lane

Hook End

Diddlington Lane

Marsh Lane

M42

Old Station Rd

Lane

19   20   21

E   F   G   H

I

2

3

4

5

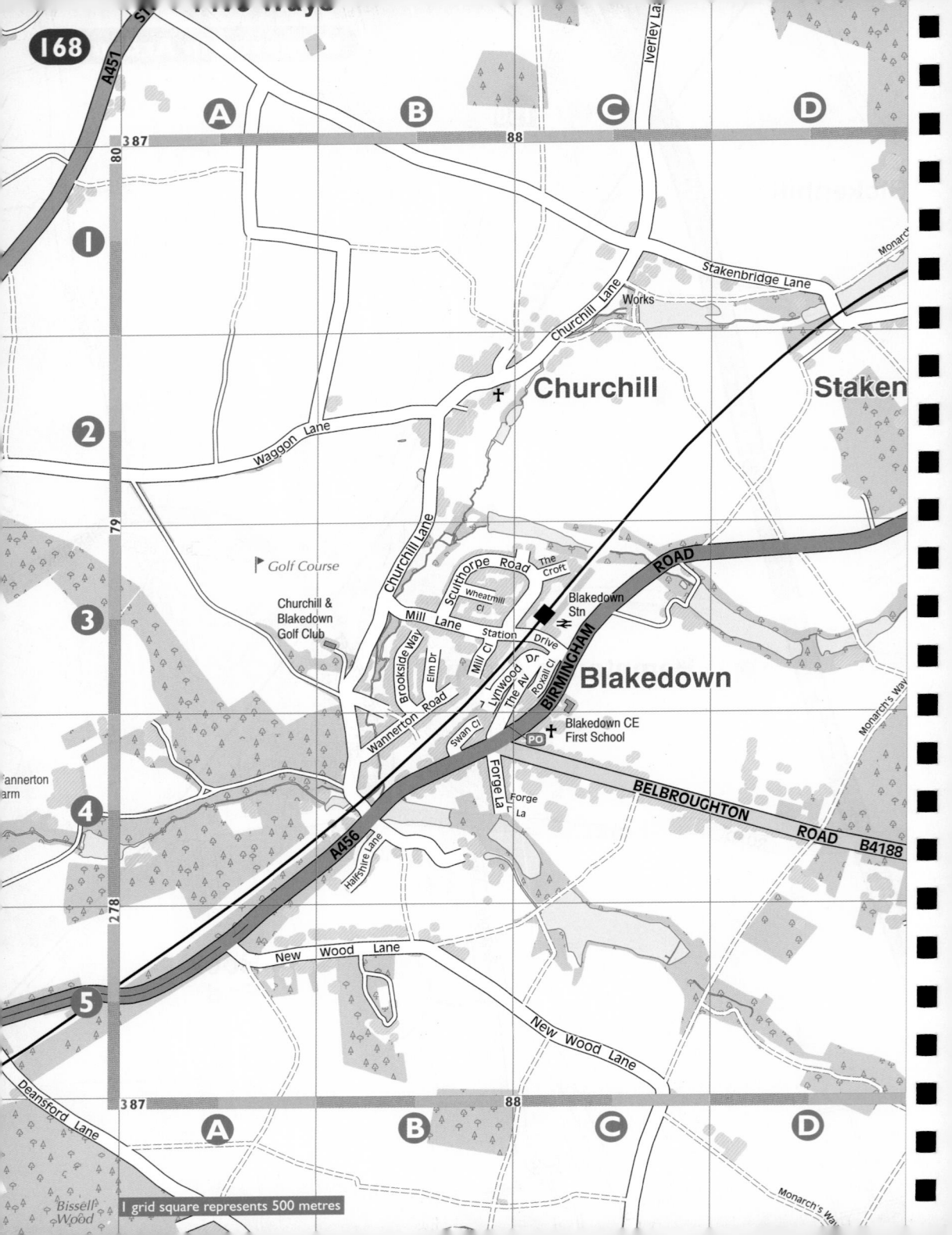

168

A451

St. The Ways

A   B   C   D

3 87   88

80

1

Iverley La

Monarch

Stakenbridge Lane

Churchill Lane

Works

Churchill

Staken

79

2

Waggon Lane

Golf Course

Churchill Lane

3

Churchill &
Blakedown
Golf Club

Scuthorpe Road

The Croft

Wheatmill Cl

Mill Lane

Station

Blakedown Stn

ROAD

Brookside Way

Elm Dr

Mill Cl

Station Drive

Lynwood Dr

The Av

Roxall Cl

BIRMINGHAM

Blakedown

278

4

Wannerton Road

Swan Cl

PO

Blakedown CE
First School

annerton
arm

Forge La

Forge
La

BELBROUGHTON   ROAD   B4188

A456

Halfshire Lane

Monarch's Way

5

New   Wood   Lane

New   Wood   Lane

Deansford Lane

3 87   88

A   B   C   D

Bissell
Wood

I grid square represents 500 metres

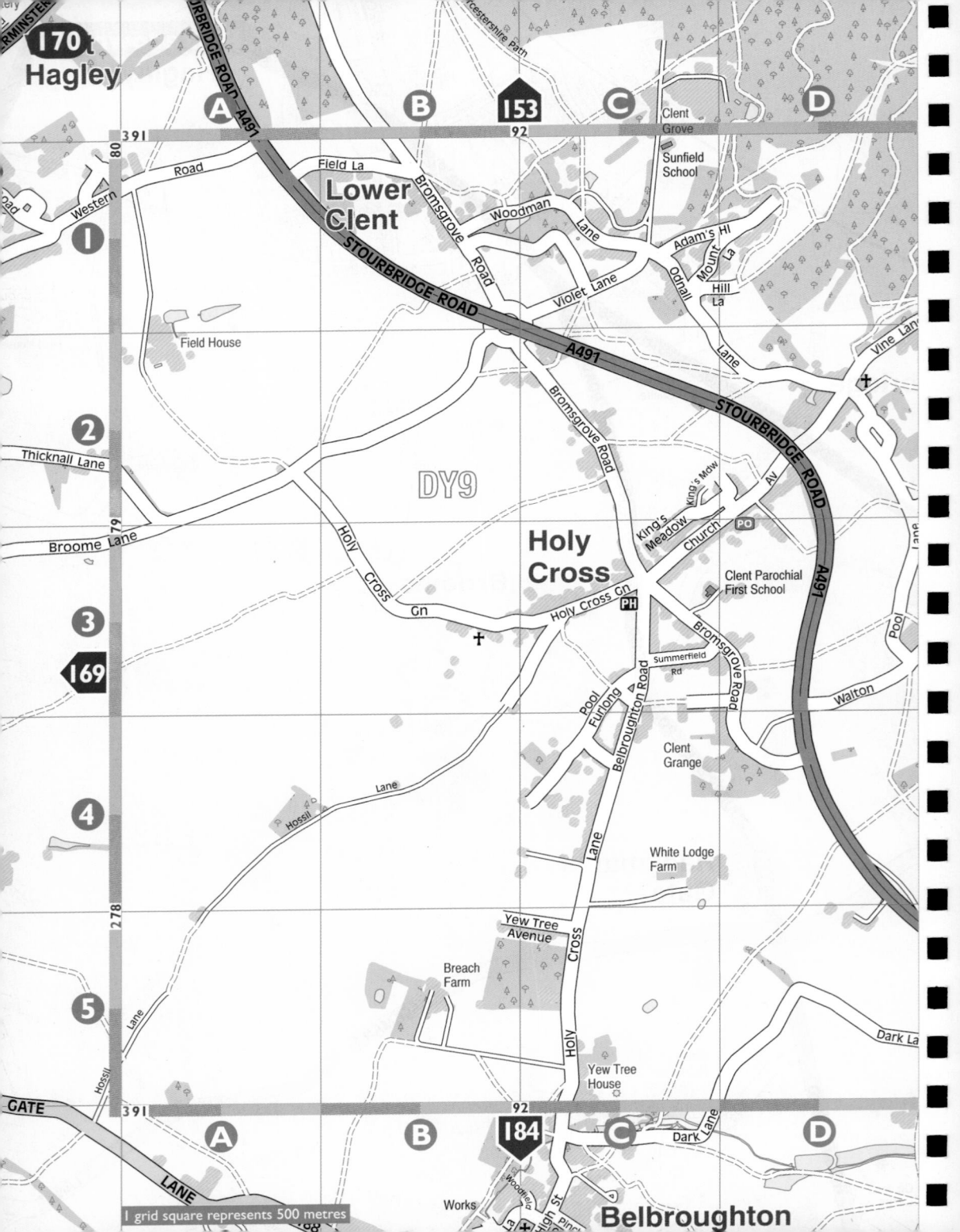

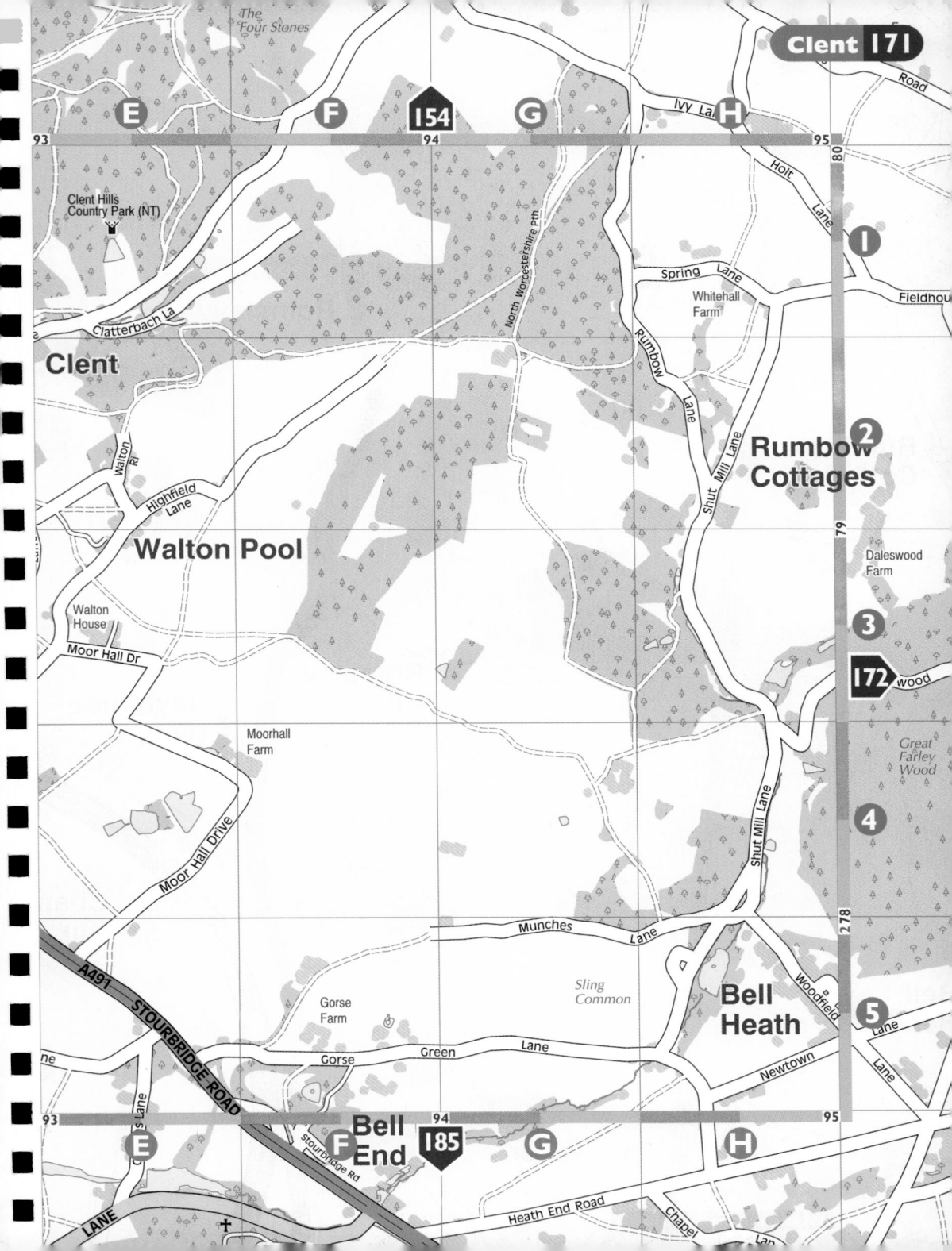

The Four Stones

E   F   **154**   G   Ivy La.   H

93   94   95   80

Holt Lane

Clent Hills
Country Park (NT)

Spring   Lane

Whitehall
Farm

Fieldhou

I

Clatterbach La.

North Worcestershire Pth

Rumbow   Lane

Clent

Shut Mill Lane

**Rumbow
Cottages**   **2**

Walton Rd

Highfield
Lane

Walton Pool

79

Daleswood
Farm

3

Walton
House

172 wood

Moor Hall Dr

*Great
Farley
Wood*

Moorhall
Farm

4

Moor Hall Drive

Shut Mill Lane

278

Munches   Lane

*Sling
Common*

Woodfield

A491

Gorse
Farm

**Bell
Heath**

5

Lane

STOURBRIDGE ROAD

Gorse   Green   Lane

Newtown

Lane

ne

93   94   95

E   **Bell
End**   **185**   F   G   H

Stourbridge Rd

LANE   Heath End Road   Chapel   Lan

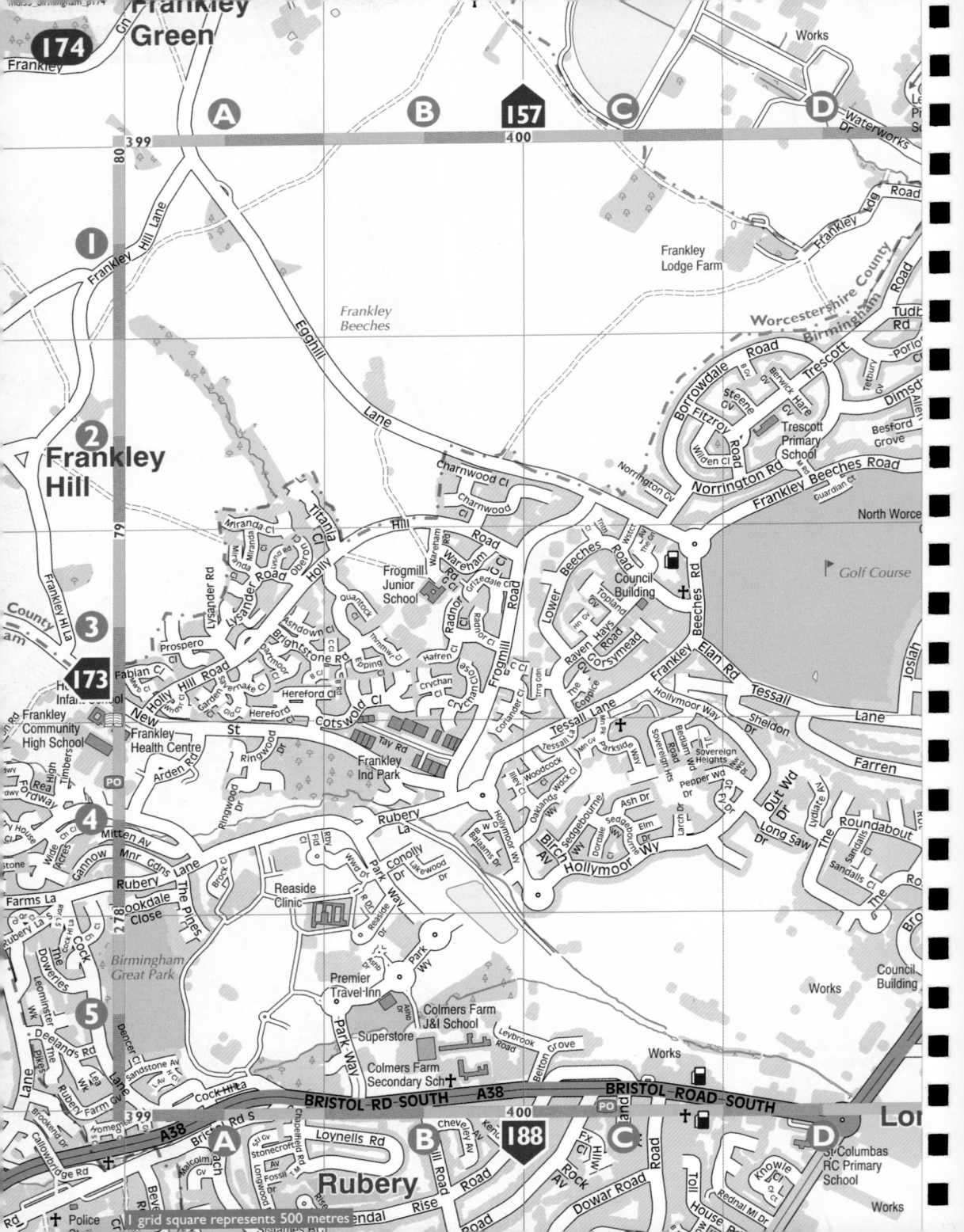

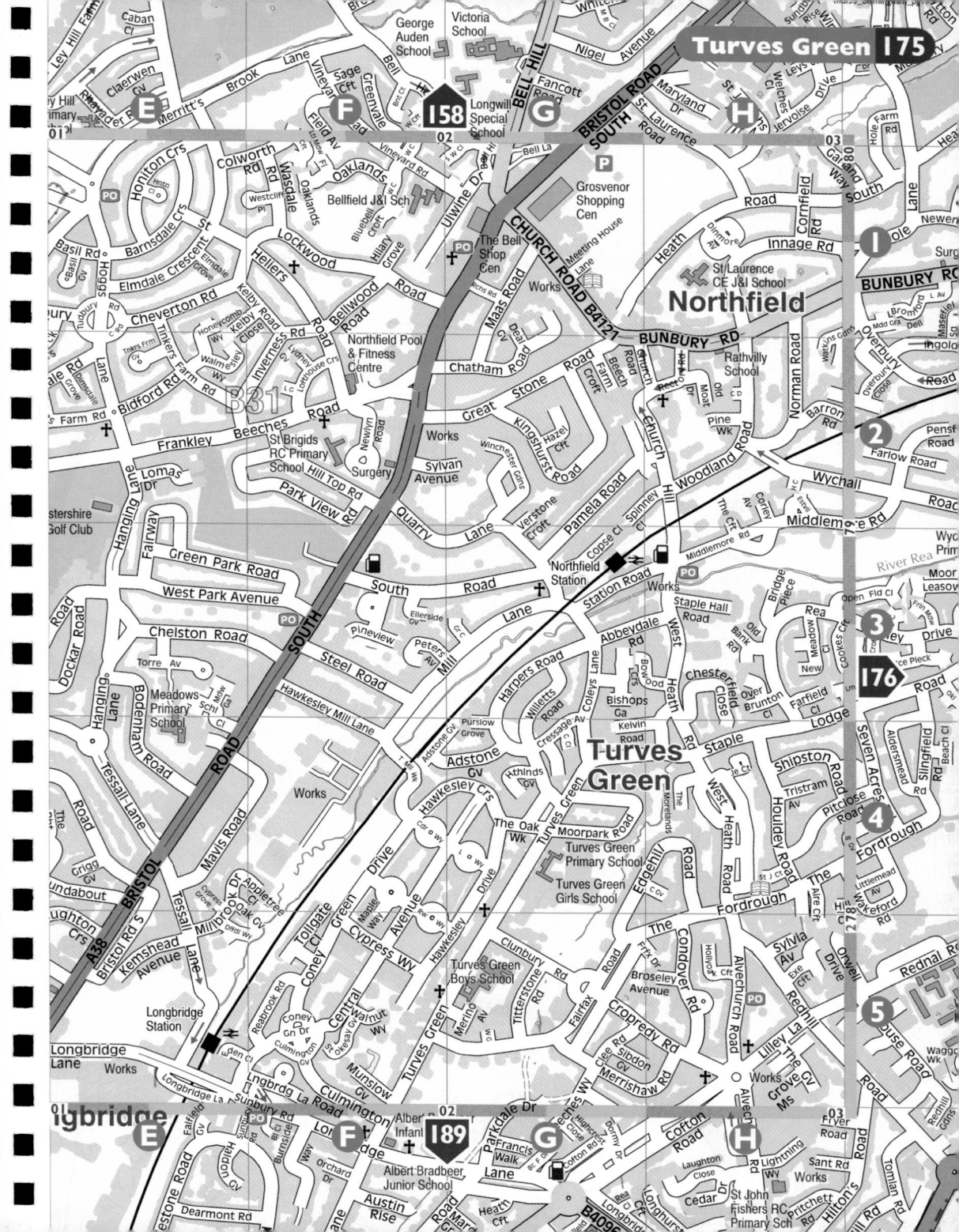

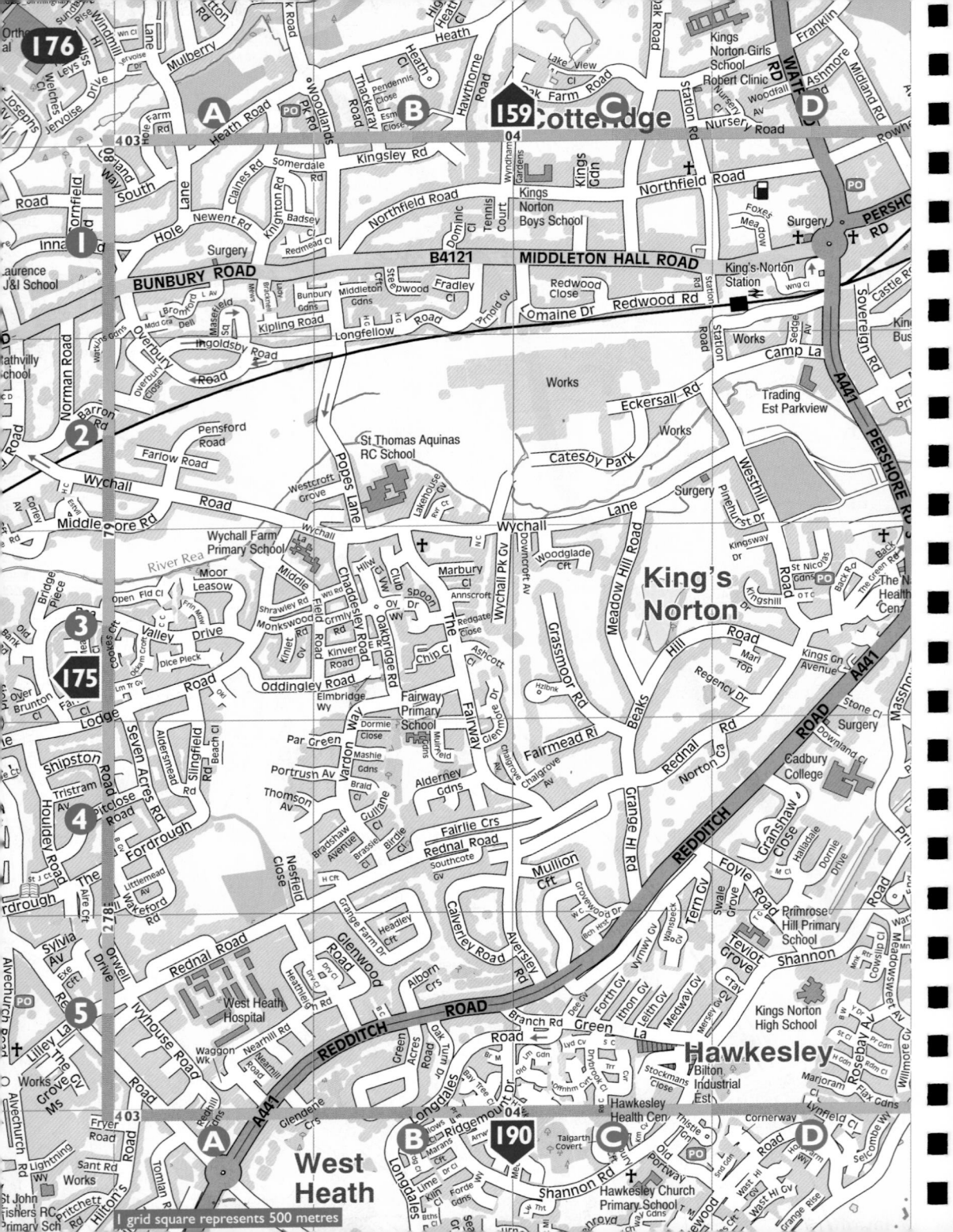

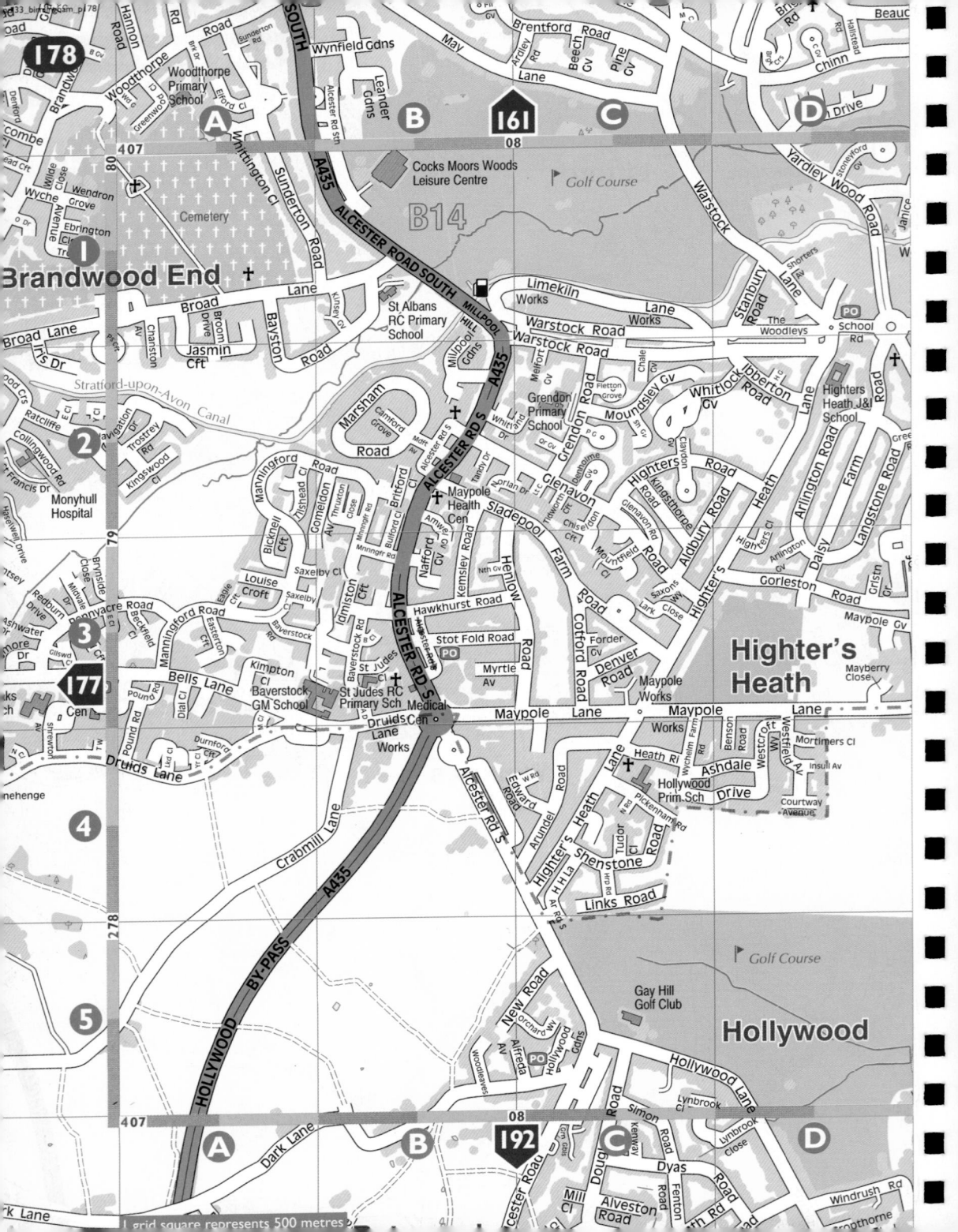

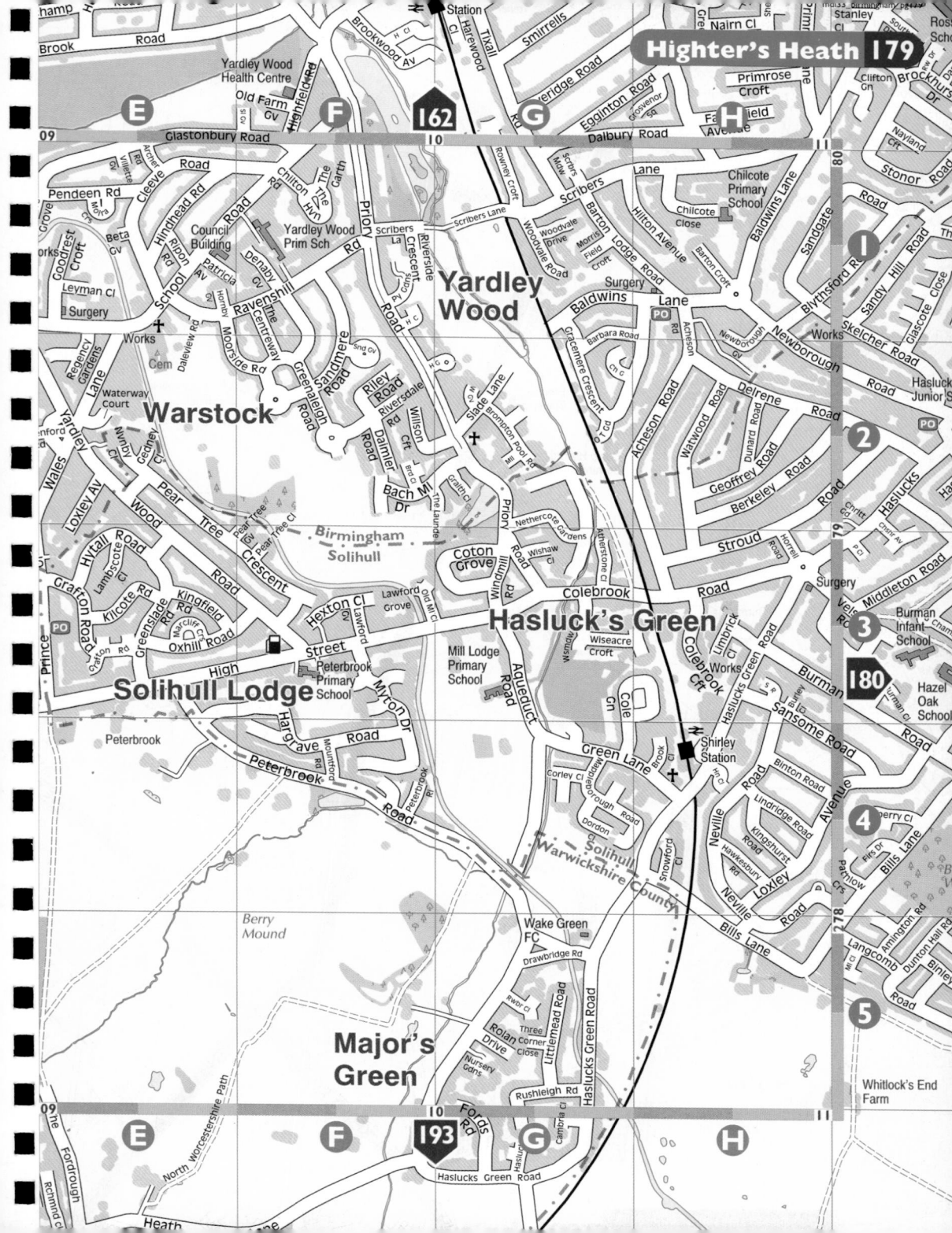

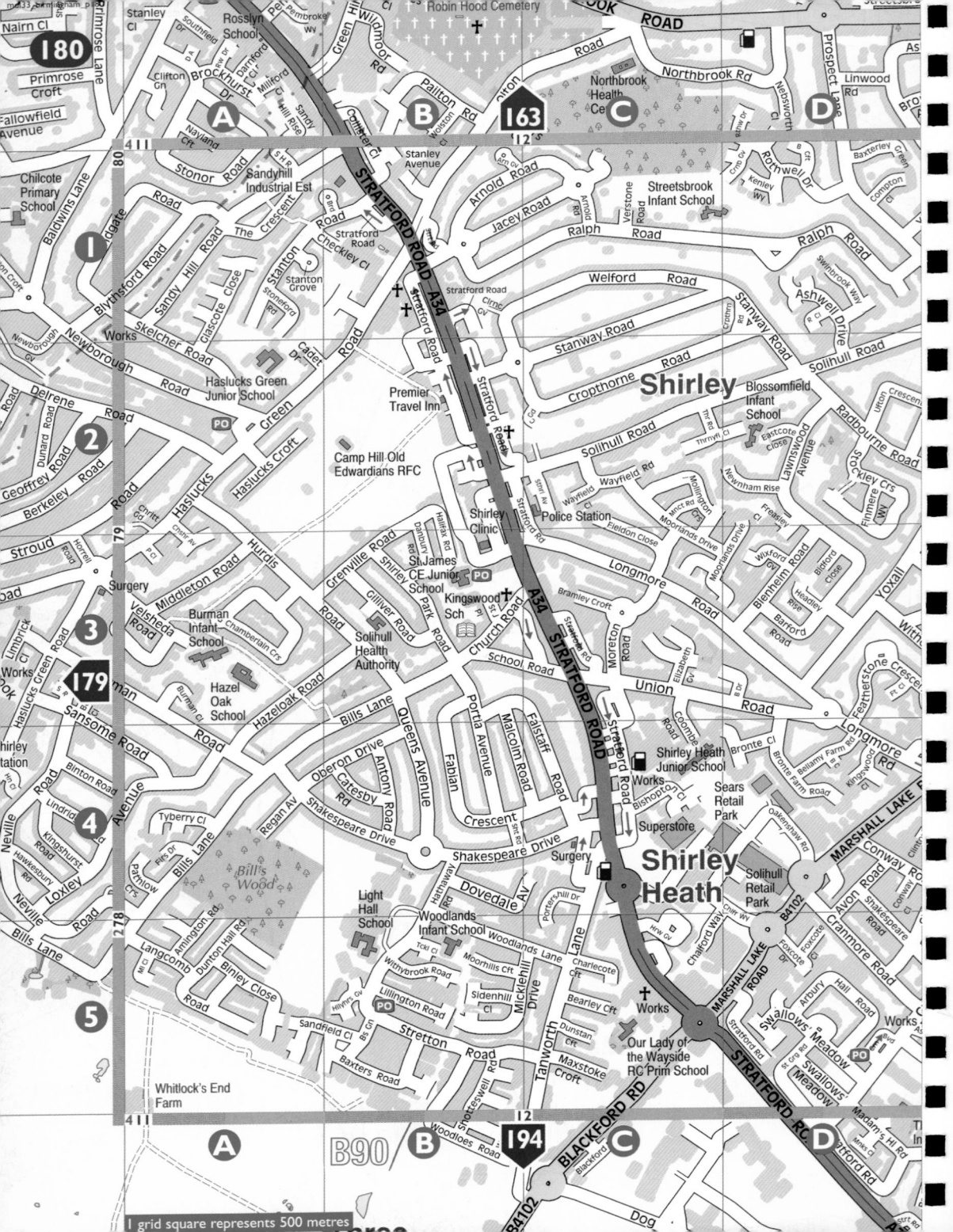

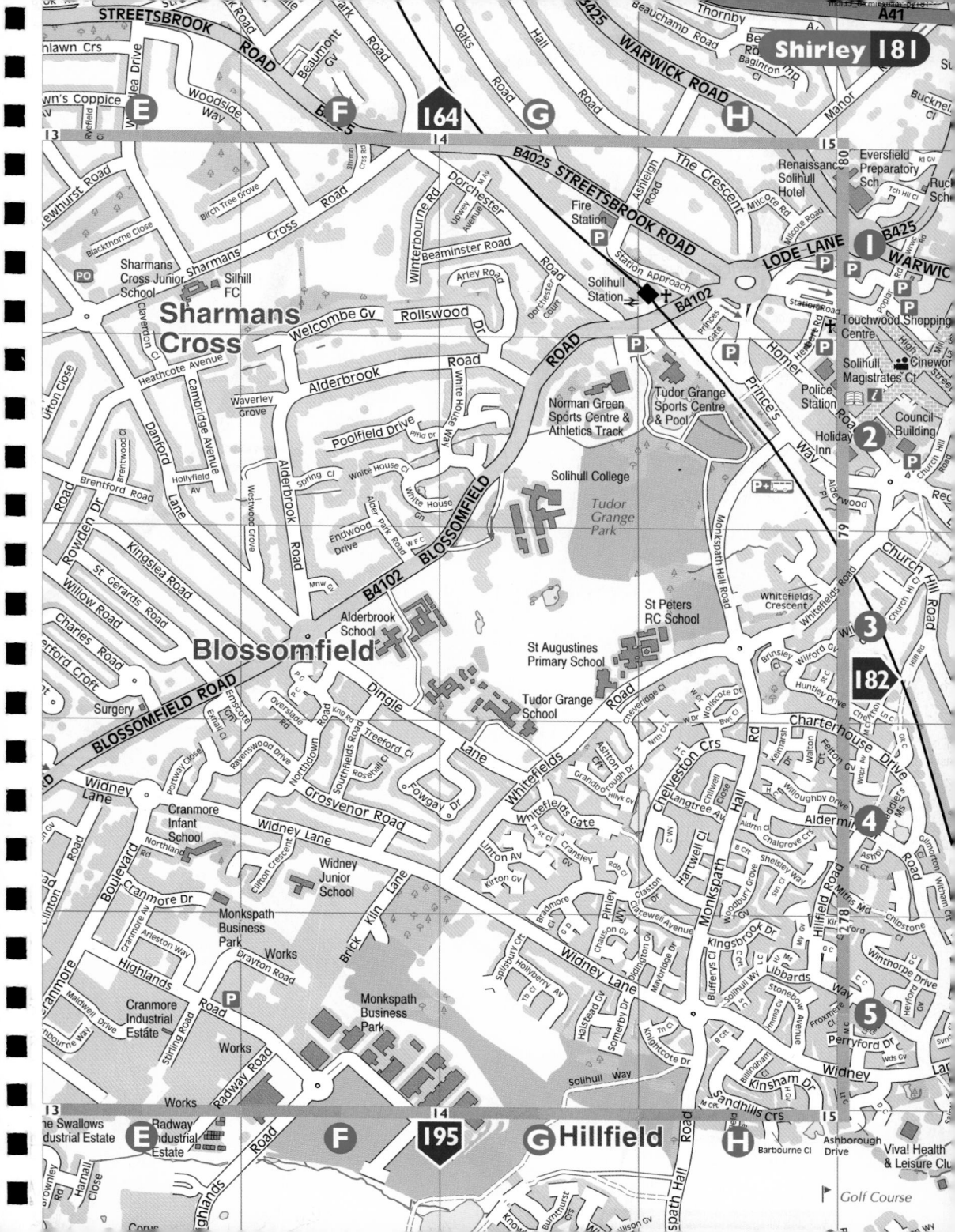

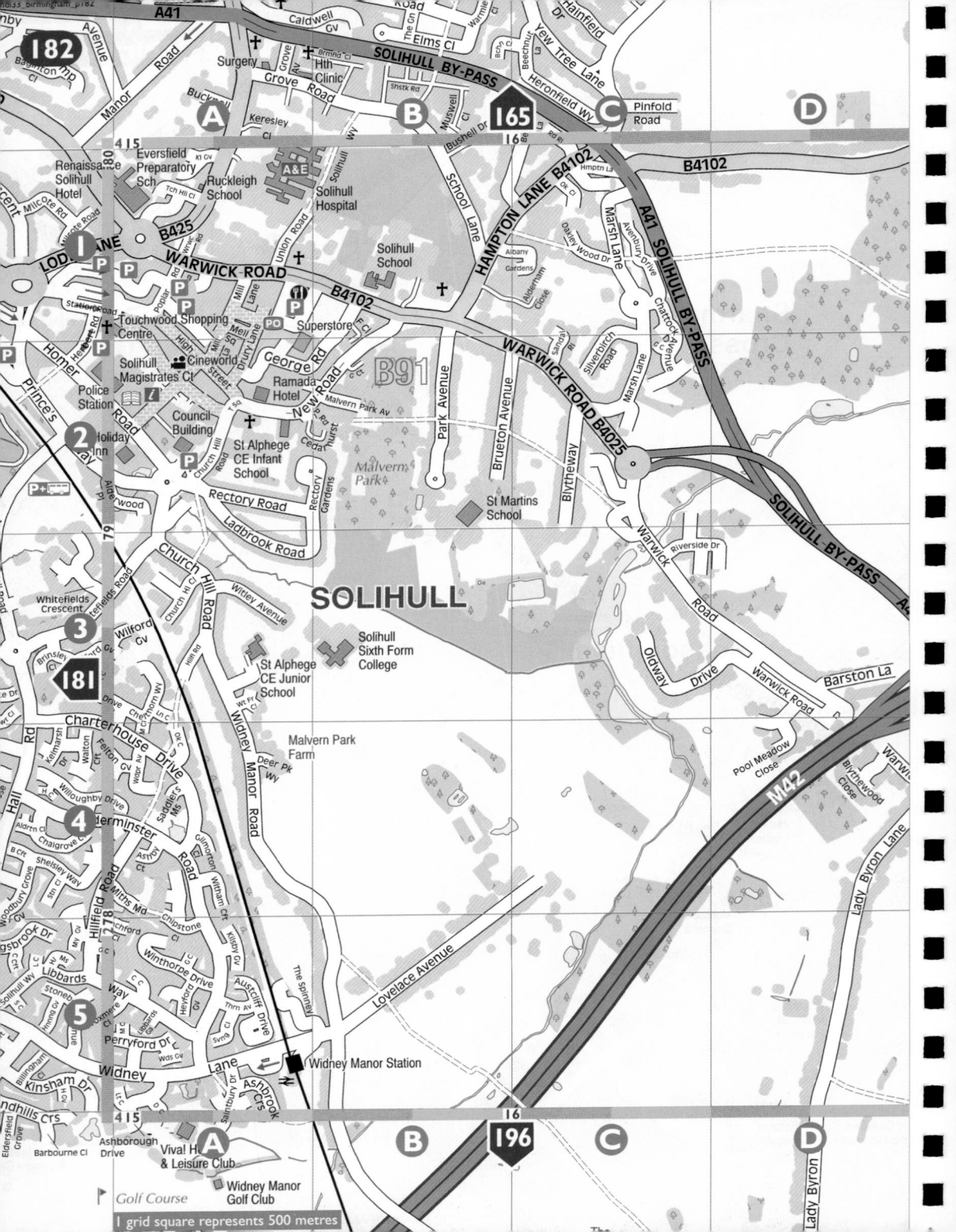

Catherine de-Barnes

HAMPTON

Walford Hall Farm

Berry Hall Lane

Ravenshaw Lane

Catherines Cl

Henwood Lane

River Blythe

Friday Lane

Grand Union Canal Walk

Cow Hayes

Works

Ravenshaw Way

Barston Lane

M42

Barston Lane

Barston Lane

Barston Lane

Barston Lane

Eastco

Henwood Hall Farm

Junction 5

Copt Heath

Jacobean Lane

Grove Farm

Knowle

River Blythe

Grand Union Canal Walk

A4141 WARWICK ROAD

Copt Heath Golf Club

Jacobean Lane

Queen Minster Cl

Queen Eleanors Dr

Warwick Rd

Golf Course

Broadfern Road

Holland Av

Hampton Road

Longdon Hall

Longdon Croft

Wychwood Avenue

Alveston Grove

High Trees Rd

Barnbrook Rd

Ragley Close

Arden Vale Road

Hampton Rd

Knowle FC

Knowle Village

Kixley

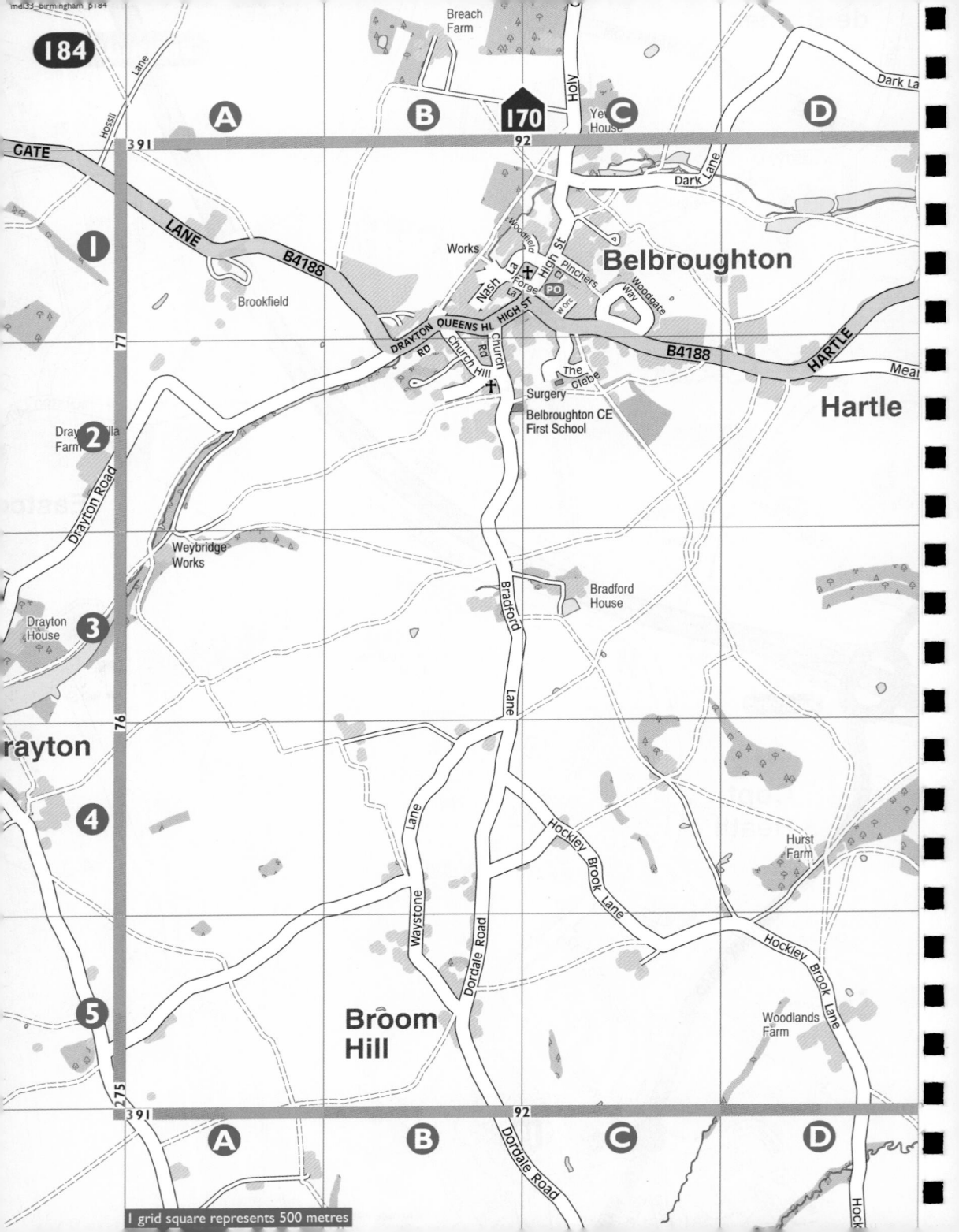

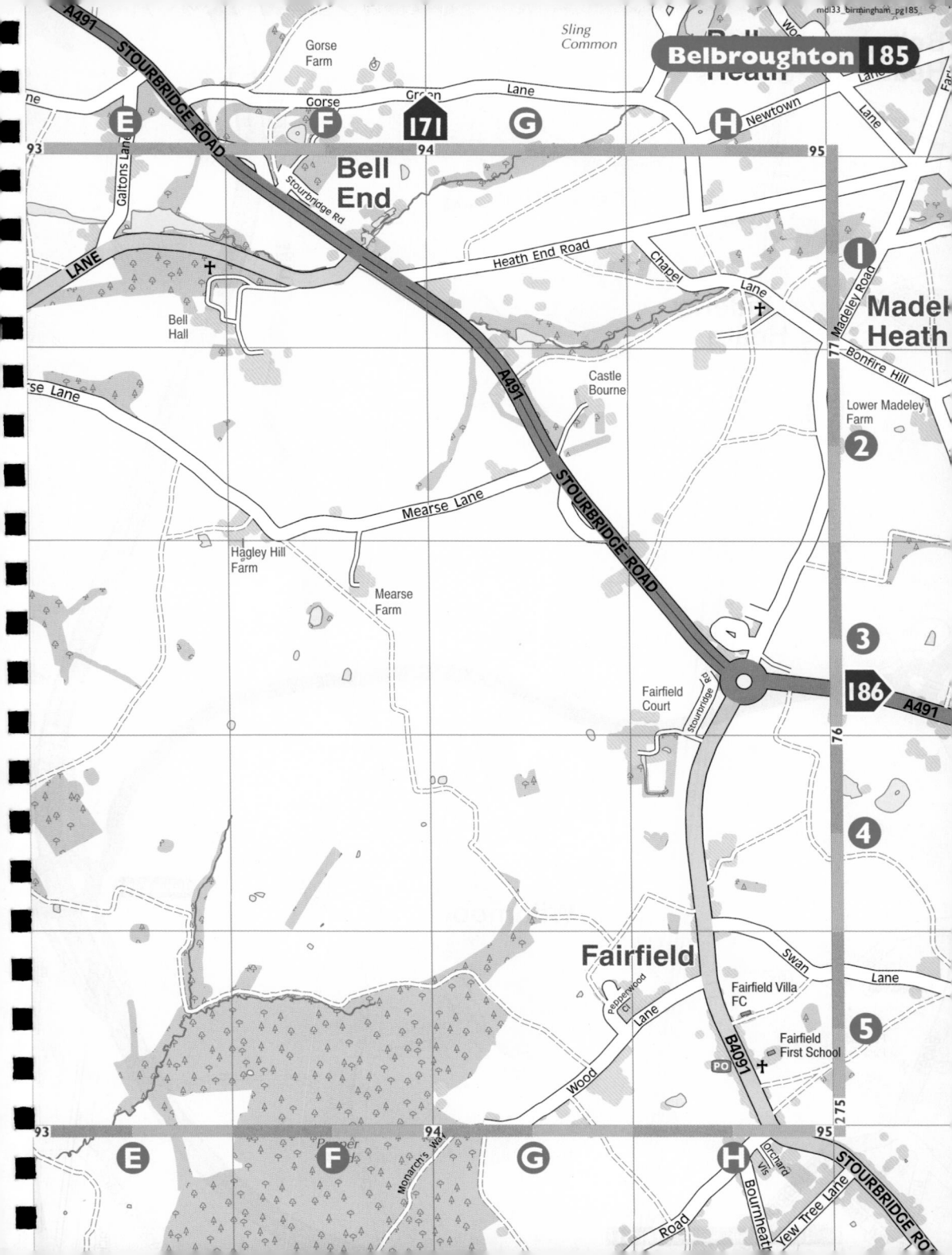

A491 STOURBRIDGE ROAD

Gorse Farm

Sling Common

Bell Heath

Gorse

Green Lane

Lane

Newtown

E

F

171

G

H

93

94

95

Galtons Lane

Stourbridge Rd

Bell End

Heath End Road

Chapel

Madeley Road

I

Madel Heath

LANE

Bell Hall

Lane

77

Bonfire Hill

se Lane

A491

Castle Bourne

Lower Madeley Farm

2

Mearse Lane

STOURBRIDGE ROAD

Hagley Hill Farm

Mearse Farm

Stourbridge Rd

3

186

A491

76

Fairfield Court

4

Fairfield

Swan Lane

Pepperwood Cl

Fairfield Villa FC

5

Lane

Fairfield First School

275

B4091

PO

Wood Lane

Monarch's Way

E

F

G

H

Orchard Vis

Bournheath

Yew Tree Lane

STOURBRIDGE RO

Road

93

94

95

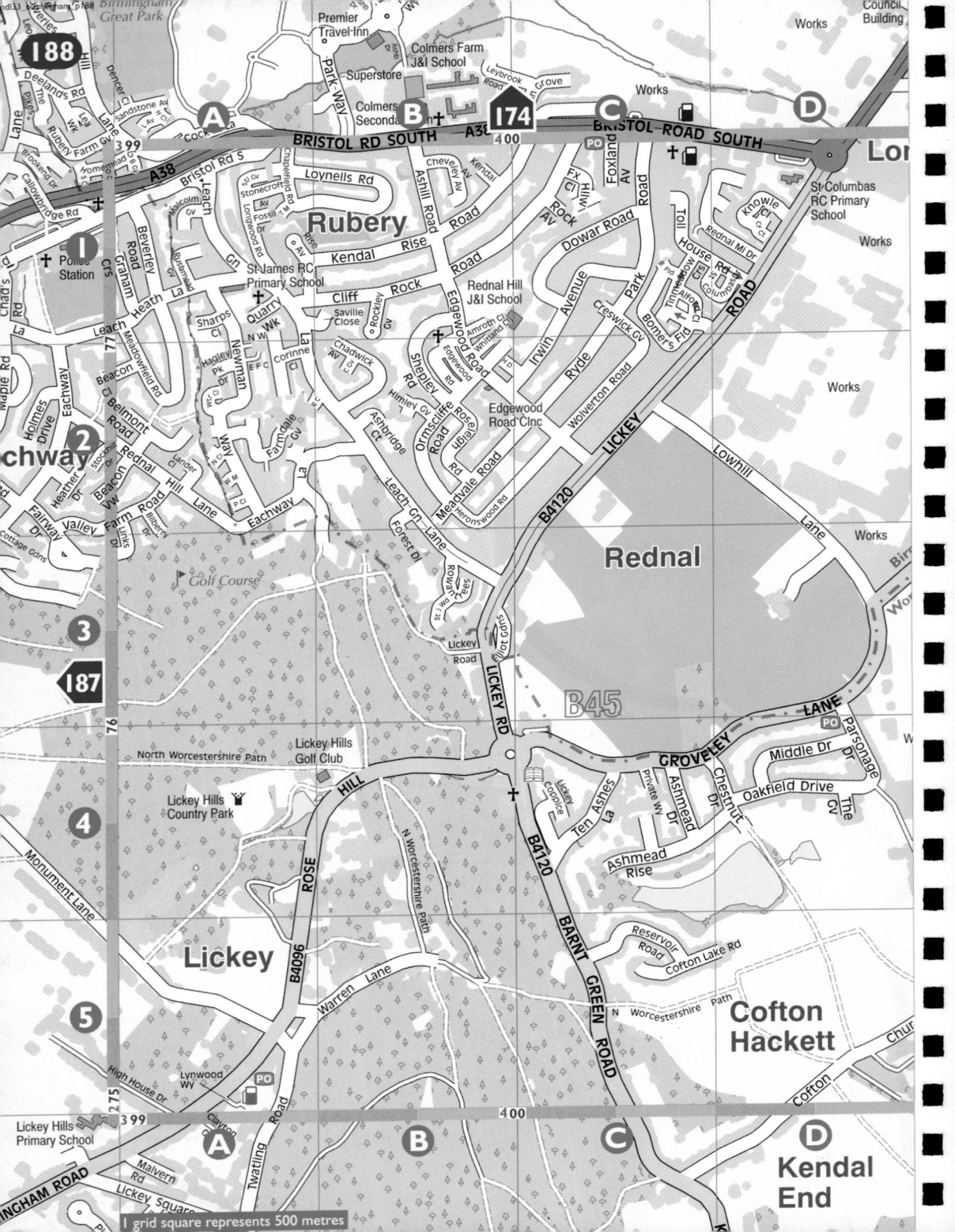

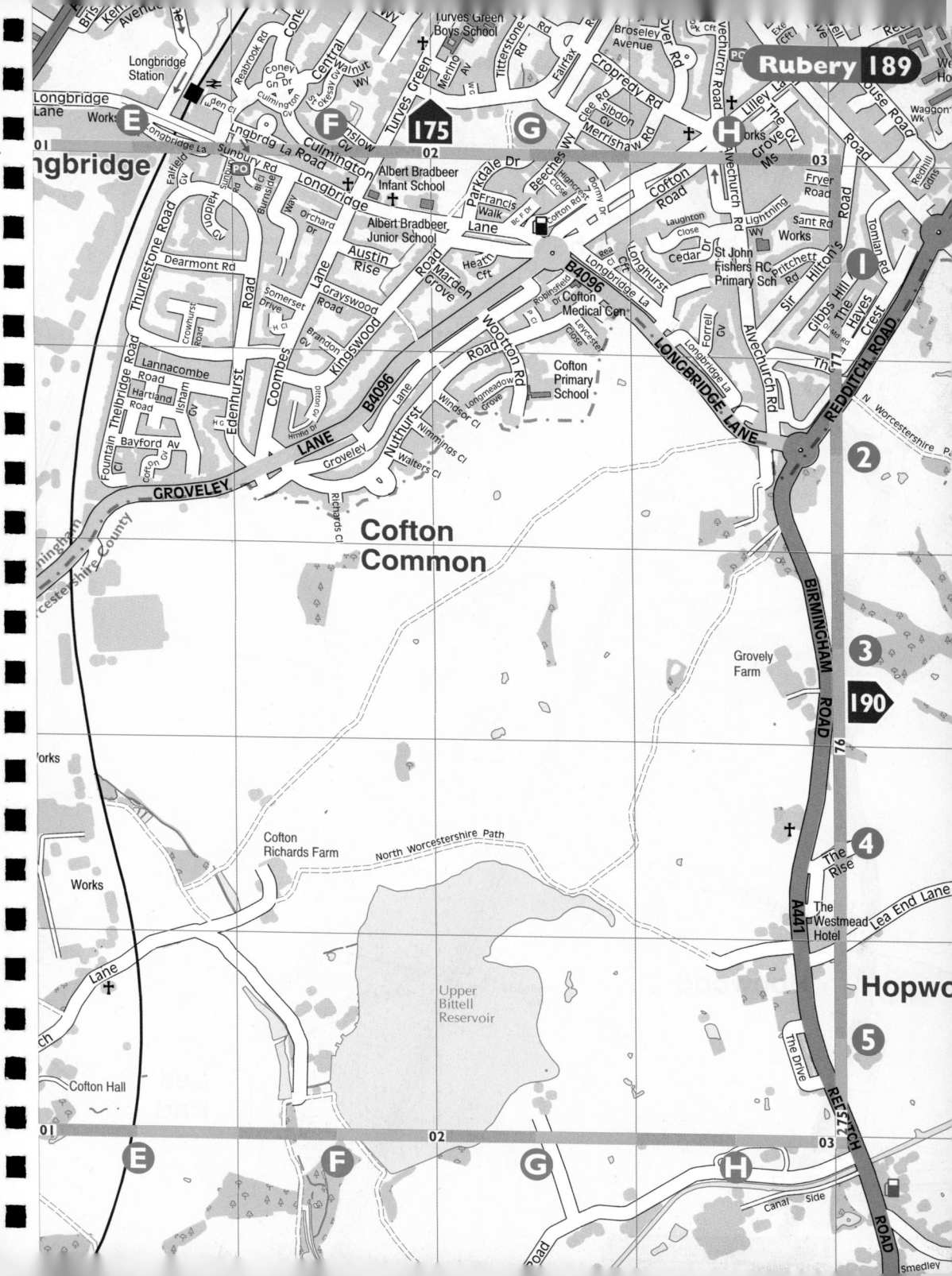

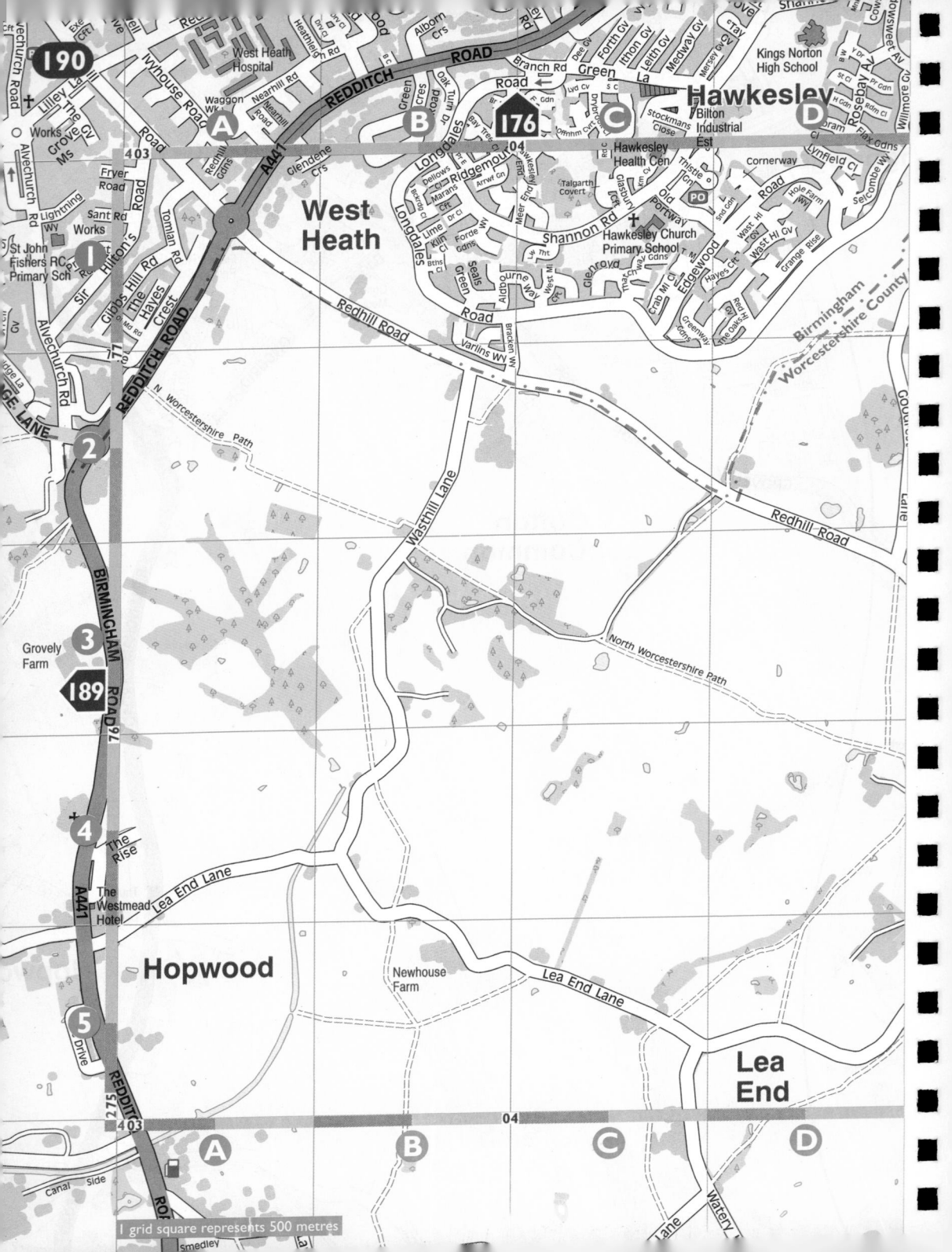

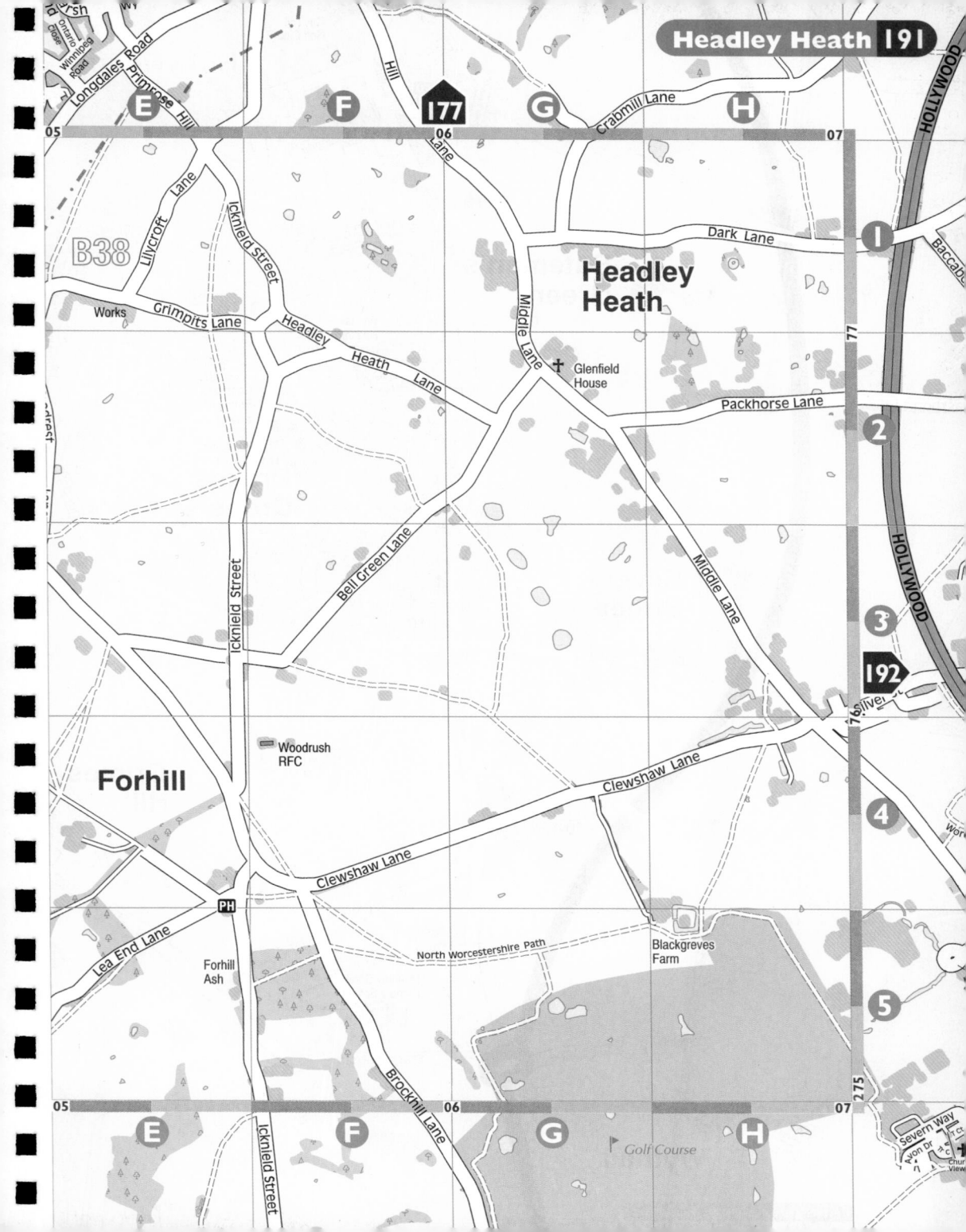

177

Headley Heath

† Glenfield House

Forhill

Woodrush RFC

PH

Forhill Ash

Blackgreves Farm

North Worcestershire Path

B38

Works

Longdales Road

Primrose Hill

Lilycroft Lane

Icknield Street

Grimpits Lane

Headley Heath Lane

Hill Lane

Middle Lane

Crabmill Lane

Dark Lane

Packhorse Lane

Middle Lane

Bell Green Lane

Icknield Street

Clewshaw Lane

Clewshaw Lane

Lea End Lane

Brockhill Lane

Icknield Street

HOLLYWOOD

Baccabox

HOLLYWOOD

192

Golf Course

Severn Way

E F G H I 2 3 4 5

05 06 07

77

275

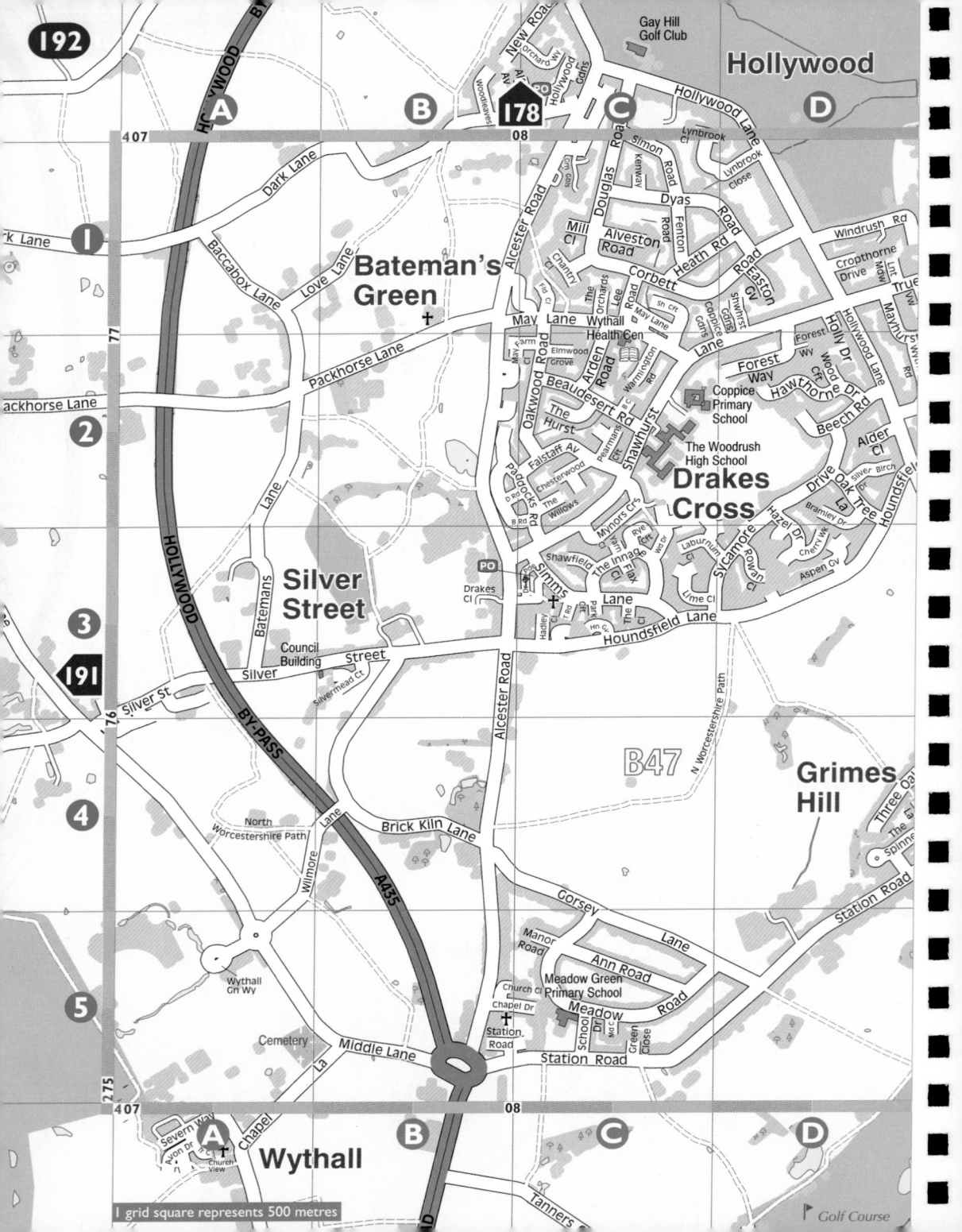

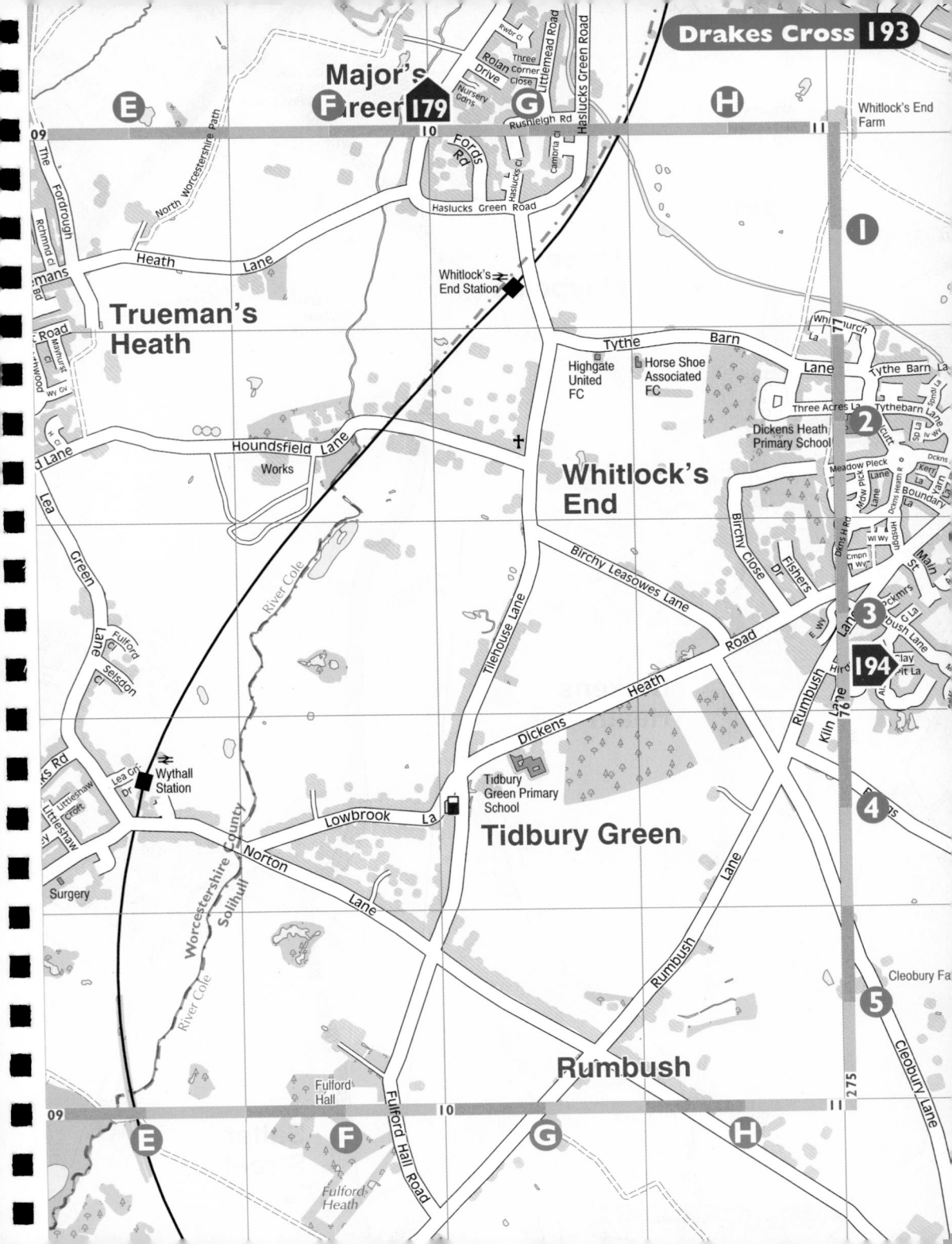

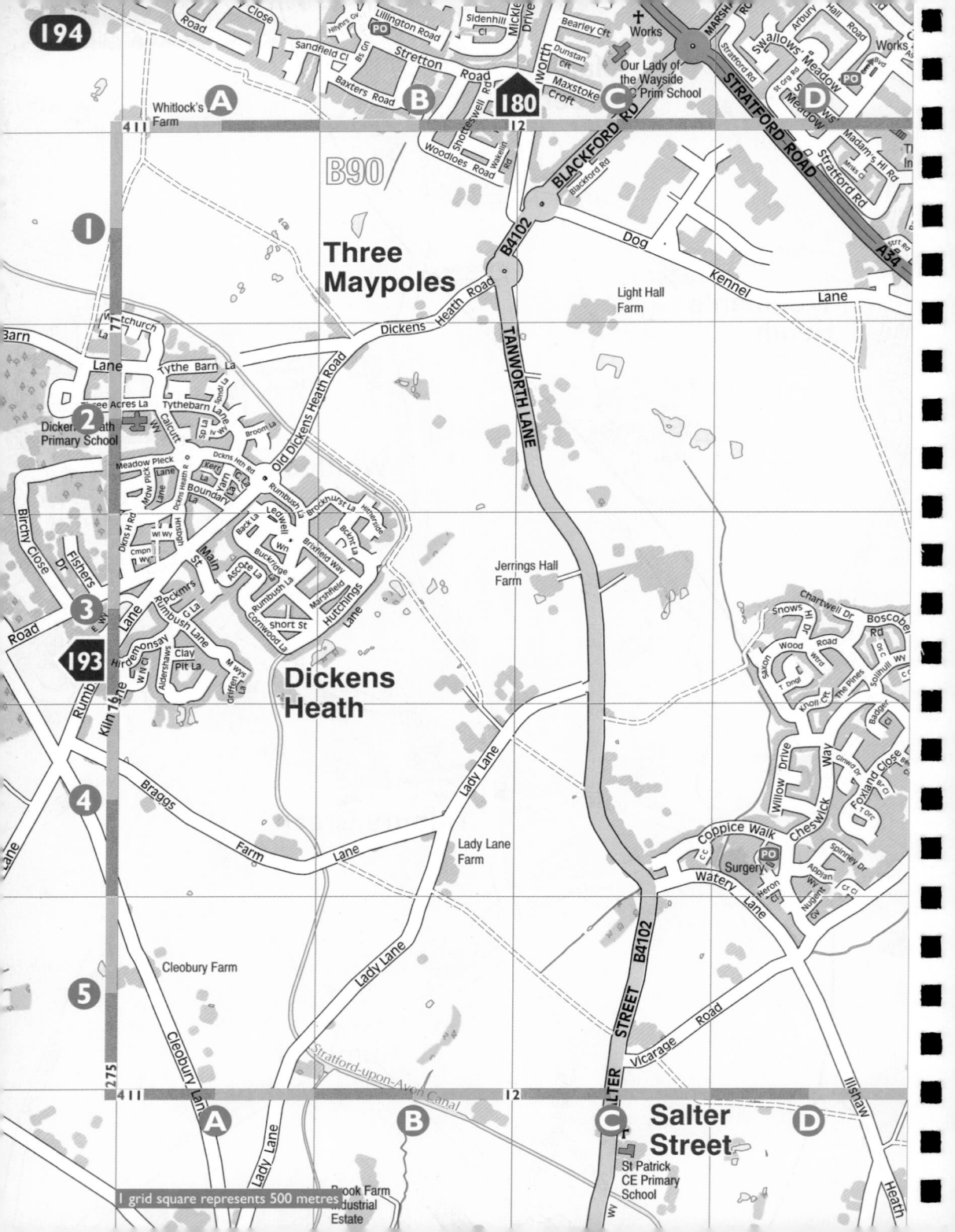

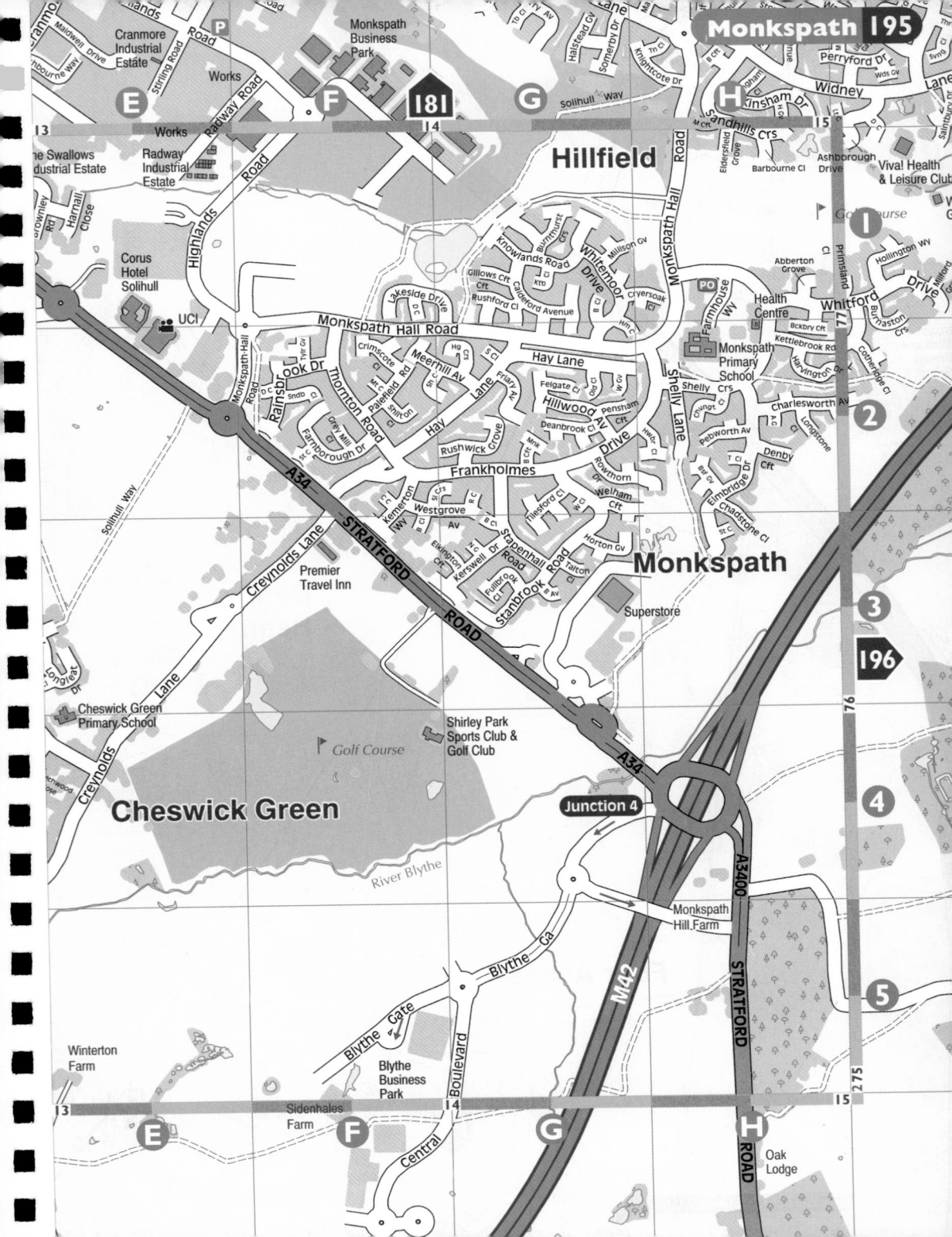

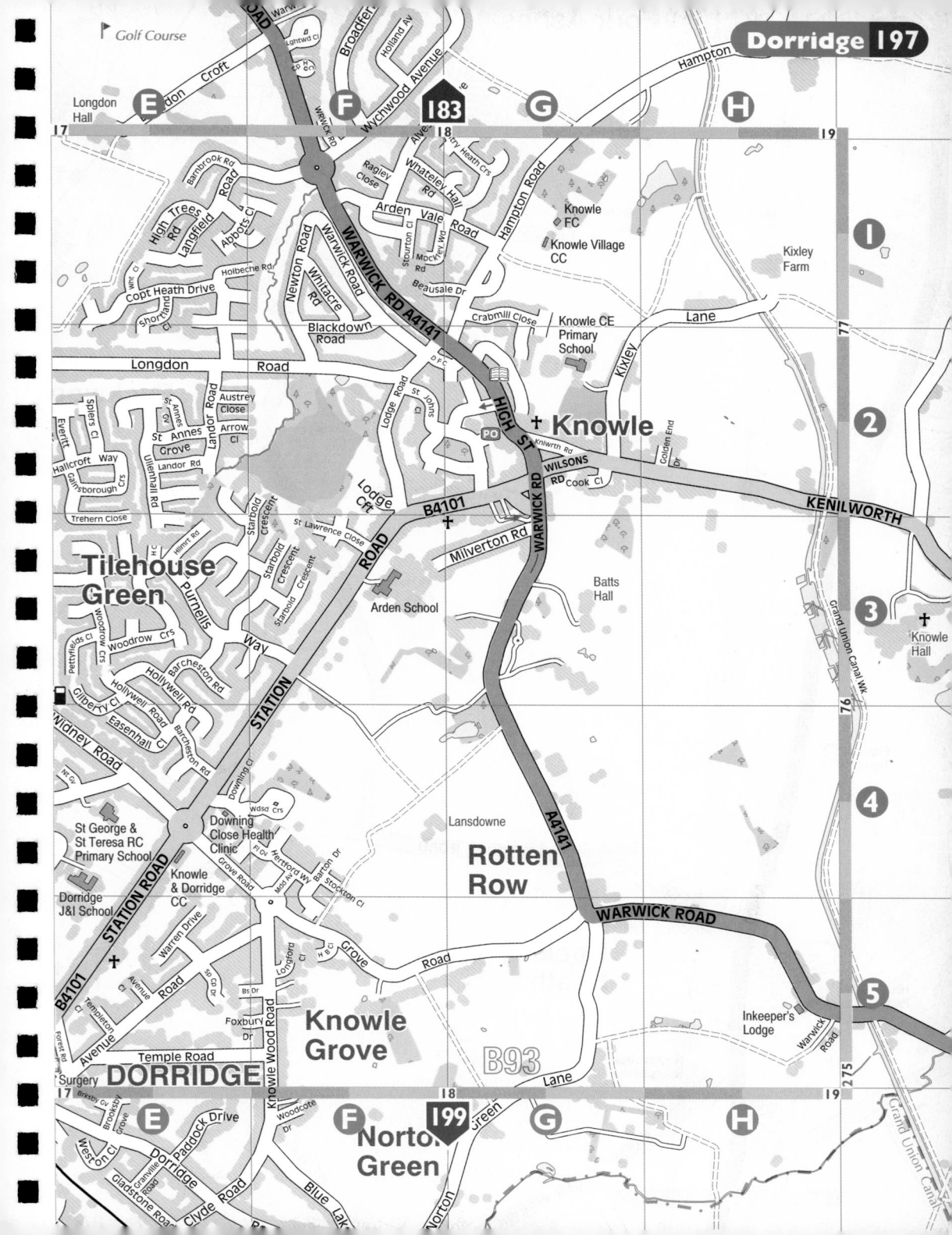

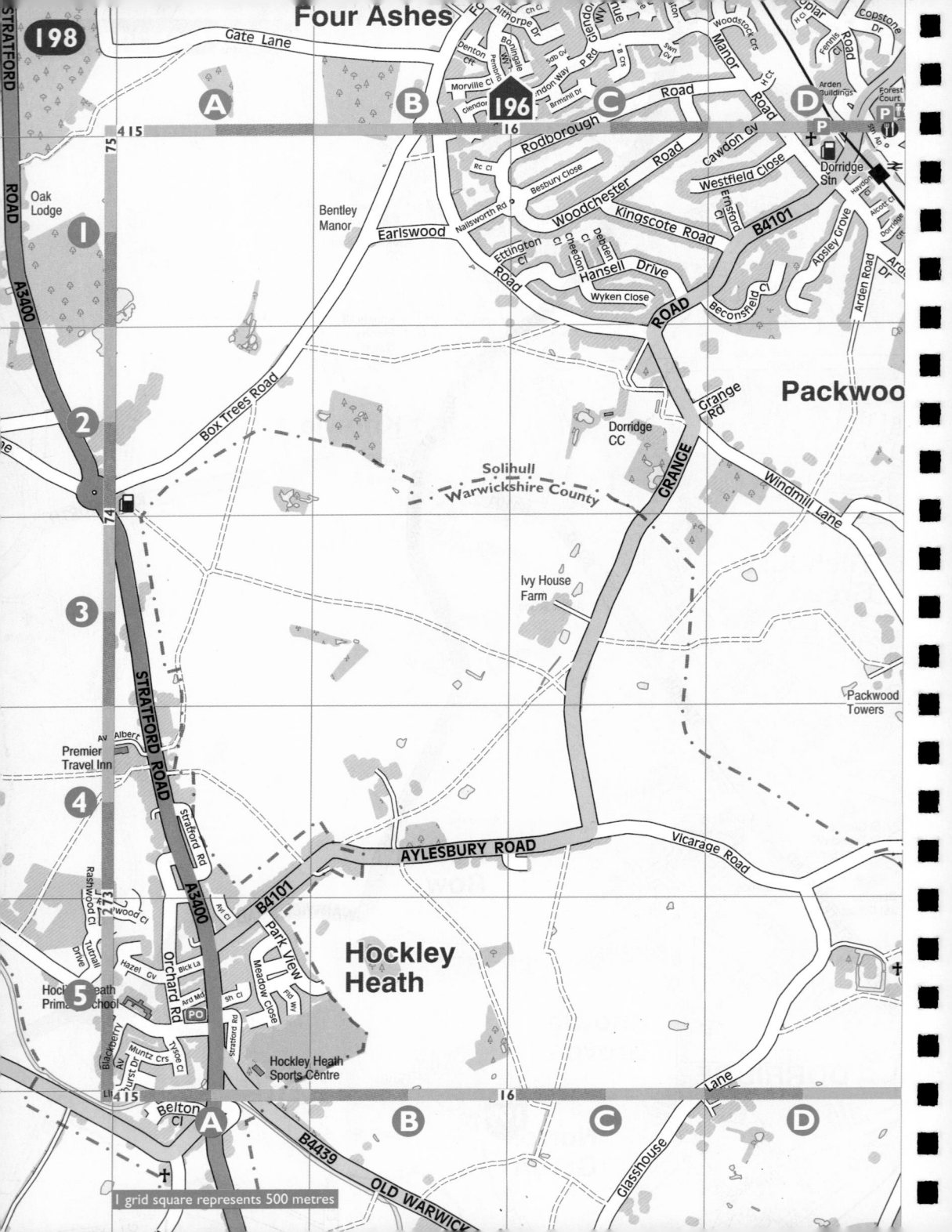

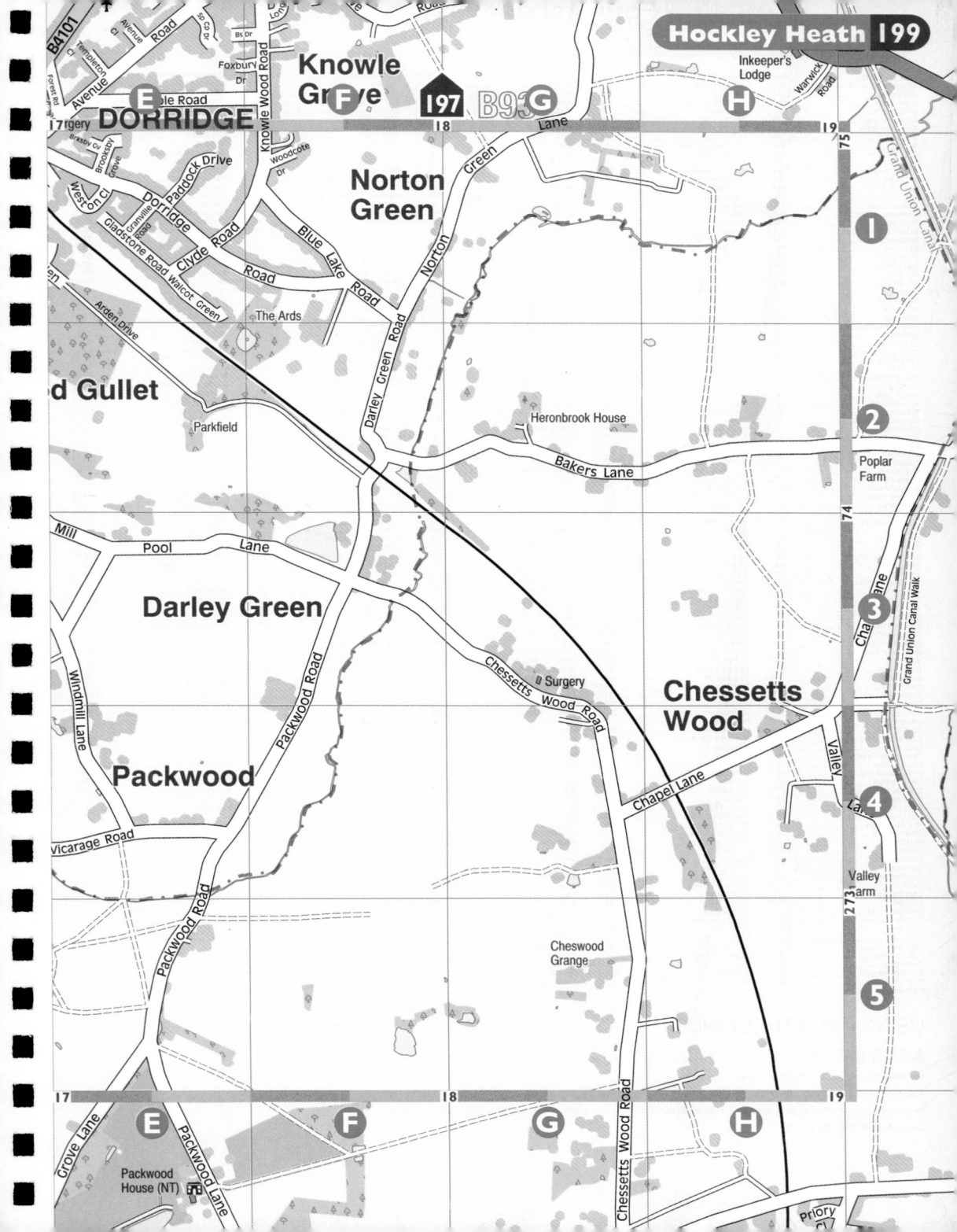

B4101

Templeton Cl

Avenue Road

Bs Dr

Foxbury Dr

Knowle Grove

Knowle Wood Road

Woodcote Dr

197 B93 **G**

Lane

Inkeeper's Lodge

Warwick Road

H

Grand Union Canal

Forest Rd

West Cn Cl

Brooksby Grove

Granville Road

E ole Road

rgery **DORRIDGE**

17

Dorridge

Gladstone Road

Walcot Green

Clyde Road

Paddock Drive

Blue Lake Road

Norton Green

Norton Green

Lane

18

19

75

I

Arden Drive

The Ards

Darley Green Road

d **Gullet**

Parkfield

Heronbrook House

Bakers Lane

Poplar Farm

74

2

Mill

Pool Lane

Darley Green

Chessetts Wood Road

Surgery

Chessetts Wood

Cha Lane

Grand Union Canal Walk

75

3

Windmill Lane

Packwood Road

Packwood

Chapel Lane

Valley Lane

4

Vicarage Road

Cheswood Grange

Valley Farm

273

5

Grove Lane

Packwood Lane

E

Packwood House (NT)

17

F

18

G

Chessetts Wood Road

H

19

Priory Cl

Acock's Green 146 A4
Alcester Lane's End 160 D4
Aldridge 30 A4
Alum Rock 129 E1
Amblecote 118 B5
Ashmore Lake 39 H1
Ashmore Park 25 F1
Ashwood 98 C4
Aston 109 F3
Bacon's End 114 C5
Balls Hill 71 E2
Balsall Heath 144 A2
Banners Gate 60 C4
Baptist End 102 C3
Barr Common 44 C2
Bartley Green 157 H2
Bateman's Green 192 B1
Bearwood 124 C3
Beech Lanes 124 A5
Belbroughton 184 C1
Bell End 185 F1
Belle Vale 138 B2
Bell Heath 171 H5
Bentley 40 B2
Bentley Heath 196 C3
Bescot 56 C1
Bickenhill 166 D1
Bilbrook 11 E5
Billesley 162 A4
Billesley Common 161 G3
Bilston 53 G1
Birch End 72 A4
Birches Green 93 E5
Birchfield 90 D5
Birchills 41 H2
Birmingham 2 C7
Blackheath 121 H2
Black Lake 71 E4
Blakedown 168 C3
Blakeley 81 E1
Blakenall Heath 41 H1
Blakenhall 51 H1
Bloomfield 69 F5
Blossomfield 181 E3
Bloxwich 27 E1
Boldmere 77 E2
Bordesley 127 G2
Bordesley Green 128 C3
Bournbrook 143 E5
Bourne Vale 44 C2
Bournville 159 H5
Bowling Green 120 D1
Brades Village 86 B5
Bradley 53 H5
Bradmore 36 A5
Bramford 68 A4
Brandwood End 177 H1
The Bratch 64 D3
Brierley Hill 119 E2
Bristnall Fields 123 F1
Brockmoor 100 D5
Bromford 94 A5
Bromley 100 C4
Broome 169 G5
Broom Hill 184 B5
Brownhills 9 G4
Brown's Green 89 H2
Buckland End 112 C2
Buckpool 118 B2
Burnt Tree 85 F4
Bushbury 13 E4
Caldmore 4 B7
California 141 F5
Carroway Head 48 D1
Castle Bromwich 113 E1
Castlecroft 35 E5
Castle Vale 94 C3
Catherine-de-Barnes 166 A5
Catshill 119 G1
Causeway Green 122 D1
Chad Valley 125 H5
Chapman's Hill 172 D4
Charlemont 71 H4
Chattle Hill 97 E4
Chelmsley Wood 132 C3
Chessetts Wood 199 H3
Cheswick Green 195 E4
The Chuckery 5 J4
Churchfield 88 A1
Church Hill 56 A4
Churchill 168 C2
Cinder Hill 67 H2
Claregate 21 H4
Clayhanger 18 D1
Clent 171 E2
Coal Pool 28 B5
Codsall 12 B1
Cofton Common 189 F2
Cofton Hackett 188 D5
Cole End 115 F1
Colehall 112 D4
Coleshill 115 G3
Colton Hills 51 G5
Compton 35 H3
Coombeswood 139 E1
Copt Heath 183 E4
Coseley 68 C2

Cotteridge 159 G5
Coven Heath 12 C1
Cradley 137 G1
Cradley Heath 120 C4
Dam Mill 21 F1
Darby End 102 D5
Darby's Hill 103 H2
Darlaston 54 D1
Darlaston Green 55 G1
Darley Green 199 E5
Daw End 28 D5
Dayhouse Bank 172 D3
Deepfields 68 B2
The Delves 57 G4
Dickens Heath 194 A3
Digbeth 3 J6
Doe Bank 62 C1
Dorridge 197 E5
Drakes Cross 192 C2
Druids Heath 30 C1
Dudley 84 D4
Dudley Port 86 A2
Dudley's Fields 26 D2
Dudley Wood 120 C2
Dunstall Hill 22 D5
Eachway 187 H2
Edgbaston 142 D1
Elmdon 149 E4
Elmdon Heath 165 G3
Erdington 93 E3
Essington 14 D4
Ettingshall 52 D3
Ettingshall Park 52 D5
Eve Hill 84 A4
Fairfield 185 G5
Falcon Lodge 63 H2
Fallings Heath 55 G3
Fishley 17 E3
Fordbridge 132 A1
Fordhouses 12 B4
Forhill 191 E4
Four Ashes 196 A5
Four Oaks 46 C2
Four Oaks Park 46 D5
Frankley 157 F5
Frankley 173 H3
Frankley Green 157 E5
Frankley Hill 173 H2
Friar Park 56 D5
Garrets Green 130 C3
Gib Heath 108 A2
Giggetty 80 C1
Gilbertstone 147 F1
Gilson 97 E5
Glebe Farm 112 B5
Golds Green 70 C3
Goldthorn Park 52 B4
Gornalwood 83 E3
Goscote 28 B2
Gospel End Village 66 B3
Gothersley 116 C2
Gravelly Hill 92 D4
Great Barr 73 H1
Great Bridge 69 H5
Greensforge 98 B3
Griffiths Hill 159 F5
Grimes Hill 192 D4
Grove Vale 73 E2
Gunstone 10 C1
Guns Village 87 E2
The Gutter 186 A1
Hackman's Gate 169 F4
Haden Cross 121 G4
Hagley 153 F4
Halesowen 139 E3
Hall Green 71 G3
Hall Green 163 E3
Hampton in Arden 167 F3
Hamstead 73 G3
Handsworth 89 F4
Handsworth Wood 90 B3
Harborne 141 G1
Harden 28 B3
Hardwick 45 F5
Hartle 184 D2
Hart's Hill 101 G4
Harvills Hawthorn 70 B4
Hasbury 138 A4
Hasluck's Green 179 G3
Hateley Heath 71 G5
Hawkesley 176 C5
Hawne 138 C2
Hayley Green 154 C1
Hay Mills 146 B1
Headley Heath 191 G1
Heath End 28 B1
Heath Town 38 A1
Highbridge 58 A4
Highbury Park 160 D1
Highgate 127 F4
High Heath 18 C5
High Heath 48 D5
Highter's Heath 178 D3
Hill 47 E1
Hillfield 195 G1
Hill Hook 32 C4
Hill Top 71 E3

Hill Wood 33 C5
Himley 81 F3
Hinksford 98 D1
Hockley Heath 198 B5
Hodgehill 111 H4
Holly Bank 19 H4
Hollywood 178 D5
Holy Cross 170 C3
Hook End 167 H5
Hopwood 190 A5
Horseley Heath 86 A1
Hunnington 155 H5
Hurst Green 122 D4
Hurst Hill 67 H3
Illey 156 C2
Katies Hill 85 E5
Kineton Green 163 H2
King's Heath 161 E3
King's Hill 55 H5
Kingshurst 114 A2
King's Norton 176 C3
Kingstanding 75 G2
Kingswinford 99 F3
Kitt's Green 113 E5
Kitwell 157 E3
Knowle 197 G2
Knowle Grove 197 F5
The Knowle 103 G4
Ladywood 126 A2
Lambert's End 87 E3
Lane Green 11 E4
Lane Head 26 A4
Lanesfield 53 F2
Langley 104 D4
Langley Green 105 F5
Lapal 139 H4
Lawns Wood 117 F1
Lea End 190 D5
Lea Hall 130 C2
Leamore 27 E4
Lee Bank 126 C4
Leighswood 30 A2
Ley Hill 47 E4
Lickey 188 A5
Lifford 177 F1
Little Aston 32 A5
Little Bloxwich 17 F4
Little Bromwich 128 D2
Little Hay 33 G1
Little Norton 8 B2
Little Packington 150 D1
Littleworth End 49 E5
Lode Heath 165 G4
Lodge Hill 141 H5
Londonderry 105 G5
London Fields 83 G4
Longbridge 188 D1
Lower Bradley 54 B4
Lower Clent 170 B1
Lower Cornal 83 G2
Lower Illey 156 C3
Lower Moor 159 H5
Lozells 108 C2
The Lunt 54 C1
Lutley 137 F5
Lydiate Ash 187 E5
Lye 136 C1
Lyndon Green 130 B5
Madeley Heath 186 A1
Major's Green 179 F5
Maney 62 B4
Marston Green 132 A4
Maw Green 57 H2
Mayer's Green 88 A5
Mere Green 47 E2
Merridale 36 A3
Merry Hill 50 C1
Merry Hill 119 H1
Mesty Croft 56 A4
Middle Bickenhill 150 C4
Mill Green 31 G3
Minworth 95 E1
Monkspath 195 G3
Monmore Green 38 B5
Moor Hall 47 H4
Moseley 38 B4
Moseley 144 B5
Moxley 54 D4
Mushroom Green 120 D3
Nechells 110 B1
Nechells Green 109 H5
Netherton 102 B4
Newbolds 24 A4
Newbridge 35 H2
New Invention 26 A2
New Oscott 76 B1
Newton 73 E3
New Town 146 C3
New Town 86 B2
Newtown 16 C2
Newtown 108 C4
Northfield 175 H1
Norton 135 E5
Norton Green 199 F1
Oakham 103 F2
Ocker Hill 70 A2
Oldbury 105 E4

Old Fallings 23 H3
Old Hill 121 G3
Old Perton 34 A2
Old Swinford 135 G4
Olton 147 G5
Orton Hill 65 E1
Ounsdale 64 D5
Overend 138 A1
Over Green 79 H2
Oxbarn 51 E1
Oxley 22 D2
Packwood 199 E4
Packwood Gullet 198 D2
Palfrey 56 D2
Priestfield 53 F2
Parkfield 52 D3
Park Village 23 H5
Pedmore 153 F2
Pelsall 18 B4
Pelsall Wood 17 H2
Pendeford 11 G5
Penn 51 E2
Pennsett 100 D2
Perry Barr 90 B1
Perry Beeches 74 A3
Perry Common 75 H3
Perton 34 C1
Pheasey 59 G4
Pleck 56 B2
Portobello 39 E3
Portway 104 A3
Prestwood 116 C3
Primrose Hill 102 D5
Princes End 69 E2
Pype Hayes 93 H1
Quarry Bank 119 H4
Queslett 74 C1
Quinton 140 A1
Reddicap Heath 63 G4
Rednal 188 C3
Ridgacre 140 A5
Romsley 172 C1
Romsley Hill 172 C3
Rood End 105 G3
Roseville 68 A3
Rotton Row 197 G4
Rotton Park 107 G5
Roughley 47 G2
Round Oak 101 G5
Round's Green 104 C1
Rowley Regis 103 H4
Rubery 188 A1
Ruiton 83 F2
Rumbow Cottages 171 H2
Rumbush 193 G5
Rushall 29 E3
Russell's Hall 101 G1
Saltley 110 C5
Sandwell 88 D3
Scotlands 24 A2
Sedgley 67 G3
Selly Oak 159 F1
Selly Park 160 A1
Shard End 113 F4
Sharmans Cross 181 E1
Sheldon 147 H2
Shelfield 29 E2
Shenley Fields 158 A3
Shenstone Woodend 33 E5
Shire Oak 19 F1
Shire Oak Hill 19 H2
Shirley 180 C2
Shirley Heath 180 C4
Short Cross 138 C3
Short Heath 26 C4
Short Heath 76 D5
Silver End 118 D3
Silver Street 192 A3
Small Heath 128 B5
Smestow 80 A2
Smethwick 106 A4
Soho 107 E3
Solihull 182 A5
Solihull Lodge 179 E3
South Yardley 146 D1
Sparkbrook 127 H5
Sparkhill 145 E4
Springfield 7 K1
Springfield 103 F4
Springfield 162 A1
Springhill 15 H2
Spring Hill 50 C4
Stakenbridge 168 D2
Stambermill 136 A2
Stechford 130 A1
Stirchley 160 A3
Stockfield 146 C5
Stockland Green 92 A2
Stockwell End 21 G5
Stonebridge 150 D5
Stone Cross 71 H2
Stourbridge 134 D3
Stourton 116 D5
Stow Lawn 38 D5
The Straits 82 D1
Streetly 45 H4

Stubber's Green 29 G2
Summer Hill 69 G2
Sutton Coldfield 62 D3
Swan Village 86 D2
Swindon 80 D4
Tansley Hill 103 F2
Tat Bank 105 E2
Ten Acres 160 B2
Tettenhall 21 G5
Tettenhall Wood 35 H1
Thimble End 78 C2
Three Maypoles 194 B1
Tidbury Green 193 G4
Tile Cross 131 G2
Tilehouse Green 197 E5
Tipton 69 G4
Tipton Green 68 D5
Tividale 85 H5
Toll End 69 H5
Tower Hill 74 A5
Trueman's Heath 193 E1
Trysull 64 A2
Tudor Hill 62 A2
Turves Green 175 G4
Tyburn 94 A3
Tyseley 146 A2
Ulverley Green 164 A2
Upper Gornal 67 G5
Upper Witton 76 A5
Vauxhall 127 H1
Vigo 19 F5
The Village 100 A2
Wake Green 161 G1
Walker's Heath 177 F4
Wallbrook 68 C4
Wall Heath 99 F1
Wallington Heath 16 C4
Walmer 78 B5
Walmley Ash 78 D4
Walsall 5 F7
Walsall Wood 19 F3
Walton Pool 171 E3
Ward End 111 E4
Warley Woods 124 A3
Warstock 179 E2
Washwood Heath 110 C3
Water Orton 96 B3
Watford Gap 32 D5
Wednesbury 70 B1
Wednesbury Oak 69 F2
Wednesfield 26 C4
Weoley Castle 158 B1
Wergs 20 D4
West Bromwich 87 F5
Westcroft 15 H4
West Hagley 152 D5
West Heath 190 A1
Whiteheath Gate 104 C5
Whitehouse Common 63 G1
Whitlock's End 193 G2
Wightwick 34 D4
Wildmoor 186 B4
Willenhall 39 H2
Winson Green 108 A4
Withymoor Village 119 G3
Witton 91 E3
Wollaston 135 E1
Wollescote 136 C3
Wolverhampton 7
Wombourne 64 B5
Woodcock Hill 158 A2
Wood End 24 C3
Woodgate 156 D1
Woodgate Valley 140 C4
Wood Green 55 G4
Wood Hayes 24 B1
Woods Bank 55 F3
Woodsetton 67 G4
Woodside 101 H5
The Woods 56 C4
Wordsley 118 A1
Worlds End 164 C3
Wylde Green 77 H2
Yardley 129 H4
Yardley Wood 179 G1
Yew Tree 57 H5

USING THE STREET INDEX

Street names are listed alphabetically. Each street name is followed by its postal town or area locality, the Postcode District, the page number, and the reference to the square in which the name is found.

Standard index entries are shown as follows:

Abberley Cl *HALE* B63 .... **138** B5

Street names and selected addresses not shown on the map due to scale restrictions are shown in the index with an asterisk:

Aaron Manby Ct *TPTN/OCK* DY4 * ..**69** F3

GENERAL ABBREVIATIONS

ACC......ACCESS	CTYD......COURTYARD	HLS......HILLS	MWY......MOTORWAY	SE......SOUTH EAST
ALY......ALLEY	CUTT......CUTTINGS	HO......HOUSE	N......NORTH	SER......SERVICE AREA
AP......APPROACH	CV......COVE	HOL......HOLLOW	NE......NORTH EAST	SH......SHORE
AR......ARCADE	CVN......CANYON	HOSP......HOSPITAL	NW......NORTH WEST	SHOP......SHOPPING
ASS......ASSOCIATION	DEPT......DEPARTMENT	HRB......HARBOUR	O/P......OVERPASS	SKWY......SKYWAY
AV......AVENUE	DL......DALE	HTH......HEATH	OFF......OFFICE	SMT......SUMMIT
BCH......BEACH	DM......DAM	HTS......HEIGHTS	ORCH......ORCHARD	SOC......SOCIETY
BLDS......BUILDINGS	DR......DRIVE	HVN......HAVEN	OV......OVAL	SP......SPUR
BND......BEND	DRO......DROVE	HWY......HIGHWAY	PAL......PALACE	SPR......SPRING
BNK......BANK	DRY......DRIVEWAY	IMP......IMPERIAL	PAS......PASSAGE	SQ......SQUARE
BR......BRIDGE	DWGS......DWELLINGS	IN......INLET	PAV......PAVILION	ST......STREET
BRK......BROOK	E......EAST	IND EST......INDUSTRIAL ESTATE	PDE......PARADE	STN......STATION
BTM......BOTTOM	EMB......EMBANKMENT	INF......INFIRMARY	PH......PUBLIC HOUSE	STR......STREAM
BUS......BUSINESS	EMBY......EMBASSY	INFO......INFORMATION	PK......PARK	STRD......STRAND
BVD......BOULEVARD	ESP......ESPLANADE	INT......INTERCHANGE	PKWY......PARKWAY	SW......SOUTH WEST
BY......BYPASS	EST......ESTATE	IS......ISLAND	PL......PLACE	TDG......TRADING
CATH......CATHEDRAL	EX......EXCHANGE	JCT......JUNCTION	PLN......PLAIN	TER......TERRACE
CEM......CEMETERY	EXPY......EXPRESSWAY	JTY......JETTY	PLNS......PLAINS	THWY......THROUGHWAY
CEN......CENTRE	EXT......EXTENSION	KG......KING	PLZ......PLAZA	TNL......TUNNEL
CFT......CROFT	F/O......FLYOVER	KNL......KNOLL	POL......POLICE STATION	TOLL......TOLLWAY
CH......CHURCH	FC......FOOTBALL CLUB	L......LAKE	PR......PRINCE	TPK......TURNPIKE
CHA......CHASE	FK......FORK	LA......LANE	PREC......PRECINCT	TR......TRACK
CHYD......CHURCHYARD	FLD......FIELD	LDG......LODGE	PREP......PREPARATORY	TRL......TRAIL
CIR......CIRCLE	FLDS......FIELDS	LGT......LIGHT	PRIM......PRIMARY	TWR......TOWER
CIRC......CIRCUS	FLS......FALLS	LK......LOCK	PROM......PROMENADE	U/P......UNDERPASS
CL......CLOSE	FM......FARM	LKS......LAKES	PRS......PRINCESS	UNI......UNIVERSITY
CLFS......CLIFFS	FT......FORT	LNDG......LANDING	PRT......PORT	UPR......UPPER
CMP......CAMP	FTS......FLATS	LTL......LITTLE	PT......POINT	V......VALE
CNR......CORNER	FWY......FREEWAY	LWR......LOWER	PTH......PATH	VA......VALLEY
CO......COUNTY	FY......FERRY	MAG......MAGISTRATE	PZ......PIAZZA	VIAD......VIADUCT
COLL......COLLEGE	GA......GATE	MAN......MANSIONS	QD......QUADRANT	VIL......VILLA
COM......COMMON	GAL......GALLERY	MD......MEAD	QU......QUEEN	VIS......VISTA
COMM......COMMISSION	GDN......GARDEN	MDW......MEADOWS	QY......QUAY	VLG......VILLAGE
CON......CONVENT	GDNS......GARDENS	MEM......MEMORIAL	R......RIVER	VLS......VILLAS
COT......COTTAGE	GLD......GLADE	MI......MILL	RBT......ROUNDABOUT	VW......VIEW
COTS......COTTAGES	GLN......GLEN	MKT......MARKET	RD......ROAD	W......WEST
CP......CAPE	GN......GREEN	MKTS......MARKETS	RDG......RIDGE	WD......WOOD
CPS......COPSE	GND......GROUND	ML......MALL	REP......REPUBLIC	WHF......WHARF
CR......CREEK	GRA......GRANGE	MNR......MANOR	RES......RESERVOIR	WK......WALK
CREM......CREMATORIUM	GRG......GARAGE	MS......MEWS	RFC......RUGBY FOOTBALL CLUB	WKS......WALKS
CRS......CRESCENT	GT......GREAT	MSN......MISSION	RI......RISE	WLS......WELLS
CSWY......CAUSEWAY	GTWY......GATEWAY	MT......MOUNT	RP......RAMP	WY......WAY
CT......COURT	GV......GROVE	MTN......MOUNTAIN	RW......ROW	YD......YARD
CTRL......CENTRAL	HGR......HIGHER	MTS......MOUNTAINS	S......SOUTH	YHA......YOUTH HOSTEL
CTS......COURTS	HL......HILL	MUS......MUSEUM	SCH......SCHOOL	

POSTCODE TOWNS AND AREA ABBREVIATIONS

ACGN......Acock's Green	CBHAM......Central Birmingham	ERDE/BCHGN......Erdington east/Birches Green	LDYWD/EDGR......Ladywood/Edgbaston Reservoir	SHLY......Shirley
ALDR......Aldridge	CBHAMNE......Central Birmingham northeast	ERDW/GRVHL......Erdington west/Gravelly Hill	LGLYGN/QTN......Langley Green/Quinton	SLYOAK......Selly Oak
ALE/KHTH/YWD......Alcester Lane's End/King's Heath/Yardley Wood	CBHAMNW......Central Birmingham northwest	ETTPK/GDPK/PENN......Ettingshall Park/Goldthorn Park/Penn	LGN/SDN/BHAMAIR......Lyndon Green/Sheldon/Birmingham Airport	SMHTH......Small Heath
ALVE......Alvechurch	CBHAMW......Central Birmingham west	FOAKS/STRLY......Four Oaks/Streetly	LICHS......Lichfield south	SMTHWK......Smethwick
AST/WIT......Aston/Witton	CBROM......Castle Bromwich	GTB/HAM......Great Barr/Hamstead	LOZ/NWT......Lozells/Newtown	SMTHWKW......Smethwick west
BDMR/CCFT......Bradmore/Castlecroft	CDSL......Codsall	GTWY......Great Wyrley	MGN/WHC......Mere Green/Whitehouse Common	SOLH......Solihull
BFLD/HDSWWD......Birchfield/Handsworth Wood	CDYHTH......Cradley Heath	HAG/WOL......Hagley/Wollescote	MOS/BIL......Moseley/Billesley	SPARK......Sparkhill/Sparkbrook
BHAMNEC......Birmingham N.E.C.	CHWD/FDBR/MGN......Chelmsley Wood/Fordbridge/Marston Green	HALE......Halesowen	NFLD/LBR......Northfield/Longbridge	STETCH......Stetchford
BHTH/HG......Balsall Heath/Highgate	CNCK/NC......Cannock/Norton Canes	HDSW......Handsworth	OLDBY......Oldbury	STRBR......Stourbridge
BILS/COS......Bilston/Coseley	COVEN......Coven	HHTH/SAND......Hateley Heath/Sandwell	PBAR/PBCH......Perry Bar/Perry Beeches	TPTN/OCK......Tipton/Ocker Hill
BKDE/SHDE......Buckland End/Shard End	CSCFLD/WYGN......Central Sutton Coldfield/Wylde Green	HIA/OLT......Hampton in Arden/Olton	POL/KGSB/FAZ......Polesworth/Kingsbury/Fazeley	VAUX/NECH......Vauxhall/Nechells
BKHL/PFLD......Blakenhall/Priestfield	CSHL/WTROR......Coleshill/Water Orton	HLGN/YWD......Hall Green/Yardley Wood	RBRY......Rubery	WALM/CURD......Walmley/Curdworth
BLKHTH/ROWR......Blackheath/Rowley Regis	CVALE......Castle Vale	HLYWD......Hollywood	RCOVN/BALC/EX......Rural Coventry north/Balsall Common/Exhall	WASH/WDE......Washwood Heath/Ward End
BLOX/PEL......Bloxwich/Pelsall	DARL/WED......Darlaston/Wednesbury	HOCK/TIA......Hockley Heath/Tanworth-in-Arden	RIDG/WDGT......Ridgacre/Woodgate	WBROM......West Bromwich
BNTWD......Burntwood	DIG/EDG......Digbeth/Edgbaston	HRBN......Harborne	RMSLY......Romsley	WLNHL......Willenhall
BORD......Bordesley	DOR/KN......Dorridge/Knowle	HWK/WKHTH......Hawkesley/Walker's Heath	RUSH/SHEL......Rushall/Shelfield	WMBN......Wombourne
BRGRVE......Bromsgrove east	DSYBK/YTR......Daisy Bank/Yew Tree	KGSTG......Kingstanding	SCFLD/BOLD......Sutton Coldfield/Boldmere	WNSFLD......Wednesfield
BRGRVW......Bromsgrove west	DUDN......Dudley north	KGSWFD......Kingswinford	SEDG......Sedgley	WOLV......Wolverhampton
BRLYHL......Brierley Hill	DUDS......Dudley south	KIDD......Kidderminster	SHHTH......Short Heath	WOLVN......Wolverhampton north
BRWNH......Brownhills	DUNHL/THL/PER......Dunstall Hill/Tettenhall/Perton	KINVER......Kinver		WSL......Walsall
BVILLE......Bournville	EDG......Edgbaston			WSLW......Walsall west
				WSNGN......Winson Green
				YDLY......Yardley

Index - streets

A

Aaron Manby Ct
TPTN/OCK DY4 * 69 F3
Abberley Rd
LGLYGN/QTN B68 ......123 F4
SEDG DY3......83 E2
Abberley St DUDS DY2 ......102 C1
SMTHWK B66 ......107 F4
Abberton Cl HALE B63......139 E4
Abberton Gv SHLY B90 ......195 H1
Abbess Gv YDLY B25......130 A3
Abbey Cl HHTH/SAND B71 ......87 C1
Abbey Crs HALE B63......137 H3
LGLYGN/QTN B68 ......123 H3
Abbeydale Rd NFLD/LBR B31 ......175 G3
Abbey Dr BLOX/PEL WS3 ......18 A2
Abbeyfield Rd
ERDW/GRVHL B23 ......56 C3
WOLVN WV10 ......13 E3
Abbey Rd DUDS DY2 ......102 D3
ERDW/GRVHL B23 ......92 B4
HALE B63 ......137 G3
HRBN B17 ......142 B2
SEDG DY3......83 E3
SMTHWK B67 ......123 H3
Abbey Sq BLOX/PEL WS3 ......16 A5
Abbey St SEDG DY3......83 E3
WSNGN B18......108 A4
Abbey St North WSNGN B18......108 A4
Abbot Rd HALE B63......154 C2
Abbots Cl DOR/KN B93 ......197 E1
RUSH/SHEL WS4 ......29 E4
Abbotsford Av GTB/HAM B43 ......73 H1
Abbotsford Dr DUDN DY1 ......101 G2
Abbotsford Rd SPARK B11......145 E1
Abbots Ms BRLYHL DY5......119 F3

Abbots Rd
ALE/KHTH/YWD B14......161 E3
Abbots Wy BDMR/CCFT WV3......36 A4
WSNGN B18......108 A4
Abbotts Pl BLOX/PEL WS3 ......27 H1
Abbotts Rd ERDE/BCHGN B24 ......92 D5
Abbotts St BLOX/PEL WS3 ......17 F5
Abdon Av SLYOAK B29......158 D3
Aberdeen St WSNGN B18 ......107 G5
Aberford Cl SHHTH WV12 ......40 B1
Abigails Cl
LGN/SDN/BHAMAIR B26 ......130 D5
Abingdon Cl WOLV WV1 ......38 B3
Abingdon Rd BLOX/PEL WS3 ......16 B5
DUDS DY2 ......120 C1
ERDW/GRVHL B23 ......75 H4
WOLV WV1 ......38 B3
Abingdon Wy BLOX/PEL WS3 ......16 B5
CVALE B35......94 C3
Ablewell St WSL WS1......5 F4
Ablow St BKHL/PFLD WV2 ......6 E7
Abney Dr BILS/COS WV14 ......67 H2
Aboyne Cl DIG/EDG B5......143 H1
Ab Rw CBHAMNE B4......3 K3
Acacia Av
CHWD/FDBR/MGN B37 ......113 H5
DUDN DY1 ......84 A3
Acacia Cl
CHWD/FDBR/MGN B37 ......113 H5
DUDN DY1 ......84 A3
Acacia Crs CDSL WV8......10 D4
Acacia Dr BILS/COS WV14 ......68 A4
Acacia Rd BVILLE B30......159 G2
Accord Ms DARL/WED WS10 ......55 F1
Acfold Rd BFLD/HDSWWD B20......89 G1
Acheson Rd HLCN/YWD B28......179 H2
Ackleton Gdns
BDMR/CCFT WV3......51 F1
Ackleton Gv SLYOAK B29......158 B2

Acorn Cl ACGN B27 ......146 B2
BVILLE B30......159 G2
WBROM B70......87 F4
Acorn Gdns SLYOAK B29 ......160 A2
Acorn Gv CBHAMW B1 ......2 A4
CDSL WV8......10 A5
STRBR DY8......118 A3
Acorn Rd RMSLY B62......122 A4
WNSFLD WV11......25 H5
Acorn St WLNHL WV13 ......40 A3
Acre Ri SHHTH WV12 ......25 H5
Acres Rd BRLYHL DY5......119 G4
Acton Dr SEDG DY3 ......82 C5
Acton Gv BILS/COS WV14 ......53 F4
KGSTG B44......75 G1
Adams Brook Dr
RIDG/WDGT B32......157 F1
Adams Cl SMTHWK B66......105 H2
TPTN/OCK DY4 ......69 F2
Adam's Hl HAG/WOL DY9......170 C1
RIDG/WDGT B32......157 G1
Adams Rd BDMR/CCFT WV3 ......36 B5
BRWNH WS8......19 G2
Adams St VAUX/NECH B7 ......3 K1
WBROM B70......87 E3
WSLW WS2......4 B2
Ada Rd SMTHWK B66 ......124 D1
YDLY B25......146 B1
Ada Wrighton Cl SHHTH WV12 ......26 A3
Addenbrooke Dr
SCFLD/BOLD B73 ......77 F1
Addenbrooke Rd
SMTHWK B67 ......124 B1
Addenbrooke St
BLOX/PEL WS3 ......27 G3
DARL/WED WS10 ......40 B5
Addenbrooke Wy
TPTN/OCK DY4 ......70 B3
Adderley Gdns
WASH/WDE B8......110 B5

Adderley Park Cl
WASH/WDE B8 * 110 C5
Adderley Rd WASH/WDE B8......128 A1
Adderley Rd South
WASH/WDE B8......128 A1
Adderley St BORD B9......127 G3
Addington Wy OLDBY B69......86 B3
Addison Cl DARL/WED WS10 ......72 A1
Addison Cft SEDG DY3 ......82 C1
Addison Gv WNSFLD WV11......24 B1
Addison Pl BILS/COS WV14 ......54 B1
CSHL/WTROR B46......96 B3
Addison Rd
ALE/KHTH/YWD B14......161 F3
BDMR/CCFT WV3......36 B5
BRLYHL DY5......118 D2
DARL/WED WS10 ......70 D1
VAUX/NECH B7......110 A1
Addison St DARL/WED WS10 ......70 D1
Adelaide Av WBROM B70......71 E4
Adelaide St BHTH/HG B12......127 F4
BRLYHL DY5......119 F1
Adelaide Wk BKHL/PFLD WV2 ......7 J7
Adey Rd WNSFLD WV11......25 F2
Adkins La SMTHWKW B67......124 B3
Admington Rd STETCH B33......131 E4
Admiral Pl MOS/BIL B13......144 B3
Admirals Wy
BLKHTH/ROWR B65......121 H2
Adria Rd SPARK B11......144 C5
Adrian Cft MOS/BIL B13......162 A1
Adshead Rd DUDS DY2......102 C2
Adstone Gv NFLD/LBR B31......175 G4
Advent Gdns WBROM B70 *......87 E5
Adwalton Rd
DUNHL/THL/PER WV6......34 D2
Agenoria Dr STRBR DY8......135 F2
Ainsdale Cl STRBR DY8......135 F5
Ainsdale Gdns HALE B63......137 H5

Ainsworth Rd WOLVN WV10 ......13 E3
Aintree Gv BKDE/SHDE B34......113 F5
Aintree Rd WOLVN WV10......12 D5
Aintree Wy DUDN DY1......83 G4
Aire Cft NFLD/LBR B31 ......175 H4
Airfield Dr ALDR WS9......43 C2
Airport Wy HIA/OLT B92......149 G4
Akrill Cl WBROM B70 *......87 F1
The Akrill Cottage Homes
WBROM B70 *......87 F1
Alamein Rd WLNHL WV13......39 E4
Albany Crs BILS/COS WV14......53 C2
Albany Gdns SOLH B91......182 B1
Albany Gv KGSWFD DY6......100 A2
WNSFLD WV11......26 A1
Albany Rd HRBN B17......142 A1
Albemarle Rd STRBR DY8......135 E1
Albermarle Rd KGSWFD DY6......100 C4
Albert Av BHTH/HG B12......144 C1
Albert Clarke Dr SHHTH WV12 ......26 A3
Albert Cl CDSL WV8......10 A3
Albert Dr HALE B63......138 B5
SEDG DY3......80 C4
Albert Rd ALE/KHTH/YWD B14 ......161 F3
AST/WIT B6......109 E2
DUNHL/THL/PER WV6......6 A1
ERDW/GRVHL B23 ......92 B4
HALE B63......138 B5
HDSW B21......89 C5
HRBN B17......141 H2
LGLYGN/QTN B68......123 H3
OLDBY B69......105 E1
STECH B33......129 H1
Albert Rd BRLYHL DY5......101 F2
DARL/WED WS10 ......70 C1
DIG/EDG B5......3 J4
KGSWFD DY6......99 F1
OLDBY B69......105 E1
STRBR DY8......135 F2
TPTN/OCK DY4......69 F3

WBROM B70 87 G5
WSLW WS2 4 E2
Albert St East OLDBY B69 105 F2
Albion Av WLNHL WV13 40 A3
Albion Field Dr
HHTH/SAND B71 87 H2
Albion Industrial Est
WBROM B70 86 D4
Albion Rd BRWNH WS8 9 E4
HDSW B21 89 F5
HHTH/SAND B71 106 C1
SPARK B11 145 F2
WBROM B70 86 D4
Albion St BILS/COS WV14 54 A2
BRLYHL DY5 119 F1
CBHAMW B1 2 B3
KGSWFD DY6 99 F1
OLDBY B69 86 C5
TPTN/OCK DY4 85 F1
WLNHL WV13 39 H3
WOLV WV1 7 H4
Alborn Crs HWK/WKHTH B38 176 B5
Albrighton Rd HALE B63 138 A4
Albright Rd LGLYGN/QTN B68 105 H5
Albury Wk SPARK B11 127 G5
Albutts Rd CNCK/NC WS11 8 B1
Alcester Dr SCFLD/BOLD B73 61 F5
WLNHL WV13 38 D5
Alcester Rd HLYWD B47 192 B4
MOS/BIL B13 144 B4
Alcester Rd South
ALE/KHTH/YWD B14 178 B4
Alcester St BHTH/HG B12 127 F4
Alcombe Gv STETCH B33 130 A2
Alcott Cl DOR/KN B93 198 D1
Alcott Gv STETCH B33 131 F1
Alcott La
CHWD/FDBR/MGN B37 131 H4
The Alcove BLOX/PEL WS3 17 F5
Aldbourne Wy
HWK/WKHTH B38 190 B1
Aldbury Rd
ALE/KHTH/YWD B14 178 C3
Aldeburgh Cl BLOX/PEL WS3 16 C4
Aldeford Dr BRLYHL DY5 119 F4
Alderbrook Cl SEDG DY3 66 D2
Alderbrook Rd SOLH B91 181 F2
Alder Cl HLYWD B47 192 D2
WALM/CURD B76 78 A4
Alder Coppice SEDG DY3 52 A5
Alder Crs DSYBK/YTR WS5 57 H4
Alder Dl BDMR/CCFT WV3 36 A4
Alderdale Av SEDG DY3 52 A5
Alderdale Crs HIA/OLT B92 165 G3
Alder Dr
CHWD/FDBR/MGN B37 132 B3
Alderflat Pl VAUX/NECH B7 110 A4
Alderford Cl CDSL WV8 22 B2
Alder Gv RMSLY B62 139 G1
Alderham Cl SOLH B91 182 C1
Alderhithe Gv
FOAKS/STRLY B74 45 H2
Alder La BVILLE B30 159 E4
Alderlea Cl STRBR DY8 135 G5
Alderley Crs BLOX/PEL WS3 28 A5
Alderminster Rd SOLH B91 181 H4
Aldermore Dr MGN/WHC B75 * 63 F2
Alderney Gdns
HWK/WKHTH B38 176 B4
Alder Park Rd SOLH B91 181 F3
Alderpits Rd BKDE/SHDE B34 113 F3
Alder Rd DARL/WED WS10 56 A2
KGSWFD DY6 100 C4
MOS/BIL B13 144 C3
Aldersea Dr AST/WIT B6 109 F2
Aldershaw Rd
LGN/SDN/BHAMAIR B26 147 E2
Aldershaws SHLY B90 194 A3
Aldersley Av
DUNHL/THL/PER WV6 22 A3
Aldersley Cl
DUNHL/THL/PER WV6 22 B3
Aldersley Rd
DUNHL/THL/PER WV6 22 B5
Aldersmead Rd NFLD/LBR B31 176 A4
Alderson Rd WASH/WDE B8 110 D5
The Alders RMSLY B62 172 B1
Alderton Cl SOLH B91 181 H4
Alderton Dr BDMR/CCFT WV3 36 A5
Alder Wy FOAKS/STRLY B74 45 E5
Alderwood Pl SOLH B91 181 H2
Alderwood Ri SEDG DY3 83 F1
Aldgate Dr BRLYHL DY5 119 E5
Aldgate Gv LOZ/NWT B19 108 D4
Aldis Cl HLGN/YWD B28 162 C1
WSLW WS2 * 56 A1
Aldis Rd WSLW WS2 56 A1
Aldridge By-Pass ALDR WS9 30 A4
Aldridge Cl LGLYGN/QTN B68 105 G5
STRBR DY8 118 A4
Aldridge Rd ALDR WS9 31 G5
FOAKS/STRLY B74 44 D5
KGSTG B44 74 C1
LGLYGN/QTN B68 123 F4
RUSH/SHEL WS4 42 D2
Aldridge St DARL/WED WS10 55 F1
Aldwych Cl ALDR WS9 30 B2
Aldwyck Dr BDMR/CCFT WV3 35 E5
Alexander Gdns
PBAR/PBCH B42 90 D3
Alexander Hl BRLYHL DY5 119 H4
Alexander Rd ACGN B27 146 B3
CDSL WV8 11 E4
SMTHWKW B67 124 A2
WSLW WS2 40 D3
Alexander Ter
SMTHWKW B67 * 106 B3
Alexander Wy WASH/WDE B8 128 D1
Alexandra Av HDSW B21 107 F2
Alexandra Crs HHTH/SAND B71 72 A3
Alexandra Pl BILS/COS WV14 53 H2
Alexandra Rd BVILLE B30 160 A3
DARL/WED WS10 55 G2
DIG/EDG B5 144 A1
ETTPK/GDPK/PENN WV4 51 G3
HALE B63 138 B4
HDSW B21 107 F2
TPTN/OCK DY4 85 G1
WSL WS1 57 E3
Alexandra St BDMR/CCFT WV3 6 D5
DUDN DY1 84 B5
Alexandra Wy ALDR WS9 30 B5
OLDBY B69 85 G4
Alford Cl RBRY B45 188 C1
Alfreda Av HLYWD B47 178 B5
Alfred Rd HDSW B21 107 G1
SPARK B11 144 D2
Alfred St ALE/KHTH/YWD B14 161 F3
AST/WIT B6 109 H1
BHTH/HG B12 144 D2
BLOX/PEL WS3 27 F1
DARL/WED WS10 55 E3
SMTHWK B66 106 D2
WBROM B70 87 H2
Algernon Rd
LDYWD/EDGR B16 107 F5
Alice St BILS/COS WV14 53 H2
Alison Cl TPTN/OCK DY4 69 G1
Alison Dr STRBR DY8 135 E5
Alison Rd RMSLY B62 139 G4
Allan Cl STRBR DY8 118 B3
Allbut St CDYHTH B64 120 D3
Allcock St BORD B9 127 G3
TPTN/OCK DY4 70 A3
Allcroft Rd SPARK B11 145 H5
Allenby Cl KGSWFD DY6 100 C4
Allen Cl GTB/HAM B43 73 G4
Allendale Gv GTB/HAM B43 73 G3
Allendale Rd WALM/CURD B76 78 A3
YDLY B25 129 F5
Allen Dr DARL/WED WS10 55 E2
WBROM B70 88 B5
Allen Rd DARL/WED WS10 55 H3
TPTN/OCK DY4 69 F2
Allens Av WSNGN B18 * 107 H3
Allens Cl SHHTH WV12 25 H5
Allens Croft Rd
ALE/KHTH/YWD B14 160 B5
Allens Farm Rd NFLD/LBR B31 174 D2
Allens La BLOX/PEL WS3 17 H5
Allens Rd WSNGN B18 107 H3
Allen St WBROM B70 87 F3
Allerdale Rd BRWNH WS8 19 E1
Allerton La HHTH/SAND B71 71 G3
Allerton Rd YDLY B25 129 F5
Allesley Cl FOAKS/STRLY B74 62 C1
Allesley Rd HIA/OLT B92 163 H2
Allesley St AST/WIT B6 109 E4
Alleston Rd WOLVN WV10 23 F1
Alleyne Gv ERDE/BCHGN B24 93 E4
Alleyne Rd ERDE/BCHGN B24 93 E5
The Alley SEDG DY3 82 D3
Allingham Gv GTB/HAM B43 59 H4
Allington Cl DSYBK/YTR WS5 43 F5
Allison St DIG/EDG B5 3 J6
Allman Rd ERDE/BCHGN B24 93 F2
Allmyn Dr FOAKS/STRLY B74 60 C2
All Saints Dr FOAKS/STRLY B74 46 D3
All Saints Rd
ALE/KHTH/YWD B14 161 E3
BKHL/PFLD WV2 7 J7
DARL/WED WS10 55 G2
WSNGN B18 108 B4
All Saints' St WSNGN B18 108 A4
All Saints Wy HHTH/SAND B71 87 H1
Allsops Cl BLKHTH/ROWR B65 103 F5
Allwell Dr ALE/KHTH/YWD B14 178 B3
Allwood Gdns
RIDG/WDGT B32 140 A5
Alma Av TPTN/OCK DY4 69 G4
Alma Crs VAUX/NECH B7 109 H5
Alma Pl DUDS DY2 84 C5
Alma St DARL/WED WS10 55 E2
HALE B63 137 G2
LOZ/NWT B19 109 E3
SMTHWK B66 107 E3
WLNHL WV13 39 H3
WOLVN WV10 37 H2
WSLW WS2 41 H1
Alma Wy LOZ/NWT B19 108 D2
Almond Av DSYBK/YTR WS5 57 G4
WSLW WS2 40 C1
Almond Cl BLOX/PEL WS3 17 H5
SLYOAK B29 158 C4
Almond Cft PBAR/PBCH B42 73 H5
Almond Gv
DUNHL/THL/PER WV6 37 E1
Almond Rd KGSWFD DY6 100 A1
Alnwick Rd BLOX/PEL WS3 16 C3
Alperton Dr HAG/WOL DY9 136 C5
Alpha Cl BHTH/HG B12 144 A1
Alpine Dr DUDS DY2 102 B5
Alpine Wy BDMR/CCFT WV3 35 G3
Alport Cft BORD B9 127 H2
Alston Cl FOAKS/STRLY B74 47 E3
SOLH B91 165 F4
Alston Gv BORD B9 129 F1
Alston Rd BORD B9 129 F1
OLDBY B69 104 C2
SOLH B91 165 F4
Alston St LDYWD/EDGR B16 125 H2
Althorpe Dr DOR/KN B93 196 B5
Alton Av SHHTH WV12 25 H5
Alton Cl WOLVN WV10 13 E4
Alton Cottages
ETTPK/GDPK/PENN WV4 * 66 B2
Alton Gv DUDS DY2 85 E5
HHTH/SAND B71 72 A4
Alton Rd SLYOAK B29 142 D4
Alum Dr BORD B9 129 E1
Alumhurst Av WASH/WDE B8 111 F5
Alum Rock Rd WASH/WDE B8 110 B4
Alumwell Cl WSLW WS2 * 41 F4
Alum Well Rd WSLW WS2 41 F4
Alvaston Cl BLOX/PEL WS3 17 E4
Alvechurch Hwy BRGRVE B60 187 E5
Alvechurch Rd HALE B63 138 B5
NFLD/LBR B31 189 H1
Alverley Cl KGSWFD DY6 99 F1
Alverstoke Cl COVEN WV9 11 H5
Alveston Gv BORD B9 129 F2
DOR/KN B93 197 F1
Alveston Rd HLYWD B47 192 C1
Alvin Cl RMSLY B62 122 D4
Alvington Cl SHHTH WV12 40 B1
Alwen St STRBR DY8 118 B3
Alwin Rd BLKHTH/ROWR B65 121 H2
Alwold Rd SLYOAK B29 141 G5
Amanda Av
ETTPK/GDPK/PENN WV4 51 F4
Amanda Dr LGN/SDN/BHAMAIR B26
130 B3
Ambassador Rd LGN/SDN/BHAMAIR
B26 149 G3
Amber Dr OLDBY B69 * 105 E4
Ambergate Cl BLOX/PEL WS3 17 E4
Ambergate Dr KGSWFD DY6 99 G1
Amberley Gn GTB/HAM B43 73 G5
Amberley Gv AST/WIT B6 91 G3
Amberley Rd HIA/OLT B92 147 F4
Amberley Wy FOAKS/STRLY B74 45 E4
Amber Wy RMSLY B62 138 D1
Amberwood Cl WSLW WS2 40 B2
Amblecote Av KGSTG B44 75 E1
Amblecote Rd BRLYHL DY5 119 F4
Ambleside RIDG/WDGT B32 157 G1
Ambleside Cl BILS/COS WV14 54 A4
Ambleside Dr BRLYHL DY5 119 E4
Ambleside Gv SHHTH WV12 25 H1
Ambleside Wy KGSWFD DY6 99 H3
Ambrose Cl WLNHL WV13 39 E3
Ambrose Crs KGSWFD DY6 99 H1
Ambury Wy GTB/HAM B43 73 F3
Amelas Cl BRLYHL DY5 118 C4
Amersham Cl RIDG/WDGT B32 141 E2
Amesbury Rd MOS/BIL B13 144 A4
Ames Rd DARL/WED WS10 55 E1
Amherst Av
BFLD/HDSWWD B20 90 A3
Amington Cl MGN/WHC B75 47 H2
Amington Rd SHLY B90 180 A5
YDLY B25 146 B1
Amiss Gdns SMHTH B10 128 A4
Amity Cl SMTHWK B66 * 106 D4
Amos Av WNSFLD WV11 24 B3
Amos La WNSFLD WV11 24 C4
Amos Rd HAG/WOL DY9 136 D5
Amphlett Cft TPTN/OCK DY4 85 H2
Amphletts Cl DUDS DY2 121 E1
Ampleforth Dr WLNHL WV13 39 H5
Ampton Rd EDG B15 126 B5
Amroth Cl RBRY B45 188 B1
Amwell Gv
ALE/KHTH/YWD B14 178 B2
Anchorage Rd
ERDW/GRVHL B23 92 B3
FOAKS/STRLY B74 62 B2
Anchor Cl LDYWD/EDGR B16 125 G3
Anchor Crs WSNGN B18 107 H4
Anchor Dr TPTN/OCK DY4 85 G3
Anchor Hl BRLYHL DY5 119 E3
Anchor La BILS/COS WV14 68 B1
SOLH B91 165 F4
Anchor Rd ALDR WS9 30 B4
BILS/COS WV14 68 C1
Andersleigh Dr BILS/COS WV14 68 A3
Anderson Crs GTB/HAM B43 73 G1
Anderson Rd ERDW/GRVHL B23 76 C5
SMTHWK B66 124 C3
TPTN/OCK DY4 85 G1
Anderton Cl FOAKS/STRLY B74 62 A1
Anderton Park Rd
MOS/BIL B13 144 C4
Anderton Rd SPARK B11 145 E1
Anderton St CBHAMW B1 2 A4
Andover Crs KGSWFD DY6 100 B5
Andover St DIG/EDG B5 3 K5
Andrew Cl SHHTH WV12 26 B4
Andrew Dr SHHTH WV12 26 B4
Andrew Gdns HDSW B21 89 G5
Andrew Rd HALE B63 138 C4
HHTH/SAND B71 72 B1
TPTN/OCK DY4 69 G2
Andrews Cl BRLYHL DY5 119 G4
Andrews Rd ALDR WS9 19 H3
Anerley Gv KGSTG B44 60 B4
Anerley Rd KGSTG B44 60 B4
Angela Av BLKHTH/ROWR B65 104 B5
Angela Pl BILS/COS WV14 53 H2
Angelica Cl DSYBK/YTR WS5 57 G5
Angelina St BHTH/HG B12 127 F5
Angel Pas STRBR DY8 135 G2
Angel St DUDN DY1 102 B1
Anglesey Av CBROM B36 114 B3
Anglesey Crs BRWNH WS8 9 F2
Anglesey Rd BRWNH WS8 9 F2
Anglesey St LOZ/NWT B19 108 C2
Anglian Rd ALDR WS9 29 F4
Angus Cl HHTH/SAND B71 71 G5
Anita Av TPTN/OCK DY4 85 G4
Anita Cft ERDW/GRVHL B23 92 C4
Ankadine Rd STRBR DY8 135 H1
Ankerdine Ct HALE B63 138 C4
Ankermoor Cl
BKDE/SHDE B34 112 D3
Annan Av WOLVN WV10 23 G3
Ann Cft
LGN/SDN/BHAMAIR B26 148 B3
Anne Cl WBROM B70 86 C3
Anne Gv TPTN/OCK DY4 69 H2
Anne Rd BRLYHL DY5 120 A3
ETTPK/GDPK/PENN WV4 51 H3
SMTHWK B66 107 E2
Ann Rd HLYWD B47 192 C2
Annscroft HWK/WKHTH B38 176 B3
Ann St WLNHL WV13 39 H2
Ansbro Cl WSNGN B18 107 H4
Anscluff Rd BRLYHL DY5 118 D3
Ansell Rd ERDE/BCHGN B24 92 D5
SPARK B11 145 E1
Anslow Gdns WNSFLD WV11 25 F1
Anslow Rd ERDW/GRVHL B23 92 A1
Anson Cl DUNHL/THL/PER WV6 20 C5
Anson Gv ACGN B27 146 D5
Anson Rd WBROM B70 70 C4
WSLW WS2 40 C3
Anstey Cft
CHWD/FDBR/MGN B37 * 114 A5
Anstey Gv ACGN B27 163 F1
Anstey Rd KGSTG B44 75 E5
Anston Wy WNSFLD WV11 24 D3
Anstruther Rd EDG B15 125 G5
Anthony Rd WASH/WDE B8 128 C1
Anton Dr WALM/CURD B76 78 C5
Antony Rd SHLY B90 180 B4
Antringham Gdns EDG B15 125 F4
Antrobus Rd HDSW B21 89 G5
SCFLD/BOLD B73 76 C2
Anvil Crs BILS/COS WV14 68 C1
Anvil Dr OLDBY B69 104 C3
Apex Rd BRWNH WS8 8 C5
Apley Rd STRBR DY8 118 A5
Apollo Cft ERDE/BCHGN B24 93 H3
Apollo Rd HAG/WOL DY9 137 E2
LGLYGN/QTN B68 105 G3
Apollo Wy BFLD/HDSWWD B20 90 C5
Apperley Wy HALE B63 120 B5
Appian Cl ALE/KHTH/YWD B14 161 E5
Appian Wy SHLY B90 194 D4
Appleby Cl ALE/KHTH/YWD B14 160 D5
Appleby Gdns WNSFLD WV11 15 G5
Appleby Gv SHLY B90 195 H2
Applecross FOAKS/STRLY B74 46 D4
Appledore Rd DSYBK/YTR WS5 43 F5
Appledorne Gdns
BKDE/SHDE B34 112 D3
Applesham Cl SPARK B11 145 F1
Appleton Av GTB/HAM B43 73 G3
STRBR DY8 135 G5
Appleton Cl BVILLE B30 159 G2
Appleton Crs
ETTPK/GDPK/PENN WV4 51 G3
Apple Tree Cl ERDW/GRVHL B23 91 H2
Appletree Cl NFLD/LBR B31 175 E4
SOLH B91 166 B5
Appletree Gv ALDR WS9 30 B5
DUNHL/THL/PER WV6 23 E5
Applewood Gv CDYHTH B64 121 F4
April Cft MOS/BIL B13 144 D5
Apse Cl WMBN WV5 64 D4
Apsley Cl LGLYGN/QTN B68 123 E5
Apsley Gv DOR/KN B93 198 D1
ERDE/BCHGN B24 93 E4
Apsley Rd LGLYGN/QTN B68 123 E5
Aqueduct Rd SHLY B90 179 G3
Aragon Dr SCFLD/BOLD B73 62 A2
Arboretum Rd WSL WS1 5 G2
Arbor Ga ALDR WS9 19 H3
Arbor Wy
CHWD/FDBR/MGN B37 132 C3
Arbury Dr STRBR DY8 117 H1
Arbury Hall Rd SHLY B90 180 D5
Arcal St SEDG DY3 67 G4
Archer Cl DARL/WED WS10 55 G5
LGLYGN/QTN B68 * 105 F5
Archer Ct HAG/WOL DY9 136 C5
Archer Gdns CDYHTH B64 120 C3
Archer Rd
ALE/KHTH/YWD B14 179 E1
BLOX/PEL WS3 28 A4
Archers Cl ERDW/GRVHL B23 76 A3
Archer Wy BLKHTH/ROWR B65 122 B3
The Arches SMHTH B10 * 127 H4
Arch Hill St DUDS DY2 102 C4
Archibald Rd LOZ/NWT B19 108 C1
Arcot Rd HLGN/YWD B28 145 H5
Ardath Rd HWK/WKHTH B38 177 E3
Ardav Rd WBROM B70 70 D3
Arden Buildings DOR/KN B93 196 D5
Arden Cl STRBR DY8 135 E1
Ardencote Rd MOS/BIL B13 161 G4
Arden Ct HIA/OLT B92 * 167 G3
Arden Cft CSHL/WTROR B46 97 F5
HIA/OLT B92 148 A3
Arden Dr DOR/KN B93 198 D1
LGN/SDN/BHAMAIR B26 130 B5
MGN/WHC B75 63 H3
SCFLD/BOLD B73 77 F3
Arden Gv LDYWD/EDGR B16 126 A3
OLDBY B69 105 E4
Ardenleigh Wy
ERDE/BCHGN B24 93 E4
Arden Meads HOCK/TIA B94 198 A5
Arden Oak Rd
LGN/SDN/BHAMAIR B26 148 B2
Arden Pl BILS/COS WV14 54 D4
Arden Rd ACGN B27 146 B3
AST/WIT B6 108 D1
DOR/KN B93 198 D1
HLYWD B47 192 C2
RBRY B45 174 A4
SMTHWKW B67 106 C5
WASH/WDE B8 128 B1
Arden Vale Rd DOR/KN B93 197 F1
Arderne Dr
CHWD/FDBR/MGN B37 132 A3
Ardgowan Gv
ETTPK/GDPK/PENN WV4 52 D3
Ardingley Wk BRLYHL DY5 118 D5
Ardley Cl DUDS DY2 102 D1
Ardley Rd ALE/KHTH/YWD B14 161 G5
Aretha Cl KGSWFD DY6 100 C3
Argil Cl WOLVN WV10 24 A2
Argus Cl WALM/CURD B76 63 F5
Argyle Cl RUSH/SHEL WS4 5 K1
STRBR DY8 118 A3
Argyle Rd BKHL/PFLD WV2 51 H2
RUSH/SHEL WS4 5 K1
Argyle St VAUX/NECH B7 110 A1
Arkle Cft BLKHTH/ROWR B65 103 F3
CBROM B36 111 G1
Arkley Gv HLGN/YWD B28 163 F3
Arkley Rd HLGN/YWD B28 163 F3
Arkwright Rd RIDG/WDGT B32 140 C2
WSLW WS2 27 F5
Arlen Dr GTB/HAM B43 73 F2
Arlescote Cl MGN/WHC B75 47 G3
Arlescote Rd HIA/OLT B92 148 A5
Arleston Wy SHLY B90 181 E5
Arley Cl OLDBY B69 104 B4
Arley Dr STRBR DY8 135 E4
Arley Gv
ETTPK/GDPK/PENN WV4 50 D3
Arley Rd SLYOAK B29 142 D4
SOLH B91 181 G1
WASH/WDE B8 110 B3
Arley Vls WSNGN B18 * 107 F5
Arlidge Cl BILS/COS WV14 53 H4
Arlington Cl KGSWFD DY6 99 H5
Arlington Ct STRBR DY8 135 H3
Arlington Gdns STRBR DY8 * 135 H3
Arlington Gv
ALE/KHTH/YWD B14 178 D3
Arlington Rd
ALE/KHTH/YWD B14 178 D2
HHTH/SAND B71 71 H5
Armada Cl ERDW/GRVHL B23 92 B5
Armoury Rd SPARK B11 145 G1
Armside Cl BLOX/PEL WS3 18 B3
Armstead Rd COVEN WV9 12 A4
Armstrong Cl STRBR DY8 135 H1
Armstrong Dr CBROM B36 95 H5
DUNHL/THL/PER WV6 22 C4
WSLW WS2 41 E1
Armstrong Wy WLNHL WV13 39 H5
Arnhem Cl WNSFLD WV11 24 B2
Arnhem Rd WLNHL WV13 39 E5
Arnhem Wy TPTN/OCK DY4 86 A1
Arnold Cl WSLW WS2 40 D2
Arnold Gv BVILLE B30 176 B1
SHLY B90 180 B1
Arnold Rd SHLY B90 180 C1
Arnwood Cl WSLW WS2 40 D3
Arosa Dr HRBN B17 141 H4
Arps Rd CDSL WV8 10 B4
Arran Cl GTB/HAM B43 58 C5
Arran Rd BKDE/SHDE B34 112 B3
Arran Wy CBROM B36 114 A2
Arras Rd DUDN DY1 85 E4
Arrow Cl DOR/KN B93 197 E2
Arrowfield Gn
HWK/WKHTH B38 190 B1
Arrow Rd BLOX/PEL WS3 28 A4
Arrow Wk HWK/WKHTH B38 177 F4
Arsenal St BORD B9 128 A3
Arter St BHTH/HG B12 144 B1
Arthur Gunby Cl
MGN/WHC B75 * 63 F1
Arthur Harris Cl SMTHWK B66 124 D1
Arthur Pl CBHAMW B1 2 B4
Arthur Rd EDG B15 143 F1
ERDE/BCHGN B24 93 F2
HDSW B21 107 H1
TPTN/OCK DY4 69 G5
YDLY B25 146 A1
Arthur St BILS/COS WV14 * 53 H2
BKHL/PFLD WV2 52 B2
SMHTH B10 127 H3
WBROM B70 87 H5
Artillery St BORD B9 127 H2
Arton Cft ERDE/BCHGN B24 92 D4
Arundel Av DARL/WED WS10 55 H5
Arundel Crs HIA/OLT B92 164 C1
Arundel Dr OLDBY B69 103 F1
Arundel Gv
DUNHL/THL/PER WV6 35 E2
Arundel Pl SPARK B11 144 C1
Arundel Rd
ALE/KHTH/YWD B14 178 C4
SHHTH WV12 26 A3
STRBR DY8 117 G2
WOLVN WV10 12 B5
Arundel St WSL WS1 57 E1
Arun Wy WALM/CURD B76 78 C2
Asbury Rd DARL/WED WS10 72 A1
Ascot Cl LDYWD/EDGR B16 125 H2
OLDBY B69 104 C3
Ascot Dr DUDN DY1 83 H4
ETTPK/GDPK/PENN WV4 51 G4
Ascote La SHLY B90 194 A3
Ascot Gdns STRBR DY8 117 H2
Ascot Rd MOS/BIL B13 144 B5
Ash Av BHTH/HG B12 144 C2
Ashborough Dr SOLH B91 195 H1
Ashbourne Gv AST/WIT B6 * 109 E1
Ashbourne Rdg HALE B63 137 H2
Ashbourne Rd BLOX/PEL WS3 17 E4
ETTPK/GDPK/PENN WV4 52 C5
LDYWD/EDGR B16 125 F1
WOLV WV1 38 A2
Ashbourne Wy SHLY B90 180 D5
Ashbridge Ct RBRY B45 188 B2
Ashbrook Crs SOLH B91 182 A5
Ashbrook Dr RBRY B45 174 B5
Ashbrook Gv BVILLE B30 160 C2
Ashbrook Rd BVILLE B30 160 C2
Ashburn Gv WLNHL WV13 40 A3
Ashburton Rd
ALE/KHTH/YWD B14 160 D5
Ashbury Covert BVILLE B30 177 G2
Ashby Cl WASH/WDE B8 111 G3
Ashby Ct SOLH B91 182 A4
Ash Cl CDSL WV8 10 C4
Ashcombe Av
BFLD/HDSWWD B20 89 G3
Ashcombe Gdns
ERDE/BCHGN B24 93 H3
Ashcott Cl HWK/WKHTH B38 176 B3
Ash Crs
CHWD/FDBR/MGN B37 113 H3
KGSWFD DY6 100 A3
Ashcroft SMTHWK B66 * 107 E4
TPTN/OCK DY4 * 85 G4
Ashcroft Gv
BFLD/HDSWWD B20 90 D4
Ashdale Cl KGSWFD DY6 99 H1
Ashdale Dr
ALE/KHTH/YWD B14 178 C4
Ashdale Gv
LGN/SDN/BHAMAIR B26 130 C4
Ashdene Cl SCFLD/BOLD B73 62 A5
Ashdene Gdns STRBR DY8 117 G2
Ashdown Cl MOS/BIL B13 161 G1
RBRY B45 174 A3
Ashdown Dr STRBR DY8 118 A1
Ashen Cl SEDG DY3 52 A5
Ashenden Ri BDMR/CCFT WV3 35 E4
Ashenhurst Rd DUDN DY1 101 H1
Ashes Rd OLDBY B69 104 D5
Ashfern Dr WALM/CURD B76 78 B4
Ashfield Av
ALE/KHTH/YWD B14 161 F1
Ashfield Cl BLOX/PEL WS3 42 A1
Ashfield Crs DUDS DY2 120 C1
HAG/WOL DY9 136 D4
Ashfield Gv HALE B63 138 A5
WOLVN WV10 12 C4
Ashfield Rd
ALE/KHTH/YWD B14 161 F1
BDMR/CCFT WV3 35 H3
BILS/COS WV14 54 C5
WOLVN WV10 12 C4
Ashford Cl ERDE/BCHGN B24 93 H2
Ashford Dr SEDG DY3 67 G4
WALM/CURD B76 94 A1
Ashfurlong Crs MGN/WHC B75 63 E1
Ash Gn DUDN DY1 84 A1
Ash Gv BORD B9 * 127 H2

HAG/WOL DY9 .... 136 B4
SEDG DY3 .... 83 E4
Ashgrove Rd KGSTG B44 .... 74 C1
Ash Hi BDMR/CCFT WV3 .... 35 H4
Ashill Rd RBRY B45 .... 188 B1
Ashland St BDMR/CCFT WV5 ...... 6 C6
Ashlawn Crs SOLH B91 .... 163 H5

Ashleigh Dr
BFLD/HDSWWD B20 .... 90 B4
Ashleigh Gv MOS/BIL B13 ...... 161 H1
Ashleigh Rd OLDBY B69 .... 104 A1
SOLH B91 .... 181 H1
Ashley Cl EDG B15 .... 85 G6
KGSWFD DY6 .... 99 G5
STRBR DY8 .... 134 C5
Ashley Gdns CDSL WV8 .... 10 B3
WASH/WDE B8 .... 110 B5
Ashley Mt
DUNHL/THL/PER WV6 .... 21 H5
Ashley Rd BLOX/PEL WS3 .... 26 D1
ERDW/GRVHL B23 .... 92 C5
ETTPK/GDPK/PENN WV4 .... 51 E5
SMTHWK B66 .... 107 E3
Ashley St BILS/COS WV14 .... 54 A2
BLKHTH/ROWR B65 .... 122 A3
Ashley Ter SLYOAK B29 * 159 G1
Ashmead Dr RBRY B45 .... 188 C4
Ashmead Gv ERDE/BCHGN B24 .. 93 E4
Ashmead Ri RBRY B45 .... 188 C4
Ash Ms ACGN B27 .... 146 C2
Ashmole Rd WBROM B70 .... 70 D4
Ashmore Av WNSFLD WV11 ..... 25 G1
Ashmore Lake Rd SHHTH WV12 .. 39 H1
Ashmore Lake Wy
SHHTH WV12 .... 39 H1
Ashmore Rd BVILLE B30 .... 159 H5

Ashold Farm Rd
ERDE/BCHGN B24 .... 93 G4
Asholme Cl CBROM B36 .... 111 G2
Ashorne Cl HLGN/YWD B28 .... 163 F3
Ash Rd DARL/WED WS10 .... 55 H3
DUDN DY1 .... 84 B3
TPTN/OCK DY4 .... 85 E2
WASH/WDE B8 .... 110 B5
Ashstead Cl WALM/CURD B76 .. 78 D5
Ash St BDMR/CCFT WV3 .... 6 B5
BILS/COS WV14 .... 54 A5
BLOX/PEL WS3 .... 27 H1
CDYHTH B64 .... 121 E2
Ashted Circ CBHAMNE B4 ...... 109 G5
Ash Ter OLDBY B69 .... 104 A2
Ashton Cft LDYWD/EDGR B16 .. 126 A2
SOLH B91 .... 181 G4
Ashton Rd ER RUSH/SHEL WS4 .. 118 C1
Ashton Park Dr BRLYHL DY5 ..... 119 E3
Ashton Rd YDLY B25 .... 129 H1
Ashtree Cl BILS/COS WV14 ...... 54 D5
Ashtree Ri BLOX/PEL WS3 .... 18 A4
Ash Tree Rd BVILLE B30 .... 160 A4
Ashtree Rd OLDBY B69 .... 104 B1
Ashurst Rd WALM/CURD B76 .... 78 B5
Ashville Av BRDE/SHDE B34 .... 112 B2
Ashville Dr HALE B63 .... 138 C2

Ashwater Dr
ALE/KHTH/YWD B14 .... 177 H3
Ash Wy ERDW/GRVHL B23 .... 76 A3
SPARK B11 .... 144 D2
Ashwell Dr SHLY B90 .... 180 D1
Ashwells Gv COVEN WV9 .... 11 H5
Ashwin Rd HDSW B21 .... 107 H2
Ashwood Av STRBR DY8 .... 117 G2
Ashwood Cl FOAKS/STRLY B74 .. 45 G5
OLDBY B69 .... 104 D5

Ashwood Dr
CHWD/FDBR/MGN B37 .... 132 D1
Ashwood Gv
ETTPK/GDPK/PENN WV4 .... 51 G3
Ashwood Lower La
KGSWFD DY6 .... 98 C4
KINVER DY7 .... 116 D1
Ashworth Rd PBAR/PBCH B42 .. 74 B2
Askew Bridge Rd SEDG DY3 * ... 82 D3
Askew Cl SEDG DY3 .... 66 C3
Aspbury Cft CBROM B36 .... 95 F5
Aspen Cl ACGN B27 .... 146 B5
WALM/CURD B76 .... 78 B1

Aspen Dr
CHWD/FDBR/MGN B37 .... 132 C4
Aspen Gdns
BFLD/HDSWWD B20 .... 90 B5
Aspen Gv BORD B9 .... 129 E1
HLYWD B47 .... 192 D3
SHHTH WV12 .... 26 C3
Aspen Wy BDMR/CCFT WV3 ...... 6 A6
Asquith Dr OLDBY B69 .... 104 C1
Asquith Rd WASH/WDE B8 ...... 111 F4
Asra Cl SMTHWK B66 .... 106 C1
Astbury Av SMTHWKW B67 ...... 124 B1
Astbury Cl BLOX/PEL WS3 .... 16 C5
WOLV WV1 .... 38 A4
Aster Av EDG B15 * 12 A4
Aster Wy DSYBK/YTR WS5 ...... 57 G5
Astley Av RMSLY B62 .... 139 H1
Astley Cl TPTN/OCK DY4 .... 70 B5
Astley Rd HDSW B21 .... 89 F5
Aston Brook Gn AST/WIT B6 * .. 109 F4
Aston Brook St AST/WIT B6 ..... 109 E3
Aston Brook St East
AST/WIT B6 .... 109 F4
Aston Bury EDG B15 .... 125 G4
Aston Church Rd
VAUX/NECH B7 .... 110 A2
Aston Cl BILS/COS WV14 .... 54 D4
Aston Hall Rd AST/WIT B6 ..... 109 G1
Aston La BFLD/HDSWWD B20 .... 91 E4
Aston Manor Cl
BFLD/HDSWWD B20 * 91 E4
Aston Rd BLOX/PEL WS3 .... 85 G5
VAUX/NECH B7 .... 3 J1
Aston Rd North AST/WIT B6 .... 109 F3
Astons Cl BRLYHL DY5 .... 119 F5
Astons Fold BRLYHL DY5 .... 119 F5
Aston St BDMR/CCFT WV5 .... 36 C5
CBHAMNE B4 .... 3 J2
TPTN/OCK DY4 .... 70 A5
Astor Dr MOS/BIL B13 .... 162 A1
Astoria Cl SHHTH WV12 .... 26 B1

Astor Rd FOAKS/STRLY B74 ..... 45 G4
KGSWFD DY6 .... 100 B4
Athelney Ct BLOX/PEL WS3 * ... 18 A4
Athelstan Gv
DUNHL/THL/PER WV6 .... 20 C5
Atherstone Cl SHLY B90 .... 179 G3
Atherstone Rd WOLV WV1 .... 38 B3
Athlone Rd DSYBK/YTR WS5 .... 43 E5
Athol Cl RIDG/WDGT B32 ...... 157 H2
Athole St BHTH/HG B12 .... 127 G5
Atlantic Rd KGSTG B44 .... 75 F3
Atlantic Wy DARL/WED WS10 ... 70 C2
Atlas Cft WOLV WV10 .... 23 E4
Atlas Est AST/WIT B6 * 91 G4
Atlas Gv WBROM B70 .... 86 D5

Attenborough Cl
LOZ/NWT B19 .... 108 D4
Attingham Dr DUDN DY1 .... 84 B4
GTB/HAM B43 .... 73 F1
Attleborough La
CSHL/WTROR B46 .... 96 A5
Attlee Cl OLDBY B69 .... 86 B4
Attlee Crs BILS/COS WV14 .... 69 E1
Attlee Rd WSLW WS2 .... 26 D5
Attwell Pk BDMR/CCFT WV3 .... 50 C6
Attwell Rd TPTN/OCK DY4 .... 69 F2
Attwood Cl WASH/WDE B8 .... 110 C3
Attwood Gdns
ETTPK/GDPK/PENN WV4 .... 52 C3
Attwood St HAG/WOL DY9 .... 136 D2
HALE B63 .... 138 B2
Aubrey Rd RIDG/WDGT B32 .... 124 A5
SMTH B10 .... 128 D5
Auchinleck Sq EDG B15 * 126 B3
Auckland Dr CBROM B36 .... 113 H1
Auckland Rd KGSWFD DY6 ..... 100 B5
SMTHWKW B67 .... 106 A4
SPARK B11 .... 127 G5
Auden Ct DUNHL/THL/PER WV6 .. 34 D1
Audley Rd STETCH B33 .... 112 A5
Augusta Rd ACGN B27 .... 146 B3
MOS/BIL B13 .... 144 A3
Augusta Rd East MOS/BIL B13 .. 144 B3
Augusta St WSNGN B18 .... 2 C1
Augustine Gv FOAKS/STRLY B74 .. 31 E5
WSNGN B18 .... 108 B3
Augustus Cl CSHL/WTROR B46 .. 97 F5
Augustus Ct EDG B15 .... 125 H4
Augustus Rd EDG B15 .... 125 G4
Augustus St WSLW WS2 .... 4 C4
Ault St WBROM B70 .... 87 H5
Austcliff Dr SOLH B91 .... 182 A5
Austen Pl EDG B15 .... 126 B4
Austin Cl ACGN B27 .... 146 D3
DUDN DY1 .... 83 H4
Austin Cft CBROM B36 .... 95 G5
Austin Ri NFLD/LBR B31 .... 189 F1
Austin Rd HDSW B21 .... 89 E3
Austin St DUNHL/THL/PER WV6 .. 36 D1
Austin Wy BFLD/HDSWWD B20 .. 90 A1
Austrey Cl SLYOAK B29 * 158 C2
Austrey Rd KGSWFD DY6 ...... 100 C4
Austy Cl CBROM B36 .... 112 A1
Autherley Jct COVEN WV9 * 22 C1
Autumn Berry Gv SEDG DY3 ..... 67 G5
Autumn Cl RUSH/SHEL WS4 ..... 30 D5
Autumn Dr ER RUSH/SHEL WS4 .. 15 H5
SEDG DY3 .... 66 B4
Autumn Gv LOZ/NWT B19 ...... 108 C3
Avalon Cl ERDE/BCHGN B24 .... 93 F2
Avebury Gv BVILLE B30 .... 160 C3
Avebury Rd BVILLE B30 .... 160 C2
Ave Maria Cl CDYHTH B64 ..... 121 E3
Avenbury Dr SOLH B91 .... 167 E5
Avenue Albert HOCK/TIA B94 .. 198 A4
Avenue Cl DOR/KN B93 .... 197 E5
VAUX/NECH B7 .... 109 G4
Avenue Rd
ALE/KHTH/YWD B14 .... 160 D2
BDMR/CCFT WV3 .... 109 G5
BILS/COS WV14 .... 68 C3
BLKHTH/ROWR B65 .... 122 B3
DARL/WED WS10 .... 55 H3
DOR/KN B93 .... 197 E5
DUDN DY1 .... 101 G3
ERDW/GRVHL B23 .... 92 D2
HDSW B21 .... 89 F4
The Avenue ACGN B27 .... 146 D4
BDMR/CCFT WV3 .... 35 F5
BLKHTH/ROWR B65 .... 121 G1
DARL/WED WS10 .... 55 H2
ETTPK/GDPK/PENN WV4 .... 51 E4
KIDD DY10 .... 168 B3
SEDG DY3 .... 66 D4
WALM/CURD B76 .... 77 G3
Averill Pl
LGN/SDN/BHAMAIR B26 .... 130 C4
Avern Cl TPTN/OCK DY4 .... 69 H5
Aversley Rd HLW/WKHTH B38 .. 176 B5
Avery Cft CVALE B35 .... 94 B3
Avery Dell BVILLE B30 * 160 B5
Avery Dr ACGN B27 .... 146 C3
Avery Myers Cl
LGLYGN/QTN B68 .... 105 H4
Avery Rd SCFLD/BOLD B75 ..... 76 A1
Aviemore Crs GTB/HAM B43 .... 59 F4
Avington Cl SEDG DY3 .... 66 B4
Avion Cl WSL WS1 .... 57 F1
Avocet Cl STETCH B33 .... 130 A1
Avon Cl BRLYHL DY5 .... 100 D2
Avon Crs BLOX/PEL WS3 .... 28 C1
Avondale Cl KGSWFD DY6 ..... 100 A1

Avondale Rd
DUNHL/THL/PER WV6 .... 36 B2
SPARK B11 .... 145 G5
Avon Dr CBROM B36 .... 115 H2
MOS/BIL B13 .... 162 B1
WLNHL WV13 .... 40 A3
Avon Gv DSYBK/YTR WS5 .... 57 G5
Avon Ms STRBR DY8 * 117 F2
Avon Rd BLOX/PEL WS3 .... 28 A1
HALE B63 .... 137 F2
SHLY B90 .... 180 D5
STRBR DY8 .... 135 F4
Avon St SPARK B11 .... 145 E2

Avro Wy CVALE B35 .... 94 D3
Awbridge Br WMBN WV5 .... 64 C1
Awbridge Rd DUDS DY2 .... 120 C1
Awefields Crs SMTHWKW B67 .. 105 H5
Awinakers Gv BLOX/PEL WS3 .. 27 G3
Axletree Wy DARL/WED WS10 ... 56 B2
Ayala Cft CBROM B36 .... 112 A1
Aylesbury Cl HOCK/TIA B94 .... 198 A5
Aylesbury Crs KGSTG B44 .... 75 G3
Aylesbury Rd HOCK/TIA B94 ... 198 B4
Aylesford Cl SEDG DY3 .... 66 D1

Aylesford Dr
CHWD/FDBR/MGN B37 .... 132 A5
FOAKS/STRLY B74 .... 32 C5
Aylesford Rd HDSW B21 .... 89 E5
Aylesmore Cl HIA/OLT B92 .... 164 A2
RIDG/WDGT B32 .... 157 G1
Ayre Rd ERDE/BCHGN B24 ...... 93 F2
Ayres Cl BXDE/SHDE B34 ...... 113 G5
Ayrshire Cl CBROM B36 .... 111 H1
Ayrton Cl DUNHL/THL/PER WV6 .. 35 E1
Azalea Cl CDSL WV8 .... 10 D4
Azalea Gv BORD B9 .... 128 D2
Aziz Isaac Cl
LGLYGN/QTN B68 * 105 G3

B

Babington Rd HDSW B21 .... 107 G2
Bablake Cft HIA/OLT B92 ...... 164 C1
Babors Fld BILS/COS WV14 ...... 53 E5
Babworth Cl COVEN WV9 .... 12 A5
Baccabox La HLYWD B47 .... 192 A1
Bacchus Rd WSNGN B18 .... 107 H4
Bache St WBROM B70 .... 87 G5
Bach Mill Dr HLGN/YWD B28 .. 179 F2
Backhouse La WNSFLD WV11 .. 38 C1
Back La ALDR WS9 .... 31 E3
LICHS WS14 .... 19 H1
SHLY B90 .... 194 A3
Back Rd HWK/WKHTH B38 .... 176 D3
KGSWFD DY6 .... 99 G1
Baddesley Rd HIA/OLT B92 .... 147 E5
Bader Rd DUNHL/THL/PER WV6 .. 34 B2
WSLW WS2 .... 40 D3
Bader Wk CVALE B35 .... 94 B4
Badger Cl SHLY B90 .... 194 D4
Badger Dr WOLV WV10 .... 37 F1
Badgers Bank Rd
FOAKS/STRLY B74 .... 32 D5
Badgers Cl BLOX/PEL WS3 ...... 18 A2
Badgers Cft RMSLY B62 .... 121 H5
Badger St HAG/WOL DY9 ...... 136 C1
SEDG DY3 .... 83 G1
Badminton Cl DUDN DY1 ...... 83 H5
Badon Covert
ALE/KHTH/YWD B14 .... 177 H3
Badsey Cl NFLD/LBR B31 ...... 176 A1
Badsey Rd OLDBY B69 .... 104 B4
Baggeridge Cl SEDG DY3 .... 66 C5
Baggott St BKHL/PFLD WV2 .... 3 H5
Baginton Cl SOLH B91 .... 164 D5
Baginton Rd CVALE B35 .... 94 D2
Bagley St HAG/WOL DY9 ...... 136 A1
Bagnall Cl YDLY B25 .... 146 D1
Bagnall Rd BILS/COS WV14 ..... 53 G2
Bagnall St BLOX/PEL WS3 .... 27 G3
TPTN/OCK DY4 .... 70 A2
WBROM B70 .... 88 A4
Bagnall Wk BRLYHL DY5 .... 119 F3
Bagnell Rd MOS/BIL B13 ..... 161 F5
Bagot Cl CBHAMNE B4 .... 109 H5
Bagridge Cl BDMR/CCFT WV3 .. 35 F5
Bagridge Rd BDMR/CCFT WV3 .. 35 F5
Bagshawe Cft
ERDW/GRVHL B23 .... 76 B4
Bagshaw Rd STETCH B33 ..... 130 A1
Bailey Rd BILS/COS WV14 .... 53 F1
Bailey St WBROM B70 .... 87 E2
WOLV WV1 .... 7 J5
Baker Av BILS/COS WV14 .... 53 E4
Baker House Gv GTB/HAM B43 .. 73 F4
Baker Rd BILS/COS WV14 .... 54 A5
Bakers Gdns CDSL WV8 .... 10 A5
Baker's La ALDR WS9 .... 30 B4
DOR/KN B93 .... 199 G2
FOAKS/STRLY B74 .... 60 B3
Baker St HDSW B21 .... 107 H1
LOZ/NWT B19 .... 108 A3
SPARK B11 .... 145 E5
TPTN/OCK DY4 .... 85 E2
WBROM B70 .... 87 F3
Bakers Wy WLNHL WV13 .... 119 F3
Bakewell Cl BLOX/PEL WS3 ...... 17 E4
Balaams La NFLD/LBR B31 .... 174 B4
Balaams Wood Dr
NFLD/LBR B31 .... 174 B4
Balaclava Rd
ALE/KHTH/YWD B14 .... 161 E2
Balcaskie Cl EDG B15 .... 125 G5
Balden Rd RIDG/WDGT B32 ... 124 A5
Baldmoor Lake Rd
ERDW/GRVHL B23 .... 76 D4
Bald's La HAG/WOL DY9 .... 136 D2
Baldwin Cl OLDBY B69 .... 86 B4
Baldwin Rd BVILLE B30 .... 177 E2
Baldwins La HLGN/YWD B28 .. 179 H1
Baldwin St BILS/COS WV14 ..... 54 A4
SMTHWK B66 .... 106 D5
Baldwin Wy SEDG DY3 .... 80 C4
Balfour Crs
DUNHL/THL/PER WV6 .... 36 B1
Balfour Dr OLDBY B69 .... 86 B5
Balfour Rd KGSWFD DY6 ...... 100 A1
Balfour St BHTH/HG B12 ...... 144 A1
Balham Gv KGSTG B44 .... 75 G1
Balking Cl BILS/COS WV14 ...... 54 B5
Ballantine Rd COVEN WV9 ...... 11 H5
Ballard Crs DUDS DY2 .... 102 D3
Ballard Rd DUDS DY2 .... 102 D4
Ballard Wk
CHWD/FDBR/MGN B37 .... 114 A3
Ballot St SMTHWK B66 .... 106 D4
Ball La WOLV WV10 .... 12 C1
Ballot St SMTHWK B66 .... 106 D4
Balls Hi WSL WS1 .... 5 G3
Balls St WSL WS1 .... 5 G3

Balmain Crs WNSFLD WV11 ..... 24 B2
Balmoral Cl RMSLY B62 .... 121 H5
RUSH/SHEL WS4 .... 29 F3
Balmoral Dr SHHTH WV12 ...... 25 H5
WMBN WV5 .... 65 E2
Balmoral Rd CBROM B36 ..... 114 A2
ERDW/GRVHL B23 .... 92 D1
ETTPK/GDPK/PENN WV4 .... 51 G3
FOAKS/STRLY B74 .... 32 D5
RIDG/WDGT B32 .... 157 E1
STRBR DY8 .... 117 G2
Balmoral Wy
BLKHTH/ROWR B65 .... 104 B5
WSLW WS2 .... 41 E1
Balsall Heath Rd DIG/EDG B5 .. 127 E5
Baltimore Rd PBAR/PBCH B42 .. 90 A1
Balvenie Wy DUDN DY1 .... 83 H5
Bamber Cl BDMR/CCFT WV3 .... 36 A5
Bamford Cl BLOX/PEL WS3 ...... 17 E4
Bamford Rd BDMR/CCFT WV3 .. 36 C5
BLOX/PEL WS3 .... 17 E4
Bampfylde Pl PBAR/PBCH B42 *. 74 C4
Banbury Cft
CHWD/FDBR/MGN B37 .... 131 H2
Banbury St DIG/EDG B5 .... 3 J5
Bancroft Cl BILS/COS WV14 .... 68 B4
Bandywood Rd KGSTG B44 ..... 60 A4
Banfield Av DARL/WED WS10 ... 55 E4
Banfield Rd DARL/WED WS10 ... 55 F4
Bangham Pit Rd
NFLD/LBR B31 .... 174 B4
Bangor Rd BORD B9 .... 128 B2
Bangor Vls DARL/WED WS10 * .. 55 H2
Bankdale Rd WASH/WDE B8 ... 111 F5
Bank Farm Cl HAG/WOL DY9 .. 153 E1
Bankfield Rd BILS/COS WV14 ... 53 H3
TPTN/OCK DY4 .... 70 A3
Banklands Rd DUDS DY2 ...... 103 E3
Bank Rd DUDS DY2 .... 102 A5
SEDG DY3 .... 83 E3
Bankside GTB/HAM B43 .... 73 G4
MOS/BIL B13 .... 145 F5
Bankside Crs FOAKS/STRLY B74 .. 62 B1
Bankside Wy ALDR WS9 .... 19 H5
Banks St WLNHL WV13 .... 39 G3
Bank St ALE/KHTH/YWD B14 .. 161 E2
BILS/COS WV14 .... 68 D5
BRLYHL DY5 .... 101 F5
DUDS DY2 .... 120 C3
HAG/WOL DY9 .... 136 D2
WOLV WV10 .... 23 G5
WSL WS1 .... 5 G4
Bankwell St BRLYHL DY5 .... 101 F5
Bannerlea Rd
CHWD/FDBR/MGN B37 .... 113 H4
Banner La STETCH B33 .... 131 F3
Banners Ct SCFLD/BOLD B75 * . 60 D5
Banners Gate Rd
SCFLD/BOLD B75 .... 60 D5
Banners Gv ERDW/GRVHL B23 .. 77 H4
Banners La HALE B63 .... 137 H1
Banners Wk KGSTG B44 .... 75 H1
Bannister Rd DARL/WED WS10 .. 70 B1
Bannister St CDYHTH B64 ..... 102 D5
Banstead Cl BKHL/PFLD WV2 .. 52 C1
Bantams Cl STETCH B33 ...... 131 E2
Bantock Av BDMR/CCFT WV3 .. 36 B5
Bantock Gdns
BDMR/CCFT WV3 .... 36 A4
The Bantocks WBROM B70 ...... 71 E5
Banton Cl ERDW/GRVHL B23 ... 76 B3
Baptist Cl
LGN/SDN/BHAMAIR B26 .... 148 A3
Baptist End Rd DUDS DY2 .... 102 C4
Barbara Rd HLGN/YWD B28 .. 179 G2
Barbel Dr WOLV WV10 .... 38 B1
Barbers La HIA/OLT B92 ...... 166 D4
Barbourne Cl SOLH B91 ...... 195 H1
Barbrook Dr BRLYHL DY5 ..... 118 C5
Barchester Rd DOR/KN B93 .. 197 E4
SLYOAK B29 .... 158 C1
Barclay Rd SMTHWKW B67 ... 124 A3
Barcroft WLNHL WV13 .... 39 H2
Bardenholme Gdns
HAG/WOL DY9 .... 136 B4
Bardfield Cl PBAR/PBCH B42 .. 73 H3
Bardon Dr SHLY B90 .... 180 D2
Bardwell Cl CDSL WV8 .... 22 B2
Barford Cl DARL/WED WS10 ... 40 A5
WALM/CURD B76 .... 63 F3
Barford Crs HWK/WKHTH B38 . 177 G5
Barford Rd SHLY B90 .... 180 D3
HDSW B21 .... 107 G5
Barford St DIG/EDG B5 .... 127 F5
Bargate Dr
DUNHL/THL/PER WV6 .... 36 C1
Bargery Rd WNSFLD WV11 ..... 25 G1
Barham Cl SHLY B90 .... 195 G3
Barker Rd FOAKS/STRLY B74 ... 62 B1
Barker St LGLYGN/QTN B68 ... 105 E5
LOZ/NWT B19 .... 108 B2
Bark Piece RIDG/WDGT B32 .. 140 C4
Barlands Cft BKDE/SHDE B34 .. 112 D5
Barley Cl ALDR WS9 .... 31 E4
Barley Cl ALDR WS9 .... 31 E4
CDSL WV8 .... 22 A1
SEDG DY3 .... 67 H4
Barley Cft
DUNHL/THL/PER WV6 .... 34 B2
Barleyfield Rw WSL WS1 .... 4 E6
Barlow Cl LGLYGN/QTN B68 .. 123 E1
RBRY B45 .... 173 G5
Barlow Dr WBROM B70 .... 88 A5
Barlow Rd DARL/WED WS10 ... 56 A3
Barlows Rd EDG B15 .... 142 B2
Barmouth Cl SHHTH WV12 .... 26 A4
Barnabas Rd ERDW/GRVHL B23 .. 92 D1

Barnaby Sq WOLVN WV10 .... 13 F3
Barnard Cl
CHWD/FDBR/MGN B37 .... 132 D3
Barnard Pl BKHL/PFLD WV2 .... 52 B1
Barnard Rd MGN/WHC B75 .... 63 E1
WNSFLD WV11 .... 25 F1
Barn Av SEDG DY3 .... 67 E4
Barnard Cl WALM/CURD B76 .. 78 A1
HALE B63 .... 136 A3
Barn Cft RIDG/WDGT B32 .... 158 A1
Barncroft Rd OLDBY B69 ...... 103 G1
Barncroft St WBROM B70 ...... 71 E5
Barnes Cl STETCH B33 .... 131 G2
Barnes Hi SLYOAK B29 .... 141 F5
Barnes Meadow Pl
BILS/COS WV14 .... 68 B5
Barnesville Cl SMTH B10 ..... 129 E4
Barnet Rd ERDW/GRVHL B23 .. 92 B1
Barnett Cl BILS/COS WV14 ...... 53 H4
KGSWFD DY6 .... 99 H5
Barnett Gn STRBR DY8 .... 99 H4
Barnett La KGSWFD DY6 .... 99 H4
STRBR DY8 .... 117 H1
Barnett Rd WLNHL WV13 ...... 39 E4
Barnetts La BRWNH WS8 .... 9 G3
Barnett St STRBR DY8 .... 117 H1
TPTN/OCK DY4 .... 69 G5
Barney Cl TPTN/OCK DY4 .... 85 F3
Barnfield Av BILS/COS WV14 .. 54 C1
Barnfield Dr HIA/OLT B92 .... 165 H4
Barnfield Gv
BFLD/HDSWWD B20 .... 89 G1
Barnfield Rd RMSLY B62 ..... 122 B5
TPTN/OCK DY4 .... 69 E4
WOLV WV1 .... 38 A3
Barnford Cl SMTH B10 * 128 A3
Barnford Crs LGLYGN/QTN B68 . 123 E1
Barnfordhill Cl
LGLYGN/QTN B68 .... 105 F3
Barn Gn BDMR/CCFT WV3 ...... 51 G1
Barnhurst La CDSL WV8 .... 11 F4
Barn La HDSW B21 .... 107 G2
HIA/OLT B92 .... 147 E3
MOS/BIL B13 .... 145 F1
Barn Meadow YDLY B25 .... 129 H3
Barnmoor Ri SOLH B91 .... 165 E3
Barn Owl Dr BLOX/PEL WS3 .. 17 H5
Barnpark Covert
ALE/KHTH/YWD B14 .... 177 G3
Barn Piece RIDG/WDGT B32 .. 140 B3
Barnsbury Av
CSCFLD/WYGN B72 .... 77 G5
Barns Cft FOAKS/STRLY B74 ... 19 F5
Barns Cft RIDG/WDGT B32 .... 45 H2
Barnsdale Crs NFLD/LBR B31 .. 175 E1
Barns La ALDR WS9 .... 29 F3
Barnsley Rd HRBN B17 .... 124 C3
Barnstaple Rd SMTHWK B66 .. 106 D4
Barn St DIG/EDG B5 .... 5 K6
Barnswood Cl HALE B63 ...... 137 G2
Barnt Green Rd RBRY B45 .... 188 C5
Barnwood Rd CDSL WV8 ...... 22 A1
RIDG/WDGT B32 .... 141 E1
Barons Cl HRBN B17 .... 123 H5
Barrack Cl HALE B63 .... 137 F1
Barrack La HALE B63 .... 137 F1
Barracks Cl BLOX/PEL WS3 ..... 28 B3
Barracks La BLOX/PEL WS3 .... 27 H2
Barrack St VAUX/NECH B7 .... 109 G5
WBROM B70 .... 71 E3
Barra Cft CVALE B35 .... 94 D2
Barrack La BLOX/PEL WS3 ...... 28 A4
Barracks Cl BLOX/PEL WS3 ..... 85 E5
Barratts Rd HWK/WKHTH B38 .. 177 E4
Barr Common Cl ALDR WS9 .... 44 B2
Barr Common Rd ALDR WS9 .. 44 B2
Barrett Cl LDYWD/EDGR B16 .. 107 G5
Barrhill Cl GTB/HAM B43 ...... 73 G1
Barrington Cl DSYBK/YTR WS5 . 57 G5
WOLVN WV10 .... 23 E1
Barrington Rd HIA/OLT B92 .. 147 E5
RBRY B45 .... 187 G1
Barr Lakes La DSYBK/YTR WS5 . 58 C1
Barron Rd NFLD/LBR B31 ..... 175 H2
Barrow Hill Rd SEDG DY3 ...... 81 F5
Barrows La LGN/SDN/BHAMAIR B26 . 147 G2
Barrows Rd SPARK B11 .... 145 E1
Barrow Wk DIG/EDG B5 .... 127 E5
Barrs Crs CDYHTH B64 .... 121 F4
Barrs Rd CDYHTH B64 .... 121 F4
Barrs St LGLYGN/QTN B68 .... 105 E5
Barr St LOZ/NWT B19 .... 108 C4
SEDG DY3 .... 83 E5
Barry Rd DSYBK/YTR WS5 ...... 57 H5
Barsham Cl DIG/EDG B5 .... 143 H1
Barsham Dr BRLYHL DY5 ...... 119 E4
Barston La BALSH/SOLH B91 .. 182 D3
Barston Rd LGLYGN/QTN B68 . 140 B1
Bartholomew Rw DIG/EDG B5 .. 3 J4
Bartholomew St DIG/EDG B5 ... 3 J5
Bartic Av KGSWFD DY6 .... 99 H5
Bartleet Rd SMTHWK B66 .... 105 H4
Bartlett Cl TPTN/OCK DY4 ...... 69 H4
Bartley Cl HIA/OLT B92 .... 147 F5
Bartley Dr NFLD/LBR B31 ..... 158 A2
Bartley Ms NFLD/LBR B31 .... 158 A2
Bartley Woods
RIDG/WDGT B32 .... 140 B5
Barton Cft HLGN/YWD B28 .... 179 H1
Barton Dr DOR/KN B93 .... 197 H4
Barton La KGSWFD DY6 .... 99 G1
Barton Lodge Rd
HLGN/YWD B28 .... 179 G1
Barton Rd
ETTPK/GDPK/PENN WV4 .... 52 D4
Bartons Bank AST/WIT B6 ..... 109 E2
Barton St WBROM B70 .... 87 F4
Bar Wk ALDR WS9 .... 30 C1
Barwell Cl DOR/KN B93 .... 196 C4
Barwell Rd BORD B9 .... 128 B1
Barwick St CBHAMNW B3 .... 3 F4
Basalt Cl WSLW WS2 .... 41 E1
Basdar Gv NFLD/LBR B31 ..... 175 E1
Basil Gv NFLD/LBR B31 .... 175 E1
Basil Rd NFLD/LBR B31 .... 175 E1
Baslow Cl BLOX/PEL WS3 ...... 16 D4
STETCH B33 .... 112 A5

Baslow Rd BLOX/PEL WS3......16 D4
Basons La LCLYGN/QTN B68...105 G4
Bassano Rd
  BLKHTH/ROWR B65.........122 A3
Bassenthwaite Ct KGSWFD DY6..99 H3
Bassett Cl
  ETTPK/GDPK/PENN WV4.....50 C2
  SHHTH WV12................40 B1
  WALM/CURD B76............80 B5
Bassett Rd SMHTH B10......127 H4
Bassett Rd DARL/WED WS10...71 G1
  HALE B63...................137 E1
Bassetts Gv
  CHWD/FDBR/MGN B37.....113 G4
Bassett St WSLW WS2.........41 G3
Bassnage Rd HALE B63......138 A5
Batchcroft BILS/COS WV14....53 H5
  DARL/WED WS10............40 B5
Batchelor Cl STRBR DY8.....118 B4
Bateman Rd SCFLD/BOLD B75..77 F2
Bateman Rd
  CSHL/WTROR B46...........97 F5
Batemans La HLYWD B47.....192 A3
Bates Cl WALM/CURD B76......78 C4
Bates Gv WNSFLD WV11......24 A5
Bate St
  ETTPK/GDPK/PENN WV4....53 E5
  WSLW WS2...................4 D1
Bath Av WOLV WV1............6 D2
Batheaston Cl
  HWK/WKHTH B38...........190 B1
Bath Meadow HALE B63......138 A2
Bath Pas DIG/EDG B5..........3 G4
Bath Rd BDMR/CCFT WV3......6 C4
  BRLYHL DY5................120 A2
  STRBR DY8.................135 F1
  TPTN/OCK DY4.............85 G1
  WSL WS1.....................5 F4
Bath Rw BHTH/HG B12......144 A2
Batmans Hill Rd
  BILS/COS WV14.............69 E1
Batson Ri STRBR DY8........118 C4
Battenhall Av HRBN B17.....141 G2
Battery Wy SPARK B11......145 G3
Battlefield Hl WMBN WV5....65 F4
Battlefield La WMBN WV5....65 F5
Bavaro Gdns BRLYHL DY5...120 A2
Baverstock Rd
  ALE/KHTH/YWD B14.......178 C5
  WALM/CURD B76...........78 B2
Baxter Rd BRLYHL DY5......119 E2
Baxters Gn SHLY B90........180 B5
Baxters Rd SHLY B90........180 B5
Bay Av BILS/COS WV14......54 B4
Bay St BILS/COS WV14......68 C3
Bayford Av
  LGN/SDN/BHAMAIR B26...148 A3
Bayley Crs DARL/WED WS10...40 A5
Bayleys La TPTN/OCK DY4....70 A4
Baylie St STRBR DY8.........135 F3
Baylis Rd WNSFLD WV11......25 F2
Bayliss Av
  ETTPK/GDPK/PENN WV4....68 A1
Bayliss Cl BILS/COS WV14....53 C1
  NFLD/LBR B31..............158 D5
Baynton Rd SHHTH WV12.....26 A3
Bayston Av BDMR/CCFT WV3...36 A5
Bayston Rd
  ALE/KHTH/YWD B14.......178 A1
Bayswater Rd
  BFLD/HDSWWD B20.........90 D5
  SEDG DY3...................83 F4
Baytree Cl BLOX/PEL WS3....16 C5
Bay Tree Cl HWK/WKHTH B38..176 B5
Baytree Rd BLOX/PEL WS3....16 C5
Baywell Cl SHLY B90........195 G1
Beach Av BILS/COS WV14....68 A1
Beach Brook Cl SPARK B11..144 D2
Beachburn Wy
  BFLD/HDSWWD B20.........90 A3
Beach Cl NFLD/LBR B31......158 D5
Beachcroft Rd KGSWFD DY6...99 G1
Beach Dr HALE B63..........138 C2
Beach Rd BILS/COS WV14....53 H1
  SPARK B11.................144 D2
Beach St HALE B63..........138 C2
Beachwood Av KGSWFD DY6...81 G5
Beacon Cl GTB/HAM B43......73 H2
  RBRY B45..................187 H3
  SMTHWK B66...............106 C2
Beacon Dr WSL WS1...........5 J7
Beacon Hl ALDR WS9.........44 C4
  AST/WIT B6.................109 E1
  RBRY B45..................187 G3
Beacon La BRGRVE B60......187 F5
  SEDG DY3...................67 G2
Beacon Ri ALDR WS9.........44 B2
  HAG/WOL DY9..............136 B3
  SEDG DY3...................67 G2
Beacon Rd ALDR WS9.........59 F1
  DSYBK/YTR WS5.............58 B3
  KGSTG B44..................60 C4
  SCFLD/BOLD B75............77 E2
  SHHTH WV12................26 A2
Beaconsfield Av
  ETTPK/GDPK/PENN WV4....52 B3
Beaconsfield Cl WSL WS1....5 K6
Beaconsfield Crs
  BHTH/HG B12 *............144 A2
Beaconsfield Dr
  ETTPK/GDPK/PENN WV4....52 B3
Beaconsfield Rd
  BHTH/HG B12..............144 A3
  FOAKS/STRLY B74..........62 B1
Beaconsfield St
  HHTH/SAND B71............87 H1
Beacon St BILS/COS WV14....67 H2
  WSL WS1.....................5 J5
Beacon Vw RBRY B45........187 H2

Beacon View Dr
  FOAKS/STRLY B74..........60 B4
Beacon View Rd
  HHTH/SAND B71............72 B1
Beacon Wy ALDR WS9........19 G4
  RUSH/SHEL WS4............42 D1
Beakes Rd SMTHWK B67....124 B1
Beaks Hill Rd
  HWK/WKHTH B38..........176 A4
Beak St CBHAMW B1..........3 F6
Beale Cl CVALE B35.........94 C4
Beales St AST/WIT B6.......109 H1
Beale St STRBR DY8........135 F2
Bealeys Av WNSFLD WV11...24 C2
Bealeys La BLOX/PEL WS3...16 C5
Beamans Cl HIA/OLT B92...147 G5
Beaminster Rd SOLH B91...181 F1
Bean Cft RDG/WDGT B32...140 C5
Bean Rd DUDS DY2..........102 D1
  TPTN/OCK DY4.............85 E1
Beardmore Rd
  CSCFLD/WYGN B72.........77 G3
Bearing Dr WNSFLD WV11....39 E1
Bearley Cft SHLY B90.......180 C5
Bearmore Rd CDYHTH B64...121 E3
Bearnett Dr
  ETTPK/GDPK/PENN WV4...65 G3
Bearnett La WMBN WV5......65 G3
Bearwood Rd SMTHWK B66..124 C2
Beasley Gv GTB/HAM B43....74 B2
Beaton Cl WLNHL WV13......39 E3
Beaton Rd FOAKS/STRLY B74..47 E2
Beatrice St BLOX/PEL WS3...27 G4
Beatrice Wk OLDBY B69.....85 G4
Beaubrook Gdns KGSWFD DY6..117 H1
Beauchamp Av
  BFLD/HDSWWD B20.........89 H1
Beauchamp Cl
  CHWD/FDBR/MGN B37.....132 B2
  WALM/CURD B76............78 D4
Beauchamp Rd MOS/BIL B13..146 H5
  SOLH B91..................164 D5
Beaudesert Cl HLYWD B47..192 C2
Beaudesert Rd
  BFLD/HDSWWD B20........108 B1
  HLYWD B47................192 C2
  WOLV WV1....................22 D2
Beaufort Av WALD WS9......44 B1
Beaulieu Av KGSWFD DY6...100 B5
Beaumaris Cl DUDN DY1.....83 H5
Beaumont Cl TPTN/OCK DY4..69 E5
Beaumont Dr BRLYHL DY5...118 D5
  HRBN B17..................141 H3
Beaumont Gdns WSNGN B18..107 H5
Beaumont Gv SOLH B91.....164 B5
Beaumont Rd BVILLE B30....159 G4
  DARL/WED WS10............54 B1
  RMSLY B62.................122 C4
Beausale Dr DOR/KN B93....197 F1
Beauty Bank CDYHTH B64...121 F4
Beauty Bank Crs STRBR DY8..135 E1
Beaver Cl WNSFLD WV11......25 F5
Bebington Cl CDSL WV8......22 B1
Beccles Dr WLNHL WV13......39 G5
Beckbury Av
  ETTPK/GDPK/PENN WV4....50 C3
Beckbury Rd SLYOAK B29...158 C1
Beck Cl SMTHWK B66........106 C5
Beckenham Av KGSTG B44...75 G2
Beckensall Cl DUDN DY1.....84 B5
Becket Cl FOAKS/STRLY B74..32 D4
Beckett St BILS/COS WV14...54 A2
Beckfield Cl
  ALE/KHTH/YWD B14........178 A3
  RUSH/SHEL WS4............29 E2
Beckford Cft DOR/KN B93 *..196 D5
Beckman Rd HAG/WOL DY9...136 A5
Beckminster Rd BDMR/CCFT WV3..51 F1
Beconsfield Cl DOR/KN B93..196 D5
Becton Gv PBAR/PBCH B42...74 D4
Bedcote Pl STRBR DY8.......135 H2
Beddoe Cl TPTN/OCK DY4....86 B1
Beddow Av BILS/COS WV14...68 C4
Beddows Rd BLOX/PEL WS3...28 A5
Bedford Dr MGN/WHC B75....63 E2
Bedford Rd BHTH/HG B12...127 G4
  HHTH/SAND B71.............71 F4
  MGN/WHC B75..............65 E1
Bedford St TPTN/OCK DY4...85 H1
  WOLV WV1..................44 B4
Bedford Ter LOZ/NWT B19 *..108 D1
Bedlam Wood Rd
  NFLD/LBR B31..............174 C4
Bedworth Cft TPTN/OCK DY4..85 H2
Bedworth Gv BORD B9........129 F2
Beebee Rd DARL/WED WS10...55 H2
Beecham Cl ALDR WS9.......30 A2
Beech Av BHTH/HG B12.....144 C2
  CHWD/FDBR/MGN B37.....132 B3
  RIDG/WDGT B32...........140 B2
  RMSLY B62.................122 A4
Beech Cl MGN/WHC B75.....63 E1
  SEDG DY3...................67 G2
  WOLV WV10.................25 G3
Beech Ct SMTHWK B66......105 G2
  WSL WS1.....................5 H6
Beech Crs DARL/WED WS10..55 H5
  TPTN/OCK DY4.............70 A3
Beechcroft Av
  HLGN/YWD B28............162 D4
Beechcroft Crs
  FOAKS/STRLY B74.........44 D4
Beechcroft Est HALE B63...137 G1
Beechcroft Pl WOLV WV10...23 E4
Beechcroft Rd CBROM B36..112 D1
  CDYHTH B64...............121 H2
Beechdale Av KGSTG B44....75 E1
Beechdale Rd BLOX/PEL WS3..26 D2
Beech Dene Gv
  ERDW/GRVHL B23..........92 C1
Beecher Pl HALE B63........137 H2
Beecher Rd East HALE B63..137 H2
Beecher St HALE B63........137 H2
Beeches Av ACGN B27.......146 C5
Beeches Cl KGSWFD DY6.....99 H4
  RBRY B45..................187 F1

Beeches Dr ERDE/BCHGN B24..93 G2
Beeches Farm Dr
  NFLD/LBR B31..............189 G1
Beeches Ms HAG/WOL DY9..169 E1
Beeches Pl BLOX/PEL WS3...27 H3
Beeches Rd
  BLKHTH/ROWR B65........121 H3
  BLOX/PEL WS3.............28 A4
  LGLVGN/QTN B68..........123 C1
  PBAR/PBCH B42.............74 B4
  WBROM B70..................88 A4
The Beeches EDG B15.......126 C4
  WBROM B70..................88 A4
  WLNHL WV13..................6 A2
Beeches View Av HALE B63..137 G3
Beeches Wk SCFLD/BOLD B75..62 B5
Beeches Wy NFLD/LBR B31..189 G1
Beechey Cl GTB/HAM B43....59 H3
Beech Farm Cft NFLD/LBR B31..175 G2
Beechfield Cl RMSLY B62...122 A4
Beechfield Gv BILS/COS WV14..68 B4
Beechfield Rd SMTHWK B67..106 B5
  SPARK B11.................144 D1
Beech Gdns CDSL WV8.......10 D5
Beech Ga FOAKS/STRLY B74..31 H5
Beechglade
  BFLD/HDSWWD B20.........89 H2
Beech Gn DUDN DY1.........84 A1
Beech Gv ALE/KHTH/YWD B14..161 G5
Beech Hill Rd
  CSCFLD/WYGN B72.........77 C4
Beech Hurst HWK/WKHTH B38..176 C5
Beechlawn Dr KINVER DY7..116 C5
Beech Ms CDYHTH B64......121 E2
Beechmore Dr
  ERDW/GRVHL B23..........93 F2
Beechnut Cl SOLH B91......165 F5
Beechnut La SOLH B91......165 G5
Beech Rd BVILLE B30.......159 G3
  DARL/WED WS10.............55 H3
  DUDN DY1...................84 C2
  ERDW/GRVHL B23...........76 D4
  HLYWD B47.................192 D2
  KGSWFD DY6................99 H4
  OLDBY B69.................103 C1
  STRBR DY8.................135 E5
  WLNHL WV13.................39 E3
  WOLV WV1....................22 D2
Beech St BILS/COS WV14....68 C5
Beech Tree Av WNSFLD WV11..24 C2
Beech Tree Cl KGSWFD DY6..100 A3
Beech Tree La ALDR WS9....19 F5
Beech Wk HWK/WKHTH B38..176 D6
Beech Wy SMTHWK B66......106 D4
Beechwood Av WNSFLD WV11..24 B2
Beechwood Cl BLOX/PEL WS3..16 D4
  SHLY B90...................194 D4
Beechwood Ct
  DUNHL/THL/PER WV6 *.....35 G2
Beechwood Cft
  FOAKS/STRLY B74..........32 B5
Beechwood Dr
  DUNHL/THL/PER WV6.......35 E3
Beechwood Park Rd
  SOLH B91..................164 A5
Beechwood Rd
  ALE/KHTH/YWD B14.......161 F5
  DUDS DY2...................103 E5
  GTB/HAM B43...............73 H2
  SMTHWK B67...............124 A4
  WBROM B70..................87 F3
Bee La WOLV WV10..........12 D4
Beeston Cl AST/WIT B6.....109 G2
  BRLYHL DY5................119 E4
Beet St BLKHTH/ROWR B65..122 A3
Beever Rd TPTN/OCK DY4....70 D4
Beggars Bush La WMBN WV5..81 F1
Beighton Cl FOAKS/STRLY B74..32 D4
Beilby Rd BVILLE B30.......160 B4
Belbroughton Rd
  HAG/WOL DY9..............170 C4
  HALE B63..................138 B5
  KIDD DY10.................168 C4
  STRBR DY8.................135 F4
Belchers La BORD B9.......129 F1
Beldray Pk BILS/COS WV14 *..54 A2
Beldray Rd BILS/COS WV14..54 A2
Belfry Cl BLOX/PEL WS3....16 C4
Belfry Dr STRBR DY8.......135 E1
The Belfry
  DUNHL/THL/PER WV6.......34 B1
Belgrade Rd WOLV WV10....12 B5
Belgrave Ct KGSWFD DY6...100 B5
Belgrave Rd DIG/EDG B5....126 D6
Belgrave Middleway
  DIG/EDG B5.................127 E5
Belgrave Rd BHTH/HG B12..144 B1
  RMSLY B62.................108 A2
Belgrave Ter HDSW B21....108 C2
Belgrave Wk WSLW WS2.....41 F2
Belgravia Cl DIG/EDG B5...127 E5
Belgrove Cl EDG B15.......142 C1
Belinda Cl WLNHL WV13.....39 F2
Bellamy Cl SHLY B90.......180 D4
Bellamy Farm Rd SHLY B90..180 D4
Bellamy La WNSFLD WV11....24 D3
Bell Barn Rd DIG/EDG B5...126 D4
Bell Cl BORD B9............128 C1
  CBROM B36.................114 B3
  DARL/WED WS10............55 F1
Bellcroft LDYWD/EDGR B16 *..2 A6
Bell Dr DSYBK/YTR WS5.....57 G3
  WASH/WDE B8..............128 D1
Bellefield Av WSNGN B18...107 G5
Bellefield Rd WSNGN B18...107 G5
Belle Isle BRLYHL DY5.....119 E1
Bellemere Rd HIA/OLT B92..167 H5
Bell End RMSLY B62.........187 E1
Belle V HALE B63...........138 A2
Bellevue DIG/EDG B5.......126 D5
Belle Vue STRBR DY8.......117 G2
Bellevue Av
  LDYWD/EDGR B16 *........107 F5
Belle Vue Dr RMSLY B62...139 G1
Belle Vue Gdns
  BLKHTH/ROWR B65 *.......122 A1

Belle Vue Rd BRLYHL DY5..120 A3
Bellevue Rd BILS/COS WV14..67 H1
  LGN/SDN/BHAMAIR B26...130 C5
Belle Vue Ter HIA/OLT B92..167 E5
Bell Fold LGLVGN/QTN B68..105 F2
Bellflower Dr DSYBK/YTR WS5..57 F5
Bell Green La
  HWK/WKHTH B38..........191 F3
Bell Heather Rd BRWNH WS8..18 D1
Bell Heath Wy
  RIDG/WDGT B32...........140 B5
Bell Hl NFLD/LBR B31......158 D5
Bell Holloway NFLD/LBR B31..158 B5
Bellington Cft SHLY B90...195 G2
Bellis St LDYWD/EDGR B16..125 H3
Bell La BLOX/PEL WS3.......27 F1
  DSYBK/YTR WS5.............57 G4
  NFLD/LBR B31..............175 G3
  STETCH B33.................131 G3
Bellman Cl DARL/WED WS10..55 F1
Bell Meadow HAG/WOL DY9..152 D2
Bell Pl WOLV WV2...........43 H5
Bell Rd DSYBK/YTR WS5....58 B2
  DUDS DY2...................102 C4
  WMBN WV5...................64 B2
Bells Farm Cl
  ALE/KHTH/YWD B14.......177 H3
Bells La ALE/KHTH/YWD B14..177 H3
  STRBR DY8.................117 H5
Bells Moor Rd WBROM B70...71 E5
Bell St BILS/COS WV14......68 C1
  BRLYHL DY5................119 F2
  DARL/WED WS10............55 E1
  TPTN/OCK DY4.............85 E1
  WBROM B70..................87 H4
  WOLV WV1....................7 F5
Bell St South BRLYHL DY5..119 F2
Bell Vue
  BLKHTH/ROWR B65........122 A2
Bellwood Rd NFLD/LBR B31..175 F1
Belmont Av ALDR WS9......30 A3
  TPTN/OCK DY4.............69 F5
Belmont Covert
  NFLD/LBR B31..............158 D4
Belmont Crs BILS/COS WV14..54 D1
Belmont Gdns BILS/COS WV14..54 D1
Belmont Pas BORD B9......127 G2
Belmont Rd BRLYHL DY5....101 F3
  ERDW/GRVHL B23...........93 E1
  ETTPK/GDPK/PENN WV4....51 G3
  HAG/WOL DY9..............136 C3
  HDSW B21..................107 E1
  RBRY B45..................187 H2
  SMTHWK B66...............124 C2
Belmont Rd East HDSW B21..107 E1
Belmont Rw CBHAMNE B4.....3 K5
Belmont St BILS/COS WV14..54 C4
Belper Dr DUDN DY1.........84 B5
Belper Rd DUDS DY2........103 E5
Belstone Cl
  ALE/KHTH/YWD B14.......160 D5
Belton Av WNSFLD WV11....24 B1
Belton Gv RBRY B45........174 C5
Belvedere Av
  ETTPK/GDPK/PENN WV4....51 H3
Belvedere Cl KGSWFD DY6..100 B5
Belvedere Gdns
  DUNHL/THL/PER WV6.......21 H3
Belvedere Rd
  ERDE/BCHGN B24..........93 E4
Belvide Gdns CDSL WV8.....10 B3
Belvide Gv SLYOAK B29....158 D2
Belvidere Gdns SPARK B11..144 D3
Belvidere Rd WSL WS1.......5 J7
Belwell Dr FOAKS/STRLY B74..47 E5
Belwell La FOAKS/STRLY B74..47 E5
Bembridge Cl SHHTH WV12..25 H2
Bembridge Rd STETCH B33..130 C2
Benacre Dr DIG/EDG B5......3 K5
Benbeck Gv TPTN/OCK DY4..84 C1
Bencroft CDSL WV8.........10 D5
Bendall Rd KGSTG B44......75 H1
Benedon Rd
  LGN/SDN/BHAMAIR B26...130 C5
Benmore Av DIG/EDG B5...143 H1
Bennett Av DUDN DY1........84 C1
Bennett Rd FOAKS/STRLY B74..46 B2
Bennett's Hl CBHAMNW B3...3 F5
  DUDS DY2...................103 E1
Bennetts Rd WASH/WDE B8..110 B5
Bennett St LOZ/NWT B19...108 D1
Ben Nevis Wy STRBR DY8...135 C1
Benson Av
  ETTPK/GDPK/PENN WV4....52 A3
Benson Cl
  DUNHL/THL/PER WV6.......20 C5
Benson Rd
  ALE/KHTH/YWD B14.......178 D4
  WSNGN B18.................107 H3
Bent Av RIDG/WDGT B32....140 D1
Bentham Ct NFLD/LBR B31..158 B5
Bentley Bridge Pk
  WNSFLD WV11 *.............38 D1
Bentley Wy
  ETTPK/GDPK/PENN WV4....52 C4
Bentley Dr CDSL WV8........10 B3
  WSL WS2....................41 E5
Bentley Farm Cl DOR/KN B93..196 C4
Bentley Gv SLYOAK B29....158 B2
Bentley La SHHTH WV12.....26 D1
Bentley Mill Cl WSLW WS2..40 A4
Bentley Mill La WSLW WS2..40 A4
Bentley Mill Wy WSLW WS2..40 A5
Bentley New Dr WSLW WS2..41 E3
Bentley Pl WSLW WS2.......41 E5
Bentley Rd North WSLW WS2..40 B5
Bentley Rd South
  DARL/WED WS10............40 B5
Bentmead Gv
  HWK/WKHTH B38..........177 E4
Benton Av SPARK B11......145 E1
Benton Cl SHHTH WV12......40 B1

Benton Crs BLOX/PEL WS3...17 F5
Benton Rd SPARK B11......145 E1
Bentons Mill Cft
  VAUX/NECH B7.............110 A1
Bent St BRLYHL DY5........101 F5
Ben Willetts Wk
  BLKHTH/ROWR B65........122 A3
Beoley Cl CSCFLD/WYGN B72..77 G2
Beoley Gv RBRY B45........188 A2
Berberry Cl BVILLE B30....159 F4
Beresford Crs WBROM B70...87 F3
Beresford Dr SCFLD/BOLD B75..77 E2
Beresford Rd BLOX/PEL WS3..28 A2
  OLDBY B69.................105 G2
The Berets MGN/WHC B75...63 F2
Bericote Cft ACGN B27.....146 D4
Berkeley Cl
  DUNHL/THL/PER WV6.......34 D2
  WSLW WS2..................40 D2
Berkeley Dr KGSWFD DY6....99 G2
Berkeley Ms YDLY B25.....129 E5
Berkeley Rd
  YDLY B25..................129 E5
Berkeley Rd East YDLY B25..129 F5
Berkeley St WSLW WS2......56 B1
Berkley Cl WSLW WS2.......40 D2
Berkley Crs MOS/BIL B13..162 A1
Berkley St CBHAMW B1......2 C6
Berkshire Cl HHTH/SAND B71..71 F4
Berkshire Crs DARL/WED WS10..56 C4
The Berkshire BLOX/PEL WS3..16 C4
Berkswell Cl DUDN DY1.....83 G3
  FOAKS/STRLY B74..........46 C1
  SOLH B91..................164 D2
Berkswell Rd ERDE/BCHGN B24..93 F2
Bermuda Cl DUDN DY1......84 B1
Bernard Pl WSNGN B18.....107 H4
Bernard Rd HRBN B17......124 D2
  LGLVGN/QTN B68..........123 G2
  TPTN/OCK DY4.............85 H1
Bernard St HHTH/SAND B71..87 G2
  WSL WS1.....................5 H6
Berners St LOZ/NWT B19...108 C2
Bernhard Dr HDSW B21....107 G1
Bernwall Cl STRBR DY8....135 F3
Berrandale Rd CBROM B36...94 B5
Berrington Dr BILS/COS WV14..69 H1
Berrington Wk DIG/EDG B5..127 E5
Berrow Dr EDG B15........125 G5
Berrowside Rd
  BKDE/SHDE B34...........113 G3
Berry Av DARL/WED WS10...54 D3
Berrybush Gdns SEDG DY3...67 G4
Berry Cl LOZ/NWT B19.....108 D5
Berry Crs DSYBK/YTR WS5...58 A4
Berry Dr ALDR WS9.........29 G5
  SMTHWK B66...............106 C3
Berryfield Rd
  BKDE/SHDE B34...........113 G3
Berry Hall La SOLH B91....183 E1
Berrymound Vw HLYWD B47..193 E1
Berry Rd DUDN DY1........84 C1
  WASH/WDE B8..............110 C4
Berry St WOLV WV1..........7 G1
  WSNGN B18.................107 G5
Bertha Rd SPARK B11......145 F2
Bertram Cl TPTN/OCK DY4...70 A2
Bertram Rd BORD B9.......128 B3
  SMTHWK B67...............106 A3
Berwick Gv GTB/HAM B43....59 H4
  NFLD/LBR B31..............174 D2
Berwicks La
  CHWD/FDBR/MGN B37.....132 B3
Berwood Farm Rd
  ERDE/BCHGN B24..........77 G5
Berwood Gdns
  ERDE/BCHGN B24..........77 G5
Berwood La ERDE/BCHGN B24..94 D3
Berwood Pk CVALE B35......94 D4
Berwood Rd
  CSCFLD/WYGN B72.........77 H5
Besant Gv ACGN B27.......146 A5
Besbury Cl DOR/KN B93....196 C4
Bescot Cft PBAR/PBCH B42..74 B4
Bescot Dr WSLW WS2.......56 C2
Bescot Rd WSLW WS2......56 C1
Bescot St WSL WS1..........5 J7
Besford Gv NFLD/LBR B31..174 D2
  SHLY B90..................195 H2
Bessborough Rd YDLY B25..129 H4
Best Rd BILS/COS WV14.....53 H1
Best St CDYHTH B64........121 F2
Beswick Gv STETCH B33....112 C5
Beta Gv ALE/KHTH/YWD B14..179 E1
Bethesda Gdns HALE B63...120 C5
Betjeman Pl WOLV WV10....24 A1
Betley Gv STETCH B33......112 C5
Betony Cl DSYBK/YTR WS5...57 G5
Betsham Cl KGSTG B44......75 H2
Bettany Gld WOLV WV10.....13 E3
Betteridge Dr WALM/CURD B76..63 E4
Bett Rd BFLD/HDSWWD B20..89 G3
Bevan Av
  ETTPK/GDPK/PENN WV4....52 C4
Bevan Cl BILS/COS WV14....54 A4
  RUSH/SHEL WS4............29 E1
Bevan Rd BRLYHL DY5.....118 C2
  TPTN/OCK DY4.............85 H2
Bevan Wy SMTHWK B66.....106 B1
Beverley Cl CSCFLD/WYGN B72..77 G2
Beverley Court Rd
  RIDG/WDGT B32...........140 C1
Beverley Crs
  ETTPK/GDPK/PENN WV4....52 D4
Beverley Cft ERDW/GRVHL B23..92 B5
Beverley Dr KGSWFD DY6....99 G2
Beverley Gv
  LGN/SDN/BHAMAIR B26...147 G2
Beverley Rd HHTH/SAND B71..71 H2
  RBRY B45..................188 A1
Beverston Rd
  DUNHL/THL/PER WV6.......35 E1
  TPTN/OCK DY4.............69 H1
Bevington Rd AST/WIT B6...109 F1
Bevin Rd WSLW WS2.........40 C2

Bewdley Av *BHTH/HG* B12 ....144 C1
Bewdley Dr *WOLV* WV1 ....38 B3
Bewdley Rd *BVILLE* B30 ....160 B2
Bewdley Vis *WSNGN* B18 * 107 F5
Bexley Cl *BRLYHL* DY5 ....118 D5
Bexley Rd *WALM* WV13 ....40 B1
Bexley Gv *HHTH/SAND* B71 ......72 A4
Bexley Rd *KGSTG* B44 ....75 H3
Bhylls Crs *BDMR/CCFT* WV3 ......50 A1
Bhylls La *BDMR/CCFT* WV3 ......50 B1
Bibbey's Gv *WOLVN* WV10 ......13 F5
Bibsworth Av *HLGN/YWD* B13 ...162 B2
Bibury Rd *HLGN/YWD* B28 ......162 C3
Bicester Sq *CVALE* B35 ....94 C2
Bickenhill La
  CHWD/FDBR/MGN B37 ......132 C5
  HIA/OLT B92 ....166 C4
  LGN/SDN/BHAMAIR B26 ...149 C3
Bickenhill Park Rd
  HIA/OLT B92 ....163 H1
Bickenhill Pkwy
  CHWD/FDBR/MGN B37 ......149 H1
Bickford Rd *AST/WIT* B6 ....95 H1
  WOLVN WV10 ....23 H5
Bickington Rd *RIDG/WDGT* B32 ..157 H1
Bickley Av *FOAKS/STRLY* B74 ....54 C5
  SPARK B11 * 145 E1
Bickley Gv
  LGN/SDN/BHAMAIR B26 ....147 H2
Bickley Rd *BILS/COS* WV14 ......54 C2
  RUSH/SHEL WS4 ....29 E3
Bicknell Cft
  ALE/KHTH/YWD B14 ......178 A3
Bickton Cl *ERDW/BCHGN* B24 ...77 C5
Biddings La *BILS/COS* WV14 ......68 B1
Biddlestone Pl
  DARL/WED WS10 ....54 D1
Biddleston Gv *DSYBK/YTR* WS5 ..58 A5
Bideford Dr *SLYOAK* B29 ....159 F1
Bideford Rd *SMTHWK* B66 ......106 D4
Bidford Cl *SHLY* B90 ....180 D5
Bidford Rd *NFLD/LBR* B31 ......175 F2
Bierton Rd *YDLY* B25 ....129 C4
Biggin Cl *CVALE* B35 ....94 C3
  TTF/PNE WV6 ....20 C5
The Big Peg *WSNGN* B19 * 2 C2
Bigwood Dr *MGN/WHC* B75 ......63 C2
  RIDG/WDGT B32 ....157 G1
Bilberry Crs *WALM/CURD* B76 ...63 E5
Bilberry Dr *RBRY* B45 ....188 A2
Bilberry Rd
  ALE/KHTH/YWD B14 ......160 C4
Bilboe Rd *BILS/COS* WV14 ......54 B5
Bilbrook Ct *CDSL* WV8 ....10 D4
Bilbrook Gv *CDSL* WV8 ....10 D4
Bilhay La *WBROM* B70 ....87 E1
Bilhay St *WBROM* B70 ....87 E1
Billau Rd *BILS/COS* WV14 ......68 D1
Billesley La *MOS/BIL B13 ......161 G2
Billingham Cl *SOLH* B91 ......181 H5
Billingsley Rd
  LGN/SDN/BHAMAIR B26 ....130 C4
Bills La *SHLY* B90 ....179 H5
Billsmore Gn *HIA/OLT* B92 ......165 E3
Bills St *DARL/WED* WS10 ......55 G2
Billy Buns La *WMBN* WV5 ....65 F5
Billy Wright Cl
  ETTPK/GDPK/PENN WV4 ....50 D2
Bilport La *DARL/WED* WS10 ......70 D3
Bilston Rd *BKHL/PFLD* WV2 ......37 H5
  DARL/WED WS10 ....55 H4
  TPTN/OCK DY4 ....69 H1
  WLNHL WV13 ....54 C1
Bilston St *DARL/WED* WS10 ......55 F2
  SEDG DY3 ....67 E3
  WLNHL WV13 ....40 D5
Bilston Street Island *WOLV* WV1 ...7 H5
Bilton Grange Rd
  LGN/SDN/BHAMAIR B26 ....130 B5
Binbrook Rd *SHHTH* WV12 ......40 B1
Bincomb Av
  LGN/SDN/BHAMAIR B26 ....147 H1
Binfield St *TPTN/OCK* DY4 ....85 G2
Bingley Av *WASH/WDE* B8 ......111 G5
Bingley St *BDMR/CCFT* WV3 ......36 C5
Binley Cl *SHLY* B90 ....180 A5
  YDLY B25 ....146 D1
Binstead Rd *KGSTG* B44 ....75 G1
Binswood Rd *RMSLY* B62 ....123 E5
Binton Cft *MOS/BIL B13 ......161 F2
Binton Rd *SHLY* B90 ....179 H4
Birbeck Pl *BRLYHL* DY5 ......100 D3
Birchall St *BHTH/HG* B12 ......127 F3
Birch Av *BRLYHL* DY5 ....120 A2
  BRWNH WS8 ....9 E4
  NFLD/LBR B31 ....174 C4
Birch Cl *BVILLE* B30 ....159 F4
  CDSL WV8 ....10 B1
Birch Coppice *BRLYHL* DY5 ......120 B2
  WMBN WV5 ....64 C5
Birchcoppice Gdns
  SHHTH WV12 ....40 C1
Birches Cls *OLDBY* B69 ....85 H5
Birch Cft *ALDR* WS9 ....30 D2
  CHWD/FDBR/MGN B37 ......132 C5
  ERDE/BCHGN B24 ....93 H1
Birch Croft Rd *MGN/WHC* B75 ...62 D1
Birchdale *BILS/COS* WV14 ......68 A2
Birchdale Av *ERDW/GRVHL* B23 ...92 C5
Birchdale Rd *ERDW/GRVHL* B23 ...92 B3
Birch Dr *FOAKS/STRLY* B74 ......32 B5
  MGN/WHC B75 ....63 F1
  RMSLY B62 ....122 C5
  STRBR DY8 ....135 E1
Birches Av *CDSL* WV8 ....21 C1
Birches Barn Av
  BDMR/CCFT WV3 ....51 F1
Birches Barn Rd
  BDMR/CCFT WV3 ....36 B5
Birches Cl *MOS/BIL B13 ......161 F1
Birches Green Rd
  ERDE/BCHGN B24 ....93 F4

Birches Park Rd *CDSL* WV8 ......10 C5
Birches Ri *WLNHL* WV13 ....39 F4
Birches Rd *CDSL* WV8 ....10 C5
Birchfield Av
  DUNHL/THL/PER WV6 ......21 F4
Birchfield Cl *HALE* B63 ....138 A5
Birchfield Crs *HAG/WOL* DY9 ...136 D4
Birchfield Gdns *AST/WIT* B6 *....108 C1
Birchfield La *OLDBY* B69 ......104 C5
Birchfield Rd
  BFLD/HDSWWD B20 ......90 D5
  HAG/WOL DY9 ....136 D4
  RBRY B45 ....187 H3
  STRBR DY8 ....108 D1
Birchfields Rd *SHHTH* WV12 ....25 G5
Birchgate *HAG/WOL* DY9 ......136 D3
Birchglade *BDMR/CCFT* WV3 ....35 H4
Birch Gv *LGLYGN/QTN* B68 ....123 H5
Birch Hill Av *WMBN* WV5 ......80 D1
Birch Hollow *EDG* B15 ....142 D1
Birch Hollow *WMBN* WV5 ......80 D1
Birchills St *WSLW* WV5 ....4 A2
Birch La *ALDR* WS5 ....30 D1
  LGLYGN/QTN B68 ......123 H5
  RUSH/SHEL WS4 ....29 E1
Birches Park Av *OLDBY* B69 ....147 F2
Birchley Ri *HIA/OLT* B92 ......147 F2
Birchmoor Cl *HLGN/YWD* B28 ...163 F3
Birchover Rd *WSLW* WS2 ......41 E1
Birch Rd *AST/WIT* B6 ....91 G4
  LGLYGN/QTN B68 ......123 H5
  RBRY B45 ....188 C2
  SEDG DY3 ....67 H2
  WNSFLD WV11 ....25 F1
Birch Rd East *AST/WIT* B6 ......91 H4
Birch St *LGLYGN/QTN* B68 ......105 C3
  TPTN/OCK DY4 ....85 F1
  WOLV WV1 ....6 E4
  WSLW WS2 ....4 B1
Birch Ter *DUDS* DY2 ....102 C5
Birch Tree Gdns *ALDR* WS9 ......30 D5
Birchtree Gdns *BRLYHL* DY5 ...120 A3
Birch Tree Gv *SOLH* B91 ......181 E1
Birchtree Hollow *SHHTH* WV12 ...26 B5
Birchtrees Dr *ERDE/BCHGN* B24 ...93 H2
Birchtrees Cft
  LGN/SDN/BHAMAIR B26 ...146 D2
Birchtrees Dr *STECH* B33 ......131 F1
Birch Wk *LGLYGN/QTN* B68 ....123 H5
Birchwood Cl *WNSFLD* WV11 ....18 A4
Birchwood Crs *BHTH/HG* B12 ...144 C5
Birchwoods *RIDG/WDGT* B32 ...144 C1
Birchy Cl *SHLY* B90 ....193 H2
Birchy Leasowes La *SHLY* B90 ...193 G3
Birdbrook Rd *KGSTG* B44 ......75 E3
Bird End *HHTH/SAND* B71 ......72 B5
Birdie Cl *HHTH/WKHTH* B38 ...176 B4
Birdlip Gv *RIDG/WDGT* B32 ....140 C1
Birds Meadow *BRLYHL* DY5 ...100 D2
Bird St *SEDG* DY3 ....83 E3
Birdwell Cft *MOS/BIL B13 ......161 F4
Birkdale Av *SLYOAK* B29 ......159 H3
Birkdale Cl *STRBR* DY8 ......152 B1
  WOLV WV1 ....38 A3
Birkdale Dr *OLDBY* B69 ......103 G2
Birkdale Gv *SLYOAK* B29 ......160 A2
Birkdale Rd *BLOX/PEL* WS3 ....16 C4
Birkenshaw Rd *KGSTG* B44 ......75 E3
Birley Gv *HALE* B63 ....154 C2
Birmingham New Rd
  DUDN DY1 ....85 E2
  ETTPK/GDPK/PENN WV4 ....52 D1
Birmingham Rd *ALDR* WS9 ......44 A1
  BKHL/PFLD WV2 ....37 F5
  BLKHTH/ROWR B65 ......122 A2
  BRGRVW B61 ....187 E4
  CBROM B36 ....112 C1
  CHWD/FDBR/MGN B37 ....114 C4
  CSCFLD/WYGN B72 ....77 F3
  DSYBK/YTR WS5 ....57 H1
  DUDN DY1 ....85 E4
  HAG/WOL DY9 ....153 F4
  KIDD DY10 ....168 C3
  LICHS WS14 ....33 E3
  NFLD/LBR B31 ....189 H5
  OLDBY B69 ....105 F2
  RCOVN/BALC/EX CV7 ......151 F4
  WBROM B70 ....88 A5
  WSL WS1 ....5 H7
Birmingham St
  DARL/WED WS10 ....55 F2
  DUDS DY2 ....84 D5
  HALE B63 ....138 C4
  OLDBY B69 ....105 E1
  STRBR DY8 ....135 H2
  WLNHL WV13 ....39 H3
  WSL WS1 ....5 F5
Birnham Ct *TPTN/OCK* DY4 ....84 D1
Bisbrook Cft *SHLY* B91 ......165 F4
Bisell Wy *BRLYHL* DY5 ......136 B1
Bishbury Cl *EDG* B15 ....125 C4
Bishop Asbury Crs
  GTB/HAM B43 ....72 D3
Bishop Cl *RBRY* B45 ....173 C4
Bishop Rd *DARL/WED* WS10 ......71 G1
Bishops Cl *DUDS* DY2 ....103 E1
Bishop Wk *SEDG* DY3 ....107 E5
Bishop's Ct
  CHWD/FDBR/MGN B37 ......133 E4
Bishops Ga *NFLD/LBR* B31 ......175 G3
Bishopsgate St *EDG* B15 ....2 B7
Bishops Meadow
  MGN/WHC B75 ....48 A2
Bishops Rd *SCFLD/BOLD* B73 ....62 B5
Bishop St *DIG/EDG* B5 ......127 E4
Bishops Wk *CDYHTH* B64 ......138 C1
Bishopstone Cl *SHLY* B90 ......180 C5
Bishton Gv *DUDS* DY2 ....102 D5
Bissel Dr *DARL/WED* WS10 ......56 B5
Bissell Cl *HLGN/YWD* B28 ......162 D4
Bissell St *DIG/EDG* B5 ....127 E4
  RIDG/WDGT B32 ....140 A1
Bissel St *BILS/COS* WV14 ......54 B3
Biton Cl *HRBN* B17 ....141 H2
Bitteli Cl *NFLD/LBR* B31 ......189 F1

Bitterne Dr *DUNHL/THL/PER* WV6 ...36 C1
Blackacre Rd *DUDS* DY2 ......102 D1
Blackberry Av *BORD* B9 ......129 E1
Blackberry Cl *DUDN* DY1 ......101 F4
Blackberry La *ALDR* WS9 ......19 H5
  BLKHTH/ROWR B65 ......103 F4
  FOAKS/STRLY B74 ....46 C1
  HALE B63 ....138 C5
Blackbird Cft *CBROM* B36 ......114 A2
Blackboards Cl *DUDS* DY2 ......120 A1
Blackbrook Cl *DUDS* DY2 ......102 A4
Blackbrook Wy *WOLVN* WV10 ...13 E3
Blackburn Av
  DUNHL/THL/PER WV6 ......22 A3
Blackburne Rd
  HLGN/YWD B28 ....162 D4
Blackbushe Cl *HRBN* B17 ......124 B5
Blackcat Cl
  CHWD/FDBR/MGN B37 ......132 A1
Black Country New Rd
  DARL/WED WS10 ....54 C2
Black Country Route
  BILS/COS WV14 ....54 B2
  DARL/WED WS10 ....40 B4
Blackdown Cl *RBRY* B45 ......174 A3
Blackdown Rd *DOR/KN* B93 ...197 F2
Blackfirs La *BHAMNEC* B46 ....134 C3
  CHWD/FDBR/MGN B37 ......132 D5
Blackford Cl *HALE* B63 ......137 H5
Blackford Rd *SHLY* B90 ......194 C1
  SPARK B11 ....145 E3
Blackford St *WSNGN* B18 ......107 F4
Blackhalve La *WNSFLD* WV11 ...24 D2
Blackham Dr *SCFLD/BOLD* B73 ...77 E4
Blackham Rd *WNSFLD* WV11 ....25 F2
Black Haynes Rd *SLYOAK* B29 ...158 C3
Black Horse Cl
  DARL/WED WS10 ....55 F3
Blackhorse La *BRLYHL* DY5 ....119 G3
Blackhouse La *WBROM* B70 ......71 E5
Blackmoor Cft *STECH* B33 ......131 F2
Blackrock Rd
  ERDW/GRVHL B23 ....75 H5
Blackroot Rd *FOAKS/STRLY* B74 ...62 A1
Blacksmith Dr *MGN/WHC* B75 ...48 A2
Blacksmiths La *HHTH/HG* B46 ...198 A5
Blacksmith Wy *WBROM* B70 ......87 G4
Blackthorn Cl *SOLH* B91 ......181 E1
Blackthorne Rd
  DSYBK/YTR WS5 ....57 F3
  DUDN DY1 ....83 H2
  SMTHWK B67 ....105 H5
Blackthorn Rd *BVILLE* B30 ......160 A2
  CBROM B36 ....113 E1
  STRBR DY8 ....118 B3
Blackwater Cl *KGSWFD* DY6 ...100 C4
Blackwell Rd
  CSCFLD/WYGN B72 ....77 H2
Blackwood Av *WNSFLD* WV11 ....24 B2
Blackwood Dr
  FOAKS/STRLY B74 ....45 E5
Blackwood Rd
  FOAKS/STRLY B74 ....45 E4
Blades Rd *WBROM* B70 ....86 B2
Blaenwern Dr *HALE* B63 ......120 B5
Blagdon Rd *HALE* B63 ......138 C1
Blair Gv
  CHWD/FDBR/MGN B37 ......132 D3
Blakedon Rd *DARL/WED* WS10 ...55 C5
Blakedown Rd *HALE* B63 ......138 B5
Blakeland Rd *KGSTG* B44 ......75 E5
Blakeland St *BORD* B9 ......128 D2
Blake La *BORD* B9 ....128 D2
Blakeley Av
  DUNHL/THL/PER WV6 ......22 B3
Blakeley Hall Gdns *OLDBY* B69 ...105 F2
Blakeley Hall Rd *OLDBY* B69 ...105 F2
Blakeley Heath Dr *WMBN* WV5 ...81 E1
Blakeley Ri
  DUNHL/THL/PER WV6 ......22 B3
Blakeley Wood Rd
  TPTN/OCK DY4 ....70 A3
Blakely Hall Rd *OLDBY* B69 ......105 F1
Blakemere Av *YDLY* B25 ......130 A4
Blakemore Cl *RIDG/WDGT* B32 ...141 F4
Blakemore Dr *MGN/WHC* B75 ...63 F2
Blakemore Rd *ALDR* WS9 ....19 H4
  WBROM B70 ....87 E4
Blakenall Cl *BLOX/PEL* WS3 ....28 A1
Blakenall Heath *BLOX/PEL* WS3 ...27 H1
Blakenall La *BLOX/PEL* WS3 ....27 H1
Blakeney Av *HRBN* B17 ......124 C5
  STRBR DY8 ....134 B3
Blakeney Cl *SEDG* DY3 ....67 E3
Blakenhale Rd *STECH* B33 ......130 D3
Blakenhall Gdns
  BKHL/PFLD WV2 ....52 B1
Blake Pl *BORD* B9 ....128 D2
Blakesley Cl *WALM/CURD* B76 ...94 B1
Blakesley Gv *YDLY* B25 ......129 H4
Blakesley Ms *YDLY* B25 ......129 H4
Blakesley Rd *STECH* B33 ......129 C2
Blake St *FOAKS/STRLY* B74 ......32 C4
Blakewood Cl
  BKDE/SHDE B34 ....113 G4
Blandford Av *CBROM* B36 ......95 G5
Blandford Dr *STRBR* DY8 ......118 A2
Blandford Rd *RIDG/WDGT* B32 ...141 E2
Blanefield *CDSL* WV8 ....22 A1
Blay Av *WSLW* WS2 ....41 F3
Blaydon Av *MGN/WHC* B75 ......48 A3
Blaydon Rd *COVEN* WV9 ......12 A5
Blaythorn Av *HIA/OLT* B92 ......147 C4
Blaze Hill Rd *KGSWFD* DY6 ......99 E1
Blaze Pk *KGSWFD* DY6 ....99 F1
Bleakhouse Rd
  LGLYGN/QTN B68 ....123 C3
Bleak St *SMTHKW* B67 ....106 B3
Blenheim Cl *RUSH/SHEL* WS4 ...29 F3
Blenheim Dr *DARL/WED* WS10 ...55 H3
  GTB/HAM B43 ....73 H3
Blenheim Rd *KGSWFD* DY6 ......100 C3
  *MOS/BIL B13 ....161 F1
  SHHTH WV12 ....25 H4
  SHLY B90 ....180 D3

Blenheim Wy *CVALE* B35 ......94 C4
  DUDN DY1 ....83 G4
  KGSTG B44 ....75 F2
Bletchley Rd *ERDE/BCHGN* B24 ...94 A2
Blewitt Cl *CBROM* B36 ....95 F4
Blewitt St *BRLYHL* DY5 ......101 E5
Blews St *AST/WIT* B6 ....109 E4
Blithe Cl *STRBR* DY8 ....118 C4
Blithfield Dr *BRLYHL* DY5 ......118 D5
Blithfield Gv *ERDE/BCHGN* B24 ...93 C1
Blithfield Rd *BRWNH* WS8 ....8 C2
Blockall *DARL/WED* WS10 ....55 F1
Bloomfield Cl *WMBN* WV5 ......64 B5
Bloomfield Dr *SHHTH* WV12 ....26 B1
Bloomfield Pk *TPTN/OCK* DY4 ...85 F2
Bloomfield Rd *MOS/BIL B13 ....144 C4
  TPTN/OCK DY4 ....69 E4
Bloomfield St North *HALE* B63 ...138 B2
Bloomfield St West *HALE* B63 ...138 B3
Bloomfield Ter *TPTN/OCK* DY4 ...68 D5
Bloomsbury Gv
  ALE/KHTH/YWD B14 ......160 C3
Bloomsbury St *BKHL/PFLD* WV2 ...52 A1
  VAUX/NECH B7 ....109 H4
Bloomsbury Wk
  VAUX/NECH B7 ....109 H4
Bloor Mill Cl *WLNHL* WV13 ......39 F4
Blossom Av *SLYOAK* B29 * 142 D5
Blossomfield Cl
  HWK/WKHTH B38 ....176 B5
  KGSWFD DY6 ....100 A1
Blossomfield Rd *SOLH* B91 ......181 F5
Blossom Gv *CBROM* B36 ......114 A1
Blossom St *ERDE/BCHGN* B24 ...93 E2
Blossom Rd *ERDE/BCHGN* B24 ...93 C2
Blossomville Wy *ACGN* B27 ......146 B3
Blowers Green Crs *DUDS* DY2 ...102 B2
Blowers Green Rd *DUDS* DY2 ...102 B2
Bloxcidge St *LGLYGN/QTN* B68 ...105 F4
Bloxham La *WSLW* WS2 ....41 E2
Bloxwich Rd *WSLW* WS2 ....27 H4
Bloxwich Rd North
  SHHTH WV12 ....26 B4
Bloxwich Rd South
  WLNHL WV13 ....39 C2
Blucher St *CBHAMW* B11 ....2 E7
Blue Ball La *HALE* B63 ....137 G1
Bluebell Cl *STRBR* DY8 ....117 G2
Bluebell Crs *ERDW/GRVHL* B23 ...76 A4
  NFLD/LBR B31 ....175 F1
Bluebell Dr
  CHWD/FDBR/MGN B37 ......132 D2
Bluebell Rd *ALDR* WS9 ....19 H4
  CDYHTH B64 ....121 E1
  DUDN DY1 ....84 B3
Bluebellwood Cl
  FOAKS/STRLY B74 ....46 D4
  WALM/CURD B76 ....47 F3
Blue Cedar Dr
  FOAKS/STRLY B74 ....60 B1
Blue Cedars Rd *STRBR* DY8 ....134 C1
Blue Lake Rd *DOR/KN* B93 ......199 F1
Blue La East *WSLW* WS2 ....4 D1
Blue La West *WSLW* WS2 ....4 C1
Blue Rock Pl *OLDBY* B69 ......104 A3
Blundell Rd *SPARK* B11 ......145 F2
Blythefield Av *GTB/HAM* B43 ...73 E2
Blythe Gdns *CDSL* WV8 ....10 B3
Blythe Ga *SHLY* B90 ....195 G5
Blythe Gv *KGSTG* B44 ....60 B5
Blythe Rd *CSHL/WTROR* B46 ...115 H1
Blytheway *SOLH* B91 ....182 C2
Blythewood Cl *SOLH* B91 ......182 D4
Blythsford Rd *HLGN/YWD* B28 ...179 H1
Blythswood Rd *SPARK* B11 ......146 A3
Blyton Cl *LDYWD/EDGR* B16 ...107 H5
Board School Gdns *SEDG* DY3 ...67 G1
Boar Hound Cl *WSNGN* B18 * ...108 A5
Boatman's La *ALDR* WS9 ....19 E5
Bobbington Wy *DUDS* DY2 ......102 D4
Bobs Coppice Wk *BRLYHL* DY5 ...119 H5
Bodenham Rd
  LGLYGN/QTN B68 ....123 F4
  NFLD/LBR B31 ....175 E3
Boden Rd *HLGN/YWD* B28 ......163 G3
Bodens La *ALDR* WS9 ....59 E1
Bodiam Ct
  DUNHL/THL/PER WV6 ......35 G2
Bodicote Gv *MGN/WHC* B75 ......48 A2
Bodington Rd *MGN/WHC* B75 ...47 F2
Bodmin Cl *DSYBK/YTR* WS5 ......58 B1
Bodmin Gv *VAUX/NECH* B7 ....109 H4
Bodmin Ri *DSYBK/YTR* WS5 ......58 B1
Bodmin Rd *DUDS* DY2 ......120 D2
Bognop Rd *WNSFLD* WV11 ......18 A3
Boldmere Cl *SCFLD/BOLD* B73 ...74 B4
Boldmere Dr *SCFLD/BOLD* B73 ...77 E3
Boldmere Gdns
  SCFLD/BOLD B73 ....77 E3
Boldmere Rd *SCFLD/BOLD* B73 ...61 H5
Boldmere Ter *SLYOAK* B29 * ...159 C1
Boleyn Rd *RBRY* B45 ....173 C4
Bolingbroke Rd *SPARK* B11 ......145 H2
Bolton Rd *SMHTH* B10 ....128 A4
  WNSFLD WV11 ....24 C5
Bolton St *BORD* B9 ....127 H2
Bolton Wy *BLOX/PEL* WS3 ......16 B4
Bomers Fid *RBRY* B45 ......188 C1
Bond Dr *CVALE* B35 ....94 C4
Bondfield Rd *MOS/BIL B13 ......161 H4
Bond Sq *WSNGN* B18 ....108 A5
Bond St *BILS/COS* WV14 ......54 C1
  BKHL/PFLD WV2 ....7 F6
  BLKHTH/ROWR B65 ......122 C1
  BVILLE B30 ....160 A3
  LOZ/NWT B19 ....2 B2
  WBROM B70 ....87 G4
Bone Mill La *WOLV* WV1 ....37 E1
Bonfire Hi *HAG/WOL* DY9 ......186 A2
Bonham Gv *YDLY* B25 ....129 H3
Boningale Wy *DOR/KN* B93 ......196 B5
Bonner Dr *WALM/CURD* B76 ....94 B1
Bonner Gv *ALDR* WS9 ....30 B3
Bonnington Wy *GTB/HAM* B43 ...59 H4
Bonsall Rd *ERDW/GRVHL* B23 ...77 E5

Bonville Gdns *WOLVN* WV10 ...13 E3
Booth Cl *BLOX/PEL* WS3 ....27 F5
  KGSWFD DY6 ....100 C3
Booth Rd *DARL/WED* WS10 ......71 G1
Booths Farm Rd
  PBAR/PBCH B42 ....74 A4
Booth's La *PBAR/PBCH* B42 ....74 B2
Booth St *BLOX/PEL* WS3 ....27 G2
  DARL/WED WS10 ....40 B5
  HDSW B21 ....107 C2
  SMTHWK B66 ....107 E5
Bordeaux Cl *DUDN* DY1 ......83 H3
Borden Cl *CDSL* WV8 ....22 B2
Bordesley Circ *SMHTH* B10 ......127 H3
Bordesley Cl *BORD* B9 ......129 E2
Bordesley Dr *BORD* B9 ......128 C2
Bordesley Gn East
  STECH B33 ....130 A2
Bordesley Green Rd *BORD* B9 ...128 B2
Bordesley Park Rd
  SMHTH B10 ....127 H3
Bordesley St *DIG/EDG* B5 ....3 J5
Borneo St *RUSH/SHEL* WS4 ......42 B1
Borough Crs *OLDBY* B69 ......104 C4
  STRBR DY8 ....135 E2
Borrowdale Cl *BRLYHL* DY5 ....118 D4
Borrowdale Gv *NFLD/LBR* B31 ...174 C2
Borrowdale Rd *NFLD/LBR* B31 ...174 C2
Borrow St *WLNHL* WV13 ......39 G2
Borwick Av *WBROM* B70 ....87 E2
Boscobel Av *TPTN/OCK* DY4 ....85 F2
Boscobel Crs *WOLV* WV1 ....37 E1
Boscobel Rd *GTB/HAM* B43 ....75 F1
  SHLY B90 ....194 D3
  WSL WS1 ....5 K6
Boscombe Av *SPARK* B11 * 145 E1
Boscombe Rd *SPARK* B11 ......145 G3
Boss Dr *DUDS* DY2 ....102 C5
Bossgate Cl *WMBN* WV5 ....81 E1
Boston Gv *KGSTG* B44 ....75 H3
Bosty La *ALDR* WS9 ....29 F5
Boswell Cl *TPTN/OCK* DY4 ......70 A2
Boswell Rd *BILS/COS* WV14 ......69 E1
  FOAKS/STRLY B74 ....62 C2
  KGSTG B44 ....75 F5
Bosworth Cl *SEDG* DY3 ....66 D3
Bosworth Dr
  CHWD/FDBR/MGN B37 ......131 H2
Bosworth Rd
  LGN/SDN/BHAMAIR B26 ...147 E3
Botany Dr *SEDG* DY3 ....83 F1
Botany Rd *DSYBK/YTR* WS5 ......57 F3
Botany Wk
  LDYWD/EDGR B16 * 126 A2
Botha Rd *BORD* B9 ....128 D2
Botteley Rd *WBROM* B70 ....71 E5
Botterham La *SEDG* DY3 ....80 C5
Bottetourt Rd *SLYOAK* B29 ......141 C5
Botteville Rd *ACGN* B27 ......146 C5
Bott La *HAG/WOL* DY9 ......136 B5
  WSL WS1 ....5 G4
Boughton Rd *YDLY* B25 ......129 G2
The Boulevard *BRLYHL* DY5 ...119 G2
  SCFLD/BOLD B73 ....77 F3
Boultbee Rd
  CSCFLD/WYGN B72 ....77 G4
Boulton Middleway
  WSNGN B18 ....108 B4
Boulton Retreat *HDSW* B21 * ...107 G1
Boulton Rd *HDSW* B21 ....90 C4
  SOLH B91 ....165 E3
  WBROM B70 ....87 H5
Boulton Sq *WBROM* B70 ....87 H5
Boulton Wk *ERDW/GRVHL* B23 ...91 H2
Boundary Av
  BLKHTH/ROWR B65 ......122 C4
Boundary Cl *WLNHL* WV13 ......38 C4
Boundary Crs *SEDG* DY3 ......83 E3
Boundary Dr *MOS/BIL B13 ......145 H5
Boundary Hill *SEDG* DY3 ......83 E2
Boundary La *KINVER* DY7 ......116 C3
  SHLY B90 ....194 A2
Boundary Pl *HDSW* B21 ....88 D5
Boundary Rd *ALDR* WS9 ....19 F4
  ERDW/GRVHL B23 ....92 C2
  FOAKS/STRLY B74 ....60 B1
Boundary Wy
  DUNHL/THL/PER WV6 ......34 D3
  ETTPK/GDPK/PENN WV4 ....50 C2
Bourlay Cl *RBRY* B45 ....173 C3
Bournbrook Rd *SLYOAK* B29 ...142 D4
Bourne Av *RMSLY* B62 ......139 H3
  TPTN/OCK DY4 ....70 A4
Bournebrook Cl *DUDS* DY2 ....102 C4
Bournebrook Crs *RMSLY* B62 ...140 A3
Bourne Cl *HALE* B63 ....162 A4
  SOLH B91 ....165 G4
Bourne Gn *RIDG/WDGT* B32 ...141 G1
Bourne Hill Cl *DUDS* DY2 ......103 E5
Bourne Rd *AST/WIT* B6 ......109 H2
Bournes Cl *HALE* B63 ......138 B4
Bournes Crs *HALE* B63 ......138 A3
Bournes Hill *HALE* B63 ......138 A3
Bourne St *DUDS* DY2 ....84 D5
  SEDG DY3 ....68 D5
Bourne V *ALDR* WS9 ....44 D2
Bourne Way Gdns *SLYOAK* B29 ...160 A2
Bourn Mill Dr *AST/WIT* B6 ......109 E4
Bournville La *BVILLE* B30 ......159 G4
Bourton Cl *HIA/OLT* B92 ......164 B2
Bourton Rd *HIA/OLT* B92 ......164 B2
Bovey Cft *WALM/CURD* B76 ......78 C4
Bovingdon Rd *CVALE* B35 ......94 C3
Bowater Av *STECH* B33 ......129 H3
Bowater St *WBROM* B70 ....87 F3
Bowbrook Av *SHLY* B90 ......195 F2
Bowcroft Gv *ERDE/BCHGN* B24 ...77 G5
Bowden Rd *SMTHWKW* B67 ......106 A3
Bowdler Rd *BKHL/PFLD* WV2 ...37 F5
Bowen Av
  ETTPK/GDPK/PENN WV4 ....53 E5
Bowen-Cooke Av
  DUNHL/THL/PER WV6 ......20 C4
Bowen St
  ETTPK/GDPK/PENN WV4 ....52 A3
Bowercourt Cl *SOLH* B91 ......181 H4
Bower La *BRLYHL* DY5 ......119 H4
Bowes Rd *RBRY* B45 ....187 G1
Bowker St *WLNHL* WV13 ....38 C5

Bowlas Av FOAKS/STRLY B74 47 F5
Bowling Green Cl
DARL/WED WS10 55 F1
ERDW/GRVHL B23 76 C4
Bowling Green Dr
SMTHWKW B67 124 A2
Bowling Green La
BFLD/HDSWWD B20 108 A1
Bowling Green Rd DUDS DY2 120 D1
SMHTH B10 128 A3
STRBR DY8 135 E2
Bowman Rd PBAR/PBCH B42 74 B2
Bowman's Ri WOLV WV1 38 A3
Bowood Crs NFLD/LBR B31 175 G3
Bowood Dr
DUNHL/THL/PER WV6 21 H5
Bowood End WALM/CURD B76 62 D5
Bowshot Cl CBROM B36 95 F5
Bowstoke Rd GTB/HAM B43 73 E3
Bow St BILS/COS WV14 54 A2
CBHAMW B1 126 D3
WLNHL WV13 39 G4
Bowyer Rd WASH/WDE B8 110 C5
Bowyer St BORD B9 127 G3
Boxhill Cl AST/WIT B6 109 F3
Box Rd CHWD/FDBR/MGN B37 132 C4
Box St WSL WS1 5 G5
Box Trees Rd HOCK/TIA B94 198 A2
Boyd Gv ACGN B27 146 B5
Boydon Cl BKHL/PFLD WV2 53 E2
Boyleston Rd HLGN/YWD B28 163 E4
Boyne Rd
LGN/SDN/BHAMAIR B26 130 D5
Boyton Gv KGSTG B44 60 B5
Brabazon Gv CVALE B35 94 B3
Brabham Crs FOAKS/STRLY B74 60 B2
Bracadale Av ERDE/BCHGN B24 93 E2
Bracebridge Rd
ERDE/BCHGN B24 92 D5
FOAKS/STRLY B74 47 E5
Bracebridge St AST/WIT B6 109 E3
Braceby Av MOS/BIL B13 162 A3
Brace St WSL WS1 4 D7
Brackenbury Rd KGSTG B44 75 H3
Bracken Cl CDSL WV8 22 A1
Bracken Cft
CHWD/FDBR/MGN B37 132 C1
Brackendale Dr
DSYBK/YTR WS5 57 H5
Brackendale Wy
HAG/WOL DY9 136 B3
Bracken Dr MGN/WHC B75 63 G3
Brackenfield Rd HALE B63 138 A4
KGSTG B44 74 C1
Brackenfield Vw DUDN DY1 101 F1
Bracken Park Gdns
STRBR DY8 118 B2
Bracken Rd ERDE/BCHGN B24 93 G4
Bracken Wy FOAKS/STRLY B74 45 F5
HWK/WKHTH B38 190 B1
Bracken Wd DSYBK/YTR WS5 58 B3
Brackenwood Dr
WNSFLD WV11 25 F5
Brackley Av
BFLD/HDSWWD B20 90 C5
Brackleys Wy HIA/OLT B92 147 F5
Bradburne Wy VAUX/NECH B7 109 G4
Bradburn Rd WNSFLD WV11 24 B2
Bradbury Cl BRWNH WS8 19 F2
Bradbury Rd HIA/OLT B92 164 B2
Braden Rd
ETTPK/GDPK/PENN WV4 50 D4
Brades Cl HALE B63 120 B5
Brades Ri OLDBY B69 104 B1
Brades Rd OLDBY B69 104 C1
Bradewell Rd CBROM B36 95 F5
Bradfield Rd PBAR/PBCH B42 74 D4
Bradford Cl GTB/HAM B43 73 H4
Bradford La HAG/WOL DY9 184 B3
WSL WS1 4 D5
Bradford Rd BKDE/SHDE B34 112 C2
BRWNH WS8 9 E4
CBROM B36 113 E2
DUDS DY2 101 H3
Bradford St DIG/EDG B5 3 H7
WSL WS1 4 D5
Bradgate Cl SHHTH WV12 26 A4
Bradgate Dr FOAKS/STRLY B74 32 C5
Bradley La BILS/COS WV14 54 B5
Bradleymore Rd BRLYHL DY5 119 E1
Bradley Rd BKDE/SHDE B34 113 F3
BKHL/PFLD WV2 52 C1
STRBR DY8 135 F1
Bradleys Cl CDYHTH B64 121 E5
Bradley's La BILS/COS WV14 69 E3
Bradley St BILS/COS WV14 54 B4
BRLYHL DY5 100 D2
TPTN/OCK DY4 85 F4
Bradmore Cl SOLH B91 181 G5
Bradmore Gv SLYOAK B29 158 C2
Bradmore Rd BDMR/CCFT WV3 36 B5
Bradnock Cl MOS/BIL B13 162 A3
Bradshaw Av DARL/WED WS10 54 D3
HWK/WKHTH B38 176 B4
Bradshaw Cl EDG B15 126 C4
TPTN/OCK DY4 85 G3
Bradshawe Cl
HLGN/YWD B28 179 F2
Bradshaw St WOLV WV1 * 7 H4
Bradstock Rd BVILLE B30 177 G1
Bradwell Cft MGN/WHC B75 48 A2
Braemar Av STRBR DY8 117 G3
Braemar Cl SEDG DY3 67 E2
SHHTH WV12 25 G4
Braemar Dr ERDW/GRVHL B23 91 H1
Braemar Rd HIA/OLT B92 164 A1
SCFLD/BOLD B73 76 D1
Braeside Cft
CHWD/FDBR/MGN B37 132 D2
Braeside Wy BLOX/PEL WS3 17 H4
Bragg Rd BFLD/HDSWWD B20 90 D4
Braggs Farm La SHLY B90 194 A4
Braid Cl HWK/WKHTH B38 176 B4
Brailes Cl HIA/OLT B92 165 G3
Brailes Dr WALM/CURD B76 63 F5
Brailes Gv BORD B9 129 F3
Brailsford Cl WNSFLD WV11 25 E2
Brailsford Dr SMTHWK B66 106 C4
Braithwaite Dr KGSWFD DY6 99 H3
Braithwaite Rd SPARK B11 127 H5
Brake La STRBR DY8 152 A4
Bramah Wy TPTN/OCK DY4 70 A5
Bramber Dr WMBN WV5 64 D5
Bramber Wy STRBR DY8 135 F5
Bramble Cl AST/WIT B6 109 E2
BRWNH WS8 19 E2
CDYHTH B64 103 F5
CSHL/WTROR B46 115 G2
NFLD/LBR B31 158 B5
SHHTH WV12 26 A3
Bramble Dell BORD B9 129 E1
Bramble Dr
LGN/SDN/BHAMAIR B26 147 G1
Bramble Gn DUDN DY1 83 H1
Brambleside STRBR DY8 118 B3
The Brambles HAG/WOL DY9 136 B4
WALM/CURD B76 78 C3
Bramblewood WMBN WV5 65 E4
Bramblewood Dr
BDMR/CCFT WV3 36 A5
Bramblewoods
BKDE/SHDE B34 113 E4
Brambling Wk EDG B15 126 C5
Bramcote Dr SOLH B91 165 E3
Bramcote Ri FOAKS/STRLY B74 62 C1
Bramcote Rd RIDG/WDGT B32 140 C2
Bramerton Cl WNSFLD WV11 24 A5
Bramford Dr DUDN DY1 68 B5
Bramley Cl DSYBK/YTR WS5 43 F5
GTB/HAM B43 59 H5
Bramley Cft SHLY B90 180 C3
Bramley Dr
BFLD/HDSWWD B20 90 B3
HLYWD B47 192 D2
Bramley Mews Ct ACGN B27 146 C3
Bramley Rd ACGN B27 146 C2
DSYBK/YTR WS5 57 H4
Brampton Av HLGN/YWD B28 163 E4
Brampton Crs SHLY B90 163 F4
Bramshall Dr DOR/KN B93 196 C5
Bramshaw Cl
ALE/KHTH/YWD B14 178 B3
Bramstead Av
DUNHL/THL/PER WV6 35 F3
Branchal Rd ALDR WS9 30 C1
Branch Rd HWK/WKHTH B38 176 B5
Brandhall La LGLYGN/QTN B68 123 F3
Brandhall Rd
LGLYGN/QTN B68 123 F3
Brandon Cl ALDR WS9 45 F2
SEDG DY3 67 G4
WBROM B70 87 E4
Brandon Gv NFLD/LBR B31 189 F1
Brandon Pk BDMR/CCFT WV3 51 E1
Brandon Pl BKDE/SHDE B34 113 F2
Brandon Rd HLGN/YWD B28 145 G5
RMSLY B62 122 C3
SOLH B91 165 E3
Brandon Wy BRLYHL DY5 119 G4
WBROM B70 87 E4
Brandwood Crs BVILLE B30 177 H2
Brandwood Gv
ALE/KHTH/YWD B14 160 D5
Brandwood Park Rd
ALE/KHTH/YWD B14 177 G1
Brandwood Rd
ALE/KHTH/YWD B14 160 D5
Branfield Cl BILS/COS WV14 68 A2
Branksome Av HDSW B21 107 H1
Branscombe Cl
ALE/KHTH/YWD B14 160 D5
Bransdale Cl
DUNHL/THL/PER WV6 22 C5
Bransdale Rd BRWNH WS8 9 E5
Bransford Ri SOLH B91 166 B5
Brantford Rd YDLY B25 129 G4
Branthill Cft SOLH B91 181 H4
Brantley Av BDMR/CCFT WV3 35 G4
Brantley Rd AST/WIT B6 91 G4
Branton Hill La ALDR WS9 30 C5
Brasshouse La SMTHWK B66 106 B3
Brassie Cl HWK/WKHTH B38 176 B4
Brassington Av
CSCFLD/WYGN B72 62 C3
Bratch Cl DUDS DY2 120 C1
Bratch Common Rd
WMBN WV5 64 C4
Bratch Hollow WMBN WV5 65 E3
Bratch La WMBN WV5 65 E3
Bratch Pk WMBN WV5 64 C3
Bratt St WBROM B70 87 G2
Braunston Cl WALM/CURD B76 78 C1
Brayford Av BRLYHL DY5 118 D5
Braymoor Rd STETCH B33 131 G3
Brays Rd
LGN/SDN/BHAMAIR B26 147 H1
Bray St WLNHL WV13 39 H3
Bream Cl
CHWD/FDBR/MGN B37 132 C2
WOLVN WV10 38 B1
Breamore Crs DUDN DY1 83 H3
Brean Av
LGN/SDN/BHAMAIR B26 147 F2
Brearley Cl LOZ/NWT B19 108 D4
Brearley St HDSW B21 107 F1
LOZ/NWT B19 108 D4
Brecknock Rd WBROM B70 71 E5
Brecon Dr STRBR DY8 135 H1
Brecon Rd
BFLD/HDSWWD B20 108 B1
Bredon Av HAG/WOL DY9 136 A2
Bredon Ct HALE B63 138 C4
Bredon Cft WSNGN B18 108 A4
Bredon Rd OLDBY B69 104 B4
STRBR DY8 135 G1
Breech Cl FOAKS/STRLY B74 60 A1
Breedon Rd BVILLE B30 160 A5
Breedon Ter WSNGN B18 * 108 A4
Breedon Wy RUSH/SHEL WS4 29 E1
Breen Rydding Dr
BILS/COS WV14 68 B2
Brelades Cl DUDN DY1 83 G3
Brendan Cl CSHL/WTROR B46 115 G4
Brennand Rd
LGLYGN/QTN B68 123 F3
Brentford Rd
ALE/KHTH/YWD B14 161 F5
SHLY B90 181 E2
Brentmill Cl WOLVN WV10 13 F3
Brentnall Dr MGN/WHC B75 47 F2
Brenton Rd
ETTPK/GDPK/PENN WV4 51 F4
Brent Rd BVILLE B30 160 C2
Brentwood Cl SOLH B91 181 E2
Brentwood Gv KGSTG B44 75 E3
Brenwood Cl KGSWFD DY6 99 F2
Brereton Cl DUDS DY2 85 E5
Brereton Rd SHHTH WV12 26 A3
Bretby Cl DOR/KN B93 196 D3
Bretby Gv ERDW/GRVHL B23 77 E5
Bretshall Cl SHLY B90 195 F3
Brett Dr RIDG/WDGT B32 157 G2
Brettell La STRBR DY8 118 B4
Brettell St DUDS DY2 102 B2
Bretton Gdns WOLVN WV10 23 H4
Bretton Rd ACGN B27 146 D5
Brett St HHTH/SAND B71 87 F1
Brevitt Rd BKHL/PFLD WV2 52 B2
Brewers Dr BLOX/PEL WS3 28 C1
Brewer St WSLW WS2 42 A1
Brewery St AST/WIT B6 109 E4
DUDS DY2 85 E5
HDSW B21 107 F1
SMTHWKW B67 106 B3
Brewins Wy BRLYHL DY5 101 H5
Breydon Gv WLNHL WV13 39 F5
Brian Rd SMTHWKW B67 106 A3
Briar Av FOAKS/STRLY B74 45 G4
Briarbeck RUSH/SHEL WS4 29 E2
Briar Cl ERDE/BCHGN B24 93 E2
Briarfield Rd SPARK B11 146 A4
Briars Cl BRLYHL DY5 101 E5
The Briars ALDR WS9 30 A3
ERDW/GRVHL B23 76 B5
HAG/WOL DY9 * 169 F1
Briar Wy HWK/WKHTH B38 177 E5
Briar Wood Cl BKHL/PFLD WV2 53 E1
Briarwood Cl SHLY B90 194 D4
Brickbridge La WMBN WV5 80 C1
Brickfield Rd YDLY B25 146 B1
Brickheath Rd WOLV WV1 38 A2
Brickhill Dr
CHWD/FDBR/MGN B37 132 A2
Brickhouse La WBROM B70 70 D5
Brickhouse La South
TPTN/OCK DY4 70 B5
Brickhouse Rd
BLKHTH/ROWR B65 103 G5
Brickiln St BRWNH WS8 9 F5
Brick Kiln La HLYWD B47 192 B4
KGSTG B44 75 E4
SEDG DY3 82 C3
SHLY B90 181 F5
Brick Kiln St BRLYHL DY5 101 G4
TPTN/OCK DY4 69 E5
Brickkiln St WLNHL WV13 39 F4
Brick St SEDG DY3 67 F3
Brickyard Rd ALDR WS9 29 H2
Briddsland Rd STETCH B33 131 G2
Bridge Av TPTN/OCK DY4 70 A4
Bridgeburn Rd NFLD/LBR B31 158 A2
Bridge Cl MOS/BIL B13 144 D4
Bridge Cft BHTH/HG B12 144 A1
Bridgeford Rd
BKDE/SHDE B34 112 D3
Bridgelands Wy
BFLD/HDSWWD B20 90 D5
Bridgeman Cft CBROM B36 113 E1
Bridgeman St WSL WS1 4 D4
Bridgemary Cl WOLVN WV10 13 F3
Bridge Meadow Dr
DOR/KN B93 196 D3
Bridgend Cft BRLYHL DY5 100 D3
Bridge Piece NFLD/LBR B31 175 H3
Bridge Rd RUSH/SHEL WS4 28 D1
TPTN/OCK DY4 70 A4
WASH/WDE B8 128 C1
Bridgeside Cl BRWNH WS8 19 F1
Bridge St BILS/COS WV14 68 C3
BRWNH WS8 19 E1
CBHAMW B1 2 D7
DARL/WED WS10 70 D1
HALE B63 120 C5
OLDBY B69 105 E2
STRBR DY8 118 A3
WBROM B70 87 F2
WLNHL WV13 39 F4
WOLVN WV10 23 G5
WSL WS1 4 E3
Bridge St North SMTHWK B66 106 D3
Bridge St South SMTHWK B66 106 D3
Bridge St West LOZ/NWT B19 108 D3
The Bridge WSL WS1 4 E4
Bridge Vw CSHL/WTROR B46 * 115 F2
Bridge Wk ACGN B27 * 146 D4
Bridgewater Av OLDBY B69 105 E5
Bridgewater Crs DUDS DY2 85 E5
Bridgewater Dr BILS/COS WV14 68 C1
WMBN WV5 64 D4
Bridge Wy BRWNH WS8 19 E1
Bridgnorth Av WMBN WV5 80 D2
Bridgnorth Gv SHHTH WV12 25 H4
Bridgnorth Rd
DUNHL/THL/PER WV6 35 E3
SEDG DY3 80 A1
STRBR DY8 134 C1
Bridgwater Cl ALDR WS9 19 F3
Bridle Gv HHTH/SAND B71 72 B3
Bridle La ALDR WS9 59 H2
FOAKS/STRLY B74 45 F5
Bridle Md HWK/WKHTH B38 176 B5
The Bridle Pth SHLY B90 163 F5
Bridle Rd STRBR DY8 134 D1
Bridlewood
FOAKS/STRLY B74 45 F5
Brierley Hill Rd STRBR DY8 118 A2
Brierley La BILS/COS WV14 69 E1
Brier Mill Rd HALE B63 139 E4
Briery Cl CDYHTH B64 121 F5
Briery Rd HALE B63 138 A4
Brigadoon Gdns
HAG/WOL DY9 136 A5
Brigfield Crs MOS/BIL B13 161 H5
Brigfield Rd MOS/BIL B13 161 H5
Brighton Cl WSLW WS2 4 B1
Brighton Pl BDMR/CCFT WV3 6 B4
Brighton Rd BHTH/HG B12 144 B2
Bright Rd LGLYGN/QTN B68 105 F4
Brightstone Cl WOLVN WV10 13 F3
Brightstone Rd RBRY B45 174 B3
Bright St DARL/WED WS10 55 F3
STRBR DY8 134 D2
WOLV WV1 6 D1
Brightwell Crs DOR/KN B93 196 C5
Brimfield Pl DUNHL/THL/PER WV6 * 36 B1
Brindle Cl LGN/SDN/BHAMAIR B26 147 E2
Brindlefields Wy TPTN/OCK DY4 85 G4
Brindle Rd DSYBK/YTR WS5 58 A4
Brindley Av WNSFLD WV11 25 G1
Brindley Cl STRBR DY8 118 A3
WMBN WV5 64 B5
WSLW WS2 26 D5
Brindley Ct LGLYGN/QTN B68 * 123 F5
TPTN/OCK DY4 85 E1
Brindley Dr CBHAMW B1 2 C5
Brindley Pl CBHAMW B1 2 B6
Brindley Rd HHTH/SAND B71 71 E3
Brindley Wy SMTHWK B66 * 107 E4
Brineton Gv SLYOAK B29 158 C1
Brineton St WSLW WS2 4 A6
Bringewood Gv
RIDG/WDGT B32 157 F2
Brinklow Cft BKDE/SHDE B34 113 F2
Brinklow Rd SLYOAK B29 141 F5
Brinley Wy KGSWFD DY6 99 G3
Brinsford Rd WOLVN WV10 12 C4
Brinsley Cl SOLH B91 181 H3
Brinsley Rd
LGN/SDN/BHAMAIR B26 130 D4
Brisbane Rd SMTHWKW B67 106 A3
Briseley Cl BRLYHL DY5 119 E4
Bristam Cl OLDBY B69 104 C3
Bristnall Hall La
LGLYGN/QTN B68 123 G1
Bristnall Hall Rd
LGLYGN/QTN B68 123 G2
Bristol Rd DUDS DY2 120 D2
ERDW/GRVHL B23 92 C3
SLYOAK B29 159 F2
Bristol Rd South RBRY B45 188 A1
Bristol St BDMR/CCFT WV3 6 C7
BILS/COS WV14 53 H3
DIG/EDG B5 126 D4
Briston Cl BRLYHL DY5 119 E4
Britannia Gdns
BLKHTH/ROWR B65 122 A1
Britannia Pk DARL/WED WS10 * 70 B1
Britannia Rd BILS/COS WV14 54 B5
BLKHTH/ROWR B65 122 A1
Britannia St OLDBY B69 86 A4
Britannic Gdns MOS/BIL B13 143 H5
Britford Cl
ALE/KHTH/YWD B14 178 B2
Brittan Cl BKDE/SHDE B34 113 G3
Brittania Rd WSL WS1 56 D3
Britton Dr CSCFLD/WYGN B72 77 G3
Britwell Rd SCFLD/BOLD B73 77 E1
Brixfield Wy SHLY B90 194 A3
Brixham Rd LDYWD/EDGR B16 107 F5
Broad Acres NFLD/LBR B31 158 A4
Broad Cft TPTN/OCK DY4 70 A5
Broadfern Rd DOR/KN B93 183 F5
Broadfield Cl HHTH/SAND B71 72 B3
KGSWFD DY6 99 H4
Broadfields HAG/WOL DY9 152 C4
Broadfields Rd
ERDW/GRVHL B23 77 F4
Broadfield Wk
LDYWD/EDGR B16 2 B7
Broadheath Dr
RUSH/SHEL WS4 29 F2
Broadhidley Dr
RIDG/WDGT B32 157 F1
Broadlands WOLVN WV10 12 D2
Broadlands Dr BRLYHL DY5 101 G4
Broad La ALE/KHTH/YWD B14 177 H2
BDMR/CCFT WV3 36 A5
BLOX/PEL WS3 16 C5
RUSH/SHEL WS4 29 E1
WNSFLD WV11 15 H2
Broad Lane Gdns
BLOX/PEL WS3 16 C5
Broad La North WNSFLD WV11 25 H4
Broad Lanes BILS/COS WV14 53 G4
Broad La South WNSFLD WV11 25 F5
Broad Meadow ALDR WS9 30 B2
Broadmeadow Cl BVILLE B30 177 F2
Broadmeadow Gn
BILS/COS WV14 53 G1
Broad Meadow La BVILLE B30 177 F2
Broadmeadows Rd
SHHTH WV12 26 C2
Broadmoor Av
LGLYGN/QTN B68 123 H2
Broadmoor Cl BILS/COS WV14 53 G4
Broadmoor Rd BILS/COS WV14 53 G4
Broad Oaks WALM/CURD B76 78 C3
Broad Oaks Rd SOLH B91 164 B5
Broad Rd ACGN B27 146 B4
Broadstone Av BLOX/PEL WS3 27 H3
HALE B63 137 F3
Broadstone Cl
ETTPK/GDPK/PENN WV4 52 B3
Broadstone Rd
LGN/SDN/BHAMAIR B26 130 B2
Broad St BILS/COS WV14 68 C3
BRLYHL DY5 101 E3
EDG B15 2 B7
KGSWFD DY6 99 H4
OLDBY B69 105 E4
WOLV WV1 7 G3
Broad Street Jct WOLV WV1 7 H3
Broadwaters Av
DARL/WED WS10 55 E4
Broadwaters Rd
DARL/WED WS10 55 E4
Broad Wy RUSH/SHEL WS4 18 C5
Broadway BDMR/CCFT WV3 35 G4
CDSL WV8 10 A4
LGLYGN/QTN B68 123 G3
SHLY B90 180 B1
WOLVN WV10 13 E5
WSL WS1 57 G2
Broadway Av BORD B9 129 E2
HALE B63 138 C5
Broadway Cft
LGLYGN/QTN B68 123 G3
LGN/SDN/BHAMAIR B26 147 G1
Broadway North WSL WS1 5 J2
The Broadway
BFLD/HDSWWD B20 90 D4
DUDN DY1 84 A3
HHTH/SAND B71 71 E4
STRBR DY8 134 D5
WMBN WV5 81 E1
Broadway West WSL WS1 56 D2
Broadwell Rd HIA/OLT B92 147 G5
OLDBY B69 105 E1
Broadyates Gv YDLY B25 146 C1
Broadyates Rd YDLY B25 146 C1
Brobury Cft SOLH B91 180 D1
Brock Cl RBRY B45 174 A4
Brockeridge Cl SHHTH WV12 26 A1
Brockhall Gv
CHWD/FDBR/MGN B37 113 H4
Brockhill La ALVE B48 191 F5
Brockhurst Crs
DSYBK/YTR WS5 57 F4
Brockhurst Dr
DUNHL/THL/PER WV6 36 C1
HLGN/YWD B28 163 E5
Brockhurst La SHLY B90 194 B3
Brockhurst Pl DSYBK/YTR WS5 57 F3
Brockhurst Rd CBROM B36 111 G3
MGN/WHC B75 47 H4
Brockhurst St WSL WS1 57 E2
Brockley Cl BRLYHL DY5 119 F1
Brockley Gv MOS/BIL B13 160 C1
Brockley Pl VAUX/NECH B7 110 A2
Brockmoor Cl HAG/WOL DY9 136 A5
Brock Rd TPTN/OCK DY4 85 H2
Brockwell Gv KGSTG B44 60 A4
Brockwell Rd KGSTG B44 60 A4
Brockworth Rd
ALE/KHTH/YWD B14 177 G3
Brocton Cl BILS/COS WV14 53 E5
BLOX/PEL WS3 27 E2
Brogden Cl HHTH/SAND B71 72 B3
Bromfield Cl AST/WIT B6 109 E2
Bromfield Ct
DUNHL/THL/PER WV6 * 35 F2
Bromfield Crs DARL/WED WS10 56 C5
Bromford Cl ERDW/GRVHL B23 92 C1
Bromford Crs
ERDE/BCHGN B24 93 E4
Bromford Dl
DUNHL/THL/PER WV6 * 36 B2
Bromford Dell NFLD/LBR B31 176 A1
Bromford Dr CBROM B36 111 H1
Bromford Hl
BFLD/HDSWWD B20 90 C3
Bromford La ERDE/BCHGN B24 93 E5
ERDE/BCHGN B24 111 E1
WBROM B70 87 F5
Bromford Ri BDMR/CCFT WV3 36 D5
Bromford Rd CBROM B36 111 G2
CBROM B36 112 A2
DUDS DY2 102 A3
WBROM B70 87 E5
Bromley BRLYHL DY5 100 D4
Bromley Gdns CDSL WV8 10 C3
Bromley La KGSWFD DY6 100 A5
Bromley Pl
ETTPK/GDPK/PENN WV4 51 G3
Bromley St BKHL/PFLD WV2 52 A1
BORD B9 127 G3
HAG/WOL DY9 136 D1
Brompton Dr BRLYHL DY5 118 D5
Brompton Lawns
DUNHL/THL/PER WV6 35 E2
Brompton Pool Rd
HLGN/YWD B28 179 G2
Brompton Rd KGSTG B44 60 A4
Bromsgrove Rd
HAG/WOL DY9 170 B1
HALE B63 139 E4
RMSLY B62 172 C2
Bromsgrove St DIG/EDG B5 126 D3
Bromwall Rd MOS/BIL B13 161 H4
Bromwich Dr MGN/WHC B75 62 C1
Bromwich La HAG/WOL DY9 152 D3
Bromwynd Cl BKHL/PFLD WV2 51 H2
Bromyard Av WALM/CURD B76 78 C3
Bromyard Rd SPARK B11 145 G4
Bronte Cl SHLY B90 180 D4
Bronte Farm Rd SHLY B90 180 D4
Bronte Rd BKHL/PFLD WV2 52 D2
Bronwen Rd BILS/COS WV14 68 C4
Bronwen Vls
DARL/WED WS10 * 55 F2
Brookbank Av
BKDE/SHDE B34 113 F3
Brookbank Gdns SEDG DY3 82 D4
Brookbank Rd SEDG DY3 82 D4
Brook Cl ALDR WS9 19 G4
SHLY B90 179 H4
STETCH B33 112 A5
Brook Crs HAG/WOL DY9 152 D5
KGSWFD DY6 99 G2
Brook Cft
CHWD/FDBR/MGN B37 132 B5
LGN/SDN/BHAMAIR B26 130 D5
Brookdale SEDG DY3 83 E3
Brookdale Cl RBRY B45 173 H4
Brookdale Dr
ETTPK/GDPK/PENN WV4 50 D2
Brook Dr RIDG/WDGT B32 157 H1
Brookend Dr RBRY B45 187 H1
Brookes Cl OLDBY B69 103 H1
Brooke St DUDS DY2 102 C1
Brookfield Cl ALDR WS9 30 A1
Brookfield Rd ALDR WS9 30 A1
BVILLE B30 177 H2
CDSL WV8 10 D5
WSNGN B18 107 H4
Brookfields Rd
LGLYGN/QTN B68 105 G5
Brookfield Wy HIA/OLT B92 163 H3
TPTN/OCK DY4 69 G5
Brook Gv CDSL WV8 10 D5
Brookhill Cl SHHTH WV12 26 A1
Brook Hill Rd WASH/WDE B8 111 E5
Brook Holloway
HAG/WOL DY9 136 C4
Brookhouse La WOLVN WV10 13 F1
Brook House La WOLVN WV10 13 G1
Brookhouse Rd
DSYBK/YTR WS5 57 H1

Brookhus Farm Rd
  WALM/CURD B76.................78 C3
Brooking Cl *GTB/HAM* B43.......59 H4
Brookland Gv *ALDR* WS9............19 F5
Brookland Rd *ALDR* WS9............19 F4
  HAG/WOL DY9.................152 C5
Brooklands *STRBR* DY8...........118 B3
Brooklands Cl *HLGN/YWD* B28 ...162 D1
Brooklands Dr
  ALE/KHTH/YWD B14.........161 E5
Brooklands Gv *ALDR* WS9..........19 F5
Brooklands Pde *WOLV* WV1 ......38 B3
Brooklands Rd
  HLGN/YWD B28...............162 D1
The Brooklands *SEDG* DY3....80 C5
Brooklands Wy
  CHWD/FDBR/MGN B37.....132 B4
Brook La *ALDR* WS9................19 G4
  ALE/KHTH/YWD B14.........161 F2
  CDYHTH B64................121 E2
  HIA/OLT B92.................163 H2
  RIDG/WDGT B32.............141 F2
Brooklea Gv *HWK/WKHTH* B38 ..177 E4
Brooklyn Av *AST/WIT* B6..........109 F2
Brooklyn Gv *BILS/COS* WV14.....69 E5
  KGSWFD DY6...................99 F1
Brookmans Av
  RIDG/WDGT B32.............140 D3
Brookmeadow Ct
  HLGN/YWD B28...............162 B4
Brook Meadow Rd
  BKDE/SHDE B34.............112 C3
  RUSH/SHEL WS4..............29 F2
Brook Mdw *CDSL* WV8..............10 D2
Brook Rd *EDG* B15................125 C5
  LGLYGN/QTN B68.............123 E2
  RBRY B45....................187 H1
  STRBR DY8..................135 H4
  WLNHL WV13..................39 G4
  WMBN WV5....................64 D5
Brooksbank Dr *CDYHTH* B64 .....105 F5
Brooksby Gv *DOR/KN* B93........199 E1
Brooks Cft *CASE* B35..............94 C4
Brookside *DARL/WED* WS10.......56 B5
  GTB/HAM B43.................73 F5
  NFLD/LBR B31...............158 B5
  SEDG DY3....................83 F4
Brookside Av *MOS/BIL* B13......144 C5
Brookside Cl *ERDW/GRVHL* B23 ..76 A4
  HALE B63...................137 H4
  WMBN WV5....................64 B5
Brookside Wy *KGSWFD* DY6........77 G5
  KIDD DY10..................168 B3
Brooks Rd
  CSCFLD/WYGN B72...........77 C2
Brook St *BILS/COS* WV14.........54 A3
  BRLYHL DY5.................120 A4
  CBHAMNW B3..................2 D3
  HAG/WOL DY9...............136 D2
  KGSWFD DY6..................85 E5
  SEDG DY3....................83 F5
  SMTHWK B66................106 D3
  STRBR DY8..................135 E2
  TPTN/OCK DY4................69 E5
  WSL WS1.....................4 B4
Brook Ter *BILS/COS* WV14.......54 A3
Brookthorpe Dr *SHHTH* WV12....40 A1
Brookvale Gv *HIA/OLT* B92.....163 H1
Brookvale Ms *SLYOAK* B29......143 F5
Brookvale Park Rd
  ERDW/GRVHL B23............93 H2
Brookvale Rd *AST/WIT* B6........91 G3
  HIA/OLT B92................163 H1
Brookview *SMTHWKW* B67 * 124 B1
Brook View Cl *LOZ/NWT* B19...108 C5
Brook Wk *RIDG/WDGT* B32.......140 D5
Brookwillow Rd *HALE* B63.......137 H5
Brookwood Av
  HLGN/YWD B28...............162 B5
Broomcroft Rd
  CHWD/FDBR/MGN B37.......113 H4
Broomdene Av
  BKDE/SHDE B34.............112 C2
Broom Dr *ALE/KHTH/YWD* B14...178 A4
Broome Av *GTB/HAM* B43..........73 E4
Broome Cl *HALE* B63.............138 C4
Broome Gdns *MGN/WHC* B75......62 C5
Broomehill Cl *BRLYHL* DY5......119 E5
Broome La *KIDD* DY10...........169 E2
Broome Rd *WOLV* WV10............23 F3
Broomfield *SMTHWKW* B67 ......106 B4
Broomfield Rd
  DARL/WED WS10...............56 C5
  ERDW/GRVHL B23............92 B4
Broomfields Cl *SOLH* B91......165 F5
Broomhall Av *WNSFLD* WV11.....24 D4
Broom Hall Crs *ACGN* B27......163 G2
Broom Hall Gv *ACGN* B27.......163 C5
Broomhill Cl *GTB/HAM* B43.......73 E5
Broomhill Rd
  ERDW/GRVHL B23.............75 H4
Broomhurst
  LDYWD/EDGR B16...........125 G4
Broomie Cl *MGN/WHC* B75........62 D4
Broom La *SHLY* B90...............194 A2
Broomlea Cl *FOAKS/STRLY* B74...65 E5
Broom Rd *DSYBK/YTR* WS5........57 H5
  DUDN DY1....................85 E4
Broomy Cl *BKDE/SHDE* B34......112 C4
Broseley Av *NFLD/LBR* B31.....158 D5
Broseley Brook Cl *BORD* B9....128 A3
Brosil Av *BFLD/HDSWWD* B20.....89 G3
Brougham St *LOZ/NWT* B19......108 A2
Brough Cl
  BIRTCK/SBDGE/PER WV6....52 D5
  VAUX/NECH B7..............109 H3
Broughton Ct
  DUNHL/THL/PER WV6.........35 G3
Broughton Crs *NFLD/LBR* B31..174 D5
Bull St *BRLYHL* DY5.............119 H5
  BDMR/CCFT WV3...............35 G4
  BFLD/HDSWWD B20.........108 A1
  HAG/WOL DY9...............136 B4
Brownfield Rd
  BKDE/SHDE B34.............113 F2
Brownhills Rd *BRWNH* WS8.......19 F2
Browning Cl *SHHTH* WV12.........26 C3
Browning Crs *WOLV* WV10.........12 C5

Browning Gv
  DUNHL/THL/PER WV6.........34 C1
Browning Rd *DSYBK/YTR* WS5.....82 C2
Brownley Rd *SHLY* B90..........195 E1
Brown Lion St *TPTN/OCK* DY4....69 E4
Brown Rd *DARL/WED* WS10.........55 E1
Brown's Coppice Av *SOLH* B91..163 H5
Brown Dr *SCFLD/BOLD* B73........76 D5
Brownsea Dr *CBHAMW* B1..........5 F6
Browns Dr *BFLD/HDSWWD* B20....89 H3
Brownshore La *WNSFLD* WV11.....15 E4
Browns La *DOR/KN* B93...........196 C2
Brownsover Cl *CBROM* B36........94 D5
Brown St *BKHL/PFLD* WV2.........52 B1
Brownswald Rd *SEDG* DY3........66 D4
Broxwood Pk
  DUNHL/THL/PER WV6.........35 F2
Brueton Av *SOLH* B91...........182 B2
Brueton Dr *ERDE/BCHGN* B24.....93 E3
Brueton Rd *BILS/COS* WV14......54 C1
Bruford Rd *BDMR/CCFT* WV3......36 C5
Brunel Cl *BHTH/HG* B12.........144 C2
Brunel Ct *BILS/COS* WV14.......69 E5
Brunel Dr *TPTN/OCK* DY4.........69 E2
Brunel Gv
  DUNHL/THL/PER WV6.........20 C4
Brunel Rd *OLDBY* B69...........104 B5
Brunel St *CBHAMW* B1.............2 E6
Brunel Wk *DARL/WED* WS10* 55 H2
Brunel Wy *BKHL/PFLD* WV2........53 E1
Brunslow Cl *WLNHL* WV13.........40 A4
  WOLV WV10....................23 E1
Brunswick Ga *STRBR* DY8........152 C1
Brunswick Park Rd
  DARL/WED WS10...............56 A5
Brunswick Rd *BHTH/HG* B12.....144 C2
  HDSW B21...................89 H5
Brunswick Sq *CBHAMW* B1.........2 B6
Brunswick St *CBHAMW* B1.........2 B6
  WSLW WS2....................56 C1
Brunswick Ter
  DARL/WED WS10...............55 H5
Bruton Rd *SMTH* B10............128 D5
Brushfield Rd *PBAR/PBCH* B42..74 D3
Brutus Dr *CSHL/WTROR* B46......97 E5
Bryan Av
  ERDE/BCHGN B24.............93 F2
Bryan Rd *WSLW* WS2..............56 A5
Bryanston Cl *SOLH* B91.........164 B3
Bryanston Rd *SOLH* B91.........164 B4
Bryant St *WSNGN* B18...........107 G4
Bryce Rd *BRLYHL* DY5...........100 D4
Brylan Cft *KGSTG* B44............75 F5
Bryn Arden Rd
  LGN/SDN/BHAMAIR B26.....147 E2
Bryndale Av
  ALE/KHTH/YWD B14.........160 C5
Brynmawr Rd *BILS/COS* WV14....52 D5
Brynside Cl
  ALE/KHTH/YWD B14.........177 H3
Bryony Cft *ERDW/GRVHL* B23....75 H4
Bryony Gdns *DARL/WED* WS10.....55 F1
Bryony Rd *SLYOAK* B29..........158 D3
Buchanan Cl *RUSH/SHEL* WS4....42 C2
Buchanan Rd *RUSH/SHEL* WS4....42 C1
Buckbury Cl *HAG/WOL* DY9......153 F1
Buckbury Cft *SHLY* B90.........195 H2
Buckingham Cl
  DARL/WED WS10...............56 A5
Buckingham Dr *SHHTH* WV12.....25 H5
Buckingham Gv *KGSWFD* DY6......99 G2
Buckingham Ms
  SCFLD/BOLD B73..............77 E1
Buckingham Rd *DUDN* DY1........83 G4
Buckingham St
  BLKHTH/ROWR B65...........104 B5
  CBROM B36..................113 H2
  ETTPK/GDPK/PENN WV4.......1 A6
  LOZ/NWT B19.................2 E1
Buckland End
  BKDE/SHDE B34.............112 C3
Bucklands End La
  BKDE/SHDE B34.............112 B3
Buckle Cl *WSL* WS1..............4 E7
Buckley Rd
  ETTPK/GDPK/PENN WV4.......51 E3
Buckminster Dr *DOR/KN* B93...196 C4
Bucknall Crs *RIDG/WDGT* B32..157 E2
Bucknall Rd *WNSFLD* WV11......25 G1
Bucknell Cl *SOLH* B91..........165 G5
Buckridge Cl
  HWK/WKHTH B38............190 B1
Buckridge La *SHLY* B90.........194 A3
Buckston Cl *MGN/WHC* B75........48 A3
Budbrook Gv *BKDE/SHDE* B34....113 G3
Budden Rd *BILS/COS* WV14.......68 A4
Bude Rd *DSYBK/YTR* WS5.........58 B1
Buffery Rd *DUDS* DY2...........102 D3
Bufferys Cl *SOLH* B91..........181 H5
Buildwas Cl *BLOX/PEL* WS3......16 B5
Bulford Cl
  ALE/KHTH/YWD B14.........178 B3
Bulger Rd *BILS/COS* WV14.......53 C1
Bullace Cft *EDG* B15...........142 B4
Buller St
  ETTPK/GDPK/PENN WV4.......51 E4
Bullfields Cl
  BLKHTH/ROWR B65...........103 F4
Bullfinch Cl *DUDN* DY1.........101 G1
Bullivents Cl *DOR/KN* B93.....196 D3
Bull La *BILS/COS* WV14..........54 D5
  WBROM B70...................85 H4
  WMBN WV5....................65 H4
Bullmeadow La *WMBN* WV5........65 H5
Bullock's Rw *WSL* WS1...........5 F4
Bullock St *VAUX/NECH* B7......109 G4
  WBROM B70...................87 E5
Bullows Rd *BRWNH* WS8..........18 C1
Bull Ring *HALE* B63............138 D4
Bull's La *WALM/CURD* B76........79 E1
Bull St *BRLYHL* DY5.............119 H5
  CBHAM B2....................3 G4
  DARL/WED WS10...............55 C2
  DUDN DY1...................102 A1
  HRBN B17...................142 B1
  SEDG DY3....................83 E4
  WBROM B70...................87 H4
Bulrush Cl *BRWNH* WS8...........9 G5
Bulwell Cl *AST/WIT* B6.........109 G2

Bumblehole Mdw *WMBN* WV5......64 D4
Bunbury Gdns *BVILLE* B30......176 A1
Bunbury Rd *NFLD/LBR* B31......175 G2
Bundle Hi *HALE* B63............138 C5
The Bungalows *WBROM* B70 * 70 D5
Bunkers Hill La *BILS/COS* WV14..39 E5
Bunns La *DUDS* DY2..............85 F5
Burbage Cl *WOLV* WV10...........23 G4
Burbidge Rd *BORD* B9...........128 B1
Burbury St *LOZ/NWT* B19.......108 C3
Burbury St South
  LOZ/NWT B19................108 C3
Burcot Av *WOLV* WV1............38 B3
Burcote Rd *ERDE/BCHGN* B24.....93 H3
Burdock Cl *DSYBK/YTR* WS5......57 G5
Burdock Rd *SLYOAK* B29........158 C4
Burdons Cl *BKDE/SHDE* B34.....112 C4
Bure Gv *WLNHL* WV13.............40 B4
Burfield Rd *HALE* B63..........137 C1
Burford Cl *DSYBK/YTR* WS5......57 G4
  HIA/OLT B92................147 G4
Burford Rd *HLYWD* B47..........192 B2
  KGSTG B44....................74 F4
Burgess Cft *HIA/OLT* B92......165 H5
Burghley Wk *BRLYHL* DY5.......118 D4
Burgh Wy *WSLW* WS2.............41 E1
Burhill Wy
  CHWD/FDBR/MGN B37.......114 B5
Burke Av *MOS/BIL* B13..........162 B1
Burkitt Dr *TPTN/OCK* DY4.......70 A3
Burland Av
  DUNHL/THL/PER WV6.........22 A3
Burleigh Cl *SHHTH* WV12.........27 G4
Burleigh Rd *BDMR/CCFT* WV3.....51 G1
Burleigh St *WSL* WS1............5 C5
Burleton Rd *STECH* B33.........131 G2
Burley Cl *SHLY* B90............179 H3
Burlington Ar *CBHAM* B3..........3 H5
Burlington Rd *SMTH* B10........128 D5
  WBROM B70...................87 H5
Burlington St *AST/WIT* B6......109 E3
Burlish Av *HIA/OLT* B92........164 B1
Burman Cl *SHLY* B90............180 A3
Burman Dr *CSHL/WTROR* B46.....115 F4
Burman Rd *SHLY* B90............179 H3
Burmese Wy
  BLKHTH/ROWR B65...........103 F3
Burnaston Crs *SHLY* B90........196 A1
Burnaston Rd *HLGN/YWD* B28....162 C2
Burnbank Gv
  ERDE/BCHGN B24.............93 F2
Burn Cl *SMTHWK* B66...........106 C5
Burncross Wy *WOLV* WV10........13 E5
Burnell Gdns *BDMR/CCFT* WV3....36 A5
Burnel Rd *SLYOAK* B29..........141 G5
Burney La *MASH/WDE* B8........111 G5
Burnfields Wy *ALDR* WS9.........30 A5
Burnham Av *WOLV* WV10..........23 E2
Burnham Cl *KGSWFD* DY6.........100 B5
Burnham Meadow
  HLGN/YWD B28...............163 B4
Burnham Rd *KGSTG* B44...........74 D4
Burnhill Gv *SLYOAK* B29........158 C2
Burnlea Gv *NFLD/LBR* B31......176 A4
Bursnip Rd *WNSFLD* WV11........15 G3
Burntot Cl *BLOX/PEL* WS3.......16 C3
Burnside Gdns *DSYBK/YTR* WS5...58 B2
Burnside Wy *NFLD/LBR* B31.....189 F1
Burns Pl *DARL/WED* WS10.........54 C3
Burns Rd *DARL/WED* WS10........54 C3
Burnthurst Crs *SHLY* B90......195 C1
Burnt Oak Dr *STRBR* DY8.......135 G2
Burnt Tree *TPTN/OCK* DY4........85 F4
Burrington Rd
  RIDG/WDGT B32.............157 E2
Burrowes St *WSLW* WS2...........4 C1
Burrow Hill Cl *CBROM* B36.....113 E1
Burrows Rd *KGSWFD* DY6.........100 B5
Burrows St *WSLW* WS2............4 B1
The Burrow *BDMR/CCFT* WV3......35 F5
Burslem Cl *BLOX/PEL* WS3.......16 C3
Burton Av *RUSH/SHEL* WS4.......28 D3
Burton Crs *WOLV* WV10...........7 J2
Burton Farm Rd
  RUSH/SHEL WS4...............42 C4
Burton Rd *DUDN* DY1.............83 H2
  WOLV WV10...................7 K2
Burton Wood Dr
  ERDE/BCHGN B24.............94 D4
Bunbury Rd *BVILLE* B30.........164 C4
Bury Hill Rd *OLDBY* B69.........86 B2
Bush Av *SMTHWK* B66...........107 E4
Bushbury Cft
  CHWD/FDBR/MGN B37.......132 C4
Bushbury La *WOLV* WV10.........23 E4
Bushbury Rd *STECH* B33........112 C4
  WOLV WV10...................38 A1
Bushell Dr *SOLH* B91...........182 B1
Bushey Cl *FOAKS/STRLY* B74....164 C4
Bushey Fields Rd *DUDN* DY1....101 G2
Bush Gv *BLOX/PEL* WS3..........18 A5
  HDSW B21....................89 E5
Bushley Cft *SOLH* B91..........181 H5
Bushman Wy *BKDE/SHDE* B34.....113 C4
Bushmore Rd *HLGN/YWD* B28.....163 E3
Bush Rd *DUDS* DY2..............120 C2
  TPTN/OCK DY4................85 E2
Bushwood Dr *DOR/KN* B93.......197 E5
Bushwood Rd *SLYOAK* B29.......158 D1
Bustleholme Av
  HHTH/SAND B71..............72 A2
Bustleholme La
  HHTH/SAND B71..............72 B1
Butchers La *HALE* B63..........120 C5
Butchers Rd *HIA/OLT* B92......167 G4
Butcroft Gdns
  DARL/WED WS10...............55 C2

Bute Cl *RBRY* B45..............173 G4
  SHHTH WV12..................27 G4
Butler Rd *HIA/OLT* B92.........147 F4
Butlers Cl *BFLD/HDSWWD* B20....90 A5
  ERDW/GRVHL B23.............76 B2
Butlers La *DUDS* DY2............85 F5
Butlers Prec *WSL* WS1...........4 D3
Butlers Rd *BFLD/HDSWWD* B20....90 A3
Butler St *WBROM* B70............87 E2
Butlin St *VAUX/NECH* B7.........110 A2
Buttercup Cl *DSYBK/YTR* WS5....57 G5
Butterfield Cl
  DUNHL/THL/PER WV6.........34 B2
Butterfield Rd *BRLYHL* DY5....100 D2
Buttermere Cl *BRLYHL* DY5.....118 D5
  DUNHL/THL/PER WV6.........21 H2
Buttermere Ct
  DUNHL/THL/PER WV6.........34 D1
Buttermere Dr
  RIDG/WDGT B32.............141 F4
  WNSFLD WV11.................11 H4
Buttermere Gv *SHHTH* WV12.....25 H1
Butterworth Cl *BILS/COS* WV14..68 A2
Buttery Rd *SMTHWKW* B67.......106 A5
Buttons Farm Rd
  ETTPK/GDPK/PENN WV4.......50 D5
Buttress Wy *SMTHWK* B66.......106 C3
Butts Rd
  ETTPK/GDPK/PENN WV4.......51 F4
  RUSH/SHEL WS4...............42 B2
Butts St *RUSH/SHEL* WS4........42 B2
The Butts *RUSH/SHEL* WS4.......42 B2
Buxton Cl *BLOX/PEL* WS3........17 E4
Buxton Rd *BLOX/PEL* WS3........17 E4
  DUDS DY2....................85 G5
  ERDW/GRVHL B23.............75 H5
  SCFLD/BOLD B73..............77 E2
Byfield Cl *STECH* B33..........131 G3
Byfleet Cl
  ETTPK/GDPK/PENN WV4.......53 E5
Byford Wy
  CHWD/FDBR/MGN B37.......132 B4
Byland *WBROM* B65..............100 D2
Byland Wy *BLOX/PEL* WS3........16 B2
Byrchen Moor Gdns
  BRLYHL DY5.................100 D2
Byrne Rd *BKHL/PFLD* WV2........52 B1
Byron Av *ERDW/GRVHL* B23.......91 H3
Byron Cft *SCFLD/BOLD* B73......77 E1
Byron Crs *DUDN* DY1.............84 B1
Byron Cft *FOAKS/STRLY* B74.....32 D4
  SEDG DY3....................82 C2
Byron Rd *SHHTH* WV12...........26 C3
  SMTH B10...................128 C5
  WOLV WV10...................24 A1
Byron St *BRLYHL* DY5...........101 F2
  HHTH/SAND B71..............87 F1
Byways *BLOX/PEL* WS3...........17 E4

C

Caban Cl *NFLD/LBR* B31.........158 A5
Cable Dr *WSLW* WS2.............41 G1
Cable St *BKHL/PFLD* WV2........37 G5
Cabot Gv *DUNHL/THL/PER* WV6....34 C1
Cadbury Dr *CVALE* B35...........94 B5
Cadbury Rd *MOS/BIL* B13.......144 D3
Cadbury Wy *HRBN* B17..........141 H2
Caddick Crs *HHTH/SAND* B71.....71 H4
Caddick Rd *PBAR/PBCH* B42......74 B2
Caddick St *BILS/COS* WV14......68 A3
Cadet Dr *SHLY* B90.............180 A2
Cadgwith Gdns *BILS/COS* WV14...69 C1
Cadine Gdns *MOS/BIL* B13......160 C1
Cadle Rd *WOLV* WV10............23 F3
Cadman Crs *WOLV* WV10..........24 A4
Cadnam Cl *HRBN* B17...........142 A4
  WLNHL WV13..................39 H5
Caernarvon Cl *SHHTH* WV12.....27 H4
Caernarvon Wy *DUDN* DY1.......83 C4
Caesar Wy *CSHL/WTROR* B46.....97 E5
Cairn Dr *WSLW* WS2.............40 D3
Cairns St *WSLW* WS2............4 A1
Caister Dr *WLNHL* WV13.........39 F5
Cakemore Rd
  BLKHTH/ROWR B65...........122 C2
Cala Dr *EDG* B15...............126 B5
Calcot Dr *DUNHL/THL/PER* WV6....9 H4
Calcutt Wy *SHLY* B90..........194 A2
Caldecote Gv *BORD* B9.........129 G3
Calderfield Av *SHLY* B90......195 G1
Calder Av *WSL* WS1.............5 H3
Calder Dr *WALM/CURD* B76........78 A5
Calder Gv *BFLD/HDSWWD* B20.....89 H4
Calderfields Cl *RUSH/SHEL* WS4..42 C2
Calder Ri *DUDN* DY1............67 H5
Caldmore Rd *WSL* WS1...........4 E7
Caldmore Rd *WSL* WS1...........38 A1
Caldwell Gv *SOLH* B91.........165 E5
Caldwell Rd *WSLW* WS2.........129 C1
Caldwell St *HHTH/SAND* B71.....71 H3
Caledonia *BRLYHL* DY5..........119 F5
Caledonia Rd *DSYBK/YTR* WS5....55 A1
Caledonia Rd *BKHL/PFLD* WV2....37 G5
Caledonia St *BILS/COS* WV14....54 A2
Caledon St *WSLW* WS2...........56 C1
Caledon St *WSLW* WS2...........5 C5
Calewood Rd *BRLYHL* DY5.......119 F5
California Rd *RIDG/WDGT* B32...141 F4
California Wy *RIDG/WDGT* B32...141 F4
Callaghan Dr *OLDBY* B69........86 A3
Callcott Dr *BRLYHL* DY5........119 F5
Callear Rd *DARL/WED* WS10......70 B2
Calley Cl *TPTN/OCK* DY4.........85 F3
Callowbridge Rd *RBRY* B45.....187 H1
Callowbrook La *RBRY* B45......187 H1
Calshot Rd *PBAR/PBCH* B42......74 A3
Calstock Rd *SHHTH* WV12........40 B1
Calthorpe Cl *DSYBK/YTR* WS5....58 C2
Calthorpe Man *EDG* B15 * 126 B3
Calthorpe Rd
  BFLD/HDSWWD B20............90 C4
  DSYBK/YTR WS5..............58 B2
  EDG B15....................126 A4
Calver Crs *WNSFLD* WV11.........25 F5
Calver Gv *KGSTG* B44............59 H5
Calverley Rd
  HWK/WKHTH B38............176 B4

Calverton Gv *GTB/HAM* B43......73 G3
Calves Cft *WLNHL* WV13.........39 G2
Calvin Cl *WMBN* WV5.............80 D1
  WOLV WV10...................12 D4
Camberlge Ms
  CSHL/WTROR B46............115 F1
Camberley Crs
  ETTPK/GDPK/PENN WV4.......67 G1
Camberley Dr
  ETTPK/GDPK/PENN WV4.......51 G4
Camberley Gv
  ERDW/GRVHL B23.............76 C5
Camberley Ri *HHTH/SAND* B71....72 B2
Camberley Rd *KGSWFD* DY6......100 C5
Camborne Cl *AST/WIT* B6.......109 E2
Camborne Rd *DSYBK/YTR* WS5.....58 B1
Cambourne Rd
  BLKHTH/ROWR B65...........122 A1
Cambrai Dr *HLGN/YWD* B28......162 C2
Cambria Cl *SHLY* B90..........193 G1
  SOLH B91...................77 F3
Cambridge Cl *ALDR* WS9.........30 A2
Cambridge Crs *EDG* B15........126 D5
Cambridge Dr
  CHWD/FDBR/MGN B37.......131 H3
Cambridge Rd *DUDS* DY2........102 C1
  MOS/BIL B13...............161 F1
  SMTHWK B66................106 C2
Cambridge St *CBHAMW* B1.......2 D5
  WBROM B70..................87 F4
  WOLV WV10...................37 F1
  WSL WS1.....................5 F1
Cambridge Wy *ACGN* B27........146 D3
Camden Cl *CBROM* B36..........112 C1
  DSYBK/YTR WS5..............57 G4
Camden Dr *CBHAMW* B1...........2 B3
Camden St *ALDR* WS9............19 E3
  WSL WS1.....................4 A2
  WSNGN B18..................107 H5
Camden Wy *KGSWFD* DY6..........81 H5
Camelia Gdns *COVEN* WV9........11 H4
Camelot Wy *SMHTH* B10.........128 B4
Cameo Dr *STRBR* DY8...........118 B4
Cameron Rd *RUSH/SHEL* WS4.......5 J1
Camford Cv
  ALE/KHTH/YWD B14.........178 B2
Cam Gdns *BRLYHL* DY5..........100 D2
Camino Rd *RIDG/WDGT* B32......141 F4
Camomile Cl *DSYBK/YTR* WS5.....57 G5
Campbell Cl *RUSH/SHEL* WS4.....42 C2
Campbells Gn
  LGN/SDN/BHAMAIR B26.....147 E2
Campbell St *BRLYHL* DY5.......101 E5
Campden Gn *HIA/OLT* B92.......147 G4
Camp Hl *BHTH/HG* B12..........127 G4
  STRBR DY8..................118 A3
Camp Hill Circ *BHTH/HG* B12...127 G4
Camphill La *DARL/WED* WS10.....70 D1
Camp Hill Middleway
  BHTH/HG B12................127 C5
Camp La *BRLYHL* DY5............127 C5
  ERDE/BCHGN B24............77 C5
  WMBN WV5....................64 C5
Campion Gv *HALE* B63..........137 H4
Campion Wy *SHLY* B90..........194 A5
Camp La *HDSW* B21..............88 D4
  HWK/WKHTH B38............176 D2
Camplea Cft
  CHWD/FDBR/MGN B37.......132 A2
Camplin Crs
  BFLD/HDSWWD B20............89 G1
Camp Rd *MGN/WHC* B75...........33 H4
Camp St *BORD* B9...............128 A3
  DARL/WED WS10...............70 D1
  WOLV WV10...................7 F1
Campville Crs *HHTH/SAND* B71...72 A2
Campville Gv
  CHWD/FDBR/MGN B37.......113 H4
Camp Wood Cl *BVILLE* B30......159 C2
Camrose Cft *BHTH/HG* B12......144 A1
  BKDE/SHDE B34.............112 D3
Camrose Gdns *COVEN* WV9........12 A4
Canal La *ERDE/BCHGN* B24.......93 E5
Canal Side *BVILLE* B30 * 177 E3
  DUDS DY2....................85 H2
Canalside Cl *BLOX/PEL* WS3.....28 A1
  DARL/WED WS10...............72 A1
Canal Side Dr
  HWK/WKHTH B38............176 D4
Canal St *BRLYHL* DY5...........101 G4
  OLDBY B69...................86 D2
  STRBR DY8..................135 F1
Canary Cv *LOZ/NWT* B19........108 C2
Canberra Gdns
  BKDE/SHDE B34.............113 C3
Canberra Ri *DSYBK/YTR* WS5.....58 A3
Canberra Wy *BHTH/HG* B12 * ...127 F5
Canford Cl *BRLYHL* DY5.........127 F5
Canford Crs *CDSL* WV8..........10 A6
Canning Cl *DSYBK/YTR* WS5......58 B2
Canning Gdns *WSNGN* B18.......107 G5
Canning Rd *DSYBK/YTR* WS5......58 B2
Cannock Rd *SHHTH* WV12.........26 A3
  WOLV WV10...................23 H5
Cannon Dr *BILS/COS* WV14.......68 C1
Cannon Hill Gv
  BHTH/HG B12................144 A2
Cannon Hill Pl *BHTH/HG* B12 * ..144 A2
Cannon Hill Rd *BHTH/HG* B12...143 H2
Cannon Rd *WMBN* WV5...........65 C5
Cannon St *CBHAM* B2............3 G5
  WLNHL WV13..................39 G5
  WSLW WS2....................42 A1
Cannon St North *WSLW* WS2......42 A1
Canterbury Av *WLNHL* WV13......40 B3
Canterbury Cl
  BLKHTH/ROWR B65...........104 C5
  BLOX/PEL WS3...............18 A2
  ERDW/GRVHL B23.............92 B4
  HHTH/SAND B71..............72 A5
Canterbury Dr
  CHWD/FDBR/MGN B37.......132 A5
  DUNHL/THL/PER WV6.........34 B1
Canterbury Rd
  BFLD/HDSWWD B20............90 D5
  DSYBK/YTR WS5..............58 B2
  HHTH/SAND B71..............71 H3
Cantlow Rd *MOS/BIL* B13.......161 C4
Canton La *CSHL/WTROR* B46......97 H1

Canute Cl WSL WS1......57 F1
Canvey Cl RBRY B45......173 G4
Canwell Av
  CHWD/FDBR/MGN B37......113 H4
Canwell Gdns BILS/COS WV14......53 F4
Canwell Ga MGN/WHC B75......48 A1
Capcroft Rd MOS/BIL B13......161 H4
Cape Hi SMTHWK B66......106 C5
Capener Rd GTB/HAM B43......74 A1
Capern Gv RIDG/WDGT B32......141 F2
Cape Rd WBROM B70......86 C2
  WSNGN B18......108 A5
Capethorn Rd SMTHWK B66......124 C1
Capilano Rd ERDW/GRVHL B23......76 A4
Capponfield Cl BILS/COS WV14......53 F5
Capstone Av WOLV WV10......22 D2
  WSNGN B18......108 C5
Captain's Cl BDMR/CCFT WV3......35 H3
Carcroft Rd YDLY B25......129 G4
Cardale St BLKHTH/ROWR B65......122 G2
Carden Cl WBROM B70......86 D2
Carder Crs BILS/COS WV14......51 G1
Carder Dr BRLYHL DY5......119 E2
Cardiff St BDMR/CCFT WV3......6 C7
Cardigan Cl HHTH/SAND B71......71 G4
Cardigan Dr SHHTH WV12......25 H5
Cardigan St CBHAMNE B4......3 K5
Cardinal Cl HRBN B17......124 C2
Cardington Av PBAR/PBCH B42......74 B2
Cardoness Rd DUDN DY1......83 H4
Careless Gn HAG/WOL DY9......136 D5
Carhampton Rd
  MGN/WHC B75......63 G2
Carillon Gdns
  BLKHTH/ROWR B65......122 A1
Carisbrooke Av
  CHWD/FDBR/MGN B37......132 C2
Carisbrooke Cl
  DARL/WED WS10......72 A1
Carisbrooke Crs
  DARL/WED WS10......72 A1
Carisbrooke Dr RMSLY B62......139 F4
Carisbrooke Gdns
  WOLVN WV10......13 E4
Carisbrooke Rd
  BLKHTH/ROWR B65......71 H1
  DUNHL/THL/PER WV6......35 E2
  HRBN B17......124 D3
  WOLVN WV10......13 E4
Carless Av HRBN B17......124 D5
Carless St WSL WS1......4 E7
Carlisle St WSNGN B18......107 G4
Carl St WSLW WS2......27 F5
Carlton Av BILS/COS WV14......54 B1
  FOAKS/STRLY B74......45 F3
  HAG/WOL DY9......136 A1
  HDSW B21......89 C5
  WNSFLD WV11......24 A3
Carlton Cl DUDN DY1......68 C5
  MGN/WHC B75......62 D1
Carlton Cft FOAKS/STRLY B74......45 G3
Carlton Ms CBROM B36......115 H2
Carlton Rd BDMR/CCFT WV3......51 G1
  BORD B9......128 B3
  SMTHWK B66......106 C1
Carlyle Gv WOLVN WV10......24 A2
Carlyle Rd BLKHTH/ROWR B65......122 A2
  LDYWD/EDGR B16......125 G5
  LOZ/NWT B19......108 C1
  WOLV WV10......23 H2
Carmel Gv RIDG/WDGT B32......157 F1
Carmodale Av PBAR/PBCH B42......74 B5
Carnegie Av TPTN/OCK DY4......85 G2
Carnegie Dr DARL/WED WS10......56 A5
Carnegie Rd
  BLKHTH/ROWR B65......121 H2
Carnford Rd
  LGN/SDN/BHAMAIR B26......147 H1
Carnforth Cl KGSWFD DY6......99 F2
Carnoustie Cl BLOX/PEL WS3......16 C4
  MGN/WHC B75......47 G2
Carnwath Rd SCFLD/BOLD B73......76 C1
Carol Crs HALE B63......138 B2
  WNSFLD WV11......25 E4
Carol Gdns STRBR DY8......118 B4
Caroline Rd MOS/BIL B13......144 B3
Caroline St CBHAMNW B3......2 D2
  DUDS DY2......85 E5
  WBROM B70......87 E4
Carpenter Gld HALE B63......137 H2
Carpenter Rd EDG B15......126 B5
Carpenters Ct BHTH/HG B12 *......127 F4
Carpenter's Rd LOZ/NWT B19......108 C2
Carrick Cl BLOX/PEL WS3......18 A2
Carriers Cl WSLW WS2......40 D4
Carriers Fold WNSFLD WV11......25 F3
Carrington Rd
  DARL/WED WS10......71 H1
Carrisbrooke Rd
  DARL/WED WS10......71 H1
Carroway Head Hl
  MGN/WHC B75......49 E1
Carrs La CBHAMNE B4......3 H5
Carshalton Gv BKHL/PFLD WV2......37 J5
Carshalton Rd KGSTG B44......75 G1
Cartbridge Crs BLOX/PEL WS3......28 C5
Cartbridge La South
  RUSH/SHEL WS4......28 C5
Cartbridge La
  RUSH/SHEL WS4......28 C5
Carter Av CDSL WV8......10 D4
Carter Rd
  DUNHL/THL/PER WV6......22 D5
  GTB/HAM B43......73 H1
Carters Gn WBROM B70......87 E3
Carter's Gn WALM/CURD B76......63 F5
Carters La RMSLY B62......139 H4
Carters Hurst STECH B33......130 D5
Carter's La RMSLY B62......139 H4
Cartland Rd BVILLE B30......160 B3
  SPARK B11......128 A5
The Cartway
  DUNHL/THL/PER WV6......34 B1
Cartwright Gdns OLDBY B69......86 A4
Cartwright Wk WALM/CURD B76 *......47 G2
Cartwright St BKHL/PFLD WV2......37 F5
Carver Ct TPTN/OCK DY4 *......69 G2
Carver Gdns STRBR DY8......135 E5
Carver St CBHAMNW B1......2 D2
Casern Vw MGN/WHC B75......63 H5
Casewell Rd KGSWFD DY6......99 G1
Casey Av ERDW/GRVHL B23......76 B3

Cash Joynson Av
  BDMR/WED WS10......40 A5
Casion Crs STRBR DY8......134 D3
Casion Rd HALE B63......137 G1
Cassandra Cl BRLYHL DY5......83 E5
Cassowary Rd
  BFLD/HDSWWD B20......89 H3
Castello Dr CBROM B36......95 F3
The Castings BILS/COS WV14......68 D1
Castlebridge Rd WNSFLD WV11......25 G3
Castle Cl BRWNH WS8......9 F2
  CDYHTH B64......121 H3
Castle Crs CBROM B36......113 E1
Castle Cft LGLYGN/QTN B68......123 H4
Castlecroft Av
  BDMR/CCFT WV3......35 E5
Castlecroft Gdns
  BDMR/CCFT WV3......34 D5
Castlecroft La
  BDMR/CCFT WV3......34 D5
Castlecroft Rd
  BDMR/CCFT WV3......34 D5
  BILS/COS WV14......54 A1
Castle Dr CSHL/WTROR B46......115 F4
  SHHTH WV12......25 H5
Castleford Rd SPARK B11......145 E3
Castleford Rd SPARK B11......145 E3
Castlefort Rd ALDR WS9......19 G4
Castlegate Dr DUDN DY1......85 E4
Castlegate Rd DUDN DY1......85 E4
Castle Grounds DUDN DY1 *......84 D4
Castle Gv STRBR DY8......135 H4
Castle Hts CDYHTH B64 *......121 H4
Castle Hl DUDN DY1......84 D4
Castlehills Dr CBROM B36......112 C1
Castle La HIA/OLT B92......164 C1
Castle Mill Rd DUDN DY1......84 C2
Castle Ms DUDN DY1 *......84 D4
Castle Rd BLOX/PEL WS3......17 E4
  PBAR/PBCH B42......74 D4
Castleton Rd DUDS DY2......102 C4
Castle Vw DUDN DY1......84 D4
Castle View Cl
  DARL/WED WS10......54 C4
Castle View Rd
  BDMR/WED WS10......54 C4
Caswell Rd SEDG DY3......67 E3
Catalpa Gv FOAKS/STRLY B74......60 A2
Cater Dr WALM/CURD B76......78 B1
Caterham Dr KGSWFD DY6......118 B1
Catesby Dr KGSWFD DY6......99 H1
Catesby Pk HWK/WKHTH B38......176 C2
Catesby Rd SHLY B90......180 B4
Cateswell Rd HLGN/YWD B28......162 D1
  SPARK B11......145 H5
Cathcart Rd STRBR DY8......135 E2
Cathedral Cl TPTN/OCK DY4......85 E1
Cathel Dr PBAR/PBCH B42......74 A4
Catherine de Barnes La
  HIA/OLT B92......166 C4
Catherine Dr SCFLD/BOLD B73......62 A2
Catherine Rd BILS/COS WV14......68 A2
Catherines Cl SOLH B91......183 F1
Catherton Cl TPTN/OCK DY4......70 A1
Catholic La SEDG DY3......67 E4
Catisfield Crs CDSL WV8......22 B1
Cat & Kittens La WOLVN WV10......13 E1
Cat La BXDE/SHDE B34......112 D2
Cato St LDYWD/EDGR B16......109 F5
Cato St North VAUX/NECH B7......110 A4
Catshill Rd BRWNH WS8......9 G5
Cattell Dr MGN/WHC B75......63 H5
Cattell Rd BORD B9......128 A3
Cattells Gv VAUX/NECH B7......110 A3
Cattermole Gv GTB/HAM B43......59 G5
Cattock Hurst Dr
  SCFLD/BOLD B73......77 H4
Causeway BLKHTH/ROWR B65......122 A2
Causeway Green Rd
  LGLYGN/QTN B68......123 E1
Causeway Rd BILS/COS WV14......68 C2
The Causeway SHLY B90......129 H5
Causey Farm Rd HALE B63......154 D2
Cavalier Circ WOLVN WV10......12 D5
Cavalier Dr HALE B63......138 C4
Cavell Closet WSLW WS2......4 B3
Cavell Rd DUDS DY2......85 F5
Cavendish Cl
  HWK/WKHTH B38......177 E4
  KGSWFD DY6......99 H5
Cavendish Dr HAG/WOL DY9......169 F1
Cavendish Gdns WSLW WS2......41 E1
Cavendish Rd
  LDYWD/EDGR B16......125 F1
  RMSLY B62......138 D4
  WOLV WV10......38 B4
  WSLW WS2......27 E5
Cavendish Wy ALDR WS9......30 B5
Caversham Rd KGSTG B44......75 H2
Cawdon Gv DOR/KN B93......198 C1
Cawdor Crs LDYWD/EDGR B16......125 H3
Caxton Gv KGSTG B44......76 A2
Cayton Gv ERDW/GRVHL B23......76 D5
Cecil Dr OLDBY B69......86 B4
Cecil Rd ERDE/BCHGN B24......92 D3
  SLYOAK B29......160 C1
Cecil St LOZ/NWT B19......3 G1
  RUSH/SHEL WS4......28 A4
  STRBR DY8......135 F2
Cedar Av BILS/COS WV14......68 A4

BRWNH WS8......9 G4
CBROM B36......95 G4
Cedar Bridge Cft
  FOAKS/STRLY B74......47 F5
Cedar Cl BVILLE B30......159 F4
  DSYBK/YTR WS5......57 H4
  LGLYGN/QTN B68......123 G4
  STRBR DY8......135 E1
Cedar Dr ERDE/BCHGN B24......93 G1
  FOAKS/STRLY B74......45 F4
  NFLD/LBR B31......189 H1
Cedar Gv BDMR/CCFT WV3......50 D4
  DARL/WED WS10......71 H1
  DUDN DY1......84 B5
  SOLH B91......182 A2
Cedar Park Rd SHHTH WV12......26 A1
Cedar Rd BVILLE B30......159 G4
  DARL/WED WS10......71 E1
  DUDN DY1......84 B5
  WLNHL WV13......39 E3
Cedars Av ACCN B27......146 C3
  KGSWFD DY6......99 H5
  WMBN WV5......81 E1
The Cedars
  DUNHL/THL/PER WV6 *......36 B2
  YDLY B25......130 A3
Cedar Wy NFLD/LBR B31......175 F4
  WNSFLD WV11......24 C3
Cedarwood FOAKS/STRLY B74......47 F5
Cedarwood Cft
  PBAR/PBCH B42......73 H3
Cedar Wood Rd SEDG DY3......83 E2
Celandine Cl KGSWFD DY6......99 G5
Celandine Rd DUDN DY1......84 A2
The Celandines WMBN WV5......64 C5
Celts Cl BLKHTH/ROWR B65......104 A5
Cemetery La WSNGN B18......108 B4
Cemetery Rd DARL/WED WS10......40 D5
  HAG/WOL DY9......136 B2
  LGLYGN/QTN B68......105 G3
  WLNHL WV13......39 G2
Cemetery Wy BLOX/PEL WS3......27 F1
Centenary Cl NFLD/LBR B31......175 G4
Centenary Dr HDSW B21......89 G5
Centenary Sq CBHAMW B1......2 D5
Central Av BILS/COS WV14......54 A1
  BLKHTH/ROWR B65......122 A2
  CDYHTH B64......120 D5
  ETTPK/GDPK/PENN WV4......52 D1
  HAG/WOL DY9......136 C4
  HLYWD B47......175 F5
  NFLD/LBR B31......175 G1
  TPTN/OCK DY4......69 F5
Central Cl BLOX/PEL WS3......27 E1
Central Dr BILS/COS WV14......68 D4
  BLOX/PEL WS3......26 D2
  SEDG DY3......83 F4
Central Pk DUDS DY2 *......121 E1
Central Park Dr WSNGN B18......107 H4
Central Sq ERDW/GRVHL B23 *......93 C2
Central Wy BRLYHL DY5......119 H1
Centre La HALE B63......138 D4
The Centreway
  ALE/KHTH/YWD B14......179 F1
Centurion Cl CSHL/WTROR B46......97 F5
Century Pk BORD B9......128 A2
Century Rd OLDBY B69......105 E1
Cedmund Crs
  CHWD/FDBR/MGN B37......132 B1
Chaceley Gv
  ERDW/GRVHL B23 *......76 B4
Chadbury Cft SHLY B90......181 H5
Chadbury Rd HALE B63......139 E4
Chaddersley Cl RBRY B45......175 H5
Chaddesley Dr HAG/WOL DY9......152 D1
Chaddesley Rd HALE B63......138 D5
  NFLD/LBR B31......176 B3
Chadley Cl SOLH B91......164 C4
Chad Rd BDMR/CCFT WV3......35 J7
  EDG B15......125 H4
Chadshunt Cl CBROM B36......95 F4
Chadsmoor Ter
  VAUX/NECH B7......109 H3
Chadstone Cl SHLY B90......195 H2
Chad Valley Cl HRBN B17......142 B1
Chadwell Gdns CDSL WV8......10 D3
Chadwich La HAG/WOL DY9......186 A2
Chadwick Av RBRY B45......188 B2
Chadwick Cl
  ETTPK/GDPK/PENN WV4......50 C2
Chadwick Ct GTB/HAM B43 *......73 C3
Chadwick Rd MGN/WHC B75......63 F3
Chadworth Av DOR/KN B93......196 C4
Chaffcombe Rd
  LGN/SDN/BHAMAIR B26......148 A1
Chaffinch Cl SEDG DY3......67 E1
Chaffinch Dr CBROM B36......114 B2
Chaffinch Rd HAG/WOL DY9......136 A4
Chainmakers Cl BILS/COS WV14......54 A1
Chalcot Gv BFLD/HDSWWD B20......89 C1
Chaldon Cl COVEN WV9......12 A5
Chale Gv ALE/KHTH/YWD B14......178 C2
Chalfont Pl HAG/WOL DY9......136 C5
Chalfont Rd ERDW/GRVHL B23......76 A3
Chalford Wy SHLY B90......180 C5
Chalgrove Av
  HWK/WKHTH B38......176 C4
Chalgrove Crs SOLH B91......181 H4
Challenge Wy WOLVN WV10......38 D5
Challenor Av WLNHL WV13......38 D5
Chalybeate Cl RBRY B45......173 H4
Chamberlain Cl
  ETTPK/GDPK/PENN WV4......51 E5
Chamberlain Crs SHLY B90......180 D2
Chamberlain Rd MOS/BIL B13......161 F4
Chamberlain's La
  ETTPK/GDPK/PENN WV4......66 C2
Chamberlain Sq CBHAMNW B3......2 E5
Chamberlain Wk
  CSHL/WTROR B46......115 F2
  SMTHWK B66 *......106 C3
Chance Cft LGLYGN/QTN B68......123 F4

Chancellor's Cl EDG B15......125 G4
Chancel Wy RMSLY B62......139 E2
Chancery Wy BRLYHL DY5......119 H2
Chandler Dr
  ETTPK/GDPK/PENN WV4......50 D5
Chandlers Cl COVEN WV9......22 C1
  WSNGN B18......108 A3
Chandlers Keep BRWNH WS8......19 F1
Chandos Av MOS/BIL B13......144 B5
Chandos Rd BORD B9......127 H1
Chanston Av
  ALE/KHTH/YWD B14......178 A1
Chanterelle Gdns
  ETTPK/GDPK/PENN WV4......51 G4
Chantrey Crs BILS/COS WV14......54 B1
  GTB/HAM B43......59 H4
Chantry Av BLOX/PEL WS3......27 G2
Chantry Cl HLYWD B47......192 C1
Chantry Dr RMSLY B62......139 H1
Chantry Heath Crs
  DOR/KN B93......183 F5
Chantry Rd HDSW B21......107 H1
  KINVER DY7......117 C5
  MOS/BIL B13......144 A3
Chapel Ash BDMR/CCFT WV3......6 C4
Chapel Ash Island
  BDMR/CCFT WV3......6 D4
Chapel Av BRWNH WS8......9 E2
Chapel Cl CDYHTH B64......121 H4
  WMBN WV5......80 D1
Chapel Dr BRWNH WS8......9 E2
  HLYWD B47......192 B5
Chapelfield Ms RBRY B45......187 H2
  STRBR DY8......135 C3
Chapelfield Rd RBRY B45......174 A5
Chapel Fields Rd HIA/OLT B92......147 F5
Chapel Gn WLNHL WV13......39 H3
Chapel House La HALE B63......137 G2
Chapelhouse Rd
  CHWD/FDBR/MGN B37......131 H2
Chapel House St BHTH/HG B12 *......5 K7
Chapel La CDSL WV8......10 B4
  GTB/HAM B43......58 D4
  HAG/WOL DY9......185 H1
  HOCK/TIA B94......199 C4
  RMSLY B62......154 C4
  SEDG DY3......80 A2
  SLYOAK B29......142 C5
Chapel St BILS/COS WV14......54 B4
  BLOX/PEL WS3......27 H2
  BRLYHL DY5......101 E2
  BRWNH WS8......9 E2
  CBHAMNE B4......3 J4
  DARL/WED WS10......70 C1
  DUDS DY2......102 D5
  HAG/WOL DY9......152 C5
  HALE B63......138 C4
  KGSWFD DY6......100 A4
  OLDBY B69......104 C2
  TPTN/OCK DY4......85 E1
  WBROM B70......87 F1
  WMBN WV5......80 D1
Chapel Vw SMTHWKW B67......106 B5
Chapel Wk BVILLE B30......177 E3
  SEDG DY3......83 E4
Chapelwood Gn
  PBAR/PBCH B42 *......90 D1
Chapman Rd SMTHWK B10......128 A4
Chapman's Hl RMSLY B62......172 D5
Chapmans Pas CBHAMW B1 *......2 E7
Chapman St WBROM B70......87 F1
Chapter House WBROM B70......87 E1
Charfield Cl BVILLE B30......159 F3
Charingworth Rd HIA/OLT B92......148 A5
Charlbury Av
  PBAR/PBCH B37......131 H2
Charlbury Crs
  LGN/SDN/BHAMAIR B26......130 B4
Charlecote Cft SHLY B90......180 C5
Charlecote Dr DUDN DY1......83 G3
  ERDW/GRVHL B23......76 C4
Charlecote Gdns
  SCFLD/BOLD B73......77 E3
Charlecote Ri WLNHL WV13......39 E4
Charlecott Cl MOS/BIL B13......162 B3
Charlemont Av
  HHTH/SAND B71......72 B3
Charlemont Crs
  HHTH/SAND B71......72 A3
Charlemont Rd
  DSYBK/YTR WS5......57 H2
Charlemont Rd
  HHTH/SAND B71......72 B3
Charles Av BLKHTH/ROWR B65......104 A5
  ETTPK/GDPK/PENN WV4......51 H3
  WNSFLD WV11......14 D5
Charles Cl WASH/WDE B8......110 B5
Charles Crs BLOX/PEL WS3......18 A2
Charlesdale Dr ALDR WS9......44 B1
Charles Dr VAUX/NECH B7......109 H3
Charles Edward Rd
  LGN/SDN/BHAMAIR B26......146 D1
Charles Foster St
  DARL/WED WS10......55 E2
Charles Henry St
  BHTH/HG B12......127 E4
Charles Holland St
  WLNHL WV13......39 H3
Charles Rd AST/WIT B6......91 G5
  BFLD/HDSWWD B20......90 C5
  RMSLY B62......120 A3
  HALE B63......138 C5
  SMHTH B10......128 C4
  SOLH B91......181 E3
  STRBR DY8......135 E3
  TPTN/OCK DY4......69 G4
Charles St SMTHWK B66......107 H2
  WBROM B70......86 C1
  WLNHL WV13......40 A2
  WSLW WS2......4 B4
Charles Wesley Ct
  BHTH/HG B12 *......5 J7
Charlesworth Av SHLY B90......195 H2
Charleville Rd LOZ/NWT B19......108 B2
Charlotte Cl OLDBY B69......85 G4

Charlotte Gdns SHLY B90......180 A2
Charlotte Rd BVILLE B30......160 A4
  DARL/WED WS10......70 B2
  EDG B15......126 B1
Charlotte St CBHAMNW B3......2 D4
  DUDN DY1......102 B3
  WSL WS1......5 H3
Charlton Dr CDYHTH B64......120 D5
Charlton Rd KGSTG B44......75 G4
Charlton St BRLYHL DY5......118 C1
  DUDN DY1......84 B5
Charminster Av YDLY B25......129 H4
Charnwood Av SEDG DY3......67 F1
Charnwood Cl BILS/COS WV14......54 C5
  BRLYHL DY5......118 D5
  RBRY B45......174 B2
Charnwood Ct HAG/WOL DY9......136 D5
Charnwood Rd
  DSYBK/YTR WS5......57 G4
  PBAR/PBCH B42......73 H4
Charter Crs CDYHTH B64......121 H4
Charterfield Dr KGSWFD DY6......99 H1
Charterhouse Dr SOLH B91......181 H4
Charter Rd TPTN/OCK DY4......70 A2
Charters Av CDSL WV8......21 F1
Charter St BRLYHL DY5......101 G4
Chartist Rd WASH/WDE B8......110 B3
Chartley Cl DOR/KN B93......196 C5
  DUNHL/THL/PER WV6......34 D1
Chartley Rd ERDW/GRVHL B23......92 A5
  HHTH/SAND B71......71 H5
The Chartway BLOX/PEL WS3......18 B5
Chartwell Cl DUDN DY1......68 B5
Chartwell Dr FOAKS/STRLY B74......46 B1
  SHLY B90......194 D3
  WLNHL WV13......40 D1
  WOLVN WV10......23 C1
Chase Gv ERDE/BCHGN B24......77 H1
The Chase Link BRWNH WS8 *......9 G3
Chasepool Rd SEDG DY3......98 A2
Chase Rd BLOX/PEL WS3......27 E2
  BRWNH WS8......9 H5
  SEDG DY3......82 D5
The Chase
  DUNHL/THL/PER WV6......22 D4
  WALM/CURD B76......77 H4
Chase Vw
  ETTPK/GDPK/PENN WV4......67 G1
Chater Dr WALM/CURD B76......78 C2
Chatham Rd NFLD/LBR B31......175 G2
Chatsworth Av GTB/HAM B43......73 E2
Chatsworth Cl
  CSCFLD/WYGN B72......77 H4
  SHHTH WV12......25 H5
  SHLY B90......194 D5
Chatsworth Crs
  RUSH/SHEL WS4......29 F3
Chatsworth Gdns
  DUNHL/THL/PER WV6......21 E3
Chatsworth Ms RMSLY B62 *......117 G2
Chatsworth Rd RMSLY B62......121 G5
Chattock Av SOLH B91......182 C1
Chattock Cl CBROM B36......112 A2
Chatwell Gv SLYOAK B29......141 H5
Chatwin Pl BILS/COS WV14......54 A5
Chatwin St SMTHWK B66......106 B2
Chatwins Whf TPTN/OCK DY4......85 F1
Chaucer Av SEDG DY3......82 C1
  SHHTH WV12......26 C2
  TPTN/OCK DY4......85 F3
Chaucer Cl BILS/COS WV14......68 D5
  ERDW/GRVHL B23......91 H3
  STRBR DY8......118 C4
Chaucer Rd BLOX/PEL WS3......28 A2
Chauson Gv SOLH B91......181 G5
Chavasse Rd
  CSCFLD/WYGN B72......62 D5
Chawn Hill HAG/WOL DY9......136 A4
Chawnhill Cl HAG/WOL DY9......136 A4
Chawn Park Dr HAG/WOL DY9......136 A4
Chaynes Gv STECH B33......131 F2
Cheadle Dr ERDW/GRVHL B23......76 B3
Cheam Gdns
  DUNHL/THL/PER WV6......22 A2
Cheapside BHTH/HG B12......127 F4
  WLNHL......39 G4
Cheatham St WASH/WDE B8......110 B3
Checketts St WSLW WS2......4 A3
Checkley Cl SHLY B90......180 A1
Checkley Cft WALM/CURD B76......78 B3
Cheddar Rd BHTH/HG B12......144 A1
Chedworth Cl SLYOAK B29......158 D4
Cheedon Cl DOR/KN B93......198 C1
Chelford Crs KGSWFD DY6......118 C1
Chells Gv MOS/BIL B13......161 H5
Chelmar Cl CBROM B36......113 H1
Chelmar Dr BRLYHL DY5......100 C3
Chelmarsh Av
  BDMR/CCFT WV3......35 E4
Chelmscote Rd HIA/OLT B92......164 B1
Chelmsley Av
  CSHL/WTROR B46......115 F3
Chelmsley Cir
  CHWD/FDBR/MGN B37......132 B2
Chelmsley Gv STETCH B33......131 G1
Chelmsley La
  CHWD/FDBR/MGN B37......131 H4
Chelsea Cl RIDG/WDGT B32......141 F5
Chelsea Dr FOAKS/STRLY B74......46 D1
Chelsea Wy KGSWFD DY6......99 G3
Chelston Dr
  DUNHL/THL/PER WV6......36 A1
Chelston Rd NFLD/LBR B31......175 E3
Cheltenham Cl
  DUNHL/THL/PER WV6......22 D5
Cheltenham Dr CBROM B36......111 H1
  KGSWFD DY6......99 F3
Cheltenham Ms
  FOAKS/STRLY B74......47 E4
Chelthorn Wy SOLH B91......182 A3
Cheltondale Rd SOLH B91......164 B5
Chelveston Rd SOLH B91......181 H4
Chelwood Gdns
  BILS/COS WV14......53 F3

Chelworth Rd
HWK/WKHTH B38 177 F3
Chem Rd BILS/COS WV14 53 F3
Cheniston Rd SHHTH WV12 26 A4
Chepstow Cl
DUNHL/THL/PER WV6 34 D1
Chepstow Gv RBRY B45 188 B2
Chepstow Rd BLOX/PEL WS3 26 D1
WOLVN WV10 12 D2
Chepstow Vls BHTH/HG B12 * 144 D2
Chequerfield Dr
BDMR/CCFT WV3 51 G2
Chequers Av WMBN WV5 65 E2
Chequer St BDMR/CCFT WV3 51 G2
Cherhill Covert
ALE/KHTH/YWD B14 177 G3
Cherington Rd SLYOAK B29 160 A2
Cheriton Gv
DUNHL/THL/PER WV6 34 C2
Cherrington Cl NFLD/LBR B31 158 A3
Cherrington Gdns
DUNHL/THL/PER WV6 35 F3
HAG/WOL DY9 153 E2
Cherrington Wy SOLH B91 181 H4
Cherry Crs ERDE/BCHGN B24 92 D3
Cherrydale Ct DUDN DY1 83 H4
Cherry Dr BORD B9 127 H3
Cherry Gn DUDN DY1 83 H2
Cherry Gv SMTHWK B66 107 E4
STRBR DY8 135 E3
Cherry Hill Wk DUDN DY1 102 A1
Cherry La DARL/WED WS10 71 E1
SCFLD/BOLD B73 77 E4
SEDG DY3 81 F3
Cherry Lea BKDE/SHDE B34 112 D3
Cherry Orch CDSL WV8 10 B3
CDYHTH B64 121 F3
Cherry Orchard Av HALE B63 138 B2
Cherry Orchard Crs HALE B63 138 B2
Cherry Orchard Rd
BFLD/HDSWWD B20 89 H1
Cherry Rd TPTN/OCK DY4 69 F4
Cherry St BDMR/CCFT WV3 6 C5
CBHAM B2 3 G5
HALE B63 138 B2
STRBR DY8 135 E3
Cherry Tree Av DSYBK/YTR WS5 57 H4
Cherrytree Ct HAG/WOL DY9 136 C4
Cherry Tree Cft ACGN B27 146 C2
Cherry Tree Gdns CDSL WV8 10 D4
Cherry Tree La CDSL WV8 10 D4
HALE B63 154 D1
Cherry Tree Rd KGSWFD DY6 100 A1
Cherry Wk HLYWD B47 192 D3
Cherrywood Cl BILS/COS WV14 68 C2
Cherrywood Crs SOLH B91 182 A5
Cherrywood Gn
BILS/COS WV14 38 D5
Cherrywood Rd BORD B9 128 B2
FOAKS/STRLY B74 44 D4
Cherrywood Wy
FOAKS/STRLY B74 46 B1
Chervil Cl PBAR/PBCH B42 74 C4
Chervil Ri WOLVN WV10 37 H2
Cherwell Dr BRWNH WS8 8 C2
CBROM B36 113 H1
Cherwell Gdns AST/WIT B6 * 108 D1
Cheshire Av SHLY B90 180 A2
Cheshire Cl STRBR DY8 117 H4
Cheshire Gv
DUNHL/THL/PER WV6 34 C1
Cheshire Rd AST/WIT B6 91 G4
SMTHWKW B67 106 C5
WSLW WS2 40 D3
Cheshunt Pl
ALE/KHTH/YWD B14 * 161 E2
Chessetts Gv MOS/BIL B13 161 G4
Chessetts Wood Rd
HOCK/TIA B94 199 G3
Chester Av
DUNHL/THL/PER WV6 22 B3
Chester Cl
CHWD/FDBR/MGN B37 132 A2
WLNHL WV13 40 B3
Chesterfield Cl NFLD/LBR B31 175 H3
Chesterfield Ct ALDR WS9 * 19 F3
Chester Gdns SCFLD/BOLD B73 76 C2
Chestergate Cft
ERDE/BCHGN B24 93 H2
Chester Pl WSLW WS2 41 F4
Chester Ri LGLYGN/QTN B68 123 G4
Chester Rd ALDR WS9 45 F2
BRWNH WS8 19 H2
CBROM B36 112 D1
CDYHTH B64 120 C4
CHWD/FDBR/MGN B37 133 E3
DUDS DY2 120 D2
ERDE/BCHGN B24 93 G1
FOAKS/STRLY B74 60 C1
HHTH/SAND B71 71 F2
HIA/OLT B92 150 D3
SCFLD/BOLD B73 76 C3
Chester Rd North BRWNH WS8 8 D3
SCFLD/BOLD B73 61 E5
Chester St
DUNHL/THL/PER WV6 36 D1
VAUX/NECH B7 109 F4
Chesterton Cl SOLH B91 164 A5
Chesterton Rd BHTH/HG B12 144 C2
WOLVN WV10 24 A2
Chesterwood ALDR WS9 45 E3
HLYWD B47 192 C2
Chesterwood Gdns
BFLD/HDSWWD B20 90 D4
Chesterwood Rd
MOS/BIL B13 161 F4
Chestnut Av DUDN DY1 84 C3
TPTN/OCK DY4 69 F4
Chestnut Cl ACGN B27 146 C3
CDSL WV8 10 B5
FOAKS/STRLY B74 45 G3
HIA/OLT B92 163 H2
STRBR DY8 134 C5
Chestnut Ct BKDE/SHDE B34 113 G2
Chestnut Dr CBROM B36 112 C1
ERDE/BCHGN B24 93 G2
HAG/WOL DY9 169 F1
RBRY B45 188 C4
RUSH/SHEL WS4 28 D2
WMBN WV5 81 E1
Chestnut Gv
CSHL/WTROR B46 115 G2
HRBN B17 142 B2
KGSWFD DY6 100 B3
Chestnut Pl BLOX/PEL WS3 27 H4
Chestnut Rd BLOX/PEL WS3 28 A4
DARL/WED WS10 71 E1
LGLYGN/QTN B68 123 G5
MOS/BIL B13 144 C3
Chestnuts Av
LGN/SDN/BHAMAIR B26 130 D5
Chestnut Wy BDMR/CCFT WV3 35 H5
Chestom Rd
ETTPK/GDPK/PENN WV4 53 F3
Cheston Rd VAUX/NECH B7 109 G3
Cheswell Cl
DUNHL/THL/PER WV6 35 F3
Cheswick Cl WLNHL WV13 39 F5
Cheswick Wy SHLY B90 194 D5
Cheswood Dr WALM/CURD B76 78 D5
Chetland Cft HIA/OLT B92 165 H3
Chettle Rd BILS/COS WV14 54 B5
Chetton Gn WOLVN WV10 12 B4
Chetwood Cl
DUNHL/THL/PER WV6 22 C5
Chetwynd Cl WSLW WS2 40 A2
Chetwynd Rd BKHL/PFLD WV2 51 H2
WASH/WDE B8 111 F4
Cheveley Av RBRY B45 188 B1
Chevening Cl SEDG DY3 67 G4
Cheveridge Cl SOLH B91 181 G4
Cheverton Rd NFLD/LBR B31 175 E2
Cheviot Rd BKHL/PFLD WV2 52 D1
STRBR DY8 135 G1
Cheviot Wy HALE B63 137 H4
Cheylesmore Cl
SCFLD/BOLD B73 62 B4
Cheyne Gdns HLGN/YWD B28 179 G2
Cheyne Wk BRLYHL DY5 119 E5
Cheyney Cl
DUNHL/THL/PER WV6 22 C5
Chichester Av DUDS DY2 102 D4
Chichester Ct
SCFLD/BOLD B73 * 62 B3
Chichester Dr RIDG/WDGT B32 140 A2
Chichester Gv
CHWD/FDBR/MGN B37 132 B3
Chigwell Cl CVALE B35 94 C3
Chilcote Cl HLGN/YWD B28 179 H1
Childs Av BILS/COS WV14 68 A1
Chilgrove Gdns
DUNHL/THL/PER WV6 21 G5
Chilham Dr
CHWD/FDBR/MGN B37 132 C2
Chillinghome Rd CBROM B36 111 H1
Chillington Dr CDSL WV8 10 B3
DUDN DY1 83 H3
Chillington Flds WOLV WV1 38 A4
Chillington Pl BILS/COS WV14 53 G3
Chillington Rd TPTN/OCK DY4 70 A2
Chillington St BKHL/PFLD WV2 37 H5
Chiltern Cl HALE B63 137 G5
SEDG DY3 83 F3
Chiltern Dr WLNHL WV13 38 D4
Chiltern Rd STRBR DY8 135 H1
Chilton Rd
ALE/KHTH/YWD B14 179 F1
Chilwell Cl SOLH B91 181 H4
Chilwell Cft LOZ/NWT B19 109 E3
Chilworth Av WNSFLD WV11 25 F3
Chilworth Cl AST/WIT B6 109 F3
Chimes Cl STETCH B33 131 G3
Chimney Rd TPTN/OCK DY4 70 B4
Chingford Cl STRBR DY8 99 G5
Chingford Rd KGSTG B44 75 G3
Chinley Gv KGSTG B44 76 A2
Chinn Brook Rd MOS/BIL B13 161 H5
Chip Cl HWK/WKHTH B38 176 B3
Chipperfield Rd CBROM B36 112 A1
Chipstead Rd
ERDW/GRVHL B23 76 B4
Chipstone Cl SOLH B91 182 A5
Chirbury Gv NFLD/LBR B31 175 H4
Chirton Gv
ALE/KHTH/YWD B14 160 D4
Chiseldon Cft
ALE/KHTH/YWD B14 178 C2
Chisholm Gv ACGN B27 163 G2
Chiswell Rd WSNGN B18 107 G5
Chivington Cl SHLY B90 195 H2
Chorley Av BKDE/SHDE B34 112 B2
Chorley Gdns BILS/COS WV14 53 F3
Christchurch Cl EDG B15 125 G4
Christ Church Gv WSL WS1 57 G1
Christina Ct HHTH/SAND B71 87 H2
Christine Cl TPTN/OCK DY4 70 A1
Christopher Rd
BKHL/PFLD WV2 37 G5
RMSLY B62 139 G4
SLYOAK B29 142 B5
Chubb St WOLV WV1 7 H3
Chuckery Rd WSL WS1 5 H4
Chudleigh Gv GTB/HAM B43 73 F3
Chudleigh Rd
ERDW/GRVHL B23 92 C2
Church Av
BFLD/HDSWWD B20 * 90 C5
HAG/WOL DY9 170 C3
MOS/BIL B13 * 144 B4
STRBR DY8 118 C5
Churchbridge OLDBY B69 104 D3
Church Cl
CHWD/FDBR/MGN B37 114 A3
HLYWD B47 192 B5
Church Cft HALE B63 138 C3
HRBN B17 141 H3
Church Cross Vw DUDN DY1 101 F1
Churchdale Rd KGSTG B44 59 H5
Church Dr BVILLE B30 160 B3
Churchfield Av TPTN/OCK DY4 69 F3
Churchfield Cl VAUX/NECH B7 110 A3
Churchfield Rd WOLVN WV10 22 D2
Churchfields Rd
DARL/WED WS10 55 H5
Churchfield St DUDS DY2 102 C1
Church Gdns SMTHWKW B67 * 124 C1
Church Gn BFLD/HDSWWD B20 89 H4
BILS/COS WV14 38 C5
Church Gv
BFLD/HDSWWD B20 * 90 B5
MOS/BIL B13 162 A5
Church Hl BRLYHL DY5 119 F2
CDSL WV8 10 B2
CSHL/WTROR B46 115 G2
DARL/WED WS10 55 H5
ETTPK/GDPK/PENN WV4 51 E4
HAG/WOL DY9 184 B2
NFLD/LBR B31 175 G2
RIDG/WDGT B32 157 E5
WSL WS1 5 F4
Church Hill Cl SOLH B91 182 A3
Church Hill Rd
BFLD/HDSWWD B20 90 B5
DUNHL/THL/PER WV6 21 H4
SOLH B91 182 A3
Church Hill St SMTHWKW B67 106 B3
Churchill Cl OLDBY B69 86 A4
Churchill Dr
BLKHTH/ROWR B65 121 H2
STRBR DY8 118 C5
Churchill Gdns SEDG DY3 67 E4
Churchill La KIDD DY10 168 C2
Churchill Pl
LGN/SDN/BHAMAIR B26 130 D3
Churchill Rd BORD B9 128 D2
HALE B63 138 B5
MGN/WHC B75 63 G3
SCFLD/BOLD B73 76 A1
WSLW WS2 40 D2
Church La AST/WIT B6 109 G1
BFLD/HDSWWD B20 89 H4
BKHL/PFLD WV2 6 E6
CDSL WV8 10 B3
HALE B63 138 D3
HHTH/SAND B71 87 F1
HIA/OLT B92 166 D1
STETCH B33 130 B1
WALM/CURD B76 79 H2
Church Moat Wy
BLOX/PEL WS3 27 F2
Churchover Cl
WALM/CURD B76 77 H5
Church Pl BLOX/PEL WS3 27 H2
Church Rd AST/WIT B6 109 G1
BDMR/CCFT WV3 51 E1
BILS/COS WV14 68 D2
BLKHTH/ROWR B65 122 A1
BLOX/PEL WS3 18 A4
BRWNH WS8 9 F5
CDSL WV8 10 B3
DUDS DY2 102 B4
DUNHL/THL/PER WV6 34 C1
EDG B15 143 F1
ERDE/BCHGN B24 93 E2
HAG/WOL DY9 136 C2
HAG/WOL DY9 184 B1
HALE B63 137 G1
LGN/SDN/BHAMAIR B26 148 A2
MOS/BIL B13 144 C4
NFLD/LBR B31 175 G2
PBAR/PBCH B42 90 D1
SCFLD/BOLD B73 76 D3
SEDG DY3 80 C4
SHHTH WV12 26 B4
SHLY B90 180 B3
SMTHWKW B67 106 B5
STETCH B33 130 B2
STRBR DY8 135 H4
WMBN WV5 65 F4
WOLVN WV10 23 E1
YDLY B25 146 D1
Churchside Vw ALDR WS9 19 H5
Church Sq OLDBY B69 105 E2
Church St BILS/COS WV14 53 H3
BKHL/PFLD WV2 6 E6
BLOX/PEL WS3 27 G2
BRLYHL DY5 119 E2
BRWNH WS8 19 E2
CBHAMNW B3 3 F4
CDYHTH B64 121 E3
DARL/WED WS10 54 D4
DUDS DY2 102 C1
HAG/WOL DY9 152 C5
LOZ/NWT B19 108 C2
OLDBY B69 105 E1
RMSLY B62 122 B3
SEDG DY3 83 F3
STRBR DY8 135 G2
TPTN/OCK DY4 85 G4
WBROM B70 87 G3
WLNHL WV13 39 H3
WOLVN WV10 38 A1
WSL WS1 5 F5
Church Ter MGN/WHC B75 * 47 G2
STETCH B33 * 130 A3
Church V BFLD/HDSWWD B20 90 B5
HHTH/SAND B71 71 H5
Church Vw ALDR WS9 19 F4
Church View Cl BLOX/PEL WS3 27 G2
Church View Dr CDYHTH B64 121 F3
Church Vls
BFLD/HDSWWD B20 * 89 G4
Church Wk BDMR/CCFT WV3 51 F1
DUNHL/THL/PER WV6 22 A5
WASH/WDE B8 111 E3
Churchward Cl STRBR DY8 135 H1
Churchward Gv WMBN WV5 65 E3
Church Wy RUSH/SHEL WS4 18 B5
Churchyard Rd TPTN/OCK DY4 85 H1
Churnet Gv
DUNHL/THL/PER WV6 34 D1
Churn Hill Rd ALDR WS9 44 A1
Churns Hill La SEDG DY3 81 F3
Churston Cl BLOX/PEL WS3 16 C4
Cider Av BRLYHL DY5 119 G4
Cinder Bank DUDS DY2 102 C3
Cinder Rd SEDG DY3 82 D4
Cinder Wy DARL/WED WS10 55 G5
Cinquefoil Leasow
TPTN/OCK DY4 70 A5
Circuit Cl WLNHL WV13 39 H2
Circular Rd ACGN B27 163 G1
Circus Av
CHWD/FDBR/MGN B37 132 C2
City Plaza CBHAM B2 * 3 G5
City Rd LDYWD/EDGR B16 125 E2
OLDBY B69 103 H2
City Vw ERDW/GRVHL B23 92 C3
WASH/WDE B8 110 B5
Civic Cl CBHAMW B1 2 C5
Claerwen Gv NFLD/LBR B31 158 A5
Claines Rd HALE B63 137 H2
NFLD/LBR B31 176 A1
Clairvaux Gdns HIA/OLT B92 163 H5
Clandon Cl ALE/KHTH/YWD B14 177 F3
Clanfield Av WNSFLD WV11 25 F2
Clapgate Gdns BILS/COS WV14 53 E5
Clap Gate Gv WMBN WV5 64 C5
Clapgate La RIDG/WDGT B32 140 C5
Clap Gate Rd WMBN WV5 64 C4
Clapton Gv KGSTG B44 75 H2
Clare Av WNSFLD WV11 25 F1
Clare Crs BILS/COS WV14 67 H1
Clare Dr EDG B15 125 H4
Clarel Av WASH/WDE B8 128 A1
Claremont Ms
BDMR/CCFT WV3 51 G1
Claremont Pl WSNGN B18 * 108 A4
Claremont Rd BDMR/CCFT WV3 51 G1
SEDG DY3 67 G3
SMTHWK B66 106 D5
SPARK B11 127 H5
WSNGN B18 108 A3
Claremont St BILS/COS WV14 53 G2
CDYHTH B64 121 E3
Claremont Wy HALE B63 138 C4
Clarence Av HDSW B21 * 107 E1
Clarence Ct LGLYGN/QTN B68 123 G2
Clarence Gdns
FOAKS/STRLY B74 46 D3
Clarence Gv SHLY B90 180 B1
Clarence Rd BILS/COS WV14 54 A1
DUDS DY2 102 D3
ERDW/GRVHL B23 92 B3
FOAKS/STRLY B74 32 C5
HDSW B21 107 E1
HRBN B17 142 B1
MOS/BIL B13 161 G2
SPARK B11 145 E3
WOLV WV1 6 E3
Clarence St SEDG DY3 83 G1
WOLV WV1 6 E4
Clarenden Pl HRBN B17 142 A2
Clarendon Dr TPTN/OCK DY4 70 B3
Clarendon Pl BLOX/PEL WS3 17 H3
RMSLY B62 139 H1
Clarendon Rd
LDYWD/EDGR B16 125 G3
MGN/WHC B75 47 G2
RUSH/SHEL WS4 18 C5
SMTHWKW B67 106 B5
Clarendon St BDMR/CCFT WV3 6 B4
BLOX/PEL WS3 27 F1
Clare Rd BLOX/PEL WS3 28 B4
WOLVN WV10 23 G3
Clarewell Av SOLH B91 181 G4
Clarkes Gv TPTN/OCK DY4 70 A5
Clarke's La HHTH/SAND B71 71 G4
WLNHL WV13 40 A3
Clark Rd BDMR/CCFT WV3 36 B3
Clarksland Gv
CHWD/FDBR/MGN B37 132 A4
Clarks La SHLY B90 194 A2
Clarkson Rd DARL/WED WS10 56 A5
Clark St LDYWD/EDGR B16 125 H2
STRBR DY8 135 E2
Clarry Dr FOAKS/STRLY B74 46 D5
Clary Gv DSYBK/YTR WS5 57 G5
Clatterbach La HAG/WOL DY9 171 E1
Claughton Rd DUDS DY2 84 D5
Claughton Rd North DUDS DY2 84 D5
Clausen Cl GTB/HAM B43 60 A4
Clavedon Cl NFLD/LBR B31 158 A3
Claverdon Cl BRWNH WS8 9 G4-
SOLH B91 181 E1
Claverdon Dr FOAKS/STRLY B74 45 H1
GTB/HAM B43 73 F3
Claverdon Gdns ACGN B27 146 B2
Claverley Dr
ETTPK/GDPK/PENN WV4 50 D3
Claybrook St DIG/EDG B5 127 E3
Claycroft Ter DUDN DY1 68 B5
Claydon Gv
ALE/KHTH/YWD B14 178 C2
Claydon Rd KGSWFD DY6 81 G5
Clay Dr RIDG/WDGT B32 140 A2
Clayhanger La BRWNH WS8 18 D1
Clayhanger Rd BRWNH WS8 19 F1
Clay La
LGN/SDN/BHAMAIR B26 147 E3
OLDBY B69 105 E5
Claypit Cl WBROM B70 87 E3
Clay Pit La SHLY B90 194 A3
Claypit La WBROM B70 87 E3
Clayton Cl BKHL/PFLD WV2 52 A1
Clayton Dr CBROM B36 113 E1
Clayton Rd BILS/COS WV14 68 B4
WASH/WDE B8 110 B4
Clear Vw KGSWFD DY6 99 F3
Clearwell Gdns DUDN DY1 83 H3
Clee Hill Dr BDMR/CCFT WV3 34 D4
Clee Hill Rd SEDG DY3 83 E2
Clee Rd DUDN DY1 102 A2
LGLYGN/QTN B68 105 G5
NFLD/LBR B31 175 G5
STRBR DY8 135 G1
Cleeve Dr FOAKS/STRLY B74 32 D4
Cleeve Rd ALE/KHTH/YWD B14 179 E1
BLOX/PEL WS3 16 B4
Cleeve Wy BLOX/PEL WS3 16 B5
Clee View Meadow SEDG DY3 67 F1
Clee View Rd WMBN WV5 80 C1
Clematis Dr COVEN WV9 11 H4
Clement Pl BILS/COS WV14 * 53 H1
Clement Rd BILS/COS WV14 53 H1
RMSLY B62 122 B3
Clements Cl OLDBY B69 104 D5
Clements Rd YDLY B25 129 H4
Clement St CBHAMW B1 2 B4
WSLW WS2 4 B5
Clemson St WLNHL WV13 39 G3
Clent Dr HAG/WOL DY9 153 E4
Clent Hill Dr
BLKHTH/ROWR B65 103 G4
Clent Rd HDSW B21 89 F5
LGLYGN/QTN B68 123 G4
RBRY B45 173 G5
STRBR DY8 135 G1
Clent View Rd HALE B63 137 G3
RIDG/WDGT B32 157 E1
STRBR DY8 134 D5
Clent Vls BHTH/HG B12 * 144 D3
Clent Wy RIDG/WDGT B32 156 D2
Cleobury La HOCK/TIA B94 194 A5
Cleton St TPTN/OCK DY4 85 H3
Clevedon Av CBROM B36 113 G1
Clevedon Rd BHTH/HG B12 144 A1
Cleveland Cl WLNHL WV13 38 D4
WNSFLD WV11 25 F1
Cleveland Pas WOLV WV1 7 F5
Cleveland Rd BKHL/PFLD WV2 7 H6
Cleveland St DUDN DY1 84 B5
STRBR DY8 135 E3
WOLV WV1 7 F5
Cleves Dr RBRY B45 187 G1
Cleves Rd RBRY B45 173 G5
Clewley Dr COVEN WV9 12 A4
Clewley Gv RIDG/WDGT B32 140 B2
Clews Cl WSL WS1 57 E1
Clewshaw La
HWK/WKHTH B38 191 G4
Cley Cl DIG/EDG B5 143 H1
Cliff Dr DARL/WED WS10 70 B3
Cliffe Dr STETCH B33 130 D1
Clifford Rd DOR/KN B93 196 D4
SMTHWKW B67 124 B3
WBROM B70 87 E4
Clifford St DUDN DY1 102 B1
DUNHL/THL/PER WV6 6 A1
LOZ/NWT B19 108 D2
Clifford Wk LOZ/NWT B19 108 D2
Cliff Rock Rd RBRY B45 188 B1
Clift Av SHHTH WV12 26 B3
Clift Cl SHHTH WV12 26 A4
Clifton Av ALDR WS9 30 C2
BRWNH WS8 18 D1
Clifton Cl AST/WIT B6 109 F2
OLDBY B69 104 D5
Clifton Crs SOLH B91 181 F4
Clifton Gdns CDSL WV8 11 E4
Clifton Gn HLGN/YWD B28 163 E5
Clifton La HHTH/SAND B71 72 A3
Clifton Rd AST/WIT B6 109 F2
BHTH/HG B12 144 C2
CBROM B36 113 G1
DUNHL/THL/PER WV6 21 H5
RMSLY B62 122 B4
SCFLD/BOLD B73 62 A4
SMTHWKW B67 106 B5
Clifton St BDMR/CCFT WV3 6 C4
BILS/COS WV14 67 H2
CDYHTH B64 121 F3
STRBR DY8 135 F3
Clifton Ter ERDW/GRVHL B23 * 92 D2
Clinic Dr HAG/WOL DY9 136 C2
Clinton Gv SHLY B90 180 D4
Clinton Rd BILS/COS WV14 54 C1
CSHL/WTROR B46 115 F3
SHLY B90 181 E5
Clinton St WSNGN B18 107 G4
Clipper Vw LDYWD/EDGR B16 125 G3
Clipston Rd WASH/WDE B8 110 D4
Clissold Cl BHTH/HG B12 127 E5
Clissold Pas WSNGN B18 108 A5
Clissold St WSNGN B18 108 A5
Clive Cl MGN/WHC B75 47 H3
Cliveden Av ALDR WS9 30 B1
PBAR/PBCH B42 90 C2
Cliveden Coppice
FOAKS/STRLY B74 46 D4
Clivedon Wy RMSLY B62 121 G5
Cliveland St LOZ/NWT B19 3 G1
Clive Rd RIDG/WDGT B32 123 H5
Clive St HHTH/SAND B71 87 G1
Clockfields Dr BRLYHL DY5 118 C3
Clock La HIA/OLT B92 149 H5
Clockmill Av BLOX/PEL WS3 17 G4
Clockmill Pl BLOX/PEL WS3 17 H4
Clockmill Rd BLOX/PEL WS3 17 G4
Clodeshall Rd WASH/WDE B8 110 C5
Cloister Dr RMSLY B62 139 F4
The Cloisters RUSH/SHEL WS4 5 F1
Clonmel Rd BVILLE B30 160 A4
Clopton Crs
CHWD/FDBR/MGN B37 114 C5
Clopton Rd STETCH B33 131 E4
The Close DARL/WED WS10 55 G5
HALE B63 137 H1
HIA/OLT B92 164 B2
HLYWD B47 192 C3
HRBN B17 124 B5
RMSLY B62 155 C3
SEDG DY3 80 C4
SEDG DY3 83 E2
SLYOAK B29 * 159 F2
Clothier Gdns WLNHL WV13 39 G2
Clothier St WLNHL WV13 39 G2
Cloudbridge Dr HIA/OLT B92 165 H3
Cloudsley Gv HIA/OLT B92 147 F4
Clover Av
CHWD/FDBR/MGN B37 132 D2
Cloverdale
DUNHL/THL/PER WV6 34 B1
Clover Dr RIDG/WDGT B32 140 C5
Clover Hl DSYBK/YTR WS5 43 G5
Clover La KGSWFD DY6 99 E2
Clover Lea Sq WASH/WDE B8 111 E3
Clover Ley WOLVN WV10 37 H2
Clover Piece TPTN/OCK DY4 70 A5
Clover Rd SLYOAK B29 158 C3
Club La WOLVN WV10 12 C1
Club Rw SEDG DY3 83 G1
Club Vw HWK/WKHTH B38 176 B3
Clunbury Cft BKDE/SHDE B34 112 D4
Clunbury Rd NFLD/LBR B31 175 G5
Clun Cl OLDBY B69 85 F5
Clun Rd NFLD/LBR B31 158 B4
Clyde Av RMSLY B62 122 C4
Clyde Ms BRLYHL DY5 100 D3
Clyde Rd DOR/KN B93 199 E1
Clydesdale
LGN/SDN/BHAMAIR B26 147 G2
Clydesdale Rd
RIDG/WDGT B32 140 B1
Clyde St BHTH/HG B12 127 G3
CDYHTH B64 121 E3
Coalbourn La STRBR DY8 118 B5
Coalheath La RUSH/SHEL WS4 29 E2
Coal Pool La BLOX/PEL WS3 28 B5
Coalport Rd WOLV WV1 38 A4

Coalway Av *BDMR/CCFT* WV3......51 G2
   LGN/SDN/BHAMAIR B26 ...148 A3
Coalway Gdns
   BDMR/CCFT WV3 ....50 D2
Coalway Rd *BORD* B9.............128 B2
   DARL/WED WS10 ....72 A1
   HALE B63.........................138 D3
   SPARK B11.......................135 G5
Cob La *BVILLE* B30................159 E4
Cobs Fld *BVILLE* B30.............159 E4
Coburg Cft *TPTN/OCK* DY4 ....70 A5
Coburn Dr *MGN/WHC* B75 ......47 H5
Cochrane Cl *HAC/WOL* DY9 ...153 E2
   TPTN/OCK DY4 * 70 A5
Cochrane Rd *DUDS* DY2.........101 H4
Cock Hill La *RBRY* B45..........173 H5
Cocksheds La *RMSLY* B62......122 A4
Cockshut Hl
   LGN/SDN/BHAMAIR B26 ...130 C4
Cockshutt La *BKHL/PFLD* WV2 . 52 B1
Cockshutts La *BKHL/PFLD* WV2.. 52 B1
Cocksmead Cft
   ALE/KHTH/YWD B14..........160 D5
Cockthorpe Cl *HRBN* B17 ....124 B5
Cocton Cl
   DUNHL/THL/PER WV6..........20 C5
Codsall Gdns *CDSL* WV8..........21 G1
Codsall Rd *CDSL* WV8 ....21 G4
   CDYHTH B64.....................121 E4
Cofield Rd *SCFLD/BOLD* B73 ....76 D2
Cofton Cr *RBRY* B45...............188 D1
Cofton Gv *NFLD/LBR* B31 ......189 E2
Cofton Lake Rd *RBRY* B45.......188 C5
Cofton Rd *NFLD/LBR* B31 ....189 H1
Cokeland Pl *CDYHTH* B64........120 D4
Colaton Cl *WOLVN* WV10 ....37 G1
Colbourne Rd *TPTN/OCK* DY4 ...85 G2
Coldbath Rd *MOS/BIL* B13 ......161 H2
Coldridge Cl *CDSL* WV8 ....22 B1
Coldstream Dr *STRBR* DY8 ......118 A1
Coldstream Rd
   WALM/CURD B76 ....78 A3
Cole Bank Rd *HLGN/YWD* B28..162 C2
Colebourne Rd *MOS/BIL* B13 ...162 B4
Coleridge Crs
   CSHL/WTROR B46..............115 F1
Colebrook Cft *SHLY* B90.........179 H5
Colebrook Rd *SHLY* B90..........179 G5
   SPARK B11.......................142 C1
Cole Ct *CHWD/FDBR/MGN* B37..132 B2
Coleford Cl *STRBR* DY8..........117 G2
Coleford Dr
   CHWD/FDBR/MGN B37......132 A2
Cole Gn *SHLY* B90.................179 G5
Cole Hall La *BKDE/SHDE* B34...112 D4
Colehurst Cft *SHLY* B90..........195 F2
Coleman Rd *DARL/WED* WS10 ..56 A3
Coleman St
   DUNHL/THL/PER WV6..........36 C1
Colemeadow Rd
   CSHL/WTROR B46..............115 F2
   MOS/BIL B13.....................161 H5
Colenso Rd *LDYWD/EDGR* B16..107 F5
Coleraine Rd *PBAR/PBCH* B42...74 A5
Coleridge Cl *BLOX/PEL* WS3 *...18 A2
   SHHTH WV12.......................26 C3
Coleridge Dr
   DUNHL/THL/PER WV6..........34 C1
Coleridge Pas *CBHAMNE* B4 ....3 H3
Coleridge Ri *SEDG* DY3............82 C2
Coleridge Rd *GTB/HAM* B43......73 G4
Colesbourne Av
   ALE/KHTH/YWD B14..........177 G3
Colesbourne Rd *HIA/OLT* B92..147 H4
Coleshill Heath Rd
   CHWD/FDBR/MGN B37......149 G1
Coleshill Rd *CBROM* B36.........112 D2
   CHWD/FDBR/MGN B37......132 A5
   MGN/WHC B75.....................62 D3
   WALM/CURD B76 ....62 C5
Coleshill St *CSCFLD/WYGN* B72..62 C5
Coleside Av *MOS/BIL* B13.......163 E5
Coles La *CSCFLD/WYGN* B72 ....62 C5
   HHTH/SAND B71 ....71 E4
The Colesleys
   CSHL/WTROR B46..............115 G3
Cole St *DUDS* DY2.................105 E5
Cole Valley Rd *HLGN/YWD* B28..162 B4
Coleview Crs *STETCH* B33.......131 G1
Coleville Rd *WALM/CURD* B76...78 D5
Coleys La *NFLD/LBR* B31 ....175 G3
Colgreave Av *MOS/BIL* B13.....145 H4
Colindale Rd *KGSTG* B44..........60 C5
Colleen Av *BVILLE* B30............177 F2
College Cl *DARL/WED* WS10 .....71 E1
College Dr *BFLD/HDSWWD* B20..89 H4
College Farm Dr
   BFLD/HDSWWD B20 ....75 B3
College Ga *WASH/WDE* B8......110 C5
College Gv
   BFLD/HDSWWD B20 * 108 B2
College Hl *SCFLD/BOLD* B73 .....62 B4
College Rd *BFLD/HDSWWD* B20..89 G4
   DUNHL/THL/PER WV6..........35 H1
   KGSTG B44.........................60 C5
   MOS/BIL B13.....................145 E5
   RMSLY B62.......................140 A1
   STRBR DY8.......................135 G3
   WASH/WDE B8.....................8 D4
College St *WSNGN* B18..........108 A5
College Vw
Collet Rd *DUNHL/THL/PER* WV6..20 C5
Colletts Brook *MGN/WHC* B75 ...48 C5
Collett Cl *STRBR* DY8.............135 G1

Colletts Gv
   CHWD/FDBR/MGN B37......113 H5
Colley Av *WOLVN* WV10 ....23 H2
Colley Ga *HALE* B63 ....137 G1
Colley La *HALE* B63 ....137 G1
Colley Orch *HALE* B63 ....137 G1
Colley St *WBROM* B70 ....87 H2
Collier Cl *BRWNH* WS8 ....8 C5
Colliers Cl *SHHTH* WV12 ....25 H4
Colliers Fold *BRLYHL* DY5 ......100 D4
Colliery Dr *BLOX/PEL* WS3........16 B4
Colliery Rd *HHTH/SAND* B71 ..106 C1
   WOLV WV1.........................37 H3
Collindale Ct *KGSWFD* DY6......81 H5
Collingbourne Av *CBROM* B36...111 H2
Collingdon Av
   LGN/SDN/BHAMAIR B26 ...148 A1
Collingtree Ct *ACGN* B27 ....146 D5
Colling Wk
   CHWD/FDBR/MGN B37......114 A4
Collingwood Dr *GTB/HAM* B43...59 H5
Collingwood Rd *BVILLE* B30....177 H2
   WOLVN WV10 ....13 E5
Collins Cl *RIDG/WDGT* B32......140 A2
Collins Rd *BRWNH* WS8...........19 G2
   DARL/WED WS10 ....56 B5
Collins St *WBROM* B70.............86 C5
   WSL WS1...........................57 E1
Collis Cl *STRBR* DY8...............118 C4
Collister Cl *SHLY* B90.............163 F5
Colly Cft
   CHWD/FDBR/MGN B37......113 H4
Collycroft Pl *ACGN* B27..........146 B2
Colman Av *WNSFLD* WV11 ....25 F4
Colman Crs *LGLYGN/QTN* B68 ..123 G2
Colman Hill *HALE* B63............137 H2
Colman Hill Av *HALE* B63.......137 H1
Colmore Av
   ALE/KHTH/YWD B14..........160 D3
Colmore Circ Queensway
   CBHAMNW B3 ....3 G3
Colmore Crs *MOS/BIL* B13......161 H1
Colmore Dr *MGN/WHC* B75.......63 G3
Colmore Flats *LOZ/NWT* B19 * ...3 F1
Colmore Rd
   ALE/KHTH/YWD B14..........160 D3
Colmore Rw *CBHAMNW* B3 ....3 G4
Coln Cl *NFLD/LBR* B31 ....158 B4
Colonial Rd *BORD* B9.............135 E3
Colshaw Rd *STRBR* DY8.........135 E4
Colston Rd *ERDE/BCHGN* B24...93 F4
Colt Cl *FOAKS/STRLY* B74.........60 A1
Coltham Rd *SHHTH* WV12 ....26 A4
Coltishall Cft *HALE* B63 ....94 B4
Coltsfoot Cl *WNSFLD* WV11 ......25 E5
Columbia Cl *DIG/EDG* B5 ....143 H1
Columbine Cl *DSYBK/YTR* WS5..119 H1
Columbus Av *BRLYHL* DY5 ......119 H1
Colville Cl *TPTN/OCK* DY4 ....70 B3
Colville Rd *BHTH/HG* B12.......144 D2
Colwall Rd *SEDG* DY3..............83 F2
Colwall Wk *ACGN* B27 ....146 D5
Colworth Rd *NFLD/LBR* B31 ....174 D3
Colyns Gv *STETCH* B33 ....112 B4
Colyshall Cft *STRLY* B74 ....94 D2
Colyns Gv *STETCH* B33 ....112 B4
Comberford Ct
   DARL/WED WS10 * 56 A5
Comberford Dr
   DARL/WED WS10 ....56 D4
Comberton Rd
   LGN/SDN/BHAMAIR B26 ...130 D5
Combine Cl *MGN/WHC* B75.......47 H1
Comet Rd
   LGN/SDN/BHAMAIR B26 ...149 G3
Commercial Rd *WOLV* WV1 ....7 K5
   WSLW WS2.........................27 E3
Commercial St *CBHAMW* B1.....2 D7
Commissary Rd
   LGN/SDN/BHAMAIR B26 ...149 E4
Commonfield Cft
   WASH/WDE B8 ....110 B4
Common La
   CHWD/FDBR/MGN B37......147 G2
   WASH/WDE B8...................110 D3
Common Rd *WMBN* WV5..........80 D2
Commonside *BLOX/PEL* WS3.....18 A5
   BRLYHL DY5 ....101 E3
Common Side *BRWNH* WS8......19 G2
Communication Rw *EDG* B15...126 C5
Compton Cl *SOLH* B91............180 D1
Compton Cft
   CHWD/FDBR/MGN B37......132 D5
Compton Dr *DUDS* DY2..........103 F1
   FOAKS/STRLY B74...............60 A1
   KGSWFD DY6......................99 H4
Compton Gv *HALE* B63............137 G3
   KGSWFD DY6......................99 H4
Compton Hill Dr
   BDMR/CCFT WV3.................35 H3
Compton Pk *BDMR/CCFT* WV3..36 A3
Compton Rd *BDMR/CCFT* WV3..36 B3
   CDYHTH B64.....................120 C3
   ERDW/GRVHL B23................92 C5
   HAG/WOL DY9...................153 F1
   RMSLY B62.......................159 H2
Compton Rd West
   BDMR/CCFT WV3.................35 H3
Comsey Rd *GTB/HAM* B43........59 F5
Comwall Cl *BLOX/PEL* WS3......27 G5
Conchar Cl *CSCFLD/WYGN* B72..77 G2
Conchar Rd *CSCFLD/WYGN* B72..77 G1
Concorde Dr *CVALE* B35...........94 B4
Concorde Rd
   LGN/SDN/BHAMAIR B26 ...149 G3
Condover Cl *WSLW* WS2..........40 B2
Condover Rd *NFLD/LBR* B31 ...175 H5
Coneyford Rd
   BKDE/SHDE B34 ....113 E3
Coney Gn *STRBR* DY8............135 H2
Coney Green Dr
   NFLD/LBR B31 ....175 F5
Coneygree Rd *TPTN/OCK* DY4..85 G3
Conifer Cl *BRLYHL* DY5 ....119 H5
Conifer Ct *MOS/BIL* B13.........144 A5
Conifer Dr *HDSW* B21.............107 G2
   NFLD/LBR B31 ....175 H2
Conifer Paddock *RMSLY* B62...122 C4
Conifer Rd *FOAKS/STRLY* B74...45 E5
Conington Gv *HRBN* B17.........141 G2

Coniston Av *HIA/OLT* B92.......147 F3
Coniston Cl *HLGN/YWD* B28....162 D3
Coniston Crs *GTB/HAM* B43......73 H4
Coniston Dr *KGSWFD* DY6.........99 F2
Coniston Rd
   DUNHL/THL/PER WV6..........21 H2
   ERDW/GRVHL B23................92 B1
   FOAKS/STRLY B74...............45 F2
Connaught Av
   DARL/WED WS10 ....56 C5
Connaught Cl *DSYBK/YTR* WS5..58 A1
Connaught Dr *WMBN* WV5........65 E2
Connaught Rd *BILS/COS* WV14..54 B1
   WOLV WV1...........................6 B3
Connops Wy *HAG/WOL* DY9 ...136 C2
Connor Rd *HHTH/SAND* B71......72 A5
Conolly Dr *RBRY* B45.............174 B4
Conrad Cl *BHTH/HG* B12.........127 G5
Consort Crs *BRLYHL* DY5 ....101 E3
Consort Dr *DARL/WED* WS10 ....40 A5
Consort Rd *BVILLE* B30...........177 E2
Constable Cl *GTB/HAM* B43......59 G5
The Constables
   LGLYGN/QTN B68...............123 F2
Constance Av *WBROM* B70.......87 E5
Constance Rd *DIG/EDG* B5......143 H2
Constantine La
   CSHL/WTROR B46................97 F5
Constantine Wy
   BILS/COS WV14....................69 C1
Constitution Hl *DUDS* DY2......102 D1
   LOZ/NWT B19 ....2 E1
Constitution Hl East
   DUDS DY2.........................102 D1
Convent Cl *BKHL/PFLD* WV2 .....7 G5
Conway Av *HHTH/SAND* B71.....71 F2
   LGLYGN/QTN B68...............123 F2
   RIDG/WDGT B32................140 B1
Conway Cl *DUDN* DY1............100 B5
   KGSWFD DY6....................100 D5
   SHLY B90.........................180 C4
Conway Crs *SHHTH* WV12 ....26 A3
Conway Dr
   BLKHTH/ROWR B65............122 A2
Conway Gv *GTB/HAM* B43........73 F4
Conway Rd
   CHWD/FDBR/MGN B37......132 B1
   DUNHL/THL/PER WV6..........21 E2
   SHLY B90.........................180 D4
   SPARK B11.......................145 E1
Conwy Cl *WSLW* WS2...............41 E1
Conybere St *BHTH/HG* B12.....127 F5
Conyworth Cl *ACGN* B27.........146 D2
Cook Av *DUDS* DY2...............102 D2
Cook Cl *DOR/KN* B93.............197 G2
   DUNHL/THL/PER WV6..........34 C1
Cookes Cft *NFLD/LBR* B31 ......174 B4
Cookesley Cl *GTB/HAM* B43......59 H4
Cooke St *BKHL/PFLD* WV2 ....52 A1
Cookley Cl *HALE* B63..............138 B5
Cooknell Dr *STRBR* DY8.........118 A2
Cook Rd *BLOX/PEL* WS3...........17 H1
Cooksey La *KGSTG* B44............60 D4
Cooksey Rd *SMHTH* B10.........127 H4
Cooks La
   CHWD/FDBR/MGN B37......114 B4
Cook St *DARL/WED* WS10 ....55 H2
   VAUX/NECH B7 ....110 A2
Coombe Cft *COVEN WV9 * 12 A4
Coombe Hl *CDYHTH* B64.........121 H4
Coombe Pk *FOAKS/STRLY* B74..61 H1
Coombe Rd
   BFLD/HDSWWD B20.............91 E5
   SHLY B90.........................180 C3
Coombes La *NFLD/LBR* B31 ....189 F2
Coombs Rd *RMSLY* B62..........122 C4
Coombswood Wy *RMSLY* B62..121 H4
Cooper Av *BRLYHL* DY5 ....118 C2
Cooper Cl *WBROM* B70.............87 H3
Coopers Bank Rd *BRLYHL* DY5..101 E1
Coopers La *SMTHWK* B66.......106 C4
Coopers Rd
   BFLD/HDSWWD B20.............90 A3
Cooper St *BKHL/PFLD* WV2 ......37 H5
   WBROM B70 ....87 G5
Copes Crs *WOLVN* WV10 ....24 A4
Cope St *BLOX/PEL* WS3 ....27 G4
   DARL/WED WS10 ....55 G2
   WSNGN B18......................108 A5
Cophall St *TPTN/OCK* DY4 ....86 B1
Cophams Cl *NFLD/LBR* B31 ....148 A5
Coplow Cottages
   LDYWD/EDGR B16 * 125 H1
Coplow St *LDYWD/EDGR* B16 ..125 H1
Copnor Gv
   LGN/SDN/BHAMAIR B26 ...147 E1
Coppenhall Gv *STECH* B33......130 C1
Copperbeach Dr
   BHTH/HG B12....................144 C2
Copperbeech Cl
   RIDG/WDGT B32................141 F2
Copperbeech Dr
   BHTH/HG B12 * 144 C2
Copper Beech Dr *KGSWFD* DY6..81 H5
   WMBN WV5..........................65 F5
Copper Beech Gdns
   BFLD/HDSWWD B20.............89 H4
Coppice Av *HAG/WOL* DY9 .....136 D4
Coppice Cl *ERDE/BCHGN* B24...92 D3
   SEDG DY3...........................67 E4
   SHLY B90.........................194 C4
Coppice Crs *BRWNH* WS8..........9 H5
Coppice Dr *BRWNH* WS8...........8 D5
   DUNHL/THL/PER WV6..........21 G3
   POL/KGSB/FAZ B78.............49 E5
   SPARK B11.......................145 H1
Coppice Farm Wy *SHHTH* WV12..25 H4
Coppice Hollow
   RIDG/WDGT B32................157 F1
Coppice La *ALDR* WS9 ....9 H5
   BRLYHL DY5 ....82 D5
   BRWNH WS8........................8 D4
   DUNHL/THL/PER WV6..........21 G3
   POL/KGSB/FAZ B78.............49 E5
Coppice Ri *ALDR* WS9.............19 F3
Coppice Rd *BILS/COS* WV14.....54 B5
   BDMR/CCFT WV3.................35 H5

Coppice Side *TPTN/OCK* DY4....69 E5
Coppice Side Industrial Est
   BRWNH WS8........................87 E2
The Coppice
   BFLD/HDSWWD B20.............90 A4
   NFLD/LBR B31 ....174 C3
   SHHTH WV12.......................24 C3
   STRBR DY8.......................152 B5
   TPTN/OCK DY4...................70 A2
Coppice View Rd
   SCFLD/BOLD B73 ....60 C4
Coppice Wk *SHLY* B90............194 C4
Coppy Hall Gv *ALDR* WS9.........30 B1
Copse Cl *NFLD/LBR* B31 ....175 G3
Copse Crs *BLOX/PEL* WS3.........18 A3
Copse Rd *DUDS* DY2...............120 D1
The Copse *FOAKS/STRLY* B74....46 D4
   MOS/BIL B13.....................144 D5
Copson Cl *WBROM* B70...........87 E3
Copstone Dr *DOR/KN* B93......196 D5
Copston Gv *SLYOAK* B29.........158 D2
Copthall Rd *HDSW* B21............91 E1
Copt Heath Cft *DOR/KN* B93...183 F5
Copt Heath Dr *DOR/KN* B93....197 F1
Copthorne Rd
   BDMR/CCFT WV3.................51 G1
   KGSTG B44.........................60 A5
Coralin Cl
   CHWD/FDBR/MGN B37......132 B2
Corbett Crs *STRBR* DY8..........135 G1
Corbett Rd *BRLYHL* DY5 ....119 G5
   HLYWD B47.......................192 C1
Corbetts Cl *HIA/OLT* B92.......167 H5
Corbett St *SMTHWK* B66........106 D5
Corbridge Av *KGSTG* B44.........75 F2
Corbridge Rd *SCFLD/BOLD* B73..76 D1
Corbyn Rd *BORD* B9...............129 F1
   DUDN DY1........................101 H1
Corbyns Cl *BRLYHL* DY5 ....100 D2
Corbyns Hall La *BRLYHL* DY5..100 D2
Corbyns Hall Rd *BRLYHL* DY5..100 D2
Cordley St *WBROM* B70............87 G2
Corfe Cl *DUNHL/THL/PER* WV6..34 D2
   RIDG/WDGT B32................141 F2
Corfe Dr *OLDBY* B69...............85 G4
Corfe Rd *BILS/COS* WV14.........68 A3
Corfton Dr
   DUNHL/THL/PER WV6..........21 H5
Coriander Cl *RBRY* B45...........174 B4
Corinne Cl *RBRY* B45.............188 A2
Corinne Cft
   CHWD/FDBR/MGN B37......114 A4
Corisande Rd *SLYOAK* B29......142 A5
Corley Av *NFLD/LBR* B31 ....175 H2
Corley Cl *SHLY* B90................179 F4
Cornbrook Rd *SLYOAK* B29.....158 B4
Cornbury Gv *SOLH* B91..........180 C1
Corncrake Cl
   CSCFLD/WYGN B72..............77 H1
Corncrake Dr *CBROM* B36.......114 H1
Corncrake Rd *DUDN* DY1..........83 G3
Cornel Cl
   CHWD/FDBR/MGN B37......114 A4
Cornerway Rd *HWK/WKHTH* B38..190 D1
Cornfield *CDSL* WV8..................9 F2
Cornfield Cl *KGSWFD* DY6.......99 E1
Cornfield Cft
   CHWD/FDBR/MGN B37......114 B4
   WALM/CURD B76 ....63 F5
Cornfield Rd
   BLKHTH/ROWR B65............103 F5
   NFLD/LBR B31 ....115 H1
   WALM/CURD B76 ....78 B2
Cornflower Crs *DUDS* DY2......103 F1
Cornflower Rd *BRWNH* WS8.....18 D1
Cowgreaves Rd *CDYHTH* B64..120 D4
The Corngreaves
   BKDE/SHDE B34 ....113 E3
Corngreaves Wk *CDYHTH* B64..121 E5
Corn Hl *DSYBK/YTR* WS5.........43 G5
   WOLV WV1...........................7 H4
Cornhill Gv *BVILLE* B30..........160 C4
Corn Mill Cl *RIDG/WDGT* B32..158 A1
   WALM/CURD B76 ....78 B2
Cornmill Cl *WSL* WS1...............56 C3
Cornmill Gv
   DUNHL/THL/PER WV6..........34 B2
Cornovian Cl
   DUNHL/THL/PER WV6..........20 C5
Corns Gv *WMBN* WV5...............80 D1
Cornwall Cl *ALGR* WS9.............30 A1
Cornwall Pl *WSLW* WS2............40 C2
Cornwall Rd
   BFLD/HDSWWD B20.............89 H4
   DSYBK/YTR WS5 ....57 H1
   DUNHL/THL/PER WV6..........20 C2
   RBRY B45.........................173 G5
   SMTHWK B66....................106 D2
   STRBR DY8.......................117 H4
Cornwall St *CBHAMNW* B3 ....2 E4
Cornwell Cl *TPTN/OCK* DY4......85 G1
Cornwood La *SHLY* B90..........158 A3
Corngie La *SOLH* B91.............165 F4
Coronation Av *WNSFLD* WV11..40 B3
Coronation Rd *ALDR* WS9.........19 F4
   BILS/COS WV14....................54 C5
   GTB/HAM B43.....................58 C4
   RUSH/SHEL WS4.................18 B3
   SLYOAK B29.....................142 D5
   TPTN/OCK DY4...................70 A1
   WASH/WDE B8...................110 D3
   WNSFLD WV11....................24 A5
Corporation Rd *DUDS* DY2.......85 F5
Corporation St *CBHAM* B2..........3 G5
   DARL/WED WS10 ....56 D1
   WOLV WV1...........................6 E4
   WSL WS1...........................4 D7
Corporation St West *WSLW* WS2..4 B7

Corrie Cft
   LGN/SDN/BHAMAIR B26 ...130 D5
   RIDG/WDGT B32................99 G1
Corrin Gv *KGSWFD* DY6...........99 G1
Corron Hl *HALE* B63 * 138 D3
Corser St *DUDN* DY1...............83 H4
   STRBR DY8.......................135 G4
   WOLV WV1.........................26 C3
Corsican Cl *SHHTH* WV12 ....26 C3
Corvedale Rd *SLYOAK* B29.....158 C4
Corve Gdns
   DUNHL/THL/PER WV6..........22 A5
Corve Vw *SEDG* DY3 * 67 E2
Corville Gdns
   LGN/SDN/BHAMAIR B26 ...147 H3
Corville Rd *RMSLY* B62...........139 H1
Corwen Cft *NFLD/LBR* B31 ......157 H5
Cory Cft *TPTN/OCK* DY4...........85 G1
Coseley Rd *BILS/COS* WV14.....53 G5
Cosford Crs *CVALE* B35............94 C3
Cosford Dr *DUDS* DY2............103 E4
Cossington Rd
   ERDW/GRVHL B23................76 B4
Costock Cl
   CHWD/FDBR/MGN B37......132 B4
Cosyli Gdns *DUDN* DY1...........102 B3
Cotford Rd
   ALE/KHTH/YWD B14..........178 C3
Cotheridge Cl *SHLY* B90.........196 A2
Cot La *KGSWFD* DY6...............99 G4
Coteigh Gv *GTB/HAM* B43.........59 H5
Cotman Cl *GTB/HAM* B43..........59 G5
Coton Gv *SHLY* B90................179 F2
Coton La *ERDW/GRVHL* B23......92 D2
Coton Rd
   ETTPK/GDPK/PENN WV4......51 H3
Cotsdale Rd
   ETTPK/GDPK/PENN WV4......51 H3
Cotsford *SOLH* B91 * 181 G2
Cotswold Cl *ALDR* WS9............30 C1
   OLDBY B69.......................104 C4
   RBRY B45.........................174 A4
Cotswold Cft *BKHL/PFLD* WV2..51 G5
Cotswold Cft *HALE* B63..........154 C1
Cotswold Gv *SHHTH* WV12 ......25 H1
Cotswold Rd *BKHL/PFLD* WV2..52 D1
   STRBR DY8.......................135 H1
Cottage Cl *WNSFLD* WV11 ....24 C4
Cottage Gdns *RBRY* B45.........187 H2
Cottage La *WALM/CURD* B76....79 F5
   WOLVN WV10 ....13 E1
Cottage Ms *ALDR* WS9 * 30 D4
Cottage St *BRLYHL* DY5 ....119 F1
   KGSWFD DY6......................99 G3
Cottage Vw *CDSL* WV8............10 D3
Cotteridge Rd *BVILLE* B30.......177 E1
Cotterills Av *WASH/WDE* B8....111 F5
Cotterills La *WASH/WDE* B8 ....111 G5
Cotterills Rd *TPTN/OCK* DY4....69 H4
Cottesbrook Rd *ACGN* B27......146 C3
Cottesfield Cl *WASH/WDE* B8...111 F5
Cottesmore Cl *HHTH/SAND* B71..72 B3
Cottle Cl *WSLW* WS2................40 D2
Cotton La *MOS/BIL* B13..........144 C5
Cottrell St *HHTH/SAND* B71......87 H2
Cottsmeadow Dr
   WASH/WDE B8...................111 G5
Cotwall End Rd *SEDG* DY3.......82 D2
Cotysmore Rd *MGN/WHC* B75...62 D1
Couchman Rd *WASH/WDE* B8..110 C5
Coulter Gv
   DUNHL/THL/PER WV6..........34 B1
Counterfield Dr
   BLKHTH/ROWR B65............103 F4
Countess Dr *RUSH/SHEL* WS4...29 F3
Countess St *WSL* WS1.............56 D1
Country Park Vw
   WALM/CURD B76 ....78 A2
County Cl *BVILLE* B30.............160 C4
   RIDG/WDGT B32................140 C4
County Park Av *RMSLY* B62.....139 F4
Court Crs *KGSWFD* DY6............99 G4
Courtenay Gdns *GTB/HAM* B43..73 G1
Courtenay Rd *KGSTG* B44.........75 F4
Court Farm Rd
   ERDW/GRVHL B23................76 C5
Courtland Rd *KGSWFD* DY6....100 A1
Courtlands Cl *DIG/EDG* B5......143 G1
The Courtlands
   DUNHL/THL/PER WV6..........36 A1
Court La *ERDW/GRVHL* B23......76 C5
Court Oak Gv *RIDG/WDGT* B32..141 F1
Court Oak Rd *RIDG/WDGT* B32..141 E1
Court Pas *DUDN* DY1...............84 C5
Court Rd *BHTH/HG* B12..........144 A1
   DUNHL/THL/PER WV6..........36 B1
   ETTPK/GDPK/PENN WV4......53 E4
   SPARK B11.......................145 E3
Court St *CDYHTH* B64.............121 E5
Court Wy *WSLW* WS2.................4 C2
Courtway Av
   ALE/KHTH/YWD B14..........178 D4
The Courtyard
   CSHL/WTROR B46................97 F1
Cousins St *BKHL/PFLD* WV2 .....52 B1
Coveley Gv *WSNGN* B18.........108 A4
Coven Cl *BLOX/PEL* WS3...........18 A2
Coven Gv *SLYOAK* B29...........141 H5
Coven St *WOLVN* WV10 ....37 F1
Coventry Rd
   CSHL/WTROR B46..............133 G3
   HIA/OLT B92.....................150 D4
   LGN/SDN/BHAMAIR B26 ...147 E1
   SMHTH B10......................127 H3
   STRBR DY8.......................135 G2
Coventry St *DIG/EDG* B5 ....3 J6
Cover Cft *WALM/CURD* B76......78 C2
Coverdale Rd *HIA/OLT* B92......147 G3
Covers La *KINVER* DY7...........116 C3
The Covert *CDSL* WV8..............22 A1
Cowles Cft *YDLY* B25..............130 A3
Cowles Cft *CBROM* B36............95 H5
Cowley Dr *ACGN* B27..............146 D3
   DUDN DY1........................145 G2
Cowper Cl *SHHTH* WV12 ....26 C3
Cowslip Cl *HWK/WKHTH* B38...176 C5
   SLYOAK B29.....................158 C3
Coxcroft Av *BRLYHL* DY5 ....119 H4

Coxmoor Cl BLOX/PEL WS3 * 16 B4
Cox Rd BILS/COS WV14 .....69 E2
Cox's La CDYHTH B64 .....121 F2
Cox St CBHAMNW B3.....2 E5
Coxwell Av WOLVN WV10 .....23 E5
Coxwell Gdns
  LDYWD/EDGR B16.....125 H2
Coyne Cl TPTN/OCK DY4.....84 D1
Coyne Rd WBROM B70 .....87 F4
Crabbe St HAG/WOL DY9 .....136 D2
Crab La SHHTH WV12.....26 D1
Crabmill Cl DUDS DY2.....197 C1
Crab Mill Cl HWK/WKHTH B38.....190 C1
Crabmill La WALM/CURD B76.....177 C5
Crabourne Rd DUDS DY2.....120 C2
Crabtree Cl HAG/WOL DY9.....152 D4
  HHTH/SAND B71.....72 B3
  NFLD/LBR B31.....176 A5
Crabtree Dr
  CHWD/FDBR/MGN B37.....131 H1
Crabtree Rd WSL WS1.....5 J3
  WSNGN B18.....108 A4
Crackley Wy DUDS DY2.....102 A3
Craddock Rd SMTHWKW B67.....106 A3
Craddock St
  DUNHL/THL/PER WV6.....36 C1
Cradley Cft HDSW B21.....89 F3
Cradley Flds HALE B63.....137 F2
Cradley Forge HALE B63.....120 A4
Cradley Park Rd DUDS DY2.....120 C2
Cradock Rd ASH/WDE B8.....110 C4
Craig Cft
  CHWD/FDBR/MGN B37.....132 D2
Crail Gv GTB/HAM B43.....59 F5
Cranbrook Rd
  CHWD/FDBR/MGN B37.....131 G1
Cramlington Rd
  PBAR/PBCH B42.....74 A3
Cranmore Cl TPTN/OCK DY4.....69 G5
Cramp Hl DARL/WED WS10.....55 F2
Cranbourne Av
  ETTPK/GDPK/PENN WV4.....52 C5
Cranbourne Gv KGSTG B44.....75 C3
Cranbourne Pl
  HHTH/SAND B71 *.....87 H2
Cranbourne Rd KGSTG B44.....75 F2
  STRBR DY8.....135 G3
Cranbrook Gv
  DUNHL/THL/PER WV6.....34 D2
Cranbrook Rd HDSW B21.....89 E5
Cranby St WASH/WDE B8.....110 A4
Craneberry Rd
  CHWD/FDBR/MGN B37.....131 G5
Crane Hollow WMBN WV5.....80 C1
Cranehouse Rd KGSTG B44.....75 G1
Cranmoor CE
  VAUX/NECH B7 *.....110 A3
Crane Rd BILS/COS WV14.....54 B5
Cranesbill Rd SLYOAK B29.....158 C4
Cranes Park Rd
  LGN/SDN/BHAMAIR B26.....148 A2
Crane Ter
  DUNHL/THL/PER WV6.....22 A5
Cranfield Gv
  LGN/SDN/BHAMAIR B26.....130 B4
Cranfield Pl DSYBK/YTR WS5.....57 F4
Cranford Gv SOLH B91 *.....182 A4
Cranford Rd BDMR/CCFT WV3 .....35 G5
Cranford St SMTHWK B66.....107 E4
Cranham Dr KGSWFD DY6.....99 H4
Cranhill Cl HIA/OLT B92.....164 D1
Crankhall La DARL/WED WS10.....71 G1
Cranleigh Cl ALVE B48.....30 E5
  SHHTH WV12.....26 C1
Cranleigh Pl KGSTG B44.....91 E1
Cranley Dr CDSL WV8.....10 B3
Cranmer Av SHHTH WV12.....26 B3
Cranmere Av
  DUNHL/THL/PER WV6.....21 E4
Cranmere Ct
  DUNHL/THL/PER WV6 *.....21 E4
Cranmer Gv FOAKS/STRLY B74.....32 C4
Cranmoor Crs HALE B63.....138 C2
Cranmore Av HDSW B21.....107 F2
  SHLY B90.....181 E5
Cranmore Bvd SHLY B90.....180 D5
Cranmore Dr SHLY B90.....181 E4
Cranmore Rd BDMR/CCFT WV3 .....36 D2
  CBROM B36.....95 C5
  SHLY B90.....180 D5
Cransley Gv SOLH B91.....181 G4
Crantock Cl WINSFLD WV11.....26 A1
Crantock Rd PBAR/PBCH B42.....90 C2
Cranwell Gn WMBN WV5.....80 D1
Cranwell Gv ERDE/BCHGN B24.....93 H5
Cranwell Wy CVALE B35.....94 C3
Cranmorne Av WOLVN WV10.....23 E1
Craufurd St STRBR DY8.....135 G4
Craven St
  ETTPK/GDPK/PENN WV4.....52 D2
Crawford Av DARL/WED WS10.....55 F1
  ETTPK/GDPK/PENN WV4.....52 D5
  SMTHWKW B67.....106 A4
Crawford Rd BDMR/CCFT WV3 .....36 D5
  WALM/CURD B76.....78 B3
Crawshaws Rd CBROM B36.....95 G2
Crayford Rd KGSTG B44.....75 G2
Craythorne Av
  BFLD/HDSWWD B20.....89 G1
Crecy Cl WALM/CURD B76.....63 E4
Credenda Rd WBROM B70.....87 E5
Credon Gv EDG B15.....142 D2
Creed Wy WBROM B70.....87 F3
Cregoe St EDG B15.....2 C6
Cremore Av WASH/WDE B8.....110 C4
Cremore Rd MGN/WHC B75.....47 F5
Cremore Wk MGN/WHC B75 *.....47 F5
Crendon Rd
  BLKHTH/ROWR B65.....103 G3
Crescent Av SOLH B91 *.....182 A1
Crescent Rd BRLYHL DY5.....119 E2
The Crescent Grange Rd
  HAG/WOL DY9 *.....136 A3
Crescent Rd DARL/WED WS10.....55 F2
  DUDS DY2.....102 A4
  WLNHL WV13.....40 A3
Crescent Studios WSNGN B18 * .108 B3
The Crescent BILS/COS WV14.....53 H2

CDYHTH B64.....121 G5
CHWD/FDBR/MGN B37.....133 E4
DARL/WED WS10.....56 A4
DUDN DY1.....85 E2
DUNHL/THL/PER WV6.....35 F2
GTB/HAM B43.....74 A2
HIA/OLT B92.....167 H3
SHLY B90.....180 A1
SOLH B91.....181 H1
STRBR DY8.....152 B5
WLNHL WV13.....40 A4
WSL WS1.....5 J5
WSNGN B18.....108 B3
Cressage Av NFLD/LBR B31.....175 G4
Cressett Av BRLYHL DY5.....100 D5
Cressett La BRLYHL DY5.....101 E5
Cressington Dr
  FOAKS/STRLY B74.....47 E4
Cresswell Crs BLOX/PEL WS3 ....16 B5
Cresswell Gv ERDE/BCHGN B24.....93 H2
Cressy Cl ALE/KHTH/YWD B14 ..177 C1
The Crest NFLD/LBR B31.....189 H2
Crestwood Av FOAKS/STRLY B74.....45 F4
Crestwood Dr KGSTG B44.....75 F4
Crestwood Gin
  DUNHL/THL/PER WV6.....22 A3
Creswell Rd HLGN/YWD B28.....163 F3
Creswick Gv RBRY B45.....188 C1
Crew Dr TPTN/OCK DY4.....85 G4
Crew Rd DARL/WED WS10.....56 A4
Creynolds Cl SHLY B90.....194 D4
Creynolds La SHLY B90.....195 F3
Cricket Cl DSYBK/YTR WS5.....57 H1
Cricketers Meadow
  CDYHTH B64.....121 G5
Cricket Meadow SEDG DY5.....83 G1
  WOLVN WV10.....12 D5
Crick La BFLD/HDSWWD B20.....108 A1
Cricklewood Dr RMSLY B62.....139 F4
Crimmond Ri HALE B63.....138 A2
Crimscote Cl SHLY B90.....195 C1
Cripps Ri WOLVN WV10 *.....40 C2
Crocketts Av HDSW B21 *.....107 F2
Crocketts La SMTHWK B66.....106 C4
Crocketts Rd HDSW B21.....107 F2
Crockett St DUDN DY1.....84 A4
Crockford Dr MGN/WHC B75 *.....47 H5
Crockford Rd HHTH/SAND B71.....71 G2
Crocus Crs COVEN WV9.....12 A4
Croft Cl YDLY B25.....130 A4
Croft Ct CBROM B36 *.....112 D1
Croft Crs BRWNH WS8.....8 D5
Croft Down Rd HIA/OLT B92.....148 B3
Croftdown Rd HRBN B17.....141 F1
Crofters Cl STRBR DY8.....135 C4
Crofters Ct EDG B15.....142 C1
Crofters La MGN/WHC B75.....48 A2
Croft La WOLVN WV10.....23 H3
Croftleigh Gdns SOLH B91 *.....181 E3
Croft Rd
  LGN/SDN/BHAMAIR B26.....130 A4
The Crofts WALM/CURD B76.....78 C4
Croft St WLNHL WV13.....39 G3
  WSLW WS2.....41 H2
The Croft DSYBK/YTR WS5.....43 F5
  DUDS DY2.....101 H5
  KIDD DY10.....168 C5
  NFLD/LBR B31.....175 H2
  SEDG DY5.....67 G2
  WLNHL WV13.....39 G3
  WMBN WV5.....80 B1
The Croftway
  BFLD/HDSWWD B20.....73 G5
Croftwood Rd HAG/WOL DY9.....136 B3
Cromdale Dr HALE B63.....137 H4
Cromer Gdns
  DUNHL/THL/PER WV6.....22 B5
Cromer Rd GTB/HAM B43.....59 H5
Crompton Av
  BFLD/HDSWWD B20 *.....90 C5
Crompton Cl WSLW WS2.....27 E5
Crompton Ct CDSL WV8.....10 D3
Crompton Rd
  BFLD/HDSWWD B20.....108 C1
  RBRY B45.....173 F4
  TPTN/OCK DY4.....85 G2
  VAUX/NECH B7.....110 A1
Cromwell Cl
  BLKHTH/ROWR B65.....103 F4
  WSLW WS2.....40 C1
Cromwell Dr DUDS DY2.....103 H5
Cromwell La NFLD/LBR B31.....157 H2
Cromwell Rd WOLVN WV10.....13 E4
Cromwell St DUDS DY2.....103 E1
  HHTH/SAND B71.....87 G1
  VAUX/NECH B7.....109 H4
Crondal Pl EDG B15.....126 B5
Cronehills Linkway
  WBROM B70.....87 H3
Cronehills St WBROM B70.....87 H2
Crookham Cl HRBN B17.....124 B5
Crookhay La HHTH/SAND B71.....71 E3
Crook La ALDR WS9.....59 E2
Croome Cl SPARK B11.....144 D4
Cropredy Rd NFLD/LBR B31.....189 H2
Cropthorne Dr HLYWD DY7.....192 D1
Cropthorne Gdns SHLY B90.....180 C2
Cropthorne Rd SHLY B90.....180 D1
Crosbie Rd HRBN B17.....141 H1
Crosby Cl CBHAMNW B1.....2 B5
  DUNHL/THL/PER WV6.....22 B5
Cross Cl CDYHTH B64.....121 F2
Cross Farm Rd HRBN B17.....142 B3
Cross Farms La RBRY B45.....173 H4
Crossfield Rd STETCH B33.....130 C1
Crossfield Wy BILS/COS WV14.....54 A3
Crossgate Cl DUDS DY2.....101 H3
Crosskey Cl STETCH B33.....131 G2
Crossland Crs
  DUNHL/THL/PER WV6.....22 B4
Cross La GTB/HAM B43.....73 G2
  SEDG DY5.....67 F3
Crossley St DUDS DY2.....102 D5
Cross Pl SEDG DY5.....67 G2
Cross St BILS/COS WV14.....69 F1
  BLKHTH/ROWR B65.....122 A3
  BLOX/PEL WS3.....28 C1
  DARL/WED WS10.....55 G5
  DUDN DY1.....84 C5

HALE B63.....138 C4
HDSW B21.....107 E1
KGSWFD DY6.....99 F1
LGLYGN/QTN B68.....105 E5
SMTHWK B66.....106 D5
STRBR DY8.....135 G2
WLNHL WV13.....37 H4
WOLV WV1.....37 H4
Cross St North WOLV WV1 *.....37 F1
Cross St South BKHL/PFLD WV2.....52 A1
Cross Walks Rd HAG/WOL DY9 .136 C2
Crossway La KGSTG B44.....75 F5
Crossways Gn KGSTG B44.....75 H4
Crosswells Rd
  LGLYGN/QTN B68.....105 F4
Crowberry Cl BRWNH WS8.....18 D1
Crowesbridge Ms
  BILS/COS WV14.....68 B3
Crowhurst Rd NFLD/LBR B31.....189 E1
Crowland Av
  DUNHL/THL/PER WV6.....34 C1
Crowle Dr HAG/WOL DY9.....136 A2
Crown Cl BLKHTH/ROWR B65 ..104 B5
  SEDG DY5.....67 F2
Crown Ct DARL/WED WS10.....40 A5
Crown La FOAKS/STRLY B74.....46 C3
  STRBR DY8.....135 F1
Crownmeadow Dr
  TPTN/OCK DY4.....70 B4
Crownoakes Dr STRBR DY8.....118 A2
Crown Rd BORD B9.....128 B2
  YDLY B25.....130 A2
Crown St WOLV WV1 *.....37 F1
Crown Wk TPTN/OCK DY4.....85 G4
Crows Nest Cl WALM/CURD B76.....63 C5
Crown Gdns HALE B63.....120 C5
Crowther Gv
  DUNHL/THL/PER WV6.....36 B1
Crowther Rd
  DUNHL/THL/PER WV6.....36 A1
  ERDE/BCHGN B23.....92 B1
Crowther St WOLVN WV10.....37 C1
Croxall Wy SMTHWK B66.....106 D4
Croxdene Av BLOX/PEL WS3.....26 D1
Croxley Gdns WLNHL WV13.....39 F5
Croxstalls Av BLOX/PEL WS3.....27 E2
Croxstalls Cl BLOX/PEL WS3.....27 E1
Croxstalls Pl BLOX/PEL WS3.....27 E1
Croxton Gv STETCH B33.....112 C5
Croyde Av PBAR/PBCH B42.....74 A5
Croydon Dr ERDE/BCHGN B24.....93 E5
  SLYOAK B29.....142 A4
Croy Dr CVALE B35.....94 D2
The Crucible BILS/COS WV14 ....68 C1
Crusader Cl OLDBY B69.....104 A5
Crychan Cl RBRY B45.....174 B5
Cryersoak Cl SHLY B90.....195 G1
Crystal Av SMTHWK B66.....106 D4
Crystal Dr SMTHWK B66.....105 C1
Cubley Rd HLGN/YWD B28.....162 C1
Cuckoo Cl STETCH B33.....112 B5
Cuckoo Rd VAUX/NECH B7.....110 B4
Culford Dr RIDG/WDGT B32.....157 H2
Culham Cl ACGN B27.....146 D5
Cullwick St WOLV WV1 *.....37 H3
Culmington Gv NFLD/LBR B31 .175 F5
Culmington Rd NFLD/LBR B31 .175 F5
Culmore Cl SHHTH WV12.....40 B1
Culmore Rd RMSLY B62.....122 C3
Culverhouse Dr BRLYHL DY5 ..118 C5
Culverley Crs DOR/KN B93.....196 D2
Culvert Wy SMTHWK B66.....105 H2
Culwell St WOLVN WV10.....7 H2
Cumberland Av STETCH B33.....131 G3
Cumberland Cl KGSWFD DY6 ..100 A5
Cumberland Rd BILS/COS WV14.....53 H1
  HHTH/SAND B71.....71 H5
  LGLYGN/QTN B68.....123 F4
  WLNHL WV13.....39 H5
Cumberland St CBHAMNW B1.....2 C6
Cumbrian Cft HALE B63.....137 H5
Cumbria Wy WASH/WDE B8.....110 B3
Cunningham Rd
  DUNHL/THL/PER WV6.....34 C1
  WSLW WS2.....40 C3
Cupfields Av TPTN/OCK DY4.....70 A3
Cupfields Crs TPTN/OCK DY4.....70 A4
Curbar Rd PBAR/PBCH B42.....74 C5
Curdale Rd RIDG/WDGT B32 ..157 F2
Curdworth La
  WALM/CURD B76.....79 H2
Curlew Dr BRWNH WS8.....9 E5
Curlews Cl ERDW/GRVHL B23 ..76 A3
Curral Rd BLKHTH/ROWR B65 ..103 H3
Curtin Dr DARL/WED WS10.....54 D4
Curtis Cl SMTHWK B66.....107 E5
Curzon Circ CBHAMNE B4.....127 C1
Curzon St BKHL/PFLD WV2.....52 B1
  CBHAMNE B4.....127 G1
Cuthbert Rd WSNGN B18.....107 C5
Cutlers Rough Cl
  NFLD/LBR B31.....158 B5
Cutshill Cl CBROM B36.....96 C4
Cutsdean Cl NFLD/LBR B31.....158 B4
Cutshill Cl CBROM B36.....113 C1
The Cutting RUSH/SHEL WS4 ....44 B2
Cutworth Cl WALM/CURD B76 ..63 C5
Cygnet Cl WMBN WV5.....80 A1
Cygnet Dr BRWNH WS8.....9 E5
Cygnet Gv KGSTG B44.....75 H5
Cygnet La BRLYHL DY5.....101 E2
Cygnet Rd WBROM B70.....87 E1
Cygnus Wy WBROM B70.....88 D1
Cypress Av SEDG DY5.....67 F3
Cypress Gdns
  FOAKS/STRLY B74.....62 A1
  KGSWFD DY6.....99 C5
Cypress Gv NFLD/LBR B31.....175 E4
Cypress Rd DSYBK/YTR WS5.....58 A4
  DUDS DY2.....85 F5
Cypress Sq ACGN B27.....146 C2
Cypress Wy NFLD/LBR B31.....158 C5
Cyprus Cl SLYOAK B29.....158 C4
Cyprus St BKHL/PFLD WV2.....51 H2
  OLDBY B69.....105 E1
Cyril Gv SMHTH B10 *.....128 A4
Cyril Rd SMHTH B10.....128 B4

D

Dacer Cl BVILLE B30.....160 B5
Dace Rd WOLVN WV10.....38 B1
Dadford Vw BRLYHL DY5.....118 D2
Dad's La MOS/BIL B13.....160 D1
Daffodil Cl SEDG DY5.....67 F2
Daffodil Pl DSYBK/YTR WS5.....43 F5
Daffodil Rd DSYBK/YTR WS5.....43 F5
Daffodil Wy NFLD/LBR B31.....175 E5
Dagger La HHTH/SAND B71.....88 A1
Dahlia Cl WOLV WV1.....38 C4
Daimler Cl CBROM B36.....95 H5
Daimler Rd
  ALE/KHTH/YWD B14.....179 F2
Dainton Gv RIDG/WDGT B32 ..157 G1
Dairy Cl TPTN/OCK DY4.....85 H1
Dairy Ct LGLYGN/QTN B68.....123 H5
Daisy Bank Cl BLOX/PEL WS3 ..18 B5
Daisy Bank Crs DSYBK/YTR WS5.....57 H1
Daisy Farm Rd
  ALE/KHTH/YWD B14.....178 D3
Daisy Meadow TPTN/OCK DY4 ..70 A5
Daisy Rd LDYWD/EDGR B16.....125 H2
Daisy St BILS/COS WV14.....69 E1
  DUNHL/THL/PER WV6.....36 C1
Daisy Wk COVEN WV9.....12 A4
Dalbeg Cl CDSL WV8.....22 A2
Dalbury Rd HLGN/YWD B28.....162 C5
Dale Cl GTB/HAM B43.....73 F2
Daleby Cl BLOX/PEL WS3 *.....28 B4
Dale End CBHAMNE B4.....3 H5
  DARL/WED WS10.....55 F2
Dale Rd RMSLY B62.....122 D4
  SLYOAK B29.....142 C4
  STRBR DY8.....135 E3
Dales Cl DUNHL/THL/PER WV6 ..22 D4
Dalesman Cl KGSWFD DY6.....99 F2
Dale St BDMR/CCFT WV3.....6 D6
  BILS/COS WV14.....54 B5
  DARL/WED WS10.....55 G5
  SMTHWK B66.....124 C1
  WSL WS1.....57 E1
Daleswood Pk RMSLY B62.....172 B3
Dale Ter OLDBY B69.....104 A1
Daleview Rd
  ALE/KHTH/YWD B14.....179 E3
Dalewood Cft
  LGN/SDN/BHAMAIR B26.....147 F1
Dalewood Rd
  CHWD/FDBR/MGN B37.....113 H4
Daley Cl CBHAMNW B1.....2 A4
Daley Rd BILS/COS WV14.....69 F1
Dalkeith Rd SCFLD/BOLD B73 ..76 C1
Dalkeith St WSLW WS2.....4 A1
Dallas Rd ERDW/GRVHL B23.....92 A2
Dallimore Cl HIA/OLT B92.....147 H4
Dalloway Cl DIG/EDG B5.....144 A1
Dalston Cl DUDS DY2.....102 D3
Dalston Rd ACGN B27.....146 C3
Dalton Ct HRBN WV5.....64 C4
Dalton Rd WSLW WS2.....41 E2
Dalton St BDMR/CCFT WV3 *.....3 H4
  CBHAMNE B4.....3 H4
Dalton Wy CBHAMNE B4.....3 H4
Dalvine Rd DUDS DY2.....120 C1
Dalwood Cl BILS/COS WV14.....68 B4
Damar Cft
  ALE/KHTH/YWD B14.....177 H1
Damien Cl SMTHWKW B67.....106 B5
Dam Mill Cl CDSL WV8.....21 G1
Damson Cl SHHTH WV12.....25 G4
Damson Pkwy HIA/OLT B92.....165 H5
Damson Wy TPTN/OCK DY4 ....85 H3
Danbury Cl WALM/CURD B76 ..78 C1
Danbury Gdns WOLVN WV10 .....12 C5
Danbury Rd SHLY B90.....180 B2
Danby Gv ERDE/BCHGN B24 ....93 F4
Dando Rd DUDS DY2.....102 D1
Dandy Bank Rd KGSWFD DY6 .100 C1
Dandy's Wk WSL WS1.....5 F6
Dane Gv BVILLE B30.....160 D2
Danesbury Crs KGSTG B44.....75 G3
Danes Cl WINSFLD WV11.....14 D3
Danescourt Rd
  DUNHL/THL/PER WV6.....21 G4
Danescroft Dr ALDR WS9.....19 F4
Dane Ter BLKHTH/ROWR B65 ..104 A4
Daneways Cl FOAKS/STRLY B74 ..45 G5
Danford Cl STRBR DY8.....135 G3
Danford Gdns SMHTH B10.....128 A3
Danford La SOLH B91.....181 E2
Danford Rd HLYWD B47.....192 B2
Danford Wy GTB/HAM B43.....73 F3
Dangerfield La
  DARL/WED WS10.....55 E3
Daniels La ALDR WS9.....44 C1
Daniels Rd BORD B9.....129 E2
Danks St TPTN/OCK DY4.....85 G4
Danzey Green Rd CBROM B36 .94 D5
Danzey Gv
  ALE/KHTH/YWD B14.....177 G2
Darby Cl BILS/COS WV14.....68 A1
Darby End Rd DUDS DY2.....103 E5
Darby Rd DARL/WED WS10.....56 B5
  LGLYGN/QTN B68.....104 C4
Darbys Hill Rd OLDBY B69.....103 H2
Darby St BLKHTH/ROWR B65 ..122 A3
Darbys Wy TPTN/OCK DY4.....85 H1
Darell Cft WALM/CURD B76.....63 E5
Daren Cl CBROM B36.....95 H4
Dare Rd ERDW/GRVHL B23.....92 C2
Darfield Wk BNTH/HG B12 *.....127 F4
Darkhouse La BILS/COS WV14 ..68 C1
Dark La HAG/WOL DY9.....184 C1
  HWK/WKHTH B38.....191 F4
  RMSLY B62.....172 B1
Darlaston La BILS/COS WV14 ....54 C1
Darlaston Rd DARL/WED WS10 ..55 F1
  WSLW WS2.....41 E5
Darley Av BKDE/SHDE B34.....112 B3
Darleydale Av KGSTG B44.....75 E2

Darley Dr DUNHL/THL/PER WV6 .22 D5
Darley Green Rd DOR/KN B93 .199 F2
Darley Wy FOAKS/STRLY B74 ....60 B1
Darlington Rd DARL/WED WS10 ..55 F3
Darlington St WOLV WV1.....6 E4
Darnel Cft SMHTH B10.....127 H3
Darnel Hurst Rd MGN/WHC B75..47 G2
Darnford Cl CSCFLD/WYGN B72...77 H4
  HLGN/YWD B28.....163 E5
Darnick Rd SCFLD/BOLD B73 ....76 B1
Darnley Rd LDYWD/EDGR B16 .125 H2
Darris Rd SLYOAK B29.....160 A2
Dartford Rd BLOX/PEL WS3.....26 D1
Dartmoor Dr RBRY B45.....174 A3
Dartmouth Av BLOX/PEL WS3 ....28 A5
  STRBR DY8.....117 H1
  WLNHL WV13.....39 H3
Dartmouth Circ AST/WIT B6.....109 F4
Dartmouth Crs BILS/COS WV14 ..54 C1
Dartmouth Dr ALDR WS9.....29 H5
Dartmouth Middleway
  VAUX/NECH B7.....3 K1
Dartmouth Rd SLYOAK B29.....142 D5
  SMTHWK B66.....106 D1
Dartmouth St BKHL/PFLD WV2 ..7 H7
  WBROM B70.....87 F3
Dart St BORD B9.....127 H5
Darvel Rd SHHTH WV12.....40 B3
Darwin Ct
  DUNHL/THL/PER WV6.....34 C1
Darwin Pl WSLW WS2.....27 F4
Darwin Rd WSLW WS2.....27 F4
Darwin St BNTH/HG B12.....127 F4
Dassett Gv BORD B9.....129 G2
Dassett Rd DOR/KN B93.....196 D4
Dauntsey Covert
  ALE/KHTH/YWD B14.....177 H3
Davena Dr RIDG/WDGT B32 ....141 E5
Davena Gv BILS/COS WV14.....53 H5
Davenport Rd DR CVALE B35.....95 E3
Davenport Rd
  DUNHL/THL/PER WV6.....21 F5
  WNSFLD WV11.....25 E4
Daventry Gv RIDG/WDGT B20 .140 C1
Davey Rd BFLD/HDSWWD B20 ...91 E5
Davey Rd BORD B9.....87 E2
David Harman Dr
  HHTH/SAND B71.....72 B4
David Peacock Cl
  TPTN/OCK DY4.....85 C1
David Rd BFLD/HDSWWD B20 ....90 B4
  WSLW WS2.....69 G4
The Davids NFLD/LBR B31.....159 E4
Davies Av BILS/COS WV14.....53 H5
Davis Av TPTN/OCK DY4.....85 E2
Davis Gv YDLY B25.....146 D1
Davis Rd SMTHWKW B67.....124 B1
Davy Rd WSLW WS2.....26 B2
Daw Dr WSLW WS2.....27 E5
Dawberry Cl
  ALE/KHTH/YWD B14.....160 D5
Dawberry Fields Rd
  ALE/KHTH/YWD B14.....160 C5
Dawberry Rd
  ALE/KHTH/YWD B14.....160 C5
Daw End RUSH/SHEL WS4.....29 E4
Daw End La RUSH/SHEL WS4 ....28 D4
Dawes Av WBROM B70.....87 G5
Dawley Brook Rd KGSWFD DY6 .99 H2
Dawley Cl WSLW WS2.....56 B1
Dawley Crs
  CHWD/FDBR/MGN B37.....132 B3
Dawley Rd KGSWFD DY6.....99 G1
Dawlish Rd DUDN DY1.....84 C1
  SLYOAK B29.....142 D5
  SMTHWK B66.....106 D4
Dawn Dr TPTN/OCK DY4.....70 A1
Dawney Dr MGN/WHC B75.....47 E1
Dawn Rd NFLD/LBR B31.....158 A4
Dawson Av BILS/COS WV14.....67 H1
Dawson Rd HDSW B21.....107 G1
Dawson Sq BILS/COS WV14 * 53 G3
Dawson St BLOX/PEL WS3.....27 H2
Day Av WNSFLD WV11.....25 E3
Dayhouse Bank RMSLY B62.....172 D4
Daylesford Rd HIA/OLT B92.....147 G4
Day St WSLW WS2.....4 D1
Deakin Av BRWNH WS8.....9 F3
Deakin Rd ERDW/GRVHL B23 ....92 D1
  MGN/WHC B75.....47 H3
Deakins Rd YDLY B25.....129 F5
Deal Dr OLDBY B69.....85 F5
Deal Gv NFLD/LBR B31.....175 G1
Deanbrook Cl SHLY B90.....195 G2
Dean Ct CSCFLD/WYGN B72 ....77 F4
  KGSTG B44.....35 H1
  STRBR DY8.....135 H1
Dean Ct DUNHL/THL/PER WV6 ..20 C5
Deanery Rd WOLV WV1 *.....7 F5
Dean Rd ERDW/GRVHL B23.....92 D1
  RUSH/SHEL WS4.....29 E3
  WMBN WV5.....80 D1
Deansfield Rd WOLV WV1.....38 A3
Deans Pl BLOX/PEL WS3.....28 B4
Dean's Rd WOLV WV1.....38 B3
Dean St DIG/EDG B5.....3 H7
  SEDG DY5.....67 F3
Dearman Rd SPARK B11.....127 H5
Dearmont Rd NFLD/LBR B31 ....189 E1
Dearne Ct SEDG DY5.....68 A5
Debden Cl DOR/KN B93.....198 C1
Debenham Crs YDLY B25.....129 H5
Debenham Rd HDSW B21.....129 H5
Deblen Dr LDYWD/EDGR B16 ..125 F3
Deborah Cl BKHL/PFLD WV2 ....52 A2
Dee Gv HWK/WKHTH B38.....176 C5
Deelands Rd RBRY B45.....173 H5
Deeley Cl CDYHTH B64.....121 G5
  EDG B15.....126 C5
Deeley Dr TPTN/OCK DY4.....70 A5
Deeley Pl BLOX/PEL WS3.....27 F2
Deeley St BLOX/PEL WS3.....27 F2
  BRLYHL DY5.....119 G3

Deepdale Av LCN/SDN/BHAMAIR B26....147 H3
Deepdale La DUDN DY1....83 C3
Deepdales WMBN WV5....64 C5
Deeplow Cl CSCFLD/WYGN B72 *....62 C4
Deepmoor Rd STECH B33....130 B1
Deepmore Av WSLW WS2....41 F3
Deepwood Cl RUSH/SHEL WS4....28 D2
Deer Cl BLOX/PEL WS3....27 C1
Deerhurst Rd BFLD/HDSWWD B20....89 H1
Dee Rd BLOX/PEL WS3....28 A1
Deer Park Wy SOLH B91....182 A4
Defford Av RUSH/SHEL WS4....29 E1
Defford Dr LGLYGN/QTN B68....105 F5
De Havilland Dr CVALE B35....40 B4
Deighton Rd DSYBK/YTR WS5....55 F5
Delamere Cl CROM B36....95 H5
Delamere Dr DSYBK/YTR WS5....73 G1
Delamere Rd HLGN/YWD B28....162 D3
SHHTH WV12....26 A3
Delancey Keep MGN/WHC B75....63 G3
Delhurst Av ETTPK/GDPK/PENN WV4....52 C5
Delhurst Rd KGSTG B44....74 D2
Delia Dr RIDG/WDGT B32....157 H2
Dell Farm Cl DRLH WS9....127 F2
Dellows Cl HWK/WKHTH B38....190 B1
Dell Rd BRLYHL DY5....100 D4
BVILLE B30....160 A5
The Dell HIA/OLT B92....164 C1
LDYWD/EDGR B16 *....125 H2
NFLD/LBR B31....157 H4
STRBR DY8....135 E1
Delmore Wy WALM/CURD B76....78 D5
Delph Dr BRLYHL DY5....119 G5
Delphinium Cl BORD B9....128 D1
Delph La BRLYHL DY5....119 F4
Delph Rd BRLYHL DY5....119 F3
Delrene Rd HLGN/YWD B28....179 H2
Delves Crs DSYBK/YTR WS5....57 G3
Delves Green Rd DSYBK/YTR WS5....57 G2
Delves Rd WALS WS1....57 F1
Delville Rd DARL/WED WS10....55 H5
De Marnham Cl WBROM B70....88 A5
De Moram Gv HIA/OLT B92....165 H3
Demuth Wy OLDBY B69....104 D4
Denaby Gv ALE/KHTH/YWD B14....179 F1
Denbigh Cl DUDN DY1....83 H4
Denbigh Crs HHTH/SAND B71....71 F5
Denbigh Dr DARL/WED WS10....56 C4
HHTH/SAND B71....71 F5
Denbigh Rd TPTN/OCK DY4....86 A2
Denbigh St BORD B9....128 B2
Denby Cl VAUX/NECH B7....109 H4
Denby Cft SHLY B90....195 H2
Dencer Cl RBRY B45....173 H5
Dencil Cl HALE B63....137 H2
Dene Av KGSWFD DY6....99 C5
Dene Court Rd HIA/OLT B92....164 B1
Denegate Cl WALM/CURD B76....78 D5
Dene Hollow MOS/BIL B13....162 A4
Dene Rd STRBR DY8....135 F4
Denewood Av BFLD/HDSWWD B20....90 B4
Denford Gv ALE/KHTH/YWD B14....160 D5
Denham Gdns BDMR/CCFT WV3....35 F5
Denham Rd ACGN B27....146 B2
Denholme Gv ALE/KHTH/YWD B14....178 C2
Denholm Rd SCFLD/BOLD B73....61 F5
Denise Dr BILS/COS WV14....68 D3
CHWD/FDBR/MGN B37....113 H5
HRBN B17....142 A3
Denleigh Rd KGSWFD DY6....100 B5
Denmark Cl DUNHL/THL/PER WV6....36 C1
Denmead Dr WNSFLD WV11....25 F2
Denmore Gdns WOLV WV1....38 B3
Dennis Hall Rd STRBR DY8....118 C4
Dennis Rd BHTH/HG B12....144 D3
Dennis St STRBR DY8....118 B4
Denshaw Rd ALE/KHTH/YWD B14....160 D4
Denton Cft DOR/KN B93....196 B5
Denton Gv GTB/HAM B43....73 F4
STETCH B33....129 H2
Denton Rd HAC/WOL DY9....137 E3
Denver Rd ALE/KHTH/YWD B14....178 C3
Denville Cl BILS/COS WV14....54 C1
Denville Crs BORD B9....129 F1
Depwo Gv RIDG/WDGT B32....157 F2
Derby Av WOLV WV6....22 A3
Derby Dr CHWD/FDBR/MGN B37....132 B2
Derby St BORD B9....127 G2
WSLW WS2....41 H1
Dereham Cl WASH/WDE B8....110 A5
Dereham Wk BILS/COS WV14....69 E1
Dereton Cl DUDN DY1....101 G2
Derron Av LCN/SDN/BHAMAIR B26....147 G2
Derry Cl HRBN B17....141 G4
Derrydown Cl ERDW/GRVHL B23....92 C3
Derrydown Rd PBAR/PBCH B42....90 B1
Derry St BKHL/PFLD WV2....37 G5
BRLYHL DY5....119 E2
Derwent Cl BRLYHL DY5....100 D3
FOAKS/STRLY B74....45 F3
WLNHL WV13....40 A3
Derwent Gv BVILLE B30....160 C2
Derwent Rd BVILLE B30....160 C2
DUNHL/THL/PER WV6....21 H2
Desford Av PBAR/PBCH B42....74 C4
Dettonford Rd RIDG/WDGT B32....157 F2
Devereux Cl CBROM B36....113 E1
Devereux Rd MGN/WHC B75....47 C4
WBROM B70....88 A5
Devey Dr TPTN/OCK DY4....70 B5
Devine Cft TPTN/OCK DY4....85 C1
Devitts Cl SHLY B90....195 F1

Devon Crs ALDR WS9....30 A1
DUDS DY2....101 H2
HHTH/SAND B71....71 C5
Devon Rd DARL/WED WS10....56 C4
RBRY B45....173 H4
SMTHWKW B67....124 A5
STRBR DY8....117 H5
WLNHL WV13....40 A4
WOLV WV1....6 D1
Devonshire Av BORD B10....107 H3
Devonshire Dr WBROM B70....88 A3
Devonshire Rd BFLD/HDSWWD B20....89 H4
SMTHWKW B67....106 A3
Devonshire St WSNGN B18....107 H3
Devon St VAUX/NECH B7....110 A5
Devoran Cl DUNHL/THL/PER WV6....36 D1
Dewberry Dr DSYBK/YTR WS5....57 C5
Dewberry Rd STRBR DY8....118 B3
Dewhurst Cft STETCH B33....130 D1
Dewsbury Cl STRBR DY8....118 A1
Dewsbury Dr ETTPK/GDPK/PENN WV4....51 C5
Dewsbury Gv PBAR/PBCH B42....90 C1
Deykin Av AST/WIT B6....110 A1
D'Eyncourt Rd WOLV WV10....24 A3
Dial Cl ALE/KHTH/YWD B14....178 A3
Dial La STRBR DY8....118 A4
WBROM B70....70 D5
Diamond Park Dr STRBR DY8....118 A3
Diana Cl ALDR WS9....19 H4
Diane Cl TPTN/OCK DY4....69 H1
Dibble Cl SHHTH WV12....26 B5
Dibble Rd SMTHWKW B67....106 B3
Dibdale Rd DUDN DY1....83 H5
Dibdale Rd West DUDN DY1....83 C3
Dibdale St DUDN DY1....83 H4
Dice Pleck NFLD/LBR B31....176 A3
Dickens Cl SEDG DY3....82 D1
Dickens Heath Rd SHLY B90....193 C4
Dickens Rd BILS/COS WV14....68 C1
WOLV WV10....24 A2
Dickinson Av WOLV WV10....23 H5
Dickinson Dr WALM/CURD B76....63 E4
WSLW WS1....56 C2
Dickinson Rd WMBN WV5....81 E2
Dick Sheppard Av TPTN/OCK DY4....69 H3
Diddington Av HLGN/YWD B28....163 E5
Didgley Gv CHWD/FDBR/MGN B37....114 A4
Digbeth DIG/EDG B5....3 J7
WSL WS1....4 C4
Digby Crs CSHL/WTROR B46....96 B3
Digby Dr CHWD/FDBR/MGN B37....149 F1
Digby Rd CSHL/WTROR B46....115 F3
KGSWFD DY6....99 H1
SCFLD/BOLD B73....62 A5
Dilke Rd ALDR WS9....29 H5
Dilloways La WLNHL WV13....39 E4
Dimberline Bank RIDG/WDGT B32....140 C3
Dimmingsdale WLNHL WV13....39 C4
Dimmocks Av BILS/COS WV14....68 D3
Dimmock St ETTPK/GDPK/PENN WV4....52 C3
Dimsdale Gv NFLD/LBR B31....175 E2
Dimsdale Rd NFLD/LBR B31....174 D2
Dingle Av CDYHTH B64....121 E4
Dingle Cl BVILLE B30....103 E2
DUDS DY2....102 C2
Dingle Hollow OLDBY B69....104 B1
Dingle La SOLH B91....181 H1
WLNHL WV13....39 C1
Dingle Mdw DUDS DY2....102 C2
KGSWFD DY6....100 C5
WMBN WV5....81 E5
Dingle St OLDBY B69....104 B1
The Dingle BDMR/CCFT WV3....35 H4
OLDBY B69....104 B1
SHLY B90....194 D3
SLYOAK B29....142 C5
Dingle Vw SEDG DY3....67 E4
Dingley Rd DARL/WED WS10....56 A3
Dinham Gdns DUDN DY1....83 C3
Dinmore Av NFLD/LBR B31....175 H1
Dippons Dr DUNHL/THL/PER WV6....35 E3
Dippons Mill Cl DUNHL/THL/PER WV6....35 E2
Dirtyfoot La ETTPK/GDPK/PENN WV4....50 A3
Discovery Cl TPTN/OCK DY4....86 A1
The Ditch WSL WS1....5 F4
Ditton Gv NFLD/LBR B31....189 F2
Dixon Cl CVALE B35....94 C4
TPTN/OCK DY4....70 A5
Dixon Rd SMTHWK B10....127 H4
Dixon's Green Rd DUDS DY2....103 E1
Dixon St BKHL/PFLD WV2....52 C2
Dobbins Oak Rd HAC/WOL DY9....153 F1
Dobbs Mill Cl SLYOAK B29....143 F5
Dobbs St BKHL/PFLD WV2....7 F7
Dockar Rd NFLD/LBR B31....175 E3
Dock La DUDN DY1....84 B5
Dock Meadow Dr ETTPK/GDPK/PENN WV4....53 E4
Dock Rd STRBR DY8....118 B2
The Dock HAG/WOL DY9....136 D2
Doctors Hi HAC/WOL DY9....136 A4
Doctors La KGSWFD DY6....98 D4
Doctor's Piece WLNHL WV13....39 H3
Doddington Gv RIDG/WDGT B32....157 F2
Dodford Cl RBRY B45....187 H1
Doe Bank La ALDR WS9....59 H2
Doe Bank Rd TPTN/OCK DY4....70 A2
Dogge Lane Cft ACGN B27....146 B5
Dog Kennel La HALE B63....138 D4
Dogkennel La LGLYGN/QTN B68....105 G4
Dog Kennel La SHLY B90....195 H1
WSL WS1....5 C3
Dogpool La BVILLE B30....160 B1

Doidge Rd ERDW/GRVHL B23....92 B3
Doilery Dr DIG/EDG B5....145 G2
Dollis Gv KGSTG B44....60 B5
Dolman St VAUX/NECH B7....127 H1
Dolman Rd AST/WIT B6....109 E1
Dolobran Rd SPARK B11....127 H5
Dolphin Cl BLOX/PEL WS3....28 B1
Dolphin La ACGN B27....163 G1
Dolphin Rd SPARK B11....145 F2
Dolton Wy TPTN/OCK DY4....85 E1
Dominic Cl BVILLE B30....176 B1
Doncaster Wy CBROM B36....111 G1
Don Cl EDG B15....125 F4
Donegal Rd FOAKS/STRLY B74....60 C3
Donibristle Cft CVALE B35....94 C2
Donovan Dr SCFLD/BOLD B75....62 A2
Dooley Cl WLNHL WV13....39 E5
Doran Cl HALE B63....154 D1
Doranda Wy HHTH/SAND B71....88 B5
Dora Cl HDSW B21....107 G2
SMHTH B10....87 G5
Dora St WSLW WS2....56 B1
Dorchester Cl SHHTH WV12....26 A2
Dorchester Ct SOLH B91....181 G1
Dorchester Dr HRBN B17....141 H5
Dorchester Rd HAG/WOL DY9....136 D5
SOLH B91....181 G1
Dordale Cl NFLD/LBR B31....174 C4
Dordale Rd HAG/WOL DY9....184 B5
Dordon Cl SHLY B90....179 G4
Doreen Gv ERDE/BCHGN B24....93 F4
Doris Rd BORD B9....128 B3
CSHL/WTROR B46....115 F1
SPARK B11....144 D3
Dorlcote Rd WASH/WDE B8....111 E5
Dormie Cl HWK/WKHTH B38....184 A1
Dormington Rd KGSTG B44....60 B5
Dormston Cl SOLH B91....182 A5
Dormston Dr SEDG DY3....82 B3
SLYOAK B29....141 F5
Dormy Dr NFLD/LBR B31....189 C1
Dorncliffe Av STETCH B33....131 F5
Dornie Dr HWK/WKHTH B38....176 D4
Dornton Rd BVILLE B30....160 C2
Dorothy Adams Cl CDYHTH B64....121 E4
Dorothy Rd SMTHWKW B67....124 C1
SPARK B11....146 B2
Dorothy St WSL WS1....56 D1
Dorridge Cft DOR/KN B93....198 D1
Dorridge Rd DOR/KN B93....198 D2
Dorrington Gn PBAR/PBCH B42....90 A1
Dorrington Rd PBAR/PBCH B42....90 A1
Dorset Cl RBRY B45....173 H5
Dorset Dr ALDR WS9....30 B1
Dorset Rd HRBN B17....124 D1
STRBR DY8....135 E1
WASH/WDE B8....110 B3
Dorset Tower WSNGN B18 *....2 A2
Dorsett Pl BLOX/PEL WS3....27 G3
Dorsett Rd DARL/WED WS10....55 H3
Dorsett Road Ter DARL/WED WS10....55 E2
Dorsheath Gdns ERDW/GRVHL B23....92 D2
Dorsington Rd ACGN B27....163 H1
Dorstone Covert ALE/KHTH/YWD B14....177 G3
Dorville Cl HWK/WKHTH B38....176 B5
Douay Rd ERDW/GRVHL B23....77 F5
Double Rw DUDS DY2....103 E5
Doughty St TPTN/OCK DY4....86 A4
Douglas Av CBROM B36....111 H5
LGLYGN/QTN B68....105 H4
Douglas Davies Cl SHHTH WV12....40 A1
Douglas Rd ACGN B27....146 A4
BILS/COS WV14....68 D3
CSCFLD/WYGN B72....62 C5
HDSW B21....107 C2
HLYWD B47....192 C1
LGLYGN/QTN B68....105 H5
RMSLY B62....122 C3
Douglas Turner Wy BDMR/CCFT WV3....36 A2
Doulton Cl ALE/KHTH/YWD B14....178 C2
Doulton Dr SMTHWK B66....106 C3
Doulton Rd BLKHTH/ROWR B65....103 G5
Dovebridge Cl WALM/CURD B76....63 F4
Dove Cl DARL/WED WS10....56 B4
WSL WS1....5 H5
YDLY B25....130 A4
Dovecote Cl DUNHL/THL/PER WV6....35 G1
SEDG DY3....67 G5
SOLH B91....164 D2
TPTN/OCK DY4....86 A1
The Dovecotes MGN/WHC B75....47 F2
Dovedale Av BLOX/PEL WS3....18 A2
SHHTH WV12....26 D3
SHLY B90....180 B4
Dovedale Ct ETTPK/GDPK/PENN WV4....67 H1
Dovedale Dr HLGN/YWD B28....162 D4
Dovedale Rd ERDW/GRVHL B23....76 A5
ETTPK/GDPK/PENN WV4....67 G1
KGSWFD DY6....100 A1
Dove Dr STRBR DY8....118 C4
Dove Gdns HWK/WKHTH B38....177 F5
Dove House La SOLH B91....164 B5
Dovehouse Pool Rd AST/WIT B6....109 E1
Dover Cl RIDG/WDGT B32....157 E3
Dovercourt Rd LCN/SDN/BHAMAIR B26....148 A2
Doverdale Cl HALE B63....137 H2
Dove Rdg STRBR DY8....118 C5
Doveridge Cl SOLH B91....164 A4
Doveridge Pl WSL WS1....5 F7
Doveridge Rd HLGN/YWD B28....162 C5
Doversley Rd ALE/KHTH/YWD B14....160 C5
Dover St BILS/COS WV14....53 E5
WSNGN B18....107 H3
Dove Wy CBROM B36....113 H1
Dovey Dr WALM/CURD B76....78 C4

Dovey Gv BLKHTH/ROWR B65....121 H2
Dovey Rd MOS/BIL B13....144 D4
SPARK B11....144 D4
Dovey Tower VAUX/NECH B7 *....109 C5
Dowar Rd RBRY B45....188 C1
Dowells Cl MOS/BIL B13....144 B5
Dowells Gdns STRBR DY8....117 H1
The Doweries RBRY B45....173 H5
Dower Rd MGN/WHC B75....47 G5
Dowles Cl SLYOAK B29....158 D4
Downcroft Av HWK/WKHTH B38....176 C5
Downend Cl WOLV WV10....13 F3
Downes Ct TPTN/OCK DY4....85 E1
Downey Cl SPARK B11....127 H5
Downfield Cl BLOX/PEL WS3....16 C3
Downfield Dr SEDG DY5....67 G5
Downham Cl DSYBK/YTR WS5....43 C4
Downham Pl BDMR/CCFT WV3....36 B5
Downie Rd CDSL WV8....11 E4
Downing Cl BLKHTH/ROWR B65....122 A3
DOR/KN B93....197 E4
WNSFLD WV11....25 C3
Downing St HALE B63....138 C2
SMTHWK B66....107 E2
Downsfield Rd LCN/SDN/BHAMAIR B26....130 D5
Downside Rd ERDE/BCHGN B24....92 C5
Downs Rd WLNHL WV13....40 A5
The Downs ALDR WS9....45 E3
WOLV WV10....23 E4
Downton Crs STETCH B33....131 G1
Dowty Wy COVEN WV9....12 A4
Drake Cl BLOX/PEL WS3....27 F1
Drake Cft CHWD/FDBR/MGN B37....114 D5
Drake Rd BLOX/PEL WS3....27 C1
ERDW/GRVHL B23....92 A3
SMTHWK B66....105 H2
Drakes Cl HLYWD B47....192 C1
Drakes Cross Pde HLYWD B47....192 C3
Drake's Gn BILS/COS WV14....54 B5
Drakes Hill Cl STRBR DY8....134 B3
Drake St HHTH/SAND B71....87 C1
Drancy Av SHHTH WV12....26 B4
Drawbridge Rd SHLY B90....179 C5
Draycote Cl HIA/OLT B92....165 F3
Draycott Av ERDW/GRVHL B23....92 B2
Draycott Cl ETTPK/GDPK/PENN WV4....50 C3
Draycott Dr NFLD/LBR B31....158 A3
Draycott Rd SMTHWK B66....106 A2
Drayman Cl WSL WS1....5 F6
Draycott Cl MGN/WHC B75....47 F2
Drayton Rd ALE/KHTH/YWD B14....161 G2
HAC/WOL DY9....184 B2
SHLY B90....180 A5
SMTHWK B66....124 C3
Drayton St BKHL/PFLD WV2....37 E5
WSLW WS2....41 G3
Dreadnought Rd BRLYHL DY5....100 D2
The Dreel EDG B15....125 C5
Dreghorn Rd CBROM B36....112 A1
Drem Cft CVALE B35....94 C4
Dresden Cl ETTPK/GDPK/PENN WV4....53 E4
Drew Crs HAC/WOL DY9....136 B4
Drew Rd HAC/WOL DY9....136 B4
Drews Holloway HALE B63....137 H2
Drews Holloway South HALE B63....137 H2
Drews Meadow Cl ALE/KHTH/YWD B14....177 G3
Driffold SCFLD/BOLD B73....62 B1
Driftwood Cl HWK/WKHTH B38....190 B1
Drive Flds ETTPK/GDPK/PENN WV4....50 B2
The Drive ALVE B48....90 A4
BFLD/HDSWWD B20....17 C5
BLOX/PEL WS3....10 B4
BRLYHL DY5....101 C4
CDSL WV8....10 B4
CSHL/WTROR B46....115 F1
DUNHL/THL/PER WV6 *....21 C5
ERDW/GRVHL B23....92 C4
HALE B63....137 H2
RUSH/SHEL WS4....29 E1
The Droveway COVEN WV9....11 H5
Druid Park Rd SHHTH WV12....26 A1
Druids Av ALDR WS9....30 C2
BLKHTH/ROWR B65....104 B5
Druids La ALE/KHTH/YWD B14....177 H4
Druids Wk ALDR WS9....30 C2
Drummond Cl WNSFLD WV11....15 E5
Drummond Gv GTB/HAM B43....59 G5
Drummond Rd BORD B9....128 D2
HAG/WOL DY9....136 D3
Drummond Wy COLV WV1....6 E2
Drury La CDSL WV8....10 B3
SOLH B91....181 H2
STRBR DY8....135 G2
Drybrook Cl HWK/WKHTH B38....176 C5
Dryden Cl SHHTH WV12....26 C2
TPTN/OCK DY4....69 G4
Dryden Gv ACGN B27....146 A5
Dryden Pl BLOX/PEL WS3....28 A5
Dryden Rd BLOX/PEL WS3....28 A3
WOLV WV10....23 H1
Drylea Gv CBROM B36....112 B1
Dubarry Av KGSWFD DY6....99 G2
Duchess Pde WBROM B70 *....87 H3
Duchess Rd LDYWD/EDGR B16...126 A1
WSL WS1....56 C3
Duck La CDSL WV8....11 H3
Duddeston Dr WASH/WDE B8....110 B5
Duddeston Manor Rd VAUX/NECH B7....109 G4
Duddeston Mill Rd VAUX/NECH B7....109 H5
Dudding Rd ETTPK/GDPK/PENN WV4....52 B3

Dudhill Rd BLKHTH/ROWR B65....121 C1
Dudley Cl BLKHTH/ROWR B65....103 F3
Dudley Crs WNSFLD WV11....25 E4
Dudley Park Rd ACGN B27....146 C4
Dudley Port TPTN/OCK DY4....85 C3
Dudley Rd BKHL/PFLD WV2....52 B1
BLKHTH/ROWR B65....103 F3
BRLYHL DY5....136 C1
HAC/WOL DY9....136 D2
HALE B63....138 D2
KGSWFD DY6....99 C1
OLDBY B69....104 C1
SEDG DY3....67 F3
TPTN/OCK DY4....84 D1
WSNGN B18....107 F2
Dudley Rd East OLDBY B69....86 A4
Dudley Rd West OLDBY B69....85 H4
Dudley Rw DUDS DY2....84 B5
Dudley Southern By-Pass DUDS DY2....102 A2
Dudley St BILS/COS WV14....53 H4
DARL/WED WS10....70 C1
DIG/EDG B5....3 C6
SEDG DY3....67 F3
STRBR DY8....135 C2
WBROM B70....87 F2
WNSFLD WV11....24 D5
WOLV WV1....7 F4
WSL WS1....7 F4
Dudley Wk ETTPK/GDPK/PENN WV4....52 A3
Dudley Wood Av DUDS DY2....120 C2
Dudley Wood Rd DUDS DY2....120 C3
Dudmaston Wy DUDN DY1....83 G3
Dudnill Gv RIDG/WDGT B32....157 E2
Duffield Cl CDSL WV8....22 E1
Dufton Rd RIDG/WDGT B32....141 E2
Dugdale Crs MGN/WHC B75....47 G2
Dugdale St WSNGN B18....107 F5
Dukes Rd BVILLE B30....177 C2
Duke St SDMR/CCFT WV3 *....51 C1
BLKHTH/ROWR B65....121 H2
CSCFLD/WYGN B72....62 B4
SEDG DY3....83 F1
STRBR DY8....135 G2
WBROM B70....87 F2
WNSFLD WV11....24 D5
WOLV WV1....7 J5
Dulvern Gv ALE/KHTH/YWD B14....160 D3
Dulverton Rd AST/WIT B6....91 C5
Dulwich Gv KGSTG B44....75 H3
Dulwich Rd KGSTG B44....75 G3
Dumbleberry Av SEDG DY3....67 E4
Dumblederry La ALDR WS9....29 C2
Dunard Rd SHLY B90....179 H2
Dunbar Gv GTB/HAM B43....59 F4
Duncalfe Dr MGN/WHC B75....47 F4
Duncan Edwards Cl DUDN DY1....102 A1
Duncan St BKHL/PFLD WV2....52 A1
Dunchurch Crs SCFLD/BOLD B73....61 E5
Dunchurch Dr NFLD/LBR B31....158 A3
Duncombe Gn CSHL/WTROR B46....115 F2
Duncombe Gv HRBN B17....124 B5
Duncombe St STRBR DY8....134 D1
Duncroft Rd LCN/SDN/BHAMAIR B26....130 B4
Duncumb Rd MGN/WHC B75....63 G5
Dundalk La BLOX/PEL WS3....60 A5
Dundas Av DUDS DY2....103 F1
Dunedin Rd KGSTG B44....60 A5
Dunham Cft DOR/KN B93....196 B5
Dunkirk Av WBROM B70....86 C2
Dunkley St WOLV WV1....6 C3
Dunley Cft SHLY B90....195 F2
Dunlin Cl ERDW/GRVHL B23....93 G4
KGSWFD DY6....100 C3
Dunlop Wy CVALE B35....94 A5
Dunnerdale Rd BRWNH WS8....18 D1
Dunnigan Rd RIDG/WDGT B32....140 C4
Dunns Bank BRLYHL DY5....119 H5
Dunoon Dr ETTPK/GDPK/PENN WV4....52 D3
Dunsfold Cl BILS/COS WV14....53 E5
Dunsfold Cft AST/WIT B6....109 F3
Dunsford Cl BRLYHL DY5....118 D5
Dunsford Rd SMTHWK B66....124 C2
Dunsink Rd AST/WIT B6....91 F5
Dunslade Crs BRLYHL DY5....119 H4
Dunslade Rd ERDW/GRVHL B23....76 D4
Dunsley Dr STRBR DY8....118 A1
Dunsley Gv ETTPK/GDPK/PENN WV4....51 C4
Dunsmore Dr BRLYHL DY5....119 H4
Dunsmore Gv SOLH B91....164 B3
Dunsmore Rd HLGN/YWD B28....162 C1
Dunstall Av DUNHL/THL/PER WV6....37 F1
Dunstall Gv SLYOAK B29....158 B2
Dunstall Hi DUNHL/THL/PER WV6....23 E3
Dunstall La DUNHL/THL/PER WV6....22 D5
Dunstall Rd DUNHL/THL/PER WV6....36 D1
HALE B63....137 H4
Dunstan Cft SHLY B90....180 C5
Dunstan St SEDG DY3....177 F1
Dunster Gv DUNHL/THL/PER WV6....34 D2
Dunster Rd CHWD/FDBR/MGN B37....132 C1
Dunston Cl KGSWFD DY6....99 C1
Dunton Cl MGN/WHC B75....47 E1
Dunton Hall Rd SHLY B90....180 A5
Dunton Rd CHWD/FDBR/MGN B37....113 H5
Dunvegan Rd ERDE/BCHGN B24....93 G2
Durant Cl RBRY B45....173 F4
Durban Rd SMTHWK B66....107 E3
D'Urberville Rd BKHL/PFLD WV2....52 C2
Durham Av WLNHL WV13....40 A2
Durham Cft CHWD/FDBR/MGN B37....132 A2
Durham Dr HHTH/SAND B71....71 H4
Durham Pl WSLW WS2....41 F4
Durham Rd BLKHTH/ROWR B65....104 C3

  DARL/WED WS10 .....56 D4
  DUDS DY2 .....120 D2
  SPARK B11 .....144 D3
  STRBR DY8 .....117 H4
  WSLW WS2 .....41 F5
Durley Dean Rd SLYOAK B29 .....142 A5
Durley Dr SCFLD/BOLD B73 .....61 E5
Durley Rd YDLY B25 .....146 C2
Durlston Gv HIA/OLT B92 .....163 E2
Durnford Cft
  ALE/KHTH/YWD B14 .....178 A4
Dursley Rd HIA/OLT B92 .....164 D2
  SHHTH WV12 .....40 B1
Dutton's La MGN/WHC B75 .....48 A1
Duxford Rd PBAR/PBCH B42 .....74 B3
Dwellings La RIDG/WDGT B32 .....140 B2
Dyas Av PBAR/PBCH B42 .....74 A4
Dyas Rd HLYWD B47 .....192 C1
  .....74 D5
Dyce CI CVALE B35 .....74 D5
Dymoke St BHTH/HG B12 .....127 F4
Dynes Wk SMTHWKW B67 .....106 C4
Dyott Rd MOS/BIL B13 .....161 G1
Dyson CI WSLW WS2 .....40 D2
Dysons Gdns WASH/WDE B8 .....110 C4

E

Eachelhurst Rd
  ERDE/BCHGN B24 .....94 A2
Eachus Rd BILS/COS WV14 .....68 D3
Eachway RBRY B45 .....187 H2
Eachway Farm CI RBRY B45 .....188 A2
Eachway La RBRY B45 .....188 A2
Eagle CI BLKHTH/ROWR B65 .....105 F5
  DUDN DY1 .....83 H5
Eagle Cft BDMR/CCFT WV3 * 51 G1
Eagle Ct ALE/KHTH/YWD B14 .....178 A5
Eagle Gdns ERDE/BCHGN B24 .....93 G4
Eagle Gv CBROM B36 .....114 A1
Eagle La TPTN/OCK DY4 .....70 B5
Eagle St BDMR/CCFT WV3 .....51 G1
  BKHL/PFLD WV2 .....7 K7
  TPTN/OCK DY4 .....70 A5
Ealing Gv KGSTG B44 .....75 G2
Earlsbury Gdns
  BFLD/HDSWWD B20 .....90 D5
Earls Court Rd HRBN B17 .....141 G1
Earls Ferry Gdns
  RIDG/WDGT B32 .....157 F3
Earls Rd RUSH/SHEL WS4 .....29 E3
Earlston Wy GTB/HAM B43 .....105 F5
Earl St BILS/COS WV14 .....68 C5
  KGSTG B44 .....99 H5
  WBROM B70 .....87 F2
  WSL WS1 .....56 D1
Earls Wy HALE B63 .....138 D3
Earlswood Cft
  BFLD/HDSWWD B20 .....90 A4
Earlswood Crs COVEN WV9 .....12 A4
Earlswood Dr
  FOAKS/STRLY B74 .....62 C1
Earlswood Rd DOR/KN B93 .....198 D3
  KGSWFD DY6 .....100 A2
Easby Wy BLOX/PEL WS3 .....16 B5
  WASH/WDE B8 .....110 C4
Easenhall CI DOR/KN B93 .....197 E4
Easmore CI
  ALE/KHTH/YWD B14 .....177 H3
East Acre WLNHL WV13 .....59 G4
East Av WOLVN WV11 .....104 A2
  WNSFLD WV11 .....24 C4
Eastbourne Av
  BKDE/SHDE B34 .....111 H3
Eastbourne St
  RUSH/SHEL WS4 .....42 B2
Eastbrook CI WALM/CURD B76 .....62 D4
Eastbury Dr HIA/OLT B92 .....147 G5
East Car Park Rd
  BHAMNEC B40 .....150 B3
Eastcote CI SHLY B90 .....180 C2
Eastcote La HIA/OLT B92 .....167 G5
Eastcote Rd ACGN B27 .....163 E1
  WOLVN WV10 .....23 H5
East Croft Rd
  ETTPK/GDPK/PENN WV4 .....50 C4
Eastdean CI ERDW/GRVHL B23 .....76 B5
Eastern Av BRLYHL DY5 .....119 E5
East Dr DIG/EDG B5 .....142 C4
Eastern Rd DARL/WED WS10 .....155 H5
Eastern Rd SCFLD/BOLD B73 .....77 F2
  SLYOAK B29 .....159 H2
Easterton Cft
  ALE/KHTH/YWD B14 .....178 A3
East Farm Cft SMHTH B10 .....128 B4
Eastfield CI ALDR WS9 .....30 A4
Eastfield Dr HIA/OLT B92 .....165 G2
Eastfield Gv WOLV WV1 .....37 H5
Eastfield Retreat WOLV WV1 .....37 H5
Eastfield Rd BORD B9 .....128 C2
  TPTN/OCK DY4 .....69 G3
  WOLV WV1 .....37 H5
East Ga LDYWD/EDGR B16 .....125 G1
East Gn
  ETTPK/GDPK/PENN WV4 .....50 C4
Eastham Rd MOS/BIL B13 .....162 A4
East Holme BORD B9 .....128 A2
Easthope Rd STETCH B33 .....112 C5
Eastlake CI GTB/HAM B43 .....105 H2
Eastlands Rd MOS/BIL B13 .....161 G1
Eastleigh SEDG DY3 .....66 D3
Eastleigh Cft WALM/CURD B76 .....78 C4
Eastleigh Dr RMSLY B62 .....172 C1
Eastleigh Gv YDLY B25 .....129 H4
East Meadway STETCH B33 .....131 H1
East Ms KGSTG B44 .....74 D1
Eastmoor CI FOAKS/STRLY B74 .....45 H5
Eastney Crs CDSL WV8 .....22 A2
Easton Gdns WNSFLD WV11 .....25 F5
Easton Gv ACGN B27 .....163 G1
  HLYWD B47 .....192 D1
East Park Wy WOLV WV1 .....38 A4
East Pathway HRBN B17 .....142 A1
East Ri MGN/WHC B75 *
East Rd
  ETTPK/GDPK/PENN WV4 .....52 D4

TPTN/OCK DY4 .....69 H5
  WOLVN WV10 .....13 H5
East St BRLYHL DY5 .....120 A4
  DUDS DY2 .....103 E1
  SEDG DY3 .....83 E3
  WOLV WV1 .....37 F5
  WSL WS1 .....57 F1
East View Rd
  CSCFLD/WYGN B72 .....62 D5
Eastville NFLD/LBR B31 .....175 H3
Eastward Glen CDSL WV8 .....21 G1
East Wy BHAMNEC B40 .....150 B4
Eastway HRBN B17 .....142 A1
Eastwood Rd BHTH/HG B12 .....143 H2
  DUDS DY2 .....103 E3
  GTB/HAM B43 .....73 G3
Eatesbrook Rd STETCH B33 .....131 E1
Eathorpe CI BKDE/SHDE B34 .....113 F5
Eaton Av WBROM B70 .....87 E2
Eaton Ct FOAKS/STRLY B74 .....62 D1
Eaton Crs SEDG DY3 .....82 D3
Eaton PI KGSWFD DY6 .....100 A4
Eaton Ri SHHTH WV12 .....25 H4
Eaton Wood Dr
  LGN/SDN/BHAMAIR B26 .....146 D2
Eaves Court Dr SEDG DY3 .....67 E1
Eaves Green Gdns ACGN B27 .....163 F2
Ebenezer St BILS/COS WV14 .....68 B5
  WBROM B70 .....70 D5
Ebley Rd BFLD/HDSWWD B20 .....90 A2
Ebmore Dr
  ALE/KHTH/YWD B14 .....177 H3
Ebrington Av HIA/OLT B92 .....147 H4
Ebrington CI
  ALE/KHTH/YWD B14 .....177 H1
Ebrington Rd HHTH/SAND B71 .....71 H5
Ebrook Rd CSCFLD/WYGN B72 .....62 D5
Ebury Rd BVILLE B30 .....177 F1
Ecclesall Av WOLVN WV10 .....23 E2
Ecclestone Rd WNSFLD WV11 .....25 G2
Echo Wy
  ETTPK/GDPK/PENN WV4 .....53 E4
Eckersall Rd HWK/WKHTH B38 .....176 C2
Edale CI
  ETTPK/GDPK/PENN WV4 .....52 C5
  KGSWFD DY6 .....99 F2
Edale Rd PBAR/PBCH B42 .....74 C4
Eddish Rd STETCH B33 .....112 D5
Eddison Rd CSHL/WTROR B46 * 97 F2
Edelweiss CI DSYBK/YTR WS5 * 57 H5
Edenbridge Rd
  HLGN/YWD B28 .....163 F2
Edenbridge Vw DUDN DY1 .....83 G3
Eden CI NFLD/LBR B31 .....175 E5
  OLDBY B69 .....86 B4
Edendale Rd
  LGN/SDN/BHAMAIR B26 .....147 H1
Eden Gdns
  BLKHTH/ROWR B65 .....121 H2
  SEDG DY3 .....67 H3
Eden Gv
  CHWD/FDBR/MGN B37 .....132 D3
  HHTH/SAND B71 .....87 G1
Edenhall Rd RIDG/WDGT B32 .....140 B2
Edenhurst Rd NFLD/LBR B31 .....189 F2
Eden PI CBHAMNW B3 .....2 E5
Eden Rd HIA/OLT B92 .....148 A4
Edensor CI WOLVN WV10 .....37 G1
Edgbaston Park Rd EDG B15 .....143 E2
Edgbaston Rd BHTH/HG B12 .....144 A3
  DIG/EDG B5 .....143 G2
  SMTHWK B66 .....124 D1
Edgbaston Rd East
  BHTH/HG B12 .....144 B3
Edgcombe Rd HLGN/YWD B28 .....162 D1
Edge Hill Av WOLVN WV10 .....24 B1
Edge Hill Dr
  DUNHL/THL/PER WV6 .....34 C2
  SEDG DY3 .....67 E1
Edge Hill Rd FOAKS/STRLY B74 .....46 C1
Edgehill Rd NFLD/LBR B31 .....175 G4
Edgemond Av
  ERDE/BCHGN B24 .....94 B2
Edge St BILS/COS WV14 .....68 C5
Edgewood CI CDYHTH B64 .....121 F4
Edgewood Rd
  HWK/WKHTH B38 .....190 C1
  RBRY B45 .....188 B2
Edgeworth CI SHHTH WV12 .....40 A1
Edgware Rd ERDW/GRVHL B23 .....92 B1
Edinburgh Av WSLW WS2 .....40 C2
Edinburgh Ct
  ERDE/BCHGN B24 .....93 H2
Edinburgh Crs STRBR DY8 .....117 H3
Edinburgh Dr RUSH/SHEL WS4 .....29 F1
  SHHTH WV12 .....25 H4
Edinburgh La WSLW WS2 * 41 E1
Edinburgh Rd BILS/COS WV14 .....54 B5
  DSYBK/YTR WS5 .....42 D5
  DUDS DY2 .....102 D3
  LGLYGN/QTN B68 .....123 F4
Edison Gv RIDG/WDGT B32 .....140 A1
Edison Rd CSHL/WTROR B46 .....97 F3
  WSLW WS2 .....27 E5
Edith Rd SMTHWK B66 .....124 D1
Edith St WBROM B70 .....87 F3
Edmonds CI STETCH B33 .....130 D3
Edmonds Rd LGLYGN/QTN B68 .....123 G2
Edmonton Av KGSTG B44 .....75 H2
Edmoor CI SHHTH WV12 .....26 A4
Edmund Rd SEDG DY3 .....67 H3
  WASH/WDE B8 .....110 C5
Edmund St CBHAMNW B3 .....3 F4
Ednam CI WBROM B70 .....71 H3
Ednam Gv WMBN WV5 .....69 F3
Ednam Rd BILS/COS WV14 .....54 A1
  DUDN DY1 .....84 C4
Edsome Wy CBROM B36 .....112 B1
Edstone CI BVILLE B30 .....177 H2
Edstone Ms CBROM B36 .....112 B1
Edward Av ALDR WS9 .....30 A3
Edward CI BILS/COS WV14 .....54 A5
Edward Fisher Dr
  TPTN/OCK DY4 * 85 G1
Edward Rd
  ALE/KHTH/YWD B14 .....178 B4
  BHTH/HG B12 .....144 A2
  CSHL/WTROR B46 .....96 C5

DIG/EDG B5 .....143 H1
  DUNHL/THL/PER WV6 .....20 C5
  HALE B63 .....138 B3
  LGLYGN/QTN B68 .....123 G4
  SMTHWKW B67 .....106 B5
  TPTN/OCK DY4 .....69 G4
  WOLV WV1 .....37 F5
Edwards Rd DUDS DY2 .....102 C5
  ERDE/BCHGN B24 .....93 E1
  MGN/WHC B75 .....47 H2
Edward St CBHAMW B1 .....2 C5
  DARL/WED WS10 .....55 G2
  DUDN DY1 .....84 B4
  ETTPK/GDPK/PENN WV4 .....52 D2
  LGLYGN/QTN B68 .....105 E5
  WBROM B70 .....87 G3
  WSLW WS2 .....41 F2
Edwin Phillips Dr
  HHTH/SAND B71 .....71 F3
Edwin Rd BVILLE B30 .....160 B5
Edwinstowe CI BRLYHL DY5 .....120 A2
Eel St OLDBY B69 .....104 C2
Effingham Rd MOS/BIL B13 .....162 A4
Egbert CI AST/WIT B6 .....109 H1
Egelwin CI
  DUNHL/THL/PER WV6 .....20 C5
Egerton Rd ERDE/BCHGN B24 .....93 H3
  FOAKS/STRLY B74 .....45 E4
  WOLVN WV10 .....11 E4
Egghill La RBRY B45 .....174 A1
Egginton Rd HGLN/YWD B28 .....117 H5
Egginton Rd HLGN/YWD B28 .....162 C5
Egmont Gdns WNSFLD WV11 .....25 F5
Eileen Gdns
  CHWD/FDBR/MGN B37 .....114 A5
Eileen Rd SPARK B11 .....144 D4
Elan CI SEDG DY3 .....83 F3
Elan Rd NFLD/LBR B31 .....174 C5
  SEDG DY3 .....67 E3
Elbow St CDYHTH B64 .....121 F2
Elbury Cft DOR/KN B93 .....196 D5
Elcock Dr PBAR/PBCH B42 .....90 D1
Eldalade Wy DARL/WED WS10 .....71 G2
Elderberry CI DSYBK/YTR WS5 .....57 F5
  STRBR DY8 .....134 C4
Elderfield Rd BVILLE B30 .....177 F2
Elder Gv WMBN WV5 .....64 D5
  WNSFLD WV11 .....24 A4
Eldersfield Gv SOLH B91 .....195 H1
Elderside CI BRWNH WS8 .....9 F4
Elder Wy ERDW/GRVHL B23 .....92 B4
Eldon Dr WALM/CURD B76 .....62 B4
Eldon Rd LDYWD/EDGR B16 .....125 H3
  RMSLY B62 .....140 A4
Eldon St DARL/WED WS10 .....55 F1
  WSL WS1 .....57 G1
Eldridge CI COVEN WV9 .....11 H5
Eleanor Rd BILS/COS WV14 .....53 H2
Electric Av AST/WIT B6 .....109 H3
Elford CI ALE/KHTH/YWD B14 .....161 G5
  FOAKS/STRLY B74 .....45 G5
Elford Gv BILS/COS WV14 .....53 G4
  CHWD/FDBR/MGN B37 .....132 B3
Elford Rd HHTH/SAND B71 .....72 A2
  HRBN B17 .....141 H4
Elgar CI DSYBK/YTR WS5 .....57 H4
Elgin CI SEDG DY3 .....67 G2
  STRBR DY8 .....118 C5
Elgin Ct DUNHL/THL/PER WV6 .....34 C1
Elgin Gv YDLY B25 .....146 A5
Elgin Rd BLOX/PEL WS3 .....16 C3
Eliot Cft BILS/COS WV14 .....68 D1
Eliot St VAUX/NECH B7 .....110 A1
Elizabeth Av BILS/COS WV14 .....54 B5
  DARL/WED WS10 .....56 C5
  ETTPK/GDPK/PENN WV4 .....51 G5
Elizabeth Crs
  LGLYGN/QTN B68 .....123 H2
Elizabeth Gv DUDS DY2 .....103 F2
  SHLY B90 .....181 H1
Elizabeth Rd HALE B63 .....138 B4
  MOS/BIL B13 .....143 G5
  SCFLD/BOLD B73 .....76 A2
  STETCH B33 .....129 H1
  WBROM B70 .....86 B2
Elizabeth Wk TPTN/OCK DY4 .....69 G2
Elkington Crt SHLY B90 .....195 F3
Elkington St AST/WIT B6 .....109 E4
Elkstone CI HIA/OLT B92 .....147 H4
Elkstone Covert
  ALE/KHTH/YWD B14 .....177 G3
Elland Gv ACGN B27 .....146 C5
Ellards Dr WNSFLD WV11 .....25 F5
Ellen St WSNGN B18 .....2 A1
Ellenvale CI BILS/COS WV14 .....68 A3
Ellerby Gv ERDE/BCHGN B24 .....94 A2
Ellerslie CI BRLYHL DY5 .....119 F4
Ellerside Rd MOS/BIL B13 .....162 A3
Ellerton Rd KGSTG B44 .....75 H2
Ellerton Wk WOLVN WV10 .....23 H3
Ellesboro' Rd HRBN B17 .....124 D4
Ellesmere Rd WASH/WDE B8 .....110 B5
Ellice Dr CBROM B36 .....114 B2
Elliot Gdns RBRY B45 .....188 B3
Elliot Rd SLYOAK B29 .....159 G2
Elliotts La CDSL WV8 .....10 C4
Elliott's Rd TPTN/OCK DY4 .....85 E1
Elliott Wy AST/WIT B6 .....91 F2
Ellis Av BRLYHL DY5 .....118 C2
Ellison St WBROM B70 .....87 F4
Ellis St CBHAMW B1 .....2 E7
Elliston Av KGSTG B44 .....75 E3
Ellowes Rd SEDG DY3 .....83 E2
Elm Av BHTH/HG B12 .....144 C3
  BILS/COS WV14 .....54 A4
  DARL/WED WS10 .....55 H4
  WNSFLD WV11 .....24 B2
Elmay Rd
  LGN/SDN/BHAMAIR B26 .....130 C5
Elm Bank MOS/BIL B13 .....144 C4
Elmbank Gv
  BFLD/HDSWWD B20 .....89 G1
Elmbank Rd DSYBK/YTR WS5 .....58 B1
Elmbridge CI HALE B63 .....137 H2
Elmbridge Dr SHLY B90 .....195 H2
Elmbridge Rd KGSTG B44 .....75 E5
Elmbridge Wy
  HWK/WKHTH B38 .....176 B3

SEDG DY3 .....67 G5
Elm CI SEDG DY3 .....82 D4
  STRBR DY8 .....134 C5
Elm Cft LGLYGN/QTN B68 .....123 G5
Elmcroft Av WOLVN WV10 .....13 E4
Elmcroft Gdns WOLVN WV10 .....13 E4
Elmcroft Rd
  LGN/SDN/BHAMAIR B26 .....130 B5
Elmdale Crs NFLD/LBR B31 .....175 E1
Elmdale Dr ALDR WS9 .....30 C2
Elmdale Gv NFLD/LBR B31 .....175 E1
Elm Dale Rd
  ETTPK/GDPK/PENN WV4 .....51 G3
Elmdon CI HIA/OLT B92 .....148 B5
  WOLVN WV10 .....22 C1
Elmdon Coppice HIA/OLT B92 .....165 H3
Elmdon La
  LGN/SDN/BHAMAIR B26 .....149 E4
Elmdon Park Rd HIA/OLT B92 .....148 B5
Elmdon Rd ACGN B27 .....146 C3
  CHWD/FDBR/MGN B37 .....131 H5
  NFLD/LBR B31 .....175 E5
  WOLVN WV10 .....22 C1
Elm Dr GTB/HAM B43 .....73 F2
  KIDD DY10 .....168 B3
  NFLD/LBR B31 .....174 C4
  RMSLY B62 .....122 C3
Elm Farm Av
  CHWD/FDBR/MGN B37 .....131 H5
Elm Farm Rd BKHL/PFLD WV2 .....52 B1
Elmfield Av ERDE/BCHGN B24 .....94 A2
Elmfield Crs MOS/BIL B13 .....144 B5
Elmfield Rd CBROM B36 .....113 G2
Elmfield Vw DUDN DY1 .....84 A3
Elm Gn DUDN DY1 .....84 A1
Elm Gv CDSL WV8 .....10 C4
  CHWD/FDBR/MGN B37 .....132 B3
Elmhurst Av
  BLKHTH/ROWR B65 .....122 A1
Elmhurst Dr KGSWFD DY6 .....100 B5
Elmhurst Rd HDSW B21 .....89 G5
Elmley CI BILS/COS WV14 .....68 B4
Elmley Gv BVILLE B30 .....176 C5
  DUNHL/THL/PER WV6 .....34 D2
Elm Ldg HIA/OLT B92 * 167 G3
Elmore CI
  CHWD/FDBR/MGN B37 .....114 A5
Elmore Green CI BLOX/PEL WS3 .....27 E1
Elmore Green Rd
  BLOX/PEL WS3 .....27 E1
Elmore Rd STETCH B33 .....130 C1
Elmore Rw BLOX/PEL WS3 .....27 F1
Elm Rd BLOX/PEL WS3 .....27 H4
  DUDN DY1 .....84 C3
  KGSWFD DY6 .....100 A3
  WALM/CURD B76 .....78 C4
Elms CI SOLH B91 .....165 F5
Elmsdale DUNHL/THL/PER WV6 .....34 D3
Elmsdale Rw WLNHL WV13 .....59 G4
Elmstead Av STETCH B33 .....131 F5
Elmstead CI DSYBK/YTR WS5 .....43 G5
Elmstead Wd DSYBK/YTR WS5 .....43 G5
The Elms LDYWD/EDGR B16 .....125 H1
Elmstone CI DUDN DY1 .....83 H2
Elm St DUNHL/THL/PER WV6 .....34 C1
  WOLV WV1 .....39 H5
  WLNHL WV13 .....39 H5
Elmsworth Rd NFLD/LBR B31 .....176 B3
Elm Ter OLDBY B69 .....85 G5
Elm Tree CI WMBN WV5 .....80 D1
Elm Tree Gv HALE B63 .....137 H1
Elm Tree Ri HIA/OLT B92 .....167 H4
Elm Tree Rd HRBN B17 .....141 G1
  BVILLE B30 .....160 A4
Elmtree Rd FOAKS/STRLY B74 .....44 D5
Elm Tree Wy CDYHTH B64 * 121 F3
Elmwood Av WNSFLD WV11 .....15 E4
Elmwood Gdns
  BFLD/HDSWWD B20 .....90 B1
Elmwood Rd SEDG DY3 .....66 D2
Elmwood Rd ERDE/BCHGN B24 .....93 G4
  FOAKS/STRLY B74 .....60 C2
  STRBR DY8 .....117 G1
Elmwoods RIDG/WDGT B32 .....140 B5
Elphinstone End
  ERDE/BCHGN B24 .....77 G5
Elsma Rd LGLYGN/QTN B68 .....123 G4
Elston Hall La WOLVN WV10 .....23 G1
Elston Hall Ter WOLVN WV10 .....23 G1
Elstree Rd ERDW/GRVHL B23 .....92 B1
Elswick Gv KGSTG B44 .....75 H3
Elsworth Gv YDLY B25 .....146 C1
Elton CI WOLVN WV10 .....13 E5
Elton Crt DOR/KN B93 .....196 D4
Elton Gv ACGN B27 .....146 A5
Eltonia Cft
  LGN/SDN/BHAMAIR B26 .....147 H1
Elva Cft CBROM B36 .....95 H5
Elvaston Wy SHLY B90 .....193 H5
Elvetham Rd EDG B15 .....126 C5
Elviron Dr
  DUNHL/THL/PER WV6 .....21 F5
Elwell Crs DUDN DY1 .....67 H5
Elwells CI BILS/COS WV14 .....53 G5
Elwell St DARL/WED WS10 .....56 B5
  WBROM B70 .....70 C4
Elwyn Rd SCFLD/BOLD B73 .....62 A5
Ely CI BLKHTH/ROWR B65 .....104 C5
  CHWD/FDBR/MGN B37 .....132 B2
Ely Gv RIDG/WDGT B32 .....141 F5
Ely PI WSLW WS2 .....41 F4
Ely Rd WSLW WS2 .....41 F4
Emay CI WBROM B70 .....70 D3
The Embankment
  BRLYHL DY5 .....119 G2
Embassy Dr EDG B15 .....126 A4
  OLDBY B69 .....104 C1
Embassy Rd OLDBY B69 .....104 C1
Embleton Gv BKDE/SHDE B34 .....112 C5
Emerald Ct WASH/WDE B8 .....111 G4
Emerson CI SEDG DY3 .....82 C2
Emerson Gv WOLVN WV10 .....23 H1
Emerson Rd HRBN B17 .....142 A1
  WOLVN WV10 .....23 H1

Emery CI ERDW/GRVHL B23 .....92 B5
  STRBR DY8 .....134 C5
Emery St WSL WS1 .....5 F6
Emily Gdns
  LGN/SDN/BHAMAIR B26 .....146 D1
Emily Rd
  LGN/SDN/BHAMAIR B26 .....146 D1
Emily St BHTH/HG B12 .....127 F5
  WBROM B70 .....87 F4
Emmanuel Rd SCFLD/BOLD B73 .....77 F4
Emmeline St BORD B9 .....127 H3
Empire CI ALDR WS9 .....29 E2
Empress Wy DARL/WED WS10 .....40 B5
Emscote Dr SCFLD/BOLD B73 .....77 E5
Emscote Rd AST/WIT B6 .....91 F5
Emsworth Crs COVEN WV9 .....12 A5
Emsworth Gv ALE/KHTH/YWD B14 .....160 D4
Enderby CI DOR/KN B93 .....196 D4
Enderby Dr
  ETTPK/GDPK/PENN WV4 .....51 F4
Enderley CI BLOX/PEL WS3 * 16 D4
Enderley Dr BLOX/PEL WS3 .....16 D4
End Hall Rd
  DUNHL/THL/PER WV6 .....35 E2
Endhill Rd KGSTG B44 .....60 C5
Endicott Rd AST/WIT B6 .....91 H5
Endmoor Gv ERDW/GRVHL B23 .....76 B5
Endsleigh Gv HLGN/YWD B28 .....163 E2
Endwood Court Rd
  BFLD/HDSWWD B20 .....90 A4
Endwood Dr FOAKS/STRLY B74 .....46 A1
  SOLH B91 .....181 F3
Enfield CI ERDW/GRVHL B23 .....76 D5
Enfield Rd BLKHTH/ROWR B65 .....122 B1
  CHWD/FDBR/MGN B37 .....132 B2
Enford CI BKDE/SHDE B34 .....113 F5
Engine La BRLYHL DY5 .....119 H1
  BRWNH WS8 .....8 C4
  DARL/WED WS10 .....54 C4
  HAG/WOL DY9 .....136 B2
Engine St OLDBY B69 .....104 A1
  SMTHWK B66 .....106 D3
Englestede CI BFLD/HDSWWD B20 .....89 H3
Englewood Dr HLGN/YWD B28 .....163 E2
Ennerdale CI BRWNH WS8 .....9 E5
Ennersdale Dr
  DUNHL/THL/PER WV6 .....34 D1
  HALE B63 .....137 H5
Ennerdale Rd
  DUNHL/THL/PER WV6 .....21 H2
  GTB/HAM B43 .....73 G4
Ennersdale Bungalows
  CSHL/WTROR B46 .....97 F5
Ennersdale CI CSHL/WTROR B46 .....97 F5
Ennersdale Rd CSHL/WTROR B46 .....97 F5
Ensall Dr STRBR DY8 .....118 A3
Ensbury CI SHHTH WV12 .....40 B1
Ensdale Rw WLNHL WV13 .....59 G4
Ensdon Gv KGSTG B44 .....75 H2
Ensford CI FOAKS/STRLY B74 .....46 C1
Enstone Rd DUDN DY1 .....101 H1
  HIA/OLT B92 .....166 C5
Enterprise Dr FOAKS/STRLY B74 .....60 A1
  HAG/WOL DY9 .....136 D1
Enterprise Gv BLOX/PEL WS3 .....18 B2
Enterprise Wy VAUX/NECH B7 .....3 J1
Enville CI BLOX/PEL WS3 .....16 C4
  CHWD/FDBR/MGN B37 .....132 D3
Enville Gv SPARK B11 .....145 F2
Enville PI STRBR DY8 * 135 F2
Enville Rd
  ETTPK/GDPK/PENN WV4 .....50 C3
  KGSWFD DY6 .....99 F1
  SEDG DY3 .....83 F1
Enville St STRBR DY8 .....135 F2

Epping Gv KGSTG B44 .....75 G4
Epsom CI DUNHL/THL/PER WV6 .....34 D1
Epsom Gv KGSTG B44 .....75 H5
Epwell Gv KGSTG B44 .....75 F5
Epwell Rd KGSTG B44 .....75 F5
Epworth Ct BRLYHL DY5 .....118 C3
Erasmus Rd SPARK B11 .....127 G5
Ercall CI ERDW/GRVHL B23 .....77 G5
Erdington Hall Rd
  ERDE/BCHGN B24 .....92 D4
Erdman CI ALDR WS9 .....44 C3
Erica CI SLYOAK B29 .....158 C2
Erica Rd DSYBK/YTR WS5 .....43 H5
Erington Crs CBROM B36 .....112 A2
Ermington Rd
  ETTPK/GDPK/PENN WV4 .....52 B3
Ernest Clarke CI SHHTH WV12 .....40 B1
Ernest Crt HWK/WKHTH B38 .....177 E4
Ernest Rd BHTH/HG B12 .....144 D3
  DUDS DY2 .....85 F5
  SMTHWKW B67 .....106 A3
Ernest St CBHAMW B1 .....126 D5
Ernsford CI DOR/KN B93 .....198 D3
Erskine St VAUX/NECH B7 .....127 H1
Esher Rd HHTH/SAND B71 .....71 H5
  KGSTG B44 .....60 B4
Eskdale CI WOLV WV1 .....38 B5
Eskdale Wk BRLYHL DY5 .....118 D4
Esme Rd SPARK B11 .....144 D5
Esmond CI NFLD/LBR B31 .....159 F5
Essendon Rd WASH/WDE B8 .....111 F5
Essex Av DARL/WED WS10 .....56 B1
  HHTH/SAND B71 .....71 G4
  KGSWFD DY6 .....99 H5
Essex Gdns STRBR DY8 .....118 A4
Essex Rd DUDS DY2 .....103 H5
Essex St DIG/EDG B5 .....127 E5
  WSLW WS2 .....56 A2
Essington CI STRBR DY8 .....118 A4
Essington Rd SHHTH WV12 .....25 H1
Essington St LDYWD/EDGR B16 .....2 B7
Essington Wy WOLV WV1 .....38 B4
Este Rd
  LGN/SDN/BHAMAIR B26 .....130 C4
Estone Wk AST/WIT B6 .....109 H2
Estria Rd EDG B15 .....142 C3

Ethelfleda Ter DARL/WED WS10...55 H5
Ethelred Cl FOAKS/STRLY B74...47 E2
Ethel Rd HRBN B17...142 B2
Ethel St CBHAM B2...5 H5
  LGLYGN/QTN B68...105 E5
  SMTHWKW B67...124 B2
Etheridge Rd BILS/COS WV14...53 H1
Eton Cl SEDG DY3...67 H4
Eton Dr STRBR DY8...135 C4
Eton Rd BHTH/HG B12...144 D5
Eton Wk HAG/WOL DY9...152 C4
Etruria Wy BILS/COS WV14...54 A1
Etta Gv KGSTG B44...60 A4
Ettingshall Park Farm La
  ETTPK/GDPK/PENN WV4...
Ettingshall Rd BILS/COS WV14...68 A2
  BKHL/PFLD WV2...53 E1
Ettington Cl AST/WIT WR B95...198 D1
Ettington Rd AST/WIT B6...109 E1
Ettymore Cl SEDG DY3...67 F3
Ettymore Rd SEDG DY3...67 F3
Ettymore Rd West SEDG DY3...67 G5
Etwall Rd HLGN/YWD B28...162 A1
Euan Cl HRBN B17...125 E4
Europa Av WBROM B70...88 B4
Evans Cl TPTN/OCK DY4...84 C1
Evans Pl BILS/COS WV14...54 A2
Evans St BILS/COS WV14...67 H2
  DUNHL/THL/PER WV6...36 C1
  WLNHL WV13...38 D4
Eva Rd LGLYGN/QTN B68...123 C2
  WSNCN B19...
Eve La OLDBY B69...83 H1
Evelyn Cft SCFLD/BOLD B73...77 E3
Evelyn Rd SPARK B11...145 E3
Evenlode Gv WLNHL WV13...40 B4
Evenlode Rd HIA/OLT B92...147 G4
Everest Cl SMTHWK B66...106 B1
Everest Rd BFLD/HDSWWD B20...90 A3
  WSLW WS2...40 D2
Evergreen Cl BILS/COS WV14...68 B5
Everitt Dr DOR/KN DY6...197 E2
Eversley Dr ERDE/BCHGN B24...93 E4
Eversley Gv SEDG DY3...67 E1
  WNSFLD WV11...24 C4
Eversley Rd BORD B9...128 B3
Evers St BRLYHL DY5...120 A4
Everton Rd WASH/WDE B8...111 G5
Evesham Crs BLOX/PEL WS3...16 D3
Evesham Ri DUDS DY2...120 D1
Eveson Ct STRBR DY8...135 E4
Eveson Rd STRBR DY8...134 D5
Evington Pl YDLY B25 *...123 E5
Ewart Rd WSLW WS2...40 C2
Ewell Rd ERDE/BCHGN B24...93 F2
Ewhurst Av SLYOAK B29...159 H1
Ewhurst Cl WLNHL WV13...39 F5
Exbury Cl COVEN WV9...11 H1
Excelsior Gv BLOX/PEL WS3...18 B2
Exchange St BRLYHL DY5...101 F5
The Exchange WSL * ...27 F1
Exe Cft NFLD/LBR B31...175 H5
Exeter Dr
  CHWD/FDBR/MGN B37...131 H4
Exeter Pas CBHAMW B1...126 D3
Exeter Rd DUDS DY2...120 D5
  SLYOAK B29...142 D5
  SMTHWK B66...106 D4
Exeter St CBHAMW B1...2 E7
Exford Cl BRLYHL DY5...118 D5
Exhall Cl SOLH B91...181 E3
Exhibition Wy BHAMNEC B40...149 H3
Exmoor Gn WNSFLD WV11...24 C3
The Expressway WBROM B70...87 G2
Exton Cl WNSFLD WV11...25 E3
Exton Wy WASH/WDE B8...110 B4
Eyland Gv WSL WS1...5 F5
Eymore Cl SLYOAK B29...158 D4
Eyre St WSNCN B18...114 A4
Eyston Av TPTN/OCK DY4...70 B3
Eyton Cft BHTH/HG B12...127 F5
Ezekiel La SHHTH WV12...26 A4

F

Fabian Cl RBRY B45...173 H3
Fabian Crs SHLY B90...180 B4
Facet Rd HWK/WKHTH B38...177 E3
Factory Rd TPTN/OCK DY4...69 E5
  WSNCN B18...107 H5
Factory St DARL/WED WS10...55 E2
Fairbourne Av
  BLKHTH/ROWR B65...104 C5
  KGSTG B44...60 D4
Fairburn Crs BLOX/PEL WS3...18 E2
Faircroft Av WALM/CURD B76...78 B5
Faircroft Rd CBROM B36...95 F5
Fairfax Dr NFLD/LBR B31...175 G5
  NFLD/LBR B31...175 G5
  WOLVN WV10...12 D4
Fairfield Dr BLOX/PEL WS3...18 B3
  CDSL WV8...10 A4
  RMSLY B62...122 C3
Fairfield Gv RMSLY B62...122 C3
Fairfield Mt WSL WS1...5 F7
Fairfield Rd STRBR DY8...134 C2
Fairfield Rd
  ALE/KHTH/YWD B14...161 E2
  DUDS DY2...102 D2
  HALE B63...138 C5
  RMSLY B62...122 C3
Fairford Gdns STRBR DY8...118 A1
Fairford Rd KGSTG B44...75 F5
Fairgreen Gdns BRLYHL DY5...101 E4
Fairgreen Wy
  FOAKS/STRLY B74...45 G4
  SLYOAK B29...159 H1
Fairgreen Wy WSL WS1...4 C6
Fairhaven Cft RMSLY B62...122 C3
Fairhills SEDG DY3...67 F3
Fairhill Wy SPARK B11...127 H5
Fairholme Rd CBROM B36...111 F2

Fairlawn EDG B15 *...126 A5
Fairlawn Cl SHHTH WV12...26 A1
Fairlawn Dr KGSWFD DY6...99 H5
Fairlawns
  LGN/SDN/BHAMAIR B26...130 B3
  WALM/CURD B76...78 C3
Fairlie Crs HWK/WKHTH B38...176 B4
Fairmead Ri HWK/WKHTH B38...176 C4
Fairmile Rd HALE B63...138 B1
Fairoak Dr
  DUNHL/THL/PER WV6...35 E2
Fairview Av PBAR/PBCH B42...74 B5
Fairview Cl WNSFLD WV11...24 D3
Fairview Crs KGSWFD DY6...100 B3
  WNSFLD WV11...24 B3
Fairview Gv WNSFLD WV11...24 B3
Fairview Ms
  WTROR B46 *...115 F2
Fairview Rd DUDN DY1...84 A4
  ETTPK/GDPK/PENN WV4...50 C4
  WNSFLD WV11...24 B3
Fairway RBRY/... B31...175 E5
  RUSH/SHEL WS4...29 F1
Fairway Av OLDBY B69...103 C1
Fairway Dr RBRY B45...187 H2
Fairway Gv WV14...53 C1
Fairway Rd LGLYGN/QTN B68...103 D4
Fairways Av STRBR DY8...135 E5
Fairways Cl STRBR DY8...135 E5
The Fairways HWK/WKHTH B38...78 B5
The Fairway HWK/WKHTH B38...176 B5
Fairfield Av CTB/HAM B43...73 F2
Fakenham Cft HRBN B17...124 B5
Falcon Crs BILS/COS WV14...67 H1
Falcondale Rd SHHTH WV12...26 A1
Falconhurst Rd SLYOAK B29...142 A5
Falcon Lodge Crs
  MGN/WHC B75...63 G3
Falcon Pl OLDBY B69...104 A2
Falcon Ri STRBR DY8...134 C1
Falcon Rd LGLYGN/QTN B68...122 D2
The Falcons MGN/WHC B75...63 H3
Falcon Wy DUDN DY1...83 H5
Falfield Cl BLKHTH/ROWR B65...104 B3
Falfield Gv NFLD/LBR B31...174 D4
Falkland Cft BVILLE B30...160 B4
Falklands Cl SEDG DY3...80 C4
Falkland Wy CBROM B36...114 B4
Falkwood Gv DOR/KN B93...196 D2
Fallindale Rd
  LGN/SDN/BHAMAIR B26...147 H1
Fallings Heath Cl
  DARL/WED WS10...55 H1
Fallowfield CDSL WV8...11 C5
  DUNHL/THL/PER WV6...34 B1
Fallow Fld FOAKS/STRLY B74...45 H2
Fallowfield Av HLGN/YWD B28...162 D5
Fallow Field Rd
  BLKHTH/ROWR B65...121 C1
Fallowfield Rd DSYBK/YTR WS5...43 C5
  HALE B63...137 H4
  HIA/OLT B92...148 A5
Fallows Rd SPARK B11...127 H1
Falmouth Rd BKDE/SHDE B34...112 A4
  DSYBK/YTR WS5...58 B1
Falstaff Av HLYWD B47...192 C2
Falstaff Cl WALM/CURD B76...78 C4
Falstaff Rd SHLY B90...180 C3
Falstone Rd SCFLD/BOLD B73...76 B1
Fancott Rd NFLD/LBR B31...158 C5
Fancourt Av
  ETTPK/GDPK/PENN WV4...50 D3
Fane Rd WNSFLD WV11...25 G1
Fanshawe Rd ACGN B27...163 G1
Faraday Av RIDG/WDGT B32...140 D2
  WALM/CURD B76...78 B5
Faraday Wf WSLW WS2...27 F4
Farbrook Wy SHHTH WV12...25 H4
Farcroft Av HDSW B21...107 F1
Farcroft Gv HDSW B21...89 F5
Farcroft Rd HDSW B21...89 F5
Fardon Wy ERDW/GRVHL B23...76 B3
Fareham Crs
  ETTPK/GDPK/PENN WV4...50 C2
Farfield Cl NFLD/LBR B31...175 H5
Far High Dr TPTN/OCK DY4...85 H1
Far Highfield WALM/CURD B76...62 D4
Far Hill Cl HHTH/SAND B71...72 B3
Farlands Dr STRBR DY8...135 C4
Farlands Gv CTB/HAM B43...73 H4
Farlands Rd STRBR DY8...135 C4
Farleigh Dr BDMR/CCFT WV3...35 E5
Farleigh Rd
  DUNHL/THL/PER WV6...35 E2
Farley La RMSLY B62...172 B4
Farley Rd ERDW/GRVHL B23...91 H2
Farley St TPTN/OCK DY4...86 B1
Farlow Cft
  CHWD/FDBR/MGN B37...131 H5
Farlow Rd NFLD/LBR B31...176 A2
Farmacre BORD B9...127 H2
Farm Av LGLYGN/QTN B68...123 E1
Farmbridge Cl WSLW WS2...40 B2
Farmbridge Rd WLNHL WV13...40 B3
Farmbrook Av WOLVN WV10...12 D4
Farm Cl CDSL WV8...10 D5
  HIA/OLT B92...148 A5
  SEDG DY3...66 C4
  STRBR DY8...130 B1
Farmcote Rd STECH B33...112 C5
Farm Cft LOZ/NWT B19...108 C3
Farmcroft Rd HAG/WOL DY9...136 C5
Farmdale Gv RBRY B45...188 C2
Farm End Cl HHTH/SAND B71...72 B2
Farmer Rd SMHTH B10...129 E5
Farmers Cl WALM/CURD B76...63 E4
Farmers Ct HALE B63...138 B3
Farmers Fold WOLV WV1...2 F4
Farmers Wk HDSW B21...107 F2
Farm House La MGN/WHC B75...48 A2
Farm House Rd SHHTH WV12...26 B5
Farm House Wy GTB/HAM B43...73 E4
Farmhouse Wy SHHTH WV12...26 B5
Farmoor Gv BKDE/SHDE B34...113 G3
Farmoor Wy WOLVN WV10...13 E5
Farm Rd BDMR/CCFT WV3...35 B5
  BLKHTH/ROWR B65...105 C5
  BRLYHL DY5...119 C3
  DUDS DY2...102 A5
  LGLYGN/QTN B68...123 E1
  SMTHWKW B67...124 A1
  SPARK B11...144 D1
  TPTN/OCK DY4...69 G4
Farmside Cl HAG/WOL DY9...137 E4
Farmside Gn COVEN WV9...11 H5
Farmstead Cl WSL WS1...57 E3
Farmstead Rd HIA/OLT B92...148 A5
Farm St LOZ/NWT B19...108 C3
  WBROM B70...87 G5
Farnborough Ct
  MGN/WHC B75...47 G3
Farnborough Dr SHLY B90...195 F2
Farnborough Rd CVALE B35...94 D3
Fanbury Cft
  HWK/WKHTH B38...177 F3
Farncote Dr FOAKS/STRLY B74...46 D2
Farndale Av
  DUNHL/THL/PER WV6...36 C1
Farndon Av
  CHWD/FDBR/MGN B37...132 B5
Farndon Rd WASH/WDE B8...110 D4
Farnham Cl GTB/HAM B43...73 H5
Farnham Rd HDSW B21...89 F4
Farnhurst Rd WASH/WDE B8...111 F2
Farnol Rd
  LGN/SDN/BHAMAIR B26...130 B4
Farnworth Gv CBROM B36...95 G5
Farquhar Rd EDG B15...142 D1
  MOS/BIL B13...144 B4
Farquhar Rd East EDG B15...142 D1
Farren Rd NFLD/LBR B31...174 D4
Farrier Cl WALM/CURD B76...78 D3
Farrier Rd GTB/HAM B43...59 H5
Farriers Mi BLOX/PEL WS3...17 C5
The Farriers
  LGN/SDN/BHAMAIR B26...147 H3
Farrier Wy KGSWFD DY6...99 E2
Farrington Rd
  ERDW/GRVHL B23...91 H1
  ETTPK/GDPK/PENN WV4...67 G1
Farrow Rd KGSTG B44...60 A5
Farthing La CSCFLD/WYGN B72...62 B4
Farthing Pools Cl
  CSCFLD/WYGN B72...62 C4
Farthings La DUDS DY2...102 A2
The Farthings HRBN B17...142 B1
Farvale Rd WALM/CURD B76...79 E5
Fashoda Rd SLYOAK B29...160 B1
Fastlea Rd RIDG/WDGT B32...157 H3
Fastmoor Ov STECH B33...131 C3
Fast Pits Rd YDLY B25...129 F4
Fatherless Barn Crs HALE B63...137 G3
Faulkland Crs WOLV WV1...7 G2
Faulkner Cl STRBR DY8...135 F3
Faulkner Rd HIA/OLT B92...148 A5
Faulkners Farm Dr
  ERDW/GRVHL B23...91 H1
Faulknor Dr BRLYHL DY5...100 D5
Faversham Cl WALM/CURD B76...63 E5
  WSLW WS2...40 B2
Fawdry Cl SCFLD/BOLD B73...62 B3
Fawdry St SCBHAMNE B4...127 G2
  SMTHWK B66...107 E4
  WOLV WV1...2 A4
Fawley Cl WLNHL WV13...39 F5
Fawley Gv BVILLE B30...160 B5
Fazeley Cl SOLH B91...182 B1
Fazeley St DIG/EDG B5...3 K6
Fearon Pl SMTHWK B66...106 C5
Featherstone Cl SHLY B90...180 D3
Featherstone Crs SHLY B90...180 D4
Featherstone Rd
  ALE/KHTH/YWD B14...161 E4
Featherston Rd
  FOAKS/STRLY B74...45 G3
Feilansill Rd SEDG DY3...80 B3
Felbrigg Cl BRLYHL DY5...119 C5
The Feldings ERDE/BCHGN B24...93 G2
Feldon La RMSLY B62...122 C5
Felgate Cl SHLY B90...195 G2
Fellbrook Cl STETCH B33...112 B5
Fell Gv HDSW B21...89 H5
Fellmeadow Rd STECH B33...130 C2
Fellmeadow Wy SEDG DY3...67 G5
Fellows Av KGSWFD DY6...99 G1
Fellows La HRBN B17...141 G1
Fellows Park Gdns
  WSLW WS2...56 B2
Fellows Rd BILS/COS WV14...53 H1
Fellows St BKHL/PFLD WV2...37 E5
Felsted Wy VAUX/NECH B7...109 G3
Felstone Rd KGSTG B44...75 E2
Feltham Cl STETCH B33...131 G3
Felton Cft STETCH B33...131 H2
Felton Gv SOLH B91...181 H4
Fenbourne Cl RUSH/SHEL WS4...29 E2
Fenchurch Cl WSLW WS2...41 H1
Fencote Av
  CHWD/FDBR/MGN B37...114 A5
Fenmere Cl
  ETTPK/GDPK/PENN WV4...52 B5
Fennel Cft BKDE/SHDE B34...112 D2
Fennel Rd BRLYHL DY5...119 E5
Fennis Cl DOR/KN B93...196 D5
Fen Ri SHHTH WV12...25 H4
Fens Crs BRLYHL DY5...101 E4
Fens Pool Av BRLYHL DY5...101 F4
Fenter Cl MOS/BIL B13...144 B2
Fentham Cl HIA/OLT B92...167 H4
Fentham Ct HIA/OLT B92...164 B1
Fentham Gn HIA/OLT B92...167 G3
Fentham Rd AST/WIT B6...108 D3
  ERDE/BCHGN B24...93 F2
  HIA/OLT B92...167 G3
Fenton St ACGN B27...144 B5
  HLYWD B47...192 C1
Fenton St BRLYHL DY5...119 F1
  SMTHWK B66...106 A2
Fenton Wy ACGN B27...146 B3
Fereday Rd ALDR WS9...19 H4

Fereday's Cft SEDG DY3...67 F4
Fereday St TPTN/OCK DY4...69 F3
Ferguson Dr TPTN/OCK DY4...69 H5
Ferguson Rd LGLYGN/QTN B68...105 H4
Ferguson St WNSFLD WV11...25 C2
Fern Av TPTN/OCK DY4...69 F4
Fernbank Cl HALE B63...137 H5
Fernbank Crs DSYBK/YTR WS5...58 A4
Fernbank Rd WASH/WDE B8...111 E5
Ferncliffe Rd HRBN B17...141 H3
Fern Cl BILS/COS WV14...68 B5
  RUSH/SHEL WS4...29 F1
Ferndale Av CTB/HAM B43...73 H4
Ferndale Cl HAG/WOL DY9...152 C5
Ferndale Crs CSHL/WTROR B46...115 C4
Ferndale Crs BHTH/HG B12...127 C4
Ferndale Ms
  CSHL/WTROR B46...115 C4
Ferndale Pk HAG/WOL DY9...153 E2
Ferndale Rd CSHL/WTROR B46...115 C4
  BHTH/HG B12...162 D2
  HLGN/YWD B28...162 D2
  LGLYGN/QTN B68...119 E4
  WNSFLD WV11...15 F4
Ferndene Rd SPARK B11...145 H4
Ferndown Av SEDG DY3...67 E4
Ferndown Cl BLOX/PEL WS3...16 D5
  LGN/SDN/BHAMAIR B26...130 C3
Ferndown Gdns WNSFLD WV11...25 F5
Ferndown Rd SOLH B91...164 D4
Fernhill Gv KGSTG B44...60 B1
Fernhill Rd HIA/OLT B92...147 E5
Fernhurst Dr BRLYHL DY5...100 D2
Fernhurst Rd WASH/WDE B8...129 E1
Fernleigh Gdns STRBR DY8...117 C1
Fernleigh Rd RUSH/SHEL WS4...42 D2
Fernley Rd SPARK B11...145 E3
Fern Leys BDMR/CCFT WV3...35 H4
Fern Rd BDMR/CCFT WV3...35 H4
  DUDN DY1...84 C2
  ERDE/BCHGN B24...93 E2
Fernside Gdns MOS/BIL B13...144 D4
Fernside Rd WLNHL WV13...39 E4
Fern Vis DARL/WED WS10 *...55 C2
Fernwood Cl SCFLD/BOLD B73...76 C2
Fernwood Cft
  ALE/KHTH/YWD B14...161 E4
  TPTN/OCK DY4...85 C4
Fernwood Rd SCFLD/BOLD B73...76 C3
Fernwoods RIDG/WDGT B32...140 B5
Ferrers Cl MGN/WHC B75...47 H3
Ferrie Gv BRWNH WS8...8 D2
Ferris Gv ACGN B27...163 E1
Festival Av DARL/WED WS10...55 E4
Festival Wy
  DUNHL/THL/PER WV6...22 D5
Fernfall Ct ERDW/GRVHL B23...92 C1
Fibbersley WLNHL WV13...39 F1
Fibbersley Bank WLNHL WV13...39 F1
Fiddlers Gn HIA/OLT B92...167 C3
Field Cl BLOX/PEL WS3...27 C2
  LGN/SDN/BHAMAIR B26...147 C1
  RUSH/SHEL WS4...18 B5
  STRBR DY8...118 C2
Field Cottage Dr STRBR DY8...135 H4
Fieldfare Cl DUDS DY2...103 F5
Fieldfare Cft CBROM B36...114 A1
Fieldfare Rd HAG/WOL DY9...136 D5
Field Head Pl
  DUNHL/THL/PER WV6...35 F1
Fieldhead Rd SPARK B11...146 A4
Fieldhouse La RMSLY B62...172 A1
Fieldhouse Rd
  ETTPK/GDPK/PENN WV4...52 C4
  YDLY B25...129 C4
Field La HAG/WOL DY9...170 A1
  RIDG/WDGT B32...157 E2
  RUSH/SHEL WS4...18 B5
  SOLH B91...166 A5
Field Maple Rd
  FOAKS/STRLY B74...60 B2
Field Ms DUDS DY2...121 E2
Fieldon Cl SHLY B90...180 C2
Field Rd BLOX/PEL WS3...27 C1
  DUDS DY2...102 B3
  TPTN/OCK DY4...69 F3
The Fields CDSL WV8...10 D5
Fieldstone Vw SEDG DY3...83 F2
Field St BILS/COS WV14...54 A5
  WLNHL WV13...39 G3
  WOLVN WV10...7 J2
Field View Dr
  BLKHTH/ROWR B65...122 D3
Field Wk ALDR WS9...198 A5
Field Wy HOCK/TIA B94...60 B5
Fieldways Cl HLYWD B47...192 C1
Fifield Gv STETCH B33...130 B2
Fifth Av BORD B9...128 D2
  WOLVN WV10...23 F3
Filey Rd WOLVN WV10...12 B5
Fillingham Cl
  CHWD/FDBR/MGN B37...132 D3
Fillon Cft CVALE B35...94 C2
Fimbrell Cl BRLYHL DY5...118 C4
Finbury Cl HIA/OLT B92...164 B1
Fincham Cl WOLVN WV10...13 F5
Finch Cl BLKHTH/ROWR B65...104 B4
Finchdene Gv BDMR/CCFT WV3...35 H4
Finch Dr FOAKS/STRLY B74...60 C3
Finchfield Cl RIDG/WDGT B32...140 A3
Finchfield Gdns
  BDMR/CCFT WV3...36 A4
Finchfield La BDMR/CCFT WV3...50 C1
Finchfield Rd West
  BDMR/CCFT WV3...35 G4
Finchley Av LOZ/NWT B19 *...108 C1
Finchley Cl SEDG DY3...84 F4
Finchley Rd KGSTG B44...75 H1
Finchmead Rd STETCH B33...131 G2
Finch Rd LOZ/NWT B19...108 C1
Findlay Rd
  ALE/KHTH/YWD B14...161 G1

Findon Rd WASH/WDE B8...111 F3
Finger Post Dr BLOX/PEL WS3...18 A2
Finlarigg Dr EDG B15...142 D1
Finmere Rd HLGN/YWD B28...162 D2
Finmere Wy SHLY B90...180 D3
Finnemore Rd BORD B9...129 E2
Finney Well Cl BILS/COS WV14...53 F5
Finsbury Dr BRLYHL DY5...117 G1
Finstall Cl CSCFLD/WYGN B72...77 G2
  VAUX/NECH B7...109 C5
Finwood Cl HIA/OLT B92...165 G2
Firbank Cl BVILLE B30...159 G3
Firbank Wy BLOX/PEL WS3...17 H5
Firbeck Gv KGSTG B44...62 D5
Firbeck Rd KGSTG B44...75 F5
Fir Cft BRLYHL DY5...119 E4
Fircroft NFLD/LBR B31...158 B2
  SOLH B91...164 B4
Firecrest Cl ERDW/GRVHL B23...75 H4
Fir Gv ALE/KHTH/YWD B14...161 F5
  BDMR/CCFT WV3...
  SOLH B91...134 C1
Firhill Cft ALE/KHTH/YWD B14...177 H5
Firmstone St STRBR DY8...118 A5
Firsbrook Cl
  DUNHL/THL/PER WV6...22 C5
Firsby Rd RIDG/WDGT B32...141 E2
Firs Cl SMTHWKW B67...106 C4
Firs Dr RBRY B45...180 A4
Firs Farm Dr CBROM B36...112 B2
Firsholm Cl SCFLD/BOLD B73...77 E4
Firs Rd KGSWFD DY6...100 A3
Firs St DUDS DY2...84 D5
First Av BORD B9...128 C3
  BRWNH WS8...9 G4
  KGSWFD DY6...82 C5
  SLYOAK B29...143 F4
  WALM/CURD B76...94 C1
  WOLVN WV10...23 G4
First Exhibition Av
  BHAMNEC B40...149 H5
First Meadow Piece
  RIDG/WDGT B32...141 E3
Fir St SEDG DY3...66 B4
Firsvale Rd WNSFLD WV11...25 F5
Firsway DUNHL/THL/PER WV6...35 E4
Firswood Rd STETCH B33...131 E5
Firth Dr ALE/KHTH/YWD B14...161 H5
  RMSLY B62...122 C4
Firth Park Crs RMSLY B62...122 C4
Fir Tree Cl KGSTG B44...75 E4
Fir Tree Dr DSYBK/YTR WS5...57 C4
  SEDG DY3...67 G4
Fir Tree Gv SCFLD/BOLD B73...76 D2
Fir Tree Rd BDMR/CCFT WV3...50 D1
Firtree Rd ERDE/BCHGN B24...93 F4
Fir Tree Rd BLOX/PEL WS3...26 D1
  BLOX/PEL WS3...105 G2
Fishers Dr SHLY B90...193 H5
Fisher St BDMR/CCFT WV3...6 C7
  BRLYHL DY5...118 D1
  DUDN DY1...84 D2
  TPTN/OCK DY4...85 C5
  WLNHL WV13...40 A3
Fishley Cl BLOX/PEL WS3...17 E5
Fishley La BLOX/PEL WS3...17 E5
Fishpool Cl CBROM B36...111 G1
Fishpool La
  RCOVN/BALC/EX CV7...150 D1
Fistral Gdns BDMR/CCFT WV3...51 F1
Fitters Mill Cl DIG/EDG B5 *...144 A1
Fitton Av KGSWFD DY6...100 C4
Fitzgerald Pl BRLYHL DY5...135 H1
Fitzguy Cl WBROM B70...88 A5
Fitzmaurice Rd WNSFLD WV11...25 F3
Fitz Roy Av HRBN B17...124 B5
Fitzroy Rd NFLD/LBR B31...174 C2
Five Broadway EDG B15 *...126 B3
Five Fields Rd SHHTH WV12...25 E5
Five Oaks Rd WLNHL WV13...39 F3
Five Ways LGLYGN/EDGR D16...126 B3
Flackwell Rd ERDW/GRVHL B23...76 C5
Fladbury Cl DUDS DY2...120 D1
Fladbury Crs SLYOAK B29...142 B5
Fladbury Gdns
  LOZ/NWT B19...108 C1
Fladbury Pl LOZ/NWT B19 *...108 C2
Flamborough Cl
  BKDE/SHDE B34...112 C2
Flamborough Wy
  BILS/COS WV14...68 A4
Flanders Dr KGSWFD DY6...99 H1
Flash La
  ETTPK/GDPK/PENN WV4...66 C1
Flash Rd OLDBY B69...105 C2
Flatlea NFLD/LBR B31...175 G5
The Flatts DARL/WED WS10...55 C1
Flavell Av BILS/COS WV14...68 D2
Flavell Rd RIDG/WDGT B32...157 F1
Flavells La SEDG DY3...67 E3
  YDLY B25...129 G4
Flavell St DUDN DY1...68 B5
Flax Cl HLYWD B47...192 C3
Flax Gdns HWK/WKHTH B38...41 F5
Flaxhall St WSLW WS2...54 C5
Flaxley Pkwy STETCH B33...112 A5
Flaxley Rd STETCH B33...130 B1
Flaxton Gv STETCH B33...112 C5
Fleace Gv CBROM B36...95 F5
Fledburgh Dr WALM/CURD B76...62 D5
Fleet St CBHAMNW B1...2 D4
Fleetwood Gv
  LGN/SDN/BHAMAIR B26...130 C3
Fleming Pl WSLW WS2...27 E4
Fleming Rd RIDG/WDGT B32...140 D2
  WSLW WS2...27 E4
Flemmynge Cl CDSL WV8...10 A3
Fletcher Gv DOR/KN B93...197 F4
Fletcher Rd SHHTH WV12...26 D2
Fletcher's La WLNHL WV13...40 A3
Fletcher St HAG/WOL DY9...136 D2
Fletton Gv
  ALE/KHTH/YWD B14...178 C2
Flinkford Cl DSYBK/YTR WS5...58 A3
Flint Green Rd ACGN B27...146 B4
Flintham Cl ACGN B27...147 H4

The Flintway STETCH B33 ....112 A5
Floodgate St DIG/EDG B5 ....3 K7
Flood St DUDS DY2 ....84 D5
Flora Rd YDLY B25 ....129 F5
Florence Av
  ETTPK/GDPK/PENN WV4 ....52 C4
  SPARK B11 ....144 D2
Florence Gv HHTH/SAND B71 ......72 A2
  WSNGN B18 ....107 G5
Florence Rd ACCN B27 ....146 D3
  ALE/KHTH/YWD B14 ....160 C1
  CDSL WV8 ....10 D4
  ERDW/GRVHL B23 ....77 F4
  HDSW B21 ....107 F1
  OLDBY B69 ....104 B2
  SMTHWK B66 ....106 D5
  TPTN/OCK DY4 ....69 G4
Florence St CBHAMW B1 ....126 D5
  WSL WS1 ....5 F3
Florence Vls SPARK B11 * 128 A5
Florian Gv DARL/WED WS10 ......55 G1
Florida Wy KGSWFD DY6 ....100 C4
Flowerdale Cl BILS/COS WV14 ....54 A4
Floyds La RUSH/SHEL WS4 ....29 E4
Floyer Rd SMHTH B10 ....128 C3
Flyford Cft SLYOAK B29 ....141 F5
Foden Rd PBAR/PBCH B42 ....74 A3
Foinavon Cl
  BLKHTH/ROWR B65 ....103 F3
Fold St WOLV WV1 ....6 E5
The Fold DARL/WED WS10 ....51 F4
  ETTPK/GDPK/PENN WV4 ....51 F4
Foldyard Cl WALM/CURD B76 ......78 C5
Foley Av DUNHL/THL/PER WV6 ....35 F2
Foley Church Cl
  FOAKS/STRLY B74 ....45 C3
Foley Dr DUNHL/THL/PER WV6 ....45 G2
Foley Gv WMBN WV5 ....80 D1
Foley Rd HAG/WOL DY9 ....135 H5
  WASH/WDE B8 ....111 F5
Foley Rd East
  FOAKS/STRLY B74 ....45 F4
Foley Rd West
  FOAKS/STRLY B74 ....44 D4
Foley St DARL/WED WS10 ....56 A5
Foley Wood Cl
  FOAKS/STRLY B74 ....45 E4
Foliot Flds YDLY B25 ....129 H4
Folkestone Cft CBROM B36 ....112 A1
Follett Rd STETCH B33 ....130 C1
Follyhouse Cl WSL WS1 ....57 F1
Follyhouse La WSL WS1 ....57 F1
  WSL WS1 ....57 F1
Fontley Cl
  LGN/SDN/BHAMAIR B26 ....130 C3
Fontwell Rd WOLVN WV10 ....12 D3
Footherley La LICHS WS14 ....32 D1
Forcebridge Rd
  CHWD/FDBR/MGN B37 ....113 H5
Ford Brook La BLOX/PEL WS3 ....28 D1
Forder Gv
  ALE/KHTH/YWD B14 ....178 C3
Forde Way Gdns
  HWK/WKHTH B38 ....190 B1
Fordfield Rd STETCH B33 ....113 E5
Fordhouse La BVILLE B30 ....160 B4
Fordhouse Rd WOLVN WV10 ......23 F1
Fordraught La RMSLY B62 ....172 D4
The Fordrift
  CHWD/FDBR/MGN B37 ....149 E2
Fordrough YDLY B25 ....128 D5
Fordrough La BORD B9 ....128 C1
Fordrough La BORD B9 ....128 C2
The Fordrough
  FOAKS/STRLY B74 ....47 E4
  NFLD/LBR B31 ....175 H5
  SHLY B90 ....193 E5
Fords Rd SHLY B90 ....193 C1
Ford St SMTHWKW B67 ....106 B3
  WSLW WS2 ....56 C1
  WSNGN B18 ....108 B4
Fordwater Rd
  FOAKS/STRLY B74 ....60 B2
Foredraft Cl HRBN B17 ....124 B4
Foredraft St HALE B63 ....137 G2
Foredrove La HIA/OLT B92 ....165 G4
Forest Av BLOX/PEL WS3 ....27 H5
Forest Cl FOAKS/STRLY B74 ......46 A2
  SMTHWK B66 ....106 A2
Forest Ct DOR/KN B93 ....196 D5
Forest Dl RBRY B45 ....188 B2
Forest Dr CDYHTH B64 ....121 F2
  HRBN B17 ....142 B1
Forest Ga SHHTH WV12 ....26 B2
Forest Hill Rd
  LGN/SDN/BHAMAIR B26 ....148 A2
Forest Pk BLOX/PEL WS3 ....28 A5
  WSLW WS2 ....27 H5
Forest Pk WALM/CURD B76 ....63 E4
Forest Pl BLOX/PEL WS3 ....28 A4
Fore St CBHAM B2 ....3 G5
Forest Rd DOR/KN B93 ....197 E5
  DUDN DY1 ....84 C2
  LGLYGN/QTN B68 ....125 G5
  MOS/BIL B13 ....144 C4
  YDLY B25 ....146 C1
Forest Wy HLYWD B47 ....192 D2
Forge Cft WALM/CURD B76 ....78 D5
Forge La ALDR WS9 ....31 F4
  CDYHTH B64 ....120 B4
  FOAKS/STRLY B74 ....32 A4
  HAG/WOL DY9 ....184 B1
  HHTH/SAND B71 ....72 C5
  KGSWFD DY6 ....100 D5
  KIDD DY10 ....168 B4
  RMSLY B62 ....139 E2
  WALM/CURD B76 ....94 D1
Forge Leys WMBN WV5 ....64 B5
Forge Rd BLOX/PEL WS3 ....17 H2
  DARL/WED WS10 ....54 D2
  SHHTH WV12 ....40 A1
  STRBR DY8 ....135 E1
Forge St DARL/WED WS10 ....55 G4
The Forge HALE B63 ....120 A3
Forge Valley Wy WMBN WV5 .....64 C5
Forge Wy OLDBY B69 ....104 C3

Formans Rd SPARK B11 ....145 G4
Formby Av
  DUNHL/THL/PER WV6 ....34 B1
Formby Wy BLOX/PEL WS3 ....16 C4
Forrell Gv NFLD/LBR B31 ....189 H1
Forrest Av WNSFLD WV11 ....15 E3
Forrester St WSLW WS2 ....4 A3
Forrester Street Prec
  WSLW WS2 ....4 A3
Forster St SMTHWKW B67 ....106 A2
  VAUX/NECH B7 ....127 G1
Forsythia Cl NFLD/LBR B31 ......158 B2
Forsythia Gv CDSL WV8 ....10 C4
Fort Crs ALDR WS9 ....19 G4
Forth Dr
  CHWD/FDBR/MGN B37 ....114 B5
Forth Gv HWK/WKHTH B38 ....176 C5
Forth Wy RMSLY B62 ....122 C4
Fortnum Cl STETCH B33 ....131 E2
Forton Cl DUNHL/THL/PER WV6 ...35 F3
Fort Pkwy ERDE/BCHGN B24 .....95 H5
Forward Rd
  LGN/SDN/BHAMAIR B26 ....149 E4
Fosbrooke Rd SMHTH B10 ....129 E4
Fosseway Dr ERDW/GRVHL B23 ...76 C3
Fossil Dr RBRY B45 ....188 A1
Foster Av BILS/COS WV14 ....68 B2
Foster Gdns WNSGN B18 * 107 H5
Foster Gn
  DUNHL/THL/PER WV6 ....34 C2
Foster Pl STRBR DY8 ....135 E1
Foster Rd WOLVN WV10 ....23 G4
Foster St DUDN DY1 ....85 G5
  DARL/WED WS10 ....55 F1
Foster St East STRBR DY8 ......135 G2
Foster Wy DIG/EDG B5 ....143 G2
Fotherley Brook Rd ALDR WS9 ...31 F5
Foundry La BLOX/PEL WS3 ....17 G4
  SMTHWK B66 ....107 F2
Foundry Rd KGSWFD DY6 ....99 F1
  WSNGN B18 ....107 F4
Foundry St BILS/COS WV14 ......68 C2
  KGSWFD DY6 ....99 G1
  TPTN/OCK DY4 ....69 E3
Fountain Arcade Chambers
  DUDN DY1 * 84 C5
Fountain Cl NFLD/LBR B31 ......189 E2
Fountain Ct CBHAMNE B4 * 3 G3
Fountain La BILS/COS WV14 .....68 D3
  OLDBY B69 ....86 D5
Fountain Rd HRBN B17 ....124 D3
Fountains Rd BLOX/PEL WS3 .....16 A5
Fountains Wy BLOX/PEL WS3 .....16 A5
Four Acres RIDG/WDGT B32 .....140 C3
Four Ashes Rd DOR/KN B93 ....196 C4
Four Crosses Rd
  RUSH/SHEL WS4 ....29 E1
Fourlands Av
  CSCFLD/WYGN B72 ....77 H2
Fourlands Rd NFLD/LBR B31 ....158 A4
Four Oaks Common Rd
  FOAKS/STRLY B74 ....46 C2
Four Oaks Rd FOAKS/STRLY B74..46 D3
Four Stones Cl SOLH B91 ....181 G4
Four Stones Gv DIG/EDG B5 ....143 H1
Fourth Av BORD B9 ....128 C2
  BRWNH WS8 ....9 G4
  SLYOAK B29 ....143 G4
  WOLVN WV10 ....23 F4
Four Winds Rd DUDS DY2 ....103 E4
Fowey Cl WALM/CURD B76 ......78 C4
Fowey Rd BKDE/SHDE B34 ......112 B5
Fowgay Dr SOLH B91 ....181 F4
Fowler Cl
  DUNHL/THL/PER WV6 ....20 C4
  SMTHWK B66 ....106 C1
Fowler Rd MGN/WHC B75 ....63 G3
Fowler St BKHL/PFLD WV2 ....52 A2
  VAUX/NECH B7 ....109 H4
Fowlmere Rd
  PBAR/PBCH B42 ....74 B3
Foxbury Dr DOR/KN B93 ....197 E5
Fox Cl MGN/WHC B75 ....63 F1
Foxcote Av HDSW B21 ....107 G2
Foxcote Cl SHLY B90 ....180 D5
Foxcote Dr SHLY B90 ....180 D5
Foxcote La HAG/WOL DY9 ....137 F4
Foxdale Dr BRLYHL DY5 ....118 D4
Foxdale Gv STETCH B33 ....131 E2
Foxes Meadow BVILLE B30 ......176 D1
  WALM/CURD B76 ....78 C3
Foxes Rdg CDYHTH B64 ....121 E4
Foxfield Dr STRBR DY8 ....135 G4
Fox Foot Dr BRLYHL DY5 ....101 E5
Foxford Cl CBROM B36 ....95 F5
  CSCFLD/WYGN B72 ....77 G4
Foxglove Cl ACCN B27 ....163 F1
  BLOX/PEL WS3 ....18 A2
  WNSFLD WV11 ....25 E5
Foxglove Crs
  CHWD/FDBR/MGN B37 ....131 G1
Foxglove Rd DUDN DY1 ....83 H2
Foxglove Wy
  ERDW/GRVHL B23 ....75 H4
  HDSW B21 ....107 F2
Fox Green Crs ACCN B27 ....146 A5
Fox Gv ACGN B27 ....146 A5
Fox HI SLYOAK B29 ....159 E2
Fox Hill Cl SLYOAK B29 ....159 E2
Fox Hill Rd MGN/WHC B75 ....48 C5
Foxhills Rd DUDS DY2 ....102 C5
Foxhills Rd
  ETTPK/GDPK/PENN WV4 ....50 C5
  STRBR DY8 ....117 H3
Foxhollies Dr HALE B63 ....138 A3
Fox Hollies Rd ACGN B27 ......146 B4
  WALM/CURD B76 ....78 B3
Fox Hollow
  DUNHL/THL/PER WV6 ....35 G3
Fox Hollow Ct RBRY B45 ....188 C2
Foxhope Cl HWK/WKHTH B38 ....177 F4
Foxhunt Rd HALE B63 ....138 A5
Foxland Av RBRY B45 ....188 C1
Foxland Cl
  CHWD/FDBR/MGN B37 ....132 D2
  SHLY B90 ....194 D4
Foxlands Av
  ETTPK/GDPK/PENN WV4 ....50 D5

Foxlands Crs
  ETTPK/GDPK/PENN WV4 ....50 C5
Foxlands Dr CSCFLD/WYGN B72..77 H4
  ETTPK/GDPK/PENN WV4 ....50 C5
  SEDG DY3 ....83 F1
Foxlea Rd HALE B63 ....154 D1
Foxley Dr SOLH B91 ....166 B5
Foxmeadow Cl SEDG DY3 ....66 D4
Foxoak St CDYHTH B64 ....120 C5
Fox's La WOLV WV1 ....23 F5
Fox St DIG/EDG B5 ....3 J4
  DUDN DY1 ....68 C5
Foxton Rd WASH/WDE B8 ....110 D4
Fox Wk ALDR WS9 ....19 H4
Foxwell Gv BORD B9 ....129 F2
Foxwell Rd BORD B9 ....129 F2
Foxwood Av GTB/HAM B43 ....59 F5
Foxwood Gv
  CHWD/FDBR/MGN B37 ....113 H4
Foxwood Rd
  CHWD/FDBR/MGN B37 ....113 H4
Foxyards Ct TPTN/OCK DY4 * 84 D1
Foxyards Rd TPTN/OCK DY4 .....84 D1
Foyle Rd HWK/WKHTH B38 ......176 D4
Fozdar Crs BILS/COS WV14 ......68 A2
Fradley Cl BVILLE B30 ....176 B1
Framefield Dr SOLH B91 ....165 G4
Framlingham Gv
  DUNHL/THL/PER WV6 ....35 E2
Frampton Cl BVILLE B30 ....159 F5
  CHWD/FDBR/MGN B37 ....132 D1
Frampton Wy GTB/HAM B43 ......59 H4
Frances Dr BLOX/PEL WS3 ....16 D5
Frances Rd BVILLE B30 ....160 A5
  ERDW/GRVHL B23 ....92 B3
  LOZ/NWT B19 ....108 C1
Franchise Gdns
  SMTHWK B66 ....55 H2
Franchise St DARL/WED WS10 ...55 G4
  PBAR/PBCH B42 ....55 G4
Francis Cl FOAKS/STRLY B74 .....45 F5
  KGSWFD DY6 ....99 H1
Francis Rd LDYWD/EDGR B16 ....126 A3
  SMTHWKW B67 ....105 H4
  STETCH B33 ....129 H1
  STRBR DY8 ....134 C2
  YDLY B25 ....146 A1
Francis St VAUX/NECH B7 ......109 G5
  WBROM B70 ....87 F1
  WOLV WV1 ....37 E1
Francis Wk NFLD/LBR B31 ......189 G1
Francis Ward Cl
  HHTH/SAND B71 ....71 E3
Frankburn Rd
  FOAKS/STRLY B74 ....45 E5
Frank Fisher Wy WBROM B70 ....87 G4
Frankfort St LOZ/NWT B19 .....108 D4
Frankholmes Dr SHLY B90 .....195 G2
Frankley Av RMSLY B62 ....139 H2
Frankley Beeches Rd
  NFLD/LBR B31 ....174 D2
Frankley Gn RIDG/WDGT B32 ...156 B5
Frankley Green La
  RIDG/WDGT B32 ....156 D5
Frankley Hl La
  RIDG/WDGT B32 ....173 H5
Frankley La RIDG/WDGT B32 ....157 G4
Frankley Lodge Rd
  NFLD/LBR B31 ....174 A2
Frankley Rd LGLYGN/QTN B68 ..123 E4
Frankley Ter HRBN B17 * 141 H2
Franklin Rd BVILLE B30 ....159 H5
Franklin St WSNGN B18 ....107 G4
Franklin Wy BVILLE B30 ....159 H3
Franklyn Cl
  DUNHL/THL/PER WV6 ....20 C5
Frank Rd SMTHWKW B67 ....106 A3
Frank St SMHTH B10 ....127 F5
Franks Wy STETCH B33 ....130 A2
Frank Tommey Cl
  BLKHTH/ROWR B65 * 122 A5
Frankton Cl HIA/OLT B92 ....147 H5
Frankton Gv BORD B9 ....129 F2
Fraser Rd SPARK B11 ....145 E2
Fraser St BILS/COS WV14 ....54 A2
Frayne Av KGSWFD DY6 ....99 G2
Freasley Cl SHLY B90 ....180 D2
Freasley Rd BKDE/SHDE B34 ...113 F4
Freda Rd OLDBY B69 ....104 B1
Freda Rd WBROM B70 ....87 F5
Fredas Gv HRBN B17 ....141 G5
Frederick Rd AST/WIT B6 ....109 F1
  EDG B15 ....126 B4
  ERDW/GRVHL B23 ....92 B4
  LGLYGN/QTN B68 ....123 H5
  SCFLD/BOLD B73 ....62 D5
  SLYOAK B29 ....142 B5
  SPARK B11 ....145 E3
  STETCH B33 ....129 H1
  WNSFLD WV11 ....25 E5
Fredericks Cl STRBR DY8 ....135 E3
Frederick St BKHL/PFLD WV2 ....7 F4
  CBHAMW B1 ....2 C2
  WBROM B70 ....87 G2
  WSLW WS2 ....4 B4
Frederick William St
  WLNHL WV13 ....39 H3
Fred Smith Cl DARL/WED WS10 ..56 B3
Freeland Gv KGSWFD DY6 ......100 B5
Freeman Dr WALM/CURD B76 ....63 F4
Freeman Pl BILS/COS WV14 .....39 E5
Freeman Rd DARL/WED WS10 ....57 H4
  VAUX/NECH B7 ....109 H4
Freeman St DIG/EDG B5 ....3 H5
  WBROM B70 ....87 H2
Freemantle Dr
  BKDE/SHDE B34 ....113 G3
Freer Rd AST/WIT B6 ....90 B5
Freer St WSL WS1 ....4 E3
Freeth Rd BRWNH WS8 ....9 G2
Freeth St LDYWD/EDGR B16 ....126 A2
  OLDBY B69 ....104 D1
Freezeland St BILS/COS WV14 ...53 F2
Fremont Dr DUDN DY1 ....83 G5
French Rd DUDS DY2 ....85 G5
Frensham Cl
  CHWD/FDBR/MGN B37 ....132 C2
Frensham Wy HRBN B17 ....142 A1
Frenshaw Gv KGSTG B44 ....75 F3
Freshwater Dr BRLYHL DY5 ....118 D3

Friardale Cl DARL/WED WS10 ....56 D5
Friar Park Rd DARL/WED WS10 ..57 E5
Friars Cl STRBR DY8 ....117 G1
Friars Gorse KINVER DY7 ....117 G1
Friar St DARL/WED WS10 ....56 B5
Friary Av SHLY B90 ....195 G2
Friary Crs RUSH/SHEL WS4 ......29 E4
Friary Dr FOAKS/STRLY B74 .....46 D2
Friary Gdns HDSW B21 ....89 H5
Friary Rd BFLD/HDSWWD B20 ...89 G4
Friday La HIA/OLT B92 ....183 H1
Friesland Dr WOLV WV1 ....38 B2
Friezeland Rd WSLW WS2 ....41 F5
Friezland La BRWNH WS8 ....19 G2
Friezland Wy BRWNH WS8 ....19 G2
Frinton Gv HDSW B21 ....107 E2
Friston Av LDYWD/EDGR B16 ...2 A7
Frodesley Rd
  LGN/SDN/BHAMAIR B26 ....130 D4
Froggatt Rd BILS/COS WV14 ....53 H1
Froggatts Ride
  WALM/CURD B76 ....63 F5
Frogmill Rd RBRY B45 ....174 B5
Frome Cl SEDG DY3 ....83 F4
Frome Dr WNSFLD WV11 ....24 C5
Frome Wy
  ALE/KHTH/YWD B14 ....160 D4
Frost St BKHL/PFLD WV2 ....53 E2
Froxmere Cl SOLH B91 ....181 H5
Froysell St WLNHL WV13 ....39 H3
Fryer Rd NFLD/LBR B31 ....189 H1
Fryers Cl BLOX/PEL WS3 ....27 F3
Fryers Rd WSLW WS2 ....27 E4
Fryer St WOLV WV1 ....7 C5
Fuchsia Dr COVEN WV9 ....11 H4
Fugelmere Cl HRBN B17 ....124 B5
Fulbrook Gv SLYOAK B29 ....158 B2
Fulbrook Rd DUDN DY1 ....84 A5
Fulford Cl HLYWD B47 ....193 E5
Fulford Dr WALM/CURD B76 .....94 D1
Fulford Gv
  LGN/SDN/BHAMAIR B26 ....131 E1
Fulham Rd SPARK B11 ....144 D2
Fullbrook Cl SHLY B90 ....195 G3
Fullbrook Rd DSYBK/YTR WS5 ...57 E3
Fulleylove Rd BRWNH WS8 ......19 G1
Fullerton Cl CDSL WV8 ....10 D4
Fullwood Crs DUDS DY2 ....101 G3
Fullwoods End BILS/COS WV14 ..68 C3
Fulmer Wk WSNGN B18 * 126 A1
Fulwell Gv KGSTG B44 ....75 G3
Fulwell Ms
  CHWD/FDBR/MGN B37 ....132 B4
Fulwood Av RMSLY B62 ....122 D4
Furber Pl KGSWFD DY6 ....100 B3
Furlong La HALE B63 ....137 G1
Furlong Meadow
  NFLD/LBR B31 ....176 A3
Furlongs Rd SEDG DY3 ....67 F5
The Furlongs STRBR DY8 ....135 E4
  WNSFLD WV11 ....24 B5
The Furlong DARL/WED WS10 ...55 G3
  SEDG DY3 ....83 F2
Furnace Cl WMBN WV5 ....80 C1
Furnace Hl HALE B63 ....138 D2
Furnace La HALE B63 ....138 D2
Furnace Pde TPTN/OCK DY4 .....69 E5
Furnace Rd DUDS DY2 ....102 C1
Furness Cl BLOX/PEL WS3 ......16 B4
Furst St BRWNH WS8 ....9 G1
Furzebank Wy SHHTH WV12 .....40 C1
Furze Wy DSYBK/YTR WS5 ....43 F5

G

The Gables ERDE/BCHGN B24 ...93 H2
  WNSFLD WV11 ....15 E3
Gaddesby Rd
  ALE/KHTH/YWD B14 ....161 F2
Gadds Dr BLKHTH/ROWR B65 ...104 B5
Gads Gv WNSFLD WV11 ....25 G5
Gads Gn DUDS DY2 ....102 D4
Gads Green Crs DUDS DY2 .....103 E3
Gads La DUDN DY1 ....84 C5
  WBROM B70 ....87 E5
Gadwall Cft ERDW/GRVHL B23 ..91 H5
Gail Cl ALDR WS9 ....30 D3
Gailey Cft KGSTG B44 ....60 A5
Gailey Pk BDLWR/CCFT WV3 ....50 D1
Gainford Cl CDSL WV8 ....22 B1
Gainford Rd KGSTG B44 ....76 A2
Gainsborough Crs
  DOR/KN B93 ....197 E2
  GTB/HAM B43 ....59 H4
Gainsborough Dr
  DUNHL/THL/PER WV6 ....34 D1
Gainsborough Hl STRBR DY8 ...135 G4
Gainsborough Pl DUDN DY1 .....83 G4
Gainsborough Rd
  PBAR/PBCH B42 ....74 B5
Gainsford Dr RMSLY B62 ....138 D1
Gairloch Rd SHHTH WV12 ....25 H1
Gaitskell Ter OLDBY B69 ....86 C4
Gaitswell Wy SMTHWK B66 .....106 B2
Galahad Wy DARL/WED WS10 ...71 E1
Galbraith Cl BILS/COS WV14 ....68 D3
Galena Wy AST/WIT B6 ....109 E3
Gale Wk BLKHTH/ROWR B65 ...105 F4
Gallery Sq WSLW WS2 ....4 D3
Galloway Av BKDE/SHDE B34 ...112 B3
Galton Cl ERDE/BCHGN B24 .....94 B2
  TPTN/OCK DY4 ....70 A5
Galton Dr DUDS DY2 ....102 B2
  GTB/HAM B43 ....73 H2
Galton Rd SMTHKWW B67 ......124 B3
Galtons La HAG/WOL DY9 ......185 E1
Gamesfield Gn
  BDMR/CCFT WV3 ....36 B4
Gammage St DUDS DY2 ....102 B1
Gandy Rd SHHTH WV12 ....25 G4
Gannahs Farm Cl
  WALM/CURD B76 ....63 F5
Gannow Green La RBRY B45 .....173 E4
Gannow Manor Crs RBRY B45 ..173 G4

Gannow Manor Gdns
  RBRY B45 ....173 H4
Gannow Rd RBRY B45 ....187 G1
Gannow Wk RBRY B45 ....187 G1
Ganton Rd BLOX/PEL WS3 ....16 C3
Garden Cl DOR/KN B93 ....196 D2
  RBRY B45 ....174 A3
  WASH/WDE B8 ....111 E4
Garden Crs BLOX/PEL WS3 .....17 H4
Garden Ct ALDR WS9 ....30 B5
Gardeners Wy WMBN WV5 ......80 D2
Garden Gv BFLD/HDSWWD B20 ..73 G5
The Gardens
  CSCFLD/WYGN B72 ....77 E3
  ERDW/GRVHL B23 ....92 C3
Garden St WSLW WS2 ....4 D1
Garden Wk BILS/COS WV14 .....54 B2
  SEDG DY3 ....83 E4
Garfield Rd
  LGN/SDN/BHAMAIR B26 ....130 D3
Garland Crs RMSLY B62 ....122 C4
Garland St BORD B9 ....128 A2
Garland Wy NFLD/LBR B31 .....175 H1
Garman Cl GTB/HAM B43 ....73 G1
Garner Cl BILS/COS WV14 .....53 H5
Garnet Av GTB/HAM B43 ....59 F5
Garnett Dr MGN/WHC B75 ......63 E2
Garrard Gdns SCFLD/BOLD B73 ..62 B3
Garrat St BRLYHL DY5 ....101 G4
Garratt Cl LGLYGN/QTN B68 ...105 G5
Garratt's La CDYHTH B64 ....121 F2
Garret Cl KGSWFD DY6 ....81 H5
Garretts Green La
  LGN/SDN/BHAMAIR B26 ....130 C5
Garrick Cl DUDN DY1 ....83 H5
Garrick St WOLV WV1 ....7 C5
Garrington St DARL/WED WS10 ..55 E1
Garrison Circ CBHAMNE B4 ....127 C2
Garrison La BORD B9 ....127 H2
Garrison St BORD B9 ....127 H2
The Garth ALE/KHTH/YWD B14 ..179 F1
Garway Gv YDLY B25 ....146 B1
Garwood Rd
  LGN/SDN/BHAMAIR B26 ....130 B2
Gas St CBHAMW B1 ....2 C6
Gatacre St SEDG DY3 ....83 F5
Gatcombe Cl WOLVN WV10 ......13 F3
Gatcombe Rd DUDN DY1 ....83 G4
Gatehouse Fold DUDS DY2 .....84 D5
Gate La DOR/KN B93 ....196 A5
  SCFLD/BOLD B73 ....76 D1
Gateley Rd LGLYGN/QTN B68 ...123 H5
Gate St SEDG DY3 ....67 G4
  TPTN/OCK DY4 ....85 G4
  WASH/WDE B8 ....110 B4
Gatis St DUNHL/THL/PER WV6 ...36 C1
Gatwick Rd CVALE B35 ....94 D2
Gauden Rd HAG/WOL DY9 ......153 F5
Gavin Wy AST/WIT B6 ....91 F2
Gawne La CDYHTH B64 ....103 E5
Gaydon Cl
  DUNHL/THL/PER WV6 ....20 C5
Gaydon Gv SLYOAK B29 ....141 G5
Gaydon Pl SCFLD/BOLD B73 ....62 B4
Gaydon Rd ALDR WS9 ....44 A1
  HIA/OLT B92 ....148 B4
Gayer St BKDE/SHDE B34 ......119 F4
Gay Hill La HWK/WKHTH B38 ...177 F5
Gayhurst Dr YDLY B25 ....130 A4
Gayle Gv ACGN B27 ....163 G2
Gaynor Ash HHTH/SAND B71 ....75 H5
Geach St LOZ/NWT B19 ....108 D3
Gedney Cl SHLY B90 ....179 E2
Geeson Cl CVALE B35 ....94 D2
Gee St LOZ/NWT B19 ....108 D3
Gem Vls SPARK B11 * 128 A5
Geneva Rd TPTN/OCK DY4 ......84 D2
Genge Av
  ETTPK/GDPK/PENN WV4 ....52 C4
Genners Ap NFLD/LBR B31 .....157 H2
Genners La NFLD/LBR B31 .....157 H3
Genthorn Cl
  ETTPK/GDPK/PENN WV4 ....52 D4
Gentian Cl NFLD/LBR B31 ......158 B4
Geoffrey Cl WALM/CURD B76 ....78 D4
Geoffrey Pl SPARK B11 * 145 E4
Geoffrey Rd SHLY B90 ....179 H2
  SPARK B11 ....145 E4
George Arthur Rd
  WASH/WDE B8 ....110 B5
George Av BLKHTH/ROWR B65 ..122 B2
George Bird Cl SMTHWK B66 *..106 C3
George Cl DUDS DY2 ....103 E1
George Frederick Rd
  SCFLD/BOLD B73 ....60 C4
George Henry Rd
  TPTN/OCK DY4 ....70 C4
George Rd CSHL/WTROR B46 ....96 C3
  EDG B15 ....126 B4
  ERDW/GRVHL B23 ....73 H1
  GTB/HAM B43 ....73 H1
  HALE B63 ....138 B3
  LGLYGN/QTN B68 ....123 G2
  SCFLD/BOLD B73 ....76 B2
  SOLH B91 ....182 A2
  TPTN/OCK DY4 ....68 D5
  YDLY B25 ....146 A1
George St BHTH/HG B12 ....4 D7
  BKHL/PFLD WV2 ....7 F6
  CBHAMW B1 ....2 D5
  DUDN DY1 ....68 B5
  HALE B63 ....107 E1
  LOZ/NWT B19 ....108 B2
  STRBR DY8 ....118 B3
  WBROM B70 ....87 H4
  WLNHL WV13 ....39 G1
  WSL WS1 ....5 F3
George St West WSNGN B18 ...108 A5
Georgina Av BILS/COS WV14 ...53 H5
Geraldine Rd YDLY B25 ....129 F5
Gerald Rd STRBR DY8 ....118 A5
Geranium Gv BORD B9 ....129 E1
Geranium Rd DUDS DY2 ....103 F1
Gerardsfield Rd STETCH B33 ..131 F1
Germander Dr DSYBK/YTR WS5 ..57 G5
Gerrard Cl LOZ/NWT B19 ......108 C2
Gerrard Rd WLNHL WV13 ....39 E4
Gerrard St LOZ/NWT B19 ......108 C3

Gervase Dr DUDN 84 C3
Geston Rd DUDN DY1 ....101 H1
Gibbet La KINVER DY7 ....134 A3
Gibbins Rd SLYOAK B29 ....159 E1
Gibbons Gv
  DUNHL/THL/PER WV6 ....36 A1
Gibbons Hill Rd SEDG DY3 ....67 F1
Gibbons La BRLYHL DY5 ....100 C2
Gibbons Rd
  MGN/WHC B75 ....36 B1
  MGN/WHC B75 ....47 F2
Gibbs Hill Rd NFLD/LBR B31 ....189 H1
Gibbs Rd HAG/WOL DY9 ....137 E2
Gibbs St DUNHL/THL/PER WV6 ....36 C1
Gibbet St BORD B9 ....3 K7
Gibson Dr BFLD/HDSWWD B20 ...108 B1
Gibson Rd
  BFLD/HDSWWD B20 ....108 B1
  DUNHL/THL/PER WV6 ....36 C1
Gideon Cl OLDY B25 ....146 D1
Gideons Cl SEDG DY3 ....85 F1
Giffard Rd WOLV WV1 ....53 F1
  WOLVN WV10 ....15 E4
Giggetty La WMBN WV5 ....64 C5
Gigmill Wy STRBR DY8 ....135 E3
Gilbanks Rd STRBR DY8 ....117 H5
Gilberry Cl DOR/KN B93 ....197 E3
Gilbert Av OLDBY B69 ....103 H2
Gilbert Cl WNSFLD WV11 ....25 G4
Gilbert La WMBN WV5 ....65 F4
Gilbert Rd SMTHWK B66 ....106 D5
Gilbertstone Av
  LGN/SDN/BHAMAIR B26 ....147 E2
Gilbert St TPTN/OCK DY4 ....85 F4
Gilbeys Cl STRBR DY8 ....118 A3
Gilby Rd LDYWD/EDGR B16 ....126 A3
Gilchrist Dr EDG B15 ....125 C4
Gildas Av HAW/WKHTH B38 ......177 E4
Giles Cl HIA/OLT B92 ....165 H5
  STETCH B33 ....130 A1
Giles Rd LGLYGN/QTN B68 ....105 F4
Gilldown Pl EDG B15 ....125 C4
Gillespie Cft AST/WIT B6 ....109 F2
Gillhurst Rd HRBN B17 ....124 D5
Gilling Gv WALM/CURD B76 ......112 C3
Gillingham Cl DARL/WED 42 D5
Gillity Av DSYBK/YTR WS5 ....42 D5
Gillity Cl DSYBK/YTR WS5 ....42 D5
Gilliver Rd SHLY B90 ....180 B3
Gilman Cl
  LGN/SDN/BHAMAIR B26 ....148 B3
Gillott Cl SOLH B91 ....182 C2
Gillott Rd LDYWD/EDGR B16 ....125 F2
Gillows Cft SHLY B90 ....195 G1
Gillscroft Rd STETCH B33 ....130 C1
Gill St DUDS DY2 ....121 E1
  WBROM B70 ....87 G5
Gilmorton Cl HRBN B17 ....124 D5
  SOLH B91 ....182 A4
Gilpin Cl WASH/WDE B8 ....111 G3
Gilpin Crs BLOX/PEL WS3 ....18 A5
Gilson Dr CSHL/WTROR B46 ......114 D1
Gilson Rd CSHL/WTROR B46 ......115 E1
Gilson St TPTN/OCK DY4 ....70 A3
Gilson Wy
  CHWD/FDBR/MGN B37 ....114 A4
Gilwell Rd BKDE/SHDE B34 ......113 G3
Gimble Wk HRBN B17 ....124 B4
Gipsy La ERDW/GRVHL B23 ....93 H1
  WLNHL WV13 ....39 H4
Gisborn Cl SMHTH B10 * 127 H4
Gladeside CI ALDR WS9 ....30 B3
The Glades CDSL WV8 ....22 A1
The Glade CDSL WV8 ....22 A1
  FOAKS/STRLY B74 ....45 E1
  HAG/WOL DY9 ....136 C2
  LGN/SDN/BHAMAIR B26 ....148 B3
Gladstone Dr OLDBY B69 ....86 A3
Gladstone Gv KGSWFD DY6 ....82 C1
Gladstone Rd DOR/KN B93 ......199 E1
  ERDW/GRVHL B23 ....92 B3
  LGN/SDN/BHAMAIR B26 ....146 D1
  SPARK B11 ....144 C1
  STRBR DY8 ....134 D1
Gladstone St AST/WIT B6 ....109 C1
  DARL/WED WS10 ....55 G2
  HHTH/SAND B71 ....87 C1
  WSLW WS2 ....2 A5
Gladys Rd SMTHKW B67 ....124 B2
  YDLY B25 ....129 F5
Gladys Ter HHTH/SAND B71 * ...124 C2
Glaisdale Gdns
  DUNHL/THL/PER WV6 ....22 C5
Glaisdale Rd HLGN/YWD B28 ....163 E2
Glaisher Dr WOLVN WV10 ....23 E4
Glamis Rd SHHTH WV12 ....37 C4
Glanville Dr MGN/WHC B75 ....47 E1
Glasbury Cfr HWK/WKHTH B38 ..190 C1
Glascote Cl SHLY B90 ....180 A2
Glascote Gv BKDE/SHDE B34 ....113 G3
Glaslyn Av BLKHTH/ROWR B65 ..121 H2
Glassford Dr
  DUNHL/THL/PER WV6 ....22 A4
Glasshouse HI STRBR DY8 ......135 H4
Glastonbury Crs BLOX/PEL WS3 ..16 A5
Glastonbury Rd
  ALE/KHTH/YWD B14 ....162 A5
  HHTH/SAND B71 ....71 H5
Glastonbury Wy BLOX/PEL WS3 ..26 C1
Glaston Dr SOLH B91 ....181 G5
Gleads Cft RMSLY B62 ....138 A3
Gleave Rd SLYOAK B29 ....159 C1
Glebe Dr SCFLD/BOLD B73 ....76 D3
Glebe Farm Rd
  BKDE/SHDE B34 ....112 C4
Glebefields Rd TPTN/OCK DY4 ....69 G3
Glebeland Cl LDYWD/EDGR B16 ..125 F3
Glebe La STRBR DY8 ....135 E3
Glebe Pl DARL/WED WS10 ....54 D2
Glebe Rd HIA/OLT B92 ....164 D1
  WLNHL WV13 ....39 F5
Glebe St WSL WS1 ....4 D6
The Glebe HAG/WOL DY9 ....184 C2
Glenavon Rd
  ALE/KHTH/YWD B14 ....178 C2
Glen CI RUSH/SHEL WS4 ....42 A3
Glencoe Rd LDYWD/EDGR B16 ..107 E5
Glen Ct BDMR/CCFT WV3 ....36 A3
  CDSL WV8 ....10 C3

Glencroft Rd HIA/OLT B92 ....148 B4
Glendale CI BDMR/CCFT WV3 .....35 G5
  HALE B63 ....138 D3
Glendale Dr STETCH B33 ....130 B1
  WMBN WV5 ....65 E5
Glendene Crs
  DUNHL/THL/PER WV6 ....36 A1
Glendon Rd ERDW/GRVHL B23 ...76 B5
Glendon Wy DOR/KN B93 ....196 C5
Glendower Rd ALDR WS9 ....30 B1
  RBAR/PBCH B42 ....90 C1
Gleneagles Dr GTB/HAM B43 .....58 C5
  MGN/WHC B75 ....62 C1
  OLDBY B69 ....103 G2
Gleneagles Rd BLOX/PEL WS3 ....16 B4
  DUNHL/THL/PER WV6 ....20 B5
  LGN/SDN/BHAMAIR B26 ....130 C4
Glenelg Dr STRBR DY8 ....135 H5
Glenelg Ms DSYBK/YTR WS5 ....58 B3
Glenfern Rd BILS/COS WV14 .....68 A3
Glenfield CDSL WV8 ....11 G5
Glenfield CI SOLH B91 ....182 A5
  WALM/CURD B76 ....63 E5
Glenfield Gv SLYOAK B29 ....160 A1
Glengarry CI RIDG/WDGT B32 ...157 F3
Glengarry Gdns
  BDMR/CCFT WV3 ....36 B4
Glenhill Dr HWK/WKHTH B38 ....177 E5
Glenhurst Cl WSLW WS2 ....40 B2
Glenmead Rd KGSTG B44 ....74 D3
Glenmore Cl BDMR/CCFT WV3 ....36 A3
Glenmore Dr HWK/WKHTH B38 ..176 B4
Glen Park Rd SEDG DY3 ....83 F4
Glenpark Rd WASH/WDE B8 .....110 C4
Glen Ri MOS/BIL B13 ....162 A4
Glen Rd SEDG DY3 ....67 C5
  STRBR DY8 ....135 F4
Glenroyde HWK/WKHTH B38 ....190 C1
Glen Side WALM/CURD B32 ......140 D5
Glenside Av HIA/OLT B92 ......147 H4
Glenthorne Rd
  ERDE/BCHGN B24 ....93 E4
Glenthorne Wy ERDE/BCHGN B24 .78 C1
Glentworth Gdns
  DUNHL/THL/PER WV6 ....22 D5
Glenville Dr ERDW/GRVHL B23 ...92 C1
Glenwood Cl BRLYHL DY5 ....119 F4
Glenwood Dr SHLY B90 ....194 D4
Glenwood Rd
  HWK/WKHTH B38 ....176 B5
Globe St DARL/WED WS10 ....70 D2
Gloucester Pl WNSFLD WV13 ....40 B3
Gloucester Rd DARL/WED WS10 ..56 C5
  DSYBK/YTR WS5 ....42 D5
  DUDS DY2 ....120 D2
Gloucester St
  DUNHL/THL/PER WV6 ....36 D1
Gloucester Wy
  CHWD/FDBR/MGN B37 ....132 A3
Glover Cl HLGN/YWD B28 ....162 D4
Glover Rd MGN/WHC B75 ....63 F3
Glovers Cft
  CHWD/FDBR/MGN B37 ....131 H1
Glovers Field Dr
  VAUX/NECH B7 ....110 A2
Glovers Rd SMHTH B10 ....128 A4
Glover St BORD B9 ....127 G2
  WBROM B70 ....87 H5
Glyme Dr DUNHL/THL/PER WV6 ..22 A5
Glyn Av BILS/COS WV14 ....54 D5
Glyn Dr BILS/COS WV14 ....54 D5
Glyn Farm Rd RIDG/WDGT B32 ..157 F2
Glynn Crs HALE B63 ....120 B5
Glynne Av KGSWFD DY6 ....99 H5
Glyn Rd RIDG/WDGT B32 ....140 D1
Glynside Av RIDG/WDGT B32 ....140 C2
Goffs Cl RIDG/WDGT B32 ....141 F4
Goldborough Cl
  BILS/COS WV14 ....53 H5
Goldby Dr DARL/WED WS10 ......55 G4
Goldcrest Cl DUDS DY2 ....102 B4
Goldcrest Cft CBROM B36 ......114 A1
Goldencrest Dr OLDBY B69 .....104 C1
Golden Cft
  BFLD/HDSWWD B20 ....89 H5
Goldencross Wy BRLYHL DY5 ...118 D3
Golden End Dr DOR/KN B93 .....197 G2
Golden Hillock Rd DUDS DY2 ...120 C1
  SMHTH B10 ....128 B5
  SPARK B11 ....145 F2
Goldfinch Cl BVILLE B30 ......159 F2
Goldfinch Rd HAG/WOL DY9 * ..136 A4
Goldicroft Rd DARL/WED WS10 ..56 A4
Goldieslie Cl SCFLD/BOLD B73 ..77 F1
Goldieslie Rd SCFLD/BOLD B73 ..77 F1
Golds Hill Gdns HDSW B21 .....107 H2
Golds Hill Rd HDSW B21 ....107 H1
Golds Hill Wy TPTN/OCK DY4 ...70 B4
Goldsmith Rd
  ALE/KHTH/YWD B14 ....161 F2
Goldstar Wy STETCH B33 ......131 E2
Goldthorn Av
  ETTPK/GDPK/PENN WV4 ....51 H3
Goldthorn Crs
  ETTPK/GDPK/PENN WV4 ....51 C2
Goldthorne Av
  LGN/SDN/BHAMAIR B26 ....148 A3
Goldthorne Wk BRLYHL DY5 ....119 F4
Goldthorn Hl BDMR/CCFT WV3 ..51 H2
Goldthorn PI BDMR/CCFT WV3 ..51 H2
Goldthorn Rd BDMR/CCFT WV3 ..51 H1
Golf La BILS/COS WV14 ....53 H1
Golson Cl MGN/WHC B75 ....63 C2
Gomeldon Av
  ALE/KHTH/YWD B14 ....178 B2
Gomer St WLNHL WV13 ....39 C3
Gomer St West WLNHL WV13 .....39 C3
Gooch Cl STRBR DY8 ....135 C1
Gooch St DIG/EDG B5 ....127 E4
Gooch St North DIG/EDG B5 ....127 E5
Goodall Gv CTB/HAM B43 ....60 A3
Goodall St WSL WS1 ....4 D4
Goodby Rd MOS/BIL B13 ....143 H4
Goode Av WSNGN B18 ....108 A4
Goode CI LGLYGN/QTN B68 .....105 G4
Goodeve Wk MGN/WHC B75 .....63 H5
Goodison Gdns
  ERDE/BCHGN B24 ....93 F1
Goodman CI HLGN/YWD B28 ....162 D4
Goodman St CBHAMW B1 ....2 A4

Goodrest Av RMSLY B62 ....140 A2
Goodrest Cft
  ALE/KHTH/YWD B14 ....179 E1
Goodrest La HWK/WKHTH B38 ..190 D2
Goodrich Av
  DUNHL/THL/PER WV6 ....35 E2
Goodrich Covert
  ALE/KHTH/YWD B14 ....177 C3
Goodrick Wy VAUX/NECH B7 * ..109 H5
Goodway Ct CBHAMNE B4 ....3 C2
Goodway Rd HIA/OLT B92 ......148 C4
  KGSTG B44 ....61 H5
Goodwood CI CBROM B36 ....111 H1
Goodwood Dr
  FOAKS/STRLY B74 ....60 B2
Goodwyn Av LGLYGN/QTN B68 ..123 H5
Goodyear Av WOLVN WV10 ....23 C3
Goodyear Rd SMTHWKW B67 ...123 H2
Goosemoor La
  ERDW/GRVHL B23 ....76 D4
Gopsal St CBHAMNE B4 ....127 G1
Gorcott La SHLY B90 ....194 A3
Gordon Av
  ETTPK/GDPK/PENN WV4 ....52 D5
  HHTH/SAND B71 ....71 C3
  LOZ/NWT B19 ....108 D2
Gordon Crs BRLYHL DY5 ....100 C4
Gordon CI OLDBY B69 ....86 B4
Gordon Crs BRLYHL DY5 ....101 C4
Gordon PI BILS/COS WV14 ......53 C3
Gordon Rd HRBN B17 ....142 B1
  LOZ/NWT B19 ....108 C2
Gordon St BKHL/PFLD WV2 * 7 H7
  BORD B9 ....127 H2
  DARL/WED WS10 ....55 F2
Gorey CI SHHTH WV12 ....25 H2
Gorge Rd SEDG DY3 ....67 C3
Gorleston Gv
  ALE/KHTH/YWD B14 ....178 D5
Gorleston Rd
  ALE/KHTH/YWD B14 ....178 D3
Gorsebrook Rd
  DUNHL/THL/PER WV6 ....22 D5
  WOLVN WV10 ....23 E5
Gorse CI
  CHWD/FDBR/MGN B37 ....131 H2
  SLYOAK B29 ....158 C2
Gorse Farm Rd GTB/HAM B43 ...59 C5
Gorsefield Rd BKDE/SHDE B34 ..113 G4
Gorse Green La HAG/WOL DY9 ..171 F5
Gorsemoor Wy WNSFLD WV11 ..15 F4
Gorse Rd DUDN DY1 ....84 A2
  WNSFLD WV11 ....25 C2
Gorsey La CSHL/WTROR B46 ....95 C5
Gorstie Cft GTB/HAM B43 ......73 G5
Gorsty Av BRLYHL DY5 ....101 E5
Gorsty Cl HHTH/SAND B71 .....72 B3
Gorsty Hayes CDSL WV8 ....10 B4
Gorsty Hill Rd RMSLY B62 ....121 H4
Gorsymead Gv NFLD/LBR B31 ..174 C3
Gorsy Rd RIDG/WDGT B32 ......140 D3
Gorway CI WSL WS1 ....57 F1
Gorway Gdns WSL WS1 ....57 G1
Gorway Rd WSL WS1 ....57 C1
Goscote CI BLOX/PEL WS3 .....28 B2
Goscote La BLOX/PEL WS3 .....28 B2
Goscote Lodge Crs
  BLOX/PEL WS3 ....28 C3
Goscote PI BLOX/PEL WS3 .....28 B1
Gosford St BHTH/HG B12 ......144 B1
Gospel End Rd SEDG DY3 ......66 D3
Gospel End St SEDG DY3 ....67 F4
Gospel Farm Rd ACGN B27 ....163 H2
Gospel La ACGN B27 ....163 H2
Gospel Oak Rd TPTN/OCK DY4 ..69 H2
Gosport CI WOLV WV1 ....53 F1
Goss The SLYOAK B29 ....159 F1
Gossey La STETCH B33 ....131 E2
Goss The SLYOAK B29 ....119 F3
Gotham Rd
  LGN/SDN/BHAMAIR B26 ....147 E1
Gothersley La KINVER DY7 ....116 A5
Goths Cl BLKHTH/ROWR B65 ...104 A5
Gough Av WNSFLD WV11 ....24 B2
Gough Dr TPTN/OCK DY4 ....86 A1
Gough Rd BILS/COS WV14 ......68 C2
  EDG B15 ....126 C5
  SPARK B11 ....145 F2
Gough St CBHAMW B1 ....2 E7
  WLNHL WV13 ....40 A3
  WOLV WV1 ....7 J4
Gould Firm La ALDR WS9 ....31 E4
Gowan Rd WASH/WDE B8 ....110 C5
Gower Av KGSWFD DY6 ....100 B5
Gower Rd RMSLY B62 ....121 H4
  SEDG DY3 ....66 D2
Gower St BKHL/PFLD WV2 * 7 J7
  LOZ/NWT B19 ....108 C2
  WLNHL WV13 ....39 C3
  WSLW WS2 ....56 B1
Gozzard St BILS/COS WV14 .....54 A3
Gracemere Crs
  HLGN/YWD B28 ....180 A1
Grace Rd OLDBY B69 ....104 A1
  SPARK B11 ....145 E1
  TPTN/OCK DY4 ....69 C4
Gracewell Rd MOS/BIL B13 ....162 B1
Grafton Dr WLNHL WV13 ....38 D4
Grafton Gdns SEDG DY3 ....82 D3
Grafton Gv LOZ/NWT B19 * ...108 C2
Grafton PI BILS/COS WV14 ....54 A1
Grafton Rd HDSW B21 ....89 F5
  HHTH/SAND B71 ....87 H2
  LGLYGN/QTN B68 ....122 D2
  SHLY B90 ....195 G2
  SPARK B11 ....127 H5
Graham Cl TPTN/OCK DY4 ......69 H2
Graham Crs RBRY B45 ....187 H1
Graham Rd HHTH/SAND B71 ....87 H2
  MOS/BIL B13 ....143 H4
  STRBR DY8 ....99 H5
  WASH/WDE B8 ....128 D1
  YDLY B25 ....146 C1
Graham St CBHAMW B1 ....2 C3
  LOZ/NWT B19 ....108 C2
Grainger CI TPTN/OCK DY4 .....70 B5

Grainger's La CDYHTH B64 ....120 C4
Grainger St DUDS DY2 ....102 D2
Graiseley Ct BDMR/CCFT WV3 ...6 D6
Graiseley HI BDMR/CCFT WV3 ..36 D5
  BKHL/PFLD WV2 ....37 E5
Graiseley La WNSFLD WV11 ....24 C5
Graiseley Rw BKHL/PFLD WV2 ...7 E5
Graiseley St BDMR/CCFT WV3 ...6 D6
Graith Cl HLGN/YWD B28 ......179 G2
Grammar School La HALE B63 ..138 C3
Grampian Rd STRBR DY8 ......135 C3
Granary CI KGSWFD DY6 ....99 E1
Granary La WALM/CURD B76 ....63 F5
Granary Rd CDSL WV8 ....22 A1
The Granary ALDR WS9 ....30 D5
Granbourne Rd SHHTH WV12 ...40 B1
Granby Av STETCH B33 ....131 E3
Granby CI HIA/OLT B92 ....164 A5
Grandborough Dr SOLH B91 ...181 G4
Grand CI SMTHWK B66 ....124 D1
Grand Junction Wy WSL WS1 ..56 D3
Grand Union Canal Wk
  ACGN B27 ....147 E4
  CBHAMNE B4 ....3 F2
  DOR/KN B93 ....197 H3
  SPARK B11 ....128 A5
  VAUX/NECH B7 ....3 K1
  YDLY B25 ....146 A1
Grandys Cft
  CHWD/FDBR/MGN B37 ....131 H2
Grange Av ALDR WS9 ....30 A1
  MGN/WHC B75 ....47 C2
  WASH/WDE B8 ....111 F3
Grange Crs HALE B63 ....138 D4
  RBRY B45 ....173 C5
  RUSH/SHEL WS4 ....28 D2
Grange Dr FOAKS/STRLY B74 ...45 F3
Grange Farm Dr
  HWK/WKHTH B38 ....176 B3
Grangefield CI CDSL WV8 .....22 B1
Grange HI RMSLY B62 ....139 E5
Grange Hill Rd
  HWK/WKHTH B38 ....176 C4
Grange La HAG/WOL DY9 ....136 B3
  KGSWFD DY6 ....99 G5
  MGN/WHC B75 ....47 C3
Grange Ri HWK/WKHTH B38 ....190 D1
Grange Rd
  ALE/KHTH/YWD B14 ....160 D2
  AST/WIT B6 ....109 E1
  BILS/COS WV14 ....68 B4
  BKHL/PFLD WV2 ....51 F2
  CDYHTH B64 ....121 H4
  DOR/KN B93 ....198 C2
  DUDN DY1 ....84 B4
  DUNHL/THL/PER WV6 ....35 C1
  ERDE/BCHGN B24 ....93 E2
  HAG/WOL DY9 ....136 A3
  HALE B63 ....138 D4
  SLYOAK B29 ....142 D4
  SMTHWK B66 ....124 D1
  SOLH B91 ....164 A3
  WBROM B70 ....87 F3
Grange St DUDN DY1 ....84 B5
  WSL WS1 ....57 F2
The Grange WMBN WV5 ....65 E4
Grangewood Ct HIA/OLT B92 * ..164 A3
Granshaw CI
  HWK/WKHTH B38 ....176 D4
Grant CI HHTH/SAND B71 ......87 F1
  KGSWFD DY6 ....99 H1
Grantham Rd BILS/COS WV14 ..118 D5
Grantham St SMTHWK B66 ....124 D1
  SPARK B11 ....144 D1
Grantley Crs KGSWFD DY6 .....99 G2
Grantley Dr
  CHWD/FDBR/MGN B37 ....132 A2
Granton Cl
  ALE/KHTH/YWD B14 ....160 D5
Granton Rd
  ALE/KHTH/YWD B14 ....160 D5
Granville CI BKHL/PFLD WV2 * ..7 J7
  DOR/KN B93 ....199 E1
Granville Dr KGSWFD DY6 .....100 B5
Granville Rd CDYHTH B64 .....121 H4
  DOR/KN B93 ....199 E1
Granville Sq EDG B15 ....2 C7
Granville St BKHL/PFLD WV2 * ..7 J7
  CBHAMW B1 ....2 D7
  WLNHL WV13 ....39 C3
Grasdene Gv HRBN B17 ....142 A3
Grasmere Av
  DUNHL/THL/PER WV6 ....34 D1
  FOAKS/STRLY B74 ....45 G2
Grasmere CI
  DUNHL/THL/PER WV6 ....21 H2
  GTB/HAM B43 ....73 H4
  KGSWFD DY6 ....99 F2
  WNSFLD WV11 ....24 C3
Grasmere Rd HDSW B21 ....107 G2
Grassington Dr
  CHWD/FDBR/MGN B37 ....131 H3
Grassmere Dr STRBR DY8 .....135 E3
Grassmoor Rd
  HWK/WKHTH B38 ....176 C3
Grassy La WNSFLD WV11 ....24 B1
Grattidge Rd ACGN B27 ......146 D5
Gravel Bank RIDG/WDGT B32 ..140 B3
Gravel Hl WMBN WV5 ....65 F5
Gravelly Hl ERDE/BCHGN B24 ..92 C4
Gravelly Hill North
  ERDW/GRVHL B23 ....92 C3
Gravelly La ERDW/GRVHL B23 ..92 D2
Gravelly Ms LGLYGN/QTN B68 ..123 E2
Grayfield Av MOS/BIL B13 ....144 B4
Grayland CI ACGN B27 ....146 B5
Grayling CI DARL/WED WS10 ...54 B5
Grayling Rd BRLYHL DY5 ......118 D1
Grayling Wk
  CHWD/FDBR/MGN B37 ....132 C2
  WOLVN WV10 ....38 D1
Grayshott CI
  ERDW/GRVHL B23 ....92 C1
Grays Rd HRBN B17 ....142 D1

Gray St BORD B9 ....127 H2
Grayswood Park Rd
  NFLD/LBR B31 ....189 C1
Grayswood Rd NFLD/LBR B31 ..189 F1
Grazebrook Cft
  RIDG/WDGT B32 ....157 H2
Grazebrook Rd DUDS DY2 .....102 C2
Grazewood CI SHHTH WV12 ....25 H3
Greadier St SHHTH WV12 .....26 A5
Great Arthur St SMTHWK B66 ..106 D2
Great Barr St BORD B9 ......127 G2
Great Bricklin St
  BDMR/CCFT WV3 ....6 C6
Great Br TPTN/OCK DY4 ....86 B1
Great Bridge Rd
  BILS/COS WV14 ....54 C4
Great Bridge St WBROM B70 ..86 D1
Great Brook St VAUX/NECH B7 .109 G5
Great Charles St BRWNH WS8 ..9 F4
Great Charles Street Queensway
  CBHAMW B3 ....2 E4
Great Colmore St EDG B15 ...126 D4
Great Cornbow HALE B63 ......138 D4
Great Farley Dr NFLD/LBR B31 .174 D4
Great Francis St
  VAUX/NECH B7 ....109 H5
Great Hampton Rw
  LOZ/NWT B19 ....2 D1
Great Hampton St WOLV WV1 ...6 D1
  WSNGN B18 ....108 C4
Great King St LOZ/NWT B19 ..108 C4
Great King St North
  LOZ/NWT B19 ....108 C3
Great Lister St VAUX/NECH B7 ..3 K1
Great Meadow TPTN/OCK DY4 ..85 H1
Greatrex Cl HHTH/SAND B71 ...71 F3
Great Stone Rd NFLD/LBR B31 .175 C2
Great Tindal St
  LDYWD/EDGR B16 ....126 A2
Great Western Ar CBHAM B2 ...3 G4
Great Western CI WSNGN B18 ..107 G3
Great Western Dr
  CDYHTH B64 ....121 G3
Great Western St
  DARL/WED WS10 ....70 C1
  WOLV WV1 ....7 C1
Great Western Wy
  TPTN/OCK DY4 ....70 B5
Great Wood Rd BORD B9 ......128 A3
Greaves Av DSYBK/YTR WS5 ...43 E5
Greaves CI DSYBK/YTR WS5 ...43 E5
Greaves Crs SHHTH WV12 .....26 A2
Greaves Rd DUDS DY2 ....121 E5
Greaves Sq HWK/WKHTH B38 ..177 F4
The Greaves WALM/CURD B76 ..79 H5
Grebe CI ERDW/GRVHL B23 ....91 H3
Greenacre Dr CDSL WV8 ....69 C2
Greenacre Rd TPTN/OCK DY4 ..85 F5
Green Acres ACGN B27 ....146 B5
Greenacres
  DUNHL/THL/PER WV6 ....21 F5
Green Acres RIDG/WDGT B32 ..157 H1
Greenacres SEDG DY3 ....66 D2
  WALM/CURD B76 ....78 C3
Green Acres WMBN WV5 ....80 D1
Greenacres Av WOLVN WV10 ...24 B1
Greenacres Cl
  FOAKS/STRLY B74 ....45 E3
Green Acres Rd
  HWK/WKHTH B38 ....176 B5
Greenaleigh Rd
  ALE/KHTH/YWD B14 ....179 F2
Green Av HLGN/YWD B28 ......162 C1
Greenaway CI GTB/HAM B43 ...59 G5
Green Bank Av
  HLGN/YWD B28 ....162 C1
Greenbank Gdns STRBR DY8 ..118 A2
Green Barns La LICHS WS14 ...33 G1
Greenbush Dr HALE B63 ....138 C2
Green CI HLYWD B47 ....192 C5
Green Ct HLGN/YWD B28 ......162 D2
Greencroft BILS/COS WV14 ...53 H2
Green Cft BORD B9 ....129 E1
Greencroft KGSWFD DY6 ....99 H5
Greencroft Rd RIDG/WDGT B32 .157 C1
Greendene Rd CDSL WV8 ......23 E3
Greendred Rd MOS/BIL B13 ..103 F1
Greenfels Ri DUDS DY2 ....103 F1
Greenfield Av CDYHTH B64 ...120 B3
  STRBR DY8 ....135 F2
Greenfield Crs EDG B15 ......126 A4
Greenfield La BILS/COS WV14 ..53 H4
Greenfield La WOLVN WV10 ....12 D2
Greenfield Rd GTB/HAM B43 ...73 F1
  HRBN B17 ....142 A2
  SMTHWK B66 ....106 A5
Greenfields ALDR WS9 ....44 D5
Greenfields Rd KGSWFD DY6 ..100 A4
  RUSH/SHEL WS4 ....18 D5
  SHHTH WV12 ....81 E1
Greenfield Vw SEDG DY3 ......66 D4
Greenfinch Rd CBROM B36 ....114 A2
  HAG/WOL DY9 ....136 B4
Greenford Rd
  ALE/KHTH/YWD B14 ....178 D2
Green Gables
  FOAKS/STRLY B74 * 45 E2
  HLYWD B47 ....192 C5
Green Gables Dr HLYWD B47 * .192 C1
Greenhill WMBN WV5 ....65 F5
Greenhill CI SHHTH WV12 .....25 H5
Green Hill Wy SHLY B90 ......163 F5
Greenholm Rd KGSTG B44 .....74 B5
Greening Dr EDG B15 ....126 D5
Greenland CI KGSWFD DY6 ....100 A1
Greenland Ct BORD B9 * 128 B2
Greenland Ri SOLH B91 ......165 F3
Greenland Rd SLYOAK B29 ....160 B1
Greenlands WMBN WV5 ....64 D3

Greenlands Rd
CHWD/FDBR/MGN B37......**132** C2
Green La ALDR WS9.............. **31** E5
BLOX/PEL WS3...................**18** A3
BLOX/PEL WS3...................**27** C4
BORD B9.........................**128** A5
BRWNH WS8........................**9** G2
CBROM B36.......................**113** C1
CSHL/WTROR B46.................**115** C4
DUDN DY1........................**153** E1
DUNHL/THL/PER WV6..............**22** A3
GTB/HAM B43......................**73** F4
HAG/WOL DY9....................**136** B2
HDSW B21........................**105** H3
HWK/WKHTH B38..................**176** C5
KGSWFD DY6.......................**99** H2
RIDG/WDGT B32...................**140** C1
RMSLY B62.......................**122** B3
RUSH/SHEL WS4...................**18** D4
SHLY B90........................**179** C4
WSLW WS2..........................**3** G2
Green Lanes BILS/COS WV14....**53** C1
SCFLD/BOLD B73...................**77** F4
Greenleas Gdns HALE B63.......**139** E3
Green Leigh ERDW/GRVHL B23...**76** D3
Greenleighs SEDG DY3............**52** B5
Greenly Rd
ETTPK/GDPK/PENN WV4............**52** B3
Green Meadow HAG/WOL DY9...**152** D2
WNSFLD WV11.....................**24** D5
Green Meadow Rd WMBN WV5.....**64** C5
Green Meadow Rd
SHHTH WV12......................**25** H3
SLYOAK B29 *.....................**72** B5
Greenoak Crs BILS/COS WV14....**68** A5
BVILLE B30.......................**160** C2
Green Oak Rd CDSL WV8.........**10** D5
Greenock Crs
ETTPK/GDPK/PENN WV4............**52** B3
Green Park Av BILS/COS WV14....**38** B5
Green Park Dr BILS/COS WV14...**38** B5
Green Park Rd DUDS DY2.........**85** F5
NFLD/LBR B31....................**175** E3
Greenridge Rd
BFLD/HDSWWD B20..................**89** C1
Green Rd DUDS DY2..............**102** D2
MOS/BIL B13.....................**162** B1
Green Rock La BLOX/PEL WS3....**27** H1
Greenroyde HAG/WOL DY9.......**152** D1
Greensand BHTH/HG B12.........**144** A2
Greensforge La KINVER DY7....**116** B4
Greenside HRBN B17..............**142** A2
Greenside Rd
ERDE/BCHGN B24...................**93** C2
Greenside Wy DSYBK/YTR WS5...**57** G4
Greensill Av TPTN/OCK DY4......**69** F5
Greenslade Cft NFLD/LBR B31...**174** C3
Greenslade Rd DSYBK/YTR WS5...**58** A1
SEDG DY3..........................**66** D1
SHLY B90........................**179** C4
Greensleeves FOAKS/STRLY B74..**46** D3
Greenstead Rd MOS/BIL B13....**162** B1
The Greens
DUNHL/THL/PER WV6 *..............**34** C2
Green St BHTH/HG B12..........**127** F3
BILS/COS WV14....................**68** C3
OLDBY B69.......................**105** E2
STRBR B70.......................**135** F2
WBROM B70.......................**106** A1
WSLW WS2..........................**2** E1
Greensway WNSFLD WV11.........**24** B2
The Green ALDR WS9............**30** C4
BLOX/PEL WS3....................**27** F1
CBROM B36.......................**112** D2
CSCFLD/WYGN B72..................**72** A4
DARL/WED WS10...................**55** F1
HWK/WKHTH B38..................**176** D3
LGLYGN/QTN B68..................**123** F2
NFLD/LBR B31....................**174** C3
RIDG/WDGT B32...................**140** A1
SOLH B91........................**165** F5
STRBR B70.......................**117** G2
Grenvale NFLD/LBR B31.........**158** B5
Greenvale Av
LGN/SDN/BHAMAIR B26............**148** B1
Green Wk HRBN B17.............**124** B5
Greenway ALDR WS9.............**19** H5
BFLD/HDSWWD B20..................**89** H2
SEDG DY3.........................**67** G2
Greenway Av STRBR DY8.........**118** A3
Greenway Dr SCFLD/BOLD B73...**61** E5
Greenway Gdns
HWK/WKHTH B38..................**190** C1
SEDG DY3.........................**67** G2
Greenway Rd BILS/COS WV14....**54** A4
Greenways HALE B63............**137** G2
NFLD/LBR B31....................**158** B2
STRBR B70.......................**117** G3
Greenway St BORD B9...........**128** A3
The Greenway
CHWD/FDBR/MGN B37..............**149** E1
HAG/WOL DY9....................**152** B5
SCFLD/BOLD B73...................**62** B5
Greenwood Av ACGN B27.........**146** A5
BLKHTH/ROWR B65.................**122** B2
LGLYGN/QTN B68..................**105** F4
Greenwood Cl
ALE/KHTH/YWD B14................**161** C5
Greenwood Pk ALDR WS9.........**30** C1
Greenwood Pl KGSTG B44........**75** H2
Greenwood Rd ALDR WS9........**19** H5
HHTH/SAND B71....................**71** F5
WOLVN WV10......................**23** E3
The Greenwoods STRBR DY8....**135** E2
Greethurst Dr MOS/BIL B13....**145** E5
Greets Green Rd WBROM B70....**86** C2
Greetville Cl STETCH B33......**112** C4
Gregory Av SLYOAK B29.........**158** C2
Gregory Cl DARL/WED WS10....**70** D1
Gregory Dr DUDN DY1..........**84** A4
Gregory Rd STRBR DY8..........**134** C2
Grendon Dr SCFLD/BOLD B73....**61** F5
Grendon Gdns
BDMR/CCFT WV3 *..................**50** D2
Grendon Rd
ALE/KHTH/YWD B14................**178** C2
HIA/OLT B92.....................**164** A2
Grenfell Dr EDG B15...........**125** H4
Grenfell Rd BLOX/PEL WS3......**17** F4

Grenville Dr WSLW WS2.........**40** B2
Grenville Dr ERDW/GRVHL B23...**91** H3
SMTHWK B66.......................**105** H1
Grenville Pl WBROM B70.........**86** C5
Grenville Rd DUDN DY1..........**83** G5
SHLY B90........................**180** B5
Gresham Rd HLGN/YWD B28......**162** D4
LGLYGN/QTN B68..................**105** F3
Gresley Cl FOAKS/STRLY B74....**47** E1
Gressel La STETCH B33.........**131** E1
Grestone Av
BFLD/HDSWWD B20..................**89** G3
Greswolde Dr
ERDE/BCHGN B24...................**93** F2
Greswolde Park Rd ACGN B27...**146** B4
Greswolde Rd SOLH B91.........**164** A4
SPARK B11.......................**145** E4
Greswold Gdns
BKDE/SHDE B34...................**112** C4
Greswold Rd HHTH/SAND B71....**87** C1
Gretton Crs ALDR WS9..........**29** H5
Gretton Rd ALDR WS9...........**29** H5
ERDW/GRVHL B23...................**76** B4
Greville Dr EDG B15...........**143** C1
Grevis Cl MOS/BIL B13.........**143** C5
Grevis Rd ALE/KHTH/YWD B14...**162** D1
Greyfort Crs HIA/OLT B92......**164** B1
Greyfriars Cl DUDN DY1........**83** C3
Greyfriars Cl LOZ/NWT B19.....**88** D2
Greyhound La STRBR DY8........**134** D5
Greyhurst Cft SOLH B91........**181** H5
Grey Mill Cl SHLY B90.........**195** F2
Greystoke Av CBROM B36........**111** H2
Greystoke Dr KGSWFD DY6.......**99** H3
Greystone Pas DUDN DY1........**84** B5
Greystone St DUDN DY1.........**84** C5
Grey Tree Crs DOR/KN B93......**196** C5
Grice St WBROM B70............**105** G1
Griffen La SHLY B90...........**194** A4
Griffin Cl NFLD/LBR B31.......**158** D4
Griffin Gdns HRBN B17.........**142** B3
Griffin Rd ERDW/GRVHL B23....**76** C1
Griffins Brook Cl BVILLE B30...**159** F4
Griffins Brook La BVILLE B30...**159** E4
Griffin St DUDS DY2...........**102** C5
WBROM B70.......................**87** H3
WOLV WV1........................**37** H4
Griffiths Dr WMBN WV5.........**37** H4
WNSFLD WV11.....................**25** F2
Griffiths Rd DUDN DY1.........**68** A5
HHTH/SAND B71....................**71** G2
SHHTH WV12......................**26** B2
Grigg Gv NFLD/LBR B31.........**175** E4
Grimley Rd NFLD/LBR B31.......**176** B3
Grimpits La HWK/WKHTH B38....**191** E1
Grimshaw Rd HLGN/YWD B28....**163** E1
Grimstock Hl
CSHL/WTROR B46 *................**115** F3
Grimstone St WOLVN WV10......**7** H2
Grindleford Rd
PBAR/PBCH B42...................**74** D4
Gristhorpe Rd SLYOAK B29.....**160** A2
Grizedale Cl RBRY B45.........**174** B3
Grocott Rd DARL/WED WS10....**54** D4
Grosmont Av BHTH/HG B12......**144** C1
Grosvenor Av
BFLD/HDSWWD B20..................**90** C4
FOAKS/STRLY B74..................**45** F4
Grosvenor Cl MGN/WHC B75....**47** G4
WOLVN WV10......................**12** D5
Grosvenor Crs WOLVN WV10....**12** D5
Grosvenor Pk
ETTPK/GDPK/PENN WV4............**51** F3
Grosvenor Rd AST/WIT B6......**109** H1
BFLD/HDSWWD B20..................**90** C4
ETTPK/GDPK/PENN WV4............**52** C5
HRBN B17........................**141** G1
LGLYGN/QTN B68..................**105** E5
SEDG DY3.........................**83** F4
SOLH B91........................**181** H4
WOLVN WV10......................**12** D5
Grosvenor Sq HLGN/YWD B28....**162** C5
Grosvenor St DIG/EDG B5.......**3** J4
WOLVN WV10......................**37** H2
Grosvenor St West EDG B15.....**2** A7
Grosvenor Wy BRLYHL DY5......**119** F5
Grotto La
DUNHL/THL/PER WV6..............**22** A2
Groucutt St BILS/COS WV14....**68** C3
Grounds Dr FOAKS/STRLY B74...**46** D2
Grounds Rd FOAKS/STRLY B74...**46** D2
Grout St WBROM B70...........**86** C2
Grove Av HALE B63.............**138** B4
HDSW B21........................**107** H1
MOS/BIL B13.....................**144** C5
SLYOAK B29 *....................**159** G1
SOLH B91........................**165** E5
Grove Cottage Rd BORD B9....**128** B2
Grove Cft PBAR/PBCH B42 *....**73** H2
Grove Crs BLOX/PEL WS3.......**17** H4
BRLYHL DY5......................**101** E4
Grove Farm Dr MCN/WHC B75...**63** F3
Grove Gdns HDSW B21..........**89** H4
Grove Hl DSYBK/YTR WS5.......**49** C5
Grove Hill Rd HDSW B21.......**89** H5
Grove House WSL WS1 *........**5** F5
Groveland Rd TPTN/OCK DY4....**85** C4
Grovelands Crs WOLVN WV10...**12** C4
Grove La BFLD/HDSWWD B20....**89** H4
DUNHL/THL/PER WV6..............**35** F3
HRBN B17........................**142** A4
SMTHWK B66......................**107** F5
WALM/CURD B76....................**79** H1
Groveley La NFLD/LBR B31......**189** F2
RBRY B45........................**188** C4
Grove Ms NFLD/LBR B31........**175** H5
Grove Pk KGSWFD DY6..........**99** F5
Grove Rd ALE/KHTH/YWD B14...**160** D3
DOR/KN B93......................**197** F5
HAG/WOL DY9....................**136** D3
LGLYGN/QTN B68..................**123** H5
SOLH B91........................**165** E5
SPARK B11.......................**145** E4
Groveside Wy BLOX/PEL WS3...**18** A2
Grove St DUDS DY2............**103** E1
SMTHWK B66......................**108** C1
WSNGN B18......................**107** F5
Grove Ter WSL WS1............**5** H3
The Grove BLKHTH/ROWR B65..**122** A2
BRLYHL DY5......................**119** E3

CSHL/WTROR B46..................**115** F5
DSYBK/YTR WS5 *.................**57** H5
ETTPK/GDPK/PENN WV4............**52** B5
FOAKS/STRLY B74..................**32** B5
GTB/HAM B43.....................**58** C4
HIA/OLT B92.....................**167** G2
LDYWD/EDGR B16 *................**125** H2
NFLD/LBR B31....................**175** H5
RBRY B45........................**188** D4
WASH/WDE B8.....................**110** A5
WNSFLD WV11.....................**24** B4
Grove Vale Av GTB/HAM B43....**73** E2
Grove Wy FOAKS/STRLY B74....**60** B1
Grovewood Dr
HWK/WKHTH B38..................**176** C4
Guardian Cl NFLD/LBR B31.....**174** D2
SOLH B91........................**182** B2
Guardians Wy NFLD/LBR B31...**158** A2
Guernsey Dr CBROM B36........**114** B3
Guest Av WNSFLD WV11........**25** E2
Guest Gv LOZ/NWT B19........**108** C3
Guild Av BLOX/PEL WS3.........**27** H3
Guild Cl LDYWD/EDGR B16......**126** A2
Guild Cft LOZ/NWT B19........**108** D3
Guildford Cft
CHWD/FDBR/MGN B37..............**131** H4
Guildford Dr LOZ/NWT B19.....**108** C3
Guildford St LOZ/NWT B19.....**108** D2
Guillswood Cl
ALE/KHTH/YWD B14................**177** H3
Gumbleberrys Cl
WASH/WDE B8.....................**111** C5
Gunmakers Wk LOZ/NWT B19....**108** A2
Gunner Gv MGN/WHC B75.......**63** C2
Gunner La RBRY B45...........**187** F1
Gunns Wy HIA/OLT B92.........**163** H3
Gunstock Cl FOAKS/STRLY B74..**60** A1
Gunstone La CDSL WV8.........**10** B2
Gunter Rd ERDE/BCHGN B24....**94** A3
Gurnard Cl SHHTH WV12........**25** H1
Gurney Pl WSLW WS2............**27** F5
Gurney Rd WSLW WS2...........**27** E5
Guthrie Cl LOZ/NWT B19.......**108** D3
Guthrum Cl
DUNHL/THL/PER WV6..............**20** D5
ERDW/GRVHL B23...................**76** C3
The Gutter HAG/WOL DY9......**186** A1
Guy Av WOLVN WV10...........**23** C4
Guys Cliffe Av WALM/CURD B76..**78** B2
Guys La SEDG DY3.............**82** D4
Gwalia Gv ERDW/GRVHL B23 *..**92** D2
Gwendoline Wy ALDR WS9......**19** H3
Gypsy La CSHL/WTROR B46......**96** D4

H

Habberley Rd
BLKHTH/ROWR B65.................**122** B2
Habberley Cft SOLH B91........**181** H4
Hackett Cl BILS/COS WV14.....**67** H2
Hackett Dr SMTHWK B66........**105** H2
Hackett Rd
BLKHTH/ROWR B65.................**122** C1
Hackett St TPTN/OCK DY4......**70** A4
Hackford Rd
ETTPK/GDPK/PENN WV4............**52** D4
Hackman's Gate La
HAG/WOL DY9....................**169** C5
Hack St BORD B9..............**127** G3
Hackwood Rd DARL/WED WS10...**71** F1
Hadcroft Gra HAG/WOL DY9....**136** B3
Hadcroft Rd HAG/WOL DY9.....**136** A3
Haddock Rd BILS/COS WV14....**53** C1
Haddon Crs SHHTH WV12.......**26** A3
Haddon Rd KGSTG B44.........**68** A5
Haddon Rd PBAR/PBCH B42....**154** C1
Haden Circ BRTH/HG B12......**127** F5
Haden Cl CDYHTH B64.........**121** F5
STRBR DY8.......................**117** H2
Haden Crs WNSFLD WV11......**25** H4
Haden Cross Dr CDYHTH B64...**121** C5
Hadendale CDYHTH B64........**121** C5
Haden Hl BDMR/CCFT WV3......**6** A4
Haden Hill Rd CDYHTH B64....**121** C5
HALE B63........................**121** C5
Haden Park Rd CDYHTH B64....**121** E5
Haden Rd CDYHTH B64.........**121** E2
TPTN/OCK DY4....................**69** C2
Haden St SHHTH B12..........**144** B1
Haden Wy BHTH/HG B12........**144** B1
Hadfield Cl ERDE/BCHGN B24...**94** A3
Hadfield Cft LOZ/NWT B19.....**108** C4
Hadfield Wy
CHWD/FDBR/MGN B37..............**114** A5
Hadland Rd STETCH B33.......**130** D5
Hadleigh Cft
WALM/CURD B76...................**78** C5
Hadley Cl DUDS DY2...........**103** E5
HLYWD B47.......................**192** C5
Hadley Cft SMTHWK B66.......**106** C2
Hadley Pl BILS/COS WV14.....**53** C5
Hadley Rd BILS/COS WV14.....**53** G1
WSLW WS2........................**26** C4
Hadley St LGLYGN/QTN B68....**105** C5
Hadlow Cft STETCH B33.......**131** F5
Hadrian Dr CSHL/WTROR B46..**97** E5
Hadyn Gv
LGN/SDN/BHAMAIR B26............**147** H1
Hadzor Rd LGLYGN/QTN B68....**123** H4
Hafren Cl RBRY B45...........**174** B3
Hafton Gv BORD B9............**128** B3
Hagger St BKHL/PFLD WV2.....**52** A2
Hagley Cswy HAG/WOL DY9....**153** H3
Hagley Cl HAG/WOL DY9.......**153** E4
Hagley Gra HAG/WOL DY9......**152** D4
Hagley Ml HALE B63..........**138** D4
Hagley Park Dr RBRY B45.....**188** C2
Hagley Rd HAG/WOL DY9......**153** C2
HALE B63........................**154** D1
HRBN B17........................**142** C3
STRBR DY8.......................**135** H4
Hagley Rd West HRBN B17.....**125** H3
RIDG/WDGT B32...................**140** B1
RMSLY B62.......................**139** H1
Hagley View Rd DUDS DY2....**102** C5

Hagley Vls BHTH/HG B12 *....**144** D3
Hagley Wood La RMSLY B62....**154** B4
Haig Cl MGN/WHC B75.........**62** C1
Haig Rd DUDS DY2............**85** F5
Haig St HHTH/SAND B71.......**87** G1
Hailes Park Cl
ETTPK/GDPK/PENN WV4............**52** B2
Hailsham Rd ERDW/GRVHL B23..**92** D1
Hailstone Cl
BLKHTH/ROWR B65.................**103** C5
Haines Cl TPTN/OCK DY4......**85** H2
Haines St WBROM B70.........**87** H4
Hainfield Dr SOLH B91.......**165** C5
Hainge Rd OLDBY B69.........**86** A4
Hainult Cl STRBR DY8........**99** H5
Halas Ct CDYHTH B64.........**121** E2
Halberton St WSNGN B18.....**107** F5
Haldon Gv NFLD/LBR B31.....**189** E1
Hale Ct WSL WS1 *..........**5** J6
Halecroft Av WNSFLD WV11...**24** D5
Hale Gv ERDE/BCHGN B24.....**93** H2
Hales Crs SMTHWK B67.......**106** B5
Halescroft Sq NFLD/LBR B31..**158** A4
Hales Gdns ERDW/GRVHL B23..**76** A3
Hales La SMTHWK B67........**106** B5
Halesmere Wy HALE B63......**138** C4
Halesowen Rd BRGRVW B61....**186** D5
CDYHTH B64......................**121** E3
DUDS DY2........................**102** C4
HALE B63........................**139** G1
Halesowen St
BLKHTH/ROWR B65.................**122** A4
OLDBY B69.......................**104** D2
Hales Rd DARL/WED WS10.....**56** A4
HALE B63........................**138** B4
Hales Wy OLDBY B69.........**104** D2
Halewood Gv HLGN/YWD B28....**163** E3
Haley St SHHTH WV12........**26** A5
Halfcot Av HAG/WOL DY9.....**152** A5
Halford Crs BLOX/PEL WS3...**28** B5
Halford Gv ERDE/BCHGN B24..**94** A2
Halford Rd SOLH B91.........**164** A4
Halfords La HHTH/SAND B71...**87** H1
SMTHWK B66......................**106** C2
Halfpenny Cl BLOX/PEL WS3..**17** H5
Halford St BILS/COS WV14....**54** A3
Hall Green St BILS/COS WV14..**54** A5
Hallgreen St BILS/COS WV14..**54** A5
Hall Gv BILS/COS WV14.......**68** C2
Hall Hays Rd BKDE/SHDE B34..**113** C2
Hall La ALDR WS9............**19** E5
BILS/COS WV14...................**67** H2
BLOX/PEL WS3....................**17** H4
HAG/WOL DY9....................**153** C5
TPTN/OCK DY4....................**69** H5
Hall Meadow HAG/WOL DY9....**153** F3
Hallmoor Rd STETCH B33......**130** D1
Hallot Cl ERDW/GRVHL B23....**76** B3
Halloughton Rd
FOAKS/STRLY B74..................**62** A1
Hallow Cl NFLD/LBR B31......**176** B3
Hall Park St BILS/COS WV14..**53** F2
Hall Rd BFLD/HDSWWD B20....**108** A2
CBROM B36.......................**112** A1
SMTHWKW B67.....................**106** A5
WASH/WDE B8.....................**110** B5
Hallstead Rd MOS/BIL B13....**161** H5
Hall St BILS/COS WV14.......**54** A3
CDYHTH B64......................**121** F2
DUDS DY2........................**84** D5
LGLYGN/QTN B68..................**105** F4
SEDG DY3........................**67** F3
STRBR DY8.......................**85** E1
TPTN/OCK DY4....................**85** F1
WBROM B70.......................**87** H3
WLNHL WV13......................**39** H4
WSLW WS2........................**42** A1
WSNGN B18......................**107** H5
Hall St East
DARL/WED WS10...................**55** E1
Hall St South WBROM B70....**105** H1
Hallswelle Gv GTB/HAM B43...**58** A4
Hall Wk CSHL/WTROR B46....**115** F5
Halsbury Gv KGSTG B44.......**75** H3
Halstead Gv SOLH B91.......**181** G5
Halton Rd SCFLD/BOLD B73....**61** F5
Halton St DUDS DY2..........**102** C4
Hamar Wy
CHWD/FDBR/MGN B37..............**132** B4
Hamberley Ct WSNGN B18.....**107** F5
Hamble Cl WBROM B70........**85** H5
CBROM B36.......................**113** H1
Hambledon Cl COVEN WV9......**12** A5
Hamble Gv
DUNHL/THL/PER WV6..............**34** C1
Hamble Rd
ETTPK/GDPK/PENN WV4............**50** C2
GTB/HAM B43.....................**73** H2
Hambleton Rd HALE B63......**137** H5
Hambletts Rd WBROM B70....**86** D5
Hambrook Cl
DUNHL/THL/PER WV6..............**22** C5

Hambury Dr
ALE/KHTH/YWD B14................**160** D3
Hamilton Av HRBN B17........**124** C4
HAG/WOL DY9....................**139** E4
STRBR DY8.......................**134** D1
Hamilton Cl SEDG DY3........**67** E3
STRBR DY8.......................**99** E1
Hamilton Dr OLDBY B69.......**86** A4
SLYOAK B29 *....................**159** E2
STRBR DY8.......................**117** G2
Hamilton Gdns WOLVN WV10...**13** F4
Hamilton Rd HDSW B21........**107** F1
SMTHWK B67......................**106** A4
TPTN/OCK DY4....................**124** A2
WOLVN WV10......................**13** F4
Hamilton St BLOX/PEL WS3....**70** A5
Ham La HAG/WOL DY9.........**136** A5
KGSWFD DY6......................**82** A5
Hamlet Gdns HLGN/YWD B28...**162** D2
Hamlet Rd HLGN/YWD B28.....**162** D3
Hammer Bank HALE B63.......**138** A4
Hammersley Cl HALE B63......**120** C5
Hammond Av WOLVN WV10....**23** G2
Hammond Dr
ERDW/GRVHL B23...................**92** D1
Hammond Wy STRBR DY8......**118** C5
Hampden Cl BRLYHL DY5......**120** A4
Hampden Retreat
BHTH/HG B12....................**144** A1
Hampshire Dr EDG B15.......**125** G4
Hampshire Rd HHTH/SAND B71..**71** E2
Hampson Cl SPARK B11.......**144** D1
Hampstead Cl WNSFLD WV11..**24** D4
Hampstead Gld HALE B63.....**139** E4
Hampton Cl WNSFLD WV10....**13** H3
Hampton Court Rd HRBN B17..**141** C1
Hampton Dr FOAKS/STRLY B74..**47** F5
Hampton Gdns HAG/WOL DY9..**136** A4
Hampton Gv BLOX/PEL WS3...**17** H5
Hampton La SOLH B91........**165** H4
Hampton Rd AST/WIT B6.....**108** D1
DOR/KN B93......................**197** C1
ERDW/GRVHL B23...................**92** B2
WOLVN WV10......................**22** D1
Hampton St BILS/COS WV14...**54** A4
DUDS DY2........................**102** B4
LOZ/NWT B19.....................**2** E1
Hams La CSHL/WTROR B46....**97** F1
Hams Rd WASH/WDE B8........**110** B5
Hamstead Hall Av
BFLD/HDSWWD B20..................**89** G1
Hamstead Hall Rd
BFLD/HDSWWD B20..................**89** G2
Hamstead Hl
BFLD/HDSWWD B20..................**89** H2
Hamstead Rd
BFLD/HDSWWD B20..................**90** B5
GTB/HAM B43.....................**73** E4
Hamstead Ter DARL/WED WS10..**71** E1
Hanam Cl MCN/WHC B75........**63** F2
Hanbury Cl HALE B63.........**138** B5
Hanbury Crs
ETTPK/GDPK/PENN WV4............**51** E2
Hanbury Cft ACGN B27.......**147** E4
Hanbury Dr OLDBY B69.......**104** B5
Hanbury Hl STRBR DY8.......**135** G3
Hanbury Rd BRWNH WS8......**9** E2
DOR/KN B93......................**197** C4
WBROM B70.......................**87** E5
Hanch Pl WSL WS1 *........**5** C6
Hancock Rd WASH/WDE B8....**110** D5
Hancox St LGLYGN/QTN B68..**123** C3
Handley Gv NFLD/LBR B31....**174** C3
Handley St DARL/WED WS10...**56** A4
Handsworth Cl HDSW B21.....**107** F2
Handsworth Dr GTB/HAM B43..**74** A2
Handsworth New Rd
WSNGN B18......................**107** G4
Handsworth Wood Rd
BFLD/HDSWWD B20..................**89** H3
Hangar Rd
LGN/SDN/BHAMAIR B26............**149** E4
Hanging La NFLD/LBR B31.....**175** E4
Hangleton Dr SPARK B11......**145** F1
Hanley Cl HALE B63..........**138** A3
Hanley St LOZ/NWT B19......**3** F1
Hannafore Rd
LDYWD/EDGR B16.................**125** F1
Hannah Rd BILS/COS WV14....**54** C5
Hanney Hay Rd BNTWD WS7....**9** H1
Hannon Rd
ALE/KHTH/YWD B14................**160** D5
Hanover Cl AST/WIT B6.......**108** D1
Hanover Ct
DUNHL/THL/PER WV6..............**35** G1
ERDE/BCHGN B24.................**110** D1
Hanover Rd
BLKHTH/ROWR B65.................**104** A5
Hansell Dr DOR/KN B93.......**198** C1
Hanson Gv RIDG/WDGT B32...**140** C2
Hanson Ct SMTHWK B66......**107** E3
Hanson Gv HIA/OLT B92.....**147** F2
Hanson's Bridge Rd
ERDE/BCHGN B24.................**94** C2
Hanwell Cl WALM/CURD B76...**78** D4
Hanwood Cl BHTH/HG B12....**127** F4
Harald Cl DUNHL/THL/PER WV6..**20** C5
Harbeck Av KGSTG B44.......**75** F3
Harberrow Cl HAG/WOL DY9..**152** C4
Harbet Dr BHAMNEC B40.....**150** A3
Harbinger Rd
HWK/WKHTH B38..................**177** F3
Harborne La SLYOAK B29.....**142** B5
Harborne Park Rd HRBN B17..**142** B3
Harborne Rd EDG B15........**142** C1
LGLYGN/QTN B68..................**123** H3
Harborough Wk
HAG/WOL DY9....................**135** H5
Harbours Hl HAG/WOL DY9...**186** A2
Harbury Cl WALM/CURD B76..**78** C3
Harbury Rd BHTH/HG B12....**143** H2
Harby Cl
CHWD/FDBR/MGN B37..............**132** B4
Harcourt Dr FOAKS/STRLY B74..**46** C1
DUDN DY1........................**84** A3
Harcourt Rd CDYHTH B64.....**121** F4
DARL/WED WS10...................**71** H1
ERDW/GRVHL B23...................**76** C5

Harden Cl BLOX/PEL WS3 ... 28 A3
Harden Gv BLOX/PEL WS3 ... 28 A3
Harden Manor Ct HALE B63 * ... 139 E4
Harden Rd BLOX/PEL WS3 ... 27 H3
Harden V HALE B63 * ... 138 A2
Harding St BILS/COS WV14 ... 68 D2
Hardon Rd
ETTPK/GDPK/PENN WV4 ... 52 D3
Hardware St WBROM B70 ... 87 H2
Hardwick Dr CDYHTH B64 ... 121 G5
Hardwicke Wy HAG/WOL DY9 ... 136 B2
Hardwick Rd FOAKS/STRLY B74 ... 45 F3
LGN/SDN/BHAMAIR B26 ... 147 E3
Hardy Rd BLOX/PEL WS3 ... 28 A2
DARL/WED WS10 ... 56 A5
Hardy Sq BKHL/PFLD WV2 * ... 52 D2
Harebell Cl DSYBK/YTR WS5 ... 57 G5
Harebell Crs DUDN DY1 ... 84 A2
Harebell Gdns
HWK/WKHTH B38 ... 176 D5
Hare Gv NFLD/LBR B31 ... 174 D2
Hare St BILS/COS WV14 ... 54 B3
Harewell Dr MGN/WHC B75 ... 47 G4
Harewood Av DARL/WED WS10 ... 56 C5
GTB/HAM B43 ... 73 E1
Harewood Cl HLGN/YWD B28 ... 162 C5
Harford St WSNGN B18 ... 2 D1
Hargate La HHTH/SAND B71 ... 72 B2
Hargrave Cl CSHL/WTROR B46 ... 96 B3
Hargrave Rd SHLY B90 ... 179 F3
Hargreave Cl WALM/CURD B76 ... 78 B4
Hargreaves St BKHL/PFLD WV2 ... 53 E1
Harland Rd FOAKS/STRLY B74 ... 47 E2
Harlech Cl DUDS DY2 ... 85 G5
RIDG/WDGT B32 ... 157 E4
Harlech Rd SHHTH WV12 ... 26 A4
Harlech Wy DUDN DY1 ... 83 H4
Harlequin Dr MOS/BIL B13 ... 144 A5
Harleston Rd KGSTG B44 ... 75 F3
Harley Cl BRWNH WS8 ... 19 G1
Harley Dr BILS/COS WV14 ... 53 F4
Harley Gra DUDS DY2 ... 102 D1
Harlow Gv HLGN/YWD B28 ... 163 E4
Harlstones Cl STRBR DY8 ... 118 C5
Harlyn Cl BILS/COS WV14 ... 69 G1
Harman Rd ERDW/GRVHL B23 ... 77 F4
Harmer St WSNGN B18 ... 108 A4
Harmon Rd STRBR DY8 ... 134 C2
Harnall Cl SHLY B90 ... 195 E1
Harness Cl DSYBK/YTR WS5 ... 57 E4
Harold Rd LDYWD/EDGR B16 ... 125 H3
SMTHWKW B67 ... 124 A1
Harold Ter LOZ/NWT B19 * ... 108 C1
Harper Av WNSFLD WV11 ... 24 C3
Harper Gv TPTN/OCK DY4 ... 84 D1
Harper Rd BILS/COS WV14 ... 53 H2
Harpers Rd
ALE/KHTH/YWD B14 ... 178 C4
NFLD/LBR B31 ... 175 G3
Harper St WLNHL WV13 ... 39 G3
Harpur Cl RUSH/SHEL WS4 ... 42 C1
Harpur Rd RUSH/SHEL WS4 ... 42 C1
Harrier Rd ACGN B27 ... 146 D5
Harriet Cl BRLYHL DY5 ... 100 D4
Harringay Dr STRBR DY8 ... 135 E4
Harringay Rd KGSTG B44 ... 75 F1
Harrington Cft
HHTH/SAND B71 ... 72 B4
Harris Dr PBAR/PBCH B42 ... 74 A3
SMTHWK B66 ... 124 D1
Harrison Cl BLOX/PEL WS3 ... 27 G1
Harrison Rd ERDE/BCHGN B24 ... 92 D2
FOAKS/STRLY B74 ... 32 C5
RUSH/SHEL WS4 ... 18 C5
STRBR DY8 ... 118 C3
Harrison's Fold DUDS DY2 ... 102 C4
Harrisons Gn EDG B15 ... 142 C1
Harrisons Pleck MOS/BIL B13 ... 144 B4
Harrison's Rd EDG B15 ... 142 C1
Harrison St BLOX/PEL WS3 ... 27 G1
Harrold Av
BLKHTH/ROWR B65 ... 122 C1
Harrold Rd
BLKHTH/ROWR B65 ... 122 C1
Harrold St TPTN/OCK DY4 ... 70 A4
Harrop Wy STRBR DY8 ... 118 A4
Harrowby Dr TPTN/OCK DY4 ... 85 G2
Harrowby Pl WLNHL WV13 ... 40 A4
Harrowby Rd BILS/COS WV14 ... 54 C4
WOLVN WV10 ... 12 B4
Harrow Cl HAG/WOL DY9 ... 152 C4
Harrowfield Rd STETCH B33 ... 112 A5
Harrow Rd KGSWFD DY6 ... 81 H5
SLYOAK B29 ... 142 D4
Harrow St
DUNHL/THL/PER WV6 ... 36 D1
Harry Perks St WLNHL WV13 ... 39 G2
Hart Dr SCFLD/BOLD B73 ... 77 E3
Hartfield Crs ACGN B27 ... 163 E1
Hartford Cl HRBN B17 ... 124 C5
Hartill Rd
ETTPK/GDPK/PENN WV4 ... 50 D5
Hartill St WLNHL WV13 ... 39 H5
Hartington Cl DOR/KN B93 ... 196 C5
Hartington Rd LOZ/NWT B19 ... 108 D1
Hartland Av BILS/COS WV14 ... 68 A3
Hartland Rd HHTH/SAND B71 ... 72 B4
NFLD/LBR B31 ... 189 E2
TPTN/OCK DY4 ... 84 D1
Hartland St BRLYHL DY5 ... 101 F2
Hartlebury Cl DOR/KN B93 ... 196 D5
Hartlebury Rd HALE B63 ... 138 B5
OLDBY B69 ... 104 B4
Hartledon Rd HRBN B17 ... 141 H2
Hartle La HAG/WOL DY9 ... 184 D2
Hartley Dr ALDR WS9 ... 44 B1
Hartley Gv KGSTG B44 ... 60 D5
Hartley Pl EDG B15 ... 125 H4
Hartley Rd KGSTG B44 ... 60 C5
Hartley St BDMR/CCFT WV3 ... 6 A4
Harton Wy
ALE/KHTH/YWD B14 ... 160 C5
Hartopp Rd FOAKS/STRLY B74 ... 46 D5
WASH/WDE B8 ... 110 C5
Hart Rd ERDE/BCHGN B24 ... 93 E1
WNSFLD WV11 ... 38 D1
Hartsbourne Dr RMSLY B62 ... 139 F3
Harts Cl HRBN B17 ... 142 B1
Harts Green Rd HRBN B17 ... 141 G2
Hartshill Cl BKDE/SHDE B34 ... 112 C3
Hartshill Rd ACGN B27 ... 146 D5
BKDE/SHDE B34 ... 112 C3
Hartshorn St BILS/COS WV14 ... 53 H3
Hartside Cl HALE B63 ... 137 G5
Harts Rd WASH/WDE B8 ... 110 C4
Hart St WSL WS1 ... 4 E6
Hartswell Dr MOS/BIL B13 ... 161 F4
Hartwell Cl SOLH B91 ... 181 H4
Hartwell Rd ERDE/BCHGN B24 ... 93 F4
Hartwood Crs
ETTPK/GDPK/PENN WV4 ... 51 F4
Harvard Cl DUDN DY1 ... 83 H2
Harvard Rd HIA/OLT B92 ... 147 H3
Harvest Cl BVILLE B30 ... 160 B5
SEDG DY3 ... 83 G1
Harvesters Cl ALDR WS9 ... 45 E3
Harvesters Rd SHHTH WV12 ... 26 B5
Harvester Wy KGSWFD DY6 ... 99 E1
Harvest Fields Wy
MGN/WHC B75 ... 47 H1
Harvest Rd
BLKHTH/ROWR B65 ... 121 G1
SMTHWKW B67 ... 123 H1
Harvey Ct STETCH B33 * ... 131 F1
Harvey Dr MGN/WHC B75 ... 47 G3
Harvey Rd
LGN/SDN/BHAMAIR B26 ... 129 H5
WSLW WS2 ... 27 F5
Harvills Hawthorn WBROM B70 ... 70 D4
Harvine Wk STRBR DY8 ... 135 E4
Harvington Dr SHLY B90 ... 195 H2
Harvington Rd BILS/COS WV14 ... 68 B2
HALE B63 ... 138 B5
LGLYGN/QTN B68 ... 123 E4
SLYOAK B29 ... 158 C2
Harvington Wy
WALM/CURD B76 ... 78 B3
Harwin Cl
DUNHL/THL/PER WV6 ... 22 B3
Harwood Gv SHLY B90 ... 180 C5
Harwood St WBROM B70 ... 87 F3
Hasbury Cl HALE B63 ... 138 A5
Hasbury Rd RIDG/WDGT B32 ... 157 E2
Haseley Rd HDSW B21 ... 107 G2
SOLH B91 ... 164 A4
Haselor Rd SCFLD/BOLD B73 ... 76 C2
Haselour Rd
CHWD/FDBR/MGN B37 ... 113 H4
Haselwell Dr BVILLE B30 ... 177 H2
Haskell St WSL WS1 ... 57 F1
Haslucks Cl SHLY B90 ... 193 G1
Haslucks Cft SHLY B90 ... 180 A2
Haslucks Green Rd SHLY B90 ... 193 G1
Hassop Rd PBAR/PBCH B42 ... 74 D4
Hastings Ct DUDN DY1 ... 83 G4
Hastings Rd ERDW/GRVHL B23 ... 75 H4
Haswell Rd HALE B63 ... 137 H4
Hatcham Rd KGSTG B44 ... 76 A1
Hatchett St LOZ/NWT B19 ... 109 E4
Hatchford Av HIA/OLT B92 ... 148 A4
Hatchford Brook Rd
HIA/OLT B92 ... 148 A4
Hatch Heath Cl WMBN WV5 ... 64 D4
Hateley Dr
ETTPK/GDPK/PENN WV4 ... 52 C4
Hatfield Cl ERDW/GRVHL B23 ... 76 B4
Hatfield Rd HAG/WOL DY9 ... 136 A3
LOZ/NWT B19 ... 108 D1
Hathaway Cl WLNHL WV13 ... 39 F5
Hathaway Ms STRBR DY8 * ... 117 G1
Hathaway Rd MGN/WHC B75 ... 47 E1
SHLY B90 ... 180 B4
Hatherden Dr WALM/CURD B76 ... 78 C1
Hathersage Rd
PBAR/PBCH B42 ... 74 D4
Hatherton Gdns WOLVN WV10 ... 13 E5
Hatherton Gv SLYOAK B29 ... 158 B1
Hatherton Pl ALDR WS9 ... 30 A3
Hatherton Rd BILS/COS WV14 ... 54 B2
WSL WS1 ... 4 E3
Hatherton St WSL WS1 ... 4 E2
Hattersley Gv SPARK B11 ... 146 A4
Hatton Crs WOLVN WV10 ... 24 A3
Hatton Gdns PBAR/PBCH B42 ... 74 B4
Hatton Rd
DUNHL/THL/PER WV6 * ... 36 B2
Hattons Gv CDSL WV8 ... 10 D5
Hatton St BILS/COS WV14 ... 54 A4
Haughton Rd
BFLD/HDSWWD B20 ... 90 C5
Haunch La MOS/BIL B13 ... 161 G5
Haunchwood Dr
WALM/CURD B76 ... 78 B4
Havacre La BILS/COS WV14 ... 68 C1
Havelock Cl BDMR/CCFT WV3 ... 51 E1
Havelock Rd
BFLD/HDSWWD B20 ... 90 C4
SPARK B11 ... 145 G3
WASH/WDE B8 ... 110 C4
Haven Cft GTB/HAM B43 ... 73 F3
Haven Dr ACGN B27 ... 146 B4
The Haven
ALE/KHTH/YWD B14 ... 179 F1
BKHL/PFLD WV2 ... 37 E5
STRBR DY8 ... 117 H2
Haverford Dr RBRY B45 ... 188 B2
Havergal Wk HALE B63 ... 137 F3
Haverhill Cl BLOX/PEL WS3 ... 16 C4
Hawbridge Cl SHLY B90 ... 195 H2
Hawbush Gdns STRBR DY8 ... 118 C3
Hawbush Rd BLOX/PEL WS3 ... 28 A4
BRLYHL DY5 ... 118 C2
Hawcroft Gv BKDE/SHDE B34 ... 113 E3
Hawes Cl WSL WS1 ... 57 F2
Hawes La BLKHTH/ROWR B65 ... 103 H5
Hawes Rd WSL WS1 ... 57 F2
Haweswater Dr KGSWFD DY6 ... 99 H3
Hawfield Cl OLDBY B69 ... 104 A2
Hawfield Gv
CSCFLD/WYGN B72 ... 77 G4
Hawfield Rd OLDBY B69 ... 104 A2
Hawker Dr CVALE B35 ... 94 B4
Hawkesbury Rd SHLY B90 ... 179 H4
Hawkes Cl BVILLE B30 ... 160 A2
Hawkesford Cl CBROM B36 ... 112 C1
FOAKS/STRLY B74 ... 47 F4
Hawkesford Rd STETCH B33 ... 131 F1
Hawkes La WBROM B70 ... 71 E4
Hawkesley Crs NFLD/LBR B31 ... 175 F4
Hawkesley Dr NFLD/LBR B31 ... 175 F5
Hawkesley End
HWK/WKHTH B38 ... 176 B5
Hawkesley Mill La
NFLD/LBR B31 ... 175 F3
Hawkesley Rd DUDN DY1 ... 101 H1
Hawkes St SMHTH B10 ... 128 B4
Hawkestone Crs WBROM B70 ... 70 D5
Hawkestone Rd SLYOAK B29 ... 158 C3
Hawkeswell Cl HIA/OLT B92 ... 164 A2
Hawkeswell Dr KGSWFD DY6 ... 99 H1
Hawkeswell La
CSHL/WTROR B46 ... 133 H1
Hawkesyard Rd
ERDE/BCHGN B24 ... 92 C5
Hawkhurst Rd
ALE/KHTH/YWD B14 ... 178 B3
Hawkinge Dr CVALE B35 ... 94 C2
Hawkins Cl DIG/EDG B5 ... 144 A1
Hawkins Cft TPTN/OCK DY4 ... 85 G3
Hawkin's Pl BILS/COS WV14 ... 54 B5
Hawkins St WBROM B70 ... 71 E3
Hawkley Cl WOLV WV1 ... 38 B3
Hawkley Rd WOLV WV1 ... 38 B3
Hawkmoor Gdns
HWK/WKHTH B38 ... 177 E5
Hawksford Crs WOLVN WV10 ... 23 F3
Hawkshead Dr DOR/KN B93 ... 196 D2
Hawksmoor Dr
DUNHL/THL/PER WV6 ... 34 B2
Hawkstone Ct
DUNHL/THL/PER WV6 ... 20 B5
Hawkswell Av WMBN WV5 ... 81 E1
Hawkswell Dr WLNHL WV13 ... 39 F5
Hawkswood Dr
BILS/COS WV14 ... 54 D5
Hawkswood Gv
ALE/KHTH/YWD B14 ... 178 D2
Hawksworth Crs
CHWD/FDBR/MGN B37 ... 132 C1
Hawley Cl RUSH/SHEL WS4 ... 42 B1
Hawnby Gv WALM/CURD B76 ... 78 C1
Hawne Cl HALE B63 ... 138 A1
The Hawnelands HALE B63 ... 138 B2
Hawne La HALE B63 ... 138 A1
Hawskford Crs WOLVN WV10 ... 23 F3
Hawthorn Brook Wy
ERDW/GRVHL B23 ... 76 C3
Hawthorn Cl BORD B9 ... 127 H3
ERDW/GRVHL B23 ... 76 D4
Hawthorn Coppice
HAG/WOL DY9 ... 152 C4
Hawthorn Cft
LGLYGN/QTN B68 ... 123 H5
Hawthorne Dr HLYWD B47 ... 192 D2
Hawthorne Gv SEDG DY3 ... 83 F4
Hawthorne La CDSL WV8 ... 20 D1
Hawthorne Rd
BKHL/PFLD WV2 ... 52 B2
BVILLE B30 ... 159 F5
CBROM B36 ... 113 G2
DUDN DY1 ... 84 C2
EDG B15 ... 125 G5
HALE B63 ... 138 A5
SHHTH WV12 ... 26 B3
WNSFLD WV11 ... 15 E4
Hawthorn Gv LOZ/NWT B19 * ... 108 C1
Hawthorn Pk
BFLD/HDSWWD B20 ... 89 G3
Hawthorn Pl WSLW WS2 ... 40 C2
Hawthorn Rd BRLYHL DY5 ... 119 G4
CSCFLD/WYGN B72 ... 77 G2
DARL/WED WS10 ... 55 H4
DSYBK/YTR WS5 ... 57 F5
FOAKS/STRLY B74 ... 45 G4
KGSTG B44 ... 75 G4
RUSH/SHEL WS4 ... 28 D2
TPTN/OCK DY4 ... 69 G3
WOLV WV1 ... 38 B5
The Hawthorns
HAG/WOL DY9 * ... 169 F1
MOS/BIL B13 * ... 144 D4
Hawthorn Ter DARL/WED WS10 ... 55 H4
Haxby Av BKDE/SHDE B34 ... 112 C3
The Haybarn WALM/CURD B76 ... 78 C2
Haybridge Av STRBR DY8 ... 152 B5
Haybrook Dr SPARK B11 ... 145 H3
Haycock Pl DARL/WED WS10 ... 55 E1
Haycroft Av WASH/WDE B8 ... 110 C4
Haycroft Dr FOAKS/STRLY B74 ... 47 E1
Haydn Sanders Sq WSL WS1 ... 4 D6
Haydock Cl CBROM B36 ... 111 G1
DUNHL/THL/PER WV6 ... 22 D5
Haydon Cl DOR/KN B93 ... 198 D1
Haydon Cft STETCH B33 ... 130 C1
Haye House Gv CBROM B36 ... 112 A2
Hayes Crs LGLYGN/QTN B68 ... 105 H4
Hayes Cft HWK/WKHTH B38 ... 190 C1
Hayes Dr ERDE/BCHGN B24 ... 93 H1
Hayes Gv ERDE/BCHGN B24 ... 77 H5
Hayes La HAG/WOL DY9 ... 137 E1
Hayes Meadow
CSCFLD/WYGN B72 ... 77 H4
Hayes Rd LGLYGN/QTN B68 ... 105 H4
Hayes St WBROM B70 ... 87 E2
The Hayes HAG/WOL DY9 ... 137 E2
NFLD/LBR B31 ... 190 A1
SHHTH WV12 ... 25 H4
Hayfield Ct MOS/BIL B13 ... 144 D5
Hayfield Gdns MOS/BIL B13 ... 144 D5
Hayfield Rd MOS/BIL B13 ... 144 D5
Hay Gn HAG/WOL DY9 ... 136 B2
Hay Green La BVILLE B30 ... 159 F4
Hay Hall Rd SPARK B11 ... 145 H2
Hay Hl DSYBK/YTR WS5 ... 43 G5
Hayland Rd ERDW/GRVHL B23 ... 76 C5
Hay La SHLY B90 ... 195 G2
Hayle Cl HWK/WKHTH B38 ... 177 F3
Hayley Green Rd
RIDG/WDGT B32 ... 157 F2
Hayley Park Rd HALE B63 ... 154 C2
Hayling Cl RBRY B45 ... 173 H4
Hayling Gv BDMR/CCFT WV3 ... 51 H2
The Hayloft HALE B63 ... 154 C1
Haynes La DSYBK/YTR WS5 ... 57 H4
Hay Pk DIG/EDG B5 ... 143 H1
Haypits Cl HHTH/SAND B71 ... 72 A4
Hayrick Dr KGSWFD DY6 ... 99 F2
Hay Rd YDLY B25 ... 129 E5
Hayseech CDYHTH B64 ... 121 G5
Hayseech Rd HALE B63 ... 138 B1
The Hays Kent's Moat
LGN/SDN/BHAMAIR B26 ... 130 C3
Haytor Av
ALE/KHTH/YWD B14 ... 160 D5
Haywain Cl COVEN WV9 ... 11 H5
Hayward Rd MGN/WHC B75 ... 62 C1
Haywards Cl BLOX/PEL WS3 ... 17 H4
ERDW/GRVHL B23 ... 92 C1
Hayward St BILS/COS WV14 ... 68 B3
Haywharf Rd BRLYHL DY5 ... 100 D4
Haywood Dr
DUNHL/THL/PER WV6 ... 35 G1
RMSLY B62 ... 122 A4
Haywood Rd STETCH B33 ... 131 F2
Haywood's Farm
HHTH/SAND B71 ... 72 B1
Hazel Av DARL/WED WS10 ... 56 A4
SCFLD/BOLD B73 ... 76 A2
Hazelbank HWK/WKHTH B38 ... 176 C3
Hazelbeach Rd WASH/WDE B8 ... 110 D4
Hazelbeech Rd WBROM B70 ... 87 F4
Hazel Cft
CHWD/FDBR/MGN B37 ... 132 B3
NFLD/LBR B31 ... 175 G2
Hazeldene Gv AST/WIT B6 * ... 109 E1
Hazeldene Rd HALE B63 ... 138 A5
STETCH B33 ... 131 F5
Hazel Dr HLYWD B47 ... 192 D2
SLYOAK B29 ... 158 B3
Hazeley Cl HRBN B17 ... 124 B5
Hazel Gdns ACGN B27 * ... 146 C3
CDSL WV8 ... 10 C3
Hazel Gv BILS/COS WV14 ... 54 A1
HOCK/TIA B94 ... 198 A5
STRBR DY8 ... 134 C4
WBROM B70 ... 87 G5
WMBN WV5 ... 65 E4
Hazelhurst Rd
ALE/KHTH/YWD B14 ... 161 E3
CBROM B36 ... 113 G2
Hazelmere Dr BDMR/CCFT WV3 ... 35 E4
Hazelmere Rd HLGN/YWD B28 ... 162 D2
Hazeloak Rd SHLY B90 ... 180 A4
Hazel Rd BDMR/CCFT WV3 ... 51 E1
DUDN DY1 ... 84 C4
KGSWFD DY6 ... 100 A4
RBRY B45 ... 187 H2
TPTN/OCK DY4 ... 70 A2
Hazelton Cl SOLH B91 ... 181 H4
Hazeltree Cft ACGN B27 ... 146 B5
Hazeltree Gv DOR/KN B93 ... 196 C5
Hazelville Gv HLGN/YWD B28 ... 163 E4
Hazelville Rd HLGN/YWD B28 ... 163 E4
Hazelwell Crs BVILLE B30 ... 160 B4
Hazelwell Dr
ALE/KHTH/YWD B14 ... 160 D4
Hazelwell Fordrough
BVILLE B30 ... 160 B3
Hazelwell La BVILLE B30 ... 160 A3
Hazelwell Rd BVILLE B30 ... 160 A4
Hazelwood Dr WNSFLD WV11 ... 24 A5
Hazelwood Gv SHHTH WV12 ... 26 B5
Hazelwood Rd ACGN B27 ... 146 B5
DUDN DY1 ... 83 H1
FOAKS/STRLY B74 ... 44 D4
Hazlemere Dr
FOAKS/STRLY B74 ... 47 E4
Hazlitt Gv BVILLE B30 ... 176 B1
Headborough Wk ALDR WS9 ... 30 B1
Headingley Dr KINVER DY7 ... 116 D3
Headingley Rd HDSW B21 ... 89 G4
Headland Dr WASH/WDE B8 ... 110 B4
Headland Rd BDMR/CCFT WV3 ... 34 D4
The Headlands
FOAKS/STRLY B74 ... 46 A2
Headley Cft HWK/WKHTH B38 ... 176 B5
Headley Heath La
HWK/WKHTH B38 ... 191 F1
Headley Ri SHLY B90 ... 180 D3
Headway Rd WOLVN WV10 ... 12 C4
Heale Cl HALE B63 ... 120 A5
Heanor Cft AST/WIT B6 ... 109 H1
Heantun Ri WOLV WV1 * ... 37 E1
Heantun Rw WNSFLD WV11 * ... 15 F5
Heartland Ms
BLKHTH/ROWR B65 ... 121 H2
Heartlands Pkwy
WASH/WDE B8 ... 110 A4
Heartlands Pl WASH/WDE B8 ... 110 C5
Heath Acres DARL/WED WS10 ... 55 E4
Heath Bridge Cl
RUSH/SHEL WS4 ... 28 C2
Heathbrook Av KGSWFD DY6 ... 99 F2
Heathcliff Rd DUDS DY2 ... 103 F2
SPARK B11 ... 145 H3
Heath Cl BVILLE B30 ... 159 F5
MGN/WHC B75 ... 63 F1
TPTN/OCK DY4 ... 85 H1
Heathcote Av SOLH B91 ... 181 E2
Heathcote Rd BVILLE B30 ... 160 A5
Heath Cft NFLD/LBR B31 ... 189 G1
Heath Croft Rd MGN/WHC B75 ... 47 G4
Heath End Rd HAG/WOL DY9 ... 185 G1
Heather Av DSYBK/YTR WS5 ... 57 H4
Heather Cl CBROM B36 ... 114 A1
WNSFLD WV11 ... 25 E5
Heather Court Gdns
FOAKS/STRLY B74 ... 47 E5
Heather Cft KGSTG B44 ... 75 F2
Heather Dl MOS/BIL B13 ... 143 G5
Heather Dr RBRY B45 ... 187 H2
Heather Gv SHHTH WV12 ... 40 C1
SOLH B91 ... 165 G4
Heatherleigh Rd CBROM B36 ... 113 H1
Heather Rd BLOX/PEL WS3 ... 26 D2
DUDN DY1 ... 84 C2
GTB/HAM B43 ... 73 E3
SMHTH B10 ... 128 D4
SMTHWKW B67 ... 106 A4
Heath Farm Rd CDSL WV8 ... 10 D5
STRBR DY8 ... 135 E4
Heathfield Av
BFLD/HDSWWD B20 ... 108 B1
Heathfield Cl CDYHTH B64 ... 121 F2
DOR/KN B93 ... 197 E3
Heathfield Dr BLOX/PEL WS3 ... 16 D5
Heathfield Gdns STRBR DY8 ... 135 F3
Heathfield La DARL/WED WS10 ... 55 E2
Heathfield La West
DARL/WED WS10 ... 54 D3
Heathfield Rd
ALE/KHTH/YWD B14 ... 161 E2
FOAKS/STRLY B74 ... 46 D2
HALE B63 ... 138 A4
LOZ/NWT B19 ... 108 B2
Heathfields CDSL WV8 ... 20 C1
Heathfield Wy CDYHTH B64 ... 121 F3
Heath Gdns SOLH B91 ... 165 F4
Heath Gn DUDN DY1 ... 83 H1
Heathgreen Cl
CHWD/FDBR/MGN B37 ... 132 D1
Heath Green Gv WSNGN B18 * ... 107 G5
Heath Green Rd WSNGN B18 ... 107 G5
Heath Gv CDSL WV8 ... 10 D4
Heath Hill Rd
DUNHL/THL/PER WV6 ... 34 C4
Heath House Dr WMBN WV5 ... 80 B1
Heath House La CDSL WV8 ... 20 C2
Heathland Av BKDE/SHDE B34 ... 112 C2
Heathlands WMBN WV5 ... 80 B1
Heathlands Cl KGSWFD DY6 ... 100 A1
Heathlands Gv NFLD/LBR B31 ... 175 G4
Heathlands Rd
SCFLD/BOLD B73 ... 76 D1
The Heathlands
BLKHTH/ROWR B65 ... 122 A3
STRBR DY8 ... 135 H3
WMBN WV5 ... 80 B1
Heath La HHTH/SAND B71 ... 71 H4
STRBR DY8 ... 135 G3
Heathleigh Rd
HWK/WKHTH B38 ... 176 A5
Heathmere Av YDLY B25 ... 129 H4
Heathmere Dr
CHWD/FDBR/MGN B37 ... 131 H2
Heath Mill Cl WMBN WV5 ... 80 B2
Heath Mill La BORD B9 ... 127 G3
Heath Mill Rd WMBN WV5 ... 80 B2
Heath Pk WOLVN WV10 * ... 12 C1
Heath Ri ALE/KHTH/YWD B14 ... 178 C4
Heath Rd BVILLE B30 ... 176 A1
DARL/WED WS10 ... 40 C5
DUDS DY2 ... 120 B2
HLYWD B47 ... 192 C1
SHHTH WV12 ... 26 B2
SOLH B91 ... 165 F4
Heath Rd South
NFLD/LBR B31 ... 175 H1
Heathside Dr BLOX/PEL WS3 ... 18 A3
HWK/WKHTH B38 ... 177 F4
Heath St BLKHTH/ROWR B65 ... 122 A3
STRBR DY8 ... 135 F2
WSNGN B18 ... 107 F4
Heath St South WSNGN B18 * ... 107 H5
Heath Wy BKDE/SHDE B34 ... 112 B2
Heathway Cl BKDE/SHDE B34 ... 112 C3
Heathy Farm Cl
RIDG/WDGT B32 ... 157 F1
Heathy Ri RIDG/WDGT B32 ... 140 A5
Heaton Cl WOLVN WV10 ... 13 E2
Heaton Dr EDG B15 ... 125 H4
Heaton Rd SOLH B91 ... 164 B3
Heaton St WSNGN B18 ... 108 B3
Hebden Gv HLGN/YWD B28 ... 179 F2
SHHTH WV12 ... 25 H1
Heddon Pl VAUX/NECH B7 * ... 127 G1
Hedera Cl DSYBK/YTR WS5 ... 57 H5
Hedgefield Gv HALE B63 ... 137 G3
Hedgerow Dr KGSWFD DY6 ... 81 H5
The Hedgerows RMSLY B62 ... 172 B1
The Hedges WMBN WV5 ... 64 C5
Hedgetree Cft
CHWD/FDBR/MGN B37 ... 132 C2
Hedgley Gv STETCH B33 ... 112 C5
Hedingham Gv
CHWD/FDBR/MGN B37 ... 132 D2
Hedley Cft CVALE B35 ... 94 D2
Hednesford Rd BRWNH WS8 ... 8 C2
Heeley Rd SLYOAK B29 ... 142 D5
Hefford Dr SMTHWK B66 ... 106 C3
Helena St CBHAMW B1 ... 2 C4
Helenny Cl WNSFLD WV11 ... 24 A5
Helford Cl TPTN/OCK DY4 ... 84 D2
Hellaby Cl CSCFLD/WYGN B72 ... 62 B4
Hellier Av TPTN/OCK DY4 ... 85 H2
Hellier Dr WMBN WV5 ... 64 C4
Hellier Rd WOLVN WV10 ... 13 E5
Hellier St DUDS DY2 ... 102 C1
Helming Dr WOLV WV1 ... 38 B2
Helmsdale Wy SEDG DY3 ... 68 A4
Helmsley Cl BRLYHL DY5 ... 119 E4
Helmsley Rd WNSFLD WV11 ... 24 C2
Helmswood Dr
CHWD/FDBR/MGN B37 ... 132 C4
Helston Cl DSYBK/YTR WS5 ... 58 B1
STRBR DY8 ... 117 G2
Helstone Gv SPARK B11 ... 146 A3
Helston Rd DSYBK/YTR WS5 ... 58 A2
Hembs Crs GTB/HAM B43 ... 73 E3
Hemlingford Cft
CHWD/FDBR/MGN B37 ... 132 A5
Hemlingford Rd
CHWD/FDBR/MGN B37 ... 113 G3
WALM/CURD B76 ... 78 B4
Hemmings Cl STRBR DY8 ... 135 E2
WOLVN WV10 ... 7 K1
Hemmings St DARL/WED WS10 ... 40 A5
Hemplands Rd STRBR DY8 ... 135 F2
Hempole La TPTN/OCK DY4 ... 70 B5
Hemyock Rd SLYOAK B29 ... 158 D2
Henbury Dr
CHWD/FDBR/MGN B37 ... 114 D5
Henbury Rd ACGN B27 ... 146 D4
Henderson Wk TPTN/OCK DY4 ... 69 H3
Henderson Wy
BLKHTH/ROWR B65 ... 122 A3
Hendon Cl SEDG DY3 ... 83 F4
WOLVN WV10 ... 23 G2
Hendon Rd SPARK B11 ... 144 D2
Heneage Pl VAUX/NECH B7 * ... 109 G5
Heneage St VAUX/NECH B7 ... 3 K1
Heneage St West
VAUX/NECH B7 ... 3 K2
Henfield Cl WNSFLD WV11 ... 24 D4
Hengham Rd
LGN/SDN/BHAMAIR B26 ... 130 C3
Henley Cl BLOX/PEL WS3 ... 28 A1
SCFLD/BOLD B73 ... 77 F3
TPTN/OCK DY4 ... 86 B1
Henley Crs SOLH B91 ... 164 D3

Henley Dr *MGN/WHC* B75 ....47 E2
Henley Rd *WOLVN* WV10............22 D1
Henley St *SPARK* B11................127 G5
Henley Vls *BHTH/HG* B12 * 144 D2
Henlow Cl *TPTN/OCK* DY4...........84 D1

Henlow Rd
  ALE/KHTH/YWD B14..........178 B3
The Hennalls *CBROM* B36............112 B2
Henn Dr *TPTN/OCK* DY4..............69 G3
Henne Dr *BILS/COS* WV14............68 C2
Henn St *TPTN/OCK* DY4..............69 G3
Henrietta St *LOZ/NWT* B19..............2 E2
Henry Rd *YDLY* B25.................146 C1
Henry St *WSLW* WS2....................4 B4
Hensborough *SHLY* B90............194 A3
Hensel Dr *BDMR/CCFT* WV3........35 G5
Henshaw Gv *YDLY* B25.............129 G5
Henshaw Rd *SMHTH* B10...........128 B4
Henstead St *DIG/EDG* B5..........126 D4

Henwood Cl
  DUNHL/THL/PER WV6..........35 H2
Henwood La *SOLH* B91............185 F1

Henwood Rd
  DUNHL/THL/PER WV6..........35 H2
Hepburn Cl *ALDR* WS9.................44 A1
Hepburn Edge
  ERDE/BCHGN B24...................93 F2
Hepworth Cl
  DUNHL/THL/PER WV6..........34 D1
Herbert Rd *ALDR* WS9................30 A1
  HDSW B21..........................89 H5
  SMHTH B10........................128 A3
  SMTHWKW B67...................126 C3
  SOLH B91.........................181 H2

Herberts Park Rd
  DARL/WED WS10..................54 D2
Herbert St *BILS/COS* WV14.........53 F2
  WBROM B70........................87 H3
  WOLV WV1............................7 G2
Herbill Cl
  ETTPK/GDPK/PENN WV4......52 B4
Hereford Cl *BHTH/HG* B12......144 C1
Hereford Cl *ALDR* WS9...............30 A2
  RBRY B45..........................174 A3
Hereford Rd *HHTH/SAND* B71....71 F4
Hereford Rd *DUDS* DY2.............121 E1
  LGLYGN/QTN B68................123 F5
Hereford Sq *WASH/WDE* B8.....110 A4
Hereford St *WSLW* WS2.............42 A1
Hereward Ri *HALE* B63...............68 A5
  RMSLY B62........................139 E2
Heritage Cl *LGLYGN/QTN* B68...105 G5
Heritage Wy *STETCH* B33.........131 F1
  TPTN/OCK DY4.....................85 H1
Hermes Rd
  LGN/SDN/BHAMAIR B26......149 G3
Hermitage Dr
  WALM/CURD B76...................63 C4
Hermitage Rd *EDG* B15...........125 E4
  ERDW/GRVHL B23...............92 E5
  SOLH B91.........................165 E5
The Hermitage *SOLH* B91.........165 E4
Hermit St *SEDG* DY3..................83 F2
Hernall Cft
  LGN/SDN/BHAMAIR B26......130 C5
Herne Cl *WSNGN* B18..............108 A5
Hernefield Rd
  BKDE/SHDE B34.................112 C2
Hernhurst *RIDG/WDGT* B32.....140 C1
Hern Rd *BRLYHL* DY5...............136 A1
Heron Cl *BRWNH* WS8...............9 H3
  SHLY B90.........................194 D5
Herondale Rd
  LGN/SDN/BHAMAIR B26......147 F1
  STRBR DY8.......................134 C3
Heronfield Dr *NFLD/LBR* B31....189 F2
Heronfield Wy *SOLH* B91.........165 G5
Heron MI *BLOX/PEL* WS3..........17 G4
Heron Rd *LGLYGN/QTN* B68....123 E2
The Heronry
  DUNHL/THL/PER WV6............34 D3
Herons Av *HRBN* B17.............142 A4
Heronswood Dr *BRLYHL* DY5...119 F5
Heronswood Rd *RBRY* B45.......188 B2
Heronville Dr *WBROM* B70........71 E4
Heronville Rd *WBROM* B70........71 E5
Heron Wy *RBRY* B45................187 G1
Herrick Rd *WASH/WDE* B8......110 C4
Herrick St *BDMR/CCFT* WV3.......6 D5

Herringshaw Cft
  WALM/CURD B76...................63 E5
Hertford St *BHTH/HG* B12.......144 C2
Hertford Wy *DOR/KN* B93.......197 F4
Hervey Gv *ERDE/BCHGN* B24....77 H5
Hesket Av *LGLYGN/QTN* B68...123 G3
Hesketh Crs
  ERDW/GRVHL B23.................92 A1
Hessian Cl *BILS/COS* WV14.......68 B1
Hestia Dr *SLYOAK* B29............159 G2
Heston Av *PBAR/PBCH* B42.......74 A3
Hever Av *KGSTG* B44.................75 C2
Hever Cl *DUDN* DY1....................83 G4
Heweli Cl *KGSWFD* DY6.............81 H5
  NFLD/LBR B31...................189 F1
Hewitson Gdns
  SMTHWKW B67* 124 B2
Hewitt St *DARL/WED* WS10.......55 E2
Hexham Wy *DUDN* DY1.............83 H4
Hexton Cl *SHLY* B90................179 F3
Heybarnes Rd *SMHTH* B10......129 E5
Heycott Gv *HWK/WKHTH* B38..177 G3
Heydon Rd *BRLYHL* DY5..........100 D4
Heyford Gv *SOLH* B91.............182 A5
Heyford Wy *CVALE* B35.............94 D1
Heygate Wy *ALDR* WS9..............30 B3
Hibberd Ct *SHLY* B90 * 194 A5
The Highlands *SHLY* B90 * 181 E5
High Leasowes *HALE* B63.......138 C3
High Meadow Rd
  HWK/WKHTH B38................177 E3
High Mdw
  DUNHL/THL/PER WV6..........35 G3
  WMBN WV5...........................55 H3
Highmoor Cl *BILS/COS* WV14.....53 H5
  SHHTH WV12.......................25 H3
Highmoor Rd
  BLKHTH/ROWR B65............121 H2
Highmore Dr *RIDG/WDGT* B32.157 G2

Hidcote Gv
  CHWD/FDBR/MGN B37........132 A5
  STETCH B33......................131 E4
Hidson Rd *ERDW/GRVHL* B23....92 A2
Higgins Av *BILS/COS* WV14........68 D1
Higgins La *RIDG/WDGT* B32.....140 C2
Higgins Wk *SMTHWK* B66.........106 D3
Higgs Field Crs *CDYHTH* B64...121 H5
Higham's Cl
  BLKHTH/ROWR B65............121 H1
Higham Wy *WOLVN* WV10.........23 C4
High Arcal Dr *SEDG* DY3...........67 H4
High Arcal Rd *SEDG* DY3..........82 D2
High Av *CDYHTH* B64...............122 D5
High Beeches *GTB/HAM* B43.....73 F2
Highbridge Rd *DUDS* DY2.......102 B5
  SCFLD/BOLD B73...................77 E2
High Brink Rd
  CSHL/WTROR B46...............115 F2
Highbrook Cl *COVEN* WV9.........12 A5
Highbullen *DARL/WED* WS10.....70 D1
Highbury Av
  BLKHTH/ROWR B65............122 B1
  HDSW B21 * 107 H1
Highbury Cl
  BLKHTH/ROWR B65............122 B1
Highbury Rd
  ALE/KHTH/YWD B14..........160 D2
  FOAKS/STRLY B74...............46 A2
  LGLYGN/QTN B66...............105 F4
High Clere *CDYHTH* B64...........121 H5
Highcrest Cl *NFLD/LBR* B31.....189 G1
High Cft *ALDR* WS9....................19 H5
Highcroft *BLOX/PEL* WS3 * 18 B1
High Cft *GTB/HAM* B43..............75 E2
Highcroft Av *STRBR* DY8..........117 F1
Highcroft Cl *HIA/OLT* B92........148 A5
Highcroft Dr *FOAKS/STRLY* B74..45 G2
Highcroft Rd *ERDW/GRVHL* B23..92 C5
Highdown Crs *SHLY* B90..........195 C2
High Ercal Av *BRLYHL* DY5......119 E2
High Farm Rd *HALE* B63..........138 B4
  RMSLY B62.......................122 D4
Highfield Av *BILS/COS* WV14.....54 A4
  RUSH/SHEL WS4..................29 E2
  WOLV WV10..........................13 G5
Highfield Cl *HLGN/YWD* B28....162 B5
Highfield Crs
  BLKHTH/ROWR B65............121 H4
  HALE B63..........................137 H2
  WNSFLD WV11.....................24 B4
Highfield Dr *SCFLD/BOLD* B73...76 D4
Highfield La *HAG/WOL* DY9......171 E2
  HALE B63..........................138 C3
  RIDG/WDGT B32................140 C3
Highfield Ms *HALE* B63............137 H1
Highfield Rd
  ALE/KHTH/YWD B14..........162 B5
  BLKHTH/ROWR B65............121 H3
  BLOX/PEL WS3....................18 A3
  DUDS DY2..........................85 E5
  EDG B15..........................124 B4
  GTB/HAM B43......................73 E4
  HALE B63..........................137 H1
  MOS/BIL B13.....................144 C4
  SEDG DY3..........................66 C5
  SMTHWKW B67.................106 D4
  STRBR DY8........................118 C2
  TPTN/OCK DY4....................69 H3
  WASH/WDE B8...................110 C4
Highfield Rd North
  BLOX/PEL WS3....................17 H2
Highfields Ct
  ETTPK/GDPK/PENN WV4 * ...50 D2
Highfields Dr *BILS/COS* WV14....53 H5
  WMBN WV5..........................81 E1
Highfields Rd *BILS/COS* WV14...53 H5
The Highfields
  DUNHL/THL/PER WV6..........35 E3
Highfield Wy *ALDR* WS9.............19 H5
Highgate *FOAKS/STRLY* B74......45 H4
  SEDG DY3............................83 G1
Highgate Av
  ETTPK/GDPK/PENN WV4.......5 C7
  WSL WS1............................57 F1
Highgate Cl *BHTH/HG* B12......127 F5
  WSL WS1............................57 F1
Highgate Dr *WSL* WS1...............57 F1
Highgate Middleway
  BHTH/HG B12....................127 F5
Highgate Pl *BHTH/HG* B12......127 C5
Highgate Rd *BHTH/HG* B12......127 F5
  DUDS DY2.........................101 H3
  WSL WS1............................57 F1
Highgate Sq *BHTH/HG* B12.....127 F5
Highgate St *BHTH/HG* B12......127 F5
  CDYHTH B64.....................121 F2
Highgrove
  DUNHL/THL/PER WV6..........35 C2
Highgrove Cl *SHHTH* WV12.......25 H4
Highgrove Pl *DUDN* DY1...........83 H4
High Haden Crs *CDYHTH* B64..121 G4
High Haden Rd *CDYHTH* B64...121 H4
High Heath Cl *BVILLE* B30.......159 F5
High Hill *WNSFLD* WV11............15 G5
High Holborn *SEDG* DY3...........67 F4
High House Dr *RBRY* B45........187 H5
Highland Ms *BILS/COS* WV14....68 D2
Highland Rdg *RMSLY* B62........139 F2
High Land Rd *ALDR* WS9...........19 H4
Highland Rd *CDYHTH* B64.......121 E2
  DUDN DY1..........................84 A3
  ERDW/GRVHL B23...............92 D1
  GTB/HAM B43......................73 G1
Highlands Rd *BDMR/CCFT* WV3..35 H5
  SHLY B90.........................195 E1

High Oak *BRLYHL* DY5.............101 E3
Highover Dr *MGN/WHC* B75.......47 E1
Highpark Av *STRBR* DY8..........134 D2
High Park Cl *SEDG* DY3.............67 F2
  SMTHWK B66.....................106 D4
High Park Crs *SEDG* DY3...........67 F2
High Park Rd *HALE* B63...........137 F2
High Park St *VAUX/NECH* B7...109 H5
High Rdg *ALDR* WS9.................29 H5
High Ridge Cl *ALDR* WS9...........29 G5
  DARL/WED WS10..................54 C4
High Ridge *SHHTH* WV12...........26 A5
High St *ALDR* WS9....................30 B4
  ALKHTH/YWD B14..............161 E2
  BILS/COS WV14....................54 A3
  BLKHTH/ROWR B65............122 A3
  BLOX/PEL WS3.....................18 A4
  BRLYHL DY5........................27 F1
  BRWNH WS8.........................19 E1
  CBHAMNE B4..........................3 G5
  CDYHTH B64.....................120 D3
  CSCFLD/WYGN B72...............62 C3
  CSHL/WTROR B46..............115 F2
  CVALE B35..........................94 D3
  DARL/WED WS10..................54 C4
  SEDG DY3............................55 E2
  DOR/KN B93......................197 G2
  DUDN DY1.........................102 C1
  DUNHL/THL/PER WV6..........35 H1
  ERDW/GRVHL B23...............92 D2
  HAG/WOL DY9....................184 C1
  HALE B63.........................138 D3
  HIA/OLT B92.....................167 G4
  HRBN B17.........................142 A2
  KGSWFD DY6........................99 F1
  LOZ/NWT B19...................109 F2
  RIDG/WDGT B32................140 A1
  SEDG DY3............................67 F2
  SEDG DY3............................80 C4
  SHLY B90.........................179 E3
  SMTHWKW B67.................106 B3
  SOLH B91.........................182 A1
  STRBR DY8........................135 E1
  TPTN/OCK DY4....................85 E1
  WASH/WDE B8...................110 B4
  WMBN WV5..........................65 F5
  WNSFLD WV11.....................24 C5
  WSL WS1..............................4 E4
High Street Bordesley
  BHTH/HG B12....................127 G3
High Street Deritend
  BHTH/HG B12......................3 K7
High Street Prec
  DARL/WED WS10..................55 F2
Highters Cl
  ALE/KHTH/YWD B14..........178 D3
Highters Heath La
  ALE/KHTH/YWD B14..........178 C4
Highters Rd
  ALE/KHTH/YWD B14..........178 C2
High Timbers *RBRY* B45..........175 H4
High Tower *VAUX/NECH* B7 * ...109 H4
Hightree Cl *RIDG/WDGT* B32...157 F1
High Trees *BFLD/HDSWWD* B20..89 H3
High Trees Rd *DOR/KN* B93.....197 F3
High Vw *BILS/COS* WV14............67 H2
Highview Dr *KGSWFD* DY6.......100 B5
Highview St *DUDS* DY2..............85 E5
Highwater Cl *MGN/WHC* B75.....47 E1
Highville Gdns *STRBR* DY8.......135 H4
Hillwood Av *SHLY* B90.............195 G2
Hillwood Cl *KGSWFD* DY6..........99 G5
Hillwood Common Rd
  LICHS WS14..........................33 F4
Hill Wood Rd *MGN/WHC* B75....53 G5
Hillwood Rd *NFLD/LBR* B31......158 A3
Hillyard Rd *HAG/WOL* DY9........79 G5
Hilsea Cl *CDSL* WV8.................122 A5
Hilton Av
  ETTPK/GDPK/PENN WV4.......50 C4
  HLGN/YWD B28..................179 G1
Hilton Cl *BLOX/PEL* WS3...........26 D1
Hilton Cross *WOLVN* WV10........13 H2
Hilton Dr *CSCFLD/WYGN* B72...77 G3
Hilton La *BILS/COS* WV14...........38 A5
Hilton Pk
  ETTPK/GDPK/PENN WV4......52 D4
  OLDBY B69........................104 A1
  WOLVN WV10......................26 A2
Hilton St *WBROM* B70................87 E3
  WOLV WV10...........................7 J1
Himbleton Cft *SHLY* B90.........195 G2
Himley Av *DUDN* DY1................83 H4
Himley Cl *CTB/HAM* B43...........73 E1
  SHHTH WV12.......................26 A5
Himley Crs
  ETTPK/GDPK/PENN WV4......52 A3
Himley Gdns *SEDG* DY3..............82 B3
Himley Gv *RBRY* B45...............188 B2
Himley La *SEDG* DY3.................80 D4
Himley Rd *DUDN* DY1................83 G5
  DUDS DY2..........................84 A5
Hinchliffe Av *BILS/COS* WV14....67 G5
Hinchwick Ct *DOR/KN* B93.....196 D5
Hinckes Rd
  DUNHL/THL/PER WV6..........21 F5
Hinckley Ct *LGLYGN/QTN* B68 * .123 F5
Hinckley St *DIG/EDG* B5..............3 F7
Hincks St *BKHL/PFLD* WV2........54 D1
Hindhead Rd
  ALE/KHTH/YWD B14..........179 E1
Hindlip Cl *HALE* B63...............138 B5
Hindlow Cl *VAUX/NECH* B7......109 H5
Hindon Gv *ACGN* B27.............163 F3
Hindon Sq *EDG* B15...............125 H4
Hingeston St *WSNGN* B18.........2 A4
Hingley Cft *ALDR* WS9..............45 F2
Hingley Rd *HALE* B63..............121 G5
Hingley St *CDYHTH* B64..........120 D3
Hinksford Gdns *SEDG* DY3........80 C4
Hinksford La *SEDG* DY3.............80 A5

Hillhampton Cl *HIA/OLT* B92...148 A5
Hill Hook Rd *FOAKS/STRLY* B74..32 C4
Hill House La *STECH* B33...........130 B1
Hillhurst Gv *CBROM* B36............95 F5
Hilliard Cft *NFLD/LBR* B31.........60 D5
Hilliards Cft *PBAR/PBCH* B42.....74 A5
Hillingford Av *GTB/HAM* B43.....59 H4
Hill La *GTB/HAM* B43.................73 G1
  HAG/WOL DY9...................170 C1
  HHTH/SAND B71...................71 F3
Hillman Dr *DUDS* DY2..............103 E2
Hillman Gv *CBROM* B36.............95 G5
Hillmeads Dr *DUDS* DY2..........103 E2
Hillmeads Rd
  HWK/WKHTH B38................177 E4
Hillmorton Rd *DOR/KN* B93....197 E5
  FOAKS/STRLY B74................45 H1
Hillmount Cl *HLGN/YWD* B28...145 G5
Hill Pk *ALDR* WS9......................19 G3
Hill Pas *CDYHTH* B64..............121 E2
Hill Pl *WNSFLD* WV11................25 G1
Hillrise *ALDR* WS9.....................19 H3
Hill Rd *OLDBY* B69.....................85 G4
  WLNH. WV13.......................40 A2
Hillside *BRWNH* WS8..................19 G1
Hill Side *SEDG* DY3....................83 E2
Hillside *WMBN* WV5...................64 C4
Hillside Av *BLKHTH/ROWR* B65..121 H4
  BRLYHL DY5........................137 H1
Hillside Cl *RIDG/WDGT* B32.....157 E2
Hillside Cft *HIA/OLT* B92.........148 C3
Hillside Dr
  CHWD/FDBR/MGN B37........113 H5
  FOAKS/STRLY B74................60 B1
  PBAR/PBCH B42..................74 A5
Hillside Gdns
  CHWD/FDBR/MGN B37 * 113 H5
  WOLV WV1..........................38 A2
Hillside Rd *DUDN* DY1...............84 A2
  ERDW/GRVHL B23...............92 B4
  FOAKS/STRLY B74................46 C1
  ERDW/GRVHL B23...............75 F1
Hillstone Gdns *WOLVN* WV10....23 H2
Hillstone Rd *BKDE/SHDE* B34..113 F4
Hill St *BILS/COS* WV14...............54 A5
  CBHAM B2..........................2 E5
  DARL/WED WS10..................55 C2
  DIG/EDG B5............................3 F6
  HAG/WOL DY9...................136 D2
  HALE B63.........................138 C4
  SEDG DY3............................83 G1
  SMTHWK B66.....................106 C3
  STRBR DY8........................135 F5
  TPTN/OCK DY4....................85 F4
  WNSFLD WV11.....................14 D4
  WSL WS1..............................5 F5
The Hill *RIDG/WDGT* B32..........96 C5
Hilltop *HAG/WOL* DY9.............136 C4
Hill Top *WBROM* B70.................71 E4
Hill Top Av *RMSLY* B62............122 C5
Hill Top Cl *KGSTG* B44...............75 F5
Hill Top Dr *CBROM* B36...........111 F2
Hilltop Rd *DUDS* DY2...............103 E1
Hill Top Rd *LGLYGN/QTN* B68..123 E2
  NFLD/LBR B31...................175 F2
Hill Top Wk *ALDR* WS9..............30 C1
Hill Vw *ALDR* WS9.....................30 C5
Hillview Cl *HALE* B63...............138 A1
Holbeache Rd *KGSWFD* DY6.....81 H5
Holbeach Rd *BKDE/SHDE* B34..113 E4
Hill Village Rd *MGN/WHC* B75...47 E1
Holbeche Gdns *STRBR* DY8.....130 D2
Holbeche Rd *DOR/KN* B93.......197 E1
  MGN/WHC B75.....................47 H4
Holberg Gv *WNSFLD* WV11.......25 F5
Holborn Hl *AST/WIT* B6...........109 H1
Holbrook Gv
  CHWD/FDBR/MGN B37........132 B4
Holbury Cl *COVEN* WV9.............12 A5
Holcombe Rd *SPARK* B11.........146 A4
Holcroft Rd *HAG/WOL* DY9.....136 A3
  HALE B63..........................137 G2
  KGSWFD DY6........................81 G5
Holcroft St *BKHL/PFLD* WV2.......53 F1
  TPTN/OCK DY4....................85 G4
Holden Cl *ERDW/GRVHL* B23....92 A5
Holden Crs *BLOX/PEL* WS3........28 A5
Holden Cft *TPTN/OCK* DY4........85 G3
Holden Rd *DARL/WED* WS10......71 E1
  ETTPK/GDPK/PENN WV4......52 A3
The Holdens *HLGN/YWD* B28...162 C4
Holder Rd *SPARK* B11.............145 E1
  YDLY B25..........................145 H1
Holders Gdns *MOS/BIL* B13.....143 G5
Holders La *MOS/BIL* B13..........143 G5
Holdford Rd *AST/WIT* B6...........91 F4
Holdgate Rd *SLYOAK* B29........158 D3
Hole Farm Wy
  HWK/WKHTH B38................190 D1
Hole La *NFLD/LBR* B31............176 A1
Holendene Wy *WMBN* WV5........64 C4
Holford Dr *PBAR/PBCH* B42.......91 E2
Holford Wy *AST/WIT* B6...........91 G3
Holifast Rd *CSCFLD/WYGN* B72..77 G4
Holland Av *DOR/KN* B93..........183 F5
  LGLYGN/QTN B68...............105 G3
Holland Rd *BILS/COS* WV14.......54 A2
  CSCFLD/WYGN B72...............62 D5
  GTB/HAM B43......................73 H3
Holland Rd West *AST/WIT* B6..109 F3
Hollands Pl *BLOX/PEL* WS3........27 H1
Hollands Rd *BLOX/PEL* WS3......27 H1
Holland St *CBHAMNW* B3...........2 C2
  CSCFLD/WYGN B72...............62 D1
  DUDN DY1.........................102 B1
  TPTN/OCK DY4....................70 A4
Hollemeadow Av
  BLOX/PEL WS3....................27 H5
Hollers Cv
  CHWD/FDBR/MGN B37........113 H4
Holliday Rd
  ERDE/BCHGN B24..................93 E2
  HDSW B21........................107 H2
Hollie Lucas Rd *MOS/BIL* B13..161 F3
Hollies Cft *DIG/EDG* B5...........143 G2
Hollies Dr *DARL/WED* WS10.......55 H5

RMSLY B62 .... 139 G1
Hollies Ri CDYHTH B64 .... 121 F4
Hollies Rd OLDBY B69 .... 103 G1
Hollies St BRLYHL DY5 .... 101 F2
The Hollies AST/WIT B6 .... 109 H1
  BKHL/PFLD WV2 .... 6 E7
  SMTHWK B66 .... 107 E5
Hollin Brow Cl DOR/KN B93 ...... 197 F5
Hollingberry La
  WALM/CURD B76 .... 63 F5
Hollings Gv SOLH B91 .... 181 H5
Hollington Rd WOLV WV1 .... 38 B5
Hollington Wy SHLY B90 .... 196 A1
Holliwell Cl BLOX/PEL WS3 .... 16 C4
Hollister Dr RIDG/WDGT B32 .... 141 F4
Holloway NFLD/LBR B31 .... 158 A4
Holloway Bank
  DARL/WED WS10 .... 70 D3
Holloway Circ Queensway
  CBHAMW B1 .... 3 F7
Holloway Dr WMBN WV5 .... 80 C1
Holloway Head EDG B15 .... 126 D5
Holloway St BKHL/PFLD WV2 .... 196 A1
  SEDG DY3 .... 83 F2
Holloway St West SEDG DY3 ...... 83 F2
The Holloway
  DUNHL/THL/PER WV6 .... 35 F3
  SEDG DY3 .... 80 B5
  STRBR DY8 .... 118 B5
Hollow Cft NFLD/LBR B31 .... 175 H2
Hollow Croft Rd SHHTH WV12 ..... 25 H3
The Hollow MOS/BIL B13 .... 144 B3
Holly Av BHTH/HG B12 .... 144 C2
  SLYOAK B29 .... 160 B1
Hollybank Av WNSFLD WV11 .... 15 E4
Hollybank Cl BLOX/PEL WS3 .... 27 H1
Hollybank Rd MOS/BIL B13 .... 161 G4
Hollyberry Av SOLH B91 .... 181 G5
Hollyberry Cl HALE B63 .... 138 C4
Hollyberry Cft
  BKDE/SHDE B34 .... 113 E3
Hollybrow SLYOAK B29 .... 158 C3
Holly Bush Gv
  RIDG/WDGT B32 .... 123 H5
Hollybush La
  ETTPK/GDPK/PENN WV4 .... 50 D4
  STRBR DY8 .... 118 B5
Holly Cl SHHTH WV12 .... 26 A4
  WALM/CURD B76 .... 78 B3
Hollycot Gdns BHTH/HG B12 .... 144 B1
Holly Ct DSYBK/YTR WS5 .... 57 G4
Hollycroft Rd HDSW B21 .... 89 F5
Hollydale Rd
  BKLHTH/ROWR B65 .... 122 B1
  ERDE/BCHGN B24 .... 93 C3
Holly Dell HWK/WKHTH B38 .... 177 F3
Holly Dr ACGN B27 .... 146 B5
  HLYWD B47 .... 192 D1
Hollyfaste Rd STETCH B33 .... 130 D5
Hollyfield Av SOLH B91 .... 181 E2
Hollyfield Ct MGN/WHC B75 .... 63 E3
Hollyfield Crs MGN/WHC B75 ...... 63 E4
Hollyfield Dr MGN/WHC B75 ...... 63 E3
Hollyfield Rd MGN/WHC B75 .... 63 E3
Holly Gv BDMR/CCFT WV5 .... 51 F1
  BVILLE B30 .... 159 H2
  LOZ/NWT B19 .... 91 F3
  STRBR DY8 .... 135 F2
Holly Hall Rd DUDS DY2 .... 102 A3
Hollyhedge Cl NFLD/LBR B31 ... 157 H4
  WSLW WS2 .... 4 A2
Hollyhedge La WSLW WS2 .... 4 A1
Hollyhedge Rd
  HHTH/SAND B71 .... 72 A4
Holly Hill Rd RBRY B45 .... 174 D1
Hollyhock Rd ACGN B27 .... 162 D1
  DUDS DY2 .... 85 F5
Hollyhurst CSHL/WTROR B46 ..... 96 C4
  SHLY B90 .... 180 B5
Hollyhurst Rd SCFLD/BOLD B73 .. 147 E1
Holly La ALDR WS9 .... 31 F2
  CHWD/FDBR/MGN B37 .... 131 H4
  ERDE/BCHGN B24 .... 93 F3
  FOAKS/STRLY B74 .... 47 E2
  SMTHWK B66 .... 106 A2
  SMTHWKW B67 .... 105 H5
Hollymoor Wy NFLD/LBR B31 .... 174 A4
Hollymount RMSLY B62 .... 123 E5
Hollyoak Cft NFLD/LBR B31 ...... 175 H5
Hollyoake LGLYGN/QTN B68 ..... 123 E2
Hollyoak Rd FOAKS/STRLY B74 .. 60 B2
Hollyoak St HHTH/SAND B71 ...... 87 H2
Holly Park Dr ERDE/BCHGN B24 .. 93 F3
Holly Pl AST/WIT B6 .... 91 F5
  SLYOAK B29 .... 145 F5
Holly Rd BILS/COS WV14 .... 107 H1
  BLKHTH/ROWR B65 .... 121 H3
  BVILLE B30 .... 177 E1
  DARL/WED WS10 .... 54 B3
  HHTH/SAND B71 .... 72 A3
  LDYWD/EDGR B16 .... 125 E3
  LGLYGN/QTN B68 .... 123 G4
Holly St DUDN DY1 .... 101 E2
  SMTHWKW B67 .... 106 B4
Hollywell Rd DOR/KN B93 .... 197 E3
  LGN/SDN/BHAMAIR B26 .... 147 H1
Hollywell St BILS/COS WV14 .... 68 A2
Holly Wd GTB/HAM B43 .... 74 A2
Hollywood By-Pass
  HLYWD B47 .... 192 A3
Hollywood Cft PBAR/PBCH B42 .. 73 H5
Hollywood Gdns HLYWD B47 .... 178 C5
Hollywood La HLYWD B47 .... 192 D1
Holman Cl WLNHL WV13 .... 39 E3
Holman Rd WLNHL WV13 .... 38 D3
Holmbridge Gv
  RUSH/SHEL WS4 .... 18 D5
Holme Mi WOLV WV1 .... 12 D3
Holmes Dr RBRY B45 .... 187 H2
Holmesfield Rd
  PBAR/PBCH B42 .... 74 C4
Holmes Rd SHHTH WV12 .... 26 B4
The Holmes WOLV WV10 .... 12 D4

Holme Wy RUSH/SHEL WS4 .... 28 D3
Holmwood Rd BORD B9 .... 128 B5
Holt Ct North VAUX/NECH B7 * ... 3 K2
Holt Ct South VAUX/NECH B7 * ... 3 K2
Holte Dr MGN/WHC B75 .... 47 H5
Holte Rd AST/WIT B6 .... 109 G1
  SPARK B11 .... 145 F2
Holte Wy AST/WIT B6 * 109 H1
Holt La RMSLY B62 .... 171 H1
Holt Rd RMSLY B62 .... 122 C3
Holtshill La WSL WS1 .... 5 C3
Holt St VAUX/NECH B7 .... 3 J1
Holy Cross Gn HAG/WOL DY9 .... 170 C3
Holy Cross La HAG/WOL DY9 .... 170 C5
Holyhead Rd CDSL WV8 .... 20 B2
  DARL/WED WS10 .... 70 D1
  HDSW B21 .... 107 F1
Holyhead Wy HDSW B21 .... 107 F1
Holyoak Cl AST/WIT B6 .... 91 F5
Holyrood Gv AST/WIT B6 .... 109 E1
Holy Well Cl LDYWD/EDGR B16 . 126 A2
Holywell La RBRY B45 .... 187 F2
Homecroft Rd YDLY B25 .... 130 A4
Homedene Rd NFLD/LBR B31 .... 158 A3
Homefield Rd LDSL WV8 .... 10 D4
Homelands PBAR/PBCH B42 .... 74 B4
The Homelands WOLV WV10 * 12 C1
Homelea Rd YDLY B25 .... 129 H4
Homemead Gv RBRY B45 .... 187 H1
Homer Hill Rd HALE B63 .... 120 B5
Homer Rd MGN/WHC B75 .... 47 C5
  SOLH B91 .... 181 H2
Homers Fold BILS/COS WV14 ...... 53 H5
Homer St BHTH/HG B12 .... 144 B4
Homerton Rd KGSTG B44 .... 75 H2
Homestead Cl SEDG DY3 .... 83 G1
Homestead Dr MGN/WHC B75 ..... 47 C2
Homestead Rd STETCH B33 ...... 130 D3
Homewood Cl
  WALM/CURD B76 .... 63 E5
Honesty Ct BRWNH WS8 .... 8 D5
Honeswode Cl
  BFLD/HDSWWD B20 .... 108 A1
Honeyborne Cl HALE B63 .... 62 D1
Honeybourne Cl HALE B63 .... 138 C4
Honeybourne Crs WMBN WV5 ..... 80 C1
Honeybourne Rd HALE B65 .... 139 E4
  STETCH B33 .... 131 E4
Honeybourne Wy
  WLNHL WV13 .... 40 A3
Honeycomb Wy
  NFLD/LBR B31 .... 175 E2
Honeysuckle Av KGSWFD DY6 ... 100 A2
Honeysuckle Cl
  RIDG/WDGT B32 .... 140 B2
Honeysuckle Dr
  DSYBK/YTR WS5 .... 57 C5
Honeysuckle Gv ACGN B27 ...... 146 C2
Honeytree Cl KGSWFD DY6 ...... 118 B1
Honiley Dr KGSTG B44 .... 76 A1
Honiley Rd STETCH B33 .... 130 C2
Honister Cl BRLYHL DY5 .... 119 H3
Honiton Cl NFLD/LBR B31 .... 175 E1
Honiton Crs NFLD/LBR B31 ...... 175 E1
Honiton Wy ALDR WS9 .... 29 H5
Honnington Ct SLYOAK B29 * 158 B1
Honor Av
  ETTPK/GDPK/PENN WV4 .... 52 A3
Hood Gv BVILLE B30 .... 176 B1
Hook Dr FOAKS/STRLY B74 .... 46 C1
Hooper St WSNGN B18 .... 107 H5
Hoosen Cl RMSLY B62 .... 140 A1
Hopedale Rd RIDG/WDGT B32 .. 140 C2
Hope Pl SLYOAK B29 * 142 D5
Hope Rd TPTN/OCK DY4 .... 70 A5
Hope St DIG/EDG B5 .... 126 D4
  DUDS DY2 .... 102 C1
  RMSLY B62 .... 122 B4
  STRBR DY8 .... 117 H1
  WBROM B70 .... 88 A1
  WSL WS1 .... 4 E6
Hopkins Dr HHTH/SAND B71 ...... 72 A4
Hopkins St TPTN/OCK DY4 .... 85 G4
Hopstone Gdns
  ETTPK/GDPK/PENN WV4 .... 51 F3
Hopstone Rd SLYOAK B29 .... 158 C1
Hopton Cl
  DUNHL/THL/PER WV6 .... 34 D2
  TPTN/OCK DY4 .... 70 A1
Hopton Crs WNSFLD WV11 .... 25 E4
Hopton Gdns DUDN DY1 .... 84 A3
Hopton Gv MOS/BIL B13 .... 162 A5
Hopwas Gv
  CHWD/FDBR/MGN B37 .... 113 H4
Hopwood Cl HALE B63 .... 138 C5
Hopwood Gv NFLD/LBR B31 ...... 189 E2
Hopyard Cl SEDG DY3 .... 82 D3
Hopyard Gdns BILS/COS WV14 .. 53 F5
Hopyard La SEDG DY3 .... 82 D4
Hopyard Rd WSLW WS2 .... 40 C3
Horace Partridge Rd
  DARL/WED WS10 * 54 C3
Horace St BILS/COS WV14 .... 68 A3
Horatio Dr MOS/BIL B13 .... 144 B3
Hordern Cl
  DUNHL/THL/PER WV6 .... 22 B5
Hordern Crs BRLYHL DY5 .... 119 F4
Hordern Rd
  DUNHL/THL/PER WV6 .... 22 B5
Hordern Pk WOLV WV10 * 12 C1
Hordern Rd
  DUNHL/THL/PER WV6 .... 36 C1
Hornbeam Cl SLYOAK B29 .... 158 D5
Hornbeam Wk BDMR/CCFT WV3 . 35 H5
Hornbrook Gv HLY/OLT B92 ...... 163 G3
Hornby Gv
  ALE/KHTH/YWD B14 .... 179 E1
Hornby Rd
  ETTPK/GDPK/PENN WV4 .... 52 A4
Horne Wy BKDE/SHDE B34 .... 113 C4
Horning Dr BILS/COS WV14 .... 53 G5
Hornsey Gv KGSTG B44 .... 75 G1
Hornsey Rd KGSTG B44 .... 75 G1
Hornton Cl FOAKS/STRLY B74 .... 32 B5
Horrell Rd
  LGN/SDN/BHAMAIR B26 .... 147 H1
  SHLY B90 .... 179 H4
Horsecroft Dr HHTH/SAND B71 . 72 B1
Horsehills Dr BDMR/CCFT WV3 .. 36 A3
Horselea Cft WASH/WDE B8 ..... 111 G5

Horseley Flds WOLV WV1 .... 7 H4
Horseley Heath TPTN/OCK DY4 .. 85 H2
Horseley Rd TPTN/OCK DY4 .... 69 H5
Horseshoe Cl WSLW WS2 .... 56 B1
Horse Shoes La
  LGN/SDN/BHAMAIR B26 .... 147 H2
The Horseshoe
  LGLYGN/QTN B68 .... 123 C2
Horsfall Rd MGN/WHC B75 .... 63 G3
Horsham Av STRBR DY8 .... 117 G1
Horsley Rd FOAKS/STRLY B74 ... 45 H5
  GTB/HAM D43 .... 59 H4
Horton Cl DARL/WED WS10 .... 55 F1
  SEDG DY3 .... 67 E3
Horton Gv SHLY B90 .... 195 G3
Horton Pl DARL/WED WS10 .... 55 F1
Horton Sq BHTH/HG B12 .... 127 E5
Horton St DARL/WED WS10 .... 55 F1
  TPTN/OCK DY4 .... 86 B1
Hospital La BILS/COS WV14 .... 68 B4
Hospital St BKHL/PFLD WV2 .... 7 H6
  ERDW/GRVHL B23 .... 92 C2
  LOZ/NWT B19 .... 3 F1
Hossil La HAG/WOL DY9 .... 169 H5
Hothersall Dr SCFLD/BOLD B73 . 76 D3
Hotspur Rd KGSTG B44 .... 75 F2
Hough Pl WSL WS2 .... 56 B1
Hough Rd
  ALE/KHTH/YWD B14 .... 160 D4
  WSLW WS2 .... 56 A1
Houghton Cl HLGN/YWD B28 .... 179 F1
Houghton St OLDBY B69 .... 104 D3
  WBROM B70 .... 105 H1
Houldey Rd NFLD/LBR B31 .... 175 H4
Houliston Cl DARL/WED WS10 .... 56 B3
Houndel Gv WMBN WV5 .... 64 D4
Houndsfield Cl HLYWD B47 .... 193 E2
Houndsfield Gv HLYWD B47 ..... 192 D3
Houndsfield La HLYWD B47 ...... 193 E3
The Houx STRBR DY8 .... 118 A4
Hove Rd ACGN B27 .... 163 F1
Howard Rd
  ALE/KHTH/YWD B14 .... 160 D3
  BFLD/HDSWWD B20 .... 90 B4
  BILS/COS WV14 .... 68 B3
  GTB/HAM B43 .... 73 E3
  HIA/OLT B92 .... 147 E4
  WNSFLD WV11 .... 25 F2
  YDLY B25 .... 146 A1
Howard Rd East
  ALE/KHTH/YWD B14 .... 161 E3
Howard St BKHL/PFLD WV2 .... 7 G7
  LOZ/NWT B19 .... 2 E1
  TPTN/OCK DY4 .... 85 H1
  WBROM B70 .... 70 D4
Howarth Wy AST/WIT B6 .... 109 G2
Howden Pl BKDE/SHDE B34 ...... 112 C4
Howdle's La BRWNH WS8 .... 9 F2
Howe Crs SHHTH WV12 .... 26 A4
Howell Rd BKHL/PFLD WV2 .... 52 C1
Howes Cft CVALE B35 .... 94 C4
Howe St CBHAMNE B4 .... 3 K3
Howford Gv VAUX/NECH B7 .... 3 K1
Howland Cl COVEN WV9 .... 11 H5
Howley Av KGSTG B44 .... 75 E2
Howley Grange Rd
  RMSLY B62 .... 139 H3
Hoylake Cl BLOX/PEL WS3 .... 16 D4
Hoylake Dr OLDBY B69 .... 103 G2
Hoylake Rd
  DUNHL/THL/PER WV6 .... 20 B5
Hoyland Wy BVILLE B30 .... 159 G2
Hubert Cft SLYOAK B29 .... 142 D5
Hubert Rd SLYOAK B29 .... 159 H1
Hubert St AST/WIT B6 .... 109 F4
The Hub SOLH B91 .... 182 A2
Hucker Cl WSLW WS2 .... 56 A1
Hucker Rd WSLW WS2 .... 56 A1
Huddlestone Cl WOLV WV10 ...... 13 C1
Huddlestown Wy SLYOAK B29 ... 159 E1
Huddocks Vw BLOX/PEL WS3 .... 17 H2
Hudson Av CSHL/WTROR B46 .... 115 F3
Hudson Gv
  DUNHL/THL/PER WV6 .... 20 C5
Hudson Rd
  BFLD/HDSWWD B20 .... 90 A2
  TPTN/OCK DY4 .... 70 A3
Hudson's Dr BVILLE B30 .... 177 E1
Hudswell Dr BRLYHL DY5 .... 119 F4
Hughes Av BDMR/CCFT WV3 ...... 36 B5
Hughes Pl BILS/COS WV14 .... 53 H1
Hughes Rd BILS/COS WV14 .... 53 H1
  DARL/WED WS10 .... 54 C3
Hugh Porter Wy
  DUNHL/THL/PER WV6 .... 22 B3
Hugh Rd SMHTH B10 .... 128 C3
Hugh Wy SMHTH B10 * 128 C3
Hulbert Dr DUDS DY2 .... 102 B3
Hulland Pl BRLYHL DY5 .... 119 E1
Hullbrook Rd MOS/BIL B13 .... 162 A5
Humber Av WALM/CURD B76 .... 78 C4
Humber Gdns HALE B63 .... 137 F2
Humber Rd BDMR/CCFT WV3 ...... 35 H5
Humberstone Rd
  ERDE/BCHGN B24 .... 94 A2
Humpage Rd BORD B9 .... 128 C2
Humphrey Middlemore Dr
  HRBN B17 .... 142 B3
Humphrey St SEDG DY3 .... 83 F3
Humphries Crs
  BILS/COS WV14 .... 69 F1
Humphries Rd WOLV WV10 .... 23 F5
Hundred Acre Rd
  FOAKS/STRLY B74 .... 60 B1
Hungary Cl HAG/WOL DY9 .... 136 A2
Hungary Hl HAG/WOL DY9 .... 136 A2
Hungerfield Rd CBROM B36 .... 95 E5
Hungerford Rd STRBR DY8 .... 133 C2
Hunningham Gv SOLH B91 .... 181 H5
Hunnington Cl
  RIDG/WDGT B32 .... 157 E1
Hunnington Crs HALE B63 .... 138 D5
Hunscote Cl SHLY B90 .... 180 A5
Hunslet Cl RIDG/WDGT B32 ...... 141 F5
Hunslet Rd RIDG/WDGT B32 ..... 141 F5
Hunstanton Av HRBN B17 .... 124 B4

Hunstanton Cl BRLYHL DY5 ...... 119 E4
Hunter Crs BLOX/PEL WS3 .... 28 B4
Hunters Cl WLNHL WV13 .... 54 C1
Hunter's Ride KINVER DY7 .... 117 F2
Hunters Rd LOZ/NWT B19 .... 108 B3
Hunter St
  DUNHL/THL/PER WV6 .... 36 C1
Hunters V LOZ/NWT B19 .... 108 B3
Huntingdon Rd
  HHTH/SAND B71 .... 71 F4
Huntington Rd SHHTH WV12 ..... 26 A3
Huntingtree Rd HALE B63 .... 138 A3
Huntlands Rd HALE B63 .... 138 A3
Huntley Dr SOLH B91 .... 181 H3
Huntly Rd LDYWD/EDGR B16 .... 126 A3
Hunton Hl ERDW/GRVHL B23 ..... 92 B3
Hunton Rd ERDW/GRVHL B23 .... 92 C3
Hunt's La SHHTH WV12 .... 26 B4
Huntsman Cl BILS/COS WV14 ..... 68 D1
Hunts Mill Dr BRLYHL DY5 .... 83 E5
Hunts Rd BVILLE B30 .... 160 A3
Hurdis Rd SHLY B90 .... 180 A3
Hurdlow Av WSNGN B18 .... 108 A4
Hurley Cl CSCFLD/WYGN B72 ..... 77 G1
  DSYBK/YTR WS5 .... 58 B2
Hurley Gv
  CHWD/FDBR/MGN B37 .... 113 H4
Hurleys Fold DUDS DY2 .... 102 B4
Hurlingham Rd KGSTG B44 .... 75 G2
Hurricane Wy CVALE B35 .... 95 G2
Hursey Dr TPTN/OCK DY4 .... 85 H5
Hurstbourne Crs WOLV WV1 ...... 38 B4
Hurst Cl CBROM B36 .... 113 C2
Hurstcroft Rd STETCH B33 .... 130 D1
Hurst Green Rd DOR/KN B93 ... 196 D4
  RMSLY B62 .... 138 B1
  WALM/CURD B76 .... 79 F5
Hurst La BKDE/SHDE B34 .... 113 F3
  BRLYHL DY5 .... 99 H1
  TPTN/OCK DY4 .... 84 D1
Hurst La North
  BKDE/SHDE B34 .... 113 G2
Hurst Rd BILS/COS WV14 .... 67 H2
  SMTHWKW B67 .... 123 H2
Hurst St DIG/EDG B5 .... 133 G1
  MOS/BIL D13 .... 162 A3
The Hurstway
  ERDW/GRVHL B23 .... 76 A3
Hurstwood Rd KGSTG B44 .... 76 A1
Huskinson Cl OLDBY B69 .... 85 H5
Hussey Rd BRWNH WS8 .... 9 E4
Hutchings La SHLY B90 .... 194 B3
Hutton Av WASH/WDE B8 .... 110 B4
Hutton Rd BFLD/HDSWWD B20 .. 90 B5
  WASH/WDE B8 .... 110 B4
Huxbey Dr HIA/OLT B92 .... 165 H2
Huxley Cl COVEN WV9 .... 12 A4
Hyacinth Cl DSYBK/YTR WS5 ..... 57 F5
Hyatt Sq BRLYHL DY5 .... 119 E5
Hyde Rd WNSFLD WV11 .... 24 D4
  HAG/WOL DY9 .... 136 B5
The Hyde HAG/WOL DY9 .... 136 B5
Hyett Wy BILS/COS WV14 .... 54 D1
Hylda Rd BFLD/HDSWWD B20 .... 90 B5
Hylstone Crs WNSFLD WV11 ...... 24 D4
Hylton St LOZ/NWT B18 .... 108 C4
Hyperion Dr
  ETTPK/GDPK/PENN WV4 .... 51 C5
Hyperion Rd CBROM B36 .... 94 A5
  KINVER DY7 .... 117 C5
Hyron Hall Rd ACGN B27 .... 146 C5
Hyssop Cl VAUX/NECH B7 .... 109 F4
Hytall Rd SHLY B90 .... 179 E3
Hythe Gv YDLY B90 .... 129 H4

I

Ibberton Rd
  ALE/KHTH/YWD B14 .... 178 D2
Ibis Gdns KGSWFD DY6 .... 100 C3
Ibstock Dr STRBR DY8 .... 135 G3
Icknield Cl FOAKS/STRLY B74 ..... 45 G4
Icknield Port Rd
  LDYWD/EDGR B16 .... 125 G1
Icknield Sq LDYWD/EDGR B16 .. 126 A1
Icknield St LDYWD/WKHTH B38 . 191 E3
  WSNGN B18 .... 2 A2
Ida Rd WBROM B70 .... 87 H5
  WSLW WS2 .... 41 C4
Idbury Rd KGSTG B44 .... 75 C4
Idmiston Cft
  ALE/KHTH/YWD B14 .... 178 D3
Idonia Rd
  DUNHL/THL/PER WV6 .... 20 C5
Ilford Rd ERDW/GRVHL B23 .... 76 B5
Iliffe Wy HRBN B17 .... 142 B3
Ilkley Gv
  CHWD/FDBR/MGN B37 .... 131 H2
Illey Cl NFLD/LBR B31 .... 174 B4
Illey La RMSLY B62 .... 156 A1
Illshaw COVEN WV9 .... 12 A4
Illshaw Heath Rd
  HOCK/TIA B94 .... 194 D5
Ilmington Dr SCFLD/BOLD B73 ... 61 E5
Ilmington Rd SLYOAK B29 .... 158 B1
Ilsham Gv NFLD/LBR B31 .... 189 E2
Ilsley Rd ERDW/GRVHL B23 .... 92 D1
Imperial Ri CSHL/WTROR B46 ... 97 F4
Imperial Rd BORD B9 .... 128 C2
Impsley Cl CBROM B36 .... 112 D1
Ince Rd DARL/WED WS10 .... 53 G3
Incestre Cl BLOX/PEL WS3 .... 16 B4
Incestre Gr GTB/HAM B43 .... 73 E2
Inge St DIG/EDG B5 .... 126 D3
Ingestre Rd HLGN/YWD B28 ..... 162 D3
  WOLV WV10 .... 23 E1
Ingham Wy HRBN B17 .... 124 D5
Ingleby Gdns
  DUNHL/THL/PER WV6 .... 22 C5

Ingledew Cl WSLW WS2 .... 40 B2
Inglefield Rd STETCH B33 .... 130 B1
Inglemere Gv SLYOAK B29 .... 158 B3
Inglenook Dr
  BFLD/HDSWWD B20 .... 90 B4
Ingleside Vls SPARK B11 * 145 E2
Ingleton Rd WASH/WDE B8 .... 111 E2
Inglewood Av BDMR/CCFT WV3 .. 36 B5
Inglewood Cl KGSWFD DY6 * 99 H4
Inglewood Gv
  FOAKS/STRLY B74 .... 45 F4
Inglewood Rd SPARK B11 .... 145 E2
Ingoldsby Rd NFLD/LBR B31 .... 176 A2
Ingot Cl WSLW WS2 .... 27 F4
Ingram Dr GTB/HAM B43 .... 73 E3
Ingram Gv ACGN B27 .... 146 A5
Ingram Pl BLOX/PEL WS3 .... 27 H1
Ingram Rd BLOX/PEL WS3 .... 27 H1
Inhedge St SEDG DY3 .... 83 G1
The Inhedge DUDN DY1 .... 84 C5
Inkberrow Cl OLDBY B69 .... 104 C5
Inkberrow Rd HALE B63 .... 138 B5
Inkerman St VAUX/NECH B7 ...... 127 H1
  WOLV WV10 .... 37 H2
Inland Rd ERDE/BCHGN B24 .... 93 F4
Innage Rd NFLD/LBR B31 .... 175 H1
The Innage HLYWD B47 .... 192 C3
Innsworth Dr CVALE B35 .... 94 D2
Inshaw Cl STETCH B33 .... 130 A1
Institute Rd
  ALE/KHTH/YWD B14 .... 161 F2
Instone Rd HALE B63 .... 138 A4
Instow Cl SHHTH WV12 .... 25 H2
Insull Av ALE/KHTH/YWD B14 ... 178 D4
Intended St HALE B63 .... 120 C5
International Dr
  LGN/SDN/BHAMAIR B26 .... 149 G3
International Sq
  CHWD/FDBR/MGN B37 * 149 G1
Intown WSL WS1 .... 5 F3
Intown Rw WSL WS1 * 5 F3
Inverclyde Dr
  ETTPK/GDPK/PENN WV4 .... 52 D3
Inverclyde Rd
  BFLD/HDSWWD B20 .... 90 A3
Inverclyde Wk
  ETTPK/GDPK/PENN WV4 .... 52 D3
Inverness Rd NFLD/LBR B31 .... 175 F2
Inworth COVEN WV9 .... 12 B4
Ipsley Cv ERDW/GRVHL B23 .... 91 G1
Ipstones Av STETCH B33 .... 112 B5
Ipswich Crs PBAR/PBCH B42 .... 74 B4
Ireland Green Rd WBROM B70 .... 87 E5
Ireton Rd BFLD/HDSWWD B20 ... 90 A2
  WOLV WV10 .... 12 D4
Iris Cl DUDS DY2 .... 102 C2
  SLYOAK B29 .... 158 D2
Iris Dr ALE/KHTH/YWD B14 .... 177 H1
Irnham Rd FOAKS/STRLY B74 ...... 47 E3
Iron Bridge Wk HAG/WOL DY9 . 152 D2
Iron La STETCH B33 .... 111 H5
Irvan Av WBROM B70 .... 86 D1
Irvine Cl BLOX/PEL WS3 .... 27 F3
Irvine Rd BLOX/PEL WS3 .... 27 F3
Irving Cl SEDG DY3 .... 66 C2
Irving Rd HIA/OLT B92 .... 148 C3
  TPTN/OCK DY4 .... 69 G2
Irving St DIG/EDG B5 .... 126 D3
Isaac Walton Pl WBROM B70 ...... 70 A4
Isbourne Wy BORD B9 .... 127 H1
Isis Gv CBROM B36 .... 113 H1
  WLNHL WV13 .... 40 A3
Island Rd HDSW B21 .... 89 E5
Islington HALE B63 .... 138 C3
Islington Rw LDYWD/EDGR B16 . 126 B3
Ismere Rd ERDE/BCHGN B24 ...... 93 H4
Itchen Gv
  DUNHL/THL/PER WV6 .... 34 C2
Ithon Gv HWK/WKHTH B38 .... 176 C5
Ivanhoe Rd BKHL/PFLD WV2 .... 52 D2
  DARL/WED WS10 .... 54 B3
  SHLY B90 .... 59 F5
Ivanhoe St DUDS DY2 .... 102 A2
Ivatt Cl RUSH/SHEL WS4 .... 28 D3
Iverley Rd HALE B63 .... 139 E4
Iverley Wk HAG/WOL DY9 .... 135 H5
Ivor Rd SPARK B11 .... 144 D5
Ivy Av BHTH/HG D12 .... 144 C2
Ivybridge Gv PBAR/PBCH B42 .. 74 B5
Ivy Cft COVEN WV9 .... 11 H4
Ivydale Av
  LGN/SDN/BHAMAIR B26 .... 148 A2
Ivyfield Rd ERDW/GRVHL B23 .... 91 H1
Ivy Gv BRWNH WS8 .... 19 G5
Ivyhouse La BILS/COS WV14 ...... 68 C5
Ivyhouse Rd HWK/WKHTH B38 .. 176 A5
Ivy House Rd OLDBY B69 .... 104 B5
Ivy La CBHAMNE B4 .... 127 G2
  RMSLY B62 .... 154 D5
Ivy Lodge Cl
  CHWD/FDBR/MGN B37 .... 132 A4
Ivy Rd DUDN DY1 .... 160 A4
  DUDN DY1 .... 84 A2
  HDSW B21 .... 108 A2
  OLDBY B69 .... 76 D2
  TPTN/OCK DY4 .... 69 G2
Ivy Wy SHLY B90 .... 194 A2
Izons La WBROM B70 .... 87 E5
Izons Rd WBROM B70 .... 87 G3

J

Jacamar Av STETCH B33 .... 112 B5
Jacey Rd LDYWD/EDGR B16 ...... 125 F2
  SHLY B90 .... 180 B1
Jackdaw Cl SEDG DY3 .... 67 E1
Jackdaw Dr CBROM B36 .... 113 H1
Jack Hayward Wy WOLV WV1 .... 6 E1
Jack Holden Av BILS/COS WV14 . 68 A1
Jackson Cl LGLYGN/QTN B68 ... 105 F4
  SPARK B11 * 127 H5
  TPTN/OCK DY4 .... 85 F2
  WOLV WV10 .... 13 C1
Jackson Dr SMTHWKW B67 .... 105 H4
Jackson Rd WASH/WDE B8 .... 110 D5
Jackson St
  DUNHL/THL/PER WV6 .... 36 D1

HAG/WOL DY9.....136 C2
LCLYGN/QTN B68.....105 F5
Jackson Wy RIDG/WDGT B32.....140 A2
Jacmar Crs SMTHWKW B67.....106 A3
Jacobean La DOR/KN B93.....183 F4
Jacoby Pl DIC/EDG B5.....143 G2
Jaffray Crs ERDE/BCHGN B24.....92 D3
Jaffray Rd ERDE/BCHGN B24.....92 D3
Jakeman Rd BHTH/HG B12.....144 A2
James Bridge Cl WSLW WS2 *.....56 B1
James Cl DARL/WED WS10.....55 H1
SMTHWKW B67.....106 C4
James Dee Cl BRLYHL DY5.....119 H3
James Eaton Cl
HHTH/SAND B71.....87 G1
Jameson Rd AST/WIT B6.....110 A1
Jameson St
DUNHL/THL/PER WV6.....36 D1
James Rd CSHL/WTROR B46.....115 F1
GTB/HAM B43.....73 C4
SPARK B11.....145 H1
James Samuel Pl
BHTH/HG B12.....127 F5
James Scott Rd HALE B63.....137 E1
James St BILS/COS WV14.....54 A2
CBHAMNW B3.....2 D5
WLNHL WV13.....39 G3
James Turner St WSNGN B18.....107 G5
James Watt Dr LOZ/NWT B19.....108 B1
James Watt Queensway
CBHAMNE B4.....3 H3
James Watt St HHTH/SAND B71.....71 F5
Jane Lane Cl WSLW WS2.....40 D1
Janice Gv CDSL WV8.....10 D4
Janine Av WNSFLD WV11.....25 E5
Jaques Cl CSHL/WTROR B46.....96 D4
Jardine Rd AST/WIT B6.....109 F1
Jarvis Cl ERDW/GRVHL B23.....76 D5
Jarvis Crs OLDBY B69.....105 E5
Jarvis Rd ERDW/GRVHL B23.....76 D5
Jarvis Wy ERDE/BCHGN B24.....110 C1
Jasmin Cft
ALE/KHTH/YWD B14.....178 A2
Jasmine Cl COVEN WV9.....11 H4
Jasmine Gv CDSL WV8.....10 D4
Jasmine Rd DUDS DY2.....103 E1
Jasmine Wy DARL/WED WS10.....55 F1
Jason Rd HAG/WOL DY9.....136 D3
Javelin Av CVALE B35.....94 D4
Javelin Pk DARL/WED WS10.....70 B1
Jayne Cl HHTH/SAND B71.....72 A2
WNSFLD WV11.....24 C5
Jay Rd KGSWFD DY6.....99 H1
Jays Av TPTN/OCK DY4.....85 H2
Jayshaw Av GTB/HAM B43.....73 G3
Jean Dr TPTN/OCK DY4.....70 B5
Jeavons Pl BILS/COS WV14.....69 E2
Jedburgh Av
DUNHL/THL/PER WV6.....34 C1
Jeddo St BKHL/PFLD WV2.....6 E7
Jeffcock Rd BDMR/CCFT WV3.....36 C5
Jefferson Cl HHTH/SAND B71.....71 F3
Jeffrey Av
ETTPK/GDPK/PENN WV4.....52 A3
Jeffrey Rd BLKHTH/ROWR B65.....122 C1
Jeffs Av BKHL/PFLD WV2.....37 C5
Jenkins Cl BILS/COS WV14.....54 C5
Jenkinson Rd DARL/WED WS10.....70 B2
Jenkins St SMHTH B10.....128 A4
Jenks Av WOLVN WV10.....23 G2
Jenks Rd WMBN WV5.....80 D1
Jennens Rd CBHAMNE B4.....3 J5
Jenner Cl WSLW WS2.....27 E4
Jenner Rd WSLW WS2.....26 D4
Jenner St BKHL/PFLD WV2.....7 J6
Jennings St CDYHTH B64.....121 F2
Jenny Cl BILS/COS WV14.....69 E2
Jenny Walkers La
DUNHL/THL/PER WV6.....34 B5
Jephcott Rd WASH/WDE B8.....129 E1
Jephson Dr
LGN/SDN/BHAMAIR B26.....130 D5
Jeremy Gv HIA/OLT B92.....147 H3
Jeremy Rd
ETTPK/GDPK/PENN WV4.....52 A3
Jerome Rd CSCFLD/WYGN B72.....62 D4
WSLW WS2.....41 F4
Jerrard Dr MGN/WHC B75.....62 C3
Jerrard Ms MGN/WHC B75 *.....62 C5
Jerry's La ERDW/GRVHL B23.....76 B4
Jersey Cft CBROM B36.....114 B3
Jersey Rd WASH/WDE B8.....110 B5
Jervis Cft BRLYHL DY5.....101 E2
Jervis Crs FOAKS/STRLY B74.....46 B2
Jervis Pk FOAKS/STRLY B74.....46 A1
Jervis Ter HDSW B21 *.....107 F1
Jervoise Dr NFLD/LBR B31.....158 D5
Jervoise La HHTH/SAND B71.....72 A2
Jervoise Rd SLYOAK B29.....158 B1
Jervoise St WBROM B70.....87 E2
Jesmond Gv ERDE/BCHGN B24.....93 H2
Jessel Rd WSLW WS2.....4 A2
Jessie Rd ALDR WS9.....30 A4
Jesson Cl WSL WS1.....57 G1
Jesson Rd MGN/WHC B75.....63 G3
SEDG DY3.....68 A5
WSL WS1.....57 H1
Jesson St WBROM B70.....88 A4
Jevons Rd SCFLD/BOLD B73.....61 E5
Jevon St BILS/COS WV14.....68 C3
Jew's La SEDG DY3.....85 G2
Jiggins La RIDG/WDGT B32.....157 F3
Jill Av GTB/HAM B43.....73 E2
Jillcot Rd HIA/OLT B92.....147 H4
Jinnah Cl BHTH/HG B12.....127 F4
Joan St WOLVN WV10.....24 A2
Jockey Fld SEDG DY3.....52 C2
Jockey La DARL/WED WS10.....56 A4
Jockey Rd SCFLD/BOLD B73.....76 B1
Joeys La CDSL WV8.....11 E4
John Bright Cl TPTN/OCK DY4.....69 F3
John Bright St CBHAMW B1.....3 F7
John Fletcher Cl
DARL/WED WS10.....56 B4
John Harper St WLNHL WV13.....39 H5
John Howell Dr TPTN/OCK DY4.....85 G1
John Kempe Wy
BHTH/HG B12.....127 G5
John Padden Ct
BLKHTH/ROWR B65.....121 H3
John Riley Dr SHHTH WV12.....26 A2

John Rd RMSLY B62.....139 H3
Johns Gv GTB/HAM B43.....73 E3
John's La OLDBY B69.....86 A4
TPTN/OCK DY4.....85 H2
John Rous Av WNSFLD WV11.....25 F3
Johnson Cl DARL/WED WS10.....71 F3
SPARK B11.....145 G2
WASH/WDE B8.....111 G3
Johnson Dr CVALE B35.....94 B5
Johnson Pl BILS/COS WV14.....54 B1
Johnson Rd DARL/WED WS10.....71 G1
ERDW/GRVHL B23.....92 D1
WNSFLD WV11.....26 B3
Johnsons Bridge Rd
HHTH/SAND B71.....71 G5
Johnson Gv LCLYGN/QTN B68.....123 G4
Johnston St BKHL/PFLD WV2.....37 F5
VAUX/NECH B7.....110 A5
Johnstone St LOZ/NWT B19.....108 D1
Johnston St WBROM B70.....87 H5
John St BKHL/PFLD WV2.....53 E2
BLKHTH/ROWR B65.....122 A3
BRLYHL DY5.....101 F5
LOZ/NWT B19.....108 B2
OLDBY B69.....105 E2
STRBR DY8.....118 B3
WBROM B70.....86 D1
WLNHL WV13.....39 G4
WS2.....4 D1
John St North HHTH/SAND B71.....87 F1
John Wesley Wy
DARL/WED WS10.....71 E2
Joiners Cft HIA/OLT B92.....165 G2
Joinings Bank
LCLYGN/QTN B68.....105 F5
Jones Field Crs WOLV WV1.....38 E3
Jones Rd SHHTH WV12.....26 B1
WOLVN WV10.....23 G1
Jones Wood Cl
WALM/CURD B76.....78 B4
Jonquil Cl ERDW/GRVHL B23.....76 A4
Jordan Cl MGN/WHC B75.....47 F4
WALM/CURD B76.....106 D4
Jordan Leys TPTN/OCK DY4.....85 H1
Jordan Pl BILS/COS WV14.....54 A5
Jordan Rd MGN/WHC B75.....47 F4
Jordan Wy ALDR WS9.....30 B1
Joseph St OLDBY B69.....104 B5
Josiah Houses BILS/COS WV14 *.....68 C3
Josiah Rd NFLD/LBR B31.....175 H3
Jowett's La HHTH/SAND B71.....71 F3
Joyberry Dr STRBR DY8.....135 F4
Joynson St DARL/WED WS10.....55 G3
Jubilee Av HHTH/SAND B71.....71 H4
Jubilee Cl BLOX/PEL WS3.....28 A4
Jubilee Ct NFLD/LBR B31.....175 H4
Jubilee Gdns ERDW/GRVHL B23.....75 H4
Jubilee Rd BILS/COS WV14.....54 C4
RBRY B45.....173 G5
TPTN/OCK DY4.....85 H3
Jubilee St HHTH/SAND B71.....71 H4
Judge Cl OLDBY B69.....105 E2
Judge Rd BRLYHL DY5.....119 H5
Julia Av ERDE/BCHGN B24.....94 C1
Julia Gdns HHTH/SAND B71.....72 B3
Julian Cl WOLV WV1.....38 B3
Julian Rd WOLV WV1.....38 B3
Julie Cft BILS/COS WV14.....69 E3
Juliet Rd RMSLY B62.....139 G5
Julius Dr CSHL/WTROR B46.....97 F5
Junction Rd BKHL/PFLD WV2.....53 F1
HDSW B21.....107 E1
STRBR DY8.....118 D3
Junction St DUDS DY2.....102 B1
OLDBY B69.....86 C5
WSL WS1.....57 G4
Junction St South OLDBY B69.....105 E4
The Junction STRBR DY8.....118 A4
June Cft
LGN/SDN/BHAMAIR B26.....148 B2
Juniper Cl ACCN B27.....146 B2
WALM/CURD B76.....63 F5
Juniper Dr DSYBK/YTR WS5.....57 H4
WALM/CURD B76.....78 C4
Juniper Ri HALE B63.....137 G2
Jury Rd BRLYHL DY5.....119 H5
Jutland Rd MOS/BIL B13.....161 H5

K

Karen Wy BRLYHL DY5.....119 F4
Katherine Rd SMTHWKW B67.....124 B2
Kathleen Rd
CSCFLD/WYGN B72.....62 C4
YDLY B25.....129 C5
Katie Rd SLYOAK B29.....159 G1
Katsura Cl FOAKS/STRLY B74.....60 B2
Kayne Cl KGSWFD DY6.....99 G2
Keanscott Dr
LCLYGN/QTN B68.....105 G5
Keasdon Gv WLNHL WV13.....40 A2
Keating Gdns MGN/WHC B75.....47 E1
Keats Av SMHTH B10.....128 B5
Keats Cl FOAKS/STRLY B74.....32 D4
SEDG DY3.....82 C1
STRBR DY8.....118 C4
Keats Dr BILS/COS WV14.....68 D1
Keats Gv ACCN B27.....163 F1
WOLVN WV10.....24 A2
Keats Rd BLOX/PEL WS3.....28 A3
SHHTH WV12.....26 C3
WOLVN WV10.....24 A1
Keble Gv
LGN/SDN/BHAMAIR B26.....147 H1
WSL WS1.....57 G1
Kedleston Cl BLOX/PEL WS3 *.....16 C4
Kedleston Rd
HLGN/YWD B28.....162 D4
Keel Dr MOS/BIL B13.....162 B1
Keeley St BORD B9.....127 H2
Keelinge St TPTN/OCK DY4.....85 H1
Keen St SMTHWK B66.....107 E5
Keepers Cl ALDR WS9.....19 F4
CSHL/WTROR B46.....115 G5
KGSWFD DY6.....99 F1
WSNGN B18.....107 H4

Keepers Gate Cl
FOAKS/STRLY B74.....62 C1
Keepers La CDSL WV8.....21 E1
Keepers Rd FOAKS/STRLY B74.....32 A5
Keer Ct BORD B9 *.....127 H1
Kegworth Rd
ERDW/GRVHL B23.....92 A4
Keir Pl STRBR DY8.....118 A4
Keir Rd DARL/WED WS10.....71 G1
Kelby Cl NFLD/LBR B31.....175 G3
Kelby Rd NFLD/LBR B31.....175 E1
Keldy Cl DUNHL/THL/PER WV6.....22 B5
Kelfield Av HRBN B17.....141 H3
Kelia Dr SMTHWKW B67.....106 B3
Kellett Rd VAUX/NECH B7.....3 K2
Kelling Cl BRLYHL DY5 *.....119 E4
Kellington Cl ERDW/GRVHL B23.....110 D5
Kelmarsh Dr SOLH B91.....181 H4
Kelmscott Rd HRBN B17.....124 D5
Kelsall Cl WOLV WV1.....38 E3
Kelsall Cft CBHAMW B1.....2 A4
Kelsey Cl VAUX/NECH B7 *.....109 H5
Kelso Gdns
DUNHL/THL/PER WV6.....34 B1
Kelsull Cft
CHWD/FDBR/MGN B37.....132 A2
Kelton Ct EDG B15.....126 A5
Kelvedon Gv SOLH B91.....182 A1
Kelverdale Gv
ALE/KHTH/YWD B14.....177 G1
Kelverley Gv HHTH/SAND B71.....72 C2
Kelvin Pl WSLW WS2.....27 F4
Kelvin Rd NFLD/LBR B31.....175 G4
WSLW WS2.....27 E4
Kelvin Wy WBROM B70.....87 G5
Kelway Av GTB/HAM B43.....59 F5
Kelwood Dr HALE B63.....138 B2
Kelynmead Rd STETCH B33.....130 C2
Kemberton Cl BDMR/CCFT WV3.....35 G4
Kemberton Rd
BDMR/CCFT WV3.....35 G4
SLYOAK B29.....141 G5
Kemble Cl SHHTH WV12.....40 B1
Kemble Cft DIG/EDG B5.....127 E5
Kemble Dr CVALE B35.....94 C3
Kemelstowe Crs HALE B63.....154 C2
Kemerton Wy SHLY B90.....195 E3
Kempe Rd STETCH B33.....112 C5
Kempsey Cl HALE B63.....138 A5
HIA/OLT B92.....147 H4
Kempsey Covert
ALE/KHTH/YWD B14.....178 B3
Kempson Av
CSCFLD/WYGN B72.....77 G2
HHTH/SAND B71.....87 F1
Kempson Rd CBROM B36.....112 B1
Kempsons Gv BILS/COS WV14.....53 F5
Kempthorne Av WOLVN WV10.....23 G2
Kempthorne Gdns
BLOX/PEL WS3.....16 C5
Kempthorne Rd
BILS/COS WV14.....54 B2
Kempton Park Rd CBROM B36.....111 H1
Kempton Wy STRBR DY8.....135 E4
Kemsey Dr BILS/COS WV14.....54 B4
Kemshead Av NFLD/LBR B31.....175 E5
Kemsley Rd
ALE/KHTH/YWD B14.....178 B3
Kendal Av CSHL/WTROR B46.....115 F2
RBRY B45.....188 B1
Kendal Cl DUNHL/THL/PER WV6.....22 B4
WOLVN WV10.....22 B4
Kendal Gv ALDR WS9.....19 F3
Kendal Gv HIA/OLT B92.....165 H2
Kendal Rd KGSWFD DY6.....100 B4
Kendal Ri
DUNHL/THL/PER WV6.....22 B4
LCLYGN/QTN B68.....123 F1
Kendal Rise Rd RBRY B45.....188 B1
Kendal Rd SPARK B11.....128 A5
Kendrick Av BKDE/SHDE B34.....113 F5
Kendrick Cl HIA/OLT B92.....165 H4
Kendrick Pl BILS/COS WV14.....54 C4
Kendrick Rd BILS/COS WV14.....54 C4
WALM/CURD B76.....94 B1
WOLVN WV10.....23 C4
Kendricks Rd DARL/WED WS10.....55 H1
Kendrick St DARL/WED WS10.....56 A5
RMSLY B62.....172 C1
Kenelm Rd BILS/COS WV14.....68 C2
LCLYGN/QTN B68.....123 E1
SCFLD/BOLD B73.....62 B4
SMHTH B10.....128 C4
Kenilworth Cl
FOAKS/STRLY B74.....47 E5
STRBR DY8.....117 H2
TPTN/OCK DY4.....84 D2
Kenilworth Ct
ETTPK/GDPK/PENN WV4.....52 C4
WSLW WS2.....41 E1
Kenilworth Rd
BFLD/HDSWWD B20.....91 E5
DOR/KN B93.....197 H2
DUNHL/THL/PER WV6.....34 D1
LCLYGN/QTN B68.....123 H4
RCOVN/BALC/EX CV7.....151 E5
Kenley Gv BVILLE B30.....177 E3
Kenley Wy SOLH B91.....180 D1
Kenmare Wy WNSFLD WV11.....38 C1
Kenmure Rd STETCH B33.....131 E5
Kennedy Crs DARL/WED WS10.....55 E1
SEDG DY3.....83 F2
Kennedy Gv
LGN/SDN/BHAMAIR B26.....130 C5
Kennedy Rd BVILLE B30.....160 B4
Kennedy Rd WOLVN WV10.....7 H2
Kennegy Ms SLYOAK B29.....142 D5
Kennerley Rd YDLY B25.....146 D1
Kennet Cl BRWNH WS8.....8 C2
Kennet Gv CBHAMW B1.....113 H1
Kenneth Gv
ERDW/GRVHL B23.....91 G1
Kennford Cl
BLKHTH/ROWR B65.....104 A3
Kennington Rd WOLVN WV10.....23 H5
Kenrick Cft CVALE B35.....94 B4
Kenrick Wy HHTH/SAND B71.....88 B5
SMTHWK B66.....106 B1

Kensington Dr
FOAKS/STRLY B74.....32 D5
Kensington Gdns STRBR DY8.....117 G3
Kensington Rd SHHTH WV12.....25 H3
SLYOAK B29.....160 A1
Kensington St LOZ/NWT B19.....108 D3
Kenswick Dr HALE B63.....155 E1
Kent Av BILS/COS WV14.....54 C3
Kent Av WSLW WS2.....41 F2
Kent Cl ALDR WS9.....30 B1
HHTH/SAND B71.....71 F4
WSLW WS2.....28 A5
Kentish Rd HDSW B21.....107 E1
Kenton Av
DUNHL/THL/PER WV6.....36 B1
Kent Pl DUDS DY2.....102 A3
Kent Rd DARL/WED WS10.....52 C1
DARL/WED WS10.....55 H1
RBRY B45.....173 H4
RMSLY B62.....139 G1
STRBR DY8.....117 H4
WSLW WS2.....40 D2
Kent's Cft HIA/OLT B92.....147 F4
Kent St DIG/EDG B5.....127 E4
SEDG DY3.....85 G1
WSLW WS2.....28 A5
Kent St North WSNGN B18.....107 F4
Kenward Cft HRBN B17.....124 D5
Kenway HLYWD B47.....192 B1
Kenwick Rd HRBN B17.....141 H3
Kenwood Rd BORD B9.....129 F2
Kenyon Cl STRBR DY8.....135 G1
Kenyon St CBHAMNW B3.....2 D2
Kerby Rd ERDW/GRVHL B23.....92 A2
Keresley Cl SOLH B91.....165 G5
Keresley Gv SLYOAK B29.....158 B1
Kernthorpe Rd
ALE/KHTH/YWD B14.....177 G1
Kerr Dr TPTN/OCK DY4.....69 E3
Kerridge Cl COVEN WV9.....11 G3
Kerr La SHLY B90.....194 A2
Kerry Cl BRLYHL DY5.....101 E5
NFLD/LBR B31.....158 B4
Kersley Gdns WNSFLD WV11.....25 F4
Kerswell Dr SHLY B90.....195 G3
Kesterton Rd FOAKS/STRLY B74.....32 C5
Kesteven Cl EDG B15.....143 F1
Kesteven Rd HHTH/SAND B71.....71 G4
Keston Rd KGSTG B44.....60 B2
Kestrel Av HLYWD B47.....206 B1
Kestrel Cl ERDE/BCHGN B24.....93 F2
Kestrel Dr FOAKS/STRLY B74.....32 D5
Kestrel Gv BVILLE B30.....159 F2
SHHTH WV12.....26 A2
Kestrel Ri
DUNHL/THL/PER WV6.....22 B5
Kestrel Rd DUDN DY1.....102 A1
HALE B63.....120 B5
LCLYGN/QTN B68.....122 D2
Keswick Dr KGSWFD DY6.....99 H5
Keswick Gv FOAKS/STRLY B74.....45 F5
Keswick Rd HIA/OLT B92.....147 F3
Ketley Cft BHTH/HG B12.....127 F5
Ketley Flds KGSWFD DY6.....100 D4
Ketley Hill Rd DUDN DY1.....101 H1
Ketley Rd KGSWFD DY6.....100 B5
Kettlebrook Rd SHLY B90.....195 H2
Kettlehouse Rd KGSTG B44.....60 B5
Kettlesbank Rd SEDG DY3 *.....83 E4
Kettles Wood Dr
RIDG/WDGT B32.....140 C5
Kettlewell Wy
CHWD/FDBR/MGN B37.....131 H2
Ketton Gv STETCH B33.....130 D1
Kew Cl CHWD/FDBR/MGN B37.....131 H1
Kew Dr DUDN DY1.....86 D4
Kew Gdns STETCH B33.....130 A3
Kewstoke Cl SHHTH WV12.....25 H1
Kewstoke Cft NFLD/LBR B31.....158 A4
Kewstoke Rd SHHTH WV12.....26 A1
Keyes Dr KGSWFD DY6.....99 E5
Key Hl WSNGN B18.....108 B4
Key Hill Circ WSNGN B18.....108 B4
Key Hill Dr WSNGN B18.....108 B4
Keynell Covert BVILLE B30.....177 G5
Keynes Dr BILS/COS WV14.....54 A2
Keys Crs HHTH/SAND B71.....71 G5
Keyse Rd MGN/WHC B75.....63 F1
Keysmith Cl WLNHL WV13.....40 A4
Keyte Cl TPTN/OCK DY4.....85 G1
The Keyway WLNHL WV13.....39 G5
Keyworth Cl DARL/WED WS10.....85 H1
Khyber Cl DARL/WED WS10.....40 A5
Kidd Cft TPTN/OCK DY4.....70 A1
Kidderminster Rd
KIDD DY10.....169 E2
Kidderminster Rd South
KIDD DY10.....169 E2
Kielder Cl DSYBK/YTR WS5.....58 A5
Kielder Gdns HAG/WOL DY9.....152 D1
Kier's Bridge Cl TPTN/OCK DY4.....85 H3
Kilburn Dr KGSWFD DY6.....83 E4
Kilburn Gv KGSTG B44.....60 B5
Kilburn Pl DUDS DY2.....102 D5
Kilburn Rd KGSTG B44.....60 B5
Kilbys Gv BFLD/HDSWWD B20.....126 A2
Kilcote Rd SHLY B90.....179 E5
Kilmet Wk SMTHWKW B67 *.....106 B4
Kilmore Cft CBROM B36.....94 A5
Kilmorie Rd ACCN B27.....146 C2
Kiln Cl BLKHTH/ROWR B65.....105 E3
Kiln La SHLY B90.....193 H4
YDLY B25.....146 B1
Kilsby Gv SOLH B91.....182 A5
Kilvert Rd DARL/WED WS10.....55 H3
Kimberley Av WASH/WDE B8.....110 C4
Kimberley Cl FOAKS/STRLY B74.....45 G3
Kimberley Pl BILS/COS WV14.....68 B4
Kimberley Rd HIA/OLT B92.....147 G5
SMTHWK B66.....106 C2
Kimberley St BDMR/CCFT WV3.....6 B6
Kimble Gv ERDE/BCHGN B24.....93 H3
Kimbley Ri HHTH/SAND B71.....71 E4
Kimpton Cl
ALE/KHTH/YWD B14.....178 A3
Kimsan Cft FOAKS/STRLY B74.....60 C1
Kinchford Cl SOLH B91.....181 H5

Kineton Cft RIDG/WDGT B32.....157 H2
Kineton Green Rd
HIA/OLT B92.....163 H2
Kineton Ri SEDG DY3.....67 E1
Kineton Rd RBRY B45.....187 G1
SCFLD/BOLD B73.....76 C2
Kinfare Dr
DUNHL/THL/PER WV6.....35 F1
Kinfare Ri SEDG DY3.....83 G2
King Charles Av WSLW WS2.....40 C3
King Charles Rd RMSLY B62.....139 H3
King Charles St DUDN DY1.....84 B4
King Edward Rd
BHTH/HG B12 B13.....144 B4
King Edwards Cl
BFLD/HDSWWD B20 *.....108 B1
King Edwards Gdns
BFLD/HDSWWD B20 *.....108 B2
King Edward's Rd CBHAMW B1.....2 B5
CBHAMW B1.....2 A3
King Edward's Rw
BKHL/PFLD WV2 *.....37 E5
King Edward's Sq
SCFLD/BOLD B73.....62 C3
King Edward St
DARL/WED WS10.....55 F3
Kingfield Rd SHLY B90.....179 E3
Kingfisher Cl BRWNH WS8.....9 E5
LGN/SDN/BHAMAIR B26.....147 G1
SEDG DY3.....67 E1
Kingfisher Dr CBROM B36.....114 A1
STRBR DY8.....134 C3
Kingfisher Gv SHHTH WV12.....25 H2
Kingfisher Rd
ERDW/GRVHL B23.....76 A4
Kingfisher Velw
BRDE/SHDE B34.....112 C4
Kingfisher Wy BVILLE B30.....159 F2
King George Crs
RUSH/SHEL WS4.....28 D4
King George Dr
RUSH/SHEL WS4.....28 D4
King George Vi Av WSL WS1.....57 G3
Kingham Cl SEDG DY3.....83 E4
Kingham Covert
ALE/KHTH/YWD B14.....177 H3
King's Av OLDBY B69.....85 H4
Kingsbridge Rd
RIDG/WDGT B32.....157 H1
Kingsbrook Dr SOLH B91.....181 H5
Kingsbury Av
ERDE/BCHGN B24.....93 H3
Kingsbury Cl RUSH/SHEL WS4.....42 D1
WALM/CURD B76.....95 F1
Kingsbury Rd
ERDE/BCHGN B24.....93 G3
TPTN/OCK DY4.....69 G3
WALM/CURD B76.....78 D4
Kingsclere Wk
BDMR/CCFT WV3.....50 C1
Kingscliff Rd SMHTH B10.....129 E4
Kings Cl ALE/KHTH/YWD B14.....160 C4
Kingscote Rd DOR/KN B93.....198 C1
EDG B15.....142 B2
King's Ct
CHWD/FDBR/MGN B37.....133 E3
STRBR DY8.....135 E2
Kings Crt CBROM B36.....113 H2
LGN/SDN/BHAMAIR B26.....147 G2
Kingscroft Cl FOAKS/STRLY B74.....45 G5
Kingscroft Rd
FOAKS/STRLY B74.....60 C1
Kingsdene Av KGSWFD DY6.....99 G5
Kingsdown Av HWK/WKHTH B42.....73 H5
Kingsdown Rd NFLD/LBR B31.....158 A1
Kingsfield Rd
ALE/KHTH/YWD B14.....161 G2
Kingsford Cl CBROM B36.....95 F5
Kingsford Nouveau
KGSWFD DY6.....100 C3
Kings Gdn BVILLE B30.....177 H1
Kings Green Av
HWK/WKHTH B38.....176 D3
Kingshayes Rd ALDR WS9.....30 B1
Kingshill Dr HWK/WKHTH B38.....176 D3
Kings Hill Fld DARL/WED WS10.....55 G5
Kingshurst Rd NFLD/LBR B31.....175 G2
SHLY B90.....179 H4
Kingshurst Wy
CHWD/FDBR/MGN B37.....113 H4
Kingsland Dr DOR/KN B93.....196 C5
Kingsland Rd KGSTG B44.....60 A4
WOLV WV1.....6 C1
Kingslea Rd SOLH B91.....181 E3
Kingsleigh Cft MGN/WHC B75.....47 F3
Kingsleigh Dr CBROM B36.....113 H1
Kingsleigh Rd
BFLD/HDSWWD B20.....90 B4
Kingsley Av
DUNHL/THL/PER WV6.....35 F1
Kingsley Bank Wy
LGN/SDN/BHAMAIR B26.....130 D5
Kingsley Ct YDLY B25 *.....130 A4
Kingsley Gdns CDSL WV8.....10 C1
Kingsley Gv SEDG DY3.....82 C1
Kingsley Rd BHTH/HG B12.....144 C2
BVILLE B30.....177 G2
KGSWFD DY6.....99 G4
Kingsley St DUDS DY2.....102 D5
WSLW WS2.....56 B1
Kingslow Av
ETTPK/GDPK/PENN WV4.....50 D2
King's Meadow HAG/WOL DY9.....170 C3
Kingstanding Ct CVALE B35.....96 D4
ERDW/GRVHL B23.....92 C4
Kings Mill Cl DARL/WED WS10.....55 C3
Kingsoak Gdns DUDS DY2.....103 G2
Kings Rd ALE/KHTH/YWD B14.....160 C4
BFLD/HDSWWD B20.....92 A2
RUSH/SHEL WS4.....75 H1
SEDG DY3.....67 G3
SPARK B11.....146 A2
Kings Sq BILS/COS WV14.....54 B5
Kings Street Prec
DARL/WED WS10.....55 F2
Kingstanding Rd KGSTG B44.....60 C4
KGSTG B44.....75 F5
Kings Ter
ALE/KHTH/YWD B14.....160 C4

Kingsthorpe Rd
ALE/KHTH/YWD B14..........178 C2
Kingston Rd BORD B9...........127 H5
MGN/WHC B75......................63 F2
Kingston Rw CBHAMW B1........2 C5
Kingsway Rd KGSWFD DY6......99 G2
King St ALDR WS9.................19 F5
BILS/COS WV14..................68 A3
BRLYHL DY5.......................118 H4
CDYHTH B64.....................121 F3
DARL/WED WS10..................70 C1
DUDS DY2............................9 D3
HAG/WOL DY9....................136 D3
HALE B63..........................138 C5
SMTHWK B66.....................106 D2
SPARK B11........................144 C1
STRBR DY8.........................135 E1
WLNHL WV13........................7 F4
WOLV WV1...........................50 D4
WSL WS1............................56 D1
King Street Pas BRLYHL DY5...120 A4
DUDS DY2.............................9 D3
Kingsway LGLYGN/QTN B68...125 F5
STRBR DY8.........................117 H4
WNSFLD WV11......................15 E3
WOLV WV10.........................24 A4
Kingsway Av TPTN/OCK DY4...69 G3
Kingsway Dr
HWK/WKHTH B38.................176 D3
Kingsway North ALDR WS9 *...29 G4
Kingsway Rd WOLV WV10.......24 A4
Kingsway South ALDR WS9 *...29 G4
Kingsway Ter WNSFLD WV11 *..15 E3
Kingswear Av
DUNHL/THL/PER WV6............34 C2
Kingswinford Rd DUDN DY1...101 G2
Kingswood Cl BVILLE B30......178 A2
SHLY B90..........................180 D4
Kingswood Cft
VAUX/NECH B7...................110 A2
Kingswood Dr SLYOAK B29....177 G2
FOAKS/STRLY B74................60 B4
Kingswood Gdns
ETTPK/GDPK/PENN WV4........51 F2
Kingswood Rd KGSWFD DY6....99 G5
MOS/BIL B13......................143 C3
NFLD/LBR B31....................189 F2
Kingswood Ter YDLY B25 *......25 H2
Kington Cl SHHTH WV12........25 H2
Kington Gdns
CHWD/FDBR/MGN B37.........131 H2
Kington Wy STETCH B33.......130 A3
King William St STRBR DY8...118 B4
Kiniths Crs HHTH/SAND B71...88 A2
Kiniths Wy HHTH/SAND B71....88 A2
RMSLY B62.........................122 C3
Kinlet Cl BDMR/CCFT WV3.....35 E5
Kinlet Gv NFLD/LBR B31........176 A3
Kinnerley St WSL WS1.............5 H5
Kinnersley Crs OLDBY B69....104 B4
Kinnerton Crs SLYOAK B29...141 F5
Kinross Crs GTB/HAM B43.......43 G4
Kinsey Gv ALE/KHTH/YWD B14..178 C3
Kinsham Dr SOLH B91............181 H5
Kintore Cft RIDG/WDGT B32...157 F3
Kintyre Cl RBRY B45..............173 G4
Kinver Av SHHTH WV12...........25 H4
Kinver Crs ALDR WS9.............30 C1
Kinver Cft BHTH/HG B12.......144 A1
WALM/CURD B76....................78 B3
Kinver Dr
ETTPK/GDPK/PENN WV4........50 C5
HAG/WOL DY9...................153 E3
Kinver Rd NFLD/LBR B31......176 B3
Kinver St STRBR DY8............101 H5
Kinwarton Cl YDLY B25..........146 D1
Kipling Av BILS/COS WV14......68 B2
Kipling Cl TPTN/OCK DY4.......69 G3
Kipling Rd NFLD/LBR B31......176 A1
SEDG DY3.............................8 D1
SHHTH WV12........................26 C3
WOLV WV10.........................12 D5
Kirby Cl BILS/COS WV14.........54 A5
Kirby Dr DUDN DY1...............83 E3
Kirkby Gn ERDW/GRVHL B23..107 C3
Kirkby Gn SCFLD/BOLD B75....62 A5
Kirkham Gdns BRLYHL DY5...101 E3
Kirkham Gv STETCH B33.......112 B5
Kirkham Wy TPTN/OCK DY4....85 C1
Kirkside Gv BRWNH WS8.........9 F5
Kirkstall Cl BLOX/PEL WS3....16 B5
Kirkstall Crs BLOX/PEL WS3...16 B5
Kirkstone Ct BRLYHL DY5.....118 D4
Kirkstone Crs GTB/HAM B43....43 H5
WMBN WV5.........................64 D5
Kirkstone Wy BRLYHL DY5....118 D4
Kirkwall Rd RIDG/WDGT B32..157 H1
Kirkwood Av ERDW/GRVHL B23...76 D4
Kirstead Gdns
DUNHL/THL/PER WV6............35 F2
Kirton Gv
DUNHL/THL/PER WV6............35 G1
SOLH B91..........................181 G4
STETCH B33......................112 B5
Kitchener Rd DUDS DY2.........85 F5
SLYOAK B29......................160 B1
Kitchen St WSNGN B18.........107 F5
Kitchen La WNSFLD WV11.......25 E2
Kitchen Rd Cl SHLY B90........195 G1
Kitegreen Cl
CHWD/FDBR/MGN B37.........114 D5
Kitsland Rd BKDE/SHDE B34..113 G3
Kitswell Gdns RIDG/WDGT B32..157 E4
Kittiwake Dr BRLYHL DY5.....119 E5
Kittoe Rd FOAKS/STRLY B74...46 D2
Kitt's Green Rd STETCH B33..130 D1
Kitwell La RIDG/WDGT B32.....157 E3
Kitwell La DOR/KN B93..........197 G2
Knaresdale Cl BRLYHL DY5...119 E4
Knaves Castle Av BRWNH WS8...9 F2
Knebworth Cl KGSTG B44......181 H5
Knightcote Dr SOLH B91.......181 H5
Knightley Rd SOLH B91.........181 F5
Knightlow Rd HRBN B17........124 D4
Knighton Cl FOAKS/STRLY B74...46 D3
Knighton Dr FOAKS/STRLY B74...46 D3
Knighton Rd DUDS DY2.........102 D5
FOAKS/STRLY B74................46 B1

NFLD/LBR B31....................176 A1
Knights Av
DUNHL/THL/PER WV6............22 A4
Knightsbridge Cl
FOAKS/STRLY B74................46 D1
Knightsbridge La SHHTH WV12..25 H4
Knightsbridge Rd
HIA/OLT B92......................164 B1
Knights Cl ERDW/GRVHL B23..92 C4
WLNHL WV13........................39 H5
Knights Ct
CHWD/FDBR/MGN B37.........133 E4
Knights Crs
DUNHL/THL/PER WV6............22 A3
Knightsfield Cl
SCFLD/BOLD B73..................61 E5
Knights Hl ALDR WS9.............44 B2
Knights Rd SMTH B25...........146 A1
Knightstone Av WSNGN B18..108 A5
Knights Wood Cl
MGN/WHC B75.....................62 D1
Knightwick Crs
ERDW/GRVHL B23................92 A1
Knipersley Rd
ERDW/GRVHL B23................77 E5
Knoll Cft ALDR WS9..............30 C1
LDYWD/EDGR B16 *.............126 A2
SHLY B90..........................194 D4
The Knoll KGSWFD DY6.......100 A4
RIDG/WDGT B32.................157 G1
Knottsall La LGLYGN/QTN B68..123 F1
Knotts Farm Rd KGSWFD DY6..100 C5
Knowlands Rd SHLY B90.......195 G1
Knowle Cl RBRY B45.............188 D1
Knowle Hill Rd DUDS DY2.....102 B5
Knowle Rd
BLKHTH/ROWR B65............103 F5
SPARK B11........................145 F4
Knowles Dr FOAKS/STRLY B74..62 A1
Knowles Rd WOLV WV1..........37 H4
Knowles St DARL/WED WS10...56 A5
Knowle Wood Rd
DOR/KN B93......................199 F1
Knox Rd BKHL/PFLD WV2.......52 A2
Knutswood Rd MOS/BIL B13 *..162 B3
Kohima Dr STRBR DY8..........135 E2
Kossuth Rd BILS/COS WV14....68 A2
Kyle Cl WOLV WV10...............22 D1
Kyles Wy RIDG/WDGT B32.....157 F3
Kynaston Crs CDSL WV8........10 D5
Kyngsford Rd STETCH B33...131 F1
Kyotts Lake Rd SPARK B11...127 G5
Kyrwicks La BHTH/HG B12.....127 G5
SPARK B11........................144 C1
Kyter La CBROM B36............112 D1

L

Laburnham Rd KGSWFD DY6...100 A3
Laburnum Av
CHWD/FDBR/MGN B37.........113 H3
SMTHWKW B67...................106 A5
Laburnum Cl BLOX/PEL WS3 *..17 H5
CHWD/FDBR/MGN B37.........113 H5
HLYWD B47........................192 C3
Laburnum Cft OLDBY B69......85 H4
Laburnum Dr WALM/CURD B76..78 B1
Laburnum Gv MOS/BIL B13 *..144 B4
WSLW WS2..........................40 D2
Laburnum Rd ALDR WS9........19 G4
BVILLE B30.......................159 H5
DARL/WED WS10..................56 B5
DSYBK/YTR WS5...................58 A3
DUDN DY1...........................84 B2
ETTPK/GDPK/PENN WV4........52 C5
TPTN/OCK DY4.....................52 C5
WOLV WV1..........................38 B5
Laburnum St BDMR/CCFT WV3..6 B6
STRBR DY8........................118 A5
Laburnum Vls SPARK B11 *...145 E2
Laburnum Wy NFLD/LBR B31..176 C4
Ladbroke Dr WALM/CURD B76..78 B1
Ladbroke Gv ACGN B27.........163 G2
Ladbrook Gv SEDG DY3..........82 C3
Ladbrook Rd SOLH B91........182 A2
Ladbury Gv DSYBK/YTR WS5...57 G4
Ladbury Rd DSYBK/YTR WS5...57 G4
Ladeler Gv STETCH B33.......131 F2
Ladies Wk SEDG DY3.............67 F3
Lady Bank RIDG/WDGT B32...157 F3
Lady Bracknell Ms
HIA/OLT B92......................176 A1
Lady Byron La DOR/KN B93...196 D1
Lady Grey's Wk STRBR DY8...134 D2
Lady La SHLY B90................194 B5
Ladymoor Rd BILS/COS WV14..68 C1
Ladypool Av SPARK B11 *......144 D1
Ladypool Cl RMSLY B62........139 E3
RUSH/SHEL WS4...................28 C5
Ladypool Rd BHTH/HG B12...144 C2
Ladysmith Rd HALE B63.......137 G1
Ladywell Cl WMBN WV5.........65 E3
Ladywell Wk DIG/EDG B5.........3 G7
Ladywood Circ
LDYWD/EDGR B16................126 A2
Ladywood Cl BRLYHL DY5....119 H2
Ladywood Middleway
LDYWD/EDGR B16................126 A2
Ladywood Rd
FOAKS/STRLY B74................47 E5
LDYWD/EDGR B16................125 H3
Lake Av DSYBK/YTR WS5........57 H1
Lake Cl DSYBK/YTR WS5.........58 A1
Lakedown Cl
ALE/KHTH/YWD B14............178 A4
Lakefield Cl HLGN/YWD B28..163 F3
Lakefield Rd WNSFLD WV11....25 E5
Lakehouse Gv
HWK/WKHTH B38................176 B2
Lakehouse Rd SCFLD/BOLD B73..76 C3
Laker Cl STRBR DY8............118 C5
Lakeside
CHWD/FDBR/MGN B37.........133 E4
FOAKS/STRLY B74................47 E5
Lakeside Cl WLNHL WV13.......39 E2
Lakeside Ct BRLYHL DY5......118 D4
Lakeside Dr ERDW/GRVHL B23..91 H1

SHLY B90..........................195 F1
Lakeside Rd WBROM B70......71 E5
Lakes Rd ERDW/GRVHL B23....75 C5
Lake St SEDG DY3.................83 F3
Lake View Cl BVILLE B30......159 C5
Lakewood Dr RBRY B45.......174 D4
Lakey La HLGN/YWD B28.......163 F5
Lambah Cl BILS/COS WV14.....54 A1
Lamb Cl BKDE/SHDE B34......113 G4
Lamb Crs WMBN WV5.............80 D1
Lambert Cl ERDW/GRVHL B23..76 B5
Lambert Ct KGSWFD DY6.......99 H1
Lambert End WBROM B70.......87 F3
Lambert Fold DUDS DY2.......103 E1
Lambert Rd WOLV WV10........23 H4
Lambert St WBROM B70.........87 F3
Lambeth Cl
CHWD/FDBR/MGN B37.........114 B5
Lambeth Rd BILS/COS WV14...53 F1
KGSTG B44.........................60 A5
Lambourne Gv
CHWD/FDBR/MGN B37.........131 G2
Lambourne Wy BRLYHL DY5..118 D4
Lambourn Rd
ERDW/GRVHL B23................92 B2
WLNHL WV13........................40 B4
Lambscote Cl SHLY B90.......179 E5
Lammas Cl HIA/OLT B92......146 C1
Lammas Rd STRBR DY8........117 C1
Lammermoor Av GTB/HAM B43..73 H1
Lamont Av RIDG/WDGT B32...141 F4
Lamorna Cl BDMR/CCFT WV3..35 F5
Lanark Cl KGSWFD DY6........100 D4
Lanark Crt CVALE B35...........94 B3
Lancaster Av ALDR WS9.........30 B2
DARL/WED WS10..................56 C5
RBRY B45..........................174 A5

Lancaster Circ Queensway
CBHAMNE B4.........................3 H2
Lancaster Cl BVILLE B30......160 A4
Lancaster Dr CVALE B35........94 D4
Lancaster Gdns
ETTPK/GDPK/PENN WV4........51 E3
Lancaster Pl BLOX/PEL WS3...17 E5
Lancaster Rd BRLYHL DY5....119 E2
Lancaster St CBHAMNE B4......3 H1
Lancelot Cl WASH/WDE B8...128 C1
Lanchester Rd
HWK/WKHTH B38................177 E4
Lanchester Wy CBROM B36...95 H5
Lander Cl RBRY B45.............188 A2
Lander Rd HDSW B21...........89 E4
Land La
CHWD/FDBR/MGN B37.........132 A5
Landor Rd DOR/KN B93.......199 C2
Landor St BORD B9..............127 H1
Landrake Rd KGSWFD DY6...100 B4
Landsdown Pl WSNGN B18...108 A4
Landseer Gv GTB/HAM B43....59 H4
Landsgate STRBR DY8.........152 C1
Landswood Cl KGSTG B44.......75 C2
Landswood Rd
LGLYGN/QTN B68................105 G5
Lane Av WSLW WS2.............41 F2
Lane Cl WSLW WS2..............41 F2
Lane Cft WALM/CURD B76......78 C3
Lane Green Av CDSL WV8.......21 G1
Lane Green Rd CDSL WV8......11 E5
Lane Rd
ETTPK/GDPK/PENN WV4........53 E5
Lanes Cl WMBN WV5.............80 B1
Lanesfield Dr
ETTPK/GDPK/PENN WV4........53 E4
Laneside Av FOAKS/STRLY B74..60 B1
Laneside Gdns WSLW WS2....41 E3
Lane St BILS/COS WV14.........53 H5
Langcomb Rd SHLY B90......180 A5
Langdale Cl BRWNH WS8.......19 E1
Langdale Cft HDSW B21......107 C2
Langdale Dr BILS/COS WV14...53 H1
Langdale Rd GTB/HAM B43....73 H4
Langdale Wy HAG/WOL DY9..136 B3
Langdon St BORD B9...........127 H2
Langfield Rd DOR/KN B93....197 F1
Langford Av GTB/HAM B43....58 C4
Langford Cl WSL WS1.............5 C5
Langford Cft SOLH B91........182 A3
Langham Cl
LGN/SDN/BHAMAIR B26.......130 C5
Langham Gn FOAKS/STRLY B74..45 F4
Langholm Dr KGSTG B44.......75 C3
Langley Av BILS/COS WV14....68 C3
Langley Cl ALDR WS9............19 G4
Langley Crs LGLYGN/QTN B68..105 F5
Langley Dr CVALE B35...........94 C3
Langley Gdns BDMR/CCFT WV3..50 D1
Langley Green Rd OLDBY B69..105 E5
Langley Hall Dr MGN/WHC B75..63 H2
Langley Hall Rd HIA/OLT B92..163 G3
MGN/WHC B75.....................63 H2
Langley Heath Dr
WALM/CURD B76..................63 F5
Langley High St OLDBY B69...105 E5
Langley Pkwy MGN/WHC B75..63 F2
Langley Ri HIA/OLT B92........148 B4
Langley Rd
ETTPK/GDPK/PENN WV4........50 C1
LGLYGN/QTN B68................105 E5
SMHTH B10.......................128 A4
Langleys Rd SLYOAK B29.....159 C1
Langmead Cl WSLW WS2.......40 B2
Langsett Rd WOLV WV10........37 G1
Langstone Rd
ALE/KHTH/YWD B14............178 D3
DUDN DY1...........................83 C5
Langton Cl CBROM B36.......114 B5
Langton Pl BILS/COS WV14....54 D1
Langton Rd WASH/WDE B8..110 C5
Langtree Av SOLH B91........181 H4
Langwood Ct CBROM B36....112 D1
Langworth Av ACGN B27......146 C2
Lannacombe Rd
NFLD/LBR B31....................189 C2
Lansbury Av DARL/WED WS10..55 G4
Lansbury Gn CDYHTH B64...121 H4
Lansbury Rd CDYHTH B64....121 H4

Lansdale Av HIA/OLT B92.....165 H2
Lansdowne Av CDSL WV8......10 A5
Lansdowne Cl BILS/COS WV14..68 A4
DUDS DY2..........................103 F3
Lansdowne Rd BILS/COS WV14..54 A1
ERDW/GRVHL B23................137 H5
HALE B63..........................137 H5
HDSW B21........................122 D4
RMSLY B62..........................6 D2
Lansdowne St WSNGN B18..107 H5
Lansdown Pl WSNGN B18 *...108 A4
Lantern Rd DUDS DY2.........120 C2
Lanton Cl BLOX/PEL WS3......16 C5
Lapal La North RMSLY B62...139 G4
Lapal La South RMSLY B62..139 G4
Lapley Cl WOLV WV1.............38 B5
Lapper Av
ETTPK/GDPK/PENN WV4........67 H1
Lapwing Cl BRWNH WS8.........9 E5
Lapwing Cft ERDW/GRVHL B23..76 A4
Lapwing Dr HIA/OLT B92.....167 H3
Lapwood Av KGSWFD DY6....100 C4
Lapworth Dr SCFLD/BOLD B75..61 E5
Lapworth Gv BHTH/HG B12..144 A1
Lara Cl HRBN B17...............124 D4
Lara Gv TPTN/OCK DY4.........85 G4
Larch Av HDSW B21.............108 C1
Larch Cft
CHWD/FDBR/MGN B37.........132 B2
OLDBY B69..........................69 E5
Larch Dr NFLD/LBR B31......174 C4
Larches La BDMR/CCFT WV3...6 A4
Larches St SPARK B11.........144 C1
Larchfield Cl
BFLD/HDSWWD B20..............90 B3
Larch Gdns BILS/COS WV14...54 C4
Larch Gv SEDG DY3..............67 G4
Larchmere Dr HLGN/YWD B28..162 D2
WNSFLD WV11......................15 E4
Larch Rd KGSWFD DY6.........100 D4
Larchwood Crs
FOAKS/STRLY B74................45 E5
Larchwood Gn DSYBK/YTR WS5..57 G4
Larchwood Rd DSYBK/YTR WS5..57 G4
Larcombe Dr
ETTPK/GDPK/PENN WV4........52 B3
Large Av DARL/WED WS10.....55 E4
Lark Cl ALE/KHTH/YWD B14...178 C3
Larkfield Av CBROM B36......112 D1
Larkfield Rd STRBR DY8......134 C3
Larkhill Rd STRBR DY8.........24 A1
Lark Meadow Dr
CHWD/FDBR/MGN B37.........131 G1
Larksfield Ms BRLYHL DY5...119 E5
Larks Ml BLOX/PEL WS3........17 G3
Larkspur Cft CBROM B36....111 H1
Larkspur Rd DUDS DY2........100 C3
Larkswood Dr
ETTPK/GDPK/PENN WV4........50 C5
SEDG DY3............................8 B3
Larne Rd
LGN/SDN/BHAMAIR B26.......130 C5
Latches Cl DARL/WED WS10...55 G2
Latelow Rd STETCH B33......130 C2
Latham Av GTB/HAM B43.......73 G4
Latham Crs TPTN/OCK DY4....85 G3
Lath La SMTHWK B66..........106 C1
Lathom Gv STETCH B33......112 B4
Latimer Gdns EDG B15........126 D5
Latimer Pl WSNGN B18.......107 G5
Latimer St WLNHL WV13........39 G4
Latymer Cl WALM/CURD B76...78 C4
Lauder Cl SEDG DY3............67 E2
WLNHL WV13........................38 D4
Lauderdale Cl BRWNH WS8....19 E1
Lauderdale Gdns WOLV WV10..13 E4
Laughton Cl NFLD/LBR B31..189 H1
Launceston Cl DSYBK/YTR WS5..58 B1
Launceston Rd
DSYBK/YTR WS5...................58 B1
The Launde HLGN/YWD B28..179 F2
Laundry Rd SMTHWK B66....125 E1
Laural Dr SMTHWK B66........106 D1
Laureates Wk
FOAKS/STRLY B74................47 F4
Laurel Av BHTH/HG B12.......144 C2
Laurel Dr FOAKS/STRLY B74...45 E5
SMTHWK B66......................106 C1
Laurel Gdns ACGN B27........146 C2
HDSW B21..........................89 G5
Laurel Gv BDMR/CCFT WV3....54 C4
BVILLE B30........................159 G4
Laurel La HALE B63.............138 D4
Laurel Rd BVILLE B30.........177 E1
DSYBK/YTR WS5...................57 H5
DUDN DY1...........................84 B3
HDSW B21...........................89 H5
TPTN/OCK DY4.....................69 F4
The Laurels
LGN/SDN/BHAMAIR B26.......148 A2
SMTHWK B66 *...................107 E5
Laurence Gv
DUNHL/THL/PER WV6............22 A3
Lauriston Cl DUDN DY1.........83 H5
Lavender Cl COVEN WV9.......11 H4
DSYBK/YTR WS5...................57 F5
Lavender Gdns
ERDW/GRVHL B23................75 H4
Lavender Gv BILS/COS WV14...68 D4
BLOX/PEL WS3.....................28 A5
Lavender La STRBR DY8......134 C4
Lavender Rd DUDN DY1........84 B5
Lavendon Rd PBAR/PBCH B42..90 A1
Lavinia Rd RMSLY B62........139 G4
Law Cliff Rd PBAR/PBCH B42..74 B5
Law Cl OLDBY B69...............86 B4
Lawden Rd SMHTH B10........127 H4
Lawford Cl VAUX/NECH B7...127 G1
Lawford Gv DIG/EDG B5.......127 F4
SHLY B90..........................179 F3
Lawfred Av WNSFLD WV11....24 D5
Lawley Cl RUSH/SHEL WS4....28 D1
Lawley Middleway
CBHAMNE B4......................127 G1
Lawley Rd BILS/COS WV14.....68 A5
Lawley St DUDN DY1.............84 A5
WBROM B70........................86 D3

The Lawley HALE B63..........154 C1
Lawn Av STRBR DY8...........135 E3
Lawn La COVEN WV9...........11 H2
Lawnoaks Cl BRWNH WS8.......8 D2
Lawn Rd BKHL/PFLD WV2.....52 C2
Lawnsdale Cl
CSHL/WTROR B46................115 F3
Lawnsdown Rd BRLYHL DY5..120 B5
Lawnsfield Gv
ERDW/GRVHL B23................76 B4
Lawnside Gn BILS/COS WV14..53 H1
Lawn St STRBR DY8............135 E3
Lawnswood KINVER DY7......117 E2
WALM/CURD B76...................78 C3
Lawnswood Av
DUNHL/THL/PER WV6............22 A2
ETTPK/GDPK/PENN WV4.......180 C2
SHLY B90..........................199 C5
STRBR DY8........................135 E3
Lawnswood Dr ALDR WS9.....19 G4
KINVER DY7.......................117 E2
Lawnswood Gv HDSW B21....89 E5
Lawnswood Rd
DUNHL/THL/PER WV6............22 B2
SEDG DY3..........................117 C1
Lawnwood Rd DUDS DY2.....120 C2
Lawrence Av WNSFLD WV11...58 A1
WOLV WV10.........................38 A1
Lawrence Dr WALM/CURD B76..79 F5
Lawrence La CDYHTH B64....121 E3
Lawrence St HAG/WOL DY9..136 A1
WLNHL WV13........................39 G2
Lawrence Wk GTB/HAM B43...59 H4
Lawson Cl ALDR WS9............44 B1
Lawson St CBHAMNE B4.........3 H2
Law St HHTH/SAND B71........87 G1
Lawton Cl BLKHTH/ROWR B65..104 A3
Laxey Rd LDYWD/EDGR B16..125 E2
Laxford Cl BHTH/HG B12.....144 A1
Laxton Cl KGSWFD DY6......100 C4
Laxton Gv SOLH B91...........165 E3
YDLY B25..........................129 H3
Lazy Hill Rd ALDR WS9........30 C1
Lazy Hill Rd ALDR WS9..........30 C1
Lea Av DARL/WED WS10........70 B2
Lea Bank Rd DUDS DY2.......120 B1
Leabon Gv HRBN B17..........142 A3
Lea Cft
CHWD/FDBR/MGN B37.........131 H2
Lea Hill Rd BFLD/HDSWWD B20..90 C4
Leaholme Gdns HAG/WOL DY9..135 H5
Leahouse Gdns
LGLYGN/QTN B68................105 F5
Lea House Rd BVILLE B30....160 A3
Leahouse Rd LGLYGN/QTN B68..123 E1
Leahurst Crs HRBN B17.......142 A3
Lea Manor Dr
ETTPK/GDPK/PENN WV4........51 E5
Leam Crs HIA/OLT B92........164 D1
Leamington Rd BHTH/HG B12..144 C2
Leamore Cl WSLW WS2.........27 E3
Leamore La WSLW WS2.........27 E5
Leamount Dr KGSTG B44......75 H4
Leander Gdns
ALE/KHTH/YWD B14............161 F5
Leander Rd HAG/WOL DY9...136 D3
Lea Rd BDMR/CCFT WV3.......51 G1
SPARK B11........................145 E5
Lea Rd WMBN WV5...............65 F4
Leasow Dr EDG B15............142 A4
Leasowe Rd RBRY B45........173 H5
TPTN/OCK DY4.....................52 C5
Leasowes Ct HALE B63........138 B5
Leasowes Dr
DUNHL/THL/PER WV6............34 B1
ETTPK/GDPK/PENN WV4........51 E5
Leasowes La HALE B63........139 E2
Leasowes Rd
ALE/KHTH/YWD B14............161 F1
The Leasowes TPTN/OCK DY4..86 A4
The Leasow ALDR WS9.........29 G5
The Lea STETCH B33...........130 C1
Leatherhead Cl AST/WIT B6..109 F3
Lea Vale Rd STRBR DY8......117 G5
Leavesden Gv
LGN/SDN/BHAMAIR B26.......147 C2
Lea Vw ALDR WS9...............29 G5
SHHTH WV12........................25 F5
Lea Village STETCH B33......130 D2
Lea Wk RBRY B45...............173 H5
Lea Yield Cl BVILLE B30......160 A3
Lechlade Rd GTB/HAM B43....58 B5
Leckie Rd WSLW WS2...........42 A1
Ledbury Cl ALDR WS9...........30 C1
LDYWD/EDGR B16...............126 A4
Ledbury Dr WOLV WV1..........38 B4
Ledbury Wy WALM/CURD B76..78 C4

Ledsam Gv RIDG/WDGT B32 ..... 141 F1
Ledsam St LDYWD/EDGR B16 .... 126 A2
Ledwell SHLY B90 ..... 194 A3
Lee Bank Middleway EDG B15 ... 126 C4
Leebank Rd HALE B63 ..... 138 A5
Leech St TPTN/OCK DY4 ..... 86 A1
Lee Crs EDG B15 ..... 126 C4
Lee Gdns SMTHWKW B67 ..... 106 A4
Lee Mt EDG B15 * 126 C4
Lee Rd CDYHTH B64 ..... 121 F4
HLYWD B47 ..... 192 C1
Leeson Wk HRBN B17 ..... 142 B2
Lees Rd BILS/COS WV14 ..... 54 B5
Lees St WSNGN B18 ..... 107 H4
Lees Ter WBROM B70 ..... 71 E3
Legge La BILS/COS WV14 ..... 68 D1
Legge St BKHL/PFLD WV2 ..... 2 C3
CBHAMNE B4 ..... 3 J1
WBROM B70 ..... 87 H5
Legion Rd RBRY B45 ..... 187 C1
Legs La WOLVN WV10 ..... 13 F4
Leicester Rd SMTHWKW B67 ... 124 A3
Leicester Pl HHTH/SAND B71 .... 71 G4
Leicester St
DUNHL/THL/PER WV6 ..... 36 D1
WSL WS1 ..... 4 E3
Leigham Dr HRBN B17 ..... 124 B3
Leigh Cl RUSH/SHEL WS4 ..... 42 C1
Leigh Rd MGN/WHC B75 ..... 46 A2
RUSH/SHEL WS4 ..... 42 C1
WASH/WDE B8 ..... 110 C3
Leighs Cl RUSH/SHEL WS4 ..... 29 E1
Leighs Rd RUSH/SHEL WS4 ..... 28 D1
Leighswood Av ALDR WS9 ..... 30 B3
Leighswood Cl ALDR WS9 ..... 30 A3
Leighswood Gv ALDR WS9 ..... 30 A3
Leighswood Rd ALDR WS9 ..... 30 A3
Leighton Cl DUDN DY1 ..... 83 G4
Leighton Rd BILS/COS WV14 .... 54 C4
ETTPK/GDPK/PENN WV4 ..... 51 F2
MOS/BIL B13 ..... 144 D4
Leith Gv HWK/WKHTH B38 ..... 176 C5
Lilanc Av HRBN B17 ..... 141 G2
Leilow St HHTH/SAND B71 ..... 71 G3
Le More FOAKS/STRLY B74 ..... 47 E3
Lemox Rd WBROM B70 ..... 71 F3
Lench Cl RMSLY B62 ..... 122 A5
Lench's Cl MOS/BIL B13 ..... 144 B5
Lenchs Gn DIG/EDG B5 ..... 127 E5
Lench St CBHAMNE B4 ..... 3 G2
Lenchs Trust Houses
BHTH/HG B12 * 127 F5
Len Davies Rd SHHTH WV12 ..... 25 C3
Lennard Gdns SMTHWK B66 * ... 107 F3
Lennox Gdns BDMR/CCFT WV4 .. 6 A7
Lennox Gv BILS/COS WV14 ..... 68 A1
Lennox St LOZ/NWT B19 ..... 108 D5
Lenton Cft
LGN/SDN/BHAMAIR B26 ..... 147 E3
Lenwade Rd LGLYGN/QTN B68 .123 H4
Leominster Rd SHLY B90 ..... 195 G4
Leominster Wk RBRY B45 ..... 175 H5
Leonard Gv LOZ/NWT B19 ..... 108 D1
Leonard Rd LOZ/NWT B19 ..... 108 C1
STRBR DY8 ..... 134 C2
Leopold Av BFLD/HDSWWD B20..89 G1
Leopold St BHTH/HG B12 ..... 127 F4
Lepid Gv SLYOAK B29 ..... 142 B5
Lerryn Cl KGSWFD DY6 ..... 100 B4
Lerwick Cl KGSWFD DY6 ..... 100 B4
Lesley Dr KGSWFD DY6 ..... 100 B5
Leslie Dr TPTN/OCK DY4 ..... 69 G2
Leslie Ri OLDBY B69 ..... 104 A1
Leslie Rd BFLD/HDSWWD B20....90 D4
FOAKS/STRLY B74 ..... 45 H3
LDYWD/EDGR B16 ..... 115 G2
WOLVN WV10 ..... 37 H1
Lesscroft Cl COVEN WV9 ..... 12 A4
Lester Gv ALDR WS9 ..... 45 E3
Lester St BILS/COS WV14 ..... 54 B3
Levante Gdns STETCH B33 ..... 130 H2
Leve La WLNHL WV13 ..... 39 H4
Level St BRLYHL DY5 ..... 119 C1
Leven Cft WALM/CURD B76 ..... 78 C4
Leven Dr SHHTH WV12 ..... 13 G4
Levenwick Wy KGSWFD DY6 .... 100 C4
The Leverretts HDSW B21 ..... 89 E3
Lever St BKHL/PFLD WV2 ..... 7 G7
Leverton Ri WOLVN WV10 ..... 23 E4
Leveson Cl DUDS DY2 ..... 108 E1
Leveson Dr TPTN/OCK DY4 ..... 69 E5
Leveson Rd WNSFLD WV11 ..... 25 F2
Leveson St WLNHL WV13 ..... 39 C3
Levington Cl
DUNHL/THL/PER WV6 ..... 20 D5
Lewis Av WOLV WV1 ..... 38 B2
Lewis Cl SHHTH WV12 ..... 26 B5
Lewis Gv WNSFLD WV11 ..... 24 D4
Lewisham Rd SMTHWK B66 ..... 106 C2
WOLVN WV10 ..... 12 D5
Lewisham St HHTH/SAND B71 ...87 H2
Lewis Rd BVLLE B30 ..... 160 C3
HAG/WOL DY9 ..... 136 B2
LGLYGN/QTN B68 ..... 123 F5
Lewis St BILS/COS WV14 ..... 54 A2
TPTN/OCK DY4 ..... 86 B1
WSLW WS2 ..... 41 H2
Lewthorn Ri
ETTPK/GDPK/PENN WV4 ..... 52 B4
Lexington Gn BRLYHL DY5 ..... 119 E5
Leybourne Crs COVEN WV9 ..... 11 H5
Leybourne Gv YDLY B25 ..... 146 B1
Leybrook Rd RBRY B45 ..... 174 B5
Leyburn Cl SHHTH WV12 ..... 26 B5
Leyburn Rd LDYWD/EDGR B16 ..126 A2
Leycester Cl NFLD/LBR B31 ..... 189 C1
Leycroft Av STECH B33 ..... 131 F1
Ley Hill Farm Rd
NFLD/LBR B31 ..... 158 A5
Ley Hill Rd MGN/WHC B75 ..... 47 C5
Leyland Av WOLV WV3 ..... 36 B4
Leyland Cft BLOX/PEL WS3 ..... 17 H5
Leyman Cl
ALE/KHTH/YWD B14 ..... 179 E1
Ley Ri SEDG DY3 ..... 67 E2
Leys Cl HAG/WOL DY9 ..... 136 A5
Leys Crs BRLYHL DY5 ..... 118 D1

Leysdown Gv ACGN B27 ..... 163 G2
Leysdown Rd ACGN B27 ..... 163 G2
Leys Rd BRLYHL DY5 ..... 118 D1
The Leys DARL/WED WS10 ..... 55 G2
Leys Wd Cft
LGN/SDN/BHAMAIR B26 ..... 147 G1
Leyton Cl BRLYHL DY5 ..... 119 F4
Leyton Gv KGSTG B44 ..... 75 C2
Leyton Rd HDSW B21 ..... 107 H1
Libbards Ga SOLH B91 ..... 182 A5
Libbards Wy SOLH B91 ..... 181 H5
Library Wy RBRY B45 ..... 187 H1
Lich Av WNSFLD WV11 ..... 25 E3
Lichfield Rd ALDR WS9 ..... 19 G3
AST/WIT B6 ..... 109 G3
BLOX/PEL WS3 ..... 17 E5
BRWNH WS8 ..... 19 C1
CSHL/WTROR B46 ..... 115 F1
FOAKS/STRLY B74 ..... 62 B1
RUSH/SHEL WS4 ..... 42 C1
WNSFLD WV11 ..... 24 D5
WOLV WV1 ..... 7 F4
WSL WS1 ..... 4 E3
Lichwood Rd WNSFLD WV11 ..... 25 F3
Lickey Coppice RBRY B45 ..... 188 C4
Lickey Rd RBRY B45 ..... 188 C2
STRBR DY8 ..... 135 H1
Liddon Gv ACGN B27 ..... 163 G2
Liddon Rd ACGN B27 ..... 163 G2
Lifford Cl ALE/KHTH/YWD B14...177 F1
Lifford La BVLLE B30 ..... 177 F1
Lifton Cft KGSWFD DY6 ..... 100 B4
Lightwoode Av
LDYWD/EDGR B16 ..... 126 A1
Lighthorne Rd SOLH B91 ..... 164 D4
Lightning Wy NFLD/LBR B31 ... 189 H1
Lightwood Cl DOR/KN B93 ..... 183 F5
Lightwood Rd DUDN DY1 ..... 84 A3
Lightwoods Hi SMTHWKW B67..124 A4
Lightwoods Rd HAG/WOL DY9 .153 E1
SMTHWK B67 ..... 124 B3
Lilac Av BHTH/HG B12 ..... 144 C2
DYSBK/YTR WS5 ..... 57 C4
FOAKS/STRLY B74 ..... 60 A1
KGSTG B44 ..... 75 E4
Lilac Dr WMBN WV5 ..... 64 D5
Lilac Gv DARL/WED WS10 ..... 71 C1
WSLW WS2 ..... 40 C2
Lilac Rd DUDN DY1 ..... 84 B2
SHHTH WV12 ..... 13 C5
WOLV WV1 ..... 38 D5
Lilac Wy RMSLY B62 ..... 122 D4
Lilian Gv BILS/COS WV14 ..... 69 E2
Lilleshall Crs BKHL/PFLD WV2 ...52 C2
Lilleshall Rd
LGN/SDN/BHAMAIR B26 ..... 130 D5
Lilley La NFLD/LBR B31 ..... 175 H5
Lillington Gv BKDE/SHDE B34..133 F4
Lillington Rd SHLY B90 ..... 180 B5
Lilycroft La HWK/WKHTH B38..191 E1
Lily Rd
LGN/SDN/BHAMAIR B26 ..... 146 D1
Lily St HHTH/SAND B71 ..... 87 G1
Limberlost Cl
BFLD/HDSWWD B20 ..... 90 A3
Limbrick Cl SHLY B90 ..... 179 H3
Limbury Gv HIA/OLT B92 * 165 H2
Lime Av SLYOAK B29 ..... 142 D5
WSLW WS2 ..... 27 H5
Lime Cl HLYWD B47 ..... 192 C3
TPTN/OCK DY4 ..... 85 E1
WBROM B70 ..... 87 E2
WSLW WS2 ..... 27 H5
Lime Ct SPARK B11 ..... 145 E3
Lime Gv BHTH/HG B12 ..... 144 B2
BILS/COS WV14 ..... 38 C5
CHWD/FDBR/MGN B37 ..... 132 B5
LGN/SDN/BHAMAIR B26 ..... 146 D5
LOZ/NWT B19 ..... 108 C1
RUSH/SHEL WS4 ..... 29 E4
SCFLD/BOLD B73 ..... 77 F4
SMTHWK B66 ..... 106 D5
Limehurst Av WOLV WV3 ..... 35 G4
Limehurst Rd RUSH/SHEL WS4..29 E5
Lime Kiln Wk HWK/WKHTH B38.190 B1
Limekiln La
ALE/KHTH/YWD B14 ..... 178 C1
Lime La BLOX/PEL WS3 ..... 8 A3
Limepit La DUDN DY1 ..... 84 A3
Lime Rd DARL/WED WS10 ..... 55 H4
SEDG DY3 ..... 67 H2
Limes Av BLKHTH/ROWR B65 ....101 E4
BRLYHL DY5 ..... 101 F4
Limes Rd DUDN DY1 ..... 84 B3
DUNHL/THL/PER WV6 ..... 21 H5
The Limes ERDE/BCHGN B24 ....92 D3
LDYWD/EDGR B16 * 125 H1
SPARK B11 ..... 145 E1
WSL WS1 ..... 5 J3
Lime St BDMR/CCFT WV3 ..... 6 B7
BILS/COS WV14 ..... 54 B4
WSLW WS2 ..... 5 G4
Limes Vw SEDG DY3 ..... 67 F4
Lime Tree Av
DUNHL/THL/PER WV6 ..... 35 E2
Lime Tree Gdns CDSL WV8 ..... 10 D4
Lime Tree Gv NFLD/LBR B31 ... 176 A3
Lime Tree Rd ACGN B27 ..... 146 C2
CDSL WV8 ..... 10 D4
DYSBK/YTR WS5 ..... 57 G4
WASH/WDE B8 ..... 110 D3
Limetree Rd FOAKS/STRLY B74...44 D4
Linchmere Rd HDSW B21 ..... 89 E4
Lincoln Av WLNHL WV13 ..... 40 B3
Lincoln Cl ACGN B27 ..... 147 E4
Lincoln Gn WOLVN WV10 ..... 12 D5
Lincoln Gv
CHWD/FDBR/MGN B37 ..... 132 A4
Lincoln Rd ACGN B27 ..... 146 D5
DUDS DY2 ..... 120 D1
HHTH/SAND B71 ..... 71 H2
SMTHWKW B67 ..... 124 A2
WSL WS1 ..... 5 H5
Lincoln Rd North ACGN B27 .... 147 E4
Lincoln St BHTH/HG B12 ..... 144 A1

WOLVN WV10 ..... 7 K2
Lindale Av CBROM B36 ..... 111 G3
Lindale Crs BRLYHL DY5 ..... 135 H1
Lindale Dr WMBN WV5 ..... 64 D5
Linden Av CGTB/HAM B43 ..... 73 G3
OLDBY B69 ..... 104 B1
RMSLY B62 ..... 122 C5
Linden Cl WSLW WS2 * 40 B3
Linden Dr STRBR DY8 ..... 135 G1
Linden La SHHTH WV12 ..... 26 D1
Linden Lea BDMR/CCFT WV3 ....35 H4
Linden Rd BVLLE B30 ..... 159 G3
DUDN DY1 ..... 84 B4
SMTHWK B66 ..... 106 D5
Lindens Dr FOAKS/STRLY B74....60 A5
The Lindens
DUNHL/THL/PER WV6 ..... 36 A2
RIDG/WDGT B32 ..... 140 C5
Lindenwood SCFLD/BOLD B73 ...62 B2
Lindford Wy HWK/WKHTH B38..177 F3
Lindley Av TPTN/OCK DY4 ..... 85 F3
Lindon Cl BRWNH WS8 ..... 19 G1
Lindon Dr BRWNH WS8 ..... 19 F1
Lindon Rd BRWNH WS8 ..... 19 F1
Lindrick Cl BLOX/PEL WS3 ..... 16 B4
Lindridge Dr WALM/CURD B76 ...79 E5
Lindridge Rd ERDW/GRVHL B23..92 A1
MGN/WHC B75 ..... 63 F1
SHLY B90 ..... 179 G4
Lindrosa Rd FOAKS/STRLY B74...45 F2
Lindsay Rd PBAR/PBCH B42 .....74 B2
Lindsey Av NFLD/LBR B31 ..... 176 B1
Lindsey Pl BRLYHL DY5 ..... 119 E1
Lindsey Rd HHTH/SAND B71 .....71 G2
Lindsworth Ap BVLLE B30 ..... 177 C2
Lindsworth Cl BVLLE B30 ..... 177 H2
Lindsworth Rd BVLLE B30 ..... 177 F2
Linfield Gdns SEDG DY3 ..... 67 E2
Linford Gv YDLY B25 ..... 129 C1
Linforth Dr FOAKS/STRLY B74...60 A1
Lingard Cl VAUX/NECH B7 ..... 109 H4
Lingard Rd MGN/WHC B75 ..... 63 F5
Lingfield Av KGSTG B44 ..... 75 E2
WOLVN WV10 ..... 12 D2
Lingfield Gdns
BKDE/SHDE B34 ..... 112 D3
Lingfield Gv
DUNHL/THL/PER WV6 ..... 34 D1
Lingham Cl HIA/OLT B92 ..... 165 F3
Lingmoor Gv RUSH/SHEL WS4 ...30 A3
Lingwood Dr KGSWFD DY6 ..... 100 C4
Link Rd ALDR WS9 ..... 19 H4
LDYWD/EDGR B16 ..... 125 G1
WMBN WV5 ..... 65 E4
Linkswood Cl MOS/BIL B13 ..... 161 H1
The Link RBRY B45 ..... 162 D1
Linley Cl ALDR WS9 ..... 29 G5
Linley Dr WOLVN WV10 ..... 23 G1
Linley Gv ALE/KHTH/YWD B14..160 C4
SEDG DY3 ..... 82 A4
Linley Rd RUSH/SHEL WS4 ..... 29 F3
Linley Wood Rd ALDR WS9 ..... 29 G5
Linnet Cl BVLLE B30 ..... 159 G2
RMSLY B62 ..... 122 A2
Linnet Gv ERDW/GRVHL B23.....75 H5
SHHTH WV12 ..... 26 A2
Linsey Rd HIA/OLT B92 ..... 148 A5
Linslade Cl
ETTPK/GDPK/PENN WV4 ..... 52 B4
Linthouse La WNSFLD WV11 ....24 D2
Lint Meadow HLYWD B47 ..... 192 D1
Linton Av SOLH B91 ..... 181 G4
Linton Cl HALE B63 ..... 137 G2
Linton Cft BILS/COS WV14 ..... 53 H4
Linton Rd CDYHTH B64 ..... 121 F1
ETTPK/GDPK/PENN WV4 ..... 51 E3
GTB/HAM B43 ..... 73 F1
SPARK B11 ..... 146 A3
Linwood Rd DUDN DY1 ..... 84 B1
HDSW B21 ..... 107 G1
SOLH B91 ..... 163 H5
Lionel St CBHAMNW B3 ..... 2 E3
Lion Pas STRBR DY8 ..... 135 F2
Lion St STRBR DY8 ..... 135 F2
Liskeard Rd DYSBK/YTR WS5 ....58 B1
Lisko Cl BRLYHL DY5 ..... 118 C4
Lismore Cl RBRY B45 ..... 175 G4
Lismore Dr HRBN B17 ..... 141 G5
Lissimore Dr TPTN/OCK DY4 ....85 G4
Lisson Gv KGSTG B44 ..... 60 B4
Listelow Cl CBROM B36 ..... 112 D1
Lister Cl TPTN/OCK DY4 ..... 85 G2
WSLW WS2 ..... 27 F5
Lister Rd DUDS DY2 ..... 102 C2
WSLW WS2 ..... 27 F5
Lister St VAUX/NECH B7 ..... 3 J1
WLNHL WV13 ..... 39 H4
Listowel Rd
ALE/KHTH/YWD B14 ..... 160 D4
Lisures Dr WALM/CURD B76 ......62 D4
Little Albert St WSLW WS2 * 4 E2
Little Ann St DIG/EDG B5 ..... 3 K6
Little Aston Hall Dr
FOAKS/STRLY B74 ..... 31 G5
Little Aston La
FOAKS/STRLY B74 ..... 32 C4
Little Aston Park Rd
FOAKS/STRLY B74 ..... 45 C2
Little Aston Rd ALDR WS9 ..... 30 C4
Little Barr St DIG/EDG B5 ..... 127 G2
Little Bell Hall Cottages
HAG/WOL DY9 * 184 B2
Little Birches BDMR/CCFT WV3..36 B5
Little Bricklin St
BDMR/CCFT WV3 ..... 6 E6
Little Bromwich Rd BORD B9 ..129 F5
Little Broom St BHTH/HG B12 ..127 G4
Little Caldmore WSL WS1 ..... 4 E6

Little Checkhill La KINVER DY7 ..98 B5
Little Clothier St WLNHL WV13 ..39 G3
Little Clover Cl VAUX/NECH B7 ..110 A3
Little Cornbow HALE B63 ..... 138 D4
Littlecote Cft
ALE/KHTH/YWD B14 ..... 178 C2
Littlecote Dr ERDW/GRVHL B23 .76 D4
Little Cottage St BRLYHL DY5 ..119 F2
Little Cft GTB/HAM B43 ..... 58 D5
Little Cross St DARL/WED WS10 .55 H1
Little Edward St BORD B9 ..... 127 G2
Little Fields Wy OLDBY B69.....104 D2
Little Francis Gv
VAUX/NECH B7 ..... 109 H4
Little Gorway WSL WS1 ..... 57 F1
Little Green La BORD B9 ..... 128 B3
Little Gn Lanes
SCFLD/BOLD B73 ..... 77 F4
Little Hall Rd VAUX/NECH B7 ..109 H5
Little Hardwick Rd ALDR WS9 ...44 D5
Little Hay La LICHS WS14 ..... 33 F5
Little Heath Cft
BKDE/SHDE B34 ..... 112 D3
Littlehill Crs CDYHTH B64 ..... 120 C5
Little Hill Wy HWK/WKHTH B38..177 E2
Little Hill Wy RIDG/WDGT B32..140 D5
Little Johnson's La ALDR WS9...44 B4
Little John St BRLYHL DY5 ..... 101 F5
Little La HHTH/SAND B71 ..... 87 H1
WLNHL WV13 ..... 26 E5
Little Lawns Cl BRWNH WS8 ....19 F2
Little London WSL WS1 ..... 57 F1
Littlemead Av NFLD/LBR B31 ...176 A4
Little Meadow Cft
NFLD/LBR B31 ..... 158 B5
Little Moor Hi SMTHWKW B67...105 H5
Little Newport St WSL WS1 .....4 D4
Little Oaks Rd AST/WIT B6 ..... 109 F1
Littleover Av HLGN/YWD B28...162 D4
Little Pk RIDG/WDGT B32 ..... 140 B5
Little Park St WOLV WV1 * 7 H4
Little Pitts Cl ERDE/BCHGN B24...93 H1
Little Potter St BRLYHL DY5 ....119 F3
Little Pountney St
BKHL/PFLD WV2 * 7 F7
Little Shadwell St
CBHAMNE B4 ..... 3 G2
Littleshaw Cft HLYWD B47 ..... 193 E4
Littleshaw La HLYWD B47 ..... 193 E4
Little's La WOLV WV1 ..... 7 G2
Little Station St WSLW WS2 .....4 D3
Little St DUDS DY2 ..... 84 D5
Little Sutton Cl WALM/CURD B76..78 C1
Little Sutton Rd MGN/WHC B75..47 H5
Littleton Cl WALM/CURD B76 ....78 D1
Littleton St East WSL WS1 ..... 4 D2
Littleton St West WSL WS2 .....4 D2
Littlewood Cl SOLH B91 ..... 181 H5
Littlewood La GTWY WS6 ..... 16 C3
Littlewood Rd GTWY WS6 ..... 16 C3
Littleworth Av DUDN DY1 ..... 68 B5
Littleworth Gv
WALM/CURD B76 ..... 63 F4
Litttleton Rd SHHTH WV12 ..... 26 A3
Liverpool Cft
CHWD/FDBR/MGN B37 ..... 131 H3
Liverpool St BORD B9 ..... 127 G2
Livery St CBHAMNW B3 ..... 2 E2
Livingstone Av
DUNHL/THL/PER WV6 ..... 20 C5
Livingstone Rd
ALE/KHTH/YWD B14 ..... 161 E4
BFLD/HDSWWD B20 ..... 90 C5
BILS/COS WV14 ..... 54 B4
BLOX/PEL WS3 ..... 17 F5
WBROM B70 ..... 87 F5
Lloyd Dr
ETTPK/GDPK/PENN WV4 ..... 65 G1
Lloyd Hl
ETTPK/GDPK/PENN WV4 * 50 C5
Lloyd Rd DUNHL/THL/PER WV6..21 H5
BFLD/HDSWWD B20 ..... 90 A2
Lloyd Sq EDG B15 ..... 125 G5
Lloyds Rd RMSLY B62 ..... 122 A5
Lloyd St DARL/WED WS10 ..... 55 G5
DUDS DY2 ..... 102 D1
DUNHL/THL/PER WV6 ..... 36 B1
HHTH/SAND B71 ..... 128 B2
Locarno Rd TPTN/OCK DY4 .....69 F5
Lochalsh Gv SHHTH WV12 .....25 H1
Lochranza Cft GTB/HAM B43 ....73 C1
Lock Dr STETCH B33 ..... 129 H1
Locke Pl VAUX/NECH B7 ..... 127 G1
Locket Cl WSLW WS2 ..... 40 D1
Lockfield Cl STRBR DY8 ..... 118 B2
Lockhart Dr MGN/WHC B75 .....47 G4
Locking Cft CVALE B35 ..... 94 D3
Lockington Cft RMSLY B62 ..... 139 H1
Lockley Cl WOLVN WV10 ..... 37 H1
Lockside ALDR WS9 ..... 29 H1
WMBN WV5 ..... 64 C4
Lockside Cl BRLYHL DY5 ..... 119 F3
Locks Vw STRBR DY8 ..... 118 A2
Lockwood Rd NFLD/LBR B31 ...175 F1
Lode La HIA/OLT B92 ..... 148 C1
SOLH B91 ..... 148 C4
Lodge Cl ALDR WS9 ..... 31 E5
RMSLY B62 ..... 139 F4
Lodge Crs DUDS DY2 ..... 102 A5
HAG/WOL DY9 ..... 152 D5
Lodge Cft DOR/KN B93 ..... 197 F2
NFLD/LBR B31 ..... 158 A3
Lodge Dr
LGN/SDN/BHAMAIR B26 ..... 130 A4
Lodge Farm Cl
WALM/CURD B76 ..... 63 F5
Lodgefield Rd RMSLY B62 ..... 121 H5
Lodge Gv ALDR WS9 ..... 30 A3
Lodge Hill Rd SLYOAK B29 ..... 159 F1
Lodge La KGSWFD DY6 ..... 99 F3
Lodgepool Cl KGSTG B44 ..... 75 E5
Lodge Rd AST/WIT B6 ..... 109 E1
BILS/COS WV14 ..... 54 B4
DARL/WED WS10 ..... 55 F5

DOR/KN B93 ..... 197 F2
DSYBK/YTR WS5 ..... 58 B3
RUSH/SHEL WS4 ..... 28 C1
SMTHWKW B67 ..... 106 A2
WBROM B70 ..... 87 F3
WOLVN WV10 ..... 12 C2
WSNGN B18 ..... 108 A4
Lodge St OLDBY B69 ..... 103 C2
SHHTH WV12 ..... 26 A5
Loeless Rd STETCH B33 ..... 130 C1
Lofthouse Crs NFLD/LBR B31 ...175 F2
Lofthouse Gv NFLD/LBR B31 ...175 F2
Lofthouse Rd
BFLD/HDSWWD B20 ..... 89 H4
Loftus Cl SLYOAK B29 ..... 158 B2
Logan Gv WOLVN WV10 ..... 23 E4
Lomaine Dr BVLLE B30 ..... 176 C1
Lomas Dr NFLD/LBR B31 ..... 175 C2
Lomas St WOLV WV1 ..... 37 E1
Lombard Av DUDS DY2 ..... 120 D1
Lombard St BHTH/HG B12 ..... 127 F4
WBROM B70 ..... 87 G3
Lombard St West
WBROM B70 * 87 G3
Lombardy Crt RMSLY B62 ..... 140 A1
Lombardy Gdns SHHTH WV12 ...26 C3
Lomond Cl BKDE/SHDE B34 ..... 113 G5
Lomond Rd SEDG DY3 ..... 67 E2
Londonderry Gv
SMTHWKW B67 ..... 106 B4
Londonderry La
SMTHWKW B67 ..... 105 H5
London Hts DUDN DY1 ..... 84 A4
London La BDMR/CCFT WV3 ....6 E5
London Rd BFLD/HDSWWD B20..91 E4
MGN/WHC B75 ..... 48 C1
London St SMTHWK B66 ..... 107 E4
Lones Rd HHTH/SAND B71 ..... 106 D1
Long Acre CDSL WV8 ..... 10 A5
VAUX/NECH B7 ..... 109 C3
Longacre WLNHL WV13 ..... 39 G5
Long Acre St WSLW WS2 ..... 4 C1
Longbank Rd OLDBY B69 ..... 104 A1
Longboat La STRBR DY8 ..... 118 A4
Longboat Quay DUDS DY2 ..... 102 D5
Longbow Rd SLYOAK B29 ..... 158 B3
Longbridge La NFLD/LBR B31 ...175 F5
NFLD/LBR B31 ..... 189 F1
Long Cl HAG/WOL DY9 ..... 169 G1
Long Close Wk CVALE B35 ..... 94 C3
Long Compton Dr
HAG/WOL DY9 ..... 152 C4
Longcroft Cl CVALE B35 ..... 94 A3
The Longcroft HALE B63 ..... 138 A3
Rush/SHEL WS4 ..... 29 E3
Longdales Rd
HWK/WKHTH B38 ..... 190 B1
Longdon Av
ETTPK/GDPK/PENN WV4 ..... 52 B3
Longdon Cft DOR/KN B93 ..... 183 E5
Longdon Dr FOAKS/STRLY B74 ..46 C1
Longdon Rd DOR/KN B93 ..... 197 E2
Longfellow Rd NFLD/LBR B31...176 B2
SEDG DY3 ..... 82 C1
Longfield Cl HLGN/YWD B28 ....162 D4
Longfield Dr FOAKS/STRLY B74 .46 A1
Longfield Rd HAG/WOL DY9 ....136 B2
NFLD/LBR B31 ..... 158 A3
Longford Cl DOR/KN B93 ..... 197 F5
RIDG/WDGT B32 ..... 157 E3
WMBN WV5 ..... 80 B1
Longford Gv KGSTG B44 ..... 60 C5
Longford Rd KGSTG B44 ..... 75 C1
WOLVN WV10 ..... 37 H1
Longham Cft RIDG/WDGT B32..141 F3
Longhurst Cft NFLD/LBR B31 ...189 G1
Long Hyde Rd SMTHWKW B67..124 B3
Long Innage HALE B63 ..... 137 E5
Long Knowle La WNSFLD WV11..24 B2
Longlake Av
DUNHL/THL/PER WV6 ..... 35 E2
Longlands Rd RMSLY B62 ..... 139 G4
The Longlands WMBN WV5 .....65 E5
Long La BLKHTH/ROWR B65 ....122 A3
GTWY WS6 ..... 16 B1
WNSFLD WV11 ..... 15 H2
Long Leasow SLYOAK B29 ..... 158 C3
Longleat GTB/HAM B43 ..... 73 F1
Longleat Gv DUDN DY1 ..... 126 C4
Longleat Rd ALDR WS9 ..... 19 G5
Long Ley WOLVN WV10 ..... 37 H2
Longley Av WALM/CURD B76 ....95 F1
Long Leys Ct
LGN/SDN/BHAMAIR B26 ..... 147 G3
Long Leys Cft
CSHL/WTROR B46 ..... 96 B4
Longmeadow Cl
MGN/WHC B75 ..... 63 G3
Longmeadow Crs
BKDE/SHDE B34 ..... 113 G3
Longmeadow Gv
NFLD/LBR B31 ..... 189 G2
Longmeadow Rd
DSYBK/YTR WS5 ..... 43 G5
Long Mill Av WNSFLD WV11 .....24 B3
Long MI North WNSFLD WV11 ...24 B3
Long MI South WNSFLD WV11 ..24 B3
Longmoor Cl WNSFLD WV11 .....25 G4
Longmoor Rd HALE B63 ..... 138 A4
SCFLD/BOLD B73 ..... 76 C3
Longmore Av WSLW WS2 ..... 40 D4
Longmore Rd SHLY B90 ..... 180 B4
Longmore St BHTH/HG B12 .....127 F5
DARL/WED WS10 ..... 55 H5
Long Mynd HALE B63 ..... 154 D1
Long Mynd Rd NFLD/LBR B31...175 H4
Long Mynd Cl SHHTH WV12 .....25 H1
Longnor Rd NFLD/LBR B31 ..... 175 H4
Long Saw Dr NFLD/LBR B31 ....174 D4
Longshaw Gv BKDE/SHDE B34 .113 F3
Longstone Cl SHLY B90 ..... 195 F3
Longstone Rd PBAR/PBCH B42..74 C1
Long St SPARK B11 ..... 144 C1

WOLV WV1.........................7 G3
WSLW WS2...........................4 C4
Long Wd BVILLE B30.........159 C5
Longwood La RUSH/SHEL WS4...45 C3
Longwood Ri SHHTH WV12.........26 B5
Longwood Rd ALDR WS9..........44 B3
  RBRY B45..........................188 A1
Lonicera Cl DSYBK/YTR WS5....57 H5
Lonsdale Cl SHHTH WV12........129 H5
  STETCH DS5........................23 E5
Lonsdale Rd BDMR/CCFT WV3...36 D5
  BILS/COS WV14....................54 B2
  DSYBK/YTR WS5...................58 A2
  HRBN B17.........................141 H1
  SMTHWK B66......................105 H2
Lord's Dr WSLW WS2................4 E1
Lords La KINVER DY7.............116 C5
Lordsmore Cl BILS/COS WV14...45 G5
Lord St BDMR/CCFT WV3...........6 C5
  BILS/COS WV14....................54 A5
  DSYBK/YTR WS5....................57 E5
  WSL /NECH B7.....................56 D2
Lord St West BILS/COS WV14....54 A5
Lordswood Rd HRBN B17........141 H1
Lordswood Sq HRBN B17 *.....124 D5
Lorimer Wy GTB/HAM B43........3 F5
Lorne St TPTN/OCK DY4...........69 F5
Lorrainer Av BRLYHL DY5.......118 C4
Lothians Rd BLOX/PEL WS3.....18 A2
  DUNHL/THL/PER WV6............21 H4
Lottie Rd SLYOAK B29...........159 G1
Lotus Cft SMTHWK B67..........106 B5
Lotus Dr CDYHTH B64............121 F2
Lotus Wy BLKHTH/ROWR B65...105 F5
Loughton Gv HALE B63..........138 B3
Louisa St CBHAMW B4.............3 F2
Louise Cft
  ALE/KHTH/YWD B14............178 A3
Louise Lorne Rd MOS/BIL B13..144 B3
Louise Rd HDSW B21............107 H2
Louise St SEDG DY3................82 D5
Lount Wk LOZ/NWT B19..........109 E4
Lovat Av BDMR/CCFT WV3........70 A2
Lovatt Cl TPTN/OCK DY4............5 J5
Loveday St CBHAMNE B4...........3 G2
Lovelace Av SOLH B91..........182 B5
Love La DUNHL/THL/PER WV6...21 H4
  HAG/WOL DY9......................99 E1
  HLYWD B47........................192 A1
  OLDBY B69.........................85 C5
  STRBR DY8.........................135 C4
  VAUX/NECH B7......................3 J5
  WSL WS1..............................5 H3
Lovell Cl SLYOAK B29..........158 C4
Loveridge Cl CDSL WV8............10 A4
Lovett Av OLDBY B69...........104 B4
Low Av GTB/HAM B43..............3 G5
Lowbridge Cl SHHTH WV12.......26 A5
Lowbrook La HLYWD B47........193 H4
Lowden Cft
  LGN/SDN/BHAMAIR B26......147 E3
Lowe Av DARL/WED WS10.........54 D1
Lowe Dr KGSWFD DY6...........100 A5
  SCFLD/BOLD B73...................61 F5
Lower Beeches Rd RBRY B45...174 C3
Lower Chapel St OLDBY B69....86 A4
Lower Church La
  TPTN/OCK DY4......................85 H1
Lower City Rd OLDBY B69........86 A5
Lowercroft Wy
  FOAKS/STRLY B74................32 C4
Lower Dartmouth St
  BORD B9..........................127 H2
Lower Darwin St
  BHTH/HG B12.....................127 F4
Lower Derry St BRLYHL DY5...119 F2
Lower Essex St DIG/EDG B5...127 E5
Lower Forster St WSL WS1.......5 F2
Lower Gn
  DUNHL/THL/PER WV6...........22 A5
  TPTN/OCK DY4 *...................85 E1
Lower Ground Cl AST/WIT B6 *..91 F5
Lower Hall La WSL WS1............4 E4
Lower Hall St WSL WS1.............4 F3
Lower High St CDYHTH B64....120 C4
  DARL/WED WS10....................70 D1
  STRBR DY8........................135 F1
Lower Higley Cl
  RIDG/WDGT B32.................141 E3
Lower Horseley Flds WOLV WV1..7 K4
Lower Lichfield St
  WLNHL WV13........................39 H3
Lower Loveday St LOZ/NWT B19..3 F1
Lower Moor BVILLE B30 *......159 G2
Lower North St
  RUSH/SHEL WS4..................42 B2
The Lower Pde
  CSCFLD/WYGN B72................62 C3
Lower Prestwood Rd
  WNSFLD WV11.....................24 C3
Lower Queen St
  CSCFLD/WYGN B72................62 C4
Lower Reddicroft
  SCFLD/BOLD B73...................62 C3
Lower Rushall St WSL WS1......5 F3
Lower Severn St CBHAMW B1...2 E6
Lowerstack Cft
  CHWD/FDBR/MGN B37........131 H1
Lower St
  DUNHL/THL/PER WV6...........22 A5
Lower Temple St CBHAM B2......2 E4
Lower Tower St LOZ/NWT B19..108 D4
Lower Trinity St BORD B9.......127 G3
Lower Valley Rd BRLYHL DY5..118 C2
Lower Vauxhall WOLV WV1........6 A3
Lower Villiers St
  BKHL/PFLD WV2....................52 A1
Lower Walsall St WOLV WV1....37 H4
Lower White Rd
  RIDG/WDGT B32.................140 D2
Lowesmoor Rd
  LGN/SDN/BHAMAIR B26......130 D5
Lowe St SHTH/HG B12...........127 C4
  DUNHL/THL/PER WV6............36 C1
Loweswater Dr SEDG DY3.......83 F3
Lowfield Cl RMSLY B62..........140 A4
Low Hill Crs WOLV N WV10......23 C2
Lowhill La RBRY B45.............188 C2
Lowland Cl CDYHTH B64........119 F3

Lowlands Av
  DUNHL/THL/PER WV6............22 A4
  FOAKS/STRLY B74................45 E5
Lowndes Rd STRBR DY8.........135 E1
Lowry Cl DUNHL/THL/PER WV6..34 D1
  SMTHWKW B67....................106 B5
  WLNHL WV13.......................38 D3
Low Thatch HWK/WKHTH B38..190 C1
Low Town OLDBY B69............105 E2
Low Wood Rd
  ERDW/GRVHL B23...................92 C2
Loxdale Sidings BILS/COS WV14..54 B4
Loxdale St BILS/COS WV14......54 B4
  DARL/WED WS10.....................70 D1
Loxley Av SHLY B90...............179 H4
Loxley Cl NFLD/LBR B31........158 A2
Loxley Rd MGN/WHC B75.........47 H2
  SMTHWKW B67....................124 B3
Loxton Cl STRBR DY8..............32 B5
Loynells Rd RBRY B45...........188 A1
Loyns Cl
  CHWD/FDBR/MGN B37.........131 C1
Lozells Rd LOZ/NWT B19........108 B2
Lozells St LOZ/NWT B19.........108 C2
Lozells Wood Cl LOZ/NWT B19..108 B2
Luanne Cl CDYHTH B64..........121 C3
Lucas Circ LOZ/NWT B19.........108 C3
Luce Cl CVALE B35.................94 D2
Luce Rd WOLV WV10..............21 H4
Lucknow Rd SHHTH WV12.........25 H5
Luddington Rd HIA/OLT B92....165 C3
Ludford Cl MGN/WHC B75........63 E1
Ludford Rd RIDG/WDGT B32....157 E1
Ludgate Cl CSHL/WTROR B46...96 A5
Ludgate Hl CBHAMNW B3...........2 E3
Ludgate St DUDN DY1 *...........84 B5
Ludlow Cl
  CHWD/FDBR/MGN B37.........132 C2
  SHHTH WV12.......................25 H4
Ludlow La WSLW WS2..............41 E1
Ludlow Rd WASH/WDE B8........128 D1
Ludlow Wy DUDN DY1.............83 C4
Ludmer Wy
  BFLD/HDSWWD B20...............90 C4
Ludstone Av
  ETTPK/GDPK/PENN WV4........50 D3
Ludstone Rd SLYOAK B29......158 B1
Ludworth Av
  CHWD/FDBR/MGN B37.........132 B4
Lugtrout La SOLH B91............165 H4
The Lukes SOLH B91.............120 C3
Lulworth Cl HALE B63............137 C1
Lulworth Rd HLGN/YWD B28...163 E2
Lumley Gv
  CHWD/FDBR/MGN B37.........132 D2
Lumley Rd WSL WS1.................5 J5
Lundy Vw CBROM B36............114 B3
Lunt Gv RIDG/WDGT B32........140 D2
Lunt Pl BILS/COS WV14............54 C2
Lunt Rd BILS/COS WV14...........54 C2
Lupin Gv BORD B9................128 D1
  DSYBK/YTR WS5....................57 H4
Lupin Rd DUDS DY2................85 F5
Lusbridge Cl HALE B63..........137 F3
Lutley Av HALE B63...............138 A3
Lutley Cl BDMR/CCFT WV3.......51 E1
Lutley Dr HAG/WOL DY9.........136 A4
Lutley Gv RIDG/WDGT B32.....157 F1
Lutley La HALE B63...............137 C5
Lutley Mill Rd HALE B63........138 A3
Luton Rd SLYOAK B29............142 D4
Luttrell Rd FOAKS/STRLY B74...46 D5
Lyall Gdns RBRY B45............175 C4
Lyall Gv ACGN B27................146 A5
Lychgate Av HAG/WOL DY9....155 E1
Lydate Rd HALE B63..............138 B2
Lydbrook Covert
  HWK/WKHTH B38................176 C5
Lydbury Gv STETCH B33.........112 C5
Lydd Cl WNSFLD WV11.............24 B5
Lydd Cft CVALE B35...............94 D2
Lyddington Dr RMSLY B62......121 H5
Lyde Gn HALE B63................120 C5
Lydford Gv ERDE/BCHGN B24...93 E4
Lydford Rd BLOX/PEL WS3.......16 D5
Lydgate Rd KGSWFD DY6.......100 B4
Lydget Gv ERDW/GRVHL B23....76 B4
Lydham Cl BILS/COS WV14.......53 F4
  HRBN B17...........................75 C5
Lydia Cft FOAKS/STRLY B74....32 C4
Lydian Cl DUNHL/THL/PER WV6..36 D1
Lydiate Ash Rd BRGRVW B61...187 E5
Lydiate Av NFLD/LBR B31.......174 D4
Lydiates Cl SEDG DY3.............66 D4
Lydney Cl SHHTH WV12...........40 B1
Lydney Gv NFLD/LBR B31.......175 F2
Lye Av RIDG/WDGT B32..........140 A5
Lye By-Pass HAG/WOL DY9.....136 C1
Lye Close La RIDG/WDGT B32..139 H5
Lyecroft Av
  CHWD/FDBR/MGN B37.........132 D2
Lye Cross Rd OLDBY B69.......103 H2
Lygon Gv RIDG/WDGT B32......141 E5
Lymedene Rd PBAR/PBCH B42..90 B1
Lyme Green Rd STETCH B33...112 B5
Lymer Rd WOLV WV10..............23 E1
Lymington Rd WLNHL WV13......40 B5
Lymsey Cft STRBR DY8..........117 C1
Lynbrook Cl DUDS DY2..........102 D3
  HLYWD B47........................192 D1
Lyncourt Gv RIDG/WDGT B32..140 B1
Lyncroft Rd SPARK B11..........145 H5
Lyndale Dr WNSFLD WV11........25 F5
Lyndale Rd DUDS DY2............103 E3
  SEDG DY3............................66 D1
Lyndhurst Dr BDMR/CCFT WV3..36 D5
  STRBR DY8........................118 B5
Lyndhurst Rd BDMR/CCFT WV3..36 D5
  ERDE/BCHGN B24...................92 D4
  HHTH/SAND B71...................72 A4
Lyndon HHTH/SAND B71..........87 H1
Lyndon Cl BFLD/HDSWWD B20..90 C4
  CBROM B36.........................113 E4
  HALE B63...........................138 A2
  SEDG DY3............................67 G2
Lyndon Cft
  CHWD/FDBR/MGN B37.........132 B5
Lyndon Gv HHTH/SAND B71......87 H2
  KGSWFD DY6........................99 F1
Lyndon Rd HIA/OLT B92.........147 F5

  RBRY B45..........................187 G1
  SCFLD/BOLD B73...................62 B3
  STETCH B33........................112 A5
Lyndworth Rd BVILLE B30......160 C3
Lyneham Gdns
  CHWD/FDBR/MGN B37...........78 D5
Lyneham Wy CVALE B35..........94 B3
Lynfield Cl HWK/WKHTH B38...190 D1
Lyng La WBROM B70................87 G4
Lynmouth Cl ALDR WS9...........29 H2
Lynn Gv SLYOAK B29............142 A4
Lynton Av
  DUNHL/THL/PER WV6...........22 A3
  HHTH/SAND B71...................71 G4
  SMTHWK B66.......................106 C3
Lynton Rd AST/WIT B6...........109 G2
Lynval Rd BRLYHL DY5..........119 H5
Lynwood Av KGSWFD DY6........99 F1
Lynwood Cl SHHTH WV12.........26 C2
Lynwood Dr KIDD DY10..........168 B3
Lynwood Wk HRBN B17..........142 A5
Lynwood Wy RBRY B45..........188 A5
Lyons Gv SPARK B11.............145 E4
Lysander Rd RBRY B45..........174 A5
Lysander Wy CVALE B35..........94 D4
Lysways St WSL WS1.................5 F6
Lytham Cl STRBR DY8...........135 C5
  WALM/CURD B76...................78 D5
Lytham Cft DIG EDG B15.......126 D5
Lytham Gv BLOX/PEL WS3.......16 C3
Lytham Rd
  DUNHL/THL/PER WV6............34 D1
Lythwood Dr BRLYHL DY5.....119 E4
Lytham Red
  LDYWD/EDGR B16...............125 F3
  STETCH B33......................129 H2
  STRBR DY8.........................134 D2
Lyttelton Av RMSLY B62.........122 C5
Lyttleton Cl DUDS DY2..........102 C5
Lyttleton St WBROM B70.........87 G4
Lytton Av
  ETTPK/GDPK/PENN WV4........50 D4
Lytton Gv ACGN B27.............163 F1
Lytton La RIDG/WDGT B32.....141 F4

M

Maas Rd NFLD/LBR B31..........175 G1
Macarthur Rd CDYHTH B64.....120 C4
Macdonald Cl OLDBY B69........86 B4
Macdonald St DIG/EDG B5.....126 D4
Mace St CDYHTH B64.............121 E5
Machin Rd ERDW/GRVHL B23....92 D2
Mackadown La STETCH B33....131 F3
Mackay Rd BLOX/PEL WS3.......17 F5
Mackenzie Rd SPARK B11......145 E5
Mackmillan Rd
  BLKHTH/ROWR B65..............122 A4
Macmillan Cl OLDBY B69.........86 A4
Macrome Rd
  DUNHL/THL/PER WV6............22 A2
Madam's Hill Rd SHLY B90.....194 D1
Maddocks HI
  CSCFLD/WYGN B72................77 F1
Madehurst Rd
  ERDW/GRVHL B23...................76 C5
Madeira Av CDSL WV8..............10 C5
Madeley Rd HAG/WOL DY9.....186 A1
  KGSWFD DY6........................99 E5
  SPARK B11.........................145 E2
Madin Rd TPTN/OCK DY4..........85 E2
Madison Av BRLYHL DY5........119 H1
  CBROM B36........................111 H3
  WSLW WS2..........................4 C3
Madley Cl RBRY B45.............175 C5
Madresfield Dr HALE B63.......138 D5
Maer Cl BLKHTH/ROWR B65....122 A1
Mafeking Rd SMTHWK B66.....106 C2
Mafeking Vls RMSLY B62 *.....121 H5
Magdala St WSNGN B18........107 G4
Magdalen Cl DUDN DY1...........84 A4
Magdalene Rd WSL WS1...........57 G1
Magness Crs SHHTH WV12......26 A5
Magnolia Cl SOLH B91..........158 C3
Magnolia Gv CDSL WV8..............9 H5
  SHHTH WV12.......................26 A5
Magnolia Wy STRBR DY8.......118 B4
Magnum Cl FOAKS/STRLY B74..60 D1
Magpie Cl DUDS DY2............121 E1
Maidendale Rd KGSWFD DY6...99 F3
Maidensbridge Gdns
  KGSWFD DY6.........................81 F5
Maidensbridge Rd
  KGSWFD DY6.........................81 F5
Maidstone Dr STRBR DY8.......118 A1
Maidstone Rd
  BFLD/HDSWWD B20................91 E5
Maidwell Dr SHLY B90...........181 H5
Mainstream Wy
  VAUX/NECH B7......................110 A5
Main St SHLY B90................194 A3
  SPARK B11.........................127 G5
Main Ter SPARK B11 *...........127 G5
Mainwaring Dr MGN/WHC B75...48 A3
Maisonettes CDSL WV8 *........100 D4
The Maisonettes
  ERDE/BCHGN B24 *................92 C4
Maitland Dr BKDE/SHDE B34..113 G3
Maitland Rd DUDS DY2............83 F5
  WASH/WDE B8....................110 D5
Majestic Wy
  BLKHTH/ROWR B65..............104 A5
Majuba Rd LDYWD/EDGR B16..107 F5
Malcolm Av
  ERDE/BCHGN B24...................93 C1
Malcolm Gv RBRY B45...........188 A1
Malcolm Rd SHLY B90...........180 B3
Malcolmson Cl EDG B15........125 H4
Malfield Dr ACGN B27...........147 E4
Malins Rd
  ETTPK/GDPK/PENN WV4........52 B3
  HRBN B17...........................142 B2
Malkit Cl WSLW WS2..............40 C1
Mallaby Cl SHLY B90.............180 A5
Mallard Cl ACGN B27.............146 C4

  BLOX/PEL WS3......................18 A1
  BRLYHL DY5........................119 E5
Mallard Dr ERDW/GRVHL B23...75 H4
  OLDBY B69.........................122 D1
Mallender Dr DOR/KN B93......196 D1
Mallen Dr OLDBY B69.............85 H5
Mallin Gdns DUDN DY1.........101 G1
Mallin St SMTHWK B66..........106 A2
Mallory Crs BLOX/PEL WS3......17 F5
Mallory Ri MOS/BIL B13........162 A1
Mallory Rd
  DUNHL/THL/PER WV6............34 C2
Mallow Cl DSYBK/YTR WS5......57 H5
Mallow Ct
  DUNHL/THL/PER WV6............22 D5
Mallow Ri ERDW/GRVHL B23....75 H4
Mallows Cl DARL/WED WS10 *...55 F2
Malmesbury Rd SMHTH B10....145 G1
Malpas Dr RIDG/WDGT B32....157 G2
Malpass Gdns CDSL WV8.........10 A3
Malpass Rd BRLYHL DY5........119 H5
Malpas Wk WOLV WV10............38 A1
Malt Cl HRBN B17................142 B1
Malthouse Cft AST/WIT B6....109 E1
Malthouse Gdns
  LOZ/NWT B19.....................108 D2
Malthouse Gv
  DUNHL/THL/PER WV6 *.........34 C2
Malthouse La
  DUNHL/THL/PER WV6............21 H4
  PBAR/PBCH B42...................74 D3
  WASH/WDE B8....................110 C5
Malthouse Meadow SOLH B91..181 H4
Malthouse Rd TPTN/OCK DY4...85 E1
Malthouse Rw
  CHWD/FDBR/MGN B37.........132 A4
The Maltings ALDR WS9 *.........30 C4
Malton Av OLDBY B69...........104 B3
Malton Gv MOS/BIL B13........161 H5
Malvern Av HAG/WOL DY9......136 A3
Malvern Cl DUNHL/THL/PER WV6..36 C1
  HHTH/SAND B71....................39 H1
  WOLV WV10.........................23 F2
Malvern Crs DUDS DY2..........101 H5
Malvern Dr ALDR WS9.............30 C2
  WALM/CURD B76...................78 C3
  WOLV WV1...........................38 B4
Malvern Hill Rd
  VAUX/NECH B7....................110 A2
Malvern Rd ACGN B27...........146 C3
  LGLYGN/QTN B68..................123 F4
  MOS/BIL B13.....................144 C2
Malvern St BHTH/HG B12......144 A1
Malvern View Rd SEDG DY3.....83 F2
Malvern Wy STRBR DY8........135 C2
Mamble Rd STRBR DY8...........117 F5
Mammoth Dr WOLV WV10..........23 H5
Manby Cl DUNHL/THL/PER WV6..36 C1
Manby Rd CVALE B35..............94 C2
Manby St TPTN/OCK DY4.........69 F3
Mancetter Rd SHLY B90........180 C2
Manchester St AST/WIT B6....109 E4
  OLDBY B69...........................86 B5
Mancroft Cl KGSWFD DY6........99 F2
Mancroft Gdns
  DUNHL/THL/PER WV6............21 G5
Mancroft Rd
  DUNHL/THL/PER WV6............21 G5
Mandale Rd WOLV WV10..........23 H4
Manderley Cl SEDG DY3..........67 E1
Manders Est WOLV WV1..........37 H2
Manderston Cl DUDN DY1.......83 G3
Mander St BDMR/CCFT WV3......6 D7
Man Der Ville Gdns
  KGSWFD DY6........................99 G3
Mandeville Gdns WSL WS1.......5 G6
Maney Cnr CSCFLD/WYGN B72..62 B4
Maney Hill Rd
  CSCFLD/WYGN B72................77 H1
Manfield Rd WLNHL WV13........38 C2
Manifold Wy DARL/WED WS10...57 E5
Manilla Rd BVILLE B30..........160 B1
Manitoba Cft
  HWK/WKHTH B38................176 D5
Manley Cl WBROM B70............87 E3
Manlove St BDMR/CCFT WV3.....6 B7
Manningford Rd
  ALE/KHTH/YWD B14............178 B3
Manor Abbey Dr RMSLY B62...138 C3
Manor Abbey Rd RMSLY B62...139 G3
Manor Cl CDSL WV8................10 D4
  ETTPK/GDPK/PENN WV4........39 F2
Manor Ct DOR/KN B93 *.........198 D1
  WSLW WS2............................41 G4
Manor Dr NFLD/LBR B31.........55 E3
  SCFLD/BOLD B73...................62 B4
  SEDG DY3............................80 C4
  SEDG DY3............................82 D5
Manor Farm Dr SHHTH WV12...26 B5
Manor Farm Rd SPARK B11....145 F3
Manorford Av HHTH/SAND B71..72 C2
Manor Gdns STETCH B33......129 H3
  WMBN WV5 *.......................65 F4
Manor Gv NFLD/LBR B31.......174 C4
Manor HI SCFLD/BOLD B73......62 B4
Manor House La SLYOAK B29..158 B1
Manor House Dr
  NFLD/LBR B31....................174 D4
Manor House La
  CSHL/WTROR B46..................96 B3
  LGN/SDN/BHAMAIR B26......147 E1
Manor House Pk CDSL WV8.....10 D3
Manor House Rd
  DARL/WED WS10....................55 H4
Manor Houses RMSLY B62 *...139 H2
Manorial Rd MGN/WHC B75.....48 A2
Manor La BRGRVW B61..........187 E3
  RMSLY B62.........................138 C3
  STRBR DY8.........................134 D4
Manor Pk KGSWFD DY6...........99 H5
  NFLD/LBR B31....................175 E3
Manor Park Cl MOS/BIL B13...144 C5
Manor Park Rd CBROM B36....113 F2
  DARL/WED WS10....................71 H1

Mallard Dr ERDW/GRVHL B23...51 F4
  ETTPK/GDPK/PENN WV4........51 F4
  ETTPK/GDPK/PENN WV4........53 E3
  FOAKS/STRLY B74................45 C5
  HLYWD B47........................192 C5
  LDYWD/EDGR B16..................62 B5
  SCFLD/BOLD B73...................62 B5
  SOLH B91..........................164 C5
  STETCH B33......................130 A1
  STRBR DY8........................117 H2
  TPTN/OCK DY4......................85 F1
  WSLW WS2............................41 C5
Manor Rd North
  LDYWD/EDGR B16...............125 F3
Manor Road Prec WSLW WS2...41 G3
Manor St DUNHL/THL/PER WV6..21 G5
Manor Wy HALE B63..............139 F4
  RMSLY B62.........................139 F4
Mansard Ct BDMR/CCFT WV3...70 B4
  WOLV WV10...........................6 A3
Manse Cl CL HALE B63...........120 B5
Mansel Rd TPTN/OCK DY4........69 G3
Mansel Rd SMHTH B10..........128 C4
Mansfield Rd AST/WIT B6......108 D1
  TPTN/OCK DY4......................85 F1
  YDLY B25...........................146 C2
Mansion Cl DUDN DY1.............84 A3
Mansion Crs SMTHWK B67......106 A5
Mansion Dr TPTN/OCK DY4......86 A1
Manson Dr CDYHTH B64.........121 C3
Manston Dr
  DUNHL/THL/PER WV6............20 C5
Manston Rd
  LGN/SDN/BHAMAIR B26......130 D5
Manwoods Cl
  BFLD/HDSWWD B20................56 C4
Maple Av DARL/WED WS10.......56 C4
Maple Bank EDG B15...............58 B5
Maplebeck Ct SOLH B91 *.......165 E5
Maple Cl BILS/COS WV14.........68 A4
  HDSW B21............................89 C5
  STRBR DY8.........................134 C5
Maple Cft MOS/BIL B13..........161 H4
Mapledene Rd
  LGN/SDN/BHAMAIR B26......148 B1
Maple Dr DSYBK/YTR WS5.......57 H4
  RUSH/SHEL WS4...................75 H5
  SEDG DY3............................82 D4
Maple Gn DUDN DY1...............84 A1
Maple Gv BDMR/CCFT WV3.....113 H5
  KGSWFD DY6.......................100 A3
  LOZ/NWT B19.....................108 C1
Maple Leaf Dr
  CHWD/FDBR/MGN B37.........132 B4
Maple Leaf Rd
  DARL/WED WS10....................70 A2
Maple Ri HLGN/OTN D68.........123 F4
Maple Rd BDMR/CCFT WV3......36 A5
  BLOX/PEL WS3......................32 A2
  BVILLE B30........................159 G2
  DUDN DY1............................84 C3
  RBRY B45..........................187 H2
  RMSLY B62.........................122 B4
Maple St BLOX/PEL WS3...........18 A3
Mapleton Gv HLGN/YWD B28..163 F3
Mapleton Rd HLGN/YWD B28..163 F3
Maple Tree La HALE B63........137 C1
Maple Wy NFLD/LBR B31........158 A3
Maplewood WALM/CURD B76....78 C5
Mapperley Gdns MOS/BIL B13..143 G4
Mappleborough Rd SHLY B90..179 G4
Mapps Cl HALE B63..............137 G1
Marans Cft HWK/WKHTH B38..190 B1
Marbury Cl HWK/WKHTH B38..176 C5
Marbury Dr BILS/COS WV14.....54 C2
Marbury Ms BRLYHL DY5.......119 F3
Marchant Rd BDMR/CCFT WV3..36 B5
  BILS/COS WV14....................24 D5
March End Rd WNSFLD WV11...24 D5
Marchmont Rd
  CSCFLD/WYGN B72................77 G5
March Wy ALDR WS9.............30 C1
Marcliff Crs SHLY B90...........179 E3
Marcot Rd HIA/OLT B92..........147 G3
Marcroft Rd WLNHL WV13.......39 F4
Marden Cl NFLD/LBR B31.......175 G2
Marden Gv NFLD/LBR B31......175 C5
Mardol Cl
  LGN/SDN/BHAMAIR B26......147 F2
Maree Gv WNSFLD WV11..........25 H1
Marfield Cl WALM/CURD B76....78 C5
Margam Crs BLOX/PEL WS3.....16 B5
Margam Ter BLOX/PEL WS3.....16 B5
Margam Wy BLOX/PEL WS3.....16 B5
Margaret Av BRLYHL DY5.......119 C4
  RBRY B45..........................135 H5
Margaret Gdns SMTHWKW B67..106 A5
Margaret Gv HRBN B17..........125 E5
Margaret Rd DARL/WED WS10..55 F4
  HRBN B17...........................142 A2
  WSL WS1..............................76 B2
  WSLW WS2............................40 C2
Margaret V TPTN/OCK DY4......70 A2
Marholm Cl COVEN WV9.........11 H5
Marian Cft
  LGN/SDN/BHAMAIR B26......148 B5
Maria St WBROM B70............105 H1
Marigold Cr DUDN DY1...........84 A2
Marigold Crs DUDN DY1..........84 A2
Marine Crs STRBR DY8..........118 A3
Marine Dr KGSTG B44.............75 E5
Marine Gdns STRBR DY8.......118 A3
Mariner Av LDYWD/EDGR B16..125 C5
Marion Cl BRLYHL DY5..........119 H2
Marion Rd SMTHWKW B67......105 H3
Marion Wy HLGN/YWD B28.....162 C3
Marita Cl DUDS DY2.............121 E1
Marjoram Cl HWK/WKHTH B38..176 D5
Marjorie Av BVILLE B30.........177 G2

Mark Av *DARL/WED* WS10 ....**55** G5
Markby Rd *WSNGN* B18 ....**107** G3
Market Pl
  BLKHTH/ROWR B65 * **122** A3
  BLOX/PEL WS3 ....**27** F1
  DARL/WED WS10 ....**70** D1
  TPTN/OCK DY4 ....**86** B1
  WLNHL WV13 ....**39** G5
Market Sq *KGSWFD* DY6 ....**99** H5
  OLDBY B69 ....**105** E1
  STRBR DY8 ....**135** G2
  WOLV WV1 ....**7** G4
Market Wy *HAG/WOL* DY9 ....**153** G5
Markfield Rd
  LGN/SDN/BHAMAIR B26 ....**130** D4
Markford Wk *LOZ/NWT* B19 ....**108** D3
Markham Crs *HIA/OLT* B92 ....**165** H1
Markham Rd *COVEN* WV9 ....**12** A5
Markham Dr *KGSWFD* DY6 ....**100** A5
Marklew Cl *BRWNH* WS8 ....
Marklin Av *WOLVN* WV10 ....**23** F1
Mark Rd *DARL/WED* WS10 ....**55** G5
Marksbury Cl
  DUNHL/THL/PER WV6 ....**22** C5
Marlbank Rd *STRBR* DY8 ....**118** C3
Marlborough Cl
  FOAKS/STRLY B74 ....**32** C4
Marlborough Dr *STRBR* DY8 ....**135** G4
Marlborough Gdns
  DUNHL/THL/PER WV6 ....**36** A1
  STRBR **117** G2
Marlborough Gv *YDLY* B25 ....**129** H5
Marlborough Rd *CBROM* B36 ....**113** F1
  SEDG DY3 ....**67** H5
  SMHTH B10 ....**128** A1
  SMTHWK B66 ....**124** C1
Marlborough St *BLOX/PEL* WS3 ....**27** F1
Marlbrook Cl *HIA/OLT* B92 ....**148** A3
Marlbrook Dr
  ETTPK/GDPK/PENN WV4 ....**51** H2
Marlburn Wy *WMBN* WV5 ....**64** C5
Marcliff Gv *HIA/OLT* B92 ....**161** G4
Marldon Rd
  ALE/KHTH/YWD B14 ....**160** D4
Marlene Cft
  CHWD/FDBR/MGN B37 ....**132** C3
Marley Rd *KGSWFD* DY6 ....**100** C5
Marling Cft *HIA/OLT* B92 ....**165** G3
Marlow Dr *DUDS* DY2 ....**120** D1
Marlowe Dr *SHHTH* WV12 ....**25** G5
Marlow Rd *ERDW/GRVHL* B23 ....**92** A1
Marlow St *BLKHTH/ROWR* B65 ....**121** H3
  WSLW WS2 ....**42** A1
Marlpit La *MGN/WHC* B75 ....**47** H2
Marlpit Ri *MGN/WHC* B75 ....**48** A2
Marlpool Dr *BLOX/PEL* WS3 ....**28** B1
Marl Rd *DUDS* DY2 ....**102** B5
Marl Top *HWK/WKHTH* B38 ....**161** E5
Marmion Dr *GTB/HAM* B43 ....**73** H1
Marmion Gv *DUDLEY* DY1 ....**102** A1
Marmion Wy *WBROM* B70 ....**70** D5
Marnel Dr *BDMR/CCFT* WV3 ....**35** H5
Marquis Dr *CDYHTH* B64 ....**121** G5
Marriott Rd *DUDS* DY2 ....**102** C5
  SMTHWK B66 ....**105** H2
Marroway St
  LDYWD/EDGR B16 ....**125** H1
Marrowfat La *HDSW* B21 ....**107** H2
Marsden Cl *HIA/OLT* B92 ....**164** A1
Marshall Cl *ALDR* WS9 ....**44** B1
Marshall Gv *KGSTG* B44 ....**75** F4
Marshall Lake Rd *SHLY* B90 ....**180** D4
Marshall Rd *GLYLGYN/QTN* B68 ....**123** G5
  WLNHL WV13 ....**38** C4
Marshall St *CBHAMW* B1 ....**2** E7
  SMTHWK B66 ....**105** H2
Marsham Court Rd *SOLH* B91 ....**164** B3
Marsham Rd
  ALE/KHTH/YWD B14 ....**178** B2
Marshbrook Cl
  ERDE/BCHGN B24 ....**94** A2
Marshbrook Rd
  ERDE/BCHGN B24 ....
Marsh Cl *ERDW/GRVHL* B23 ....**92** D1
Marsh Crs *STRBR* DY8 ....**117** F1
Marsh End *HWK/WKHTH* B38 ....**177** E5
Marshfield *SHLY* B90 ....**194** A3
Marshfield Gdns
  ERDE/BCHGN B24 ....**92** C4
Marsh Hl *ERDW/GRVHL* B23 ....**92** C4
Marshland Wy *WSLW* WS2 ....**40** C4
Marsh La *CSHL/WTROR* B46 ....**96** B5
  ERDW/GRVHL B23 ....**92** D1
  HHTH/SAND B71 ....**71** H5
  SOLH B91 ....**182** C2
  WOLVN WV10 ....**12** B5
  WSLW WS2 ....
Marsh Lane Pde *WOLVN* WV10 ....**12** C5
Marshmont Wy
  ERDW/GRVHL B23 ....**76** B3
Marsh St *WSLW* WS2 ....
The Marsh *DARL/WED* WS10 ....**55** G5
Marshwood Cft *RMSLY* B62 ....**140** A4
Marsland Cl *HRBN* B17 ....**125** E4
Marsland Rd *HIA/OLT* B92 ....**164** A3
Marston Av *DARL/WED* WS10 ....**54** D5
Marston Cl *STRBR* DY8 ....**134** C3
Marston Cft
  CHWD/FDBR/MGN B37 ....**131** H4
Marston Dr
  CHWD/FDBR/MGN B37 ....
Marston Gv *GTB/HAM* B43 ....**73** E5
Marston La *BKHL/PFLD* WV2 ....**52** A4
  DUDN DY1 ....**101** F1
  SLYOAK B29 ....**158** C2
Marston St *WLNHL* WV13 ....**40** A3
Martham Dr
  DUNHL/THL/PER WV6 ....**35** F3
Martin Cl *BILS/COS* WV14 ....**68** D4
  YDLY B25 ....
Martindale Wk *BRLYHL* DY5 ....**135** H1
Martin Dr *SHHTH* WV12 ....**26** C5
Martineau Pl *CBHAM* B2 ....**3** G5
Martineau Sq *CBHAM* B2 ....
Martingale Cl *DSYBK/YTR* WS5 ....**57** F4
Martin Hill St *DUDS* DY2 ....**102** C1

Martin Ri
  CHWD/FDBR/MGN B37 ....**131** H4
Martin Rd *BILS/COS* WV14 ....**54** B5
  DSYBK/YTR WS5 ....**45** G5
  TPTN/OCK DY4 ....**85** G1
Martin St
  ETTPK/GDPK/PENN WV4 ....**52** D2
Martlesham Sq *HLWD* B47 ....**192** D1
Martley Crs *RIDG/WDGT* B32 ....**141** E3
  SOLH B91 ....**181** H5
Martley Dr *HAG/WOL* DY9 ....**136** A3
Martley Rd *OLDBY* B69 ....**104** B5
  RUSH/SHEL WS4 ....**29** E1
Marton Cl *VAUX/NECH* B7 ....**109** H5
Marwood Dr *FOAKS/STRLY* B74 ....**45** G3
Mary Ann St *CBHAMNW* B3 ....**2** E3
  WOLV WV1 * J5
Maryland Av *BKDE/SHDE* B34 ....**112** A4
Maryland Dr *NFLD/LBR* B31 ....**158** D5
Maryland Rd *BRLYHL* DY5 ....**119** H5
Marylebone Cl *STRBR* DY8 ....**118** C5
Mary Macarthur Dr
  CDYHTH B64 ....**120** C3
Mary Rd *HDSW* B21 ....**107** G2
  OLDBY B69 ....**104** A1
  STECH B33 ....**129** H1
  WBROM B70 ....**87** H5
Mary St *BHTH/HG* B12 ....**144** A2
  CBHAMNW B3 ....**2** D2
  WSLW WS2 ....**41** H2
Mary Vale Rd *BVILLE* B30 ....**159** G4
Maryvell Cl *RIDG/WDGT* B32 ....**157** F3
Masefield Av *DUDN* DY1 ....**68** C4
Masefield Cl *BILS/COS* WV14 ....**69** F1
Masefield Ri *RMSLY* B62 ....**159** F4
Masefield Rd *BLOX/PEL* WS3 ....**28** A2
  SEDG DY3 ....**82** C2
  WOLVN WV10 ....**24** A1
Masefield Sq *NFLD/LBR* B31 ....**176** A1
Masham Cl *STETCH* B33 ....**130** A2
Mashie Gdns
  HWK/WKHTH B38 ....**176** B4
Maslen Pl *HALE* B63 ....**138** D4
Maslin Dr *BILS/COS* WV14 ....**68** A2
Mason Crs
  ETTPK/GDPK/PENN WV4 ....**51** E3
Masonleys Rd *NFLD/LBR* B31 ....**174** D2
Mason Rd *ERDE/BCHGN* B24 ....**93** E2
  WSLW WS2 ....**27** F5
Masons Cl *HALE* B63 ....**137** G1
Masons Cottages
  ERDE/BCHGN B24 * **93** F1
Mason St *BILS/COS* WV14 ....**68** B4
  BKHL/PFLD WV2 ....**52** A1
  WBROM B70 ....**87** F2
Masons Wy *HIA/OLT* B92 ....**147** E5
Massbrook Gv *WOLVN* WV10 ....**23** H4
Massbrook Rd *WOLVN* WV10 ....**23** H4
Masshouse La *EDG/EDG* B5 ....**3** J4
  BKDE/SHDE B34 ....**112** A4
Masters La
  BLKHTH/ROWR B65 ....**121** G5
Math Meadow
  RIDG/WDGT B32 ....**141** F2
Matlock Cl *BLOX/PEL* WS3 ....**17** E4
  DUDS DY2 ....**120** D1
Matlock Rd *BLOX/PEL* WS3 ....**17** E4
  SPARK B11 ....**145** H4
Matlock Vls *BHTH/HG* B12 * **144** D2
Matthews Cl
  BLKHTH/ROWR B65 ....**121** H3
Mattox Rd *WNSFLD* WV11 ....**24** B4
Matty Rd *LGLYGYN/QTN* B68 ....**105** G5
Maud Rd *CSHL/WTROR* B46 ....**96** D3
  WBROM B70 ....**87** G5
Maughan St *BRLYHL* DY5 ....**120** A4
  DUDN DY1 ....**84** A5
Maurice Gv *WOLVN* WV10 ....**24** A3
Maurice Rd
  ALE/KHTH/YWD B14 ....**161** E4
  SMTHWKW B67 ....**104** D4
Mavis Gdns *LGLYGYN/QTN* B68 ....**123** H5
Mavis Rd *NFLD/LBR* B31 ....**175** E4
Maw St *WSL* WS1 ....**57** F2
Maxholm Rd *FOAKS/STRLY* B74 ....**45** E5
Max Rd *RIDG/WDGT* B32 ....**140** D2
Maxstoke Cl *BLOX/PEL* WS3 ....**16** C4
Maxstoke Cft *SHLY* B90 ....**180** C5
Maxstoke La
  CSHL/WTROR B46 ....**76** C1
Maxstoke Rd *SBORD* B90 ....**127** H2
Maxted Rd *ERDW/GRVHL* B23 ....**76** D1
Maxwell Av
  BFLD/HDSWWD B20 ....**90** B5
Maxwell Rd *BKHL/PFLD* WV2 ....**7** H7
Mayall Dr *MGN/WHC* B75 ....**47** G1
May Av *BHTH/HG* B12 ....**144** C2
Maybank *BORD* B9 ....**128** D1
Maybank Pl *KGSTG* B44 ....**75** E5
Maybank Rd *DUDS* DY2 ....**120** C1
Mayberry Cl
  ALE/KHTH/YWD B14 ....**178** D3
Maybridge Dr *SOLH* B91 ....**181** H5
Maybrook Rd *BRWNH* WS8 ....**9** F3
  WALM/CURD B76 ....**94** C1
Maybury Cl *CDSL* WV8 ....**10** A3
Maybush Gdns *WOLVN* WV10 ....**23** E1
Maydene Cft *BHTH/HG* B12 ....**144** B5
Mayfair *HAG/WOL* DY9 ....**136** B5
Mayfair Cl *DUDN* DY1 ....**84** A4
  KGSTG B44 ....**75** H4
Mayfair Dr *KGSWFD* DY6 ....**99** G2
Mayfair Gdns *BDMR/CCFT* WV3 ....**35** H5
  TPTN/OCK DY4 ....**85** F4
May Farm Cl *HLYWD* B47 ....**192** B2
Mayfield Cl *SOLH* B91 ....**182** A4
Mayfield Crs
  BLKHTH/ROWR B65 ....**121** G1
Mayfield Rd *BVILLE* B30 ....**160** A4
  DUDN DY1 ....**84** B2
  FOAKS/STRLY B74 ....**45** F5
  HALE B63 ....**137** H5
  LOZ/NWT B19 ....**108** C5
  MOS/BIL B13 ....**144** C5
  RMSLY B62 ....**122** D3
  SCFLD/BOLD B73 ....**77** E1
  SPARK B11 ....**146** A3
  WOLV WV1 ....**38** B4

Mayfields Dr *BRWNH* WS8 ....**8** B2
Mayflower Cl *LOZ/NWT* B19 ....**108** D3
Mayflower Dr *BRLYHL* DY5 ....**100** C2
Mayford Gv *MOS/BIL* B13 ....**161** H4
Maygrove Rd *KGSWFD* DY6 ....**99** G2
Mayhurst Cl *HLYWD* B47 ....**193** E2
  TPTN/OCK DY4 ....**69** G5
Mayhurst Rd *HLYWD* B47 ....**192** D1
Maryland Rd
  LDYWD/EDGR B16 ....**125** E2
May La *ALE/KHTH/YWD* B14 ....**161** F5
  HLYWD B47 ....**192** C1
Maynard Av *STRBR* DY8 ....**134** C3
Maypole Cl *CDYHTH* B64 ....**120** D4
Maypole Ct *WMBN* WV5 ....**65** E5
Maypole Dr *STRBR* DY8 ....**135** E2
Maypole Flds *HALE* B63 ....**120** A5
Maypole Gv
  ALE/KHTH/YWD B14 ....**178** D3
Maypole Hl *HALE* B63 ....**120** A4
Maypole La
  ALE/KHTH/YWD B14 ....**178** C3
Maypole Rd *LGLYGYN/QTN* B68 ....**123** F5
Maypole St *WMBN* WV5 ....**65** F4
May St *BLOX/PEL* WS3 ....**27** H4
Mayswood Dr
  DUNHL/THL/PER WV6 ....**34** D4
Mayswood Rd *HIA/OLT* B92 ....**148** A5
Maythorn Av *WALM/CURD* B76 ....**78** C5
Maythorn Gdns *CDSL* WV8 ....**10** C5
Maythorn Gv *SOLH* B91 ....**181** H5
Maytree Cl
  CHWD/FDBR/MGN B37 ....**132** A2
May Tree Gv
  BFLD/HDSWWD B20 ....**89** H3
Maywood Dr *HIA/OLT* B92 ....**165** H2
Maywell Ct *KGSWFD* DY6 ....**99** F3
McBean Rd
  DUNHL/THL/PER WV6 ....**36** B1
McDougall Rd *DARL/WED* WS10 ....**56** C5
McGregor Cl *AST/WIT* B6 ....**91** F5
McKean Rd *OLDBY* B69 ....**105** E1
McKen Ct *WBROM* B70 * **87** C4
McLean Rd *WOLVN* WV10 ....**12** C5
Meaburn Cl *SLYOAK* B29 ....**158** C3
Mead Cl *ALDR* WS9 ....**30** B4
Mead Crs *BORD* B9 ....**129** F1
Meadfoot Av
  ALE/KHTH/YWD B14 ....**178** B2
Meadfoot Dr *KGSWFD* DY6 ....**99** F2
The Meadlands *WMBN* WV5 ....**64** A5
Meadowbrook Gdns *CDSL* WV8 ....**10** D5
Meadowbrook Rd *NFLD/LBR* B31 ....**137** H4
Meadow Brook Rd
  NFLD/LBR B31 ....**158** B5
Meadow Cl *FOAKS/STRLY* B74 ....**45** F4
  HOCK/TIA B94 ....**198** A5
  HRBN B17 ....**124** D3
  RUSH/SHEL WS4 ....**29** E2
  STRBR DY8 ....**78** B2
Meadow Cft
  DUNHL/THL/PER WV6 ....**34** B2
  HLYWD B47 ....**192** C5
  HLYWD B47 ....
Meadow Dr *HIA/OLT* B92 ....**167** G4
Meadowfield Rd *RBRY* B45 ....**188** A4
Meadowfields Cl *STRBR* DY8 ....**118** A2
Meadow Gra Dr *NFLD/LBR* B31 ....**175** E3
Meadow Grange Dr
  SHHTH WV12 ....**25** H5
Meadow Gv *HWK/WKHTH* B38 ....**163** H1
Meadowhill Dr *STRBR* DY8 ....**118** A2
Meadow Hill Rd
  HWK/WKHTH B38 ....**176** C3
Meadowlands Dr
  RUSH/SHEL WS4 ....**29** E2
Meadow La *BILS/COS* WV14 ....**68** B1
  SHHTH WV12 ....**25** G5
  WMBN WV5 ....**65** E5
  WOLVN WV10 ....**12** C1
Meadowpark Rd *STRBR* DY8 ....**117** H4
Meadow Pleck La *SHLY* B90 ....**193** H2
Meadow Ri *NFLD/LBR* B31 ....**175** E3
Meadow Rd *ALDR* WS9 ....**44** A1
  BDMR/CCFT WV3 ....**35** G5
  DUDN DY1 ....**84** A2
  HALE B63 ....**137** H4
  HRBN B17 ....**124** D3
  LGLYGYN/QTN B68 ....**123** F2
  RIDG/WDGT B32 ....**140** A1
  SMTHWK B67 ....**122** A4
Meadows Cv *CDSL* WV8 ....**10** C5
Meadowside Rd *GTB/HAM* B43 ....**73** G2
Meadowside Rd
  FOAKS/STRLY B74 ....**46** D1
The Meadows *ALDR* WS9 ....**29** G5
  STRBR DY8 ....**152** D5
Meadowsweet Av
  HWK/WKHTH B38 ....**176** D5
Meadowsweet Wy
  KGSWFD DY6 ....**100** C3
Meadow St *CDSL* WV8 ....**21** F1
Meadow Vw *MOS/BIL* B13 ....**162** A2
  SEDG DY3 ....**66** C2
Meadow View Whf
  DUNHL/THL/PER WV6 ....**36** A1
Meadow Wk *CDYHTH* B64 ....**120** D4
Meadow Wy *CDSL* WV8 ....**10** A5
  STRBR DY8 ....**117** G2
Mead Ri *EDG* B15 ....**142** D1
The Mead *SEDG* DY3 ....**66** D3
Meadthorpe Rd *KGSTG* B44 ....**74** D3
Meadvale Rd *RBRY* B45 ....**188** B2
Meadway *STECH* B33 ....**130** C2
The Meadway
  DUNHL/THL/PER WV6 ....**21** G5
Mears Cl *ERDW/GRVHL* B23 ....**76** B3
Mears Coppice *BRLYHL* DY5 ....**136** C1
Mears Dr *STECH* B33 ....**111** H5
Mearse Cl *WSNGN* B18 ....**108** A4
Mearse La *HAG/WOL* DY9 ....**184** D2

Mease Cft *BORD* B9 ....**127** H2
Measham Gv
  LGN/SDN/BHAMAIR B26 ....**147** E2
Measham Wy *WNSFLD* WV11 ....**25** E5
Medcroft Av
  BFLD/HDSWWD B20 ....**89** G2
Medina Cl *SPARK* B11 ....**145** G3
Medina Wy *KGSWFD* DY6 ....**99** G3
Medley Rd *SPARK* B11 ....**145** F2
Medlicott Rd *SPARK* B11 ....**145** G2
Medway Cl *KGSWFD* DY6 ....**100** C3
Medway Cft *CBROM* B36 ....**113** H2
Medway Gv *HWK/WKHTH* B38 ....**176** C5
Medway Rd *BRWNH* WS8 ....**8** C2
Medwin Gv *ERDW/GRVHL* B23 ....**76** B4
Meer End *HWK/WKHTH* B38 ....**190** C1
Meerhill Av *SHLY* B90 ....**195** F2
Meeting House La
  NFLD/LBR B31 ....**175** G1
Meeting La *BRLYHL* DY5 ....**118** C3
Meeting St *DARL/WED* WS10 ....**55** G5
  DUDS DY2 ....**102** C5
Mehdi Rd *OLDBY* B69 ....**104** C4
Melbourne Av *BRWNH* WS8 ....**8** C2
  LOZ/NWT B19 ....**108** C3
  SMTHWK B66 ....**106** D2
Melbourne Cl *KGSWFD* DY6 ....**100** A5
Melbourne Gdns
  DSYBK/YTR WS5 ....**57** H2
Melbourne Rd
  BKDE/SHDE B34 ....**113** G3
  HALE B63 ....**138** C1
  SMTHWK B66 ....**106** D2
Melbourne St *BKHL/PFLD* WV2 ....**7** G6
Melbury Cl *BDMR/CCFT* WV3 * **6** B5
Melbury Gv
  ALE/KHTH/YWD B14 ....**161** E5
Melchett Rd *BVILLE* B30 ....**176** D2
Melcote Gv *KGSTG* B44 ....**75** E3
Meldon Dr *BILS/COS* WV14 ....**69** C1
Melford Cl *SEDG* DY3 ....**67** E1
Melford Hall Rd *SOLH* B91 ....**164** B5
Melfort Gv
  ALE/KHTH/YWD B14 ....**178** C2
Melksham Sq *CVALE* B35 ....**94** C3
Mellis Gv *ERDW/GRVHL* B23 ....**91** G1
Mellish Dr *RUSH/SHEL* WS4 ....**42** D2
Mellish Rd *RUSH/SHEL* WS4 ....**42** D2
Mellor Dr *FOAKS/STRLY* B74 ....**46** C2
Mellors Cl *HRBN* B17 ....**141** H4
Mellowdew Rd *STRBR* DY8 ....**117** C1
Mell Sq *SOLH* B91 ....**182** A1
Melplash Av *SOLH* B91 ....**181** G1
Melrose Av *BHTH/HG* B12 ....**71** H2
  HHTH/SAND B71 ....
  SCFLD/BOLD B73 ....**76** C1
  STRBR **152** C1
Melrose Cl *HWK/WKHTH* B38 ....**176** D4
Melrose Dr
  DUNHL/THL/PER WV6 ....**34** B1
Melrose Gv *LOZ/NWT* B19 ....**108** B2
Melrose Pl *SMTHWK* B66 ....**105** H1
Melstock Cl *TPTN/OCK* DY4 ....**84** D1
Melstock Rd
  ALE/KHTH/YWD B14 ....**160** D3
Melton Av *HIA/OLT* B92 ....**147** G3
Melton Dr *EDG* B15 ....**126** C5
Melton Rd
  ALE/KHTH/YWD B14 ....**161** F2
Melverley Gv *KGSTG* B44 ....**75** F4
Melverton Av *WOLVN* WV10 ....**23** G2
Melville Hall
  LDYWD/EDGR B16 * **125** F3
Melville Rd *LDYWD/EDGR* B16 ....**125** F3
Melvina Rd *VAUX/NECH* B7 ....**109** H5
Membury Rd *WASH/WDE* B8 ....**110** B5
Memorial Cl *WLNHL* WV13 ....**39** G3
Memory La *DARL/WED* WS10 ....**40** B5
  WNSFLD WV11 ....**24** B5
Menai Cl *SHHTH* WV12 ....**26** A4
Mendip Av *WASH/WDE* B8 ....**110** A4
Mendip Cl *BKHL/PFLD* WV2 ....**52** D2
  SEDG DY3 ....**83** F3
Mendip Rd *HALE* B63 ....**154** D1
  STRBR **135** H1
  WASH/WDE B8 ....**110** A4
Menin Crs *MOS/BIL* B13 ....**161** H5
Menin Rd *MOS/BIL* B13 ....**161** H5
  TPTN/OCK DY4 ....**84** D1
Meon Gv
  DUNHL/THL/PER WV6 ....**34** C1
  STETCH B33 ....**130** D4
Meon Ri *HAG/WOL* DY9 ....**136** A4
Meon Wy *WNSFLD* WV11 ....**25** F3
Meranti Cl *SHHTH* WV12 ....**26** A3
Mercer Av *CSHL/WTROR* B46 ....**96** A3
Mercer Gv *WNSFLD* WV11 ....**24** D3
Merchants Wy *ALDR* WS9 ....**30** A3
Mercia Dr
  ALE/KHTH/YWD B14 ....**160** D4
  DUNHL/THL/PER WV6 ....**20** C5
Mere Av *CVALE* B35 ....**94** C3
Mere Cl *SHHTH* WV12 ....**25** G4
Merecote Rd *HIA/OLT* B92 ....**163** H5
Meredith Pool Cl
  WSNGN B18 ....**107** H3
Meredith Rd *DUDS* DY2 ....**82** C1
  WNSFLD WV11 ....**24** C2
Meredith St *CDYHTH* B64 ....**120** D5
Mere Dr *MGN/WHC* B75 ....**47** C5
Mere Green Rd *MGN/WHC* B75 ....**47** C5
Mere Oak Rd
  DUNHL/THL/PER WV6 ....**20** C5
Mere Pool Rd *MGN/WHC* B75 ....**47** H5
Mere Rd *ERDW/GRVHL* B23 ....**92** C5
  STRBR DY8 ....**135** E3
Mereside Wy *HIA/OLT* B92 ....**164** A4
Meres Rd *HALE* B63 ....**137** G2
Merevale Rd *HIA/OLT* B92 ....**147** H5
Mere Vw *RUSH/SHEL* WS4 ....**29** E2
Mereways *SHLY* B90 ....**194** A3
Meriden Av *STRBR* DY8 ....**134** D1
Meriden Cl *STRBR* DY8 ....**134** D1
  YDLY B25 ....**129** F5
Meriden Dr
  CHWD/FDBR/MGN B37 ....**114** A4

Meriden Ri *HIA/OLT* B92 ....**148** B4
Meriden Rd *HIA/OLT* B92 ....**167** H5
  WOLVN WV10 ....**22** C2
Meriden St *DIG/EDG* B5 ....**3** J6
Merino Av *NFLD/LBR* B31 ....**175** E5
Merion Cl *CVALE* B35 ....**94** C3
  DUDN DY1 ....**101** H1
Merlin Gv
  LGN/SDN/BHAMAIR B26 ....**147** G2
Merrick Cl *HALE* B63 ....**137** H5
Merrick Rd *WNSFLD* WV11 ....**25** F4
Merridale Av *BDMR/CCFT* WV3 ....**36** B5
Merridale Crs *BDMR/CCFT* WV3 ....**6** A4
Merridale Gdns
  BDMR/CCFT WV3 ....**6** A5
Merridale La *BDMR/CCFT* WV3 ....**6** A4
Merridale Rd *BDMR/CCFT* WV3 ....**6** A4
Merridale St *BDMR/CCFT* WV3 ....**6** D6
Merridale St West
  BDMR/CCFT WV3 ....**6** A7
Merrill's Hall La *WNSFLD* WV11 ....**39** E1
Merrington Cl *SOLH* B91 ....**182** A5
Merrion's Cl *GTB/HAM* B43 ....**58** C4
Merrishaw Rd *NFLD/LBR* B31 ....**175** G5
Merritts Brook Cl *SLYOAK* B29 ....**158** C5
Merritt's Brook La
  NFLD/LBR B31 ....**158** A5
Merritt's Hl *NFLD/LBR* B31 ....**158** A5
Merrivale Rd *RMSLY* B62 ....**122** D4
  SMTHWK B66 ....**124** C2
Merryfield Cl *HIA/OLT* B92 ....**165** F3
Merryfield Gv *HRBN* B17 ....**142** A3
Merryfield Rd *DUDN* DY1 ....**83** E5
Merry Hl *BRLYHL* DY5 ....**119** H5
Merryhill Dr *WSNGN* B18 ....**107** H3
Mersey Gv *HWK/WKHTH* B38 ....**176** C5
Mersey Rd *BLOX/PEL* WS3 ....**28** A1
Merstal Dr *HIA/OLT* B92 ....**165** G4
Merstone Cl *BILS/COS* WV14 ....**53** C2
Merstowe Cl *ACGN* B27 ....**146** B4
Merton Cl *LGLYGYN/QTN* B68 ....**123** F2
Merton Rd *MOS/BIL* B13 ....**145** F4
Mervyn Pl *BILS/COS* WV14 ....**54** B5
Mervyn Rd *BILS/COS* WV14 ....**54** B5
  HDSW B21 ....**107** H1
Meryhurst Rd *DARL/WED* WS10 ....**56** B4
Messenger La *WBROM* B70 ....**87** H3
Messenger Rd *SMTHWK* B66 ....**106** D3
Metchley Cft *SHLY* B90 ....**195** F2
Metchley Ct *HRBN* B17 ....**142** B3
Metchley Dr *HRBN* B17 ....**142** A2
Metchley La *HRBN* B17 ....**142** B3
Metchley Park Rd *EDG* B15 ....**142** A2
Metchley Ri *HRBN* B17 ....**142** B2
Metfield Cft *HRBN* B17 ....**142** A4
  KGSWFD DY6 ....**100** B5
Metlin Gv *STETCH* B33 ....**131** C1
Metric Wk *SMTHWK* B67 ....**106** C4
Metro Wy *SMTHWK* B66 ....**107** E2
The Mews *BLKHTH/ROWR* B65 * ....
Mey Coppice *CBROM* B36 ....**113** H2
Meyrick Rd *HHTH/SAND* B71 ....**71** E5
Meyrick Wk *HLGN/EDGR* B16 ....**125** H3
Miall Park Rd *SOLH* B91 ....**164** A5
Miall Rd *HLGN/YWD* D28 ....**162** C1
Michael Dr *EDG* B15 ....**126** C5
Michael Rd *DARL/WED* WS10 ....**54** D1
  SMTHWK B66 ....**106** A3
Michelle Cl *MOS/BIL* B13 ....**161** G5
Mickleton Cl *EDG* B15 ....
Mickle Acre Rd
  RIDG/WDGT B32 ....**141** E5
Middle Av *WLNHL* WV13 ....**39** G4
Middle Bickenhill La
  HIA/OLT B92 ....**150** C3
Middle Crs *BLOX/PEL* WS3 ....**28** B5
Middle Cross *WOLV* WV1 ....**7** J5
Middle Dr *RBRY* B45 ....**188** D4
Middlefield *CDSL* WV8 ....**11** G5
Middlefield Av *RMSLY* B62 ....**122** D3
Middlefield La *HAG/WOL* DY9 ....**152** D4
Middle Field Rd *NFLD/LBR* B31 ....**175** C1
Middlefield Rd *OLDBY* B69 ....**103** G1
Middlehill Ri *RIDG/WDGT* B32 ....**139** H5
Middle La *HLYWD* B47 ....**192** B5
  HWK/WKHTH B38 ....**191** G1
Middle Leaford
  BKDE/SHDE B34 ....**112** C4
Middle Leasowe
  RIDG/WDGT B32 ....**140** C3
Middle Meadow Av
  RIDG/WDGT B32 ....**140** C2
Middlemist Gv *GTB/HAM* B43 ....**73** H5
Middlemore La *ALDR* WS9 ....**29** H4
Middlemore La West *ALDR* WS9 ....**29** G4
Middlemore Rd *NFLD/LBR* B31 ....**175** H5
  SMTHWK B66 ....**106** C2
Middle Park Cl *SLYOAK* B29 ....**158** D2
Middlepark Dr *NFLD/LBR* B31 ....**158** D4
Middlepark Rd *DUDN* DY1 ....**101** G1
Middle Park Rd *SLYOAK* B29 ....**158** D2
Middle Rd *BRGRVW* B61 ....**186** B4
Middleton Gdns *DSYBK/YTR* WS5 ....**57** F3
Middleton Hall Rd *BVILLE* B30 ....**176** A1
Middleton Rd
  ALE/KHTH/YWD B14 ....**161** C2
  BRWNH WS8 ....**9** G3
  SHLY B90 ....**180** A3
Middletree Rd *HALE* B63 ....**120** C5
Middle Vauxhall *WOLV* WV1 ....**6** B5
Middleway Av *STRBR* DY8 ....**117** G1
Middleway Rd *BILS/COS* WV14 ....**38** C5
Middleway Vw *WSNGN* B18 ....**126** A1
Middlewood Cl *SOLH* B91 ....**165** H4

Midgley Dr *FOAKS/STRLY* B74 ...... 47 E3
Midhill Dr *BLKHTH/ROWR* B65 .... 104 A3
Midhurst Cv
  DUNHL/THL/PER WV6 .... 21 G5
Midhurst Rd *BVILLE* B30 .... 177 F2
Midland Cl *HDSW* B21 .... 107 H2
Midland Dr *SCFLD/WYGN* B72 ... 62 C5
Midland Rd *BVILLE* B30 .... 159 H5
  DARL/WED WS10 .... 40 A5
  FOAKS/STRLY B74 .... 42 B5
  WSL WS1 .... 4 D5
Midland St *BORD* B9 .... 128 A1
Midpoint Bvd *WALM/CURD* B76 .. 95 E1
Midpoint Pk *WALM/CURD* B76 * .. 95 E1
Midvale Dr
  ALE/KHTH/YWD B14 .... 177 H3
Milburn Rd *KGSTG* B44 .... 60 C5
Milcote Dr *SCFLD/BOLD* B73 ...... 61 G5
  WLNHL WV13 .... 38 D4
Milcote Rd *SLYOAK* B29 .... 158 C2
  SMTHWKW B67 .... 124 B2
  SOLH B91 .... 181 H1
Milcote Wy *KGSWFD* DY6 .... 99 F2
Mildenhall Rd *PBAR/PBCH* B42 ... 74 A2
Mildred Rd *CDYHTH* B64 .... 121 E2
Mildred Wy
  BLKHTH/ROWR B65 .... 104 A3
Milebrook Gv *RIDG/WDGT* B32 ... 157 F2
Milebush Av *CBROM* B36 .... 95 F5
Mile Flat *KGSWFD* DY6 .... 98 A5
Miles Gv *DUDS* DY2 .... 103 F2
Miles Meadow Cl *SHHTH* WV12 .. 26 A2
Milestone Dr *HAG/WOL* DY9 ...... 169 C1
Milestone La *HDSW* B21 .... 107 F1
Milestone Wy *SHHTH* WV12 ...... 25 C5
Milford Av *SHHTH* WV12 .... 25 C5
Milford Cl *STRBR* DY8 .... 118 A1
Milford Copse *HRBN* B17 .... 141 H2
Milford Ct *LOZ/NWT* B19 .... 108 D4
Milford Cft
  BLKHTH/ROWR B65 .... 103 F5
Milford Gv *SHLY* B90 .... 196 A1
Milford Pl
  ALE/KHTH/YWD B14 .... 161 G2
Milford Rd *BKHL/PFLD* WV2 .... 52 A1
  HRBN B17 .... 141 H2
Milholme Gn *HIA/OLT* B92 .... 165 F3
Milking Bank *DUDN* DY1 .... 83 G4
Milk St *DIG/EDG* B5 .... 3 K7
Millard Rd *BILS/COS* WV14 .... 68 A2
Mill Bank *SEDG* DY3 .... 67 F3
Millbank Gv *BKDW/GRVHL* B23 .. 75 H5
Millbank St *WNSFLD* WV11 .... 26 C1
Millbrook Dr *NFLD/LBR* B31 ...... 175 E5
Millbrook Rd
  ALE/KHTH/YWD B14 .... 160 C4
Millbrook Wy *BRLYHL* DY5 .... 118 D4
Mill Burn Wy *BORD* B9 .... 127 H2
Mill Cl *HLYWD* B47 .... 192 C1
  KIDD DY10 .... 168 D3
  SEDG DY3 .... 67 F3
Mill Cft *BILS/COS* WV14 .... 54 A2
Millcroft Cl *RIDG/WDGT* B32 ..... 141 E5
Milldale Crs *WOLVN* WV10 .... 12 D4
Milldale Rd *WOLVN* WV10 .... 12 D4
Mil Dr *SMTHWK* B66 .... 106 D4
Millenium Pk *WODG* B70 .... 87 E1
Millenium Cl *BLOX/PEL* WS3 ...... 16 B5
Millenium Gdns *CDYHTH* B64 ... 121 F2
Millenium Pk *WBROM* B70 * 87 E1
Millenium Wy *CDSL* WV8 .... 10 D3
Miller Crs *BILS/COS* WV14 .... 68 A2
Millers Cl *WSLW* WS2 .... 41 G3
Millersdale Dr *HHTH/SAND* B71 .. 72 B1
Millers Green Dr *KGSWFD* DY6 ... 99 E1
Miller St *AST/WIT* B6 .... 109 E4
Millers V *WMBN* WV5 .... 80 B1
Millers Wk *BLOX/PEL* WS3 .... 17 G4
Mill Farm Rd *HRBN* B17 .... 142 A4
Millfield *NFLD/LBR* B31 * 175 G1
Millfield Av *BLOX/PEL* WS3 .... 17 F5
  RUSH/SHEL WS4 .... 28 D1
Millfield Rd
  BFLD/HDSWWD B20 .... 89 H1
  WMBN WS8 .... 9 G5
Millfields *STETCH* B33 .... 131 G1
Millfields Rd
  ETTPK/GDPK/PENN WV4 .... 53 E3
  HHTH/SAND B71 .... 71 F2
Millfields Wy *WMBN* WV5 .... 80 B1
Millfield Vw *HALE* B63 .... 138 A3
Millford Cl *HLGN/YWD* B28 ...... 163 E5
Mill Gdns *SMTHWKW* B67 * 124 B3
Mill Gn *WOLVN* WV10 .... 12 D3
Mill Gv *CDSL* WV8 .... 11 E4
Millhaven Av *BVILLE* B30 .... 160 B4
Mill HI *SMTHWKW* B67 .... 124 B3
Mill House Rd *YDLY* B25 .... 129 G4
Millichip Rd *WLNHL* WV13 .... 39 E4
Millington Rd *CBROM* B36 .... 112 A1
  TPTN/OCK DY4 .... 69 H4
  WOLVN WV10 .... 23 C4
Mill La *SHLY* B90 .... 195 G1
Mill La *ALDR* WS9 .... 31 C4
  BRGRVW B61 .... 186 B5
  CDSL WV8 .... 8 A5
  DIG/EDG B5 .... 3 J7
  DOR/KN B93 .... 196 D4
  DUNHL/THL/PER WV6 .... 35 E3
  HALE B63 .... 139 E3
  KIDD DY10 .... 168 D3
  NFLD/LBR B31 .... 175 F3
  OLDBY B69 .... 87 F4
  RIDG/WDGT B32 .... 141 E5
  RUSH/SHEL WS4 .... 42 B1
  SEDG DY3 .... 80 D1
  SHHTH WV12 .... 26 A5
  SOLH B91 .... 182 A2
  WMBN WV5 .... 65 F4
  WNSFLD WV11 .... 24 D3
Mill Lane Ar *SOLH* B91 * 182 A2
Millmead Rd
  RIDG/WDGT B32 .... 141 E5
Mill Pl *BLOX/PEL* WS3 .... 42 A1
Mill Pool Cl *HAG/WOL* DY9 ...... 169 G1
  WMBN WV5 .... 80 B1
Millpool Gdns
  ALE/KHTH/YWD B14 .... 178 B2

Millpool Hill Alcester Rd South
  ALE/KHTH/YWD B14 .... 178 B1
Mill Pool La *DOR/KN* B93 .... 199 E3
Millpool Wy *SMTHWK* B66 .... 106 C5
Mill Race La *STRBR* DY8 .... 135 G1
Mill Rd *BRWNH* WS8 .... 9 G5
  CDYHTH B64 .... 121 E5
  WALM/CURD WS4 .... 28 D1
Mills Av *WALM/CURD* B76 .... 63 E4
Mills Cl *WNSFLD* WV11 .... 24 B2
Mills Crs *BKHL/PFLD* WV2 .... 37 G5
Millside *HLGN/YWD* B28 .... 179 G2
  WMBN WV5 * 80 C1
Mills Rd *BKHL/PFLD* WV2 .... 37 G5
Millstone Cl *WALM/CURD* B76 .... 78 B2
Mill Stream Cl *CDSL* WV8 .... 10 D3
Mill St *AST/WIT* B6 .... 109 F4
  BILS/COS WV14 .... 53 G3
  BRLYHL DY5 .... 119 F2
  CDYHTH B64 .... 120 C5
  CSCFLD/WYGN B72 .... 62 C4
  DARL/WED WS10 .... 55 E2
  STRBR DY8 .... 118 A2
  BORD B9 .... 86 B1
  WBROM B70 .... 87 G2
  WLNHL WV13 .... 40 A3
  WSLW WS2 .... 42 A2
Millthorpe Cl *WASH/WDE* B8 .... 110 D4
Mill Vw *STETCH* B33 .... 113 E5
Millwalk Dr *COVEN* WV9 .... 11 H2
The Mill Wk *NFLD/LBR* B31 .... 175 F4
Millward St *BORD* B9 .... 128 A3
  WBROM B70 .... 87 E3
Millwright Cl *TPTN/OCK* DY4 .... 85 H1
Milner Av *SLYOAK* B29 .... 160 A1
Milner Rd *MOS/BIL* B13 .... 162 B2
Milsom Gv *BKDE/SHDE* B34 ...... 113 F3
Milstead Rd
  LGN/SDN/BHAMAIR B26 .... 130 C3
Milston Cl *ALE/KHTH/YWD* B14 .. 178 A4
Milton Av *DOR/KN* B93 .... 196 D4
  SHHTH WV12 .... 26 C5
  STRBR DY8 .... 118 C5
  WSL WS1 .... 5 H4
Milton Ct *DUNHL/THL/PER* WV6 .. 34 C1
Milton Crs *SEDG* DY3 .... 82 C1
  YDLY B25 .... 129 H5
Milton Dr *HAG/WOL* DY9 .... 153 F3
Milton Gv *HDSW* B21 .... 107 E1
Milton Pl *WSL* WS1 .... 56 D2
Milton Rd *BILS/COS* WV14 .... 68 D4
  DOR/KN B93 .... 196 D4
  SMTHWKW B67 .... 105 H4
  WOLVN WV10 .... 24 A5
Milton St *BRLYHL* DY5 .... 101 F2
  HHTH/SAND B71 .... 87 F1
  STRBR DY8 .... 109 E3
  WSL WS1 .... 4 C7
Milverton Cl *HALE* B63 .... 138 C1
  WALM/CURD B76 .... 78 B4
Milverton Rd *DOR/KN* B93 .... 197 G3
  ERDW/GRVHL B23 .... 90 C4
Mimosa Cl *SLYOAK* B29 .... 158 D2
Mimosa Wk *KGSWFD* DY6 .... 100 A1
Mincing La
  BLKHTH/ROWR B65 .... 122 A1
Mindelsohn Wy *HRBN* B17 .... 142 B3
Minden Gv *SLYOAK* B29 .... 158 D1
Minehead Rd *DUDN* DY1 .... 101 F1
  WOLVN WV10 .... 12 B5
Miner St *WSLW* WS2 .... 41 G2
Minerva Cl *SHHTH* WV12 .... 40 D1
Minewood Cl *BLOX/PEL* WS3 ..... 16 B4
Minith Rd *BILS/COS* WV14 .... 68 D5
Miniva Dr *WALM/CURD* B76 ...... 78 C1
Minivet Dr *BHTH/HG* B12 .... 144 A1
Minley Av *HRBN* B17 .... 124 B5
The Minories *CBHAMNE* B4 .... 3 G4
  DUDS DY2 .... 84 D5
Minstead Rd *ERDE/BCHGN* B24 .. 92 B5
Minster Cl *BLKHTH/ROWR* B65 .. 122 C1
  DOR/KN B93 .... 183 F5
Minster Ct *MOS/BIL* B13 * 144 C3
Minster Dr *SMHTH* B10 .... 128 A5
Minsterley Cl *BDMR/CCFT* WV3 .. 36 A5
The Minster *BDMR/CCFT* WV3 .. 51 F1
Mintern Rd *YDLY* B25 .... 129 G3
Minton Cl *WOLV* WV1 .... 38 A4
Minton Rd *RIDG/WDGT* B32 ...... 141 F5
Minworth Rd *CSHL/WTROR* B46 .. 96 B3
Miranda Cl *RBRY* B45 .... 174 A3
Mirfield Cl *COVEN* WV9 .... 12 A4
Mirfield Rd *SOLH* B91 .... 164 C4
  STETCH B33 .... 130 D2
Mission Cl *CDYHTH* B64 .... 121 C3
Mission Dr *TPTN/OCK* DY4 .... 85 G2
Mistletoe Dr *DSYBK/YTR* WS5 ... 57 C5
Mitcham Gv *KGSTG* B44 .... 75 H2
Mitcheldean Covert
  ALE/KHTH/YWD B14 .... 177 H3
Mitchel Av *BILS/COS* WV14 .... 68 B2
Mitchel Rd *KGSWFD* DY6 .... 100 B5
Mitford Dr *HIA/OLT* B92 .... 165 F3
Mitre Cl *SHHTH* WV12 .... 26 B5
  WNSFLD WV11 .... 15 E4
Mitre Fold *WOLV* WV1 .... 6 E5
Mitre Rd *HAG/WOL* DY9 .... 156 C2
Mitten Av *RBRY* B45 .... 173 H4
Mitton Rd *BFLD/HDSWWD* B20 .. 89 G4
Moat Brook Av *CDSL* WV8 .... 10 A3
Moat Coppice
  RIDG/WDGT B32 .... 157 E1
Moat Cft
  CHWD/FDBR/MGN B37 .... 132 A2
  WALM/CURD B76 .... 78 D4
Moat Dr *BKDE/SHDE* B34 .... 112 C3
Moat Farm Dr *RIDG/WDGT* B32 .. 157 E1
Moat Farm Wy *BLOX/PEL* WS3 ... 18 A2
Moatfield Ter *DARL/WED* WS10 .. 56 A5
Moat Green Av *WNSFLD* WV11 ... 25 E3
Moat House La East
  WNSFLD WV11 .... 24 D3
Moathouse La West
  WNSFLD WV11 .... 24 D3
Moat House Rd
  WODG B8 .... 111 E5
Moat La *DIG/EDG* B5 .... 3 H6
  LGN/SDN/BHAMAIR B26 .... 130 A5
  SOLH B91 .... 165 E4

The Moatway
  HWK/WKHTH B38 .... 190 C1
Mobberley Rd *BILS/COS* WV14 ... 68 A2
Mob La *RUSH/SHEL* WS4 .... 18 C5
Mockley Wood Rd
  DOR/KN B93 .... 197 F1
Modbury Av *RIDG/WDGT* B32 ... 157 H1
Moden Cl *SEDG* DY3 .... 83 F1
Moden HI *SEDG* DY3 .... 70 A1
Mogul La *HALE* B63 .... 120 A5
Moilliett St *WSNGN* B18 .... 107 F5
Moilliett Ct *SMTHWK* B66 .... 107 E5
Moira Crs *ALE/KHTH/YWD* B14 .. 179 E1
Moises Hall Rd *WMBN* WV5 ...... 65 F5
Moland St *CBHAMNE* B4 .... 3 H1
Mole St *BHTH/HG* B12 .... 144 D1
Molineux St *WOLV* WV1 .... 6 E2
Mollington Crs *SHLY* B90 .... 180 C2
Molyneux Rd *DUDS* DY2 .... 121 E2
Monarch Dr *TPTN/OCK* DY4 ...... 70 A5

Monarch's Wy
  BLKHTH/ROWR B65 .... 121 G2
  BRGRVW B61 .... 186 B5
  CDSL WV8 .... 20 A5
  CDYHTH B64 .... 121 F1
  COVEN WV9 .... 11 G2
  DARL/WED WS10 .... 54 D5
  ETTPK/GDPK/PENN WV4 .... 64 D1
  HAG/WOL DY9 .... 153 F2
  KGSWFD DY6 .... 98 C5
  KIDD DY10 .... 168 D4
  KINVER DY7 .... 116 C2
  OLDBY B69 .... 86 A4
  RBRY B45 .... 187 E2
  RMSLY B62 .... 173 E2
  SEDG DY3 .... 66 C4
  SHHTH WV12 .... 26 C4
  STRBR DY8 .... 135 E1
  TPTN/OCK DY4 .... 70 B5
  WMBN WV5 .... 80 A1
  WNSFLD WV11 .... 24 D2
  WOLVN WV10 .... 12 C1
  WSLW WS2 .... 41 E2
Monarch Wy *DUDS* DY2 .... 102 B5
Mona Rd *ERDW/GRVHL* B23 ...... 92 D1
Monastery Dr *SOLH* B91 .... 164 A4
Monckton Rd
  LGLYGN/QTN B68 .... 123 E5
Moncrieffe Cl *DUDS* DY2 .... 103 E1
Moncrieffe St *WSL* WS1 .... 5 H5
Money La *BRGRVW* B61 .... 186 C2
Monica Rd *SMHTH* B10 .... 128 D4
Monins Av *TPTN/OCK* DY4 .... 85 F3
Monk Rd *TPTN/OCK* DY4 .... 85 H3
Monkgate Dr *HHTH/SAND* B71 .. 71 F5
Monk Rd *WASH/WDE* B8 .... 111 F4
Monks Cl *WMBN* WV5 .... 64 C5
Monkseaton Rd
  SCFLD/WYGN B72 .... 77 F1
Monksfield Av *GTB/HAM* B43 .... 73 F2
Monkshood Ms
  ERDW/GRVHL B23 .... 75 H4
Monkshood Retreat
  HWK/WKHTH B38 .... 176 D5
Monks Kirby Rd
  WALM/CURD B76 .... 63 F5
Monkspath *SHLY* B90 .... 195 G2
  SHLY B90 .... 78 B3
Monkspath Cl *SHLY* B90 .... 194 D1
Monkspath Hall Rd *SHLY* B90 .. 195 F2
Monksway *HWK/WKHTH* B38 ... 177 F3
Monkswell Cl *BRLYHL* DY5 ...... 119 F3
  SMHTH B10 .... 128 B5
Monkswood Rd
  NFLD/LBR B31 .... 176 A3
Monkton Rd *SLYOAK* B29 .... 141 G4
Monmer Cl *WLNHL* WV13 .... 39 H2
Monmer La *WLNHL* WV13 .... 39 H2
Monmore Rd *WOLV* WV1 .... 38 A5
Monmouth Dr
  HHTH/SAND B71 .... 71 F4
  SCFLD/BOLD B73 .... 61 E4
Monmouth Rd
  RIDG/WDGT B32 .... 157 H2
  SMTHWKW B67 .... 124 A4
  WSLW WS2 .... 40 C2
Monsal Av *WOLVN* WV10 .... 23 C5
Monsaldale Cl *BRWNH* WS8 ...... 18 D1
Monsal Rd *PBAR/PBCH* B42 ...... 74 C4
Mons Rd *DUDS* DY2 .... 85 E5
Montague Rd
  ERDE/BCHGN B24 .... 93 E5
  HDSW B21 .... 107 H1
  LDYWD/EDGR B16 .... 125 G3
  SMTHWK B66 .... 124 D1
Montague St *AST/WIT* B6 .... 3 H1
  BORD B9 .... 127 G1
Montana Av *PBAR/PBCH* B42 ..... 90 A1
Monteagle Dr *KGSWFD* DY6 ...... 81 H5
Montford Gv *SEDG* DY3 * 67 F4
Montfort Rd
  CSHL/WTROR B46 .... 115 F4
  WALM/CURD B76 .... 56 B2
Montgomery Crs *BRLYHL* DY5 .. 119 H5
Montgomery Cft *SPARK* B11 .... 128 A5
Montgomery Rd *WSLW* WS2 ...... 40 C5
Montgomery St *SPARK* B11 ..... 127 H5
Montgomery Wy
  WASH/WDE B8 .... 111 E5
Montpelier Rd
  ERDE/BCHGN B24 .... 93 E5
Montpellier Gdns *DUDN* DY1 ... 83 G4
Montpellier St *BHTH/HG* B12 ... 144 C1
Montrose Dr *CVALE* B35 .... 93 H3
  DUDN DY1 .... 102 A1
Montsford Cl *DOR/KN* B93 .... 196 D2
Monument Av *HAG/WOL* DY9 ... 136 C3
Monument La *HAG/WOL* DY9 ... 153 F5
  RBRY B45 .... 187 H4
  SEDG DY3 .... 67 G2
Monument Rd
  LDYWD/EDGR B16 .... 125 H3
Monway Ter *DARL/WED* WS10 ... 55 G5
Monwood Gv *SOLH* B91 .... 181 F3

Moat Mdw *RIDG/WDGT* B32 ..... 141 E3
Moat Rd *LGLYGN/QTN* B68 ...... 123 F1
  TPTN/OCK DY4 .... 69 G4
  WSLW WS2 .... 41 G3
Moatside Cl *BLOX/PEL* WS3 .... 18 A2
Moat St *WLNHL* WV13 .... 39 G3

Monyhull Hall Rd *BVILLE* B30 ... 177 F2
Moodyscroft Rd *STECH* B33 .... 131 E1
Moorcroft Dr *DARL/WED* WS10 .. 70 A1
Moorcroft Pl *VAUX/NECH* B7 *.. 109 G5
Moorcroft Rd *MOS/BIL* B13 ..... 143 H4
Moordown Av *HIA/OLT* B92 ...... 147 E3
Moore Cl *FOAKS/STRLY* B74 ...... 32 D4
  DUNHL/THL/PER WV6 .... 34 D1
Moore Crs *LGLYGN/QTN* B68 ... 123 G1
Moorend Av
  CHWD/FDBR/MGN B37 .... 132 A3
Moor End La *ERDE/BCHGN* B24 .. 93 E2
Moore Rd *SHHTH* WV12 .... 26 B2
Moore's Rw *DIG/EDG* B5 .... 3 K7
Moore St *WOLV* WV1 .... 37 H4
Moorfield Av *DOR/KN* B93 .... 196 D2
Moorfield Dr *HALE* B63 .... 138 C2
  SCFLD/BOLD B73 .... 76 D3
Moorfield Rd *BKDE/SHDE* B34 .. 112 C3
  BKHL/PFLD WV2 .... 51 H1
Moorfields Cl *ALDR* WS9 .... 30 A3
Moorfoot Av *HALE* B63 .... 137 G2
Moor Green La *MOS/BIL* B13 ... 160 C1
Moor Hall Pk *HAG/WOL* DY9 ... 171 E4
  MGN/WHC B75 .... 47 G4
Moorhen Cl *BRWNH* WS8 .... 9 F5
Moorhills Cft *RBRY* B45 .... 180 B5
The Moorings *BRLYHL* DY5 .... 101 H5
  COVEN WV9 * 11 H5
  OLDBY B69 .... 104 C3
  WOLV WV1 .... 107 H4
Moorland Av *WOLVN* WV10 .... 23 E4
Moorland Rd *BLOX/PEL* WS3 ...... 27 E2
  LDYWD/EDGR B16 .... 125 F3
Moorlands Dr *SHLY* B90 .... 180 C1
Moorlands Rd *HHTH/SAND* B71 .. 71 G2
The Moorlands
  FOAKS/STRLY B74 .... 46 D5
Moor La *AST/WIT* B6 .... 91 G3
  BLKHTH/ROWR B65 .... 121 H5
  LICHS WS14 .... 32 C1
Moor Leasow *NFLD/LBR* B31 .... 176 A3
Moor Meadow Rd
  MGN/WHC B75 .... 62 D1
Moor Pk *BLOX/PEL* WS3 .... 20 B5
  DUNHL/THL/PER WV6 .... 34 D1
Moorpark Rd *NFLD/LBR* B31 .... 175 G4
Moor Pool Av *HRBN* B17 .... 142 A1
Moors Cft *RIDG/WDGT* B32 ...... 157 F1
Moorside Gdns *WSLW* WS2 .... 41 F2
Moorside Rd
  ALE/KHTH/YWD B14 .... 179 E1
Moors La *NFLD/LBR* B31 .... 158 A2
Moors Mill La *TPTN/OCK* DY4 ... 70 A4
Moorsom St *AST/WIT* B6 .... 108 E4
The Moors *CBROM* B36 .... 112 B1
Moor St *BRLYHL* DY5 .... 118 C1
  CBHAMNE B4 .... 3 H6
  DARL/WED WS10 .... 71 F1
  WBROM B70 .... 87 G4
Moor St Queensway
  CBHAMNE B4 .... 3 H6
Moor St South *BKHL/PFLD* WV2 .. 52 A1
The Moor *WALM/CURD* B76 .... 78 C3
Moorville Wk *SPARK* B11 .... 127 G5
Morar Cl *CVALE* B35 .... 94 D2
Moray Cl *RMSLY* B62 .... 122 A3
Morcom Rd *SPARK* B11 .... 145 G2
Morcroft *BILS/COS* WV14 .... 54 C5
Mordaunt Dr *MGN/WHC* B75 ... 47 H3
Morden Rd *STETCH* B33 .... 129 H1
Moreland Cft *WALM/CURD* B76 .. 78 D5
The Morelands *NFLD/LBR* B31 .. 175 H4
Morestead Av
  LGN/SDN/BHAMAIR B26 .... 148 A2
Moreton Av
  ETTPK/GDPK/PENN WV4 .... 52 C4
  GTB/HAM B43 .... 74 C1
Moreton Cl *RIDG/WDGT* B32 ... 141 F2
  TPTN/OCK DY4 .... 69 H5
  YDLY B25 .... 129 F5
Moreton Rd *SHLY* B90 .... 180 C3
  WOLVN WV10 .... 23 F1
Moreton St *CBHAMW* B1 .... 2 A2
Morford Rd *ALDR* WS9 .... 30 B3
Morgan Cl *CDYHTH* B64 .... 121 E5
  OLDBY B69 .... 87 G5
  SHHTH WV12 .... 39 H1
Morgan Gv *CBROM* B36 .... 95 H5
Morgrove Av *DOR/KN* B93 .... 196 D2
Morjon Dr *GTB/HAM* B43 .... 73 H1
Morland Rd *GTB/HAM* B43 .... 59 C4
Morley Gv
  DUNHL/THL/PER WV6 .... 37 E1
Morley Rd *WASH/WDE* B8 .... 111 F3
Morlich Ri *BRLYHL* DY5 .... 135 E3
Morning Pines *STRBR* DY8 ...... 135 E3
Morningside *SCFLD/BOLD* B73 .. 62 B2
Mornington Rd *SMTHWK* B66 ... 106 D2
Morris Av *WSLW* WS2 .... 40 C3
Morris Cl *CBROM* B36 .... 95 G5
Morris Fld Cft
  HLGN/YWD B28 .... 179 G1
Morrison Av *WOLVN* WV10 .... 23 F2
Morrison Rd *TPTN/OCK* DY4 ...... 86 B2
Morris Rd *WASH/WDE* B8 .... 111 F3
Morris St *WBROM* B70 .... 87 G5
Mortimers Cl
  ALE/KHTH/YWD B14 .... 178 D4
Morton Rd *BRLYHL* DY5 .... 119 F5
Morvale Gdns *HAG/WOL* DY9 ... 136 C2
Morvale St *HAG/WOL* DY9 .... 136 C2
Morven Rd *SCFLD/BOLD* B73 ..... 76 D1
Morville Cl *DOR/KN* B93 .... 196 D4
Morville Cft *BILS/COS* WV14 ..... 53 F4
Morville Rd *DUDS* DY2 .... 102 D5
Morville St *LDYWD/EDGR* B16 .. 2 A7
Mosborough Crs
  LOZ/NWT B19 .... 108 C4
Mosedale Dr *WNSFLD* WV11 ..... 25 F5
Moseley Ct *WNSFLD* WV11 .... 14 D4
Moseley Dr
  CHWD/FDBR/MGN B37 .... 131 H4
Moseley Old Hall La
  WOLVN WV10 .... 13 G2
Moseley Rd *BHTH/HG* B12 .... 144 B2
  BILS/COS WV14 .... 39 E5
  WLNHL WV13 .... 38 D4
  WOLVN WV10 .... 13 H2

Moseley St *DIG/EDG* B5 .... 127 F3
  TPTN/OCK DY4 .... 70 A4
  WOLV WV10 .... 37 E1
Moss Cl *ALDR* WS9 .... 42 C2
  RUSH/SHEL WS4 .... 42 C2
Mossdale Wy *SEDG* DY3 .... 67 G4
Moss Dr *SCFLD/WYGN* B72 ...... 62 C5
Mossfield Rd
  ALE/KHTH/YWD B14 .... 161 E3
Moss Gdns *BILS/COS* WV14 ...... 53 F5
Moss Gv *ALE/KHTH/YWD* B14 .. 160 D4
  KGSWFD DY6 .... 99 H2
Moss House Cl *EDG* B15 .... 126 B3
Mossley Cl *BLOX/PEL* WS3 .... 26 D1
Mossley La *BLOX/PEL* WS3 .... 16 B5
Mossvale Cl *CDYHTH* B64 .... 121 E3
Mossvale Gv *WASH/WDE* B8 ... 110 D4
Moss Wy *FOAKS/STRLY* B74 ...... 60 B1
Mostyn Crs *HHTH/SAND* B71 .... 71 E4
Mostyn Pl *AST/WIT* B6 .... 107 H1
Mostyn Rd *HDSW* B21 .... 107 H1
  LDYWD/EDGR B16 .... 125 G5
Mostyn St *WOLV* WV1 .... 36 D1
Mott Cl *TPTN/OCK* DY4 * 70 A3
Mottram Cl *WBROM* B70 .... 87 E4
Mottrams Cl
  SCFLD/WYGN B72 .... 77 G1
Mott St *LOZ/NWT* B19 .... 2 E1
Mott's Wy *CSHL/WTROR* B46 ... 115 G3
Moundsley Gv
  ALE/KHTH/YWD B14 .... 178 C2
Mountain Ash Dr
  HAG/WOL DY9 .... 136 A5
Mountain Ash Rd *BRWNH* WS8 .. 19 E2
Mount Av *BRLYHL* DY5 .... 101 E5
Mountbatten Cl *WBROM* B70 ..... 88 B4
Mountbatten Rd *WSLW* WS2 ...... 40 C5
Mount Cl *MOS/BIL* B13 .... 144 B3
  SEDG DY3 .... 83 E4
  WMBN WV5 .... 65 E4
Mount Cottages
  ETTPK/GDPK/PENN WV4 * 51 F5
Mount Ct
  DUNHL/THL/PER WV6 * 35 F2
  WMBN WV5 .... 65 E4
Mountfield Cl
  ALE/KHTH/YWD B14 .... 178 C3
Mountford Cl
  BLKHTH/ROWR B65 .... 122 A1
Mountford Crs *ALDR* WS9 .... 30 B2
Mountford Dr *MGN/WHC* B75 ... 47 G5
Mountford Rd *SHLY* B90 .... 179 F4
Mountford St *SPARK* B11 .... 145 G2
Mount Gdns *CDSL* WV8 .... 10 D3
Mountjoy Crs *HIA/OLT* B92 ...... 148 A4
Mount La *HAG/WOL* DY9 .... 170 C1
  SEDG DY3 .... 83 E4
Mount Pleasant
  ALE/KHTH/YWD B14 .... 161 E1
  BILS/COS WV14 .... 54 A2
  BKHL/PFLD WV2 .... 52 D1
  BRLYHL DY5 .... 118 A3
  ETTPK/GDPK/PENN WV4 * 51 F5
  KGSWFD DY6 .... 99 G5
  LGLYGN/QTN B68 * 105 F5
  SMHTH B10 .... 127 H3
  TPTN/OCK DY4 .... 70 B5
Mount Pleasant Av *HDSW* B21 .. 89 C5
  WMBN WV5 .... 64 D4
Mount Pleasant St
  BILS/COS WV14 .... 68 B3
  WBROM B70 .... 87 C4
Mountrath St *WSL* WS1 .... 5 C4
Mount Rd *BLKHTH/ROWR* B65 .. 122 C1
  BLOX/PEL WS3 .... 18 A3
  DUNHL/THL/PER WV6 .... 35 E3
  HDSW B21 .... 107 F2
  OLDBY B69 .... 104 A1
  STRBR DY8 .... 135 H2
  TPTN/OCK DY4 .... 70 A5
  VAUX/NECH B7 .... 110 A5
  WSL WS1 .... 4 C6
Mounts Wy *VAUX/NECH* B7 ..... 110 A5
The Mount *CDYHTH* B64 .... 121 G3
  ERDW/GRVHL B23 .... 92 D5
  WALM/CURD B76 .... 96 C1
Mount Vw *MGN/WHC* B75 .... 63 G4
Mountwood Covert
  DUNHL/THL/PER WV6 .... 35 F2
Mousehall Farm Rd
  BRLYHL DY5 .... 119 F5
Mouse HI *BLOX/PEL* WS3 .... 17 H4
Mousesweet Cl *DUDS* DY2 .... 103 E5
Mousesweet La *DUDS* DY2 ...... 103 E5
Mowbray Cl *RBRY* B45 .... 174 A3
Mowbray St *DIG/EDG* B5 .... 127 E4
Mowe Cft
  CHWD/FDBR/MGN B37 .... 132 A5
Moxhull Cl *SHHTH* WV12 .... 26 A1
Moxhull Dr *WALM/CURD* B76 .... 78 A3
Moxhull Gdns *SHHTH* WV12 ..... 26 A1
Moxhull Rd
  CHWD/FDBR/MGN B37 .... 114 A4
Moxley Rd *DARL/WED* WS10 .... 54 D4
Moyle Dr *HALE* B63 .... 120 B5
Moyses Cft *SMTHWK* B66 .... 106 C1
Muchall Rd
  ETTPK/GDPK/PENN WV4 .... 51 C3
Mucklow HI *RMSLY* B62 .... 138 D3
Mucklow Hill Rd *RMSLY* B62 .... 16 C4
Muirfield Crs *OLDBY* B69 .... 103 G2
Muirfield Gdns
  HWK/WKHTH B38 .... 176 B4
Muirville Cl *STRBR* DY8 .... 117 H1
Mulberry Dr *MOS/BIL* B13 ...... 161 H1
Mulberry Gn *DUDN* DY1 .... 83 H1
Mulberry Pl *BLOX/PEL* WS3 ...... 26 D1
Mulberry Rd *BLOX/PEL* WS3 .... 159 E5
Mull Cl *RBRY* B45 .... 173 G4
Mull Cft *CBROM* B36 .... 94 D2
Mullensgrove Rd
  CHWD/FDBR/MGN B37 .... 114 A4
Mullett Rd *WNSFLD* WV11 .... 24 B3
Mullett St *BRLYHL* DY5 .... 100 D4

Mulliners Cl
CHWD/FDBR/MGN B37 * 132 D2
Mullion Cft HWK/WKHTH B38 176 C4
Mulroy Rd FOAKS/STRLY B74 62 B2
Mulwych Rd STETCH B33 131 G2
Munches La RMSLY B62 171 G5
Munslow Gv NFLD/LBR B31 175 F5
Muntz Crs HOCK/TIA B94 198 A5
Muntz St SMHTH B10 128 B4
Murcroft Rd HAG/WOL DY9 153 F1
Murdoch Dr KGSWFD DY6 99 G2
Murdoch Rd BILS/COS WV14 54 B2
Murdock Gv HDSW B21 107 G2
Murdock Rd SMTHWK B66 107 F3
Murdock Wy WSLW WS2 26 D5
Murray Ct SCFLD/BOLD B73 62 A5
Murrell Cl DIG/EDG B5 126 D5
Musborough Cl CBROM B36 95 E5
Muscott Gv HRBN B17 141 G2
Muscovy Rd ERDW/GRVHL B23 92 A3
Musgrave Cl WALM/CURD B76 63 E5
Musgrave Rd WSNGN B18 107 H4
Mushroom Hall Rd
LGLYGN/QTN B68 105 G4
Musk La SEDG DY3 82 D3
Musk La West SEDG DY3 82 D3
Musson Cl
CHWD/FDBR/MGN B37 132 B4
Muswell Cl SOLH B91 165 F5
Muxloe Cl BLOX/PEL WS3 16 C4
Myatt Av ALDR WS9 29 H5
BKHL/PFLD WV2 52 C2
Myatt Cl BKHL/PFLD WV2 52 C2
Myddleton St WSNGN B18 108 A5
Myles Ct BRLYHL DY5 101 F5
Mynors Crs HLYWD B47 192 C3
Myring Dr MGN/WHC B75 63 F3
Myrtle Av ALE/KHTH/YWD B14 178 B3
BHTH/HG B12 144 C2
Myrtle Cl SHHTH WV12 26 C3
Myrtle Gv BDMR/CCFT WV3 51 E2
LOZ/NWT B19 * 108 C1
Myrtle Pl SLYOAK B29 * 143 F5
Myrtle Rd DUDN DY1 84 A3
Myrtle St BKHL/PFLD WV2 52 D2
Myrtle Ter TPTN/OCK DY4 69 H1
Myton Dr SHLY B90 179 F3
Mytton Cl DUDS DY2 85 E5
Mytton Gv TPTN/OCK DY4 85 E1
Mytton Rd BVILLE B30 159 E5
CSHL/WTROR B46 95 H3
Myvod Rd DARL/WED WS10 56 A3

N

Naden Rd LOZ/NWT B19 108 B3
Nadin Rd SCFLD/BOLD B73 77 E3
Naesby Rd
DUNHL/THL/PER WV6 34 D2
Nafford Gv
ALE/KHTH/YWD B14 178 B3
Nagersfield Rd BRLYHL DY5 118 C1
Nailers Cl RIDG/WDGT B32 139 H5
Nailers Fold BILS/COS WV14 68 C1
Nailors Rw WMBN WV5 * 80 D1
Nailstone Crs ACGN B27 163 G2
Nailsworth Rd DOR/KN B93 198 B1
Nairn Cl HLGN/YWD B28 162 D5
Nairn Rd BLOX/PEL WS3 16 C3
Nally Dr BILS/COS WV14 68 A1
Nanaimo Wy KGSWFD DY6 100 C5
Nansen Rd SPARK B11 145 E4
WASH/WDE B8 110 C4
Nantmel Gv RIDG/WDGT B32 157 G2
Naomi Wy ALDR WS9 19 H3
Napier Dr TPTN/OCK DY4 70 A5
Napier Rd BKHL/PFLD WV2 52 B1
WSLW WS2 27 E5
Napton Gv SLYOAK B29 141 F5
Narraway Gv TPTN/OCK DY4 70 B3
Narrowboat Wy BRLYHL DY5 102 A4
Narrow La BRWNH WS8 9 F4
RMSLY B62 122 C5
WSLW WS2 56 B1
Naseby Dr HALE B63 137 H5
Naseby Rd SOLH B91 164 D4
WASH/WDE B8 110 D4
Nash Av DUNHL/THL/PER WV6 34 C2
Nash Cl BLKHTH/ROWR B65 122 A3
Nash Cft
CHWD/FDBR/MGN B37 132 B4
Nash La HAG/WOL DY9 184 B1
Nash Sq PBAR/PBCH B42 90 D2
Nash Wk SMTHWK B66 * 107 E4
Nately Gv SLYOAK B29 141 H4
Nathan Cl MGN/WHC B75 47 G5
Naunton Cl SLYOAK B29 158 C3
Naunton Rd WSLW WS2 41 E2
Navenby Cl
ALE/KHTH/YWD B14 179 E2
Navigation Dr BRLYHL DY5 102 A5
BVILLE B30 177 H2
Navigation La HHTH/SAND B71 72 B1
Navigation St CBHAMW B1 2 E6
WOLV WV1 7 J6
WSLW WS2 4 C3
Navigation Wy WBROM B70 86 D4
WSNGN B18 107 H4
Nayland Cft HLGN/YWD B28 163 E5
Naylors Gv SEDG DY3 83 G2
Neachells Ct WLNHL WV13 39 E4
Neachells La WLNHL WV13 38 D2
WNSFLD WV11 24 D5
Neachless Av WMBN WV5 81 E1
Neachley Gv STETCH B33 112 B5
Neale St WSLW WS2 4 A2
Near High Dr TPTN/OCK DY4 85 H1
Nearhill Rd HWK/WKHTH B38 176 A5
Near Lands Cl RIDG/WDGT B32 140 B3
Nearmoor Rd BKDE/SHDE B34 113 F4
Neasden Gv KGSTG B44 75 H3
Neath Rd BLOX/PEL WS3 16 B5
Neath Wy BLOX/PEL WS3 16 B5
SEDG DY3 68 A5
Nebsworth Cl SHLY B90 163 H5
Nechells Park Rd
VAUX/NECH B7 110 A2
Nechells Pkwy VAUX/NECH B7 109 G5
Nechells Pl VAUX/NECH B7 109 H3
Needham St VAUX/NECH B7 110 A2
Needhill Cl DOR/KN B93 196 D2
Needless Aly CBHAM B2 * 3 G5
Needwood Cl BKHL/PFLD WV2 51 H2
Needwood Dr
ETTPK/GDPK/PENN WV4 52 D4
Needwood Gv HHTH/SAND B71 72 A2
Nelson Av BILS/COS WV14 53 G1
Nelson Rd AST/WIT B6 91 F5
DUDN DY1 84 B5
Nelson St CBHAMW B1 2 B4
HHTH/SAND B71 87 G1
OLDBY B69 105 F3
WLNHL WV13 39 H2
Nene Cl STRBR DY8 135 G3
Nene Wy CBROM B36 113 H1
Neptune St TPTN/OCK DY4 84 D1
Nesbit Gv BORD B9 129 F1
Nesfield Cl HWK/WKHTH B38 176 A4
Nesfield Gv HIA/OLT B92 167 H3
Nesscliffe Gv ERDW/GRVHL B23 76 B4
Nest Common BLOX/PEL WS3 17 H2
Neston Gv STETCH B33 129 H2
Netheravon Cl
ALE/KHTH/YWD B14 177 H4
Netherby Rd SEDG DY3 67 E3
Nethercote Gdns SHLY B90 179 G2
Netherdale Cl
CSCFLD/WYGN B72 77 G4
Netherdale Rd
ALE/KHTH/YWD B14 178 C4
Netherend Cl HALE B63 120 A5
Netherend La HALE B63 120 B5
Netherend Sq HALE B63 120 A5
Netherfield Gdns ACGN B27 146 B4
Nethergate SEDG DY3 83 H1
Netherhouse Cl KGSTG B44 60 A5
Netherstone Gv
FOAKS/STRLY B74 32 D5
Netherton Gv STETCH B33 131 E1
Netherwood Cl SOLH B91 164 A4
Nethy Dr DUNHL/THL/PER WV6 21 F5
Netley Gv SPARK B11 145 H4
Netley Rd BLOX/PEL WS3 16 A5
Netley Wy BLOX/PEL WS3 16 A5
Nevada Wy
CHWD/FDBR/MGN B37 132 C3
Neve Av WOLVN WV10 23 H1
Neville Av
ETTPK/GDPK/PENN WV4 52 B2
Neville Rd CBROM B36 95 C5
ERDW/GRVHL B23 92 A3
SHLY B90 179 H4
Nevin Gv PBAR/PBCH B42 90 C1
Nevis Ct BDMR/CCFT WV3 36 A3
Nevis Gv SHHTH WV12 25 H1
Nevison Gv GTB/HAM B43 59 F4
Newark Cft
LGN/SDN/BHAMAIR B26 147 H1
Newark Rd DUDS DY2 120 D2
SHHTH WV12 26 A3
Newbank Gv BORD B9 129 E1
New Bartholomew St
DIG/EDG B5 3 J5
New Birmingham Rd
DUDS DY2 85 G5
OLDBY B69 104 B1
Newbold Cl DOR/KN B93 196 D3
Newbold Cft VAUX/NECH B7 109 H4
Newbolds Rd WOLVN WV10 24 A4
Newbolt Rd BILS/COS WV14 54 A2
Newbolt St DSYBK/YTR WS5 57 E3
New Bond St BORD B9 127 H3
DUDS DY2 102 D1
Newborough Gv
HLGN/YWD B28 179 H1
Newborough Rd
HLGN/YWD B28 179 H1
Newbridge Av
BDMR/CCFT WV3 36 A2
Newbridge Crs
DUNHL/THL/PER WV6 36 A1
Newbridge Gdns
DUNHL/THL/PER WV6 36 A1
Newbridge Ms
DUNHL/THL/PER WV6 * 36 B1
Newbridge Rd BORD B9 129 F4
KGSWFD DY6 99 G1
Newbridge St
DUNHL/THL/PER WV6 36 B1
Newburn Cft RIDG/WDGT B32 140 B2
Newbury Cl RMSLY B62 139 F4
Newbury La OLDBY B69 104 B3
Newbury Rd STRBR DY8 117 G2
WOLVN WV10 12 C5
Newby Gv
CHWD/FDBR/MGN B37 114 B5
New Canal St DIG/EDG B5 3 J6
Newcastle Cft CVALE B35 95 E3
New Church Rd
SCFLD/BOLD B73 77 E3
New College Cl WSL WS1 57 G1
Newcombe Rd HDSW B21 89 F4
Newcome Cl ERDE/BCHGN B24 93 H2
Newcomen Dr TPTN/OCK DY4 85 F3
Newcott Cl COVEN WV9 11 H5
New Coventry Rd
LGN/SDN/BHAMAIR B26 147 F2
New Cft LOZ/NWT B19 109 E2
Newcroft Gv
LGN/SDN/BHAMAIR B26 130 A5
New Cross Av WOLVN WV10 38 B1
New Cross St DARL/WED WS10 55 F3
TPTN/OCK DY4 85 E1
New Crown St DUDN DY1 102 B1
Newdigate Rd MGN/WHC B75 63 G4
New Dudley Rd KGSWFD DY6 99 C1
Newells Dr TPTN/OCK DY4 70 B4
Newells Rd
LGN/SDN/BHAMAIR B26 130 C4
New England RMSLY B62 122 C5
New England Cl OLDBY B69 86 C5
Newent Cl SHHTH WV12 40 B1
Newent Rd NFLD/LBR B31 176 A1
Newey Cl RBRY B45 188 A2
Newey Rd HLGN/YWD B28 162 D4
WNSFLD WV11 25 G2
Newey St DUDN DY1 84 A4
New Farm Rd HAG/WOL DY9 136 A2
Newfield Cl SOLH B91 165 F4
WSLW WS2 27 G5
Newfield Crs HALE B63 138 C2
Newfield Dr KGSWFD DY6 100 A5
Newfield Gdns HAG/WOL DY9 169 G1
Newfield La HALE B63 138 C2
Newfield Pl HAG/WOL DY9 169 G1
Newfield Rd HAG/WOL DY9 169 G1
OLDBY B69 104 D1
New Forest Rd BLOX/PEL WS3 28 A4
New Gas St WBROM B70 71 E5
Newhall Ct CBHAMNW B3 * 2 C3
New Hall Dr MGN/WHC B75 62 D4
WALM/CURD B76 78 A2
Newhall Farm Cl
WALM/CURD B76 62 D4
Newhall Hl CBHAMW B1 2 C3
New Hall Pl DARL/WED WS10 * 56 A5
Newhall Rd
BLKHTH/ROWR B65 122 A1
New Hall St WLNHL WV13 39 G3
Newhall St CBHAMNW B3 2 E4
TPTN/OCK DY4 69 E3
WBROM B70 87 G4
WSL WS1 4 E6
New Hampton Rd East
WOLV WV1 6 C1
New Hampton Rd West
DUNHL/THL/PER WV6 36 C1
Newhaven Cl VAUX/NECH B7 109 G5
Newhay Cft LOZ/NWT B19 108 C2
New Heath Cl WNSFLD WV11 24 B5
New Henry St
LGLYGN/QTN B68 105 E5
Newhome Wy BLOX/PEL WS3 27 H3
Newhope Cl EDG B15 126 D4
New Hope Rd SMTHWK B66 107 E5
Newhouse Farm Cl
WALM/CURD B76 * 63 F5
Newhouse Farm Dr
NFLD/LBR B31 158 D4
Newick Av FOAKS/STRLY B74 45 H2
Newick Gv
ALE/KHTH/YWD B14 * 160 C5
Newick St DUDS DY2 102 C5
Newington Rd
CHWD/FDBR/MGN B37 132 B4
New Inn Rd LOZ/NWT B19 108 D1
New Inns Cl HDSW B21 107 F1
New Inns La RBRY B45 173 G4
New John St AST/WIT B6 109 E4
RMSLY B62 122 A3
New John St West
LOZ/NWT B19 108 B3
New King St DUDS DY2 * 84 C5
Newland Cl RUSH/SHEL WS4 18 C5
Newland Gdns CDYHTH B64 121 E4
Newland Gv DUDS DY2 101 H2
Newland Rd BORD B9 128 D3
Newlands Cl HAG/WOL DY9 153 E4
WLNHL WV13 39 G4
Newlands Dr RMSLY B62 122 C5
Newlands La
CHWD/FDBR/MGN B37 149 E1
Newlands Rd BVILLE B30 160 B3
DOR/KN B93 196 C4
Newlands Wk
LGLYGN/QTN B68 * 105 F5
New Landywood La
WNSFLD WV11 16 A1
Newlyn Rd CDYHTH B64 120 D4
NFLD/LBR B31 175 F2
Newman Av
ETTPK/GDPK/PENN WV4 52 D4
Newman College Cl
RIDG/WDGT B32 * 157 G2
Newman Pl BILS/COS WV14 54 B1
Newman Rd
ERDE/BCHGN B24 92 D2
TPTN/OCK DY4 70 A2
WOLVN WV10 24 A1
Newmans Cl SMTHWK B66 * 107 E5
Newman Wy RBRY B45 188 A1
Newmarket Cl
DUNHL/THL/PER WV6 22 C5
New Market St CBHAMW B3 * 2 E4
Newmarket Wy CBROM B36 111 F2
Newmarsh Rd
WALM/CURD B76 78 C5
New Meadow Cl
NFLD/LBR B31 175 H3
New Meeting St OLDBY B69 105 E1
New Mills St WSL WS1 56 D1
New Mill St DUDS DY2 84 C5
Newmore Gdns
DSYBK/YTR WS5 58 A2
New Moseley Rd
BHTH/HG B12 127 G4
Newnham Gv
ERDW/GRVHL B23 76 C5
Newnham Ri SHLY B90 180 D2
Newnham Rd
LDYWD/EDGR B16 125 E2
New Pool Rd CDYHTH B64 120 B4
Newport Rd BHTH/HG B12 144 C3
CBROM B36 112 B1
Newport St WOLVN WV10 37 G1
WSL WS1 4 D4
Newquay Cl DSYBK/YTR WS5 58 C1
Newquay Rd DSYBK/YTR WS5 58 B1
New Railway St WLNHL WV13 39 H3
New Rd ALDR WS9 30 A5
BRWNH WS8 9 F5
CSHL/WTROR B46 96 B3
DUDS DY2 102 C2
DUNHL/THL/PER WV6 36 A1
HALE B63 138 D3
HLYWD B47 178 B5
RBRY B45 187 G1
SEDG DY3 80 A3
SOLH B91 182 A2
STRBR DY8 135 G2
TPTN/OCK DY4 70 B5
WLNHL WV13 39 G4
WOLVN WV10 24 B2
New Rowley Rd DUDS DY2 103 E2
New Shipton Cl
WALM/CURD B76 78 B2
New Spring Gdns WSNGN B18 108 A5
New Spring St WSNGN B18 108 A5
New Spring St North
WSNGN B18 108 A4
Newstead Rd KGSTG B44 60 C5
New St BDMR/CCFT WV3 50 D2
BKHL/PFLD WV2 53 E2
BLOX/PEL WS3 27 F1
BRLYHL DY5 120 A4
CBHAM B2 3 G5
CBROM B36 112 D1
DARL/WED WS10 70 D2
DUDN DY1 84 C5
ERDW/GRVHL B23 92 D1
ETTPK/GDPK/PENN WV4 52 C3
KGSWFD DY6 99 G1
RBRY B45 174 A3
RUSH/SHEL WS4 28 D3
SEDG DY3 83 E3
SMTHWK B66 106 D3
STRBR DY8 135 G2
TPTN/OCK DY4 85 E1
WBROM B70 87 H3
WLNHL WV13 39 E4
WNSFLD WV11 15 E4
WSL WS1 5 F5
New St North HHTH/SAND B71 87 H3
New Summer St LOZ/NWT B19 3 F1
New Swan La WBROM B70 87 E1
Newton Cl GTB/HAM B43 73 E3
Newton Gdns GTB/HAM B43 72 D3
Newton Gv SLYOAK B29 * 142 D5
Newton Manor Cl
GTB/HAM B43 73 F3
Newton Pl WSLW WS2 27 F4
WSNGN B18 107 H2
Newton Rd DOR/KN B93 197 F1
GTB/HAM B43 73 F2
SPARK B11 144 D2
WSLW WS2 27 F5
Newton Sq GTB/HAM B43 73 G2
Newton St CBHAMNE B4 3 H3
HHTH/SAND B71 72 A4
New Town BRLYHL DY5 100 D5
DUDS DY2 120 D3
Newtown Dr LOZ/NWT B19 108 C3
Newtown La CDYHTH B64 120 D3
HAG/WOL DY9 171 H5
RMSLY B62 173 F3
Newtown Middleway
AST/WIT B6 109 E4
New Town Rw AST/WIT B6 109 E4
Newtown St CDYHTH B64 120 D2
New Village DUDS DY2 120 C3
New Vls WNSFLD WV11 * 24 A5
New Wood Cl KINVER DY7 117 G4
New Wood Dr NFLD/LBR B31 174 D4
New Wood Gv ALDR WS9 19 G4
New Wood La KIDD DY10 168 A5
Niall Cl EDG B15 125 H4
Nicholas Rd FOAKS/STRLY B74 45 E5
Nicholds Cl BILS/COS WV14 68 B2
Nicholls Fold WNSFLD WV11 24 D5
Nicholls Rd TPTN/OCK DY4 69 E2
Nicholls St WBROM B70 87 H4
Nichols Cl HIA/OLT B92 165 H3
Nigel Av NFLD/LBR B31 158 C5
Nigel Rd DUDN DY1 83 H4
WASH/WDE B8 110 C3
Nightingale Av CBROM B36 114 A1
Nightingale Cl
ERDW/GRVHL B23 76 A4
Nightingale Crs BRLYHL DY5 119 F5
SHHTH WV12 25 H2
Nightingale Dr TPTN/OCK DY4 86 A1
Nightingale Pl BILS/COS WV14 53 H1
Nightingale Wk EDG B15 126 C5
Nightjar Gv ERDW/GRVHL B23 76 A5
Nighwood Dr FOAKS/STRLY B74 60 B1
Nijon Cl HDSW B21 89 E5
Nimmings Cl NFLD/LBR B31 189 F2
Nimmings Rd RMSLY B62 122 B3
Nineacres Dr
CHWD/FDBR/MGN B37 132 A2
Nine Elms La WOLVN WV10 37 G1
Nine Leasowes SMTHWK B66 106 A2
Nine Locks Rdg BRLYHL DY5 119 F2
Nineveh Av HDSW B21 107 H2
Nineveh Rd HDSW B21 107 G2
Ninfield Rd ACGN B27 146 A3
Nith Pl DUDN DY1 84 B4
Nocke Rd WNSFLD WV11 25 F1
Nock St TPTN/OCK DY4 * 70 A4
Noddy Pk ALDR WS9 30 B3
Noddy Park Rd ALDR WS9 30 B3
Noele Gordon Gdns WSL WS1 * 4 D7
Noel Rd LDYWD/EDGR B16 125 H3
Nolton Cl GTB/HAM B43 73 F3
Nooklands Cft STETCH B33 130 C2
The Nook BRLYHL DY5 100 D4
Noose Crs WLNHL WV13 39 E3
Noose La WLNHL WV13 39 F2
Nora Rd SPARK B11 145 E4
Norbiton Rd KGSTG B44 75 G3
Norbreck Cl GTB/HAM B43 73 F3
Norbury Av BLOX/PEL WS3 17 H4
Norbury Crs
ETTPK/GDPK/PENN WV4 52 D4
Norbury Dr BRLYHL DY5 119 F3
Norbury Gv HIA/OLT B92 147 G4
Norbury Rd BILS/COS WV14 54 B2
KGSTG B44 60 B5
WBROM B70 70 D4
WOLVN WV10 23 H4
Norcombe Gv SHLY B90 195 G3
Nordley Rd WNSFLD WV11 24 C5
Norfolk Av HHTH/SAND B71 71 H4
Norfolk Cl BVILLE B30 160 B4
Norfolk Crs ALDR WS9 30 B2
Norfolk Dr DARL/WED WS10 56 D4
Norfolk Gdns MGN/WHC B75 47 F5
Norfolk New Rd WSLW WS2 41 E1
Norfolk Pl WSLW WS2 27 H5
Norfolk Rd BDMR/CCFT WV3 36 C5
DUDS DY2 102 A2
EDG B15 125 F4
ERDW/GRVHL B23 92 D1
LGLYGN/QTN B68 123 F5
MGN/WHC B75 62 C1
RBRY B45 173 H4
STRBR DY8 117 H4
Norgrave Rd HIA/OLT B92 148 A5
Norlan Dr ALE/KHTH/YWD B14 178 B2
Norland Rd ACGN B27 163 G1
Norley Gv MOS/BIL B13 162 A3
Norman Av RIDG/WDGT B32 124 A5
Normandy Rd
BFLD/HDSWWD B20 90 D5
Norman Rd DSYBK/YTR WS5 58 A1
NFLD/LBR B31 175 H2
SMTHWK B67 123 H3
Norman St DUDS DY2 102 D1
WSNGN B18 107 G4
Norman Ter
BLKHTH/ROWR B65 104 A5
Normanton Av
LGN/SDN/BHAMAIR B26 148 B2
Norrington Gv RBRY B45 174 C2
Norrington Rd NFLD/LBR B31 174 C2
Norris Dr STETCH B33 130 A1
Norris Rd AST/WIT B6 91 F5
Norris Wy MGN/WHC B75 62 D3
Northampton St WSNGN B18 2 C1
Northam Wk
DUNHL/THL/PER WV6 36 D1
Northanger Rd ACGN B27 146 B5
North Av BHAMNEC B40 150 B2
WNSFLD WV11 24 C4
Northbrook Rd SHLY B90 163 G5
Northbrook St
LDYWD/EDGR B16 107 H5
Northcote Rd STETCH B33 111 H5
Northcote St WSLW WS2 41 H1
Northcott Rd BILS/COS WV14 54 A4
DUDS DY2 102 D5
Northcroft Wy
ERDW/GRVHL B23 92 B3
Northdown Rd SOLH B91 181 F4
North Dr BFLD/HDSWWD B20 108 B1
DIG/EDG B5 143 G2
MGN/WHC B75 62 C2
Northfield Gv BDMR/CCFT WV3 50 C1
Northfield Rd BVILLE B30 176 C1
DUDS DY2 102 D4
HRBN B17 141 G4
Northfields Wy BRWNH WS8 8 D5
Northgate ALDR WS9 30 A3
CDYHTH B64 120 D4
North Ga HRBN B17 125 E5
Northgate Wy ALDR WS9 30 A2
North Gn
ETTPK/GDPK/PENN WV4 50 D2
North Holme BORD B9 128 A2
Northland Rd SHLY B90 181 E4
Northlands Rd MOS/BIL B13 161 G1
Northleach Av
ALE/KHTH/YWD B14 177 H3
Northleigh Rd WASH/WDE B8 111 E3
Northolt Dr CVALE B35 94 C2
Northolt Gv PBAR/PBCH B42 73 H2
North Ov SEDG DY3 83 G1
Northover Cl COVEN WV9 12 A5
North Park Rd
ERDW/GRVHL B23 91 H3
North Pathway HRBN B17 124 D5
North Rd BFLD/HDSWWD B20 91 E4
ETTPK/GDPK/PENN WV4 52 D3
HRBN B17 142 B1
TPTN/OCK DY4 69 H3
WOLV WV1 37 E1
North Roundhay STETCH B33 112 C5
Northside Dr FOAKS/STRLY B74 45 F5
North Springfield SEDG DY3 67 G2
North St BRLYHL DY5 119 E2
DARL/WED WS10 55 H5
DUDS DY2 84 D5
SMTHWKW B67 106 B4
WOLV WV1 7 F3
WSLW WS2 42 A1
Northumberland St
VAUX/NECH B7 127 G1
North View Dr BRLYHL DY5 101 G4
North Warwick St BORD B9 * 128 B3
Northway BHAMNEC B40 150 B2
SEDG DY3 66 D2
North Western Ar CBHAM B2 3 G4
North Western Rd
SMTHWK B66 106 B3
North Western Ter
WSNGN B18 107 H2
Northwick Crs SOLH B91 181 H4
Northwood Park Cl
WOLVN WV10 13 E4
Northwood Park Rd
WOLVN WV10 13 E5
Northwood St CBHAMNW B3 2 D2
North Wood St CBHAMW B1 2 C3
Northwood Wy BRLYHL DY5 118 D4
North Worcestershire Pth
ALVE B48 191 F5
RBRY B45 187 F1
SHLY B90 193 E1
Northycote La WOLVN WV10 13 F3
Norton Cl
ETTPK/GDPK/PENN WV4 50 C5
SMTHWK B66 107 E4
Norton Crs BILS/COS WV14 68 D2
BORD B9 129 F1
DUDS DY2 121 E1
Norton Ga HWK/WKHTH B38 176 C4
Norton Green La DOR/KN B93 199 F1
Norton La SHLY B90 193 F4
Norton Rd BLOX/PEL WS3 18 A2
CSHL/WTROR B46 115 F1
STRBR DY8 135 E5
Norton St WSNGN B18 107 H4
Norton Ter BVILLE B30 * 160 A4
Norton Vw
ALE/KHTH/YWD B14 160 D4
Nortune Cl HWK/WKHTH B38 176 B3
Norwich Cft
CHWD/FDBR/MGN B37 131 H3
Norwich Dr HRBN B17 124 B4
Norwich Rd DUDS DY2 120 D2
WSLW WS2 41 F4
Norwood Av CDYHTH B64 121 E5
Norwood Gv LOZ/NWT B19 108 B2
Norwood Rd BORD B9 128 C2
BRLYHL DY5 119 E1
Nottingham Dr SHHTH WV12 26 A3
Nottingham Wy BRLYHL DY5 119 H2

Nova Ct GTB/HAM B43 ....74 B2
Nova Scotia St DIG/EDG B5 ....3 J4
Nowell St DARL/WED WS10 ....55 C3
Nugent Cl AST/WIT B6 ....108 C2
Nugent Dr WBROM B70 ....194 D5
Nursery Av ALDR WS9 ....30 B5
BHTH/HG B12 ....144 B2
Nursery Cl BVILLE B30 ....159 H5
HAG/WOL DY9 ....152 C5
Nursery Dr BFLD/HDSWWD B20 ..90 A5
WMBN WV5 ....80 D2
Nursery Gdns CDSL WV8 ....10 B3
SHLY B90 ....118 B3
STRBR DY8 ....118 E5
Nursery La FOAKS/STRLY B74 ......47 E3
Nursery Rd BLOX/PEL WS3 ....27 F2
BVILLE B30 ....159 G5
EDG B15 ....125 F5
LOZ/NWT B19 ....108 B3
Nursery View Cl ALDR WS9 ....45 E3
Nursery Wk
DUNHL/THL/PER WV6 ....21 H5
Nutbush Dr NFLD/LBR B31 ....157 H4
Nutfield Wk RIDG/WDGT B32 ....141 F2
Nutgrove Cl
ALE/KHTH/YWD B14 ....161 F3
Nuthatch Dr RMSLY DY5 ....119 E5
Nuthurst MGN/WHC B75 ....63 C4
Nuthurst Gv
ALE/KHTH/YWD B14 ....178 B3
DOR/KN B93 ....197 E4
Nuthurst Rd NFLD/LBR B31 ......189 F2
Nutley Dr TPTN/OCK DY4 ....76 B5
Nutmeg Gv WSL WS1 ....5 J3
Nuttall Gv HDSW B21 ....107 E2

O

Oak Av BHTH/HG B12 ....144 C2
WBROM B70 ....87 F3
WSLW WS2 ....40 C2
Oak Bank WSNGN B18 ....90 B5
Oak Barn Rd RMSLY B62 ....122 B4
Oakbridge Rd SHHTH WV12 ....176 B3
Oak Cl HRBN B17 ....141 G1
TPTN/OCK DY4 ....69 C2
Oak Ct HALE B63 ....138 B5
Oak Crs BLOX/PEL WS3 ....85 H5
OLDBY B69 ....85 H5
Oak Cft
CHWD/FDBR/MGN B37 ....131 C1
Oakcroft Rd MOS/BIL B13 ....161 H3
Oakdale Cl BRLYHL DY5 ....100 C2
LGLYGN/QTN B68 ....123 E2
Oakdale Rd CBROM B36 ....112 A1
LGLYGN/QTN B68 ....122 D2
Oak Dr ERDW/GRVHL B23 ....76 A4
Oaken Covert CDSL WV8 ....10 A5
Oaken Dr CDSL WV8 ....10 A4
SHHTH WV12 ....26 C5
SOLH B91 ....181 H5
Oaken Gv CDSL WV8 ....10 A5
Oakenhayes Crs BRWNH WS8 ....9 F3
Oakenhayes Dr BRWNH WS8 ....9 F3
Oaken Lanes CDSL WV8 ....10 A5
Oaken Pk CDSL WV8 ....10 C5
Oakenshaw Rd SHLY B90 ....180 D4
Oakeswell St DARL/WED WS10 .....2 A5
Oakeywell St DUDS DY2 ....84 D5
Oak Farm Cl WALM/CURD B76 ......78 C4
Oak Farm Rd BVILLE B30 ....159 G5
Oakfield Av BHTH/HG B12 ....144 C2
DUDN DY1 ....84 B3
KGSWFD DY6 ....100 A4
Oakfield Cl SMTHWK B66 ....107 E3
STRBR DY8 ....118 B3
Oakfield Dr BLOX/PEL WS3 ....18 A2
RBRY B45 ....188 D4
Oakfield Rd BHTH/HG B12 ....144 A3
CDSL WV8 ....10 D5
ERDE/BCHGN B24 ....92 D3
HAG/WOL DY9 ....152 C5
SLYOAK B29 ....143 E4
SMTHWK B66 ....107 E4
STRBR DY8 ....118 C3
Oakfields Wy SOLH B91 ....166 B5
Oak Gn DUDN DY1 ....84 A1
DUNHL/THL/PER WV6 ....35 F2
Oak Green Wy
LGLYGN/QTN B68 ....105 E5
Oak Gv NFLD/LBR B31 ....175 E4
WNSFLD WV11 ....25 H1
Oakhall Dr DOR/KN B93 ....196 D4
Oakham Av DUDS DY2 ....103 E2
Oakham Ct DUDS DY2 ....103 E1
Oakham Crs DUDS DY2 ....103 E2
Oakham Dr DUDS DY2 ....103 E2
Oakham Rd DUDS DY2 ....103 E2
HRBN B17 ....124 D5
Oak Hl BDMR/CCFT WV3 ....35 C5
Oakhill Cl HRBN B17 ....141 G2
Oakhill Crs ACGN B27 ....163 F2
Oakhill Dr BRLYHL DY5 ....118 D5
Oak Hill Dr EDG B15 ....125 G5
Oakhurst Rd ACGN B27 ....163 F1
CSCFLD/WYGN B72 ....77 F5
Oakland Cl SOLH B91 ....182 C1
Oakland Dr SEDG DY3 ....82 D4
Oakland Rd BLOX/PEL WS3 ....28 A3
HDSW B21 ....107 G1
MOS/BIL B13 ....144 C4
Oaklands NFLD/LBR B31 ....175 F1
RMSLY B62 ....140 A3
WALM/CURD B76 ....96 B1
Oaklands Av HRBN B17 ....141 G2
Oaklands Cft WALM/CURD B76 ...78 B4
Oaklands Dr
BFLD/HDSWWD B20 ....89 H4
Oaklands Gn BILS/COS WV14 ......69 F1
Oaklands Rd BDMR/CCFT WV3 ....35 C5
FOAKS/STRLY B74 ....47 F5
The Oaklands
BDMR/CCFT WV5 * 36 D5
CHWD/FDBR/MGN B37 ....132 A5
Oaklands Wy BLOX/PEL WS3 ......18 B4

NFLD/LBR B31 ....174 C4
Oak La KGSWFD DY6 ....82 A5
WBROM B70 ....87 F3
Oak Leasow RIDG/WDGT B32 .....140 C5
Oakleaf Cl RIDG/WDGT B32 ......140 C5
Oak Leaf Dr MOS/BIL B13 ....144 C4
Oakleigh NFLD/LBR B31 ....176 A5
Oakleigh Dr CDSL WV8 ....10 C4
SEDG DY3 ....67 E4
Oakleigh Rd STRBR DY8 ....135 G5
Oak Leigh Rd STRBR DY8 ....135 H5
Oakleighs STRBR DY8 ....117 C3
Oakley Av ALDR WS9 ....30 A5
WALM/CURD WS9 ....69 C5
Oakley Gv
ETTPK/GDPK/PENN WV4 ....50 D3
Oakley Rd BVILLE B50 ....160 B5
ETTPK/GDPK/PENN WV4 ....50 D3
SMHTH B10 ....128 A5
Oak Leys BDMR/CCFT WV3 ....35 C4
Oakley Wood Dr SOLH B91 ......182 C1
Oakmeadow Av
ERDE/BCHGN B24 ....93 H3
Oakmeadow Cl
LGN/SDN/BHAMAIR B26 ......146 D2
STETCH B33 ....131 F2
Oakmeadow Wy
ERDE/BCHGN B24 ....93 H5
Oakmount Cl BLOX/PEL WS3 .....17 H4
Oakmount Rd
FOAKS/STRLY B74 ....60 C1
Oak Park Rd STRBR DY8 ....118 B3
Oakridge Cl SHHTH WV12 ....40 A1
Oakridge Dr SHHTH WV12 ....40 A1
Oak Rd CSHL/WTROR B46 ....115 F4
Oak Rd ALDR WS9 ....19 C4
BLOX/PEL WS3 ....17 H2
DUDN DY1 ....84 C3
LGLYGN/QTN B68 ....123 E2
RUSH/SHEL WS4 ....29 E2
TPTN/OCK DY4 ....69 E5
WBROM B70 ....87 F3
WLNHL WV13 ....39 E3
Oakthorpe Dr
CHWD/FDBR/MGN B37 ....113 H4
Oakthorpe Gdns OLDBY B69 ....85 C4
Oak Tree Cl DOR/KN B93 ....196 C4
Oak Tree Crs RBRY B45 ....139 H1
Oak Tree Gdns HLGN/YWD B28 ..179 C2
STRBR DY8 ....118 C3
Oak Tree La BVILLE B30 ....159 G5
HLYWD B47 ....192 D2
Oaktree Rd DARL/WED WS10 ......56 B5
Oak Tree Rd WASH/WDE B8 ......110 A3
Oak Turn Dr HWK/WKHTH B38 ..176 B5
The Oak Wk NFLD/LBR B31 ......175 C4
Oak Wy WALM/CURD B76 ....78 B1
Oakwood Cl ALDR WS9 ....19 E3
WNSFLD WV11 ....15 H4
Oakwood Crs DUDS DY2 ....101 H5
Oakwood Cft SOLH B91 ....182 A4
Oakwood Dr
ALE/KHTH/YWD B14 ....177 H1
FOAKS/STRLY B74 ....45 E5
Oakwood Pl ALDR WS9 ....19 F4
Oakwood Rd BLOX/PEL WS3 ....28 A3
HLYWD B47 ....192 C2
SCFLD/BOLD B73 ....76 C2
SMTHWK B67 ....106 C5
SPARK B11 ....145 E4
Oakwood St WBROM B70 ....87 F1
The Oasis HAG/WOL DY9 ....152 B5
Oasthouse Cl KGSWFD DY6 ....99 E2
Oaston Rd CBROM B36 ....113 F1
Oatlands Wy
DUNHL/THL/PER WV6 ....34 B2
Oatmill Cl DARL/WED WS10 * 55 C3
Oban Rd HIA/OLT B92 ....164 B1
Oberon Cl RBRY B45 ....174 A3
Oberon Dr SHLY B90 ....180 A4
Occupation Rd BRWNH WS8 ....19 C3
Occupation St DUDN DY1 ....84 A4
Ocean Dr DARL/WED WS10 ....70 B2
Ocean Cft NFLD/LBR B31 ....176 A3
Ocker Hill Rd TPTN/OCK DY4 ....69 H2
O'Connor Dr TPTN/OCK DY4 ......70 A2
Oddingley Rd NFLD/LBR B31 ....175 H5
Odell Crs BLOX/PEL WS3 ....27 C3
Odell Pl DIG/EDG B5 ....143 G2
Odell Rd BLOX/PEL WS3 ....27 F5
Odensil Gn HIA/OLT B92 ....147 H5
Odnall La HAG/WOL DY9 ....170 C1
Offa's Dr DUNHL/THL/PER WV6 ..20 C5
Offenham Covert
HWK/WKHTH B38 ....176 C5
Offini Cl WBROM B70 ....88 B4
Offmoor Rd RIDG/WDGT B32 ....157 F2
Ogbury Cl HWK/WKHTH B38 ....177 C5
Ogley Crs BRWNH WS8 ....9 C5
Ogley Dr MGN/WHC B75 ....63 C3
Ogley Hay Rd BNTWD WS7 ....9 C1
Ogley Rd BRWNH WS8 ....9 C5
O'Keeffe Cl SPARK B11 ....144 D1
Okehampton Dr
HHTH/SAND B71 ....71 G5
Okement Dr WNSFLD WV11 ....24 B5
Old Abbey Gdns HRBN B17 ......142 B5
Old Acre Cl WALM/CURD B76 ......77 H5
Old Acre Dr HDSW B21 ....107 G2
Oldacre Rd NFLD/LBR B31 ....189 F2
Old Bank Rd NFLD/LBR B31 .....159 H5
Old Barn Rd BVILLE B30 ....159 E3
STRBR DY8 ....118 C3

Old Beeches ERDW/GRVHL B23 ....76 A3
Old Bell Rd ERDW/GRVHL B23 ....77 F5
Old Bush St BRLYHL DY5 ....100 C1
Old Bridge Wk
BLKHTH/ROWR B65 ....103 F4
Old Bromford La
WASH/WDE B8 ....111 F3
Old Brookside STETCH B33 ....130 A2
Old Bridge St LOZ/NWT B19 ....108 B3
Old Bury Ring NV OLDBY B69 ....104 D2
Oldbury Rd
BLKHTH/ROWR B65 ....122 B2
BRLYHL DY5 ....105 G2
SMTHWK B66 ....106 C3
WBROM B70 ....86 D3
Oldbury Road Industrial Est 86 D4
Oldbury St DARL/WED WS10 ......56 B5
Old Bush St BRLYHL DY5 ....119 G1
Old Camp Hl BHTH/HG B12 .....127 G4
Old Castle Gv BRWNH WS8 ....9 F2
Old Chapel Rd SMTHWK B67 ....124 D1
Old Church Gn STETCH B33 .....130 A2
Old Church Rd
CSHL/WTROR B46 ....96 B3
HRBN B17 ....141 H2
Old College Dr HHTH/SAND B71 ..71 E2
Old Croft La CBROM B36 ....112 D2
Old Cross St TPTN/OCK DY4 ......85 E1
Old Crown Cl RIDG/WDGT B32 ..157 F1
Old Damson La HIA/OLT B92 ....148 D5
Old Dickens Heath Rd
SHLY B90 ....194 A3
Old End La BILS/COS WV14 ......68 C4
Old Fallings Crs WOLV WV10 .....23 H4
Old Fallings La WOLV WV10 ......23 H2
Old Farm Dr CDSL WV8 ....10 C3
Old Farm Gv
ALE/KHTH/YWD B14 ....162 B5
Old Farm Meadow
BDMR/CCFT WV3 ....35 G5
Old Farm Rd STETCH B33 ....112 A5
Oldfield Dr STRBR DY8 ....135 G4
Oldfield Rd BHTH/HG B12 ......144 C1
BILS/COS WV14 ....68 A3
Oldfields CDYHTH B64 ....120 D4
HAG/WOL DY9 ....152 D4
Old Flour Mills WBROM B70 ......87 G4
Fordrove WALM/CURD B76 ....62 D5
Old Forest Wy
BKDE/SHDE B34 ....112 D3
Old Grange Rd SPARK B11 ......145 E3
Old Grove Gdns HAG/WOL DY9 ..136 B4
Old Hall Cl STRBR DY8 ....118 C5
Old Hall La ALDR WS9 ....59 F3
Old Hall St BKHL/PFLD WV2 ....7 G5
Old Ham La HAG/WOL DY9 ....110 A5
Old Hampton La WOLV WV10 ....14 A5
Old Hawne La HALE B63 ....138 C2
Old Heath Crs WOLV WV1 ....38 A4
Old Heath Rd WOLV WV1 ....38 A3
Old High St BRLYHL DY5 ....119 H5
Old Hl DUNHL/THL/PER WV6 .....21 H5
Old Hobicus La
LGLYGN/QTN B68 ....105 F4
Old Horns Crs GTB/HAM B43 .....74 C1
Oldhouse Farm Cl
HLGN/YWD B28 ....162 D4
Old House La RMSLY B62 ....117 G4
Oldington Gv SOLH B91 ....181 G5
Old Kingsbury Rd
WALM/CURD B76 ....47 H5
Oldknow Rd SMHTH B10 ....145 G1
Old Landywood La
WNSFLD WV11 ....15 G1
Old La BLOX/PEL WS3 ....27 G3
DUNHL/THL/PER WV6 ....34 D3
Old Level Wy DUDS DY2 ....102 D5
Old Lime Gdns
HWK/WKHTH B38 ....176 C5
Old Lindens Cl
FOAKS/STRLY B74 ....60 A1
Old Lode La HIA/OLT B92 ....147 H5
The Old Mnr
DUNHL/THL/PER WV6 * 21 H5
Old Masters Cl WSL WS1 ....5 H4
Old Meadow Rd
NFLD/LBR B31 ....189 H1
Old Meeting Rd BILS/COS WV14 ..68 C3
Old Meeting St WBROM B70 ......87 F3
Old Mill Cl SHLY B90 ....179 F3
Old Mill Gdns RUSH/SHEL WS4 ..18 C5
Old Mill Gv
BFLD/HDSWWD B20 * 90 C4
Old Mill House Cl
RUSH/SHEL WS4 ....28 D1
Old Mill Rd CSHL/WTROR B46 ..115 F2
Old Moat Dr NFLD/LBR B31 ....175 H2
Old Moat Wy WASH/WDE B8 ....111 F3
Oldnall Cl HAG/WOL DY9 ....136 D5
Oldnall Rd HAG/WOL DY9 ......137 E3
Old Oak Cl ALDR WS9 ....30 B2
Old Oak Rd HWK/WKHTH B38 ...177 E3
Old Oscott La KGSTG B44 ....75 E3
Old Pk SLYOAK B29 ....158 C5
Old Park La OLDBY B69 ....105 E4
Old Park Rd DARL/WED WS10 .....55 G4
Old Penns La
CSHL/WTROR B46 ....115 F2
Old Pleck Rd WSLW WS2 ....56 C1
Old Port Cl TPTN/OCK DY4 * 85 H4
Old Portway
HWK/WKHTH B38 ....190 C1
Old Postway LOZ/NWT B19 .....108 D2
Old Quarry Cl RBRY B45 ....173 H5
Old Quarry Dr SEDG DY3 ....83 E1
Old Rectory Gdns ALDR WS9 .....30 C4
Old School Cl WLNHL WV13 ....39 G3
Old School Dr
BLKHTH/ROWR B65 ....121 H1
Old Scott Cl STETCH B33 ....131 E2
Old Smithy Pl WSNGN B18 ......108 A4
Old Snow Hl LOZ/NWT B19 ....3 F2
Old Sq CBHAMNW B4 ....3 G4
Old Stables Wk
VAUX/NECH B7 ....110 A2
Old Station Rd HIA/OLT B92 ....167 G2

STETCH B33 ....111 H5
Old Stone Cl RBRY B45 ....173 H4
Old Stowheath La WOLV WV1 * ..38 C4
Old Tokengate HRBN B17 ....142 B1
Old Town Cl HWK/WKHTH B38 ..176 D3
Old Town La BLOX/PEL WS3 ......17 H4
Old Vicarage Cl BLOX/PEL WS3 ..18 A5
WMBN WV5 ....65 F4
Old Walsall Rd PBAR/PBCH B42 ..73 H5
Old Warwick Ct HIA/OLT B92 ...164 A1
Old Warwick Rd HIA/OLT B92 ...164 A1
Oldway Dr SOLH B91 ....182 C3
Old Well Cl RUSH/SHEL WS4 ......28 D3
Old Wharf Rd STRBR DY8 ....135 F1
Olga Dr TPTN/OCK DY4 ....69 H2
Olinthus Av WNSFLD WV11 ....25 E3
Olive Av
ETTPK/GDPK/PENN WV4 ....52 C3
Olive Hill Rd RMSLY B62 ....122 B4
Olive La RMSLY B62 ....122 A4
Olive Pl ALE/KHTH/YWD B14 ....161 F3
Oliver Cl DUDS DY2 ....103 E1
Oliver Ct BLKHTH/ROWR B65 ....69 E1
Oliver Rd ERDW/GRVHL B23 ......76 D5
SMTHWK B66 ....125 E1
Oliver St VAUX/NECH B7 ....109 G4
Ollerton Rd
LGN/SDN/BHAMAIR B26 ......130 B5
Ollison St FOAKS/STRLY B74 .....45 F3
Olliver Cl RMSLY B62 ....139 H5
Olorenshaw Rd
LGN/SDN/BHAMAIR B26 ......148 B2
Olton Bvd East ACGN B27 ......146 C5
Olton Bvd West SPARK B11 .....145 H4
Olton Cft ACGN B27 ....146 D4
Olton Mere HIA/OLT B92 * 146 D5
Olton Rd SHLY B90 ....164 A1
Olton Whf HIA/OLT B92 ....164 A1
Olympus Dr TPTN/OCK DY4 ......70 B5
Ombersley Cl OLDBY B69 ....104 D1
Ombersley Rd BHTH/HG B12 ....144 C1
HALE B63 ....138 D5
Ombersley Wy NFLD/LBR B31 ..176 B3
Onibury Rd HDSW B21 ....89 F5
Onslow Crs HIA/OLT B92 ....164 C1
Onslow Rd SPARK B11 ....146 A3
Ontario Cl HWK/WKHTH B38 ...177 E5
Oozells Sq CBHAMW B1 ....2 B6
Oozells St CBHAMW B1 ....2 C6
Opal Gdns LGLYGN/QTN B68 ....105 F4
Open Field Cl NFLD/LBR B31 ...175 H5
Openfield Cft
CSHL/WTROR B46 ....96 C4
Orchard Av SOLH B91 ....165 F5
Orchard Cl BLKHTH/ROWR B65 ..115 F2
CSHL/WTROR B46 ....169 H1
HAG/WOL DY9 ....137 C1
HALE B63 ....138 B5
HDSW B21 ....107 G1
RUSH/SHEL WS4 ....29 E5
WLNHL WV13 ....39 H4
Orchard Crs BDMR/CCFT WV3 ....50 B1
KGSWFD DY6 ....100 B1
Orchard Dr LOZ/NWT B19 ....108 C3
Orchard Gv ALDR WS9 ....44 B1
ETTPK/GDPK/PENN WV4 ....51 G4
FOAKS/STRLY B74 ....45 E5
SEDG DY3 ....82 D3
Orchard La CDSL WV8 ....10 C4
The Orchard FOAKS/STRLY B74 ..47 E5
HLYWD B47 ....192 C1
SHLY B90 ....194 D4
Orchard St BRLYHL DY5 ....101 F5
Orchards Wk BHTH/HG B12 .....144 A1
The Orchard BILS/COS WV14 ....54 A3
BLOX/PEL WS3 ....17 H4
CHWD/FDBR/MGN B37 ....131 H4
DUNHL/THL/PER WV6 ....22 A4
Orchard Wy ACGN B27 ....146 D3
CTB/HAM B43 ....73 H2
HLYWD B47 ....178 C5
Orchid Cl SMTHWK B66 ....105 H2
Orchid Dr LOZ/NWT B19 ....108 C3
Oregon Cl KGSWFD DY6 ....100 B3
Oregon Dr SHHTH WV12 ....26 C5
Orford Gv HDSW B21 ....107 E2
Oriel Cl DUDN DY1 ....84 B5
Oriel Dr WOLV WV10 ....12 D4
Oriel Vls SPARK B11 ....145 E2
Orion Cl WASH/WDE B8 ....111 F5
Orkney Av BKDE/SHDE B34 .....112 D2
Orkney Cft CBROM B36 ....114 B2
Orlando Cl WSL WS1 ....4 E6
Ormande Cl HALE B63 ....155 H4
Orme Cl STRBR DY8 ....118 C4
Ormes La DUNHL/THL/PER WV6 ..35 F2
Ormond Pl BILS/COS WV14 ......54 A2
Ormond Rd RBRY B45 ....173 G4
Ormsby Gv ACGN B27 ....163 F3
Ormscliffe Rd RBRY B45 ....188 B2
Orphanage Rd
ERDE/BCHGN B24 ....93 F1
Orpington Rd KGSTG B44 ....60 A5
Orpwood Rd STETCH B33 ....130 C2
Orton Av WALM/CURD B76 ....78 B4
Orton Cv
ETTPK/GDPK/PENN WV4 ....50 D4
Orton La WMBN WV5 ....65 E2
Orton Wy CVALE B35 ....114 C4
Orwell Cl DUDS DY2 ....120 B2
STRBR DY8 ....134 C2
WNSFLD WV11 ....25 F5
Orwell Dr HHTH/SAND B71 ......71 H5
HWK/WKHTH B38 ....176 B5
Orwell Pas DIG/EDG B5 ....5 K6
Orwell Rd WSL WS1 ....57 F1
Osberton Dr DUDN DY1 ....83 H4
Osborne Cl AST/WIT B6 ....109 C2
BRLYHL DY5 ....119 H5

Osborne Dr DARL/WED WS10 .....40 B5
Osborne Cv LOZ/NWT B19 * 108 C2
Osborne Rd ERDW/GRVHL B23 ...92 D1
ETTPK/GDPK/PENN WV4 ....51 F3
HDSW B21 ....107 H1
WBROM B70 ....87 C5
Osborn Rd SPARK B11 ....145 E1
Oscott Cft Cft SHLY B90 ....194 D5
Oscott Gdns PBAR/PBCH B42 ....91 E3
Oscott School La KGSTG B44 .....75 E1
Oscott Rd PBAR/PBCH B42 ....75 H5
Osier Pl WOLV WV1 ....37 H5
Osier St WOLV WV1 ....37 H5
Osier St LDYWD/EDGR B16 .....125 H2
Osmaston Rd HRBN B17 ....141 G4
STRBR DY8 ....135 E5
Osmington Gv HALE B63 ....137 H1
Osprey Dr DUDN DY1 ....83 H5
Osprey Rd ACGN B27 ....146 D5
ERDW/GRVHL B23 ....76 A5
Oswald Pl BILS/COS WV14 ....69 F2
Oswin Rd BLOX/PEL WS3 ....28 B5
Oswin Rd BLOX/PEL WS3 ....28 B5
Othello Rd WOLV WV10 ....23 C5
Otley Gv BORD B10 ....129 G1
Otter Cft BKDE/SHDE B34 ......113 F4
Otterstone Cl DUDN DY1 ....67 E1
Oughton Rd BHTH/HG B12 ......127 G5
Oundle Rd KGSTG B44 ....75 C4
Ounsdale Crs WMBN WV5 ....65 G4
Ounsdale Dr DUDS DY2 ....102 C5
Ounsdale Rd WMBN WV5 ....64 D4
Ousterley Gv CDSL WV8 ....10 A5
Outmore Rd STETCH B33 ....131 F2
Out Wood Dr NFLD/LBR B31 ...174 D4
Oval Rd ERDE/BCHGN B24 ....92 C5
TPTN/OCK DY4 ....69 F5
The Oval DARL/WED WS10 ....55 H4
DUDN DY1 ....101 G1
SMTHWKW B67 ....123 H2
Overbrook Cl SEDG DY3 ....83 E4
Over Brunton Cl
NFLD/LBR B31 ....175 H3
Overbury Cl HALE B63 ....138 D5
NFLD/LBR B31 ....176 A2
Overdale Av WALM/CURD B76 ...40 A2
Overdale Cl WLNHL WV13 ....40 A2
Overdale Dr WLNHL WV13 ....40 A2
Overdale Rd RIDG/WDGT B32 ..141 E3
Overend Rd HALE B63 ....137 H1
Overend St WBROM B70 ....87 H5
Overfield Dr BILS/COS WV14 .....53 E5
Overfield Rd DUDN DY1 ....101 G1
RIDG/WDGT B32 ....158 A1
Over Green Dr
CHWD/FDBR/MGN B37 ....113 H4
Overlea Av ACGN B27 ....146 B4
Over Mill Dr SLYOAK B29 ......143 F5
Overmoor Cl LOZ/NWT B19 .....108 B2
Over Pool Rd WASH/WDE B8 ...111 E3
Overseal Rd WNSFLD WV11 ......25 E2
Overslade Rd SOLH B91 ....181 F5
Oversley Rd WALM/CURD B76 ...78 C5
Overstrand COVEN WV9 ....11 G5
Overton Cl HLGN/YWD B28 ....163 E4
Overton Dr CSHL/WTROR B46 ...96 C2
Overton Gv ACGN B27 ....163 G2
VAUX/NECH B7 *..................110 B2
Overton Rd ACGN B27 ....163 F2
Overwood Cft WASH/WDE B8 ...128 C1
Owen Pl BILS/COS WV14 ....53 H2
Owen Rd BDMR/CCFT WV3 ....6 C7
BILS/COS WV14 ....54 A3
WLNHL WV13 ....39 H4
Owens Cft HWK/WKHTH B38 ...177 E4
Owen St DARL/WED WS10 ....55 F1
DUDS DY2 ....84 D5
TPTN/OCK DY4 ....69 H2
Owens Wy CDYHTH B64 ....121 C3
Ownall Rd BKDE/SHDE B34 .....112 D3
Oxbarn Av BDMR/CCFT WV3 ......51 E1
Oxendon Wy BHTH/HG B12 * 137 H5
Oxford Cl WASH/WDE B8 ....111 F4
Oxford Ct ACGN B27 ....146 D3
STRBR DY8 ....135 F5
Oxford Rd ACGN B27 ....146 C4
ERDW/GRVHL B23 ....92 D2
MOS/BIL B13 ....144 C5
SMTHWK B66 ....106 C1
WBROM B70 ....87 F3
Oxford St BILS/COS WV14 ....54 A3
BVILLE B30 ....160 A5
DARL/WED WS10 ....71 F1
DIG/EDG B5 ....4 D5
DUDN DY1 ....84 B5
WOLV WV1 ....7 H1
WSLW WS2 ....56 C1
Oxford Wy TPTN/OCK DY4 ....84 D2
Oxhill Rd HDSW B21 ....89 F4
HDSW B21 ....107 E1
SHLY B90 ....179 H4
Ox Leasow RIDG/WDGT B32 ....140 C5
Oxley Av WOLV WV10 ....23 E4
Oxley Cl DUDS DY2 ....120 B2
Oxley Cl SLYOAK B29 ....158 C2
Oxley La WOLV WV1 ....6 C1
Oxley Links Rd WOLV WV10 ......12 C2
Oxley Moor Rd COVEN WV9 ......22 C2
Ox Leys Rd MGN/WHC B75 ....63 H4
Oxley St WOLV WV1 ....37 E1
Oxlip Cl DSYBK/YTR WS5 ....57 G5
Oxpiece Dr CBROM B36 ....111 H1
Oxstall Cl WALM/CURD B76 ......95 F1
Ox St SEDG DY3 ....81 F1
Oxted Cl WNSFLD WV11 ....25 F5
Oxted Cft ERDW/GRVHL B23 .....92 C5
Oxwood La RIDG/WDGT B32 ....173 E1

P

Pace Crs BILS/COS WV14 ....69 F1
Pacific Av DARL/WED WS10 ......70 B2
Packhorse La HLYWD B47 ....192 A2
HWK/WKHTH B38 ....191 H2
Packington Av
BKDE/SHDE B34 ....113 E4

Packington La
CSHL/WTROR B46 .... 115 C5
RCOVN/BALC/EX CV7 .... 150 D2
Packmores SHLY B90 .... 194 A3
Packwood Cl
BFLD/HDSWWD B20 .... 90 A4
DOR/KN B93 .... 196 C4
WLNHL WV13 .... 39 F5
Packwood Cottages
DOR/KN B93 * 198 D2
Packwood Ct SLYOAK B29 ..... 142 D4
Packwood Dr GTB/HAM B43 ... 73 F2
Packwood Rd HOCK/TIA B94 ... 199 F4
LGN/SDN/BHAMAIR B26 .... 130 D4
OLDBY B69 .... 85 G5
Padarn Cl SEDG DY3 .... 67 E2
Padbury COVEN WV9 .... 12 B4
Paddington Rd HDSW B21 ...... 89 E5
Paddock Dr DOR/KN B93 .... 199 E1
LGN/SDN/BHAMAIR B26 .... 130 C5
Paddock La ALDR WS9 .... 30 A5
WSL WS1 .... 5 G4
Paddocks Gn WSNGN B18 ...... 108 A4
Paddocks Rd HLYWD B47 .... 192 C2
The Paddock BILS/COS WV14 .. 68 D2
CDSL WV8 .... 10 C5
DUNHL/THL/PER WV6 .... 34 B1
HAG/WOL DY9 .... 152 D2
SEDG DY3 .... 83 G1
WMBN WV5 .... 64 C5
Paddock Vw
DUNHL/THL/PER WV6 .... 22 D5
Padgate Cl CVALE B35 .... 94 D5
Padstow Rd ERDE/BCHGN B24 . 93 H2
Paganal Dr WBROM B70 .... 88 A5
Paganel Dr DUDN DY1 .... 84 C3
Paganel Rd SLYOAK B29 .... 141 C5
Pages Cl CSCFLD/WYGN B72 ... 62 C5
Pages La GTB/HAM B43 .... 73 G2
Paget Cl BILS/COS WV14 * 68 B5
Paget Rd DUNHL/THL/PER WV6 . 36 B2
ERDE/BCHGN B24 .... 93 H5
Paget St WOLV WV1 .... 6 D1
Pagham Cl COVEN WV9 .... 11 H5
Pagnell Gv MOS/BIL B13 .... 162 A4
Pagoda Cl FOAKS/STRLY B74 ... 60 B2
Paignton Rd
LDYWD/EDGR B16 .... 125 F1
Pailton Cl SLYOAK B29 .... 158 D1
Pailton Rd SHLY B90 .... 163 F5
Painswick Cl DSYBK/YTR WS5 .. 57 H5
Painswick Rd HLGN/YWD B28 .. 162 C5
Paint Cup Rw DUDS DY2 .... 120 C2
Painters Cft BILS/COS WV14 ... 69 E2
Pakefield Rd BVILLE B30 .... 177 F2
Pakenham Cl WALM/CURD B76 . 78 B3
Pakenham Dr WALM/CURD B76 . 78 B5
Pakenham Rd EDG B15 .... 126 C5
Pakfield Wk AST/WIT B6 * 91 F5
Palace Cl BLKHTH/ROWR B65 .. 108 B5
Palace Dr SMTHWK B66 .... 105 G1
Palace Rd BORD B9 .... 128 C3
Palefield Rd SHLY B90 .... 195 F2
Pale La HRBN B17 .... 124 B4
Pale St SEDG DY3 .... 83 G1
Palethorpe Rd TPTN/OCK DY4 . 69 G3
Palfrey Rd STRBR DY8 .... 134 D2
Palmcourt Av HLGN/YWD B28 .. 162 C5
Palm Cft BRLYHL DY5 .... 119 E4
Palmer Cl WNSFLD WV11 .... 25 F1
SHLY B90 .... 163 F5
Palmers Gv CBROM B36 .... 112 A1
Palmerston Dr OLDBY B69 ..... 86 B4
Palmerston Rd SPARK B11 ..... 144 D1
Palmer St BORD B9 .... 127 G2
Palmers Wy CDSL WV8 .... 11 G1
Palmvale Cft
LGN/SDN/BHAMAIR B26 .... 147 G1
Palomino Pl
LDYWD/EDGR B16 .... 125 H2
Pamela Rd NFLD/LBR B31 .... 175 G3
Pan Cft CBROM B36 .... 111 G2
Panjab Gdns SMTHWK B67 * .. 106 B3
Pannel Cft LOZ/NWT B19 .... 108 D5
Panther Cft BKDE/SHDE B34 .. 113 F4
Paper Mill End KGSTG B44 ..... 74 D5
Papyrus Wy CBROM B36 .... 94 B5
The Parade BRWNH WS8 .... 9 E5
CDYHTH B64 .... 120 D4
DUDN DY1 .... 84 B4
KGSWFD DY6 .... 99 F2
WNSFLD WV11 * 24 A2
Paradise DUDS DY2 .... 102 D1
Paradise Circ Queensway
CBHAMNW B3 .... 2 D4
Paradise Gv BLOX/PEL WS3 .... 17 H4
Paradise La BLOX/PEL WS3 .... 17 H4
HLGN/YWD B28 .... 162 C4
Paradise Pl CBHAMNW B3 * 2 E5
Paradise St CBHAMW B1 .... 2 E5
WSLW WS2 .... 41 G3
Pardington Cl HIA/OLT B92 ..... 145 G2
Pargeter Rd SMTHWK B67 ..... 124 D2
Pargeter St STRBR DY8 .... 135 F3
WSLW WS2 .... 41 G3
Par Gn HWK/WKHTH B38 .... 176 D4
Parish Gdns HAG/WOL DY9 .... 153 D1
Park Ap ERDW/GRVHL B23 ..... 92 A4
Park Av BLKHTH/ROWR B65 .... 122 A1
BVILLE B30 .... 160 A5
CSHL/WTROR B46 .... 115 F3
ETTPK/GDPK/PENN WV4 ...... 52 A3
LGLYGN/QTN B68 .... 123 F1
SMTHWK B67 * 106 B5
SOLH B91 .... 182 B2
TPTN/OCK DY4 .... 85 E1
WLNHL WV13 .... 39 F3
WMBN WV5 .... 80 D1
WOLV WV1 .... 6 D3
WSNGN B18 .... 108 A2
Park Cl BRWNH WS8 .... 9 F4
DUDN DY1 .... 68 B4
ERDE/BCHGN B24 .... 93 H1
HIA/OLT B92 .... 148 B5
OLDBY B69 .... 104 A2
Park Crs HHTH/SAND B71 ...... 87 H2
WOLV WV1 .... 6 C3
Park Cft HLYWD B47 .... 192 C3
Parkdale Av DARL/WED WS10 .. 56 A4
Parkdale Cl ERDE/BCHGN B24 .. 92 D4

Park Dale Ct WOLV WV1 .... 6 A2
Parkdale Dr NFLD/LBR B31 .... 189 G1
Park Dl East WOLV WV1 .... 6 A2
Parkdale Rd
LGN/SDN/BHAMAIR B26 .... 148 A1
Park Dl West WOLV WV1 .... 6 A2
Park Dr
ETTPK/GDPK/PENN WV4 ...... 52 A3
FOAKS/STRLY B74 .... 46 A1
Park Edge HRBN B17 .... 125 E5
Park End DR RIDG/WDGT B32 .. 157 H1
Parker Rd WNSFLD WV11 .... 25 E1
Parker St BLOX/PEL WS3 .... 27 E1
LDYWD/EDGR B16 .... 125 H3
Parkes Av CDSL WV8 .... 10 D5
Parkes Hall Rd DUDN DY1 ..... 84 A1
Parkes La SEDG DY3 .... 68 A4
TPTN/OCK DY4 .... 69 F3
Parkes St BRLYHL DY5 .... 119 F1
SMTHWK B67 .... 106 B5
WLNHL WV13 .... 39 H4
Park Farm Rd GTB/HAM B43 ... 75 H2
Parkfield RIDG/WDGT B32 ..... 139 H5
Parkfield Chalet Land
BKHL/PFLD WV2 * 52 B2
Parkfield Cl EDG B15 .... 126 C5
RMSLY B62 .... 140 A2
Parkfield Colliery
ETTPK/GDPK/PENN WV4 ...... 52 D3
Parkfield Crs BKHL/PFLD WV2 . 52 C2
Parkfield Dr CBROM B36 .... 95 E5
Parkfield Gv BKHL/PFLD WV2 .. 52 C2
Parkfield Rd
CSHL/WTROR B46 .... 115 F2
DUDS DY2 .... 102 D5
ETTPK/GDPK/PENN WV4 ...... 52 C2
LGLYGN/QTN B68 .... 123 E1
STRBR DY8 .... 135 H2
WASH/WDE B8 .... 128 C1
Park Gv CSHL/WTROR B46 ..... 115 F3
Park Hall Cl DSYBK/YTR WS5 .. 58 A2
Park Hall Crs CBROM B36 ...... 112 D1
Parkhall Cft BKDE/SHDE B34 .. 113 E2
Park Hall Rd DSYBK/YTR WS5 . 58 B2
ETTPK/GDPK/PENN WV4 ...... 52 B2
Park Head Crs DUDS DY2 * 102 B1
Parkhead Locks DUDS DY2 * .. 102 A3
Park Head Rd DUDS DY2 .... 102 B1
Park Hl BLKHTH/ROWR B65 .... 121 H5
DARL/WED WS10 .... 56 C4
MOS/BIL B13 .... 144 A3
Park Hill Dr
BFLD/HDSWWD B20 .... 89 H2
Park Hill Rd HRBN B17 .... 142 A1
SMTHWK B67 .... 106 B4
Parkhill Rd WALM/CURD B76 ... 78 B5
Park Hill St DUDS DY2 .... 103 E1
Parkhouse Av WNSFLD WV11 .. 25 H4
Parkhouse Dr
ERDW/GRVHL B23 .... 91 G1
Parkhouse Gdns SEDG DY3 .... 83 E2
Parklands Av
BFLD/HDSWWD B20 .... 90 A5
Parklands Dr FOAKS/STRLY B74 . 46 D5
Parklands Gdns WSL WS1 ...... 5 J7
Parklands Rd BILS/COS WV14 .. 53 H5
DARL/WED WS10 .... 56 C4
WSNGN B18 .... 38 B5
The Parklands
BDMR/CCFT WV3 .... 35 H5
ERDW/GRVHL B23 .... 76 B5
WOLV WV1 .... 36 D2
Park La AST/WIT B6 .... 109 E2
CVALE B35 .... 94 D1
DARL/WED WS10 .... 55 H4
HALE B63 .... 137 E1
HDSW B21 .... 88 D2
KGSWFD DY6 .... 100 A2
OLDBY B69 .... 105 E3
WOLV WV10 .... 23 H5
Park La East TPTN/OCK DY4 .... 85 H2
Park La West TPTN/OCK DY4 ... 85 E2
Park Lime Dr RUSH/SHEL WS4 .. 42 D1
Park Meadow Av
BILS/COS WV14 .... 38 C5
Park Ms SLYOAK B29 * 158 D1
Park Pl VAUX/NECH B7 .... 110 A2
Park Retreat SMTHWK B66 .... 106 C5
Park Rdg FOAKS/STRLY B74 .... 62 A1
Park Ridge Dr HALE B63 .... 137 F1
Park Ri BDMR/CCFT WV3 .... 36 A3
Park Rd AST/WIT B6 .... 109 G2
BILS/COS WV14 .... 53 G5
BLOX/PEL WS3 .... 27 F1
BRLYHL DY5 .... 119 H4
CSHL/WTROR B46 .... 115 H3
DARL/WED WS10 .... 54 D2
DSYBK/YTR WS5 .... 58 B3
DUDN DY1 .... 68 B5
DUDS DY2 .... 102 C3
ERDW/GRVHL B23 .... 92 A4
HAG/WOL DY9 .... 152 D5
HALE B63 .... 137 F1
MOS/BIL B13 .... 144 B3
OLDBY B69 .... 104 A1
RUSH/SHEL WS4 .... 29 E5
SCFLD/BOLD B75 .... 62 B5
SEDG DY3 .... 82 D2
SMTHWK B67 .... 124 B3
SOLH B91 .... 182 A2
SPARK B11 .... 145 E4
STRBR DY8 .... 134 D2
WLNHL WV13 .... 39 F2
WSNGN B18 .... 107 H2
Park Rd East WOLV WV1 .... 6 A1
Park Rd South WSNGN B18 .... 108 A4
Park Rd West STRBR DY8 .... 134 C2
WOLV WV1 .... 6 A1
Park Crs WNSFLD WV11 .... 15 E5
Parkside RIDG/WDGT B32 ...... 157 G1
Parkside Av WLNHL WV13 .... 38 D1
Parkside Cl DARL/WED WS10 .. 56 B5
Parkside Rd
BFLD/HDSWWD B20 .... 89 G1
HALE B63 .... 137 H2
Parkside Wy
FOAKS/STRLY B74 .... 45 G4
NFLD/LBR B31 .... 174 C4

Park Sq
CHWD/FDBR/MGN B37 .... 132 C4
Parkstone Cl RUSH/SHEL WS4 .. 29 E1
Park St AST/WIT B6 .... 109 G2
BLKHTH/ROWR B65 .... 122 B3
CDYHTH B64 .... 120 D2
DARL/WED WS10 .... 55 E5
DIG/EDG B5 .... 3 J5
HAG/WOL DY9 .... 136 D2
KGSWFD DY6 .... 99 H3
OLDBY B69 .... 104 D5
STRBR DY8 .... 135 G5
TPTN/OCK DY4 .... 85 G1
WBROM B70 .... 87 H3
Park St South BKHL/PFLD WV2 . 52 A2
Park St West
BLKHTH/ROWR B65 .... 122 B3
Park Ter DARL/WED WS10 ...... 54 D2
HDSW B21 .... 107 G1
Park Tree Wy
ERDE/BCHGN B24 .... 93 H2
HOCK/TIA B94 .... 198 A5
SCFLD/BOLD B75 .... 62 A2
Parkview Ct KGSWFD DY6 ...... 99 F1
Parkview Cl WSLW WS2 .... 41 E1
Parkview Dr BRWNH WS8 .... 9 F2
WASH/WDE B8 .... 111 E5
Parkview Rd BILS/COS WV14 ... 38 C5
HAG/WOL DY9 .... 136 D3
Park View Rd FOAKS/STRLY B74 . 46 D2
Park Vis BORD B9 * 127 H2
Parkville Av HRBN B17 .... 141 H4
Park Wk BRLYHL DY5 .... 119 H4
Park Wy RBRY B45 .... 174 B5
Parkway WASH/WDE B8 .... 111 E4
Park Wy WNSFLD WV11 .... 25 G1
Parkway Rd DUDN DY1 .... 84 A4
The Parkway
DUNHL/THL/PER WV6 .... 34 C2
RUSH/SHEL WS4 .... 29 E2
Parkwood Cl BRWNH WS8 ...... 9 G2
Parkwood Cft GTB/HAM B43 ... 74 B2
Parkwood Dr KGSTG B44 ...... 76 A1
Parkyn St BKHL/PFLD WV2 ..... 37 G5
Parliament St AST/WIT B6 ..... 109 F3
SMTH B10 .... 128 A4
WBROM B70 .... 87 H5
Parlows End
HWK/WKHTH B38 .... 190 B1
Parry Rd WNSFLD WV11 .... 25 G2
Parsonage Dr HALE B63 .... 120 A5
RBRY B45 .... 188 D4
Parsonage St HHTH/SAND B71 . 71 H5
OLDBY B69 .... 105 F3
Parson's Hl BVILLE B30 .... 177 F5
LGLYGN/QTN B68 .... 123 F3
Parsons Dr DUDN DY1 .... 84 C5
Parsons St DUDN DY1 .... 84 C5
Partons Rd
ALE/KHTH/YWD B14 .... 160 D4
Partridge Av
DARL/WED WS10 .... 54 D2
Partridge Cl
CHWD/FDBR/MGN B37 .... 132 C5
Partridge MI BLOX/PEL WS3 ... 17 G4
Partridge Rd
LGN/SDN/BHAMAIR B26 .... 130 C3
STRBR DY8 .... 134 C3
Passey Rd MOS/BIL B13 .... 145 F5
Passfield Rd STETCH B33 ...... 130 B1
The Pastures
DUNHL/THL/PER WV6 .... 34 B1
Pasture Vw BLOX/PEL WS3 ..... 28 B1
Patent Dr DARL/WED WS10 .... 70 A1
Paternoster Rw DIG/EDG B5 * . 3 H5
WOLV WV1 .... 6 C2
Paterson Pl BRWNH WS8 .... 19 H2
Pathlow Crs SHLY B90 .... 180 A4
Patina Cl BRLYHL DY5 .... 119 H4
Paton Gv MOS/BIL B13 .... 144 B5
Patricia Av
ALE/KHTH/YWD B14 .... 179 E1
ETTPK/GDPK/PENN WV4 ...... 52 A3
Patricia Crs DUDN DY1 .... 68 B5
Patricia Dr TPTN/OCK DY4 ..... 85 G4
Patrick Gregory Rd
WNSFLD WV11 .... 25 F3
Patrick Rd
LGN/SDN/BHAMAIR B26 .... 130 A5
Patriot Cl WSL WS1 .... 56 D5
Patshull Av WOLV WV10 .... 12 C4
Patshull Cl GTB/HAM B43 ...... 73 F2
Patshull Gv WOLV WV10 .... 12 C4
Patshull Pl LOZ/NWT B19 * 108 C2
Pattenham Cl SHHTH WV12 .... 40 B1
Patterdale Rd
ERDW/GRVHL B23 .... 92 B2
Pattingham Rd
DUNHL/THL/PER WV6 .... 34 A3
Pattison Gdns
ERDW/GRVHL B23 .... 92 B4
Pattison St DSYBK/YTR WS5 ... 57 E3
Paul Byrne Ct
BFLD/HDSWWD B20 .... 90 B5
Paul Pursehouse Rd
BILS/COS WV14 .... 53 H5
Pauls Coppice BRWNH WS8 ... 19 F2
Paul St BILS/COS WV14 .... 68 A2
BKHL/PFLD WV2 .... 6 E7
DARL/WED WS10 .... 56 C3
Paul's TPTN/OCK DY4 .... 85 H1
Pavenham Dr DIG/EDG B5 ..... 143 G3
Pavilion Av SMTHWK B67 .... 124 A1
Pavilion Dr AST/WIT B6 .... 110 A2
Pavilion End KIDW WV7 .... 116 C5
Pavilion Gdns DUDS DY2 ...... 120 C2
Pavilion Rd AST/WIT B6 .... 110 A2
The Pavilions CBHAMNE B4 * .. 3 H5
CHWD/FDBR/MGN B37 .... 132 D4
Pavilion Cl ALDR WS9 .... 30 B2
Paxford Wy NFLD/LBR B31 ..... 158 B4
Paxton Av
DUNHL/THL/PER WV6 .... 34 C2
Paxton Rd HAG/WOL DY9 ...... 136 C3
WSNGN B18 .... 108 A4
Payne St BLKHTH/ROWR B65 .. 122 A3
Payton Cl OLDBY B69 .... 86 C5

Payton Rd HDSW B21 .... 107 F1
Peach Av DARL/WED WS10 ..... 55 E2
Peachley Cl HALE B63 .... 138 D5
Peach Ley Rd SLYOAK B29 ..... 158 B5
Peach Rd SHHTH WV12 .... 25 G4
Peacock Cl TPTN/OCK DY4 ..... 85 E5
Peacock Ct DARL/WED WS10 .. 54 D1
MOS/BIL B13 .... 161 F4
Peacocks Est CDYHTH B64 * ... 120 C3
Peak Cft CBROM B36 .... 111 H1
Peak Dr SEDG DY3 .... 83 F5
Peake Crs BRWNH WS8 .... 19 F2
Peake Rd BRWNH WS8 .... 19 F2
Peak House Rd GTB/HAM B43 . 58 C5
Peakman Cl RBRY B45 .... 188 A2
Peak Rd STRBR DY8 .... 135 H1
Peal St WSL WS1 .... 5 F4
Pearce Cl DUDN DY1 .... 101 G1
Pearl Gv ACGN B27 .... 146 B2
WSNGN B18 .... 107 G5
Pearman Rd RBRY B45 .... 173 F4
SMTHWK B66 .... 124 C1
Pearsall Dr OLDBY B69 .... 86 B3
Pearson St BKHL/PFLD WV2 .... 37 G5
BRLYHL DY5 .... 119 F1
CDYHTH B64 .... 121 E3
WBROM B70 .... 105 G1
WOLV WV2 .... 36 D3
Pear Tree Av TPTN/OCK DY4 ... 85 F1
Peartree Av WLNHL WV13 .... 39 H4
Pear Tree Cl GTB/HAM B43 ..... 73 D2
Pear Tree Cl
SHLY B90 .... 179 F5
STETCH B33 .... 129 H2
Pear Tree Ct
BLKHTH/ROWR B65 .... 122 B1
GTB/HAM B43 .... 73 E2
Peartree Dr STRBR DY8 .... 135 G5
Pear Tree Gv SHLY B90 .... 179 F5
Pear Tree La BILS/COS WV14 .. 68 D5
BRWNH WS8 .... 8 C2
Peartree La CDYHTH B64 ...... 121 E5
DUDS DY2 .... 102 D1
Pear Tree La WOLV WV10 .... 24 B1
Pear Tree Rd BKDE/SHDE B34 . 113 E3
GTB/HAM B43 .... 73 D2
SMTHWK B67 .... 106 A5
Peascroft La BILS/COS WV14 .. 54 A1
Peasefield Cl HDSW B21 .... 107 E1
Pebble Cl STRBR DY8 .... 135 H2
Pebble Mill Rd DIG/EDG B5 .... 143 F3
Pebworth Av SHLY B90 .... 195 H2
Pebworth Cl SLYOAK B29 .... 159 E1
Pebworth Gv DUDN DY1 .... 84 A3
STETCH B33 .... 131 E4
Peckover Cl
BLKHTH/ROWR B65 .... 121 H3
Peddimore La
WALM/CURD B76 .... 79 F5
Pedmore Court Rd STRBR DY8 . 152 D1
Pedmore Gv KGSTG B44 .... 74 D5
Pedmore Hall La
HAG/WOL DY9 .... 153 E2
Pedmore Rd BRLYHL DY5 ...... 120 B2
DUDS DY2 .... 103 H1
HAG/WOL DY9 .... 136 B2
Peel Cl DARL/WED WS10 .... 40 B5
HIA/OLT B92 .... 167 H4
WLNHL WV13 .... 39 G4
Peel St BDMR/CCFT WV3 .... 6 E5
DUDS DY2 .... 103 E1
HHTH/SAND B71 .... 87 G1
TPTN/OCK DY4 .... 85 G2
WLNHL WV13 .... 39 H5
WSNGN B18 .... 107 G4
Peel Wk HRBN B17 .... 124 B5
Peel Wy OLDBY B69 .... 86 A4
Pegasus Wk SLYOAK B29 .... 159 F4
Pelham Dr DUDN DY1 .... 84 A4
Pelham Rd WASH/WDE B8 ..... 111 F5
Pelham St BDMR/CCFT WV3 ... 6 B6
Pelsall La BLOX/PEL WS3 .... 17 F4
RUSH/SHEL WS4 .... 28 C2
Pelsall Rd BRWNH WS8 .... 9 G3
Pemberley Rd ACGN B27 .... 163 E1
Pemberton Cl SMTHWK B66 ... 124 D1
Pemberton Crs
DARL/WED WS10 .... 56 C4
Pemberton Rd BILS/COS WV14 . 68 D2
WBROM B70 .... 71 E5
Pemberton St WSNGN B18 ..... 2 B2
Pembridge Cl BRLYHL DY5 .... 119 H5
RIDG/WDGT B32 .... 157 E5
Pembridge Rd DOR/KN B93 ... 196 C5
Pembroke Av BKHL/PFLD WV2 . 53 E1
Pembroke Cl SHHTH WV12 ..... 25 H4
Pembroke Gdns STRBR DY8 ... 117 G2
Pembroke Rd BHTH/HG B12 ... 144 C5
HHTH/SAND B71 .... 71 F2
Pembroke Wy HHTH/SAND B71 . 71 F4
HLGN/YWD B28 .... 162 D5
Pembury Cl FOAKS/STRLY B74 . 60 B2
Pembury Cft KGSTG B44 .... 75 G2
Pencombe Dr
ETTPK/GDPK/PENN WV4 ...... 52 B3
Pencroft Rd BKDE/SHDE B34 .. 112 D2
Penda Gv
DUNHL/THL/PER WV6 .... 20 D5
Pendeen Rd
ALE/KHTH/YWD B14 .... 179 E1
Pendeford Av
DUNHL/THL/PER WV6 .... 22 A2
Pendeford Cl
DUNHL/THL/PER WV6 .... 22 A2
Pendeford Hall La COVEN WV9 . 11 F2
Pendeford La COVEN WV9 ...... 12 A3
Pendeford Mill La CDSL WV8 ... 11 E4
Pendennis Cl BVILLE B30 .... 159 F5
Pendennis Dr OLDBY B69 ...... 86 B3
Penderel St BLOX/PEL WS3 ..... 27 G1
Pendigo Wy BHAMNEC B40 .... 150 B4

Pendinas Dr CDSL WV8 .... 10 D4
Pendleton Gv ACGN B27 .... 163 F2
Pendragon Rd PBAR/PBCH B42 . 90 C2
Pendrell Cl
CHWD/FDBR/MGN B37 .... 132 A1
Pendrell Ct CDSL WV8 * 10 C4
Pendrill Rd WOLV WV10 .... 13 F4
Penfields Rd STRBR DY8 .... 135 G1
Penge Gv KGSTG B44 .... 60 A5
Penhallow Dr
ETTPK/GDPK/PENN WV4 ...... 52 C3
Penhurst Av
BFLD/HDSWWD B20 .... 90 D5
Penkridge Cl WSLW WS2 .... 41 H1
Penkridge Gv STETCH B33 ...... 112 B5
Penkridge St WSLW WS2 .... 41 H2
Penk Ri DUNHL/THL/PER WV6 .. 35 F1
Penleigh Gdns WMBN WV5 .... 64 B4
Penley Gv WASH/WDE B8 .... 111 F3
Pennant Cl BDMR/CCFT WV3 .. 36 D5
Pennant Gv SLYOAK B29 .... 141 G5
Pennant Rd
BLKHTH/ROWR B65 .... 121 H1
CDYHTH B64 .... 120 D3
Pennard Gv RIDG/WDGT B32 .. 141 E3
Penn Cl BLOX/PEL WS3 .... 27 G1
Penn Common Rd
ETTPK/GDPK/PENN WV4 ...... 66 A2
Penncricket La
LGLYGN/QTN B68 .... 122 C1
Penn Croft La
ETTPK/GDPK/PENN WV4 ...... 66 C2
Penndale Cl ERDE/BCHGN B24 . 77 G5
Pennhouse Av
ETTPK/GDPK/PENN WV4 ...... 51 F3
Pennine Dr SEDG DY3 .... 83 F5
Pennine Wy SHHTH WV12 ...... 40 B1
STRBR DY8 .... 133 G5
WASH/WDE B8 .... 110 B5
Penn La WOLN WV10 .... 24 B1
Penn Rd BLKHTH/ROWR B65 ... 122 C1
ETTPK/GDPK/PENN WV4 ...... 51 E4
SEDG DY3 .... 66 B2
Penn Road Island
BDMR/CCFT WV3 .... 6 E6
Penns Lake Rd
WALM/CURD B76 .... 78 A4
Penns La CSCFLD/WYGN B72 .. 77 H4
Penns St BDMR/CCFT WV3 ..... 5 F1
CBHAMNE B4 .... 127 G1
CDYHTH B64 .... 127 G2
Penns Wood Cl SEDG DY3 ...... 67 E1
Penns Wood Dr
WALM/CURD B76 .... 78 B4
Pennwood La
ETTPK/GDPK/PENN WV4 ...... 51 F5
Pennyacre Rd
ALE/KHTH/YWD B14 .... 177 H3
Pennyfield Crs STETCH B33 .... 130 A1
Pennyhill La HHTH/SAND B71 .. 72 A4
Pennyroyal Cl DSYBK/YTR WS5 . 57 G5
Penny Royal Cl SEDG DY3 ...... 83 E4
Penrice Dr OLDBY B69 .... 85 F5
Penrith Cl BRLYHL DY5 .... 118 D4
Penrith Cft RIDG/WDGT B32 ... 157 H2
Penrith Gv
CHWD/FDBR/MGN B37 .... 132 C2
Penryn Cl DSYBK/YTR WS5 ..... 58 B1
Penryn Rd DSYBK/YTR WS5 .... 58 B1
Pensarn Vls DARL/WED WS10 * . 55 F2
Pensby Cl MOS/BIL B13 .... 162 A2
Pens Cl SMTHWK B66 .... 106 D5
Pensford Rd NFLD/LBR B31 .... 176 A2
Pensham Cft SHLY B90 .... 195 G2
Penshaw Cl COVEN WV9 .... 12 A5
Penshaw Gv MOS/BIL B13 ..... 162 B1
Pensnett Rd DUDN DY1 .... 101 G2
Penstock Dr OLDBY B69 .... 104 D5
Pentland Cft BHTH/HG B12 .... 127 F5
Pentland Dr BDMR/CCFT WV3 . 36 A3
Pentos Dr SPARK B11 .... 145 E2
Pentridge Cl WALM/CURD B76 . 78 A5
Penwood Gdns BILS/COS WV14 . 68 C3
Penzer St KGSWFD DY6 .... 99 H2
Peolsford Rd BLOX/PEL WS3 ... 18 B5
Peplins Wy BVILLE B30 .... 177 F2
Peplow Rd STETCH B33 .... 112 C5
Pepperbox Dr TPTN/OCK DY4 . 85 G1
Pepper HI STRBR DY8 .... 135 G3
Pepperwood Cl BRGRVW B61 .. 185 H5
Pepper Wood Dr
NFLD/LBR B31 .... 174 C4
Perch Av
CHWD/FDBR/MGN B37 .... 132 A1
Perch Cl WOLN WV10 .... 23 H2
Perch Rd WSLW WS2 .... 41 E1
Percival Rd LDYWD/EDGR B16 . 125 F4
Peregrine Cl DUDN DY1 .... 83 H5
Pereira Rd HRBN B17 .... 124 B3
Perimeter Rd BHAMNEC B40 .. 149 H5
Perivale Gv BILS/COS WV14 .... 68 D3
Perivale Wy STRBR DY8 .... 118 C4
Periwinkle Cl BRWNH WS8 ..... 18 D1
Perkins Cl DUDN DY1 .... 84 C5
Perks Rd WNSFLD WV11 .... 25 G1
Perrins La HAG/WOL DY9 .... 136 C5
Perrins Rd HAG/WOL DY9 ...... 136 D5
Perrott Gdns BRLYHL DY5 ...... 118 D5
Perrott St WSNGN B18 .... 107 F5
Perry Av PBAR/PBCH B42 .... 90 C2
WOLN WV10 .... 23 H2
Perry Barr Locks
PBAR/PBCH B42 * 74 B5
Perry Cl DUDS DY2 .... 102 D1
Perry Common Rd
ERDW/GRVHL B23 .... 75 H5
Perry Ct LGLYGN/QTN B68 ..... 123 F5
Perry Hall Dr SHHTH WV12 .... 25 H5
Perry Hall Rd WNSFLD WV11 .. 25 F4
Perry Hill Crs LGLYGN/QTN B68 . 123 F5
Perry Hill La
LGLYGN/QTN B68 * 123 F5
Perry Hill Rd LGLYGN/QTN B68 . 123 F5
Perry Park Rd
BLKHTH/ROWR B65 .... 121 H3

Perry St BILS/COS WV14 ....54 A5
DARL/WED WS10 ....40 B5
DARL/WED WS10 ....70 D2
SMTHWK B66 ....106 C2
TPTN/OCK DY4 ....
Perry Villa Dr PBAR/PBCH B42 ....90 D1
Perry Wk ERDW/GRVHL B23 ....75 H5
Perrywell Rd AST/WIT B6 ....91 G2
Perry Wood Rd
PBAR/PBCH B42 ....74 A3
Persehouse St WSL WS1 ....5 G3
Pershore Ct BLOX/PEL WS3 ....16 B5
Pershore Rd BLOX/PEL WS3 ....16 B5
BVILLE B30 ....176 D1
HALE B63 ....138 C5
Pershore Rd South
BVILLE B30 ....176 D2
Pershore St DIG/EDG B5 ....5 G6
Perth Rd SHHTH WV12 ....25 H4
Perton Brook V
DUNHL/THL/PER WV6 ....34 D3
Perton Gv
DUNHL/THL/PER WV6 ....34 D3
SLYOAK B29 ....158 C1
Perton Rd
DUNHL/THL/PER WV6 ....34 D3
Petchells Ct BRLYHL DY5 ....100 D4
Peter Av BILS/COS WV14 ....69 F1
Peterbrook Ri SHLY B90 ....179 F4
Peterbrook Rd SHLY B90 ....179 F4
Peterdale Dr
ETTPK/GDPK/PENN WV4 ....51 F5
Peters Av NFLD/LBR B31 ....175 F3
Petersfield Ct
HLGN/YWD B28 * 162 D2
Petersfield Dr
BLKHTH/ROWR B65 ....122 C1
Petersfield Rd HLGN/YWD B28 ....162 C3
Petersham PI EDG B15 ....142 C1
Peter's Hill Rd BRLYHL DY5 ....119 E5
Petershouse Dr
FOAKS/STRLY B74 ....32 D5
Peters St WBROM B70 ....71 E4
Petford St CDYHTH B64 ....121 E3
Pettyfield Ct
LGN/SDN/BHAMAIR B26 ....147 G1
Pettyfields Cft DOR/KN B93 ....197 E3
Petworth Cl WLNHL WV13 ....39 F5
Petworth Gv
LGN/SDN/BHAMAIR B26 ....147 E1
Pevensey Cl OLDBY B69 ....103 F1
Peverell Dr HLGN/YWD B28 ....162 D5
Peveril Gv WALM/CURD B76 ....63 E4
Peveril Rd
DUNHL/THL/PER WV6 ....34 D1
ETTPK/GDPK/PENN WV4 ....52 C5
Pevrn Wy GTB/HAM B43 ....73 H1
Pheasant St CBROM B36 ....114 A1
Pheasant Rd SMTHWKW B67 ....123 H2
Pheasant St BRLYHL DY5 ....119 E1
Philip Rd HALE B63 ....138 C1
TPTN/OCK DY4 ....86 B1
Philip Sidney Rd SPARK B11 ....144 D4
Philip St BILS/COS WV14 ....68 D2
Philip Victor Rd
BFLD/HDSWWD B20 ....89 H5
Phillimore Rd WASH/WDE B8 ....110 B4
Phillip Rd WSLW WS2 ....56 C2
Phillips Av SHHTH WV11 ....25 F1
Phillips St AST/WIT B6 ....109 E5
Phipson Rd MOS/BIL B13 ....144 D4
Phoenix Gn EDG B15 ....125 C5
Phoenix Pk
BLKHTH/ROWR B65 ....122 B3
Phoenix Ri DARL/WED WS10 ....55 F4
ERDW/GRVHL B23 ....75 H4
Phoenix Rd TPTN/OCK DY4 ....69 F5
WNSFLD WV11 ....38 D2
Phoenix St BKHL/PFLD WV2 ....52 B2
WBROM B70 ....86 D1
Piccadilly Ar CBHAM B2 ....3 F5
Piccadilly Cl
CHWD/FDBR/MGN B37 ....132 C3
Pickenham Rd
ALE/KHTH/YWD B14 ....178 C4
Pickering Cft RIDG/WDGT B32 ....157 G1
Pickering Rd WNSFLD WV11 ....24 D5
Pickersleigh Cl HALE B63 ....138 C4
Pickford St DIG/EDG B5 ....3 K6
Pickrell Rd BILS/COS WV14 ....68 C2
Pickwick Gv MOS/BIL B13 ....145 E5
Pickwick Pl BILS/COS WV14 ....54 A4
Picton Cft
CHWD/FDBR/MGN B37 ....132 D3
Picton Gv MOS/BIL B13 ....161 H5
Picturedrome Wy
DARL/WED WS10 ....55 F2
Piddock Rd SMTHWK B66 ....106 C4
Pierce Av HIA/OLT B92 ....147 E4
Piercy St WBROM B70 ....87 E5
Piers Rd HDSW B21 ....108 A2
Piggots Cft
CHWD/FDBR/MGN B37 ....131 H1
Pike Dr CHWD/FDBR/MGN B37 .132 C1
Pikehelve St TPTN/OCK DY4 ....70 C4
Pikehorne Cft CBROM B36 ....95 F4
Pike Rd WSLW WS2 ....41 E1
The Pikes RBRY B45 ....173 H5
Pikewater Rd BORD B9 ....111 E1
Pilkington Av
CSCFLD/WYGN B72 ....62 B5
Pilson Cl CBROM B36 ....112 B1
Pimbury Rd SHHTH WV12 ....26 B3
Pimlico Ct SEDG DY3 ....83 F3
Pimpernel Dr DSYBK/YTR WS5 ....57 G5
Pinbury Cft
CHWD/FDBR/MGN B37 ....132 B4
Pinchers Cl HAG/WOL DY9 ....184 C1
Pineapple Cl
ALE/KHTH/YWD B14 ....160 C4
Pineapple Gv BVILLE B30 ....160 C3
Pineapple Rd BVILLE B30 ....160 C3
Pine Av DARL/WED WS10 ....55 H5
SMTHWK B66 ....106 A2
Pine Cl BDMR/CCFT WV5 ....6 A5
KGSWFD DY6 ....91 H3
SOLH B91 ....

Pine Gn DUDN DY1 ....84 A1
Pine Gv ALE/KHTH/YWD B14 ....161 G5
Pinehurst Dr
HWK/WKHTH B38 ....176 D2
Pine Leigh FOAKS/STRLY B74 ....47 F4
Pineneedle Cft SHHTH WV12 ....40 C1
Pine Rd DUDN DY1 ....84 C1
OLDBY B69 ....105 C1
The Pines BDMR/CCFT WV5 ....35 H4
RBRY B45 ....174 A4
SHLY B90 ....194 D5
WSL WS1 ....5 F6
Pine St BLOX/PEL WS3 ....27 G1
Pinetree Dr FOAKS/STRLY B74 ....44 D4
Pineview NFLD/LBR B31 ....158 A4
Pine Wk CDSL WV8 ....10 B5
HAG/WOL DY9 ....136 B4
NFLD/LBR B31 ....175 H2
Pinewall Av HWK/WKHTH B38 ....176 D4
Pineways FOAKS/STRLY B74 ....46 A2
STRBR DY8 ....117 G2
Pineways Dr
DUNHL/THL/PER WV6 ....34 A4
The Pineways OLDBY B69 ....104 A4
Pinewood Cl BDMR/CCFT WV5 ....35 E5
BRWNH WS8 ....9 E2
DSYBK/YTR WS5 ....57 H4
KGSTG B44 ....75 E4
RBRY B45 ....173 F5
SHHTH WV12 ....26 B3
WMBN WV5 ....65 G5
Pinewood Gv RIDG/WDGT B32 .157 E2
Pinewood Cl SOLH B91 ....181 E3
Pine Woods RIDG/WDGT B32 ....140 A5
Pinewoods NFLD/LBR B31 ....158 B2
HALE B63 ....123 E5
Pinewoods Av HAG/WOL DY9 ....169 F1
Pinewoods Cl HAG/WOL DY9 ....169 F1
Pinfold BLOX/PEL WS3 ....27 G2
Pinfold Ct DARL/WED WS10 ....55 E3
Pinfold Crs
ETTPK/GDPK/PENN WV4 ....50 D2
Pinfold Gdns WNSFLD WV11 ....24 D5
Pinfold Gv
ETTPK/GDPK/PENN WV4 ....51 E3
Pinfold La ALDR WS9 ....59 E3
ETTPK/GDPK/PENN WV4 ....50 D3
Pinfold Rd SOLH B91 ....165 G5
Pinfold St BILS/COS WV14 ....54 A4
CBHAM B2 ....3 F5
DARL/WED WS10 ....55 E3
OLDBY B69 ....105 E1
Pingle Cl HWK/SAND B71 ....72 B2
Pinkney Pl LGLYGN/QTN B68 ....123 C1
Pinley Gv GTB/HAM B43 ....59 F5
Pinley Wy SOLH B91 ....181 G5
Pinner Gv RIDG/WDGT B32 ....141 E5
Pinson Rd WLNHL WV13 ....39 F4
Pintail Dr ERDW/GRVHL B23 ....92 A4
Pinto Cl LDYWD/EDGR B16 ....125 H2
Pinza Cft CBROM B36 ....111 H1
Pioli PI WSLW WS2 ....27 H5
Pioneer Wy CVALE B35 ....94 D4
Piper Cl DUNHL/THL/PER WV6 ....34 D1
Piper PI STRBR DY8 ....118 B4
Piper Rd BDMR/CCFT WV3 ....35 F5
Pipers Gn HLGN/YWD B28 ....162 D5
Pipers Rw WOLV WV1 ....7 H4
Pipes Meadow
BILS/COS WV14 ....54 A3
Pippin Av HALE B63 ....120 B5
Pirbright Cl BILS/COS WV14 ....54 A5
Pirrey Cl BILS/COS WV14 ....68 D2
Pitcairn Cl BVILLE B50 ....160 B4
Pitcairn Dr RMSLY B62 ....138 D1
Pitcairn Rd SMTHWKW B67 ....123 H5
Pitclose Rd NFLD/LBR B31 ....175 H4
Pitfield Rd STETCH B33 ....131 F3
Pitfield Rw DUDN DY1 ....84 B5
Pitfields Cl LGLYGN/QTN B68 ....123 C4
Pitfields Rd LGLYGN/QTN B68 ....123 E4
Pitfield St DUDN DY1 * 84 B5
Pithall Rd BKDE/SHDE B34 ....113 F4
Pit Leasow Cl BVILLE B30 ....160 B2
Pitman Rd RIDG/WDGT B32 ....140 C2
Pitmaston Rd HLGN/YWD B28 ....165 E4
Pitsford St WSNGN B18 ....2 A1
Pitt La HIA/OLT B92 ....149 H5
Pitts Farm Rd
ERDE/BCHGN B24 ....93 C3
Pitt St CBHAMNE B4 ....127 G1
Pixall Dr EDG B15 ....143 F1
Pixhall Wk CVALE B35 ....94 D3
Plainview Cl ALDR WS9 ....45 E3
Plaistow Av CBROM B36 ....111 G2
Plane Cv
CHWD/FDBR/MGN B37 ....132 B3
Planetary Rd WLNHL WV13 ....38 C2
Plane Tree Rd DSYBK/YTR WS5 ....57 H4
Planetree Rd FOAKS/STRLY B74 ....44 D5
Planet Rd BRLYHL DY5 ....101 F5
Plank La CSHL/WTROR B46 ....96 A4
Planks La WMBN WV5 ....64 D5
Plantation La SEDG DY3 ....81 F2
Plantation Rd DSYBK/YTR WS5 ....57 G4
The Plantation BRLYHL DY5 ....100 D2
Plants Brook Rd
WALM/CURD B76 ....78 B5
Plants Cl ERLD/BOLD B73 ....76 B2
Plants Gv ERDE/BCHGN B24 ....77 H5
Plants Hollow BRLYHL DY5 ....119 F3
Plant St CDYHTH B64 ....120 D3
STRBR DY8 ....118 A2
Plant Wy BLOX/PEL WS3 ....17 H3
Plascom Rd WOLV WV1 ....38 A4
Platts Crs STRBR DY8 ....118 A4
Platts Dr STRBR DY8 ....118 B4
Platts Rd STRBR DY8 ....118 A4
Platt St DARL/WED WS10 ....55 F3
Playdon Gv
ALE/KHTH/YWD B14 ....178 C2
Pleasant Cl KGSWFD DY6 ....99 G5
Pleasant St WBROM B70 ....87 G5
Pleasant Vw SEDG DY3 ....83 F4
Pleck Rd WSLW WS2 ....41 C5
Pleck Wk HWK/WKHTH B38 ....178 E4
Plestowes Cl SHLY B90 ....165 F5
Plimsoll Gv RIDG/WDGT B32 .140 C2
Plough Av RIDG/WDGT B32 ....140 C5

Plough & Harrow Rd
LDYWD/EDGR B16 ....125 H3
Ploughmans Pl MGN/WHC B75 ....47 H1
Ploughmans Wk KGSWFD DY6 ....99 E2
Ploverdale Crs KGSWFD DY6 ....100 C3
Plowden Rd STETCH B33 ....112 B5
Plume St AST/WIT B6 ....110 A1
Plumstead Rd KGSTG B44 ....75 C3
Plym Cl WNSFLD WV11 ....24 C5
Plymouth Cl NFLD/LBR B31 ....189 G1
Plymouth Rd BVILLE B30 ....160 B3
Pocklington Pl
NFLD/LBR B31 * 159 E4
Pointon Cl BILS/COS WV14 ....68 A1
Polden Cl HALE B63 ....154 C1
Polesworth Gv
BKDE/SHDE B34 ....112 C3
Pollard Rd ACGN B27 ....163 G1
The Pollards ERDW/GRVHL B23 .76 C3
Polo Flds HAG/WOL DY9 ....152 D1
Pomeroy Rd GTB/HAM B43 ....59 H4
RIDG/WDGT B32 ....157 C1
Pommel Cl DSYBK/YTR WS5 ....57 F4
Pond Crs BKHL/PFLD WV2 ....52 C1
Pond Gv BKHL/PFLD WV2 ....52 C1
Pond La BKHL/PFLD WV2 ....52 C1
Poole Crs BILS/COS WV14 ....68 D1
BRWNH WS8 ....8 C2
HRBN B17 ....142 A4
Poolehouse Rd GTB/HAM B43 ....58 C5
Pool End Cl DOR/KN B93 ....196 D2
Pooles La SHHTH WV12 ....26 C3
Poole St STRBR DY8 ....135 E3
Pool Farm Rd ACGN B27 ....163 C1
Poolfield Dr SOLH B91 ....181 F2
Pool Furlong HAG/WOL DY9 ....170 C4
Pool Gn ALDR WS9 ....30 A5
Pool Hall Crs BDMR/CCFT WV3 .34 D5
Pool Hall Rd BDMR/CCFT WV3 .34 C5
Pool Hayes La SHHTH WV12 ....25 C5
Pool House Rd WMBN WV5 ....64 B5
Pool La OLDBY B69 ....104 D5
Pool Meadow WALM/CURD B76 .78 C3
Pool Meadow Cl MOS/BIL B13 .162 A1
SOLH B91 ....182 D4
Pool Rd BRWNH WS8 ....9 E2
HALE B63 ....138 D4
SMTHWK B66 ....106 D4
WNSFLD WV11 ....24 D5
Pool St AST/WIT B6 ....109 F3
BKHL/PFLD WV2 ....52 B2
DUDN DY1 ....68 A5
WSL WS1 ....5 G5
Pool Vw RUSH/SHEL WS4 ....29 F5
Pope Rd WOLV WV10 ....24 A2
Popes La DUNHL/THL/PER WV6 .21 E4
HWK/WKHTH B38 ....176 B2
OLDBY B69 ....105 F3
Pope St SMTHWK B66 ....106 D2
WSNGN B18 ....2 A2
Poplar Ar SOLH B91 * 182 A1
Poplar Av ALE/KHTH/YWD B14 .161 E2
BHTH/HG B12 ....144 C3
BRWNH WS8 ....8 D5
CHWD/FDBR/MGN B37 .132 C4
DSYBK/YTR WS5 ....57 G4
ERDW/GRVHL B23 * 92 D2
HRBN B17 ....124 D2
LOZ/NWT B19 * 108 C1
MGN/WHC B75 ....63 F1
OLDBY B69 ....105 H1
TPTN/OCK DY4 ....85 H4
WBROM B70 ....88 A4
WNSFLD WV11 ....24 B3
WSLW WS2 ....40 C1
Poplar Cl OLDBY B69 ....86 A5
WSLW WS2 ....65 F5
WSLW WS2 ....40 C1
Poplar Crs DUDN DY1 ....84 B3
STRBR DY8 ....135 E4
Poplar Dr AST/WIT B6 ....91 F1
WASH/WDE B8 ....110 B3
Poplar Gn DUDN DY1 ....68 A5
Poplar Gv LOZ/NWT B19 * 108 C1
SMTHWK B66 ....124 D1
Poplar La RMSLY B62 ....172 C2
Poplar Ri ALDR WS9 ....44 B4
OLDBY B69 ....104 A1
PBAR/PBCH B42 ....91 E1
Poplar Rd ALE/KHTH/YWD B14 .161 E2
BDMR/CCFT WV3 ....51 C2
BILS/COS WV14 ....54 B1
BRWNH WS8 ....9 G4
DARL/WED WS10 ....55 C3
DSYBK/YTR WS5 ....57 G4
KGSWFD DY6 ....100 A4
OLDBY B69 ....105 H1
SMTHWK B66 ....124 C5
SOLH B91 ....181 H2
SPARK B11 ....144 D2
STRBR DY8 ....135 E4
Poplars Dr CBROM B36 ....111 D1
CDSL WV8 ....10 B5
The Poplars
LDYWD/EDGR B16 * 125 H1
STRBR DY8 ....118 B2
Poplar St BKHL/PFLD WV2 ....52 B2
SMTHWK B66 ....107 E4
Poplarwoods RIDG/WDGT B32 .140 B5
Poppy Dr DSYBK/YTR WS5 ....57 F4
Poppy Gv WASH/WDE B8 ....110 D5
Poppy La ERDE/BCHGN B24 ....93 C1
Poppymead ERDW/GRVHL B23 .75 H3
Porchester Cl ALDR WS9 ....19 C5
Porchester Dr LOZ/NWT B19 ....108 D1
Porlock Crs NFLD/LBR B31 ....174 D2
Porlock Rd STRBR DY8 ....135 C1
Portal Rd WSLW WS2 ....40 D5
Portchester Dr WNSFLD WV11 .24 D5
Porters Cft HRBN B17 ....124 A4
Porters Dr
ALE/KHTH/YWD B14 ....177 G1
Porters Fld DUDS DY2 ....84 D3
Portersfield Rd CDYHTH B64 ....120 C4
Portershill Dr SHLY B90 ....180 C5
Porter St DUDS DY2 ....84 D5
Porter St South DUDS DY2 ....84 D5
Porters Wy BORD B9 ....128 C2

Portfield Dr TPTN/OCK DY4 ....85 G3
Portfield Gv ERDW/GRVHL B23 .77 E5
Porthkerry Gv SEDG DY3 ....66 A4
Port Hope Rd SPARK B11 ....127 C5
Porthouse Gv BILS/COS WV14 * .53 F5
Portia Av SHLY B90 ....180 B3
Portland Av ALDR WS9 ....30 B5
Portland Crs HAG/WOL DY9 ....152 D1
Portland Dr HAG/WOL DY9 ....152 D1
OLDBY B69 ....86 B5
Portland Pl BILS/COS WV14 ....68 C5
Portland Rd ALDR WS9 ....30 B4
LDYWD/EDGR B16 ....125 E2
Portland St AST/WIT B6 ....109 G2
WSLW WS2 ....28 A4
Portland Ter WSNGN B18 ....108 A4
Port La COVEN WV9 ....10 D1
Portman Rd MOS/BIL B13 ....161 H1
Portobello Cl WLNHL WV13 ....38 D4
Portobello Rd WBROM B70 ....70 D3
Portrush Av HWK/WKHTH B38 .176 A4
Portrush Rd
DUNHL/THL/PER WV6 ....21 C5
Portsdown Cl WOLV WV10 ....23 H3
Portsdown Rd HALE B63 ....154 D1
Portsea St BLOX/PEL WS3 ....27 E3
Portswood Cl COVEN WV9 ....22 B1
Portway Cl KGSWFD DY6 ....100 A4
SOLH B91 ....181 E4
Portway HI OLDBY B69 ....86 B3
Portway Rd BILS/COS WV14 ....54 A1
BLKHTH/ROWR B65 ....103 H5
DARL/WED WS10 ....70 C1
OLDBY B69 ....104 C2
The Portway KGSWFD DY6 ....100 A4
Posey Cl HDSW B21 ....89 E3
Poston Cft
ALE/KHTH/YWD B14 ....177 H1
Potter Cl ERDW/GRVHL B23 ....76 B5
Potters La AST/WIT B6 ....109 E2
DARL/WED WS10 ....70 C1
Potterton Wy SMTHWK B66 ....106 A5
Pottery Rd LGLYGN/QTN B68 .123 H5
Pouk HIll Cl WSLW WS2 ....41 E2
Poultney St WBROM B70 ....87 E4
Poulton Cl MOS/BIL B13 ....144 C5
Pound Cl LGLYGN/QTN B68 ....122 D1
Pound La CSHL/WTROR B46 ....115 C5
RIDG/WDGT B32 ....158 D1
Poundley Cl CBROM B36 ....113 E1
Pound Rd ALE/KHTH/YWD B14 .178 A4
DARL/WED WS10 ....56 A5
LGLYGN/QTN B68 ....122 D1
Pountney St BKHL/PFLD WV2 ....7 F6
Powell Av RIDG/WDGT B32 ....140 A1
Powell Pl BILS/COS WV14 ....54 A5
TPTN/OCK DY4 ....86 A1
Powell Rd
DUNHL/THL/PER WV6 * 21 G5
Powell St CBHAMNE B4 ....3 G2
Powells of CSCFLD/WYGN B72 .71 G1
Powell St HALE B63 ....138 D4
WSNGN B18 ....125 G2
WSNGN B18 ....2 A2
Power Crs
LDYWD/EDGR B16 * 126 A3
Power Wy TPTN/OCK DY4 ....70 D5
Powick Pl LOZ/NWT B19 * 108 C2
Powick Rd ERDW/GRVHL B23 .92 E5
Powis Av TPTN/OCK DY4 ....69 H4
Powke La CDYHTH B64 ....121 F1
Powlers Cl HAG/WOL DY9 ....136 C5
Powlett St BKHL/PFLD WV2 ....7 G6
Poxon Rd ALDR WS9 ....19 C3
The Poynings
DUNHL/THL/PER WV6 ....21 C5
The Precinct SHHTH WV12 * 25 H5
Premier Ct EVILLE B30 ....177 G2
Premier St VAUX/NECH B7 ....110 B1
Prescot Rd HAG/WOL DY9 ....136 A4
Prestbury Rd AST/WIT B6 ....109 E1
Presthope Rd SLYOAK B29 ....158 D5
Preston Av WALM/CURD B76 ....63 G5
Preston Rd
LGN/SDN/BHAMAIR B26 ....146 D1
WSNGN B18 ....107 G4
Prestons Rw BILS/COS WV14 * .53 E5
Prestwick Cl MGN/WHC B75 ....62 C1
Prestwick Rd CVALE B35 ....94 D2
KGSWFD DY6 ....100 A1
Prestwood Av WNSFLD WV11 .24 D2
Prestwood Dr KINVER DY7 ....116 D4
Prestwood Rd SLYOAK B29 ....158 D3
WNSFLD WV11 ....24 A5
Prestwood Rd West
WNSFLD WV11 ....24 B4
Pretoria Rd BORD B9 ....128 C1
Priam Gv BLOX/PEL WS3 ....18 B2
Price Crs BILS/COS WV14 ....53 H1
Price Rd DARL/WED WS10 ....56 C5
HAG/WOL DY9 ....137 E1
Price St BILS/COS WV14 ....68 B3
CBHAMNE B4 ....3 C3
DUDS DY2 ....105 E1
SMTHWK B66 ....106 D4
WBROM B70 ....87 G5
Priestfield Cl KGSTG B44 ....74 D1
Priestfield St BILS/COS WV14 ....53 F1
Priestland Rd BKDE/SHDE B34 .112 D2
Priestley Cl
BFLD/HDSWWD B20 ....90 A5
HALE B63 ....137 F1
Priestley Rd SPARK B11 ....127 C5
WSLW WS2 ....27 F5
Priest St CDYHTH B64 ....121 F3
Primley Av CBROM B36 ....111 H2
WSLW WS2 ....42 A1
Primley Cl WSLW WS2 ....41 F3
Primrose Av SPARK B11 ....145 E2
TPTN/OCK DY4 ....69 G1
WOLV WV10 ....12 D4
Primrose Bank
LGLYGN/QTN B68 ....105 F5
Primrose Cl BLOX/PEL WS3 ....18 A2
CDYHTH B64 ....120 D5
Primrose Crs DUDN DY1 ....84 C2
Primrose Cft ERDW/GRVHL B23 .76 B5
HLGN/YWD B28 ....162 D5
Primrose Gdns CDSL WV8 ....10 C4
HWK/WKHTH B38 ....176 D4
Primrose HI HWK/WKHTH B38 .176 D4
SMTHWKW B67 ....105 H5

STRBR DY8 ....118 A2
WOLV WV10 ....23 H2
Primrose La HLGN/YWD B28 ....162 D5
WOLV WV10 ....23 H2
Primrose Pk BRLYHL DY5 ....101 E2
Primrose Rd DUDS DY2 ....102 C5
The Primroses DSYBK/YTR WS5 .57 H4
Primrose Woods
RIDG/WDGT B32 ....140 B5
Primsland Cl SHLY B90 ....196 A1
Prince Albert St BORD B9 ....128 B3
Prince Andrew Crs RBRY B45 .173 G3
Prince Charles Cl RBRY B45 ....173 G3
Prince Charles Rd
BILS/COS WV14 ....54 B5
Prince Edward Dr RBRY B45 .173 G3
Prince George Rd
DARL/WED WS10 ....56 A3
Prince of Wales La
ALE/KHTH/YWD B14 ....179 E3
Princep Cl GTB/HAM B43 ....59 H4
Prince Philip Cl RBRY B45 ....173 G3
Prince Rd BVILLE B30 ....176 D2
Prince's Av WSL WS1 ....5 J6
Princes Dr CDSL WV8 ....10 C4
Princes Gdns CDSL WV8 ....10 B4
Princes Ga SOLH B91 ....181 H1
WBROM B70 ....88 A4
Prince's Rd OLDBY B69 ....85 G4
STRBR DY8 ....134 C5
Princess Alice Dr
SCFLD/BOLD B73 ....76 B1
Princess Aly WOLV WV1 ....7 G4
Princess Anne Rd
BILS/COS WV14 ....54 B5
WSLW WS2 ....40 D2
Princess Crs HALE B63 ....138 A1
Princess Rd HWK/SAND B71 ....71 H4
LGLYGN/QTN B68 ....123 H2
Princes Rd DIG/EDG B5 ....144 A1
Princess Sq BILS/COS WV14 * .68 C1
Princess Wy DARL/WED WS10 .40 A5
Prince St ALDR WS9 ....19 F5
CDYHTH B64 ....120 D3
DUDS DY2 ....84 D5
WSLW WS2 ....41 G5
Prince's Wy SOLH B91 ....181 H2
Princethorpe Cl
BKDE/SHDE B34 ....113 F2
SHLY B90 ....180 A3
Princethorpe Rd SLYOAK B29 .158 D1
Prince Thorpe Rd WLNHL WV13 .39 H5
Princeton Gdns COVEN WV9 ....11 H1
Prince William Cl
ERDW/GRVHL B23 ....92 B4
Princip St CBHAMNE B4 ....3 G2
Printing House St CBHAMNE B4 .3 G3
Priors MI SEDG DY3 ....
Priors Wy ERDW/GRVHL B23 ....76 A5
Priory Av SLYOAK B29 ....143 F5
Priory Chambers DUDN DY1 * .84 C5
Priory Cl CSHL/WTROR B46 ....115 G4
DUDN DY1 ....84 C5
SMTHWK B66 ....107 E5
WBROM B70 ....88 B4
Priory Dr LGLYGN/QTN B68 ....105 G4
Priory Field Cl BILS/COS WV14 .67 H2
Priory Gdns HLGN/YWD B28 ....179 F1
Priorygate Wy BORD B9 ....111 C5
Priory La SEDG DY3 ....67 F4
The Priory Queensway
CBHAMNE B4 ....3 H4
Priory Rd ALE/KHTH/YWD B14 .160 C3
AST/WIT B6 ....109 H1
DUDN DY1 ....84 C4
EDG B15 ....143 F1
HLGN/YWD B28 ....179 F1
RMSLY B62 ....
STRBR DY8 ....135 H4
Priory Sq CBHAMNE B4 ....3 H3
Priory St DUDN DY1 ....84 C5
The Priory SEDG DY3 ....67 F3
Pritchard Av WNSFLD WV11 ....25 E4
Pritchard Cl SMTHWK B66 ....106 D4
Pritchard St BRLYHL DY5 ....118 D1
DARL/WED WS10 ....55 H1
Pritchatts Rd EDG B15 ....142 D2
Pritchett Av
ETTPK/GDPK/PENN WV4 ....52 D5
Pritchett Rd NFLD/LBR B31 ....190 B1
Pritchett St AST/WIT B6 ....109 E4
Private Wy RBRY B45 ....188 C4
Privet Cl KGSTG B44 ....60 A5
Probert Rd WOLV WV10 ....22 D1
Proctor St VAUX/NECH B7 ....109 G4
Proffitt Cl WSLW WS2 ....42 A1
Proffitt St WSLW WS2 ....42 A1
Prole St WOLV WV10 ....37 G1
The Promenade BRLYHL DY5 .119 F2
Prospect Gdns STRBR DY8 ....135 G3
Prospect Hl STRBR DY8 ....135 G3
Prospect La SOLH B91 ....163 H5
Prospect Rd BHTH/HG B12 * .144 B2
Prospect Rd MOS/BIL B13 ....161 F1
RMSLY B62 ....139 E2
SEDG DY3 ....82 D4
Prospect Rw DUDS DY2 ....102 C2
STRBR DY8 ....135 G4
Prospect St BILS/COS WV14 ....54 A2
TPTN/OCK DY4 ....70 A3
Prosper Meadow
KGSWFD DY6 ....100 B2
Prosperity Cl RBRY B45 ....174 A3
Prosser St BILS/COS WV14 ....53 G5
WOLV WV10 ....23 C5
Prossers Wk
CSHL/WTROR B46 ....115 F2
Proud's La BILS/COS WV14 ....53 H1
Provence Cl WOLV WV10 ....37 H1
Providence Cl BLOX/PEL WS3 .27 G3
Providence Dr HAG/WOL DY9 .136 C1
Providence La BLOX/PEL WS3 .27 G3
Providence Rw
BILS/COS WV14 ....68 B3
Providence St CDYHTH B64 ....120 D3
HAG/WOL DY9 ....136 C1
TPTN/OCK DY4 ....86 A1

Providence Ter
DARL/WED WS10 * ...55 G2
Pruden Av
ETTPK/GDPK/PENN WV4...52 D5
Pryor Rd *LGLYGN/QTN* B68...123 G1
Pudsey Dr *MGN/WHC* B75...47 G2
Pugh Crs *WSLW* WS2...40 C3
Pugh Rd *AST/WIT* B6...109 G2
BILS/COS WV14...67 H1
Pugin Cl *DUNHL/THL/PER* WV6...34 B2
Pugin Gdns *ERDW/GRVHL* B23...76 B3
Pumphouse Wy *OLDBY* B69...104 D5
Pump St *BKHL/PFLD* WV2...53 E1
Puppy Gn *TPTN/OCK* DY4...85 H1
Purbeck Cl *HALE* B63...154 D1
Purbeck Cft *RIDG/WDGT* B32...141 F2
Purbrook Rd *WOLV* WV1...38 A5
Purcell Rd *WOLVN* WV10...23 G2
Purdy Rd *BILS/COS* WV14...69 E2
Purefoy Rd *MOS/BIL* B13...162 A5
Purley Gv *ERDW/GRVHL* B23...91 G1
Purlin Whf *DUDS* DY2...121 E1
Purnells Wy *DOR/KN* B93...197 E3
Purslet Rd *WOLV* WV1...38 A4
Purslow Gv *NFLD/LBR* B31...175 G4
Putney Av *BFLD/HDSWWD* B20...90 C5
Putney La *RMSLY* B62...172 D3
Putney Rd *BFLD/HDSWWD* B20...90 C5
Pype Hayes Cl
ERDE/BCHGN B24...93 H2
Pype Hayes Rd
ERDE/BCHGN B24...93 H2
Pytman Dr *WALM/CURD* B76...78 C4

Q

The Quadrangle *BVILLE* B30 *...159 H4
The Quadrant *SEDG* DY3...67 F2
Quadrille Lawns *COVEN* WV9...11 H5
Quail Gn *DUNHL/THL/PER* WV6...34 D3
Qualcast Rd *WOLV* WV1...37 H3
Quantock Cl *BRWNH* WS8...19 G2
HALE B63...137 H5
RBRY B45...174 B3
Quantock Rd *STRBR* DY8...135 H1
Quantry La *HAG/WOL* DY9...186 A1
Quarrington Gv
ALE/KHTH/YWD B14...178 C2
Quarry Brow *SEDG* DY3...83 G1
Quarry Hl *HALE* B63...138 B5
Quarry House Cl *RBRY* B45...173 H4
Quarry La *HALE* B63...138 B5
NFLD/LBR B31...175 F2
Quarry Park Rd *STRBR* DY8...152 C2
Quarry Ri *OLDBY* B69...103 H1
Quarry Rd *DUDS* DY2...120 B2
SLYOAK B29...158 B1
Quarry Wk *RBRY* B45...188 A1
Quasar Centre *WSL* WS1...4 D3
Quayle Gv *STRBR* DY8...117 H1
Quayside *WSNGN* B18...108 A4
Quayside Cl *OLDBY* B69...104 C1
Quayside Dr *WSLW* WS2...4 A6
Queen Eleanors Dr
DOR/KN B93...183 F5
Queen Elizabeth Av *WSLW* WS2...40 D3
Queen Elizabeth Rd *RBRY* B45...173 G3
Queen Mary St *WSL* WS1...56 D2
Queens Ar *WOLV* WV1...7 F4
Queens Av
ALE/KHTH/YWD B14 *...161 E2
OLDBY B69...85 H5
SHLY B90...180 B3
WSNGN B18 *...107 H3
Queensbridge Rd *MOS/BIL* B13...143 H5
Queens Cl *ERDE/BCHGN* B24...92 D4
SMTHWKW B67...106 C4
Queens Ct *RIDG/WDGT* B32...141 G2
SOLH B91 *...182 C1
Queens Crs *BILS/COS* WV14...68 A2
STRBR DY8...118 C5
Queen's Cross *DUDN* DY1...102 B1
Queens Dr *BLKHTH/ROWR* B65...104 B5
BVILLE B30...177 E1
DIG/EDG B5...3 G6
Queens Gdns *BILS/COS* WV14...53 H1
CDSL WV8...10 B4
DUDS DY2...102 B5
ERDW/GRVHL B23...75 H4
Queens Head Rd *HDSW* B21...107 G2
Queens Hl *HAG/WOL* DY9...184 B1
Queens Hospital Cl *EDG* B15...126 C3
Queen's Lea *SHHTH* WV12...26 A5
Queens Md *SMTHWKW* B67 *...106 C4
Queen's Park Rd
RIDG/WDGT B32...141 F1
Queen Sq *WOLV* WV1...7 F4
Queen's Ride *DIG/EDG* B5...143 G3
Queens Rd *AST/WIT* B6...109 G1
DSYBK/YTR WS5...57 H2
ERDW/GRVHL B23...92 A3
LGN/SDN/BHAMAIR B26...130 B3
RUSH/SHEL WS4...29 E3
SEDG DY3...67 G3
SMTHWKW B67...105 H5
STRBR DY8...135 F1
Queens Tower
VAUX/NECH B7 *...109 H4
Queen St *ALDR* WS9...19 F5
BHTH/HG B12...144 D2
BILS/COS WV14...54 A3
BRLYHL DY5...120 A4
CSCFLD/WYGN B72...62 B4
HALE B63...138 C3
KGSWFD DY6...99 H2
OLDBY B69...105 E1
STRBR DY8...135 F1
TPTN/OCK DY4...69 F3
WBROM B70...87 H3
WOLV WV1...7 G4
WSLW WS2...4 B5
Queensway *FOAKS/STRLY* B74...45 G5
HAG/WOL DY9...136 C5
HALE B63...138 D4
LGLYGN/QTN B68...123 F4
Queensway Cl
LGLYGN/QTN B68...123 F4
Queensway Ml *HALE* B63 *...138 D4
Queenswood Rd
MGN/WHC B75...47 F4
MOS/BIL B13...144 C3
Quenby Dr *DUDN* DY1...84 A3
Quendale *WMBN* WV5...64 C5
Quentin Dr *DUDN* DY1...101 H2
Queslade Cl *GTB/HAM* B43...73 H2
Queslett Rd *GTB/HAM* B43...74 B2
Queslett Rd East
FOAKS/STRLY B74...60 A3
Quicksand La *ALDR* WS9...43 H1
Quigley Av *BORD* B9...127 H2
Quillets Rd *STRBR* DY8...117 G1
Quilter Cl *BILS/COS* WV14...68 A3
WSLW WS2...40 D2
Quilter Rd *ERDE/BCHGN* B24...93 F4
Quincey Dr *ERDE/BCHGN* B24...93 G3
Quincy Ri *BRLYHL* DY5...119 E5
Quinton Cl *HIA/OLT* B92...148 B3
Quinton Expy
RIDG/WDGT B32...140 B3
Quinton La *RIDG/WDGT* B32...140 D1
Quinton Rd *HRBN* B17...141 H4
Quinton Rd West *RIDG/WDGT* B32...140 B2
Quorn Crs *STRBR* DY8...117 G1
Quorn Gv *ERDE/BCHGN* B24...93 F4

R

Rabone La *SMTHWK* B66...106 D3
Raby Cl *OLDBY* B69...103 F1
Raby St *BKHL/PFLD* WV2...7 H7
Racecourse La *STRBR* DY8...152 A1
Racecourse Rd
DUNHL/THL/PER WV6...22 C5
Racemeadow Crs *DUDS* DY2...120 C3
Rachael Gdns *DARL/WED* WS10...56 C4
Rachel Cl *TPTN/OCK* DY4...70 A2
Rachel Gdns *SLYOAK* B29...142 B5
Radbourn Dr *FOAKS/STRLY* B74...62 D2
Radbourne Dr *HALE* B63...120 A5
Radbourne Rd *SHLY* B90...180 D2
Radcliffe Dr *RMSLY* B62...139 G1
Raddens Rd *RMSLY* B62...139 H4
Raddington Dr *HIA/OLT* B92...163 H2
Raddlebarn Farm Dr
SLYOAK B29...159 H1
Raddlebarn Rd *SLYOAK* B29...159 H1
Radford Cl *DSYBK/YTR* WS5...57 G5
Radford Dr *RUSH/SHEL* WS4...18 C5
Radford Ri *SOLH* B91...165 G5
Radford Rd *SLYOAK* B29...158 C3
Radley Gv *SLYOAK* B29...141 G5
Radley Rd *HAG/WOL* DY9...136 D3
RUSH/SHEL WS4...29 E4
The Radleys *STETCH* B33...131 G4
Radlow Crs
CHWD/FDBR/MGN B37...132 B4
Radnor Cl *RBRY* B45...174 B3
Radnor Cft *DSYBK/YTR* WS5...58 A5
Radnor Gn *HHTH/SAND* B71...71 G4
Radnor Rd
BFLD/HDSWWD B20...108 B1
LGLYGN/QTN B68...123 F5
SEDG DY3...67 E3
Radnor St *WSNGN* B18...107 H3
Radstock Av *CBROM* B36...111 G2
Radstock Rd *SHHTH* WV12...26 A1
Radway Rd *SHLY* B90...195 E1
Raeburn Rd *GTB/HAM* B43...59 G4
Raford Rd *ERDW/GRVHL* B23...76 B5
Ragees Rd *KGSWFD* DY6...118 B1
Raglan Av
DUNHL/THL/PER WV6...34 D2
SMTHWK B66...107 E5
Raglan Cl *ALDR* WS9...45 F2
SEDG DY3...66 D4
Raglan Rd *DIG/EDG* B5...143 H1
SMTHWK B66...107 E5
Raglan St *BDMR/CCFT* WV3...6 D4
BRLYHL DY5...101 E5
Raglan Wy
CHWD/FDBR/MGN B37...132 D2
Ragley Cl *BLOX/PEL* WS3...27 E1
DOR/KN B93...197 F1
Ragley Dr *GTB/HAM* B43...73 F1
LGN/SDN/BHAMAIR B26...148 A1
WLNHL WV13...39 F5
Ragnall Av *STETCH* B33...131 F5
Railswood Dr *BLOX/PEL* WS3...18 A4
Railway Dr *BILS/COS* WV14...54 A3
WOLV WV1...7 H3
Railway Rd
BFLD/HDSWWD B20...91 F4
SCFLD/BOLD B73...62 B3
Railwayside Cl *SMTHWK* B66...106 A2
Railway St *BILS/COS* WV14...54 A3
TPTN/OCK DY4...86 A1
WBROM B70...87 F2
WOLV WV1...7 H3
Railway Ter *DARL/WED* WS10...70 D1
PBAR/PBCH B42 *...73 H5
VAUX/NECH B7...109 H2
Railwharf Sidings *DUDS* DY2...102 D5
Rainbow St *BILS/COS* WV14...53 H5
BKHL/PFLD WV2...52 B1
Rainham Cl *TPTN/OCK* DY4...84 D1
Rainsbrook Dr *SHLY* B90...195 F2
Rake Wy *EDG* B15...2 B7
Raleigh Cl *HDSW* B21...88 D5
Raleigh Cft *GTB/HAM* B43...58 C5
Raleigh Rd *BILS/COS* WV14...54 B5
BORD B9...128 B2
Raleigh St *HHTH/SAND* B71...87 G2
WSLW WS2...41 G3
Ralph Rd *SHLY* B90...180 D1
WASH/WDE B8...110 B5
Ralphs Meadow
RIDG/WDGT B32...140 D5
Ralston Cl *BLOX/PEL* WS3...16 C3
Ramp Rd
CHWD/FDBR/MGN B37...149 G2
Ramsay Cl *HHTH/SAND* B71...72 B3
Ramsay Rd *LGLYGN/QTN* B68...123 G4
TPTN/OCK DY4...69 E4
WSLW WS2...27 E5
Ramsden Cl *SLYOAK* B29...158 D3
Ramsey Cl *RBRY* B45...173 G4
Ramsey Rd *VAUX/NECH* B7...110 A2
Randall Cl *KGSWFD* DY6...100 B5
Randle Dr *MGN/WHC* B75...47 G2
Randle Rd *HAG/WOL* DY9...136 A3
Randwick Gv *KGSTG* B44...74 D2
Ranelagh Rd *BKHL/PFLD* WV2...52 A2
Rangeview Cl
FOAKS/STRLY B74...60 B2
Rangeways Rd *KGSWFD* DY6...118 B1
Rangoon Rd *HIA/OLT* B92...148 C3
Ranleigh Av *KGSWFD* DY6...100 B5
Rann Cl *LDYWD/EDGR* B16...126 A3
Rannoch Cl *BRLYHL* DY5...118 D4
Ranscombe Dr *SEDG* DY3...83 E4
Ransom Rd *ERDW/GRVHL* B23...92 A2
Ranworth Ri
ETTPK/GDPK/PENN WV4...52 B4
Ratcliffe Av *BVILLE* B30...177 H2
Ratcliffe Cl *SEDG* DY3...67 H4
Ratcliffe Dr *WLNHL* WV13...39 G5
Ratcliffe Rd *SOLH* B91...165 E3
WNSFLD WV11...25 G4
Ratcliff Wk *OLDBY* B69 *...104 D2
Ratcliff Wy *TPTN/OCK* DY4...70 A5
Rathbone Cl *BILS/COS* WV14...53 H3
DIG/EDG B5...127 E5
Rathbone Rd *SMTHWKW* B67...124 B2
Rathlin Cl *COVEN* WV9...12 A4
Rathlin Cft *CBROM* B36...114 B4
Rathmore Cl *STRBR* DY8...135 E5
Rathwell Cl *COVEN* WV9...12 A5
Rattle Cft *STETCH* B33...130 A1
Ravenall Cl *BKDE/SHDE* B34...112 D2
Raven Crs *WNSFLD* WV11...25 F2
Ravenfield Cl *WASH/WDE* B8...110 D4
Ravenhayes La
RIDG/WDGT B32...157 E4
Raven Hays Rd *NFLD/LBR* B31...174 C3
Ravenhill Dr *CDSL* WV8...10 C4
Ravenhurst Dr *GTB/HAM* B43...58 C5
Ravenhurst Ms
ERDW/GRVHL B23...92 C3
Ravenhurst Rd *HRBN* B17...125 E5
Ravenhurst St *BHTH/HG* B12...127 G4
Raven Rd *DSYBK/YTR* WS5...57 H2
Ravensbourne Gv
WLNHL WV13...40 A3
Ravenscroft *STRBR* DY8...134 C1
Ravenscroft Rd *HIA/OLT* B92...164 C2
SHHTH WV12...25 H5
Ravensdale Cl *DSYBK/YTR* WS5...57 H1
Ravensdale Gdns
DSYBK/YTR WS5...57 H2
Ravensdale Rd *SMHTH* B10...128 D5
Ravenshaw La *SOLH* B91...183 E1
Ravenshaw Rd
LDYWD/EDGR B16...125 E2
Ravenshaw Wy *DOR/KN* B93...183 E3
Ravenshill Rd
ALE/KHTH/YWD B14...179 E1
Ravensholme
DUNHL/THL/PER WV6...34 D3
Ravensitch Wk *BRLYHL* DY5...119 G3
Ravenswood *EDG* B15...125 G4
Ravenswood Cl
FOAKS/STRLY B74...47 F5
Ravenswood Dr *SOLH* B91...181 E4
Ravenswood Hl
CSHL/WTROR B46...115 F2
Rawdon Gv *KGSTG* B44...75 H3
Rawlings Rd *SMTHWKW* B67...124 C2
Rawlins Cft *CVALE* B35...94 D3
Rawlins St *LDYWD/EDGR* B16...126 A3
Raybolds Bridge Rd *WSLW* WS2...41 G1
Raybolds Bridge St *WSLW* WS2...41 G1
Raybon Cft *RBRY* B45 *...188 A2
Raybould's Fold *DUDS* DY2...102 C4
Rayford Dr *HHTH/SAND* B71...72 B1
Ray Hall La *GTB/HAM* B43...72 D3
Rayleigh Rd *BDMR/CCFT* WV3...36 C5
Raymond Av *PBAR/PBCH* B42...74 B5
Raymond Cl *WSLW* WS2...27 H5
Raymond Gdns *WNSFLD* WV11...25 E5
Raymond Rd *WASH/WDE* B8...110 C5
Raymont Gv *GTB/HAM* B43...59 F4
Rayners Cft
LGN/SDN/BHAMAIR B26...130 B2
Raynor Rd *WOLVN* WV10...23 H4
Rea Av *RBRY* B45...173 G5
Reabrook Rd *NFLD/LBR* B31...175 F5
Rea Cl *NFLD/LBR* B31...189 G1
Readers Wk *GTB/HAM* B43...73 H2
Rea Fordway *RBRY* B45...173 H4
Reansway Sq
DUNHL/THL/PER WV6...36 C1
Reapers Cl *SHHTH* WV12...26 B5
Reaside Crs
ALE/KHTH/YWD B14...160 B5
Reaside Cft *BHTH/HG* B12 *...144 A1
Reaside Dr *RBRY* B45...174 B5
Rea St *DIG/EDG* B5...127 F3
Rea St South *DIG/EDG* B5...127 E4
Rea Ter *DIG/EDG* B5...3 K6
Rea Valley Dr *NFLD/LBR* B31...175 H3
Reaview Dr *SLYOAK* B29...143 F5
Reaymer Cl *WSLW* WS2...27 F4
Reay Nadin Dr
SCFLD/BOLD B73...60 D4
Rebecca Dr *SLYOAK* B29...142 C5
Rebecca Gdns
ETTPK/GDPK/PENN WV4...51 F4
Recreation St *DUDS* DY2...102 D4
Rectory Av *DARL/WED* WS10...55 F2
Rectory Cl *STRBR* DY8...135 H4
Rectory Gdns *SOLH* B91...182 B2
STRBR DY8...135 H4
Rectory Gv *WSNGN* B18...107 G3
Rectory La *CBROM* B36...112 C1
Rectory Park Av
MGN/WHC B75...63 E4
Rectory Park Cl *MGN/WHC* B75...63 E4
Rectory Park Rd
LGN/SDN/BHAMAIR B26...148 A2
Rectory Rd *MGN/WHC* B75...62 C3
NFLD/LBR B31...175 H2
SOLH B91...182 A2
STRBR DY8...135 H4
Rectory St *STRBR* DY8...117 H1
Redacre Rd *SCFLD/BOLD* B73...76 D1
Redacres *DUNHL/THL/PER* WV6...22 A4
Redbank Av *ERDW/GRVHL* B23...92 A3
Redbourn Rd *BLOX/PEL* WS3...16 C3
Red Brick Cl *CDYHTH* B64...120 D5
Redbrook Covert
HWK/WKHTH B38...190 C1
Red Brook Rd *WSLW* WS2...27 E5
Redbrooks Cl *SOLH* B91...181 G4
Redburn Dr
ALE/KHTH/YWD B14...177 H3
Redcar Cft *CBROM* B36...111 G1
Redcar Rd *WOLVN* WV10...12 D3
Redcliffe Dr *WMBN* WV5...65 F5
Redcotts Cl *WOLVN* WV10...24 A3
Redcroft Dr *ERDE/BCHGN* B24...93 E5
Redcroft Rd *DUDS* DY2...103 E3
Reddal Hill Rd *CDYHTH* B64...121 E3
Reddicap Heath Rd
MGN/WHC B75...63 F4
Reddicap Hl *WALM/CURD* B76...62 D4
Reddicroft *SCFLD/BOLD* B73...62 C3
Reddings La *HLGN/YWD* B28...145 G5
Reddings Rd *MOS/BIL* B13...143 H5
The Reddings *HLYWD* B47...192 C3
Redditch Rd *ALVE* B48...189 H5
HWK/WKHTH B38...176 C4
NFLD/LBR B31...190 A2
Redfern Cl *HIA/OLT* B92...164 D1
Redfern Park Wy *SPARK* B11...146 A2
Redfern Rd *SPARK* B11...146 A2
Redfly La *BRLYHL* DY5...101 E3
Redford Cl *MOS/BIL* B13...144 D5
Redgate Cl *HWK/WKHTH* B38...176 B3
Redhall Rd *RIDG/WDGT* B32...124 A5
SEDG DY3...83 E4
Red Hl *STRBR* DY8...135 H3
Redhill Av *WMBN* WV5...65 E5
Redhill Cl *STRBR* DY8...135 H3
Redhill Gdns *NFLD/LBR* B31...190 A1
Red Hill Gv *HWK/WKHTH* B38...190 D1
Redhill La *BRGRVW* B61...187 E3
Red Hill Pl *RMSLY* B62...155 G3
Redhill Rd *HWK/WKHTH* B38...190 B1
NFLD/LBR B31...175 H5
YDLY B25...146 A1
Red Hill St *WOLV* WV1...7 F1
Red House Av *DARL/WED* WS10...56 B5
Redhouse Cl *DOR/KN* B93...196 C3
Red House La *ALDR* WS9...29 G5
Red House Park Rd
GTB/HAM B43...73 G1
Redhouse Rd
DUNHL/THL/PER WV6...21 F5
Red House Rd *STETCH* B33...130 A1
Redhouse St *WSL* WS1...57 E1
Redhurst Dr *WOLVN* WV10...12 B4
Redlake Dr *HAG/WOL* DY9...152 D2
Redlake Rd *HAG/WOL* DY9...152 D1
Redlands Cl *SOLH* B91...165 F5
Redlands Rd *SOLH* B91...165 E5
Redlands Wy *FOAKS/STRLY* B74...45 G4
Red La *SEDG* DY3...66 D3
WNSFLD WV11...15 G5
Red Leasowes Rd *HALE* B63...138 B4
Redliff Av *CBROM* B36...95 F5
Red Lion Cl *OLDBY* B69...85 G5
Red Lion St *WOLV* WV1...6 E3
Redmead Cl *NFLD/LBR* B31...176 A1
Redmoor Gdns
ETTPK/GDPK/PENN WV4...51 G3
Redmoor Wy *WALM/CURD* B76...79 F5
Rednal Hill La *RBRY* B45...188 A2
Rednall Dr *MGN/WHC* B75...47 G2
Rednal Mill Dr *RBRY* B45...188 C1
Rednal Rd *HWK/WKHTH* B38...176 A5
Redpine Crest *SHHTH* WV12...40 B1
Red River Rd *WSLW* WS2...27 E5
Red Rock Dr *CDSL* WV8...10 B5
Redruth Cl *DSYBK/YTR* WS5...58 B1
KGSWFD DY6...99 H1
Redruth Rd *DSYBK/YTR* WS5...58 B1
Redstone Dr *WNSFLD* WV11...25 F5
Redstone Farm Rd
HLGN/YWD B28...163 F4
Redthorn Gv *STETCH* B33...129 H1
Redvers Rd *BORD* B9...128 C3
Redwing Gv *ERDW/GRVHL* B23...75 H4
Redwood Av *DUDN* DY1...83 H1
Redwood Cl *BVILLE* B30...176 C1
FOAKS/STRLY B74...45 F3
Redwood Cft
ALE/KHTH/YWD B14...161 E3
Redwood Dr *OLDBY* B69...85 H4
Redwood Gdns *ACGN* B27...146 B2
Redwood Rd *BILS/COS* WV14...68 D1
BVILLE B30...176 C1
DSYBK/YTR WS5...57 H4
Redwood Wy *SHHTH* WV12...25 H2
Reedham Gdns
ETTPK/GDPK/PENN WV4...50 D2
Reedly Rd *SHHTH* WV12...26 A1
Reedmace Cl
HWK/WKHTH B38...176 D5
Reedswood Cl *WSLW* WS2...41 G2
Reedswood Gdns *WSLW* WS2...41 G2
Reedswood La *WSLW* WS2...41 G2
Reedswood Wy *WSLW* WS2...41 E1
Rees Dr *WMBN* WV5...65 F4
Reeves Cl *TPTN/OCK* DY4...85 H4
Reeves Gdns *CDSL* WV8...10 C3
Reeves Rd
ALE/KHTH/YWD B14...160 C4
Reeves St *BLOX/PEL* WS3...27 F2
Reform St *WBROM* B70...87 H3
Regal Cft *CBROM* B36...111 F1
Regal Dr *WSLW* WS2...4 A7
Regan Av *SHLY* B90...180 A4
Regan Crs *ERDW/GRVHL* B23...76 C5
Regan Dr *OLDBY* B69...104 B1
Regency Cl *BORD* B9...128 B3
Regency Ct *WSL* WS1...57 G1
Regency Dr *HWK/WKHTH* B38...176 C3
Regency Gdns
ALE/KHTH/YWD B14...179 E2
Regency Wk *FOAKS/STRLY* B74...32 B5
Regent Av *OLDBY* B69...85 G5
Regent Cl *DIG/EDG* B5...143 H1
HALE B63...138 C3
KGSWFD DY6...99 G3
OLDBY B69...103 G1
Regent Ct *SMTHWK* B66...106 C4
Regent Dr *OLDBY* B69...85 G5
Regent Pde *CBHAMW* B1...2 C2
Regent Park Rd *SMHTH* B10...128 A4
Regent Pl *CBHAMW* B1...2 C2
OLDBY B69...85 H4
Regent Rd
ETTPK/GDPK/PENN WV4...51 E3
HDSW B21...107 F1
HRBN B17...142 A1
OLDBY B69...85 G5
Regents Ct *BKHL/PFLD* WV2 *...7 F6
Regent St *BILS/COS* WV14...53 H2
BVILLE B30...160 A3
CBHAMW B1...2 C2
CDYHTH B64...121 F2
DUDN DY1...68 C5
SMTHWK B66...106 C3
TPTN/OCK DY4...69 E3
WLNHL WV13...39 G2
Regents Wy *MGN/WHC* B75...63 F2
Regina Av *KGSTG* B44...74 D3
Regina Cl *RBRY* B45...173 G4
Regina Crs
DUNHL/THL/PER WV6...35 F1
Regina Dr *PBAR/PBCH* B42...90 D3
RUSH/SHEL WS4...42 C1
Reginald Rd *SMTHWKW* B67...124 B2
WASH/WDE B8...110 B5
Regis Beeches
DUNHL/THL/PER WV6 *...21 G5
Regis Gdns
BLKHTH/ROWR B65...122 A3
Regis Heath Rd
BLKHTH/ROWR B65...122 B2
Regis Rd *BLKHTH/ROWR* B65...122 A2
DUNHL/THL/PER WV6...21 F5
Reid Av *SHHTH* WV12...26 B4
Reid Rd *LGLYGN/QTN* B68...123 G3
Reigate Av *WASH/WDE* B8...111 G5
Relko Dr *CBROM* B36...111 G2
Remembrance Rd
DARL/WED WS10...56 C5
Remington Pl *WSLW* WS2...27 G5
Remington Rd *WSLW* WS2...27 F4
Renfrew Cl *STRBR* DY8...117 G1
Renfrew Sq *CVALE* B35...94 D2
Rennie Gv *RIDG/WDGT* B32...140 D2
Rennison Dr *WMBN* WV5...65 E5
Renown Cl *BRLYHL* DY5...100 D2
Renton Gv *WOLVN* WV10...22 C1
Renton Rd *WOLVN* WV10...22 C1
Repington Wy *MGN/WHC* B75...63 H3
Repton Av
DUNHL/THL/PER WV6...34 B2
Repton Gv *BORD* B9...129 F1
Repton Rd *BORD* B9...129 F1
Reservoir Cl *WSLW* WS2...41 F5
Reservoir Pas *DARL/WED* WS10...55 H5
Reservoir Pl *WSLW* WS2...41 F5
Reservoir Retreat
LDYWD/EDGR B16...125 H3
Reservoir Rd
BLKHTH/ROWR B65...122 B1
ERDW/GRVHL B23...92 B2
HIA/OLT B92...164 B2
LDYWD/EDGR B16...125 H2
LGLYGN/QTN B68...105 G5
RBRY B45...188 C5
SLYOAK B29...142 A4
Reservoir St *WSLW* WS2...41 F5
Retallack Cl *SMTHWK* B66...106 D1
Retford Dr *WALM/CURD* B76...63 E4
Retford Gv *YDLY* B25...146 C1
Retreat Gdns *SEDG* DY3...67 G4
The Retreat *CDYHTH* B64...121 E5
Revesby Wk *VAUX/NECH* B7...109 G5
Revival St *BLOX/PEL* WS3...27 F1
Reynards Cl *SEDG* DY3...68 A4
Reynolds Cl *SEDG* DY3...80 C5
Reynolds Gv
DUNHL/THL/PER WV6...20 D5
Reynolds Rd *HDSW* B21...107 G2
Reynoldstown Rd
CBROM B36...111 G1
Reynolds Wk *WNSFLD* WV11...25 G2
Rhayader Rd *NFLD/LBR* B31...158 A5
Rhodes Cl *SEDG* DY3...82 C2
Rhone Cl *SPARK* B11...145 E4
Rhoose Cft *CVALE* B35...94 D4
Rhys Thomas Cl *SHHTH* WV12...40 B1
Rian Ct *CDYHTH* B64...120 D4
Ribbesford Av *WOLVN* WV10...22 D2
Ribbesford Cl *HALE* B63...137 H2
Ribbesford Crs *BILS/COS* WV14...68 D2
Ribblesdale Rd *BVILLE* B30...160 A3
Richard Pl *DSYBK/YTR* WS5...43 E5
Richard Rd *DSYBK/YTR* WS5...43 E5
Richards Cl
BLKHTH/ROWR B65...104 C5
NFLD/LBR B31...189 F2
Richardson Dr *STRBR* DY8...118 A4
Richards Rd *TPTN/OCK* DY4...69 F2
Richards St *DARL/WED* WS10...55 F1
Richard St *VAUX/NECH* B7...109 F4
WBROM B70...87 F3
Richard St West *WBROM* B70...87 F4
Richard Watts Dr
DARL/WED WS10...55 H3
Richard Williams Rd
DARL/WED WS10...71 F1
Richborough Dr *DUDN* DY1...83 G3
Riches St *DUNHL/THL/PER* WV6...36 B2
Richford Gv *STETCH* B33...131 F2
Richmond Aston Dr
TPTN/OCK DY4...85 G1
Richmond Av *BDMR/CCFT* WV3...36 B4
BHTH/HG B12 *...144 B2
Richmond Cl
BFLD/HDSWWD B20...90 A4
Richmond Cft *PBAR/PBCH* B42...73 H5
Richmond Dr *BDMR/CCFT* WV3...36 A4
DUNHL/THL/PER WV6...34 D2
MGN/WHC B75...63 F2
Richmond Gdns *WMBN* WV5...81 E1
Richmond Gv *STRBR* DY8...118 A4
Richmond Hl *LGLYGN/QTN* B68...105 G4
Richmond Hill Gdns *EDG* B15...142 C1

Richmond Hill Rd *EDG* B15.......... 142 D1
Richmond Pk *KGSWFD* DY6.......... 99 G1
Richmond Pl
ALE/KHTH/YWD B14.......... 161 F2
Richmond Rd
BDMR/CCFT WV3.......... 36 A4
DUDN DY1.......... 102 B1
HIA/OLT B92.......... 147 E5
HLYWD B47.......... 193 E1
RBRY B45.......... 188 C2
SCFLD/BOLD B73.......... 62 B2
SEDG DY3.......... 67 G4
SMTHWK B66.......... 124 C2
STETCH B33.......... 108 B3
WSNGN B18.......... 108 B3
Richmond St *HALE* B63.......... 138 C3
WBROM B70.......... 86 C1
WSL WS1.......... 5 G5
Richmond St South
WBROM B70.......... 86 C1
Richmond Wy
CHWD/FDBR/MGN B37.......... 132 C1
Rickard Cl *DOR/KN* B93.......... 196 C5
Rickman Dr *EDG* B15.......... 126 D4
Rickyard Cl *SLYOAK* B29.......... 158 C4
YDLY B25.......... 129 H5
Rickyard Piece
RIDG/WDGT B32.......... 141 E3
Riddfield Rd *CBROM* B36.......... 112 A1
Ridding La *ALDR* WS9.......... 70 D1
Riddings Crs *BLOX/PEL* WS3.......... 17 H5
The Riddings *HAG/WOL* DY9.......... 136 D5
STETCH B33.......... 112 A5
WALM/CURD B76.......... 78 C5
WOLVN WV10.......... 24 A3
Ridgacre La *RIDG/WDGT* B32.......... 140 C2
Ridgacre Rd *HHTH/SAND* B71.......... 71 F5
RIDG/WDGT B32.......... 140 B1
Ridgacre Rd West
RIDG/WDGT B32.......... 140 A1
Ridge Cl *MOS/BIL* B13.......... 146 A2
WSLW WS2.......... 40 B2
Ridgefield Rd *RMSLY* B62.......... 122 A4
Ridge Gv *HAG/WOL* DY9.......... 136 A2
Ridge La *WNSFLD* WV11.......... 24 D3
Ridgemont Dr
HWK/WKHTH B38.......... 190 B1
Ridge St *STRBR* DY8.......... 134 C1
Ridgewater Cl *RBRY* B45.......... 188 B2
Ridge Wy *ALDR* WS9.......... 44 B1
Ridgeway *HRBN* B17.......... 124 C2
RIDG/WDGT B32.......... 140 A2
SEDG DY3.......... 67 F4
The Ridgeway
ERDW/GRVHL B23.......... 91 G1
Ridgewood *BKDE/SHDE* B34.......... 112 D3
Ridgewood Av *STRBR* DY8.......... 134 C1
Ridgewood Cl *WSL* WS1.......... 5 F6
Ridgewood Dr *ERDW/GRVHL* B75.......... 47 F4
Ridgewood Gdns *KGSTG* B44.......... 75 F4
Ridgmont Pk *ERDW/GRVHL* B32.......... 141 E2
Riding Cl *HHTH/SAND* B71.......... 72 B4
Riding Wy *SHHTH* WV12.......... 26 B4
Ridley St *CBHAMW* B1.......... 126 C5
Ridpool Rd *STETCH* B33.......... 130 D1
Rifle St *BILS/COS* WV14.......... 68 A3
Rigby St *DARL/WED* WS10.......... 70 C2
Riland Rd *MGN/WHC* B75.......... 62 D3
Riley Crs *BDMR/CCFT* WV3.......... 51 G2
Riley Dr *CBROM* B36.......... 96 A5
Riley Rd *ALE/KHTH/YWD* B14.......... 179 F2
Riley St *WLNHL* WV13.......... 39 H3
Rilstone Rd *RIDG/WDGT* B32.......... 141 F2

Rindleford Av
ETTPK/GDPK/PENN WV4.......... 50 C2
Ringhills Rd *CDSL* WV8.......... 10 D5
Ringinglow Rd *KGSTG* B44.......... 74 C1
Ringmere Av *CBROM* B36.......... 112 D1
Ring Rd North *EDG* B15.......... 142 D5
Ring Road St Andrews
WOLV WV1.......... 6 D4
Ring Road St Davids
WOLV WV1.......... 7 H3
Ring Road St Georges
BKHL/PFLD WV2.......... 7 G6
Ring Road St Johns
BKHL/PFLD WV2.......... 6 E6
Ring Road St Marks
BDMR/CCFT WV3.......... 6 D5
Ring Road St Patricks
WOLV WV1.......... 7 G2
Ring Rd South *EDG* B15.......... 142 D5
Ringswood Rd *HIA/OLT* B92.......... 147 E3
The Ring *YDLY* B25.......... 129 G4
Ringwood Av *ALDR* WS9.......... 30 B5
Ringwood Dr *RBRY* B45.......... 174 A4
Ringwood Rd *WOLVN* WV10.......... 23 F1
Ripley Gv *ERDW/GRVHL* B23.......... 91 H1
Ripon Dr *HHTH/SAND* B71.......... 71 H2
Ripon Rd *ALE/KHTH/YWD* B14.......... 179 E1
WOLVN WV10.......... 23 G5
WSLW WS2.......... 41 F5
Rippingille Rd *GTB/HAM* B43.......... 59 G4
Ripple Rd *BVILLE* B30.......... 160 B3
Rischale Wy *RUSH/SHEL* WS4.......... 29 E2
Rise Av *RBRY* B45.......... 188 A1
Riseley Crs *DIG/EDG* B5.......... 143 H5
The Rise *ALVE* B48.......... 189 H4
CHWD/FDBR/MGN B37.......... 132 A5
KGSWFD DY6.......... 100 A4
PBAR/PBCH B42.......... 74 A3
Rising Brook
DUNHL/THL/PER WV6.......... 35 F1
Rissington Av *SLYOAK* B29.......... 160 A2
Ritchie Cl *MOS/BIL* B13.......... 161 G1
Rivendell Gdns
DUNHL/THL/PER WV6.......... 21 F5
Riverbank Rd *WLNHL* WV13.......... 40 B3
River Brook Dr *BVILLE* B30.......... 160 B3
River Lee Rd *SPARK* B11 *.......... 145 G2
Rivermead Pk
BKDE/SHDE B34.......... 112 C4

Riversdale Rd
ALE/KHTH/YWD B14.......... 179 F2
Riverside Ct *HWK/WKHTH* B38.......... 176 B2
Riverside Crs *HLGN/YWD* B28.......... 179 F1
Riverside Dr *SOLH* B91.......... 182 C5
STETCH B33.......... 111 H5
Riverside Gdns *CDSL* WV8.......... 10 D2
Riversleigh Dr *STRBR* DY8.......... 118 A4
River St *DIG/EDG* B5.......... 127 G2
River Wk *DARL/WED* WS10.......... 71 F1
Riverway *DARL/WED* WS10.......... 71 F1
Rivington Cl *STRBR* DY8.......... 135 E3
Rivington Crs *KGSTG* B44.......... 76 A2
Roach Cl *BRLYHL* DY5.......... 119 H1
CHWD/FDBR/MGN B37.......... 132 C1
Roach Crs *WNSFLD* WV11 *.......... 25 F2
Roach Pool Cft
LDYWD/EDGR B16.......... 125 E2
Robert Av *ERDW/GRVHL* B23.......... 76 C5
Robert Rd *BFLD/HDSWWD* B20.......... 90 B5
TPTN/OCK DY4.......... 69 F5
Roberts Cl *ALDR* WS9.......... 19 F5
Roberts Green Rd *SEDG* DY3.......... 83 G2
Roberts La *HAG/WOL* DY9.......... 152 D2
Robertson Knoll *CBROM* B36.......... 112 B2
Robertsons Gdns
VAUX/NECH B7.......... 110 A2
Roberts Rd *ACGN* B27.......... 146 C4
BLOX/PEL WS3.......... 28 B5
DARL/WED WS10.......... 57 E5
Robert St *SEDG* DY3.......... 83 G2
Robert Wynd *BILS/COS* WV14.......... 67 H2
Robeson Cl *TPTN/OCK* DY4.......... 84 D1
Robin Cl *CBROM* B36.......... 114 A1
KGSWFD DY6.......... 100 C3
Robin Hood Crs
HLGN/YWD B28.......... 162 C3
Robin Hood Cft
HLGN/YWD B28.......... 162 D5
Robin Hood La
HLGN/YWD B28.......... 162 C3
Robin Hood Rd *BRLYHL* DY5.......... 119 H2
Robin's Cl *STRBR* DY8.......... 135 G4
Robinsfield Dr *NFLD/LBR* B31.......... 189 G1
Robinson's Wy
WALM/CURD B76.......... 95 F1
Robottom Cl *WSLW* WS2.......... 27 F4
Rocester Av *WNSFLD* WV11.......... 25 F3
Rochdale Wk *SMHTH* B10.......... 128 A5
Roche Rd *BLOX/PEL* WS3.......... 26 D1
Rochester Cft *WSLW* WS2.......... 41 E1
Rochester Rd *NFLD/LBR* B31.......... 175 C1
Roche Wy *BLOX/PEL* WS3.......... 26 D1
Rochford Cl *HALE* B63.......... 138 B5
RBRY B45.......... 187 G1
WALM/CURD B76.......... 78 C3
Rochford Ct *SHLY* B90.......... 56 C1
Rochford Gv
ETTPK/GDPK/PENN WV4.......... 50 D3
Rock Av *RBRY* B45.......... 188 C1
Rocket Pool Dr *BILS/COS* WV14.......... 68 C4
Rockford Rd *PBAR/PBCH* B42.......... 74 A4
Rock Gv *HIA/OLT* B92.......... 147 E4
Rockingham Cl
BLOX/PEL WS3 *.......... 27 F1
DOR/KN B93.......... 198 B1
SEDG DY3.......... 82 D3
Rockingham Dr
DUNHL/THL/PER WV6.......... 34 C2
Rockingham Gdns
FOAKS/STRLY B74.......... 62 B2
Rockingham Hall Gdns
HAG/WOL DY9.......... 153 F5
Rockingham Rd *YDLY* B25.......... 129 H4
Rockland Dr *STETCH* B33.......... 112 A5
Rockland Gdns *WLNHL* WV13.......... 39 G5
Rocklands Dr *MGN/WHC* B75.......... 47 F5
Rockley Gv *RBRY* B45.......... 188 B1
Rockley Rd
BLKHTH/ROWR B65.......... 103 G3
Rockmead Av *KGSTG* B44.......... 75 F1
Rockmoor Cl
CHWD/FDBR/MGN B37.......... 131 G1
Rock Rd *BILS/COS* WV14.......... 67 H5
HIA/OLT B92.......... 147 E4
Rock St *SEDG* DY3.......... 67 H5
The Rock *DUNHL/THL/PER* WV6.......... 21 H5
Rockville Rd *WASH/WDE* B8.......... 111 E5
Rockwood Rd *ACGN* B27.......... 147 E4
Rocky La *AST/WIT* B6.......... 109 G3
PBAR/PBCH B42.......... 73 H5
Rodborough Rd *DOR/KN* B93.......... 198 C1
CHWD/FDBR/MGN B37.......... 131 H1
Rodbourne Rd *HRBN* B17.......... 142 A4
Roddis Cl *ERDW/GRVHL* B23.......... 76 B3
Roderick Dr *WNSFLD* WV11.......... 24 D5
Roderick Rd *SPARK* B11.......... 145 E2
Rodlington Av *KGSTG* B44.......... 75 F1
Rodman Cl *EDG* B15.......... 125 F4
Rodney Cl *HIA/OLT* B92 *.......... 164 D1
LDYWD/EDGR B16.......... 126 A2
Rodney Rd *HIA/OLT* B92.......... 164 D1
Rodway Cl *BRLYHL* DY5.......... 119 F5
ETTPK/GDPK/PENN WV4.......... 52 B5
LOZ/NWT B19.......... 108 D2
Rodwell Gv *KGSTG* B44.......... 75 F5
Roebuck Cl *BKDE/SHDE* B34.......... 113 G5
Roebuck Gld *SHHTH* WV12.......... 40 C1
Roebuck La *SMTHWK* B66.......... 106 B2
WBROM B70.......... 88 A5
Roebuck Pl *BLOX/PEL* WS3.......... 28 A4
Roebuck Rd *BLOX/PEL* WS3.......... 28 A4
Roebuck St *WBROM* B70.......... 88 B5
Roedean Cl *KGSTG* B44.......... 75 H4
Roford Cl *SEDG* DY3.......... 83 G1
Rogerfield Rd
ERDW/GRVHL B23.......... 77 E5
Rogers Cl *WNSFLD* WV11.......... 25 G1
Rogers Rd *WASH/WDE* B8.......... 111 F4
Rokeby Cl *WALM/CURD* B76.......... 63 E4
Rokeby Rd *GTB/HAM* B43.......... 73 H1
Rokewood Cl *KGSWFD* DY6.......... 81 H5
Rolan Dr *SHLY* B90.......... 179 G5
Roland Rd *LOZ/NWT* B19.......... 108 C1
Roland Vernon Wy
TPTN/OCK DY4.......... 70 A4
Rolfe St *SMTHWK* B66.......... 106 C3

Rollason Rd *DUDS* DY2.......... 102 D1
ERDE/BCHGN B24.......... 92 E3
Rollesby Dr *WLNHL* WV13.......... 39 F5
Rolling Mill Cl *DIG/EDG* B5 *.......... 127 E5
Rolling Mill Rd *CNCK/NC* WS11.......... 8 A1
Rollingmill St *WSLW* WS2.......... 4 A5
Rollswood Dr *SOLH* B91.......... 181 F1
Roman Cl *BRWNH* WS8.......... 9 E2
Roman Gra *FOAKS/STRLY* B74.......... 32 A5
Roman La *FOAKS/STRLY* B74.......... 45 H2
Roman Pk *FOAKS/STRLY* B74.......... 45 H1
Roman Rd *FOAKS/STRLY* B74.......... 46 A1
STRBR DY8.......... 134 D3
Romany Cl
BFLD/HDSWWD B37.......... 90 B3
Romany Rd *FOAKS/STRLY* B74.......... 134 C4
Roma Rd *SPARK* B11.......... 145 G2
Romford Cl
LGN/SDN/BHAMAIR B26.......... 147 H1
Romilly Av *BFLD/HDSWWD* B20.......... 90 B4
Romilly Cl *STRBR* DY8.......... 135 E1
WALM/CURD B76.......... 64 A2
Romney Cl *HLGN/YWD* B28.......... 162 D3
Romney Wy *GTB/HAM* B43.......... 59 H4
Romsey Gv *WOLVN* WV10.......... 12 C4
Romsey Rd *WOLVN* WV10.......... 12 C4
Romsey Wy *BLOX/PEL* WS3.......... 16 B4
Romsley Rd *HALE* B63.......... 138 D5
RBRY B45.......... 173 G5
Rush/Shel WS4.......... 18 C5
Romsley Rd *HAG/WOL* DY9.......... 136 A2
LGLYGN/QTN B68.......... 123 F2
RIDG/WDGT B32.......... 157 F2
Romulus Cl
BFLD/HDSWWD B20.......... 90 B3
Ronald Gv *CBROM* B36.......... 95 F5
Ronald Pl *BORD* B9.......... 128 C2
Ronald Rd *BORD* B9.......... 128 B2
Ron Davis Cl *SMTHWK* B66 *.......... 106 D4
Rood End Rd
LGLYGN/QTN B68.......... 105 G3
Rooker Av *BKHL/PFLD* WV2.......... 52 C2
Rooker Crs *BKHL/PFLD* WV2.......... 52 C2
Rookery Av *BRLYHL* DY5.......... 118 C2
ETTPK/GDPK/PENN WV4.......... 53 E5
Rookery Cl
ETTPK/GDPK/PENN WV4.......... 53 E5
HDSW B21.......... 89 C3
SLYOAK B29.......... 159 G5
WMBN WV5.......... 65 F5
Rookery Rd
ETTPK/GDPK/PENN WV4.......... 53 E5
HDSW B21.......... 89 G3
SLYOAK B29.......... 159 G5
WMBN WV5.......... 65 F5
Rookery St *WNSFLD* WV11.......... 24 C5
The Rookery *RMSLY* B62.......... 140 A5
Rooks Meadow *HAG/WOL* B75.......... 152 D4
Rookwood Dr
DUNHL/THL/PER WV6.......... 34 D4
Rooth St *DARL/WED* WS10.......... 56 B4
Roper Wy *SEDG* DY3.......... 67 H5
Rope Wk *DARL/WED* WS10.......... 56 A4
Rosafield Av *RMSLY* B62.......... 139 H1
Rosalind Av *DUDN* DY1.......... 85 G5
Rosamond St *WSL* WS1.......... 56 D1
Rosary Rd *ERDW/GRVHL* B23.......... 92 B4
Rosary Vls *SPARK* B11 *.......... 145 G1
Rose Av *KGSWFD* DY6.......... 100 B4
LGLYGN/QTN B68.......... 122 D1
Rose Bank *BLOX/PEL* WS3 *.......... 42 A1
Rosebay Av *HWK/WKHTH* B38.......... 176 D5
Roseberry Rd *HHTH/SAND* B66.......... 107 E5
Rosebery St *BDMR/CCFT* WV3.......... 6 A6
SMTHWK B66.......... 107 E4
WSNGN B18.......... 108 A5
Rosebury Gv *WMBN* WV5.......... 64 C5
Rose Cl *SMTHWK* B66.......... 107 E4
Rose Cottage Dr *STRBR* DY8.......... 117 H1
Rose Cottages *SLYOAK* B29 *.......... 142 D5
Rosecroft Rd
LGN/SDN/BHAMAIR B26.......... 148 A1
Rosedale Av *ERDW/GRVHL* B23.......... 92 C3
SMTHWK B66.......... 107 E4
Rosedale Gv *YDLY* B25.......... 129 G4
Rosedale Pl *WLNHL* WV13.......... 39 G5
Rosedene Dr
BFLD/HDSWWD B20.......... 89 H4
Rose Dr *BRWNH* WS8.......... 19 E2
Rosefield Cft *AST/WIT* B6.......... 109 F2
Rosefield Rd *SMTHWKW* B67.......... 106 C5
Rosehall Cl *SOLH* B91.......... 181 F4
Rose Hi *BRLYHL* DY5.......... 120 A3
RBRY B45.......... 188 A4
WLNHL WV13.......... 39 G4
Rose Hill Cl *CBROM* B36.......... 112 D1
Rose Hill Gdns *WLNHL* WV13.......... 39 G4
Rose Hill Rd *HDSW* B21.......... 108 A2
Roseland Av *DUDS* DY2.......... 85 F5
Roseland Wy *EDG* B15.......... 126 B3
Roseleigh Rd *RBRY* B45.......... 188 B2
Rosemary Av *BILS/COS* WV14.......... 54 B2
ETTPK/GDPK/PENN WV4.......... 52 A3
Rosemary Crs *DUDN* DY1.......... 101 F3
ETTPK/GDPK/PENN WV4.......... 52 A3
Rosemary Crs West
ETTPK/GDPK/PENN WV4.......... 51 H3
Rosemary Dr *FOAKS/STRLY* B74.......... 46 A2
Rosemary Hill Rd
FOAKS/STRLY B74.......... 46 A3
Rosemary La *STRBR* DY8.......... 134 D4
Rosemary Nook
FOAKS/STRLY B74.......... 32 B5
Rosemary Rd *HALE* B63.......... 137 H5
STETCH B33.......... 130 B2
TPTN/OCK DY4.......... 85 G1
Rosemoor Dr *BRLYHL* DY5.......... 118 B5
Rose Rd *CSHL/WTROR* B46.......... 115 F1
HRBN B17.......... 142 B1
Rose St *BILS/COS* WV14.......... 69 F1
Rose Vls *SPARK* B11 *.......... 129 E5
Roseville Gdns *CDSL* WV8.......... 10 B3
Roseville Prec *BILS/COS* WV14 *.......... 68 C5
Rosewood Dr
ERDW/GRVHL B23.......... 92 B4
SHHTH WV12.......... 25 H2
Rosewood Gdns *WNSFLD* WV11.......... 13 F5
Royal Cl *BLKHTH/ROWR* B65.......... 104 A4
BRLYHL DY5.......... 119 G4

Rosewood Rd *DUDN* DY1.......... 84 B1
Roshven Rd *MOS/BIL* B12.......... 144 C3
Roslin Gv *LOZ/NWT* B19.......... 108 C2
Roslyn Cl *SMTHWK* B66.......... 106 C5
Ross *BLKHTH/ROWR* B65.......... 121 H2
Ross Cl *BDMR/CCFT* WV3.......... 36 A3
Ross Dr *KGSWFD* DY6.......... 99 G2
Rosse Ct *HIA/OLT* B92.......... 165 H2
Rossendale Cl *HALE* B63.......... 137 H1
Ross Hls *BLKHTH/ROWR* B65.......... 121 H1
Rosslyn Rd *WALM/CURD* B76.......... 78 B5
Ross Rd *BLOX/PEL* WS3.......... 28 B2
Rostrevor Rd *SMHTH* B10.......... 128 D3
Rotherby Gv
CHWD/FDBR/MGN B37.......... 132 B5
Rotherfield Rd
LGN/SDN/BHAMAIR B26.......... 130 D4
Rothesay Cft *RIDG/WDGT* B32.......... 157 F3
Rothesay Dr *STRBR* DY8.......... 117 G1
Rothesay Gdns
ETTPK/GDPK/PENN WV4.......... 52 C3
Rothesay Wy *SMHTH* WV12.......... 25 H4
Rothwell Dr *SOLH* B91.......... 180 D1
Rotton Park Rd
LDYWD/EDGR B16.......... 125 F3
Rotton Park St
LDYWD/EDGR B16.......... 125 G3
Rough Hay Rd *DARL/WED* WS10.......... 55 E1
Rough Hay Rd
BLKHTH/ROWR B65.......... 103 F5
Rough Hill Dr
BLKHTH/ROWR B65.......... 103 F5
Rough Hills Rd *BKHL/PFLD* WV2.......... 52 D2
Roughlea Av *CBROM* B36.......... 112 B2
Roughley Farm Rd
MGN/WHC B75.......... 47 G3
The Roundabout
NFLD/LBR B31.......... 174 D4
Round Hill *WLNHL* WV13.......... 39 F3
Round Hi *SEDG* DY3.......... 67 F1
Round Hill Av *HAG/WOL* DY9.......... 153 E1
Roundhill Cl *WALM/CURD* B76.......... 64 A1
Roundhill Rd *RMSLY* B62.......... 122 C5
Roundhill Ter *RMSLY* B62.......... 122 C5
Roundhill Wy *BRWNH* WS8.......... 9 G2
Round House Rd *SEDG* DY3.......... 83 G2
Roundlea Cl *SHHTH* WV12.......... 25 H5
Roundlea Rd *NFLD/LBR* B31.......... 158 B4
Round Rd *ERDE/BCHGN* B24.......... 93 F4
Round Saw Cft *RBRY* B45.......... 173 H5
Rounds Green Rd *OLDBY* B69.......... 104 D2
Rounds Hill Rd *BILS/COS* WV14.......... 68 D5
Rounds Rd *BILS/COS* WV14.......... 68 C2
Round St *DUDS* DY2.......... 102 C3
Roundway Down
DUNHL/THL/PER WV6.......... 34 C2
Rousay Cl *RBRY* B45.......... 173 H4
Rousdon Gv *GTB/HAM* B43.......... 73 F3
Rover Dr *ACGN* B27.......... 146 D3
CBROM B36.......... 96 A5
Rowallan Rd *MGN/WHC* B75.......... 47 H3
Rowan Cl *HLWD* B47.......... 192 D5
WALM/CURD B76.......... 78 B1
Rowan Ct *BVILLE* B30.......... 177 E3
Rowan Crs *BDMR/CCFT* WV3.......... 51 E1
BILS/COS WV14.......... 68 D2
Rowan Dr *HLGN/YWD* B28.......... 163 E5
WNSFLD WV11.......... 15 F4
Rowan Ri *KGSWFD* DY6.......... 100 A3
Rowan Rd *CSCFLD/WYGN* B72.......... 77 C1
DSYBK/YTR WS5.......... 57 E2
SEDG DY3.......... 67 H2
Rowantrees *RBRY* B45.......... 188 B3
Rowan Wy
CHWD/FDBR/MGN B37.......... 132 C3
NFLD/LBR B31.......... 175 F4
Roway La *OLDBY* B69.......... 86 C5
Rowbrook Cl *SHLY* B90.......... 179 G5
Rowchester Ct *CBHAMNE* B4 *.......... 3 K3
Rowcroft Covert
ALE/KHTH/YWD B14.......... 177 G2
Rowdale Rd *PBAR/PBCH* B42.......... 74 B4
Rowden Dr *ERDW/GRVHL* B23.......... 77 E5
SOLH B91.......... 181 H4
Rowena Gdns *SEDG* DY3.......... 67 E1
Rowheath Rd *BVILLE* B30.......... 176 D1
Rowington Av
BLKHTH/ROWR B65.......... 122 B1
Rowington Rd
BKDE/SHDE B34.......... 113 G3
Rowington Ter *YDLY* B25 *.......... 129 F5
Rowland Gdns *WSLW* WS2.......... 41 G2
Rowland Hill Dr
TPTN/OCK DY4 *.......... 86 A2
Rowlands Av *WOLV* WV1.......... 38 B3
WSLW WS2.......... 40 C2
Rowlands Cl *WSLW* WS2.......... 40 C1
Rowlands Crs *SOLH* B91.......... 164 D2
Rowlands Rd
LGN/SDN/BHAMAIR B26.......... 130 A5
Rowland St *WSLW* WS2.......... 41 G2
Rowley Cl *WSL* WS1.......... 5 G5
Rowley Gv *STETCH* B33.......... 131 F1
Rowley Hall Av
BLKHTH/ROWR B65.......... 122 A1
Rowley Hill Vw *CDYHTH* B64.......... 121 F4
Rowley Pl *RUSH/SHEL* WS4.......... 28 D3
Rowley Regis Blf
DARL/WED WS10.......... 55 E4
WBROM B70.......... 87 F3
Rowley Village
BLKHTH/ROWR B65.......... 122 A1
Rowney Crt *HLGN/YWD* B28.......... 179 G1
Rowood Dr *HIA/OLT* B92.......... 165 E3
Rowthorn Cl *FOAKS/STRLY* B74.......... 60 C1
Rowthorn Dr *SHLY* B90.......... 195 G2
Rowton Av
DUNHL/THL/PER WV6.......... 34 C4
Rowton Dr *FOAKS/STRLY* B74.......... 60 B3
Roxall Cl *KIDD* DY10.......... 168 C3
Roxburgh Gv *GTB/HAM* B43.......... 59 G4
Roxburgh Rd *SCFLD/BOLD* B73.......... 62 B2
Roxby Gdns
DUNHL/THL/PER WV6.......... 22 C5

Royal Gv *ERDW/GRVHL* B23.......... 75 H4
Royal Mail St *CBHAMW* B1.......... 2 E6
Royal Oak Rd
BLKHTH/ROWR B65.......... 103 F4
RMSLY B62.......... 139 H5
Royal Rd *CSCFLD/WYGN* B72.......... 62 C3
Royal Scot Gv *WSL* WS1.......... 56 D3
Royal Star Cl *STETCH* B33.......... 131 E2
Roydon Rd *ACGN* B27.......... 163 G2
Roylesden Crs
SCFLD/BOLD B73.......... 76 A1
Royston Cha *FOAKS/STRLY* B74.......... 45 G2
Royston Cft *BHTH/HG* B12.......... 144 B1
Royston Wy *SEDG* DY3.......... 67 E3
Rubens Cl *SEDG* DY3.......... 83 F1
Rubery Farm Gv *RBRY* B45.......... 173 H5
Rubery Field Cl *RBRY* B45.......... 174 A4
Rubery La *RBRY* B45.......... 173 H4
Rubery La South *RBRY* B45.......... 173 H5
Rubery St *DARL/WED* WS10.......... 40 B5
Ruckley Av *LOZ/NWT* B19.......... 108 C2
Ruckley Rd *SLYOAK* B29.......... 158 D2
Rudder Cl *WOLVN* WV10.......... 38 B1
Ruddington Wy *LOZ/NWT* B19.......... 109 E4
Rudge Av *WOLV* WV1.......... 38 B2
Rudge Cl *SHHTH* WV12.......... 40 A1
Rudge Gv *STETCH* B33.......... 112 C5
Rudge Wk *WSNGN* B18 *.......... 126 A4
Rudgewick Cft *AST/WIT* B6.......... 109 F3
Rudyard Cl *WOLVN* WV10.......... 13 E3
Rudyard Gv *STETCH* B33.......... 130 D1
Rudyngfield Dr *STETCH* B33.......... 130 B1
Rufford Cl *ERDW/GRVHL* B23.......... 76 B3
Rufford Rd *HAG/WOL* DY9.......... 136 A3
Rufford St *HAG/WOL* DY9.......... 136 B1
Rufford Wy *ALDR* WS9.......... 29 G3
Rugby St *WOLV* WV1.......... 117 H5
Rugby St *WOLV* WV1.......... 6 C1
Rugeley Av *SHHTH* WV12.......... 26 B2
Rugeley Cl *TPTN/OCK* DY4.......... 85 E1
Ruislip Cl *CVALE* B35.......... 95 H2
Ruiton St *SEDG* DY3.......... 83 F2
Rumbow *HALE* B63.......... 138 D3
Rumbow La *RMSLY* B62.......... 171 H1
Rumbush La *HOCK/TIA* B94.......... 193 H5
Runcorn Cl
CHWD/FDBR/MGN B37.......... 114 C5
Runcorn Rd *BHTH/HG* B12.......... 144 C3
Runnymede Rd *SPARK* B11.......... 145 G4
Rupert St *BDMR/CCFT* WV3.......... 6 A3
VAUX/NECH B7.......... 109 G4
Rushall Cl *RUSH/SHEL* WS4.......... 42 D1
STRBR DY8.......... 118 A4
Rushall Manor Cl
RUSH/SHEL WS4.......... 42 D1
Rushall Manor Rd
RUSH/SHEL WS4.......... 42 D1
Rushall Rd *WOLVN* WV10.......... 13 E5
Rushbrook Cl *ALDR* WS9.......... 19 E1
RUSH/SHEL WS4.......... 42 D1
HIA/OLT B92.......... 147 E5
Rushbrooke Cl *MOS/BIL* B13.......... 144 B3
Rushbrooke Dr
SCFLD/BOLD B73.......... 61 G4
Rushbrook Gv
ALE/KHTH/YWD B14.......... 177 G2
Rushbury Cl *BILS/COS* WV14.......... 53 F3
SHLY B90.......... 180 D1
Rushden Cft *KGSTG* B44.......... 75 F1
Rushes MI *BLOX/PEL* WS3.......... 17 C4
Rushey La *SPARK* B11.......... 146 A2
Rushford Av *WMBN* WV5.......... 65 E5
Rushford Cl *SHLY* B90.......... 195 G1
Rush Gn *RIDG/WDGT* B32.......... 141 E5
Rushleigh Rd *SHLY* B90.......... 179 C5
Rushmead Gv *RBRY* B45.......... 188 A1
Rushmere Rd *TPTN/OCK* DY4.......... 69 C3
Rushmoor Cl *FOAKS/STRLY* B74.......... 62 B2
Rushwater Cl *WMBN* WV5.......... 64 A5
Rushwick Gv *SHLY* B90.......... 195 G2
Rushwood Cl *RUSH/SHEL* WS4.......... 42 C2
Rushy Piece *RIDG/WDGT* B32.......... 140 D4
Ruskin Av *BLKHTH/ROWR* B65.......... 104 A3
ETTPK/GDPK/PENN WV4.......... 67 H1
SEDG DY3.......... 82 C1
Ruskin Cl *AST/WIT* B6.......... 109 F1
Ruskin Gv *ACGN* B27.......... 146 B5
Ruskin Hall Gv *AST/WIT* B6.......... 109 F2
Ruskin Rd *WOLVN* WV10.......... 23 H2
Ruskin St *HHTH/SAND* B71.......... 87 C1
Russell Bank Rd
FOAKS/STRLY B74.......... 46 C1
Russell Cl *OLDBY* B69.......... 86 B4
TPTN/OCK DY4.......... 70 A2
WNSFLD WV11.......... 25 F1
Russell Rd *BILS/COS* WV14.......... 54 B1
HLGN/YWD B28.......... 145 G5
MOS/BIL B13.......... 144 B4
Russell's Hall Rd *DUDN* DY1.......... 83 G5
The Russells *MOS/BIL* B13.......... 143 H4
Russell St *BDMR/CCFT* WV3.......... 6 D6
DUDN DY1.......... 84 B5
WLNHL WV13.......... 39 H5
Russett Cl *DSYBK/YTR* WS5.......... 43 F5
Russett Wy *BRLYHL* DY5.......... 100 C2
Russ Hall Av *NFLD/LBR* B31.......... 158 A4
Ruston St *LDYWD/EDGR* B16.......... 126 A5
Ruthall Cl *SLYOAK* B29.......... 159 E3
Ruth Cl *TPTN/OCK* DY4.......... 70 A1
Rutherford Rd
ERDW/GRVHL B23.......... 76 C4
WSLW WS2.......... 27 E4
Rutland Av
ETTPK/GDPK/PENN WV4.......... 50 D4
Rutland Crs *ALDR* WS9.......... 30 A3
BILS/COS WV14.......... 53 H1
Rutland Dr
LGN/SDN/BHAMAIR B26.......... 130 A5
Rutland Pl *STRBR* DY8.......... 117 H4
Rutland Rd *DARL/WED* WS10.......... 56 C4
HHTH/SAND B71.......... 71 H5
SMTHWK B66.......... 124 C3
Rutland St *BLOX/PEL* WS3.......... 28 A5
Rutley Gv *RIDG/WDGT* B32.......... 141 F3
Rutters Meadow
RIDG/WDGT B32.......... 140 B3
Rutter St *WSL* WS1.......... 57 E1
Ryan Av *WNSFLD* WV11.......... 25 G3

Ryan Pl DUDS DY2 ....102 C3
Rycroft Gv STETCH B33 ....131 E2
Rydal Cl FOAKS/STRLY B74 ....45 F3
  WNSFLD WV11 ....24 C3
Rydal Dr DUNHL/THL/PER WV6...34 D1
Rydding La HHTH/SAND B71 ....71 C3
Rydding Sq HHTH/SAND B71 ....71 F3
Ryde Gv ACGN B27 ....163 E1
Ryde Park Rd RBRY B45 ....188 C2
Ryders Green Rd WBROM B70 ...86 C2
Ryders Hayes La
  BLOX/PEL WS3 ....18 A3
Ryder St CBHAMNE B4 * 3 H3
  STRBR DY8 ....117 H2
  WBROM B70 ....86 D1
Ryebank Cl BVILLE B30 ....159 E5
Ryeclose Cft
  CHWD/FDBR/MGN B37 ....132 D1
Rye Cft ACGN B27 ....146 C2
  HAG/WOL DY9 ....136 C5
  HLYWD B47 ....192 C4
Ryecroft Av
  ETTPK/GDPK/PENN WV4 ....51 H3
Ryecroft Cl SEDG DY3 ....67 E5
Ryecroft Pl BLOX/PEL WS3 ....28 B4
Ryecroft St WSLW WS2 ....4 D5
Ryefield CDSL WV8 ....22 A1
Ryefield Cl HAG/WOL DY9 ....169 G1
  SOLH B91 ....164 A5
Ryefield Wy KGSWFD DY6 ....99 C3
Rye Grass Wk CVALE B35 ....94 D3
Rye Gv SPARK B11 ....145 H5
Ryknild Cl FOAKS/STRLY B74 ...32 C4
Ryknild Dr FOAKS/STRLY B74 ...60 C1
Ryland Cl HALE B63 ....138 A5
  TPTN/OCK DY4 ....85 H1
Ryland Rd EDG B15 ....126 C5
  ERDE/BCHGN B24 ....92 D5
  STRBR DY8 ....145 F3
Rylands Dr
  ETTPK/GDPK/PENN WV4 ....51 C4
Ryland St LDYWD/EDGR B16....2 A7
Ryle St BLOX/PEL WS3 ....17 F5
Rymond Rd BKDE/SHDE B34 ...112 A3
Ryton Cl SCFLD/BOLD B75 ....62 B3
  WNSFLD WV11 ....24 A3
Ryton Gv BKDE/SHDE B34 ....113 F2

S

Sabell Rd SMTHWKW B67 ....106 B3
Sabrina Rd
  DUNHL/THL/PER WV6 ....34 C4
Saddlers Cl HALE B63 ....157 F2
Saddlers Ms SOLH B91 ....182 A4
The Saddlestones
  DUNHL/THL/PER WV6 ....34 B1
Saddleworth Rd
  BLOX/PEL WS3 ....16 C3
Sadler Rd BRWNH WS8 ....9 G4
  MGN/WHC B75 ....63 F1
Sadlers Cl WSLW WS2 ....56 B1
Sadlers Ml BRWNH WS8 * 9 G5
Sadlers Wk LDYWD/EDGR B16...126 A3
Saffron Gdns
  ETTPK/GDPK/PENN WV4 ....51 G4
Sage Cft NFLD/LBR B31 ....158 B5
St Agatha's Rd WASH/WDE B8 ..111 F4
St Agnes Cl KNOS/BIL B13 ....144 D5
St Agnes Rd MOS/BIL B13 ....144 D5
St Aidans Wk SMHTH B10 * ...128 A4
St Albans Cl SMTHWKW B67 *..106 A3
  WNSFLD WV11 ....25 C2
St Albans Rd MOS/BIL B13 ....144 C3
  SMTHWKW B67 ....106 A3
St Alphege Cl SOLH B91 * 182 A2
St Ambrose Cl RMSLY B62 ....121 H4
St Andrews Av BLOX/PEL WS3 ...18 A2
St Andrews Cl
  DUNHL/THL/PER WV6 ....36 C1
  RIDG/WDGT B32 ....141 C4
  SEDG DY3 ....82 C3
  STRBR DY8 ....135 F5
St Andrews Dr
  DUNHL/THL/PER WV6 ....34 B1
  OLDBY B69 ....103 H2
  MGN/WHC B75 ....62 C1
St Andrew's St BORD B9 ....127 H2
  DUDS DY2 ....102 C4
St Annes Cl
  BFLD/HDSWWD B20 ....89 H2
St Anne's Ct MOS/BIL B13 ....144 A3
St Annes Gv DOR/KN B93 ....197 E2
St Anne's Rd DUDS DY2 ....120 C3
  WLNHL WV13 ....39 H2
  WOLVN WV10 ....22 D1
St Annes Wy KGSTG B44 ....75 G4
St Anthonys Dr BLOX/PEL WS3...18 B2
St Athan Cft CVALE B35 ....94 D3
St Augustine's Rd
  LDYWD/EDGR B16 ....125 F3
St Augustus Cl WBROM B70 ....88 B4
St Austell Rd DSYBK/YTR WS5 ..58 B1
St Bartholomew Ter
  DARL/WED WS10 ....55 H5
St Benedict's Cl WBROM B70 ....88 B4
St Benedicts Rd SMHTH B10 ...128 D4
Saint Benedicts Rd WMBN WV5..65 E4
St Bernards Rd
  CSCFLD/WYGN B72 ....77 C1
  HIA/OLT B92 ....163 H5
St Blaise Av CSHL/WTROR B46...96 C4
St Blaise Rd MGN/WHC B75 ....47 H2
St Brades Cl OLDBY B69 ....104 A2
St Brides Cl SEDG DY3 ....67 E3
  WMBN WV5 ....64 D5
Saintbury Dr SOLH B91 ....196 A1
St Caroline Cl WBROM B70 ....88 B4
St Catherines Cl WSL WS1 ....57 C1
St Catherines Cl DUDS DY2 * ...85 H5
  MGN/WHC B75 ....63 F1
St Catherine's Crs
  ETTPK/GDPK/PENN WV4 ....51 F5
St Chad's Circ CBHAMNW B3....3 F3
St Chad's Cl SEDG DY3 ....82 D5

St Chads Queensway
  CBHAMNE B4 ....3 G2
St Chads Rd BILS/COS WV14 ....54 B1
  MOS/BIL B13 ....63 E5
  RBRY B45 ....187 H1
  WOLVN WV10 ....23 H3
St Christopher Cl WBROM B70...88 A4
St Christophers
  BFLD/HDSWWD B20 ....89 H2
St Clement's Av BLOX/PEL WS3 ..27 G5
St Clement's La
  HHTH/SAND B71 ....87 H2
St Clements Rd
  VAUX/NECH B7 ....110 A3
St Columbas Dr RBRY B45 ....188 D1
St Cuthbert's Cl WBROM B70....88 A4
St Davids Cl BLOX/PEL WS3 ....18 B2
  WBROM B70 ....88 B4
St Davids Dr RIDG/WDGT B32 ..140 B2
St Davids Gv
  BFLD/HDSWWD B20 ....89 H2
St Davids Pl BLOX/PEL WS3 ....17 F5
St Denis Rd SLYOAK B29 ....158 C4
St Dominic's Rd
  ERDE/BCHGN B24 ....92 C5
St Edburghs Rd YDLY B25 ....130 A3
St Edmund's Cl
  WBROM B70 ....88 B4
St Edward's Rd SLYOAK B29 ...142 D5
St Eleanor Cl WBROM B70 ....88 B3
St Francis Av SOLH B91 ....164 A4
St Francis Cl BLOX/PEL WS3 ....18 B2
St Francis Dr BVILLE B30 ....177 H2
St George Dr SMTHWK B66 * ..106 C2
St Georges Av
  ERDW/GRVHL B23 ....76 D4
St Georges Cl DARL/WED WS10...55 F1
  EDG B15 ....126 A5
  MGN/WHC B75 ....63 F2
St Georges Ct
  FOAKS/STRLY B74 ....32 C5
St George's Pde BKHL/PFLD WV2..7 G5
St Georges Pl WBROM B70 ....87 G2
St Georges Rd DUDS DY2 ....102 D3
  SHLY B90 ....180 D5
  STRBR DY8 ....134 D5
St Georges St DARL/WED WS10...55 F1
  LOZ/NWT B19 ....2 A1
St Gerards Rd SOLH B91 ....181 E3
St Giles Av BLKHTH/ROWR B65..105 H5
St Giles Cl BLKHTH/ROWR B65 ..105 H5
St Giles Crs WOLV WV1 ....38 A3
St Giles Rd STETCH B33 ....131 F2
  WLNHL WV13 ....38 A3
  WOLV WV1 ....38 A3
St Giles Rw STRBR DY8 * 135 G1
St Helen's Rd SOLH B91 ....164 A1
St Heliers Rd NFLD/LBR B31 ...175 E1
St Ives Rd DSYBK/YTR WS5 ....58 B1
St James Av
  BLKHTH/ROWR B65 ....105 G5
St James Cl BLOX/PEL WS3 * ...18 B2
  WBROM B70 ....88 B4
St James Pl SHLY B90 ....180 B3
  VAUX/NECH B7 ....127 G1
St James Rd EDG B15 ....126 B4
  HDSW B21 ....88 D3
  MGN/WHC B75 ....47 G3
  OLDBY B69 ....104 B1
St James's Rd DUDN DY1 ....84 B4
St James's Ter DUDN DY1 ....84 A4
St James St DARL/WED WS10 ...70 C1
  SEDG DY3 ....83 F3
  WOLV WV1 ....7 J5
Saint James Wk BRWNH WS8 ....9 F5
St John Bosco Ct
  HHTH/SAND B71 ....71 F4
St John Cl MGN/WHC B75 ....47 H2
St Johns Av
  BLKHTH/ROWR B65 ....103 H5
St John's Ct ALDR WS9 ....19 F4
  DOR/KN B93 ....197 F2
  WBROM B70 ....80 B4
St Johns Cl NFLD/LBR B31 ....175 H4
St Johns Gv
  CHWD/FDBR/MGN B37 ....131 H1
St Johns Rd BILS/COS WV14 ....18 B2
  BRWNH WS8 ....19 C2
  DARL/WED WS10 ....55 E5
  DUDS DY2 ....102 D1
  HALE B63 ....138 A3
  HRBN B17 ....142 B1
  LGLYGN/QTN B68 ....105 C4
  SPARK B11 ....145 E2
  STRBR DY8 ....135 C1
  TPTN/OCK DY4 ....69 F4
  WNSFLD WV11 ....15 E4
St John's Sq BKHL/PFLD WV2....7 F6
St Paul's St WSL WS1 ....4 E3
St John St DUDS DY2 ....102 C4
St Johns Wk PBAR/PBCH B42 ...90 D2
St Johns Wd RBRY B45 ....188 B3
St Josephs Av NFLD/LBR B31 ...158 D5
St Josephs Cl BLOX/PEL WS3 ....18 A3
St Josephs Rd WASH/WDE B8 ..111 F4
St Joseph St DUDS DY2 ....84 D5
St Judes Cl
  ALE/KHTH/YWD B14 ....178 B3
  MGN/WHC B75 ....63 F2
St Jude's Pas DIG/EDG B5 * 3 F7
St Jude's Rd
  DUNHL/THL/PER WV6 ....36 B2
St Jude's Rd West
  DUNHL/THL/PER WV6 ....36 B2
St Katherine's Rd
  LGLYGN/QTN B68 ....105 G4
St Kenelms Av HALE B63 ....154 D1
St Kenelm's Cl WBROM B70 ....88 B4
St Kenelm's Rd RMSLY B62 ....152 C5
St Kilda's Rd WASH/WDE B8 *..110 C4
St Lawrence Rd
  NFLD/LBR B31 ....158 C5
St Lawrence Cl DIG/EDG B5 ...126 D5
  DOR/KN B93 ....197 F3
St Lawrence Wy
  DARL/WED WS10 ....55 F2

St Leonards Cl
  CHWD/FDBR/MGN B37 ....132 A5
St Loye's Cl RMSLY B62 ....122 B5
St Lukes Cl
  BLKHTH/ROWR B65 ....103 H5
St Lukes Rd DARL/WED WS10 ...56 B5
Saint Lukes Rd
  DARL/WED WS10 ....71 E1
St Luke's Rd DIG/EDG B5 ....127 E5
St Luke's St CDYHTH B64 ....120 D3
St Margaret's FOAKS/STRLY B74..46 A2
St Margarets Av
  WASH/WDE B8 ....111 F3
St Margarets Dr HALE B63 ....138 B5
St Margarets Rd BLOX/PEL WS3..17 H3
  GTB/HAM B43 ....73 G3
  HIA/OLT B92 ....164 A1
  WASH/WDE B8 ....111 E3
St Marks Crs CBHAMW B1 ....126 A1
St Mark's Rd BDMR/CCFT WV3 ..6 C5
  BLOX/PEL WS3 ....18 B3
  BRWNH WS8 ....19 G2
  DUDS DY2 ....85 F5
  HAG/WOL DY9 ....136 B3
  SMTHWKW B67 ....123 H1
  TPTN/OCK DY4 ....69 G3
St Mark's St BDMR/CCFT WV3 ..6 D5
St Martin's Cl BKHL/PFLD WV2...52 C2
  WBROM B70 ....88 B3
St Martin's Queensway (Below)
St Martins Rd MGN/WHC B75 ...63 F5
St Martin's St EDG B15 ....126 B3
St Martin's Ter BILS/COS WV14...54 A5
St Marys Cl ACGN B27 ....146 B4
  ERDE/BCHGN B24 ....93 H2
St Marys Ct WLNHL WV13 * 39 C3
St Mary's La STRBR DY8 ....135 H4
St Mary's Rd HDSW B21 ....88 A3
  SMTHWKW B67 ....105 H5
  HRBN B17 ....142 B2
St Mary's Rw CBHAMNE B4 ....3 G3
  MOS/BIL B13 ....144 B4
St Mary's Vw ERDW/GRVHL B23..76 B3
St Mary's Wy ALDR WS9 ....30 A5
St Matthews Cl
  BLOX/PEL WS3 * 18 B2
  WSL WS1 ....5 F5
Saint Matthews Rd
  LGLYGN/QTN B68 ....123 E2
St Matthews Rd SMTHWK B66..107 E4
St Matthew St WOLV WV1 ....37 H4
St Mawes Rd
  DUNHL/THL/PER WV6 ....34 D2
St Mawgen Cl CVALE B35 ....95 E2
St Michael's Cl BLOX/PEL WS3 ..17 H5
St Michael's Cr
  DUNHL/THL/PER WV6 ....22 A5
St Michael's Crs OLDBY B69 ...104 D3
St Michael's Gv DUDS DY2 ....85 F5
St Michael's Rd
  SCFLD/BOLD B73 ....76 D3
  SEDG DY3 ....82 B1
  WSNGN S18 ....108 A2
St Michael St WSL WS1 ....4 E7
St Michael St West
  WBROM B70 ....87 G3
St Michaels Wy TPTN/OCK DY4..85 G3
St Nicholas Cl BLOX/PEL WS3 ...18 A3
St Nicolas Gdns
  HWK/WKHTH B38 ....176 D3
St Oswalds Rd SMHTH B10 ....128 C4
St Patricks Cl
  ALE/KHTH/YWD B14 ....161 E4
St Paul's Av BHTH/HG B12 ....144 C2
St Pauls Crs BLOX/PEL WS3 ....18 B2
  CSHL/WTROR B46 ....115 C2
  WBROM B70 ....70 C4
St Pauls Dr RMSLY B62 ....122 B3
  TPTN/OCK DY4 ....85 H2
St Paul's Rd BHTH/HG B12 ....144 B1
  DARL/WED WS10 ....56 B3
  DUDS DY2 ....102 D4
  SMTHWK B66 ....105 H2
St Paul's Sq CBHAMNW B3 ....2 D1
St Paul's St WSL WS1 ....4 E3
St Peter Cft DARL/WED WS10 ...57 E5
St Peters Cl CSCFLD/WYGN B72..82 D5
  CSHL/WTROR B46 ....96 B4
Saint Peters Cl
  HLGN/YWD D28 ....162 B4
St Peter's Ct TPTN/OCK DY4 ...86 B2
St Peters Ct BLOX/PEL WS3 ....27 F1
St Peter's Cft
  SCFLD/BOLD B73 * 62 B5
St Peters La HIA/OLT B92 ....166 D2
St Peter's Rd
  BFLD/HDSWWD B20 ....90 C5
  DUDS DY2 ....102 D4
  HAG/WOL DY9 ....153 C1
  HRBN B17 ....141 H2
St Peters Sq WOLV WV1 * 7 F3
St Peters Ter WSLW WS2 ....42 A1
St Philips Av BDMR/CCFT WV3 ..51 G1
St Phillips Av BDMR/CCFT WV3 ..51 F1
St Phillips Gv BDMR/CCFT WV3 ..51 F1
St Quentin St WSLW WS2 ....41 G5
St Saviour's Cl BKHL/PFLD WV2..52 D2
St Saviour's Rd WASH/WDE B8..128 C1
St Silas' Sq LOZ/NWT B19 ....108 B2
St Simons Cl MGN/WHC B75 ....63 F2
St Stephen's Av WLNHL WV13 ...39 F3
St Stephens Gdns
  WLNHL WV13 * 39 C4
St Stephens Rd
  HHTH/SAND B71 ....106 D1
  SLYOAK B29 ....160 B2
St Stephens St AST/WIT B6 ....109 E3
St Thomas' Cl ALDR WS9 ....30 D1
  WSL WS1 ....5 J5
St Thomas' Rd
  ERDW/GRVHL B23 ....76 B3
St Thomas St DUDS DY2 ....102 C4
St Valentines Cl WBROM B70 ...88 B4
St Vincent Crs WBROM B70 ....70 D5
St Vincent St LDYWD/EDGR B16..2 A5

St Vincent St West
  LDYWD/EDGR B16 ....126 A2
Saladin Av OLDBY B69 ....104 C4
Salcombe Av
  LGN/SDN/BHAMAIR B26 ....148 A2
Salcombe Cl BRLYHL DY5 ....119 E4
Salcombe Gv BILS/COS WV14 ...68 D2
Salcombe Rd SMTHWK B66 ...106 D4
Salem St TPTN/OCK DY4 ....86 B1
Salford St AST/WIT B6 ....110 A1
Salisbury Chambers
  MOS/BIL B13 * 144 B3
Salisbury Cl DUDN DY1 ....83 H5
  MOS/BIL B13 ....144 A4
Salisbury Dr CSHL/WTROR B46....96 C1
Salisbury Rd LOZ/NWT B19 ....108 D1
  MOS/BIL B13 ....144 A4
  SMTHWK B66 ....106 D5
  WASH/WDE B8 ....111 C5
  WBROM B70 ....88 A5
Salisbury St BDMR/CCFT WV3 ....6 C6
  DARL/WED WS10 ....55 G1
Sallow Cv BRWNH WS8 ....19 C3
Sally Ward Dr ALDR WS9 ....19 G5
Salop Dr HHTH/SAND B71 ....71 F5
Salop Dr LGLYGN/QTN B68 ...123 C2
Salop Rd LGLYGN/QTN B68 ....123 C1
Salop St BHTH/HG B12 ....127 G5
  BILS/COS WV14 ....54 A4
  DUDN DY1 ....84 A4
  OLDBY B69 ....86 C5
  WBROM B70 ....86 C5
Salstar Cl AST/WIT B6 ....109 E3
Saltash Gv YDLY B25 ....129 C3
Saltbrook Rd HALE B63 ....120 A5
Saltel La HHTH/SAND B71 ....88 B2
Salter's Rd ALDR WS9 ....19 C4
Salters V WBROM B70 ....88 A5
Saltley Cottages
  ERDE/BCHGN B24 * 110 D1
Saltley Rd VAUX/NECH B7 ....109 H4
Saltley Vlad VAUX/NECH B7 ...110 A4
Saltney Cl ERDE/BCHGN B24 ....93 H1
Saltwells La BRLYHL DY5 ....120 A2
Saltwells Rd DUDS DY2 ....120 B2
Salwarpe Gv SLYOAK B29 ....141 F5
Sambourn Cl SOLH B91 ....165 C4
Sambourne Dr
  BKDE/SHDE B34 ....113 F2
Sambrook Rd WOLVN WV10 ....24 A4
Sampson Cl HDSW B21 ....89 E5
  OLDBY B69 ....104 A2
Sampson Rd North
  SPARK B11 ....127 H5
Sampson Rd SPARK B11 ....127 C5
Sampson St DARL/WED WS10 ...56 B5
Samuel St WSLW WS2 ....4 A3
Samuels Rd RIDG/WDGT B32 ..140 A2
Samuel St BLOX/PEL WS3 ....27 F1
Sanda Cft CBROM B36 ....114 B3
Sandals Cl NFLD/LBR B31 ....174 D4
Sandalls Rd SOLH B91 ....182 C2
Sandals Ri RMSLY B62 ....139 F4
Sandalwood Cl SHHTH WV12 ...25 H2
Sand Bank BLOX/PEL WS3 ....27 F1
Sandbarn Cl SHLY B90 ....195 F2
Sandbeds Rd SHHTH WV12 ....40 A1
Sandbourne Rd
  WASH/WDE B8 ....111 E5
Sanderling Ri KGSWFD DY6 ....100 C3
Sanders Cl DUDS DY2 ....103 F2
Sanders Crs TPTN/OCK DY4 ....85 H1
Sandfield Br BRLYHL DY5 ....82 D5
Sandfield Rd SHLY B90 ....180 A5
  WBROM B70 ....88 A1
Sandfields Av SMHTH B10 ....127 H4
Sandfields Rd
  LGLYGN/QTN B68 ....123 C2
Sandford Av
  BLKHTH/ROWR B65 ....122 A1
Sandford Ri
  DUNHL/THL/PER WV6 ....22 A4
Sandford Rd DUDN DY1 ....83 C5
  MOS/BIL B13 ....144 C4
Sandgate Rd HLGN/YWD D28 ..179 H1
  TPTN/OCK DY4 ....69 C3
Sandhills Crs SOLH B91 ....181 H5
Sandhill St BLOX/PEL WS3 ....27 E1
Sandhurst Av CBROM B36 ....114 B3
  HAG/WOL DY9 ....136 B5
Sandhurst Dr
  ETTPK/GDPK/PENN WV4 ....51 C4
Sandhurst Gv STRBR DY8 ....118 A1
Sandhurst Rd
  FOAKS/STRLY B74 ....32 D5
  KGSWFD DY6 ....100 C5
  MOS/BIL B13 ....144 A5
Sandland Cl BILS/COS WV14 ....54 B2
Sandland Rd SHHTH WV12 ....26 A2
Sandmartin Cl DUDS DY2 ....120 C2
Sandmeadow Pl KGSWFD DY6 ..99 C4
Sandmere Gv
  ALE/KHTH/YWD B14 ....179 F2
Sandmere Rd
  ALE/KHTH/YWD B14 ....179 F2
Sandon Gv ERDE/BCHGN B24 ...92 B3
Sandon Rd HAG/WOL DY9 ....136 D3
  HRBN B17 ....124 D3
  WOLVN WV10 ....12 B5
Sandown
  DUNHL/THL/PER WV6 ....34 D1
Sandown Rd CBROM B36 ....111 H4
Sandpiper Cl HAG/WOL DY9 ...136 D2
Sandpiper Gdns
  HWK/WKHTH B38 ....190 D1
Sandpiper Wy
  ERDW/GRVHL B23 ....76 A5
Sandpit BVILLE B30 ....159 G2
Sand Pits Pde CBHAMW B1 ....2 B4
Sandport Ms DUDS DY2 * 102 C4
Sandra Cl ALDR WS9 ....30 B5
Sandringham Av SHHTH WV12 ..25 H4
Sandringham Dr ALDR WS9 ....30 B1

  BLKHTH/ROWR B65 ....104 A5
Sandringham Pl STRBR DY8 ...117 H3
Sandringham Rd
  ETTPK/GDPK/PENN WV4 ....51 C4
  PBAR/PBCH B42 ....74 D3
  RMSLY B62 ....121 H5
  STRBR DY8 ....117 C3
  WMBN WV5 ....65 F5
Sandringham Wy BRLYHL DY5..119 E4
Sandstone Av RBRY B45 ....174 A5
Sandstone Cl SEDG DY3 ....83 F2
Sand St WBROM B70 ....86 C2
Sandway Gdns WASH/WDE B8 ..110 B3
Sandway Gv MOS/BIL B13 ....162 A3
Sandwell Av DARL/WED WS10 ...54 D3
Sandwell Pl SHHTH WV12 ....26 B3
Sandwell Rd HDSW B21 ....88 F5
  WBROM B70 ....87 G2
  WOLVN WV10 ....22 D1
Sandwell Rd North
  HHTH/SAND B71 ....87 H2
Sandwell St WSL WS1 ....5 F6
Sandwell Wk WSL WS1 ....5 F7
Sandwood Dr KGSTG B44 ....75 F3
Sandyacre Wy STRBR DY8 ....135 H2
Sandy Crt CSCFLD/WYGN B72 ...62 C5
  MOS/BIL B13 ....162 A3
Sandyfields Rd SEDG DY3 ....82 B1
Sandy Gv BRWNH WS8 ....9 F5
Sandy Hill Ri SHLY B90 ....180 A5
Sandy Hill Rd SHLY B90 ....180 A5
Sandy Hollow
  DUNHL/THL/PER WV6 ....35 C3
Sandy La AST/WIT B6 ....109 G2
  BRGRVW B61 ....186 B3
  CDSL WV8 ....10 B5
  DSYBK/YTR WS5 ....57 E4
  DUNHL/THL/PER WV6 ....22 A4
  PBAR/PBCH B42 ....74 D5
  WOLVN WV10 ....23 G1
Sandy Mt WMBN WV5 ....65 F4
Sandy Mount Rd WSL WS1 ....5 C7
Sandy Rd TPTN/OCK DY4 ....85 E1
Sandy Wy EDG B15 ....2 C7
Sangwin Rd BILS/COS WV14 ....68 C4
Sansome Rd SHLY B90 ....179 H5
Sansome Rd SHLY B90 ....179 H5
Sanstone Cl BLOX/PEL WS3 ....17 E4
Sanstone Rd BLOX/PEL WS3 ....16 D4
Santolina Dr DSYBK/YTR WS5 ...57 C5
Sant Rd NFLD/LBR B31 ....189 H1
The Saplings WALM/CURD B76..78 C5
Saracen Dr MGN/WHC B75 ....63 F2
Sara Cl FOAKS/STRLY B74 ....47 E2
Sarah Cl BILS/COS WV14 ....69 E2
Sarah Gdns DSYBK/YTR WS5 ....57 F4
Sarah St BORD B9 ....127 H2
Saredon Cl BLOX/PEL WS3 ....28 C1
Sarehole Rd HLGN/YWD D28 ..162 C2
Sargent Cl GTB/HAM B43 ....59 H4
Sark Dr CBROM B36 ....114 B5
Saunton Wy SLYOAK B29 ....159 E1
Saveker Dr WALM/CURD B76 ....63 E4
Savernake Cl RBRY B45 ....174 A5
Saville Cl RBRY B45 ....188 B1
Savoy Cl RIDG/WDGT B32 ....141 F2
Saw Mill Cl RUSH/SHEL WS4 ....4 F1
Saxelby Cl
  ALE/KHTH/YWD B14 ....178 A3
Saxoncourt
  DUNHL/THL/PER WV6 ....21 C5
Saxondale Av
  LGN/SDN/BHAMAIR B26 ....147 F1
Saxon Dr BLKHTH/ROWR B65 ..104 A5
Saxonfields
  DUNHL/THL/PER WV6 ....21 C5
Saxons Wy
  ALE/KHTH/YWD B14 ....178 C5
Saxon Wy
  CHWD/FDBR/MGN B37 ....131 H1
Saxon Wood Cl NFLD/LBR B31..175 C1
Saxon Wood Rd SHLY B90 ....194 D3
Saxton Dr FOAKS/STRLY B74 ....32 C4
Scafell Dr BILS/COS WV14 ....54 B1
  ERDW/GRVHL B23 ....92 A1
Scafell Rd STRBR DY8 ....135 H1
Scampton Cl
  DUNHL/THL/PER WV6 ....20 C5
Scarborough Cl WSLW WS2 ....47 F5
Scarborough Rd WSLW WS2 ....41 C5
Scarecrow La MGN/WHC B75 ...48 A1
Scarsdale Rd PBAR/PBCH B42 ...74 D3
Schofield Av HHTH/SAND B71 ...71 F5
Schofield Rd
  CHWD/FDBR/MGN B37 ....113 H4
Scholars Ga STETCH B33 ....130 D2
Scholars Rd HDSW B21 ....107 H2
Schoolacre Ri
  FOAKS/STRLY B74 ....45 E4
Schoolacre Rd
  BKDE/SHDE B34 ....112 D3
School Av BRWNH WS8 ....9 F4
School Cl BDMR/CCFT WV3 ....50 B1
  CDSL WV8 ....10 C3
  CHWD/FDBR/MGN B37 ....114 A3
  CVALE B35 ....94 D3
  NFLD/LBR B31 ....175 E3
  OLDBY B69 ....104 A2
  WMBN WV5 ....64 A2
School Cottages
  WOLVN WV10 * 12 B5
School Dr BILS/COS WV14 * 68 C2
  BKDE/SHDE B34 ....113 G4
  HLYWD B47 ....192 C5
  STRBR DY8 ....118 B4
The School Dr DUDS DY2 ....102 D2
Schoolgate Cl RUSH/SHEL WS4..29 F1
  STECH B33 ....112 B4
School Gn BILS/COS WV14 ....38 C5
Schoolhouse Cl
  HWK/WKHTH B38 ....177 F3
School La BKDE/SHDE B34 ....112 D3
  BLOX/PEL WS3 ....17 H3
  BRLYHL DY5 ....101 F5
  HAG/WOL DY9 ....153 F4
  HIA/OLT B92 ....146 B3
  SOLH B91 ....182 B1
  STETCH B33 ....130 B3
  WOLVN WV10 ....12 D5

School Rd
ALE/KHTH/YWD B14......178 D1
BRLYHL DY5......120 A2
DARL/WED WS10......71 H1
DUNHL/THL/PER WV6......35 E1
HLGN/YWD B28......162 D2
MOS/BIL B13......161 F1
RBRY B45......81 F5
SEDG DY3......180 B3
SHLY B90......180 B3
WMBN WV5......64 A2
WNSFLD WV11......24 C4
School St BDMR/CCFT WV3......
BRLYHL DY5......101 F2
CDYHTH B64......120 D3
DARL/WED WS10......55 F3
DUDN DY1......84 B5
RUSH/SHEL WS4......9 G7
SEDG DY3......67 G3
STRBR DY8 *......135 F1
WLNHL WV13......39 F5
School St West BILS/COS WV14......38 C5
School Ter SLYOAK B29 *......142 D5
School Wk BILS/COS WV14......38 C5
Scorers Cl SHLY B90......163 F4
The Scotchings CBROM B36......112 A1
Scotland La RIDG/WDGT B32......157 G3
Scotland St CBROM B36......2 C4
Scott Av DARL/WED WS10......71 F1
ETTPK/GDPK/PENN WV4......51 E4
Scott Gv HIA/OLT B92......147 E4
Scott Rd DSYBK/YTR WS5......58 B2
GTB/HAM B43......73 H1
HIA/OLT B92......147 E5
Scott's Green Cl DUDN DY1......101 H1
Scott's Rd STRBR DY8......135 F1
Scotts St TPTN/OCK DY4......86 A1
Scotwell Cl
BLKHTH/ROWR B65......121 H1
Scout Cl STETCH B33......131 H1
Scribbans Cl SMTHWK B66......106 D5
Scribers La HLGN/YWD B28......179 G1
Scribers Meadow
HLGN/YWD B28......179 G1
Sculthorpe Rd KIDD DY10......168 B3
Seacroft Av YDLY B25......130 A3
Seafield Cl KGSWFD DY6......100 A5
Seaforth Gv SHHTH WV12......25 H1
Seagar St BRLYHL DY5......119 F2
Seager's La BRLYHL DY5......119 F2
Seagull Bay Dr BILS/COS WV14......68 D2
Seal Cl WALM/CURD B76......63 E5
Seals Gn HWK/WKHTH B38......190 B1
Seamless Dr WNSFLD WV11......25 F5
Seaton Cl WNSFLD WV11......25 F5
Seaton Gv MOS/BIL B13......160 D1
Seaton Pl STRBR DY8......117 G2
Seaton Rd SMTHWK B66......106 D4
Second Av BORD B9......128 C3
BRWNH WS8......9 G4
KGSWFD DY6......100 C2
SLYOAK B29......143 F4
WOLVN WV10......23 H4
Second Exhibition Av
BHAMNEC B40......149 H3
Sedge Av HWK/WKHTH B38......176 D2
Sedgeborrow Covert
HWK/WKHTH B38......176 C5
Sedgeborrow Rd HALE B63......138 C5
Sedgeborrow Wy
DUNHL/THL/PER WV6......174 C4
Sedgefield Cl DUDN DY1......83 C3
Sedgefield Gv
DUNHL/THL/PER WV6......34 D1
Sedgeford Rd BRLYHL DY5......119 F4
Sedgehill Av HRBN B17......141 H3
Sedgemere Av RUSH/SHEL WS4......29 E2
Sedgemere Rd
LGN/SDN/BHAMAIR B26......130 B3
Sedgley Av BFLD/HDSWWD B20......89 G2
Sedgley Hall Av SEDG DY3......67 E3
Sedgley Rd
ETTPK/GDPK/PENN WV4......66 B1
Sedgley Rd East TPTN/OCK DY4......85 G2
Sedgley Rd West
SEDG DY3......68 C5
Sedgley St BKHL/PFLD WV2......52 A1
Seedhouse Ct CDYHTH B64......121 C4
Seeds La BRWNH WS8......9 F4
Seeleys Rd SPARK B11......145 G2
Sefton Dr BLKHTH/ROWR B65......103 F5
Sefton Gv TPTN/OCK DY4......70 A1
Sefton Rd LDYWD/EDGR B16......125 H3
Segbourne Rd RBRY B45......173 G5
Segundo Cl DSYBK/YTR WS5......57 F4
Segundo Rd DSYBK/YTR WS5......57 F4
Selborne Cl WSL WS1 *......5 H4
Selborne Gv MOS/BIL B13......162 A5
Selborne Rd
BFLD/HDSWWD B20......90 A4
DUDS DY2......102 D2
Selborne St WSL WS1......5 H4
Selbourne Crs WOLV WV1......38 B4
Selby Cl
LGN/SDN/BHAMAIR B26......130 B3
Selby Gv MOS/BIL B13......162 A5
Selby Wy BLOX/PEL WS3......16 A5
Selcombe Wy
HWK/WKHTH B38......190 D1
Selco Wy WALM/CURD B76......94 C1
Selcroft Av RIDG/WDGT B32......141 F2
Selecta Av KGSTG B44......74 D1
Selkirk Cl HHTH/SAND B71......71 G5
Selly Av SLYOAK B29......143 G5
Selly Cl SLYOAK B29......143 F5
Selly Hall Cft BVILLE B30......159 H4
Selly Hill Rd SLYOAK B29......142 D5
Selly Oak Rd BVILLE B30......159 G5
Selly Wharf SLYOAK B29......143 F5
Selly Wick Dr SLYOAK B29......143 F5
Selly Wick Rd SLYOAK B29......143 F5
Sellywood Rd BVILLE B30......159 G5
Selman's Hill BLOX/PEL WS3......17 E4
Selman's Pde BLOX/PEL WS3 *......17 E5
Selsdon Cl HLYWD B47......193 E5
Selsdon Rd BLOX/PEL WS3......16 A5
Selsey Av HRBN B17......124 D1
Selsey Rd HRBN B17......124 D1

Selston Rd AST/WIT B6......109 E2
Selvey Av GTB/HAM B43......59 F5
Selworthy Rd CBROM B36......113 H2
Selwyn Cl BKHL/PFLD WV2......52 A1
Selwyn Rd BILS/COS WV14......54 B2
LDYWD/EDGR B16......125 F1
Selwyn Wk FOAKS/STRLY B74......46 A1
Senneleys Park Rd
NFLD/LBR B31......158 B1
Sennen Cl WLNHL WV13......39 F4
Sensall Rd HAG/WOL DY9......136 D4
Sentry Wy MGN/WHC B75......63 E5
Serpentine Rd AST/WIT B6......91 G5
HRBN B17......142 A2
SLYOAK B29......143 E4
Sheen Rd KGSTG B44......60 A4
Sheepcose Dr
CHWD/FDBR/MGN B37......132 A1
Sheepcote St LDYWD/EDGR B16......2 A5
Sheepfold Cl
BLKHTH/ROWR B65......103 G5
Sheepmoor Cl HRBN B17......124 B4
Sheepwash La TPTN/OCK DY4......86 B1
Sheerwater Dr BRLYHL DY5......77 E4
Sheffield Rd SCFLD/BOLD B73......77 E4
Sheffield St BRLYHL DY5......120 A3
Shefford Rd AST/WIT B6......109 F4
Sheila Av WNSFLD WV11......25 E5
Shelah Rd HALE B63......138 C1
Shelbourne Cl OLDBY B69......86 B4
Sheldon Av DARL/WED WS10......56 A4
Sheldon Cl BILS/COS WV14......53 H5
Sheldon Dr NFLD/LBR B31......174 D4
Sheldonfield Rd
LGN/SDN/BHAMAIR B26......148 B3
Sheldon Gv
LGN/SDN/BHAMAIR B26......147 H2
Sheldon Hall Av STETCH B33......131 F1
Sheldon Heath Rd
LGN/SDN/BHAMAIR B26......130 C2
Sheldon Rd HHTH/SAND B71......72 A3
WOLVN WV10......22 C1
Shelfield Rd
ALE/KHTH/YWD B14......177 G2
Shelley Av TPTN/OCK DY4......69 G3
Shelley Cl SEDG DY3......66 D2
STRBR DY8......118 C4
Shelley Dr ERDW/GRVHL B23......91 H5
FOAKS/STRLY B74......32 D4
WOLVN WV10......26 C5
Shelly Cl
CHWD/FDBR/MGN B37......131 H2
Shelly Crs SHLY B90......195 H2
Shelly Cft STETCH B33......130 C1
Shelly La SHLY B90......195 H2
Shelsley Av OLDBY B69......104 B4
Shelsley Dr MOS/BIL B13......161 H4
Shelsley Wy SOLH B91......181 H4
Shelton Cl DARL/WED WS10......56 C3
Shelton La HALE B63......138 A2
Shelwick Gv DOR/KN B93......196 D4
Shenley Av DUDN DY1......68 B5
Shenley Fields Dr
NFLD/LBR B31......158 A2
Shenley Fields Rd SLYOAK B29......158 B3
Shenley Gdns SLYOAK B29......158 C4
Shenley Hl NFLD/LBR B31......158 B3
Shenley La NFLD/LBR B31......158 B3
Shenstone Av RMSLY B62......159 C3
STRBR DY8......118 A5
Shenstone Cl FOAKS/STRLY B74......32 C4
Shenstone Ct BDMR/CCFT WV3......51 G2
Shenstone Dr ALDR WS9......30 A2
Shenstone Rd
ALE/KHTH/YWD B14......178 C4
GTB/HAM B43......73 G3
LDYWD/EDGR B16......125 E1
Shenstone Valley Rd
RMSLY B62......139 H1
Shenton Wk
CHWD/FDBR/MGN B37......113 H4
Shepheard Rd
LGN/SDN/BHAMAIR B26......148 B2
Shepherd Dr SHHTH WV12......25 H5
Shepherds Brook Rd
HAG/WOL DY9......136 B2
Shepherds Fold
BLKHTH/ROWR B65......121 H2
Shepherds Gdns EDG B15......126 B3
Shepherds Green Rd
ERDE/BCHGN B24......92 D4
Shepherds Pool Rd
MGN/WHC B75......48 A3
Shepherds Standing
BKDE/SHDE B34......112 D3
Shepwell Gn
ERDW/GRVHL B23......76 A3
Shepley Rd RBRY B45......188 B2
Sheppey Dr CBROM B36......114 B4
Shepwell Gn WLNHL WV13......40 A4
Sherard Cft CBROM B36......114 B3
Sheraton Cl ALDR WS9......30 D4
Sheraton Gra STRBR DY8......135 F5
Sherborne Cl BLOX/PEL WS3......27 G3
CSHL/WTROR B46......115 C5
Sherborne Gdns CDSL WV8......10 C4
Sherborne Gv CBHAMW B1......126 A1
Sherborne Rd WOLVN WV10......23 F1
Sherborne St LDYWD/EDGR B16......2 A6
Sherbourne Dr ACGN B27......146 A1
Sherbourne Rd ACGN B27......146 B3
BHTH/HG B12......144 B1
CDYHTH B64......121 G4
STRBR DY8......135 H3
Sherdmore Cft SHLY B90......195 F2
Sheridan Cl WSLW WS2......56 B1
Sheridan Gdns SEDG DY3......82 B1
Sheridan St HHTH/SAND B71......71 F4
WSLW WS2......56 B1
Sheriff Dr BRLYHL DY5......119 H2
Sherifoot La MGN/WHC B75......47 F2
Sheringham EDG B15......125 G2
Sheringham Rd BVILLE B30......177 F2
Sherington Dr
ETTPK/GDPK/PENN WV4......52 B3
Sherlock Cl SHHTH WV12......26 B5
Sherlock St DIG/EDG B5......127 E4

Shawsdale Rd CBROM B36......112 B2
Shaw's Pas DIG/EDG B5......3 J5
Shaw St WBROM B70......70 C3
WSLW WS2......4 D3
Shayler Gv BKHL/PFLD WV2......52 B1
Sheaf La
LGN/SDN/BHAMAIR B26......147 H3
Shearers Pl MGN/WHC B75......48 A2
Shearwater Cl RBRY B45......187 H2
Shearwater Wk
ERDW/GRVHL B23......75 H5
Sheaves Cl BILS/COS WV14......53 E5
Shedden St DUDS DY2......102 D1
Sheddington Rd
ERDW/GRVHL B23......76 B4
Sheepcote St LDYWD/EDGR B16......2 A5
Sheffield Wk
FOAKS/STRLY B74......46 A1

Sherrans Dell
ETTPK/GDPK/PENN WV4......52 B5
Sherratt Cl WALM/CURD B76......78 B3
Sherringham Dr WNSFLD WV11......26 A1
Sherron Gdns BHTH/HG B12......144 B2
Sherston Covert BVILLE B30......177 G3
Shervale Cl
ETTPK/GDPK/PENN WV4......51 G2
Sherwin Av BILS/COS WV14......68 A1
Sherwood Av TPTN/OCK DY4......85 F2
Sherwood Cl HIA/OLT B92......164 B2
HLGN/YWD B28......162 D5
Sherwood Dr BRLYHL DY5......119 H3
Sherwood Ms HLGN/YWD B28......162 C4
Sherwood Rd HLGN/YWD B28......162 C4
SMTHWK B67......105 E5
STRBR DY8......118 A5
Sherwood St WOLV WV1......6 E1
Sherwood Wk ALDR WS9......29 F3
Shetland Cl
DUNHL/THL/PER WV6......22 D4
LDYWD/EDGR B16......125 H2
Shetland Dr SMTHWK B66......105 H2
Shidas La OLDBY B69......104 C2
Shifnal Wy MGN/WHC B75......63 F1
Shillcock Gv LOZ/NWT B19......109 E4
Shilton Cl SHLY B90......195 F2
Shilton Gv SLYOAK B29......158 A2
Shinwell Crs OLDBY B69......86 B4
Shipbourne Cl
RIDG/WDGT B32......141 F2
Shipley Flds ERDE/BCHGN B24......93 G5
Shipley Gv SLYOAK B29......158 C2
Shipston Rd NFLD/LBR B31......175 H4
Shipton Cl DUDN DY1......83 C3
Shipton Rd SCFLD/WYGN B72......62 C5
Shipway Rd YDLY B25......129 E5
Shirebrook Cl AST/WIT B6......109 H1
Shire Cl LDYWD/EDGR B16......125 H2
LGLYGN/QTN B68......123 F2
Shireland Brook Gdns
WSNGN B18 *......107 F3
Shireland Cl
BFLD/HDSWWD B20......89 G3
Shire Rdg ALDR WS9......19 G5
Shirestone Rd STETCH B33......131 G2
Shireview Gdns
BLOX/PEL WS3 *......18 B3
Shireview Rd BLOX/PEL WS3......18 B3
Shirland Rd
CHWD/FDBR/MGN B37......132 A3
Shirley Dr SCFLD/WYGN B72......62 C4
Shirley Park Rd SHLY B90......180 B3
Shirley Rd ACGN B27......146 B3
BVILLE B30......160 A5
DUDS DY2......103 E1
HLGN/YWD B28......163 E2
LGLYGN/QTN B68......123 F2
Shirral Gv
CHWD/FDBR/MGN B37......113 H4
Shirrall Dr MGN/WHC B75......49 F1
Sholing Cl CDSL WV8......22 B1
Shooters Cl EDG B15......143 H1
Shooters Hl CSCFLD/WYGN B72......77 H1
Shop La CDSL WV8......20 B1
Shopton Rd BKDE/SHDE B34......112 C2
Shoreham Cl WLNHL WV13......38 D4
Short Acre St WSLW WS2......4 D1
Shorters Av
ALE/KHTH/YWD B14......178 D1
Short Heath Rd
ERDW/GRVHL B23......76 C5
ERDW/GRVHL B23......76 C5
Shortlands Cl ERDE/BCHGN B24......92 B4
Shortlands Cl BVILLE B30......177 E3
Shortlands La BLOX/PEL WS3......17 H5
Short Rd SMTHWK B67......123 H1
WOLVN WV10......23 E3
Short St BILS/COS WV14......53 H2
BLKHTH/ROWR B65......122 A3
BRWNH WS8......9 F5
DARL/WED WS10......84 A4
DUDN DY1......84 C4
HALE B63......138 B3
SHHTH WV12......26 A5
SHLY B90......194 A3
STRBR DY8......135 F2
TPTN/OCK DY4......69 E5
WOLV WV1......6 D4
WSLW WS2......4 B4
Short St Vw
BLKHTH/ROWR B65......121 H1
Six Acres RIDG/WDGT B32......140 C3
Skelcher Rd SHLY B90......180 A1
Skemp Cl BILS/COS WV14......53 H4
Sketchley Cl SMTHWK B66......106 C4
Skidmore Av BDMR/CCFT WV3......36 B5
Skidmore Dr WBROM B70......69 H4
Skidmore Rd BILS/COS WV14......68 D1
Skinner La DIG/EDG B5......127 E3
Skinner St WOLV WV1......6 E4
Skip La DSYBK/YTR WS5......58 C3
Skipton Gn
DUNHL/THL/PER WV6......22 C5
Skipton Rd LDYWD/EDGR B16......126 A3
Skomer Cl RBRY B45......173 C4
Sky Lark Cl BRLYHL DY5......118 C5
Skylark Cl BRLYHL DY5......83 E5
ERDW/GRVHL B23......76 A4
Sladefield Rd WASH/WDE B8......111 E4
Slade Gv DOR/KN B93......165 G5
Slade Hl
DUNHL/THL/PER WV6......36 B2
Slade La HLGN/YWD B28......179 G2
MGN/WHC B75......48 A2
Slade Lanker BKDE/SHDE B34......112 C4
Sladepool Farm Rd
ALE/KHTH/YWD B14......178 B2
Slade Rd ERDW/GRVHL B23......92 B4
HALE B63......137 G1
MGN/WHC B75......48 A2
WOLVN WV10......12 C4

Sidenhill Cl SHLY B90......180 B5
Sidestrand COVEN WV9......11 H4
The Sidings STRBR DY8......152 C4
WBROM B70......87 C4
Sidlaw Cl HALE B63......137 G5
Sidney St BKHL/PFLD WV2......6 E7
Sidwick Crs BKHL/PFLD WV2......53 F2
Sigmund Cl WOLV WV1......38 B2
Signal Gv BLOX/PEL WS3......27 E1
Signal Hayes Rd
WALM/CURD B76......78 C2
Silesbourne Cl CBROM B36 *......95 E5
Silhill Hall Rd SOLH B91......164 C3
Silva Av KGSWFD DY6......100 B5
Silver Birch Cl WASH/WDE B8......110 B3
Silver Birch Coppice
FOAKS/STRLY B74......32 B5
Silver Birch Dr HLYWD B47......192 D2
Silver Birch Rd BKHL/PFLD WV2......53 F2
CHWD/FDBR/MGN B37......113 H5
ERDW/GRVHL B23......77 F5
KGSWFD DY6......45 F4
Silverbirch Rd B24......182 C2
Silvercroft Av HDSW B21......89 C2
Silverdale Dr WOLVN WV10......37 G1
Silverdale Gdns STRBR DY8......117 C1
Silverdale Rd ERDE/BCHGN B24......93 H2
Silverfield Cl
ALE/KHTH/YWD B14......161 G2
Silver Innage HALE B63......120 C5
Silverlands Av
LGLYGN/QTN B68......123 F4
Silverlands Cl HLGN/YWD B28......162 D1
Silvermead Ct HLYWD B47......192 A3
Silvermead Rd
SCFLD/BOLD B73......77 E2
Silvermere Rd
LGN/SDN/BHAMAIR B26......148 B1
Silver's Cl BLOX/PEL WS3......17 H2
Silverstone Cl WSLW WS2......40 B2
Silverstone Dr
FOAKS/STRLY B74......60 B2
Silver St ALE/KHTH/YWD B14......161 G2
BRLYHL DY5......118 D5
BRWNH WS8......9 E5
HLYWD B47......193 C2
Silverthorne Av TPTN/OCK DY4......84 D1
Silverthorne La CDYHTH B64......120 D3
Silverton Crs MOS/BIL B13......162 B1
Silverton Hts SMTHWK B67 *......106 D3
Silverton Rd SMTHWK B66......106 A3
Silverton Wy WNSFLD WV11......25 E3
Silvertrees Rd TPTN/OCK DY4......85 F1
Silvester Rd BILS/COS WV14......118 D4
Silvester Wy BRLYHL DY5......118 D4
Silvington Cl SLYOAK B29......159 E3
Simcox Gdns RIDG/WDGT B32......140 D5
Simcox Rd DARL/WED WS10......55 H3
Simeon Bissell Cl
TPTN/OCK DY4......85 C1
Simeon's Wk BRLYHL DY5......120 B1
Simmonds Cl BLOX/PEL WS3......17 F4
Simmonds Pl DARL/WED WS10......55 H1
Simmonds Rd BLOX/PEL WS3......17 F4
Simmonds Wy BRWNH WS8......19 G2
Simmons Dr RIDG/WDGT B32......140 C4
Simmons Leasow
RIDG/WDGT B32......140 D5
Simms La DUDS DY2......102 C4
HLYWD B47......192 C3
Simon Cl HHTH/SAND B71......72 A2
Simon Rd HLYWD B47......192 C1
Simpkins Cl ALDR WS9......19 G4
Simpson Gv WOLVN WV10......23 G4
Simpson Rd CSCFLD/WYGN B72......77 G5
WOLVN WV10......23 G4
Simpson St OLDBY B69......105 E2
Singer Cft CBROM B36......95 H5
Sir Alfreds Wy
WALM/CURD B76......43 E5
Sir Harrys Rd DIG/EDG B5......143 G1
Sir Hilton's Rd NFLD/LBR B31......189 H1
Sir John's Rd SLYOAK B29......143 F1
Sir Richards Dr HRBN B17......124 D5
Sisefield Rd HWK/WKHTH B38......177 E4
Siskin Cl LGLYGN/QTN B68......123 G2
Siskin Dr BHTH/HG B12......144 A1
Siskin Rd STRBR DY8......135 H4
Sister Dora Buildings WSL WS1 *......5 H4
Sister Dora Gdns WSL WS1......4 D5
Sivite's Cl BLKHTH/ROWR B65 *......121 H1
Siviter's La
BLKHTH/ROWR B65......121 H1

Shambles DARL/WED WS10......70 D1
Shandon Cl RIDG/WDGT B32......141 F4
Shannon Dr BRWNH WS8......8 C2
Shannon Rd HWK/WKHTH B38......190 C1
Shapinsay Dr RBRY B45......173 H4
Shard End Crs
BKDE/SHDE B34......113 G4
Shardlow Rd WNSFLD WV11......25 E2
The Shardway
BKDE/SHDE B34......113 G4
Sharesacre St WLNHL WV13......39 H2
Sharington Cl DUDS DY2......103 E1
Sharman Rd WOLVN WV10......23 H5
Sharmans Cross Rd SOLH B91......181 F1
Sharon Cl
LGN/SDN/BHAMAIR B26......52 C3
Sharps Cl RBRY B45......188 A1
Sharrat Fld MGN/WHC B75......47 H3
Sharrocks St WOLV WV1......7 J6
Shawberry Av CVALE B35......94 D5
Shawberry Rd
CHWD/FDBR/MGN B37 *......113 H4
Shawbrook Gv
ALE/KHTH/YWD B14......178 C2
Shawbury Gv BHTH/HG B12......127 F4
DUNHL/THL/PER WV6......20 C5
Shawbury Rd WOLVN WV10......23 H5
Shaw Dr STETCH B33......130 A2
Shawfield HLYWD B47......192 C1
Shawhellier Av BRLYHL DY5......119 G2
Shaw Hill Rd WASH/WDE B8......111 E5
Shawhurst Cft HLYWD B47......192 C1
Shawhurst Gdns HLYWD B47......192 D1
Shawhurst La HLYWD B47......192 C2
Shaw La DUNHL/THL/PER WV6......35 F2
Shawley Crt ACGN B27......147 E3
Shaw Rd BILS/COS WV14......68 B2
BKHL/PFLD WV2......52 A2
DUDS DY2......102 B2
TPTN/OCK DY4......86 A2
WOLVN WV10......23 H4

Slaithwaite Rd
HHTH/SAND B71 ....87 H2
Slaney Ct *WSLW* WS2 ....56 C1
Slaney Rd *WSLW* WS2 ....56 C1
Slatch House Rd
SMTHWK B67 ....124 A2
Slateley Crs *SHLY* B90 ....195 F2
Slater Ct *CDYHTH* B64 ....121 F3
Slater Rd *DOR/KN* B93 ....196 C4
Slaters La *WSLW* WS2 ....56 B1
Slater St *BILS/COS* WV14 ......54 A5
DARL/WED WS10 ....55 F2
TPTN/OCK DY4 ....85 G2
WLNHL WV13 ....40 A2
Sleaford Gv *HLGN/YWD* B28 .163 E5
Sleaford Rd *HLGN/YWD* B28 .163 E5
Sledmore Rd *DUDS* DY2 ....102 D2
The Slieve *BFLD/HDSWWD* B20 .90 A3
Slim Av *BILS/COS* WV14 ....54 A5
Slim Rd *WSLW* WS2 ....40 C3
Slims Ga *HALE* B63 ....138 C3
Slingfield Rd *NFLD/LBR* B31 ..176 A4
The Sling *DUDS* DY2 ....102 C3
Sloane St *CBHAMW* B1 ....2 C4
Smallbrook La *WMBN* WV5 ......65 F4
Smallbrook Queensway
DIG/EDG B5 ....3 G7
Small Cl *SMTHWK* B67 ....105 H4
Smalldale Rd *PBAR/PBCH* B42 .74 D4
Small Heath Br *SPARK* B11 ....127 H5
Small Heath Hwy *SMHTH* B10 .145 H1
Smallshire Cl *WNSFLD* WV11 ..25 F5
Smallshire Wy *STRBR* DY8 .....117 H4
Small St *HHTH/SAND* B71 ....87 F1
WSL WS1 ....4 D6
Smallwood Cl
ERDE/BCHGN B24 ....93 H3
WALM/CURD B76 ....63 E5
Smallwood Rd *CDSL* WV8 ....11 C5
Smarts Av *LICHS* WS14 ....33 E3
Smeaton Gdns *WSNGN* B18 ...107 G5
Smeed Gv *ERDE/BCHGN* B24 ...93 E5
Smestow La *SEDG* DY5 ....80 A2
Smestow St *WOLVN* WV10 ....37 F1
Smirrells Rd *HLGN/YWD* B28 ..162 C5
Smith Av *DARL/WED* WS10 ......55 F4
Smith Cl *BILS/COS* WV14 ....68 A4
SMTHWKW B67 ....123 H1
Smithfield Rd *BLOX/PEL* WS3 ..27 H1
Smithmoor Crs
HHTH/SAND B71 ....72 B3
Smith Pl *TPTN/OCK* DY4 ....85 H2
Smith Rd *DARL/WED* WS10 .....70 D2
WSLW WS2 ....56 C2
Smiths Cl *RIDG/WDGT* B32 ....157 F1
Smiths La *DOR/KN* B93 ....196 C2
Smith St *BILS/COS* WV14 ....53 H3
DUDS DY2 ....102 D2
LOZ/NWT B19 ....108 C4
Smithy Dr *BLOX/PEL* WS3 ....18 A3
Smithy La *BRLYHL* DY5 ....100 D1
The Smithy
LGN/SDN/BHAMAIR B26 ......147 H1
Smout Crs *BILS/COS* WV14 ......67 H1
Snapdragon Dr
DYSBK/YTR WS5 ....57 F5
Snape Rd *WNSFLD* WV11 ....25 G1
Sneyd Hall Cl *BLOX/PEL* WS3 * ..27 E2
Sneyd Hall Rd *BLOX/PEL* WS3 ..26 D1
Sneyd La *WNSFLD* WV11 ....25 H1
Snowberry Dr *BRLYHL* DY5 .....83 E5
Snowberry Gdns *ACGN* B27 * .146 C2
Snowdon Gv *HALE* B63 ....154 D1
Snowdon Rd *SEDG* DY5 ....67 F5
Snowdon Wy *SHHTH* WV12 .....25 H1
WOLVN WV10 ....22 D4
Snowdrop Cl *BRWNH* WS8 ......18 D1
Snowford Cl *SHLY* B90 ....179 F1
Snow Hl *BKHL/PFLD* WV2 ....7 G5
Snow Hill Jct *BKHL/PFLD* WV2 * .7 G6
Snow Hl Queensway
CBHAMNE B4 ....3 F3
Snows Hill Dr *SHLY* B90 ....194 D3
Snowshill Gdns *DUDN* DY1 .....83 H2
Soberton Cl *WNSFLD* WV11 .....25 F5
Soho Cl *SMTHWK* B66 ....108 A2
Soho Cl *SMTHWK* B66 ....107 E5
Soho Hl *HDSW* B21 ....108 A2
Sohopoolway *WSNGN* B18 .....108 A3
Soho Rd *HDSW* B21 ....107 H2
Soho Wy *SMTHWK* B66 ....106 D3
Solari Cl *TPTN/OCK* DY4 ....70 A5
Solent Cl *COVEN* WV9 ....11 H5
Solihull By-Pass *SOLH* B91 ....182 D2
Solihull La *HLGN/YWD* B28 ....163 E4
Solihull Pkwy
CHWD/FDBR/MGN B37 ....133 E5
Solihull Rd *HIA/OLT* B92 ....166 D4
SHLY B90 ....180 D2
SPARK B11 ....145 F4
Solihull Vw *CBROM* B36 ....112 C1
HIA/OLT B92 ....194 D3
SHLY B90 ....194 D3
Solly Gv *TPTN/OCK* DY4 ....70 B4
Solva Cl *WOLV* WV1 ....38 B4
Solway Cl *DARL/WED* WS10 .....56 C4
Somerby Dr *BILS/COS* WV14 ..181 G5
Somercotes Rd
PBAR/PBCH B42 ....74 D3
Somerdale Rd *NFLD/LBR* B31 .176 A1
Somerfield Cl *WNSFLD* WV11 ..25 F4
Somerfield Rd *BLOX/PEL* WS3 .27 F2
Somerford Gdns *WOLVN* WV10 .13 E5
Somerford Pl *WLNHL* WV13 .....39 F4
Somerford Rd *SLYOAK* B29 ....158 B2
Somerford Wy *BILS/COS* WV14 .68 D3
Somerland Rd
LGN/SDN/BHAMAIR B26 ......130 C3
Somerset Crs *DARL/WED* WS10 .56 D4
Somerset Dr *NFLD/LBR* B31 ...189 F1
STRBR DY8 ....117 H5
Somerset Rd
BFLD/HDSWWD B20 ....89 H4
EDG B15 ....142 C3
ERDW/GRVHL B23 ....76 C5
HHTH/SAND B71 ....71 H5

RUSH/SHEL WS4 ....42 C1
WLNHL WV13 ....40 B3
Somers Rd *RMSLY* B62 ....139 E2
Somerton Dr
CHWD/FDBR/MGN B37 ....132 B5
ERDW/GRVHL B23 ....77 E5
Somerville Rd *SCFLD/BOLD* B73 .62 A4
SMHTH B10 ....128 D4
Somery Rd *DUDN* DY1 ....84 C3
RIDG/WDGT B32 ....141 G5
Sommerfield Rd
RIDG/WDGT B32 ....140 D4
Sommerville Dr
SCFLD/BOLD B73 ....62 A4
Sonning Dr *COVEN* WV9 ....11 H5
Sopwith Cft *CVALE* B35 ....94 C4
Sorrel Cl *OLDBY* B69 ....85 H4
Sorrel Dr *ACGN* B27 ....146 B5
DYSBK/YTR WS5 ....57 G5
Sorrel Gv *ERDE/BCHGN* B24 ...93 H5
Southacre Av *DIG/EDG* B5 .....127 E4
Southall Crs *BILS/COS* WV14 ..68 C2
Southall Rd *WNSFLD* WV11 .....25 G2
Southall's La *DUDN* DY1 ....84 B5
Southam Cl *HLGN/YWD* B28 ..162 C2
Southam Dr *SCFLD/BOLD* B73 .77 F2
Southampton St *WOLV* WV1 .....7 G2
Southam Rd *HLGN/YWD* B28 .162 C2
South Av *STRBR* DY8 ....135 F3
WNSFLD WV11 ....24 C5
South Bank Rd *CDYHTH* B64 ...111 G1
Southbank Vw *KGSWFD* DY6 ..100 A5
Southbourne Av
BKDE/SHDE B34 ....111 H3
WSLW WS2 ....41 F4
Southbourne Cl *SLYOAK* B29 .143 E5
Southbourne Rd *WOLVN* WV10 .12 C4
Southcote Gv
HWK/WKHTH B38 ....176 B4
Southcott Av *BRLYHL* DY5 ....119 E4
South Crs *WOLVN* WV10 ....14 A1
Southcroft Rd
ERDW/GRVHL B23 ....92 C3
South Dene *SMTHWK* B67 * ...106 B4
Southdown Av *WSNGN* B18 ...108 A3
South Dr *CSHL/WTROR* B46 ...115 E3
DIG/EDG B5 ....145 G3
MGN/WHC B75 ....62 C2
Southend Rd *KGSWFD* DY6 ....118 B1
Southendown Rd *SEDG* DY5 ....66 D3
Southern Dr
ALE/KHTH/YWD B14 ....177 H3
Southern Rd *WASH/WDE* B8 ..111 G4
Southey Cl *DARL/WED* WS10 ..55 E5
Southey Cl *SHHTH* WV12 ....26 C2
SOLH B91 ....181 H5
Southfield Av *CBROM* B36 .....112 D1
LDYWD/EDGR B16 ....25 F5
Southfield Cl *ALDR* WS9 ....30 A5
Southfield Gv *HLGN/YWD* B28 .163 E5
Southfield Rd *BDMR/CCFT* WV3 .50 C1
Southfield Rd
LDYWD/EDGR B16 ....125 F1
WNSFLD WV11 ....25 F5
Southfields Cl
CSHL/WTROR B46 ....115 G4
Southfields Rd *SOLH* B91 ......181 F4
South Gdns *HAG/WOL* DY9 ....169 G1
Southgate *CDYHTH* B64 ....120 D4
WOLV WV1 ....6 D3
Southgate Rd *KGSTG* B44 ....75 E1
South Gn
ETTPK/GDPK/PENN WV4 ....50 D3
South Gv *ERDW/GRVHL* B23 ....92 D1
LOZ/NWT B19 ....108 B1
South Holme *BORD* B9 ....128 A3
Southlands Rd *MOS/BIL* B13 ..161 G1
Southminster Dr
ALE/KHTH/YWD B14 ....161 E4
South Oval *SEDG* DY5 ....83 G1
South Pde *CSCFLD/WYGN* B72 .62 C4
South Park Ms *BRLYHL* DY5 ...119 E2
South Range *SPARK* B11 ....144 D1
South Rd *ALE/KHTH/YWD* B14 .161 E2
ERDW/GRVHL B23 ....92 D2
ETTPK/GDPK/PENN WV4 ....52 D4
HAG/WOL DY9 ....169 G1
NFLD/LBR B31 ....175 F3
SMTHWKW B67 ....106 B4
SPARK B11 ....127 H5
TPTN/OCK DY4 ....69 H3
WSNGN B18 ....108 A3
South Road Av *WSNGN* B18 ..108 A3
South Roadway *STETCH* B33 ..130 C1
South St *BRLYHL* DY5
HRBN B17 ....142 B1
WLNHL WV13 ....39 E4
WOLVN WV10 ....23 E4
South View Gdns *WSL* WS1 ......4 C7
South Tower *VAUX/NECH* B7 * .109 H5
South Vw *GTB/HAM* B43 ....73 C4
Southview Rdg *BRLYHL* DY5 ..119 F5
South View Rd *SEDG* DY5 ....66 D3
Southville Bungalows
ALE/KHTH/YWD B14 * 178 D1
Southway Cl *WBHAMNEC* B40 ..150 B4
Southway Ct *KGSWFD* DY6 ....100 B5
Southwick Pl *BILS/COS* WV14 ..53 H1
Southwick Rd *RMSLY* B62 .....122 B4
Southwold Av *BVILLE* B30 ......177 G2
Southwood Av
BKDE/SHDE B34 ....112 C2
Southwood Cl *KGSWFD* DY6 ..100 A4
Southwood Covert
ALE/KHTH/YWD B14 ....177 G3
Sovereign Dr *DUDN* DY1 ....83 F4
Sovereign Hts *NFLD/LBR* B31 ..174 C4
Sovereign Rd *BVILLE* B30 .....176 D1
Sovereign Wk *WSL* WS1 ....5 G3
Sovereign Wy *MOS/BIL* B13 ..144 B3
Sowerby March
ERDE/BCHGN B24 ....93 H2

SHHTH WV12 ....39 H1
Spark St *SPARK* B11 ....144 C1
Sowers Cl *SHHTH* WV12 ....26 B5
Sowers Ct *MCN/WHC* B75 ......47 H1
Sowers Gdns *SHHTH* WV12 .....26 B5
Spa Gv *BVILLE* B30 ....177 F4
Sparkbrook St *COVE WV? 70 A5
Sparrey Dr *BVILLE* B30 ....160 A2
Sparrow Cl *DARL/WED* WS10 ..56 B3
Speakers Cl *OLDBY* B69 ....103 H2
Spearhill Rd *TPTN/OCK* DY4 ...69 E5
Speedwell Cl *ALDR* WS9 ....29 H5
WNSFLD WV11 ....25 E5
Speedwell Gdns *BRLYHL* DY5 ..115 H5
Speedwell Rd *DIG/EDG* B5 ....146 A1
YDLY B25 ....129 H3
Spencer Av *BILS/COS* WV14 ....53 H2
Spencer Cl *ERDE/BCHGN* B24 ..93 H2
HHTH/SAND B71 ....72 B5
OLDBY B69 ....103 H1
SEDG DY2 ....82 C2
Spencer St *WSNGN* B18 ....2 F3
STRBR DY8 ....117 F1
Spernal Gv *SLYOAK* B29 ....158 C1
Spey Cl *DIG/EDG* B5 ....143 H1
Spiceland Rd *NFLD/LBR* B31 ..158 B4
Spiers Cl *DOR/KN* B93 ....197 E2
Spies Cl *RMSLY* B62 ....139 H1
Spies La *RMSLY* B62 ....139 H2
Spills Meadow *SEDG* DY3 ....85 G1
Spilsbury Cft *SOLH* B91 ....181 G5
Spindle La *SHLY* B90 ....194 A2
Spinners End Dr *CDYHTH* B64 ..120 D5
Spinney Cl *BLOX/PEL* WS3 .....18 A5
NFLD/LBR B31 ....175 G2
STRBR DY8 ....117 F1
Spinney Dr *SHLY B90 ....194 D4
The Spinney *BDMR/CCFT* WV3 ..35 H4
BFLD/HDSWWD B20 ....89 G2
FOAKS/STRLY B74 ....31 H4
HLYWD B47 ....192 D4
SEDG DY3 ....81 H4
SOLH B91 ....182 A5
Spiral Cl *RMSLY* B62 ....122 C4
Spiral Gn *ERDE/BCHGN* B24 ...93 G4
Spitfire Rd *ERDE/BCHGN* B24 ..94 C4
Spitfire Wy *CVALE* B35 ....94 C4
Spondon Gv *BKDE/SHDE* B34 .113 E4
Spondon Rd *WNSFLD* WV11 ....25 E2
Spon La *WBROM* B70 ....87 H5
Spon La South *SMTHWK* B66 ..105 H1
Spoon Dr *HWK/WKHTH* B38 ..176 B3
Spooner Cft *DIG/EDG* B5 ......127 E4
Spout La *WSL* WS1 ....4 E7
Spreadbury Cl *HRBN* B17 ......124 B4
Sprig Cft *CBROM* B36 ....112 A1
Springavon Cft *HRBN* B17 .....142 A2
Springbank Rd *EDG* B15 ....126 C5
Springbrook Cl *CBROM* B36 ...93 H5
Springcroft *HAG/WOL* DY9 ....169 F1
RUSH/SHEL WS4 ....18 B1
SOLH B91 ....181 F2
Spring Coppice Dr
DOR/KN B93 ....197 E5
Spring Gv *WSL* WS1 ....5 J7
Spring Crs *CDYHTH* B64 ....121 F5
Springcroft *ERDW/GRVHL* B23 .92 B5
Springfield Av *BHTH/HG* B12 ..144 C1
HAG/WOL DY9 ....136 C3
SEDG DY3 ....67 G2
Springfield Cl
BLKHTH/ROWR B65 ....103 F4
Springfield Crs *DUDS* DY2 .....103 E3
HIA/OLT B92 ....148 A4
WALM/CURD B76 ....63 G4
WBROM B70 ....88 C5
Springfield Dr
ALE/KHTH/YWD B14 ....161 E1
Springfield Gdns *DUDS* DY2 ...103 E3
Springfield Gv *SEDG* DY3 ....67 F2
Springfield La
BLKHTH/ROWR B65 ....103 F4
WOLVN WV10 ....12 D3
Springfield Rd
ALE/KHTH/YWD B14 ....161 E1
BILS/COS WV14 ....54 A1
CBROM B36 ....113 F1
LGLYGN/QTN B68 ....105 G5
MOS/BIL B13 ....122 B5
RMSLY B62 ....122 A1
WALM/CURD B76 ....78 B1
WOLVN WV10 ....37 G1
Springfield Ter
BLKHTH/ROWR B65 ....103 F4
Springs Gdns *DUDS* DY2 ......102 D1
HDSW B21 ....107 H2
Spring Gv *LOZ/NWT* B19 * 108 B3
Spring Grove Gdns
WSNGN B18 ....107 H3
Spring Head *DARL/WED* WS10 .70 D1
Spring Hl *ERDE/BCHGN* B24 ...92 D3
WSNGN B18 ....108 A5
Springhill Av
ETTPK/GDPK/PENN WV4 ....50 C5
Spring Hill Gdns *WSNGN* B18 ....2 A5
Springhill Cl *RUSH/SHEL* WS4 ..29 F1
SHHTH WV12 ....26 B3
Springhill Gv
ETTPK/GDPK/PENN WV4 ....50 C4
Springhill La
ETTPK/GDPK/PENN WV4 ....50 A4
Springhill Pk
ETTPK/GDPK/PENN WV4 ....50 C4
Springhill Rd *BRLYHL* DY5 .....83 E3
Spring Hill Pas *WSNGN* B18 ..126 A1
Springhill Rd *BRWNH* WS8 ......9 G3
WNSFLD WV11 ....24 D3
Spring La *ERDE/BCHGN* B24 ...93 E3
RMSLY B62 ....171 H3
RUSH/SHEL WS4 ....18 C5

Spring Meadow *CDYHTH* B64 ..39 H1
Spring Meadow *HALE* B63 .....138 B5
Springmeadow Gv
LOZ/NWT B19 ....108 D3
Springmeadow Rd *DUDS* DY2 .102 C5
Spring Meadows *CDSL* WV8 ....10 D5
Spring Parklands *DUDN* DY1 ..102 A1
Spring Rd *DUDS* DY2 ....102 D3
EDG B15 ....126 D5
ETTPK/GDPK/PENN WV4 ....55 E5
RUSH/SHEL WS4 ....29 F1
SMTHWK B66 ....105 H1
SPARK B11 ....145 H4
Springslade *RIDG/WDGT* B32 .141 F2
Springslade Dr
ERDE/BCHGN B24 ....93 H3
The Springs *CDYHTH* B64 .....121 G3
Spring St *EDG* B15 ....126 D4
HALE B63 ....136 C5
HALE B63 ....137 G1
TPTN/OCK DY4 ....85 G1
Springthorpe Gn
ERDE/BCHGN B24 ....93 G2
Springthorpe Rd
ERDE/BCHGN B24 ....93 F2
Springvale Av *BILS/COS* WV14 .53 F4
DYSBK/YTR WS5 ....57 G4
Spring Vale Rd
BLKHTH/ROWR B65 ....103 G4
Springvale Wy *BILS/COS* WV14 .68 A2
Spring Wk *HALE* B63 ....154 D1
OLDBY B69 ....105 E4
WSL WS2 ....41 F2
Sproat Av *DARL/WED* WS10 ....55 E3
Spruce Gv *ERDE/BCHGN* B24 ..94 F4
Spruce Rd *DYSBK/YTR* WS5 ....73 G4
Spruce Wy *BDMR/CCFT* WV3 ..35 H4
Spur Tree Av *BDMR/CCFT* WV3 .35 E4
Squadron Cl *CVALE* B35 ....95 E2
Square La *RIDG/WDGT* B32 ...140 C4
The Square *BKHL/PFLD* WV2 ...7 F5
CDSL WV8 ....11 E1
HRBN B17 ....141 H1
SHHTH WV12 * 26 D2
SOLH B91 ....182 A2
TPTN/OCK DY4 ....85 G1
Squires Ct *BRLYHL* DY5 ....119 E3
Squires Cft *WALM/CURD* B76 ..78 C2
Squires Gate Rd *WLNHL* WV13 .39 H3
Squirrel Hollow
WALM/CURD B76 ....78 C3
Squirrels Hollow
LGLYGN/QTN B68 ....123 H5
Squirrel Wk
ETTPK/GDPK/PENN WV4 ....51 G4
FOAKS/STRLY B74 ....32 A5
Stable Cft *HHTH/SAND* B71 ....72 B4
Stableford Cl *RIDG/WDGT* B32 .141 F4
The Stables *SLYOAK* B29 ......143 E5
Stacey Cl *CDYHTH* B64 ....121 E3
Stacey Grange Gdns
RBRY B45 * 188 A2
Stackhouse Cl *BLOX/PEL* WS3 ..19 G4
Stackhouse Dr *BLOX/PEL* WS3 ..18 B2
Stadium Cl *WLNHL* WV13 ....39 E3
Stadium Dr *DUDS* DY2 ....120 C3
Stafford Cl *BLOX/PEL* WS3 .....17 E5
Stafford Dr *HHTH/SAND* B71 ..71 F4
Stafford La *CDSL* WV8 ....20 D5
Stafford Rd *DARL/WED* WS10 ..54 D2
GTWY WS6 ....16 C1
HDSW B21 ....107 H1
WOLVN WV10 ....37 G1
Staffordshire Pool Cl
AST/WIT B6 ....91 F5
Staffordshire Wy *CDSL* WV8 ...10 B2
Stafford St *BILS/COS* WV14 ....53 H3
DARL/WED WS10 ....70 C1
DUDN DY1 ....84 B5
WLNHL WV13 ....39 E4
WOLV WV1 ....7 G3
WSLW WS2 ....4 D2
Stafford Street Jct *WOLV* WV1 ..7 F2
Stafford Wy *GTB/HAM* B43 .....73 C2
Staff Wy *ERDW/GRVHL* B23 ....92 C2
Stag Crs *BLOX/PEL* WS3 ....28 A4
Stag Hill Rd *BLOX/PEL* WS3 ....28 A3
Stag Wk *WALM/CURD* B76 ......77 H4
Stainsby Av *LOZ/NWT* B19 ....108 C2
Stainsby Cft *SHLY* B90 ....195 H3
Stakenbridge La *KIDD* DY10 ..168 C1
Stalling's La *KGSWFD* DY6 .....82 C5
Stambermill Cl *HAG/WOL* DY9 ..136 B2
Stambermill Cft *SOLH* B91 ....181 H5
Stamford Gv
BFLD/HDSWWD B20 ....90 C5
BFLD/HDSWWD B20 ....90 C5
BRLYHL DY5 ....99 H2
STRBR DY8 ....135 H2
Stamford St *STRBR* DY8 ....118 B5
Stanbrook Rd *SHLY* B90 ....195 G5
Stanbury Av *DARL/WED* WS10 .54 D2
Stanbury Rd
ALE/KHTH/YWD B14 ....178 D1
Stancroft Gv
LGN/SDN/BHAMAIR B26 ......130 C4
Standbridge Wy
TPTN/OCK DY4 ....69 E4
Standhills Rd *KGSWFD* DY6 ..100 B4
Standlake Av *CBROM* B36 .....111 H2
Stanfield Rd *GTB/HAM* B43 .....73 F1
RIDG/WDGT B32 ....124 A5
Stanford Av *PBAR/PBCH* B42 ..74 A4
Stanford Cl *BRLYHL* DY5 ....100 B1
Stanford Gv *HALE* B63 ....153 H1
Stanford Rd *BKHL/PFLD* WV2 ...7 K7
Stanhoe Cl *BRLYHL* DY5 ....119 F4
Stanhope Rd *SMTHWKW* B67 .124 D1
Stanhope St *BDMR/CCFT* WV3 .6 A5
BHTH/HG B12 ....127 F5
DUDS DY2 ....103 E5

Stanhope Wy *GTB/HAM* B43 ...59 H4
Stanhurst Wy *HHTH/SAND* B71 .72 C1
Stanier Av *CBHAMNE* B4 ....28 D5
Stanier Gv *BFLD/HDSWWD* B20 .90 A4
Staniforth St *CBHAMNE* B4 ......3 H1
Stanley Av *MGN/WHC* B75 ......63 F4
RIDG/WDGT B32 ....124 A5
SHLY B90 ....180 B1
Stanley Cl *HLGN/YWD* B28 ....163 E5
WNSFLD WV11 ....25 F2
Stanley Ct
ALE/KHTH/YWD B14 ....160 D3
DARL/WED WS10 ....55 F3
HHTH/SAND B71 ....72 A4
Stanley Dr *CUN* B68 ....123 G5
RUSH/SHEL WS4 ....28 C1
STRBR DY8 ....135 F4
VAUX/NECH B7 ....110 A2
WOLVN WV10 ....23 G2
Stanley St *BLOX/PEL* WS3 ......27 G2
Stanmore Gv *HALE* B63 ....154 A4
Stanmore Rd
BFLD/HDSWWD B20 ....125 E3
Stanton Av *DUDN* DY1 ....67 H5
Stanton Gv
LGN/SDN/BHAMAIR B26 ......130 B4
SHLY B90 ....180 A1
TPTN/OCK DY4 ....85 G1
Stanton Rd *GTB/HAM* B43 ......73 F3
SHLY B90 ....180 A1
WOLV WV1 ....37 H3
Stanville Rd
LGN/SDN/BHAMAIR B26 ......148 A1
Stanway Gdns *HHTH/SAND* B71 .72 A4
Stanway Gv *KGSTG* B44 ....60 D5
Stanway Rd *HHTH/SAND* B71 ..71 H5
SHLY B90 ....180 D1
Stanwell Gv *ERDW/GRVHL* B23 .76 C5
Stanwick Av *STETCH* B33 ......131 G1
Stapenhall Rd *SHLY* B90 ......195 E5
Stapleford Cft
ALE/KHTH/YWD B14 ....177 C3
Stapleford Gv *STRBR* DY8 .....118 A2
Staple Hall Rd *NFLD/LBR* B31 .175 H5
Staplehurst Rd
HLGN/YWD B28 ....162 D2
Staple Lodge Rd
NFLD/LBR B31 * 175 H4
Stapleton Dr
CHWD/FDBR/MGN B37 ....132 A1
Stapleton Rd *ALDR* WS9 ....29 H5
Stapleton Av *HHTH/SAND* B71 .141 H2
Starbank Rd *SMHTH* B10 ......129 E4
Starbold Crs *DOR/KN* B93 .....197 F5
Star Cl *TPTN/OCK* DY4 ....86 A1
WSLW WS2 ....40 D1
Starcross Rd *ACGN* B27 ....146 C5
Star Hl *EDG* B15 ....126 B4
Starkey Cft
CHWD/FDBR/MGN B37 ....149 G1
Starkie Dr *LGLYGN/QTN* B68 ..105 G5
Starley Wy
CHWD/FDBR/MGN B37 ....149 G3
Star St *BDMR/CCFT* WV3 ....36 A5
HAG/WOL DY9 ....136 D2
Statham Dr *LDYWD/EDGR* B16 .125 E2
Station Ap *DOR/KN* B93 ....196 D5
FOAKS/STRLY B74 ....32 D4
SCFLD/BOLD B73 ....62 B2
SOLH B91 ....181 H1
Station Av *LDYWD/EDGR* B16 .125 E3
Station Buildings
DUNHL/THL/PER WV6 * 36 A1
Station Cl *BLOX/PEL* WS3 ....27 F2
CDSL WV8 ....10 A4
Station Dr *BRLYHL* DY5 ....118 C3
FOAKS/STRLY B74 ....47 F5
HAG/WOL DY9 ....152 C5
SHLY B90 ....164 A1
Station Link Rd
CHWD/FDBR/MGN B37 ....149 H3
Station Rd *BLOX/PEL* WS3 .....146 C3
ACGN B27 ....30 A5
ALDR WS9 ....30 A5
ALE/KHTH/YWD B14 ....160 D2
AST/WIT B6 ....91 F5
BILS/COS WV14 ....54 A3
BLKHTH/ROWR B65 ....103 F5
BLOX/PEL WS3 ....18 A4
BRLYHL DY5 ....99 G5
BVILLE B30 ....176 C1
CDSL WV8 ....10 A4
CDYHTH B64 ....121 G4
CHWD/FDBR/MGN B37 ....131 H5
DOR/KN B93 ....197 F4
ERDW/GRVHL B23 ....115 F1
HDSW B21 ....107 E1
HIA/OLT B92 ....167 G3
HLYWD B47 ....192 D5
HRBN B17 ....142 A1
HWK/WKHTH B38 ....175 C3
KGSWFD DY6 ....105 G4
RUSH/SHEL WS4 ....29 E1
SCFLD/BOLD B73 ....77 E2
SOLH B91 ....181 H1
STETCH B33 ....129 H1
WMBN WV5 ....65 E3
Station St *BLOX/PEL* WS3 ....16 C4
CBHAMW B1 ....3 F7
CDYHTH B64 ....120 C4
TPTN/OCK DY4 ....55 G2
SCFLD/BOLD B73 ....62 C3
TPTN/OCK DY4 ....85 H1
WSLW WS2 ....4 D5
Staunton Rd *BLOX/PEL* WS3 ...16 C4
Staveley Rd
ALE/KHTH/YWD B14 ....160 D4
WOLV WV1 ....37 G1

Stead Cl *TPTN/OCK* DY4 ....69 H2
.... WSLW WS2 ....27 G5
Steadman Cft *TPTN/OCK* DY4 *....70 B3
Stechford La *WASH/WDE* B8....117 H4
Stechford Rd *BKDE/SHDE* B34..111 H4
Steel Bright Rd *SMTHWK* B66...107 E3
Steel Dr *WOLVN* WV10 ....23 F2
Steel Gv *YDLY* B25 ....129 G5
Steelhouse La *BKHL/PFLD* WV2....7 F7
.... CBHAMNE B4 ....7 F7
Steelmans Rd *DARL/WED* WS10...55 H1
Steelpark Rd *RMSLY* B62 ....121 H5
Steelpark Wy *WNSFLD* WV11 ....58 D1
Steel Rd *NFLD/LBR* B31 ....175 F3
Steene Gv *NFLD/LBR* B31 ....174 C2
The Steeples *STRBR* DY8 ....135 H4
Steepwood Cft *BVILLE* B30 .....176 B1
Stella Cft
.... CHWD/FDBR/MGN B37 ....132 C2
Stella Gv *CTB/HAM* B43 ....73 E3
Stella Rd *TPTN/OCK* DY4 ....69 F5
Stencills Dr *WOLVN* WV10 ....13 F3
Stencills Rd *RUSH/SHEL* WS4 .....42 D1
Stennels Av *RUSH/SHEL* WS4 .....42 D1
Stennels Crs *RMSLY* B62 ....139 G3
Stephens Cl *WNSFLD* WV11 ......25 F2
Stephenson Av *WSLW* WS2 ....27 E4
Stephenson Dr
.... CHWD/FDBR/MGN B37 ....132 B2
.... DUNHL/THL/PER WV6..........20 C5
Stephenson Pl *CBHAM* B2 ....3 G4
Stephenson Sq *WSLW* WS2 ....27 F5
Stephenson St *BDMR/CCFT* WV3...6 D5
.... CBHAM B2 ....3 F5
Stephens Rd *WALM/CURD* B76....63 G4
Stepping Stone Cl *WSLW* WS2....40 D1
Stepping Stones *STRBR* DY8....135 H2
Steppingstone St *DUDN* DY1 ....84 B5
Sterling Pk *BRLYHL* DY5 * 101 H5
Sterndale Rd *PBAR/PBCH* B42..74 C3
Steven Dr *BILS/COS* WV14 ....69 E2
Stevens Av *BKHL/PFLD* WV2 .....82 D5
Stevens Ga *BKHL/PFLD* WV2 .....37 E5
Stevens Rd *HAC/WOL* DY9 ......136 C5
Stewart St *WSNGN* B18 ....126 A1
Stewart Rd *WOLVN* WV10 ....19 C4
.... KGSWFD DY6 ....99 H5
Stewarts Rd *RMSLY* B62 ....122 B5
Stewkins *BKHL/PFLD* WV2 ....7 F7
Stewkins *STRBR* DY8 ....118 A4
Steyning Rd
.... LGN/SDN/BHAMAIR B26 ......147 E2
Stickley La *SEDG* DY3 ....83 E2
Stilehouse Crs
.... BLKHTH/ROWR B65 ....122 A2
Stilthouse Gv *RBRY* B45 ....188 A1
Stirling Crs *SHHTH* WV12 ....13 G5
Stirling Rd *BILS/COS* WV14 ....54 B5
.... DUDS DY2 ....103 E3
.... LDYWD/EDGR B16 ....125 H3
.... SCFLD/BOLD B73 ....76 B1
.... SHLY B90 ....180 D5
Stirrup Cl *DSYBK/YTR* WS5 ....57 F4
Stockbridge Cl
.... DUNHL/THL/PER WV6...........34 D5
Stockdale Pl *EDG* B15 ....125 F4
Stock Exchange Buildings
.... CBHAMNW B3 * 2 E4
Stockfield Rd *ACGN* B27 ....146 B3
Stockhill Dr *RBRY* B45 ....187 H2
Stocking St *HAC/WOL* DY9 ......136 D2
Stockland Rd
.... ERDW/GRVHL B23 ....92 B2
Stockley Crs *SHLY* B90 ....180 D2
Stockmans Cl
.... HWK/WKHTH B38 ....176 C5
Stockton Cl *DOR/KN* B93 ....197 H4
.... WALM/CURD B76 ....95 G1
.... WSLW WS2 ....41 H1
Stockton Gv *STETCH* B33 ....131 F3
Stockwell Av *BRLYHL* DY5 ....119 F4
Stockwell End
.... DUNHL/THL/PER WV6...........21 H4
Stockwell Ri *HIA/OLT* B92 ....165 F3
Stockwell Rd
.... DUNHL/THL/PER WV6............21 F5
.... HDSW B21 ....89 G4
Stokes Av *TPTN/OCK* DY4 ....69 G3
.... WLNHL WV13 ....39 F5
Stokes Av
.... DUNHL/THL/PER WV6...........34 D2
Stokesay Cl *OLDBY* B69 ....103 G1
Stokesay Gv *RI DUDN* DY1 ....83 G3
Stokes St *BLOX/PEL* WS3 ....27 F2
Stoke Wy *EDG* B15 ....2 C7
Ston Rd *BILS/COS* WV14 ....53 F3
Stoneacre Cl *BARTT/CCFT* WV3...35 E4
Stone Av *MOS/NHC* B75 ....63 G3
Stonebow Av *SOLH* B91 ....194 D5
Stonebridge Crs
.... CHWD/FDBR/MGN B37 ....113 H5
Stonebridge Rd
.... CSHL/WTROR B46 ....133 G4
Stonebrook Wy *SLYOAK* B29...141 F5
Stonechat Dr
.... ERDW/GRVHL B23 ....92 A4
Stone Cl *HWK/WKHTH* B38.....176 D3
Stonecroft Av *RBRY* B45 ....188 A1
Stonecrop Cl *BRWNH* WS8 ....18 D1
.... HWK/WKHTH B38 ....176 D5
Stone Cross *CSHL/WTROR* B46...96 B3
Stonedown Cl *BILS/COS* WV14...54 B5
Stonefield Dr *BRLYHL* DY5 ....100 C2
Stonefield Rd *BILS/COS* WV14 *..53 H3
Stoneford Rd *SHLY* B90 ....180 A1
Stonehaven Gv
.... HLGN/YWD B28 ....163 F2
Stonehenge Cft
.... CSHL/WTROR B46 ....195 F2
Stonehouse Av *WLNHL* WV13 ....39 F2
Stonehouse Crs
.... DARL/WED WS10 ....71 F1
Stonehouse Dr
.... FOAKS/STRLY B74 ....45 H1
Stonehouse Hl *SLYOAK* B29...141 G5
Stonehouse La
.... RIDG/WDGT B32 ....140 D5

Stonehouse Rd
.... SCFLD/BOLD B73 ....61 H5
Stonehurst Rd *GTB/HAM* B43....59 G5
Stonelea Av *DUDN* DY1 ....30 E5
Stonelea Cl *HHTH/SAND* B71....72 A3
Stoneleigh Cl *FOAKS/STRLY* B74..46 D5
Stoneleigh Gdns *CDSL* WV8 .....10 B3
Stoneleigh Rd
.... BFLD/HDSWWD B20 ....91 E5
.... SOLH B91 ....163 H5
Stoneleigh Wy *SEDG* DY3 ....67 F5
Stonepine Pl *SEDG* DY3 ....67 G5
Stone Rd *EDG* B15 ....126 D5
Stonerwood Av
.... HLGN/YWD B28 ....162 C3
Stones Gn *ERDW/GRVHL* B23....76 D5
Stone St *DUDN* DY1 ....84 C5
.... OLDBY B69 ....104 A2
Stoneton Gv *SLYOAK* B29 ......158 C2
Stone Yd *BHTH/HG* B12 ....3 K7
Stoney Brook Leys *WMBN* WV5..80 C1
Stoney Cl *HIA/OLT* B92 ....165 G3
Stoneyford Gv
.... ALE/KHTH/YWD B14 ....178 D1
Stoneyhurst Rd
.... ERDE/BCHGN B24 ....92 D5
Stoney La *BHTH/HG* B12 ....144 D2
.... BLOX/PEL WS3 ....17 F4
.... DUDS DY2 ....120 C1
.... HHTH/SAND B71 ....87 H2
.... KIDD DY10 ....98 D2
.... RIDG/WDGT B32 ....140 B1
.... STETCH B33 ....130 A3
Stoneymoor Dr *CBROM* B36 ......95 F5
Stoneythorpe Cl *SOLH* B91 ....181 H4
Stonnal Gv *ERDW/GRVHL* B23...77 E5
Stonnall Ga *ALDR* WS9 ....30 B2
Stonnall Rd *ALDR* WS9 ....30 C2
Stonor Park Rd *SOLH* B91 ......164 B4
Stonor Rd *HLGN/YWD* B28 ......180 A1
Stony La *SMTHWK* B67 ....106 B3
Stornoway Rd *CVALE* B35 ....94 D2
Storrs Cl *BORD* B9 ....128 A3
Storrs Pl *SHHTH* B10 ....128 B3
The Storrs Wy
.... RIDG/WDGT B32 ....157 F3
Stot Fold Rd
.... ALE/KHTH/YWD B14 ....178 B3
Stourbridge Rd *BRGRVW* B61..185 H5
.... BRLYHL DY5 ....101 C4
.... DUDN DY1 ....102 A1
.... ETTPK/GDPK/PENN WV4.50 C5
.... HAG/WOL DY9 ....81 E2
.... HALE B63 ....138 B3
.... WMBN WV5 ....81 C2
Stour Cl *HALE* B63 ....138 A4
Stourdale Rd *CDYHTH* B64 .....120 C5
Stourdell Rd *HALE* B63...........138 A1
Stour Hl *BRLYHL* DY5 ....120 A5
Stourmore Cl *SHHTH* WV12 ....26 B4
Stour St *WBROM* B70 ....86 C3
.... WSNGN B18 ....108 B3
Stourton Cl *DOR/KN* B93 ....197 F1
.... WALM/CURD B76 ....63 F4
Stourton Dr
.... ETTPK/GDPK/PENN WV4.......50 C3
Stourton Rd *RIDG/WDGT* B32..140 B2
Stour Vale Rd *HAG/WOL* DY9..136 D1
Stour Valley Cl *BRLYHL* DY5 ....119 F5
Stow Dr *BRLYHL* DY5 ....135 H1
Stow Heath La *WOLV* WV1 ....54 D1
Stowe St *BLOX/PEL* WS3 ....27 C3
Stow Gv *CBROM* B36 ....102 A1
Stow Heath La *WOLV* WV1 ....53 F1
Stow Heath Pl *WOLV* WV1 ....53 F1
Stowmans Cl *BILS/COS* WV14...53 F5
Straight Rd *SHHTH* WV12 ....26 A4
Straits Gn *SEDG* DY3 ....82 D2
Straits Rd *SEDG* DY3 ....82 D3
The Straits *SEDG* DY3 ....82 C2
Stratford Cl *DUDN* DY1 ....83 G4
Stratford Dr *ALDR* WS9 ....30 C2
Stratford Pl *BHTH/HG* B12 ......127 G4
Stratford Rd *HLGN/YWD* B28...162 D3
.... HOCK/TIA B94 ....198 A5
.... SHLY B90 ....194 D1
.... SPARK B11 ....144 D1
Stratford St *SPARK* B11 ....144 D1
Stratford St North *SPARK* B11..127 G4
Strathern Dr *BILS/COS* WV14 ...53 E5
Strathmore Crs *WMBN* WV5 ......65 E2
Strathmore Rd *TPTN/OCK* DY4...69 G3
Stratton St *WOLVN* WV10 ....37 C1
Strawberry Cl *OLDBY* B69 ......104 A2
Strawberry La *WLNHL* WV13 .....13 G5
Stream Meadow
.... RUSH/SHEL WS4 ....29 E1
Stream Rd *KGSWFD* DY6 ....99 H5
Streamside Wy *HIA/OLT* B92...148 B5
.... RUSH/SHEL WS4 ....29 F2
Streatham Gv *KGSTG* B44 ....68 D2
Streather Rd *MGN/WHC* B75.....47 G2
Streetly Crs *FOAKS/STRLY* B74..46 B2
Streetly Dr *FOAKS/STRLY* B74....46 B3
Streetly La *FOAKS/STRLY* B74 ....46 C3
Streetly Rd *ERDW/GRVHL* B23...92 B1
Streetly Wd *FOAKS/STRLY* B74 ..45 G3
Streetsbrook Rd *SOLH* B91 .....181 G1
Strensham Hl *BHTH/HG* B12 ...144 B2
Strensham Rd *BHTH/HG* B12 ..144 A3
Stretton Gdns *CDSL* WV8 ....10 B3
Stretton Gv *LOZ/NWT* B19 * 108 C2
.... SPARK B11 ....145 E1
.... WASH/WDE B8 ....111 F3
Stretton Pl *BILS/COS* WV14 ......68 A2
.... DUDS DY2 ....102 D5
Stretton Rd *SHHTH* WV12 ....26 A2
.... SHLY B90 ....180 B5
Stringer Cl *MGN/WHC* B75 ....47 E1
Stringes Cl *WLNHL* WV13 ....39 H2
Stringes La *WLNHL* WV13 ....39 H3
Strode Rd *BKHL/PFLD* WV2 ....52 A2
Stronsay Cl *RBRY* B45 ....173 H4
Stroud Av *SHHTH* WV12 ....40 B1
Stroud Cl *SHHTH* WV12 ....40 A1
Stroud Rd *SHLY* B90 ....179 H3

Strutt Cl *EDG* B15 ....125 F4
Stuart Crs *DUDS* DY2 ....85 E5
Stuart Rd
.... BLKHTH/ROWR B65 ....104 A5
.... RMSLY B62 ....139 H2
Stuarts Dr *STETCH* B33 ....129 H5
Stuarts Gn *HAG/WOL* DY9 ....136 D2
Stuarts Rd *STETCH* B33 ....129 H2
Stuart St *BLOX/PEL* WS3 ....27 F2
.... VAUX/NECH B7 ....110 A2
Stuarts Wy *RIDG/WDGT* B32...157 F3
Stubbers Green Rd
.... RUSH/SHEL WS4 ....29 F2
Stubbington Cl *WLNHL* WV13 ...38 D4
Stubbs Rd *BDMR/CCFT* WV3 .....51 G1
Stubby La *WNSFLD* WV11 ....25 G4
Stubley Dr *WOLVN* WV10 ....23 G5
Studland Rd *HLGN/YWD* B28...163 E2
Studland La *STETCH* B33 ....130 B1
Studley Cft *HIA/OLT* B92 ....148 A4
Studley Dr *BRLYHL* DY5 ....119 E4
Studley Ga *STRBR* DY8 ....134 D2
Studley Rd *BDMR/CCFT* WV3 ....35 C5
Studley St *BHTH/HG* B12 ....144 D2
Sturman Dr
.... BLKHTH/ROWR B65 ....121 H3
Suckling Green La *CDSL* WV8 ....10 B5
Sudbury Cl *WNSFLD* WV11 ....25 E2
Sudbury Gv *KGSTG* B44 ....75 H1
Sudeley Cl *CBROM* B36 ....94 D5
Sudeley Gdns *DUDN* DY1 ....83 E4
Suffield Gv *ERDW/GRVHL* B23...91 H1
Suffolk Cl *LGLYGN/QTN* B68....105 F5
.... WNSFLD WV11 ....24 C4
Suffolk Dr *BRLYHL* DY5 ....119 E5
Suffolk Gv *ALDR* WS9 ....30 B2
Suffolk Pl *CBHAM* B1 * 3 F7
.... WSLW WS2 ....27 H5
Suffolk Rd *DARL/WED* WS10 .....56 C5
.... DUDS DY2 ....102 A2
Suffolk St Queensway
.... CBHAM B1 ....2 E6
Suffrage St *SMTHWK* B66 ......106 D4
Sugden Gv *DIG/EDG* B5 ....127 E4
Sulgrave Cl *DUDN* DY1 ....84 A3
Sumburgh Cft *CVALE* B35 ....94 C5
Summercourt Dr *KGSWFD* DY6..99 C4
Summercourt Sq *KGSWFD* DY6..99 B4
Summer Cft *LOZ/NWT* B19 ......108 D3
Summerdale Dr *SEDG* DY3 ....83 F3
Summergate Dr *DUDN* DY1 ....83 F3
Summer Hl Rd *CBHAMW* B1 ....2 A3
.... KGSWFD DY6 ....99 C3
Summer Hill St *CBHAMW* B1 ....2 B4
Summer Hill Ter *CBHAMW* B1 .....2 B4
Summerhouse Rd
.... BILS/COS WV14 ....68 A2
Summer La *LOZ/NWT* B19 ....3 F1
.... RUSH/SHEL WS4 ....18 B5
.... SEDG DY3 ....83 E3
.... WALM/CURD B76 ....76 F5
Summerlee Rd
.... ERDE/BCHGN B24 ....93 H4
Summer Rd *ACGN* B27 ....146 A5
.... BLKHTH/ROWR B65 ....122 B1
.... DUDN DY1 ....84 A2
.... EDG B15 ....126 C5
.... ERDW/GRVHL B23 ....92 D2
Summer Rw *BKHL/PFLD* WV2 ......7 F5
.... CBHAMNW B3 ....2 D4
Summerton Rd *OLDBY* B69 .....104 B1
Summervale Cl *HAG/WOL* DY9..152 C5
Summervale Rd
.... HAG/WOL DY9 ....152 C5
Summerville Ter *HRBN* B17 * ...142 A2
Summit Crs *SMTHWK* B66 ......106 A1
Summit Gdns *HALE* B63 ....138 B4
Summit Pl *SEDG* DY3 ....82 D4
The Summit *HAG/WOL* DY9 .....152 C5
Sumner Rd *CSHL/WTROR* B46..115 C3
Sunbeam Cl *CBROM* B36 ....95 H5
Sunbeam Dr *BKHL/PFLD* WV2....52 A1
Sunbeam St *BKHL/PFLD* WV2 ......7 G7
Sunleigh Gv *ACGN* B27 ....147 E3
Sunningdale *RMSLY* B62 ....139 G3
Sunningdale Av *DUNHL/THL/PER* WV6....6 B1
Sunningdale Cl
.... BFLD/HDSWWD B20 ....89 C2
.... SCFLD/BOLD B73 ....77 E1
.... STRBR DY8 ....135 F5
Sunningdale Dr *OLDBY* B69 ....103 G2
Sunningdale Rd *SEDG* DY3.......83 C2
.... SPARK B11 ....146 A4

Sunnybank Av *ALDR* WS9 ....45 E3
Sunny Bank Rd
.... LGLYGN/QTN B68 ....123 G5
Sunnybank Rd
.... SCFLD/BOLD B73 ....77 E3
.... SEDG DY3 ....83 G1
Sunnydene *WASH/WDE* B8......111 E4
Sunny Hill Cl *WMBN* WV5 ....65 F5
Sunnymead Rd
.... LGN/SDN/BHAMAIR B26 ......147 F1
Sunnymead Wy
.... FOAKS/STRLY B74 ....60 B1
Sunnymede Rd *KGSWFD* DY6..100 C5
Sunnyside *ALDR* WS9 ....19 E5
.... OLDBY B69 ....103 H2
Sunnyside Av
.... ERDW/GRVHL B23 ....92 C5
Sunridge Av *LOZ/NWT* B19 ....108 D3
.... WMBN WV5 ....65 E3
Sunset Pl
.... ETTPK/GDPK/PENN WV4 .....52 D5
Sun St *BRLYHL* DY5 ....119 H3
.... WOLVN WV10 ....7 J2
.... WSL WS1 ....56 D1
Surfeit Hl *CDYHTH* B64 ....121 E4
Surrey Cl *CDYHTH* B64 ....120 D4
Surrey Crs *HHTH/SAND* B71 .....71 E3
Surrey Dr *BDMR/CCFT* WV3 ......36 A4
.... KGSWFD DY6 ....100 A5
Surrey Rd *DUDS* DY2 ....102 A2
.... KGSTG B44 ....60 A4
Surrey Wk *ALDR* WS9 ....30 A2
Sussex Av *ALDR* WS9 ....30 A2
.... DARL/WED WS10 ....56 D4
.... HHTH/SAND B71 ....71 G5
Sussex Dr *BDMR/CCFT* WV3 .....35 E5
Sutherland Av *BKHL/PFLD* WV2..37 H5
.... SHLY B90 ....180 C4
Sutherland Cl *GTB/HAM* B43.....59 H4
Sutherland Dr *MOS/BIL* B13 ...144 B3
.... WMBN WV5 ....65 E3
Sutherland Gv
.... DUNHL/THL/PER WV6..........34 D1
Sutherland Pl *BKHL/PFLD* WV2..7 H6
Sutherland Rd *CDYHTH* B64 ...121 E4
.... ETTPK/GDPK/PENN WV4..51 E5
Sutherland St *AST/WIT* B6......109 H1
Sutton Ap *WASH/WDE* B8 ....111 E5
Sutton Cl
.... ETTPK/GDPK/PENN WV4 ......67 C1
.... RDN/WHC B75 ....62 E1
Sutton Crs *WBROM* B70 ....87 E3
Sutton New Rd
.... ERDW/GRVHL B23 ....92 D2
Sutton Oak Rd
.... SCFLD/BOLD B73 ....60 C4
Sutton Rd *ALDR* WS9 ....44 B4
.... DARL/WED WS10 ....54 C3
.... ERDW/GRVHL B23 ....93 E1
.... WSL WS1 ....43 E4
Sutton's Dr *GTB/HAM* B43 ....56 A1
Sutton Sq *WALM/CURD* B76 .....79 C5
Sutton St *AST/WIT* B6 ....108 C7
.... CBHAMW B1 ....2 B6
.... STRBR DY8 ....118 A3
Swallow Av *CBROM* B36 ....95 H5
Swale Gv *HWK/WKHTH* B38 ....176 D5
.... WLNHL WV13 ....40 B5
Swallow Cl *BHTH/HG* B12 ......144 D2
.... DARL/WED WS10 ....56 D4
Swallow Dr *HDSW* WS8 ....10 D2
Swalcliffe Rd *STRBR* DY8 ....134 C3
Swallowdale *ALDR* WS9 ....19 G3
Swallowfields Rd *SEDG* DY3 ....52 A5
Swallows Cl *BLOX/PEL* WS3 ......18 A2
Swallows' Meadow *SHLY* B90..180 D5
Swan Av *SMTHWK* B66 ....106 A2
Swanage Rd *SMTHWK* B66 ......128 B4
Swan Bank
.... ETTPK/GDPK/PENN WV4 .....51 F4
Swan Cl *KIDD* DY10 ....168 B4
.... WASH/WDE B8 ....110 D3
Swan Copse *YDLY* B25 ....146 C2
Swancote Dr
.... ETTPK/GDPK/PENN WV4 .....50 C3
Swancote Rd *DUDN* DY1 ....102 A1
.... STETCH B33 ....112 B4
Swan Ctyd
.... LGN/SDN/BHAMAIR B26 ......146 D1
Swan Dr *BRWNH* WS8 ....9 E5
Swanfield Rd *STRBR* DY8 ....118 C3
Swan Gdns *ERDW/GRVHL* B23...92 D2
Swan La *BRGRVW* B61 ....185 H5
.... STRBR DY8 ....118 C2
.... WBROM B70 ....85 H5
Swanley Cl *RMSLY* B62 ....140 A4
Swanmore Cl *BDMR/CCFT* WV3.51 E1
Swann Rd *BILS/COS* WV14 ....68 A1
Swan Pool Gv *RUSH/SHEL* WS4..29 F1
Swansbrook Gdns
.... HWK/WKHTH B38 ....177 C5
Swanshurst La *MOS/BIL* B13...162 A2
Swan St *DUDN* DY1 ....101 E3
.... DUDS DY2 ....102 C5
.... STRBR DY8 ....135 E2
.... WOLV WV1 ....37 H3
Swanswell Rd *HIA/OLT* B92 .....163 H3
Swanswood Gv
.... CHWD/FDBR/MGN B37 * 132 C1
Swarthmore Rd *SLYOAK* B29..158 D3
Swarthmore La *SHHTH* WV12 ...26 B5
Sweetbriar Rd *BKHL/PFLD* WV2.53 E1
Sweetbrier Dr *STRBR* DY8 ......118 A3
Sweetman Pl
.... DUNHL/THL/PER WV6.............6 B1
Sweetman St
.... DUNHL/THL/PER WV6...........36 C1
Sweetmoor Cl *CBROM* B36 .....113 E1
Sweetpool La *STRBR* DY8 ....152 B5
Swift Cl *CBROM* B36 ....114 A1
Swinbrook Gv *KGSTG* B44 ....75 E2
Swinbrook Wy *SHLY* B90 ....180 D1

Swincross Rd *STRBR* DY8 ....135 H4
Swindell Rd *HAG/WOL* DY9 .....153 E1
Swindon Rd *HRBN* B17 ....124 D1
.... KGSWFD DY6 ....196 C5
Swinford Dr *DOR/KN* B93 ....196 B5
Swinford Leys *WMBN* WV5 ....80 B1
Swinford Rd *SLYOAK* B29 ....141 G4
.... STRBR DY8 ....135 G5
.... WOLVN WV10 ....23 G5
Swin Forge Wy *SEDG* DY3 ....80 C4
Swinnerton Dr *WNSFLD* WV11...14 D3
Swiss Dr *STRBR* DY8 ....118 B2
Swynnerton Dr *WNSFLD* WV11..14 D3
Sycamore Av *CBROM* B36 ....92 D3
.... RUSH/SHEL WS4 ....44 B2
.... STRBR DY8 ....134 D5
.... WALM/CURD B76 ....78 B1
Sycamore Crs
.... CHWD/FDBR/MGN B37 ....132 A4
.... ERDE/BCHGN B24 ....92 D5
Sycamore Dr *BDMR/CCFT* WV3..35 H4
.... HLYWD B47 ....192 D3
Sycamore Gn *DUDN* DY1 ....83 H1
Sycamore Paddock
.... STRBR DY8 ....118 C3
Sycamore Pl *BILS/COS* WV14 ...54 G5
Sycamore Rd *AST/WIT* B6 ....109 C1
.... BILS/COS WV14 ....53 G5
.... BORD B9 ....159 H5
.... DARL/WED WS10 ....71 E1
.... DSYBK/YTR WS5 ....57 F5
.... ERDW/GRVHL B23 ....76 D4
.... GTB/HAM B43 ....58 C5
.... HDSW B21 ....107 F1
.... KGSWFD DY6 ....100 A3
.... OLDBY B69 ....105 E5
.... RUSH/SHEL WS4 ....28 D2
.... SMTHWK B66 ....124 D1
.... TPTN/OCK DY4 ....69 F4
The Sycamores *STRBR* DY8 ....152 B5
.... WOLVN WV10 ....23 H2
Sycamore Ter
.... ALE/KHTH/YWD B14 * 160 C3
Sycamore Wy *ACGN* B27 ....146 C3
Sydenham Rd *SMTHWK* B66 ...106 C3
.... SPARK B11 ....145 E1
.... WOLV WV1 ....38 A3
Sydney Cl *WBROM* B70 ....70 E4
Sydney Rd *BORD* B9 ....128 A2
.... CDYHTH B64 ....120 B5
.... SMTHKW B67 ....124 A2
Sydney Wy *BKDE/SHDE* B34 ...113 G3
Sylvan Av *NFLD/LBR* B31 ....175 F2
Sylvan Gn *RMSLY* B62 ....139 F2
Sylvia Av *NFLD/LBR* B31 ....175 H5
Symphony Ct
.... LDYWD/EDGR B16 ....2 B6
Sytch La *WMBN* WV5 ....81 E1

Tack Farm Rd *STRBR* DY8 ....117 H3
Tackford Cl *CBROM* B36 ....95 E5
Tackley Cl *SHLY* B90 ....180 B5
Tadmore Cl *BILS/COS* WV14 .....53 G3
Tadworth Cl *WOLV* WV1 ....38 A3
Tainsh Dr *DYSBK/YTR* WS5 ....38 A2
Talaton Cl *COVEN* WV9 ....13 G4
Talbot Av *FOAKS/STRLY* B74 .....45 H2
Talbot Cl *ERDW/GRVHL* B23 .....76 B3
.... WSLW WS2 ....27 C4
Talbot Rd *BKHL/PFLD* WV2 ....52 A2
.... DUDS DY2 ....102 B5
.... SMTHWK B66 ....124 C1
Talbots La *BRLYHL* DY5 ....119 F5
Talbot St *BRLYHL* DY5 ....119 F1
.... HAG/WOL DY9 ....136 D2
.... HALE B63 ....137 G1
.... STRBR DY8 ....135 G2
.... WSNGN B18 ....107 H3
Talbot Wy *SMTHTH* B10 ....128 D5
Talfourd St *BORD* B9 ....128 B3
Talgarth Covert
.... HWK/WKHTH B38 ....190 C1
Talke Rd *DSYBK/YTR* WS5 ......120 C5
Talladale *RIDG/WDGT* B32 ......157 F3
Tallington Rd *STETCH* B33 ......131 E5
Tall Trees Cl *FOAKS/STRLY* B74..46 B1
.... SHHTH WV12 ....26 A4
Tall Trees Dr *HAG/WOL* DY9 ....136 B5
Talton Cl *SHLY* B90 ....195 D3
Tamar Cl *BRWNH* WS8 ....8 C2
Tamar Dr *CBROM* B36 ....113 H1
.... DUDS DY2 ....67 H5
.... WALM/CURD B76 ....78 D4
Tamar Gv *DUNHL/THL/PER* WV6.34 C1
.... WLNHL WV13 ....40 A3
Tamarisk Cl *SLYOAK* B29 ....158 D2
Tamar Ri *STRBR* DY8 ....118 C4
Tame Av *DARL/WED* WS10 ....56 C4
Tame Cl *WSL* WS1 ....57 E2
Tame Crs *HHTH/SAND* B71 ....71 G5
Tame Dr *BLOX/PEL* WS3 ....28 C1
Tame Ri *LGLYGN/QTN* B68......123 F4
Tame Rd *AST/WIT* B6 ....91 G4
.... LGLYGN/QTN B68 ....123 E4
.... OLDBY B69 ....86 A1
Tamerton Rd *RIDG/WDGT* B32..157 H3
Tameside Cl *WLNHL* WV13 ....39 F3
Tameside Dr *AST/WIT* B6 ....91 F2
.... CVALE B35 ....94 C5
Tame St *BILS/COS* WV14 ....54 B3
.... WBROM B70 ....70 D5
.... WSL WS1 ....57 E2
Tame St East *WSL* WS1 ....57 F2
Tamworth Cl *BRWNH* WS8 ....9 F2
Tamworth Rd *MGN/WHC* B75 ....62 D1
Tanacetum Dr *DSYBK/YTR* WS5..57 G5
Tandy Dr *ALE/KHTH/YWD* B14..178 B2
Tanfield Cl
.... DUNHL/THL/PER WV6...........35 F2
Tanfield Rd *DUDS* DY2 ....102 B2
.... STETCH B33 ....130 B1
Tanford Rd *HIA/OLT* B92 ....148 A4
Tanglewood Cl
.... BKDE/SHDE B54 ....113 E4
.... RIDG/WDGT B32 ....140 B3
Tanglewood Gv *SEDG* DY3 ....67 E1

Tangmere Cl
 DUNHL/THL/PER WV6................20 C5
Tangmere Dr CVALE B35................94 C3
Tanhouse Av GTB/HAM B43........73 E4
Tanhouse Farm Rd
 HIA/OLT B92....................148 A3
Tanhouse La HALE B63........137 G2
Tanners Cl MGN/WHC B75............63 E1
Tannery Cl WSLW WS2.....................4 C1
Tansey Green Rd BRLYHL DY5...100 D1
Tansley Cl DOR/KN B93.............196 D4
Tansley Gv KGSTG B44.................75 F2
Tansley Hill Av DUDS DY2........103 E1
Tansley Hill Rd DUDS DY2........103 E1
Tansley Rd KGSTG B44..................75 F3
Tansley Vw BKHL/PFLD WV2........52 B1
Tantany La HHTH/SAND B71........87 G2
Tantarra St WSL WS1...................24 C5
Tanwood Cl SOLH B91.............181 H5
Tanworth Hn BRLYHL B12........144 B1
Tanworth La SHLY B90.............194 B2
Tanyards ACGN B27.....................146 D4
Tapestrie Av WBROM B70............87 E2
Tapton Cl BLOX/PEL WS3................17 E4
Tarmac Rd
 ETTPK/GDPK/PENN WV4........53 F3
Tarragon Gdns RBRY B45.........174 C3
Tarrant Gv RIDG/WDGT B32........141 F2
Tarrington Covert
 HWK/WKHTH B38................176 C5
Tarry Hollow Rd BRLYHL DY5...100 D1
Tarry Rd WASH/WDE B8..............109 G2
Tarvin Ms BRLYHL DY5................119 F5
Taryn Dr DARL/WED WS10..........55 F1
Tasker St WBROM B70.................86 C2
 WSL WS1...........................4 C6
Tasman Gv
 DUNHL/THL/PER WV6................20 C5
Tat Bank Rd OLDBY B69.............105 F3
Taunton Av WOLVN WV10..............12 D5
Taunton Cl NFLD/LBR B31........114 C2
Taunton Rd BHTH/HG B12........144 C3
Taverners Cl SHHTH WV12............26 A1
Taverner's Gn
 BFLD/HDSWWD B20................89 H3
Tavistock Rd ACGN B27.............163 G3
Taw Cl CBROM B36...................113 H2
Tay Cft CHWD/FDBR/MGN B37...114 D5
Tay Gv HWK/WKHTH B38.............176 C5
 RMSLY B62.......................122 C4
Taylor Av BLOX/PEL WS3.............27 H2
Taylor Cl BLOX/PEL WS3.............121 E2
 ETTPK/GDPK/PENN WV4........52 D5
 MOS/BIL B13.......................105 E3
Taylor's La HHTH/SAND B71........87 H2
 OLDBY B69.......................104 C2
 SMTHWKW B66....................106 B4
Taylors Orch ERDW/GRVHL B23...91 H2
Taylor St WOLV WV1.....................17 F5
Taylor Wy OLDBY B69.................103 H1
Tay Rd RBRY B45.....................174 B4
Taysfield Rd NFLD/LBR B31........158 A4
Taywood Dr SMHTH B10.............128 A5
Tealby Gv SLYOAK B29................142 D5
Teal Dr ERDW/GRVHL B23..........91 H3
Teal Gv DARL/WED WS10..............54 D5
Teall Rd WASH/WDE B8..............110 C4
Tean Cl AMBIS WS1....................146 A4
Teasdale Wy HAG/WOL DY9........119 H3
Teasel Rd WNSFLD WV11................25 E5
Teazel Av BVILLE B30.................159 F4
Tebworth Cl COVEN WV9................11 H5
Tedbury Crs ERDW/GRVHL B23...76 C5
Tedder Rd WSLW WS2....................27 E5
Teddesley Gv STETCH B33........113 E5
Teddesley St RUSH/SHEL WS4........5 F1
Teddington Gv PBAR/PBCH B42...90 C3
Tedstone Rd RIDG/WDGT B32...141 E2
Teesdale Av BKDE/SHDE B34........112 B3
Teesdale Cl WOLV WV1..................38 A3
Tees Gv HWK/WKHTH B38.............176 D5
Teignmouth Rd SLYOAK B29...142 D5
Telford Cl HHTH/SAND B71..........71 E3
 SMTHWKW B67....................123 H3
 WSLW WS2..........................27 E5
Telford Gdns BDMR/CCFT WV3...50 D1
Telford Rd WSLW WS2....................27 E5
Telford Wy SMTHWKW B66.........106 B2
Teme Gv WLNHL WV13..................40 B3
Teme Rd HALE B63....................137 F2
 STRBR DY8........................135 F4
Tempest St BKHL/PFLD WV2..........3 F5
The Templars OLDBY B69.........104 C4
Templars Wk WLNHL WV13............39 G3
Templefield Gdns BORD B9.........128 C1
Templefield Sq EDG B15............126 B5
Templefield St BORD B9.............128 A3
Temple Meadows Rd
 HHTH/SAND B71....................88 A1
Templemore Dr GTB/HAM B43...73 E4
Temple Pas CBHAM B2....................3 F5
Temple Rd DOR/KN B93.............197 E5
 WLNHL WV13.......................39 G2
Temple Rw CBHAM B2....................3 G5
Temple Rw West CBHAM B2.........3 F5
Temple Sq WLNHL WV13..............39 G2
Temple St BILS/COS WV14............54 A3
 BKHL/PFLD WV2.....................7 F5
 DUDE B9.............................3 F5
 SEDG DY3..........................85 F3
 WBROM B70........................87 G2
Templeton Rd KGSTG B44..........75 E1
Templeton Rd KGSTG B44............75 F1
Temple Wy CSHL/WTROR B46........97 F1
Tenacre La SEDG DY3.................83 G1
Ten Acres End BVILLE B30.........160 B2
Ten Acres Ms SLYOAK B29........160 B2
Ten Ashes La RBRY B45.............158 C4
Tenbury Cl ALDR WS9..................30 C2
 WSLW WS2............................40 B2
Tenbury Ct
 ETTPK/GDPK/PENN WV4........50 D3
Tenbury Gdns
 ETTPK/GDPK/PENN WV4........50 D4
Tenbury Rd
 ALE/KHTH/YWD B14.............160 C4
Tenby St MOS/BIL B13.............145 F5

Tenby St CBHAMW B1......................2 B2
Tenby St North CBHAMW B1..........2 B2
Tenlands Rd HALE B63..............138 B4
Tennal Rd RIDG/WDGT B32.......141 E1
Tennal Gv RIDG/WDGT B32........141 E1
Tennal La RIDG/WDGT B32........141 E2
Tennal Rd RIDG/WDGT B32........141 E1
Tennant St EDG B15..................126 B3
Tennis Ct BVILLE B30.................176 B1
Tennis Cts EDG B15...................126 B3
Tennyson Av FOAKS/STRLY B74...32 D4
Tennyson Rd BLOX/PEL WS3......28 B3
 SEDG DY3............................82 C1
 SHHTH WV12........................26 C2
 SMHTH B10........................128 C5
 WOLVN WV10.........................24 A1
Tennyson St BRLYHL DY5...........101 F3
Tenter Cl HALE B63...................138 D3
Tenter Dr HALE B63..................139 E4
Tenterfields HALE B63..............138 D3
Terminal Rd
 DUNHL/THL/PER WV6................36 B2
Tern Cl ETTPK/GDPK/PENN WV4...52 B5
Tern Gv HWK/WKHTH B38.........176 C5
Terrace Rd LOZ/NWT B19.........108 A2
Terrace St BRLYHL DY5.............101 G4
 CDYHTH B64.......................121 H3
 DARL/WED WS10...................55 H5
The Terrace BDMR/CCFT WV3...35 G4
 CDYHTH B64.......................121 H3
Terrence Vls DARL/WED WS10 * ...55 F1
Terret Cl WSL WS1.......................5 F2
Terry Dr WALM/CURD B76..............78 B2
Terrys La ERDE/BCHGN B24.........93 G3
Terry St DUDS DY2....................84 D5
Tessall La NFLD/LBR B31...........174 D3
Tetbury Gv NFLD/LBR B31........174 D2
Tetley Av RUSH/SHEL WS4...........42 C1
Tetley Rd SPARK B11................145 E4
Tetnall St DUDS DY2...................102 D1
Tettenhall Rd BDMR/CCFT WV3...6 A2
 DUNHL/THL/PER WV6................36 B2
Teviot Gdns BRLYHL DY5............100 B4
 CDSL WV8...........................10 C2
Teviot Gv HWK/WKHTH B38......176 D5
Tewkesbury Dr DUDS DY2.........120 D1
Tewkesbury Rd
 BFLD/HDSWWD B20................91 E5
 BLOX/PEL WS3......................16 A5
Tew Park Rd HDSW B21.............107 G2
Thackeray Rd BVILLE B30........159 F5
Thames Cl BRLYHL DY5.............100 D2
Thames Ct SCFLD/BOLD B73 *....62 B5
Thames Rd BLOX/PEL WS3..........27 H2
Thanet Cl KGSWFD DY6................99 G3
Thanet Gv PBAR/PBCH B42........90 B2
The Thatchers RMSLY B62.........122 C4
Thatchway Gdns
 HWK/WKHTH B38................176 D5
Thaxted Rd STETCH B33.............131 G1
Theatre Ap DIG/EDG B5..................3 G7
Thelbridge Rd NFLD/LBR B31...189 E2
Thelma Rd SHLY B90..................180 A2
Thelma St WSL WS1.....................56 D1
Thelsford Wy HIA/OLT B92........165 F2
Theodore Cl HRBN B17.............142 B3
 OLDBY B69.........................86 C5
Theresa Rd SPARK B11.............127 H5
Thetford Cl TPTN/OCK DY4..........84 D1
Thetford Gdns WNSFLD WV11...24 D4
Thetford Rd PBAR/PBCH B42......74 B4
Thetford Wy DSYBK/YTR WS5...58 A5
Thickett Cl WOLV WV1..................41 F5
Thicknall Dr HAG/WOL DY9.......135 H5
Thicknall La HAG/WOL DY9.......169 H2
Thicknall Ri HAG/WOL DY9.......169 G1
Thimble Dr WALM/CURD B76........78 B2
Thimble End Rd
 WALM/CURD B76....................78 C1
Thimble Mill La AST/WIT B6......109 H2
Thimblemill Rd
 SMTHWKW B67....................124 B1
Third Av BORD B9.....................128 C2
 BRWNH WS8........................10 B1
 KGSWFD DY6.......................100 B1
 SLYOAK B29........................143 G4
 WOLVN WV10........................23 H3
Third Exhibition Av
 BHAMNEC B40......................149 H2
Third Rd BRGRVW B61................186 A4
Thirlmere Cl
 DUNHL/THL/PER WV6..............21 H2
Thirlmere Dr MOS/BIL B13........162 A2
 WNSFLD WV11.......................15 E5
Thirlmere Gv
 DUNHL/THL/PER WV6..............34 D1
Thirlmere Wk BRLYHL DY5........118 D5
Thirsk Cft CBROM B36..............111 G1
Thirston Cl WNSFLD WV11..........25 G5
Thistle Cl SEDG DY3...................67 H5
Thistle Cft WNSFLD WV11..........24 D5
Thistle Down Cl
 FOAKS/STRLY B74...................45 G3
Thistledown Rd
 BKDE/SHDE B34..................113 E2
Thistle Gn HWK/WKHTH B38....190 C1
Thistlegreen Cl
 BLKHTH/ROWR B65...............103 F4
Thistlegreen Rd DUDS DY2.......103 E5
Thistle La RIDG/WDGT B32.......157 F2
Thomas Benson Pl
 BHTH/HG B12......................127 F5
Thomas Crs SMTHWK B66..........107 E4
Thomas Guy Rd WBROM B70......70 C4
Thomas Mason Cl
 WNSFLD WV11........................24 D3
Thomas St AST/WIT B6.............109 F3
 BKHL/PFLD WV2.......................7 F7
 SMTHWK B66......................106 D4
 WBROM B70.........................87 H4
 WSLW WS2............................27 E5
Thompson Av BKHL/PFLD WV2...52 B1
Thompson Cl DUDS DY2...........120 B2
Thompson Dr
 ERDE/BCHGN B24..................110 D1
Thompson Gdns
 SMTHWKW B67....................106 B5
Thompson Rd
 LGLYGN/QTN B68.................105 F5

SMTHWKW B67......................106 B5
Thompson St BILS/COS WV14...53 H3
 WLNHL WV13.........................39 G2
Thomson Av HWK/WKHTH B38...176 A4
Thoresby Cft DUDN DY1............119 H2
Thornberry Dr DUDN DY1..........101 F1
Thornberry Wk
 VAUX/NECH B7....................110 A3
Thornbridge Av
 PBAR/PBCH B42.....................74 D4
Thornbridge Gv ALDR WS9..........19 F4
Thornbury Ct
 DUNHL/THL/PER WV6..............35 E2
Thornbury Rd
 BFLD/HDSWWD B20................90 D4
Thornby Av SOLH B91...............164 D5
Thornby Rd ERDW/GRVHL B23...76 A3
Thorncliffe Rd NFLD/LBR B31......75 E1
Thorne Cl DARL/WED WS10.........55 H4
Thorne Av WOLVN WV10..............23 C5
Thorne Rd WLNHL WV13.............39 G1
Thorne St BKHL/PFLD WV2..........53 C1
Thorneycroft La WOLVN WV10...24 A5
Thorneycroft Rd
 BILS/COS WV14.....................54 C5
Thornfield Cft SEDG DY3...........45 F4
Thornfield Cft SEDG DY3............67 F2
Thornfield Rd ACGN B27...........146 C5
Thorngrove Av SOLH B91.........182 A5
Thornham Wy
 ALE/KHTH/YWD B14.............177 H4
Thornhill Gv HDSW B21............107 H1
Thornhill Pk FOAKS/STRLY B74...45 G5
Thornhill Rd BRLYHL DY5..........119 C3
 DUDN DY1............................84 C2
 FOAKS/STRLY B74................45 G4
 HALE B63...........................138 A4
 HDSW B21..........................107 H1
 SOLH B91...........................165 E3
 SPARK B11...........................145 F4
Thornhurst Av
 RIDG/WDGT B32..................124 A5
Thornleigh SEDG DY3..................83 F1
Thornley Cl MOS/BIL B13.........161 G1
 WNSFLD WV11........................25 F1
Thornley St WOLV WV1.................25 E1
Thorns Av BRLYHL DY5.............119 G3
Thorns Rd BRLYHL DY5.............119 G5
Thornsett Gv SHLY B90.............163 F4
Thorntree Rd BLOX/PEL WS3.....18 A1
Thorntree Wk ROWR B65...........104 A4
Thornton Cl OLDBY B69..............86 A4
Thornton Dr BRLYHL DY5 *........119 G3
Thornton Rd SHLY B90.............195 F2
 WOLV WV1............................38 A4
Thornwood Cl
 LGLYGN/QTN B68.................105 G4
Thornyfield Cl SHLY B90............180 C2
Thornyfield Rd SHLY B90...........180 D2
Thorpe Cl MGN/WHC B75.............62 C1
Thorpe Rd WSL WS1....................57 E1
Thorp St CBHAMW B1....................3 F7
Three Acres La SHLY B90.........179 H5
Three Broadway EDG B15 *........126 B3
Three Corner Cl SHLY B90........179 G5
Three Oaks Rd HLYWD B47.......192 D4
Three Shires Oak Rd
 SMTHWK B66......................124 B2
Three Tuns La WOLVN WV10........12 C5
Threshers Dr SHHTH WV12..........26 B4
Throne Cl BLKHTH/ROWR B65...104 A4
Throne Crs
 BLKHTH/ROWR B65...............104 B5
Throne Rd BLKHTH/ROWR B65...104 A4
Throstles Cl GTB/HAM B43..........73 G4
Thrush Rd LGLYGN/QTN B68.....122 D2
Thruxton Cl
 ALE/KHTH/YWD B14.............178 B2
Thunderbolt Wy
 TPTN/OCK DY4......................68 D5
Thurcroft Cl WASH/WDE B8.......110 D5
Thuree Rd SMTHWK B67............123 H2
Thurleigh Cl HAG/WOL DY9.......135 H5
Thurlestone Rd NFLD/LBR B31...189 E1
Thurloe Crs RBRY B45...............173 G4
Thurlston Av HIA/OLT B92.........147 F3
Thurstone Dr
 ETTPK/GDPK/PENN WV4...........51 F4
Thurstone Rd BLOX/PEL WS3....16 D4
Thursfield Rd HHTH/SAND B71...72 A4
 TPTN/OCK DY4.......................85 E2
Thurston Av OLDBY B69..............86 D5
Thynne St WBROM B70.................88 A4
Tibbats Cl RIDG/WDGT B32.......140 C4
Tibberton Cl BDMR/CCFT WV3...50 D1
 HALE B63...........................137 H5
 SOLH B91...........................181 G5
Tibbets La HRBN B17................141 G5
Tibbington Rd TPTN/OCK DY4....69 E4
Tibbington Ter TPTN/OCK DY4....69 F4
Tiberius Cl CSHL/WTROR B46......97 E1
Tibland Rd ACGN B27.................163 H1
Tiddington Cl CBROM B36............94 D5
Tideswell Rd PBAR/PBCH B42.....74 C5
Tidworth Cft
 ALE/KHTH/YWD B14.............178 C2
Tierney Dr TPTN/OCK DY4...........70 A5
Tiffany La COVEN WV9.................11 H5
Tiffield Rd YDLY B25.................146 C2
Tilbury Cl BDMR/CCFT WV3........35 E5
Tilbury Gv MOS/BIL B13............160 D1
Tildasley St WBROM B70.............87 F1
Tildesley Dr SHHTH WV12...........25 H5
Tile Cross Rd STETCH B33.........131 G3
Tiled House La BRLYHL DY5......100 D3
Tile Gv
 CHWD/FDBR/MGN B37...........114 A4
Tilehouse Green La
 DOR/KN B93........................196 D1
Tilehouse La SHLY B90..............193 G5
Tilesford Cl SHLY B90...............195 G5
Tiller Gv MGN/WHC B75................47 H1
Tilley St DARL/WED WS10............55 G2
Tillyard Cft SLYOAK B29............159 E1

Tilshead Cl
 ALE/KHTH/YWD B14.............178 A2
Tilsley Gv ERDW/GRVHL B23........91 H1
Tilston Dr BRLYHL DY5.............119 F5
Tilton Rd BORD B9....................128 A3
Timberline Cl HALE B63............137 H1
Timberlake Cl SHLY B90...........195 H2
Timberley Cft
 BKDE/SHDE B34...................113 F2
Timberley La BKDE/SHDE B34...113 F2
Timbers Wy ERDE/BCHGN B24...94 B2
 SPARK B11.........................144 C1
Timbertree Crs CDYHTH B64...121 E5
Timbertree Rd CDYHTH B64.....121 E5
Times Square Av BRLYHL DY5...119 H2
Timmins Cl SOLH B91...............165 G5
Timmis Cl BILS/COS WV14...........53 F5
Timmis Rd HAG/WOL DY9..........136 A1
Timothy Rd OLDBY B69.............104 A2
Tinacre Hl
 DUNHL/THL/PER WV6..............34 C2
Tinchbourne St DUDN DY1..........84 C5
Tindal St BHTH/HG B12...........144 B2
Tinkers Farm Gv
 NFLD/LBR B31....................175 E2
Tinkers Farm Rd
 NFLD/LBR B31....................175 E1
Tinmeadow Crs RBRY B45.........188 C1
Tinsley St TPTN/OCK DY4............86 C1
Tintagel Cl
 DUNHL/THL/PER WV6..............34 D2
Tintagel Dr DUDN DY1................83 G4
Tintagel Wy ALDR WS9................29 G4
Tintern Cl FOAKS/STRLY B74.......60 C1
Tintern Ct
 DUNHL/THL/PER WV6..............34 C2
Tintern Crs BLOX/PEL WS3..........16 B5
Tintern Rd BFLD/HDSWWD B20...91 E5
Tintern Vls BHTH/HG B12 *.......144 D2
Tintern Wy BLOX/PEL WS3..........16 B5
Tipperary Cl CBROM B36...........112 A1
Tipps Stone Cl TPTN/OCK DY4....85 E2
Tipton Rd DUDN DY1...................85 H5
 OLDBY B69...........................86 A4
 SEDG DY3.............................67 G4
Tirley Rd STETCH B33................112 C5
Titania Cl RBRY B45..................174 A2
Titchfield Cl WOLVN WV10............13 E5
Titford Cl OLDBY B69...............104 B4
Titford La BLKHTH/ROWR B65...104 B4
Titford Rd OLDBY B69...............104 B4
Tithe Cft WOLVN WV10................37 H2
Tithe Rd WNSFLD WV11...............25 G2
Titterstone Rd NFLD/LBR B31...175 G5
Tiverton Cl KGSWFD DY6...........118 C1
Tiverton Dr HHTH/SAND B71.......71 F4
Tiverton Gv SMTHWKW B67 *....106 B3
Tiverton Rd SLYOAK B29...........142 D5
 SMTHWKW B66...................106 D4
Tividale Hl
 OLDBY B69...........................85 H4
Tividale Rd OLDBY B69...............85 C4
Tividale St TPTN/OCK DY4...........85 H3
Tixall Rd HLGN/YWD B28...........162 C5
Toberland WSLW WS2 *.................27 F3
Toll End Rd TPTN/OCK DY4..........70 A3
Tollgate Cl NFLD/LBR B31.........175 F5
Tollgate Dr
 BFLD/HDSWWD B20................108 A2
Toll House Rd RBRY B45............188 D1
Tollhouse Wy SMTHWK B66.......106 D2
 WMBN WV5...........................64 C4
Tolworth Hall Rd
 ERDE/BCHGN B24...................93 F3
Tomey Rd SPARK B11................145 F2
Tomlan Rd NFLD/LBR B31.........190 A1
Tomlinson Rd CBROM B36...........94 B5
Tompstone Rd HHTH/SAND B71...72 B3
Tonadine Cl WNSFLD WV11........25 G1
Tonbridge Rd
 ERDE/BCHGN B24...................93 E5
Tong St WSL WS1..........................5 J4
Top Croft Rd ERDW/GRVHL B23...76 A5
Topland Gv NFLD/LBR B31........174 C3
Top Rd BRGRVW B61.................186 C4
Topsham Cft
 ALE/KHTH/YWD B14.............160 D5
Topsham Rd SMTHWKW B67.....106 A3
Torfield CDSL WV8.....................11 C5
Toronto Gdns RIDG/WDGT B32...141 E1
Torre Av NFLD/LBR B31............175 E3
Torrey Gv WASH/WDE B8...........111 C5
Torridge Dr WNSFLD WV11..........24 C5
Torridon Cft MOS/BIL B13........143 H4
Torridon Rd SHHTH WV12...........12 D4
Torvale Rd
 DUNHL/THL/PER WV6..............35 G3
Tor Wy BLOX/PEL WS3................17 H4
Totnes Gv SLYOAK B29.............142 D5
Totnes Rd WNSFLD WV11............25 G1
Tottenham Crs KGSTG B44.........75 H1
Touchwood Hall Cl SOLH B91...182 A1
Towcester Cft CBROM B36........111 H1
Tower Cft
 CHWD/FDBR/MGN B37...........114 B5
Tower Hl PBAR/PBCH B42...........74 B5
Tower Rd AST/WIT B6................109 F2
 ERDW/GRVHL B23...................92 C3
 MGN/WHC B75.......................63 F3
 OLDBY B69..........................104 A2
Tower St DUDN DY1.....................84 C5
 LOZ/NWT B19......................108 A2
 SEDG DY3.............................67 F2
 WOLV WV1..............................7 G4
 WSL WS1...............................56 D1
Townend St WSLW WS2...............4 D5
Townfold BLOX/PEL WS3............18 A3
Townley Gdns AST/WIT B6..........91 E5
Townsend Av SEDG DY3...............67 F2
Townsend Dr WALM/CURD B76...78 B4
Townsend Wy CBHAM B3 *...........2 C3
Townshend Gv
 CHWD/FDBR/MGN B37...........113 H5
Townwell Fold WOLV WV1 *.........25 F2
Towpath Cl BORD B9.................127 H3
Towpath Cl BORD B9..................127 G2
Towyn Rd MOS/BIL B13.............162 B2
Toys La HALE B63.....................137 G2

Tozer St TPTN/OCK DY4...............69 F4
Traceys Meadow RBRY B45.......188 A1
Trafalgar Gv YDLY B25................146 A1
Trafalgar Rd ERDE/BCHGN B24...92 D5
 HDSW B21..........................107 C1
 MOS/BIL B13......................144 B4
 OLDBY B69...........................85 H5
 SMTHWK B66.......................106 D5
Trajan Hl CSHL/WTROR B46........97 E5
Tram Wy SMTHWK B66..............105 G2
Tramway Cl BILS/COS WV14.........54 B1
 WSL WS10..............................55 G1
Tranter Rd WASH/WDE B8.........111 F4
Tranwell Cl COVEN WV9.............11 H5
Traquain Dr DUDN DY1...............84 A3
Treaford La WASH/WDE B8........111 F5
Tredington Cl SLYOAK B29.......158 C3
Tree Acre Gv HALE B63.............137 E1
Treeford Cl SOLH B91...............181 F4
Trees Rd WSL WS1.......................57 F2
Treeton Cft STETCH B33...........130 C2
The Tops WMBN WV5..................64 C5
Treetops Dr SHHTH WV12...........26 C5
Trefoil Cl SLYOAK B29...............158 C3
Trefoil Gdns STRBR DY8...........135 G1
Tregarron Rd HALE B63............137 G2
Tregea Ri GTB/HAM B43..............73 F4
Trehern Cl DOR/KN B93.............197 E5
Trehernes Dr HAG/WOL DY9.....152 D1
Trehurst Av PBAR/PBCH B42.......74 C4
Trejon Rd CDYHTH B64.............121 E4
Tremont St WOLV WV1...................7 K2
Trenchard Cl MGN/WHC B75.......63 F5
Trent Cl DUNHL/THL/PER WV6...34 C1
 STRBR DY8.........................135 G3
Trent Dr CBROM B36................113 H1
Trentham Av SHHTH WV12..........25 G5
Trentham Gv
 LGN/SDN/BHAMAIR B26........147 E2
Trentham Ri BKHL/PFLD WV2.....52 D1
Trent Pl BLOX/PEL WS3..............18 C1
Trent Rd BLOX/PEL WS3.............28 C1
Trent St DIG/EDG B5......................3 K6
Trenville Av BHTH/HG B12........144 D2
Tresco Cl RBRY B45..................173 G4
Prescott Rd NFLD/LBR B31.......158 A4
Tresham Rd KGSTG B44...............75 E2
 KGSWFD DY6.........................99 H1
Trevanie Av RIDG/WDGT B32....140 C1
Treverne Cl BHTH/HG B12.........144 B1
Trevor Av GTB/HAM B43..............57 H2
Trevor Rd BLOX/PEL WS3............17 H3
Trevor St VAUX/NECH B7............110 A3
Trevor St West VAUX/NECH B7...110 A2
Trevose Cl BLOX/PEL WS3 *........16 B4
Trevose Retreat
 BHTH/HG B12......................144 B2
Trewman Cl WALM/CURD B76......78 B3
Treyamon Rd DSYBK/YTR WS5....58 B1
Treynham Cl WOLV WV1...............38 B4
The Triangle WSNGN B18...........107 H5
Trickley Dr MGN/WHC B75 *.........63 F2
Trident Bvd CVALE B35................94 D4
Trident Cl ERDW/GRVHL B23.......77 E4
 WALM/CURD B76....................78 B4
Trident Ct
 CHWD/FDBR/MGN B37...........133 E4
Trident Dr DARL/WED WS10........55 F5
 LGLYGN/QTN B68.................105 F4
Trident Rd
 LGN/SDN/BHAMAIR B26........149 C5
Trigo Cft CBROM B36................112 A1
Trimpley Cl DOR/KN B93...........196 C5
Trimpley Gdns
 ETTPK/GDPK/PENN WV4...........51 F2
Trimpley Rd RIDG/WDGT B32....157 F2
Trinder Rd SMTHWKW B67.......123 H3
Trindle Rd DUDN DY1.................84 D4
Tring Ct DUNHL/THL/PER WV6...36 B1
Trinity Cl HIA/OLT B92..............164 D1
 STRBR DY8.........................117 H2
Trinity Gv
 LGN/SDN/BHAMAIR B26........147 E2
Trinity Hi SCFLD/WYGN B72.......62 C3
Trinity Pk HIA/OLT B92 *...........149 H4
Trinity Pl SCFLD/WYGN B72 *....62 D3
Trinity Rd AST/WIT B6.................91 F5
 BILS/COS WV14.....................54 B5
 DUDN DY1............................83 G1
 MGN/WHC B75.......................47 F4
 SHHTH WV13........................38 C3
 STRBR DY8.........................118 C4
Trinity Rd North WBROM B70......87 H4
Trinity Rd South WBROM B70.....87 H4
Trinity St ACGN B27..................119 F1
 CDYHTH B64.......................121 E3
 OLDBY B69.........................105 E4
 SMTHWK B66......................106 C3
 WBROM B70..........................87 H5
Trinity Ter BHTH/HG B12...........127 G4
Trinity Wy BFLD/HDSWWD B20...90 B5
 WBROM B70..........................87 H5
Trippleton Av RIDG/WDGT B32...157 F3
Tristram Av NFLD/LBR B31.......175 H4
Trittiford Rd MOS/BIL B13........162 A4
Tromans Cl CDYHTH B64...........121 E5
Troon Cl BLOX/PEL WS3..............30 A5
 MGN/WHC B75.......................47 H5
Troon Ct DUNHL/THL/PER WV6...20 D5
Troon Pl STRBR DY8..................117 G1
Trostrey Rd BVILLE B30............178 A2
Trotter's La HHTH/SAND B71......71 E4
Troughton Crs BVILLE B30........159 F5
Troutbeck Dr BRLYHL DY5........118 D4
Troy Gv ALE/KHTH/YWD B14......177 H1
Truda St WSL WS1.......................56 D1
Truemans Heath La
 HLYWD B47........................192 D1
Truro Cl BLKHTH/ROWR B65.....104 C5
Truro Rd DSYBK/YTR WS5...........58 B1
Trustin Crs HIA/OLT B92.............54 A2
Tryon Pl BILS/COS WV14..............54 A2
Trysull Av
 LGN/SDN/BHAMAIR B26........148 A3
Trysull Gdns BDMR/CCFT WV3...50 D1
Trysull Rd BDMR/CCFT WV3.......50 D1
 WMBN WV5...........................64 A3
Trysull Wy DUDS DY2...............102 C5
Tudbury Rd NFLD/LBR B31........174 D1
Tudman Cl WALM/CURD B76........78 B4
Tudor Cl ALE/KHTH/YWD B14....178 C4
 MOS/BIL B13......................161 F4

SCFLD/BOLD B73 76 B1
Tudor Ct TPTN/OCK DY4 85 G2
WNSFLD WV11 14 D3
Tudor Crs BKHL/PFLD WV2 51 H2
Tudor Cft
CHWD/FDBR/MGN B37 131 H3
Tudor Gdns ERDW/GRVHL B23 92 C3
STRBR DY8 135 E2
Tudor Gv FOAKS/STRLY B74 45 G5
Tudor Hl SCFLD/BOLD B73 62 A2
Tudor Pl SEDG DY3 67 G5
Tudor Rd BILS/COS WV14 54 D4
BLKHTH/ROWR B65 104 A4
LGLYGN/QTN B68 105 G5
MOS/BIL B13 144 B4
SCFLD/BOLD B73 62 B3
SEDG DY3 67 G5
WOLVN WV10 38 A1
Tudors Cl SMTHH B10 * 128 A4
Tudor St TPTN/OCK DY4 85 G2
WSNGN B18 107 F5
Tudor Ter DUDS DY2 85 E5
HRBN B17 * 142 A1
Tudor V SEDG DY3 67 G5
Tudor Wy CSCFLD/WYGN B72 77 F1
Tufnell Gv WASH/WDE B8 111 E2
Tugford Rd SLYOAK B29 159 E3
Tulip Gv FOAKS/STRLY B74 60 B2
Tulyar Cl CBROM B36 111 G1
Tunnel La ALE/KHTH/YWD B14 177 G1
Tunnel Rd WBROM B70 71 E3
Tunnel St BILS/COS WV14 68 C3
Tunstall Rd KGSWFD DY6 100 C4
Turchill Dr WALM/CURD B76 78 C3
Turfpits La ERDW/GRVHL B23 76 B5
Turf Pitts La MGN/WHC B75 48 B2
Turks Headway WBROM B70 87 G4
Turley St DUDN DY1 68 A5
Turls Hill Rd BILS/COS WV14 67 H3
Turls St SEDG DY3 67 G4
Turnberry Gv
DUNHL/THL/PER WV6 20 B5
Turnberry Rd BLOX/PEL WS3 16 D3
PBAR/PBCH B42 74 B3
Turner Av
ETTPK/GDPK/PENN WV4 67 H1
Turner Dr BRLYHL DY5 119 F5
Turner Gv
DUNHL/THL/PER WV6 35 E1
Turners Cft HHTH/SAND B71 72 C3
Turner's Gv SEDG DY3 83 E2
Turner's Hl
BLKHTH/ROWR B65 103 H3
Turners Hill Rd SEDG DY3 83 E2
Turner's La BRLYHL DY5 119 E4
Turner St DUDN DY1 102 B1
SEDG DY3 83 F3
SPARK B11 144 C1
TPTN/OCK DY4 69 F4
WBROM B70 87 F3
Turney Rd STRBR DY8 135 F1
Turnham Gn
DUNHL/THL/PER WV6 34 C2
Turnhouse Rd CVALE B35 94 D2
Turnley Rd BKDE/SHDE B34 113 E3
Turnpike Cl SPARK B11 144 C1
Turnpike Dr CSHL/WTROR B46 96 C3
Turton Cl BLOX/PEL WS3 16 C3
Turton Rd TPTN/OCK DY4 69 F2
WBROM B70 87 E4
Turtons Cft BILS/COS WV14 53 F5
Turves Gn NFLD/LBR B31 175 G4
Turville Rd
BFLD/HDSWWD B20 90 C5
Tustin Gv ACGN B27 163 G2
Tutbury Av
DUNHL/THL/PER WV6 34 D2
Tuxford Cl WOLVN WV10 37 G1
Tweeds Well RIDG/WDGT B32 157 F3
Twickenham Ct STRBR DY8 117 G5
Twickenham Dr MOS/BIL B13 144 A5
Twickenham Rd KGSTG B44 75 H2
Two Gates HALE B63 137 F2
Two Gates La HALE B63 137 G2
Two Locks BRLYHL DY5 101 H5
Two Woods La BRLYHL DY5 119 G3
Twycross Gv CBROM B36 111 H2
Twydale Av OLDBY B69 85 H5
Twyford Cl ALDR WS9 30 B5
Twyford Gv WNSFLD WV11 25 F5
Twyford Rd WASH/WDE B8 111 G4
Twyning Rd BVILLE B30 160 B3
LDYWD/EDGR B16 107 F5
Tyber Dr BFLD/HDSWWD B20 90 B3
Tyberry Cl SHLY B90 180 A4
Tyburn Gv ERDE/BCHGN B24 93 H3
Tyburn Rd ERDE/BCHGN B24 92 B5
WOLV WV1 38 C4
Tyburn Sq ERDE/BCHGN B24 93 H3
Tyebeams BKDE/SHDE B34 113 E4
Tye Gdns HAG/WOL DY9 152 D1
Tyler Ct ERDE/BCHGN B24 92 D3
Tyler Gdns WLNHL WV13 39 H4
Tyler Gv GTB/HAM B43 74 A2
Tyler Rd WLNHL WV13 39 G5
Tylers Gn HWK/WKHTH B38 177 F4
Tylers Gv SHLY B90 195 F2
Tylney Cl DIG/EDG B5 126 D5
Tyndale Crs GTB/HAM B43 59 G5
Tyne Cl BRWNH WS8 8 C2
CHWD/FDBR/MGN B37 114 B5
Tynedale Crs
ETTPK/GDPK/PENN WV4 52 C5
Tynedale Rd SPARK B11 145 H4
Tyne Gv YDLY B25 129 H4
Tyne Pl BRLYHL DY5 119 H2
Tyning Cl COVEN WV9 12 A5
Tyninghame Av
DUNHL/THL/PER WV6 21 H4
Tynings La ALDR WS9 30 A5
Tyrley Cl DUNHL/THL/PER WV6 35 F3
Tyrol Cl STRBR DY8 134 D1
Tyseley Hill Rd SPARK B11 146 A3
Tyseley La SPARK B11 146 A3
Tysoe Cl HOCK/TIA B94 198 A5
Tysoe Dr WALM/CURD B76 63 F4
Tysoe Rd KGSTG B44 75 F4
Tythebarn Dr KGSWFD DY6 99 E2
Tythe Barn La SHLY B90 193 G2
SHLY B90 194 A2
Tythebarn La SHLY B90 194 A2
Tyzack Cl BRLYHL DY5 119 E2

U

Udall Rd BILS/COS WV14 53 H5
Uffculme Rd BVILLE B30 160 D2
Uffmoor Est HALE B63 155 E1
Uffmoor La HALE B63 155 E1
RMSLY B62 154 D4
Ufton Cl SHLY B90 181 E2
Ufton Crs SHLY B90 180 D2
Ullenhall Rd DOR/KN B93 197 E2
WALM/CURD B76 78 B3
Ullenwood HDSW B21 107 F2
Ulleries Rd HIA/OLT B92 147 G5
Ullrik Gn ERDE/BCHGN B24 92 D4
Ullswater Cl RIDG/WDGT B32 141 F5
Ullswater Gdns KGSWFD DY6 99 H3
Ullswater Ri BRLYHL DY5 101 F4
Ullswater Rd SHHTH WV12 25 H1
Ulster Dr KGSWFD DY6 100 A5
Ulverley Crs HIA/OLT B92 164 B2
Ulverley Green Rd
HIA/OLT B92 164 C2
Ulwine Dr NFLD/LBR B31 175 G1
Umberslade Rd SLYOAK B29 160 A2
Uncle Ben's Cl OLDBY B69 104 D5
Underhill La WOLVN WV10 13 G5
Underhill Rd TPTN/OCK DY4 70 A5
WASH/WDE B8 128 D1
Underhill St OLDBY B69 105 E4
Underley Cl KGSWFD DY6 99 F2
The Underpass BHAMNEC B40 150 A3
Underwood Cl EDG B15 142 B4
ERDW/GRVHL B23 92 A2
Underwood Rd
BFLD/HDSWWD B20 89 G1
Unett St LOZ/NWT B19 108 C4
SMTHWK B66 107 E5
Unett St North LOZ/NWT B19 108 C4
Unett Wk LOZ/NWT B19 108 C4
Union La WMBN WV5 64 B2
Union Mill St WOLV WV1 7 J4
Union Pas CBHAM B2 3 G5
Union Pl SLYOAK B29 143 F5
Union Rd AST/WIT B6 109 H1
OLDBY B69 86 C4
SHLY B90 180 C3
SOLH B91 182 A1
Union Rw HDSW B21 107 H1
Union St BILS/COS WV14 53 G3
BLKHTH/ROWR B65 122 A3
CBHAM B2 3 G5
DARL/WED WS10 70 D1
DUDN DY1 84 C5
HAG/WOL DY9 136 C2
STRBR DY8 135 G3
TPTN/OCK DY4 85 F1
WBROM B70 105 H1
WLNHL WV13 39 G3
WOLV WV1 7 H4
WSL WS1 5 G3
Unitt Dr CDYHTH B64 121 E4
Unity Cl DARL/WED WS10 55 E4
Unity Pl OLDBY B69 * 105 E1
SLYOAK B29 * 142 D5
Unketts Rd SMTHWKW B67 124 A1
Unwin Crs STRBR DY8 135 E2
Upavon Cl CVALE B35 94 C2
Upland Rd SLYOAK B29 143 E5
Uplands HALE B63 137 H5
Uplands Av BDMR/CCFT WV3 35 H5
BLKHTH/ROWR B65 122 B1
WLNHL WV13 38 D4
Uplands Cl DUDS DY2 103 E2
Uplands Dr BDMR/CCFT WV3 36 A5
SEDG DY3 67 F3
Uplands Gv WLNHL WV13 38 C4
Uplands Rd DUDS DY2 103 E2
HDSW B21 89 F4
WLNHL WV13 38 C4
The Uplands SMTHWKW B67 106 B5
Upper Ashley St RMSLY B62 122 A3
Upper Balsall Heath Rd
BHTH/HG B12 144 B1
Upper Brook St WSLW WS2 4 B4
Upper Chapel St OLDBY B69 85 H4
Upper Church La TPTN/OCK DY4 69 F4
Upper Clifton Rd
SCFLD/BOLD B73 62 B3
Upper Cl RIDG/WDGT B32 140 D4
Upper Coneybere St
BHTH/HG B12 127 F5
Upper Dean St DIG/EDG B5 3 G7
Upper Ettingshall Rd
BILS/COS WV14 68 A3
Upper Forster St
RUSH/SHEL WS4 5 F1
Upper Gough St CBHAMW B1 126 D3
Upper Gn
DUNHL/THL/PER WV6 21 H5
Upper Green La WSLW WS2 41 G1
Upper Grosvenor Rd
BFLD/HDSWWD B20 90 B4
Upper Hall La WSL WS1 4 E5
Upper Highgate St
BHTH/HG B12 127 F5
Upper High St CDYHTH B64 120 D3
DARL/WED WS10 55 H5
Upper Holland Rd
CSCFLD/WYGN B72 62 C4
Upper Lichfield St
WLNHL WV13 39 G3
Upper Marshall St
CBHAMW B1 2 E7
Upper Meadow Rd
RIDG/WDGT B32 140 C2
Upper Navigation St
WSLW WS2 4 C3
Upper Rushall St WSL WS1 5 F4
Upper Russell St
DARL/WED WS10 70 D1
Upper St Mary's Rd
SMTHWKW B67 124 B3
Upper Short St WSLW WS2 4 B4
Upper Sneyd Rd WNSFLD WV11 15 F5
Upper Stone Cl
WALM/CURD B76 63 E4
Upper St
DUNHL/THL/PER WV6 21 H5
Upper Sutton St AST/WIT B6 109 F2
Upper Thomas St AST/WIT B6 109 F3
Upper Trinity St BORD B9 127 G3
Upper Vauxhall WOLV WV1 6 B3
Upper Villiers St
BKHL/PFLD WV2 51 H2
Upper William St CBHAMW B1 2 C7
Upper Zoar St
BDMR/CCFT WV3 6 C7
Upton Gdns BILS/COS WV14 53 G3
Upton Gn WOLVN WV10 12 B4
Upton Gv STETCH B33 129 G3
Upton Rd STETCH B33 129 G2
Upton St DUDS DY2 102 C4
Upwey Av SOLH B91 181 G1
Usk Cl BLOX/PEL WS3 27 H2
Usk Wy CBROM B36 113 H1
Uttoxeter Cl
DUNHL/THL/PER WV6 22 D5
Uxbridge Cl SEDG DY3 83 F4
Uxbridge St LOZ/NWT B19 108 D4

V

Valbourne Rd
ALE/KHTH/YWD B14 177 G1
Vale Av ALDR WS9 44 D3
SEDG DY3 67 F5
Vale Cl RIDG/WDGT B32 141 F4
Vale Ct CDYHTH B64 * 120 D5
Vale Head Dr
DUNHL/THL/PER WV6 35 E3
Valencia Cft CVALE B35 94 D2
Valentine Cl FOAKS/STRLY B74 60 B2
Valentine Rd
ALE/KHTH/YWD B14 161 E1
LGLYGN/QTN B68 123 G2
Valepits Rd STETCH B33 131 E3
Valerie Gv GTB/HAM B43 73 E3
Vale Rd DUDS DY2 103 E5
Vale Rw SEDG DY3 83 F1
Vales Cl WALM/CURD B76 78 A4
Vale St BKHL/PFLD WV2 53 E2
HHTH/SAND B71 72 A5
SEDG DY3 83 F1
STRBR DY8 118 B4
The Vale SPARK B11 144 D5
Vale Vw ALDR WS9 44 B2
Valley Farm Rd RBRY B45 187 H2
Valley La HOCK/TIA B94 199 H4
Valley Rd BLOX/PEL WS3 27 H2
CDYHTH B64 121 E5
FOAKS/STRLY B74 60 B1
GTB/HAM B43 73 E4
HAG/WOL DY9 136 D1
HIA/OLT B92 148 A3
RMSLY B62 122 D4
SEDG DY3 67 G5
SMTHWKW B67 124 B1
WOLVN WV10 23 H5
Valley Side BLOX/PEL WS3 17 H5
Valley Vw BRWNH WS8 9 G5
Vallian Cft CBROM B36 112 B2
Vanborough Wk DUDN DY1 84 A4
Vanbrugh Ct
DUNHL/THL/PER WV6 34 C2
Van Diemans Rd WMBN WV5 80 C1
Vanguard Cl CBROM B36 112 A1
Vanguard Rd
LGN/SDN/BHAMAIR B26 149 G3
Vann Cl SMTHH B10 128 A4
Vantage Point WBROM B70 * 87 G4
Varden Cft DIG/EDG B5 126 D5
Vardon Wy HWK/WKHTH B38 176 B4
Varley Rd ERDE/BCHGN B24 93 H2
Varley V ERDE/BCHGN B24 93 H2
Varlins Wy HWK/WKHTH B38 190 B2
Varney Av WBROM B70 87 H4
Vaughan Cl FOAKS/STRLY B74 32 D4
Vaughan Gdns CDSL WV8 10 B3
Vaughan Rd WLNHL WV13 38 D4
Vaughton Dr MGN/WHC B75 63 E2
Vaughton St BHTH/HG B12 127 F4
Vaughton St South
BHTH/HG B12 127 E5
Vauxhall Av WOLV WV1 6 B3
Vauxhall Crs CBROM B36 95 H5
Vauxhall Gdns DUDS DY2 103 E2
Vauxhall Gv VAUX/NECH B7 127 H1
Vauxhall Pl VAUX/NECH B7 * 127 G1
Vauxhall Rd STRBR DY8 135 G2
VAUX/NECH B7 127 G1
Vauxhall St DUDN DY1 102 B1
Velsheda Rd SHLY B90 180 A3
Venetia Rd BORD B9 128 A2
Venning Gv GTB/HAM B43 73 F4
Ventnor Av CBROM B36 111 H2
LOZ/NWT B19 108 C2
Ventnor Cl LGLYGN/QTN B68 123 G5
Ventnor Rd HIA/OLT B92 148 A4
Venture Wy VAUX/NECH B7 3 K1
Vera Rd
LGN/SDN/BHAMAIR B26 130 A5
Verbena Gdns VAUX/NECH B7 109 G4
Verbena Rd NFLD/LBR B31 158 B5
Vercourt FOAKS/STRLY B74 45 H2
Verdun Crs DUDS DY2 85 F5
Vere St DIG/EDG B5 126 D4
Verity Wk STRBR DY8 118 A3
Verney Av STETCH B33 131 F5
Vernier Av KGSWFD DY6 100 C4
Vernolds Cft DIG/EDG B5 * 127 E4
Vernon Av BFLD/HDSWWD B20 89 H2
BRWNH WS8 9 G5
TPTN/OCK DY4 85 E2
Vernon Cl FOAKS/STRLY B74 32 C5
RMSLY B62 122 A4
WLNHL WV13 39 E4
WNSFLD WV11 14 D3
Vernon Ct LDYWD/EDGR B16 125 G3
LGLYGN/QTN B68 * 123 F5
Vernon Rd BILS/COS WV14 54 B2
LDYWD/EDGR B16 125 F3
LGLYGN/QTN B68 105 G3
RMSLY B62 122 A4
Vernon St WBROM B70 86 C3
Vernon Wy BLOX/PEL WS3 26 C1
Veronica Av
ETTPK/GDPK/PENN WV4 52 C3
Veronica Cl SLYOAK B29 158 B4
Veronica Rd KGSWFD DY6 100 C3
Verstone Cft NFLD/LBR B31 175 G3
Verstone Rd SHLY B90 180 C1
Verwood Cl WLNHL WV13 38 D4
Vesey Cl CSHL/WTROR B46 96 B4
FOAKS/STRLY B74 46 D3
Vesey Rd SCFLD/BOLD B73 77 F2
Vesey St CBHAMNE B4 3 G2
Vestry Cl CDYHTH B64 121 F3
Vestry Ct STRBR DY8 135 E1
Viaduct Dr
DUNHL/THL/PER WV6 22 D4
Viaduct St VAUX/NECH B7 127 G1
Vibart Rd
LGN/SDN/BHAMAIR B26 130 B4
Vicarage Cl BRLYHL DY5 119 E5
BRWNH WS8 9 G4
BVILLE B30 160 B3
PBAR/PBCH B42 74 D4
TPTN/OCK DY4 85 E1
Vicarage Gdns RMSLY B62 122 B3
WALM/CURD B76 78 B4
Vicarage Gv ACGN B27 163 F2
Vicarage La BRLYHL DY5 101 F1
CSHL/WTROR B46 96 B4
Vicarage Pl WSL WS1 4 D5
Vicarage Prospect DUDN DY1 84 B5
Vicarage Rd
ALE/KHTH/YWD B14 160 D3
AST/WIT B6 109 G2
BILS/COS WV14 68 C4
BKHL/PFLD WV2 7 H7
BLOX/PEL WS3 18 A5
BRWNH WS8 9 F5
DARL/WED WS10 55 H5
EDG B15 125 H4
ETTPK/GDPK/PENN WV4 51 E5
HAG/WOL DY9 136 D2
HHTH/SAND B71 71 H5
HOCK/TIA B94 198 D4
HRBN B17 141 H2
LGLYGN/QTN B68 105 G4
RMSLY B62 122 A4
SEDG DY3 83 G1
SMTHWKW B67 106 B4
STRBR DY8 117 H5
WNSFLD WV11 24 B4
WSNGN B18 108 A2
YDLY B25 130 A3
Vicarage Rd West DUDN DY1 68 C5
Vicarage St LGLYGN/QTN B68 105 F4
Vicarage Ter WSLW WS2 41 G5
Vicarage Wk WSL WS1 4 D5
Vicar St DARL/WED WS10 56 A5
DUDS DY2 102 C1
SEDG DY3 67 F3
Vicars Wk HAG/WOL DY9 136 C5
Viceroy Cl DIG/EDG B5 143 G1
KGSWFD DY6 100 C4
Victor Cl BKHL/PFLD WV2 53 F2
Victoria Ar WOLV WV1 7 F4
Victoria Av BLOX/PEL WS3 27 G1
RMSLY B62 139 H1
SMTHH B10 * 128 B5
SMTHWK B66 106 C4
Victoria Gdns CDYHTH B64 * 121 F2
Victoria Gv WMBN WV5 65 E3
WSNGN B18 107 G5
Victoria Ms OLDBY B69 122 D1
RUSH/SHEL WS4 42 C2
Victoriana Wy
BFLD/HDSWWD B20 90 A5
Victoria Park Rd
SMTHWK B66 106 D4
Victoria Pas WOLV WV1 7 F4
Victoria Pl DARL/WED WS10 * 40 B5
Victoria Rd ACGN B27 146 C5
AST/WIT B6 109 E2
BDMR/CCFT WV3 51 E1
BLOX/PEL WS3 18 A4
BRLYHL DY5 120 A3
BVILLE B30 160 A3
CDYHTH B64 121 F2
CSCFLD/WYGN B72 62 C4
DARL/WED WS10 55 F2
DUNHL/THL/PER WV6 22 A5
ERDW/GRVHL B23 92 B3
HDSW B21 107 G2
HRBN B17 141 H2
LGLYGN/QTN B68 105 G3
RMSLY B62 122 B4
SEDG DY3 67 G3
STETCH B33 129 H1
TPTN/OCK DY4 85 F1
WNSFLD WV11 24 B4
WOLVN WV10 23 H5
Victoria Sq CBHAMNW B3 2 E5
Victoria St BORD B9 128 B2
BRLYHL DY5 119 F1
DARL/WED WS10 70 C1
HALE B63 138 C3
KGSWFD DY6 99 E1
STRBR DY8 135 G2
WBROM B70 86 D1
WLNHL WV13 39 G2
WOLV WV1 7 F5
Victoria Ter RUSH/SHEL WS4 42 B2
Victor Rd HIA/OLT B92 148 A4
WSNGN B18 107 G3
Victor St BLOX/PEL WS3 28 C1
WSL WS1 57 E1
Victory Av DARL/WED WS10 55 E4
Victory La WSLW WS2 41 E1
Victory Ri HHTH/SAND B71 87 H1
View Dr DUDS DY2 103 E1
Viewfield Crs SEDG DY3 67 F4
Viewlands Dr
DUNHL/THL/PER WV6 35 E3
View Point OLDBY B69 103 H1
Vigo Cl ALDR WS9 19 F5
Vigo Pl ALDR WS9 30 A3
Vigo Rd ALDR WS9 19 F5
Vigo Ter ALDR WS9 19 F4
Viking Ri BLKHTH/ROWR B65 104 A5
Village Ms RIDG/WDGT B32 140 A1
Village Rd AST/WIT B6 91 G5
The Village KGSWFD DY6 100 A2
Village Wy BILS/COS WV14 53 F3
Villa Rd LOZ/NWT B19 108 B2
Villa St LOZ/NWT B19 108 C3
STRBR DY8 118 C4
Villa Wk LOZ/NWT B19 108 C3
Villette Gv
ALE/KHTH/YWD B14 179 E1
Villiers Av BILS/COS WV14 53 H2
Villiers Sq BILS/COS WV14 53 H1
Villiers St WLNHL WV13 39 G3
WSL WS1 57 E1
WSNGN B18 107 G4
Vimy Rd DARL/WED WS10 56 A4
MOS/BIL B13 161 H2
Vincent Cl BHTH/HG B12 144 B1
Vincent Dr EDG B15 142 B4
Vincent Pde BHTH/HG B12 144 B1
Vincent Rd MGN/WHC B75 63 E1
Vincent St BHTH/HG B12 144 B2
WSL WS1 57 F1
Vince St SMTHWK B66 124 C1
Vinculum Wy WLNHL WV13 39 H5
Vine Av BHTH/HG B12 144 C2
Vine Cl WOLVN WV10 12 D4
Vine Crs HHTH/SAND B71 71 H5
Vine Gdns CDYHTH B64 121 F2
Vine La HAG/WOL DY9 170 D2
HALE B63 138 D4
STRBR DY8 * 118 A3
The Vineries ACGN B27 147 E3
Vine St AST/WIT B6 109 H2
BRLYHL DY5 101 G4
STRBR DY8 118 A3
Vineyard Rd NFLD/LBR B31 175 F1
Vinnall Gv RIDG/WDGT B32 157 F2
Vintage Cl BKDE/SHDE B34 112 C4
Vinyard Cl HDSW B21 107 H2
Violet Cft TPTN/OCK DY4 69 H2
Violet La HAG/WOL DY9 170 C1
Virginia Dr
ETTPK/GDPK/PENN WV4 51 F4
Viscount Cl CVALE B35 94 C4
Viscount Dr CVALE B35 94 D4
Vista Gn HWK/WKHTH B38 177 F4
The Vista SEDG DY3 67 F2
Vittoria St CBHAMW B1 2 C2
SMTHWK B66 107 F5
Vivian Cl HRBN B17 142 A2
Vivian Rd HRBN B17 142 A2
Vixen Cl WALM/CURD B76 77 H4
Vowles Rd HHTH/SAND B71 71 H5
Vulcan Rd BILS/COS WV14 54 B3
SOLH B91 165 E4
Vyrnwy Gv HWK/WKHTH B38 176 C5
Vyse St AST/WIT B6 109 H1
WSNGN B18 2 C1

W

Wadbarn SHLY B90 194 A3
Waddams Pool DUDS DY2 84 D5
Waddell Cl BILS/COS WV14 67 H2
Waddens Brook La
WNSFLD WV11 25 E5
Waddington Av GTB/HAM B43 73 G2
Wades Cl TPTN/OCK DY4 85 E1
Wadesmill Lawns WOLVN WV10 13 E3
Wadham Cl
BLKHTH/ROWR B65 104 A3
Wadhurst Rd HRBN B17 124 D2
Wadleys Rd SOLH B91 164 B4
Waen Cl TPTN/OCK DY4 69 H3
Waggon La KIDD DY10 168 A2
Waggon St CDYHTH B64 121 F2
Waggon Wk HWK/WKHTH B38 176 A5
Wagoners Cl WASH/WDE B8 110 D3
Wagon La HIA/OLT B92 147 F3
Wagstaff Cl BILS/COS WV14 68 D3
Wagstaff Wy
CHWD/FDBR/MGN B37 132 A4
Wainwright Cl KGSWFD DY6 99 E2
Wainwright St AST/WIT B6 109 G2
Waite Rd WLNHL WV13 39 E5
Wakefield Cl SCFLD/BOLD B73 77 E1
Wakefield Ct MOS/BIL B13 * 144 D5
Wakefield Gv CSHL/WTROR B46 96 B3
Wakeford Rd NFLD/LBR B31 176 A4
Wake Green Pk MOS/BIL B13 144 D5
Wake Green Rd MOS/BIL B13 144 C5
MOS/BIL B13 162 A1
TPTN/OCK DY4 69 G2
Wakelam Gdns GTB/HAM B43 73 F2
Wakeley Hl
ETTPK/GDPK/PENN WV4 51 G5
Wakelin Rd SHLY B90 194 B1
Wakeman Ct WNSFLD WV11 14 D4
Wakeman Dr OLDBY B69 103 H1
Wakeman Gv STETCH B33 131 F5
Wakes Cl WLNHL WV13 39 H4
Wakes Rd DARL/WED WS10 71 E1
Walcot Cl MGN/WHC B75 47 F2
Walcot Dr GTB/HAM B43 73 G5
Walcot Gdns BILS/COS WV14 53 F3
Walcot Gn DOR/KN B93 199 E1
Waldale Cl SHHTH WV12 26 A1
Walden Gdns
ETTPK/GDPK/PENN WV4 51 E2
Walden Rd SPARK B11 146 A4
Waldeve Gv HIA/OLT B92 165 H2
Waldley Gv ERDE/BCHGN B24 93 G3
Waldron Av BRLYHL DY5 118 D2
Waldron Cl DARL/WED WS10 55 H2
Waldrons Moor
ALE/KHTH/YWD B14 160 C5
Walford Av BDMR/CCFT WV3 36 B5
Walford Dr HIA/OLT B92 148 B4
Walford Rd SPARK B11 144 D1
Walford St OLDBY B69 85 F4
Walhouse Cl WSL WS1 5 G3
Walhouse Rd WSL WS1 5 G3
Walker Av BRLYHL DY5 119 F5
HAG/WOL DY9 136 B4
OLDBY B69 104 A2

WOLVN WV10 .... 23 G2
Walker Dr *ERDE/BCHGN* B24 .... 110 C1
Walker Pl *BLOX/PEL* WS3 .... 28 A2
Walker Rd *BLOX/PEL* WS3 .... 27 H2
Walkers Fold *SHHTH* WV12 .... 26 B4
Walkers Heath Rd
HWK/WKHTH B38 .... 177 F4
Walker St *DUDS* DY2 .... 102 C5
TPTN/OCK DY4 .... 70 A4
Walkers Wy *CSHL/WTROR* B46 .. 115 G3
Walk La *WMBN* WV5 .... 65 E5
The Walk *SEDG* DY3 .... 67 F2
Wallace Cl *OLDBY* B69 .... 104 B3
Wallace Ri *CDYHTH* B64 .... 121 E5
Wallace Rd *BILS/COS* WV14 .... 54 C5
BILS/COS WV14 .... 69 F1
BRWNH WS8 .... 9 E4
OLDBY B69 .... 104 B3
SLYOAK B29 .... 143 F5
Wall Av *CSHL/WTROR* B46 .... 115 F4
Wallbank Rd *WASH/WDE* B8 .... 111 E3
Wallbrook St *BILS/COS* WV14 .... 68 D3
Wall Cl *SMTHWKW* B67 .... 105 H5
Wall Cft *ALDR* WS9 .... 30 B3
Wall Dr *FOAKS/STRLY* B74 .... 46 D1
Wall End Cl *WSLW* WS2 .... 27 E3
Wallface *HHTH/SAND* B71 .... 71 E4
Walling Cft *BILS/COS* WV14 .... 53 F5
Wallington Cl *BLOX/PEL* WS3 .... 16 D5
Wallington Heath
BLOX/PEL WS3 .... 16 D5
Wallows La *WSL* WS1 .... 56 C2
Wallows Pl *BRLYHL* DY5 .... 101 E4
Wallows Rd *BRLYHL* DY5 .... 101 E5
Wallows Wd *SEDG* DY3 .... 82 C2
Wall St *WOLV* WV1 .... 38 A3
Wall Well *HALE* B63 .... 138 B4
Wall Well La *HALE* B63 .... 138 B4
Walmead Cft *HRBN* B17 .... 124 B5
Walmer Gv *ERDW/GRVHL* B23 .... 91 H1
Walmer Meadow *ALDR* WS9 .... 30 B3
The Walmers *ALDR* WS9 .... 30 B3
Walmer Wy
CHWD/FDBR/MGN B37 .... 132 C1
Walmesley Wy *NFLD/LBR* B31 ... 175 E2
Walmley Ash Rd
WALM/CURD B76 .... 78 B4
Walmley Cl *HALE* B63 .... 120 B5
WALM/CURD B76 .... 78 B3
Walmley Rd *WALM/CURD* B76 .... 63 F5
Walnut Av *CDSL* WV8 .... 10 D4
Walnut Cl
CHWD/FDBR/MGN B37 .... 132 B3
HAG/WOL DY9 .... 152 D1
Walnut Dr *BDMR/CCFT* WV3 .... 35 H4
SMTHWK B66 .... 106 D4
Walnut La *DARL/WED* WS10 .... 71 E1
Walnut Rd *DSYBK/YTR* WS5 .... 57 G5
Walnut Wy *NFLD/LBR* B31 .... 175 F5
Walpole St
DUNHL/THL/PER WV6 .... 6 B1
Walpole Wk *WBROM* B70 .... 87 H5
Walsall Rd *ALDR* WS9 .... 30 A5
ALDR WS9 .... 43 H1
BLOX/PEL WS3 .... 18 A5
DARL/WED WS10 .... 55 G2
DSYBK/YTR WS5 .... 57 F4
FOAKS/STRLY B74 .... 46 C2
HHTH/SAND B71 .... 72 A4
PBAR/PBCH B42 .... 74 A3
RUSH/SHEL WS4 .... 19 E5
WLNHL WV13 .... 40 A3
Walsall St *BILS/COS* WV14 .... 53 H3
DARL/WED WS10 .... 55 F2
WBROM B70 .... 87 H3
WLNHL WV13 .... 39 H4
WOLV WV1 .... 7 J5
Walsall Wood Rd *ALDR* WS9 .... 30 B3
Walsgrave Dr *HIA/OLT* B92 .... 165 F3
Walsham Cft *BKDE/SHDE* B34 .... 113 E4
Walsh Dr *WALM/CURD* B76 .... 63 F4
Walsh Gv *ERDW/GRVHL* B23 .... 76 B3
Walsingham St *WSL* WS1 .... 5 H5
Walstead Rd *DSYBK/YTR* WS5 .... 57 H3
Walstead Rd West
DSYBK/YTR WS5 .... 57 E3
Waltdene Cl *GTB/HAM* B43 .... 73 G1
Walter Cobb Dr
SCFLD/BOLD B73 .... 77 E2
Walter Rd *BILS/COS* WV14 .... 54 A5
SMTHWKW B67 .... 106 A3
Walters Cl *NFLD/LBR* B31 .... 189 F2
Walters Rd *LGLYGN/QTN* B68 .... 123 E5
Walters Rw *DUDN* DY1 .... 84 A5
Walter St *BLOX/PEL* WS3 .... 28 C1
VAUX/NECH B7 .... 109 H3
WBROM B70 .... 87 H4
Waltham Gv *KGSTG* B44 .... 75 H1
Walthamstow Ct *BRLYHL* DY5 .... 119 F3
Walton Av *BLKHTH/ROWR* B65 .. 121 H4
Walton Cl *BLKHTH/ROWR* B65 .... 103 G5
HALE B63 .... 138 B5
Walton Crs
ETTPK/GDPK/PENN WV4 .... 52 C3
Walton Cft *SOLH* B91 .... 181 H4
Walton Dr *HAG/WOL* DY9 .... 136 A2
Walton Gdns *CDSL* WV8 .... 10 B3
Walton Gv *BVILLE* B30 .... 177 F3
Walton Heath *BLOX/PEL* WS3 .... 16 B4
Walton Pool La *HAG/WOL* DY9 .. 170 D3
Walton Ri *HAG/WOL* DY9 .... 171 E2
Walton Rd *ALDR* WS9 .... 30 A1
DARL/WED WS10 .... 71 G1
ETTPK/GDPK/PENN WV4 .... 52 D3
LGLYGN/QTN B68 .... 123 G3
STRBR DY8 .... 135 G1
Walton St *TPTN/OCK* DY4 .... 85 F1
Wanderers Av *BKHL/PFLD* WV2 .... 52 A2
Wanderer Wk *CBROM* B36 .... 94 A5
Wandle Gv *SPARK* B11 .... 146 A4
Wandsworth Rd *KGSTG* B44 .... 60 A5
Wannerton Rd *KIDD* DY10 .... 168 B4
Wansbeck Gv
HWK/WKHTH B38 .... 176 C5
Wansbeck Wk *SEDG* DY3 .... 67 H5
Wanstead Gv *KGSTG* B44 .... 75 G2
Wantage Rd
CSHL/WTROR B46 .... 97 E5
Ward Cl *WASH/WDE* B8 .... 111 E4
Warden Av *SCFLD/BOLD* B73 .... 76 D3
Ward End Cl *WASH/WDE* B8 .... 110 D3
Ward End Hall Gv
WASH/WDE B8 .... 111 E3
Ward End Park Rd
WASH/WDE B8 .... 110 D4
Wardend Rd *WASH/WDE* B8 .... 111 E3
Warden Rd *SCFLD/BOLD* B73 .... 76 D3
Ward Gv
ETTPK/GDPK/PENN WV4 .... 52 D5
Wardle Cl *MGN/WHC* B75 .... 47 E1
Wardlow Cl
ETTPK/GDPK/PENN WV4 .... 51 H2
Wardlow Rd *VAUX/NECH* B7 .... 109 G4
Wardour Dr
CHWD/FDBR/MGN B37 .... 132 C2
Wardour Gv *KGSTG* B44 .... 76 A3
Ward Rd *CDSL* WV8 .... 10 B4
ETTPK/GDPK/PENN WV4 .... 52 B3
Ward St *BILS/COS* WV14 .... 68 B3
BKHL/PFLD WV2 .... 53 F2
ERDW/GRVHL B23 .... 92 C2
LOZ/NWT B19 .... 3 G1
WLNHL WV13 .... 39 H2
WOLV WV1 .... 7 J4
WSL WS1 .... 5 G2
Wareham Cl *BLOX/PEL* WS3 .... 28 B5
Wareham Rd *RBRY* B45 .... 174 B3
Wareing Dr *ERDW/GRVHL* B23 .... 76 B3
Warewell Cl *WSL* WS1 .... 5 F3
Warewell St *WSL* WS1 .... 5 F4
Waring Cl *TPTN/OCK* DY4 .... 69 E3
Waring Rd *TPTN/OCK* DY4 .... 69 G3
The Warings *WMBN* WV5 .... 80 D2
War La *HRBN* B17 .... 141 H2
Warley Cft *LGLYGN/QTN* B68 .... 123 H4
Warley Hall Rd
LGLYGN/QTN B68 .... 123 H3
Warley Rd *LGLYGN/QTN* B68 .... 105 G4
Warmington Dr
SCFLD/BOLD B73 .... 62 B4
Warmington Rd *HLYWD* B47 .... 192 C2
LGN/SDN/BHAMAIR B26 .... 148 A2
Warmley Cl
DUNHL/THL/PER WV6 .... 22 D5
SOLH B91 .... 165 F5
Warner Dr *BRLYHL* DY5 .... 119 F3
Warner Pl *BLOX/PEL* WS3 .... 28 B4
Warner Rd *BLOX/PEL* WS3 .... 28 C4
CDSL WV8 .... 10 B4
DARL/WED WS10 .... 71 G1
Warner St *BHTH/HG* B12 .... 127 G4
Warners Wk *SMTHWK* B10 .... 128 A4
Warple Rd *RIDG/WDGT* B32 .... 140 C2
Warren Av *WOLVN* WV10 .... 23 H5
Warren Cl *TPTN/OCK* DY4 .... 69 F4
Warren Dr *BLKHTH/ROWR* B65 .. 103 F5
DOR/KN B93 .... 197 E5
SEDG DY3 .... 67 E1
Warren Farm Rd *KGSTG* B44 .... 75 F3
Warren Gdns *KGSWFD* DY6 .... 99 G3
Warren Gv *WASH/WDE* B8 * 110 C3
Warren Hill Rd *KGSTG* B44 .... 75 G4
Warren House Wk
WALM/CURD B76 .... 78 B2
Warren La *RBRY* B45 .... 188 B5
Warren Pl *BRWNH* WS8 .... 9 G5
Warren Rd *BVILLE* B30 .... 160 A3
KGSTG B44 .... 75 G5
WASH/WDE B8 .... 110 C3
Warrens Cft *DSYBK/YTR* WS5 .... 58 B3
Warrens End
HWK/WKHTH B38 .... 176 D5
Warrens Hall Rd *DUDS* DY2 .... 103 E2
Warrington Cl
WALM/CURD B76 .... 78 C2
Warrington Dr
ERDW/GRVHL B23 .... 76 B4
Warsash Cl *WOLV* WV1 .... 38 B5
Warstock La
ALE/KHTH/YWD B14 .... 178 C1
Warstock Rd
ALE/KHTH/YWD B14 .... 178 C1
Warston Av *RIDG/WDGT* B32 .... 140 D4
Warstone Dr *HHTH/SAND* B71 .... 88 A2
Warstone La *WSNGN* B18 .... 2 C2
Warstone Ms *WSNGN* B18 * 2 C2
Warstone Pde East *WSNGN* B18 ... 2 B2
Warstones Crs
ETTPK/GDPK/PENN WV4 .... 50 D3
Warstones Dr
ETTPK/GDPK/PENN WV4 .... 50 C3
Warstones Gdns
ETTPK/GDPK/PENN WV4 .... 50 C2
Warstones Rd
ETTPK/GDPK/PENN WV4 .... 50 D4
Warstone Ter *HDSW* B21 .... 107 G1
Wartell Bank *KGSWFD* DY6 .... 99 H2
Warwards La *SLYOAK* B29 .... 160 A1
Warwell La
LGN/SDN/BHAMAIR B26 .... 146 D1
Warwick Av *DARL/WED* WS10 .... 56 C5
DUNHL/THL/PER WV6 .... 34 D2
WLNHL WV13 .... 40 B3
Warwick Cl *LGLYGN/QTN* B68 .... 123 F2
WBROM B70 .... 70 C4
Warwick Crest *EDG* B15 * 126 B5
Warwick Dr *CDSL* WV8 .... 10 A4
Warwick Gdns *OLDBY* B69 .... 86 A4
Warwick Gra *SOLH* B91 .... 164 B3
Warwick Gv *HIA/OLT* B92 .... 163 H1
Warwick Pas *CBHAM* B2 .... 3 G5
Warwick Rd *DOR/KN* B93 .... 183 F5
DOR/KN B93 .... 197 F1
DUDS DY2 .... 121 E1
LGLYGN/QTN B68 .... 123 H5
SCFLD/BOLD B73 .... 76 A1
SOLH B91 .... 164 B3
SPARK B11 .... 145 G3
STRBR DY8 .... 117 H3
Warwick St *BHTH/HG* B12 .... 127 G3
BILS/COS WV14 .... 54 A3
RUSH/SHEL WS4 .... 5 F1
WOLV WV1 .... 7 J5
Warwick Wy *ALDR* WS9 .... 30 A1
Wasdale Dr *KGSWFD* DY6 .... 100 A3
Wasdale Rd *BRWNH* WS8 * 18 D1
NFLD/LBR B31 .... 175 F1
Waseley Rd *RBRY* B45 .... 173 G5
Washbrook Rd
WASH/WDE B8 .... 111 E3
Washford Gv *YDLY* B25 .... 129 F4
Washington Dr
BFLD/HDSWWD B20 .... 90 B3
Washington St *CBHAMW* B1 .... 2 D7
DUDS DY2 .... 120 D1
Washington Whf *CBHAMW* B1 .... 2 D7
Wash La *YDLY* B25 .... 129 G5
Washwood Heath Rd
WASH/WDE B8 .... 110 C3
Wasperton Cl *CBROM* B36 .... 112 D1
Wassell Ct *HALE* B63 .... 138 A5
Wassell Grove La
HAG/WOL DY9 .... 137 E5
Wassell Grove Rd
HAG/WOL DY9 .... 153 H1
Wassell Rd *BILS/COS* WV14 .... 53 H1
HAG/WOL DY9 .... 136 C5
HALE B63 .... 138 A5
Wast Hill Gv *HWK/WKHTH* B38 .... 190 D1
Wasthill La *HWK/WKHTH* B38 .... 190 B3
Wastwater Ct
DUNHL/THL/PER WV6 .... 34 D1
Watchbury Cl *CBROM* B36 .... 95 E5
Watchman Av *BRLYHL* DY5 .... 119 H5
Waterbridge La *WMBN* WV5 .... 64 C4
Water Dl *BDMR/CCFT* WV3 .... 36 A3
Waterdale *SHLY* B90 .... 194 D3
WMBN WV5 .... 80 C1
Waterfall Cl *SMTHWK* B66 .... 106 A2
Waterfall La *CDYHTH* B64 .... 121 G3
Waterfall Rd *BRLYHL* DY5 .... 119 E5
Waterfield Cl *TPTN/OCK* DY4 .... 84 C1
Waterfield Wy
LGN/SDN/BHAMAIR B26 .... 131 E5
Waterford Pl *STETCH* B33 .... 131 E1
Waterford Rd *KGSWFD* DY6 .... 99 H2
Waterfront East *BRLYHL* DY5 .... 101 G5
The Waterfront *BRLYHL* DY5 * ... 101 G5
Waterfront Wy *BRLYHL* DY5 .... 119 G1
WSLW WS2 .... 4 B3
Waterfront West *BRLYHL* DY5 .... 119 G1
Waterglade La *WLNHL* WV13 .... 39 G4
Waterhaynes Cl *RBRY* B45 .... 188 A2
Waterhead Cl *WOLVN* WV10 .... 13 G5
Waterhead Dr *WOLVN* WV10 .... 13 H5
Water La *HHTH/SAND* B71 .... 72 B4
Water Lily Gv *BRWNH* WS8 .... 8 D5
Waterlinks Bvd *AST/WIT* B6 .... 109 G2
Waterloo Av
CHWD/FDBR/MGN B37 .... 114 B5
Waterloo Rd
ALE/KHTH/YWD B14 .... 161 E2
SMTHWK B66 .... 124 D1
WOLV WV1 .... 6 E3
YDLY B25 .... 146 B1
Waterloo St *CBHAM* B2 .... 3 F5
DUDN DY1 .... 102 A1
TPTN/OCK DY4 .... 85 F1
Waterloo St East
TPTN/OCK DY4 .... 85 F1
Watermead Gra *BRWNH* WS8 .... 9 E5
Watermeadow Dr
RUSH/SHEL WS4 .... 29 F1
Watermere *RUSH/SHEL* WS4 .... 29 F2
Water Mill Cl *SLYOAK* B29 .... 142 B4
Watermill Cl *WOLVN* WV10 .... 12 D4
Water Mill Crs *WALM/CURD* B76 .. 78 B2
Water Orton La
WALM/CURD B76 .... 95 F1
Water Orton Rd *CBROM* B36 .... 113 F1
Water Rd *SEDG* DY3 .... 83 E4
Waters Dr *FOAKS/STRLY* B74 .... 46 B2
The Waters Edge *CBHAMW* B1 .... 2 B6
Waterside *GTB/HAM* B43 .... 73 G4
Waterside Av *DARL/WED* WS10 .... 71 E2
Waterside Cl *BKHL/PFLD* WV2 .... 52 B1
BORD B9 .... 127 H2
ERDE/BCHGN B24 .... 94 C2
Waterside Ct *OLDBY* B69 .... 104 D5
Waterside Dr *WSNGN* B18 .... 107 H4
Waterside Orch *ALVE* B48 * 189 H5
Waterside Pk *TPTN/OCK* DY4 * 70 B4
Waterside Vw *BRLYHL* DY5 .... 118 D3
WSNGN B18 .... 108 A4
Waterside Wy *BRWNH* WS8 .... 8 C2
Water Side Wy *COVEN* WV9 .... 12 A5
Waterson Cft
CHWD/FDBR/MGN B37 .... 132 D1
Water St *CBHAMNW* B3 .... 2 E3
KGSWFD DY6 .... 99 H2
WBROM B70 .... 87 H4
WOLVN WV10 .... 7 H1
Waters Vw *BLOX/PEL* WS3 .... 18 B2
Waterward Cl *HRBN* B17 .... 142 A2
Waterway Ct
ALE/KHTH/YWD B14 .... 179 E2
Waterways Dr *OLDBY* B69 .... 86 C5
Waterways Gdns *STRBR* DY8 .... 118 A3
Waterworks Dr *NFLD/LBR* B31 .. 157 H5
Waterworks Rd
LDYWD/EDGR B16 .... 125 H3
Waterworks St *AST/WIT* B6 .... 109 H1
Watery La *CDSL* WV8 .... 10 C2
SHLY B90 .... 194 C4
SMTHWKW B67 .... 106 C4
STRBR DY8 .... 118 A2
TPTN/OCK DY4 .... 85 F1
WLNHL WV13 .... 39 E2
WSL WS1 .... 4 D7
Watery La Middleway
BORD B9 .... 127 H3
Watford Gap Rd *LICHS* WS14 .... 33 E3
Watford Rd *BVILLE* B30 .... 159 H5
Wathan Av *BILS/COS* WV14 .... 67 H1
The Wathecroft *HRBN* B17 .... 141 H1
Watkins Gdns *NFLD/LBR* B31 .... 175 H2
Watkins Rd *SHHTH* WV12 .... 26 A5
Watland Gn *BKDE/SHDE* B34 .... 112 C4
Watling St *CNCK/NC* WS11 .... 8 A2
Watney Gv *KGSTG* B44 .... 76 A3
Watson Cl *CSCFLD/WYGN* B72 .... 77 F1
Watson Rd *BILS/COS* WV14 .... 67 H1
DARL/WED WS10 .... 54 C3
WASH/WDE B8 .... 110 B2
WOLVN WV10 .... 12 B5
Watson Rd East
VAUX/NECH B7 .... 110 B2
Watsons Cl *DUDS* DY2 .... 103 E1
Watson's Green Flds
DUDS DY2 .... 103 F1
Watson's Green Rd *DUDS* DY2 .... 103 E1
Wattisham Sq *CVALE* B35 .... 94 C2
Wattis Rd *SMTHWKW* B67 .... 124 C2
Wattle Rd *WBROM* B70 .... 87 E3
Watton Cl *BILS/COS* WV14 .... 68 A2
Watton Gn *CVALE* B35 .... 94 C4
Watton La *CSHL/WTROR* B46 .... 96 C4
Watton St *WBROM* B70 .... 87 G4
Watt Rd *ERDW/GRVHL* B23 .... 92 C2
TPTN/OCK DY4 .... 69 H3
Watts Cl *TPTN/OCK* DY4 .... 84 C1
Watt's Rd *SMHTH* B10 .... 128 B4
Watt St *HDSW* B21 .... 107 F2
SMTHWK B66 .... 106 D3
Wattville Av *HDSW* B21 * 107 E1
Wattville Rd *HDSW* B21 .... 107 E1
Watwood Rd *HLGN/YWD* B28 .... 179 H2
Waugh Cl
CHWD/FDBR/MGN B37 .... 132 B2
Waugh Dr *HALE* B63 .... 154 D2
Wavell Rd *BRLYHL* DY5 .... 119 H5
WASH/WDE B8 .... 110 C4
WSLW WS2 .... 40 C3
Waveney Av
DUNHL/THL/PER WV6 .... 34 C1
Waveney Cft *CBROM* B36 .... 113 H1
Waverhill Rd *HDSW* B21 .... 107 H2
Waverley Av *GTB/HAM* B43 .... 59 F4
Waverley Crs *BKHL/PFLD* WV2 .... 51 H2
ETTPK/GDPK/PENN WV4 .... 52 D5
RMSLY B62 .... 172 B1
Waverley Gv *SOLH* B91 .... 181 E2
Waverley Rd *BLOX/PEL* WS3 .... 16 B5
DARL/WED WS10 .... 55 F2
SMHTH B10 .... 145 G1
Waverley St *DUDN* DY1 .... 102 A1
Wavers Marston *CHWD/FDBR/MGN*
B37 .... 132 A4
Waxland Rd *HALE* B63 .... 138 D5
Wayfield Cl *SHLY* B90 .... 180 C2
Wayfield Rd *SHLY* B90 .... 180 C2
Wayford Dr *CSCFLD/WYGN* B72 .... 77 H4
Wayford Gld *WLNHL* WV13 .... 39 F5
Waynecroft Rd *GTB/HAM* B43 .... 73 G1
Wayside
CHWD/FDBR/MGN B37 .... 132 A4
Wayside Acres *CDSL* WV8 .... 10 B5
Wayside Dr *FOAKS/STRLY* B74 .... 46 A2
Wayside Gdns *SHHTH* WV12 .... 26 C5
Wayside Wk *WSLW* WS2 .... 41 E2
Waystone La *HAG/WOL* DY9 .... 184 B5
Wealden Hatch *WOLVN* WV10 .... 13 E3
Wealdstone Dr *SEDG* DY3 .... 83 F4
Weaman St *CBHAMNE* B4 .... 3 G3
Weatheroak Rd *SPARK* B11 .... 145 E2
Weatheroaks *ALDR* WS9 .... 19 H3
Weather Oaks *HRBN* B17 .... 141 H2
Weatheroaks *RMSLY* B62 .... 123 E5
Weaver Av
LGN/SDN/BHAMAIR B26 .... 147 H1
WALM/CURD B76 .... 78 C2
Weaver Cl *BRLYHL* DY5 .... 100 D3
Weaver Gv *WLNHL* WV13 .... 40 B3
Weavers Ri *DUDS* DY2 .... 120 D1
Webb Av *DUNHL/THL/PER* WV6 ... 20 C5
Webbcroft Rd *STETCH* B33 .... 112 A5
Webb La *HLGN/YWD* B28 .... 162 C4
Webb Rd *TPTN/OCK* DY4 .... 70 A4
Webb St *BILS/COS* WV14 .... 68 C1
WLNHL WV13 .... 39 F3
Webley Ri *WOLVN* WV10 .... 13 F3
Webster Cl *CSCFLD/WYGN* B72 .... 77 F4
SPARK B11 .... 144 D1
Webster Rd *WLNHL* WV13 .... 39 G2
WSLW WS2 .... 27 H5
Webster Wy *WALM/CURD* B76 .... 78 D4
Weddell Wynd *BILS/COS* WV14 .... 69 E2
Wedgbury Cl *DARL/WED* WS10 .... 71 E2
Wedgbury Wy *BRLYHL* DY5 .... 118 D3
Wedge St *WSL* WS1 .... 5 G3
Wedgewood Av *WBROM* B70 .... 70 D4
Wedgewood Dr
BFLD/HDSWWD B20 .... 90 B4
Wedgewood Pl *WBROM* B70 .... 70 D4
Wedgewood Rd
RIDG/WDGT B32 .... 140 C2
Wedgwood Cl *WMBN* WV5 .... 64 D4
WOLV WV1 .... 38 A4
Wedmore Rd *SCFLD/BOLD* B73 .... 76 D3
Wednesbury Oak Rd
TPTN/OCK DY4 .... 69 G2
Wednesbury One
DARL/WED WS10 * 55 F5
Wednesbury Rd *WSL* WS1 .... 4 C6
WSLW WS2 .... 56 C1
Wednesfield Rd *WLNHL* WV13 .... 39 G2
WOLVN WV10 .... 7 K2
Wednesfield Wy *WNSFLD* WV11 .. 25 E5
WOLVN WV10 .... 38 A1
Weeford Dell *MGN/WHC* B75 .... 48 A2
Weeford Dr
BFLD/HDSWWD B20 .... 89 H2
Weeford Rd *MGN/WHC* B75 .... 48 A4
Weirbrook Cl *SLYOAK* B29 .... 158 D3
Welbeck Av *WOLVN* WV10 .... 23 F3
Welbeck Cl *RMSLY* B62 .... 139 G2
Welbeck Dr *RUSH/SHEL* WS4 .... 29 F3
Welbeck Gv *ERDW/GRVHL* B23 .... 91 H1
Welbury Gdns
DUNHL/THL/PER WV6 .... 22 B5
Welby Rd *HLGN/YWD* B28 .... 162 D1
Welch Cl *TPTN/OCK* DY4 .... 69 H4
Welches Cl *NFLD/LBR* B31 .... 158 D5
Welcombe Dr *WALM/CURD* B76 .. 78 A3
Welcombe Gv *SOLH* B91 .... 181 F2
Welford Av
LGN/SDN/BHAMAIR B26 .... 130 B4
Welford Gv *FOAKS/STRLY* B74 .... 46 D2
Welford Rd
BFLD/HDSWWD B20 .... 108 A1
SCFLD/BOLD B73 .... 76 C2
SHLY B90 .... 180 C1
Welham Cft *SHLY* B90 .... 195 G2
Welland Cl *CSHL/WTROR* B46 .... 96 B4
Welland Dr *STRBR* DY8 .... 118 C4
Welland Gv *ERDE/BCHGN* B24 .... 93 G3
WLNHL WV13 .... 40 A3
Welland Rd *HALE* B63 .... 138 C5
Welland Wy *WALM/CURD* B76 .... 78 C4
Well Cl *CBROM* B36 * 112 A1
Wellcroft Rd *BKDE/SHDE* B34 .... 112 C2
Wellcroft St *DARL/WED* WS10 .... 55 H5
Wellesbourne Cl
BDMR/CCFT WV3 .... 35 F5
Wellesbourne Dr
BILS/COS WV14 .... 68 B4
Wellesbourne Rd
BFLD/HDSWWD B20 .... 90 B5
Wellesley Dr *TPTN/OCK* DY4 .... 85 F1
Wellesley Gdns *MOS/BIL* B13 .... 162 B1
Wellesley Rd *LGLYGN/QTN* B68 .. 105 F3
Wellfield Gdns *DUDS* DY2 .... 103 E3
Wellfield Rd *ALDR* WS9 .... 30 B2
HLGN/YWD B28 .... 163 F4
Wellhead La *PBAR/PBCH* B42 .... 91 E4
Wellington Av
BDMR/CCFT WV3 .... 51 F1
Wellington Cl *KGSWFD* DY6 .... 100 A5
Wellington Gv *SOLH* B91 .... 164 B4
Wellington Pl *WLNHL* WV13 .... 39 F2
Wellington Rd
BFLD/HDSWWD B20 .... 90 B4
BILS/COS WV14 .... 53 G2
DSYBK/YTR WS5 .... 58 A2
DUDN DY1 .... 84 B5
EDG B15 .... 143 G1
SMTHWKW B67 .... 124 C1
TPTN/OCK DY4 .... 85 G1
Wellington St *CDYHTH* B64 .... 121 F2
HHTH/SAND B71 .... 87 G2
OLDBY B69 .... 105 F3
SMTHWK B66 .... 107 F4
WSLW WS2 .... 56 B1
Wellington St South
WBROM B70 .... 87 G2
Wellington Ter
LOZ/NWT B19 * 108 B2
WLNHL WV13 * 39 G2
Wellington Wy *CVALE* B35 .... 94 D4
Well La *BLOX/PEL* WS3 .... 28 A3
DIG/EDG B5 .... 3 H6
WNSFLD WV11 .... 38 C1
Wellman Cft *SLYOAK* B29 .... 159 F1
Wellman's Rd *WLNHL* WV13 .... 40 A4
Well Meadow *RBRY* B45 .... 188 A2
Well Pl *BLOX/PEL* WS3 .... 28 A2
Wells Av *DARL/WED* WS10 .... 54 D2
Wells Cl *DUNHL/THL/PER* WV6 .... 34 B1
HHTH/SAND B71 .... 71 H3
TPTN/OCK DY4 .... 69 G2
Wellsford Av *HIA/OLT* B92 .... 147 G3
Wells Green Rd *HIA/OLT* B92 .... 147 G3
Wells Rd *BILS/COS* WV14 .... 54 A5
BLKHTH/ROWR B65 .... 122 C1
BRLYHL DY5 .... 118 D1
ETTPK/GDPK/PENN WV4 .... 51 F3
HIA/OLT B92 .... 148 A3
Well St *DARL/WED* WS10 .... 55 G2
LOZ/NWT B19 .... 108 C4
Welney Gdns *COVEN* WV9 .... 12 A4
Welsby Av *GTB/HAM* B43 .... 73 G4
Welsh House Farm Rd
RIDG/WDGT B32 .... 141 F3
Welshmans Hl *KGSTG* B44 .... 75 H1
SCFLD/BOLD B73 .... 61 E5
Welton Cl *WALM/CURD* B76 .... 78 C1
Welwyndale Rd
CSCFLD/WYGN B72 .... 77 G5
Wembley Gv *YDLY* B25 .... 129 G4
Wem Gdns *WNSFLD* WV11 .... 24 D4
Wendell Crest *WOLVN* WV10 .... 13 F4
Wendover Rd
BLKHTH/ROWR B65 .... 103 G3
ERDW/GRVHL B23 .... 76 A4
ETTPK/GDPK/PENN WV4 .... 67 G1
Wendron Gv
ALE/KHTH/YWD B14 .... 177 H1
Wenlock Av *BDMR/CCFT* WV3 .... 36 A5
Wenlock Cl *HALE* B63 .... 137 H5
SEDG DY3 .... 67 E4
Wenlock Gdns *BLOX/PEL* WS3 .... 28 A5
Wenlock Rd
BFLD/HDSWWD B20 .... 91 E5
STRBR DY8 .... 135 H1
Wenman St *BHTH/HG* B12 .... 144 B1
Wensley Cft *HLGN/YWD* B28 .... 163 F4
Wensleydale Rd
PBAR/PBCH B42 .... 74 B5
Wensley Rd
LGN/SDN/BHAMAIR B26 .... 147 F1
Wentbridge Rd *WOLV* WV1 .... 38 C4
Wentworth Av *CBROM* B36 .... 112 D1
Wentworth Dr *OLDBY* B69 .... 103 G2
Wentworth Ga *HRBN* B17 .... 141 H1
Wentworth Gv
DUNHL/THL/PER WV6 .... 20 B5
Wentworth Park Av
HRBN B17 .... 141 H1
Wentworth Ri *RMSLY* B62 .... 139 F4
Wentworth Rd *BLOX/PEL* WS3 .... 16 B3
FOAKS/STRLY B74 .... 47 E5
HIA/OLT B92 .... 147 F4
HRBN B17 .... 141 H1
STRBR DY8 .... 117 H5
WOLVN WV10 .... 13 F5
Wentworth Wy
RIDG/WDGT B32 .... 141 F4
Wenyon Cl *TPTN/OCK* DY4 .... 85 H2
Weoley Av *SLYOAK* B29 .... 142 A5
Weoley Castle Rd *SLYOAK* B29 .... 158 C1
Weoley Hl *SLYOAK* B29 .... 159 E2
Weoley Park Rd *SLYOAK* B29 .... 158 D1
Wergs Dr *DUNHL/THL/PER* WV6 .. 21 E3
Wergs Gdns *CDSL* WV8 * 20 D1
Wergs Hall Rd *CDSL* WV8 .... 20 D1
Wergs Rd
DUNHL/THL/PER WV6 .... 21 E4
Werneth Gv *BLOX/PEL* WS3 .... 16 C3
Wesley Av *CDSL* WV8 .... 10 D5
HALE B63 .... 120 B5
Wesley Cl *CDYHTH* B64 .... 121 F3
Wesley Gv *DARL/WED* WS10 .... 55 G5
Wesley Pl *TPTN/OCK* DY4 .... 70 A4
Wesley Rd *BRLYHL* DY5 .... 100 D4
CDSL WV8 .... 10 C5
ERDW/GRVHL B23 .... 92 D1
Wesleys Fold *DARL/WED* WS10 .... 55 F2
Wesley St *BILS/COS* WV14 .... 69 E1
BKHL/PFLD WV2 .... 53 E2
OLDBY B69 .... 105 E1

WBROM B70 87 F3
Wessex Cl BRWNH WS8 9 F5
Wessex Rd BKHL/PFLD WV2 52 D2
Wesson Gdns HALE B63 138 C4
Wesson Rd DARL/WED WS10 55 E1
West Acre WLNHL WV13 39 F4
Westacre Crs BDMR/CCFT WV3 35 F5
Westacre Dr BRLYHL DY5 119 H4
Westacre Gdns STETCH B33 130 B2
West Av BFLD/HDSWWD B20 89 H2
CBROM B36 113 F1
OLDBY B69 103 H1
WNSFLD WV11 24 C4
Westbook Wy WMBN WV5 80 D1
West Bvd RIDG/WDGT B32 141 E1
Westbourne Av
BKDE/SHDE B34 112 A3
Westbourne Crs EDG B15 126 A4
Westbourne Gdns EDG B15 126 A5
Westbourne Gv HDSW B21 * 107 H2
Westbourne Rd
DARL/WED WS10 55 H1
EDG B15 125 H4
ETTPK/GDPK/PENN WV4 51 G3
HDSW B21 89 F5
HIA/OLT B92 164 B3
RMSLY B62 139 G1
RUSH/SHEL WS4 42 B1
WBROM B70 87 F5
Westbourne St
RUSH/SHEL WS4 42 B2
West Bromwich Ringway
WBROM B70 87 H3
West Bromwich Rd
DSYBK/YTR WS5 57 E2
West Bromwich St OLDBY B69 86 D5
WSL WS1 4 E7
Westbrook Av ALDR WS9 29 H5
Westbury Av DARL/WED WS10 55 H2
Westbury Rd DARL/WED WS10 55 H2
HRBN B17 124 D1
Westbury St WOLV WV1 7 G3
Westcliff Pl NFLD/LBR B31 175 F1
Westcombe Gv
RIDG/WDGT B32 157 E1
West Coppice Rd BRWNH WS8 8 C4
Westcote Av NFLD/LBR B31 174 C3
Westcote Cl HIA/OLT B92 147 G5
Westcott Cl KGSWFD DY6 118 B1
Westcott Rd
LGN/SDN/BHAMAIR B26 130 C4
Westcroft Av WOLVN WV10 24 A1
Westcroft Gv
HWK/WKHTH B38 176 A2
Westcroft Rd
DUNHL/THL/PER WV6 20 D4
SEDG DY3 66 D1
Westcroft Wy
ALE/KHTH/YWD B14 178 D4
Westdean Cl RMSLY B62 139 E3
West Dr BFLD/HDSWWD B20 108 B1
DIG/EDG B5 143 G3
West End Av SMTHWK B66 105 H2
Westerdale Cl SEDG DY3 68 A4
Westerham Cl DOR/KN B93 196 D2
Westeria Cl CBROM B36 113 E1
Westering Pkwy WOLVN WV10 13 E3
Westerings
BFLD/HDSWWD B20 90 C4
Western Av BRLYHL DY5 118 D2
RMSLY B62 139 G3
SEDG DY3 66 D3
WSLW WS2 40 B2
Western Cl WSLW WS2 40 B2
Western Rd CDYHTH B64 120 D4
ERDE/BCHGN B24 93 E3
HAG/WOL DY9 169 H1
OLDBY B69 105 F4
SCFLD/BOLD B73 77 E2
STRBR DY8 135 F3
WSNGN B18 107 H5
Western Wy DARL/WED WS10 55 E5
Westfield Av
ALE/KHTH/YWD B14 178 D3
Westfield Cl DOR/KN B93 198 C1
Westfield Dr ALDR WS9 30 A4
WMBN WV5 64 D4
Westfield Gra
ALE/KHTH/YWD B14 161 E1
Westfield Gv BDMR/CCFT WV3 35 G5
Westfield Mnr MGN/WHC B75 47 E1
Westfield Rd ACGN B27 146 B4
ALE/KHTH/YWD B14 160 D2
BILS/COS WV14 53 F1
BRLYHL DY5 119 H4
DUDS DY2 102 D2
EDG B15 125 F5
RMSLY B62 122 C3
SEDG DY3 67 F2
SMTHWKW B67 106 B5
WLNHL WV13 39 E5
Westford Gv HLGN/YWD B28 179 G2
Westgate ALDR WS9 29 G3
EDG B15 142 D3
West Ga LDYWD/EDGR B16 125 G1
Westgate Cl SEDG DY3 67 G4
West Gn
ETTPK/GDPK/PENN WV4 50 C3
West Green Cl EDG B15 126 B4
Westgrove Av SHLY B90 195 F2
Westhaven Dr NFLD/LBR B31 158 A3
Westhaven Rd
CSCFLD/WYGN B72 62 C2
Westhay Rd HLGN/YWD B28 163 F3
West Heath Rd NFLD/LBR B31 175 H4
WSNGN B18 107 F5
Westhill BDMR/CCFT WV3 35 G3
Westhill Cl HIA/OLT B92 164 A2
SLYOAK B29 159 F1
Westhill Rd HWK/WKHTH B38 176 D2
West Holme BORD B9 128 A2
Westholme Cft BVILLE B30 159 G3
Westhouse Gv
ALE/KHTH/YWD B14 177 H1
Westland Av BDMR/CCFT WV3 36 B3
Westland Cl ERDW/GRVHL B23 92 D1
Westland Gdns
BDMR/CCFT WV3 36 B3
STRBR DY8 118 B5
Westland Rd BDMR/CCFT WV3 36 B3
Westlands Rd MOS/BIL B13 161 G1
WALM/CURD B76 78 B5
Westleigh Rd WMBN WV5 80 D1
Westley Brook Cl
LGN/SDN/BHAMAIR B26 147 H2
Westley Cl HLGN/YWD B28 163 F4
Westley Rd ACGN B27 146 B4
Westley St BORD B9 127 G2
DUDN DY1 102 B1
Westmead Crs
ERDE/BCHGN B24 93 G2
West Mead Dr
ALE/KHTH/YWD B14 161 E4
Westmead Dr
LGLYGN/QTN B68 105 F5
West Ms KGSTG B44 74 D1
West Mill Cft
HWK/WKHTH B38 190 C1
Westminster Av
ETTPK/GDPK/PENN WV4 51 H3
Westminster Cl DUDN DY1 84 A4
Westminster Dr
ALE/KHTH/YWD B14 160 D4
Westminster Rd
BFLD/HDSWWD B20 90 C4
HHTH/SAND B71 71 H2
RUSH/SHEL WS4 28 D3
SLYOAK B29 160 A1
STRBR DY8 117 G2
Westmore Wy
DARL/WED WS10 56 D3
Westmorland Rd
HHTH/SAND B71 71 G5
Weston Av LOZ/NWT B19 * 108 C2
OLDBY B69 85 H5
Weston Cl DOR/KN B93 199 E1
WSL WS1 57 E2
Weston Crs ALDR WS9 44 B1
Weston Dr BILS/COS WV14 53 G4
TPTN/OCK DY4 70 A1
Weston La SPARK B11 145 G3
Weston Rd LOZ/NWT B19 108 B2
SMTHWKW B67 124 B3
Weston St WSL WS1 57 E2
Weston Ter LOZ/NWT B19 * 108 D1
Westover Rd
BFLD/HDSWWD B20 89 G2
West Park Av NFLD/LBR B31 175 E3
West Park Cl ALDR WS9 29 G5
West Park Rd SMTHWKW B67 105 H3
West Pathway HRBN B17 142 A1
Westport Crs WNSFLD WV11 25 F5
Westray Cl RBRY B45 173 G4
Westridge SEDG DY3 67 E3
Westridge Rd MOS/BIL B13 162 A4
West Ri MGN/WHC B75 62 C2
West Rd
ETTPK/GDPK/PENN WV4 52 D3
GTB/HAM B43 73 G4
HALE B63 137 F1
TPTN/OCK DY4 69 H3
West Rd South HALE B63 137 F1
Westside Dr RIDG/WDGT B32 157 H1
West St BLKHTH/ROWR B65 122 A3
BLOX/PEL WS3 27 G3
BRLYHL DY5 119 H4
DUDN DY1 84 B4
DUNHL/THL/PER WV6 23 E5
STRBR DY8 135 F2
VAUX/NECH B7 * 3 K2
Westthorpe Gv LOZ/NWT B19 108 C4
West Vw WASH/WDE B8 111 G5
West View Ct MGN/WHC B75 63 E2
West View Dr KGSWFD DY6 100 A4
West View Rd MGN/WHC B75 63 E2
Westville Rd WSLW WS2 41 E2
Westward Cl KGSTG B44 75 F3
West Wy RUSH/SHEL WS4 18 B5
Westwood Av SPARK B11 145 G3
STRBR DY8 134 D4
Westwood Dr RBRY B45 174 B4
Westwood Gv SOLH B91 181 F2
Westwood Rd AST/WIT B6 91 G4
SCFLD/BOLD B73 60 C4
Westwood St BRLYHL DY5 118 C3
Westwood Vw
ERDE/BCHGN B24 93 G3
Wetherby Cl CBROM B36 111 H1
WOLVN WV10 12 D3
Wetherby Rd ACGN B27 146 C5
BLOX/PEL WS3 16 C3
Wetherfield Rd SPARK B11 146 A4
Wexford Cl DUDN DY1 83 H4
Weybourne Rd KGSTG B44 75 E1
Weycroft Rd ERDW/GRVHL B23 75 H4
Weyhill Cl COVEN WV9 11 G5
Weymoor Rd HRBN B17 141 G4
Weymouth Dr
FOAKS/STRLY B74 46 D1
Wharf Ap ALDR WS9 29 H3
Wharfdale Rd SPARK B11 146 B2
Wharfedale Cl KGSWFD DY6 99 F2
Wharfedale St
DARL/WED WS10 70 D1
Wharf La SOLH B91 165 F4
WSNGN B18 108 A4
Wharf Rd BVILLE B30 177 E3
SPARK B11 146 B2
Wharfside OLDBY B69 104 D2
Wharfside St CBHAMW B1 2 D7
Wharf St AST/WIT B6 109 G2
WOLV WV1 7 J5
WSLW WS2 4 A5
WSNGN B18 108 A3
Whar Hall Rd HIA/OLT B92 165 G2
Wharton Av HIA/OLT B92 165 G3
Wharton St VAUX/NECH B7 110 B1
Whatcote Gn HIA/OLT B92 165 F2
Whateley Av BLOX/PEL WS3 28 B4
Whateley Crs CBROM B36 113 F1
Whateley Gn FOAKS/STRLY B74 47 E5
Whateley Hall Cl
DOR/KN B93 * 197 G1
Whateley Hall Rd
DOR/KN B93 197 F1
Whateley Pl BLOX/PEL WS3 * 28 B4
Whateley Rd BLOX/PEL WS3 28 B4
HDSW B21 107 G1
Wheatcroft Cl MGN/WHC B75 48 A2
RMSLY B62 122 D4
Wheatcroft Dr
CHWD/FDBR/MGN B37 132 D3
Wheatcroft Gv DUDS DY2 85 F5
Wheatcroft Rd STETCH B33 130 B2
Wheaten Cl
CHWD/FDBR/MGN B37 132 D1
Wheatfield Cl CBROM B36 114 A2
Wheatfield Vw NFLD/LBR B31 157 H5
Wheat Hl DSYBK/YTR WS5 43 G5
Wheathill Cl
ETTPK/GDPK/PENN WV4 51 E5
Wheatland Gv ALDR WS9 44 C1
Wheatlands Cft STETCH B33 131 G1
The Wheatlands
DUNHL/THL/PER WV6 34 B2
Wheatley Cl HIA/OLT B92 165 G2
LGLYGN/QTN B68 123 G4
MGN/WHC B75 47 G2
Wheatley Gra
CSHL/WTROR B46 115 F3
Wheatley Rd LGLYGN/QTN B68 123 G4
Wheatley St BKHL/PFLD WV2 52 C2
WBROM B70 87 E2
Wheatmill Cl KIDD DY10 168 B3
Wheatmoor Ri MGN/WHC B75 63 E2
Wheatmoor Rd MGN/WHC B75 63 F1
Wheaton Cl WOLVN WV10 23 E3
Wheaton V
BFLD/HDSWWD B20 89 G3
Wheatridge Cl KGSWFD DY6 99 E2
Wheats Av HRBN B17 141 H4
Wheatsheaf Cl MGN/WHC B75 48 A1
Wheatsheaf Rd CDSL WV8 22 A1
LDYWD/EDGR B16 125 F2
OLDBY B69 103 G1
Wheatstone Cl SEDG DY3 67 G5
Wheatstone Gv STETCH B33 112 B4
Wheel Av CDSL WV8 10 B4
The Wheel Ct CDSL WV8 10 B4
Wheeler Cl CDSL WV8 10 A3
Wheeler Rd WNSFLD WV11 24 C2
Wheeler's Fold WOLV WV1 7 G4
Wheelers La MOS/BIL B13 161 E4
Wheeler St LOZ/NWT B19 108 D3
STRBR DY8 135 F2
Wheeley Moor Rd
CHWD/FDBR/MGN B37 114 A4
Wheeley Rd HIA/OLT B92 165 F3
Wheeleys La EDG B15 126 C4
Wheeleys Rd EDG B15 126 B5
Wheelock Cl FOAKS/STRLY B74 60 B1
Wheelwright Cl
DARL/WED WS10 55 E2
Wheelwright Rd
ERDE/BCHGN B24 92 C4
Wheldrake Av
BKDE/SHDE B34 113 E4
Whernside Dr
DUNHL/THL/PER WV6 22 C5
Wherretts Well La SOLH B91 165 G5
Whetstone Cl EDG B15 * 142 D2
Whetstone Gn WOLVN WV10 * 23 F1
Whetstone Gv WOLVN WV10 23 F2
Whetstone La ALDR WS9 44 B1
Whetstone Rd WOLVN WV10 23 F2
Whettybridge Rd RBRY B45 187 G2
Whetty La RBRY B45 187 G1
Whichford Cl WALM/CURD B76 77 H5
Whichford Gv BORD B9 129 F2
While Rd CSCFLD/WYGN B72 62 B4
Whilmot Cl WOLVN WV10 13 H1
Whinberry Ri BRLYHL DY5 83 E5
Whisley Brook La
HLGN/YWD B28 145 H5
Whiston Av WNSFLD WV11 25 G3
Whiston Gv SLYOAK B29 158 D2
Whitacre Rd BORD B9 128 C1
DOR/KN B93 197 F1
Whitbourne Cl BHTH/HG B12 144 D2
Whitburn Av PBAR/PBCH B42 90 A1
Whitburn Cl COVEN WV9 12 A5
Whitby Cl BLOX/PEL WS3 16 B4
Whitby Rd BHTH/HG B12 144 C3
Whitchurch La SHLY B90 193 H1
Whitcot Gv NFLD/LBR B31 * 175 F5
Whitebeam Cl BRWNH WS8 19 E1
SEDG DY3 83 E2
Whitebeam Cft
HWK/WKHTH B38 176 C5
White Beam Rd
CHWD/FDBR/MGN B37 132 D3
White City Rd BRLYHL DY5 120 A3
White Cl HAG/WOL DY9 136 A5
Whitecrest GTB/HAM B43 73 H1
Whitecroft Rd
LGN/SDN/BHAMAIR B26 148 B2
White Falcon Ct SOLH B91 181 F3
White Farm Rd
FOAKS/STRLY B74 46 C1
White Field Av HRBN B17 141 G1
Whitefield Cl CDSL WV8 10 D5
Whitefields Crs SOLH B91 181 H3
Whitefields Ga SOLH B91 181 G4
Whitefields Rd SOLH B91 181 H3
Whitefriars Dr HALE B63 138 C3
Whitegates Rd BILS/COS WV14 68 D1
Whitehall Dr DUDN DY1 84 A4
HALE B63 138 D3
Whitehall Rd BORD B9 128 B3
CDYHTH B64 120 C3
ETTPK/GDPK/PENN WV4 51 H4
HALE B63 138 D3
HDSW B21 108 A2
KGSWFD DY6 99 G3
STRBR DY8 135 H5
TPTN/OCK DY4 86 B1
WSL WS1 57 E1
Whitehead Dr
WALM/CURD B76 79 F5
Whitehead Rd AST/WIT B6 109 E2
White Hl NFLD/LBR B31 158 D5
Whitehill La SLYOAK B29 158 C5
White Hollies BLOX/PEL WS3 17 G3
White Horse Rd BRWNH WS8 9 E2
Whitehouse Av
BDMR/CCFT WV3 35 G5
DARL/WED WS10 54 D1
White House Av
WNSFLD WV11 25 F3
White House Cl SOLH B91 181 F2
Whitehouse Common Rd
MGN/WHC B75 63 E1
Whitehouse Crs MGN/WHC B75 48 A5
WNSFLD WV11 25 F1
Whitehouse Dr SMTHWK B66 106 C2
White House Gn SOLH B91 181 F2
Whitehouse La CDSL WV8 10 C2
Whitehouse Pl RBRY B45 187 H2
White Houses La WOLVN WV10 13 G1
Whitehouse St AST/WIT B6 109 F3
BILS/COS WV14 68 C3
TPTN/OCK DY4 85 G4
Whitehouse Wy ALDR WS9 43 H1
White House Wy SOLH B91 181 G2
Whitemoor Dr SHLY B90 195 G1
White Oak Dr BDMR/CCFT WV3 35 G4
KGSWFD DY6 99 G3
Whitepoplars Cl BRLYHL DY5 101 E5
White Rd RIDG/WDGT B32 140 D1
SMTHWKW B67 106 B3
SPARK B11 128 A5
White Rw WMBN WV5 64 A2
White's Dr SEDG DY3 67 G3
Whiteslade Cl DOR/KN B93 197 E1
Whitesmith Cl SEDG DY3 67 F3
White's Rd HHTH/SAND B71 71 G5
Whitestone Rd HALE B63 138 C1
White St BHTH/HG B12 144 C2
WSL WS1 4 D6
Whites Wd WMBN WV5 81 E1
Whitethorn Crs
FOAKS/STRLY B74 44 D4
Whitethorn Rd STRBR DY8 118 C3
Whitewood Gld SHHTH WV12 40 C1
Whitford Dr SHLY B90 195 H1
Whitgreave Av WOLVN WV10 23 G2
Whitgreave Ct WBROM B70 86 C3
WOLVN WV10 * 13 H1
Whitgreave St WBROM B70 86 C3
Whitland Cl RBRY B45 188 B2
Whitland Dr
ALE/KHTH/YWD B14 178 B2
Whitley Cl
DUNHL/THL/PER WV6 35 F3
Whitley Court Rd
RIDG/WDGT B32 140 C1
Whitley Dr FOAKS/STRLY B74 45 G5
Whitley St DARL/WED WS10 55 G5
Whitlock Gv
ALE/KHTH/YWD B14 178 C2
Whitminster Av
ERDE/BCHGN B24 93 F3
Whitminster Cl SHHTH WV12 40 A1
Whitmore Hl WOLV WV1 6 E3
Whitmore Rd SMHTH B10 128 A4
STRBR DY8 134 D2
Whitmore St WOLV WV1 7 G3
WSL WS1 56 D1
WSNGN B18 108 B4
Whitney Av STRBR DY8 134 D1
Whittaker St BKHL/PFLD WV2 52 C1
Whittall St CBHAMNE B4 3 G3
Whittimere St WSL WS1 5 F3
Whittingham Gv
WNSFLD WV11 25 F4
Whittingham Rd HALE B63 138 C2
Whittington Cl
ALE/KHTH/YWD B14 161 E5
HHTH/SAND B71 72 B3
Whittington Gv STETCH B33 130 B2
Whittington Hall La
KINVER DY7 134 B4
Whittington Ov STETCH B33 130 C2
Whittington Rd STRBR DY8 134 D4
Whittle Cft CVALE B35 94 B3
Whittleford Gv CBROM B36 95 E5
Whitton St DARL/WED WS10 55 G2
Whitwell Cl SHLY B90 195 G2
Whitworth Cl DARL/WED WS10 55 G1
Whitworth Dr HHTH/SAND B71 72 A2
Whyley St WBROM B70 87 E2
Whyley Wk OLDBY B69 105 E4
Whynot St HALE B63 137 F2
Wibert Cl SLYOAK B29 160 A1
Wichnor Rd HIA/OLT B92 147 F2
Wicket La KINVER DY7 116 C3
Wickham Gdns WNSFLD WV11 24 A4
Wicklow Cl HALE B63 154 D1
Wideacre Dr KGSTG B44 75 E4
Wide Acres RBRY B45 173 H4
Widney Av ALDR WS9 30 B1
SLYOAK B29 142 A5
Widney Cl DOR/KN B93 196 D3
Widney La SOLH B91 181 F4
Widney Manor Rd
DOR/KN B93 196 B1
SOLH B91 182 A3
Widney Rd DOR/KN B93 196 D4
Wiggins Cft WALM/CURD B76 63 F5
Wiggins Hill Rd
WALM/CURD B76 79 H3
Wigginsmill Rd
DARL/WED WS10 70 B2
Wiggin St LDYWD/EDGR B16 125 H1
Wight Cft CBROM B36 114 B3
Wightwick Bank
DUNHL/THL/PER WV6 34 D3
Wightwick Cl BLOX/PEL WS3 27 F1
Wightwick Gv
DUNHL/THL/PER WV6 35 E3
Wightwick Hall Rd
DUNHL/THL/PER WV6 34 C4
Wigmore Gv KGSTG B44 75 H3
Wigmore La HHTH/SAND B71 72 C3
Wigorn La HAG/WOL DY9 152 D2
Wigorn Rd SMTHWKW B67 124 B3
Wilberforce Wy HIA/OLT B92 165 G3
Wilbraham Rd WSLW WS2 41 G4
Wilcote Gv ACGN B27 163 G2
Wildacres STRBR DY8 134 C1
Wilday Cl TPTN/OCK DY4 85 G1
Wilde Cl ALE/KHTH/YWD B14 177 H1
Wilden Cl NFLD/LBR B31 174 C2
Wilderness La
GTB/HAM B43 58 B5
Wildfell Rd ACGN B27 146 D5
Wildmoor La BRGRVW B61 186 C4
Wildmoor Rd SHLY B90 163 F5
Wildtree Av WOLVN WV10 13 G5
Wiley Av DARL/WED WS10 55 E2
Wiley Av South
DARL/WED WS10 55 E3
Wilford Gv SOLH B91 181 H3
WALM/CURD B76 78 D5
Wilford Rd HHTH/SAND B71 71 H5
Wilkes Av WSLW WS2 40 D3
Wilkes Cl BLOX/PEL WS3 17 G4
Wilkes Cft SEDG DY3 67 F4
Wilkes Rd CDSL WV8 10 B4
Wilkes St HHTH/SAND B71 72 A4
WLNHL WV13 39 G4
Wilkin Rd BRWNH WS8 8 C2
Wilkinson Av BILS/COS WV14 69 E1
Wilkinson Cl SCFLD/BOLD B73 77 F1
Wilkinson Cft WASH/WDE B8 111 G3
Wilkinson Rd DARL/WED WS10 54 C3
Wilkins Rd BILS/COS WV14 53 H1
Willard Rd YDLY B25 146 C1
Willaston Rd STETCH B33 131 F5
Willclare Rd
LGN/SDN/BHAMAIR B26 147 G1
Willcock Rd BKHL/PFLD WV2 52 C1
Willenhall La SHHTH WV12 26 D3
Willenhall Rd BILS/COS WV14 54 B2
DARL/WED WS10 40 B5
WOLV WV1 38 B4
Willenhall St DARL/WED WS10 55 E2
Willerby Fold WOLVN WV10 13 F3
Willersey Rd MOS/BIL B13 162 B2
Willes Rd WSNGN B18 107 G3
Willett Rd HHTH/SAND B71 72 A3
Willetts Dr HALE B63 137 F3
Willetts Rd NFLD/LBR B31 175 G4
Willetts Wy CDYHTH B64 121 F2
Willey Gv ERDE/BCHGN B24 93 F4
William Booth La CBHAMNE B4 3 F2
William Cook Rd
WASH/WDE B8 111 F4
William Edward St
BHTH/HG B12 127 F5
William Green Rd
DARL/WED WS10 56 C5
William Harper Rd
WLNHL WV13 39 H4
William Henry St
VAUX/NECH B7 109 G3
William Ker Rd TPTN/OCK DY4 86 A1
William Rd SMTHWKW B67 123 H1
Williams Cl SHHTH WV12 26 A5
Williamson St BDMR/CCFT WV3 6 D7
William St BRLYHL DY5 119 F1
EDG B15 126 C3
RUSH/SHEL WS4 42 B2
WBROM B70 86 C1
William St North LOZ/NWT B19 3 F1
William St West SMTHWK B66 106 D2
William Wiggin Av
BLOX/PEL WS3 16 D5
Willingsworth Rd
DARL/WED WS10 70 A2
Willingworth Cl BILS/COS WV14 53 E5
Willis Pearson Av
BILS/COS WV14 69 F1
Willmore Gv HWK/WKHTH B38 176 D5
Willmore Rd
BFLD/HDSWWD B20 90 D4
Willmott Cl MGN/WHC B75 47 H2
Willmott Rd MGN/WHC B75 47 H2
Willoughby Dr SOLH B91 181 H4
Willoughby Gv SLYOAK B29 158 C1
Willow Av DARL/WED WS10 55 H4
HRBN B17 124 C2
WNSFLD WV11 24 B2
Willow Bank BDMR/CCFT WV3 35 G4
Willow Bank Rd DOR/KN B93 196 D2
Willow Cl CDYHTH B64 121 E3
HAG/WOL DY9 152 B5
Willow Coppice
RIDG/WDGT B32 157 G1
Willow Ct SMTHWK B66 105 H1
Willowdale Gra
DUNHL/THL/PER WV6 22 A5
Willow Dr CDSL WV8 10 D4
HDSW B21 89 E5
OLDBY B69 104 A2
SHLY B90 194 D4
Willow End HAG/WOL DY9 136 B4
Willow Gdns
LDYWD/EDGR B16 107 H5
Willow Gv WLNHL WV13 39 H4
WNSFLD WV11 15 F4
Willow Hts CDYHTH B64 121 G4
Willowherb Cl DSYBK/YTR WS5 57 G5
Willowherb Wy SHLY B90 194 A3
Willow Ms SLYOAK B29 158 D1
Willow Park Dr STRBR DY8 135 G5
Willow Ri BRLYHL DY5 119 E3
Willow Rd BDMR/CCFT WV3 35 H5
BVILLE B30 159 H2
DUDN DY1 84 A2
GTB/HAM B43 73 H2
SOLH B91 181 E3
Willowsbrook Rd RMSLY B62 122 D4
Willows Crs BHTH/HG B12 143 H2
Willowside RUSH/SHEL WS4 29 E2
Willows Rd BHTH/HG B12 144 A2
RUSH/SHEL WS4 29 E2
WSL WS1 5 J4
The Willows ACGN B27 146 B5
DUDS DY2 103 E4
HLYWD B47 192 C2
WALM/CURD B76 78 B1
WMBN WV5 80 D1
Willow Wy
CHWD/FDBR/MGN B37 132 B2
Wills Av HHTH/SAND B71 71 F4
Willsbridge Covert
ALE/KHTH/YWD B14 177 G2
Willson Cft HLGN/YWD B28 179 F2
Wills St LOZ/NWT B19 108 C2
Wills Wy SMTHWK B66 107 E5
Wilmcote Cl BHTH/HG B12 144 A1
Wilmcote Dr MGN/WHC B75 47 F2
Wilmcote Rd SOLH B91 164 B4
Wilmington Rd
RIDG/WDGT B32 140 B1
Wilmore La HLYWD B47 192 A4
Wilmot Av CSHL/WTROR B46 115 F3
Wilmot Dr ERDW/GRVHL B23 77 E5
TPTN/OCK DY4 69 E5

Wilmot Gdns DUDN DY1....84 A4
Wilnecote Gv
  PBAR/PBCH B42....90 C2
Wilner's Vw BLOX/PEL WS3....17 H2
Wilsford Cl
  ALE/KHTH/YWD B14....177 H4
  RUSH/SHEL WS4....29 E2
Wilson Dr MGN/WHC B75....63 G3
  OLDBY B69....84 B4
Wilson Rd BILS/COS WS14....68 C4
  BRLYHL DY5....101 E5
  HRBN B17....124 D1
  TPTN/OCK B68....123 H4
  LOZ/NWT B19....108 D1
Wilsons Rd DOR/KN B93....197 G2
Wilson St TPTN/OCK DY4....85 E2
Wilton Cl SEDG DY3....67 G4
Wilton Rd BFLD/HDSWWD B20....90 B5
  ERDW/GRVHL B23....92 D1
  SPARK B11....144 D2
Wilton St LOZ/NWT B19....108 D1
Wiltshire Cl WSLW WS2....41 H1
Wiltshire Dr HALE B63....120 B5
Wiltshire Wy HHTH/SAND B71....71 G4
Wimbledon Dr STRBR DY8....135 H5
Wimborne Rd WOLVN WV10....24 A4
Wimborne Rd
  LDYWD/EDGR B16....125 F1
  WALM/CURD B76....78 B5
Wimperis Wy GTB/HAM B43....59 G4
Wimperley Gv KGSTG B44....75 H5
Wimshurst Meadow
  WOLVN WV10....13 F3
Wincanton Cft CBROM B36....111 G1
Winceby Rd
  DUNHL/THL/PER WV6....34 D2
Winchcombe Cl DUDN DY1....83 G3
  HIA/OLT B92....147 H5
Winchcombe Rd HIA/OLT B92....147 H5
Winchester Cl
  BLKHTH/ROWR B65....104 C5
  HAG/WOL DY9....152 C3
Winchester Dr
  CHWD/FDBR/MGN B37....132 A2
  STRBR DY8....135 G4
Winchester Gdns
  NFLD/LBR B31....175 G2
Winchester Gv HDSW B21 *....107 E1
Winchester Ms ALDR WS9....44 B1
Winchester Ri DUDN DY1....84 A4
Winchester Rd
  BFLD/HDSWWD B20....90 D5
  HHTH/SAND B71....71 F5
  WOLVN WV10....12 C5
Winchfield Dr HRBN B17....124 B5
Wincote Dr
  DUNHL/THL/PER WV6....35 G1
Wincrest Wy BKDE/SHDE B34....113 E4
Windermere Dr
  FOAKS/STRLY B74....45 F2
  KGSWFD DY6....99 H3
Windermere Rd
  DUNHL/THL/PER WV6....21 H2
  HRBN B17....89 G4
  MOS/BIL B13....161 H1
Windfall Ct ERDE/BCHGN B24....93 H2
Winding Mill North
  BRLYHL DY5 *....119 G5
Winding Mill South
  BRLYHL DY5 *....119 G5
Windlass Cft NFLD/LBR B31....175 F1
Windleaves Rd CBROM B36....113 G2
Windmill Av
  CSHL/WTROR B46....115 F2
  RBRY B45....173 G5
Windmill Bank WMBN WV5....65 E4
Windmill Cl NFLD/LBR B31....159 G5
Windmill Cottages
  PBAR/PBCH B42 *....90 A1
Windmill Crs BDMR/CCFT WV3....35 E4
  SMTHWK B66....107 E4
Windmill End DUDS DY2....103 E4
Windmill Gv KGSWFD DY6....99 E1
Windmill Hl HALE B63....137 H2
  NFLD/LBR B31....158 D5
Windmill La BDMR/CCFT WV3....35 E4
  DOR/KN B93....198 D2
  HOCK/TIA B94....199 E3
  SMTHWK B66....106 D5
Windmill Prec SMTHWK B66....106 D4
Windmill Rd SHLY B90....179 G3
Windmill St CBHAMW B1....126 D3
  DARL/WED WS10....55 H5
  DUDN DY1....84 A4
  SEDG DY3....83 F1
  WSL WS1....4 E6
Windmill Vw BILS/COS WS14....68 B4
Windridge Crs HIA/OLT B92....165 H2
The Windrow
  DUNHL/THL/PER WV6....34 B1
Windrush Cl ERDW/GRVHL PE WS3....28 C1
Windrush Gv SLYOAK B29....160 A2
Windrush Rd HLYWD B47....192 D1
Windsor Av
  ETTPK/GDPK/PENN WV4....51 E2
  LGLYGN/QTN B68....123 E1
Windsor Cl
  BLKHTH/ROWR B65....104 A5
  HALE B63....138 A4
  NFLD/LBR B31....189 C2
  RBRY B45....174 A3
  SEDG DY3....82 D5
Windsor Crs DUDS DY2....102 D3
Windsor Dr ERDE/BCHGN B24....93 C1
  HIA/OLT B92....147 H5
Windsor Gdns BDMR/CCFT WV3....30 A1
  CDSL WV8....10 B4
Windsor Ga SHHTH WV12....40 A1
Windsor Gv RUSH/SHEL WS4....18 C5
  STRBR DY8....118 A3
Windsor Pl ERDW/GRVHL B23....92 C5
  VAUX/NECH B7....127 C1
Windsor Rd
  BLKHTH/ROWR B65....104 A4
  BVILLE B30....160 B5
  CBROM B36....113 H2
  ETTPK/GDPK/PENN WV4....52 D3
  HALE B63....138 A3
  HHTH/SAND B71....71 F5
  LGLYGN/QTN B68....123 E1

SCFLD/BOLD B73....76 B2
STRBR DY8....134 D4
TPTN/OCK DY4....69 G3
WMBN WV5....64 D5
Windsor St BILS/COS WV14....53 G2
  VAUX/NECH B7....109 G5
  WSL WS1....57 E1
Windsor St South
  VAUX/NECH B7....109 G5
Windsor Ter
  LDYWD/EDGR B16 *....125 H3
Windsor Vw RIDG/WDGT B32....157 F3
Windsor Wk DARL/WED WS10....40 B5
Windsor Wy RUSH/SHEL WS4....29 F5
Winds Point HAG/WOL DY9....152 C4
Windward Wy CBROM B36....113 H2
Windyridge Rd
  WALM/CURD B76....78 B5
Winfield Rd ARLY KGSWFD DY6....100 A5
Wingate Cl HWK/WKHTH B38....176 D1
Wingate Rd WSLW WS2....40 D1
Wingfield Cl
  CHWD/FDBR/MGN B37....131 H1
Wingfield Rd
  CSHL/WTROR B46....115 F4
  PBAR/PBCH B42....74 C4
Wingfoot Av WOLVN WV10....23 F2
Winleigh Rd
  BFLD/HDSWWD B20....89 H4
Winnall Cl BILS/COS WV14....68 D1
Winnie Rd SLYOAK B29....159 G1
Winnington Rd
  WASH/WDE B8....111 E2
Winnipeg Rd
  HWK/WKHTH B38....177 E5
Winrush Cl SEDG DY3....83 F3
Winscar Cft SEDG DY3....83 G3
Winsford Cl HALE B63....138 C1
  WALM/CURD B76....63 E5
Winsham Gv HDSW B21....107 F1
Winslow Dr
  DUNHL/THL/PER WV6....36 A1
Winson Green Rd WSNGN B18....107 G4
Winson St WSNGN B18....107 F5
Winstanley Rd STETCH B33....129 H2
Winster Av DOR/KN B93....196 C4
Winster Gv KGSTG B44....74 D1
Winster Rd GTB/HAM B43....73 F3
  WOLV WV1....38 B4
Winston Dr
  BFLD/HDSWWD B20....90 B5
  RMSLY B62....172 C1
Winston Rd SEDG DY3....83 G3
Winterbourne Cft
  ALE/KHTH/YWD B14....177 G3
Winterbourne Rd SOLH B91....181 F1
Winterley Gdns SEDG DY3....67 G5
Winterley La RUSH/SHEL WS4....29 E5
Winterton Rd KGSTG B44....60 C5
Winthorpe Dr SOLH B91....182 A5
Wintney Ct HRBN B17....124 C5
Winton Gv WALM/CURD B76....62 D5
Winwood Heath Rd
  RMSLY B62....172 A3
Winwood Rd
  BLKHTH/ROWR B65....122 C1
Winwoods Gv
  RIDG/WDGT B32....157 G2
Wiremill Cl KGSTG B44....75 E5
Wirral Rd NFLD/LBR B31....158 B4
Wiseacre Cft SHLY B90....179 G3
Wiseman Gv KGSTG B44....76 B2
Wisemeadow SHLY B90....179 C3
Wisemore WSL WS2....4 D2
Wishaw Cl SHLY B90....179 G3
Wishaw Gv
  CHWD/FDBR/MGN B37....113 H4
Wishaw La WALM/CURD B76....79 G4
Wisley Wy RIDG/WDGT B32....141 F2
Wistaria Cl NFLD/LBR B31....158 C4
Wisteria Dr DSYBK/YTR WS5....57 F4
Wisteria Gv KGSTG B44....75 E1
Wistmans Cl DUDN DY1....83 F5
Wistwood Hayes
  WOLVN WV10....13 F3
Witham Cl WALM/CURD B76....78 C2
Witham Cft SOLH B91....182 A4
Withdean Cl SPARK B11....145 F2
Witherford Cl SLYOAK B29....159 E2
Witherford Cft SOLH B91....180 D3
Witherford Wy SLYOAK B29....159 F2
Withern Wy SEDG DY3....83 F3
Withers Rd CDSL WV8....10 C4
Withers Wy HHTH/SAND B71....87 H2
Withington Covert
  ALE/KHTH/YWD B14....177 H3
Withington Gv DOR/KN B93....196 C4
Withybrook Rd SHLY B90....180 B5
Withy Gv
  CHWD/FDBR/MGN B37....113 G4
Withy Hill Rd MGN/WHC B75....63 H3
Withymere La WMBN WV5....65 G3
Withymoor Rd DUDS DY2....105 E5
  STRBR DY8....118 C5
Withy Rd BILS/COS WV14....53 G5
Withywood Cl SHHTH WV12....25 H1
Witley Av HALE B63....138 A3
  SOLH B91....182 A5
Witley Crs OLDBY B69....104 C4
Witley Farm Cl SOLH B91....182 A3
Witley Rd NFLD/LBR B31....176 B3
Witney Dr
  CHWD/FDBR/MGN B37....131 H2
Witney Gv WOLVN WV10....11 H5
Witton Bank RMSLY B62....139 H1
Witton La AST/WIT B6....94 D1
  HHTH/SAND B71....71 E3
Witton Lodge Rd
  ERDW/GRVHL B23....75 H4
Witton Rd AST/WIT B6....109 E1
  ETTPK/GDPK/PENN WV4....51 G2
Witton St BORD B9....127 H2
  STRBR DY8....135 E3
Wixford Gv SHLY B90....168 C5
Wobaston Rd CDSL WV8....11 H4
Woburn Av SHHTH WV12....25 H4

Woburn Crs GTB/HAM B43....73 F2
Woburn Dr BRLYHL DY5....118 D4
  RMSLY B62....121 G5
Wodehouse Cl WMBN WV5....80 C1
Wodehouse La SEDG DY3....66 A5
Woden Av WNSFLD WV11....24 C4
Woden Cl WMBN WV5....64 D4
Woden Crs WNSFLD WV11....24 C4
Woden Rd BD WOLVN WV10....37 H1
Woden Rd East
  DARL/WED WS10....56 B3
Woden Rd North
  DARL/WED WS10....55 G3
Woden Rd South
  DARL/WED WS10....55 G5
Woden Rd West
  DARL/WED WS10....70 D2
Wold Wk MOS/BIL B13....161 H4
Wolfsbane Dr DSYBK/YTR WS5....57 C5
Wolfson Dr RBRY B45....190 B2
Wollaston Ct STRBR DY8....134 C1
Wollaston Crs WNSFLD WV11....24 D4
Wollaston Rd KINVER DY7....117 C5
  STRBR DY8....134 C2
Wollerton Gv MGN/WHC B75....63 F2
Wollescote Dr SOLH B91....181 H4
Wollescote Rd HAG/WOL DY9....136 B4
Wolmer Rd WNSFLD WV11....14 D5
Wolseley Av SLYOAK B29....160 B1
Wolseley Bank WOLVN WV10....23 H3
Wolseley Cl CBROM B36....96 A5
Wolseley Dr WASH/WDE B8....111 E2
Wolseley Rd BILS/COS WV14....53 H1
  WBROM B70....70 D5
Wolseley St BORD B9....127 H2
Wolston Cl SHLY B90....165 F5
Wolverhampton Rd
  BLOX/PEL WS3....17 G4
  CDSL WV8....27 F1
  COL DVE WV9....10 D4
  KGSWFD DY6....99 C1
  KINVER DY7....116 D5
  LGLYGN/QTN B68....123 E1
  OLDBY B69....105 E5
Wolverhampton Rd East
  ETTPK/GDPK/PENN WV4....52 C4
Wolverhampton Rd South
  RIDG/WDGT B32....124 A5
Wolverhampton Rd West
  WLNHL WV13....40 B3
Wolverhampton St
  BILS/COS WV14....53 C2
  DARL/WED WS10....54 D2
  DUDN DY1....84 B5
  WLNHL WV13....39 F4
  WSL WS2....4 C3
Wolverley Av
  ETTPK/GDPK/PENN WV4....50 D3
  STRBR DY8....134 C1
Wolverley Rd HALE B63 *....138 B5
  HIA/OLT B92....148 B5
  RIDG/WDGT B32....157 F2
Wolverson Cl SHHTH WV12....40 A1
Wolverson Rd ALDR WS9....19 G3
Wolverton Rd
  CHWD/FDBR/MGN B37....132 B5
  DUDS DY2....85 E5
  RBRY B45....188 C2
Wombourne Cl SEDG DY3....67 E5
Wombourne Pk WMBN WV5....80 D2
Wombourne Rd SEDG DY3....80 D3
Wombrook Dr WMBN WV5....64 B5
Woodacre Rd
  ERDE/BCHGN B24....93 C2
Woodall Rd AST/WIT B6....91 F5
Woodall St BLOX/PEL WS3....27 G2
  CDYHTH B64....121 F4
Woodard Rd TPTN/OCK DY4....70 A4
Wood Av SEDG DY3....83 C2
  WNSFLD WV11....24 C4
Wood Bank Rd
  BDMR/CCFT WV3....35 E5
Woodbank Rd SEDG DY3....67 E4
Woodberry Dr
  WALM/CURD B76....78 C1
Woodberry Wk ACGN B27....146 D4
Woodbine Av SMTHWK B10 *....128 B4
Woodbine Cft
  LGN/SDN/BHAMAIR B26....147 G1
Woodbourne EDG B15....125 H4
Woodbourne Rd
  SMTHWK B67....124 A2
Woodbridge Cl BLOX/PEL WS3....16 D4
  RUSH/SHEL WS4....29 E1
Woodbrooke Gv
  NFLD/LBR B31....158 D4
Woodbrooke Rd SMTHWK B66....107 C2
Woodburn Cl BKDE/SHDE B34....112 C3
  BRLYHL DY5....119 H3
  RMSLY B62....122 D4
Woodbury Gv SOLH B91....181 H5
Woodbury Rd RMSLY B62....123 E4
Woodchester Rd DOR/KN B93....196 C5
Woodchurch Gra
  SCFLD/BOLD B73....76 D3
Wood Cl CSHL/WTROR B46....115 F2
Woodcock Cl NFLD/LBR B31....174 C4
Woodcock La ACGN B27....146 D3
  NFLD/LBR B31....158 A2
Woodcock La North
  ACGN B27....146 D3
Woodcock St CBHAMNE B4....3 J2
Woodcote Dr DOR/KN B93....199 F1
  WASH/WDE B8....110 D4
Woodcote PI LOZ/NWT B19 *....108 C2

Woodcote Rd
  DUNHL/THL/PER WV6....35 G1
  ERDE/BCHGN B24....93 H1
Woodcote Wy
  FOAKS/STRLY B74....60 B2
  WSNGN B18....108 A5
Wood Ct BFLD/HDSWWD B20....90 A4
Wood Cft HLYWD B47....192 D2
Woodcroft Av
  BFLD/HDSWWD B20....89 G3
  TPTN/OCK DY4....84 C1
Woodcroft Cl BLOX/PEL WS3....18 A3
  CDYHTH B64....121 F4
Woodcross La BILS/COS WV14....68 A1
Woodcross St BILS/COS WV14....67 H1
Woodend BFLD/HDSWWD B20....73 G5
Wood End La ERDE/BCHGN B24....92 D3
Woodend Pl
  DUNHL/THL/PER WV6....35 F1
Wood End Rd DSYBK/YTR WS5....43 F5
  ERDE/BCHGN B24....92 D5
  WNSFLD WV11....24 C2
Woodfall Av BVILLE B30....159 H5
Woodfield Av BRLYHL DY5....100 D2
  HAG/WOL DY9....136 D5
  OLDBY B69....105 E5
Woodfield Cl DSYBK/YTR WS5....58 C3
  FOAKS/STRLY B74....47 F5
Woodfield Crs BHTH/HG B12....144 C1
Woodfield Hts
  DUNHL/THL/PER WV6....35 H1
Woodfield La RMSLY B62....171 H5
Woodfield Rd
  ALE/KHTH/YWD B14....161 F2
  BHTH/HG B12....144 C1
  SEDG DY3....83 E3
  SOLH B91....164 D4
Woodfold Cft ALDR WS9....30 B3
Woodford Av CBROM B36....112 C1
Woodford Cl COVEN WV9....11 H5
Woodford Crs CDN
  HLGN/YWD B28....163 E2
Woodford La WMBN WV5....64 B3
Woodford Rd GTB/HAM B43....73 G4
Woodgate Dr RIDG/WDGT B32....157 E1
Woodgate Gdns
  RIDG/WDGT B32....140 A5
Woodgate La
  RIDG/WDGT B32....140 A5
Woodgate Wy HAG/WOL DY9....184 C1
Woodglade Cft
  HWK/WKHTH B38....176 C3
Woodgreen Cft
  LGLYGN/QTN B68....123 G5
Woodgreen Rd
  LGLYGN/QTN B68....123 G5
Wood Green Rd
  DARL/WED WS10....55 H5
  WSNGN B18 *....107 E3
Woodhall Cl TPTN/OCK DY4....69 G3
Woodhall Cft HIA/OLT B92....147 F4
Woodhall Rd
  ETTPK/GDPK/PENN WV4....51 E4
Woodham Cl RBRY B45....173 G4
Woodhaven RUSH/SHEL WS4....29 F1
Wood Hayes Cft WOLVN WV10....14 A5
Wood Hayes Rd WNSFLD WV11....24 C1
  WOLVN WV10....14 B5
Woodhill Cl WMBN WV5....64 D5
Wood Hill Dr WMBN WV5....64 D5
Woodhouse Fold
  WNSFLD WV11....24 D5
Woodhouse Orch
  HAG/WOL DY9....184 C1
Woodhouse Rd
  DUNHL/THL/PER WV6....35 F2
  RIDG/WDGT B32....141 E1
Woodhouse Rd North
  DUNHL/THL/PER WV6....35 F2
Woodhouse Wy CDYHTH B64....120 C3
Woodhurst Rd MOS/BIL B13....144 C1
Wooding Crs TPTN/OCK DY4....69 H2
Woodington Rd
  MGN/WHC B75....63 G3
Woodland Av BRLYHL DY5....120 A3
  DUDN DY1....84 C5
  DUNHL/THL/PER WV6....35 F2
  STRBR DY8....152 B5
Woodland Centre
  SHHTH WV12 *....26 C5
Woodland Cl HAG/WOL DY9....153 F1
  SHHTH WV12....26 B4
Woodland Cottages
  ETTPK/GDPK/PENN WV4 *....51 E4
Woodland Ct LICHS WS14....33 E3
Woodlands Av
  BDMR/CCFT WV3....50 D1
Woodland Dr SMTHWK B66....106 A2
Woodland Gv DOR/KN B43....58 C5
  SEDG DY3....82 D3
Woodland Rl CDYHTH B64....121 F4
  SCFLD/BOLD B73....76 B1
Woodland Rd
  BLKHTH/ROWR B65....122 D2
  DARL/WED WS10....55 E3
  HDSW B21....107 E1
  NFLD/LBR B31....175 H2
  RMSLY B62....122 D4
Woodlands Av
  CSHL/WTROR B46....96 A4
  DSYBK/YTR WS5....58 C3
Woodlands Cottages
  ETTPK/GDPK/PENN WV4 *....51 E4
Woodlands Crs BLOX/PEL WS3....17 H2
Woodlands Farm Rd
  ERDE/BCHGN B24....94 B2
Woodlands La SHLY B90....180 B5
Woodlands Paddock
  ETTPK/GDPK/PENN WV4....51 E4
Woodlands Park Rd
  BVILLE B30....159 E5
Woodlands Rd RBRY B45....189 E5
  SPARK B11....145 E4
  WASH/WDE B8....128 D1
  WMBN WV5....81 E1
Woodlands St SMTHWK B66....107 E4
The Woodlands CDYHTH B64....121 C5
  MGN/WHC B75....63 F2
  STRBR DY8....135 G5

Woodlands Wy
  CHWD/FDBR/MGN B37....132 D5
Wood La ALDR WS9....31 G2
  BFLD/HDSWWD B20....90 B4
  BLOX/PEL WS3....17 H2
  BRGRVW B61....185 G5
  CHWD/FDBR/MGN B37....132 A4
  ERDE/BCHGN B24....93 F5
  FOAKS/STRLY B74....47 H5
  HRBN B17....141 C1
  HHTH/SAND B71....72 C2
  MGN/WHC B75....87 E5
  WBROM B70....87 E5
  WOLVN WV10....12 D5
Wood Lane Cl SHHTH WV12 *....26 C5
Woodlawn Gv KGSWFD DY6....99 H4
Woodlea Dr ERDE/BCHGN B24....92 D4
  SOLH B91....164 A5
Wood Leasow
  RIDG/WDGT B32....140 D5
Woodleaves HLYWD B47....178 B5
Woodleigh Av HRBN B17....142 B3
Woodleigh Cl HALE B63....138 C1
Woodleigh Rd
  CSCFLD/WYGN B72....77 F2
The Woodleys
  ALE/KHTH/YWD B14....178 D1
Woodloes Rd SHLY B90....194 B1
Woodman Cl DARL/WED WS10....56 C3
  HALE B63....139 E4
Woodman La MGN/WHC B75....48 A2
Woodman La HAG/WOL DY9....170 B1
Woodman Rd
  ALE/KHTH/YWD B14....178 C4
  HALE B65....139 E4
Woodmeadow Rd BVILLE B30....177 E2
Woodnorton Dr MOS/BIL B13....144 A5
Woodnorton Rd
  BLKHTH/ROWR B65....122 D2
Woodpecker Gv CBROM B36....114 A2
Woodpecker Rd STETCH B33....112 B5
Woodperry Av SOLH B91....182 A4
Woodridge AST/WIT B6....91 E5
Woodridge Av
  RIDG/WDGT B32....140 B3
Woodridge Rd HALE B63....138 C2
Wood Rd DUNHL/THL/PER WV6....35 F2
  SEDG DY3....83 E3
  WMBN WV5....64 D4
Woodrough Dr MOS/BIL B13....144 B5
Woodrow Crs DOR/KN B93....197 E3
Woodruff Wy DSYBK/YTR WS5....57 C5
Woodrush Dr HLYWD B47....192 C3
Woods Bank Ter
  DARL/WED WS10....55 E3
Woods Crs BRLYHL DY5....120 A3
Woodsetton Cl DUDN DY1....68 B5
Woodshires Rd HIA/OLT B92....164 A3
Woodside
  CHWD/FDBR/MGN B37....113 G5
  FOAKS/STRLY B74....46 C3
Wood Side WNSFLD WV11....24 C4
Woodside Cl DSYBK/YTR WS5....58 B3
Woodside Crs DOR/KN B93....197 E4
Woodside Dr FOAKS/STRLY B74....32 A5
Woodside Gv CDSL WV8....10 C4
Woodside Rd DSYBK/YTR WS5....58 B3
  DUDS DY2....101 H3
  SLYOAK B29....160 A1
Woodside Wy ALDR WS9....30 B5
  RIDG/WDGT B32....157 E2
  SHHTH WV12....26 B4
  SOLH B91....164 A5
Woods La BRLYHL DY5....119 F5
  CDYHTH B64....120 C4
Woodsome Gv
  ERDW/GRVHL B23....76 A4
Woodsorrel Rd DUDN DY1....83 H2
The Woods
  ALE/KHTH/YWD B14....161 F1
Woodstile BKDE/SHDE B34....113 D3
Woodstile Cl MGN/WHC B75....47 H2
Woodstock Cl DUDN DY1....102 A1
  STRBR DY8....117 C3
Woodstock Crs DOR/KN B93....196 D5
Woodstock Dr
  FOAKS/STRLY B74....46 B1
  STRBR DY8....117 C2
Woodstock Rd HDSW B21....107 H1
  MOS/BIL B13....144 C3
  WOLV WV1....38 B4
Woodston Gv SOLH B91....182 A5
Wood St DARL/WED WS10....55 H2
  DUDS DY2....101 H3
  ETTPK/GDPK/PENN WV4....51 D3
  HAG/WOL DY9....136 D2
  STRBR DY8....117 H5
  TPTN/OCK DY4....69 E5
  WSL WS1....39 G3
  WOLV WV10....37 G5
Woodthorne Cl SEDG DY3....83 F4
Woodthorne Rd
  DUNHL/THL/PER WV6....21 E4
Woodthorne Rd South
  DUNHL/THL/PER WV6....21 E5
Woodthorpe Dr
  HAG/WOL DY9....136 B4
Woodthorpe Gdns
  ALE/KHTH/YWD B14....161 E5
Woodthorpe Rd
  ALE/KHTH/YWD B14....160 D5
Woodvale Dr HLGN/YWD B28....179 G1
Woodvale Rd HLGN/YWD B28....179 E1
  RIDG/WDGT B32....157 E1
Woodview Dr EDG B15....126 C5
Woodville Gdns SEDG DY3....67 H2
Woodville Rd
  ALE/KHTH/YWD B14....161 F2
  HRBN B17....141 C1
Woodward Pl HAG/WOL DY9....136 A3
Woodwards Cl WSLW WS2....41 F5
Woodwards Pl WSLW WS2....41 F5
Woodwards Rd WSLW WS2....41 F5
Woodward St
  HHTH/SAND B71....87 H2
Woodway ERDE/BCHGN B24....93 F1
Woodway Cl WASH/WDE B8....111 E4
Woolacombe Lodge Rd
  SLYOAK B29....142 A5

Woolmore Rd
  ERDW/GRVHL B23 .... 92 A2
Woolpack Cl
  BLKHTH/ROWR B65 .... 103 C5
Wootton Gv KGSTG B44 .... 76 A3
Wootton Av WNSFLD WV11 .... 24 D3
Wootton Rd BDMR/CCFT WV3 ... 50 C1
  NFLD/LBR B31 .... 189 C1
Worcester Bar CBHAMW B1 * 2 C6
Worcester Cl HAG/WOL DY9 ..... 152 C5
  MGN/WHC B75 .... 47 H2
Worcester Ct BDMR/CCFT WV5 ... 34 A1
Worcester Gn HHTH/SAND B71 .. 71 G4
Worcester Gv
  DUNHL/THL/PER WV6 .... 34 B1
Worcester La HAG/WOL DY9 .... 152 D2
  MGN/WHC B75 .... 47 H2
Worcester Rd SLYOAK B29 .... 160 B1
Worcester Rd DUDS DY2 .... 121 E1
  HAG/WOL DY9 .... 169 G1
  LGLYGN/QTN B68 .... 123 C4
  WLNHL WV13 .... 40 B5
Worcester St BKHL/PFLD WV2 .... 3 G6
  CBHAM B2 .... 5 G6
  STRBR DY8 .... 135 G3
Worcester Wk CBHAM B2 * 3 G6
Word HI HRBN B17 .... 124 B5
Wordsworth Av
  ETTPK/GDPK/PENN WV4 .... 52 C4
Wordsworth Cl TPTN/OCK DY4 ... 69 F3
Wordsworth Ct
  SEDG DY3 .... 82 D1
  SHHTH WV12 .... 26 C3
  SMHTH B10 .... 128 B5
Wordsworth Rd BLOX/PEL WS3 ... 28 A2
  SEDG DY3 .... 82 D1
  SHHTH WV12 .... 26 C3
  SMHTH B10 .... 128 B5
Wordsworth St
  HHTH/SAND B71 .... 87 G1
Worfield Cl RUSH/SHEL WS4 ..... 42 C1
Worfield Gdns
  BDMR/CCFT WV3 .... 51 F2
Works Rd
  LGN/SDN/BHAMAIR B26 ...... 149 E4
World's End Av
  RIDG/WDGT B32 .... 140 D1
World's End La
  RIDG/WDGT B32 .... 140 D2
Worlds End Rd
  BFLD/HDSWWD B20 .... 90 A3
Worley's Wharf Av
  DARL/WED WS10 .... 72 A1
Worsey Dr DARL/WED DY4 .... 70 B5
Worthen Gv NFLD/LBR B31 ...... 175 G5
The Worthings BVILLE B30 ...... 160 B4
Worthy Down WNSFLD WV11 ...... 25 F5
Wortley Av WOLVN WV10 * 23 C4
Worton Rd HAG/WOL DY9 .... 136 C5
Wragby Cl COVEN WV9 .... 12 B4
Wrekin Cl HALE B65 .... 154 C1
Wrekin Dr BDMR/CCFT WV5 ...... 36 A5
  DUNHL/THL/PER WV6 .... 21 E5
  HAG/WOL DY9 .... 136 B3
Wrekin Gv SHHTH WV12 .... 25 H1
Wrekin La
  DUNHL/THL/PER WV6 .... 21 E5
Wrekin Rd KGSTG B44 .... 75 F5
  SCFLD/BOLD B73 .... 77 E2

Wrekin Vw BRWNH WS8 .... 19 G2
Wrekin View Rd SEDG DY3 .... 67 E3
Wren Av DUNHL/THL/PER WV6 ... 34 B2
Wrenbury Dr BILS/COS WV14 .... 54 C1
Wrens Av KGSWFD DY6 .... 100 C5
  TPTN/OCK DY4 .... 84 C1
Wrens Hill Rd DUDN DY1 .... 84 B1
Wren's Nest Cl DUDN DY1 ...... 194 A3
Wrens Nest Rd DUDN DY1 .... 84 A2
Wrens Park Av
  WALM/CURD DY4 .... 78 A4
Wren St DUDN DY1 .... 68 B5
  DUDS DY2 .... 102 B4
Wrentham St DIG/EDG B5 .... 127 E4
Wretham Rd LOZ/NWT B19 ...... 108 B3
Wrexham Av WSLW WS2 .... 40 D4
Wright Av WNSFLD WV11 .... 24 D5
Wrighton Cl SHHTH WV12 .... 26 A2
Wrighton Dr BRLYHL DY5 .... 83 E5
Wright Rd WASH/WDE B8 ...... 110 C4
Wright's La CDYHTH B64 .... 54 A4
Wright St BILS/COS WV14 .... 54 B3
  HALE B63 .... 138 D3
  SMHTH B10 .... 128 B4
  WOLVN WV10 * 37 F1
Wrottesley Park Rd
  DUNHL/THL/PER WV6 .... 34 B1
Wrottesley Rd
  DUNHL/THL/PER WV6 .... 21 F5
  GTB/HAM B43 .... 73 F2
Wrottesley Rd West
  DUNHL/THL/PER WV6 .... 20 D4
Wrottesley St DIG/EDG B5 .... 3 G7
Wroxall Cl BRLYHL DY5 .... 118 D4
Wroxall Gv MOS/BIL B13 ...... 161 C4
Wroxall Rd SOLH B91 .... 164 A4
Wroxham Gln WLNHL WV13 ...... 39 F5
Wroxton Rd YDLY B25 .... 130 A4
Wulfruna Gdns
  BDMR/CCFT WV3 .... 36 B4
Wulfruna St WOLV WV1 .... 7 F5
Wulfrun Sq WOLV WV1 .... 7 G5
Wulfrun Wy WOLV WV1 .... 7 F5
Wyatt Cl DIG/EDG B5 .... 143 G2
Wyatt Rd MGN/WHC B75 .... 63 H2
Wychall Dr WOLVN WV10 .... 13 E3
Wychall La HWK/WKHTH B38 ... 176 B3
Wychall Park Gv
  HWK/WKHTH B38 .... 176 B3
Wychall Rd NFLD/LBR B31 ..... 175 H2
Wychbold Cl SHHTH WV12 ...... 26 B1
Wychbold Ct HAG/WOL DY9 .... 153 E2
Wychbold Crs STETCH B33 ..... 131 E1
Wychbury DUNHL/WALM/CURD B76 . 78 C5
Wychbury Ct HALE B63 .... 138 C4
Wychbury Dr HAG/WOL DY9 .... 153 E5
Wychbury Rd BDMR/CCFT WV3 .. 50 C1
  BRLYHL DY5 .... 119 C4
  HAG/WOL DY9 .... 153 G1
  RIDG/WDGT B32 .... 157 E2
Wyche Av ALE/KHTH/YWD B14 .. 177 H1
Wycheim Farm Rd
  ALE/KHTH/YWD B14 .... 178 C4
Wych Elm Rd BRWNH WS8 .... 18 D2
Wycherley Wy CDYHTH B64 ...... 71 E1
Wychnor Gv HHTH/SAND B71 .... 72 A1
Wychwood Av
  DOR/KN B93 .... 183 F5

Wychwood Crs
  LGN/SDN/BHAMAIR B26 ...... 147 G1
Wyckham Cl KRBN B17 .... 141 G3
Wyckham Rd CBROM B36 .... 113 H2
Wycome Rd HLGN/YWD B28 .... 162 D4
Wye Cliff Rd
  BFLD/HDSWWD B20 .... 108 B1
Wye Cl DUNHL/THL/PER WV6 ... 34 D1
  WALM/CURD DY4 .... 78 C4
Wyegate Cl CBROM B36 .... 114 A1
Wyemanton Cl GTB/HAM B43 ... 73 E2
Wye Rd BLOX/PEL WS3 .... 28 A1
Wykeham Gv
  DUNHL/THL/PER WV6 .... 34 B2
Wyken Cl DOR/KN B93 .... 198 C1
Wyld Ct HHTH/SAND B71 .... 71 E3
Wylde Crs BLKHTH/ROWR B65 .. 104 A5
Wylde Green Rd
  CSCFLD/WYGN B72 .... 77 C2
Wymering Av WNSFLD WV11 ..... 25 F5
Wynall La HAG/WOL DY9 .... 136 D4
Wynall La South HAG/WOL DY9 . 137 E4
Wynbrook Gv SHLY B90 .... 195 C2
Wynchcombe Av
  ETTPK/GDPK/PENN WV4 .... 50 D4
Wyndcliff Rd BORD B9 .... 128 D2
Wyndham Gdns BVILLE B30 .... 176 C1
Wyndham Rd LDYWD/EDGR B16 125 H1
Wyndhurst Rd STETCH B33 ..... 112 A5
Wyndley Cl FOAKS/STRLY B74 .. 32 D4
Wyndley Dr SCFLD/BOLD B73 ... 62 B4
Wyndley Gv CSCFLD/WYGN B72 . 77 G1
Wyndley La SCFLD/BOLD B73 ... 62 A4
Wyndmill Crs HHTH/SAND B71 .. 72 B2
Wynds Covert
  ALE/KHTH/YWD B14 .... 177 G5
Wyndshiels CSHL/WTROR B46 .. 115 G3
Wynds Point NFLD/LBR B31 .... 158 D5
The Wynd SEDG DY3 .... 67 F2
Wynfield Gdns
  ALE/KHTH/YWD B14 .... 161 F5
Wynford Rd ACGN B27 .... 146 C2
Wyn-Griffith Dr TPTN/OCK DY4 . 85 E3
Wynne Crs
  ETTPK/GDPK/PENN WV4 .... 50 C5
Wynn Rd
  ETTPK/GDPK/PENN WV4 .... 51 F2
Wynn St DIG/EDG B5 .... 127 H3
Wynstead Covert
  ALE/KHTH/YWD B14 .... 177 G3
Wyre Cl ALE/KHTH/YWD B14 .... 178 A1
Wyre La HHTH/SAND B71 .... 71 F3
Wyrley Cl BRWNH WS8 .... 9 F1
  SHHTH WV12 .... 26 A3
Wyrley Rd AST/WIT B6 .... 91 G3
  CBROM B36 .... 95 F5
  WNSFLD WV11 .... 25 C4
Wyrley St WOLVN WV10 .... 37 H3
Wyrley Wy ERDW/GRVHL B23 ... 95 G5
Wythall Green Wy HLYWD B47 . 192 A5
Wythall Rd HALE B65 .... 138 C5
Wythwood Cl HAG/WOL DY9 .... 153 F1
Wythwood Gv HLYWD B47 ...... 192 D1
  TPTN/OCK DY4 .... 69 G5
Wythwood Rd HLYWD B47 ...... 192 D2
Wyton Av LGLYGN/QTN B68 .... 123 G2
Wyvern Cl FOAKS/STRLY B74 .... 62 B1

  LGLYGN/QTN B68 .... 105 F5
  SHHTH WV12 .... 25 C5
Wyvern Gv SLYOAK B29 .... 142 A5
Wyvern Rd FOAKS/STRLY B74 ... 62 B1
Wyvis Cl BDMR/CCFT WV3 .... 36 A3

Y

Yale Dr WNSFLD WV11 .... 25 E5
Yale Rd WLNHL WV13 .... 54 C1
Yardley Cl LGLYGN/QTN B68 .. 123 F3
Yardley Fields Rd STETCH B33 .. 129 F2
Yardley Green Rd BORD B9 .... 128 D3
Yardley Rd ACGN B27 .... 146 C3
Yardley St DARL/WED WS10 .... 55 F1
  HAG/WOL DY9 .... 136 A1
Yardley Wood Rd
  ALE/KHTH/YWD B14 .... 178 D1
  MOS/BIL B13 .... 161 H5
Yare Gv WLNHL WV13 .... 40 B4
Yarnborough HI STRBR DY8 ... 135 G5
Yarnbury Cl
  ALE/KHTH/YWD B14 .... 178 A4
Yarn Cl HLYWD B47 .... 192 C3
Yarner Cl DUDN DY1 .... 85 C5
Yarnfield Rd SPARK B11 ...... 146 A4
Yarningale La BVILLE B30 .... 177 H2
Yarningale Rd
  ALE/KHTH/YWD B14 .... 160 C5
Yarn La SHLY B90 .... 194 A2
Yarrow Cl BLOX/PEL WS3 .... 18 A2
  WNSFLD WV11 .... 25 F5
Yarrow Dr HWK/WKHTH B38 ... 176 D5
Yarwell Cl WOLVN WV10 .... 37 F1
Yateley Av PBAR/PBCH B42 ... 74 A4
Yateley Crs PBAR/PBCH B42 ... 74 A4
Yateley Rd EDG B15 .... 125 C5
Yatesbury Av CVALE B35 ...... 94 D3
Yates Cft FOAKS/STRLY B74 ... 32 D4
Yates La BLKHTH/ROWR B65 ... 122 C2
Yeadon Gdns BDMR/CCFT WV3 . 35 H5
Yeames Cl GTB/HAM B43 .... 59 G3
Yelverton Cl BLOX/PEL WS3 .... 16 D5
Yelverton Dr EDG B15 .... 125 G5
Yeman Rd LGLYGN/QTN B68 ... 123 H1
Yemscroft Flats
  RUSH/SHEL WS4 * 28 C4
Yenton Gv ERDE/BCHGN B24 .... 77 G5
Yeomanry Cl MGN/WHC B75 .... 63 G2
Yeomans Wy MGN/WHC B75 .... 63 F2
Yerbury Gv ERDW/GRVHL B23 .. 91 G1
Yew Croft Av HRBN B17 .... 141 G1
Yewdale HRBN B17 .... 142 A5
Yewhurst Rd SOLH B91 .... 180 D1
Yew St BDMR/CCFT WV3 .... 6 B5
Yew Tree Av HAG/WOL DY9 .... 170 B5
Yew Tree Gdns CDSL WV8 ...... 10 C3
Yew Tree Hills DUDS DY2 ..... 120 C1
Yewtree La
  BLKHTH/ROWR B65 .... 121 H2
Yew Tree La BILS/COS WV14 ... 68 D2
  DARL/WED WS10 .... 71 E1
  DUNHL/THL/PER WV6 .... 35 F1
  LGN/SDN/BHAMAIR B26 ...... 130 A5
  RIDG/WDGT B32 .... 173 H2

  SOLH B91 .... 165 C5
Yew Tree Pl RMSLY B62 .... 155 F5
Yew Tree Ri WALM/CURD B76 .. 63 F5
Yewtree Rd FOAKS/STRLY B74 .. 44 D5
  SCFLD/BOLD B73 .... 62 A4
Yew Tree Rd AST/WIT B6 ...... 91 C5
  CBROM B36 .... 113 C1
  DSYBK/YTR WS5 .... 57 G3
  DUDS DY2 .... 102 C5
  EDG B15 .... 125 F5
  HALE B63 .... 138 A4
  MOS/BIL B13 .... 145 H5
  RUSH/SHEL WS4 .... 28 D1
  SMTHWKW B67 .... 106 A5
Yew Tree Vls
  SCFLD/BOLD B73 * 77 E4
Yockleton Rd STETCH B33 ..... 131 E1
York Av BDMR/CCFT WV3 .... 36 A4
  WLNHL WV13 .... 40 B5
  WSLW WS2 .... 41 F3
Yorkbrooke Dr
  LGN/SDN/BHAMAIR B26 ...... 147 H2
York Cl BVILLE B30 .... 160 A4
  TPTN/OCK DY4 .... 69 F3
York Crs BDMR/CCFT WV3 ...... 35 H4
  BKDE/SHDE B34 .... 113 G4
  DARL/WED WS10 .... 55 F2
  STRBR DY8 .... 117 H5
  WBROM B70 .... 71 E5
Yorkdale Cl SEDG DY3 .... 83 F5
York Dr CBROM B36 .... 111 F1
Yorke Av BRLYHL DY5 .... 118 C5
York Gdns BDMR/CCFT WV3 ... 36 A4
Yorklea Cl
  CHWD/FDBR/MGN B37 .... 131 H2
Yorklea Cft
  CHWD/FDBR/MGN B37 .... 131 H2
Yorkminster Dr
  CHWD/FDBR/MGN B37 .... 132 D1
York Rd ALE/KHTH/YWD B14 .. 161 E2
  BDMR/CCFT WV3 .... 35 F5
  BLKHTH/ROWR B65 .... 122 C1
  DUDS DY2 .... 121 E1
  ERDW/GRVHL B23 .... 92 D2
  HDSW B21 .... 107 H1
  LGLYGN/QTN B68 .... 122 D1
  LDYWD/EDGR B16 .... 125 F3
  RUSH/SHEL WS4 .... 29 F3
York St HRBN B17 .... 142 B1
  WOLV WV1 .... 7 J5
Yorks Wood Dr
  CHWD/FDBR/MGN B37 .... 113 G4
York Ter WSNGN B18 .... 108 C4
Young St WBROM B70 .... 87 E3
Yoxall Gv STETCH B33 .... 130 C1
Yoxall Rd SHLY B90 .... 180 D3

Z

Zions Cl CDYHTH B64 .... 121 F5
Zion St TPTN/OCK DY4 .... 69 F5
Zoar St BDMR/CCFT WV3 .... 6 B5
  SEDG DY3 .... 83 E3
Zouche Cl STRBR DY8 .... 118 A4

Index - featured places

The 3b Business Village
  HDSW B21 .... 107 F2
A1 Trading Estate
  SMTHWK B66 .... 106 C2
  SMTHWKW B67 .... 124 C3
Abberley Industrial Centre
  SMTHWK B66 .... 107 F4
Abbey CP School
  BLOX/PEL WS3 .... 16 A4
Abbey Infant School
  SMTHWKW B67 .... 124 A2
Abbey Junior School
  SMTHWKW B67 .... 124 A3
Abbey Tutorial College
  CBHAMNW B5 .... 2 E3
Abu Bakr Girls School WSL WS1 .. 4 B7
Ace Business Park
  STETCH B33 .... 131 E2
Acupoint Magneto Clinic
  SMHTH B10 .... 128 C5
Adderley Primary School
  WASH/WDE B8 .... 128 B1
Adderley Trading Estate
  WASH/WDE B8 .... 110 A5
Albert Bradbeer Infant School
  NFLD/LBR B31 .... 189 F1
Albert Bradbeer Junior School
  NFLD/LBR B31 .... 189 F1
Albert Pritchard Infant School
  DARL/WED WS10 .... 56 A3
Albion Business Park
  SMTHWK B66 .... 106 A1
Albion Industrial Estate
  WBROM B70 .... 87 E4
Albion Junior School
  HHTH/SAND B71 .... 106 C1
Albion Road Junior School
  WLNHL WV13 .... 39 H3
Alcott Hall Primary School
  CHWD/FDBR/MGN B37 .... 132 B3
Alderbrook School SOLH B91 .. 181 F3
Alder Coppice Primary School
  SEDG DY3 .... 67 E2
Aldersley High School
  CDSL WV8 .... 22 A1
Aldersley Leisure Village
  DUNHL/THL/PER WV6 .... 22 B4
Aldridge School ALDR WS9 .... 30 A5
Alexander Industrial Estate
  BILS/COS WV14 .... 53 G4
Alexandra High School &
  Sixth Form Centre
  TPTN/OCK DY4 .... 69 H5
Alexandra Industrial Estate
  TPTN/OCK DY4 .... 69 F5

Alexandra Medical Centre
  HALE B63 .... 138 B2
Alexandra Theatre DIG/EDG B5 .. 3 F6
Al-Furqan Community College
  SPARK B11 .... 145 H3
Al Furqan Primary School
  SPARK B11 .... 145 H3
Al Hijrah School BORD B9 .... 128 B2
Al-Hira School BHTH/HG B12 .. 144 B1
Al Huda Girls School
  WASH/WDE B8 .... 110 B4
Alison Nicholas Golf Academy
  PBAR/PBCH B42 .... 74 C3
Allens Croft Primary School
  ALE/KHTH/YWD B14 .... 160 B5
All Saints CE J & I School
  HHTH/SAND B71 .... 71 G5
All Saints Industrial Estate
  WBROM B70 .... 108 A4
Alma Industrial Estate
  DARL/WED WS10 .... 55 G2
Alston Primary School
  BORD B9 .... 129 E1
Alumrock Medical Centre
  WASH/WDE B8 .... 110 C5
Alumwell Community School
  WSLW WS2 .... 41 E4
Alumwell Infant School
  WSLW WS2 .... 41 E3
Alumwell Junior School
  WSLW WS2 .... 41 E3
Amblecote Primary School
  STRBR DY8 .... 118 B4
AMC Cinema
  LDYWD/EDGR B16 .... 126 A3
Amptronik Trading Estate
  WMBN WV5 .... 80 B2
Anchor Brook Industrial Park
  ALDR WS9 .... 30 B4
Anderton Park Primary
  School
  BHTH/HG B12 .... 144 C3
Anglesey Primary School
  LOZ/NWT B19 .... 108 C2
Anglo African Industrial Estate
  OLDBY WV5 .... 86 C4
Anita Myatt Health Centre
  ETTPK/GDPK/PENN WV4 .... 50 D4
Annie Lennard Infant School .
  SMTHWKW B67 .... 124 A1
Arcadian Shopping Centre
  DIG/EDG B5 .... 3 G7
Archbishop Grimshaw
  RC School
  CHWD/FDBR/MGN B37 .... 131 H1

Archbishop Ilsey Catholic
  Technology College &
  Sixth Form Centre
  ACGN B27 .... 146 C4
Arden Hotel & Leisure Club
  HIA/OLT DY2 .... 149 F5
Arden Industrial Estate
  WASH/WDE B8 .... 111 F2
Arden Primary School
  SPARK B11 .... 145 E2
Arden School
  DOR/KN B93 .... 197 F3
Armoury Trading Estate
  SPARK B11 .... 145 F1
Arran Medical Centre
  CBROM B36 .... 114 A2
Arrow Industrial Estate
  SHHTH WV12 .... 25 H3
Arthur Terry School
  FOAKS/STRLY B74 .... 47 E3
Ashbourne Centre
  ERDW/GRVHL B23 .... 92 C3
Ashford Industrial Estate
  BKHL/PFLD WV2 .... 52 D1
Ashfurlong Health Centre
  MGN/WHC B75 .... 48 A5
Ashmore Park Clinic
  WNSFLD WV11 .... 25 G2
Ashmores Industrial Estate
  DUDN DY1 .... 84 D3
Ashtree Medical Centre
  BVILLE B30 .... 160 A4
Ashwood Park Primary School
  STRBR DY8 .... 117 H3
Aston Cross Business Park
  SHHTH WV12 .... 109 C3
Aston Expressway
  AST/WIT B6 .... 109 E4
Aston Hall AST/WIT B6 .... 109 F1
Aston Health Centre
  AST/WIT B6 .... 91 E5
Aston Manor Cricket &
  Lucas Sports Club
  PBAR/PBCH B42 .... 90 D1
Aston Manor School
  AST/WIT B6 .... 109 F3
Aston Science Park
  VAUX/NECH B7 .... 3 K2
Aston Tower Primary School
  AST/WIT B6 .... 109 F2
Aston University
  CBHAMNE B4 .... 3 J3
Aston Villa FC (Villa Park)
  AST/WIT B6 .... 91 F3

Aston Wood Golf Club
  FOAKS/STRLY B74 .... 32 C4
Astoria Hotel
  LDYWD/EDGR B16 .... 125 F3
Atlas Trading Estate
  BILS/COS WV14 .... 69 F1
  SPARK B11 .... 145 F1
Attock Community Sports & CC
  MOS/BIL B13 .... 162 A1
Attwood Business Centre
  HAG/WOL DY9 .... 136 D2
Autobase Industrial Estate
  TPTN/OCK DY4 .... 85 H3
Avery Dell Industrial Estate
  BVILLE B30 .... 159 H4
Axcess 10 Business Park
  DARL/WED WS10 .... 40 C5
Baggeridge Country Park
  SEDG DY3 .... 66 A5
Bagley Industrial Park
  DUDS DY2 .... 102 D5
Balliol Business Park
  COVEN WV9 .... 11 C4
Banners Gate Infant School
  SCFLD/BOLD B73 .... 62 B3
Banners Gate Junior School
  SCFLD/BOLD B73 .... 60 C4
Bantock House & Park
  BDMR/CCFT WV3 .... 36 B4
Barber Institute of Fine Arts
  EDG B15 .... 142 D3
Barford Primary School
  LDYWD/EDGR B16 .... 125 G1
Barnfield Trading Estate
  TPTN/OCK DY4 .... 69 E4
Baron Business Park
  HAG/WOL DY9 .... 136 C2
Barons Court Industrial Estate
  ALDR WS9 .... 19 E5
Barons Court Trading Estate
  ALDR WS9 .... 19 E5
The Barr Beacon School
  ALDR WS9 .... 59 F3
Bartley Green FC
  RIDG/WDGT B32 .... 157 G1
Bartley Green Health Centre
  RIDG/WDGT B32 .... 157 F1
Bartley Green Technology
  College RIDG/WDGT B32 .... 157 G1
Barton Industrial Estate
  BILS/COS WV14 .... 54 A1
Baskerville Special School
  HRBN B17 .... 141 C1
Bath Walk Industrial Estate
  BHTH/HG B12 .... 144 C2

Baverstock GM School
  ALE/KHTH/YWD B14 .... 178 A3
Bayer Hall Clinic
  BILS/COS WV14 .... 68 C3
Beacon CP School
  SHHTH WV12 .... 26 B2
Beacon Hill Cemetery
Beacon Hill Cemetery
  ETTPK/GDPK/PENN WV4 .... 67 G1
Beaconside Primary School
  RBRY B45 .... 187 G2
Beacon Trading Estate
  ALDR WS9 .... 29 H4
Bean Road Industrial Estate
  TPTN/OCK DY4 .... 68 C5
Bearwood Medical Centre
  SMTHWKW B67 .... 124 B2
Bearwood Primary School
  SMTHWK B66 .... 124 C2
Bearwood Shopping Centre
  SMTHWK B66 .... 124 C3
Beaufort Special School
  CBROM B36 .... 111 H4
Beaumont College
  ALE/KHTH/YWD B14 .... 160 D2
Beauty Bank Primary School
  STRBR DY8 .... 135 F1
Beechdale CP School
  WSLW WS2 .... 27 G5
Beeches Hospital
  WOLV WV1 .... 6 A2
Beeches Pool & Fitness Centre
  PBAR/PBCH B42 .... 74 B4
Belbroughton CE First School
  HAG/WOL DY9 .... 184 C2
Belfront Trading Estate
  RMSLY B62 .... 139 E3
Bell Barn Shopping Centre
  EDG B15 .... 126 C3
Belle Vue Medical Centre
  EDG B15 .... 126 D5
Belle Vue Primary School
  STRBR DY8 .... 117 G1
Bellfield J & I School
  NFLD/LBR B31 .... 175 F1
Bells Farm Primary School
  ALE/KHTH/YWD B14 .... 177 G3
The Bell Shopping Centre
  NFLD/LBR B31 .... 175 G1
Bennetts Well Primary School
  CHWD/FDBR/MGN B37 .... 131 H1
Benson Community School
  WSNGN B18 .... 107 H3
Benson Industrial Estate
  WSNGN B18 .... 107 H3

Bentley Bridge Business Park
 WNSFLD WV11 .... 24 C5
Bentley Bridge Leisure Park
 WNSFLD WV11 .... 38 B1
Bentley Cemetery
 WLNHL WV13 .... 40 B3
Bentley Drive Primary School
 WSLW WS2 .... 41 F2
Bentley Heath CE
 Primary School
 DOR/KN B93 .... 196 D3
Bentley Lane Industrial Park
 WSLW WS2 .... 41 F1
Bentley Mill Industrial Estate
 WSLW WS2 .... 40 D3
Bentley West Primary School
 WSLW WS2 .... 40 C2
Berrybrook Primary School
 WOLVN WV10 .... 24 B1
Bescot Industrial Estate
 DARL/WED WS10 .... 55 F5
Best Western Premier Moor Hall
 Hotel & Spa
 MGN/WHC B75 .... 47 H4
Best Western The Fairlawns
 at Aldridge ALDR WS9 .... 31 E4
Best Western Westley Hotel
 ACGN B27 .... 146 B4
Bevan Industrial Estate
 BRLYHL DY5 .... 118 C2
Beverley Hotel
 RUSH/SHEL WS4 .... 42 C1
Bhylls Acre Primary School
 BDMR/CCFT WV3 .... 50 B1
Bickenhill Trading Estate
 CHWD/FDBR/MGN B37 .... 149 H2
Bickford Road Industrial Estate
 AST/WIT B6 .... 91 C5
Bilbrook CE Middle School
 CDSL WV8 .... 10 D4
Bilbrook Medical Centre
 CDSL WV8 .... 10 D4
Billesley Primary School
 MOS/BIL B13 .... 162 A4
Bilston Cemetery
 BILS/COS WV14 .... 53 C1
Bilston Central Industrial Estate
 BILS/COS WV14 .... 54 A3
Bilston CE Primary School
 BKHL/PFLD WV2 .... 53 F2
Bilston Health Centre
 BILS/COS WV14 .... 53 H2
Bilston High School
 BILS/COS WV14 .... 53 H3
Bilston Industrial Estate
 BILS/COS WV14 .... 54 C4
Bingle Primary School
 BDMR/CCFT WV3 .... 36 C5
Bilston Key Industrial Estate
 BILS/COS WV14 .... 54 C4
Bilston Leisure Centre
 BILS/COS WV14 .... 54 B2
Bilston Public Library &
 Art Gallery BILS/COS WV14 ..... 54 A2
Bilston Town FC
 BILS/COS WV14 .... 54 B2
Bilton Industrial Estate
 HWK/WKHTH B38 .... 176 C5
Birches First School CDSL WV8 .. 21 F1
Birches Green J & I School
 ERDE/BCHGN B24 .... 93 F3
Birchfield Independent
 Girls School AST/WIT B6 .... 109 E1
Birchfield Primary School
 AST/WIT B6 .... 90 D5
Birchills CE Primary School
 WSLW WS2 .... 4 A1
Birchills Health Centre
 WSLW WS2 .... 4 A1
Birchley Industrial Estate
 OLDBY B69 .... 104 C4
Birch Road East
 Industrial Estate
 AST/WIT B6 .... 91 H4
Birmingham Alexander
 Stadium PBAR/PBCH B42 .... 74 C5
Birmingham Area Civil Service
 Sports Club HIA/OLT B92 .... 149 E5
Birmingham Botanical
 Gardens & Glasshouses
 EDG B15 .... 125 H5
Birmingham Business Centre
 WBROM B70 .... 88 B4
Birmingham Business Park
 CHWD/FDBR/MGN B37 .... 133 E4
Birmingham Christian Centre
 CBHAMNW B3 .... 3 F4
Birmingham City College
 BORD B9 .... 129 E1
Birmingham City FC
 (St Andrews Stadium)
 BORD B9 .... 127 H3
Birmingham College of Food,
 Tourism & Creative Studies
 CBHAMNW B3 .... 2 D4
Birmingham Community College
 CSCFLD/WYGN B72 .... 62 C3
Birmingham Conservatoire
 (University of Central England)
 CBHAMNW B3 .... 2 D4
The Birmingham Crematorium
 PBAR/PBCH B42 .... 90 C1
Birmingham Heartlands
 Hospital BORD B9 .... 129 F2
Birmingham Hebrew
 Congregation CBHAMW B1 .... 2 E7
Birmingham International
 Airport
 LGN/SDN/BHAMAIR B26 .... 149 G3
Birmingham Marriott Hotel
 EDG B15 .... 126 B4
The Birmingham & Midland
 Hospital for Woman
 SPARK B11 .... 145 E4
The Birmingham Mint
 WSNGN B18 .... 2 B1
Birmingham Museum &
 Art Gallery CBHAMNW B3 .... 2 E5
The Birmingham Nuffield
 Hospital EDG B15 .... 142 D2

Birmingham One Industrial
 Estate CBHAMW B1 .... 2 B4
Birmingham Repertory Theatre
 CBHAMW D1 .... 2 D5
Birmingham Wheels
 Adventure Park BORD B9 .... 128 A2
Birmingham Womens Hospital
 HRBN B17 .... 142 B2
Birmingham (Yardley)
 Crematorium YDLY B25 .... 146 D2
Bishop Ashbury's Cottage
 GTB/HAM B43 .... 72 D2
The Bishop Challoner RC School
 ALE/KHTH/YWD B14 .... 161 E2
Bishop Milner RC Secondary
 School DUDN DY1 .... 84 A3
Bishop Veseys Grammar School
 FOAKS/STRLY B74 .... 46 D2
Bishop Walsh Catholic School
 WALM/CURD B76 .... 77 H1
Bishop Wilson CE
 Primary School
 CHWD/FDBR/MGN B37 .... 132 C1
Bi-Tec Industrial Park
 WOLV WV1 .... 37 H4
Blackbrook Valley
 Industrial Estate
 DUDS DY2 .... 102 A3
Blackbrook Valley
 Industrial Park
 BRLYHL DY5 .... 102 A4
Black Country Living Museum
 DUDN DY1 .... 84 D3
Blackheath Primary School
 BLKHTH/ROWR B65 .... 121 H3
Blackheath Trading Estate
 BLKHTH/ROWR B65 .... 122 C2
Black Lake Industrial Estate
 WBROM B70 .... 71 E5
Blackwood School
 FOAKS/STRLY B74 .... 45 E4
Blakedown CE First School
 KIDD DY10 .... 168 C4
Blakeley Heath Primary School
 WMBN WV5 .... 81 E1
Blakenall CE BLOX/PEL WS3 .... 27 G3
Blakenall Heath Junior School
 BLOX/PEL WS3 .... 27 G2
Blakenhale Infant School
 STETCH B33 .... 130 D3
Blakenhale Junior School
 STETCH B33 .... 130 D3
Blakenhall Industrial Estate
 BDMR/CCFT WV3 .... 51 H1
Blakesley Hall YDLY B25 .... 130 A3
Blakesley Hall Primary School
 STETCH B33 .... 129 H3
Blanford Mere Primary School
 KGSWFD DY6 .... 99 G1
Bleakhouse Clinic
 LGLYGN/QTN B68 .... 123 C3
Bleakhouse Junior School
 LGLYGN/QTN B68 .... 123 C3
Blossomfield Infant School
 SHLY B90 .... 180 D2
Blowers Green Primary School
 DUDS DY2 .... 102 B1
Bloxwich Business Park
 WSLW WS2 .... 27 F5
Bloxwich CE Primary School
 BLOX/PEL WS3 .... 27 F1
Bloxwich Golf Club
 BLOX/PEL WS3 .... 16 D3
Bloxwich Hospital
 BLOX/PEL WS3 .... 27 F2
Bloxwich Lane Industrial Estate
 WSLW WS2 .... 41 E2
Bloxwich Leisure Centre
 BLOX/PEL WS3 .... 27 G2
Blue Coat CE Comprehensive
 School WSL WS1 .... 5 F5
Blue Coat CE Infant School
 WSL WS1 .... 5 F6
Blue Coat CE Junior School
 WSL WS1 .... 5 C5
The Blue Coat School
 HRBN B17 .... 142 C1
Blythe Business Park
 SHLY B90 .... 195 F5
Blythe Special School
 CSHL/WTROR B46 .... 115 C5
BMI Priory Hospital
 DIG/EDG B5 .... 143 F2
Boddis Industrial Park
 CDYHTH B64 .... 121 G2
Boldmere Clinic
 SCFLD/BOLD B73 .... 76 D2
Boldmere Golf Club
 SCFLD/BOLD B73 .... 61 C5
Boldmere J & I School
 SCFLD/BOLD B73 .... 76 D2
Boldmere St Michaels FC
 SCFLD/BOLD B73 .... 76 D3
Bordesley Green Girls School
 WASH/WDE B8 .... 128 C1
Bordesley Green Primary
 School BORD B9 .... 129 E2
Bordesley Green Trading
 Estate WASH/WDE B8 .... 128 B1
Borough Cemetery
 DUDS DY2 .... 102 B1
Bosworth Wood Primary
 School CBROM B36 .... 95 H5
Boulton Industrial Centre
 HDSW B21 .... 108 B4
The Boundary Hotel
 WSL WS1 .... 57 H1
Boundary Industrial Estate
 WOLVN WV10 .... 12 C2
Bournville Infant School
 BVILLE B30 .... 159 G3
Bournville Junior School
 BVILLE B30 .... 159 G3
Bournville College of Further
 Education SLYOAK B29 .... 159 E3
Bournville School of
 Art & Craft BVILLE B30 .... 159 G3
Bournville School &
 Sixth Form Centre
 NFLD/LBR B31 .... 159 E4

Bowlplex LDYWD/EDGR B16 .... 126 A3
Brackendale Shopping Centre
 SHHTH WV12 .... 40 B1
Bradford Street Clinic WSL WS1 .. 4 D5
Braidwood School for
 Deaf Children
 ERDW/GRVHL B23 .... 75 H5
Bramford Primary School
 BILS/COS WV14 .... 68 A5
Brandhall Clinic
 LGLYGN/QTN B68 .... 123 F4
Brandhall Golf Club
 LGLYGN/QTN B68 .... 123 E2
Brandhall Primary School
 LGLYGN/QTN B68 .... 123 F3
Brandon Way Industrial Estate
 WBROM B70 .... 86 D3
Brandwood End Cemetery
 ALE/KHTH/YWD B14 .... 178 A1
Brasshouse Infant School
 SMTHWK B66 .... 106 C2
Brasshouse Language Centre
 SMTHWK B66 .... 106 C2
Brays Special School
 LGN/SDN/BHAMAIR B26 .... 147 G1
Breener Industrial Estate
 BRLYHL DY5 .... 118 D3
Brickhouse J & I School
 BLKHTH/ROWR B65 .... 121 G1
Bridge Industrial Estate
 SOLH B91 .... 165 E2
Bridge Special School
 ERDW/GRVHL B23 .... 92 C2
Bridge Street Industrial Estate
 DARL/WED WS10 .... 70 D2
The Bridge Trading Estate
 SMTHWK B66 .... 106 D2
Brierley Hill Cemetery
 BRLYHL DY5 .... 118 D2
The Brierley Hill Health Centre
 BRLYHL DY5 .... 119 F1
Brierley Hill Primary School
 BRLYHL DY5 .... 119 F2
The Brierley Trading Estate
 BRLYHL DY5 .... 119 G1
Brierly Hill Leisure Centre
 BRLYHL DY5 .... 119 G2
The Brier Special School
 BRLYHL DY5 .... 119 G1
Brindley Place CBHAMW B1 .... 2 C6
Brinston Industrial Estate
 WSLW WS2 .... 4 A6
Bristnall Hall High School
 LGLYGN/QTN B68 .... 123 H1
Broadcott Industrial Estate
 CDYHTH B64 .... 121 G3
Broadfield House Glass Museum
 KGSWFD DY6 .... 99 H4
Broadmeadow J & I School
 BVILLE B30 .... 177 F3
Broadwalk Retail Park
 WSL WS1 .... 56 D2
Broadway Medical Centre
 WSL WS1 .... 57 F2
Broadway Plaza
 LDYWD/EDGR B16 .... 126 A3
Broadway School
 BFLD/HDSWWD B20 .... 91 E4
Broadwell Industrial Estate
 OLDBY B69 .... 87 E5
Broadwyn Trading Estate
 CDYHTH B64 .... 121 G3
Brockmoor Industrial Estate
 KGSWFD DY6 .... 118 C1
Brockmoor Primary School
 BRLYHL DY5 .... 119 E1
Bromford Road Industrial
 Estate OLDBY B69 .... 87 E5
Bromley Hills Primary School
 KGSWFD DY6 .... 100 B5
Bromley Primary School
 BRLYHL DY5 .... 100 D4
Brookfields Primary School
 WSNGN B18 .... 2 A1
Brooklands Hospital
 CHWD/FDBR/MGN B37 .... 132 B4
The Brook Primary School
 STRBR DY8 .... 118 B3
Brookside Industrial Estate
 DARL/WED WS10 .... 56 B5
Brook Street Business Centre
 ERDW/GRVHL B23 .... 69 E5
Brookvale Primary School
 ERDW/GRVHL B23 .... 91 H2
Brookvale Trading Estate
 AST/WIT B6 .... 91 G3
Brownhills Business Park
 BRWNH WS8 .... 19 F2
Brownhills Clinic BRWNH WS8 ...... 9 F5
Brownhills Comprehensive
 School BRWNH WS8 .... 9 F3
Brownhills West JMI School
 BRWNH WS8 .... 8 C2
Brownhills West Station
 BRWNH WS8 .... 8 C1
Browning Street Industrial
 Estate LDYWD/EDGR B16 .... 2 A6
Brownmead Primary School
 BKDE/SHDE B34 .... 112 D3
Brunswick Park Trading Estate
 DARL/WED WS10 .... 56 A4
Brymill Industrial Estate
 TPTN/OCK DY4 .... 69 E4
BSA Business Park SPARK B11 .... 145 F1
BT Tower CBHAMNW B3 .... 2 E3
Bullring Shopping Centre
 DIG/EDG B5 .... 3 H6
Bull Ring Trading Estate
 BHTH/HG B12 .... 3 K7
Bull Street Trading Estate
 BRLYHL DY5 .... 118 D3
Burman Infant School
 SHLY B90 .... 180 A3
Burnt Tree Industrial Estate
 TPTN/OCK DY4 .... 85 H4
Burnt Tree J & I School
 OLDBY B69 .... 85 G4
Burton Industrial Estate
 CDYHTH B64 .... 121 E4

Bushbury Baths
 WOLVN WV10 .... 23 C1
Bushbury Cemetery
 WOLVN WV10 .... 13 F5
Bushbury Health Centre
 WOLVN WV10 .... 13 E5
Bushbury Hill J & I School
 WOLVN WV10 .... 23 H1
Busill Jones JMI School
 BLOX/PEL WS3 .... 26 D2
The Business Centre
 SPARK B11 .... 145 H1
Butts JMI School
 RUSH/SHEL WS4 .... 5 F1
Cadbury College
 HWK/WKHTH B38 .... 176 D4
Cadbury World BVILLE B30 .... 159 H3
Calderfields Golf Club &
 Academy RUSH/SHEL WS4 .... 43 E3
Caldmore JMI School WSL WS1 ...... 4 E7
Caldmore Medical Centre
 WSL WS1 .... 4 E7
Calthorpe Special School
 BHTH/HG B12 .... 127 G4
Cambrian Wharf CBHAMW B1 .... 2 C5
Cambridge Tutorial College
 SMHTH B10 .... 128 B4
Campanile Hotel
 VAUX/NECH B7 .... 109 F4
Camp Hill Old Edwardians
 RFC SHLY B90 .... 180 B2
Canal Side Industrial Estate
 BRLYHL DY5 .... 118 D3
Canning Wharf CBHAMNW B3 .... 2 D4
Cannon Business Park
 BILS/COS WV14 .... 68 C2
Canterbury Cross
 Primary NC School
 BFLD/HDSWWD B20 .... 90 D4
Cape Hill Medical Centre
 SMTHWK B66 .... 107 E5
Cape Primary School
 SMTHWK B66 .... 107 E5
Cardinal Wiseman
 Catholic School KGSTG B44 ...... 75 F1
Carlton Business Centre
 VAUX/NECH B7 .... 110 A4
Carlyle Business Park
 WBROM B70 .... 86 D1
Carters Green Medical Centre
 WBROM B70 .... 87 G2
Caslon Primary School
 HALE B63 .... 137 F5
Castle Bromwich Business
 Park CVALE B35 .... 94 B5
Castle Bromwich CC
 CBROM B36 .... 113 E1
Castle Bromwich Hall
 Gardens CBROM B36 .... 112 C1
Castle Bromwich Infant
 School CBROM B36 .... 113 C1
Castle Bromwich Junior
 School CBROM B36 .... 113 F2
Castlecroft J & I School
 BDMR/CCFT WV3 .... 35 F4
Castiefort JMI School
 ALDR WS9 .... 19 H4
Castle High School
 DUDN DY1 .... 84 B4
The Castle Pool &
 Adventure Play Centre
 CVALE B35 .... 95 E4
Castle Special School
 BLOX/PEL WS3 .... 27 F3
Castle Vale Health Centre
 CVALE B35 .... 94 B3
Castle Vale Industrial Estate
 WALM/CURD B76 .... 94 C1
Castle Vale Shopping Centre
 CVALE B35 .... 94 B3
Castle View Industrial Estate
 TPTN/OCK DY4 .... 85 F3
Causeway Green
 Primary School
 LGLYGN/QTN B68 .... 122 D1
C&C Site RMSLY B62 .... 172 A1
Cemetery of St Joseph
 VAUX/NECH B7 .... 109 H2
Central Business Park
 STETCH B33 .... 131 F5
Central Clinic DUDS DY2 .... 84 D5
Central Hall CBHAMNW B3 .... 3 H3
Central Industrial Estate
 BKHL/PFLD WV2 .... 52 D1
Central Park Industrial Estate
 TPTN/OCK DY4 .... 121 E1
Central Trading Estate
 KGSWFD DY6 .... 82 B5
Centre Link Industrial Estate
 VAUX/NECH B7 .... 109 H3
Century Industrial Estate
 KGSTG B44 .... 60 A5
Chad Vale Primary School
 EDG B15 .... 125 F5
Chamber of Commerce
 WSL WS1 .... 5 G2
Chamber of Commerce &
 Industry BDMR/CCFT WV3 .... 6 A3
Chancel Industrial Estate
 DARL/WED WS10 .... 55 F5
 KGSWFD DY6 .... 81 H5
 KGSWFD DY6 .... 100 A1
 WLNHL WV13 .... 39 H5
 WOLV WV1 .... 37 H4
Chandos Primary School
 DIG/EDG B5 .... 127 E5
Chapel Fields Junior School
 HIA/OLT B92 .... 147 F4
Chapel Street Industrial Estate
 DUDS DY2 .... 102 D5
Charlemont Primary School
 HHTH/SAND B71 .... 72 A3
Charles Street Industrial Estate
 TPTN/OCK DY4 .... 86 C1
Charnwood Business Park
 BILS/COS WV14 .... 53 G3

Charterfield Shopping Centre
 KGSWFD DY6 .... 99 F1
Chase Watersports Centre
 BRWNH WS8 .... 8 C1
Cheapside Industrial Estate
 BHTH/HG B12 .... 127 F3
Chelmsley Wood Industrial
 Estate
 CHWD/FDBR/MGN B37 .... 114 A4
Chelmsley Wood Shopping
 Centre
 CHWD/FDBR/MGN B37 .... 132 B2
Chelsea Trading Estate
 AST/WIT B6 .... 109 G3
Cherry Oak Special School
 SLYOAK B29 .... 142 B5
Cherry Orchard Primary
 School BFLD/HDSWWD B20 .... 90 A3
Cherry Trees Special School
 WMBN WV5 .... 64 D5
Cherrywood Industrial Estate
 WASH/WDE B8 .... 128 B1
Cheston Industrial Estate
 AST/WIT B6 .... 109 H2
Cheswick Green Primary
 School SHLY B90 .... 195 E3
Chilcote Primary School
 HLGN/YWD B28 .... 179 H1
Chillington Works Industrial
 Estate WOLV WV1 .... 37 H4
The Chiropody Surgery
 YDLY DY5 .... 129 H3
Chivenor Primary School
 CVALE B35 .... 94 C4
Christ Church CE Infant School
 DUNHL/THL/PER WV6 .... 36 D1
Christ Church CE Junior School
 DUNHL/THL/PER WV6 .... 35 G1
Christ Church CE
 Primary School
 BLOX/PEL WS3 .... 27 H3
 OLDBY B69 .... 105 E1
 SPARK B11 .... 127 H5
Christ Church Infant School
 DUNHL/THL/PER WV6 .... 35 E2
Christ Church Primary School
 BILS/COS WV14 .... 68 D2
Christ the King RC
 Primary School KGSTG B44 .... 75 G2
Chuckery Primary School
 WSL WS1 .... 5 H4
Churchbridge Industrial Estate
 OLDBY B69 .... 104 D3
Churchfield Industrial Estate
 DUDS DY2 .... 102 C1
Churchill & Blakedown
 Golf Club KIDD DY10 .... 168 A3
Churchill Precinct DUDN DY1 .... 84 D5
Church Lane Health Centre
 STETCH B33 .... 130 B1
Church Lane Industrial Estate
 HHTH/SAND B71 .... 71 G5
Church of Ascension CE
 Primary School
 KGSWFD DY6 .... 99 F1
Cineworld SOLH B91 .... 182 A2
City College ALGN B27 .... 146 C4
City College Birmingham
 BKDE/SHDE B34 .... 113 F3
 HDSW B21 .... 108 A2
 HRBN B17 .... 142 B1
 STETCH B33 .... 130 D4
City Hospital WSNGN B18 .... 107 H5
City of Wolverhampton College
 BKHL/PFLD WV2 .... 7 C5
City Plaza Shopping Centre
 CBHAM B2 .... 3 F5
City Road Primary School
 LDYWD/EDGR B16 .... 125 F1
The City Technology College
 CHWD/FDBR/MGN B37 .... 114 A5
City Trading Estate
 LDYWD/EDGR B16 .... 125 H1
Claregate Primary School
 DUNHL/THL/PER WV6 .... 22 B3
Clarendon Medical Centre
 SCFLD/BOLD B73 .... 77 E2
Clearwater Industrial Estate
 BKHL/PFLD WV2 .... 52 D1
Clent Hills HAG/WOL DY9 .... 154 A5
Clent Hills Country Park (NT)
 HAG/WOL DY9 .... 171 E1
Clent Parochial First School
 HAG/WOL DY9 .... 170 D3
Cleton Street Business Park
 TPTN/OCK DY4 .... 85 H3
Clifton Infant School
 BHTH/HG B12 .... 144 C2
Clifton Junior School
 BHTH/HG B12 .... 144 C2
Clifton Road Industrial Estate
 BHTH/HG B12 .... 144 B2
Clothier Street Primary School
 WLNHL WV13 .... 39 G2
CMT Industrial Estate
 OLDBY B69 .... 105 E1
Coalpool Clinic BLOX/PEL WS3 ... 28 B4
Coal Pool Lane Cemetery
 BLOX/PEL WS3 .... 42 B1
Cobham Business Centre
 WASH/WDE B8 .... 128 B1
Cockshut Hill Technology
 College
 LGN/SDN/BHAMAIR B26 .... 130 C4
Cocks Moors Woods
 Leisure Centre
 ALE/KHTH/YWD B14 .... 178 B1
Codsall Cemetery
 CDSL WV8 .... 10 B2
Codsall Clinic CDSL WV8 .... 10 C4
Codsall Middle School
 CDSL WV8 .... 10 C4
Cofton Medical Centre
 NFLD/LBR B31 .... 189 G1
Cofton Primary School
 NFLD/LBR B31 .... 189 G2
Coldland Colts FC
 SOLH B91 .... 165 H4
Colebourne Primary School
 BKDE/SHDE B34 .... 112 A4

Coleshill Cemetery *CSHL/WTROR* B46 ... 115 G3
Coleshill CE Primary School *CSHL/WTROR* B46 ... 115 F3
Coleshill Clinic *CSHL/WTROR* B46 ... 115 G3
Coleshill Heath Primary School *CHWD/FDBR/MGN* B37 ... 132 C3
Coleshill Hotel *CSHL/WTROR* B46 ... 115 G3
Coleshill Industrial Estate *CSHL/WTROR* B46 ... 97 F4
Coleshill Leisure Centre *CSHL/WTROR* B46 ... 115 F3
Coleshill School *CSHL/WTROR* B46 ... 133 G1
Coleshill Town FC *CSHL/WTROR* B46 ... 133 G1
The College High School *KGSTG* B44 ... 75 G3
College of Continuing Education *WSL* WS1 ... 57 E1
Colley Lane Health Clinic *HALE* B63 ... 137 G1
Colley Lane Primary School *HALE* B63 ... 137 F1
Collingwood Primary School *WOLVN* WV10 ... 13 E5
Colmers Farm J & I School *RBRY* B45 ... 174 B5
Colmers Farm Secondary School *RBRY* B45 ... 174 B5
Colmore J & I School *ALE/KHTH/YWD* B14 ... 160 D3
Colonial Industrial Park *CDYHTH* B64 ... 120 C5
Colton Hills School *ETTPK/GDPK/PENN* WV4 ... 51 H4
Comfort Inn *LDYWD/EDGR* B16 ... 125 F3
Community High School *CDSL* WV8 ... 10 C3
Community Leisure Centre *TPTN/OCK* DY4 ... 68 D5
Coneygre Industrial Estate *TPTN/OCK* DY4 ... 85 F4
Connect Business Park *WASH/WDE* B8 ... 128 A2
Conway Primary School *SPARK* B11 ... 144 D1
Cookley Wharf Industrial Estate *BRLYHL* DY5 ... 118 C1
Cooper & Jordan CE J & I School *ALDR* WS9 ... 30 C4
Copperfield House Hotel *SLYOAK* B29 ... 143 E4
Coppice High Community School *WNSFLD* WV11 ... 25 H2
Coppice Junior School *HIA/OLT* B92 ... 165 G3
Coppice Primary School *HLYWD* B47 ... 192 C2
MGN/WHC B75 ... 47 C4
Coppice Side Industrial Estate *BRWNH* WS8 ... 8 D5
Copt Heath Golf Club *DOR/KN* B93 ... 185 E5
Copthorne Hotel *BRLYHL* DY5 ... 101 G5
BCHAMNW B3 ... 2 D5
Corbett Hospital *STRBR* DY8 ... 118 C5
Corbett Industrial Estate *DUDS* DY2 ... 102 C3
Corngreaves Hall Golf Club *CDYHTH* B64 ... 121 F4
Corngreaves J & I School *CDYHTH* B64 ... 120 D3
Corngreaves Trading Estate *CDYHTH* B64 ... 120 D5
Cornwall Industrial Estate *SMTHWK* B66 ... 107 E2
WASH/WDE B8 ... 110 A5
Cornwall Road Industrial Estate *SMTHWK* B66 ... 107 E2
Corpus Christi RC Primary School *STECH* B33 ... 129 H2
WNSFLD WV11 ... 25 G2
Corus Hotel Solihull *SHLY* B90 ... 195 E1
Coseley Medical Centre *BILS/COS* WV14 ... 68 C3
The Coseley School *BILS/COS* WV14 ... 68 B2
Coseley Swimming Pool *BILS/COS* WV14 ... 68 C3
Cotteridge Primary School *BVILLE* B30 ... 160 A5
Cotterbrooke Infant School *ACGN* B27 ... 146 D3
Cottesbrooke Infant School *ACGN* B27 ... 146 D3
Cottesbrooke Junior School *ACGN* B27 ... 146 C3
Cotwall End Primary School *SEDG* DY3 ... 67 E4
County Bridge Primary School *WLNHL* WV13 ... 40 C4
Courtfarm Primary School *ERDW/GRVHL* B23 ... 76 C5
Crabtree Clinic *CHWD/FDBR/MGN* B37 ... 131 H2
Cradley Cemetery *HALE* B63 ... 120 C5
Cradley CE Primary School *HALE* B63 ... 120 C5
Cradley Heath Community Recreation Centre *DUDS* DY2 ... 121 E2
Cradley High School *HALE* B63 ... 137 F1
Cradley Town FC *HALE* B63 ... 137 G3
Craig Croft Child Health Clinic *CHWD/FDBR/MGN* B37 ... 132 C2
Craig Croft Medical Centre *CHWD/FDBR/MGN* B37 ... 132 C2
Cranmore Industrial Estate *SHLY* B90 ... 181 E5
Cranmore Infant School *SOLH* B91 ... 181 E4
Crescent Industrial Estate *DUDS* DY2 ... 102 B2
Crescent Theatre *LDYWD/EDGR* B16 ... 2 B6

Crescent Works Industrial Park *DARL/WED* WS10 ... 40 B4
Crestwood Park Primary School *KGSWFD* DY6 ... 100 C4
The Crestwood Secondary School *KGSWFD* DY6 ... 100 B4
Crocketts Lane Primary School *SMTHWK* B66 ... 106 C4
Croft Foundry Industrial Estate *WLNHL* WV13 ... 39 G3
Croft Industrial Estate *CHWD/FDBR/MGN* B37 ... 132 B2
Croft Street JMI School *WSLW* WS2 ... 41 H1
Cromwell Primary School *VAUX/NECH* B7 ... 109 G3
Cronehill Primary School *WBROM* B70 ... 87 G2
Cronehills Health Centre *WBROM* B70 ... 87 H3
Crossings Industrial Estate *BLOX/PEL* WS3 ... 27 E2
Cross Quays Business Park *OLDBY* B69 ... 86 A4
Cross Street Health Centre *DUDN* DY1 ... 84 C5
Crossways Shopping Centre *WOLVN* WV10 ... 38 A2
Crown Wharf Shopping Centre *WSLW* WS2 ... 4 C2
Crown Wharf Shopping Park *WSLW* WS2 ... 41 G1
Crystal Leisure Centre *STRBR* DY8 ... 135 F2
Culwell Industrial Park *WOLVN* WV10 ... 7 J2
Culwell Trading Estate *WOLVN* WV10 ... 37 H1
Dadsford Bridge Industrial Estate *STRBR* DY8 ... 118 A2
Dame Elizabeth Cadbury School *BVILLE* B30 ... 159 G3
Dame Ellen Pinsent School *HRBN* B17 ... 124 D2
Damson Wood Infant School *HIA/OLT* B92 ... 165 F3
Danescourt Crematorium & Cemetery *DUNHL/THL/PER* WV6 ... 21 F4
Danesmore Park Primary School *WNSFLD* WV11 ... 25 F1
Darlaston Central Trading Estate *DARL/WED* WS10 ... 55 G1
Darlaston Clinic *DARL/WED* WS10 ... 55 F2
Darlaston Community School *DARL/WED* WS10 ... 54 D2
Darlaston FC *DARL/WED* WS10 ... 54 D3
Darlaston Road Industrial Estate *DARL/WED* WS10 ... 55 F3
Dartmouth Golf Club *HHTH/SAND* B71 ... 72 A5
Dartmouth High School *GTB/HAM* B43 ... 58 B5
David Lloyd Birmingham *RUSH/SHEL* WS4 ... 60 A5
Daw End School *RUSH/SHEL* WS4 ... 28 D4
Dawley Brook Primary School *KGSWFD* DY6 ... 99 G2
Dawley Trading Estate *KGSWFD* DY6 ... 99 H1
Daylesford Infant School *HIA/OLT* B92 ... 147 G4
Days Inn *SPARK* B11 ... 128 A5
Deanery CE Primary School *WALM/CURD* B76 ... 78 B3
Deansfield High School *WOLV* WV1 ... 38 C3
Deeleys Industrial Estate *WSLW* WS2 ... 27 F4
Deepdale Industrial Estate *DUDN* DY1 ... 83 G3
The Dell Stadium *BRLYHL* DY5 ... 100 D4
Delph Road Industrial Estate *BRLYHL* DY5 ... 119 E3
Delph Road Industrial Park *BRLYHL* DY5 ... 119 F3
Delta Trading Estate *BKHL/PFLD* WV2 ... 37 H5
Delves J & I School *DSYBK/YTR* WS5 ... 57 G3
Dental Health Centre *KGSTG* B44 ... 75 F1
Dental Hospital *CBHAMNE* B4 ... 3 G2
Department of Art (University of Central England) *CBHAMNW* B3 ... 2 E4
Devonshire J & I School *SMTHWKW* B67 ... 106 A4
Deykin Avenue J & I School *AST/WIT* B6 ... 91 G4
D'Eyncourt Primary School *WOLVN* WV10 ... 24 B3
Diana Princess of Wales Hospital (for Children) *CBHAMNE* B4 ... 3 G3
Dickens Heath Primary School *SHLY* B90 ... 193 H2
Digbeth Coach Station *DIG/EDG* B5 ... 3 J7
Dingle Primary School *KGSWFD* DY6 ... 100 C5
Dock Lane Industrial Estate *DUDN* DY1 ... 84 B5
Dock Meadow Drive Industrial Estate *ETTPK/GDPK/PENN* WV4 ... 53 E4
Doranda Way Industrial Park *HHTH/SAND* B71 ... 88 B5
Dormston Secondary School *SEDG* DY3 ... 67 G3
Dormston Trading Estate *DUDN* DY1 ... 83 H2
Dorothy Pattison Hospital *WSLW* WS2 ... 41 F4
Dorothy Purcell Junior School *BILS/COS* WV14 ... 54 D5
Dorridge CC *DOR/KN* B93 ... 198 C2

Dorridge J & I School *DOR/KN* B93 ... 197 E5
Dorrington Primary School *PBAR/PBCH* B42 ... 74 A5
Doulton Trading Estate *BLKHTH/ROWR* B65 ... 103 F5
Dovecote J & I School *DUDN* DY1 ... 22 A1
The Dovecote Surgery *LGLYGN/QTN* B68 ... 123 H5
Downing Close Health Clinic *DOR/KN* B93 ... 197 E4
Dreamwell Industrial Estate *SPARK* B11 ... 145 H1
Droicon Industrial Park *BLKHTH/ROWR* B65 ... 103 H5
Droicon Trading Estate *BLKHTH/ROWR* B65 ... 103 H4
Druids Heath Golf Club *ALDR* WS9 ... 30 C2
Duddeston Mill Trading Estate *WASH/WDE* B8 ... 110 A5
Dudley Castle & Zoological Gardens *DUDN* DY1 ... 84 D4
Dudley Central Trading Estate *DUDN* DY1 ... 102 B1
Dudley College *BRLYHL* DY5 ... 119 E1
DUDN DY1 ... 84 B5
Dudley College (Mons Hill Campus) *DUDN* DY1 ... 84 B2
Dudley Golf Club *BLKHTH/ROWR* B65 ... 103 G3
Dudley Kingswinford RFC *KGSWFD* DY6 ... 99 E2
Dudley Leisure Centre *DUDN* DY1 ... 84 B5
Dudley Museum & Art Gallery *DUDN* DY1 ... 84 C5
Dudley Town Hall *DUDN* DY1 ... 84 C4
Dudley Water Sports Centre *DUDS* DY2 ... 120 B1
Dudley Wood Primary School *DUDS* DY2 ... 120 C2
Dunstall Hill Industrial Estate *DUNHL/THL/PER* WV6 ... 23 E5
Dunstall Hill Primary School *DUNHL/THL/PER* WV6 ... 37 E1
Dunton Trading Estate *VAUX/NECH* B7 ... 110 B2
Durberville Road Industrial Estate *BKHL/PFLD* WV2 ... 52 D1
Eagle Industrial Estate *TPTN/OCK* DY4 ... 70 B4
Eagle Trading Estate *HALE* B63 ... 138 C3
Earls High School *HALE* B63 ... 138 D3
Eastbourne House School *ACGN* B27 ... 146 C3
Eastfield Primary School *WOLV* WV1 ... 37 H3
East Park J & I School *WOLV* WV1 ... 38 B5
East Park Trading Estate *BKHL/PFLD* WV2 ... 37 H5
Eaton Wood Medical Centre *ERDE/BCHGN* B24 ... 93 H5
Ebrook Adult Training Centre *CSCFLD/WYGN* B72 ... 62 D5
Eclipse Industrial Estate *TPTN/OCK* DY4 ... 85 E1
Eclipse Trading Estate *TPTN/OCK* DY4 ... 85 E1
Edgar Stammers Primary School *BLOX/PEL* WS3 ... 28 B3
Edgbaston Golf Club *EDG* B15 ... 143 F1
Edgbaston Health Clinic *EDG* B15 ... 142 C2
SOLH B91 ... 164 B4
Edgbaston High School for Girls & Preparatory Department *EDG* B15 ... 125 H5
Edgbaston Shopping Centre *LDYWD/EDGR* B16 ... 126 A4
Edgewood Road Clinic *RBRY* B45 ... 188 B2
Edward Street Hospital *WBROM* B70 ... 87 G3
Electra Park Industrial Estate *AST/WIT* B6 ... 91 H5
Electric Cinema *DIG/EDG* B5 ... 3 F6
The Ellowes Hall School *DUDS* DY2 ... 83 E1
Elmdon Trading Estate *CHWD/FDBR/MGN* B37 ... 149 G1
Elmore Green JMI School *BLOX/PEL* WS3 ... 27 E1
Elms Farm Primary School *STECH* B33 ... 131 E5
Elms Health Centre *HALE* B63 ... 137 F1
Elm Terrace Clinic *OLDBY* B69 ... 85 H5
Elston Hall Primary School *WOLVN* WV10 ... 12 D5
Embassy Industrial Estate *HAG/WOL* DY9 ... 136 D2
Emmanuel School *WSL* WS1 ... 4 E6
Empire Industrial Park *ALDR* WS9 ... 29 H2
English Martyrs RC Primary School *SPARK* B11 ... 145 E3
Enterprise Trading Estate *BRLYHL* DY5 ... 119 H1
Erdington Hall Primary School *ERDE/BCHGN* B24 ... 92 D4
Erdington Industrial Estate *ERDW/GRVHL* B23 ... 94 B3
Erdington Medical Centre *ERDW/GRVHL* B23 ... 93 E2
Erdington Pool & Turkish Suite *ERDW/GRVHL* B23 ... 93 G2
Essington Light Industrial Estate *WNSFLD* WV11 ... 14 D3
Ettingshall Primary School *BKHL/PFLD* WV2 ... 53 F1
Euro Business Park *OLDBY* B69 ... 86 C5
European Business Park *OLDBY* B69 ... 104 C2
Eversfield Preparatory School *SOLH* B91 ... 182 A1

Express by Holiday Inn *HLGN/YWD* B28 ... 163 E4
Expressway Industrial Estate *AST/WIT* B6 ... 109 E3
Eye Infirmary *BDMR/CCFT* WV3 ... 6 B4
Fairfax School *MGN/WHC* B75 ... 63 F3
Fairfield First School *BRGRVW* B61 ... 185 H5
Fairfield Villa FC *BRGRVW* B61 ... 185 H5
Fairhaven Primary School *STRBR* DY8 ... 117 H1
Fairway Primary School *NFLD/LBR* B31 ... 176 B3
Falcon Lodge Clinic *MGN/WHC* B75 ... 63 G3
Fallings Heath Cemetery *DARL/WED* WS10 ... 55 H5
Fallings Park Industrial Estate *WOLVN* WV10 ... 23 H5
Fallings Park Primary School *WOLVN* WV10 ... 24 A3
Fazeley Industrial Estate ... 3 K5
Featherstone Primary School *ERDW/GRVHL* B23 ... 92 C2
Feldon Lane Clinic *RMSLY* B62 ... 122 C5
Fernbank Medical Centre *WASH/WDE* B8 ... 111 E5
Ferndale Primary School *GTB/HAM* B43 ... 73 G3
Field Road Cemetery *BLOX/PEL* WS3 ... 27 G1
Field Road Industrial Estate *BLOX/PEL* WS3 ... 27 G2
Firs Primary School *CBROM* B36 ... 112 A1
Fir Tree Primary School *DSYBK/YTR* WS5 ... 57 G4
Five Ways Shopping Centre *EDG* B15 ... 126 B3
The Foot Clinic *CBHAMNW* B3 ... 2 E4
Fordhouse Road Industrial Estate *WOLVN* WV10 ... 23 E2
Fordhouses CC *WOLVN* WV10 ... 12 D3
Forest Oak School *CBROM* B36 ... 95 G5
Forge Trading Estate *RMSLY* B62 ... 139 E2
Formans Trading Estate *SPARK* B11 ... 145 F4
Fort Industrial Park *CVALE* B35 ... 94 B5
The Fort Shopping Park *ERDE/BCHGN* B24 ... 94 B5
Foundry Primary School *WSNGN* B18 ... 107 F3
Fountain Court Hotel *LDYWD/EDGR* B16 ... 125 E3
Four Dwellings High School *RIDG/WDGT* B32 ... 140 B2
Four Dwellings Infant School *RIDG/WDGT* B32 ... 140 B2
Four Oaks J & I School *FOAKS/STRLY* B74 ... 46 C1
Four Oaks Medical Centre *MGN/WHC* B75 ... 47 F3
Four Oaks Saints CC *FOAKS/STRLY* B74 ... 32 C5
Four Seasons Art Gallery *ERDE/BCHGN* B24 ... 93 E1
Fox & Goose Shopping Centre *WASH/WDE* B8 ... 111 G3
The Fox Hollies Leisure Centre *HLGN/YWD* B28 ... 163 E1
Fox Hollies Special School *ACGN* B27 ... 163 E1
Foxmill Estate *SPARK* B11 ... 145 F5
Foxyards Primary School *TPTN/OCK* DY4 ... 84 C1
Frank P Harrison Comprehensive School *SHHTH* WV12 ... 26 D3
Frankley Community High School *RBRY* B45 ... 173 H3
Frankley Health Centre *RBRY* B45 ... 174 A4
Frankley Industrial Park *RBRY* B45 ... 174 B4
Friar Park Clinic *DARL/WED* WS10 ... 56 D5
Frogmill Junior School *RBRY* B45 ... 174 B3
Gainsborough Trading Estate *STRBR* DY8 ... 135 H3
Garretts Green Trading Estate *STECH* B33 ... 131 E3
Gas Street Basin *CBHAMW* B1 ... 2 C6
Gatehouse Trading Estate *BRWNH* WS8 ... 9 G3
Gate Medical Centre *BDMR/CCFT* WV3 ... 6 A4
Gay Hill Golf Club *HLYWD* B47 ... 178 C5
George Auden School ... 158 B5
George Betts Primary School *SMTHWK* B66 ... 105 G2
George Dixon School & Sixth Form *HRBN* B17 ... 125 G2
George Fentham Endowed Primary School *HIA/OLT* B92 ... 167 G4
George Salter High School *WBROM* B70 ... 87 E2
Gibbons Industrial Park *KGSWFD* DY6 ... 100 C3
The Gifford RC Primary School *DUNHL/THL/PER* WV6 ... 22 B5
Gig Mill Primary School *STRBR* DY8 ... 135 E4
Gilbertstone Primary School *LGN/SDN/BHAMAIR* B26 ... 146 D2
Gis Davies Industrial Estate *HALE* B63 ... 137 E1
Glebefields Health Centre *TPTN/OCK* DY4 ... 69 G3
Glebe Fields Primary School *TPTN/OCK* DY4 ... 69 G2
Glenmead J & I School *KGSTG* B44 ... 74 D3
Glynne Primary School *KGSWFD* DY6 ... 99 G5

Golden Hillock School *SPARK* B11 ... 145 F1
Goldtel Industrial Estate *ETTPK/GDPK/PENN* WV4 ... 53 E3
Goldthorne Industrial Estate *BKHL/PFLD* WV2 ... 52 A2
Goldthorn Park Primary School *ETTPK/GDPK/PENN* WV4 ... 52 B5
Good Hope Hospital *MGN/WHC* B75 ... 62 D2
Gornal Wood Cemetery *SEDG* DY3 ... 83 E3
Gornal Wood Crematorium *SEDG* DY3 ... 82 D5
Goscote Hospital *BLOX/PEL* WS3 ... 28 B2
Goscote Industrial Estate *BLOX/PEL* WS3 ... 28 A1
Gossey Lane J & I School *STETCH* B33 ... 131 E2
Gracechurch Shopping Centre *CSCFLD/WYGN* B72 ... 62 B3
Grace Mary Primary School *OLDBY* B69 ... 104 A2
Graiseley Primary School *BKHL/PFLD* WV2 ... 37 E5
Granada Industrial Estate *OLDBY* B69 ... 104 D3
Granby Business Park *STETCH* B33 ... 131 F3
Grand Theatre *WOLV* WV1 ... 7 G4
The Grange Arts & Media Centre *WSL* WS1 ... 4 E2
The Grange Playhouse *WSL* WS1 ... 42 D4
The Grange School *HAG/WOL* DY9 ... 136 B3
Gravel Hill Surgery *WMBS* WV5 ... 65 F5
Gravelly Industrial Park *ERDE/BCHGN* B24 ... 110 C1
Grazebrook Industrial Estate *DUDS* DY2 ... 102 A3
Grazebrook Industrial Park *DUDS* DY2 ... 102 B3
Great Barr Business Park *PBAR/PBCH* B42 ... 90 A1
Great Barr Golf Club *GTB/HAM* B43 ... 58 D4
Great Barr Hotel & Conference Centre *GTB/HAM* B43 ... 72 D2
Great Bridge Industrial Estate *TPTN/OCK* DY4 ... 70 A4
Great Bridge Primary School *TPTN/OCK* DY4 ... 70 A5
Great Western Industrial Estate *WSNGN* B18 ... 107 G3
Green Acres Primary School *BILS/COS* WV14 ... 54 B2
Greenfield Primary School *RUSH/SHEL* WS4 ... 29 E2
STRBR DY8 ... 135 F2
Greenfield Surgery *STRBR* DY8 ... 135 F2
Greenholm J & I School *KGSTG* B44 ... 75 E4
Green Lane Industrial Estate *BORD* B9 ... 128 C2
Green Meadow Primary School *SLYOAK* B29 ... 158 B3
Green Rock J & I School *BLOX/PEL* WS3 ... 28 A1
Greet Primary School *SPARK* B11 ... 145 E3
Greets Green Road Industrial Estate *WBROM* B70 ... 86 D2
Gregston Industrial Estate *OLDBY* B69 ... 105 F1
Grendon Primary School *ALE/KHTH/YWD* B14 ... 178 C2
Grestone Primary School *BFLD/HDSWWD* B20 ... 89 G2
Greswold Primary School *SOLH* B91 ... 164 D4
Griffin Business Park *CHWD/FDBR/MGN* B37 ... 132 C1
Griffin Industrial Estate *BLKHTH/ROWR* B65 ... 122 D1
Griffins Brook Medical Centre *SLYOAK* B29 ... 159 E3
Grimstock Country House Hotel *CSHL/WTROR* B46 ... 97 E5
Grosvenor Shopping Centre *NFLD/LBR* B31 ... 175 G1
Grove Medical Centre *BKHL/PFLD* WV2 ... 37 G5
Grove Primary School *BKHL/PFLD* WV2 ... 52 C1
Grove School *HDSW* B21 ... 107 H1
Grove Vale Primary School *GTB/HAM* B43 ... 73 F2
Guardian Angels RC Primary School *BKDE/SHDE* B34 ... 113 F3
Guest Hospital *DUDN* DY1 ... 85 E5
Gun Barrel Industrial Centre *CDYHTH* B64 ... 138 C1
Gums Village Primary School *WBROM* B70 ... 87 E3
Gunter Primary School *ERDE/BCHGN* B24 ... 94 A2
Gupta Trading Estate *OLDBY* B69 ... 86 D5
Guru Nanak Sikh Temple *BDMR/CCFT* WV3 ... 36 D5
Guy Motors Industrial Estate *WOLVN* WV10 ... 23 G5
GWS Industrial Estate *DARL/WED* WS10 ... 70 B2
GWS Trading Estate *TPTN/OCK* DY4 ... 70 B2
Haden Hill Leisure Centre *CDYHTH* B64 ... 121 F4
Hadley Stadium *SMTHWK* B66 ... 124 C1
Hagley Cemetery *HAG/WOL* DY9 ... 152 D5
Hagley Golf & Country Club *HAG/WOL* DY9 ... 154 A2
Hagley Hall *HAG/WOL* DY9 ... 153 F4
Hagley RC High School *STRBR* DY8 ... 152 B4

Halas Industrial Estate
 HALE B63 .... 138 D2
Halcyon Gallery *CBHAM* B2 ...... 3 F6
Halesbury Special School
 RMSLY B62 .... 122 C4
Halesowen CE *HALE* B63 .... 138 D5
Halesowen Cemetery
 HALE B65 .... 138 C3
Halesowen CE Primary
 School *HALE* B63 .... 138 C3
Halesowen College *HALE* B63 ... 138 D2
Halesowen FC (The Grove
 Recreation Ground)
 HALE B63 .... 138 C2
Halesowen Golf Club
 RMSLY B62 .... 139 F2
Halesowen Harriers FC
 HALE B63 .... 137 F2
Halesowen Health Centre
 HALE B65 .... 138 D4
Halesowen Industrial Park
 RMSLY B62 .... 138 D1
Halesowen Leisure Centre
 HALE B65 .... 138 D4
Hale Trading Estate
 TPTN/OCK DY4 .... 85 H1
Halifield School *EDG* B15 .... 126 A5
Hall Green Cemetery
 BILS/COS WV14 .... 69 E1
Hall Green J & I School
 HHTH/SAND B71 .... 71 G2
Hall Green Little Theatre
 ACGN B27 .... 146 A5
Hall Green Secondary School
 HLGN/YWD B28 .... 162 C2
Hall Green Stadium
 HLGN/YWD B28 .... 162 D1
Hallmoor Special School
 STECH B33 .... 130 D1
Hall of Memory *CBHAMW* B1 ...... 2 D5
Hamd House School
 SMTH B10 .... 128 C4
Ham Dingle Primary School
 HAG/WOL DY9 .... 136 A5
Hamilton Special School
 HDSW B21 .... 107 F1
Hams Hall International Freight
 Terminal
 CSHL/WTROR B46 .... 97 G3
Hams Hall National
 Distribution Park
 CSHL/WTROR B46 .... 97 H2
Hamstead Hall School
 BFLD/HDSWWD B20 .... 75 G5
Hamstead J & I School
 GTB/HAM B43 .... 74 F4
Handsworth Boys Grammar
 School *HDSW* B21 .... 107 G1
Handsworth Cemetery
 HDSW B21 .... 88 D4
Handsworth Golf Club
 BFLD/HDSWWD B20 .... 89 F2
Handsworth Leisure Centre
 BFLD/HDSWWD B20 .... 107 H1
Handsworth RFC
 GTB/HAM B43 .... 58 B4
Handsworth Wood Girls
 School & Sixth Form Centre
 BFLD/HDSWWD B20 .... 89 H4
Harborne Church Farm Golf
 Club *HRBN* B17 .... 141 H5
Harborne Golf Club
 RIDG/WDGT B32 .... 141 G2
Harborne Hill School *EDG* B15 .. 142 C1
Harborne Pool & Fitness
 Centre *HRBN* B17 .... 141 H2
Harborne Primary School
 HRBN B17 .... 142 A1
Harden Primary School
 BLOX/PEL WS3 .... 28 A3
Hargate Primary School
 HHTH/SAND B71 .... 87 G2
The Harper Bell School
 BHTH/HG B12 .... 127 C4
Harry Mitchell Leisure Centre
 SMTHWKW B67 .... 106 B4
Harvey Road Health Centre
 LGN/SDN/BHAMAIR B26 .... 130 A5
Harvey Works Industrial
 Estate *HALE* B63 .... 138 B1
Harvills Hawthorn Primary
 School *WBROM* B70 .... 70 D4
Hasbury CE Primary School
 HALE B63 .... 138 B5
Haslucks Green Junior School
 SHLY B90 .... 180 A2
Hastingwood Industrial Park
 ERDE/BCHGN B24 .... 93 F5
Hatchford Brook Golf Club
 LGN/SDN/BHAMAIR B26 .... 148 C3
Hatchford Brook Primary
 School *HIA/OLT* B92 .... 148 A4
Hatchford Gm Primary School
 CHWD/FDBR/MGN B37 .... 131 H2
Hateley Heath Primary School
 HHTH/SAND B71 .... 71 F4
Hatherton Lane Primary
 School *WSLW* WS2 .... 26 D4
Hawbush Primary School
 BRLYHL DY5 .... 118 D2
Hawkesley Church Primary
 School *HWK/WKHTH* B38 .... 190 C1
Hawkesley Health Centre
 HWK/WKHTH B38 .... 190 C1
Hawksmill Industrial Estate
 SMTH B10 .... 128 A3
Hawthorne Primary School
 KGSTG B44 .... 75 C4
Hawthorns Business Centre
 SMTHWK B66 .... 106 C1
Hawthorns Industrial Estate
 SMTHWK B66 .... 106 D1
Haybridge High School &
 Sixth Form
 STRBR DY8 .... 152 B4
Hayes Trading Estate
 HAG/WOL DY9 .... 137 E1
The Hayes Trading Estate
 HAG/WOL DY9 .... 137 E1

Hayley Green Hospital
 HALE B63 .... 154 D2
Hayward Industrial Park
 ALDR WS9 .... 30 A3
Hazel Oak School *SHLY* B90 ..... 180 A3
Healthcare Clinic
 CSCFLD/WYGN B72 .... 84 D4
The Heartlands High School
 VAUX/NECH B7 .... 109 G5
Heath Clinic *SOLH* B91 .... 165 F5
Heathfield Foundation Technology
 College *CDYHTH* B64 .... 121 F2
Heathfield Primary School
 LOZ/NWT B19 .... 108 C1
Heartlands Primary (NC)
 School *BKDE/SHDE* B34 .... 112 B2
Heath Lane Cemetery
 HHTH/SAND B71 .... 71 H4
Heath Lane Hospital
 HHTH/SAND B71 .... 71 H4
Heath Lodge Hotel
 CHWD/FDBR/MGN B37 .... 132 D4
Heath Mount Primary School
 BHTH/HG B12 .... 144 A1
Heath Park Junior School
 WOLN WV10 .... 24 A5
Heath Street Industrial Estate
 SMTHWK B66 .... 107 F4
Heath Town Leisure Centre
 WOLVN WV10 .... 38 A1
The High Arcal Secondary
 School *SEDG* DY3 .... 67 H5
Highclare St Paul's School
 FOAKS/STRLY B74 .... 62 B1
Highclare School
 CSCFLD/WYGN B72 .... 77 G2
Highclare the Abbey School
 ERDW/GRVHL B23 .... 93 E1
Highcroft Hospital
 ERDW/GRVHL B23 .... 92 B3
Highfield Primary School
 WASH/WDE B8 .... 110 C4
Highfields Primary School
 BILS/COS WV14 .... 68 C1
 BLKHTH/ROWR B65 .... 122 A4
Highfields School
 ETTPK/GDPK/PENN WV4 .... 50 B3
Highgate Business Centre
 BHTH/HG B12 .... 144 D1
Highgate Medical Centre
 BHTH/HG B12 .... 127 F5
Highgate Primary School
 DUDS DY2 .... 101 H3
Highgate Retail Park
 BHTH/HG B12 .... 127 F5
Highgate Trading Estate
 BHTH/HG B12 .... 127 G5
High Meadow Infant School
 CSHL/WTROR B46 .... 115 F1
Highters Heath J & I School
 ALE/KHTH/YWD B14 .... 178 D2
Hillary Primary School
 WSLW WS2 .... 56 C1
Hill Avenue Primary School
 ETTPK/GDPK/PENN WV4 .... 52 D5
Hillcrest Business Park
 DUDS DY2 .... 102 C2
Hillcrest Industrial Estate
 CDYHTH B64 .... 120 D4
Hillcrest School & Community
 College *DUDS* DY2 .... 102 B4
Hillcrest School & Sixth Form
 Centre *RIDG/WDGT* B32 .... 141 E4
Hillmeads Health Centre
 HWK/WKHTH B38 .... 177 E4
Hillstone Primary School
 BKDE/SHDE B34 .... 113 F4
Hill Top Industrial Estate
 WBROM B70 .... 70 D3
Hilltop Medical Centre
 LGLYGN/QTN B68 .... 123 G2
Hilltop Public Golf Course
 HDSW B21 .... 89 E2
Hilton Cross Business Park
 WOLVN WV10 .... 13 H1
Hilton Main Industrial Estate
 WNSFLD WV11 .... 14 A2
Hilton Trading Estate
 ETTPK/GDPK/PENN WV4 .... 52 D4
Himley Country Hotel
 SEDG DY3 .... 81 F3
Himley Hall Golf Centre
 SEDG DY3 .... 82 A2
Himley Hall & Park *SEDG* DY3 ... 81 H2
Himley House Hotel *SEDG* DY3 ... 81 H2
Himley Plantation
 Nature Reserve *WMBN* WV5 ... 81 E3
Hingley Industrial Estate
 DUDS DY2 .... 120 C3
Hive Industrial Centre
 WSNGN B18 .... 108 A3
HM Prison *WSNGN* B18 .... 107 C4
Hob Green Primary School
 HAG/WOL DY9 .... 136 C5
Hobmoor Primary School
 YDLY B25 .... 129 H4
Hobs Moat Medical Centre
 HIA/OLT B92 .... 147 C5
Hockley Brook Trading Estate
 WSNGN B18 .... 108 A3
Hockley Heath Pavilion
 (Sports Centre)
 HOCK/TIA B94 .... 198 A5
Hockley Hill Industrial Estate
 WSNGN B18 .... 108 B4
Hodge Hill Girls School
 CBROM B36 .... 111 G2
Hodge Hill School
 CBROM B36 .... 111 G2
Holiday Inn *SOLH* B91 .... 181 H2
Holland House Infant School
 CSCFLD/WYGN B72 .... 62 C4
Holland Industrial Park
 DARL/WED WS10 .... 40 B5
Holliday Wharf *CBHAMW* B1 ...... 2 D7
The Hollies Clinic
 LGLYGN/QTN B68 .... 105 F5
Hollies Industrial Estate
 BDMR/CCFT WV3 .... 6 D7

Holloway Bank Trading Estate
 DARL/WED WS10 .... 70 D2
Holly Bush Medical Centre
 RIDG/WDGT B32 .... 123 H5
Hollyfield Primary School
 MGN/WHC B75 .... 63 F4
Holly Hall Clinic *DUDN* DY1 .... 101 H2
Hollyhedge Primary School
 HHTH/SAND B71 .... 72 A3
Holly Hill Infant School
 RBRY B45 .... 173 H5
Holly Lane Cemetery
 SMTHWKW B67 .... 105 H4
Holly Lodge High School
 SMTHWKW B67 .... 105 H2
Holly Park Industrial Estate
 ERDE/BCHGN B24 .... 93 G4
Hollywood Primary School
 ALE/KHTH/YWD B14 .... 178 C4
Holte School *LOZ/NWT* B19 ...... 108 D2
Holt Farm Primary School
 RBRY B62 .... 122 C3
Holy Child School *EDG* B15 ..... 143 F1
Holy Cross Catholic Primary
 School *WALM/CURD* B76 .... 63 G5
Holy Family RC Primary School
 RBRY B45 .... 173 H2
Holyhead Primary School
 DARL/WED WS10 .... 55 F5
Holyhead School *HDSW* B21 ..... 107 F1
Holy Name RC School
 WOLV WV1 .... 38 A4
Holy Souls RC Primary School
 ACGN B27 .... 146 C4
Holy Trinity Catholic Primary
 School *BILS/COS* WV14 .... 54 A2
Holy Trinity CE Primary School
 BFLD/HDSWWD B20 .... 90 C4
 BRWIH WS8 .... 18 D1
 WBROM B70 .... 87 H5
Holy Trinity RC School
 SMTH B10 .... 128 A4
Holywell Primary School
 RBRY B45 .... 187 F1
Horrell Road Health Centre
 LGN/SDN/BHAMAIR B26 .... 148 D1
Horse Shoe Associated FC
 SHLY B90 .... 193 H2
Hotel Clarine
 LDYWD/EDGR B16 .... 125 G3
Hotel du Vin & Bistro
 CBHAMNW B3 .... 3 F4
Hotel Ibis *CBHAMW* B1 .... 126 D3
 DIG/EDG B5 .... 3 G7
 SMHTH B10 .... 127 H5
Howard Street Industrial
 Estate *WBROM* B70 .... 70 D4
Howley Grange Primary
 School *RMSLY* B62 .... 140 A2
HRS Business Park
 STETCH B33 .... 130 D3
HRS Industrial Estate
 STETCH B33 .... 131 E3
Hudson Industrial Estate
 BKHL/PFLD WV2 .... 52 D1
Hulbert Industrial Estate
 DUDS DY2 .... 102 B3
Huntingtree Primary School
 HALE B63 .... 138 A3
Hurst Business Park
 BRLYHL DY5 .... 101 H5
Hurstgreen Primary School
 RMSLY B62 .... 122 C4
Hurst Hill Primary School
 BILS/COS WV14 .... 68 A3
Hydesville Tower School
 WSL WS1 .... 5 H2
IKEA store Wednesbury
 DARL/WED WS10 .... 56 A2
Ikon Gallery *CBHAMW* B1 .... 2 C6
IMAX Cinema *DIG/EDG* B5 .... 3 K4
Imex Business Park
 BKHL/PFLD WV2 .... 52 A1
 BORD B9 .... 128 B2
 SPARK B11 .... 145 H1
 STETCH B33 .... 111 H4
 TPTN/OCK DY4 .... 85 G3
Imex Industrial Estate
 WSNGN B18 .... 108 A5
Indian High Commission
 WSNGN B18 .... 2 C1
Industrial Kingston School
 BORD B9 .... 127 G3
Industrial Weston Estate
 SPARK B11 .... 145 G3
Infant Welfare Clinic
 GTB/HAM B43 .... 59 H5
Inkeepers Hotel *DOR/KN* B93 ... 197 H5
Innkeeper's Lodge
 DARL/WED WS10 .... 147 H5
 KGSWFD DY6 .... 99 C3
 RIDG/WDGT B32 .... 123 G5
The Innkeeper's Lodge Hotel
 SCFLD/BOLD B73 .... 60 C3
International Convention
 Centre *CBHAMW* B1 .... 2 C5
International School &
 Community College
 STETCH B33 .... 131 F1
Izons Lane Industrial Estate
 WBROM B70 .... 86 D5
Jack o'Watton Business Park
 CSHL/WTROR B46 .... 96 D3
Jack o'Watton Industrial
 Estate *CSHL/WTROR* B46 .... 96 D5
James Bridge Cemetery
 DARL/WED WS10 .... 40 D5
James Watt Industrial Park
 SMTHWK B66 .... 107 E3
Jamia Mosque
 DUNHL/THL/PER WV6 .... 6 A1
Jane Lane Special School
 WSLW WS2 .... 40 D2
Janet Shaw Clinic
 CHWD/FDBR/MGN B37 .... 132 A4
JAS Industrial Park
 OLDBY B69 .... 104 C5
Jerome Retail Park *WSL* WS1 ...... 4 C5

Jervoise J & I School
 SLYOAK B29 .... 158 C1
Jessons CE First & Middle
 School *DUDN* DY1 .... 84 A5
Jewellery Quarter *WSNGN* B18 ... 2 C1
The Jewellery Quarter
 Discovery Centre
 WSNGN B18 .... 108 B4
Jewish Cemetery *AST/WIT* B6 ... 91 G1
JFK Memorial *CBHAMW* B4 .... 3 G5
John Black Day Hospital
 CHWD/FDBR/MGN B37 .... 132 B4
John Willmott School
 WALM/CURD B76 .... 63 F4
Joseph Chamberlain Sixth
 Form College
 BHTH/HG B12 .... 127 F5
Joseph Leckie Comprehensive
 School *WSL* WS1 .... 57 E3
Joseph Turner Primary School
 TPTN/OCK DY4 .... 69 H4
Josiah Mason College
 CVALE B35 .... 94 D3
 DUDN DY1 .... 101 H1
 KGSTG B44 .... 74 D2
 MOS/BIL B13 .... 144 A5
Jubilee Business Park
 HAG/WOL DY9 .... 136 D2
Jubilee Park Primary School
 HAG/WOL DY9 .... 69 H3
Junction 2 Industrial Estate
 OLDBY B69 .... 104 D3
Junction 6 Industrial Park
 AST/WIT B6 .... 91 H4
Jubilee Industrial Estate
 SMTHWK B66 .... 106 B2
Jurys Inn
 CBHAMW B1 .... 2 C6
Karis Medical Centre
 LDYWD/EDGR B16 .... 125 H3
Kates Hill Primary School
 DUDS DY2 .... 103 E1
Kelvin Way Trading Estate
 WBROM B70 .... 105 F1
Key Business Park
 ERDE/BCHGN B24 .... 93 H3
Key Hill Cemetery
 WSNGN B18 .... 2 B1
Key Industrial Park
 WLNHL WV13 .... 38 D2
Keyway Retail Park
 WLNHL WV13 .... 39 H5
Khalsa Industrial Estate
 SMTHWK B66 .... 107 F5
Kineton Green Infant School
 ACGN B27 .... 163 H1
King Charles Primary School
 WSLW WS2 .... 40 D3
King David Primary School
 MOS/BIL B13 .... 144 B5
King Edwards School (Boys)
 EDG B15 .... 143 E3
King Edwards VI Aston School
 AST/WIT B6 .... 109 F1
King Edwards VI Handsworth
 School *HDSW* B21 .... 108 A2
King Edward VI Camp Hill
 School for Boys
 ALE/KHTH/YWD B14 .... 160 D3
King Edward VI Camp Hill
 School for Girls
 BVILLE B30 .... 160 D2
King Edward VI College
 STRBR DY8 .... 135 C1
King Edward VI Five Ways
 School *RIDG/WDGT* B32 .... 157 G2
King Edward VI Girls High
 School *EDG* B15 .... 143 E3
Kingfisher Industrial Estate
 WBROM B70 .... 86 C2
Kingfisher Primary School
 CBROM B36 .... 114 A1
King George V Primary School
 HHTH/SAND B71 .... 88 A3
Kingsbury Business Park
 WALM/CURD B76 .... 79 G5
Kingsbury School
 ERDE/BCHGN B24 .... 92 D4
Kings Bush Park
 GTB/HAM B43 .... 59 H5
The Kings CE School
 DUNHL/THL/PER WV6 .... 21 F5
Kings Cinema *WBROM* B70 .... 87 H3
Kings Heath Boys School
 MOS/BIL B13 .... 161 G4
Kings Heath CC
 ALE/KHTH/YWD B14 .... 161 E4
Kings Hill Business Park
 DARL/WED WS10 .... 55 G4
Kings Hill Clinic
 DARL/WED WS10 .... 55 G3
Kings Hill JMI School
 DARL/WED WS10 .... 55 G3
Kingshurst City Technology
 College
 CHWD/FDBR/MGN B37 .... 132 B1
Kingshurst Clinic
 CHWD/FDBR/MGN B37 .... 114 A4
Kingshurst J & I School
 CHWD/FDBR/MGN B37 .... 114 A3
Kingsland Primary School
 KGSTG B44 .... 60 B4
Kings Norton Boys School
 BVILLE B30 .... 176 C1
Kings Norton Business Centre
 BVILLE B30 .... 176 D1
Kings Norton Girls School
 BVILLE B30 .... 159 G5
Kings Norton High School
 HWK/WKHTH B38 .... 176 D5
Kings Norton Primary School
 BVILLE B30 .... 177 E2
Kingsrise Community Primary
 School *KGSTG* B44 .... 75 H1
Kings Road Industrial Estate
 YDLY B25 .... 145 H1
Kingstanding Leisure Centre
 KGSTG B44 .... 75 H3
Kingstanding Special School
 KGSTG B44 .... 75 E2

Kingsthorne Primary School
 KGSTG B44 .... 75 C2
The Kingswinford Secondary
 School *KGSWFD* DY6 .... 99 H2
Kingswood School
 SHLY B90 .... 180 D1
Kitwell J & I School
 RIDG/WDGT B32 .... 157 E3
Klaxon Industrial Estate
 SPARK B11 .... 145 H3
Knowle CE Primary School
 DOR/KN B93 .... 197 G1
Knowle & Dorridge CC
 DOR/KN B93 .... 197 E4
Knowle FC *DOR/KN* B93 .... 197 G1
Knowle Village CC
 DOR/KN B93 .... 197 C1
La Caverna Hotel
 LGN/SDN/BHAMAIR B26 .... 148 A3
Ladypool Primary School
 SPARK B11 .... 144 D1
Ladywood Arts & Leisure
 Centre *LDYWD/EDGR* B16 .... 126 A2
Ladywood Middleway Health
 Centre *CBHAMW* B1 .... 126 A1
Lakeside JMI School
 WLNHL WV13 .... 39 G2
Lakeside Medical Centre
 DUNHL/THL/PER WV6 .... 34 C1
Lakey Lane Primary School
 HLGN/YWD B28 .... 163 G2
Lanchester School *CBROM* B36 ... 95 G5
Lane Green First School
 CDSL WV8 .... 10 D3
The Lane Medical Centre
 BHTH/HG D12 .... 144 D2
Lanesfield Primary School
 ETTPK/GDPK/PENN WV4 .... 53 E5
The Lanes Shopping Centre
 SCFLD/BOLD B73 .... 77 F4
Langley High School
 LGLYGN/QTN B68 .... 105 F5
Langley Primary School
 HIA/OLT B92 .... 163 H4
 OLDBY B69 .... 104 D4
Langley Special School *HIA/OLT* B92 ... 163 H3
Langley Special School
 MCN/WHC B75 .... 63 G2
Langley Swimming Centre
 LGLYGN/QTN B68 .... 105 F5
Lansdowne Health Centre
 WSNGN B18 .... 107 H5
Lapal Primary School
 RMSLY B62 .... 139 H3
Lasercare Clinics *EDG* B15 .... 126 B4
Laurie Pike Health Centre
 AST/WIT B6 .... 108 D1
Leamore Industrial Estate
 WSLW WS2 .... 27 E3
Leamore Primary School
 BLOX/PEL WS3 .... 27 G3
Lea Road Medical Practice
 BDMR/CCFT WV3 .... 36 C5
Leasowes Community College
 RMSLY B62 .... 139 G3
Leaverstock Industrial Estate
 STETCH B33 .... 131 E3
Lee Bank Business Centre
 CBHAMW B1 .... 2 E7
Legg Brothers Industrial
 Estate
 ETTPK/GDPK/PENN WV4 .... 52 D3
Leigh J & I (NC) School
 WASH/WDE B8 .... 110 C3
Leighswood Junior School
 ALDR WS9 .... 30 B3
Leighswood School *ALDR* WS9 ... 30 B2
Lemar Industrial Estate
 BVILLE B30 .... 160 C1
Lennon Indoor Market
 KGSTG B44 .... 60 C5
Leona Industrial Estate
 RMSLY B62 .... 122 D3
Leviss Industrial Estate
 STETCH B33 .... 111 H5
Lewisham Industrial Estate
 SMTHWK B66 .... 106 C2
Leyhill Health Centre
 NFLD/LBR B31 .... 158 A4
Ley Hill Primary School
 NFLD/LBR B31 .... 157 H5
Leys Industrial Estate
 BRLYHL DY5 .... 118 C1
Lickey Hills Country Park
 RBRY B45 .... 188 B4
Lickey Hills Golf Club
 RBRY B45 .... 188 A4
Lifford Trading Estate
 BVILLE B30 .... 177 E1
Light Hall School *SHLY* B90 ..... 180 B4
Light House Cinema
 WOLV WV1 .... 7 G3
Lightwoods Primary School
 LGLYGN/QTN B68 .... 123 H4
Linden Road Instruction
 Swimming Pool
 BVILLE B30 .... 159 H3
Lindens Primary School
 FOAKS/STRLY B74 .... 60 B2
Lindley Lodge Industrial Estate
 ALDR WS9 .... 29 G4
Lindsworth North School
 ERDW/GRVHL B23 .... 77 E5
Lindsworth School
 BVILLE B30 .... 177 G2
Link One Industrial Park
 TPTN/OCK DY4 .... 70 C5
Linkwood Industrial Estate
 KGSWFD DY6 .... 135 F1
Lion Industrial Park *ALDR* WS9 ... 30 A1
Little Aston CP School
 FOAKS/STRLY B74 .... 32 A4
Little Aston Golf Club
 FOAKS/STRLY B74 .... 45 H1
Little Bloxwich CE (V) School
 BLOX/PEL WS3 .... 17 F4
Little London JMI School
 WLNHL WV13 .... 39 G3
Locarno Primary School
 TPTN/OCK DY4 .... 69 F5

The Lock Museum
  WLNHL WV13 ....39 F4
Lode Heath School *SOLH* B91 ..165 E4
Lodge Farm Primary School
  SHFTH WV12 ....40 C1
Lodge Farm Trading Estate
  CDYHTH B64 ....120 C5
Lodge Forge Trading Estate
  CDYHTH B64 ....120 C5
Lodge Hill Cemetery
  SLYOAK B29 ....158 D1
Lodge Hill Crematorium
  SLYOAK B29 ....141 H5
Lodge Primary School
  WBROM B70 ....87 F5
Long Acre Trading Estate
  VAUX/NECH B7 ....109 H2
Long Knowle Primary School
  WNSFLD WV11 ....24 C2
Long Lane Medical Centre
  RMSLY B62 ....122 B3
Long Lane Trading Estate
  RMSLY B62 ....122 B3
Longmoor Special School
  SCFLD/BOLD B75 ....60 D4
Longwill Special School
  NFLD/LBR B31 ....158 C5
Lordswood Boys School
  HRBN B17 ....124 C4
Lordswood Girls School
  HRBN B17 ....124 D4
Lordswood Medical Practice
  HRBN B17 ....141 H1
Lower Farm JMI School
  BLOX/PEL WS3 ....17 E3
Lower Gornal Health Centre
  SEDG DY3 ....82 D4
Low Hill Medical Centre
  WOLVN WV10 ....23 G3
Loxdale Industrial Estate
  BILS/COS WV14 ....54 A4
Loxdale Primary School
  BILS/COS WV14 ....54 B4
Lozells Primary School
  LOZ/NWT B19 ....108 D2
Lugman Medical Centre
  WSL WS1 ....56 D1
Lutley Primary School
  HALE B63 ....154 D1
Lye Business Centre
  BRLYHL DY5 ....119 H5
Lye CE *HAC/WOL* DY9 ....136 B2
Lye Town FC *HAC/WOL* DY9 ......136 B2
Lye Valley Industrial Estate
  HAC/WOL DY9 ....136 D1
Lye & Wollescote Cemetery
  HAC/WOL DY9 ....136 C3
Lyndon Green J & I School
  LGN/SDN/BHAMAIR B26 ....147 F1
Lyndon School *HIA/OLT* B92 ....147 G4
Lyng Primary School
  WBROM B70 ....87 G5
Macdonald Burlington Hotel
  CBHAM B2 ....3 F5
Magreal Industrial Estate
  LDYWD/EDGR B16 ....125 H1
Maidensbridge Primary School
  KGSWFD DY6 ....81 F5
The Mailbox *CBHAMW* B1 ....2 E6
Mainstream Forty Seven
  Industrial Park
  VAUX/NECH B7 ....110 A4
Mainstream Industrial Park
  VAUX/NECH B7 ....110 A5
Malmaison Hotel *CBHAMW* B1 ......2 E7
Malt Mill Lane Trading Estate
  RMSLY B62 ....122 B4
Mander Shopping Centre
  WOLVN WV10 ....7 F4
Manders Industrial Estate
  WOLVN WV10 ....37 H2
Maney Hill Primary School
  CSCFLD/WYGN B72 ....77 H1
The Manor General Hospital
  WSLW WS2 ....41 G4
Manor High School (Foundation)
  DARL/WED WS10 ....56 D5
Manor Industrial Estate
  WSLW WS2 ....4 A4
Manor Park Primary School
  AST/WIT B6 ....109 C1
Manor Primary School
  FOAKS/STRLY B74 ....68 B1
  OAKS/STRLY B74 ....45 G4
Manor Way Primary School
  HALE B63 ....139 E4
Mansfield Green Primary School
  AST/WIT B6 ....109 H1
Maple Business Park
  VAUX/NECH B7 ....109 H3
Maple Leaf Industrial Estate
  WSLW WS2 ....41 F2
Marlborough J & I School
  SMHTH B10 ....128 C3
Marlow Estate
  BLKHTH/ROWR B65 ....121 H3
Marshalls Industrial Estate
  BKHL/PFLD WV2 ....52 A1
Marsh Hill Primary School
  ERDW/GRVHL B23 ....91 H2
Marston Green Clinic
  CHWD/FDBR/MGN B37 ....132 A5
Marston Green Infant School
  CHWD/FDBR/MGN B37 ....132 A5
Marston Green Junior School
  CHWD/FDBR/MGN B37 ....132 A5
Marston Road Industrial Estate
  BKHL/PFLD WV2 ....52 A1
Mary Elliot Special School
  WSLW WS2 ....42 A1
Maryvale Catholic Primary
  School *KGSTG* B44 ....75 F1
Maryvale Institute *KGSTG* B44 ....75 F1
Maternity Welfare Clinic
  ETTPK/GDPK/PENN WV4 ....50 D2
Matthew Boulton College of
  Further & Higher Education
  CBHAMNE B4 ....3 J3
  DIG/EDG B5 ....126 D4
Matthew Boulton Community
  Primary School
  HDSW B21 ....107 G2

Maybrook Industrial Estate
  BRWNH WS8 ....19 F2
The Mayfair Centre *CBHAM* B2 .....3 G6
Mayfield Preparatory School
  WSL WS1 ....5 H6
Mayfield Special School
  LOZ/NWT B19 ....108 C1
Maypole Health Centre
  ALE/KHTH/YWD B14 ....178 B2
Meadow Green Primary School
  HLYWD B47 ....192 C5
Meadows Primary School
  NFLD/LBR B31 ....175 E3
Meadow View JMI School
  GTB/HAM B43 ....59 H5
Meadwood Industrial Estate
  BILS/COS WV14 ....54 A3
Media Centre *WOLV* WV1 ....7 G3
Meeting Lane Industrial
  Estate *BRLYHL* DY5 ....118 D3
Megabowl *BRLYHL* DY5 ....119 F2
Menzies High School
  HHTH/SAND B71 ....71 G3
Mere Green Combined School
  MGN/WHC B75 ....47 F3
Merridale Cemetery
  BDMR/CCFT WV3 ....6 A7
Merridale Primary School
  BDMR/CCFT WV3 ....6 A6
Merry Hill Shopping Centre
  BRLYHL DY5 ....119 H2
Mesty Croft Primary School
  DARL/WED WS10 ....56 A5
Metalloys Industrial Estate
  WALM/CURD B76 ....94 D1
Middlemore Business Park
  ALDR WS9 ....29 G4
Middlemore Industrial Estate
  HDSW B21 ....88 D5
  SMTHWK B66 ....106 D1
Middleton Trading Estate
  WLNHL WV13 ....39 E3
Middleway Industrial Estate
  BHTH/HG B12 ....127 F5
Midland House Dawley
  Trading Estate *KGSWFD* DY6 ...99 H1
Midland Institute *CBHAMNW* B3 ....2 E4
Midlands Arts Centre Cinema
  BHTH/HG B12 ....143 H5
Milking Bank Primary School
  DUDN DY1 ....83 G4
Millard Industrial Estate
  WBROM B70 ....87 E5
Millbuck Industrial Estate
  WOLVN WV10 ....23 F3
Millfield CP School *BRWNH* WS8 ...9 C5
Millfield Special School
  HHTH/SAND B71 ....71 H5
Mill Lodge Primary School
  SHLY B90 ....179 G3
Minworth Industrial Park
  WALM/CURD B76 ....78 D5
  WALM/CURD B76 ....95 E1
Minworth J & I School
  WALM/CURD B76 ....95 F1
Moat Farm J & I School
  LGLYGN/QTN B68 ....123 C1
Mobarak Health Centre
  BHTH/HG B12 ....144 A2
Monarch Industrial Estate
  SPARK B11 ....146 A2
Monkspath Business Park
  SHLY B90 ....181 E5
Monkspath Primary School
  SHLY B90 ....195 H2
Monmer Close Industrial Estate
  WLNHL WV13 ....39 H2
Monmore Business Park
  BKHL/PFLD WV2 ....52 D1
Monmore Green Greyhound Stadium
  BKHL/PFLD WV2 ....38 A5
Monmore Park Industrial Estate
  BKHL/PFLD WV2 ....52 D1
Montgomery Primary School
  SPARK B11 ....128 A5
Montgomery Street Business Centre
  SPARK B11 ....145 E1
Monway Industrial Estate
  DARL/WED WS10 ....55 F5
Monyhull Hospital *BVILLE* B30 ...177 H2
The Moore Group Business
  Centre *WSL* WS1 ....4 E7
Moor Green FC
  HLGN/YWD B28 ....162 C3
Moor Green J & I School
  MOS/BIL B13 ....160 C1
Moor Green Sports Centre
  SLYOAK B29 ....143 G5
Moor Group Business Centre
  WSL WS1 ....4 E7
Moor Hall Golf Club
  MGN/WHC B75 ....47 H4
Moorcroft School
  MGN/WHC B75 ....47 H3
Moorlands Primary School
  HHTH/SAND B71 ....71 F3
Moor Lane Trading Estate
  AST/WIT B6 ....91 F2
Moor Street Industrial Estate
  BRLYHL DY5 ....119 E2
Moreton Community School
  WBROM B70 ....23 H1
Moseley CE *SHLY* B90 ....163 G5
Moseley CE Primary School
  MOS/BIL B13 ....144 B5
Moseley Golf Club
  ALE/KHTH/YWD B14 ....161 G2
Moseley Hall Hospital
  MOS/BIL B13 ....144 A4
Moseley Old Hall (NT)
  WOLVN WV10 ....13 G2
Moseley Primary School
  BLOX/PEL WS3 ....16 B5

The Mount Hotel
  DUNHL/THL/PER WV6 ....35 E3
Mount Pleasant Primary
  School *BRLYHL* DY5 ....119 G3
Mount Street Business Centre
  VAUX/NECH B7 ....110 A3
Mount Street Business Park
  VAUX/NECH B7 ....110 B2
Moxley Industrial Centre
  DARL/WED WS10 ....55 E5
Moxley Medical Centre
  DARL/WED WS10 ....55 E2
Mucklow Hill Industrial Estate
  RMSLY B62 ....139 E2
Mucklow Hill Trading Estate
  RMSLY B62 ....139 E2
Municipal Art Gallery
  WOLV WV1 ....7 F3
Munrow Sports Centre
  EDG B15 ....142 D3
Nansen J & I School
  WASH/WDE B8 ....110 D4
National Exhibition Centre
  BHAMNEC B40 ....150 A2
National Indoor Arena
  CBHAMW B1 ....2 B5
National Institute of
  Conductive Education
  MOS/BIL B13 ....143 H3
National Motorcycle Museum
  HIA/OLT B92 ....150 C4
National Sea Life Centre
  LDYWD/EDGR B16 ....2 B3
The Natural Health Centre
  HWK/WKHTH B38 ....176 D3
Nature Park *WALM/CURD* B76 ......94 C1
Neachells Lane Industrial
  Estate *WNSFLD* WV11 ....38 D1
Nechells Primary School
  VAUX/NECH B7 ....110 A1
Nelson Mandela Primary
  School *BHTH/HG* B12 ....144 C2
Nelson Primary School
  CBHAMW B1 ....2 A4
Neptune Industrial Estate
  WLNHL WV13 ....39 H5
Netherbrook Primary School
  DUDS DY2 ....120 D3
Netherton Business Park
  DUDS DY2 ....120 D1
Netherton CC *DUDS* DY2 ....102 B5
Netherton CE Primary School
  DUDS DY2 ....102 B4
Network Park Industrial
  Estate *VAUX/NECH* B7 ....110 A5
The New Art Gallery Walsall
  WSLW WS2 ....4 C3
Newbridge Preparatory School
  DUNHL/THL/PER WV6 ....36 A1
New Cross Hospital
  WNSFLD WV11 ....24 B5
New Cross Industrial Estate
  WOLV WV1 ....38 A2
Newfield Park Primary School
  HALE B63 ....138 C2
New Hall Hotel
  WALM/CURD B76 ....78 A1
New Hall J & I School
  MGN/WHC B75 ....63 H3
Newhampton Arts Centre
  WOLV WV1 ....6 D2
New Invention Junior School
  SHFTH WV12 ....26 A4
Newman College of Higher
  Education *RIDG/WDGT* B32 ......157 G2
Newsome Industrial Estate
  SPARK B11 ....145 F1
Newton Industrial Estate
  BORD B9 ....128 B2
Newtown Health Centre
  LOZ/NWT B19 ....108 D3
Newtown Primary School
  WBROM B70 ....86 B3
Newtown Shopping Centre
  LOZ/NWT B19 ....109 E3
Ninestiles School
  ACGN B27 ....163 F1
Nonsuch Primary School
  RIDG/WDGT B32 ....140 D5
Norfolk House School
  EDG B15 ....125 F4
Norman Green Sports Centre &
  Athletics Track *SOLH* B91 ....181 G2
Northbrook Health Centre
  SHLY B90 ....163 G5
Northfield Manor Primary
  School *SLYOAK* B29 ....158 D3
Northfield Pool & Fitness
  Centre *NFLD/LBR* B31 ....175 F2
Northfield Primary School
  DUDS DY2 ....102 D4
Northicote Secondary School
  WOLVN WV10 ....13 E4
Northmoor Industrial Estate
  BRLYHL DY5 ....119 F1
Northside Business Centre
  WSNGN B18 ....107 G4
North Solihull Sports Centre
  & Track
  CHWD/FDBR/MGN B37 ....132 A1
North Street Industrial
  Estate *BRLYHL* DY5 ....119 E2
North Worcestershire Golf
  Club *NFLD/LBR* B31 ....174 D3
Novotel
  CBHAMW B1 ....2 B6
  LGN/SDN/BHAMAIR B26 ....149 G3
  WOLV WV1 ....7 H4
Oak College Primary School
  SOLH B91 ....164 A4
Oakdale Trading Estate
  KGSWFD DY6 ....81 H5
  KGSWFD DY6 ....100 A1
Oakeswell Health Centre
  DARL/WED WS10 ....56 A5
Oakham Primary School
  DUDS DY2 ....103 H2
Oak House *WBROM* B70 ....87 F4
The Oak Industrial Park
  KGSWFD DY6 ....82 A5

Oaklands Primary School
  ACGN B27 ....146 C5
Oakleigh Trading Estate
  BILS/COS WV14 ....68 B1
The Oaks Primary School
  WNSFLD WV11 ....25 G3
Oak Meadow Primary School
  WNSFLD WV11 ....25 G3
Oak Street Industrial Estate
  CDYHTH B64 ....120 D3
Oak Street Trading Estate
  BRLYHL DY5 ....119 H3
Oakwood Special School
  ALDR WS9 ....19 G4
Ocker Hill J & I School
  TPTN/OCK DY4 ....70 A3
Odeon Cinema *CBHAM* B2 ....3 G6
  CSCFLD/WYGN B72 ....62 B5
Ogley Hay Infant School
  BRWNH WS8 ....9 F4
Oldbury Business Centre
  LGLYGN/QTN B68 ....123 G2
Oldbury Green Retail Park
  OLDBY B69 ....104 D1
Oldbury Health Centre
  OLDBY B69 ....105 E1
Oldbury Leisure Centre
  OLDBY B69 ....104 C3
Oldbury Road Industrial
  Estate *SMTHWK* B66 ....105 H2
  WBROM B70 ....86 D4
Oldbury United FC
  BLKHTH/ROWR B65 ....122 C1
Old Bush Trading Estate
  BRLYHL DY5 ....119 G1
Old Church CE Primary School
  DARL/WED WS10 ....55 E2
Oldfield Trading Estate
  CDYHTH B64 ....120 C4
Old Forge Trading Estate
  DARL/WED WS10 ....55 C3
Old Halesonians RFC
  HAG/WOL DY9 ....153 H2
Old Hall Industrial Estate
  BLOX/PEL WS3 ....27 G2
Oldhall Special School
  WSLW WS2 ....26 C5
Old Hill CC *CDYHTH* B64 ....121 F4
Old Hill Primary School
  CDYHTH B64 ....121 F3
Oldknow Junior School
  SMHTH B10 ....128 C5
Old Limberlost Sports Club
  BFLD/HDSWWD B20 ....90 A3
Old Park Industrial Estate
  DARL/WED WS10 ....55 G4
Old Park Primary School
  DARL/WED WS10 ....55 C3
Old Park Special School
  DUDN DY1 ....101 H1
Old Rep Theatre *DIG/EDG* B5 ......3 F7
The Old Square Shopping
  Centre *WSL* WS1 ....4 E4
Oldswinford CE Primary
  School *STRBR* DY8 ....135 G4
Old Swinford Hospital School
  STRBR DY8 ....135 G5
Olive Hill Primary School
  RMSLY B62 ....122 B5
Orton Golf Club *SOLH* B91 ......164 C3
One Stop Retail Park
  PBAR/PBCH B42 ....90 D2
Open University *HRBN* B17 ......142 B1
Oratory RC Primary School
  LDYWD/EDGR B16 ....125 H2
Orchard Lane Clinic
  HAG/WOL DY9 ....136 C1
The Orchards School
  SMTHWK B66 ....106 A2
Orthodontists Surgery
  SPARK B11 ....146 A4
Osborne Primary School
  ERDW/GRVHL B23 ....93 E1
Ounsdale High School
  WMBN WV5 ....64 D4
Ounsdale Sports Centre
  WMBN WV5 ....64 D4
Our Lady of Compassion RC
  Primary School
  HIA/OLT B92 ....163 H3
Our Lady of Fatima RC Primary
  School *HRBN* B17 ....124 B5
Our Lady of Lourdes RC
  Primary School
  MOS/BIL B13 ....162 B5
Our Lady of the Wayside RC
  Primary School *SHLY* B90 ......180 C5
Our Lady & St Chad RC
  Secondary School
  WOLVN WV10 ....23 H2
Our Lady & St Kenelm RC
  Primary School *HALE* B63 ......138 C4
Our Lady & St Rose of Lima RC
  Primary School
  SLYOAK B29 ....158 D1
Our Ladys RC Primary School
  STETCH B33 ....131 F2
The Oval Primary School
  STETCH B33 ....130 B2
Owen Road Industrial Estate
  WLNHL WV13 ....40 A4
Owen Road Primary School
  WLNHL WV13 ....40 A4
Oxbarn Social & Sports Club
  BDMR/CCFT WV3 ....51 H5
Oxford Street Industrial Park
  BILS/COS WV14 ....54 B3
Oxley Park Golf Club
  WOLVN WV10 ....23 E3
Paddys Wide Water Industrial
  Estate *BRLYHL* DY5 ....101 E4
Paget Primary School
  ERDE/BCHGN B24 ....93 G2
Palfrey Girls School *WSL* WS1 ....4 D4
Palfrey Infant School
  WSL WS1 ....56 D1
Palfrey Junior School
  WSL WS1 ....56 D1

Pallasades Shopping Centre
  CBHAMW B1 ....3 F6
Palmers Cross Primary School
  DUNHL/THL/PER WV6 ....21 H2
Paper Mill End Industrial Estate
  KGSTG B44 ....74 D5
Parkbrook Industrial Estate
  HAG/WOL DY9 ....136 D2
Park Clinic *ERDW/GRVHL* B23 .....93 E1
Parkfield Clinic
  BKHL/PFLD WV2 ....52 B2
Parkfield High School
  ETTPK/GDPK/PENN WV4 ....52 C3
Parkfield Primary School
  ETTPK/GDPK/PENN WV4 ....52 C3
  WASH/WDE B8 ....128 C1
Park Hall Infant School
  SMHTH B10 ....128 C5
Park Hall Junior School
  DSYBK/YTR WS5 ....58 A1
Park Hall School *CBROM* B36 .....95 C5
Park Hill Primary School
  DARL/WED WS10 ....56 C4
  MOS/BIL B13 ....144 B5
Park Lane Industrial Estate
  HHTH/SAND B71 ....88 C5
Park Lane Trading Estate
  OLDBY B69 ....105 E2
  WOLVN WV10 ....23 C5
Park Medical Centre
  SMHTH B10 ....128 C5
Parkrose Industrial Estate
  SMTHWK B66 ....106 D1
Parkside Industrial Estate
  WOLV WV1 ....37 H4
Park Trading Estate
  WSNGN B18 ....108 A3
Park View School
  WASH/WDE B8 ....110 C4
Parkway Industrial Centre
  VAUX/NECH B7 ....109 G5
Pavilions Shopping Centre
  CBHAMNE B4 ....3 H5
Pdh Industrial Estate
  DARL/WED WS10 ....55 E4
  WLNHL WV13 ....38 D2
Peartree Industrial Park
  DUDS DY2 ....102 A3
Pedmore CE Primary School
  HAG/WOL DY9 ....152 D1
Pedmore Road Industrial
  Estate *BRLYHL* DY5 ....101 H5
Pegasus Primary School
  CVALE B35 ....72 B5
Pelsall Clinic *BLOX/PEL* WS3 .....18 A3
Pelsall Village School
  BLOX/PEL WS3 ....17 H3
Pendeford Business Park
  COVEN WV9 ....11 H4
Pendeford Health Centre
  COVEN WV9 ....12 A5
Pendeford High School
  WOLVN WV10 ....12 B5
Pendeford Mill Nature
  Reserve *COVEN* WV9 ....11 G3
Pendene Complimentary
  Medical Centre *WOLV* WV1 ....6 C3
Penn Cemetery
  ETTPK/GDPK/PENN WV4 ....50 D5
Pennfields Health Centre
  BDMR/CCFT WV3 ....6 A3
Penn Fields School
  BDMR/CCFT WV3 ....51 F1
Penn Golf Club
  ETTPK/GDPK/PENN WV4 ....66 C1
Penn Hall Special School
  ETTPK/GDPK/PENN WV4 ....51 E4
Penn Hospital
  ETTPK/GDPK/PENN WV4 ....51 E4
Penn Industrial Estate
  DUDS DY2 ....120 C3
Penn Manor Medical Centre
  ETTPK/GDPK/PENN WV4 ....51 F4
Penn Road Retail Park
  BKHL/PFLD WV2 ....36 D5
Penns Primary School
  CSCFLD/WYGN B72 ....77 C5
Pens Meadow Special School
  STRBR DY8 ....118 A1
The Pennsett School of
  Technology *BRLYHL* DY5 ....100 B1
Pensnett Trading Estate
  KGSWFD DY6 ....100 B1
The Pennsett Trading Estate
  KGSWFD DY6 ....100 C1
Percy Business Park
  OLDBY B69 ....104 D2
Percy Shurmer Primary
  School *DIG/EDG* B5 ....127 E5
Perry Barr Greyhound
  Stadium *PBAR/PBCH* B42 ....90 D3
Perry Beeches J & I School
  PBAR/PBCH B42 ....74 C3
Perry Common Primary
  School *ERDW/GRVHL* B23 ....75 H4
Perryfields High School
  RMSLY B62 ....123 E4
Perryfields Primary School
  RMSLY B62 ....123 E4
Perry Hall Primary School
  WNSFLD WV11 ....25 F4
Perry Street Industrial Estate
  BILS/COS WV14 ....54 A5
Personal & Child Health
  Centre *BVILLE* B30 ....160 A4
Perton Clinic
  DUNHL/THL/PER WV6 ....34 C1
Perton First School
  DUNHL/THL/PER WV6 ....20 C5
Perton Middle School
  DUNHL/THL/PER WV6 ....35 E1
Perton Park Golf Club
  DUNHL/THL/PER WV6 ....34 A2
Peterbrook Primary School
  SHLY B90 ....179 E1
Peters Hill Primary School
  BRLYHL DY5 ....119 C5

Pheasey Clinic
GTB/HAM B43 ....59 G5
Pheasey Park Farm Primary
School *CTB/HAM* B43 ....59 G4
Phillips Street
Industrial Estate
AST/WIT B6 ....109 E3
Phoenix Business Park
VAUX/NECH B7 ....109 G3
Phoenix Industrial Estate
BILS/COS WV14 ....54 B4
Phoenix International
Industrial Estate
WBROM B70 ....86 D1
Phoenix Road Industrial
Estate *WLNHL* WV13 ....38 D2
Phoenix Works Industrial
Estate *DARL/WED* WS10 ....40 C5
Piccadilly Cinema
SPARK B11 ....144 D2
The Picture House
STRBR DY8 ....135 G3
WASH/WDE B8 ....111 E4
Pines Special School
CBROM B36 ....112 B1
Pinfold Industrial Estate
BLOX/PEL WS1 ....27 G2
Pinfold Street Primary School
DARL/WED WS10 ....55 E3
Planetary Industrial Estate
WLNHL WV13 ....38 C1
Planet Ice Arena *DIG/EDG* B5 .....3 H7
Plantsbrook School
CSCFLD/WYGN B72 ....62 C4
Pleck Business Park *WSLW* WS2 ....4 A4
Pleck Industrial Estate
WSLW WS2 ....41 G5
Pool Hayes Comprehensive
School *SHHTH* WV12 ....25 H5
Pool Hayes Primary School
WNSFLD WV11 ....25 H4
Poplar Road Clinic
ALE/KHTH/YWD B14 ....161 F1
Poplar Trading Estate
AST/WIT B6 ....91 F1
Portersfield Industrial Estate
CDYHTH B64 ....120 C4
Portland Hotel
LDYWD/EDGR B16 ....125 E3
Portway Road Industrial
Estate *OLDBY* B69 ....104 C3
Powke Lane Industrial Estate
BLKHTH/ROWR B65 ....121 G2
Premier Business Centre
HAG/WOL DY9 ....136 D2
Premier Business Park
WSLW WS2 ....4 B5
Premier Lodge *MGN/WHC* B75 ...63 F1
Premier Partnership Industrial
Estate *KGSWFD* DY6 ....100 C5
Premier Trading Estate
VAUX/NECH B7 ....109 F4
Premier Travel Inn
AST/WIT B6 ....109 F4
BHAMNEC B40 ....133 F5
CBHAMW B1 ....2 D6
CNCK/NC WS11 ....8 A1
EDG B15 ....2 B7
KGSWFD DY6 ....100 B2
OLDBY B69 ....104 B2
RBRY B45 ....174 B5
SHLY B90 ....180 B2
WBROM B70 ....86 D1
WOLVN WV10 ....12 D2
WSLW WS2 ....40 C4
Preston College *WLNHL* WV13 ..39 G4
Priestley Smith Special School
ERDW/GRVHL B23 ....75 H5
Primrose Hill Primary School
HWK/WKHTH B38 ....176 D5
Primrose Hill Trading Estate
DUDS DY2 ....102 D5
Primrose Lane Health Centre
WOLVN WV10 ....24 A2
Primrose Trading Estate
DUDS DY2 ....102 C5
Prince Albert Primary School
AST/WIT B6 ....109 E1
Princes End Industrial Park
BILS/COS WV14 ....69 E2
Princethorpe J & I School
CSHLW B29 ....158 C2
Priory Clinic *DUDN* DY1 ....84 B3
Priory Courts *CBHAMNE* B4 ....3 G4
Priory Green Primary School
COVEN WV9 ....12 A5
Priory House Industrial Estate
WSNGN B18 ....108 B4
Priory Junior Mixed & Infants
School *BLOX/PEL* WS5 ....27 F5
Priory New Way Industrial
Estate *AST/WIT* B6 ....109 E4
Priory Primary School
DUDN DY1 ....84 B3
The Priory School
DARL/WED WS10 ....71 H1
Prospect Trading Estate
CBHAMW B1 ....2 C4
Providence Industrial Estate
CRAD/WED WS10 ....136 C1
Pype Hayes Golf Club
WALM/CURD B76 ....78 A5
Qualcast Road Industrial Estate
WOLV WV1 ....37 H3
Quality Hotel *BDMR/CCFT* WV3 ..36 D5
Quarry Bank Primary School
BRLYHL DY5 ....120 A3
Queen Alexandra College
HRBN B17 ....141 G1
Queen Elizabeth Hospital
EDG B15 ....142 C2
Queen Elizabeth Psychiatric
Hospital *EDG* B15 ....142 C3
Queen Marys Grammar School
WSL WS1 ....5 J6
Queen Marys High School
RUSH/SHEL WS4 ....5 G1

Queensbury Special School
ERDE/BCHGN B24 ....92 D3
Queens College *EDG* B15 ....142 D2
Queens Court Trading Estate
WBROM B70 ....86 D3
Queen Street Cemetery
WSLW WS2 ....4 A6
Queensway Trading Estate
DIG/EDG B5 ....3 J4
Queen Victoria Primary School
SEDG DY3 ....67 F5
Quinton Business Park
RIDG/WDGT B32 ....140 A2
Quinton Cemetery
RMSLY B62 ....122 D5
Quinton CE Primary School
RIDG/WDGT B32 ....140 A1
Racecourse Road Industrial Estate
DUNHL/THL/PER WV6 ....22 C5
Raddlebarn J & I School
SLYOAK B29 ....159 H1
Radleys Primary School
SHLY B90 ....29 E3
Radway Industrial Estate
SHLY B90 ....195 E1
Rainbow Business Park
WLNHL WV13 ....39 H2
Rake Gate Infant School
WOLVN WV10 ....22 D1
Rake Gate Junior School
WOLVN WV10 ....22 D1
Raleigh Industrial Estate
HDSW B21 ....88 D5
Ramada Hotel *SOLH* B91 ....182 A2
WALM/CURD B76 ....78 A4
Rathvilly School
NFLD/LBR B31 ....175 H2
Rea Business Park
VAUX/NECH B7 ....109 H5
Reaside Clinic *RBRY* B45 ....174 A4
Reaside Junior School
RBRY B45 ....173 G4
Reddal Hill Primary School
CDYHTH B64 ....121 E3
Redditch Trading Estate
MGN/WHC B75 ....62 D4
Red Hall Primary School
SEDG DY3 ....83 E3
Redhill J & I School *RDYL* B25 ..129 E5
Redhill Secondary School
STRBR DY8 ....135 H2
Red Hill Street Clinic
WOLV WV1 ....37 E1
The Red House Glass Cone
STRBR DY8 ....118 A2
Redhouse Industrial Estate
ALDR WS9 ....29 F4
Redhouse JMI School
ALDR WS9 ....29 G5
Redhill Mill J & I School
RBRY B45 ....188 B1
Red Rooster Industrial Estate
ALDR WS9 ....29 G4
Redwoods Business Park
SMTHWK B66 ....105 G2
Reedswood Retail Park
WSLW WS2 ....41 F1
Reflex Industrial Park
WLNHL WV13 ....39 F2
Regents Park Primary School
SMHTH B10 ....128 A4
Regent Special School
OLDBY B69 ....85 G5
Regis Medical Centre
BLKHTH/ROWR B65 ....122 A3
Reliance Trading Estate
ETTPK/GDPK/PENN WV4 ....53 F3
Renaissance Solihull Hotel
SOLH B91 ....181 H1
Reynalds Cross School
HIA/OLT B92 ....163 H3
The Ridge Primary School
STRBR DY8 ....134 C2
Ridgewood High School
STRBR DY8 ....134 C1
Ridpool Primary School
STETCH B33 ....130 D1
Riland Industrial Estate
MGN/WHC B75 ....62 C3
River Brook Medical Centre
BVILLE B30 ....160 B2
RMW Business Centre
HAG/WOL DY9 ....136 D2
Robert Clinic *BVILLE* B30 ....159 C5
Roberts Primary School
SEDG DY3 ....83 G2
Robin Hood Cemetery
SHLY B90 ....163 F5
Robin Hood Golf Club
HIA/OLT B92 ....163 G4
Robin Hood Primary School
HLGN/YWD B28 ....163 F4
Robins Business Park
TPTN/OCK DY4 ....70 C4
Rocky Lane Trading Estate
VAUX/NECH B7 ....109 G3
Rollinghmill Business Park
WSLW WS2 ....4 A5
Romney House Industrial
Estate *DARL/WED* WS10 ....54 D1
Rood End Cemetery
LGLYGN/QTN B68 ....105 G2
Rood End Primary School
LGLYGN/QTN B68 ....105 G3
Rookery Primary School
HDSW B21 ....89 G5
Rosary RC Primary School
WASH/WDE B8 ....128 C1
Rosedale CE Infant School
SHMTH WV13 ....26 B5
Rosewood Special School
DUDN DY1 ....83 G5
Rosslyn School
HLGN/YWD B28 ....163 E5
Rotton Park Medical Centre
LDYWD/EDGR B16 ....125 F1
Rotunda *CBHAM* B2 ....3 G6
Rough Hay Primary School
DARL/WED WS10 ....55 H1

Rough Wood Nature Reserve
....26 C4
Rounds Green Primary School
OLDBY B69 ....104 C1
Rovex Business Park
SPARK B11 ....145 H2
Rowley Hall Primary School
BLKHTH/ROWR B65 ....104 A5
Rowley Regis Cemetery &
Crematorium
BLKHTH/ROWR B65 ....121 G2
Rowley Regis College
BLKHTH/ROWR B65 ....121 H1
Rowley Regis Hospital
BLKHTH/ROWR B65 ....121 H1
Royal Birmingham Society of
Arts *CBHAMNW* B3 ....3 D2
Royal Brierley Trading Estate
BRLYHL DY5 ....119 E1
Royal Orthopaedic Hospital
NFLD/LBR B31 ....158 D5
Royal Theatre *CDYHTH* B64 ....120 D3
The Royal Wolverhampton
Junior School
BDMR/CCFT WV3 ....51 G1
The Royal Wolverhampton
School *BDMR/CCFT* WV3 ....51 H1
RSPB Sandwell Valley Nature
Reserve *GTB/HAM* B43 ....73 E5
Rubery Clinic *RBRY* B45 ....187 G1
Ruckleigh School *SOLH* B91 ....182 A1
Rufford Primary School
HAG/WOL DY9 ....136 A2
Rushall Community College
RUSH/SHEL WS4 ....28 D4
Rushall JM School & Education
Development Centre
RUSH/SHEL WS4 ....28 C1
Russell Medical Centre
DARL/WED WS10 ....70 D1
Russells Hall Hospital
BRLYHL DY5 ....101 F2
Russells Hall Primary School
DUDN DY1 ....83 G5
Ryders Green Primary School
WBROM B70 ....87 E2
Ryders Hayes JMI School
BLOX/PEL WS3 ....18 A2
Sacred Heart RC Primary
School *BFLD/HDSWWD* B20 ....90 D5
TPTN/OCK DY4 ....85 F2
Saddlers Shopping Centre
WSL WS1 ....4 A3
Sai Medical Centre *WSLW* WS2 ...4 A3
St Albans CE Primary School
WNSFLD WV11 ....25 H2
St Albans CE School
BHTH/HG B12 ....127 F5
St Albans RC Primary School
ALE/KHTH/YWD B14 ....178 B1
St Alphege CE Infant School
SOLH B91 ....182 A2
St Alphege CE Junior School
SOLH B91 ....182 A1
St Ambrose Barlow RC
Primary School
HLGN/YWD B28 ....163 E4
St Andrews CE Infant School
DUNHL/THL/PER WV6 ....36 B1
St Andrews Industrial Estate
BORD B9 ....128 A2
St Andrews CE Primary School
BORD B9 ....127 H2
St Annes RC Primary School
HIA/OLT B92 ....147 G5
St Annes Industrial Estate
WLNHL WV13 ....39 H2
St Anne's RC JMI School
FOAKS/STRLY B74 ....45 E5
St Annes RC Primary School
BHTH/HG B12 ....127 G4
CHWD/FDBR/MGN B37 ....132 A2
St Anthonys RC Primary
School
CHWD/FDBR/MGN B37 ....114 A4
WOLVN WV10 ....12 D4
St Augustines Catholic Primary
School *HDSW* B21 ....89 F4
St Augustines Primary School
SOLH B91 ....181 G3
St Barnabas CE Primary School
ERDE/BCHGN B24 ....93 F3
St Bartholomews CE Primary
School
ETTPK/GDPK/PENN WV4 ....51 E5
St Benedict Biscop CE Primary
School *WMBN* WV5 ....65 E4
St Benedicts Infant School
SMHTH B10 ....128 D5
St Bernadettes RC JMI School
BRWNH WS8 ....9 F4
St Bernadettes RC Primary
School *SMHTH* B10 ....129 F4
WMBN WV5 ....64 D5
St Bernards RC Primary School
MOS/BIL B13 ....162 A1
St Brigids RC Primary School
NFLD/LBR B31 ....175 F2
St Catherine of Siena RC
School *EDG* B15 ....126 D4
St Chads Industrial Estate
LOZ/NWT B19 ....109 H4
St Chads RC CE Cathedral
CBHAMNE B4 ....3 F2
St Chads RC Primary School
LOZ/NWT B19 ....108 D4
SEDG DY3 ....67 F4
St Christophers RC Primary
School *CDSL* WV8 ....10 C5
St Clares Primary School
BFLD/HDSWWD B20 ....90 B5
St Clements CE Primary
School *VAUX/NECH* B7 ....109 H2
St Columbas RC Primary School
SCOL RBRY* B45 ....188 D1
St Cuthberts RC Primary
School *WASH/WDE* B8 ....111 G5
St Dunstans RC
Primary School
ALE/KHTH/YWD B14 ....161 E2

St Edmund Campion RC
School *ERDW/GRVHL* B23 ....77 F5
St Edmunds Catholic School
BDMR/CCFT WV3 ....35 H2
St Edmunds RC Primary
School *WSNGN* B18 ....108 A5
St Edward's RC Primary
School *CSHL/WTROR* B46 .....115 C4
St Edwards RC Primary
School *CSHL/WTROR* B46 .....133 G1
SLYOAK B29 ....160 B1
St Francis CE Primary School
BVILLE B30 ....159 F4
St Francis of Assisi RC School
ALDR WS9 ....30 C5
St Francis RC Primary School
LOZ/NWT B19 ....108 B3
RUSH/SHEL WS4 ....29 E1
St Francis Xavier RC Primary
School *OLDBY* B69 ....105 E1
St George & St Teresa RC
Primary School
DOR/KN B93 ....197 G4
St Georges CE Primary School
LDYWD/EDGR B16 ....125 H3
St Georges RC Primary School
Edgbaston
EDG B15 ....126 B4
St Georges Sixth Form & CE
Primary School
LOZ/NWT B19 ....108 D4
St Gerards Orthopaedic
Hospital
CSHL/WTROR B46 ....115 C4
St Gerards RC Primary School
CVALE B35 ....94 D2
St Giles CE Primary School
SHLY B90 ....39 H3
St Gregorys RC Primary School
SMTHWKW B67 ....124 B2
St Huberts RC Primary School
LGLYGN/QTN B68 ....123 C3
St James CE Junior School
SHLY B90 ....180 B3
St James CE Primary School
HDSW B21 ....89 F5
SEDG DY3 ....104 B4
STRBR DY8 ....117 H5
St James Medical Centre
HDSW B21 ....107 F1
St James RC Primary School
BRWNH WS8 ....9 F4
St James RC Primary School
RBRY B45 ....188 A1
St John Bosco RC Primary
School *WNTH/SAND* B71 ....71 F4
St John Fishers RC Primary
School *NFLD/LBR* B31 ....189 H1
St John & St Monica RC
Primary School
MOS/BIL B13 ....144 A3
St Johns CE JMI School
ALDR WS9 ....19 F4
St Johns CE Primary School
DARL/WED WS10 ....70 D1
LDYWD/EDGR B16 ....126 A2
SEDG DY3 ....80 C4
SPARK B11 ....145 E4
WNSFLD WV11 ....15 E3
St Johns Retail Park
BKHL/PFLD WV2 ....7 F6
St John the Baptist RC Primary
School *CBROM* B36 ....114 A2
St John Wall RC School
HDSW B21 ....89 F4
St Josephs Catholic Primary
School *DARL/WED* WS10 ....55 F1
FOAKS/STRLY B74 ....62 C1
STRBR DY8 ....135 F5
St Josephs RC Primary School
BVILLE B30 ....159 G5
DUDS DY2 ....85 E5
VAUX/NECH B7 ....109 H3
St Judes CE Primary School
DUNHL/THL/PER WV6 ....36 B2
St Judes RC Primary School
ALE/KHTH/YWD B14 ....178 B3
St Kenelms CE First School
RMSLY B62 ....172 C1
St Laurence CE J & I School
NFLD/LBR B31 ....175 H1
St Lukes CE Aided Primary
School *BKHL/PFLD* WV2 ....51 H1
St Margaret Mary RC Primary
School *ERDW/GRVHL* B23 ....76 A5
St Margarets CE Primary
School *CTB/HAM* B43 ....58 C4
HIA/OLT B92 ....147 H5
St Margarets Hospital
DSYBK/YTR WS5 ....43 G5
St Marks CE Primary School
BRLYHL DY5 ....101 E2
St Marks RC Primary School
PBAR/PBCH B42 ....73 H4
St Martin de Porres RC
Primary School
MOS/BIL B13 ....144 C4
St Martins CE Primary School
BILS/COS WV14 ....69 C1
TPTN/OCK DY4 ....69 H5
St Martins Industrial Estate
OLDBY B69 ....85 E3
St Martins Market *DIG/EDG* B5 ....3 H7
St Martins RC Primary School
SOLH B91 ....182 B2
St Mary & Johns RC Primary
School *BKHL/PFLD* WV2 ....37 F5
St Mary Magdalene CE Primary
School *HHTH/SAND* B71 ....71 H5
St Mary of the Angels RC JMI
School *ALDR* WS9 ....30 B5
St Marys Abbey (Remains)
RMSLY B62 ....139 F5
St Mary & St John RC Primary
School *ERDW/GRVHL* B23 ....92 C3
St Mary & St Margarets CE
Primary School
CBROM B36 ....112 D1
St Marys CE Primary School
BFLD/HDSWWD B20 ....90 B4
KGSWFD DY6 ....99 H2
SLYOAK B29 ....159 F1

St Marys RC Primary School
BRLYHL DY5 ....119 G3
DARL/WED WS10 ....55 H4
HRBN B17 ....142 A2
WOLVN WV10 ....24 A3
St Marys the Mount RC School
WSL WS1 ....5 H7
St Matthews CE Primary
School *SMTHWK* B66 ....106 D4
VAUX/NECH B7 ....109 G5
St Michaels CE High School
BLKHTH/ROWR B65 ....104 B4
St Michaels CE Primary School
BLOX/PEL WS3 ....17 H5
DUNHL/THL/PER WV6 ....22 A5
HDSW B21 ....108 A2
RIDG/WDGT B32 ....157 G2
St Michaels RC Primary School
BDMR/CCFT WV3 ....50 D1
St Nicholas CE VC First School
CDSL WV8 ....10 B3
St Nicholas RC JMI School
SCFLD/DOLD B73 ....76 D1
St Patricks Catholic Primary
School
CHWD/FDBR/MGN B37 ....132 C2
WSLW WS2 ....4 C1
St Patricks RC Primary School
WNSFLD WV11 ....24 C5
WNSGN B18 ....107 H5
St Pauls CE Primary School
COVEN WV9 ....12 A5
St Pauls RC Primary School
HWK/WKHTH B38 ....177 F4
St Pauls School *BHTH/HG* B12 ...144 C2
St Pauls School for Girls
LDYWD/EDGR B16 ....125 G3
St Peter & Paul RC Primary
School *ERDE/BCHGN* B24 ....93 G3
St Peters CE Junior School
HRBN B17 ....142 A3
St Peters C JMI School
WSL WS1 ....16 D5
St Peters Collegiate Secondary
School *BDMR/CCFT* WV3 ....36 A2
St Peters RC Primary School
RIDG/WDGT B32 ....157 G1
St Peters RC School *SOLH* B91 ...181 H5
St Philips Cathedral
CBHAMNW B3 ....3 F4
St Philips RC Primary School
SMTHWK B66 ....106 D3
St Philips RC Sixth Form
College *LDYWD/EDGR* B16 ...125 H4
St Saviours CE Primary School
WASH/WDE B8 ....110 B4
St Stephens CE Primary
School *WOLVN* WV10 ....37 G1
St Teresas RC Primary School
BFLD/HDSWWD B20 ....90 A4
ETTPK/GDPK/PENN WV4 ....52 C3
St Thomas Aquinas RC School
HWK/WKHTH B38 ....176 B2
St Thomas CE Primary School
EDG B15 ....126 D4
WNSFLD WV11 ....24 D3
St Thomas Community
Network *DUDS* DY2 ....85 G3
St Thomas More Catholic
School *WLNHL* WV13 ....39 H5
St Thomas More RC Primary
School
LGN/SDN/BHAMAIR B26 ....147 H2
St Thomas of Canterbury RC
JMI School *BLOX/PEL* WS3 .....28 B4
St Vincents RC Primary
School *VAUX/NECH* B7 ....127 H1
St Wilfrids RC Primary School
CBROM B36 ....112 B1
Salafi Independent School
SMHTH B10 ....128 B4
Salford Trading Estate
AST/WIT B6 ....110 A1
Salisbury Place Industrial
Estate *BDMR/CCFT* WV3 ....6 C6
Salisbury Primary School
DARL/WED WS10 ....55 G1
Saltbrook Trading Estate
HALE B63 ....120 A5
Saltley Business Park
WASH/WDE B8 ....110 B3
Saltley Health Centre
WASH/WDE B8 ....110 C4
Saltley Industrial Estate
WASH/WDE B8 ....128 A1
Saltley Leisure Centre
BORD B9 ....129 E1
Saltley School *WASH/WDE* B8 ..129 E1
Saltley Trading Estate
WASH/WDE B8 ....110 A4
Salvation Army *CBHAMNE* B4 .....3 F3
Sandown First School
DUNHL/THL/PER WV6 ....34 D1
Sandwell Borough FC
OLDBY B69 ....104 C2
Sandwell Business
Development Centre
OLDBY B69 ....105 G2
Sandwell Business Park
SMTHWK B66 ....105 G1
Sandwell Business &
Technology Centre
WBROM B70 ....122 D2
Sandwell College
LGLYGN/QTN B68 ....123 E1
SMTHWK B66 ....106 C4
WBROM B70 ....87 G3
Sandwell District General
Hospital
HHTH/SAND B71 ....87 H1
Sandwell Health Authority
Clinic *CDYHTH* B64 ....121 E3
Sandwell Park Golf Club
HHTH/SAND B71 ....88 B4
Sandwell Park Industrial
Estate *HHTH/SAND* B71 ....88 B5
Sandwell Valley
HHTH/SAND B71 ....72 C5

Sandyhill Industrial Estate *HLGN/YWD* B28 ...180 A1
Sapcote Business Centre *SMHTH* B10 ...145 C1
Sapcote Industrial Estate *CDYHTH* B64 ...121 F1
Sapcote Trading Centre
  AST/WIT B6 ...91 G3
  CDYHTH B64 ...121 F1
  SMHTH B10 ...145 C1
Sarehole Mill *MOS/BIL* B13 ...162 B2
Sarephed Medical Centre *SMTHKWK* B67 ...106 C4
Sargent Turner Trading Estate *HAG/WOL* DY9 ...136 D1
Satellite Industrial Park *WNSFLD* WV11 ...38 C1
School of Jewellery (University of Central England) *CBHAMW* B1 ...2 C2
Scott Arms Shopping Centre *GTB/HAM* B43 ...73 C2
Sears Retail Park *SHLY* B90 ...180 A4
Sedgley Golf Centre *SEDG* DY3 ...66 D5
Selly Manor Museum *BVILLE* B30 ...159 H5
Selly Oak Health Centre *SLYOAK* B29 ...159 G1
Selly Oak Hospital *SLYOAK* B29 ...159 H1
Selly Oak Industrial Estate *SLYOAK* B29 ...159 G1
Selly Oak School *SLYOAK* B29 ...159 G2
Selly Park Technology College for Girls *SLYOAK* B29 ...160 B1
Seth Somes Track *RMSLY* B62 ...139 E5
Severne Primary School *ACGN* B27 ...163 G2
Shaftmoor Industrial Estate *HLGN/YWD* B28 ...145 H5
Sharmans Cross Junior School *SOLH* B91 ...181 C1
Shaw Hill Primary School *WASH/WDE* B8 ...110 C5
Shaw Park Business Village *WOLVN* WV10 ...23 F4
Sheldon CC *YDLY* B25 ...129 H4
Sheldon Country Park *LGN/SDN/BHAMAIR* B26 ...148 C1
Sheldon Heath Community School *LGN/SDN/BHAMAIR* B26 ...131 E4
Shefield Clinic *RUSH/SHEL* WS4 ...29 E2
Sheffield Sports & Community College *RUSH/SHEL* WS4 ...18 C1
Shell Corner Trading Estate *RMSLY* B62 ...122 B4
Shelter Waterside Industrial Estate *ETTPK/GDPK/PENN* WV4 ...53 E3
Shenley Court School *SLYOAK* B29 ...158 B3
Shenley Lane Community Association Sports Centre *SLYOAK* B29 ...158 C4
Shenstone Trading Estate *HALE* B63 ...139 E3
Sherborne Wharf *LDYWD/EDGR* B16 ...2 A1
Shireland Hall Primary School *SMTHWK* B66 ...125 E1
Shireland Language College *SMTHWK* B66 ...125 E1
Shire Oak School *BRWNH* WS8 ...19 G2
Shirestone Primary School *STETCH* B33 ...131 F2
Shirley Clinic *SHLY* B90 ...180 B2
Shirley Heath Junior School *SHLY* B90 ...180 C4
Shirley Park Sports Club & Golf Club *SHLY* B90 ...195 G4
Shirley Road Health Clinic *ACGN* B27 ...163 F1
Short Heath Clinic *SHHTH* WV12 ...26 B4
Short Heath Primary School *ERDW/GRVHL* B23 ...76 B5
Shorth Heath Junior School *SHHTH* WV12 ...
Showcase Cinema *DUDN* DY1 ...85 E5
  WSLW WS2 ...40 D4
Showcase Cinemas *ERDE/BCHGN* B24 ...93 H4
Showell Road Industrial Estate *WOLVN* WV10 ...23 F4
The Shrubbery School *WALM/CURD* B76 ...78 B4
Silhill FC *SOLH* B91 ...181 E1
Silver End Business Park *BRLYHL* DY5 ...118 D4
Silver End Industrial Estate *BRLYHL* DY5 ...118 D3
Sladefield Infant School *WASH/WDE* B8 ...111 E4
Slade Primary School *ERDW/GRVHL* B23 ...92 B4
Sledmere Primary School *DUDS* DY2 ...102 D3
Small Heath Business Park *SMHTH* B10 ...128 D5
Small Heath Lower School *SMHTH* B10 ...128 D5
Small Heath Trading Estate *SPARK* B11 ...145 F1
Smestow Bridge Industrial Estate *WMBN* WV5 ...64 A5
Smestow Secondary School *WOLV* WV3 ...35 F4
Smethwick Medical Centre *SMTHWKW* B67 ...106 C3
Smethwick Swimming Centre *SMTHWKW* B67 ...124 B2
Smith's Wood School *CBROM* B36 ...114 A3
Sneyd Community School *BLOX/PEL* WS3 ...27 G5
Snow Hill Clinic *BKHL/PFLD* WV2 ...7 G5
Soho Health Centre *HDSW* B21 ...107 H2

Soho House *WSGN* B18 ...108 A2
Solihull College *SOLH* B91 ...181 G2
Solihull Hospital *SOLH* B91 ...181 B1
Solihull Ice Rink *HIA/OLT* B92 ...147 H4
Solihull Retail Park *SHLY* B90 ...180 D4
Solihull School *SOLH* B91 ...182 B1
Solihull Sixth Form College *SOLH* B91 ...182 B3
Somerville Primary School *SMHTH* B10 ...128 B4
South Birmingham College
  BHTH/HG B12 ...3 K7
  HLGN/YWD B28 ...162 C2
Southside Business Centre *BHTH/HG* B12 ...144 C2
South Staffordshire Golf Club *DUNHL/THL/PER* WV6 ...21 G4
Sovereign Trading Centre *STRBR* DY8 ...135 E2
Sparkbrook Health Centre *SPARK* B11 ...127 H5
Sparkhill Pool & Fitness Centre *SPARK* B11 ...145 E3
Spartan Industrial Centre *WBROM* B70 ...70 C5
Speedwell Trading Estate *SPARK* B11 ...146 A1
Spines Clinic *WMBN* WV5 ...64 D5
Spinners End Industrial Estate *CDYHTH* B64 ...120 D3
Spon Lane Industrial Estate *SMTHWK* B66 ...105 H1
Spon Lane Trading Estate *WBROM* B70 ...87 G4
Springdale J & I School *ETTPK/GDPK/PENN* WV4 ...50 C3
Springfield Industrial Estate *OLDBY* B69 ...105 F2
Springfield Infant School *BLKHTH/ROWR* B65 ...145 F5
Springfield Junior School *BLKHTH/ROWR* B65 ...103 C5
Springfield Primary School *BLKHTH/ROWR* B65 ...103 C5
Spring Hill Industrial Estate *WSGN* B18 ...108 A5
Spring Lane Industrial Estate *SHHTH* WV12 ...40 A1
Spring Road Industrial Estate *ETTPK/GDPK/PENN* WV4 ...53 E4
Springvale Business Park *BILS/COS* WV14 ...53 F4
Springvale Industrial Park *BILS/COS* WV14 ...53 F4
Spring Vale Primary School *ETTPK/GDPK/PENN* WV4 ...52 C4
Stafford Road Sports Club *BILS/COS* WV14 ...16 D5
Stag Industrial Estate *BILS/COS* WV14 ...54 C4
Stambermill Industrial Estate *HAG/WOL* DY9 ...136 A1
Stanhope Road Clinic *SMTHWKW* B67 ...124 D1
Stanville Primary School *LGN/SDN/BHAMAIR* B26 ...147 H1
Starbank Primary School *SMHTH* B10 ...129 F4
Start Point Trading Estate *SPARK* B11 ...145 F3
Station Road Industrial Estate
  BLKHTH/ROWR B65 ...122 D2
  CSHL/WTROR B46 ...115 F1
Stechford Cascades *STETCH* B33 ...130 A1
Stechford Health Centre *STETCH* B33 ...130 A2
Stechford Primary School *STETCH* B33 ...129 H2
Stechford Retail Park *STETCH* B33 ...112 A5
Stechford Trading Estate *STETCH* B33 ...112 A5
Steetley Industrial Estate *BILS/COS* WV14 ...68 C4
Stephens Industrial Estate *SPARK* B11 ...145 H4
Stevens Dental Health Centre *DY8* ...135 F3
Stirchley Primary School *BVILLE* B30 ...160 A4
Stirchley Trading Estate *BVILLE* B30 ...160 B3
Stock Exchange *CBHAMNW* B3 ...2 E4
Stockland Clinic *ERDW/GRVHL* B23 ...92 B2
Stockland Green Health Centre *ERDW/GRVHL* B23 ...92 B2
Stockland Green School *ERDW/GRVHL* B23 ...92 A2
Stone Cross Clinic *HHTH/SAND* B71 ...72 A2
Stourbridge CC *STRBR* DY8 ...118 B5
Stourbridge Cemetery *STRBR* DY8 ...134 D3
Stourbridge Clinic *STRBR* DY8 ...135 H3
Stourbridge College
  HAG/WOL DY9 ...136 B2
  STRBR DY8 ...135 E2
Stourbridge Crematorium *STRBR* DY8 ...134 D3
Stourbridge Golf Club *STRBR* DY8 ...152 C1
Stourbridge Industrial Estate *STRBR* DY8 ...135 G1
Stourbridge RFC *KINVER* DY7 ...134 B1
Stourvale Industrial Estate *HAG/WOL* DY9 ...136 D1
Stourvale Trading Estate *HALE* B63 ...137 H1
Stowheath Industrial Estate & New Enterprise Centre *BKHL/PFLD* WV2 ...38 A5
Stow Heath J & I School *WLNHL* WV13 ...38 D4
Stowlawn Primary School *WOLV* WV1 ...38 C5
Straits Primary School *SEDG* DY3 ...82 D1

Stratford Road School Clinic ...145 F5
Strawberry Lane Industrial Estate *WLNHL* WV13 ...38 C2
The Streetley School *FOAKS/STRLY* B74 ...60 B2
Streetly Cemetery *ALDR* WS9 ...44 D3
Streetly Clinic *FOAKS/STRLY* B74 ...45 E5
Streetly Crematorium *ALDR* WS9 ...44 D3
Streetly Hockey & CC *FOAKS/STRLY* B74 ...45 G4
Streetly Methodist Recreation Centre *FOAKS/STRLY* B74 ...45 F3
Streetsbrook Infant School *SHLY* B90 ...180 C1
Stuart Bathurst RC High School *DARL/WED* WS10 ...56 B3
Stuart Crystal *STRBR* DY8 ...118 A3
Summerfield Hospital *WSNGN* B18 ...107 H5
Summerfield Primary School *WSNGN* B18 ...107 G5
Summer Hill Industrial Park *CBHAMW* B1 ...2 A3
The Summerhill Secondary School *KGSWFD* DY6 ...99 F4
Sundridge Primary School *KGSTG* B44 ...60 A4
Sunfield School *HAG/WOL* DY9 ...170 C1
Sunrise Business Park *STRBR* DY8 ...118 A5
Sunshine Infant School *BLOX/PEL* WS3 ...27 G2
Sutton Arts Theatre *CSCFLD/WYGN* B72 ...62 C4
Sutton Coldfield College
  ERDE/BCHGN B24 ...93 E2
  ERDW/GRVHL B23 ...92 A2
  FOAKS/STRLY B74 ...62 C2
  KGSTG B44 ...75 F2
  MGN/WHC B75 ...47 H2
  WASH/WDE B8 ...110 D2
Sutton Coldfield Crematorium *MGN/WHC* B75 ...48 C3
Sutton Coldfield Girls School *SCFLD/BOLD* B73 ...62 B5
Sutton Coldfield Golf Club *FOAKS/STRLY* B74 ...45 H4
Sutton Coldfield Hospital *SCFLD/BOLD* B73 ...62 B4
Sutton Coldfield Town FC *CSCFLD/WYGN* B72 ...62 C5
Sutton Coldfield Town Hall *SCFLD/BOLD* B73 ...62 B2
Sutton Coldfield Cemetery *MGN/WHC* B75 ...62 D2
The Sutton Special School *MGN/WHC* B75 ...101 H1
Sutton Town Sports Club *CSCFLD/WYGN* B72 ...62 C4
Sutton United FC *MGN/WHC* B75 ...63 E3
The Swallows Industrial Estate *SHLY* B90 ...194 D1
Swallows Rise Business Park *BRLYHL* DY5 ...119 G1
Swan Lane Industrial Estate *WBROM* B70 ...87 E1
Swan Medical Centre *YDLY* B25 ...129 H5
Swanpool Medical Centre *TPTN/OCK* DY4 ...69 G3
Swanshurst Girls School *MOS/BIL* B13 ...161 G3
Sycamore Green Primary School *DUDN* DY1 ...83 H1
Sycamore House Medical Centre *WSL* WS1 ...5 J7
Sycamore Industrial & Trading Estate *HDSW* B21 ...107 F2
Symphony Hall *CBHAMW* B1 ...2 C5
Talbots Lane Trading Estate *BRLYHL* DY5 ...119 G3
Tamar Medical Centre *DUNHL/THL/PER* WV6 ...34 C1
Tamebridge Industrial Estate *PBAR/PBCH* B42 ...91 E2
Tame Road Industrial Estate *AST/WIT* B6 ...91 H5
Tame Valley Primary School *CBROM* B36 ...111 H1
Tandon Medical Centre *SEDG* DY3 ...83 G1
Tansey Green Trading Estate *BRLYHL* DY5 ...100 D1
Telsen Industrial Centre *AST/WIT* B6 ...109 F3
Temple Meadow Primary School *CDYHTH* B64 ...121 F3
Tenterfields Primary School *HALE* B63 ...139 E3
Tettenhall College *DUNHL/THL/PER* WV6 ...35 H1
Tettenhall Wood Special School *DUNHL/THL/PER* WV6 ...35 F2
Thameside Primary School *DARL/WED* WS10 ...71 C1
Thinktank at Millennium Point *CBHAMNE* B4 ...3 K4
Thistle Hotel
  CBHAMNE B4 ...3 F5
  LDYWD/EDGR B16 ...125 C3
Thornleigh Trading Estate *DUDS* DY2 ...102 A2
Thorns Community College *BRLYHL* DY5 ...119 F4
Thorns Primary School *BRLYHL* DY5 ...119 F4
Thornton Junior School *WASH/WDE* B8 ...111 F4
Three Crowns Special School *DYSBK/YTR* WS5 ...43 H4
Tidbury Green Primary School *SHLY* B90 ...193 G4
Tile Cross Trading Estate *STETCH* B33 ...131 F3

Timberley Primary School *BKDE/SHDE* B34 ...113 F3
Timbertree Primary School *CDYHTH* B64 ...121 E5
Tindal Primary School *BHTH/HG* B12 ...144 B2
Tipper Trading Estate *HALE* B63 ...137 E2
Tipton Green Junior School *TPTN/OCK* DY4 ...85 F2
Tipton Sports Academy *TPTN/OCK* DY4 ...69 H2
Tiverton J & I School *SLYOAK* B29 ...142 D5
Tiverton Road Pool & Fitness Centre *SLYOAK* B29 ...159 H1
Tividale Business Park *TPTN/OCK* DY4 ...85 H3
Tividale Comprehensive School *OLDBY* B69 ...86 A5
Tividale FC *OLDBY* B69 ...85 H5
Tividale Hall Primary School *OLDBY* B69 ...85 G5
Tividale Medical Centre *OLDBY* B69 ...104 B1
Tividale Primary School *OLDBY* B69 ...85 H4
Tollgate Shopping Precinct *SMTHWKW* B67 ...106 B3
Topcliffe Primary School *CVALE* B35 ...94 C3
Touchwood Shopping Centre *SOLH* B91 ...182 A1
Tower Hill Health Centre *PBAR/PBCH* B42 ...74 A5
Tower Works Industrial Estate *BDMR/CCFT* WV3 ...6 A6
Town Gate Retail Park *DUDN* DY1 ...85 F4
Town Junior School *CSCFLD/WYGN* B72 ...62 C4
Town Wharf Business Park *WSLW* WS2 ...4 B3
T P Riley Community School *BLOX/PEL* WS3 ...17 E5
Tractor Spares Industrial Estate *WLNHL* WV13 ...38 D5
Trading Estate Parkview *HWK/WKHTH* B38 ...176 D2
Travelodge
  BRLYHL DY5 ...105 G5
  EDG B15 ...2 C7
  LGN/SDN/BHAMAIR B26 ...147 C1
  OLDBY B69 ...104 B2
  RIDG/WDGT B32 ...156 D3
  SCFLD/BOLD B73 ...76 D1
Trescott Primary School *NFLD/LBR* B31 ...174 D2
Trevor Street Industrial Estate *VAUX/NECH* B7 ...110 A3
Trident Retail Park *BORD* B9 ...127 G2
Trident Shopping Centre *DUDN* DY1 ...84 C5
Trinity Business Park *HIA/OLT* B92 ...149 H4
Trinity CE Primary School *WOLVN* WV10 ...37 H1
Tromans Industrial Estate *DUDS* DY2 ...120 D1
Truck Stop Business Park *SPARK* B11 ...146 B1
Tudor Grange School *SOLH* B91 ...181 G3
Tudor Grange Sports Centre & Pool *SOLH* B91 ...181 H2
Tudor Industrial Estate *SPARK* B11 ...146 B2
Turves Green Boys School *NFLD/LBR* B31 ...175 G5
Turves Green Girls School *NFLD/LBR* B31 ...175 G4
Turves Green Primary School *NFLD/LBR* B31 ...175 G4
Twickenham Primary School *KGSTG* B44 ...76 A2
Two Woods Industrial Estate *BRLYHL* DY5 ...119 G3
Two Woods Trading Estate *BRLYHL* DY5 ...119 H3
Tyburn Industrial Estate *ERDE/BCHGN* B24 ...93 H4
Tyseley Industrial Estate *SPARK* B11 ...145 G2
Tyseley Locomotive Works Visitor Centre *SPARK* B11 ...145 H2
UCI Cinema
  BRLYHL DY5 ...119 G2
  SHLY B90 ...195 E1
Uffculme Clinic *MOS/BIL* B13 ...143 H5
Uffculme Special School *MOS/BIL* B13 ...161 C1
Ulverley Primary School *HIA/OLT* B92 ...164 D2
Union Business Park *WSLW* WS2 ...4 C4
Unisant Trading Estate *CDYHTH* B64 ...121 F2
University of Birmingham
  CBHAMNE B4 ...3 G2
  EDG B15 ...142 D4
University of Central England
  CBHAMNW B3 ...3 J2
  CBHAMNW B3 ...2 E1
  PBAR/PBCH B42 ...90 D3
University of Central England (Institute of Art & Design) *CBHAMNE* B4 ...3 J1
University of Central England (Technology Innovation Centre) *CBHAMNE* B4 ...2 C4
University of Wolverhampton
  BDMR/CCFT WV3 ...35 H3
  WOLVN WV10 ...23 C4
  WOLVN WV10 ...38 B1
  WSL WS1 ...5 J2
  WSLW WS2 ...41 C4
University of Wolverhampton (North Site) *WOLV* WV1 ...7 F2
University of Wolverhampton (South Site) *WOLV* WV1 ...7 F3

Uplands Cemetery *SMTHWKW* B67 ...124 A1
Uplands Junior School *BDMR/CCFT* WV3 ...35 H5
Uplands Manor Primary School *SMTHWKW* B67 ...124 A1
Upper School & Sixth Form *SMHTH* B10 ...128 B4
Usam Trading Estate *WOLVN* WV10 ...12 D5
Valley Infant School *HIA/OLT* B92 ...148 B4
Valley Park Campus *DUNHL/THL/PER* WV6 ...22 B5
Vaughan Trading Estate *TPTN/OCK* DY4 ...85 H3
Vauxhall Trading Estate *VAUX/NECH* B7 ...109 H5
Vector Industrial Park *HHTH/SAND* B71 ...71 G5
Venkat Medical Centre *STETCH* B33 ...131 G1
Vernon Trading Estate *RMSLY* B62 ...122 A4
Victoria Health Centre *SMTHWK* B66 ...106 D5
Victoria Infant School *TPTN/OCK* DY4 ...85 E1
Victoria Park Primary School *SMTHWK* B66 ...106 D4
Victoria School *NFLD/LBR* B31 ...158 C5
Villiers Primary School *BILS/COS* WV14 ...53 H1
Villiers Trading Estate *BKHL/PFLD* WV2 ...7 K2
Visit Centre *WSNGN* B18 ...107 G4
Viva! Health & Leisure Club *WSL* WS1 ...196 A1
Vulcan House Industrial Estate *SOLH* B91 ...165 E4
Vulcan Industrial Estate *WSLW* WS2 ...27 G4
Wake Green FC *SHLY* B90 ...179 G5
Wallbrook Primary School *BILS/COS* WV14 ...69 E3
The Wallows Industrial Estate *BRLYHL* DY5 ...101 F4
Walmley CC *WALM/CURD* B76 ...78 A4
Walmley Golf Club *CSCFLD/WYGN* B72 ...77 C3
Walmley Infant School *SCFLD/BOLD* B73 ...78 C4
Walsall Business Park *ALDR* WS9 ...30 B5
Walsall CC *WSL* WS1 ...43 G1
Walsall College *WSLW* WS2 ...57 C1
Walsall College of Arts & Technology *WSLW* WS2 ...4 D2
Walsall FC (Bescot Stadium) *WSL* WS1 ...56 D3
Walsall Gala Baths *WSL* WS1 ...4 E3
Walsall Golf Club *WSL* WS1 ...57 H2
Walsall Leather Museum *WSL* WS2 ...4 D1
Walsall Museum & Library *WSL* WS1 ...5 F3
Walsall RFC *WSL* WS1 ...43 F4
Walsall Wood Cemetery *ALDR* WS9 ...19 F4
Walsall Wood Primary School *ALDR* WS9 ...19 F4
Ward End Medical Centre *WASH/WDE* B8 ...111 F4
Ward End Primary School *WASH/WDE* B8 ...111 F3
Warley High School *LGLYGN/QTN* B68 ...123 C2
Warley Infant School *LGLYGN/QTN* B68 ...123 C2
Warley Woods Golf Club *SMTHWKW* B67 ...124 A4
Warner Village Star City *VAUX/NECH* B7 ...110 B1
Warren Farm Primary School *KGSTG* B44 ...75 H3
Warstones Primary School *ETTPK/GDPK/PENN* WV4 ...51 E2
Wartell Bank Industrial Estate *KGSWFD* DY6 ...99 H1
Warwick Road Trading Estate *SPARK* B11 ...145 F3
Warwickshire CCC (Edgbaston) *DIG/EDG* B5 ...143 H2
Waseley Hills Country Park *BRGRVW* B61 ...173 E5
Waseley Hills High School *RBRY* B45 ...187 F1
Washington Street Industrial Estate *DUDS* DY2 ...120 D1
Washwood Heath Technology College *WASH/WDE* B8 ...111 G4
Waterfall Lane Trading Estate *CDYHTH* B64 ...121 G3
Waterfront Business Park *BRLYHL* DY5 ...119 G1
Waterlinie Industrial Estate *CHWD/FDBR/MGN* B37 ...114 B4
Watermill Primary School *SLYOAK* B29 ...142 B3
Water Orton CC *CSHL/WTROR* B46 ...96 B3
Water Orton Primary School *CSHL/WTROR* B46 ...96 A3
Waterside Industrial Estate
  BKHL/PFLD WV2 ...53 E2
  BLKHTH/ROWR B65 ...103 F5
Watery Lane Industrial Estate *WLNHL* WV13 ...38 D2
Watling Street Business Park *CNCK/NC* WS11 ...8 A2
Watling Street JMI School *BRWNH* WS8 ...9 E3
Wattville Primary School *SMTHWK* B66 ...106 D1
Wattville Road Industrial Estate *SMTHWK* B66 ...106 D2
Waverley School *SMHTH* B10 ...129 E4

Webnor Industrial Estate
BKHL/PFLD WV2 .... 53 E2
Wednesbury CC
DARL/WED WS10 .... 56 A4
Wednesbury Chiropody Surgery
DARL/WED WS10 .... 55 H5
Wednesbury Leisure Centre
DARL/WED WS10 .... 55 G5
Wednesbury Medical Centre
DARL/WED WS10 .... 70 C1
Wednesbury Oak Primary
School *TPTN/OCK* DY4 .... 69 F2
Wednesbury Rugby Club
DARL/WED WS10 .... 70 D2
Wednesbury Trading Estate
DARL/WED WS10 .... 55 G4
Wednesfield CC
WNSFLD WV11 .... 24 C4
Wednesfield High School
WNSFLD WV11 .... 25 E5
Wednesfield Village Primary
School *WNSFLD* WV11 .... 24 D5
Wednesfield Way Industrial
Estate *WNSFLD* WV11 .... 38 D1
Welford Primary School
BFLD/HDSWWD B20 .... 108 B1
Wellington industrial Estate
BILS/COS WV14 .... 68 C4
Welsh House Farm Primary
School *RIDG/WDGT* B32 ...... 141 F3
Welsh RFC *HIA/OLT* B92 .... 149 G5
Weoley Castle Health Centre
SLYOAK B29 .... 158 C1
Weoley Castle Ruins &
Museum *SLYOAK* B29 .... 141 G5
Wergs Golf Club
DUNHL/THL/PER WV6 .... 21 E3
Westacre Infant School
BDMR/CCFT WV3 .... 35 H4
West Bromwich Albion FC
(The Hawthorns)
HHTH/SAND B71 .... 88 C5
West Bromwich Dartmouth CC
HHTH/SAND B71 .... 88 B5
Westcroft Special School &
Sports College
WOLVN WV10 .... 13 H5
West Cross Shopping Centre
SMTHWK B66 .... 105 H2
Westfield Business Park
RMSLY B62 .... 121 H5
WSNGN B18 .... 107 G3
Westfield Primary School
WMBN WV5 .... 65 G4
Westgate Trading Estate
ALDR WS9 .... 29 G4
West Heath Hospital
HWK/WKHTH B38 .... 176 A5
West House School
EDG B15 .... 126 C4
The Westmead Hotel
ALVE B48 .... 189 H4
West Midlands Hospital
HALE B63 .... 137 H2
Westminster Industrial Estate
BFLD/HDSWWD B20 .... 120 D2
Westminster Primary School
BFLD/HDSWWD B20 .... 90 C5

Westminster School
TPTN/OCK DY4 .... 69 G5
West Park Hospital *WOLV* WV1 .. 6 C3
West Park Primary School
WOLV WV1 .... 6 C1
Westwood Business Park
AST/WIT B6 .... 91 H4
Wharton Street Industrial
Estate *VAUX/NECH* B7 .... 110 B1
Wheelers Lane Technology
College *MOS/BIL* B13 .... 161 F3
Wheeler Street Shopping
Centre *LOZ/NWT* B19 .... 108 C3
Whetstone Field Primary
School *ALDR* WS9 .... 44 B1
Whitecrest Primary School
GTB/HAM B43 .... 74 A1
Whitehall Industrial Park
TPTN/OCK DY4 .... 86 C1
Whitehall Infant School
WSL WS1 .... 57 F1
Whitehall Junior School
WSL WS1 .... 57 F1
Whiteheath Clinic
OLDBY B69 .... 104 B4
Whitehouse Common
Primary School
MGN/WHC B75 .... 62 D1
Whitesmore School
CHWD/FDBR/MGN B37 .... 131 H3
Whitgreave J & I School
WOLVN WV10 .... 23 G2
Whitmore Medical Centre
WOLV WV1 .... 6 E1
Whitmore Reans Health Centre
DUNHL/THL/PER WV6 .... 36 C1
Whitworth Industrial Park
BORD B9 .... 128 A2
Wholesale Markets
DIG/EDG B5 .... 3 H7
Widney Junior School
SOLH B91 .... 181 F4
Widney Manor Cemetery
DOR/KN B93 .... 196 C2
Widney Manor Golf Club
SHLY B90 .... 196 A1
Wightwick Hall Special School
DUNHL/THL/PER WV6 .... 34 C3
Wightwick Manor (NT)
DUNHL/THL/PER WV6 .... 34 D4
Wilkes Green J & I School
HDSW B21 .... 89 G5
Wilkinson Primary School
BILS/COS WV14 .... 54 B5
Willenhall Industrial Estate
WLNHL WV13 .... 40 A2
Willenhall Lane Industrial
Estate *BLOX/PEL* WS3 .... 27 E2
Willenhall Lawn Cemetery
SHHTH WV12 .... 26 C5
Willenhall Leisure Centre
WLNHL WV13 .... 39 H4
Willenhall School Sports
College *SHHTH* WV12 .... 26 C5
Willenhall Town FC
WLNHL WV13 .... 39 F2
Willenhall Trading Estate
WLNHL WV13 .... 39 F4

William Cowper Primary
School
LOZ/NWT B19 .... 109 E3
William Hanke Industrial
Estate
BRLYHL DY5 .... 119 G3
Willingsworth High School
TPTN/OCK DY4 .... 69 H1
Wilson Stuart Special School
ERDW/GRVHL B23 .... 76 A5
Windmill Hill (Look out)
RBRY B45 .... 173 E5
Windmill Works Industrial Park
DUDS DY2 .... 102 B2
Windsor High School
HALE B63 .... 138 B3
Windsor Industrial Estate
VAUX/NECH B7 .... 109 G4
Windward Way Industrial
Estate
CBROM B36 .... 113 H1
Windy Arbor Primary School
CHWD/FDBR/MGN B37 .... 132 D1
Winster Grove Industrial
Centre *KGSTG* B44 .... 74 D1
Winster Grove Industrial
Estate *KGSTG* B44 .... 75 E1
Wishaw Golf Course
WALM/CURD B76 .... 79 F1
Withymoor Primary School
BRLYHL DY5 .... 119 F3
Witton Industrial Estate
BILS/COS WV14 .... 53 C5
Witton Park Industrial Estate
AST/WIT B6 .... 91 G4
Woden Primary School
WOLVN WV10 .... 37 G1
Wodensborough Community
Technology College
DARL/WED WS10 .... 71 F1
Wodensfield Primary School
WNSFLD WV11 .... 24 B4
Wollescote Business Park
HAC/WOL DY9 .... 136 D2
Wollescote Primary School
HAC/WOL DY9 .... 136 D3
Wolverhampton Business Park
WOLVN WV10 .... 12 D2
Wolverhampton CC
DUNHL/THL/PER WV6 .... 21 G4
Wolverhampton Central Baths
WOLV WV1 .... 6 D3
Wolverhampton College
WOLV WV1 .... 53 F1
Wolverhampton Girls High
School
DUNHL/THL/PER WV6 .... 36 B2
Wolverhampton Grammar
School *BDMR/CCFT* WV3 .... 36 B3
Wolverhampton Healthcare
WOLVN WV10 .... 38 B1
The Wolverhampton Nuffield
Hospital
DUNHL/THL/PER WV6 .... 35 G2
Wolverhampton Racecourse
DUNHL/THL/PER WV6 .... 22 C4

Wolverhampton Wanderers FC
(Molineux Stadium)
WOLV WV1 .... 6 E1
Wombourne Cricket Tennis &
Bowling Club *WMBN* WV5 ..... 65 E4
Wombrook Business Centre
WMBN WV5 .... 64 C4
Wombrook Industrial Estate
WMBN WV5 .... 64 C5
Woodbourne Priory Hospital
HRBN B17 .... 125 E3
Woodcock Hill Primary
School
NFLD/LBR B31 .... 158 A3
Woodcock Sports Centre
CBHAMNE B4 .... 3 J2
Woodcross Clinic
BILS/COS WV14 .... 68 A1
Wood End Primary School
WNSFLD WV11 .... 24 C3
Woodfield J & I School
ETTPK/GDPK/PENN WV4 .... 51 F2
Woodgate Business Park
RIDG/WDGT B32 .... 140 B5
Woodgate Primary School
RIDG/WDGT B32 .... 157 F1
Woodgate Valley
RIDG/WDGT B32 .... 140 C3
Woodgate Valley Health
Centre *RIDG/WDGT* B32 ...... 140 C5
Wood Green High School
College of Sport
DARL/WED WS10 .... 56 B3
Wood Green Junior School
DARL/WED WS10 .... 55 H4
Woodhouse J & I School
RIDG/WDGT B32 .... 141 E1
Woodlands Cemetery
CBROM B36 .... 114 C4
Woodlands Hotel *HRBN* B17 ... 124 D3
Woodlands Infant School
SHLY B90 .... 180 B5
Woodlands Primary School
SHHTH WV12 .... 26 B4
Woodland's Way High School
HLYWD B47 .... 192 C2
Woodrush Rugby Club
HWK/WKHTH B38 .... 191 F4
The Woodsbank Industrial
Estate *DARL/WED* WS10 ...... 55 F4
The Woodsbank Trading
Estate *DARL/WED* WS10 ...... 55 F4
The Woodsetton Special
School *SEDG* DY3 .... 67 H4
Woodside Industrial Estate
DUDS DY2 .... 101 H4
Woodstock Girls School
MOS/BIL B13 .... 144 C3
Woodthorne Primary School
DUNHL/THL/PER WV6 .... 35 E1
Woodthorpe Primary School
ALE/KHTH/YWD B14 .... 161 E5
Woodview Primary School
WOLVN WV10 .... 38 B1
Woodville Primary School
EDG B15 .... 126 C4
Wordsley Green Health
Centre *STRBR* DY8 .... 117 H2
Wordsley Green Shopping
Centre *STRBR* DY8 .... 117 H2

Wordsley Hospital
STRBR DY8 .... 118 A1
Works Trading Estate
SMTHWK B66 .... 106 C2
Worlds End J & I School
RIDG/WDGT B32 .... 140 C2
The Worsley School
KGSWFD DY6 .... 118 B1
Wren's Nest National Nature
Reserve *DUDN* DY1 .... 84 B2
Wrens Nest Primary School
DUDN DY1 .... 84 A2
Wrottesley Hall
WOLV WV1 .... 20 A2
Wulfrun Shopping Centre
WOLV WV1 .... 7 F5
Wulfrun Trading Estate
WOLV WV1 .... 23 E5
Wychall Farm Primary School
NFLD/LBR B31 .... 176 A3
Wylde Green Primary School
SCFLD/BOLD B73 .... 77 F4
Wyndcliffe Primary School
BORD B9 .... 128 B3
Wyndley Leisure Centre
FOAKS/STRLY B74 .... 62 A3
Wyndley Swimming Baths
SCFLD/BOLD B73 .... 62 A4
Wynford Industrial Trading
Estate *ACGN* B27 .... 146 C2
Wynford Road Industrial
Estate *ACGN* B27 .... 146 C2
Wythall Cemetery
HLYWD B47 .... 192 A5
Wythall Health Centre
HLYWD B47 .... 192 C1
Yardley Cemetery
YDLY B25 .... 146 D2
Yardley Green Health Centre
SMHTH B10 .... 128 C3
Yardley Green Medical Centre
SMHTH B10 .... 128 A4
Yardley Medical Centre
YDLY B25 .... 129 F5
Yardleys School
SPARK B11 .... 145 G4
Yardleys Secondary School
SPARK B11 .... 145 H3
Yardley Wood Health Centre
MOS/BIL B13 .... 162 A5
Yardley Wood Primary School
ALE/KHTH/YWD B14 .... 179 F1
Yarnfield Primary School
SPARK B11 .... 146 A4
Yenton Junior School
ERDE/BCHGN B24 .... 77 F5
Yew Tree Community
Junior School
AST/WIT B6 .... 91 G5
Yew Tree Primary School
DSYBK/YTR WS5 .... 57 H4
SOLH B91 .... 165 G5
York Mead Primary School
HLGN/YWD B28 .... 145 G5
Yorks Wood Primary School
CHWD/FDBR/MGN B37 .... 113 H4
Zip Theatre
WOLV WV1 .... 6 D1

Acknowledgements

Schools address data provided by Education Direct

Petrol station information supplied by Johnsons

Garden centre information provided by:

Garden Centre Association ● Britains best garden centres

🌸 Wyevale Garden Centres

The statement on the front cover of this atlas is sourced, selected and quoted
from a reader comment and feedback form received in 2004

 **Street by Street** QUESTIONNAIRE

Dear Atlas User
Your comments, opinions and recommendations are very important to us.
So please help us to improve our street atlases by taking a few minutes
to complete this simple questionnaire.

You do not need a stamp (unless posted outside the UK). If you do not want to remove this page from your street atlas, then photocopy it or write your answers on a plain sheet of paper.

Send to: Marketing Assistant, AA Publishing, 14th Floor Fanum House,
Freepost SCE 4598, Basingstoke RG21 4GY

ABOUT THE ATLAS...

Please state which city / town / county you bought:

_____

Where did you buy the atlas? (City, Town, County)

_____

For what purpose? (please tick all applicable)

To use in your local area ☐   **To use on business or at work** ☐

Visiting a strange place ☐   **In the car** ☐   **On foot** ☐

Other (please state)

_____

Have you ever used any street atlases other than AA Street by Street?

Yes ☐   No ☐

If so, which ones?

_____

Is there any aspect of our street atlases that could be improved?
(Please continue on a separate sheet if necessary)

_____
_____
_____

ML33y

continued overleaf

Please list the features you found most useful:

_____
_____

Please list the features you found least useful:

_____
_____
_____

LOCAL KNOWLEDGE...

Local knowledge is invaluable. Whilst every attempt has been made to make the information contained in this atlas as accurate as possible, should you notice any inaccuracies, please detail them below (if necessary, use a blank piece of paper) or e-mail us at _streetbystreet@theAA.com_

_____
_____
_____

ABOUT YOU...

Name (Mr/Mrs/Ms) _____
Address _____
                                            Postcode _____
Daytime tel no _____
E-mail address _____

Which age group are you in?

Under 25 ☐   25-34 ☐   35-44 ☐   45-54 ☐   55-64 ☐   65+ ☐

Are you an AA member?   YES ☐   NO ☐

Do you have Internet access?   YES ☐   NO ☐

Thank you for taking the time to complete this questionnaire. Please send it to us as soon as possible, and remember, you do not need a stamp (unless posted outside the UK).

We may use information we hold about you to, telephone or email you about other products and services offered by the AA, we do NOT disclose this information to third parties.

Please tick here if you do not wish to hear about products and services from the AA. ☐

ML33y